THE MIDDLE EAST

THE MIDDLE EAST

TENTH EDITION

CQ PRESS

A DIVISION OF CONGRESSIONAL QUARTERLY INC.

WASHINGTON, D.C.

CQ Press
1255 22nd Street, NW, Suite 400
Washington, DC 20037

Phone: 202-729-1900; toll-free, 1-866-427-7737 (1-866-4CQ-PRESS)

Web: www.cqpress.com

Cover credit: Painting by Hossein Zenderoudi from *Hafez: Dance of Life* by Michael Boylan et al., copyright 1998, Mage Publishers, Washington, D.C.

Photo credits: 233, 261, 276, 298, 316, 324, 353, 359, 410, and 426 (AP/Wide World Photos); 395 (Reuters).

Separation and disengagement map on page 76 courtesy of the Foundation for Middle East Peace.

Major Middle Eastern oil fields and pipelines map on page 183 modified by International Mapping Associates based on source material courtesy of PennWell MAPSearch.

Cover design: Anne Masters Design
Composition: TechBooks
Indexer: Jan Williams
Proofreader: Inge Lockwood

♾ The paper used in this publication exceeds the requirements of the American National Standard for Information Sciences—Permanence of Paper for Printed Library Materials, ANSI Z39.48-1992.

Printed and bound in the United States of America

09 08 07 06 05   1 2 3 4 5

Library of Congress Cataloging-in-Publication Data

The Middle East / Congressional Quarterly, Inc.—10th ed.
     p.   cm.
  Includes bibliographical references and index.
  ISBN 1-933116-13-7 (hardcover : alk. paper) — ISBN 1-933116-14-5 (pbk. : alk. paper)
  1. Middle East—Politics and government—1979– I. Congressional Quarterly, Inc.

DS63.1.M484   2005
956.05—dc22
                                                    2005019604

CONTENTS

Visit www.cqpress.com/Middle-East-Supplements for biographical sketches of key figures in the Middle East and a collection of important historic documents about the region.

MAPS, BOXES, AND TABLES

CONTRIBUTORS

As'ad AbuKhalil prepared Chapter 2, "Arab-Israeli Conflict," and the country profile of Syria. He is a professor of political science at California State University, Stanislaus, and a visiting professor at the University of California, Berkeley.

Geoffrey Aronson prepared the country profile of Israel. He is director of research and publications at the Foundation for Middle East Peace in Washington, D.C.

Louay Bahry prepared the country profile of Kuwait. He is an adjunct scholar at the Middle East Institute in Washington, D.C., and adjunct professor of political science at the University of Tennessee, Knoxville. He has published extensively on the Middle East, particularly on Iraq and the Persian Gulf.

André Bank prepared the country profile of Jordan. He is a junior research fellow at the Center for Conflict Studies and a doctoral candidate in political science at the Philipps-Universität Marburg in Germany. He specializes in comparative politics, international relations, and political sociology of the Middle East, focusing on Iran, Iraq, Jordan, and Syria.

Michael Collins Dunn prepared the country profile of Egypt. He has been the editor of the *Middle East Journal* since 1998 and editor of *The Estimate* since 1989. He formerly taught at Georgetown University and Utah State Universities.

John L. Esposito prepared Chapter 6, "Fifteen Centuries of Islam." He is professor of Islamic studies and founding director of the Center for Muslim-Christian Understanding at Georgetown University.

Benedict FitzGerald prepared the country profile of Iran. He has been an observer of Iran for nearly forty years as a defense and intelligence official, contractor, and consultant.

Frederic C. Hof prepared the country profile of Lebanon. He is the chief executive officer of AALC, Ltd., an international business consulting firm based in Arlington, Virginia. He served formerly as a military attaché in the U.S. embassy in Beirut.

Benton Ives-Halperin prepared the chronology and the bibliography. He studied the Middle East at the University of Virginia and wrote about it while working at the *CQ Researcher*. He currently covers Congress for Congressional Quarterly.

David Mack prepared the country profile of Libya. He is vice president of the Middle East Institute in Washington, D.C., focusing on public policy and scholarly programs.

J. E. Peterson prepared Chapter 1, "Introduction"; Chapter 3, "U.S. Policy in the Middle East"; Chapter 4, "The Persian Gulf"; and the country profiles of Iraq and the Persian Gulf states. He is an independent historian and political analyst based in Tucson, Arizona, and has taught university courses on the Middle East. He also served in the Office of the Deputy Prime Minister for Security and Defense in the Sultanate of Oman.

David Wochner prepared Chapter 5, "Middle Eastern Oil and Gas," and the country profiles on Saudi Arabia and Yemen. He received a bachelor's degree with a certificate in Arab studies from Georgetown University's School of Foreign

Service and a law degree from the Georgetown University Law Center. He currently works in the energy practice at the law firm of Sutherland Asbill & Brennan in Washington, D.C.

The Middle East, tenth edition, was edited by CQ Press project editor Robin Surratt, who also assisted with research and writing. Olivia Rubenstein, a CQ Press intern through the Work Internship Program at the Field School in Washington, D.C., researched the key facts boxes for the country profiles. Sally Ryman handled production of the tenth edition. CQ Press would also like to acknowledge the work of those who contributed to the ninth edition of *The Middle East:* Joseph A. Davis, Daniel Diller, Max Gross, Mary King, Gretchen North, Andrew Parasiliti, Mark A. Schoeff Jr., and Mary Sebold.

PART ONE

OVERVIEW OF
THE MIDDLE EAST

Middle Eastern nations and their peoples are challenged and threatened on many fronts. Even as Israel and the Palestinians seemed again to be edging ever so slowly toward renewed peace-making efforts, the region remained one of the more potentially destabilizing parts of the world. Violence, poverty, and unresponsive governments tear at the fabric of Middle Eastern societies, but some find reason for cautious optimism in efforts to change old patterns and habits.

In 2003 a U.S.-led invasion relieved Iraqis of control by Saddam Hussein, who within a span of just ten years launched a deadly (and in the end pointless) war against Iran (in 1980) and then invaded and plundered the neighboring Arab nation of Kuwait (in 1990). Throughout his rule, Hussein heaped great hardships and sufferings upon the Iraqi people through wars, repression, and international sanctions imposed on their country as a result of his actions. The Iraqi elections in early 2005 and establishment of a government charged with drafting a constitution temporarily lifted spirits but did little to dispel the atmosphere of sectarian violence and frequent acts of terror by a persistent insurgency.

Iran just a quarter-century ago in 1979 experienced a true grassroots revolution that brought to power Islamists committed to delivering a new theological concept of governing to the world and who sometimes supported violence against individuals and governments in the name of revolution and Islam. In the two and a half decades since, the Iranian government has moderated somewhat. A number of its most zealous leaders have passed from the scene, and some new leaders appear to be attempting to move toward the mainstream of the international community, as they face significant economic problems that will require outside assistance and cooperation to resolve. Nevertheless, the limited success of the country's more liberal politicians caused some disappointment, and fears that Iran might be seeking to build nuclear weaponry rattled many. The struggle pitting Iran's hard-line religious leaders against the more moderate elements of the government remained unsettled in 2005.

The end of the al-Aqsa intifada and new leadership for the Palestinians created a sliver of hope in 2004–2005 that the fragile, decades-long peace process intended to mitigate and someday resolve the conflict between Israelis and Palestinians might be rejuvenated. Deep distrust, created by cycles of violence and dispossession, and divergent views on what a Palestinian state will entail meant that the conflict would continue to elude quick or easy resolution.

A Historically Important Region

The Middle East, situated at the crossroads of three continents, has been a rich and diverse region of enormous cultural significance throughout history. It has spawned three of the world's great religions—Christianity, Islam, and Judaism—and has provided many other contributions to civilization. In the twentieth century, the discovery of the world's largest petroleum deposits there made the Middle East vital to the

Defining the Middle East

No definitive definition exists for the term *Middle East,* as the region to which it refers is not a precisely defined area. In addition, one's location on Earth as well as issues of culture and ethnicity complicate determining the region's boundaries.

People around the world have various terms for what here is called the "Middle East." For example, some Europeans refer to it as the Near East. Indians of the subcontinent may call it Southwest Asia or West Asia. It all depends on where one stands.

The issues of culture and ethnicity further cloud the picture. If the Middle East is defined solely as the Arab states and Israel, Iran would be excluded. If it comprises Israel and the predominantly Muslim states in the area, then the North African states of Algeria, Libya, Morocco, and Tunisia, plus Afghanistan, Pakistan, the Sudan, and Turkey would have to be included.

In the academic community, the term *Middle East* refers to the Arab countries of North Africa, the Arab countries of Asia, Israel, the non-Arab countries of Iran and Turkey, and sometimes Afghanistan and Pakistan. According to some broader definitions, it also includes the Central Asian countries of Kazakhstan, Kyrgyzstan, Tajikistan, Turkmenistan, and Uzbekistan.

That said, this book focuses on those countries that Americans most often associate with the Middle East and that have had a continuing and central role in two issues of importance to U.S. foreign policy: the Arab-Israeli conflict and the security of the Persian Gulf and its oil resources. The nations covered here are Bahrain, Egypt, Iran, Iraq, Israel, Jordan, Kuwait, Lebanon, Libya, Oman, Qatar, Saudi Arabia, Syria, the United Arab Emirates, and Yemen.

This book examines a group of Middle Eastern nations and issues that for political, religious, and economic reasons hold particular significance for the United States and other Western and industrialized nations. *("Defining the Middle East," box, this page)*

Perhaps more than any other region, the Middle East has experienced conflicts that seem to defy solution. Disputes between Arabs and Israelis, Iranians and Iraqis, Kuwaitis and Iraqis, and other antagonists often extend beyond the immediate issues of territory or fears of political and economic intentions, tracing their roots to decades or centuries of mutual wariness and ethnic, religious, and cultural prejudices. Constructing long-term settlements requires not only carefully drawn compromises backed by international guarantees, but also fundamental changes in the attitudes of people and governments toward their enemies.

Many of today's Middle Eastern nations have histories dating to biblical times and beyond, but the modern history of the region can be traced to the breakup of the Ottoman Empire at the end of World War I and the subsequent responsibilities of oversight assumed by victorious Allies in the form of mandates. Post–World War I developments in the region reflected a continuation of centuries-old Western colonial expansion, though a number of today's Middle Eastern states were created during this postwar period. *(Map, p. 5)*

Even colonialism's demise in the wake of World War II, leaving behind the outlines and boundaries of today's nation-states, would contribute significantly to the region's conflicts. In addition to the increasing importance of the region—from the discovery of oil to the new geographical realities carved out of the Ottoman Empire—the proponents of the ideology of Zionism, with its roots in nineteenth-century Europe, would succeed in bringing about the creation of Israel, the dispossession of the Palestinian people, and the entrenchment of one of the twentieth century's most intractable conflicts.

international economy. Thus, what happens there affects not only the local peoples and nations, but the entire world. Because of the region's importance, during the cold war years it was often a pawn in the geopolitics of superpower conflict.

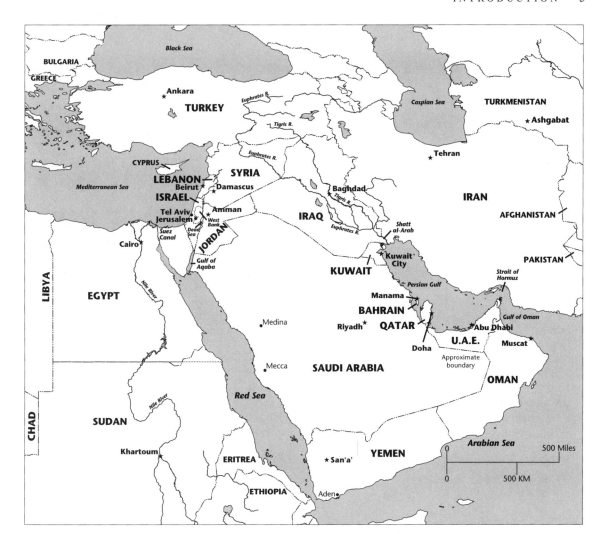

The Arab-Israeli Conflict

For half a century after the end of Word War II, Western eyes primarily viewed the Middle East as the area of the conflict between Israelis and Arabs. In more recent years, important events—including the emergence of a theocratic government in Iran and Iraq's attempt to conquer Kuwait—have added other perspectives to that view, but U.S. eyes, at least until the 2003 invasion of Iraq, usually returned reflexively to the "Arab-Israeli problem."

Israel and its Arab neighbors have fought five major wars and numerous smaller battles that exemplify the intractability of the conflict and that, at times, have threatened to involve the superpowers. *("Major Middle Eastern Wars," box, pp. 6–7)* With a complex mosaic of religion and history as backdrop, the fundamental nature of this conflict is easy to overlook: a modern struggle between two peoples making claims to the same piece of land—historic Palestine.

Key elements of the current map of the Middle East, as they apply to Israel and its immediate neighbors, date to the war fought three decades earlier, in June 1967. In that confrontation Israel captured land from Arab

Major Middle Eastern Wars

1948—First Arab-Israeli War. As Britain ends its mandate over Palestine, on May 14 Zionist leaders proclaim the state of Israel in the areas allotted to the Jews in the November 1947 UN partition plan for Palestine and other areas under Jewish control. The proclamation follows months of Jewish-Arab strife and attacks against one another and on the British. Full-scale war ensues when Egypt, Iraq, Lebanon, and Syria send forces into Palestine on May 15, as the British depart. In fighting that lasts into early 1949, Israeli forces defeat the Arab armies and take control of virtually all the territory allocated to the Jewish state in the UN partition as well as that designated to Palestinian Arabs.

1956—Suez War. Israel, in a secret agreement made with Britain and France, invades the Sinai Peninsula in an effort to topple Egyptian president Gamal Abdel Nasser, open the Israeli port of Eilat to maritime commerce, neutralize Palestinian guerrilla attacks from Gaza, and reassert European control over the Suez Canal, which Nasser had earlier nationalized. After issuing a transparent ultimatum for a cease-fire, withdrawal of forces, and British-French protection of the canal zone, Britain and France launch a coordinated attack against Egypt. Under strong U.S. and UN pressure, the British and French evacuate the area, and Israel and Egypt retreat to previous positions.

1967—June War/Six-Day War. Israel attacks Egypt, Iraq, Jordan, and Syria, capturing Syria's Golan, the Jordanian-controlled West Bank (including East Jerusalem), the Egyptian-administered Gaza Strip, and Egypt's Sinai Peninsula. Israel begins colonizing the captured territories through the establishment of Jewish settlements.

1973—October War/Yom Kippur War. In coordinated surprise attacks, Egypt and Syria overrun Israeli positions in the Sinai and Golan. Israeli forces regroup and regain lost territory after the United States launches a massive resupply of materiel. Although they were ultimately unsuccessful from a military standpoint, the Egyptian and Syrian forces performed respectably enough against the Israelis, laying the groundwork for later peace initiatives.

1975—Lebanese Civil War. Fighting erupts among militia groups for and against the Palestinian cause after the Maronite-led Lebanese government is paralyzed by disagreement over what to do about the activities of the Palestine Liberation Organization in Lebanon. In an attempt to restore order in 1976, Syrian president Hafiz al-Asad—apparently worried that a PLO victory would bring Israel

countries that it still largely occupied in 2005, including Gaza, the Golan, and, most important, the West Bank, including East Jerusalem. In the nearly forty years since the 1967 war, the Arab states have consistently insisted that Israel withdraw from these occupied lands and recognize the right of the Palestinians to statehood. Israel has just as adamantly insisted that these lands are essential to its existence and cannot be readily relinquished without a broad and permanent resolution of its security concerns. The more than 200,000 Israeli settlers on the West Bank—out of some 400,000 total settlers—further complicate the issue, as do assertions by some that the occupied lands must be retained on religious grounds.

After years of fruitless negotiations and intermittent warfare, diplomatic successes in the early 1990s began to transform the Arab-Israeli conflict. Saddam Hussein's use of the conflict to rally support during Iraq's occupation of Kuwait and the Palestinian intifada prompted the United States, with assistance from the Soviet Union, to push Arab states and Israel to meet face to face at the Madrid conference in October 1991. The parties continued discussions began at Madrid in a series of multilateral and bilateral dialogues. On September 13, 1993, PLO chairman Yasir Arafat and Israeli prime minister Yitzhak Rabin stunned the world when they shook hands at a White House ceremony marking their mutual recognition and the beginning of the so-called Oslo era.

directly into the Lebanese conflict—deploys army units to Lebanon at the request of the Maronite government. The combination of economic, sectarian, and political issues fuels violence until a 1990 Saudi-brokered reconstitution of the Lebanese government.

1980—Iran-Iraq War. Iraq, sensing Iran in a state of postrevolutionary turmoil, launches an attack against it in an effort to alter the demarcation of their border along the Shatt al-Arab waterway and to prevent the spread of Iran's Islamic revolution. In spite of initial Iraqi military successes, the war settles into an eight-year stalemate. In 1988, with Iraqi forces poised to overrun Iranian troops on the border, Iran accepts a UN-brokered cease-fire, to which Iraq also agrees.

1982—Israeli Invasion of Lebanon. Israel invades Lebanon, asserting the need to clear PLO forces from an area north of the Lebanese border. As the campaign continues, however, other Israeli goals become evident. Although the invasion appears successful initially, it ultimately fails to secure Israeli objectives: the PLO is driven from Beirut and other parts of Lebanon (but later reemerges); Bashir Gemayel, Israel's preferred candidate for Lebanese president, is elected (but then assassinated); an accord is reached with the Lebanese government (but is later abrogated). Israeli forces withdraw from most of the country but continue to occupy a ten-kilometer self-declared "security zone" on Lebanese territory. The occupation mires Israel in an eighteen-year guerrilla war with Shiite forces in south Lebanon.

1990—Persian Gulf War. Desperately in need of financial assistance after an eight-year war with Iran, Iraq invades and occupies the much wealthier Kuwait. An international coalition, led by the United States and including a number of Arab nations, launches an air- and sea-based counterattack in January 1991. In February, coalition ground forces drive the Iraqi army from Kuwait and penetrate deep into Iraqi territory before a cease-fire takes effect.

2003—Iraq War. The administration of George W. Bush, claiming that Iraqi president Saddam Hussein is developing and hiding weapons of mass destruction and supporting terrorism, threatens to attack Iraq. In March 2003, supported by Britain and a number of other countries, the United States invades Iraq despite widespread opposition and a failure to obtain an authorizing resolution from the United Nations Security Council. Coalition ground forces gain control of the country within a month of the initial air campaign, capture Hussein in December, and set up a governing authority to run the country. A determined insurgency takes shape, and ethnic and religious tensions rise, challenging the effectiveness of the government and the U.S.-led military presence.

That day, they signed a Declaration of Principles, establishing a framework for the Israeli transfer of most of Gaza and the West Bank city of Jericho to the control of the Palestinian Authority, the newly created entity through which the Palestinians would govern territories handed over by Israel. In June 1994, Arafat returned to the occupied territories for the first time in twenty-seven years.

Palestinian recognition of Israel opened the door for other Arabs to possibly establish relations with Israel. On July 25, 1994, King Hussein of Jordan and Prime Minister Rabin signed the Washington Declaration, ending the forty-six-year state of belligerence between their nations. On October 26, they signed a formal peace treaty on their border with U.S. president Bill Clinton in attendance. The rest of the 1990s did not, however, bear witness to similar progress. In fact, movement toward a permanent peace at times ground to a halt. The Israelis and Syrians failed to codify progress on the return of the Golan to Syria. Israel continued to occupy part of southern Lebanon in an effort to secure its northern border. The conservative Israeli administration of Benjamin Netanyahu moved forward aggressively with new settlement construction in the West Bank while virtually ignoring the agreements of previous Israeli governments to transfer more land to the Palestinians.

Under U.S. pressure, partly brought to bear in a meeting of Palestinian and Israeli officials convened by President Clinton at the Wye River Plantation in rural Maryland, the parties laid a foundation for getting the peace process back on track and for Israel and the PLO to fulfill already agreed upon provisions of their agreements. Although Netanyahu signed off on the Wye River Memorandum, he later reneged on it. His successor, Ehud Barak, elected in May 1999, pledged to implement the accord. In September 1999, Barak formalized this pledge in agreements signed with the PLO in Sharm al-Shaykh, Egypt. He also managed in May 2000 to extract Israeli forces from southern Lebanon.

Even as Israel's position had grown stronger because of the collapse of the Soviet Union and the decimation of Iraq's military power in 1991, its internal situation had dictated its move toward peace early in the 1990s. The Palestinian intifada, which began in late 1987 and lasted several years, took an economic and moral toll on Israelis, convincing an increasing number of them that Israel might not possess the resources to control the occupied territories permanently. In addition, the financial costs and social upheaval of the immigration and integration of hundreds of thousands of Soviet Jews made peace more urgent. The new wave of immigration was, at the same time, ironically an important factor behind the growth of settlements in the West Bank, which hindered accommodation. Israel also increasingly confronted the challenge of striking a balance between the sometimes conflicting objectives of being a Jewish state and a modern democratic nation, an issue that will continue to have some bearing on its approach to relations with the Palestinians.

A July 2000 Israeli-Palestinian summit at Camp David ended without an agreement. Two months later, Israeli hardliner Ariel Sharon inflamed Palestinian passions by making a provocative visit to Islamic holy sites in Jerusalem. Sharon's action converged with Palestinian frustration at the lack of improvement in their lives and the continued growth of the settler population under Oslo to spark the al-Aqsa intifada. Further attempts to craft the details of final status issues died as violence increased and Barak lost to Sharon in elections held in February 2001. The failure to achieve a breakthrough in Palestinian-Israeli negotiations

and the subsequent violence led to obituaries for the Oslo process.

The second Palestinian uprising was characterized by its violence, particularly that of the Islamist groups Hamas and Islamic Jihad, which carried out a series of attacks inside Israel, and of the Israeli military. Although armed wings of Palestinian organizations targeted some military installations and soldiers, their suicide bombings of buses, cafes, and other civilian targets for a time became a refrain in the rebellion. Israel responded with massive military incursions into the West Bank and Gaza, taking control of towns and cities, confining Arafat in his Ramallah headquarters after destroying most of it, assassinating actual and suspected Islamist leaders and killing scores of innocent civilians in the process, replacing Palestinian workers in Israel, and building a concrete barrier around and on confiscated territory in the West Bank to prevent Palestinians from entering Israel.

By early 2005, if not earlier, the intifada had become counterproductive: Israeli popular attitudes had hardened, and Palestinians had lost at least three times the number of lives as Israelis and seen their standard of living plummet drastically. The death of Arafat in November 2004 and his replacement by Abbas seemed to herald an opportunity for renewed negotiation, particularly as Abbas worked to persuade Hamas and Islamic Jihad (as well as the Tanzim and al-Aqsa Martyrs Brigades) to end their suicide bombings and as Sharon announced plans to evacuate Israeli settlers and the military from Gaza.

The Persian Gulf

In 1979 the Iranian Revolution drove from power Shah Mohammad Reza Pahlavi, in whom the United States had invested heavily as a defense against Soviet expansion. The revolution brought to power a regime antagonistic not only to the United States, but to Western secular democracy in general. The U.S. embassy hostage crisis in which fifty-two American diplomats were held captive for 444 days in Tehran, the oil price increases resulting from the revolution's turmoil and ideology, and the Soviet decision to invade Afghanistan while the world was distracted converged to focus attention on the Persian Gulf as never before. During the 1980s, the protracted Iran-Iraq War underscored the Gulf's volatility as well as its strategic and economic importance. Touched off in September 1980 by Iraq's invasion of Iran, the eight-year conflict threatened the flow of oil throughout the Gulf and ultimately led to the United States and other countries outside the region acting to protect the world's oil supply.

In 1988 the United Nations brokered a tense peace between Iran and Iraq, but two years later, in August 1990, Iraq again engulfed the region in war when it invaded and occupied wealthy and oil-rich Kuwait. A long-feared international economic nightmare threatened to become reality: a belligerent military power appeared to be in a position to dominate the oil reserves of the Persian Gulf.

Although Iraqi president Saddam Hussein employed pan-Arabist rhetoric to justify the invasion of Kuwait, most Arab countries, including Egypt, Saudi Arabia, and Syria, saw it as naked aggression against a fellow Arab state. The Gulf oil-producing states, in particular, feared that if Hussein were left unchecked, he would eventually move against them. In early 1991, a UN-backed, U.S.-led international coalition operating out of Saudi Arabia drove Iraqi forces from Kuwait.

The coalition destroyed much of Iraq's military might, humbling what was reputed to be the fourth-largest army in the world. The totality of the Iraqi defeat largely undercut Hussein's appeal as an Arab champion willing to defy the West. Although severely weakened, Hussein would cling tenaciously to power despite rebellions among the Kurds in northern Iraq and Shiites in the south and twelve years of international sanctions.

Following the 1991 war, the coalition that defeated Iraq attempted to carry out arms inspections, as provided in UN resolutions, to see that Iraq eliminated its weapons of mass destruction. Primarily as a result of Iraqi noncooperation, this effort failed and ultimately led to the withdrawal of UN inspection teams. That was followed in turn by the continuing, if low-profile, campaign—largely by the

United States—of bombing Iraqi targets for violations in the "no-fly" zones set up to protect Kurds and Shiites. By 1999 some nations in the coalition had tired of the aerial campaign and the sanctions, believing that they were not accomplishing their goals and that Iraqis, particularly children, were suffering terribly from the lack of food, medicine, and other necessities as the result of sanctions.

Al-Qaida's attacks of September 2001 dramatically changed American perceptions of the Middle Eastern and Islamic worlds and prompted a U.S. assault on Afghanistan, whose Taliban government had provided refuge to al-Qaida. The U.S. attack swept the Taliban from power and put al-Qaida leaders—including Osama bin Ladin—on the run. Hamid Karzai headed a new Afghan government, but hostilities continued into 2005, and the writ of the central government barely extended beyond a few principal cities.

Though Iraq was not involved in the September 11 attack, the administration of George W. Bush implied that it was and used the attack, along with other issues, in a campaign to drum up support for an invasion to overthrow the government of Saddam Hussein. After toppling Hussein, coalition forces—comprised principally of U.S. and British detachments, as well as others from several dozen countries—appear headed for a prolonged occupation of the country. In summer 2004, a provisional governing authority handed control to an interim government, which was replaced in 2005 by an elected government, but several hundred thousand coalition troops remained in Iraq to battle continuing resistance. The "insurgents," as the occupying forces called these fighters, seemed to be composed of Hussein's diehard followers, Iraqi nationalists, criminal elements, and Islamist extremists inspired to travel to Iraq to drive out the Westerners, as they had done to the Soviets in Afghanistan two decades earlier.

Iraqi Shiites, the majority of the population, dominated the elections held in 2005 and as a result formed a new government, which also included Kurds in leadership positions. The government faced the daunting task of convincing the Sunni Arab population of central Iraq, who had dominated previous Iraqi governments, to participate and thereby avoid a sectarian civil war.

Iran meanwhile experienced a slow evolution from the strident rhetoric of the early revolutionary years. The United States, along with other countries, however, still considered Iran in the early 2000s a supporter of international terrorism that should remain outside the community of nations. Although Iranians elected a moderate, Mohammad Khatami, as president in 1997, the conservative religious establishment that parallels the government remained opposed to many of his policies, highlighting the political and social tensions at work in Iran.

The Khatami government faced the challenge of reinvigorating a struggling economy and overcoming the country's lingering isolation. Khatami's election initially boosted the morale of many Iranians and gave them a sense of participating in the government. Under Khatami, Iran took some steps toward becoming a more democratic and tolerant society and resolving conflicts with other nations, including the United States. This movement slowed, however, as Khatami and fellow reformists seemed to lose ground to the renewed energy of the country's hardliners.

Elsewhere in the Gulf, memories of the Iraqi invasion of Kuwait reminded Saudi Arabia and its fellow members of the Gulf Cooperation Council that they continued to need U.S. protection despite disagreements with U.S. policies toward Israel and Iraq. The involvement of Saudi citizens in al-Qaida and the September 11 attacks created tensions in U.S.-Saudi relations but could not break the economic and political bonds between Washington and Riyadh. Just as Saudi Arabia's leaders remained dependent on U.S. support, the United States found itself increasingly dependent on Saudi Arabian oil, particularly as petroleum prices reached record levels in nominal terms during 2004 and 2005.

Outlook

The twentieth century concluded with the Middle East a marginally more stable region than at any time in the half-century since the creation of Israel plunged it into a series of costly wars. The early years of the twenty-first century produced forces and events that altered that status and will significantly have a hand in determining the region's future for years to come.

Saddam Hussein's Iraq was replaced by a fragile country under occupation and beset by violence. Iran's road to moderation appeared at least temporarily blocked, not least because of indications that the government sought to acquire a capability for nuclear weapons. The events of September 11 cast a dark shadow over the region, as extremist Islamists carried out attacks in Egypt, Iraq, Kuwait, Qatar, and Saudi Arabia. The peace process between Israel and the Palestinians, although again suffused with slight optimism in 2005, remained troubled by the deep roots of the conflict and the often fundamentally opposed objectives of the two sides. The best prognosis is that it will take years and probably decades before relations between Israel and the Arab states can be governed by mutual trust and concord. The peace process, as shown so often in the past, however, has assumed a life of its own, at least in part because all sides can see the even darker consequences of a lack of one.

Political reform and the adoption of conditions necessary for economic growth are two critical issues confronting the nations of the area. The Middle East remains the least democratized region in the world. Iran and most Arab countries are saddled with stagnant economies, while populations have mushroomed. Only the upward sweep of oil prices has rescued most Gulf states from persistent budget deficits.

While a number of faces familiar for the last twenty years continue to occupy positions of authority, a transfer of power has clearly begun to a new and younger generation. Jordan is notable in this respect, as the long-reigning and influential monarch King Hussein died of cancer in early 1999, transferring power to his thirty-seven-year-old son Abdallah II. Although young and untested in the treacherous waters of Middle Eastern politics, Abdallah moved quickly to establish ties with the Jordanian people and to reach out to contemporaries of his age in the area. Iran, too, experienced a similar evolution in leadership, though a lesser generational change, in its selection of Khatami as president.

Longtime Syrian president Hafiz al-Asad passed away in 2000 and was replaced by Bashar al-Asad, the first son to succeed his father in the "hereditary republics" of the Arab world. In the case of Syria, the son is considered to be weaker than the father. While Bashar al-Asad maintained most of the elder Asad's policies, he also enacted economic reforms and allowed space for greater political expression, within limits. The Syrian military's withdrawal from Lebanon took many by surprise, coming as it did only months after the assassination of former Lebanese prime minister Rafiq al-Hariri generated Lebanese and international pressure to do so.

In Egypt, Hosni Mubarak seemed to be grooming his son to succeed him, and in Yemen, Ali Abdallah Salih appeared to have the same intention. The situation in Saudi Arabia differs, because the existing leadership and almost all its possible replacements are well advanced in years. The normal transfer of power in Saudi Arabia would lead to a series of octogenarian kings, but at some point succession must move on to the next generation. Younger leaders in Bahrain and Qatar have already demonstrated their willingness to chart new political paths.

About This Book

Readers of *The Middle East,* tenth edition, will find in thematic chapters and country profiles a more detailed examination of the events and issues summarized above. This revision also explores the issues of security concerns, weapons of mass destruction and arms transfers, democratization efforts, and more.

Chapter two examines the Arab-Israeli conflict, providing a historical perspective of events in mandate Palestine and the nascent stages of the ensuing conflict. It discusses the creation of Israel and the ramifications for the Palestinians and the Arab states, along with Arab-Israeli and inter-Arab relations. The chapter details the wars fought between Arabs and Israelis, Palestinian responses to life under Israeli occupation after the 1967 war (including the two uprisings), and the course of attempts at peace over the years.

Chapter three reviews U.S. policy toward the Middle East, beginning with the administration of Woodrow Wilson at the end of World War I but focusing primarily on policy evolution after 1945, including changes stemming from the al-Qaida attacks of September 2001. Chapter four provides a detailed look at the Persian Gulf, with special attention paid to Iraq and Iran, the Iraqi invasion of Kuwait, the "war on terror," the overthrow of Iraqi president Saddam Hussein, and the fallout of these momentous events.

Chapter five discusses the role of oil and gas in the modern industrial world, with a focus on the influence of petroleum in the politics of the Middle East and the impact of increased global demand for these natural resources. Chapter six examines the origins of Islam, the tenets and branches of the faith, and its modern politicization.

Twelve country profiles follow these chapters and examine the history, geography, population, economy, and politics of each state. The back of the book includes a brief chronology featuring the major events between 1900 and 1944 and a more detailed chronology covering the period 1945 to 2005. A bibliography provides guidance on further reading, and a detailed index concludes the volume.

Readers can access thumbnail biographical sketches of leaders and other influential figures as well as documents pertaining to the Middle East at www.cqpress.com/Middle-East-Supplements.

CHAPTER **2**

ARAB-ISRAELI CONFLICT

P resentations of the Arab-Israeli conflict in the West have often stressed elements of ancient history and religion, but to truly grasp the situation one must discard the misperception that it is a religious conflict. Even Jimmy Carter, who devoted more time and effort than any other U.S. president to learning about this highly charged issue, portrays the conflict as the product of blood feuds and biblically induced tensions in *The Blood of Abraham.* In reality, however, this is a modern politico-national struggle between two peoples making claims to the same piece of land. That the land is holy for Jews, Christians, and Muslims alike only adds another dimension to the conflict. To discuss analytically and academically the Arab-Israeli conflict is no easy task, because people bring to the discussion a host of emotions and biases. Although this is a protracted conflict between two antagonistic nationalisms, both have resorted to religious imagery and historical motifs, and both are certain of the absolute validity of their claims.

The Arab-Israeli conflict has attracted worldwide attention because it centers on the Holy Land and because the founding of Israel is closely tied in public perception to the horrific images of the Holocaust and today increasingly to biblical prophecy . Many of the new citizens of the State of Israel were, in fact, survivors or relatives of survivors of the Holocaust. Support for Israel was and remains for peoples and governments in the West a logical step in eradicating Nazi crimes. The Palestinians, however, do not feel that they

should pay the price for a crime that they did not commit. Other Arabs agree with this position. The Palestinians eventually succeeded in attracting the world's attention to their situation through the use of political violence and since the 1970s and 1980s through diplomacy as well. A fair assessment of the Palestinian-Israeli conflict must note that both sides in the conflict have mastered the art of political violence. At the epicenter of the conflict, the Israelis as well as the Palestinians have engaged in political violence, or terrorism—their violence, often aimless and indiscriminate, demonstrating total disregard for the plight of civilians—although many in the West tend to associate terrorism only with the Arab side, perhaps because to them state violence, in this case Israel's, carries more legitimacy than violence by individuals and groups.

For more than forty years, the conflict between Israel and its Arab neighbors, and the conflict between Zionism and Palestinian Arab nationalism, remained one of the world's most dangerous and intractable confrontations, steadfastly refusing to confine itself to the Middle East. During the cold war, the Arab-Israeli conflict became an item on the agenda of superpower summits, and the Arabs and Israelis learned how to manipulate the United States and Soviet Union to their own ends. Similarly, the two superpowers manipulated the Arabs and Israelis to further their own global interests. The Arab-Israeli wars of the past often drew international intervention and brought the two superpowers to the brink of direct nuclear confrontation at least once during the war in October 1973, when President Richard Nixon, worried about possible Soviet intervention, put U.S. forces on worldwide alert.

Two events—the initiation of negotiations between Israel and its Arab neighbors in Madrid, Spain, in October 1991 and the agreement between Israel and the Palestine Liberation Organization (PLO) signed in Washington on September 13, 1993—shattered some long-held assumptions about the conflict. Like the surprise decision of Egyptian president Anwar al-Sadat to visit Jerusalem in November 1977 and the resulting Camp David process, these events signified the weak state of official Arab ranks vis-à-vis Israel, which has held the best cards during most of the conflict's history. To be sure, some people saw in the ceremonial handshake between PLO chairman Yasir Arafat and Israeli prime minister Yitzhak Rabin an end to the Arab-Israeli conflict. Those who prematurely predicted Arab-Israeli harmony were, however, surprised by the depth to which the roots of the conflict sank. All have since learned that it will take much more than photo ops to resolve this confrontation now on the verge of entering its second century.

Some type of diplomatic negotiation or peace initiative aimed at an Arab-Israeli settlement has existed, at least in theory, since the June 1967 War. Outbreaks of full-scale war, acts of terrorism, pre-emptive and retaliatory raids—both sides often justify their violence by insisting that they are merely "retaliating" for the acts of violence by the other side—civil strife, hostile propaganda, refusal to compromise, and unceasing mutual recriminations have served to make progress seemingly unsustainable.

Now that some substantial, long-maintained barriers to negotiations have been removed, an active peace process is likely to remain prominent, albeit often irrelevant as long as crucial facets of the conflict remain unaddressed and as long as Israel continues to take full advantage of its substantially superior politico-military status. Setbacks in this process are inevitable, as parties on both sides can be expected to resist compromises

and pursue maximalist solutions. As the history of this conflict has taught, optimistic outlooks are often frustrated by facts on the ground.

The Arab-Israeli conflict has uniquely haunted and frustrated successive U.S. administrations and will continue to do so into the immediate future. Some have come to power with the intent of ignoring the conflict—because its resolution has defied every U.S. peace initiative since the days of Richard Nixon (if not earlier, when John F. Kenney briefly dabbled in it)—yet violence ultimately forces their hand. The administration of George W. Bush did not originally consider the conflict a high priority, believing that the Clinton administration's intense attention to it had damaged U.S. credibility and wasted political capital by deeply involving the president in Palestinian-Israeli negotiations that ended without a settlement. Yet European pressure, UN urging, and violence resulted in the Bush administration assuming a more active role in the dispute than it would have liked. The origins of the conflict offer insight into the difficulties of addressing the situation today.

Origins of the Conflict

The modern Middle East is the inheritor of five thousand years of history. The ancient connection of the people of Israel to the land of Palestine is an integral part of this story, as is the connection to the same piece of land of the Palestinians, who trace their origins to the ancient Canaanites. The Roman destruction of the Second Temple in Jerusalem in 70 C.E. and the forced dispersal of the Jews from Palestine left the Jewish people scattered around the world. Although large numbers of Jews assimilated into the many countries of their diaspora, with many of them becoming integral members of European and other societies, for nearly two thousand years a significant number of religious Jews retained their Jewish identity and each year concluded Passover ceremonies with the prayer "Next year in Jerusalem." The prophetic concept of an eventual ingathering of the Jewish exiles into the land of their origin has for centuries

Zionism and Jewish Settlement of Palestine

Like the United States, Israel is a country founded and built by immigrants from many different ethnic and cultural backgrounds, but unlike the United States, immigrants to Israel share a common religious background. Israel has encouraged this "ingathering" of Jews from all parts of the world, counting on their common Jewish heritage to help cement their union—a task that has presented many difficulties. Bringing Jews together is the essence of Zionism, which could be called the "founding religion" of Israel.

Zionism emerged from the ferment of nationalist, socialist, populist, and utopian ideas inflaming Europe in the nineteenth century. As nationalists, the Jews were not unlike other minority groups chafing from discrimination within the Russian and Austro-Hungarian empires and beyond. Anti-Semitic persecutions, however, added a special impetus for the Jews to foster a political national movement. Anti-Semitism had afflicted enlightened and less-enlightened societies throughout Europe for centuries, often blessed (if not created and promoted) by the Church.

The Earliest Settlements

The first Jewish settlements in Palestine arose through the efforts of Jews who in 1882 formed an organization called Lovers of Zion. (Zion is the hill in Jerusalem on which King David's palace is said to have stood.) They conceived the idea of sending groups of colonists to Palestine to establish Jewish communities in their ancestral land, then a neglected but inhabited part of the Ottoman Empire. The Zionist movement, however, got its start when Theodor Herzl, a Viennese journalist, wrote *Der Judenstaat* (The Jewish state), the rationale for the creation of a Jewish state. Later, in 1897, Herzl founded the movement as it exists today. "I imagine that the Jews will always have sufficient enemies, just as every other nation," Herzl wrote. "But once settled in their own land, they can never again be scattered all over the world." Such a strong nationalist movement, born in response to the hatefulness of anti-Semitism, ironically proceeded to ignore the rights and existence of another people—the Arab population of Palestine. The poverty of the Palestinian Arabs, and the fragmented structure of their leadership, facilitated the Zionists' endeavors.

At the turn of the twentieth century, Palestine had a Jewish population of about 25,000 people, mostly descendants of refugees from the Spanish Inquisition and pious pilgrims to the Holy Land. They were poor, religious, and lived lives separate from the largely Arab Muslim population of some 600,000. Some resident Jews looked with hostility upon the new arrivals, whom they considered dangerous, radical elements and religious renegades. Despite Palestine's unpromising conditions and difficult climate, a succession of immigrants succeeded over the next few decades in founding several dozen communities.

Jewish settlement of Palestine proceeded in waves of immigration, known by the Hebrew word *aliyah,* meaning ascension (to Zion). The first aliyah, from 1882 to 1903, brought in some 25,000 to 30,000 Jews. The second aliyah, from 1905 to 1914, which led to 35,000 to 40,000 Jews arriving in Palestine, set the tone for the future state of Israel. Wrote Judah Matras in the *Integration and Development in Israel,* this wave of immigrants became "the political, social, economic, and ideological backbone of the Jewish community in Palestine, and large sectors of life in Israel . . . are organized around institutions created by immigrants arriving in the second aliyah." Indeed, this wave produced the first leaders of independent Israel, among them David Ben-Gurion and Isaac Ben-Zvi, later prime minister and president, respectively.

The members of the second aliyah were mainly Jews in their late teens and early twenties, burning to create a Jewish utopia. They believed that only through socialism could a society be created free of the evils of materialism, exploitation, and the aberrations that produced anti-Semitism. These immigrants were driven by an intense devotion to their cause. Working the soil for them represented not merely a pioneering necessity, but also a sacred mission. They combined Jewish traditions with contemporary social and political movements in developing ideologies and principles for the institutions of the society they set out to create.

Second aliyah immigrants started the kibbutzim, the collective farms that gripped the Jewish consciousness. They founded the first kibbutz, Degania, in 1910 on swampland near Lake Tiberias (Sea of Galilee); it was the cheapest land available. Soon thereafter more agricultural collectives sprouted. Although the kibbutzim never attracted more than 10 to 12 percent of the Jewish population of Palestine, they created, in Zionist mythology, the ideal of the tough, vital, selflessly dedicated Jewish farmer-soldier and patriot. The kibbutz would produce a number of Israel's governing elite and many of its best soldiers.

The World Wars and Nazi Persecution

World War I brought Jewish immigration to Palestine to a halt. Furthermore, the Ottoman government, which sided with the Central Powers, expelled scores of Jews who had come to Palestine from Allied nations. Other Jews left voluntarily because of deteriorating economic conditions. During World War I, the Jewish population of Palestine dropped from some 85,000 people to 56,000. After the war, however, the third aliyah began, encouraged by the Balfour Declaration, issued on November 2, 1917, in which the British government expressed sympathy for the Jewish goal of establishing a homeland in Palestine, as long as it did not prejudice the rights of the "non-Jewish community."

Britain in 1917 was the occupying power in Palestine and from 1920 to 1948 ruled the region under a League of Nations mandate that incorporated the Balfour Declaration in its preamble. Historians debate the reasons or motives for the declaration, but it is certain that the British felt more sympathy for the Jewish national cause than for the Arabs; they also likely thought that supporting the Zionists might benefit their imperial interests. Zionism was largely a European movement with which the Western world could easily identify. Furthermore, some anti-Semites in Britain were all too eager to support a cause that would reduce the number of Jews in their midst.

Between 1919 and 1923, the third aliyah brought 35,000 Jews to Palestine. This group was composed primarily of Russians, whose motives were a combination of insecurity and fear. The fourth aliyah, from 1924 to 1931, brought in some 82,000 immigrants, mainly middle-class Jews from Poland. An economic depression, combined with anti-Semitism, had led to economic, social, and political sanctions against the Jews there. The passage of legislation in the United States restricting immigration from Eastern Europe also played a role in Jews choosing to settle in Palestine.

The fifth aliyah, from 1932 to 1938, brought 217,000 Jews to the Holy Land. The rise of Nazism in Germany and its expansionist moves into Central Europe occasioned the first sizable influx of immigrants from Austria and Germany, as well as from Czechoslovakia, Greece, and Hungary. The Nazi threat also accounted in large part for a renewed flow of immigrants, totaling 91,000 Jews, from Poland. Unlike the earlier settlers, who were young, unattached, and eager to work the soil, the aliyah of the 1930s included large numbers of stable middle-class families headed by men who had made their mark in business and the professions.

Throughout the period of Jewish settlement, large numbers of immigrants decided not to stay on in Palestine. Nevertheless, by the end of 1938 the Jewish population had reached 413,000. The Palestinian Arabs protested the influx, and the British government eventually responded by reducing immigration quotas and restricting Jewish land purchases. This policy, set forth in a British government white paper on May 17, 1939, remained in force throughout World War II. Regardless, 75,000 Jews entered Palestine during the war years, 29,000 of them illegally. By the end of the war in 1945, the Jewish population of Palestine stood at 564,000.

The next wave of immigration drew mainly from the 200,000 homeless Jews—from Germany, Poland, and Russia—living in so-called displaced persons camps after World War II. During the years 1946 to 1948, some 61,000 Jews arrived in Palestine, nearly half of them slipping through a blockade the British had imposed to halt further immigration. The ban drew protests from a world stunned by the revelations of Hitler's death camps, and it provided an additional ingredient fueling a three-sided civil war that developed among the Jews, the British, and the Palestinian Arabs.

A hard-pressed and exasperated Britain notified the United Nations in 1947 that it could no longer continue its role in Palestine and planned to withdraw its forces. With the end of the British mandate, Jews in Palestine, despite protests by the Palestinians, declared the State of Israel in May 1948. Within three years, Israel's population doubled to 1.4 million, 75 percent of it foreign born.

influenced the beliefs and expectations of many Jews and Christians in the West.

Zionism, the political movement among European Jewry that led to increased Jewish immigration to Palestine and ultimately to the establishment of Israel in 1948, traces its roots to the social and political milieu of nineteenth-century Europe. The growth across Europe, and ultimately throughout the world, of the idea of nationalism as an ideological basis for political organization caused many to ponder the ultimate meaning of Jewish identity in an age of emerging nation-states. The anti-Semitism found throughout most of Europe—especially in Russia and the Pale of Settlement but also in liberal France, where Zionist founder Theodor Herzl worked as a correspondent—culminated in the Holocaust during World War II and finally led most Jews and a great many others in the West to look favorably upon the idea of an independent Jewish state in Palestine. More than half a million Jews had established themselves there by the end of the war. The plight of the existing inhabitants, Palestinian Arabs, was not on the agenda of the Western powers or that of Zionist leaders. Rather, they viewed this largely peasant society with indifference or contempt, which allowed Zionist leaders, in the words of Israel Zangwill, to declare Palestine "a land without a people for a people without a land."

Establishing a Jewish state in Palestine was not, however, a simple matter. Much had happened there during the nearly two thousand years of the Jewish diaspora. Since the rise of Islam in the seventh century, the Middle East had become largely an Arab-Islamic region, and the inhabitants of the Arabian Peninsula, Egypt, Iraq, Palestine, and Syria were now nearly all Arabs or Arabized peoples. Islam, which shares similarities with Judaism and Christianity, also had laid claim to Jerusalem as one of its holy cities: Jerusalem is the site of the Prophet Muhammad's nocturnal journey, a miraculous event according to which Muhammad ascended into heaven.

As Muslims, most Arabs believed that the Jews—as a "people of the book," that is, having received a divine scripture like Christians and Muslims had—should be free to live peaceably in Arab areas so long as they recognized Arab-Islamic political sovereignty. The Arabs, however, did not believe that Jews had a right to an independent state of their own on an already inhabited land that was now part of the Arab-Islamic world. Thus, the Zionist movement from its inception faced general opposition in the Middle East, not only from the Arab inhabitants of Palestine, who were Muslims and Christians, but also from the larger Arab world of which Palestine was considered a part. Their opposition was not directed at the Zionists as Jews, but at the implications of their political project.

The Arabs of Palestine were, however, ill equipped to meet the challenge posed by the Zionist movement. For four centuries, beginning in 1516, the Ottoman Empire controlled Palestine and neighboring areas. Ottoman rule, although Islamic in character, was fundamentally oppressive and aimed at extracting as much wealth as possible from an increasingly impoverished Arab peasantry. As the twentieth century began, Palestinian Arab society, like most Arab societies, was seriously underdeveloped. Moreover, long centuries of relatively oppressive foreign rule had fragmented the Palestinian Arabs politically and promoted the rule of an elite group of notables at the expense of the larger populace. As a result, the Palestinians had only a weak tradition of independent political organization, although Palestinian nationhood existed in various forms, as Rashid Khalidi shows in *Palestinian Identity: The Construction of Modern National Consciousness.* Thus, despite being greatly disturbed by the Zionist movement and its possible implications, the Palestinians lacked salient political institutions or military organizations through which to secure their rights and interests. Even if they had developed such effective institutions and organizations, it is highly unlikely that after World War II they would have been able to hold their own in the face of Western resolve fueled by concerns and aspirations that conflicted with those of the Palestinians.

In the early part of the twentieth century, European powers had competed for influence and

Palestine and Its Inhabitants

Palestinian national identity characterizes the Palestinian Arab people as Zionism characterizes the Jewish population of Israel. The Palestinians and the Jews both faced existential threats and responded by forming strong national movements to represent their aspirations as a people, and in the case of the Jews, to find a haven from historical persecution and oppression. Just as Jews developed Zionism, or Jewish nationalism, in response to anti-Semitism, the Palestinian Arab people developed and promoted Palestinian nationalism partly in response to the Zionist threat to their patrimony, although forms of Palestinian nationalism existed before the advent of Zionism. The differing aspirations of these two movements form the core of the Arab-Israeli conflict.

For Palestinian Arabs, "Palestine" today refers to the would-be state that the Palestine Liberation Organization (PLO) has been trying to establish for more than thirty years. Palestine is a full member of the Arab League and has observer status in the UN General Assembly, but it still lacks the international status of statehood, despite efforts in 1999 by PLO chairman Yasir Arafat to declare a state. Some areas of Palestine in the West Bank and Gaza are under Palestinian control, but the majority of it remains under Israeli occupation.

The word *Palestine* is of Roman origin, referring to the biblical land of the Philistines that today encompasses Israel, the West Bank, Gaza, and parts of Jordan and southern Lebanon. The territory of Palestine was recognized for centuries by Arab rulers and by the Ottoman Turks, the latter of whom distinguished Palestine from Lebanon. (The various administrative units during the Ottoman era sometimes changed names and boundaries.) The British maintained the use of *Palestine* as an official designation for the area that the League of Nations mandated to their supervision in 1920, following the dissolution of the Ottoman Empire after World War I. On July 24, 1922, the league approved the terms of the mandate, including the commitment made by Britain in the 1917 Balfour Declaration to view "with favor the establishment in Palestine of a national home for the Jewish people."

The British mandate originally also applied to Transjordan (now Jordan). Transjordan lay entirely to the east of the Jordan River, and Palestine lay entirely to the west of it (and hence the designation of part of that territory as the West Bank). Because the league's mandate applied to both regions, however, the argument was made that "Palestinian" applied to persons east as well as west of the Jordan River and that the designation applied not just to the Arab Muslim and Christian inhabitants but also to Jews living in the former mandated area.

The Palestinian people today are an Arab people who share with other Arabs the Arabic tongue, heritage, history, culture, and general Arab national aspirations. They are predominately Muslim, but many are of other faiths.

In 1947 the United Nations had voted to partition Palestine into Arab and Jewish sectors to solve the problem of these groups' competing nationalisms. Palestine as a legal entity ceased to exist in 1948, when Britain, unable to control Arab-Jewish hostilities and the influx of Jewish immigrants to Palestine, relinquished its mandate, and the Zionist movement declared the State of Israel on May 14. Large numbers of Palestinians left Palestine. Zionist troops forcibly evicted many of them, while others fled in the face of war.

During 1948–1949 Israel increased its territory in the war with the Palestinians and other Arabs, but it did not gain control of all of Palestine. One region, the West Bank, came under the control of Jordan, which later annexed the territory; another area, Gaza, found itself under Egyptian administration. These territories, however, were subsequently captured and occupied by Israel during the June 1967 War. In 1993 Israel and the PLO signed the Oslo Accords as a step toward possibly determining the final status of the occupied territories and establishing Palestinian self-rule. As part of the Oslo process, the Israelis and Palestinians agreed to the creation of the Palestinian Authority, a quasi-governmental entity, to take control of the areas over which Israel would relinquish administrative and in some cases security responsibilities.

Some Palestinians continue to live in Israel within the 1948 borders, while others remain dispersed in the Palestinian diaspora either in refugee camps in the Middle East or in various communities around the world.

domination in the various regions of the rapidly declining Ottoman Empire. European Zionists felt that they might be able to advance their cause by backing the imperial aims of the European power most likely to prevail in the contest for influence in Palestine. During the last days of World War I, after lobbying by Zionists, Great Britain concluded that supporting the Zionist movement might significantly serve its imperial interests in the Middle East. On November 2, 1917, the British government issued what has come to be known as the Balfour Declaration, named after Lord Arthur James Balfour, the British foreign minister who enunciated it:

His Majesty's Government views with favor the establishment in Palestine of a national home for the Jewish people, and will use their best endeavors to facilitate the achievement of this object, it being clearly understood that nothing shall be done which may prejudice the civil and religious rights of existing non-Jewish communities in Palestine, or the rights and political status enjoyed by Jews in any other country.

Many observers regard this statement as the beginning of the Arab-Israeli conflict. The declaration clearly established the Jews as the point of reference for Western powers, as the 91 percent of the population—the Muslim and Christian Palestinian Arabs—were described only as "existing non-Jewish communities in Palestine." It would be decades before Western officials and reporters would utter the word *Palestinian*. That the declaration omitted any mention of political rights for the Palestinian Arabs ensured the unpopularity of the Balfour Declaration among them. To this day, November 2 is a sad day for Arabs and a day marking victory for Zionists and for British (and Western) adoption of the Zionist program.

The British Mandate

With the defeat of the Ottoman Empire in World War I, the British and the French divided its former Arab holdings into spheres of influence. Palestine fell under British control. Although the Balfour Declaration called for a Jewish "national home" in

Palestine, statehood was the goal the fledgling Zionist movement had set at its first meeting in Switzerland in 1897. Other powers, including France and the United States, soon issued resolutions of support for the principles enunciated in the Balfour Declaration. (The U.S. resolution referred by name to Palestine's Christian population, some 10 percent of Palestinian Arabs, while referencing the Muslims as "others.") In July 1922, the League of Nations adopted the British mandate for Palestine, which incorporated the principles of the Balfour Declaration in its preamble. Article two of the mandate document states,

The Mandatory shall be responsible for placing the country under such political, administrative and economic conditions as will secure the establishment of the Jewish national home, as laid down in the preamble, and the development of self-governing institutions, and also for safeguarding the civil and religious rights of all the inhabitants of Palestine, irrespective of race and religion.

Thus Britain committed itself to supporting the establishment of a Jewish political entity in Palestine. The official implementation of the mandate in September 1923 opened the road for unrestricted Jewish migration to Palestine and the establishment of legally sanctioned institutions that would culminate in the State of Israel twenty-five years later. Although Jewish statehood was not the paramount thrust of British foreign policy, Britain worked to implement the terms of the mandate while allowing the Zionists substantial freedom to define the means of that implementation. Arab opposition later modified British actions and may have reduced their enthusiasm for Jewish statehood, but ultimately to no avail.

Barriers to a Jewish State

Even with international support, large-scale Jewish settlement of Palestine and the eventual establishment of an independent Jewish state were not necessarily inevitable, as early support of the Zionist movement was more idealistic than practical. After an initial surge in immigration in 1924 and 1925, the number of Jewish settlers arriving in

Who Is an Arab?

It is not easy to define accurately the term *Arab*. The British geographer W. B. Fisher in *The Middle East: A Physical, Social and Regional Geography* states that from an anthropological point of view, it is not possible to accurately speak of either an Arab or a Semitic people. According to him, both terms connote mixed populations that vary widely in their physical characteristics and origins. He suggests, therefore, that these descriptions be used purely as cultural and linguistic terms, respectively. One can say, however, that the so-called Arab countries have populations that share a common culture and primary language and have been shaped by the legacy of Arabo-Islamic civilization.

Language was a crucial element in the construction of the Arab national identity; Arabic remains the official language of all Arab countries. It is an ancient Semitic language, and also one in which Arabs take great pride, as it is the language in which God communicated with Muhammad: It is the language of the Quran.

As Islam began spreading from the Arabian Peninsula in the seventh century, Arabization and Islamization—processes that are closely linked but not identical—altered the societies of the conquered. Peter Mansfield writes in *The Arab World: A Comprehensive History* that Arabization had begun in the fourth century, some two centuries before the birth of the Prophet Muhammad, as Arabian tribes moved into Syria and Iraq and beyond. Arabization reached its farthest and deepest during the first two centuries of the vast Arabo-Islamic empire, as Muslims captured territory and spread their new religion far beyond the

bounds of its birthplace in Arabia. The process of Islamization lasted much longer and continues today, albeit at a much slower pace compared to the fast and early rise of Islam. It is especially evident in Africa.

The countries recognized as Arab on the African continent are the Comoros, Djibouti, Egypt, Somalia, Sudan, and the North African countries collectively known as the Maghrib—Algeria, Libya, Mauritania, Morocco, and Tunisia. The Arab nations in the Levant, the area at the eastern end of the Mediterranean Sea on the Asian continent, are Iraq, Jordan, Lebanon, and Syria as well as the Palestinian territories. The Arab countries of the Persian Gulf, also on the Asian continent, are Bahrain, Kuwait, Oman, Qatar, Saudi Arabia, the United Arab Emirates, and Yemen.

Islam is the dominant religion today in all of these nations, but substantial numbers of religious minorities coexist there, including Christians, Jews, Druze, and others. Religion, in this case Islam, does not, however, define Arab nationhood. For instance, Afghanistan, Indonesia, Iran, Pakistan, and Turkey are Islamic but not Arab. Similarly, not all Arabs are Muslims. Lebanon's population includes close to a million Arab Christians. Several other Middle Eastern countries have significant Arab Christian minorities, some with ancestral roots antedating the Muslim conquest and others converted by missionaries. Millions of Christian Copts still live in Egypt, for example. There are also several non-Arab Muslim minorities in the Middle East, including the Kurds in parts of Iran, Iraq, Syria, and Turkey and the Berbers in North Africa.

Palestine annually fell to an average of between 2,500 and 5,000—hardly a sufficient number to transform the basic national character of Palestine. A significant increase in Jewish immigration occurred only after the 1933 elections in Germany brought Hitler and the National Socialists to power and the subsequent issuance of the Nuremberg Laws. These events contributed significantly to the growing belief among Jews that a Jewish national home was indeed needed.

Considerable ideological conflict and political factionalism within the early yishuv, the Jewish settlement in Palestine, also threatened the Zionist movement. Socialist-labor Zionists, mainly from Eastern Europe and Russia, sought to collectivize the economic activities of the yishuv while Judaizing it. Capitalist- as well as socialist-oriented Zionists excluded the use of Arab labor based on the concept and slogan of "Hebrew labor." Both these groups were opposed by an even larger body of Orthodox Jews, who denounced the Zionist vision of a Jewish state as being inconsistent with their spiritualist view of religion, which eagerly awaited the return of the Messiah, before which a Jewish state could not be legitimated. Furthermore, some Orthodox Jews viewed with distaste the secularist and in some cases atheistic philosophies of the Zionist leadership. Conflicts also arose between the leadership of the yishuv and the Zionist leadership abroad over the Zionist enterprise.

The concurrent growth of nationalist sentiment among the Arabs was another factor inhibiting the progress of the Zionist movement in Palestine. The emergence of such thought predated World War I and had given rise first to movements opposed to continued Ottoman rule and after the war to the imposition of European rule through the League of Nations mandate system. During the war, the British had capitalized on Arab nationalist sentiment by striking an agreement with Hussein ibn Ali (Sharif Hussein), who led an Arab revolt against the Turks in support of British military operations in Palestine and Syria. In return for this support, Henry McMahon, the British high commissioner in Egypt, promised Hussein, in what later became known as the Hussein-McMahon correspondence, British support for an Arab kingdom under his rule after the war. Such a kingdom, covering present-day Syria and its capital at Damascus, did come into being briefly in 1918, with Hussein's son Faisal at its head, but it was violently suppressed in July 1920 by French forces acting to assert control in Lebanon and Syria in accordance with its League of Nations mandate over these areas. Historians still dispute the boundaries that were to have demarcated the entire area of promised Arab independence. One letter from McMahon left the impression that Palestine was to be included, but the British later denied that interpretation.

While the British were talking with Hussein in 1915 and 1916 and making promises of support for an Arab kingdom after the war, the British and French in 1916 secretly signed the Sykes-Picot Agreement, which set aside Lebanon and Syria as areas of French interest while giving Britain a free hand in the region to the south. It was only after the 1917 Bolshevik Revolution in Russia that the details and text of the agreement became known.

Sorting out the conflicting promises made in the Hussein-McMahon correspondence, the Sykes-Picot Agreement, and the Balfour Declaration occurred at the Paris peace talks after the war. During these talks, Faisal, at the time the king of the new Arab state at Damascus, expressed his willingness to collaborate with the Zionists and to accept the principle of a Jewish national home in Palestine. This brief possibility of Arab-Zionist cooperation quickly faded, however, with France's suppression of Faisal's rule.

With the demise of Faisal's kingdom, Arab nationalist hopes that had been nurtured during the war turned to bitterness. Although some Arabs collaborated with the French and British during the 1920s and 1930s, an increasingly strong nationalist movement promoted strikes, demonstrations, occasional acts of political violence, and other forms of resistance against European rule. The European division of the Middle East into several countries was perceived, correctly it would seem, as part of a larger Western strategy to divide and rule the Arab world and to prevent nationalist aspirations from being fulfilled. Many Arabs viewed Western support for Zionist aspirations in Palestine as part of this strategy, which entailed creating a Western-sponsored base in the heart of the Arab world that would legitimize a permanent Western presence under the guise of sustaining and defending the Jewish national home, even if against the interests of the native inhabitants. The struggle against European colonial domination between the world wars, therefore, included opposition to Jewish migration to Palestine as well as to the perpetuation of the European mandate system. Arab opposition to Zionist aspirations, consequently, had a pan-Arab character and influenced Arab opinion far beyond the boundaries of Palestine, which, then as now, constituted the central theater of the Arab-Israeli conflict.

Although Britain remained committed to the promises of the Balfour Declaration, successive British governments amended it verbally, albeit mildly, but not juridically, in response to Arab nationalist challenges within Palestine and beyond. The first major compromise came about in March 1921 at the Cairo Conference, which was convened by Winston Churchill, then England's colonial secretary, to seek ways to consolidate British authority in Palestine and in Iraq in the face of growing Arab nationalist opposition and the need to cut the costs of colonial administration. The conference decided to install Faisal, the recently deposed king in Damascus, as king of Iraq. In addition, to further appease Faisal's Hashimite family, the original Palestine mandate was divided at the Jordan River, and Faisal's brother, Abdallah, was installed as king in eastern Palestine, which took the name Transjordan.

This division of Palestine put Transjordan off limits to the Jewish immigration and settlement allowed concerning Palestine, a circumstance that some Zionists saw as a betrayal of the British promise in the Balfour Declaration and a contravention of Britain's responsibilities under the terms of its League of Nations mandate. Zionist protestations to the contrary, the British never seriously wavered in their support for the implementation of the idea of a Jewish national home. No matter how loud and occasionally violent Arab opposition became, the British continued for years to think that they could reconcile the goal of Jewish statehood with Arab demands for independence.

British Reassessment

In Jerusalem in August 1929, a major outbreak of Arab-Jewish violence erupted around the Western Wall, or Wailing Wall, sparked by increasing Arab fears about Jewish intentions and newly acquired Zionist confidence and public displays of political power. The violence then spread to other parts of Palestine and led the British government to take another look at its policy in the region. Two investigative reports—the Shaw Report of March 1930 and the Hope-Simpson Report of May 1930—concluded that insufficient attention was being paid to the second half of Britain's obligations under its mandate charter, namely, "ensuring the rights and positions" of the "non-Jewish communities" of Palestine, which remained the majority of the population although waves of Jewish immigration increasingly undermined their demographic strength. Both reports recommended restrictions on Jewish immigration and limitations on future land transfers to "non-Arabs." The British government accepted these recommendations in the subsequent Passfield White Paper of October 1930. This new position provoked a political furor in England, however, and appeared to threaten the survival of Prime Minister Ramsay MacDonald's government. MacDonald subsequently issued a letter repudiating the Passfield document, and the perceived threat to Zionist aspirations in Palestine passed. These events, however, indicated to Jews, but not to Arabs, that the British commitment to a Jewish national home in Palestine was not without limits.

Following the upsurge in Jewish immigration that accompanied the rise to power of the Nazis in Germany in the mid-1930s, violence again erupted in 1936 in the form of the Great Arab Revolt. Triggered by the discovery of smuggled weapons for use by the Jews and by the increasing displacement of Arab peasants by Jewish immigrants, the renewed violence led Britain to review its position in Palestine. British authorities ultimately crushed the revolt, which lasted until 1939 and was in some respects analogous to the Palestinian intifada of the late 1980s. In July 1937, the apparent irreconcilability of Zionist aspirations with Arab nationalist claims had finally led the Peel Commission, formed by the British to investigate the causes of conflict and violence in Palestine, to recommend the partition of the territory into Jewish and Arab states. It was the first official endorsement of partition as a potential solution to the emerging conflict. The Arabs rejected the commission's recommendation on partition—in part because it allocated the fertile lands of the Galilee to the Jewish section and required the "transfer" of tens of thousands of Palestinian Arabs from their homes—and Zionist leaders, although grudgingly accepting the principle of partition, objected to the limited amount of territory allotted to the Jews. Moreover, the Palestinian Arabs identified with the whole of Palestine and did not want to abandon their claim to their national territory.

Historians generally agree that with the clouds of World War II looming over Europe, Britain's perception of its strategic interests in the Middle East began to favor positions that would not alienate the Arabs. Not wanting the Arabs to look to the Nazis as potential liberators from British control, Britain reviewed its position yet again. In 1939 the government issued a white paper effectively dispensing with its open-ended commitment to the establishment of a Jewish national home in Palestine. This white paper remained the basis of British policy in Palestine until the end of the mandate in 1948 and emphasized meeting Arab demands more so than satisfying Zionist aspirations. It rejected the concept of partition and promised a vague independence, presumably for the Arabs of Palestine or for an Arab Palestine, within ten years.

The 1939 white paper enunciated the principle that the Jewish national home could be established only with Arab consent, and it proposed that such a home be established within an independent Palestine. Regarding Jewish immigration, twenty-five thousand immigrants would be admitted immediately; during the next five years, it would be restricted to fifteen thousand a year; after that period, Jewish immigration would only be allowed with Arab consent. Jewish land purchases and settlements would be restricted to the coastal and lowland areas. Meanwhile, the British proposed to develop self-governing institutions to include Arabs and Jews, even if both sides refused to collaborate. If after a ten-year period it appeared that Palestine remained unready for independence, Britain would undertake another review to determine its next course of action.

The Arabs opposed the 1939 white paper because it did not halt Jewish immigration, and it failed to grant immediate political independence to Palestine. The Zionists rejected it on the grounds that it constituted a violation of international law, that is, the League of Nations mandate,

which they believed obligated Britain to use its authority on behalf of Zionist goals. Believing that the British had abandoned their commitment to the national home, the Zionists vowed to resist the new policy, even while lending support to the British war effort in Europe and North Africa.

Jewish Infrastructure

The Jewish settlement in Palestine depended on diaspora Jewry for financial assistance, migration, and political activism in support of the Zionist cause. During the early 1920s, Zionists had actively established institutions for organizing the Jewish presence in Palestine. The most significant of these were the Jewish National Fund, which purchased land for Zionist settlement; the Keren Hayesod, another fund that financed development projects on behalf of the yishuv; the Histadrut, a labor organization that gradually became the dominant force in yishuv and later Israeli affairs; and the Haganah, a secret and illegal paramilitary force raised by the yishuv that would be the forerunner of the Israel Defense Forces (the Israeli army after 1948). The Jewish Agency, with headquarters in Jerusalem, oversaw all these activities after 1929. (The London-based World Zionist Organization, founded in the nineteenth century to lead international Zionist efforts, had previously exerted primary executive authority over the affairs of the yishuv.) Throughout the 1930s and 1940s, yishuv figures, notably David Ben-Gurion, strengthened their influence over the Jewish Agency and the Zionist movement.

The Palestinian Arabs had no counterpart to the developing Jewish infrastructure in Palestine. Divided among various factions that reflected the rivalries among traditional notable families of Jerusalem, the Arabs generally protested British rule and Jewish immigration and settlement while failing to construct a united political force. They demonstrated and signed petitions, and women organized and took to the streets in protest. Delegations and committees were formed, but family rivalries hampered their effectiveness. Although some Arabs favored collaboration with the British as a means of

The Rise of Arab Nationalism and the Arab League

Early traces of Arab nationalism can be detected in the literature of the nineteenth century, when it was advocated by educated Christian and Muslim Arabs. The Christian writers and thinkers championed Arab nationalism as a movement based on culture rather than religion. An alternative nationalism, based on Islamic identity, was for obvious reasons less appealing to them. The British occupation of Egypt in 1882 sparked the development of nationalism there, but until World War I, Islam primarily supplied the bulwark against the encroaching West.

As a popular movement, Arab nationalism first developed between 1908 and 1914 with the Young Turks' rise to power in the crumbling Ottoman Empire. The Young Turks had advocated a constitution providing for the fusion of the different ethnic and religious groups of the empire into a single, Ottoman democracy. Once in control, however, they used their power to promote Turkish national and linguistic interests and to rule the empire based on the tenet of Turkish racial supremacy. In response, Arab leaders formed clandestine societies in Beirut, Cairo, and Paris and called for Arab political autonomy within the empire. These efforts culminated in the convening of the 1913 Paris Congress, at which the Young Turks agreed to negotiate the Arabs' desire for autonomy. The defeat of the Ottomans in World War I and the occupation of the Arab Middle East by the victorious European powers led to an even stronger desire among the Arabs for autonomy.

At the beginning of the war, most Muslim Arabs had favored the Turks against the Allies, but in 1916 the British supported an Arab revolt, immortalized by the writings of T. E. Lawrence, whose role in the Arab movement has been greatly exaggerated in Western popular culture. Bedouin troops, whose leaders had been promised independence for the entire Arab East, supported the British forces advancing through Palestine and Syria, but after the war the Arabs found themselves divided into states governed by British or French mandates. As formalized by the League of Nations between 1922 and 1924, these mandates allowed the British and French to administer and develop the territories until they were "ready" for independence.

The British assumed control of Palestine, Transjordan, and Iraq. Transjordan—the area to the east of the Jordan River—and Iraq were ruled by Arab kings under the supervision of British advisers and troops. Palestine was run by a British commissioner who, under the mandate, was obliged to allow the development of a national home for the Jews. The French administered Syria, which included the territory that later became Lebanon. In 1923 the British agreed to independence for Egypt, but negotiated to retain advisers there and station troops to oversee the Suez Canal. Iraq's independence came with the end of the British mandate there in 1932. Other mandates would expire around mid-century.

The situation in the Arabian Peninsula was somewhat different because Ottoman power had never deeply penetrated the area. A struggle for power had developed in the peninsula between Hussein ibn Ali, ruler of the Hijaz, and Ibn Saud, ruler of the Najd. The French and British contentedly let them fight it out, and in 1927 Ibn Saud imposed sovereignty over the Najd as well as the Hijaz.

Between the world wars, independent Saudi Arabia focused its attention inward, having no interest in leading the movement for Arab unity that had begun during World War I. The other Arab states, under their tutelary rulers, concerned themselves with achieving a greater degree of independence from occupying powers than working for pan-Arab nationalism. It took World War II to energize the pan-Arab movement.

The Arabs of 1939 had progressed beyond the complete servitude of 1914 to semiautonomous existences based on treaties with Britain and France. The war removed the French from Syria and Lebanon and the Italians from Libya, leaving the British the only colonial power in the Middle East. Britain's eventual withdrawal, however, appeared inevitable.

Near the end of World War II, the Hashimite Arab leaders of Iraq and Syria proposed to unite several Arab countries under their leadership, but non-Hashimite Arabs and the British opposed their plans. They supported instead the formation of a loose federation of Arab states that would safeguard national sovereignties but enable them to work for the common good. The federation concept grew out of two conferences involving Egypt, Iraq, Lebanon, Saudi Arabia, Syria, Transjordan, and Yemen and became the Arab League, or the League of Arab States, as it is officially known.

The birth of the first pan-Arab organization in 1944 was not, however, cause for high hopes among many Arabs. The league was seen by some as a cynical attempt by the British to manipulate Arab public opinion, and it soon developed into an ineffective gathering of unelected leaders where promises were casually made but rarely kept. The seven original states were unequal in wealth and prestige and harbored differing political agendas. None wanted to sacrifice its own sovereignty to a federalist ideal, and destructive personal rivalries among the rulers of Egypt, Iraq, Jordan, and Saudi Arabia strained relations.

The one area in which members of the league did agree in its early years, however, was opposition to growing Jewish political claims to Palestine. After the United Nations voted to partition Palestine in 1947, the league declared its opposition to the idea because the creation of a Jewish state would displace the existing Arab population of Palestine. The first Arab-Israeli war ended in defeat for the Arabs and the influx of unwanted Palestinian refugees into their countries. Later, instead of acting in a coordinated fashion, each state sided with a particular Palestinian client group in an effort to emerge as the champion of the Palestinian cause, sometimes leading to or resulting in bitter feuds.

The 1948 war and subsequent emergence of Egypt as the leader in the Arab League destroyed Britain's hopes of a British-Hashimite plan for Arab unity and, consequently, British influence in the league. The formation in Gaza of the All-Palestine government under Egyptian aegis, Jordan's annexation of the West Bank—which the league condemned and only two countries recognized—and a collapse of the Syrian government in 1949 threatened to bring down the league. It was resuscitated, however, by the signing of a mutual security pact aimed at protecting Syria from the ambitions of the Hashimite kings, who, relishing British support,

were eager for a kingdom that extended beyond the narrow confines of Transjordan.

The factionalism of the Arab League and its failure to achieve the primary goals of unity, solidarity, and the liberation of Palestine are reflected in the history of the Arab world since World War II. As the British systematically relinquished control in the area, the newly independent nations endured dictatorships, coups, assassinations, and abdications. The population, however, never felt nostalgic for colonial times. They simply wanted to live in peace with freedom and dignity. The Arab governments themselves exacerbated the situation by continually interfering in each other's affairs. Egypt, for example, attempted to instigate or support revolutions in Iraq, Jordan, Lebanon, Saudi Arabia, and Syria. Egypt became involved in a full-scale war in Yemen during the 1960s and at one point had as many as 70,000 troops there. Saudi Arabia similarly fomented opposition in countries loyal to Egyptian president Gamal Abdel Nasser and his vision of Arab nationalism. Almost all of the Arab countries at one time or another were involved in maneuverings intended to bolster one state against another. Until 1973 attempts to achieve fruitful pan-Arab cooperation always ended in failure.

Egypt, the most populous state, sought to lead the Arab world for much of the post–World War II period. In 1952 army officers overthrew the monarchy, which was supplanted by a military dictatorship headed by the charismatic Nasser. The new Egyptian leader emerged as the champion of a new brand of politically active Arab nationalism, but his feuds with other leaders reduced his overall regional effectiveness. According to Nasser's vision of Arab nationalism, the borders of Arab countries represented artificial creations of imperialism that should be eliminated and replaced by a new Arab federation that would revive the glories of the Arab past. To nationalists, Arab nationalism represented a political necessity, not a romantic vision. The socialist Baath Party—whose rival branches dominated the governments of Syria and Iraq for more than thirty years—championed this version of Arab nationalism. In 1958 Nasser's Egypt and Baathist Syria founded the United Arab Republic, a federal union symbolizing the potential of Arab nationalism, but this vision suffered a severe blow in 1961, when the union collapsed.

Nasser's successor, Anwar al-Sadat, broke with pan-Arab ideologues and advocated an Egyptian nationalist agenda. Sadat's trip to Jerusalem in 1977 and signing of the Egyptian-Israeli peace treaty in 1979 exemplified this new tack. The Arab League, opposing the unilateral agreement with Israel, expelled Egypt in 1979 but welcomed it back in May 1989.

During the 1990–1991 Persian Gulf crisis and war, the league split over Iraq's invasion of fellow member Kuwait. Twelve of the twenty-one league members voted to commit troops to the multinational coalition created to oppose the Iraqi occupation; three voted for the resolution with reservations; three abstained or were absent; and three—Iraq, Libya, and the Palestine Liberation Organization—voted against the measure.

The governments cast their votes based on self-interest, not according to their relations or views regarding Kuwait or their desire to preserve Arab unity. The wealthy Gulf states, which had the most to fear from the invasion, followed Saudi Arabia's lead and joined with the West in opposing Iraq. Egypt, which at the time received $2.3 billion a year in aid from the United States and which had traditionally stood as an Iraqi rival for Arab leadership, also sided with Saudi Arabia and the West. President Hafiz al-Asad of Syria joined the coalition based on his personal enmity toward Iraqi president Saddam Hussein and his ambitions for Damascus to eclipse Baghdad as an Arab power center. He was also anxious to improve relations with the wealthy Gulf states and the United States. The Iraqi invasion of Kuwait and Arab reaction to it demonstrated that pan-Arab impulses, as far as the various governments were concerned, ran a distant second to the interests of individual Arab states.

In the early 2000s, the Arab League continued to suffer from a number of weaknesses, and it is not likely that the league will be rejuvenated as long as Arab leaders remain suspicious of one another. Contributing to the league's problems, the more wealthy Arab countries continue to refuse to fulfill their financial obligations, especially as the Gulf Cooperation Council has assumed more relevance for Gulf states. The league failed to arrive at a consensus on or exert any influence during the U.S. push in 2002 and 2003 to invade Iraq. Such failures reinforced the thinking of many in the region that the league is perhaps obsolete or irrelevant. At the 2005 league summit in Algiers, nine of the twenty-two leaders sent lower-ranking officials in their stead.

The academic community continues to debate whether Arab nationalism is dead or whether it has existed all along despite efforts by various Arab regimes to smash it. Nevertheless, it is clear that Arab governments have perceived and dealt with Arab nationalism as a threat because of its potential to eliminate political entities they control. Arab popular reactions to regional issues, including the Palestinian situation and the latest war against Iraq, indicate that a measure of commonality of interests and sentiments is still widely shared among Arab peoples.

co-opting British favor, they were usually intimidated into silence by leaders who favored boycotts and general strikes to demand immediate political independence. The British arrested numerous nationalists and confiscated their weapons; some nationalists fled abroad before World War II, just as British policy was becoming more supportive of Arab concerns, or less supportive of maximalist Zionist demands.

Because Arab attacks during the 1936–1939 revolt were directed against British authority as well as the Jewish presence, the British began to rely on Jews to undertake police duties on their behalf. They raised, trained, armed, and paid a Jewish police force to guard isolated yishuv settlements. Most of the Jews organized for this purpose turned out to be members of the Haganah. Established in the early 1920s, the Haganah was initially little more than a paper organization formally grouping local village defense committees. In 1936, as a consequence of the Arab revolt, however, the yishuv selected one thousand men for a standing force available for service anywhere in Palestine. Infiltration of the British police provided legal cover for the illegal Haganah to conduct military training and carry weapons, which they used in special operations of their own against Arab groups involved in the revolt. Police duties would give the Jews an important advantage in events to come.

The issuance of the 1939 white paper put Palestinian Jewry on a collision course with the British and strengthened the resolve of the yishuv to maintain and strengthen the still-secret Haganah. The restrictions on Jewish immigration to Palestine at a time of extreme anti-Semitism in Nazi-dominated Europe led the Haganah to facilitate illegal immigration in opposition to British policy. At the same time, however, the organization collaborated with the British by providing about twenty-seven thousand Jews to serve with British forces against Nazi Germany during World War II. This service provided further training and experience to the armed forces of the yishuv and gave credibility to Jewish military forces. It in addition increased British tolerance for Jewish military organization in Palestine.

Also during this period, a rival Jewish militia, the Irgun Zvai Leumi, formed under the leadership of Vladimir Jabotinsky, a political opponent of the socialist-labor Zionists who dominated the politics of the yishuv and controlled the Haganah. Less restrained than the Haganah and more racialist in its nationalist outlook, the Irgun favored using more forceful tactics, including terrorism, against the Arabs of Palestine, and later against the British.

Another result of the 1939 white paper was a decision by the World Zionist Organization to broaden its base of international support. No longer confident of British guarantees, the Zionist movement increasingly looked to the United States for funding and political support. The Biltmore Conference, held in New York City in May 1942 to mobilize the large U.S. Jewish community, adopted resolutions calling for the United States to support the opening of Palestine to Jewish immigration, to recognize the Jewish Agency in Jerusalem as the sole authority in control of immigration and the economic development of Palestine, and to recognize all of Palestine after the war as "a Jewish Commonwealth integrated in the structure of the new democratic world." This appeal had great success, and Britain soon found itself increasingly on the defensive in matters pertaining to Palestine, especially as evidence of the Holocaust grew more apparent during the second half of 1942.

End of the British Mandate

The quest for a Jewish homeland in Palestine reached a climax during the three years following the end of World War II. With thousands of displaced Jews from the war living in refugee camps, Britain came under great international pressure, encouraged by the Zionists, to admit them to Palestine, although the same Western governments advocating immigration restricted the number of Jews admitted to their own countries. At the same time, the Haganah, the Irgun, and a third breakaway Jewish militia, LEHI, or the Stern Gang (led by future Israeli prime minister Yitzhak Shamir), inaugurated a violent campaign against the British in Palestine. Britain was unable to maintain central authority and unwilling to reverse the policy enunciated in the 1939 white paper. As Arab nationalists, including those in Palestine, strove with increasing success to achieve political independence and an end to European colonial rule in the Middle East, Britain perceived its best interests to be associated with the maintenance of satisfactory relations with the newly independent Arab states. They, like the Arabs of Palestine, opposed Jewish immigration and resisted any thought that Palestine be partitioned into two states. The British saw no resolution to their predicament. Unable to satisfy Zionist aspirations as promised in the Balfour Declaration or the demands of the Palestinian Arabs, who had only the token support of their Arab neighbors (in the form of the king and princes, but not the people), Britain announced in February 1947 that it would relinquish its responsibilities under the mandate and refer the problem to the newly formed United Nations. Thus began the end of Britain's colonial enterprise in Palestine.

Partition of Palestine

In May 1947, the UN Special Committee on Palestine (UNSCOP) was established to investigate the situation in Palestine and to recommend action to the General Assembly. The committee consisted of representatives of eleven countries:

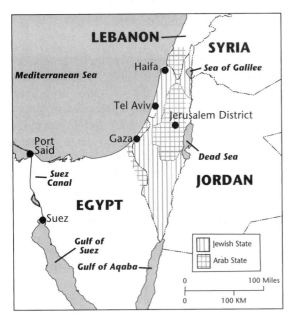

UN Partition of Palestine, 1947

The commission presented its report in August 1947, and some three months later the UN General Assembly voted on it. The newly independent Arab states in the assembly, although favoring Palestinian independence, opposed partition in any form. In the end, however, they supported the UNSCOP minority report in an effort to head off the majority recommendation. Zionist forces and their supporters favored the full partition plan and exerted pressure to obtain the votes even of countries whose delegates had gone on record against partition. Following numerous postponements and delays until the requisite two-thirds vote could be obtained, the General Assembly adopted UNSCOP's majority recommendation in Resolution 181 on November 29, 1947. The vote was 33 to 13, with 10 abstentions.

Jews around the world greeted the UN decision with joy and celebration, as it provided international legitimacy for the establishment of a Jewish state in Palestine. The vote, however, caused Arab-Jewish hostilities to erupt throughout Palestine, with Arabs struggling to prevent partition and the forces of the yishuv fighting to ensure its implementation. On December 3, 1947, Britain, which had abstained from voting on Resolution 181, announced its unwillingness to implement a policy with which it disagreed and that lacked support from both sides of the conflict. It declared that it would evacuate Palestine on May 15, 1948. Also on December 3, the two-year-old League of Arab States (or Arab League) declared its opposition to the partition and encouraged league members to intervene.

In early 1948, Palestine's Jewish population—which lived mainly in the area assigned to the Jewish state by the UN resolution—numbered slightly more than 600,000, while the Palestinian Arab population numbered about 1.3 million. At least half a million Arabs lived alongside Jews in the sector allotted to the Jewish state. The Haganah in late 1947 numbered about 43,000. Well organized to defend Jewish settlements, and better trained than the Palestinian Arab forces, the Haganah also possessed a rudimentary mobile field force of about 11,000 men, many of whom

Australia, Canada, Czechoslovakia, Guatemala, India, Iran, Mexico, the Netherlands, Peru, Sweden, and Yugoslavia. Feted and warmly received by the Zionists and boycotted completely by the Arab leadership in Palestine, the committee concluded that the British mandate should indeed be terminated and that Palestine be granted independence.

The implacable attitudes expressed by the Arabs and the Jews, however, led the commission to recommend partition as the basis for granting independence, though committee members differed on how partition should be implemented. The minority report (supported by India, Iran, and Yugoslavia) recommended "an independent federal state" composed of two autonomous political entities (Arab and Jewish) but united by a central government that would include Arab and Jewish representatives. Jerusalem would serve as its capital. The majority report recommended the establishment of two sovereign states joined in an economic federation. Jerusalem would enjoy a separate status as an international city under UN administration.

had served with the British army during World War II. In addition, the Irgun (led by future Israeli prime minister Menachem Begin) fielded a militia numbering about 5,000, while LEHI consisted of several hundred fighters. To the outside world, it seemed unlikely that the yishuv could prevail in its determination to establish a Jewish state, but their armed forces in fact significantly outnumbered the forces of the combined Arab units.

Against these elements of the yishuv, the Arabs organized what were essentially village militias, but they lacked central command, coordination, and the weaponry of the Jews. The British had confiscated Arab weapons with a zeal that it did not exhibit toward the Zionists, and the Arabs found it impossible to develop coordinated military activity until after the November 1947 partition resolution, because the British had been closely monitoring their activities since the revolt of the late 1930s. The Arabs eventually organized two military forces. The first, the Holy Jihad Army, was sponsored by the exiled mufti of Jerusalem, Hajj Amin al-Husseini, the leader of the 1936 revolt who resided in Cairo because the British had prohibited him from reentering Palestine. Never larger than 5,000 loosely coordinated fighters in various parts of the country, Husseini's forces lacked the support of the Arab League, which sponsored a second force, the Arab Salvation Army. Composed of some 3,800 volunteers from the various Arab countries, including some 1,000 from Palestine, its units entered northern Palestine between January and May 1948. Elements of Jordan's Arab Legion represented a third force, but they remained under British authority and were, therefore, officially neutral. After Britain's departure on May 15, 1948, the legion came under Jordanian control. All these forces had separate commands, and each regarded the others with suspicion and envy. The Arab governments proved to be more keen on exploiting the conflict for their own political and propaganda purposes than on helping the Palestinians retain their patrimony. The Jordanian royal family, it would later be revealed, collaborated closely not only with its British patron, but also with the Zionists.

Israel after the 1948–49 War

The fighting in Palestine during December 1947 and early 1948 consisted mainly of low-level guerrilla operations—sniping, ambushes, and acts of terrorism—as Jewish forces sought to hold the main roads linking their settlements. In February 1948, the leadership of the yishuv announced a general mobilization, and in April the Haganah went on the offensive. Operating in accordance with what was called Plan D, the Haganah set out to secure control (prior to the departure of the British) of all territory allotted to the Jewish state by Resolution 181. This involved seizing all the Palestinian Arab towns and villages in the Jewish sector and expelling as many of their Arab inhabitants as possible. The Haganah also attempted to secure the road connecting the Jewish sector to West Jerusalem, where nearly one-fifth of the Jewish inhabitants of Palestine lived.

Jewish forces quickly achieved a number of victories, seizing control of Tiberias on April 18, Haifa on April 22, Safed on May 10, and Jaffa on May 13. In the process, by May 15, some 300,000 of the half-million Arabs living in the Jewish sector became refugees, fleeing to other parts of Palestine or neighboring Arab countries. Some left voluntarily, while others were forced to flee. Increasing amounts of evidence uncovered by Israeli historians reveal that the Zionists forcibly expelled many more Palestinians from their towns and villages than previously acknowledged. Furthermore, historians now generally agree that the systematic massacre of some 250 Palestinian Arabs by the Irgun and Stern Gang on April 9 in Dayr Yassin, a village overlooking the road to Jerusalem, helped create the psychological climate that encouraged residents to flee.

Israel Proclaimed

By the time Britain's mandate formally ended and the last British forces evacuated Jerusalem on May 15, 1948, the armed forces of the yishuv had laid effective claim to virtually all the territory allocated to it under the terms of the partition resolution and in addition had seized part of the lands allocated to the Palestinian side. Some 74 percent of historic Palestine was now under Jewish control. On May 14, David Ben-Gurion, then head of the Jewish Agency, had formally proclaimed the establishment of Israel as an independent state. The United States and the Soviet Union quickly recognized Israel, as did most other members of the United Nations. Of Western states, only Britain delayed, waiting until January 30, 1949.

The Arab governments refused to recognize the new state. To do otherwise, as far as the Arab masses were concerned, would entail the acceptance of the dispossession of the Palestinians. In secret, Arab governments made it clear to the West and to Israel that they did not want confrontation with Israel, although in public speeches they promised a speedy recovery of Palestine by all means. The Arabs of Palestine could not accept what was left of "their part" of Palestine, nor could the Palestinians from areas that came under Israeli control simply abandon their traditional homes, where they and their ancestors had lived for centuries. Yet, Israel and its supporters in the West urged the Palestinians to forgive, forget, and move on. They viewed national attachments as a

characteristic of Western people, not desert dwellers, as the Arabs have been historically perceived. Earlier hostilities between Jews and Arabs along with the Arab states' verbal if not actual commitment to their Palestinian brethren made compromise impossible. As they had vowed and had been preparing to do since December 1947, Egypt, Iraq, Lebanon, and Syria sent contingents of their armies into Palestine on May 15, as the last British forces were departing.

The 1948 War

The entrance of the Arab armies into the fighting transformed what had fundamentally been an ethnic conflict with religious overtones concerning land in Palestine into a war among the newly established states of the region. Conflicting Arab objectives resulted in uncoordinated military strategies that the new Israeli state was able to exploit to its full advantage. In addition, the troops that the Arab states sent ostensibly to support the Palestinians were merely token forces with outdated weapons. The Arabs initially appeared to hold the edge (at least on paper) in terms of aircraft, armored vehicles, and artillery, but the Israeli troops, formally reincorporated as the Israel Defense Forces on May 26, 1948, held a distinct manpower and materiel advantage. Israel fielded a mobile army of nine brigades with 25,000 frontline troops that would grow to nearly 80,000 by the end of the year, because with the British departure, restrictions on Jewish immigration were lifted, allowing Israel to significantly increase its pool of available manpower.

The 1948 war developed in three phases. During the first phase (May 15 to June 11), Israel conducted primarily defensive operations that succeeded in halting Arab offensive thrusts into its territory. Unable to break through Jordanian defenses on the road to Jerusalem, Jewish forces managed to construct a secondary road, the so-called Burma Road, which allowed them to resupply and thus secure West Jerusalem. A UN-brokered cease-fire gave time to all sides to rearm, reorganize, train, and plan for the second phase of the war. When the truce ended, on July 6, primarily because of Syrian and Egyptian unwillingness to extend it, Israel had greatly improved its military position in terms of weaponry, manpower, and organization.

During the second phase (July 6–19), Israel took the offensive and delivered several crushing blows to the various Arab armies. It took Lod and Ramle in central Palestine (and expelled their populations en masse) and Nazareth in the north, all areas designated as part of the Arab state in the UN partition plan. An Israeli effort to capture Arab East Jerusalem had not succeeded by the time a second UN cease-fire was imposed on July 19, leaving Egyptian and Jordanian forces in control of the Negev, which the UN partition had assigned to Israel. This second cease-fire was meant to hold until armistice agreements could be signed, but Israel, determined not to lose the Negev, on October 15 seized upon the pretext of Egyptian sniping at an Israeli convoy to resume offensive operations that eventually isolated Egyptian forces. The withdrawal of Egyptian troops from the Negev following a new cease-fire on January 7, 1949, opened the way for Israeli occupation of the Negev, which it accomplished on March 10, 1949.

Meanwhile, from October 29 to October 31, 1948, Israel had resumed offensive operations in the north and quickly defeated Syrian, Lebanese, and Arab Salvation Army forces, most of which avoided fighting altogether, bringing all of the Galilee under Israeli control. This further usurpation of territory assigned to the proposed Arab state by the UN partition was soon followed by the de facto annexation in December 1948 of the remaining portion of Arab Palestine—the West Bank—by King Abdallah of Jordan, who had contacts with and colluded with the Zionists. As the war ended, Egyptian forces remained in occupation of the Gaza Strip, but unlike Jordan, Egypt never annexed it. Effectively defeated by Israel and unable to continue the war, the Arab states finally signed UN-sponsored armistice agreements in 1949: Egypt on February 25; Lebanon on March 23; Jordan on April 3; and Syria on July 20.

When the fighting subsided, Palestinian Arabs found themselves living under Egyptian, Israeli, and Jordanian rule or as displaced refugees in hastily constructed camps around the margins of Israel's newly established and expanded frontiers and in surrounding Arab states. Others fled even farther. Out of Palestine's prewar Arab population of 1.3 million, approximately half had become refugees. They had not only failed to keep Israel from being established, but they had also lost what had been assigned to them in the UN partition. Israel emerged as an independent and powerful state in the region, having successfully defended its newly created borders, expanded its territory, and obtained general international recognition. With Israel's acquisition of areas allotted to the proposed Arab state and Jordan's annexation of most of the rest of it, the Arab state envisioned by the United Nations was left without territory. Jerusalem emerged as a divided city, partitioned into Israeli and Jordanian sectors, rather than the united city under international administration proposed by the UN plan.

Early Arab-Israeli Relations

The nearly two decades between the establishment of Israel in 1948 and the Arab-Israeli war of June 1967 was a time of momentous change in the Middle East. The newly established Jewish state, inhabited by large numbers of European emigres, was better equipped and more effectively organized to take advantage of post–World War II developments in technology and communications than the more traditional societies of its Arab neighbors. Israel also benefited from the generous aid of Western governments that wanted to help the state that offered itself as a haven for the survivors of the Holocaust. Israel embarked on a period of nation building that with generous Western support gradually transformed it into the most technologically advanced and heavily armed state in the Middle East. Unrestricted immigration led to rapid population growth during the early years of Israeli independence, from a Jewish population of 717,000 in November 1948 to nearly

2 million by 1961. Many of these immigrants were Jews from Arab countries whom Israel worked in a variety of overt and covert ways to attract, while others immigrated seeking a safer environment.

For the Arab states surrounding Israel, the defeat of their armies in 1948 was a disaster (*nakba*). So overwhelming did the defeat appear that it seriously undermined the legitimacy of every Arab regime; it ushered in an era of general Arab political instability, and a popular desire to seek revenge for the insult of 1948 fueled Arab political rhetoric, but not action, for the next two decades. General corruption and oppression by Arab regimes only added to this crisis of political legitimacy.

Unable to force compliance with the UN partition resolution of November 1947, the UN General Assembly in December 1948 had established the Conciliation Commission for Palestine to mediate the conflict. Consisting of France, Turkey, and the United States, and headed by UN acting mediator Ralph Bunche, the commission presided over Arab-Israeli negotiations on the island of Rhodes. Its efforts led to various armistice agreements. The commission was unable, however, to transform these agreements into a broader peace settlement. The Arab states insisted on negotiating as a bloc, while Israel wanted only to negotiate with individual states. In addition, Israel rebuffed Arab demands for the repatriation of Palestinian refugees. Although some Arab leaders privately indicated their willingness to resolve the conflict in return for territorial concessions by Israel, the Israeli government adamantly refused to relinquish any land, especially after Israel's formal admission to the United Nations on May 11, 1949.

In December 1948, the UN General Assembly passed Resolution 194 calling for the return of Palestinian refugees or for their compensation. Israel's refusal to permit even a partial repatriation of Arab refugees, Arab states' refusal to grant them citizenship, and the refugees' insistence on their own independent, Palestinian identity perpetuated the enormous refugee problem. In response, in 1950 the UN Relief and Works Agency (UNRWA) was established to fund and administer refugee camps in Lebanon, Jordan, Syria, the West Bank, and Gaza. The camps, which soon became permanent, demonstrated the impotence of the international community in leading the conflicting parties toward an overall settlement. The Palestinians consistently rejected the view that their situation was a humanitarian problem, instead insisting that their plight remained a political-national one at heart.

Regional Arms Race

Given the unstable political situation that emerged after the 1948 war, Great Britain, France, and the United States in May 1950 announced the Tripartite Declaration, in which they agreed to limit arms supplies to the various parties of the Arab-Israeli conflict and to insist on a political rather than a military solution to it. This early effort to contain a potential arms race soon broke down, however, when in 1954 Israel concluded a major arms agreement with France. On February 28, 1955, Israel made use of its newly strengthened armed forces to launch a successful raid against an Egyptian position in Gaza. Ostensibly undertaken in retaliation for ongoing border violations by unspecified Arab refugees, the raid was carried out primarily to demonstrate Israeli military strength and the futility of continued Arab nonrecognition.

Instead of intimidating Egypt into recognizing the permanence of Israel, the Gaza raid, along with other similar Israeli raids into Arab territory, only served to provoke the new military leadership in Egypt, headed by Col. Gamal Abdel Nasser, to seek a reliable source of arms. Nasser preferred to obtain weapons from the West, especially from the United States, which was seeking to draw Egypt into a Western-sponsored Middle Eastern alliance, but President Dwight D. Eisenhower refused to provide arms on political terms that Egypt would accept. Nasser turned reluctantly to the Soviet bloc. A subsequent Czech-Egyptian arms agreement announced on September 27, 1955, marked the death of the Tripartite Declaration, gave impetus to the developing French-Israeli arms relationship, undercut U.S. efforts to contain Soviet influence in the Middle East, and provoked tensions that led to the Israeli attack on Egypt in October 1956.

Barriers to Peace

Despite continuing diplomatic efforts by the United Nations, the United States, and Great Britain to assuage tensions and put forth plans for an overall Arab-Israeli settlement, a variety of factors combined to thwart them. Foremost was the pattern of border clashes and incidents that developed almost from the moment the various parties signed the 1949 armistice agreements. At first the clashes were triggered by Palestinian villagers on one side of the armistice line whose lands and crops had ended up on the Israeli side of the unofficially established border. For much of the 1950s, the "infiltrators" were civilians who wanted to check on their property. Thousands of them were killed by Israeli forces. These incidents, however, gradually evolved into more organized attempts at sabotage and violence by some of the refugees who in the late 1950s had begun to coalesce into resistance groups. Arab governments sometimes supported the groups, but more often than not they sought to control them. These border clashes served as the impetus for Israel to send a message of its strength to Arab governments and to Palestinian refugees. To that end, Israel held the Arab governments responsible for patrolling their side of the border, but they generally were unable or unwilling to perform this task. Israel's adoption in 1952 of a more aggressive, self-described policy of reprisal led the Arab states to enhance their defensive postures.

During the early 1950s, a number of factors fueled Israel's sense of isolation: Arab rhetoric calling for the "liberation of Palestine," which Israel and many of its supporters interpreted only as the destruction of the Jewish state; an Arab League boycott on trade with Israel; and frequent Egyptian blockades of sea traffic to or from Israel through the Strait of Tiran and Suez Canal. The Czech-Egyptian arms agreement of September 1955 increased Israeli fears of the Arabs' potential military capacity. Pressure in Israel grew for a major strike against Egypt, mainly to secure Sharm al-Shaykh, the western flank of the Strait of Tiran, before Egypt could integrate its new weapons into its armed forces. Israel also signed another major arms agreement with France.

Israel's growing desire to attack Egypt became an increasingly feasible possibility because of developing Western hostility toward the Egyptian government. France viewed Nasser with disfavor because of the moral and material support he offered resistance fighters opposing French imperial rule in Algeria. Nasser alarmed Britain with his nationalist policies and desire to end the British military and political presence in Egypt and the Suez Canal Zone. He also resisted British efforts at organizing the Baghdad Pact, a Western-supported alliance including Iran, Iraq, Pakistan, and Turkey, ostensibly intended to check the expansion of Soviet influence in the Middle East.

The United States, whose policy was to encourage Egypt's inclusion in any Western alliance formed in the region, gradually became disenchanted with Nasser's policies as well. His official acceptance of Soviet bloc assistance in 1955, his refusal to lift a blockade against Israeli shipping, and his recognition of communist China in May 1956 were all considered blows to U.S. interests. Nasser's recognition of China, however, was the act that led U.S. secretary of state John Foster Dulles, on July 20, 1956, to withdraw assistance for building the Aswan High Dam, the principal symbol of Nasser's ambitious plans for Egypt's agricultural and economic development. Although Dulles's action was probably a maneuver aimed at forcing Nasser to take more seriously U.S. interests in the region, Nasser reacted on July 26 by nationalizing the French- and British-owned Suez Canal Company. Britain and France began preparations for a joint attack to take back the canal.

Unable to secure support for military intervention from the United States, which preferred a negotiated settlement, Britain, France, and Israel adopted a secret strategy in which Israel would launch an attack on Egyptian forces in the Sinai and appear to threaten the canal. At that point Britain and France would intervene to separate the warring parties, reoccupying the canal zone in the process. They scheduled the operation for late October 1956, when the United States would be focused on presidential elections and presumably therefore too distracted to take action against the attack.

The 1956 Suez Crisis and War

On October 29, Israel launched an offensive against Egyptian positions in the Sinai. An Israeli paratroop drop near the Mitla pass was executed to give the appearance of threatening the Suez Canal. The transparency of the allied strategy became evident the following day, when France and Britain jointly issued an ultimatum demanding an immediate cease-fire, a withdrawal of Egyptian and Israeli forces from opposite sides of the canal, and Egyptian acceptance of a temporary occupation of the canal zone by their forces to separate the Middle Eastern belligerents and to ensure freedom of shipping through the waterway. At this point, Israeli-Egyptian hostilities had barely begun near the Israeli frontier, far from the canal, and Egypt would have had to evacuate its 30,000-man force from the Sinai, according to the terms of the proposed cease-fire.

Israel quickly indicated its acceptance of the ultimatum, while Egypt rejected it. Nasser issued orders that in the event of an Anglo-French attack, all Egyptian forces in the Sinai were to be redeployed to defend the canal. The Egyptian military implemented these orders on the nights of October 31 and November 1, following French and British air attacks against Egyptian airfields on October 31. The movement of Egyptian forces toward the canal, coupled with the decimation of the Egyptian air force by the allied air attacks, opened the way for Israel's complete occupation of the Sinai, almost without a fight, by the morning of November 5.

Meanwhile, on November 1 the UN General Assembly had adopted a U.S.-sponsored resolution calling for an immediate cease-fire, a withdrawal of Israeli forces to behind the 1949 armistice lines, the reopening of the Suez Canal (which Egypt had closed), and all other UN members (that is, Britain and France) "to refrain from introducing military goods into the area." Egypt immediately accepted the call for a cease-fire, but Britain, France, and Israel would not, the first two because they had not yet introduced ground forces into the canal area. Finally succumbing to international and domestic pressure, Britain accepted the UN cease-fire effective at midnight on November 6–7, long before it had been able to achieve its military objectives in the canal zone. Israel and France also accepted the cease-fire.

Under strong pressure from the United Nations, especially from the United States and the Soviet Union, to withdraw unconditionally from all territories it had occupied during the conflict, Israel ultimately did so. The last Israeli troops left Gaza on March 9, 1957. The last French and British troops had left Egypt on December 22, 1956. In return for Israel's evacuation of the Sinai, Israel and Egypt accepted (on the Egyptian side of their armistice line) the presence of the United Nations Emergency Force (UNEF), which had begun arriving in mid-November 1956. The force's mission was to help protect Israel's southern frontier from Arab attacks as well as to ensure freedom of Israeli navigation through the Strait of Tiran. Israel alone profited from the military campaign, but it failed, however, to secure a general peace treaty as a result of the war or explicit Arab recognition of its legitimacy as a state. More important, it failed in overthrowing the regime of Nasser. Thus Israel remained technically at war with Egypt as well as with the rest of the Arab world.

Arab Rivalries

The years immediately following the Suez crisis witnessed a significant downturn in Arab-Israeli tensions primarily because of the Arab states' preoccupation with inter-Arab politics and rivalries. While anti-Israeli sentiment remained the staple of Arab political rhetoric, Israel took a back seat to the instability and other problems afflicting Arab regimes, although the Arab public remained quite concerned about the plight of the Palestinians.

Despite Egypt's military defeat in 1956, Nasser emerged afterward as a popular hero to many Arabs. The military outcome aside, Britain and France, the traditional colonial powers in the Arab world, had been politically humiliated. Moreover, Egypt's nationalization of the Suez Canal received international recognition, and Israel was denied territorial expansion. Nasser, now perceived as the only leader capable of restoring Arab dignity and pride, embarked on a period of leadership genuinely appreciated by large segments of the Arab public that would last until Egypt's humiliating defeat in the 1967 Arab-Israeli war.

Nasser's popularity and the plans of his regional and international enemies provoked crises in several Arab countries during the late 1950s and early 1960s. In Jordan, Nasserist groups and other opponents raised challenges to King Hussein's rule that led the British to intervene in support of him in 1957 and 1958. In February 1958, Syrian politicians, concerned with the rise of communism there, went to Cairo offering their country as part of a Nasser-led United Arab Republic (UAR). Nasser, initially reluctant despite his Arab nationalist declarations, decided to accept. The political union of Egypt and Syria lasted three years, until disgruntled Syrian officers reclaimed Syrian sovereignty through a military coup in September 1961. Syrian Baath Party leaders' support of "secession" from the UAR created a permanent rift between Nasser and the Baath. Nasser would never again trust the Baath, fueling what U.S. political scientist Malcolm Kerr called the Arab cold war.

Inspired by the union of Egypt and Syria, large numbers of Lebanese in 1958 demonstrated in favor of union with the UAR. The subsequent destabilization of the sitting Lebanese government—brought about by President Camille Chamoun's pro-Western policies and his manipulation of the electoral system to allow himself to remain in office counter to the terms of the constitution—led the United States to intervene during the summer in support of the pro-U.S. regime. Almost simultaneously, military officers in Iraq, influenced by the example set by Nasser's Egypt, overthrew their pro-Western monarchy and withdrew Iraq from the Baghdad Pact. Rather than join the UAR, however, the new military regime emphasized Iraqi independence and began to vie with Nasser for Arab nationalist leadership in the region.

In September 1962, pro-Nasser elements in the North Yemeni military overthrew their monarchy, leading ultimately to extensive Egyptian military intervention against the Saudi-financed royalist opposition, which the new Yemeni military regime could not subdue. The Egyptian commitment in soldiers, money, and materiel in Yemen severely drained Cairo's resources and decreased Nasser's ability to counter Israel's military challenge.

Despite continuing popular support in the Arab world, by the mid-1960s Nasser's relations with conservative Arab leaders were strained. Those with Saudi Arabia were the most hostile because of the conflict in Yemen, but Jordan and Iraq also took issue with Egypt. They strongly resented appeals by Nasser to the "Arab masses" that put strains on all the regimes unfriendly to him. One of Nasser's more frequent calls was for Arabs to rise up and overthrow the "tools of imperialism," that is, to overthrow the pro-Western regimes in the region. He financed and sometimes armed opposition groups that followed his political line.

In the midst of these disputes, any credible Arab threat to Israel seemed remote, although with Soviet support and assistance, Egypt and Syria continued to arm themselves for a potential third round of hostilities. The Israeli victories in 1948 and 1956 had provided a measure of deterrence against Arab attack. The Jewish state, however, continued its military procurement relationship with France and was developing its own arms manufacturing industry and a nuclear capability. In addition, it was gradually building its highly trained citizen army to meet any future Arab military challenge and to fulfill the goal of capturing East Jerusalem, the site of the Western Wall of the Temple, and beyond. Even as late as the spring of 1967, the possibility of an Arab-Israeli war did not appear likely. Yet, within the conflicts spawned by inter-Arab rivalries lay the seeds of the war that began on June 5, 1967.

The June 1967 War

Developments in 1964 resulted in the gradual revival of border tensions that, in turn, culminated in the June 1967 War. An Israeli project to divert water from the Sea of Galilee, or Lake Tiberias, along an aqueduct to the Negev Desert led Syria to call for joint Arab action. Nasser—under constant pressure from Baath Party questioning of his commitment to the Palestinian cause and seeking to reassert his credentials as leader of the Arab world—called for a meeting of Arab heads of state in Cairo under the auspices of the Arab League. This first Arab summit, convened in January 1964, produced two significant decisions: general Arab support for Syria to divert sections of the Jordan River in its territory (to diminish the amount of water flowing into Israel) and the formal establishment of the Palestine Liberation Organization.

Since the 1956 Suez crisis, stateless Palestinian refugees from the 1948 war had been organizing political groups and attempting to mobilize public support for their return to their homeland, now Israel. In general, they continued to look to the Arab regimes to help them achieve this goal, but many were becoming increasingly skeptical about the ability and the willingness of the Arab governments to bring about the "liberation of Palestine," a slogan that captured the dreams of millions of Palestinians and other Arabs.

Some Palestinians, such as George Habash, a leader of the Arab Nationalist Movement (ANM), which he had helped to establish in Beirut in the early 1950s, believed general popular upheaval and the achievement of Arab unity to be preconditions for overcoming Israeli intransigence. Habash and the ANM argued for the need to organize Palestinians militarily in response to popular demands for action, especially after the Fatah movement, led by Yasir Arafat, announced its existence with a series of minor military acts against targets in Israel in the mid-1960s. At the same time, other leaders and groups, including Arafat and Fatah, took the view that Palestinians must develop their own independent political capacity, distinct from the Arab states, to foster an eventual return of the lands lost in 1948. Their willingness to press for an independent Palestinian leadership and for independent Palestinian action and decision making marked a new era in the history of Palestinian nationalism.

The proliferation and appeal of such groups led Nasser to favor the establishment of a formal Palestinian organization within the Arab League structure. Fearing Palestinian organizing slipping from his control, he sought to rein in the movement. Through the establishment of the PLO, Nasser sought to channel Palestinian irredentist energies into support for himself and his leadership of the Arab world. Whereas previous gatherings of Arab officials after 1949 had called for the "application of the UN resolutions"—that is, that Israel should accept border rectifications and the return of Arab refugees—the language of the summit communique establishing the PLO called for the "liberation of Palestine."

Mounting Tensions

Nasser wanted to avoid direct confrontation with Israel in 1964 and refrained from mobilizing general Arab support against Israeli efforts, which included air strikes, to stop Syria's water diversion project. Unable to count on Nasser's backing, Syria responded by providing arms and training to Arafat's Fatah for operations against Israel. The forays caused little damage but resulted in a few Israeli casualties. The attacks continued throughout 1965 and escalated in 1966 and 1967. Meanwhile, Arafat exploited Fatah's (real and imagined) military endeavors for maximum propaganda effect. He issued declarations characterized by bombast and exaggeration to placate a public eager for quick victory. Complicating matters for Israel was the fact that although the attacks against it originated in Syria, the missions were conducted across Jordan's West Bank armistice line. In accordance with its policy, therefore, Israel held Jordan and other neighboring Arab countries responsible for failing to control its border. In November 1966, after an incident in which several Israelis were killed, Israel attacked the village of Samu, near Hebron in the West Bank, killing eighteen people and injuring more than fifty.

During this period, Syria shelled Israeli settlement areas from the elevated position of the Golan. UN observers often held Israelis responsible for provoking these incidents, because of their efforts to farm territories whose status had not been resolved in the 1949 armistice agreements. In an interview published posthumously, Israeli defense minister Moshe Dayan acknowledged that Israel sometimes deliberately advanced bulldozers into the demilitarized zone to provoke Syrian gunfire. Syrian shells often hit areas outside the disputed areas, including established Israeli settlements. A particularly intense Syrian shelling on April 7, 1967, escalated into an air skirmish in which Israeli pilots downed six Syrian aircraft.

Syrian and Jordanian reaction to mounting tensions focused on criticism of Nasser, whom they accused of hiding behind the UNEF troops along his armistice line with Israel and of being more interested in events in Yemen than in helping confront Israel, the common enemy. The Jordanian and Syrian governments, despite their own rivalry, in effect dared Nasser to assert his self-proclaimed leadership of the Arab world. Attacked from the left and the right, pressure mounted and Nasser felt compelled to do something.

Counterstrikes by Israel did not deter ongoing attacks against it, and in early May 1967 the Israeli government announced that it was considering taking more decisive action, especially against Syria. Word of Israeli preparations for war along the Syrian border, rumors apparently spread by Moscow, raised a challenge that Nasser could not avoid. On May 16, he demanded the withdrawal of the UNEF from the Sinai and began reinforcing Egyptian troops near the frontier with Israel. On May 22, Nasser, hoping for a UN-mediated diplomatic solution that never materialized,

announced his intention to reestablish the blockade of the Strait of Tiran. This action, a violation of the terms of the 1956 agreement that ended the Suez crisis, was, perhaps too conveniently, considered an act of war by Israel.

The prospect of impending war began to grip the Middle East, fueled by Jordan's decision on May 30 to join a mutual defense pact with Egypt and Syria. The latter two had entered into such an agreement in November 1966. Meanwhile, paralyzed by indecision, the Israeli government fell, and on June 1 a new national unity government under Levi Eshkol was formed that included as defense minister Moshe Dayan, the architect of Israel's 1956 military campaign.

With historical hindsight, it appears that if Israel had not launched attacks on June 5, war in 1967 would have been avoided. A diplomatic settlement of the crisis would likely have been reached at the expense of the Israeli goal of capturing all of Jerusalem and the Golan Heights. Despite Nasser's insistence that any outbreak of war would be initiated by Israel, other Arab leaders, particularly Ahmad Shuqayri, the pro-Nasser chairman of the PLO, made grandiose declarations that alarmed the Israeli public. Across the border Israel waited for a pretext to attack.

Israel Attacks

Achieving total surprise, Israel launched its military campaign on June 5 at 8:45 A.M. In the first days of the war, Israel claimed that Egypt had fired the first shots, but the United States knew otherwise, and Israel never repeated this claim, instead citing the doctrine of preemptive strike as justification for its actions.

In three hours of bombing, Israeli aircraft struck Egyptian airfields, destroying 300 of Egypt's 431 aircraft. Similar attacks would destroy the Jordanian and Syrian air forces and Iraqi aircraft at a major airfield in western Iraq. Forty-five minutes after launching air strikes against Egypt, Israel sent a message through UN mediators to Jordanian king Hussein informing him that Israel would not attack the West Bank unless Jordan attacked first. Hussein ordered his artillery to open fire on various targets in Israel, apparently before receiving the Israeli message. Hussein did so under the misperception that Egypt was destroying the Israeli air force, an impression that Nasser conveyed to him and which Nasser's commanders, in turn, had conveyed to him. Although the artillery fire did not constitute a prelude to Jordanian offensive operations, it did supply a pretext for Israel to attack the West Bank, which was treasured by many Zionists as part of the biblical Land of Israel.

Israeli military action against the West Bank began at 11:15 A.M. on June 5, shortly before its destruction of the Jordanian air force, which began around noon. The capture of East Jerusalem was Israel's first priority. Fierce fighting took place around the city on June 5 and 6. The Jordanian commander in Jerusalem, realizing the weakness of his position, withdrew his forces during the night of June 6, and unopposed Israeli forces took control of the city the next morning. Meanwhile, Israeli columns moved in from the north, west, and south against Jordanian forces concentrated at Nablus. Aided by air superiority—which provided the outmanned Israeli ground forces a decisive advantage throughout the war—they gradually overcame Jordanian resistance and converged on Nablus on June 7. Virtually surrounded by approaching Israeli forces and their morale broken, the defenders of Nablus fled across the Jordan River, leaving Israel in effective control of the West Bank. At 8 P.M. on the evening of June 7, Jordan and Israel accepted a UN appeal for a cease-fire, fully a day and a half before a cease-fire would be concluded in the Sinai.

On the first day of the war, Israeli ground forces had launched a multipronged attack into the Sinai aimed at breaking through Egyptian lines, severing communications, and destroying the Egyptian army as it tried to retreat. With complete air superiority, the strategy proved highly effective. Egypt unconditionally accepted a UN Security Council request for a cease-fire on June 9, by which time Israel had achieved full control of the peninsula.

Syria, whose actions and policies had contributed to the sparks that led to the war, performed poorly once hostilities began. After the destruction of its air force on June 5 only hours after Israel's first strike on Egypt, Syria became vulnerable to Israeli interdiction of its military movements. As the breadth of Israel's victories in the Sinai and West Bank became apparent, the Syrian government planned, at the appropriate moment, to accept the UN call for a cease-fire, which it did at 5:20 P.M. on June 8. After the outbreak of the war, Syrian artillery from the Golan Heights did manage to keep Israeli forces and settlements under constant bombardment. The Israeli government had faced strong pressure from residents in the north and from army units in its northern territorial command to do something to silence the Syrian guns that before the war had launched rocket attacks against Israel. Capture of the Golan was therefore on Israel's list of military objectives. Accordingly, Defense Minister Dayan ordered the army to attack Syria as soon as possible, which would not be until June 9, a day after Syria had accepted a cease-fire.

Despite the obstacles posed by the geography of the Golan, Israeli columns advanced up the heights under fire from dug-in Syrian positions along their routes. The Syrian government immediately protested Israel's violation of the cease-fire to the United States and issued orders for its frontline units to withdraw from the Golan to defensive positions near Damascus, the capital. The withdrawal began on the afternoon of June 9 even before the Israelis had reached the crest of the heights. When Israel resumed operations the following morning, its units consequently swept to their designated military objectives without opposition. Having achieved its military and political goals, Israel accepted the UN cease-fire at 6:30 A.M. on June 10, the sixth day of the war.

The Aftermath of War

The outcome of the 1967 war greatly complicated the Arab-Israeli conflict and exacerbated the suffering of the Palestinian people, as many more of them joined their already large number of refugees. Before the war, the key issues of the conflict were quite clear: the final settlement of Israel's borders and the ultimate disposition of the Palestinian Arab refugees. After the war, several new issues emerged. Among these were the terms by which the Sinai Peninsula would be returned to Egypt and the Golan Heights to Syria; the status of the West Bank and Gaza Strip; the status of Jerusalem, which Israel now proclaimed to be the reunited and eternal capital of Israel and not subject to negotiation. Israel did not wait long before annexing East Jerusalem, thereby settling the status of the city as far as it was concerned. Two other results of the war would also profoundly affect the conflict in the coming years. The war increased international involvement in the Middle East, especially by the United States and the Soviet Union, and heightened the sense of national identity among Palestinian refugees as well as among those Palestinians living under Israeli occupation.

Israel initially expressed an official, albeit vague, willingness to return the territories it had occupied during the war, with the exception of East Jerusalem. It also stated, however, that it would not permit a return to the prewar status quo, which it argued had created the conditions for war in the first place. Israel insisted on negotiated peace agreements with neighboring states—which would have entailed its official recognition by those states—in exchange for undefined parts of the occupied territories. Israel, did not, however, seek talks with the Palestinians, whose existence it did not recognize outside the context of systematically referring to them as "terrorists." Concerning territorial issues, in 1967 the United States, in contrast to its stance in 1956, this time supported Israel's position.

In August 1967, the Arab states convened a summit in Khartoum and adopted the position that Israel should unconditionally withdraw from the occupied territories. Because the UN Charter enshrined the principle of the "inadmissibility of the acquisition of territory by war," they expected the international community to support their posi-

Aftermath of the 1967 War

tion. Unlike the United States, the Soviet Union, which had broken diplomatic relations with Israel during the war, supported them. Moscow also agreed to rearm Egypt and Syria, a gesture that strengthened their resolve to hold fast to the principles enunciated at Khartoum: "no peace with Israel, no recognition of Israel, no negotiations with it, and insistence on the rights of the Palestinian people in their own country." France, which had been instrumental in helping Israel in the construction of its military, including its unacknowledged nuclear capabilities, began distancing itself from the Jewish state. It ended arms exports to Israel the following year. The United States would then become the most effective and consistent supplier of the most advanced weapons and aid to the Jewish state.

UN Resolution 242

The United States and the Soviet Union, now immersed in the Arab-Israeli situation, sought to reach agreement on a framework for encouraging settlement of the conflict. The result of their efforts was UN Security Council Resolution 242, adopted on November 22, 1967. Emphasizing the "inadmissibility of the acquisition of territory by war and the need to work for a just and lasting peace in which every state in the area can live in security," the resolution also stressed that a just and lasting peace should include the application of the following principles: "(i) Withdrawal of Israeli armed forces from territories occupied in the recent conflict; (ii) Termination of all claims or states of belligerency and respect for and acknowledgment of the sovereignty, territorial integrity and political independence of every State in the area and their right to live in peace within secure and recognized boundaries free from threats or acts of force." Other principles enunciated in the resolution included freedom of navigation through international waterways in the area, a just settlement of the refugee problem, and establishment of demilitarized zones, if necessary, to guarantee the territorial inviolability and the political independence of every state in the region.

Of note, the resolution's English version, but not its French or Russian versions, referred to the withdrawal of Israeli forces from "territories occupied," not from "the territories occupied," thereby leaving it entirely up to Israel to determine how much of those lands it wished to keep. Furthermore, it angered the Palestinians that the word *Palestinian* appeared not once in the resolution and that it presented their situation not as a political issue but as a humanitarian and refugee problem. In addition, although the resolution clearly linked the establishment of peace with Israeli withdrawal, it notably lacked any insistence on direct negotiations among the hostile parties. The resolution concluded, however, by requesting the appointment of a special UN representative to conduct negotiations with the various parties in accordance with its provisions.

Gunnar Jarring, Sweden's ambassador to the Soviet Union, was appointed mediator between the Arabs and Israelis, but his efforts to move the situation along soon failed. Egypt, although it grudgingly accepted Resolution 242, mainly at the Soviets' insistence, held fast to the view that Jarring should focus solely on Israeli withdrawal as a precondition for negotiations. Syria, on the other hand, led by the radical regime of Salah Jadid, who preached a "people's war against Israel and world imperialism," refused to accept the resolution and continued to support Palestinian resistance groups willing to stage raids into Israel. Such attitudes strengthened the hands of a rapidly growing body of similarly hard-line Israelis who believed in resurrecting Eretz Israel, or Greater Israel—that is, the creation of a state coinciding with the boundaries of biblical Israel, stretching from the Mediterranean to the Euphrates—and so called for retention of the occupied territories (or at the least most of them). Some Israelis felt that the territories were needed as a security buffer, because the Arabs would never agree to a peace. Others claimed that because the territories were part of historical Israel, they should not in any case be returned. Some religious Israelis believed that Greater Israel was a gift from God and not subject to diplomatic argumentation.

In the face of continued Israeli occupation of the territories, King Hussein grudgingly tolerated the growth of Palestinian resistance organizations in Jordan. He had accepted Resolution 242 but saw the Palestinian groups as a means of deterring any Israeli attempt to annex the West Bank, which technically remained part of his kingdom. Moreover, presiding over a kingdom with a majority Palestinian population, the king had no other choice at that moment.

The emergence of an increasingly significant Palestinian-based guerrilla movement against Israel proved to be one of the more salient new features of the Arab-Israeli conflict in the years following the 1967 war. The rapidly growing community of Palestinian refugees became increasingly drawn to the idea, most effectively articulated by Fatah, that the Palestinians needed to forge their own independent political identity in order to secure the liberation of Palestine. The popularity of this attitude, however, would bring them into conflict not only with Israel, but also with their Arab host states, especially those in which the guerrilla movement took root.

War of Attrition

As the ineffectiveness of the Jarring mission became clear and Israel moved to consolidate its hold on the occupied territories, Nasser decided to renew military confrontation with Israel as a means of maintaining superpower interest in the conflict. Continuing Soviet military assistance strengthened his determination to secure Israel's withdrawal from the Sinai on his terms rather than on Israel's. By the summer of 1968, Egypt had upgraded its inventory of military hardware to make it superior in quality and quantity to what it had been on the eve of the 1967 war. In September 1968, Egypt began intensive artillery barrages of Israeli positions along the length of the Suez Canal. The tactic failed, however, to elicit an international response. Israel's retaliation with air attacks against civilian targets and helicopter raids deep inside Egyptian territory indicated to Nasser the need for better defensive preparation. Meanwhile, the Israelis built stronger fortified positions, the so-called Bar-Lev Line, along the east bank of the canal.

In response, Nasser evacuated civilians from the Egyptian cities along the canal and began building, with Soviet assistance, an elaborate air defense network to counter Israeli air superiority. With these preparations in place, he formally announced and launched on March 8, 1969, the War of Attrition against Israeli forces on the canal. Nasser hoped that an extended conflict would weaken Israeli resolve by inflicting unacceptable casualties and destroying the Bar-Lev Line, making it possible for Egyptian forces to cross the canal and establish a beachhead in the Sinai.

Intense Egyptian and Israeli bombardments lasted for about eighty days. When in July an Egyptian commando unit succeeded in crossing the canal and inflicting heavy casualties, Israel decided to commit its air force. It first sent a commando unit to destroy a key radar installation controlling parts of Egypt's air defense system and then jets followed with ten days of intensive air attacks, causing great damage to Egyptian artillery and surface-to-air missile systems. The operation made it possible for Israeli warplanes to subsequently strike virtually at will against Egyptian positions.

The War of Attrition continued, however. In early 1970, Israel decided to expand the war by bombing targets in the Egyptian interior. Such attacks led Nasser to again seek increased Soviet support, which in due course Moscow provided. The Soviets sent personnel to help operate certain sectors of Egypt's air defense system and to fly newly supplied aircraft. The influx of Soviet personnel soon improved Egyptian air defenses but provoked at least one instance of aerial combat between Israeli and Soviet pilots in which the Israelis emerged victorious. Most important for Nasser, however, the Soviet role prompted a new U.S. initiative aimed at implementing a cease-fire. The Rogers Plan—named after U.S. secretary of state William Rogers, who enunciated it—was firmly grounded in UN Resolution 242, calling for a cease-fire that included a memorandum of understanding stating that Egypt and Israel accept the resolution as a basis for further negotiations.

Egypt and Jordan, though not Syria, accepted the plan, but Israel refused to make any commitment to withdrawal before negotiations and therefore rejected it. In addition, national security adviser Henry Kissinger, sympathetic to the Israeli position, had been undermining Rogers' efforts. Only after the United States applied pressure, promised continuing military assistance, and guaranteed that it would not insist on a full withdrawal to the 1967 borders did Israel finally agree to accept the Rogers proposal. Even then, the Israeli decision provoked a minor government crisis, as several cabinet members resigned rather than be associated with it. Nevertheless, a cease-fire took effect on August 8, 1970, though not before Nasser had been able to obtain from Israel a commitment, in principle and guaranteed by the United States, to withdraw its forces from the Sinai.

The October 1973 War

A few weeks after the cease-fire agreement with Israel, Nasser died, in September 1970, and Anwar al-Sadat succeeded him as president of Egypt. Although Sadat had been among the Free Officers cadre that overthrew King Farouk in 1952 and had been part of Nasser's leadership council from the start, he differed from Nasser in many ways. Sadat was less ideological and had a more relaxed (albeit no less autocratic) style of leadership. He also proved to be less wedded to the concept of pan-Arabism and more oriented toward the security of his regime, regardless of larger Arab interests and causes. Many observers at the time thought of Sadat as a transitional leader, partly because he seemed to lack Nasser's personality and charisma.

Following the Egyptian-Israeli cease-fire, the United States focused on reviving UN ambassador Jarring's efforts to secure full implementation of Resolution 242. In February 1971, Jarring asked Sadat to enter into a peace agreement with Israel on the basis of the resolution. Sadat readily agreed, accepting even the principle of settling the refugee issue on the basis of UN Resolutions 194 and 242, a stance at variance with the policy of the PLO. Israel, however, rejected Sadat's terms, indicating that it would not accept full withdrawal to the prewar borders. It also refused to accept a negotiation process mediated by a third party, instead insisting on direct negotiations with the Arabs and without preconditions. Soon after the breakdown of this round of mediation, Jarring abandoned his effort at achieving a settlement based on Resolution 242. In rejecting Sadat's offer, the Israelis gravely underestimated the new Egyptian president. He would eventually obtain what he had hoped to procure by negotiation, but it would be at a cost to Israel.

Preparations for War

Over time, Sadat concluded that the geopolitical situation produced by the 1967 war could not be reversed by diplomacy. As early as 1971, he began to prepare for war. Even as he did so, however, he continued to privately communicate to the United States his desire to achieve a negotiated settlement. Sadat also made contacts with Hafiz al-Asad, the new president of Syria, who eagerly supported the concept of a two-front war. Under the cover of talks concerning a Libyan-proposed federation of Arab republics embracing Egypt, Libya, Sudan, and Syria, they and their staffs held strategy sessions to plan an attack.

For Sadat and Asad, receiving sufficient arms from the Soviet Union would be key to their war effort. Although the two leaders excluded Libyan leader Mu'ammar al-Qadhafi from their plans, Qadhafi's generous infusion of Libyan oil wealth contributed significantly to the rearming of both their countries. Sadat became frustrated by the slowness of Soviet arms deliveries—which he blamed on U.S.-Soviet efforts at achieving detente—while U.S. arms continued to flow steadily to Israel. In July 1972, hoping to obtain full U.S. backing, Sadat took the surprising step of expelling all 21,000 Soviet military advisers and operations personnel serving in Egypt. The expulsions caused the Soviets to speed up weapons deliveries in an attempt to win back Sadat's favor and in order to retain that of Asad. The expulsions made a favorable impression in Washington and seemed to diminish the possibility that Egypt would soon launch a war against Israel. According to Sadat's memoirs, by November 30, 1972, he felt confident enough in Egypt's military preparedness to make a firm decision to go to war.

The Arabs Attack

On October 6, 1973, the high Jewish holy day of Yom Kippur, Egypt and Syria launched a joint attack against Israel at precisely 2:05 P.M. The offensive, despite sufficient intelligence and a back-channel warning from King Hussein of Jordan, caught the Israeli high command by surprise, as they misinterpreted the evidence of an impending attack until just hours before it occurred. In accordance with a meticulously planned and methodically executed operation, nearly 90,000 Egyptian troops, supported by intense artillery barrages and aerial bombardments, crossed the Suez Canal, overran Israeli defenses, and established defensive beachheads along the length of the canal's eastern bank. By the time Israel mobilized enough forces to counterattack on October 8, Egyptian defensive positions were virtually impregnable. An elaborate air defense system behind the canal effectively neutralized Israeli air strike capabilities against Egyptian positions. Meanwhile, an effective deployment of antitank weapons neutralized Israel's mobile armored units, the second principal element of its military superiority.

As it became clear that Sadat intended to consolidate his newly won defensive position rather than strike out across the Sinai, Israel turned its attention to the Syrian front. In coordination with the Egyptian offensive, Syria had sent 35,000 troops and 800 tanks to attack Israeli defenses on the Golan. Unlike the Egyptian strategy—which was to establish a strong position on the eastern bank of the Suez, defend it, and use it to consolidate its gains in subsequent negotiations—the Syrians' objective was to drive the Israelis off the Golan, recapturing the territory that it had lost in 1967. From October 6 to October 13, the Golan front became the principal theater of the war, as Israel devoted the bulk of its resources to holding its position there. In close and bitter fighting, the Syrians almost achieved their objective before halting offensive operations on October 9, after Israeli reinforcements reestablished a firm defensive line at the crest of the heights.

Ground forces played the decisive role in defending Israeli positions on the Golan. During the first days of the war, the Israeli air force faced a network of surface-to-air missiles and antiaircraft artillery similar to the one that had successfully challenged its control of the air over the Sinai. By October 8, however, as the Sinai front stabilized, the Israelis launched an effort to destroy the Syrian air defense system. By October 11, Israel once again had achieved general control of the air. That day Israeli ground forces went on the offensive to recapture territories that they had lost and to carry the battle beyond the cease-fire line of 1967 toward the Syrian capital.

Despite a respectable defense and a Soviet airlift of supplies, Syrian forces proved unable to contain the Israeli advance toward Damascus along the eastern base of Mount Hermon. Syrian troops withdrew under fire to an established defensive line at Sasa and prepared to defend the approaches to Damascus with the support of newly arrived (albeit symbolic) Iraqi and Jordanian units. Saudi Arabia and Morocco also sent token troops, but they did not have combat roles. Having reestablished control of the battlefield and created a pressure point within Syria to absorb future counterattacks, Israel after October 13 broke off offensive operations and returned its attention to the Sinai front.

The Israelis had been planning their counteroffensive at the Suez Canal even before turning back the Syrian offensive on the Golan. It called for a breakthrough and crossing of the canal at Deversoir, just north of the Great Bitter Lake. The Israeli high command had hoped that their attack would be preceded by an Egyptian thrust from the bridgehead into the Sinai. They planned to blunt the Egyptian offensive and take advantage of the confusion to drive through Egyptian lines to the designated crossing point at the canal. When Egyptian forces failed to cooperate and remained secure in their well-defended positions, Israel continued to prepare for a breakthrough on the night of October 14.

Meanwhile, as Syrian forces came under extreme Israeli pressure on October 11, President Asad had appealed to Sadat to attack in the Sinai. In their prewar planning, Asad had understood that Sadat wanted to drive deeper into the Sinai than his forces had gone at that point. When the drive did not continue, Asad felt betrayed. Egypt had indeed planned an expanded offensive across the Sinai, but not until its air defense system had been transported across the canal. Against the advice of his generals, and after it was too late to relieve the Syrian front, Sadat ordered an October 14 offensive to capture the Giddi and Mitla passes, thus providing Israeli generals with precisely the opportunity for which they had hoped.

The Egyptian forces advanced beyond their air defense cover, and under an ill-conceived plan, toward an increasingly strong and well-prepared

Israeli army. In the Sinai, nearly 1,000 Egyptian tanks and 800 Israeli tanks, the latter now supported by air cover, fought the largest armored battle since World War II. Israeli tactics and superior mobility blunted the Egyptian advance, inflicting heavy casualties and causing confusion in the Egyptian ranks that allowed Israel to implement its plan to cross to the western bank of the canal.

On the night of October 15, a small Israeli force commanded by Gen. Ariel Sharon broke through a gap in the Egyptian defenses, bridged the canal, and reached the western side by the morning of October 16. Intense fighting continued for two more days, as Egyptian forces attempted to close the gap. By the afternoon of October 17, after nearly forty-eight hours of continuous battle, a much larger Israeli force succeeded in clearing the gap, opening the way for a major crossing of the canal and the establishment of an effective Israeli beachhead on its western flank. For two more days, the Israelis fought to consolidate the beachhead and bring in more forces to strengthen their position, while Egyptian forces encircling the beachhead attempted desperately to destroy it.

On October 19, Israeli forces on the western bank of the canal drove south along the waterway toward Suez in an attempt to trap the Egyptian Third Army on the eastern bank. When a UN-sponsored cease-fire went into effect on the evening of October 22, however, Israeli forces had been able to push only halfway toward their goal because of Egyptian resistance. Despite Israeli acceptance of the cease-fire, and after an unprecedented massive U.S. airlift of military hardware on Israel's behalf, fighting continued in this sector until October 25, when Israeli units effectively cut all supply lines serving the Third Army. Shelling and several other last-ditch efforts continued on the Golan after the October 22 cease-fire, as both sides tried to secure final positions.

Cease-Fire

Egypt primarily had taken the lead in responding to international appeals for a cease-fire, though only after it had become clear that the tide was turning against the Arabs. On October 16, after the disastrous Egyptian showing in the Sinai but before receiving information about the Israeli breakthrough across the canal, Sadat, in a television and radio broadcast, expressed his willingness to accept a cease-fire if Israel withdrew from all the territories occupied in 1967. In addition, he expressed his willingness to attend a postwar peace conference with Israel and to attempt to convince the other Arab states to participate. When the war ended, none of the participants had attained the military victory it would have preferred, yet all had achieved partial success. Although Israel was victorious militarily, unlike in previous Arab-Israeli wars, there was no clear winner.

As the war had continued, it increasingly became the focus of great power concern, facilitating communication between Washington and Moscow, even as U.S.-Soviet tensions mounted. After Sadat appealed on October 19 to the Soviet Union to help him in arranging a cease-fire, the Soviets requested a visit to Moscow by Henry Kissinger, who had become U.S. secretary of state. After two days of negotiations in Moscow, the two parties agreed to procedures for a cease-fire and future negotiations. Presented to the UN Security Council, the call for a cease-fire passed unanimously on October 22 as Resolution 338.

The day before, the Organization of Arab Petroleum Exporting Countries (OAPEC), led by Saudi Arabia, had announced a general boycott of oil sales to the United States in response to the U.S. congressional decision to appropriate $2.2 billion for a major military arms package for Israel.

When Israel continued, despite the cease-fire, to consolidate its position on the western bank of the Suez, Moscow protested to Washington, suggesting the urgent dispatch of Soviet and U.S. troops to police the cease-fire and to implement the provisions of Resolution 338. If the United States disagreed, the Kremlin said, the Soviet Union was prepared to act alone. U.S. president Richard Nixon, on the advice of Kissinger, interpreted the Soviet communication as an ultimatum and placed U.S. forces on worldwide alert to face down the Soviet challenge. Although the war was effectively over, the conflict still seemed to have the potential to threaten global nuclear war. The nuclear crisis was probably more hypothetical than real, and it passed quickly, as tensions diminished after Israel halted offensive operations on October 25.

Disengagement Agreements

Despite the joint U.S.-Soviet role in bringing an end to the 1973 war, Secretary of State Kissinger emerged as the central mediator in postwar negotiations, due in part to a growing perception among the Arabs, especially Sadat, that only the United States held enough sway to extract compromises from Israel. As long as support for UN Security Council Resolution 242 remained an element of U.S. policy, a basis for achieving Israeli withdrawal from the occupied territories through diplomatic means seemed feasible.

In addition to calling for an immediate cease-fire in the 1973 war, UN Resolution 338 reiterated that the consenting parties implement Resolution 242 in all its parts. Unlike Resolution 242, however, Resolution 338 called for negotiations "between the parties concerned under appropriate auspices aimed at establishing a just and durable peace in the Middle East." Sadat was prepared to participate in such negotiations, and under the rubric of "appropriate auspices" a role was provided for Kissinger. Traveling repeatedly between Arab capitals and Israel, Kissinger engaged in what came to be called shuttle diplomacy. His efforts gradually produced a series of disengagement agreements, the first of which, on October 28, 1973, secured Israel's assent for relief of Egypt's encircled Third Army. A subsequent agreement on November 11 committed Egypt and Israel to implement Resolutions 242 and 338 and to stabilize the cease-fire.

On January 18, 1974, Kissinger's diplomacy resulted in the Disengagement of Forces Agreement, which significantly reduced the chances of a future surprise attack by either side. In it, Israel consented to withdraw its forces from the west bank of the Suez. In return, Egypt accepted stringent limitations on the number of its forces permitted on the east bank of the canal and a withdrawal of its surface-to-air missiles—a key component of its success in the war—and long-range artillery to a line thirty kilometers behind the demilitarized zone now established between Egyptian and Israeli forces. A similar limitation constrained Israeli forces near the canal. UN Disengagement Observer Forces (UNDOF) in the demilitarized zone would monitor compliance.

Following the Egyptian-Israeli agreements, Kissinger focused on negotiations between Syria and Israel. Sadat's decision to acquiesce to provisions that reduced the chances for a renewed two-front war had weakened Asad's negotiating position, as did Sadat's promise to Kissinger to encourage the Arab oil-producing states to lift their boycott on petroleum sales to the United States, which they did on March 18, 1974. As with Sadat, Kissinger's assurances to Asad that the United States would work for implementation of Resolutions 242 and 338 enabled him to secure acceptance of a Syrian-Israeli Separation of Forces agreement on May 31, 1974.

In accordance with this arrangement, Israel withdrew from the salient it had occupied during the war and relinquished a narrow strip of land it had captured in 1967, including the town of Qunaitra (after destroying most of it). This area then became a demilitarized buffer zone controlled by UNDOF. Syria and Israel were allowed to deploy restricted numbers of personnel and weapons on their respective side of the zone. In a separate agreement with Kissinger, Asad promised to prevent Palestinian guerrilla attacks on Israel along the Golan front, something he had never permitted in any case.

During summer 1974, U.S.-Soviet talks, the Turkish invasion of Cyprus, and the Watergate scandal overshadowed Kissinger's continuing efforts at furthering the Arab-Israeli peace process. Further complicating matters, the Arab League in October 1974 decided at a summit in

Rabat, Morocco, to endorse the PLO as the sole legitimate representative of the Palestinian people. Their endorsement meant that although Egypt and Syria remained free to pursue the recovery of their territories lost to Israel in 1967, collective Arab policy toward a general resolution of the Arab-Israeli conflict would focus on arrangements between the PLO and Israel. The Arab states' support of the PLO's claim to represent all Palestinians living as refugees outside of Israel or under Israeli occupation conflicted with Israel's policy, buttressed by Resolution 338, of seeking peace through direct negotiations with neighboring Arab states. In addition, Israel adamantly opposed negotiations with the PLO because of its insistence on the "liberation of Palestine," which for Israel represented a denial of its right to exist. At the same time, Israel, under no pressure to recognize Palestinian national rights, continued to dismiss the PLO as a mere terrorist organization.

Sinai II

Kissinger's shuttle diplomacy resulted in a second Israeli-Egyptian disengagement agreement, Sinai II, on September 4, 1975. In it, Israel agreed to a further withdrawal of its forces from the Mitla and Giddi passes and the Abu Rudais oil fields to a new cease-fire line. Egyptian forces were permitted to move up to the line Israel had previously occupied. In between, a new UNDOF-monitored buffer zone was established, and early-warning electronic monitoring systems operated by U.S. technicians were positioned to alert both governments to violations of the agreement.

Sinai II also imposed limitations on forces in areas abutting the buffer zone, and Israel and Egypt promised to observe their continuing cease-fire and to abjure the use of force or military blockade against one another. Egypt also agreed to allow Israel to use the Suez Canal for the passage of nonmilitary cargo, and both countries pledged to continue negotiations toward a final peace settlement. Despite Sinai II's guarantees, Israel conditioned acceptance of them on

two side memorandums signed by Kissinger. The first provided guarantees of continued and generous U.S. economic and military assistance to Israel, and the second declared that the United States agreed not to "recognize or negotiate with the PLO so long as the PLO does not recognize Israel's right to exist and does not accept Security Council Resolutions 242 and 338." With the signing of the Sinai II accord, Kissinger's ability to advance an Arab-Israeli peace process came to an end. The position of the United States and Israel not to negotiate with the PLO stood at odds with what had become a collective Arab, if not international, position.

Sinai II's implications for Syria disturbed President Asad. He feared that Egypt's agreement with Israel would hinder his attempts at securing a return of the Golan. He, therefore, refused to cooperate with U.S. peacemaking efforts, but he also refused to join with Algeria, Iraq, Libya, South Yemen, and the PLO in a front condemning Sadat's increasing accommodation with Israel and seeking to undermine it. The grouping, dubbed the Rejectionist Front, wanted to revive the old formula of the Khartoum conference after the 1967 war, which rejected peace, negotiations, and recognition of the Jewish state. It wanted to discredit all "liquidationist solutions," a reference to attempts at legitimizing Israeli occupation of Palestinian lands.

Role of the PLO

The growing importance of the PLO in the Arab-Israeli conflict in the years after 1967 represented a function of Palestinian nationalism. When formed at the Arab summit in 1964, the PLO was intended as a token bureaucratic arm of the Arab League, then effectively controlled by Nasser. Despite this effort to establish control over the Palestinian movement, the various independent resistance groups that sprang up in the 1950s and 1960s managed to avoid Arab League domination. When Fatah began operations against Israel in the mid-1960s, it had done so independently (with Syrian blessing), not as an element of the PLO.

Only in February 1969 did the various resistance groups seek and receive admission to the PLO, which hitherto comprised ineffective political organizations and various unions and syndicates. By this time, however, the newly emerged resistance groups had become strong enough to take control of the organization. Arafat, head of Fatah, the largest Palestinian organization, became PLO chairman. Under his leadership the PLO strove to become an independent political actor in inter-Arab relations and mastered the art of political maneuvering among the assorted Arab rivalries and conflicts. At the same time, the perceived need to maintain unity within the Palestinian movement, and thus the requirement of consensus among the different commando and political organizations belonging to the PLO, constrained Arafat's independence. He also needed to maintain the flow of financial and military aid from Arab governments. Some of them, fearing Palestinian radicalism, wanted to curry favor with Arafat.

The moral support, funds, and recruits that began to flow toward the various resistance groups, especially to Fatah, is what allowed them to assert their influence over the PLO in the period following the 1967 war. As the Arab states slowly recovered from their military debacle and sought to recoup their losses, the resistance groups kept the Arab-Israeli conflict alive by launching raids and committing acts of violence in Israel and the occupied territories.

The PLO in Jordan and Lebanon

The largest numbers of Palestinian refugees lived in Jordan and Lebanon. The Palestinian political movement and resistance groups thrived in these two countries in part because of the sympathy of Jordanians and Lebanese toward their plight and because of weak government. It was also in Jordan and Lebanon that tensions between the movement and Arab governments grew the most strained.

An incident in Jordan soon after the 1967 war greatly contributed to the fortunes of Arafat's Fatah. A major Israeli "reprisal" against the Jordanian town of Karameh in March 1968 encountered stiff resistance from Fatah fighters, supported by Jordanian artillery. Although the Israeli unit technically accomplished its mission, it sustained notable casualties. Arafat was able to claim, perhaps with some justification, that his fighters had fought more bravely than any of the Arab armies a few months earlier. The Battle of Karameh became legend, bringing attention to Fatah and drawing new recruits to it and other PLO member organizations, such as the Popular Front for the Liberation of Palestine (PFLP). Further Israeli reprisals and bombing raids into Jordan and Lebanon similarly served to strengthen the resistance groups, which began to take control of the Palestinian refugee camps in Lebanon and Jordan.

The PFLP, an organization led by George Habash, a major rival of Arafat at the time, espoused a far more revolutionary philosophy than did Fatah. It called for the overthrow of discredited Arab regimes and the unification of the Arab world under revolutionary leadership as a means of achieving the liberation of Palestine. Habash, who led the Arab Nationalist Movement prior to 1967, founded the PFLP in December 1967 in response to the June war defeat and endorsed, with some initial reluctance, a Marxist-Leninist ideology. In July 1968, the PFLP began hijacking El Al planes and then those of Western airlines that serviced Israel to draw the spotlight to the seriousness of the Arab-Israeli conflict and the intensity of its Palestinian dimension. Although these and subsequent such acts attracted international attention to the Palestinian cause and the plight of the refugees, they also provoked outrage and tended to discredit the Palestinian movement. They made it easier for the enemies of the Palestinians to dismiss their activism as nothing more than terrorism.

A developing pattern of PLO-Israeli violence along Lebanon's southern boundary with Israel provoked a government crisis in 1969 in Lebanon that led to a change in status for the PLO there. A large portion of Lebanese wanted their government to deal forcibly with the increasing frequency of Israeli bombing raids across the border. In 1968, when Israeli commandos attacked Beirut International Airport and burned a number of civilian airliners to protest a hijacking by a Palestinian group based in Lebanon, various political groups and personalities demanded more official support for the Palestinian resistance. At the same time, a minority sympathetic with Maronite-oriented right-wing militias opposed the PLO and feared that the presence of the Palestinian movement in Lebanon would strengthen the hand of the Muslim (and leftist) segments of the population. The conflict between the two tendencies produced political paralysis and a government crisis that was resolved only by the intervention of Egypt's Nasser. His mediation produced the October 1969 Cairo Agreement, which resolved the immediate crisis but did not address the root cause. The agreement aimed at recognizing Lebanese military control over Lebanese territory while allowing the PLO to maintain a political and military presence in the country. It remarkably specified areas of operation for the PLO in southern Lebanon and placed the refugee camps under PLO control. In short, it amounted to a significant infringement on Lebanese sovereignty by giving the PLO virtual state-within-a-state status in Lebanon. It also strengthened Arafat in his endeavor to become an independent actor in inter-Arab politics.

Between 1949 and 1967 Lebanon had remained aloof from the Arab-Israeli conflict. Its emergence as the principal arena of the Israeli-PLO conflict placed additional strains on the Lebanese political system, which eventually erupted in civil war in 1975. The war, however, primarily concerned domestic and internal issues. Sectarian tensions in the country had been exacerbated by a political system designed by the French in the 1920s that continued to favor the Maronite Christians even though their percentage of the population had long been surpassed by Muslims because of their higher birth rates. In addition, as Lebanon increasingly became the center of PLO operations, the various

PLO groups operating there, as well as Lebanese and Palestinian civilians, became targets of Israeli raids.

In Jordan, tensions between the army and the PLO had increased throughout 1970 and finally erupted in civil war in September of that year following a PFLP hijacking of four international airliners. The hijackers had forced the planes to land at a remote airfield outside the Jordanian capital, Amman. After the crisis resolved, King Hussein unleashed his army against the Palestinian guerrillas and camps in Jordan, defeating them in ten days of fighting. Thousands of Palestinians were killed. This setback for the PLO, which is remembered as Black September, made Lebanon the sole center of PLO organizational activity in its struggle against Israel and left the Palestinian movement radicalized and bitter.

Growing International Stature

During the early 1970s, the PLO's support among Palestinians outside and within Israel continued to grow. The strength and appeal of the PLO among the refugees and in the Arab world stemmed less from its proclivity to draw attention to the Palestinian cause through violence than from its political symbolism and for its husbanding of Palestinian resources. Nonetheless, its use of political violence brought it the popular legitimacy in the eyes of the Palestinian people that helped solidify its leadership. It founded charity networks and centralized the distribution of funds for the needy and for the families of martyrs, as Palestinians call those killed while fighting for their cause. It also created the Red Cross–like Palestine Red Crescent Society to attend to the health needs of the refugees.

Since 1948 the Arab states had justified their hostility toward Israel on the grounds of supporting the right of the Palestinians to return to their land. The emergence of a grassroots Palestinian political movement increasingly relieved the Arab states of some burdens related to the Palestinians' predicament, as the movement increasingly shouldered the burden. To the degree that the PLO demonstrated its viability and ability to mobilize the Palestinians, most Arab states saw it in their interest to support it with funds and diplomatic backing. Some states, such as Saudi Arabia, donated generously to PLO funds to insulate the country from Palestinian political and military activities.

By October 1974, only five years after assuming the chairmanship of the PLO, Yasir Arafat achieved the first stage of his quest to formulate an independent Palestinian agenda when the Rabat Arab League summit recognized "the right of the Palestinian people to establish an independent national authority under the command of the PLO, the sole legitimate representative of the Palestinian people, in any Palestinian territory that is liberated." One month later, on November 13, Arafat and the PLO received international recognition when he spoke before the UN General Assembly, which granted the PLO observer status. The vote to admit the PLO was 105 to 4, with 20 abstentions. Israel, the United States, Bolivia, and the Dominican Republic cast the four votes against admission. In 1976 the PLO became the twenty-first full member of the Arab League, and by 1977 more than a hundred nations had granted the PLO some form of diplomatic recognition. The organization that Israel and the United States considered an unacceptable negotiating partner had ironically garnered more diplomatic recognition than Israel.

The PLO's new international stature and recognition had several repercussions. First, it brought into question Jordan's annexation of the West Bank, which occurred in 1950 and no Arab state formally recognized. King Hussein's efforts to negotiate a return of the territory from Israel were accordingly undermined, although the concept of a joint Jordanian-PLO negotiating posture remained a possibility, at least from a non-Palestinian perspective; the Palestinians insisted on designating the PLO alone as their official representative. Despite Hussein's bitterness toward the PLO, he publicly accepted the decision of the Rabat summit though he would not abjure Jordanian claims to the West Bank until 1988.

Second, the PLO's newfound recognition produced fissures within the organization. Essentially an umbrella organization of the various resistance groups and civilian and professional syndicates and societies, each with a different political outlook, the PLO maintained its unity by accommodating the views of even its most radical members. The growing acceptance of the PLO in international affairs, however, carried with it the burden of being responsive to the basic guidelines laid down by the international community for a settlement of the Arab-Israeli conflict, namely, accepting Israel, aligning with existing UN resolutions, and abandoning the struggle for the total liberation of Palestine.

Some PLO members, such as the PFLP, withdrew from its Executive Committee at various times rather than become a party to any compromise. Arafat, ever anxious to maintain the unity of the movement, tried an approach to Israel that would be acceptable to all factions and the international community: He insisted that any compromise settlement be viewed only as a prelude to the total liberation of Palestine, although his rivals knew that he no longer demanded anything more than the West Bank and Gaza as the site for a would-be Palestinian state. Israeli leaders, who continued to perceive and portray the PLO primarily as a terrorist organization bent on destroying Israel, rejected his formula. Furthermore, some Israeli political parties wanted to retain the lands occupied in 1967. Similarly unimpressed were potential U.S. interlocutors, such as Kissinger, who sought ostensibly to facilitate an Arab-Israeli peace process, but only with parties willing to accept and make peace with Israel and largely on Israeli terms. Successive U.S. presidents endorsed the Kissinger formula, and U.S. talks with PLO officials were legally taboo.

Israel's Position Hardens

The third implication of the enhanced international status of the PLO was a hardening of attitudes in Israel, as it girded itself in the occupied territories. Two trends had dominated Zionism since its origins in the late nineteenth century. The first, the socialist-labor tendency, manifested itself in Israel's ruling Labor Party. Ideological about the economic and social life of Israel, it nevertheless remained, in the eyes of the West and in its own words, "pragmatic and flexible" in international relations and diplomacy. Until the early 1990s, however, Labor never expressed a willingness to negotiate with the PLO or, until the late 1990s, accept a Palestinian state or recognize the Palestinians as a people. The second tendency, revisionist Zionism, was influenced by racialist nationalism and focused on the historic destiny of the Zionist movement to gain control of Eretz Israel— Palestine in addition to southern Lebanon, southern Syria, Jordan, and the territories occupied in the 1967 war. The revisionist Zionists traced their ideological formulations to their founder, Vladimir Jabotinsky, whose writings were influenced by Italian and German nationalist stirrings and literature. Revisionist Zionists dominated the Herut Party, which had been led by Menachem Begin since 1948. They had opposed the 1947 UN partition plan on the grounds that Jews could never agree to the partition of historic Israel. In the post-1967 period, Herut maintained that the occupied territories were part of historic Israel that had been "redeemed." It called, therefore, for Israeli settlement of the territories and opposed any suggestion that Israel should withdraw from them. Labor would ironically become the party to inaugurate Israel's settlement activities.

The revisionists were supported by the Greater Land of Israel Movement, which emerged immediately following the 1967 war. The movement included numerous Labor Party members, including then–defense minister Dayan, who favored establishing Jewish settlements in the occupied territories. By "creating facts" on the ground, proponents of settlement hoped to avoid returning some or all of the territories. Also, Jewish settlers would need protection, thus requiring that Israel deploy its military to the occupied territories. The presence of such a force, some proponents of settlement argued, would serve to enhance Israeli security, by providing a line of defense against attack, and to strengthen

Israel's bargaining position. Even in the summer of 1967, various Israeli citizen groups independently established a number of settlements, often with the tacit support of Israeli politicians. Begin and his supporters in the Knesset used their positions of influence to demand government approval of the settlements, which are illegal under international law.

As time passed without movement toward an Arab-Israeli settlement, the view increasingly gained hold (especially in the military) that Israel should retain most or all of the occupied territories as the best guarantee of its political regional dominance and of its security. In 1974, following the first disengagement agreements with Egypt and Syria, a new organization, Gush Emunim, appeared on the scene, committed to creating illegal Israeli settlements near the main Palestinian population centers and forcing the government to accept them. Gush Emunim's efforts initially received behind-the-scenes and later overt support from ranking members of the military, making it virtually impossible for the government to stop the settlements begun by the organization. In the context of this increasingly contentious political environment, it proved impossible for Israel to consider even minor concessions to Jordan concerning the West Bank.

The Lebanese Civil War

The fourth implication of the international legitimization of the PLO involved Lebanon. With such legitimization failing to elicit a positive response in Israel, the field of PLO activity would remain in Lebanon for the foreseeable future. This posed a challenge to the Maronite-dominated Lebanese government, which became paralyzed over the issue of how to deal with the PLO. As a result, various right-wing militias, receiving covert support from Israel, began to acquire arms through the help of the Maronite-led Lebanese Army. At the same time, the PLO armed itself, as did a variety of Muslim and leftist organizations and groups.

In April 1975, the Lebanese civil war erupted. At first the PLO stayed out of the conflict, but in the winter of 1975, attacks on Palestinian refugee camps in Maronite territory led to its involvement on the side of the Lebanese National Movement (LNM), an assortment of leftist and Arab nationalist organizations that all staunchly supported the Palestinian struggle. As fighting continued into the spring of 1976, PLO involvement helped tip the balance toward the LNM forces. In response, Lebanese president Sulayman Franjiyyah, a Maronite, and other right-wing leaders requested Syrian intervention on behalf of the government. Syrian president Hafiz al-Asad, apparently worried about the possibility of Israeli intervention if he did not act, sent Syrian units into Lebanon in June 1976. The intervention was not, however, meant to assist the Maronite forces in achieving victory, but to restore balance and prevent a radical takeover of the government. Among the forces engaged by the Syrians was the PLO, whose military units were forced back into southern and coastal Lebanon. An eventual reconciliation between the PLO and Syria would later allow the organization to establish its international headquarters in Lebanon, while the Lebanese civil war continued on and off. Meanwhile, south Lebanon became a battle ground between PLO forces and their Lebanese supporters and Israeli troops.

Camp David Accords

On March 26, 1979, Egyptian president Anwar al-Sadat completed the process of normalizing relations between Egypt and Israel by signing a peace treaty in Washington. In return for peace between the two countries and the establishment of diplomatic relations, Israel agreed to withdraw completely from the Sinai within three years. Most of the Sinai became a demilitarized zone with UN and multinational forces posted to ensure compliance with the treaty. The treaty guaranteed freedom of navigation for Israeli shipping through the Strait of Tiran and the Suez Canal, and Egypt accepted limitations on the size of the military force it could keep in a fifty-mile-wide area east of the Canal.

After the signing of the Sinai II accords in September 1975, Sadat had become frustrated by

the lack of progress in achieving a final agreement on Israeli withdrawal from the Sinai. He had concluded that only a dramatic gesture could break the psychological barrier that, in his view, made the Arab-Israeli conflict so intractable. Such a gesture seemed especially necessary following Menachem Begin's assumption of the Israeli premiership in June 1977. Begin and his right-wing Likud bloc, of which Herut was a member, had campaigned on a promise never to return any portion of "Judea and Samaria," as he and others sharing this position called the West Bank. A proponent of accelerated Jewish settlement of all the occupied territories, Begin referred to the PLO as a Nazi organization with whom he would never deal, even if it accepted UN Resolution 242. Moreover, Begin adamantly opposed the "concessions" that Israel already had made to Egypt in the two disengagement agreements.

On November 9, 1977, Sadat announced his willingness to go to Israel to discuss the issue of peace with the Israeli government. Such an initiative coming from the leader of the most powerful and populous Arab state required a response, even by the recalcitrant and suspicious Begin. Preparatory contacts through Morocco were instrumental in laying the delicate groundwork for Sadat's visit. Given the history of the Arab-Israeli conflict up to that time, Sadat's announcement of his visit astonished the world.

In an address to the Knesset on November 19, Sadat expressed his desire that Egypt and Israel live together in "permanent peace based on justice" and listed the conditions he thought necessary to achieve Arab-Israeli peace. In addition to the usual references to permanent borders, mutual recognition, nonbelligerency, and settling disputes through peaceful means, he called for an Israeli withdrawal from the occupied territories and the acceptance of the fundamental rights of the Palestinian people, including their right to self-determination and to establish their own state.

Following up on Sadat's initiative, Begin, on December 25, 1977, visited Ismailia, Egypt, where he presented Israel's response to the

Egyptian proposal. He focused primarily on points related to a settlement of issues in the Sinai but also presented a proposal for settlement of West Bank and Gaza issues. He proposed replacing the military administration in the occupied territories with "administrative autonomy of the residents, by and for them." Security and public order were to remain the responsibility of Israel, however. Begin asserted that "Israel stands by its right and its claim of sovereignty of Judea, Samaria and the Gaza district," but added, "In the knowledge that other claims exist, [Israel] proposes for the sake of agreement and peace, that the question of sovereignty be left open." He proposed that the status of the holy places and Jerusalem be considered separately in other negotiations. Begin did not promise to end the Israeli occupation or recognize a Palestinian right to self-representation and a state.

Framework Agreements

Israel and Egypt, despite the disparity between their positions, agreed to establish negotiating committees to further their dialogue. Discussion continued sporadically but unsuccessfully throughout the first half of 1978. As negotiations broke down, U.S. president Jimmy Carter intervened in an effort to keep the talks alive, inviting Sadat and Begin for face-to-face talks at Camp David, the presidential retreat in Maryland.

The Camp David talks, as they came to be called, convened with Carter in attendance on September 5, 1978, and continued for thirteen days. After difficult negotiations, which apparently would have failed without the mediation of Carter and his advisers, the two sides on September 17 reached the agreement popularly known as the Camp David Accords. *(See Camp David Summit, Chapter 3, p. 97)*

The Camp David talks actually produced two agreements, neither of which was a treaty, but rather constituted an agreement to agree. Called Frameworks for Peace, the first dealt with issues relating to Egypt and Israel and provided the basis for the treaty that the two countries would sign in

March 1979. The second framework, for settling the future of the West Bank and Gaza, was an agreement among Israel, Egypt, and the United States, also a signatory to the accords, on an approach for resolving this aspect of the Arab-Israeli conflict. Pressure by Arab states against Egypt signing a separate peace with Israel made Sadat anxious to arrive at a formula that would take into account their perspective toward Israel. This annoyed Begin, who resented Sadat's insistence on including issues that in his view rightfully should be addressed in negotiations between Israel and other Arab neighbors. Nevertheless, he continued pursuing a treaty that would bring peace with Egypt. The main points of the West Bank and Gaza framework are as follows:

- Egypt, Israel, and Jordan would agree on modalities for establishing an elected self-governing authority in the West Bank and Gaza.
- Egypt, Israel, and Jordan would negotiate an agreement establishing the powers and responsibilities of the self-governing authority in the West Bank and Gaza.
- After agreement, Israeli armed forces would withdraw from the West Bank and Gaza except in specified security locations.
- During a five-year transition period, Egypt, Israel, Jordan, and the West Bank–Gaza authority would negotiate the final status of the Israeli-occupied territories.
- Israel and Jordan would negotiate a peace accord taking into account the agreement reached on the final status of the West Bank and Gaza.
- All negotiations would be based on UN Security Council Resolution 242.

This unusual document, the West Bank and Gaza framework, left every issue subject to negotiation but confined the debate within the boundaries of the original Palestine mandate (which included Jordan). It made no mention of Syria or the Golan. It provided for the principle of Israeli withdrawal from some of the occupied territories, but without specifying the extent of the withdrawal. The framework also left open the possibility of a variety of options for achieving a final settlement of the conflict, among them the following:

- Jordanian option—A West Bank–Gaza self-governing authority under Jordanian sovereignty or in confederation with Jordan.
- Israeli option—A West Bank–Gaza self-governing authority under Israeli sovereignty or in confederation with Israel.
- Independent state option—An independent state for the Palestinians of the West Bank and Gaza, expressing their right to self-determination.

Arab Response

From the perspective of the United States and Israel, the key to proceeding on the West Bank and Gaza framework was to secure the participation of Jordan. Although King Hussein appeared to consider seriously the possibility of joining the negotiations, he resented not having been invited to Camp David. He also had not been consulted during the talks, and he was, therefore, offended at the presumption that he would follow meekly. By agreeing to participate, he would have implicitly accepted the premise that Jordanian sovereignty over the West Bank was negotiable. Moreover, Hussein had to take into account the attitude of his powerful neighbors—Iraq, Saudi Arabia, and Syria—and his own large population of Palestinian citizens, who adamantly opposed the Camp David accords, which were seen as hostile to the Palestinian right to self-determination because they excluded PLO participation and rejected Palestinian statehood.

Although Hussein did not condemn Sadat's initiative, most of the Arab world did. As Arab leaders had intensely pressured Sadat not to sign a treaty with Israel, it subsequently pressured Hussein not to collaborate on it. Especially critical were Syria and the PLO, which perceived Egypt's withdrawal from the Arab-Israeli conflict as weakening their positions. After Sadat signed the treaty on March 26, 1979, nineteen members of the twenty-two-member Arab League, including Jordan, convened

West Bank and Gaza

in Baghdad the following day and agreed to a package of political and economic sanctions against Egypt. Oman and Sudan chose not to attend. Egypt had not been invited, but the league sent a delegation to Cairo, where Sadat refused to meet with its members. The league expelled Egypt and moved its headquarters from Cairo to Tunis. Arab League members with the exceptions of Oman, Sudan, and, notably, the PLO, broke diplomatic relations with Cairo. Egypt was also expelled from most regional political and economic institutions, such as the Organization of Arab Petroleum Exporting Countries, the Organization of the Islamic Conference, and the Organization of African Unity. Arab nations also endorsed a general economic boycott on trade with Egypt.

West Bank–Gaza Talks

King Hussein did not attend the first meetings on the West Bank and Gaza framework held in

Beersheba between Sadat and Begin on May 25, 1979. The nonparticipation of Jordan in this and subsequent meetings played into the hands of those Israelis who, like Prime Minister Begin, opposed Israeli withdrawal from the West Bank and Gaza. As noted, Begin encouraged accelerated Jewish settlement in the occupied territories and the development of administrative mechanisms to strengthen Israeli authority and increase Jewish ownership of land there. In 1977 only seventeen Jewish settlements existed on the West Bank, with a combined population of about 5,000. By 1982 there were approximately one hundred settlements with a combined population of more than 20,000. By the end of 1988, Israel had established one hundred fifty settlements on the West Bank and populated them with 175,000 settlers. Israel also actively continued to illegally settle Jews in East Jerusalem.

As the Begin government pursued its settlement policy, the "autonomy talks" between Egypt and Israel stalled for a number of reasons: Israel sought to limit autonomy to the Palestinian *inhabitants* of the territories, while Egypt believed that autonomy should extend to the *territory* itself. Each promoted its own version of a self-governing authority. Egypt claimed that it sought total Israeli withdrawal from the territories (including East Jerusalem), the dismantling of Israeli settlements, and the right to self-determination for the Palestinians. Israeli leaders opposed these concepts because they felt they would set in motion an irreversible process leading to the establishment of an independent Palestinian state. The talks broke down in May 1980.

In June 1981, Israelis narrowly returned Begin to office in an election he interpreted as a mandate for his policies. Sadat was assassinated later in the year, on October 6, and was succeeded by Hosni Mubarak, whose government proved no more amenable than Sadat's to Israel's autonomy proposals. The Begin cabinet responded by moving to unilaterally implement its concept of autonomy while claiming that it fulfilled the intent of the Camp David agreement. On November 8, 1981, the Israeli government established a so-called

civilian administration to replace the military administration that had governed the occupied territories since 1967. The civilian administration, actually a department of the military, began the process of constructing a powerless "self-governing authority" based on a reorganization of the "village leagues," groups of armed informants and collaborators upon whom the military administration had relied to intimidate uncooperative Palestinians.

These policies, which aimed at thwarting the Palestinian independence movement rather than aiding it, provoked strong resistance among Palestinians across the territories: The PLO, the undisputed political representative of the Palestinian people, had been excluded, while non-Palestinian voices, such as Sadat, Mubarak, and Hussein, were encouraged to claim to represent Palestinian national interests. To quell Palestinian opposition, the Israeli military instituted an "iron fist" policy. Violence in the West Bank and Gaza escalated throughout the first six months of 1982, with the Begin government blaming the disturbances on the influence of the PLO among Palestinians in the territories. Israel moved in June 1982 to attack the problem at what it considered its source by invading Lebanon.

The Israeli Invasions of Lebanon

After Egypt signed the peace treaty with Israel in March 1979, the focus of the Arab-Israeli conflict shifted to Israel's northern frontiers. Despite the continuing harsh anti-Israeli rhetoric emanating from Syria, the Golan front, monitored by UN observer forces, had been quiet since the Syrian-Israeli separation of forces agreement of 1974. Egypt's involvement in the Camp David process had prompted Syria to pursue military parity with Israel, but Syrian leaders were not contemplating a major military action until they had substantially built up their forces. Also, the Egyptian-Israeli peace treaty greatly diminished the chance that Syria would launch an attack on Israel to regain the Golan, because it could not count on Egypt to open a second front. Conversely, Israel, no longer concerned about an attack from Egypt in the south, could regroup its military and send it north. Jordan assuredly opposed war with Israel.

The 1978 Invasion

With the entry of Syrian forces into Lebanon in spring 1976 and the deployment of PLO units to southern Lebanon, Israel designated a "red line" in that country across which it warned Syria not to cross. At the same time, it began arming a southern Lebanese militia commanded by Maj. Saad Haddad, a renegade Greek Catholic Lebanese officer. Israel hoped that this force would help it control the infiltration of PLO fighters from Lebanon. Nevertheless, shortly after an attack by eight Fatah commandos on a beach between Haifa and Tel Aviv in response to Israeli attacks on Lebanon, Israel on March 14, 1978, launched a 20,000-man invasion. Ostensibly undertaken as a retaliatory raid in response to the Fatah attack, the real purpose of the invasion, code named Operation Litani and planned months in advance, was to clear an area about ten kilometers wide along Israel's northern frontier that would serve as a "security zone" controlled and patrolled by Haddad's Free Lebanon Militia (FLM).

Soon after the invasion, and before Israeli forces retreated in June 1978, the United Nations dispatched a 6,000-man peacekeeping force, the United Nations Interim Force in Lebanon (UNIFIL), to patrol the area in the south separating PLO forces from the northern Israeli border. Israel and Haddad would not permit the deployment of UNIFIL into the FLM zone, and violence was not uncommon between UNIFIL and FLM units during the first weeks of the UN mission. Despite the UNIFIL-FLM buffer, PLO units continued to find their way into Israel. They also made increasing use of rockets and long-range artillery to launch attacks on northern Israeli towns over the heads of FLM and UNIFIL troops. PLO and Israeli attacks against one another became particularly violent during the last months before the signing of the Egyptian-Israeli peace treaty in March 1979.

In addition to sponsoring Haddad's militia, Israel, at least by mid-1976, had begun to provide arms and training to the Maronite Lebanese Forces militia as another means of countering the PLO and its allies in Lebanon. As this relationship deepened following the outbreak of the Lebanese civil war, Syrian president Asad began to fear an Israeli challenge to Syrian preeminence in Lebanon. Asad responded with policies aimed at securing Syrian regional hegemony to promote his concept of strategic parity with Israel.

His policy involved combating the Lebanese Forces and asserting Syrian control over the PLO in Lebanon. To achieve the latter goal, Asad supported Palestinian groups opposed to Arafat in an attempt to weaken his leadership of the organization. In addition, Shiite public opinion in south Lebanon, formerly supportive of the PLO, began turning against the Palestinian resistance because of misconduct by PLO fighters. The Shiite movement Amal, which was closely aligned with Syria, emerged as a new political force. Amal had an anti-PLO bias, as its Shiite members had suffered greatly from PLO-Israeli violence in the south. In the early 1980s, the PLO, confronted with a variety of opponents in Lebanon, found itself increasingly isolated.

Precursors to Full Invasion

In April 1981, hostilities flared between the Syrians and the Lebanese Forces in the Bekaa Valley. Lebanese Forces leader Bashir Gemayel provoked the confrontations with the intent of dragging Israel deeper into Lebanon to help advance his political fortunes. After the outbreak of fighting, the Maronites appealed for Israeli support. When Israel responded by shooting down two Syrian helicopters, Asad installed surface-to-air missiles in Lebanon near the city of Zahle. Israeli prime minister Begin vigorously protested the installations and threatened to destroy them if Syria refused to remove them. The "missile crisis" prompted the United States to send special envoy Philip Habib to the area to negotiate a solution.

To demonstrate its force following Syria's installation of these missiles, Israel conducted a series of air raids on PLO targets, and the PLO retaliated with rocket barrages into northern Israel. An escalation of the violence over a three-week period in July prompted negotiations among the PLO, UNIFIL, Saudi Arabia, the United States, and Israel that ultimately culminated in a PLO-Israeli cease-fire on July 24, 1981.

Despite Israeli assertions that the PLO would not adhere to a cease-fire, it did. The longer the cease-fire endured, however, the more it seemed to alarm the Begin government. The cease-fire not only implied indirect Israeli recognition of the PLO, but it also gave the PLO time to strengthen its forces in Lebanon and enhance Arafat's stature as a responsible political figure who could impose discipline throughout his organization. The possibility that international pressure could build to resolve the problem of Lebanon's civil war at the expense of Israeli aspirations on the West Bank and in Gaza could not be discounted. While resistance to Israeli rule in the territories increased during the spring of 1982, Israel made preparations for a major military operation against the PLO in Lebanon.

The 1982 Invasion and Expulsion of the PLO

On June 6, 1982, Israel launched a massive invasion of Lebanon. The publicly stated purpose of Operation Peace for Galilee was to clear all PLO forces from a forty-kilometer area north of Israel's border with Lebanon, thus putting northern Israel out of range of PLO artillery. As the operation developed, however, other Israeli objectives became clear:

- the total destruction of the PLO leadership and infrastructure, thus eliminating what Israel perceived as the main obstacle to the consolidation of its rule over the West Bank and Gaza
- the election of right-wing militia leader Bashir Gemayel as president of Lebanon, so, Israel hoped, he could bring the remaining Pales-

tinians there under tight Lebanese government authority
- a peace treaty with Lebanon that would grant Israel important security and military concessions

In a rapid, three-prong advance complemented by extensive naval landing operations along Lebanon's coast, Israeli units drove PLO forces back into Beirut. In a June 9 air war in the Bekaa Valley, Israeli planes destroyed the Syrian surface-to-air missile installations. Israeli and Syrian army units on the ground engaged in heavy fighting until the two governments agreed to a cease-fire on June 11. The Syrians generally tried to avoid confrontations with Israel despite Lebanese and Palestinian pleas for action, but some Syrian units fought against Israeli troops anyway.

By June 14 Israeli forces had effectively surrounded Beirut. Instead of entering the city and engaging in risky urban fighting, they laid siege to it and demanded the surrender of the PLO. The siege—marked by massive and often indiscriminate bombing and shelling of neighborhoods, confiscation of food, and interruption of water and electric services—continued through the summer until August 12, when negotiations, mediated by U.S. special envoy Habib, achieved a cease-fire and an agreement allowing the PLO to evacuate southern and coastal Lebanon. Some 20,000 people, mostly civilian Lebanese and Palestinians, died in the invasion.

The departure of the PLO from Beirut, which was completed by September 2, deprived the organization of its last base in the Arab world from which to make direct attacks on Israeli territory. The organization was now scattered throughout a number of Arab countries. Only one of them, Syria, bordered Israel, and it refused to allow the PLO autonomy of action.

The PLO leadership regrouped in Tunis. It appeared initially that the expulsion from Lebanon had greatly diminished the organization's significance, but this was only an illusion. The strength of the PLO, although forged on the concept of armed struggle against Israel, had never rested with its military capability. The broad range of international diplomatic support that the PLO had garnered over the years as the institutional symbol of Palestinian nationalism had now become the principal basis of its legitimacy. In the years after the PLO's departure from Lebanon, it was this aspect of the organization that Arafat sought to husband and enhance.

With the PLO's expulsion, Israel had achieved the major objective of its invasion. Israel's second objective, fostering a strengthened right-wing Maronite government with which it could sign a peace treaty, was shattered by the assassination of president-elect Bashir Gemayel on September 14, 1982. The Israelis succeeded, however, in negotiating a treaty, signed May 17, 1983, with the less amenable successor government of President Amin Gemayel, Bashir's brother, but the agreement foundered because of widespread Lebanese resistance to it and the refusal of the Syrian government to withdraw its troops. The treaty, according to Gemayel, was signed under strong pressure from the U.S. government, but it became clear that U.S. support could not strengthen the Lebanese government sufficiently to enable it to overcome the resistance engendered by the agreement. The Israeli military began a series of unilateral withdrawals and by July 1985 had extricated itself from Beirut and the mountains though not from the south.

Israeli-Shiite Conflict

In its attempt to drive the PLO from Lebanon, Israel found itself mired in another conflict and one only indirectly related to the PLO or the Palestinian problem: Its foray into Lebanon opened a second front in the Arab-Israeli conflict against the Muslim militia groups who mobilized themselves to resist Israel's continuing occupation of southern Lebanon. The Shiites of the south as well as secular organizations fought Israel not so much out of solidarity with the Palestinian national movement as out of detestation for an oppressive and cruel occupation that disrupted daily lives and virtually destroyed the local economy.

Israel justified its expanded, self-declared "security zone"—partially controlled by its surrogate force, now called the South Lebanon Army, commanded by Antoine Lahd, a retired Lebanese general with right-wing leanings—by pointing to the continued presence of Syrian forces in the northern parts of Lebanon.

For the Shiite inhabitants of southern Lebanon who at first welcomed the Israeli invasion but turned against it as the Israeli occupation became prolonged and oppressive, the so-called security zone was perceived as a joint effort by Israel and Lebanon's Maronite Christians to perpetuate the second-class status that Shiite Muslims had long held in Lebanese society. Armed and funded primarily by Syria and Iran, two major Shiite militias—Amal and Hizballah, or Party of God (inspired by the religious appeals of revolutionary Iran)—attacked Israeli troops in the security zone throughout the 1980s and 1990s. Israel responded by arresting Shiites with especially strong militant reputations and by demolishing houses of suspected attackers or leaders. Israel also shelled villages throughout south Lebanon to put pressure on the inhabitants and on the Lebanese government to desist from resisting the occupation. The illegal arrest and transport of Shiites to Israeli prisons provoked acts of international violence and kidnappings to secure their release.

Diplomacy, 1982–1987

Following the evacuation of the PLO from Beirut, the focus of the Palestinian component of the Arab-Israeli conflict shifted to diplomacy rather than military confrontation. Intense debate within the PLO led most factions and groups to accept that the military option had failed and that Israel, thanks to unwavering U.S. support, had achieved unprecedented military superiority over its Arab neighbors. The 1982 invasion of Lebanon had harshly exposed Arab impotence vis-à-vis Israel. The Palestinians knew that they could no longer count on empty, official Arab promises of liberating Palestine. At the same time, the international community became more aware that, indeed, the Palestinian problem represented the heart of the Arab-Israeli conflict and that it was much more than a refugee problem. The Palestinians wanted a state with a flag, not blankets and tents. In September 1982, a flurry of international diplomacy provided some momentum to the U.S.-sponsored peace process.

The Reagan Initiative

In a national telecast on September 1, 1982, President Ronald Reagan outlined an initiative intended to provide Camp David a "fresh start." Taking advantage of the PLO's situation and clearly trying to appeal to King Hussein of Jordan, whose participation in the Camp David process was necessary for it to have any chance of meaningful success, Reagan committed the United States to the "Jordanian option." The essence of this track was to bypass the PLO by treating the king of Jordan as the representative of the Palestinians, Palestinian objections notwithstanding. While asserting that the United States would exclude the PLO from negotiations and oppose creation of an independent Palestinian state, Reagan reiterated U.S. opposition to further Israeli settlement in the West Bank, Gaza, and the Golan and to annexation or permanent control of the territories. Reagan then proposed some type of self-government by the Palestinians in the territories in association with Jordan. He also called for negotiations to decide the disposition of Jerusalem.

The Begin government immediately rejected the proposal, saying it "deviated" from Camp David in that it tended to predetermine the outcome of negotiations. On the other hand, opposition Labor leader Shimon Peres saw it as "a basis for dialogue with the United States." Hussein, who had been consulted on the substance of the Reagan initiative prior to its announcement, initially indicated interest, but also noted his need to secure general Arab support and PLO approval before entering into negotiations. Indeed, the Reagan announcement was deliberately timed to precede a forthcoming Arab summit.

The Fez Summit Peace Proposal

The Arab summit that met in Fez, Morocco, September 5–8, 1982, did not respond to the U.S. initiative as the Reagan administration had hoped but instead endorsed the first collective Arab expression of intent to reach a settlement of the Arab-Israeli conflict. Passed unanimously by all members present, including the PLO and Jordan—Libya had not attended because of the agenda; Egypt was no longer a member of the league—the Fez proposal adopted a formula that would for the first time entail recognition of Israel, provided that the Palestinians obtained statehood.

The proposal's provisions included an Israeli withdrawal from all the territories occupied in 1967; the administration of the territories by the UN Security Council for a short, transitional period not to exceed several months; the establishment of a Palestinian state with Jerusalem as its capital; and UN Security Council guarantees to protect the peace and security of states in the region, including Israel.

By continuing to designate the PLO as the sole legitimate representative of the Palestinian people and calling for the creation of an independent Palestinian state, the summit reinvigorated the PLO, so recently battered in Beirut. At the same time, it undercut any effort by King Hussein to participate in the Camp David process on behalf of the Palestinian people or even to consider Jordanian sovereignty over the West Bank as legitimate.

The Hussein-Arafat Initiative

Because the Reagan initiative failed to draw Jordan into the Camp David process, it lost momentum. The Israeli government's uncompromising position added to the initiative's demise. Although the Labor Party's Shimon Peres took over as prime minister in 1984 under a coalition agreement with the rival Likud bloc, economic problems and activities in Lebanon preoccupied the Israeli leadership. Meanwhile, King Hussein and PLO chairman Arafat held talks during late 1982 and early 1983 in an effort to find a formula that would enable Jordan to negotiate on behalf of the PLO. Two concepts dominated the dialogue: establishing a Jordanian–West Bank Palestinian confederation or creating a joint Jordanian-Palestinian delegation to participate in the Camp David process.

Arafat's efforts to reach agreement with Hussein, however, faced opposition from two sources. The first of these were PLO factions wedded to the concepts of armed struggle and the total liberation of Palestine. These had taken refuge mainly in Syria following the evacuation from Beirut and opposed Arafat's temptation to follow the path of diplomacy. They also objected to Arafat's willingness to forfeit the Palestinians' right to self-determination. The second source of opposition was Syrian president Asad, whose determination to dominate regional affairs, including the Palestine issue, clashed sharply with any Jordanian or PLO effort to pursue an independent policy.

The PLO-Syrian feud reached a crisis in May 1983, when Asad supported a mutiny against Arafat's leadership of Fatah and the PLO. Intra-PLO fighting continued in eastern and northern Lebanon throughout the summer, fall, and into winter, when in December Arafat and 4,000 followers were evacuated from Lebanon, this time from the port city of Tripoli. Asad failed, however, to dislodge Arafat and his supporters from power, in part because he was unable to produce a credible alternative to Arafat within the PLO. Pro-Syrian factions within the PLO were well-known for their corruption.

To the surprise of the world, Arafat's first stop after his departure from Lebanon was Egypt, where President Mubarak received him. This symbolic visit marked a formal split in the PLO over management of the Arab-Israeli conflict. While Arafat moved toward reconciling himself with the Camp David process and toward trying to mold the process according to Palestinian terms, the rejectionist element within the PLO subordinate to Syria argued for a comprehensive settlement and opposed attempts at settling some aspects of the conflict through bilateral talks between Israel and individual Arab states. Despite strong Israeli objection, Mubarak lent support to the idea of developing a new approach that would bring Jordan and the PLO into negotiations with Israel. So too did King Hussein, who resumed negotiations with Arafat in early 1984 to work on a joint Jordanian-Palestinian policy for talks with Israel.

Although Hussein and Arafat both wanted to formulate a common position that would secure Israeli withdrawal from the occupied territories, they did so for different reasons. During 1984 Hussein reconvened the Jordanian parliament, half of whose members were West Bank Palestinians, restored diplomatic relations with Egypt in September, and sought the support of "moderate" Arab states and the United States for an enhanced Jordanian role in the peace process. As noted, however, the 1974 Rabat summit and the 1982 Fez summit obligated Hussein to obtain a PLO mandate to negotiate on behalf of the Palestinians. He also needed its blessing to pacify the Palestinian population inside Jordan (and in the final analysis end the state of war with Israel that the Hashimites never enthusiastically endorsed). Meanwhile, Arafat sought to use his leverage to gain the approval of Egypt, Jordan, and ultimately the United States for the concept of an independent Palestinian state, to be achieved through the venue of an international conference, as stipulated by the Fez conference resolution, and recognition of the Palestinian right to self-determination. In return, Arafat expressed his willingness to recognize Israel, renounce terrorism, and accept UN Security Council Resolution 242.

Because of the opposition of Syria and Syrian-based elements in the PLO to Arafat's leadership, however, Arafat required reaffirmation of his PLO chairmanship before he could conclude an agreement with Hussein. Despite Syrian threats and a boycott by Arafat's opposition, King Hussein permitted the Palestine National Council (PNC) to convene in Jordan in November 1984. Arafat dominated its deliberations and was once again reelected PLO chairman. He obtained authorization to continue his diplomatic efforts, but not to conclude a peace settlement on the basis of Resolution 242. With his chairmanship reconfirmed, Arafat reached an agreement with Hussein on a joint diplomatic initiative, which the two signed on February 11, 1985. Its provisions included the following:

- an exchange of land for peace as provided for in the resolutions of the United Nations, including those of the Security Council
- the right of self-determination for the Palestinian people in the context of a Jordanian–Palestinian Arab confederation
- the settlement of the Palestinian refugee issue in accordance with UN resolutions
- an international peace conference in which the five permanent members of the Security Council and all parties to the conflict would participate, including the PLO

Peace Efforts Founder

King Fahd of Saudi Arabia, President Mubarak, and King Hussein followed up the announcement of the Hussein-Arafat agreement with visits to the United States in May 1985 to solicit support for it. Hussein proposed that a preliminary meeting between U.S. representatives and a joint Jordanian-Palestinian delegation, excluding PLO representatives, be held before an international conference convened. In addition, Hussein delivered a list of Palestinians recommended by the PLO for U.S. consideration as members of the joint delegation to the international conference.

The United States responded cautiously because of suspicions that hidden within the term *self-determination* lurked the seeds of an independent Palestinian state. The Reagan administration reiterated its requirement that the PLO give a public and unequivocal statement accepting UN Resolutions 242 and 338 and Israel's right to exist before the United States would meet with its representatives, but the PNC had just as unequivocally denied Arafat the authority to make such a statement during its November meeting in Jordan. In addition, the bitter opposition of the Syrian-based PLO rejectionists constrained Arafat from meeting the U.S. conditions unless the United States first declared its acceptance of the right of the Palestinian people to self-determination.

Two episodes contributed to the demise of the diplomatic process. In the first, on September 25, 1985, persons alleged to be members of Force 17, a PLO unit personally loyal to Arafat, killed three people in Larnaca, Cyprus, who were believed to be working for Mossad, the Israeli intelligence agency. Israel responded by bombing PLO headquarters in Tunis on October 1. In the second episode, on October 8, men from the Palestinian Liberation Front, a pro-Arafat PLO member, hijacked the *Achille Lauro,* an Italian cruise ship and during the operation killed Leon Klinghoffer, an American Jewish tourist confined to a wheelchair. Although the hijacking was not planned in cooperation with Arafat or with his knowledge, the association of the Palestinian movement with such acts proved gravely damaging to Arafat's attempts at bolstering international recognition and legitimacy. U.S. allies in the Arab world could not convince Washington to deal with Arafat.

Faced with Arafat's inability to enhance his political situation and image, the Reagan administration's caution, and the lack of responsiveness from a politically paralyzed Israel, King Hussein repudiated the agreement with Arafat in February 1986. Jordanian-PLO relations rapidly deteriorated, and in July 1986 Hussein ordered all PLO offices in Jordan closed. In April 1987, Arafat repudiated the accord as a first step in an attempt to effect reconciliation with his opposition in the PLO.

In November 1987 in Amman, King Hussein convened an Arab summit, the outcome of which was a personal triumph. The conference endorsed his request to hold an international peace conference, and it placed him, rather than Arafat, squarely in the position of Arab leadership regarding the Arab-Israeli conflict. It also gave leave for individual Arab countries to restore relations with Egypt, broken since the Camp David Accords, although Syrian opposition still precluded its readmission to the Arab League. The summit, with Syrian reservations, endorsed Iraq's position in the Iran-Iraq War, and Hussein was able to arrange a personal meeting between the feuding Saddam Hussein of Iraq and Asad of Syria.

The Intifada, 1987–1991

Hussein's mandate to enter the "peace process" would be short-lived, however. Within a few weeks of the summit, the intifada, a sustained general uprising by the Palestinians of the West Bank, Gaza, and East Jerusalem, transformed the Arab-Israeli conflict by shifting the focus away from the disputes between Israel and its Arab neighbors and toward Israel's relations with the Palestinians under its occupation.

The intifada was ostensibly sparked by the December 9, 1987, deaths of four Palestinian laborers from Gaza who were crushed after a day's work in Israel when an Israeli-driven truck collided with their two vans waiting to pass through an army checkpoint. Seven other workers were injured. The funeral for three of the men drew four thousand demonstrators. Other mass funerals and riots touched off a territories-wide upsurge of popular action. In the following weeks, seemingly unorganized protests by Palestinians took root across the Israeli-occupied territories.

The intifada was, however, far from unorganized. Indeed, it was a coordinated rebellion in reaction to decades of Israeli efforts to control the lives of Palestinians, often harshly, and suppress political expression in the occupied territories. For decades, Israel implemented policies and created conditions that it hoped would induce the Palestinians to fear its authority and submit to its will: it expropriated Palestinians' land and property in the West Bank, including East Jerusalem, and Gaza; built settlements for Jews on these expropriated lands; siphoned off the territories' water for the benefit of settlers and Israelis inside the Green Line; destroyed the family dwellings of individuals who resisted the occupation or who built homes without permits (which, when obtainable, usually took years); arrested and detained Palestinians arbitrarily; tortured Palestinians in

detention and committed other human rights violations against them; imposed curfews and school closings; controlled travel and deported Palestinians engaged in activities aimed at lifting or resisting the occupation. What distinguished the intifada from previous episodes of resistance were its territories-wide nature and the inability of Israeli authorities to contain it, despite the army's use of shootings, beatings, massive arrests, and curfews.

Leaflets issuing instructions to Palestinians began to appear soon after the mass protests began; their content was also broadcast by radio. The third leaflet indicated the existence of the anonymous, self-proclaimed Unified National Leadership Command and its adoption of a relatively coherent program of action based on nonviolent struggle. Its publicly expressed demands called for an end to Israeli military occupation, the right to self-determination, and the establishment of an independent Palestinian state.

The first seventeen leaflets contained an overwhelming majority of appeals for nonviolent action, including local strikes, demonstrations, marches, raising of Palestinian flags, fasting and praying, defiance of school closures, symbolic funerals, the ringing of church bells, and renaming of streets and schools, and economic sanctions, such as withholding taxes and boycotting Israeli products. During the course of the intifada, Palestinians used fourteen of fifteen categories of nonviolent direct action employed by Gandhi in India. Popular committees served as the backbone of the day-to-day infrastructural machinations of the intifada, while the political contours were shaped by East Jerusalem–based activist intellectuals who had for two decades been working to alter Palestinian political thinking.

The Palestinians' prohibition on the use of weaponry against Israelis reflected intentional restraint. As the Israel Defense Forces acknowledged, from the start of the intifada in December 1987 through 1991, only twelve Israeli soldiers were killed in the West Bank and Gaza Strip, despite their overwhelming presence on rooftops and on the ground. The few fatalities on the Israeli side contrasted with the high number of Palestinian deaths. During the same period according to the IDF, at least 706 Palestinians were killed by Israelis, sometimes four or five in one day. Some estimates place the final death toll at more than 1,000.

The adamancy of Israeli authorities in denying that the Palestinians were engaged in a predominantly nonviolent uprising against military occupation protracted the struggle and weakened the forces in Palestinian society seeking to replace armed struggle with political engagement. Rather than undermine the forces that sought to continue violent struggle, Israeli officials chose instead to lock up or deport the very Palestinian leadership that had kept the uprising nonviolent. Thus, Israel missed the opportunity to profit from the profound shifts that the intifada represented for accession to peace and security, which for decades Israeli leaders professed as their goals.

Although the Unified National Leadership Command survived four waves of arrests, no one who had weighed the costs versus the benefits of mass nonmilitary action—as had the leaflet writers of the first two years—weathered a March 1990 decapitation of the last autonomous leadership collective. Thereafter the PLO took over the command, placing its organizational control of the group ahead of local Palestinians' stated goals. The activist intellectuals who had fought for a new political consensus in the territories were unable to sustain the upper hand. A "war of the leaflets" erupted among the factions, breaching the nonviolent program of the intifada. As the leaflets changed, a debate on civil disobedience that had lasted for the entire first year of the uprising and well into its second came to an end. General strikes, which are easy to announce but have little or no effect because they are not focused on specific grievances, became frequent, reflecting the PLO's lack of familiarity with the discipline of nonviolent struggle.

Internal dissension, old ideologies, ambivalent support from Tunis for nonviolent struggle, and thwarting of the nonviolent strategy meant that Israel's use of excessive force became the

rationale for reviving the failed, violent, and desiccated tactics of armed struggle from the past, instead of being interpreted as proof that the nonviolent strategy was working. The Islamic Resistance Movement, or Hamas, grew, along with its justifications for violence. Palestinian youth formed armed bands, and Palestinians who collaborated with the Israelis began to be killed. Eventually, however, the Israeli authorities came to realize the futility of suppressing the uprising militarily and determined that political means must be sought.

The sight of Palestinian children armed with rocks facing heavily armed Israeli soldiers increased international sympathy for the cause of the Palestinians under occupation. The critical problem for Israel became that the young rock throwers, and local Palestinian leaders who had emerged to explain the intifada, regarded the PLO as their representative. The uprising, although not inspired or instigated by the PLO, thus focused international attention on Arafat as leader of the Palestinians. (The PLO was initially wary of the uprising, fearing that it would foster a local leadership strong enough to challenge it.)

The intifada represented not only a massive and popular reaction against the Israeli occupation, but also Palestinian frustration at the failure of Arab diplomacy to reach an acceptable resolution to the Arab-Israeli conflict. In an effort to revive momentum toward a peaceful settlement, in spring 1988 U.S. secretary of state George Shultz embarked on a diplomatic mission, the first official U.S. peace initiative since the Reagan plan of 1982. His initiative featured a tight timetable for completion of a negotiation process by the end of the year, but it was otherwise similar to an agreement reached in April 1987 between Israeli foreign minister Shimon Peres and King Hussein—who had been negotiating in secret for years in an attempt to bypass the PLO—for an international peace conference, for which Hussein (at the Amman summit) had obtained the mandate to pursue.

Whereas U.S. mediation of the Peres-Hussein agreement had been low key, because of the delicacy of negotiating an agreement with a foreign minister (Peres) operating without the approval of his prime minister (Likud leader Yitzhak Shamir), the urgency of the situation led Shultz to lend it the prestige of his personal involvement. Peres had accepted a token international conference that would in actuality be dominated by the United States. International sponsors would meet in a preliminary session, but then leave the parties to the conflict to negotiate directly among themselves.

Shultz's mission encountered two primary obstacles: the opposition of Shamir and the noncooperation of West Bank Palestinians because of the lack of a place in his plan for the PLO. Despite initially cautious support from Syria and Jordan, Syria eventually demanded a conference with a unified Arab delegation, and King Hussein realized that the Palestinian youth of the intifada generation would not allow him to represent them. By May 1988, it became clear that the concept of an international conference as originally conceived by Peres had no future.

A three-day emergency Arab summit confirmed the new situation on the ground. Convened by Algerian president Chadli Bendjedid in Algiers June 7–9, the assembled Arab leaders decided to withdraw from Jordan and Syria the annual funding previously allotted to them as "frontline" states bordering Israel. They also halted or rechanneled the same such funding for the PLO, for its leadership role. The summit then endorsed general Arab support for the intifada and urged that all Arab funds henceforth be distributed to the occupied territories through the PLO. These funds were to be allocated state by state, however, not by the Arab League. Rather than condemning the Shultz initiative outright, the Arab leaders reiterated their support for an international conference under UN auspices and urged the PLO to declare the establishment of an independent Palestinian state, which they proposed to designate as the principal Arab interlocutor at such a conference.

In July 1988, King Hussein relinquished Jordan's claims to the West Bank, which it had maintained since 1949. Hussein's decision appeared designed to free Jordan, with its large Palestinian population, from the potentially disruptive effects of the intifada and to force the PLO into a more conciliatory position by making it solely responsible for representing the Palestinians of the occupied territories. Although Hussein's announcement did not remove him entirely from Middle Eastern diplomacy, it was a blow to U.S. and Israeli leaders who had anticipated a prominent role for Jordan in any settlement.

As the intifada continued and the Israeli government sought unsuccessfully to contain it with force, Arafat convened a meeting of the Palestine National Council in Algiers. On November 15, 1988, the PNC took the historic step of proclaiming in principle the establishment of an independent Palestinian state and announced its recognition of UN Resolution 242, implicitly recognizing Israel. It also adopted a declaration rejecting terrorism and called for an international conference under the sponsorship of the United Nations with the purpose of negotiating a resolution of the Arab-Israeli conflict.

Because the Reagan administration maintained that the PLO's pronouncements did not satisfy its conditions for opening a dialogue with the organization, Arafat on December 14 explicitly accepted Resolutions 242 and 338, recognized Israel's right to exist, and renounced acts of violence that the United States and Israel had long condemned as terrorism. Dismissing Israeli objections, the United States responded by opening talks with the PLO in Tunis.

The U.S.-PLO Dialogue

The U.S. decision to open talks with the PLO came during the last days of the Reagan administration. The incoming administration of George Bush, Reagan's vice president, gave priority to achieving a settlement of the Arab-Israeli conflict, but Bush's election in late 1988 had followed soon after the reelection of the Likud Party to lead Israel and the selection of its leader, Yitzhak Shamir, as prime minister in June. Shamir made clear his total opposition to direct negotiations with the PLO and to accepting the principle of an independent Palestinian state. Instead, in May 1989 Shamir put forth a plan for the election in the occupied territories of a local Palestinian delegation to negotiate with Israel on some type of autonomy formula in accordance with the Israeli interpretation of the Camp David Accords. He made a halt to the intifada a precondition for holding such elections.

The PLO found Shamir's electoral proposal difficult to resist in principle and so did not reject it outright. The organization insisted, however, that before elections could take place, Israel must agree in principle to withdraw from the occupied territories and to allow the Palestinian residents of East Jerusalem to participate in the elections. Both conditions were at odds with the Israeli position, so the impasse continued.

In an effort to break the deadlock, James Baker III, the new U.S. secretary of state, sought to find ways to implement the Shamir plan while reassuring Palestinians that U.S. policy remained sensitive to their concerns. These assurances included public statements by Baker suggesting that Israel ultimately would have to negotiate with "representatives of the PLO" and urging Israel to relinquish what he called an unrealistic vision of Greater Israel and to reach out to Palestinians as neighbors deserving of political rights.

The U.S. efforts were abetted by an Egyptian ten-point plan put forth in September 1989 that, among other things, called for international observers to monitor the elections and agreement by Israel to accept any and all results of the polling. This initiative was followed by a Baker five-point plan that called for Egypt, Israel, and the United States to begin a round of negotiations aimed at finding a compromise between the Israeli and Palestinian positions. The Shamir government—interpreting these initiatives as virtually direct Israeli-PLO negotiations, even if through third parties—rejected them. Its decision came at a cost to U.S.-Israeli relations.

The Egyptian and U.S. initiatives put considerable pressure on the Israeli political system. Israel's Labor Party, which remained part of the ruling coalition, favored responding to both initia-

tives and criticized Shamir vehemently for rejecting his own plan and disrupting relations with the United States. Even hard-line figures in Shamir's own party leveled criticism at him, possibly to preempt his reaching a compromise with Labor. Pressure mounted until mid-March 1990, when the government fell. The inability of Labor leader Peres to form a new government, however, gave Shamir a second chance, and he succeeded by June in forming a government without calling for elections. Shamir's new administration, which included most of Israel's religious parties, excluded Labor and was considerably more hardline than the one it replaced. Meanwhile, the PLO, seeing the prospects for compromise and increased PLO involvement in the peace process slipping away, began altering its position. Following Israel's rejection of the Egyptian and Baker initiatives, it adopted the position that any Palestinian delegation engaged in talks with Israel should represent the PLO, a stance it previously had not insisted on, despite strong opposition from many Palestinians.

At the same time, a complex set of changes in the international environment led Arafat to develop closer relations with Iraqi president Saddam Hussein, a source of funding and diplomatic support for the PLO. These changes included the end of the Iran-Iraq War and the reemergence of Iraq as an Arab actor with an interest in the Arab-Israeli conflict; the collapse of communist regimes in Eastern Europe that previously had been reliable supporters of the PLO; the changing nature of the Soviet government, which, beginning in late 1989, permitted the immigration of large numbers of Russian Jews to Israel; the diminishing financial support from Arab Gulf states; and a late 1989 Syrian-Egyptian rapprochement that raised hopes of broadening the peace process, possibly at the PLO's expense.

An emergency Arab summit held in Baghdad May 28–30, 1990, highlighted the linkage between Arafat and the PLO's changing situation and the heightened role of Saddam Hussein in Arab politics. Convened at Iraq's initiative to discuss the status of the intifada, stagnation of the peace process, and perceived U.S.-instigated campaigns against Iraq and Libya, the summit aimed, an Iraqi spokesman stated, at forging a "new Arab order" to meet these challenges. Limitations on the U.S. role in the Middle East was a central theme of the summit's official communique. The conference also endorsed the PLO's desire to move away from a U.S.-Israeli-Egyptian setting for negotiations and called for convening an international conference on the Arab-Israeli conflict an urgent necessity.

A failed attack by dissident members of the PLO on Israeli beaches near Tel Aviv on May 30, the last day of the summit, revived tensions and undercut the initiative inaugurated by the PLO's recognition of Israel in November 1988. The United States severed its dialogue with the PLO soon thereafter, when Arafat refused to condemn the event or its perpetrator, the Palestinian Liberation Front, the same group that had been responsible for the *Achille Lauro* hijacking in October 1985. It was in this environment of heightened tension and increasingly hard-line politics that the Persian Gulf crisis of 1990 erupted.

Seeds of Agreement

The Baghdad summit and changed direction for the Arab world as reflected in the summit's communique clearly resulted from efforts by Iraqi president Saddam Hussein to assume a position of decisive leadership in the region. The rationale for his actions became apparent in early August 1990, when Iraq invaded and subsequently annexed Kuwait. Immediately challenged by an outraged international community, Hussein publicly rationalized his action by pointing to the Israeli occupation of the West Bank, East Jerusalem, Gaza, Golan (which Israel had annexed in 1981), and south Lebanon. He offered to withdraw from Kuwait in exchange for an Israeli withdrawal from these territories. His argument garnered the Iraqi leader considerable support among the Palestinians of the occupied territories and refugee camps, but rejection by the United States, which assembled a multinational coalition to confront

the Iraqi occupation. Despite U.S. resistance to any effort by Hussein to link the invasion to unresolved issues of the Arab-Israeli conflict, he persisted in doing so.

U.S. efforts at pulling together a coalition to challenge Iraq depended in part on the maintenance of a broad international consensus. Not all members of the international community, however, were as adamant as the United States in rejecting the linkage between the occupied territories and Kuwait. The Arab members of the coalition, in particular, were at least as concerned about the prospects of regional instability provoked by the unresolved Arab-Israeli conflict as they were about the Iraqi occupation. To maintain the coalition's consensus and solidarity, therefore, U.S. leaders found it necessary to coordinate activities with an array of leaders whose assorted views had to be taken into account. The Soviet Union made it known that it was prepared to cooperate fully with the United States in working toward the resolution of the Persian Gulf crisis as well as the Arab-Israeli conflict. On January 29, 1991, two weeks into the war launched to drive Iraqi forces from Kuwait, the United States and the Soviet Union issued a joint communique that not only called for Iraq to withdraw unequivocally, but also committed the two powers to working together after the war to promote Arab-Israeli peace and regional stability.

Madrid Talks

The U.S.-led coalition's victory over Iraq in January–February 1991 produced a situation quite different from that envisioned by the Iraqi-dominated Arab summit of the previous summer. Instead of limiting the U.S. role in the Middle East, the war made the United States the decisive external arbiter of Middle Eastern (if not global) affairs. The Bush administration sought to exert this leadership role, as it had in the Gulf crisis, through force and diplomacy. Thus, continuing sanctions against Iraq and efforts to contain its military reconstruction were undertaken as UN actions. Efforts to promote regional stability necessarily meant focusing immediately on the Arab-Israeli conflict as well.

The Persian Gulf War ended on February 28, 1991, and on March 7 Secretary of State Baker returned to the region with the principal aim of reviving the peace process. He made eight trips to the Middle East during the summer of 1991, successfully obtaining agreements from all the major parties to the Arab-Israeli dispute to convene for talks in Madrid, Spain, on October 30. The Madrid summit represented the first direct diplomatic encounter between Israel and neighboring Arab states since the aborted UN-sponsored peace talks on Rhodes in 1951. Several factors, including an indefatigable sense of mission, accounted for Baker's success.

First, and perhaps most important, was the change in the international order that had resulted from the collapse of communism in Eastern Europe in 1989, including reform of the ruling party in the Soviet Union and the end of the cold war. As illustrated in the Gulf crisis, the United States and the Soviet Union found that they could work cooperatively on international affairs, despite lingering disagreements over matters of substance. A key part of Baker's success stemmed from the invitation to Madrid being issued jointly by the United States and the Soviet Union, and the presidents of both countries presiding over the conference. Such cooperation would have been virtually unthinkable only a year or two earlier. In addition, the United Nations and the European Community had been mobilized as supporters of the process and sent representatives to Madrid as observers. The weight of international opinion, therefore, clearly favored a transformation of the Arab-Israeli conflict from a struggle conducted on the battlefield to one conducted in the corridors of diplomacy. The principal parties to the conflict assessed the risks of resisting such pressure to be too great.

Second, the crushing defeat of Iraq in the Gulf war represented a decisive defeat for the more radical forces in the Arab world that favored a military solution to the Arab-Israeli conflict. The defining role played by the United States in the war meant that it, together with its allies, would take the lead in formulating the shape of the peace that followed. If U.S. policy favored a diplomatic settlement of the Arab-Israeli conflict as an outcome of the crisis, few were in a position to resist diplomatically, not to mention militarily, the power so recently demonstrated by the United States. Certainly those Arab states that had fought in the multinational coalition—Saudi Arabia and the other Gulf states (in whose defense the war had been fought), Egypt (which already had a peace treaty with Israel), and Syria (which by joining the coalition had sought to escape its isolation by cultivating better relations with the United States and Arab states)—had done so for benefits they hoped to gain and were not interested in sacrificing them by not cooperating with U.S. postwar policy.

Certain anomalies of the Gulf War probably abetted Baker's success. The loyalty that PLO chairman Arafat demonstrated for Saddam Hussein ironically facilitated the peace process. Being allied with the losing side, the PLO had forfeited the support of the key Arab states that were to be represented at Madrid, a situation that made acceptance of an invitation more appealing to Israel. At the same time, the marginal role played by Israel in the Gulf crisis, and indeed even the protective role the United States had played in deploying Patriot antimissile batteries to Israel to help defend against Iraqi Scud missile attacks, had the effect of slightly weakening Israel's bargaining position with the United States.

To ensure the cooperation of key Arab states and to further bolster the consensus politics used successfully to this point, Baker insisted that the Palestinians be included at Madrid. Israeli insistence on a veto over who among the Palestinians might be included in such a delegation was not in the end sustained nor were the delegates chosen by an electoral process requested by Prime Minister Shamir a year earlier. The Palestinians were instead present as part of the Jordanian delegation; they all hailed from the occupied territories and had no official affiliation with the PLO. The inclusion of Palestinians unquestionably reflected the impact of the intifada, the continuation of which implied that no resolution of the Arab-Israeli conflict would be possible without some voice for them.

On July 18, Syria accepted the U.S.-Soviet invitation to Madrid, and within days Lebanon and Jordan announced that they too planned to attend. Saudi Arabia, participating only as an observer, announced its support of the process, and Egypt, which had worked with the United States to facilitate the diplomatic maneuvering, also accepted an invitation to attend as an observer. In the end, it was ironically the hard-line Israeli government of Shamir that proved the most hesitant party, withholding a decision to attend until October 20. Concerned mainly with the composition of the Palestinian delegation and fearing that the delegation would prove to be a de facto representative of the PLO, the Israelis sought assurances that could not be delivered. Israel also worried about the development of an international consensus at the conference that would put pressure on it to make concessions.

Eleven Rounds of Negotiations

Between the Madrid conference—held October 30–November 1, 1991—and the Israeli-PLO Declaration of Principles of September 13, 1993, eleven meetings of bilateral negotiations between Israel and its immediate Arab neighbors took place in Washington. Also flowing from Madrid, a number of other world capitals hosted a series of multilateral negotiations involving other countries to discuss wider-ranging issues, such as arms control, water sharing and the environment, and refugees. Although these meetings failed to produce diplomatic progress, that they actually took place marked a new stage in the evolution of the Arab-Israeli conflict.

It evolved gradually that the bilateral talks consisted of four sets of negotiations rather than three, as originally conceived. In addition to talking with Jordan, Lebanon, and Syria, Israel increasingly found itself negotiating separately with the Palestinian members of the joint Jordanian-Palestinian delegation. Moreover, despite efforts by Israel to avoid direct talks with the PLO, it became clear that the Palestinian members of the Jordanian-Palestinian delegation would not make decisions without first consulting PLO headquarters in Tunis. The growing indirect role of the PLO in the negotiating process presented a serious challenge to Shamir's hard-line government. In June 1992 elections, Israelis ousted his Likud Party in favor of the Labor Party, now led by Yitzhak Rabin. The elections represented, among other things, a mandate for continuing the peace process begun at Madrid, but perhaps of most significance was the status of Israel's relations with the United States.

On September 6, 1991, as the U.S. government sought Israel's agreement to attend the Madrid summit, the Shamir government had formally submitted a request for $10 billion in loan guarantees to fund the construction of housing for the overflow of immigrants arriving in Israel from the Soviet Union as a result of the latter's political opening. Coming when it did, the loan request had the appearance of pressuring President Bush to respond favorably to ensure Israel's acceptance of the invitation to Madrid. Bush reacted negatively, however, asking the U.S. Congress to defer action on the request until after the summit. Shortly thereafter he reacted even more strongly, insisting that Israel freeze all settlement construction activities in the occupied territories as a condition for receiving the guarantees. Shamir retaliated by criticizing the Bush administration for trying to pressure Israel. The impasse continued, poisoning U.S.-Israeli relations and becoming yet another issue used by Labor to weaken Likud's grip on the Israeli electorate.

The election of the Labor Party and Rabin as the new prime minister marked a departure from the hard-line policies followed by Israel under successive Likud-led governments since 1977. Although Rabin had a reputation as one of the most hard-line Labor politicians, a reputation bolstered by his role as an architect and director of Israel's iron fist policy in the occupied territories, he was eager to restore frayed U.S.-Israeli relations. In one of his first acts, he froze all new settlements (but did not stop work on settlements already under construction or on their expansion). This step proved sufficient for the Bush administration to assert that U.S. conditions had been met, and during Rabin's first state visit to the United States, in August 1992, the administration announced its decision to authorize the $10 billion in guarantees. During Rabin's first weeks in office, he announced his willingness to meet personally with Arab heads of state, and perhaps anticipating the inevitable, to negotiate with Palestinians directly affiliated with the PLO.

The Oslo Accords

In late August 1993, as Arab and Israeli delegates returned to Washington to meet for the eleventh round of the increasingly stalemated bilateral peace talks, they and the rest of the world were startled by the announcement that representatives of the Israeli government and the PLO had reached a secretly negotiated agreement. The agreement evolved from informal, indirect contacts between moderate Israelis and PLO figures concerned about the lack of progress in the bilateral talks. A changing international and regional environment unfavorable to the Palestinian cause prompted the PLO's participation, while pressure on Israel by the United States to present a working formula for a solution served as impetus for the Israelis.

While attempting to craft a statement of principles acceptable to both sides, the two parties working largely through the government of Norway discovered areas of common agreement sufficient to interest the PLO leadership and the new Rabin government in pursuing further dialogue. After the Israeli cabinet and the Knesset in early 1993 lifted a 1986 ban against official dealings with PLO representatives, Israeli-PLO contacts became direct over the course of a series of increasingly formal meetings by ever-higher levels of negotiators. Conducted at various locations outside Oslo, Norway, the negotiations continued, unknown to the rest of the world, until the breakthrough in August. In fact, the two sides reached two agreements.

In the first agreement, signed by Arafat in Tunis on September 10 and by Rabin a few hours later, the PLO formally recognized Israel's right to exist in peace and security, renounced the use of terror and violence, and pledged to remove the clauses in the PLO charter calling for the elimination of Israel as a state. In return, Rabin, by affixing his signature, formally extended Israeli recognition to the PLO as the legitimate representative of the Palestinian people. This agreement paved the way for a second accord, the Declaration of Principles on Interim Self-Government Arrangements, signed in Washington on September 13, 1993. Known also as the "Gaza-Jericho first" plan, this agreement, following closely the formula first developed at Camp David fifteen years earlier, envisioned a five-year process during which Israel gradually would militarily withdraw from parts of the occupied territories and Palestinian self-rule would be established in those areas. As a first-stage mutual confidence-building measure, both sides agreed to an initial implementation of the plan in Gaza and Jericho by December 13, 1993, three months after the signing of the agreement. The Palestinian Legislative Council, to be elected by July 1994, would then begin assuming responsibility for a variety of government services throughout the territories, as the Israeli armed forces simultaneously withdrew from major Palestinian towns and cities. The exact organization and powers of the council were not delineated but would be worked out in further negotiations before the end of the five-year period. In December 1995, negotiations were to begin on reaching a final settlement of the Israeli-Palestinian conflict. The results of these negotiations were to take effect in December 1999, five years after the withdrawal of Israel from Gaza and Jericho.

Post-Oslo

Israeli forces did not withdraw from Gaza and Jericho on December 13, 1993, as called for in the Israeli-PLO accords, because of disagreement involving two issues—whether the term *Jericho* referred to the town or the district of that name and which security forces, Israeli or PLO, would remain posted on the borders of Egypt and Gaza and of Jordan and Jericho. The delay pointed to how difficult the process of negotiating and implementing the full agreement would be. Following additional talks, the two sides signed the Cairo Agreement, leading on May 11, 1994, to Israel finally withdrawing forces from Gaza and Jericho, although not fully, opening the way for Palestinian administration of these areas. The agreement also created the Palestinian Authority (PA) to administer the territories handed over by Israel, which remained in control of the land, airspace, and people in Gaza and the bulk of the West Bank.

On September 28, 1995, in Washington, Israel and the PLO signed the Israeli-Palestinian Interim Agreement on the West Bank and Gaza Strip. Also known as Oslo II, the agreement provided for the further deployment of the Israeli army from the occupied territories and laid out the mechanisms for and extent of Palestinian authority in the areas to be evacuated by Israel. Its main feature set out the division of the West Bank into three areas with varying degrees of Palestinian and Israeli control. In Area A, consisting of the seven major Palestinian towns, Palestinians would have complete control of civil administration and security. In Area B, consisting of all other Palestinian population centers with the exception of some refugee camps, Israel would retain control of "overriding security responsibility." In Area C, consisting of all Israeli settlements, military bases, and areas declared "state lands," Israel would retain sole security authority. *(For more detail on the Oslo Accords, see the Israel profile, p. 281)*

Oslo faced many difficulties. Rejectionist forces on both sides of the conflict strongly opposed it. Hard-line groups in Israel denounced Rabin as a traitor who had sold out to the enemy. (He would be assassinated in 1996 by a Jewish zealot who accused him of treason.) Many Israelis continued to see Arafat as the primary enemy of the Jewish state and a man responsible for the killing of hundreds of Jews. Among Palestinians, members of Hamas opposed Arafat's compromise

and threatened to undermine it through violence. Even some member groups of the PLO opposed the agreement. Both sets of Palestinian rejectionists received moral and financial support from Islamist parties external to the conflict, such as from Iran, but the reasons for the opposition to Oslo were indigenous, involving distrust of Israeli intentions and lack of implementation of the terms on Israel's part. Dissent among these groups led to speculation that changed political circumstances might one day reverse the progress made toward a settlement. At the very least, their existence indicated that even a comprehensive settlement might not entirely still the violence historically associated with the conflict, but it would be an Israeli government, led by Benjamin Netanyahu, and not Palestinian rejectionists, that would derail the process in the coming years.

Netanyahu, elected prime minister in 1996, treated the Palestinians contemptuously, as he carefully courted his right-wing constituency, certain that the United States—no matter how much it may have quietly urged progress in the peace process—would never pressure him publicly and would never hold him responsible for the failure of peace efforts. In October 1998, U.S. president Bill Clinton invited the Israelis and Palestinians to direct talks at the Wye River Plantation in Maryland to move the peace process forward, as Netanyahu distrusted his Palestinian partners and was not a proponent of Oslo. After days of intensive negotiations in which U.S. officials were directly involved, the parties agreed to the Wye River Memorandum. The agreement linked further Israeli withdrawal from an additional 13 percent of the West Bank to improved security measures on the part of the Palestinian Authority to prevent acts of violence against Israel. The United States agreed that officials of the Central Intelligence Agency in the region would serve as mediators and monitor Palestinian security arrangements. Israel agreed to fulfill its obligations under Oslo by withdrawing from more territory. The Israeli government, supported by the United States, also reiterated demands that the Palestine National Council abrogate the terms of the PLO charter that referenced the "liberation of Palestine."

To assuage the United States and Israel, the PNC held a special session in December 1998, at which Clinton addressed the members, hailing them for their courage. The Israeli government, on the other hand, precariously held together in a coalition under Netanyahu, refused to implement the withdrawals to which it had agreed at Wye. Netanyahu's defense minister, Yitzhak Mordecai, launched a campaign against him. Secretary of State Madeleine Albright criticized the pace of Israeli settlement activity in the occupied territories and earlier had threatened to hold Israel responsible for the stalemate in the peace process, but congressional pressure saved Israel from public embarrassment.

Frustrated by the lack of movement in negotiations with Israel according to the terms of the Oslo Accords, Arafat threatened to officially declare a Palestinian state on May 4, 1999, the date on which, according to the accords, the final-status talks should have concluded. The Wye River agreement precluded the Palestinians from unilaterally declaring a state without prior consultation with the Israeli government and the United States. Under U.S. pressure, Arafat postponed the announcement. Such a declaration could come only after the conclusion of final-status negotiations. (The European Union officially endorsed Palestinian statehood in 1999.)

The stalemate in Israeli-Palestinian relations continued until the election of Ehud Barak as prime minister in 1999. The Clinton administration, frustrated with Netanyahu, openly threw its weigh behind Barak. (Former Clinton campaign advisers and allies even assisted him.) Although Barak promised to adhere to the Wye River agreement and to withdraw Israeli troops from Lebanon within a year, once in office he tried to impose an interpretation of Wye that would weaken the Palestinians' negotiating stance. He objected, for example, to an active U.S. role in the peace process for fear that Washington would favor the Palestinians, and he wanted to reduce the number of Palestinian prisoners slated for release. After months of intense

negotiations, the Israeli and Palestinian sides reached and signed the Sharm al-Shaykh Memorandum on September 4, 1999. According to its terms, Israel would withdraw gradually from the West Bank, increasing the area under direct and indirect Palestinian control to some 40 percent of the land, and release some Palestinian prisoners. Negotiations for the final settlement would proceed concurrently with implementation of Wye. Even if Wye were fully implemented, Israel would remain in control of the occupied territories' resources, sovereignty, security, ports, and airspace. The Palestinians would fully control less than 10 percent of the West Bank and Gaza, but that control would be subject to ultimate Israeli authority.

Establishing Palestinian Autonomy

Beyond threats from Jewish and Arab extremists, the success of the autonomy scheme established by the Israeli-Palestinian agreements rested on the ability of Chairman Arafat and the PLO to bring effective government to the territory evacuated by the Israelis. On July 1, 1994, Arafat returned to the Gaza Strip after twenty-seven years in exile, and although jubilance marked the occasion, the political future of the Palestinians remained uncertain. Arafat's large entourage and his extensive security precautions projected an imperial approach that some observers and locals found irksome, while some of the other new arrivals on occasion dealt heavy-handedly with local Palestinians. In short, numbers of the newly arrived PLO officials did not understand the public mood of the community or its sensibilities.

Under the Cairo Agreement, signed in April 1994, the Palestinian Authority, as the controlling political entity, gained the power to collect taxes and customs duties and oversee most economic matters in areas under Palestinian administration. Nevertheless, the economy of the Palestinian-controlled areas would remain closely linked through trade and currency to Israel's. The PA built a parastatal infrastructure, complete with ministries and a large security apparatus, to oversee the business of Palestinian self-rule.

International aid was critical to the development of the Palestinian-controlled areas and to the operation of Palestinian government. Although the United States and other Western countries pledged aid, the Palestinians did not receive the windfall that Egypt received when Sadat signed the peace treaty with Israel. About $2.2 billion over five years was initially pledged, but delivery was slow and uncertain. Many donors expressed the concern that their funds might be used as patronage money rather than for effective development. A 1999 European evaluation of Palestinian budget policies noted improvements in accountability but urged more transparency.

Other Tracks

The U.S.-sponsored Arab-Israeli peace process received a boost on July 25, 1994, when in Washington Jordan's King Hussein and Israeli prime minister Rabin ended the forty-six-year state of war between their two countries by signing the Washington Declaration. Their agreement was followed by a formal peace treaty, signed on October 26, 1994, at a ceremony on the Israeli-Jordanian border. The treaty resolved border and water disputes and established cooperation in a number of areas, including in trade, tourism, communications, and transportation. In addition, both sides pledged not to allow their territory to be used as a base for third-party attacks against the other.

Despite the fanfare and the premature declarations of the end of the Arab-Israeli conflict as a result of the Oslo Accords, the Israeli-Jordanian treaty, and other signs of a relaxation of tensions, the resolution to this protracted conflict failed to transpire. Negotiations between Israel and Syria and Lebanon were suspended. Although Rabin while prime minister in the 1990s had indicated in secret negotiations with Syrian president Hafiz al-Asad his willingness to abandon the Golan in return for security guarantees from Syria, the Likud government of Benjamin Netanyahu mostly ignored relations with Syria. The Syrian government felt isolated in the region. The attention that it received during the Gulf War, when it agreed to support the U.S.-led war effort, did not last. While

---

Palestinian Territories

Area: 6,220 square kilometers: West Bank (including East Jerusalem), 5,860 square kilometers; Gaza, 360 square kilometers

Intended Capital: East Jerusalem; Ramallah, on the West Bank, is the seat of the Palestinian Authority

Population: West Bank, 2,385,615 (plus 364,000 Israeli settlers, including in East Jerusalem) (2004); Gaza, 1,376,289 (plus more than 5,000 Israeli settlers, scheduled for evacuation in 2005) (2005)

Religion: West Bank—Muslim, 75 percent; Jewish, 17 percent; Christian and other, 8 percent; Gaza—Muslim, 98.7 percent; Christian, 0.7 percent; Jewish, 0.6 percent

Language: Arabic; Hebrew spoken by settlers and many Palestinians; English widely understood

Type of Government: Some Palestinian interim self-government, but Israel retains ultimates authority as an occupying power

GDP: West Bank—$1.8 billion; per capita, $800 (2003); Gaza—$768 million; per capita, $600 (2003)

Source: Figures from Central Intelligence Agency, *CIA World Factbook*, 2005.

U.S.-Syrian relations improved somewhat, U.S. bombings of Iraq in December 1998 resulted in mass demonstrations against the United States in Syria. A group of demonstrators stormed the U.S. embassy, putting the Syrian government in the position of having to pay reparations to cover the damages. The Israeli-Palestinian agreement signed at Sharm al-Shaykh in 1999 only heightened Syrian anxieties. Syria had hoped that the Israeli government under Barak would adhere to the tentative agreement reached with Rabin. President Asad continued to insist on the full withdrawal of all Israeli troops from the Golan Heights and refused to consider normalization measures until such a time. He held firm to this position when he met with President Clinton in Geneva in 2000. Clinton attended the meeting hoping to urge Asad to accept some Israeli retention of Syrian lands, specifically, Lake Tiberias (Sea of Galilee), its shoreline, and a road around it. Asad died later that year and was succeeded by his son Bashar al-Asad, whom the Israelis see as too weak at this point to deliver an agreement.

Israel continued to occupy part of south Lebanon—one-tenth of Lebanese territory—and violence between Lebanese resistance groups and Israeli occupation forces and their Lebanese surrogate militia continued to plague the area. Israel launched more than 100 bombing raids into Lebanon in 1998 alone, and, in 1999, Prime Minister Netanyahu ordered a massive bombing raid against the electrical grid serving Beirut and its environs. Hizballah continued to insist that it had the right to use violence against Israeli forces and their surrogate in Lebanon. In 1998 fighting between Israel and the Lebanese groups brought outside intervention, mostly U.S. and French.

Major movement occurred on the Lebanese front in 2000, when Israeli prime minister Barak fulfilled his campaign promise of withdrawing Israeli forces from the south. He had set July 2000 for completion of the withdrawal, but increasing attacks by the Lebanese resistance movement headed by Hizballah, the most heavily armed and best-trained militia in Lebanon, led him to move the date forward to late May. The Lebanese-Israeli conflict did not, however, end with the completion of the Israeli withdrawal on May 24, 2000. Israel asserted that its evacuation fulfilled UN Resolution 425 of 1978 calling for it to withdraw forces from Lebanon—and the United Nations backed the Israeli claim—but according to the Lebanese government, Israel had not complied because its forces continued to occupy the Shab`a Farms area. Israel and the United Nations assert, however, that the area is Syrian territory. After the Israeli withdrawal, Hizballah maintained its arms, and the Lebanese government and many Lebanese citizens continued to support its existence because, they felt, it would serve as a deterrent against further Israeli actions.

Israeli-Jordanian relations suffered a setback in early 1999, when King Hussein died. The king, with long experience in Arab and international affairs, was often willing to shatter taboos. He often broke with the Palestinian movement over the years, although the majority of his country's population was Palestinian. Hussein's successor, his son King Abdallah II, expressed his determination to respect the previous commitments of the Jordanian government, but he was and remains too weak to assume an independent political role in the region.

Upon assuming the throne, Abdallah took immediate steps to improve ties with the Syrian government, which under Hafiz al-Asad had been critical of what it considered his father's disregard for the plight of the Arabs of the Golan, the other Israeli-occupied territories, and Lebanon. He paid an official visit to Damascus, hoping to repair the damage with Asad's son and successor. For now, he is likely to stick to the Arab consensus rather than risk isolation as he did in March 2005, when he floated the idea to Arab leaders that they normalize relations with Israel before it evacuates the occupied territories. His suggestion met with official and popular disapproval.

Abdallah has maintained good relations with Israel, and the United States would like him to play a role in Israeli-Palestinian relations. In February 2005, he attended the Sharm al-Shaykh summit between the Palestinian and Israeli leaders. Abdallah's dependence on Western financial aid will limit his ability to distance himself from the United States, if that is his desire. Abdallah's priority in coming years will, however, remain his domestic situation and his status in the Arab world.

While Egyptian president Hosni Mubarak has emerged as one of the most effective Arab leaders, Egypt remains in a state of cold peace with Israel. Mubarak continues to play a leading role in Palestinian affairs and often mediates between the Palestinians on the one hand and the United States and Israel on the other. Egypt has been critical of the Israeli government, especially regarding its unwillingness to open its nuclear facilities for international inspection. The Egyptian government has also spoken out in favor of Arab cooperation and coordination. Its renewed leadership role within the Arab League, which relocated to its headquarters in Cairo, came at the price of Israeli-Egyptian rapprochement.

Camp David and the al-Aqsa Intifada

May 4, 1999, marked the end of the five-year interim period set by the Oslo Accords for reaching a final settlement of the Israeli-Palestinian conflict. During this period, Palestinians grew uneasy and frustrated over the lack of improvement in their lives despite the accords. Corruption spread throughout the Palestinian Authority, and high unemployment plagued Palestinian areas.

As punishment for Arafat's lack of action against militants who organized and launched attacks in Israel and against the settlements, Israel refused to forward to the PA taxes it had collected from Palestinians. Israeli prime minister Barak initially seemed more interested in pursuing the Syria track than in talking with the Palestinians. Meanwhile, Israel continued to expropriate Palestinian land in the occupied territories, and the settler population in the West Bank (excluding East Jerusalem) and Gaza grew from 127,800 in 1994, the year Oslo was signed, to 194,300 in 2000, the year the al-Aqsa intifada erupted. *(See Israeli Settler Population table, p. 301)*

In mid-2000, President Bill Clinton hosted Palestinian-Israeli talks at Camp David in an attempt to breathe new life into the peace process by abandoning the phased approach to negotiations in favor of a push for a final settlement. PA leader Arafat and Israeli prime minister Barak met with Clinton for approximately two weeks, July 11–24, but in the end failed to conclude an agreement. The two sides disagree on what caused the failure, but immediately after the talks, Clinton and Barak launched a public relations offensive to place the blame on Arafat. Israel repeatedly castigated the Palestinian leader for having rejected an incredibly "generous offer." The Clinton administration supported the Israeli line. The Palestinians did not find the offer particularly generous.

According to Robert Malley, Clinton's Middle East adviser on the National Security Council,

Israel never put a formal offer on the table. Rather, the Americans presented to the Palestinians the gist of Israeli ideas about a settlement:

- Israel would withdraw from the West Bank though not from all of it. (The two sides disagree on the percentage of the territory Israel would have retained according to the offer.)
- Israel would agree to a "land swap" involving the Negev to compensate for occupied territory that it would retain.
- Israel would cede part but not all of East Jerusalem as the Palestinians wanted. (Arafat felt that he could not accept any solution that did not include all of East Jerusalem as part of the Palestinian state.)
- Israel would not be required to dismantle all of the settlements in the West Bank and would retain bypass roads (for the exclusive use of settlers) that would separate Palestinian communities in the West Bank, prohibiting uninterrupted movement by Palestinians.
- Israel would "lease" land in the Jordan Valley and control the air space over the West Bank.
- Palestinian refugees would return to areas in the West Bank and Gaza under Palestinian sovereignty (thus rejecting the strongly held right of return).

Though the Palestinians felt that they could not accept the Israeli offer, they were not prepared to make a counteroffer. In fact, before agreeing to attend the summit, they had expressed reservations, informing the Clinton administration that they would prefer more time to prepare. Although the Camp David negotiations ended without a settlement, the two sides did make progress and agreed to continue talking.

At the end of September 2000, mounting Palestinian frustrations erupted in the al-Aqsa intifada, after Ariel Sharon, out of the government at the time and accompanied by hundreds of Israeli security forces, led a delegation of Likud Party legislators on a visit to the Haram al-Sharif in East Jerusalem. Palestinians viewed Sharon's visit to Islam's third holiest site as a provocation, while

Sharon claimed that he had the right as an Israeli to go anywhere he wanted in the Land of Israel. After Sharon left the compound, confrontations ensued between Palestinians and the security forces deployed for his visit. Disturbances spread across the West Bank. The following day, violence again erupted when Palestinians leaving prayers on the Haram al-Sharif threw stones at Israeli police officers, who then stormed the compound.

This second Palestinian rebellion was far more lethal, destructive, and violent than the first intifada had been. Some Palestinian groups, particularly Hamas and Islamic Jihad, resorted to terrifying suicide bombings that did not distinguish between Israeli civilians and soldiers. Israel targeted for assassination leaders of Hamas, Islamic Jihad, and the al-Aqsa Martyrs Brigades, a Fatah-affiliated group, and employed overwhelming force, such as unleashing F-16s and laser guided bombs in urban areas, leading to large numbers of civilian deaths. Many more Israelis and Palestinians died in the course of the al-Aqsa uprising than had been killed in the first uprising.

In October, Clinton gathered Israeli and Palestinian leaders at Sharm al-Shaykh and hammered out an agreement to end the uptick in violence, but the deal foundered almost immediately. One proposal raised by Clinton was, however, carried out with the dispatch of former senator George Mitchell and CIA director George Tenet to the region in December 2000 on a fact-finding mission. Mitchell was charged with investigating the underlying causes of the uprising and proposing confidence-building measures toward a deescalation, while Tenet worked on establishing a cease-fire and other security arrangements to deal with the violence.

Also in the midst of the uprising, Israeli and Palestinian representatives convened for talks in Washington in December 2000 and in Taba, Egypt, in January 2001 to further discuss issues broached earlier at Camp David. The Taba talks ended, as all such meetings had, without resolution on the status of Israeli settlements, the status of East Jerusalem, the plight of the Palestinian refugees, or what West Bank lands Israel might retain. The following month, Barak—who had resigned on December 10 in order to "seek a new mandate" to deal with the ongoing crisis—suffered electoral defeat at the hands of Likud's Ariel Sharon.

Developments in the region worsened in 2001. While the United States focused on the events of September 11 and the subsequent war in Afghanistan, the conflict between the Israelis and Palestinians raged. President George W. Bush initially did not want to waste political capital on the Palestinian-Israeli issue, having seen how the efforts of his predecessor had come to naught. After Sharon's election, the continuing violence and potential for further instability forced Bush's hand. Former Treasury secretary Paul O'Neil recounts in *The Price of Loyalty* that Bush had stunned Secretary of State Colin Powell at a cabinet meeting by praising Sharon's use of force against the Palestinians and expressing his belief that Israel's actions would be good for a settlement. The State Department believed, however, that the United States needed to engage.

In a report released in May 2001, the Mitchell Commission asserted the need for both sides to take steps to end the ongoing violence, lowering its level to a cooling-off period as quickly as possible, so they could proceed with confidence-building measures and negotiations. He notably concluded that it would be difficult to bring an end to Israeli-Palestinian violence without a halt to Israeli settlement. The Palestinian Authority was called on to make every effort to prevent the use of violence against Israelis. The commission's recommendations were ignored by all parties.

With the Bush administration focused on the "war on terror," Sharon began to portray Israel's conflict with the Palestinians as a front in that war. This approach gained support from the Bush administration, which rarely criticized Israeli violence against Palestinians. Israel also successfully used the ongoing violence as justification for its refusal to implement agreements with the Palestinians, arguing that acts of terror committed by Palestinians violated their accords. The Palestinians countered that the Israeli government had consistently violated the terms of their agreements, disregarding deadlines, failing to transfer funds to the PA, and continuing settlement activity.

Arabs throughout the region were alarmed at the level and duration of violence and the disintegration of the political process. At an Arab summit held in Beirut March 27–28, 2002, Saudi crown prince Abdallah presented a plan envisioning peace with Israel in return for its full withdrawal from the Arab lands captured in 1967. Israel dismissed the plan and on March 29 launched Operation Defensive Shield, a massive military incursion to reoccupy most of the West Bank and Gaza. Observers and politicians pronounced the Oslo process dead.

In early April 2002, the Israelis attacked the city and refugee camp of Jenin, setting off a fierce battle and great controversy over what transpired there. Demolitions of homes with people still inside them, claims of large numbers of Palestinian deaths, and widespread destruction led to calls for an investigation of Israeli actions. A UN report criticized the violence on both sides as posing a threat to civilians, while the human rights organization Amnesty International accused Israel of violating international human rights and humanitarian law and committing war crimes. A United Nations investigation put the death toll at fifty-two Palestinians (half of them civilians) and twenty-three Israeli soldiers. Some 450 families were made homeless.

Israel continued its campaign, asserting that it was engaged in dismantling the Palestinian "terrorist infrastructure." Its forces targeted PA political and military infrastructures, blasting ministries and deploying soldiers to destroy or confiscate computers and equipment containing any manner of records, including land recordations and other administrative files. They also targeted Palestinian forces entrusted with security responsibilities under Oslo, but which the Sharon government accused of not doing enough to prevent Palestinian attacks against Israelis.

The suicide bombings continued, despite Israel's massive show of force. In response to pressure from Israelis to stop Palestinian attacks, the

Fatalities of the al-Aqsa Intifada, September 2000–May 2005

More than 4,300 people died during the course of the al-Aqsa intifada.

Palestinians killed by Israelis

3,179	By security forces in the West Bank and Gaza
56	By security forces in Israel
35	By Israeli citizens in the West Bank and Gaza

17 Palestinian citizens of Israel killed
151 Palestinians killed by Palestinians

Israelis killed by Palestinians

439	Civilians in Israel
220	Civilians in the West Bank and Gaza
218	Israeli security forces in the West Bank and Gaza
83	Israeli security forces in Israel

52 Foreign citizens killed

Note: Figures do not include suicide bombers and Palestinian deaths resulting from delays in obtaining medical treatment because of Israeli-imposed restrictions on movement.
Source: B'Tselem: The Israeli Information Center for Human Rights in the Occupied Territories, http://www.btselem.org. See the B'Tselem Web site for additional statistics and breakdowns.

Israeli government approved the construction of the first phase of a 440-mile separation wall, or "security fence" as it is called in Israel, which would make it difficult for Palestinians to cross the Green Line and conduct attacks. Construction began in June.

The United Nations and various human rights organizations criticized the decision on a number of grounds: Portions of the barrier followed the Green Line, but large segments of it did not. The plan called for the barrier to be built mostly on Palestinian land, which Israel confiscated for the project, and it incorporated West Bank territory in order to include certain settlements on the "Israeli

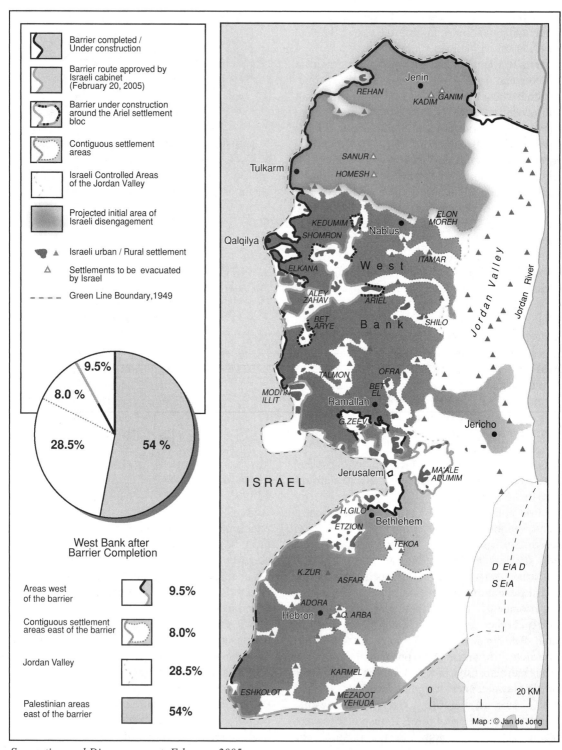

Separation and Disengagement, February 2005

side." Israel dismissed objections to what appeared to be an illegal land grab, arguing that the route of the wall was not meant to be permanent nor to affect any potential settlement with the Palestinians.

The barrier effectively sealed off some villages and towns, creating virtual prisons, and sometimes separated villagers from their agricultural lands. It further restricted Palestinians' movement, already stifled by Israeli military checkpoints. In July 2004, the International Court of Justice would declare the barrier illegal and demand that its construction be halted. The United States used its veto power to prevent the Security Council from taking up the issue.

In response to the deteriorating situation and its potential threat to the region, the European Union, Russia, the United Nations, and the United States—collectively known as the Quartet—set to work on a peace plan that would be publicly unveiled in late April 2003. The plan, consisting of three phases and popularly referred to as the "road map," became a cornerstone of the Bush administration's Middle East policy. The first phase (from immediately after its acceptance until May 2003) called for and end to the violence, Palestinian security and political reforms, an Israeli settlement freeze and withdrawal from the areas it reoccupied in 2002, and Palestinian elections. During this phase, the humanitarian conditions of the Palestinian territories would be assessed in conjunction with economic reforms within the Palestinian Authority to provide more transparency and accountability. In the second phase (June 2003–December 2003), a Palestinian state would be created with provisional borders, and a new Palestinian constitution would be promulgated in preparation for the last phase. In the third phase (2004–2005), negotiations were to begin over such permanent status issues as refugees, Jerusalem, borders, water, settlements, and so on. Though the road map was not implemented when and as planned, the Quartet remained committed to it.

Bush released the plan only after PA leader Arafat succumbed to pressure to appoint a prime minister. Israel had for decades argued that it would welcome peace talks with the Palestinians if only it had a partner with whom to negotiate. During the al-Aqsa intifada, the Bush administration embraced this line, accusing Arafat of being "tainted by terrorism," and made the isolation and disregard of Arafat an element of U.S. policy. The Israelis had essentially placed Arafat under house arrest, confining him to his mostly destroyed Ramallah compound in late 2001 and threatening periodically to deport him.

Rather than face further political isolation and financial strangulation, in March 2003 Arafat reluctantly appointed Mahmoud Abbas (Abu Mazen), a longtime member of Fatah, to the newly created post of prime minister. The Palestinian Legislative Council approved Abbas's cabinet on April 29, and the following day copies of the road map were presented to the Israeli and Palestinian leaders.

By June, Abbas had managed to convince Palestinian factions to agree to a *hudna,* a cease-fire in attacks on Israelis. It would last for seven weeks. Meanwhile, tensions soon rose between Arafat and Abbas, as Arafat resisted relinquishing any of his powers and failed to see any advantage to facilitating Abbas's job. While publicly appearing to support Abbas, Arafat continually obstructed his efforts behind the scenes. Being favored by Bush and Sharon as well as undermined by Arafat did little to boost support for Abbas among Palestinians. He resigned in September 2003, some four months after taking office, when Arafat refused to hand over control of the security forces and the financial files of the PLO. Arafat replaced him with Ahmad Qurei, Speaker of the Palestinian legislature, an architect of Oslo, and an old ally.

Outlook

The Bush administration and others who portrayed Arafat as the obstacle to a Palestinian-Israeli peace, pronounced his death in November 2004 an opportunity to pursue anew a settlement of the conflict. Despite Arafat's passing and other developments, however, there are no signs of peace on the horizon. In 2004 the Israeli government and the Bush administration officially endorsed Prime Minister Sharon's plan to relocate some 6,000 settlers from Gaza and withdraw most of the Israeli military. Although the Palestinians welcomed this development, they also expressed concerns about its implications. U.S. policy previously had opposed unilateral acts by either of the two sides, holding that both should be involved in resolving issues related to their conflict. The Bush administration's endorsement of the disengagement plan represents a shift in policy that effectively dismisses Palestinian participation in matters directly affecting them. Palestinians also worry that the withdrawal from Gaza is a harbinger of Israel's intent to redirect its energies toward tightening its grip on the West Bank.

Construction of the separation barrier continued, as did plans to effectively seal East Jerusalem from the West Bank. In April 2005, the Sharon government announced plans to expand the settlement of Ma'ale Adumim, a move that would severe Palestinian West Bank communities from those of East Jerusalem and further hamper movement between major Palestinian population centers.

In January 2005, Mahmoud Abbas, the former PA prime minister, won the election to succeed Arafat as PA president. (He had earlier succeeded Arafat as chairman of the PLO.) Shortly after taking office, he reached an agreement with Palestinian factions to suspend attacks on Israelis, and at a summit in early February in Sharm al-Shaykh, he and Sharon declared an informal truce.

Palestinians held municipal elections in the West Bank and Gaza in 2004, but Abbas indefinitely postponed legislative council elections scheduled for July 2005, stating that additional time was needed to work out issues involving electoral laws. Hamas, which had boycotted the elections held in 1996, was expected to participate (and do well) in the 2005 elections.

Abbas made his first visit to Washington as leader of the PA in May 2005. President Bush promised $50 million in direct assistance as part of an estimated $350 million package. Congress had earlier agreed to allocate funds to the PA, though in an affront to Abbas had insisted that the monies be distributed through nongovernmental organizations, rather than directly to the PA.

Other tracks in the Arab-Israeli conflict will remain on hold until the Palestinians and Israelis rejoin negotiations and make progress toward resolution of the longstanding issues confronting them. It is highly unlikely that the Holy Land and other parts of the Middle East will know real and lasting peace any time soon, as Israelis, Palestinians, and other parties have recently produced new political forces, often inspired by fundamentalist visions, that are firmly opposed to peaceful settlement. The Arab-Israeli conflict continues to defy diplomacy of every kind.

CHAPTER 3

U.S. POLICY IN THE MIDDLE EAST

In the history of U.S. foreign policy, the Middle East as a region of interest is a relative newcomer. Although Americans have traveled to the region since the late eighteenth century—Mark Twain was a famous visitor—the U.S. government paid the Middle East little attention until the end of World War II. Since then, the United States has played an increasing role in Middle Eastern politics.

U.S. policy in the region has focused on six major objectives: ensuring the security of Israel; achieving an Arab-Israeli peace settlement; maintaining access by industrialized nations to Middle Eastern oil; blocking Soviet influence in the region (until 1989); countering terrorism; and in recent years promoting regime change in certain countries. With the breakup of the Soviet Union, the U.S. interest shifted to an uneasy combination of maintaining local stability and promoting democratization. This balance becomes even more delicate when teamed with efforts to secure the United States' traditional interests in the region. Since the late 1970s, U.S. policy has been complicated by the Islamist political ideology put forth by individuals, groups, and governments that challenge the paradigms through which foreign policy is analyzed and made in the United States and other Western nations.

Following the attacks of September 11, 2001, the United States has pursued an aggressive campaign against Islamist groups engaged in terrorism. Most notably, this has resulted in the invasion of Afghanistan and the overthrow of the Islamist regime there, as well as the subsequent ouster of the Saddam Hussein government in Iraq, based in part on allegations that Iraq supported terrorism. The United States also has sought to prevent the spread of nuclear, chemical, and biological arms and has continued to promote economic and security ties with moderate Arab states.

These policy objectives have often been in conflict. In particular, the relationship between the United States and Israel has at times made other U.S. policy goals more difficult to pursue and achieve. For example, U.S. support for Israel during the 1973 Arab-Israeli war led to an Arab oil boycott against the United States. Ten years later the United States was selling tens of billions of dollars worth of advanced military hardware to the Gulf states responsible for the oil boycott. Regardless of the inherent contradictions, successive U.S. administrations have agreed that these major objectives must all be pursued, and they have retained public and congressional support. This chapter examines the mechanisms of the U.S. foreign policy making process and looks at the major events in U.S.–Middle East relations, touching briefly on the presidency of Woodrow Wilson, during which the modern era emerged, but concentrating on post–World War II events.

U.S. Foreign Policy Formation

U.S. foreign policy formation involves interplay between the president and close advisers, Congress, the foreign policy bureaucracies, and, to a lesser extent, the public. The president is the central figure in this process but is dependent on advisers. Those who contend for the president's attention include the national security adviser, the secretary of state, the director of national intelligence, and special interest groups outside the government. Other entities involved in the process include the Agency for International Development (AID), the Defense, Treasury, and Commerce Departments, other members of the intelligence community, and international organizations of which the United States is a member. These participants seldom if ever agree on all points at the same time, and often they have conflicting policies for events or regions as well as different institutional agendas. There remains, however, enough overlap among their agendas to produce significant jurisdictional and resource conflicts, especially during the congressional appropriations process.

The Executive Branch

The Presidency

The executive branch of the U.S. government encompasses the presidency and various departments and independent agencies. Those most directly involved in foreign policy formation are the State and Defense Departments, the Central Intelligence Agency and other intelligence and national-security agencies, and the Agency for International Development. Smaller foreign policy entities whose focus is information dissemination and political, economic, or humanitarian development include the Department of State's Office of International Information Programs, the National Endowment for Democracy, the Overseas Private Investment Corporation, and the Peace Corps. These agencies are more instruments of policy, but their very existence speaks to the many ways in which the United States exerts its influence abroad. The most important foreign policy forum of the executive branch is the Office of the President, represented by the president and his National Security Council, headed by the national security adviser.

Presidents face many challenges in foreign policy formation and implementation. First, as

individuals, they bring different experiences to the Oval Office that shape their view of the world, including their conception of proper foreign policy making and implementation. However, these experiences have rarely made them experts in the operation of the international system. The typical post–World War II president has come to the White House via a state governorship, a stint in Congress, or the vice presidency and usually has been more comfortable with domestic politics and campaigning than with the larger world.

Additionally, presidents are too busy to learn the complexities of all international issues that might command their attention. Time demands, therefore, leave the president reliant on advisers to present information he can use without himself becoming an expert in international relations. Advisers must summarize complex situations quickly and neatly, knowing that the situations are never so neat.

Among advisers, competition is keen for the president's attention. The secretary of state and the national security adviser are selected by the president, who tends to favor one over the other. The relationship between these two advisers often affects their reception in the Oval Office, as well.

Presidential management styles influence decisions to fill these important roles and how the individuals will be used in decision making. Some presidents like to take charge of foreign policy decisions, regardless of their knowledge of international affairs. These presidents can foster a collegial atmosphere among advisers, where everyone cooperates (or respectfully disagrees) and consensus opinions emerge. Collegiality is achieved through careful selection of advisers who share a worldview or through a clear articulation of presidential policy preferences, both of which create clarity of purpose. Presidents John F. Kennedy, George Bush, and Bill Clinton have all employed this management style.

Alternatively, presidents who want close control of policy may select one key adviser, typically the national security adviser or the secretary of state, to consult more than all others when deciding foreign policy questions. In this case, the personal relationship—perceptions of loyalty and trust—between president and adviser is crucial. Sometimes, however, advisers are more loyal than expert in the subjects about which they are to advise the president. Further, it is through this individual that policy directives are disseminated. The adviser or senior staff manager then must create a hierarchy of specialists to turn the president's directives into concrete policies and actions. The members of this hierarchy will tend to share similar worldviews, because the top leadership is interested in their activity and does not want to mediate disputes. This atmosphere fosters consensus thinking and may freeze out points of view that do not support it. Serious differences of opinion are likely to lead to the departure of one or more advisers. This was typical of the presidency of Richard M. Nixon from 1969 to 1974.

The alternative presidential managerial style is more hands-off, allowing advisers and subordinates to handle the details of foreign policy. In some cases, a president will give only general policy directives to his staff. Presidents who adopt this style tend to be more interested and competent in domestic policy. This is hardly surprising given the career path of most presidents, but it may allow policy to drift or be paralyzed by disputes between advisers. The presidency of Ronald Reagan is a notable example of this management style.

The National Security Council

The National Security Council (NSC) was established, along with the Department of Defense and the CIA, by the National Security Act of 1947. Its original purpose was to provide a coordinating mechanism for all national security and foreign policy information coming into the White House, providing comprehensive policy reviews and allowing policy officials a structured meeting forum. It functioned in this manner under the Truman and Eisenhower administrations, in the late 1940s and the 1950s, with an executive secretary and a staff of twenty. The NSC became more institutionalized under Dwight D. Eisenhower, with a staff hierarchy emerging. Two boards were created, policy planning and operations, to formulate and implement foreign and national security policy. The executive secretary became the assistant for national security affairs, or more commonly, the national security adviser.

However, bureaucratic constraints soon hampered the creative problem-solving process needed to formulate policy. Under the Kennedy administration, from 1961 to 1963, the national security advising system became more personalized. While circumventing some bureaucratic problems of the NSC, personalization created new ones. President Kennedy valued direct contact with lower-level officials and interagency working groups, believing they were more responsive to his foreign policy directives. NSC staff appointments on the basis of personal loyalty to the president, rather than expert knowledge, became more common. This trend continued under Lyndon B. Johnson, who became president on Kennedy's assassination in 1963 and remained in office until 1969, during the period when the Vietnam War dominated U.S. foreign policy decisions. Johnson went further outside the formal NSC system than had Kennedy, and the NSC became a body to circumvent rather than to consult.

President Nixon came into office in 1969 with a plan to revitalize the NSC by creating a number of new committees and interagency bodies under the leadership of his national security adviser, Henry Kissinger. In effect, this system allowed Kissinger to engage or ignore the NSC as he preferred. Jimmy Carter, who spent four years in the White House beginning in 1977, replaced the Nixon system with two committees, one for long-term projects and planning, and the other for short-term work. However, the personal dimension introduced under Kennedy persisted, and over the course of his administration, Carter shifted away from the formal NSC system to weekly meetings with select advisers.

President Reagan, a two-term president from 1981 to 1989, echoing Nixon, pledged to make the NSC system less personal but wound up with an organization that had little role in the foreign policy process and was difficult to monitor. The national security adviser took a back seat to the secretaries of state and defense and to the director of central intelligence. Reagan's lack of attention produced drift in the NSC and, when combined with the president's laissez-faire style of policy articulation, created conditions that allowed generally unaccountable officials to implement the illegal sale of arms to Iran and divert the profits to groups fighting left-wing governments in Latin America. At the same time, the NSC overall had become a bloated bureaucracy too occupied with procedure.

Presidents George H. W. Bush (1989–1993) and Clinton (1993–2001) had the most success in getting away from personalization in the NSC system. Both men created collegial teams of advisers who worked well together and avoided intramural battles typical of earlier administrations. However, collegiality is not always amenable to creative thinking and changing times. This especially was a factor for the Bush administration: the president's closest advisers agreed on their view of the world, and they liked it so well that they could not see that it was changing. Clinton led his foreign policy team through these shifts, seemingly making policy on a case-by-case basis, without the global outlook of the cold war or Bush's "new world order."

During the first term of President George W. Bush (2001–), the NSC was more subordinated to other agencies, and the role of his national security adviser was regarded as playing mediator between competing senior officials—particularly the vice president, the secretary of defense, and the secretary of state—and enjoying the personal trust of the president in providing advice on conflicting opinions from these senior officials.

The Department of State

The Department of State was formed in 1789 as the primary foreign policy organ of the new United States of America. Its employees today remain the primary representatives of the United States in foreign countries and international organizations, but its post–World War II domestic role has shifted from policy formation to information processing and dissemination. Although the secretary of state remains an important figure in policy formation, his or her position in the hierarchy of presidential foreign policy advisers is often determined by loyalty to the president or to the department. Another factor is the secretary's relationship with other foreign policy figures, in particular the national security adviser. When conflict occurs between these two individuals, usually the secretary is isolated from the decision-making process.

As organs to implement policy, U.S. embassies abroad are for the most part highly effective. However, there are logistical and personnel issues that on occasion cause problems for policy implementation. First, the embassy is home not only to Department of State personnel, but also to representatives of up to forty-five different federal departments and agencies, all with their own reporting channels and some with different, even contradictory, policy objectives. This makes the job of the ambassador, which includes managing the embassy staff and ensuring coherent policy implementation, difficult, and the problem is compounded if the ambassador is not interested in the day-to-day embassy operations. Although most ambassadors are career Foreign Service officers, a significant number are political appointees who may feel more effective as the visible embodiment of the U.S. presence in their host country than as personnel managers. Additionally, political appointees to ambassadorships are not necessarily familiar with the countries to which they are assigned, although many serve with distinction. Sometimes lack of knowledge will unfortunately damage their credibility, and by extension, that of the Department of State and the United States.

Within the Department of State, five of the six offices overseen by undersecretaries are directly involved with discharging foreign policy. In addition, the United States Agency for International Development (USAID) receives guidance from the secretary of state, and the permanent representative to the United Nations reports to him or her.

The office of Political Affairs manages bilateral and regional policy issues, integrating political, economic, and security matters into the United

States' bilateral relations. Among its regional bureaus, Near Eastern Affairs deals specifically with foreign policy and diplomatic relations toward Middle Eastern nations. The office of Arms Control and International Security concerns itself with the nonproliferation of weapons of mass destruction, disarmament, regional security arrangements, agreements on forces, and arms transfer policy.

Public Diplomacy and Public Affairs oversees the Bureaus of Education and Cultural Affairs, Public Affairs, and International Information Programs in fulfilling what was once the mission of the United States Information Agency: explaining and advocating U.S. policy to foreign populations (as well as to domestic audiences) rather than to foreign governments. It carries out its responsibilities primarily through broadcasting, print material, and the Internet. It also administers the Fulbright educational exchange program. Before a government restructuring in the late 1990s, USIA also oversaw the well-known Voice of America, but it now operates under the Broadcasting Board of Governors, as does the al-Hurra satellite network and Radio Sawa, which are directed at the Arab world, and Radio Farda, which is aimed at Iran.

The office of Global Affairs coordinates policy on a number of international issues, including democracy, labor, human rights, narcotics, the environment, and population. USAID disburses U.S. foreign aid in the form of humanitarian, economic, and political development programs, which it carries out through field offices and subcontractors.

The Intelligence Community

The intelligence community is composed of several different agencies, some autonomous, some affiliated with cabinet-level departments. They have in common a mission to gather information considered valuable to U.S. interests, analyze it, and present conclusions to policy makers. While on the surface each of these agencies has a distinct role to play, in practice they overlap, resulting in interagency conflicts. The best known of the intelligence agencies is the Central Intelligence Agency, which is responsible for general national security and foreign government information gathering. Other agencies include the National Security Agency (NSA), which is responsible for ensuring the security of sensitive U.S. signals traffic (cables, wires, and encrypted broadcasts) and for decoding and analyzing foreign communications. The Defense Intelligence Agency (DIA) is responsible for military intelligence. The National Reconnaissance Office (NRO) operates a system of reconnaissance satellites serving the intelligence community. NSA, DIA, and NRO are tied to the Department of Defense. The Federal Bureau of Investigation (FBI), a branch of the Justice Department, is responsible for foreign counterterrorism efforts, whether in the United States or abroad.

The goal of intelligence gathering is to provide forewarning to government officials, thereby limiting foreign affairs surprises, and to supply information for policy decisions. Another aspect of intelligence is covert operation, which is most closely associated with the CIA but is carried out by a number of agencies. Covert action can be a valuable and effective tool of foreign policy, but following a number of bungled operations in the 1970s and 1980s, presidents have been reluctant to use this tool to any significant degree.

Covert operations, when discovered, have also made for long-lasting anti-American sentiments abroad. In the Middle East, a well-known example occurred in Iran in 1953 when U.S. covert intervention helped ensure the failure of an attempt to replace the shah and contributed to long-lasting hostility to the United States by opponents of the shah and Iran's revolutionary government after 1979. More recently, as part of the Bush administration's "war on terror" after 2001, the CIA has assumed a more active role in operating Special Forces against military and terrorist elements in Afghanistan and Iraq. In addition, unmanned CIA aircraft have been used to assassinate terrorist leaders.

The failure of the intelligence community to ascertain that Iraq did not have weapons of mass destruction prior to the 2003 war—as well as alleged disagreement or opposition to Bush administration policy views in some sectors—produced a restructuring of intelligence leadership. A new position of director of national intelligence was created in 2005 to oversee the entire intelligence community. Previously the director of the CIA had held a supervisory role over the community.

Congress

The job of Congress is to make the laws of the land, and in pursuit of this goal it has organized itself into committees and subcommittees, allowing members to become specialists in certain fields. Most members of Congress are not on committees dealing directly with international issues and spend little time—less than 5 percent by one estimate—considering foreign policy matters before voting on them. Another reason foreign affairs receives little congressional attention is the small constituency interested in international issues; some members consider assignment to these committees as an electoral liability. That said, Congress does consider foreign policy legislation, does have executive branch oversight responsibilities, does make billions of dollars in appropriations for foreign affairs, and is accordingly an important part of U.S. foreign policy making.

The committees most responsible for foreign affairs legislation are the House International Relations Committee, the Senate Foreign Relations Committee, the House and Senate Armed Services Committees, and all of their regional and functional subcommittees, such as on economic or human rights policy. The House International Relations Committee in the 109th Congress (2005–2007) has a subcommittee on the Middle East and Central Asia. The Senate Foreign Relations Committee had a subcommittee on Near Eastern and South Asian Affairs.

Most policy initiatives originate in the executive branch. Congress, through the appropriate committee or subcommittee, deals with the legal details of the proposed initiative. Throughout this process, politics may be close to the surface, forcing participants to consider factors not directly related to the appropriateness or efficacy of the policy in question. Political factors include election considerations, public interest and percep-

tions, symbolic politics, and domestic concerns such as the presence of military personnel or manufacturing that might be affected by a policy. However, political considerations usually are essential as part of building public consensus for a policy, without which no foreign policy program will be effective, or often even possible to implement.

Relations between the legislative and executive branches also play a role. During the Clinton administration, a time of acrimonious executive-legislative relations, Congress on various occasions affected the foreign policy process by drawing out the confirmation hearings for ambassadors-designate and other appointees. One notable example was a year-long delay (including an ethics investigation from which no charges arose) in the confirmation of Richard Holbrooke as U.S. ambassador to the United Nations.

Institutional factors help and hinder Congress's ability to handle foreign policy issues. One is simply the volume of work that any Congress faces. No member is an expert on all issues on which votes occur, and most rely on leadership guidance, colleagues on specialized committees, and committee staffs and specialized agencies that provide information.

Congress plays other roles in the foreign policy process. The Constitution grants it the power to regulate foreign commerce, impose import taxes, and declare war. The latter has been a continuing source of contention between presidents, who assert their right to commit U.S. military forces as part of their power as commander in chief, and Congress, which has sought ways to limit this assertion, particularly since the Vietnam War.

The president has the right to enter into treaties, but they do not become U.S. law without the "advice and consent" of two-thirds of the Senate; this constitutional requirement allows the Senate to amend treaties and even permits Senate rejection of a treaty negotiated by the president. A notable example of the latter was the defeat of the League of Nations treaty negotiated by President Woodrow Wilson at the end of World War I. In practice, the executive branch has devised ways to circumvent this clause. There is no constitutional definition of a treaty, and presidents have claimed the right to negotiate other types of international agreements. In some cases, the president receives prior approval to negotiate and reach an agreement; this is known as a statutory agreement. Congress has fulfilled its duty of providing advice and consent, but it has no say in the content of the agreement arrived at, and the agreement has the force of U.S. law. In other cases, the president will arrive at an executive agreement with a foreign power without the prior approval of the Senate. Most of these agreements have dealt with diplomatic issues or administrative concerns surrounding prior military commitments. However, this is an area in which the Senate has been trying to win back control, so far with little success.

The Public and Foreign Policy

The American public is involved in foreign policy making primarily in two ways: through public opinion polling and through lobbying. While the foreign policy stance of a candidate may influence a voter's choice, it rarely is of primary concern; domestic issues take precedence. Except for overriding events, such as the Vietnam war in the 1960s or the Persian Gulf War in 1991, the public has limited interest in or knowledge of foreign policy matters. Americans may become interested in foreign policy when it involves other issues of concern to them, such as the environment, local jobs, or human rights abuses. When foreign policy matters do catch domestic attention, Americans tend to look for policies that will generate immediate results. All of this allows policy leaders to shape public opinion, if they choose, but at the same time establishes a public indifference that is difficult to overcome until an issue is so urgent that considered policy debate and options get lost in the crises of the moment.

Lobbying plays a much larger role in the foreign policy process than do public opinion polls. The major lobbying force in U.S. Middle East policy is the American Israel Public Affairs Committee (AIPAC), which was founded in 1954 with the express purpose of lobbying Congress on

behalf of Israel, as its needs are perceived by the American Jewish community. It is widely regarded as the most powerful ethnic lobby in Washington, D.C., and is also active in every state. It provides timely, concise information to members of Congress, financially supports pro-Israeli candidates for office, and wages media campaigns against candidates perceived to be less sympathetic to its cause.

AIPAC succeeds in its lobbying efforts for a number of reasons: it has ample funds to spend on campaign contributions and advertising; it has access to the offices of the majority of members of Congress; and it understands the power of Jewish history, the Holocaust, and sensitivity about anti-Semitism to influence public opinion and decisions of elected officials. Charges of anti-Semitism have been leveled at candidates who oppose its positions. AIPAC is aided additionally by the interests it represents. Israeli and Jewish issues are easily focused, whereas Muslim and Arab Middle Eastern issues span a range of religious and regional variables. It should be noted that AIPAC is not the only Israeli or Jewish lobby in Washington, simply the wealthiest and most powerful.

There are Arab lobbying organizations also, the best-known member of which is the American-Arab Anti-Discrimination Committee–National Association of Arab-Americans, originally two organizations. They merged in 2001. The NAAA was founded in 1972 as a response to AIPAC and served as a lobby organization and a political action committee. It did not, however, have the financial resources of AIPAC and was less successful in getting its members out in shows of support (or criticism) for policies on the Middle East. The ADC started as a grassroots organization drawing attention to issues affecting Arab Americans, and it continues to act as a watchdog group in addition to presenting Arab concerns before the executive and legislative branches. The Arab American Institute, founded in 1985, has become a vocal advocate on behalf of Arab Americans.

A problem for the Arab lobby is the diversity it represents. The Arab world comprises twenty-two states (including the North African countries and the Palestinian territories), all with their own interests that often do not coincide. One might say that they are united behind the Palestinian cause, or in opposition to U.S. policy in Iraq, but on a particular issue each country pursues its own agenda. Arab Americans are even more diverse than their countries of origin: there are Christian and Muslim Arabs, recent immigrants and those whose families have been here for generations. Finally, oil companies and Iranian Americans have interests in the region, but they are not represented by either the Arab or Jewish lobbies. Consequently, the Arab lobby does not and cannot speak with one voice, a fact that greatly diminishes its effectiveness in lobbying Congress.

U.S. Middle East Policy

The Wilson Administration

President Woodrow Wilson set the framework for U.S. policy in the Middle East when he endorsed a 1917 letter from British foreign secretary Arthur Balfour to Lord Lionel Rothschild, a British Zionist leader, pledging that Britain would support the establishment in Palestine of a "national home" for the Jewish people, on the understanding "that nothing shall be done which may prejudice the civil and religious rights of existing non-Jewish communities in Palestine." The U.S. Congress adopted a resolution approving the declaration in September 1922.

Wilson also strongly influenced the post–World War I peace settlement that established national boundaries for the Middle East. He conceived the interim League of Nations mandates, which led to the formation of most of the countries that exist in the Middle East today. In July 1922, the League of Nations approved an arrangement giving Great Britain a mandate over Palestine. The mandate, which went into force September 22, 1923, contained a preamble incorporating the Balfour Declaration and stressing the Jews' historical connection with Palestine. Britain was made responsible for placing the country under such "political, administrative, and eco-

nomic conditions as will secure the establishment of a Jewish National Home."

Between 1923 and 1939 more than four hundred thousand Jews immigrated to Palestine, causing resentment against the British among the Arabs. In 1939, however, Arab unrest and German and Italian attempts to improve relations with the Arabs led the British to issue a white paper that reduced the flow of Jewish immigrants to Palestine—primarily European Jews suffering from Nazi persecution— to fifteen thousand a year for five years. After that, no more Jewish immigration was to be allowed unless agreed upon by the local Arab population. Jews denounced the restrictions and tried to circumvent them.

The Truman Administration (1945–1953)

The United States led the post–World War II effort to lift the restrictions on Jews entering Palestine. In August 1945, President Harry S. Truman called for the free settlement of Palestine by Jews to a point consistent with maintaining civil peace. He also suggested in a letter to British prime minister Clement R. Attlee that an additional hundred thousand Jews be allowed to enter Palestine. In December both houses of Congress adopted a resolution urging U.S. aid in opening Palestine to Jewish immigrants and in building a "democratic commonwealth."

Meanwhile, Britain, eager to have the United States share responsibility for its Jewish immigration policy, joined with the United States in November to establish a commission to examine admission of European Jews to Palestine. Britain also agreed to permit an additional fifteen hundred Jews to enter Palestine each month.

In April 1946, an Anglo-American Committee of Inquiry recommended the immediate admission of a hundred thousand Jews into Palestine and continuation of the British mandate until a United Nations trusteeship was established. Truman endorsed the proposal, but Britain stipulated that before it would agree to continue its mandate, underground Jewish forces in Palestine would have to disband.

On October 4, 1946, Truman released a communication sent to the British government in which he appealed for "substantial immigration" into Palestine "at once" and expressed support for the Zionist plan for creating a "viable Jewish state" in part of Palestine. Britain said it regretted that Truman's statement had been made public before a settlement was realized, fearing that the unqualified expression of U.S. support for a Jewish state would reduce chances of a compromise between indigenous Arabs and Jewish immigrants. Britain was tired of fighting a losing guerrilla war with Jewish groups seeking an independent state, and by 1947 it had given up on finding a mediated settlement. Britain turned the question over to the United Nations.

The United Nations set up the Special Committee on Palestine (UNSCOP) to devise a solution. Its report, and the vote that the United Nations took on it, were among the first items on the young organization's agenda, and President Truman was concerned about Americans' perception of the United Nations following the vote. He was aware of U.S. sympathy for Jewish immigrants, who had suffered the horrors of the Holocaust, and was concerned also about domestic politics. The Democratic Party had lost the midterm elections of 1946, giving control of Congress to the Republicans. The next presidential elections were not far off, in 1948, and as a first-term president who had come to the office from the vice presidency on the death of Franklin Delano Roosevelt, he could not afford to alienate a potent voting bloc; nor did he wish to discredit the United Nations by having the United States, its most powerful member, vote against it on one of its first major resolutions. Therefore, when UNSCOP proposed partitioning Palestine into Arab and Jewish territories, he supported it. When the state of Israel declared its independence in May 1948, he quickly recognized it.

Throughout this period, Truman—already sympathetic to Jewish interests in Palestine—was lobbied strenuously by prominent American Jews who opposed any restrictions on immigration and wanted a Zionist state in Palestine. The Zionist lobby faced opposition from the State and Defense Departments, who believed that the creation of a Jewish state without adequate consideration of the Arab population of Palestine, as well as other Arab interests in the Levant and the Arabian Peninsula, would lead to future diplomatic and military challenges to U.S. strategic interests in the region. The Department of Defense especially opposed the partition plan, believing that such a plan was doomed to failure, that the ensuing violence would invite Russian troops into the area (the cold war was just starting to heat up), and that any Arab-Jewish fighting would be a threat to the supply of oil. However, in part because many of Truman's closest advisers were pro-Zionist, these concerns did not prevail. In addition, Congress was pro-Zionist and could be counted on to support the new state on legislative questions.

While generally successful in its goals, the American Jewish lobby did not always prevail. For example, American Jews lobbied to delay postwar development aid to Britain because of perceived slow British action on increased immigration to Palestine. Truman resisted their pressure because of the historic friendship between Britain and the United States and because Britain was pushing for the United States to assume full military and financial responsibility in Palestine. Truman even thought that, on occasion, American Jews were too strident in their lobbying efforts, actually damaging their influence with him.

Following the 1948 Arab-Israeli war, the United States tried to persuade the new state to allow repatriation of Arab refugees to their homes in what were now Israeli towns: Haifa, Jaffa, and the surrounding coastal areas. Israel resented what it felt was interference in its internal affairs, and especially resented an arms embargo that Western nations established to placate Arab states. When Israel remained adamant on refugee repatriation, the United States supported creation of the United Nations Relief and Works Agency (UNRWA) to assist settlement of Arab refugees in surrounding countries. This policy position did not help the United States with Arab states, but Washington was considering larger issues of the cold war with the Soviet Union.

In 1950, fearing an expansion of Soviet influence in the region, the United States, Britain, and France jointly declared their continued interest in the region and backed their declaration with arms supplies and security guarantees for the Arabs. Their common declaration came even though the Western powers had little reason to fear Soviet influence over Arab states at that time, which were politically dominated by Britain—Egypt, Transjordan, and Iraq—and France—Syria and Lebanon. Additionally, another problem was brewing for Western allies: the Korean War began in June 1950 and turned U.S. attention to East Asia, where it would remain through the 1952 election of Republican Dwight D. Eisenhower. Even a coup in Egypt in July 1952, which deposed King Farouk, had little impact on U.S. Middle East policy, since the revolutionaries initially maintained good relations with the Western powers.

The Eisenhower Administration (1953–1961)

President Dwight D. Eisenhower, a Republican, came into office far less beholden to the American Jewish vote than his Democratic predecessor had been. His secretary of state, John Foster Dulles, was more concerned with cold war geopolitics and the global defense of Western interests than he was with the goals of Zionism, and his view informed Eisenhower's entire eight years in office. However, the U.S. worldview during the 1950s was not deeply shared by Israel and Arab states. Israel saw her neighbors as a more serious threat than the Soviet Union, a thousand miles distant. Arab states were interested in doing business with whichever nations met their needs, but because of their Islamic heritage had no love for communism. The clash between the U.S. and Israeli worldviews led the Eisenhower administration to penalize Israel for such actions as building a canal to divert the headwaters of the Jordan River (aid funding was suspended until construction was halted in late 1953). More seriously, the U.S. worldview caused it to see in Egyptian president Gamal Abdel Nasser's turn to the nonaligned movement a

dangerous support for global communism. The U.S. perception proved incorrect because Nasser was initially willing to work with the West to achieve a peaceful settlement of Egypt's dispute with Israel over Gaza, but Egyptian willingness evaporated in the face of slow American negotiations and Nasser's need for a dramatic breakthrough to feed his revolutionary-visionary public image.

Also in 1953, and again with an eye to containing world communism, the United States oversaw the installation of Shah Mohammad Reza Pahlavi as ruler of Iran. After World War II Western interests had installed the shah as ruler, but he lost power to a right-wing nationalist, Mohammad Mossadeq, in 1951. Mossadeq, to consolidate his position, nationalized the oil industry, at that time almost totally controlled by foreign companies that had been granted generous concessions by the shah. By 1953 Iran was suffering economically from the nationalizations, and Mossadeq was taking repressive measures. In August of that year, the shah fled the country, but his supporters in the military—with apparent backing from the U.S. Central Intelligence Agency—staged a coup that deposed Mossadeq and brought him back. The shah's return with U.S. support, and his policies over the following two decades, culminated in 1979 in the Iranian revolution led by Ayatollah Ruholla Khomeini.

Nasser's attendance at the Bandung conference of unaligned nations in 1954, as well as an arms deal with the Soviet Union, via Czechoslovakia, prompted the United States on July 19, 1956, to rescind financial backing for a major Egyptian development project, the Aswan High Dam. Nasser responded on July 26—the fourth anniversary of the revolution and Farouk's departure from Egypt—by nationalizing the Suez Canal. Meanwhile, Soviet arms shipments to Egypt in 1955 and 1956 persuaded Israel that it must prepare for war against Egypt before the military balance shifted in Cairo's favor. However, Israel's request for U.S. arms was rejected by Eisenhower, who on March 7, 1956, warned that it could provoke an "Arab-Israeli arms race."

Nationalizing the canal posed an immediate threat to Israeli shipping and to Britain and France, which had controlled the canal. Israel felt perpetually at risk from her belligerent neighbors. France regarded Nasser as the inspiration for the Algerian uprising against French rule that had started in 1954. Britain accurately saw him as an anti-imperialist who had not only removed the pliant Egyptian monarchy but had influenced Jordan's King Hussein to exile the British head of the Arab Legion, in March 1956, thus greatly diminishing London's role in the Middle East. All three parties regarded Nasser's actions as a threat to their oil supplies.

The United States tried to mediate a diplomatic solution to this crisis but was distracted by the presidential elections in 1956, and Britain, France, and Israel found the confluence of circumstances too much in their interests to settle for a mediated solution. On October 29, Israel invaded the Sinai, the opening move in a planned strategy with Britain and France to recapture the Suez Canal by bringing in their troops as "peacekeepers." None of the three believed that the United States would respond as it did, by publicly denouncing the actions of three of her allies as imperialist meddling. However, the United States had other global political problems on its hands. The week before, two weeks before the presidential election, anti-communist disturbances had broken out in Poland and Hungary. The Eisenhower administration, which came into office on a strong anticommunist platform, was forced to watch Soviet troops roll into Budapest to put down the rebellion, lest it risk open confrontation with the Soviet Union.

An Anglo-French force invaded Port Said, at the northern end of the canal, on November 5, one day before the U.S. presidential election, which Eisenhower won in a landslide even in the midst of actions by friends and enemies abroad. The Soviet Union was conscious of the possibility for armed confrontation with the United States, which it was eager to avoid, and it recognized the restraint that Washington had shown in not interfering with its actions against its recalcitrant European clients. It also recognized the possibility of

the two superpowers being drawn into continued fighting at the Suez Canal. In this milieu, the Soviet and American delegates to the United Nations joined to condemn the Anglo-French-Israeli action as an imperialist challenge to world order. A United Nations Emergency Force (UNEF) was deployed, allowing the Anglo-French forces to withdraw and providing a buffer between the Egyptian and Israeli militaries.

Negotiations to demilitarize the Sinai continued into 1957. The Israelis insisted on control of part of the Sinai to guarantee Israeli shipping through the Strait of Tiran to Eilat. However, Secretary of State Dulles, always weighing cold war considerations, believed that Israeli control in the Sinai would damage U.S. credibility with the Arabs and push them toward the Soviet Union. In the end, the United States received Egyptian guarantees that Israeli shipping through the strait would not be obstructed, and Israel made clear that violation of this commitment would lead to new fighting.

The following spring, in March 1957, Eisenhower announced a new doctrine that the United States would aid any state facing armed aggression from "the agents of international communism." He made the statement in the context of the then-popular "domino theory" of geopolitics, which postulated the fall of one country to communists would inevitably lead to the fall of others nearby, like toppling dominos. His doctrine opened the door in the 1960s to U.S. involvement in Vietnam, where the Vietnamese were still fighting their French colonial rulers, but it was the Middle East that provided the first real test of the Eisenhower Doctrine. On February 1, 1958, Egypt and Syria joined to form the United Arab Republic (UAR). On July 14, followers of Egypt's Nasser overthrew the British-installed Hashimite monarchy of Iraq. Jordan and Lebanon, small states with good relations with the United States, fearing for their political stability, invoked the Eisenhower Doctrine and requested arms and troops to maintain order. Eisenhower and Dulles, seeking stable, friendly regimes to counteract Nasser's power in the region, sent U.S. Marines to Beirut on July 15; Britain sent troops to

Amman to assist King Hussein. In Lebanon, the U.S. presence quelled disturbances and facilitated the election of Fuad Chehab, a moderate, pro-Western former general, to the presidency of the country. The marines left Lebanon in October.

The Kennedy Administration (1961–1963)

President John F. Kennedy's administration was involved in a number of important international incidents, but none in the Middle East. The United States, in its continuing confrontation with international communism, faced the Soviet building of the Berlin Wall, an unsuccessful invasion of Cuba in 1961 at the Bay of Pigs, and a Soviet-U.S. crisis in 1962 over Soviet missiles installed in Cuba. Kennedy also oversaw a U.S. troop buildup in Vietnam. On the domestic front, the civil rights movement was gaining momentum. The Middle East was barely a blip on the national radar screen.

The Johnson Administration (1963–1969)

President Lyndon B. Johnson came to office on the assassination of Kennedy in November 1963. The country was in turmoil, not only from the death of the president but from escalating violence surrounding the civil rights movement and increased U.S. troop involvement in Southeast Asia.

In the Middle East, significant events were developing. At the January 1964 Arab League summit meeting in Cairo, the assembled leaders created the Palestine Liberation Organization (PLO) as an umbrella group and a means of controlling Palestinian aspirations for the liberation of Palestine. As the 1960s progressed, the low-intensity fighting increased along the Israeli-Syrian and Israeli-Jordanian borders; Palestinian guerrillas would stage a raid on Israel, and the Israel Defense Force would shell suspected guerrilla hideouts and villages on the other side of the border. These exchanges continued until 1967.

The June 1967 War. Middle East tensions poured over again on June 5, 1967, with the start of

the Six-Day War. Diplomatic efforts immediately preceding the war had failed to lift a blockade of the Gulf of Aqaba that Egypt's Nasser imposed on May 23. The blockade halted most Israeli shipping and threatened to strangle the country's economy. Nasser imposed the blockade following his demand that the UN Emergency Force be removed from the Gaza Strip and the Gulf of Aqaba outpost at Sharm al-Shaykh. Evidence suggests that Nasser provoked the confrontation with Israel, even though much of his army was engaged in Yemen at the time, based on poor intelligence information from the Soviets suggesting an Israeli troop buildup and possible preparations to strike at Damascus. The United Nations relented and withdrew the Emergency Force from the whole of Sinai, not just those areas requested. At the same time, Nasser moved a substantial Egyptian force into the Sinai Peninsula, and Syria, Iraq, and Jordan signed a treaty of mutual defense and began to mobilize their forces.

Fearing an imminent attack, Israel decided to strike first. Its warplanes surprised Egyptian airfields, destroying the bulk of the Egyptian air force on the ground. Then, in a lightning move across the Sinai Peninsula, the Israeli army broke the Egyptian blockade of the Gulf of Aqaba and once again put Israeli soldiers on the banks of the Suez Canal. The Israelis destroyed hundreds of Egyptian tanks and artillery pieces in the Sinai. In the east, Israel's forces ousted Jordanian troops from the Old City of Jerusalem and seized control of all Jordanian territory west of the Jordan River. In the north, Israel captured the strategic Golan Heights, where the raiding and shelling had been taking place.

The 1967 war fundamentally altered the political balance in the Middle East. Israel's overwhelming victory stunned the Arabs and their Soviet backers and left Israel in a position of unparalleled strength. In contrast to 1956, when Israeli forces were withdrawn under Washington's pressure, Tel Aviv quickly announced that Israel would remain in the occupied territories until decisive progress toward a permanent settlement was made.

U.S. diplomatic efforts in the Middle East during the war failed. Washington had access to every capital in the region but little influence over the belligerents, even Israel. Arab states, while respecting the United States as a superpower, received most of their military equipment from the Soviet Union. Israel also respected the United States and needed both its private and public financial support, but France was Tel Aviv's largest arms supplier at the time. The United States was powerless to do more than persuade the parties. Nor could the United States become directly involved in the war because of the possibility of confrontation with the Soviet Union and because U.S. public opinion, while supportive of Israel, was increasingly against further overseas troop commitments, as Washington's military involvement in the Vietnam war was expanding and becoming more controversial.

A few hours after Israel's initial attack on June 5, Robert J. McCloskey, deputy assistant secretary of state for public affairs, declared that the U.S. position was "neutral in thought, word, and deed." The McCloskey statement met sharp criticism in Congress and from other supporters of Israel. Later the same day, George Christian, President Johnson's press secretary, said the McCloskey statement was "not a formal declaration of neutrality." And at a news conference Dean Rusk, Johnson's secretary of state, said the term "neutral" in international law meant that the United States was not a belligerent. He said it was not "an expression of indifference." Nasser, charging that U.S.-made aircraft had contributed to Egypt's defeat, severed diplomatic relations with Washington, as did six other Arab states.

On June 19, President Johnson, in his first major statement on U.S. Middle East policy since the outbreak of the war, outlined a five-point formula for Middle East peace: "the recognized right of national life; . . . justice for the refugees; . . . innocent maritime passage; . . . limits on the wasteful and destructive arms race; and . . . political independence and territorial integrity for all." Johnson also said Israeli troops "must be withdrawn" from the lands occupied during the war, but made clear

he would not press for a withdrawal to prewar lines in every respect.

On November 22, 1967, the United States voted with the rest of the UN Security Council members in unanimously approving Resolution 242. The document called for (1) withdrawal of Israeli forces from the occupied Arab areas; (2) an end to the state of belligerency between the Arab nations and Israel; (3) acknowledgment of and respect for the sovereignty, territorial integrity, and political independence of every nation in the area; (4) the establishment of "secure and recognized boundaries;" (5) a guarantee of freedom of navigation through international waterways in the area; and (6) a just settlement of the refugee problem.

Although UN efforts to end the Arab-Israeli conflict once again foundered, the resolution remained the basis for subsequent UN peace initiatives. Before the 1967 war, Arabs had insisted that Israel return all lands in excess of the territory assigned to the Jewish state by the 1947 UN partition plan. After the 1967 war, however, Arabs gradually modified their demands by insisting only that Israel adhere to the principles of the 1967 Security Council resolution, which they interpreted as calling for Israel to return to its pre-1967 borders.

In mid-1968 the United States became Israel's leading supplier of arms through an amendment added to a congressional appropriations bill. This action reflected the increasing international isolation of Israel following the passage of Resolution 242 and Israel's subsequent noncompliance, as well as the continuing power of the American Jewish lobby to influence U.S. foreign policy.

The Nixon Administration (1969–1974)

Republican president Richard M. Nixon came into office at a turbulent moment in U.S. history. Opposition to the Vietnam war was strong and growing, and the civil rights movement, while having made enormous gains, was increasingly divisive in society and had turned violent in many cities following the assassination of a number of leaders, particularly Martin Luther King Jr. In this environment, Nixon adopted a strong, hands-on leadership style, especially in foreign policy. He deliberately set up the Department of State to be an agent of policy execution rather than formation by choosing for secretary of state a man with little foreign policy experience, William Rogers. Nixon expected his primary adviser on Middle East policy to be his national security adviser, Henry Kissinger.

Renewed sporadic fighting developed in 1969 along the Suez Canal front after Egypt repudiated the 1967 cease-fire. During this "war of attrition" period Egypt tried to wear down the Israelis and bring about territorial withdrawals. Although frequently violated, the cease-fire technically continued on the other fronts.

In a departure from previous U.S. policy, Nixon agreed early in 1969 to a series of bilateral talks on the Middle East with the Soviet Union as well as to four-power talks including Britain and France. The talks were held in Geneva throughout the year but made little progress. In December 1969, Rogers proposed a peace plan that called for the return of the Sinai Peninsula to Egypt and direct negotiations between Israel, Jordan, and Syria regarding the return of their territories (the West Bank and Golan Heights). The Rogers Plan, as it came to be known, also specified that while Israel might physically control all of Jerusalem, Jordan should have a hand in the administration of the eastern half of the city, including the Old City. The plan was immediately rejected by the Israeli government, which became even more committed to retaining the territories gained in the 1967 war. The Arab states were at best lukewarm and said little, allowing Israel to take the blame for rejecting this peace proposal.

At the same time, the United States continued to support the efforts of UN envoy Gunnar Jarring to mediate a peace settlement. On January 25, 1970, Nixon reaffirmed U.S. support for Israel's insistence on direct peace negotiations with the Arabs. A few days later he asserted that the United States was "neither pro-Arab nor pro-Israeli. We are pro-peace." With the situation highly volatile

and scattered border clashes continuing, Rogers in June 1970 submitted another cease-fire proposal and called for resumption of UN mediation efforts to implement the 1967 Security Council resolution. Egypt and Jordan and then Israel agreed to a ninety-day cease-fire, beginning August 8, in conditionally accepting the U.S. formula for peace negotiations.

Once the agreement was announced, however, protests arose in many Middle East locations. Palestinian resistance groups and the governments of Syria and Iraq rejected the peace initiative and denounced Nasser for accepting it. In Israel, six members of the minority Gahal Party resigned from the cabinet of Premier Golda Meir. Palestinian commandos carried out a series of spectacular commercial aircraft hijackings. These hijackings, on September 6 and 9, 1970, terminated at a small field in the Jordanian desert and ended in the destruction of three aircraft, although the hostages were later released. They also led to the Black September incident, which ultimately led to the PLO's expulsion from Jordan. *(Jordan profile, p. 305)*

The United States limited its response to placing naval forces on alert in the Mediterranean. The events of Black September and the failure of the Rogers Plan changed Nixon's perception of the Middle East situation. Nixon had viewed the region in cold war terms, seeing Israel and Arab states as U.S. and Soviet clients, which could be manipulated by their mentors. The hostile Israeli response to the Rogers Plan changed his opinion. Further, Henry Kissinger did not favor the plan, which had the United States making deals with enemy regimes and endangering relations with a friendly one. Nixon was unprepared to back Rogers over Kissinger, who had good personal relations with the Israeli ambassador in Washington, Yitzhak Rabin, and may have communicated to him the administration's ambivalence about the Rogers Plan. Another factor in Nixon's reassessment of U.S. policy in the region was the influence of AIPAC in Congress and public sentiment in favor of Israel and against further international military involvement.

Another significant event at this time was the death of Egypt's Nasser from a massive heart attack after mediating an end to the fighting between Jordan, Syria, and the PLO. He was succeeded by Anwar al-Sadat, one of the last of the original participants in the 1952 revolution still in the government. Sadat was widely considered a transitional figure but instead set out his own agenda for Egypt, which did not correspond neatly with the Soviet Union's regional interests. He sought to rebuild Egyptian prestige and Arab pride, while the Soviet Union was more interested in limiting Western influence in the region and avoiding a confrontation with Washington. Sadat asked repeatedly and unsuccessfully for increased Soviet military aid to prepare for a war with Israel. The Soviets continued to press for a peaceful solution of the conflict, repeatedly stating their support for UN Security Council Resolution 242.

As Sadat's differences with the Soviet Union became more acute, he concluded that Egyptian and Soviet goals were incompatible. On July 18, 1972, Sadat ordered all twenty thousand Soviet military advisers out of Egypt, severely damaging the Soviet position in the Middle East. The Soviet Union responded by expanding ties to Syria, Iraq, and the PLO. Sadat hoped that his rejection of the Soviet Union would allow for better U.S.-Egyptian relations, but 1972 was an election year and Nixon was concerned about losing the Jewish vote if he became too friendly with an enemy of Israel; however, the two countries developed informal contacts.

Gulf Security. In early 1968 the British said they would withdraw from the Arabian Peninsula and the Persian Gulf as part of a "reevaluation" of their commitments east of Suez, raising for the United States the specter of Soviet movements to obtain a warm-water port. Because U.S. commitments in Vietnam precluded replacing British troops in the Gulf, the administration of Lyndon B. Johnson looked to Iran for regional security and stability. Johnson was willing to arm Iran for this purpose, believing it necessary to ensure U.S. access to oil supplies.

During the 1970s, while pursuing an Arab-Israeli peace agreement, the United States also was strengthening its strategic relationship with Iran and Saudi Arabia. These two nations, which successive U.S. presidents saw as bulwarks against potential Soviet expansion southward, were sold billions of dollars of sophisticated U.S. military equipment.

The United States had begun an arms supply relationship with Saudi Arabia in the 1950s, but it was the Nixon administration in the early 1970s that made the oil-rich kingdom one of the "two pillars" of U.S. policy in the Persian Gulf region. Between 1950 and 1987 Saudi Arabia purchased more than $30 billion of U.S. defense articles. Much of this money was spent on sophisticated aircraft and ultra-modern air, naval, and army bases.

Washington viewed the shah as one of its most important allies because of the close proximity of his country to the Soviet Union, the growing U.S.-Iranian trade relationship, and close military and intelligence cooperation. Moreover, the U.S.-Israeli friendship was not an impediment to a relationship with the shah, as it sometimes was with Saudi Arabia and other Arab nations.

The "two pillar" policy involved a number of assumptions by Nixon and Kissinger, not all of which held up over time. One erroneous assumption was that Iran and Saudi Arabia were willing to work together to secure regional stability. By the mid-1970s, the price of oil, of vital concern to the industrialized world, increasingly was in dispute. The price rose dramatically in the wake of the next Arab-Israeli war, in 1973. Iran wanted to keep the price high, whereas Saudi Arabia was inclined toward moderation at oil pricing summits, even while supporting many events surrounding the 1973 war that helped push up the price. *(Middle Eastern Oil and Gas, p. 179)*

That both regimes were stable was another assumption later shaken by events. In 1975 King Faisal of Saudi Arabia was assassinated. Although the transition to the next in line maintained the stability of the monarchy and the Saudi regime, the event emphasized the fragility of governments in the region. Stability, however, did not prevail in

Iran when the shah's regime collapsed in 1979 in the face of a revolution led by Khomeini. *(The Persian Gulf, Chapter 4, p. 137; Iran and Saudi Arabia profiles, pp. 241, 387)*

October War (1973). The "no-war, no-peace" stalemate held until October 1973, when Arab frustrations over the deadlock triggered the fourth Arab-Israeli war. Egypt and Syria launched a coordinated attack during Yom Kippur, the holiest day of the Jewish calendar. Egyptian and Syrian troops broke through Israel's forward fortifications and advanced into the Sinai Peninsula and the Golan Heights.

The war that began on October 6, 1973, has different names. In Israel it is known as the Yom Kippur War. The Arabs sometimes call it the War of Ramadan, since it began during their month-long period of daytime fasting. Israel had good intelligence that troops were being mobilized for a possible strike, but its leaders were warned by Nixon that if Israel dealt the first blow it could not rely on U.S. assistance during the war. Further, the Israeli government was distracted and somewhat disorganized at the time. It was dealing with a terrorist incident in Europe, the foreign minister was in New York at the United Nations, the ambassador to the United States was in Israel on personal business, and the military was standing down for the holiday, a large number of troops having been granted home leave. While Israeli military action would have been possible, it is unlikely that Israel could have recreated the surprise first strike employed in 1967.

The U.S. government, dealing with its own problems at the time, wanted to avoid involvement in yet another Middle Eastern conflict. By October 1973, the initial Watergate scandal had come to light, involving charges of illegal action by Nixon and his top aides, including the use of government agencies to thwart investigations. The scandal was an all-consuming national issue that fed congressional impeachment proceedings against the president. Congress itself was in a hostile mood over the administration's conduct of the Vietnam war and had just passed the controversial War Powers

Resolution to limit presidential war-making power. Fighting continued in Southeast Asia. A U.S. rapprochement with China was barely a year old and still controversial. Henry Kissinger had recently become secretary of state, while keeping his portfolio as national security adviser, and, finally, Nixon's vice president, Spiro Agnew, was facing tax evasion charges that forced his resignation from office. All told, these events were impediments to the United States assuming more responsibilities in the Middle East.

Despite the success of the initial Egyptian and Syrian strikes into Israeli-occupied territory, Israeli forces recovered. They broke through the Egyptian lines and drove to the western bank of the Suez Canal. On the other front, they advanced to within twenty miles of the Syrian capital of Damascus. The United States carried out a massive airlift of war materiel to Israel, as the prolonged fighting stretched Tel Aviv's resources to the limits.

The United States and the Soviet Union joined in pressing for an end to the fighting. Following a visit by Kissinger to Moscow, the United States and Soviet Union jointly presented to the Security Council on October 21 Resolution 338, calling for an immediate cease-fire and implementation of the 1967 UN Resolution 242. Egypt and Israel agreed, and the cease-fire was expected to go into effect the next day. Regardless, the fighting continued, and Egyptian president Sadat, concerned for the fate of his army, called on the United States and the Soviet Union for troops to enforce the cease-fire. The main flashpoint was the city of Suez, at the southern end of the canal, where the Israeli army had surrounded the Egyptian army. On the evening of October 24 Soviet general secretary Leonid Brezhnev sent a message to Nixon proposing joint U.S.-Soviet supervision of the truce. Brezhnev warned, "If you find it impossible to act together with us in this matter, we should be faced with the necessity urgently to consider the question of taking appropriate steps unilaterally." The proposal was rejected by the United States, which preferred a UN observer force without big-power participation. In the early morning hours of October 25, the president placed

U.S. armed forces worldwide on alert in response to the possibility of a unilateral move by the Soviet Union to send troops to the Middle East. The crisis was defused later that day when Moscow agreed to a Security Council resolution establishing an international peacekeeping force without the participation of the five permanent members of the Security Council.

The oil embargo imposed on the United States and Western Europe by the members of the Organization of Arab Oil Exporting Countries had an enormous impact on national economies. The decision to cut off the flow of oil was a direct response to the U.S. airlift of war goods to Israel during the fighting.

Kissinger Diplomacy Efforts. U.S. diplomacy was instrumental in achieving a cease-fire between Egypt and Israel and, under the Ford and Carter administrations, in brokering a series of agreements that led to a peace treaty between the former belligerents. Kissinger negotiated a six-point cease-fire agreement on November 11, 1973, that Egyptian and Israeli military representatives signed at kilometer 101 on the Cairo-to-Suez road. On December 21, 1973, largely through Kissinger's efforts, the Geneva conference on an Arab-Israeli peace was convened in accordance with UN Security Council Resolution 338, which established the cease-fire. The talks were attended by Egypt, Israel, Jordan, the Soviet Union, and the United States. Syria boycotted the conference.

The first round of the conference ended the following day with an agreement to begin talks to separate Israeli and Egyptian forces along the Suez Canal. Egypt and Israel signed a troop disengagement accord January 18, 1974, and they completed their troop withdrawals on March 4. Meanwhile, efforts to negotiate a similar agreement between Israel and Syria were concluded May 31.

The Ford Administration (1974–1977)

The Nixon administration came to an end on August 9, 1974, with the president's resignation from office in the wake of the Watergate scandal. Throughout Nixon's presidency, his primary foreign policy adviser had been Henry Kissinger, and Kissinger remained secretary of state for Gerald Ford, who assumed the Oval Office from the vice presidency.

In early 1975 Kissinger sought a second-stage disengagement in the Sinai Peninsula, but after fifteen days of shuttling between Egypt and Israel he declared in March that his efforts had failed. When Kissinger returned to Washington, he and Ford made clear they were upset with Israel's negotiating position and said the United States would begin a "reassessment" of Middle East policy. Consideration of Israel's request for $2.5 billion in U.S. aid was suspended pending the reassessment, widely seen as a thinly veiled form of pressure on the Israeli government to be more forthcoming in talks with Egypt. At the same time, the United States approved the sale of Hawk air-defense missiles to Jordan. The "reassessment" touched off a firestorm of protest from the American Jewish community, which organized a lobbying effort in the Senate and in the public to pressure the Ford administration to alter its stance toward Israel.

The United States' reassessment of its Middle East policy coincided with other important events. In Saudi Arabia, King Faisal, long regarded as a U.S. ally, was assassinated in March. This sign of instability in the United States' largest supplier of oil was disconcerting but did not seriously damage U.S.-Saudi relations. The third event in the Middle East in the spring of 1975 was the outbreak of the civil war in Lebanon, which was to continue for fifteen years and take the lives of nearly three hundred American soldiers. *(Lebanon profile, p. 333)*

Second Sinai Accord. Arab-Israeli negotiations began again in June 1975. President Ford met first with Sadat in Salzburg, Austria, and then with Israeli prime minister Yitzhak Rabin in Washington. (Rabin had been elected to replace Golda Meir in June 1974). This time the talks were more successful, producing a second Sinai disengagement pact that Israel and Egypt signed on September 1. Israel agreed to withdraw from the Sinai mountain passes and to return the Abu Rudeis oil fields to Egypt in return for Egyptian political concessions. The United States agreed to station an observation force in the Sinai.

Compared with the basic issues of recognition of Israel, the future of the Palestinians, permanent boundaries, the status of Jerusalem, and peace guarantees, the issues settled in the Sinai troop disengagement accords were minor. In two respects, however, the accords accomplished a major breakthrough. First, they brought the United States into the midst of the Arab-Israeli conflict. Somewhat hesitantly, Congress approved the stationing of U.S. technicians between the Israeli and Arab armies to monitor military activities. Second, they established a modest basis of trust between the two primary actors in the Arab-Israeli dispute necessary to pursue more basic issues.

The second disengagement agreement also resulted in considerable tension among the Arab parties to the conflict. Syrian president Hafiz al-Asad and the PLO denounced Sadat for agreeing to what amounted, in their view, to a separate, though partial, peace with Israel.

By late 1976 a new Arab strategy began to emerge. By presenting a moderate image to the world, Sadat and most of the Arab leaders hoped to affect U.S. policy and create the conditions for resumption of the Geneva negotiations. Even the Palestine Liberation Organization began to make gestures, however ambiguous, indicating a willingness to accept the existence of Israel if Israel returned the occupied territories to the Palestinians.

The Carter Administration (1977–1981)

Egyptian-Israeli Peace.   By 1977 the United States had become the most influential participant in the Middle East conflict from outside the region. "The U.S. holds 99 percent of the cards," Sadat said repeatedly. Accordingly, the Arabs launched a major diplomatic effort in 1977 to persuade the United States that they no longer challenged Israel's existence, only its 1967 occupation of Arab lands and refusal to recognize "Palestinian rights." In February 1977, Sadat said in an interview, "I

want the American people to know that never before have the prospects for peace been better. Not in the last twenty-eight years—since Israel was created—have we had a better chance for a permanent settlement in the Middle East. We must not lose the chance."

In this atmosphere of renewed hope for achieving a comprehensive peace settlement, newly elected Israeli prime minister Menachem Begin came to the United States on July 19, 1977, for two days of talks with President Jimmy Carter. Although the atmosphere was cordial, it was clear that the new U.S. administration and the new Israeli government were far apart on many important issues. Begin refused even to consider agreeing to a Palestinian homeland; he had been elected on a platform of never returning the West Bank and Gaza to Arab sovereignty.

The initial Carter strategy for achieving a comprehensive peace settlement focused on reconvening the Geneva Conference, which had met in December 1973. The Soviet Union responded favorably, and the result was a joint statement on the Middle East, issued October 1, 1977, calling for a conference "not later than December 1977" to work out a full resolution of the Arab-Israeli conflict "incorporating all parties concerned and all questions."

The Israelis reacted negatively to the prospect of bringing the Soviet Union into the forefront of the peace negotiations. In addition, the radical Arab governments in Algeria, Iraq, and Libya still rejected any direct negotiations with Israel. Israeli officials opposed the idea because, among other factors, they feared the Soviets might succeed in drawing the PLO into the negotiations.

The Egyptian reaction to the joint statement was equally cool. Since 1972, when Sadat expelled Soviet military advisers from Egypt, relations between Cairo and Moscow had turned increasingly sour. A Geneva Conference co-chaired by the Soviet Union was no more appealing to Egypt than to Israel. The unpleasant prospect of another conference was seen by some observers as one reason behind Sadat's momentous decision to visit Jerusalem and proffer his terms for peace.

Initial Peace Efforts.   In addition to a desire to preempt Soviet involvement in the Middle East peace process, other reasons have been cited for Sadat's dramatic visit to Jerusalem on November 19, 1977. Analysts speculate that Sadat was motivated by a belief that another Middle East conflict would produce a 1967-type defeat for the Arabs. He also was thought to fear a radical upheaval in economically depressed Egypt, and he desperately wanted to get U.S. economic aid.

Sadat's initiative took the Carter administration by surprise. Only later did it give full support to the peace effort and abandon a comprehensive approach to back direct Egyptian-Israeli discussions for a separate agreement. Sadat's Jerusalem visit was followed by meetings between Israeli and Egyptian officials in Cairo. Then the leaders of the two nations met on December 25 in Ismailia, Egypt, where Begin presented his West Bank proposal. It offered only local "autonomy" for the Palestinians over a five-year period. Israeli troops and settlements were to remain. The plan contained no mention of eventual sovereignty for the West Bank, a critical point with Sadat.

Camp David Summit.   The talks ended in a stalemate, followed by unproductive and lower-level discussions over the next few months. As negotiations broke down, the United States took urgent steps to rescue the situation, among them sponsoring a foreign ministers' conference at Leeds Castle outside London on July 18, 1978. The meeting was attended by U.S. secretary of state Cyrus R. Vance, Israeli foreign minister Moshe Dayan, and Egyptian foreign minister Muhammad Ibrahim Kamel. Although Vance saw some flexibility in the discussions, the conference did not produce concrete results. In August, with Egypt and Israel renewing strong criticism of one another, the United States became increasingly concerned that the impasse would jeopardize the fragile relations between the two nations and wreck any chance for peace in the Middle East. President Carter then invited the two leaders to Camp David, the presidential retreat in western Maryland, for informal face-to-face talks aimed at breaking the stalemate. Both accepted immediately.

Carter's decision to call the Camp David summit was widely seen as a brash gamble that paid off beyond all expectations. The announcement of the summit came in August, when the president's popularity was at a low point. In thirteen days of arduous negotiations, Carter persuaded Sadat and Begin to make compromises that led to an agreement. Both Sadat and Begin later said Carter's firmness was the key to the breakthrough. The accords reached at Camp David represented agreements to agree, rather than an actual settlement of the issues dividing the two nations or the even broader disputes between Israel and other Arab nations. "This is one of those rare, bright moments of history," Carter declared as Begin and Sadat signed the historic accords on September 17, 1978. The parties had reached two agreements at Camp David, one dealing with Israeli withdrawal from the Sinai Peninsula and peace arrangements between Israel and Egypt, and the other a "framework" for settling the future of the West Bank and Gaza.

By the end of 1978, however, success was threatened by a renewal of discord. As negotiations continued and the euphoria of the Camp David summit dissipated, both Israeli and Egyptian leaders found that agreeing to the specifics of a treaty while under pressure from domestic groups who opposed a settlement was more difficult than agreeing to a "framework" in the seclusion of the presidential retreat in the Maryland mountains. Carter repeatedly expressed frustration that Israel and Egypt would quibble over what he viewed as minor issues, but none of the issues were minor to either side. Israeli and Egyptian leaders were being asked to resolve disputes perpetuated by years of hostility and to give up positions they considered essential to their national interests. In return for a peace treaty, Israel was asked to give up territory that for more than eleven years had served as a buffer against one of its major enemies. Egypt was pressured by other Middle East nations not to sign a separate peace treaty with what they considered to be the Arab world's common enemy.

Egyptian-Israeli Peace Treaty. Shortly after the Camp David accords were signed, Secretary of State Vance optimistically predicted that a treaty establishing peace between Egypt and Israel could be concluded by November 19—the anniversary of Sadat's 1977 visit to Jerusalem. It soon became obvious, however, that negotiating the treaty would be a slow process. Predictions of a treaty signing were pushed back to December 10, the date Sadat and Begin were to receive the Nobel Peace Prize, and then to December 17, the date specified in the Camp David agreement. As the end of the year approached, officials stopped predicting when the treaty would be concluded.

Even before treaty negotiations began, disagreements developed over what actually had been said and agreed on at Camp David. Even before Begin had left the United States after the Camp David summit, he and Carter disputed the terms of an agreement on Israeli settlements on the West Bank and Gaza. Begin said Israel could establish new settlements after a three-month moratorium, but Carter said Begin had agreed at Camp David not to establish any new settlements during the five-year transition period. While they were being pressured by the United States to reach a final agreement, both Sadat and Begin also came under intense pressure at home not to make concessions. Other Arab nations, including Jordan and Saudi Arabia, warned Sadat not to renounce Palestinian rights in the rush toward a peace treaty. In Israel, Begin was sharply criticized for his apparent willingness to abandon Israeli claims to some of the territories occupied in the 1967 war.

As negotiations proceeded, the main questions became whether, and to what extent, the peace treaty between Egypt and Israel would be linked to the West Bank and Gaza issues. The United States and Egypt insisted that the treaty be linked to the resolution of the occupied territories issue. Israel wanted the treaty but did not want to include provisions dealing with the occupied territories. Begin fueled the Palestinian controversy early in the negotiations by announcing plans to expand Israeli settlements on the West Bank. Those plans were bitterly protested by Carter and Sadat and then put aside, where they simmered throughout the peace talks.

At a summit meeting in Baghdad November 2–5, 1978, the hard-line Arab countries charged Sadat with treason, then offered Egypt $5 billion if Sadat would cut off negotiations with Israel. Sadat refused the offer, making it clear he expected assistance from the United States instead. American officials were distressed that Saudi Arabia and Jordan, two moderate Arab nations, joined in the hard-line attacks on Egypt.

The Israeli cabinet on November 21 finally accepted a vaguely worded link between the peace treaty and the West Bank–Gaza issues, but it flatly rejected any timetable for Palestinian elections. With the disagreement over a timetable unresolved, the United States early in December offered a compromise that would have put the issues in a "side letter" rather than in the treaty itself. Under that compromise, the two sides would have agreed to begin negotiations on the West Bank and Gaza within a month of ratification of the peace treaty. A target date of December 31, 1979, was proposed for elections in the territories.

Throughout the negotiations, the PLO rejected all the timetables and self-rule proposals. PLO leader Yasir Arafat said his group was the only true representative of the more than one million Palestinians on the West Bank and Gaza. He rejected Sadat's claim that the Egyptian leader was negotiating on behalf of the Palestinians. Just as important as the PLO objection was the refusal of Jordan's King Hussein to participate in the negotiations. Jordan had administered the West Bank before the 1967 war, and the Camp David accords were based on the assumption that Hussein would participate in the peace settlement.

Implicit in the negotiations was the assumption that the United States would provide substantial aid to both Egypt and Israel once a peace treaty was signed. Although peace in the Middle East generally was accepted as being in the long-term interest of all parties, the short-term costs were heavy for both Israel and Egypt. Israeli officials estimated that moving its military forces from the Sinai Peninsula to the Negev Desert in southern

Israel would cost approximately $3 billion over three years, a huge sum for that nation. To help pay for that move, and for other costs of peace, the Israelis asked the United States for an additional $3.3 billion over three years. At Camp David, Carter committed the United States to building two replacement military bases for Israel in the Negev.

For his part, Sadat quietly spread the word that he expected the United States to pay a major share of the cost of economic development in Egypt, possibly as much as $10 billion to $15 billion over five years. The United States had been providing Egypt $1 billion a year.

After preliminary discussions among Vance, Israeli foreign minister Moshe Dayan, and Egyptian prime minister Mustafa Khalil in February 1979, Carter suggested that Begin and Sadat meet with him in a second round of summit talks at Camp David. The two leaders declined. Faced with the possible collapse of the treaty talks, Carter then invited Begin to meet with him alone in Washington. Begin accepted, and the talks opened March 1. Before leaving for the United States, Begin said Israel and Egypt remained far apart and accused the Carter administration of supporting Egyptian proposals that were "totally unacceptable to us." Among the points at issue were Sadat's insistence on Israeli acceptance of Palestinian autonomy for the West Bank and Gaza within a year; deletion of a clause in the Camp David accords giving an Israeli-Egyptian peace treaty priority over Egyptian treaties with other nations; and a delay, until all other treaty issues were resolved, in discussing Israel's request that Egypt supply Israel with oil from the Sinai oil fields. On February 17, Sadat said Egypt would make no further concessions in the peace treaty negotiations and that it was "now up to the Israelis."

On March 5, Carter announced that he would press his personal mediation efforts by visiting Cairo and Jerusalem. A White House statement said: "There is certainly no guarantee of success, but . . . without a major effort such as this the prospects for failure are almost overwhelming." Carter's Middle East trip bore fruit. After agreeing to most aspects of the compromise proposals put forward by the U.S. president, the Israeli cabinet March 14 approved 15-0 the two remaining points that had blocked an agreement. The Egyptian cabinet approved them the next day. Under the terms of the agreement, Israel accepted an arrangement whereby Egypt would sell it 2.5 million tons of oil a year for an "extended period." For its part, Israel agreed to submit a detailed timetable for withdrawing its forces from the Sinai.

The Israeli Knesset gave its overwhelming approval of the treaty on March 22. The vote was 95-18. Both Carter and Sadat hailed the Knesset's action. On March 26, 1979, Israel and Egypt formally ended the state of war that had existed between them since Israel declared its independence in 1948.

The treaty provided for the normalization of relations between Egypt and Israel. It implemented the "framework" for a treaty agreed on at Camp David. Annexes to the treaty spelled out the details of further negotiations on trade, cultural, transportation, and other agreements and of a phased Israeli withdrawal from the Sinai Peninsula. Egypt and Israel were to undertake negotiations on the future of the West Bank and Gaza. The negotiations on Palestinian self-rule, to be supervised by the United States, were to begin one month after the formal exchange of treaty ratification documents and were to be completed within one year. The treaty did not mention East Jerusalem, occupied by Israel since 1967 and claimed by both Israel and Jordan. Egypt insisted that East Jerusalem was part of the West Bank and thus subject to negotiation. Israel rejected that view.

Security, Oil Agreements.   Two hours after the peace treaty was signed, Secretary of State Vance and Foreign Minister Dayan signed a "memorandum of agreement" in which the United States provided Israel with specific assurances if the treaty fell apart. The memorandum reaffirmed, and broadened, U.S. assurances given Israel at the time of the 1975 Sinai disengagement agreement.

If the treaty were violated, the memorandum stated, the United States "will consult with the parties with regard to measures to halt or prevent the violation," and the United States "will take such remedial measures as it deems appropriate, which may include diplomatic, economic and military measures."

The agreement brought a sharp protest from Egypt. In a letter to Vance, Egyptian prime minister Khalil said Egypt was "deeply disappointed to find the United States accepting to enter into an agreement we consider directed against Egypt." The agreement "assumes that Egypt is the side liable to violate the treaty," Khalil said. In a March 28 statement, Sadat said the memorandum violated the Israeli-Egyptian accord and that it "could be construed as an eventual alliance against Egypt." The Department of State issued a response saying Khalil's complaints were "based on a misreading of the document." The agreement "does not assume that Egypt is likely to violate the pact," the response said. Carter administration officials emphasized that the United States would carry out the pledges only in response to a violation of the treaty by either Israel or Egypt, and it insisted the agreement did not constitute an alliance or a mutual defense treaty with Israel.

One of the most controversial assurances given by Carter to Israel was the guarantee to supply oil. At the time of the September 1975 Sinai agreement, President Ford agreed to guarantee Israel an adequate oil supply for a five-year period if that nation's normal supplies were cut off. As an incentive to sign the peace treaty, Carter agreed to extend the guarantee to fifteen years. Under the agreement, the United States was to supply Israel with enough oil "to meet all its normal requirements for domestic consumption." The promise was contingent on the United States being able to obtain enough oil "to meet its normal requirements." Israel was to pay the United States "world market prices" for any oil supplied under the emergency agreement.

Aftermath of the Treaty. On May 25, 1979, in keeping with the agreed timetable, Sadat and Begin met in Beersheba to begin the Palestinian autonomy negotiations. The goal of the first stage was full autonomy for the West Bank and Gaza under a freely elected self-governing authority that would serve for a five-year transition period. Agreement on the region's final status was reserved for a second stage to begin not later than three years after the self-governing authority was inaugurated.

Several meetings were held in 1980, but little progress was made. Sadat suspended Egyptian participation in mid-August after the Knesset passed a law confirming Jerusalem's status as Israel's "eternal and undivided capital." Early in 1981 Israel requested a resumption of the talks, but a new U.S. administration reacted cautiously. President Ronald Reagan's position contrasted sharply with that of the Carter administration, which had placed great emphasis on the negotiations and, through its special envoy, had been instrumental in keeping the negotiations alive.

The Israeli Sinai withdrawal was more successful. Under the terms of the treaty, once withdrawal was completed in April 1982, the United States was obligated to organize a peacekeeping force if the United Nations did not do so. The United Nations subsequently declined, largely because of opposition from the Soviet Union. "Normal relations" between Egypt and Israel officially began January 26, 1980, by which time Israel had withdrawn from two-thirds of the Sinai. Borders were opened between the two countries, travel was permitted, and embassies were established.

When the peace treaty was signed in March 1979, there was little doubt that the so-called hard-line Arab states—Algeria, Iraq, Libya, South Yemen, Syria, and the Palestine Liberation Organization—would condemn the treaty. Both Egypt and the United States anticipated some criticism from traditionally pro-Western, pro-Sadat Arab nations such as Saudi Arabia, Jordan, Morocco, and the Persian Gulf states. The moderates might not like the treaty, but, it was thought, they would seek to minimize any anti-Sadat or anti-American measures that the hard-liners demanded.

A day after the Washington signing, however, nineteen members of the Arab League—Algeria, Bahrain, Djibouti, Iraq, Jordan, Kuwait, Lebanon, Libya, Mauritania, Morocco, the Palestine Liberation Organization, Qatar, Saudi Arabia, Somalia,

Syria, Tunisia, the United Arab Emirates, the Yemen Arab Republic (North Yemen), and the People's Democratic Republic of Yemen (South Yemen)—met in Baghdad and adopted a package of tough political and economic sanctions against Egypt. Of the twenty-two Arab League members, only Oman and the Sudan, close allies of Sadat, boycotted the meeting. Egypt was not invited. Within weeks, all of the Baghdad participants had severed diplomatic ties with Egypt. Egypt was also expelled from the Arab League, the Islamic Conference, and many other Arab and international organizations.

Hostage Crisis.   Late in 1979, less than eight months after the signing of the Egyptian-Israeli peace treaty, a group of Iranian students took hostage a large number of Americans, producing a crisis that paralyzed Carter's administration and creating its biggest foreign policy embarrassment.

Although U.S. arms sales had strengthened the shah militarily, by the late 1970s his repressive regime in Iran faced enormous domestic opposition. On January 16, 1979, the shah left Iran for what turned out to be a permanent exile. The revolution that led to his departure was capped by the return to Iran of the exiled charismatic religious leader Ayatollah Ruholla Khomeini on February 1. On April 1 of that year, Iranian voters approved the establishment of an Islamic republic. *(Iran profile, p. 241)*

On November 4, 1979, Iranian students seized the U.S. embassy in Tehran, taking sixty-six hostages. They released thirteen of the hostages later in the month and released one hostage in July 1980. Fifty-two Americans were held for 444 days. The students demanded that the shah, who was receiving medical treatment in the United States, be returned to Iran to stand trial. The students were backed by Khomeini and his Revolutionary Council.

Carter took several steps to pressure Iran to free the hostages. On November 14, 1979, he froze all Iranian assets in domestic and overseas branches of U.S. banks. In April 1980, he severed relations with Iran and instituted trade sanctions.

On April 25, a U.S. rescue mission ended in disaster after it was aborted because of equipment failure. Two of the departing aircraft collided on the ground and eight U.S. servicemen were killed. The shah died of cancer in Egypt on July 27, but the hostage crisis continued, fueled by the virulent anti-American sentiments of the Iranians and the exploitation of those sentiments by Iran's leaders for domestic political purposes.

The frustration of the American people at Carter's inability to free the hostages contributed to his defeat in the 1980 election by Ronald Reagan. The hostages were released January 20, 1981, a few minutes after Reagan took the presidential oath of office. Following release of the hostages, Reagan largely ignored Iran during his first term, aside from ritual denunciations of terrorism and calls for an end to the Iran-Iraq war.

Soviets in Afghanistan.   On December 24, 1979, less than two months after the U.S. embassy in Tehran was seized, the Soviet Union invaded Afghanistan to prop up a pro-Soviet government, taking the United States by surprise. Carter said in a December 31 television interview that the invasion changed his opinion of the Soviets more than any other event. On January 20, 1980, he called the invasion the "most serious threat to peace since the Second World War."

Although the Soviet invasion of Afghanistan did not constitute a strike into the heart of the Persian Gulf oil-producing region, many analysts saw it as a serious threat to the security of the Gulf and its oil supplies. With the Soviets in Afghanistan and the Iranian hostage crisis continuing, the importance of Persian Gulf security rose in the Carter administration.

On January 23, 1980, Carter announced what would become known as the Carter Doctrine. In his State of the Union address, he warned that "An attempt by any outside force to gain control of the Persian Gulf region will be regarded as an assault on the vital interests of the United States of America, and such an assault will be repelled by any means necessary, including military force." The statement was a direct challenge to the Soviet Union.

Moscow's Afghanistan adventure ironically harmed rather than advanced Soviet interests in the Middle East. Islamic nations, including Iran and Saudi Arabia, regarded the invasion as proof of Soviet aggressiveness and lack of respect for Islam. The Soviet Union retained influence with some Arab states through its arms sales and its ability to act as a counterweight to the United States, but Soviet credibility was severely damaged. Saudi Arabia and the small Gulf states, in particular, moved toward a closer relationship with the United States in response to the Soviet invasion.

The Reagan Administration (1981–1989)

During President Reagan's first term, his administration continued efforts to mediate Middle East peace. It concentrated on getting Jordan and "moderate" Palestinians into the peace process with two goals in mind: a second peace treaty between Israel and an Arab country, and an agreement giving Palestinian residents of the West Bank some form of political autonomy.

Almost from its first days in office, the Reagan administration was forced by events to focus on Lebanon, a country that had suffered nearly ten years of civil war and occupation by Syrian and Israeli troops and the forces of the Palestine Liberation Organization. U.S. prestige and power in the region suffered badly in the early 1980s when the administration's diplomatic and military efforts did not bring peace to war-torn Lebanon. Moreover, continued hostility toward Israel by the Arab states wiped out the optimism engendered by the 1979 peace treaty between Israel and Egypt. The 1981 assassination of Egyptian president Sadat removed from the scene the United States' most loyal and important ally in the Arab world. *(Egypt profile, p. 221)*

Meanwhile, domestic political consensus about policies the United States should pursue in the region disintegrated. The administration and Congress clashed repeatedly as Reagan and his advisers shifted from diplomacy and mediation to an increased reliance on the use of American troops and large arms sales to moderate Arab states.

Reagan brought to office a vigorous anticommunist view of the world. In his campaign he charged that earlier administrations were too accommodating to the Soviet Union, allowing U.S. strength and reputation to decline. He identified Moscow as the source of most major international political problems, including those in the Middle East. Reagan, in contrast to Carter, placed relatively little importance on the role of developing nations in U.S. foreign policy. The focus of Reagan policy, rather, was on countering communism.

Reagan viewed Israel as the most reliable friend in the region, and he believed Israel's democratic system made it a natural ally for the United States. Few of Reagan's senior advisers had Middle East experience, and during the first months of the administration, important Middle East policy-making posts remained vacant. An overall U.S. approach to the Middle East would not emerge until after Israel's invasion of Lebanon in June 1982. The administration placed the Arab-Israeli conflict on a back burner, partly because it wanted to wait for the June 1981 Israeli elections and partly because there was no pressing need to do otherwise.

Strained Relations with Israel. Despite Reagan's inclinations toward a close relationship with Israel, Israeli air strikes in mid-1981 against Iraq and Lebanon precipitated a temporary U.S. suspension of F-16 aircraft deliveries to Tel Aviv. The use of American-made jets in the raids raised the question of whether Israel had violated a U.S. law limiting U.S. arms to defensive purposes. Beyond that, however, the air strikes had political repercussions in the United States, raising doubts about Israel's normally unquestioned support in Congress and the country.

Using American-made F-16 bombers escorted by F-15 fighters, Israel on June 7, 1981, attacked and destroyed the Osirak nuclear reactor under construction near Baghdad, Iraq. Israeli prime minister Begin called the raid "an act of supreme, legitimate self-defense," claiming Iraq planned to use the facility to produce nuclear weapons that would threaten Israel. Critics, including many members of Congress, labeled the strike as aggression and accused Begin of launching the raid to bolster his chances in Israel's June 30 general election. The Reagan administration June 10 suspended delivery of four F-16s scheduled to be shipped to Israel June 12. Not since Eisenhower in the 1950s had an American president postponed aid in response to an Israeli action.

Nevertheless, this demonstration of U.S. displeasure did not alter the fundamental relationship between the United States and Israel. On June 16, Reagan said Israel appeared to have violated the defense-only legal requirements but added, "I do think one has to recognize that Israel had reason for concern in view of the past history of Iraq."

In July 1981, Reagan broadened the suspension of F-16 aircraft deliveries to Israel amid intense clashes between Israel and the PLO in southern Lebanon, where Israel had conducted air and commando raids to quell PLO artillery and rocket fire against Israeli border settlements. Although the attacks and counterattacks spanned nearly two weeks, the catalyst for Reagan's action was Israel's July 17 bombing of a PLO headquarters in downtown Beirut, an air strike that reportedly killed more than three hundred persons and wounded eight hundred.

The most direct U.S. criticism of Israel came July 23 from Deputy Secretary of State William P. Clark, who said Begin "is making it difficult for us to help Israel. Our commitments are not to Mr. Begin, but to the nation he represents." Defense secretary Caspar W. Weinberger said Begin's actions "cannot really be described as moderate at this point." The Beirut attack also damaged, at least temporarily, Israel's support in Congress.

On August 24, U.S.-Israeli relations were strained further when Reagan formally notified Congress of his intention to sell Saudi Arabia five airborne warning and control system (AWACS) planes. He had first signaled the possibility of such a sale on April 21.

Nevertheless, propelled by the desire of Secretary of State Alexander M. Haig Jr. to form a "strategic consensus" to counter Soviet expansion in the region, Israeli prime minister Begin met with Reagan in September 1981 to discuss improved ties.

At the end of November, Israeli defense minister Ariel Sharon met with Secretary of Defense Weinberger to make final a "strategic memorandum of understanding." The memorandum was designed to counter Soviet-inspired political instability and pledged the signatories to meet threats in the Middle East "caused by the Soviet Union or Soviet-controlled forces from outside the region." It provided for military cooperation and coordination between Israel and the United States, but it did not obligate the United States to aid Israel if the Jewish state were attacked by the Arab states.

Although the Likud Party in Israel hailed the agreement, the opposition Labor Party was critical, claiming that it did nothing to ensure Israel's security and only committed Israel to defending U.S. interests in the region.

Debate over the merits of the agreement would soon become irrelevant. On December 14, 1981, the Israeli Knesset voted 63-21 to extend Israeli law to the Golan Heights, thereby annexing the territory it had occupied since 1967. Reagan strongly criticized the action and, in response, ordered that the memorandum of understanding with Israel not be implemented.

Israel Invades Lebanon. On June 6, 1982, Israeli armed forces invaded Lebanon with the stated purpose of creating a twenty-five-mile-wide buffer zone in southern Lebanon free of Palestinian guerrillas. In the initial stages of the war the United States appeared ambivalent toward the Israeli moves. After Israel went beyond its self-declared twenty-five-mile limit, however, the administration began to voice opposition.

The administration's immediate concerns were to prevent the war from expanding to include Syria. Philip Habib, Reagan's special envoy, who had already conducted a number of the negotiations between the Arabs and Israelis vis-à-vis Lebanon, returned in an effort to prevent hostilities from expanding. On June 9, Israel and Syria fought a massive air battle over Lebanon's Bekaa Valley, in which Israel destroyed Syrian surface-to-air missiles and decimated the Syrian air force. After this crippling blow, Moscow and Washington engaged Syria and Israel, respectively, in intense dialogue to prevent an all-out ground war. On June 11, Israel and Syria signed a cease-fire, thus ending the brief encounter between the two. Even though the administration opposed Israel's invasion, it seemed to support some of its goals. U.S. officials said they would seek the withdrawal of all foreign forces from Lebanon. This expansion of the original U.S. request that Israel pull out of the country reflected Israel's goal of ending the PLO and Syrian presence in Lebanon.

In spite of Israel's original claim to only a twenty-five-mile buffer zone, its armed forces continued their advance until they reached the outskirts of Beirut and surrounded thousands of PLO guerrillas in West Beirut. Quiet opposition to Israeli actions ended when the Israelis reached Beirut. Reagan made clear that the United States did not want Israel to enter Beirut, an Arab capital.

Divisions within the Reagan administration over Middle East policy widened during the war. Although opposed to the invasion, Haig saw benefits in the Israelis' eliminating the PLO presence in Lebanon and in their pressuring the Syrians to leave. This, he thought, would change the political conditions in Lebanon, enabling the Lebanese government to regain control of the country. Then, on June 24, 1982, Haig abruptly resigned. Most analysts suggest that internal administration conflict over Lebanon war policy was the final dispute in a long list of disputes for Haig.

The nomination of George P. Shultz as Haig's replacement was widely seen as portending changes in the administration's view of the Middle East. During Reagan's presidential bid in 1980, Shultz, who had been advising on other issues, was critical of the candidate's views toward Israel. Shultz stated often that the United States should have a "balanced approach" to the Arab-Israeli conflict.

With the Israelis on the outskirts of Beirut, the administration tried to reassure friendly Arab states that Israel would not enter Beirut. In attempting to negotiate an end to the crisis, Habib

managed to conclude a number of cease-fire agreements, all of which were broken almost immediately. Habib eventually secured agreement for PLO forces to leave Beirut, but the evacuation did not occur until after the Israelis engaged in a day-long bombardment of the city on August 12.

Although the PLO had agreed in principle to leave Beirut, the final agreement was delayed while negotiators hammered out details of the evacuation and searched for a destination. President Hafiz al-Asad of Syria refused to allow the PLO to come to his country. Jordan also refused to take the PLO because of tensions dating back to the Jordanian civil war in 1970, when factions of the PLO attempted to overthrow King Hussein.

Finally, Habib got all the parties to agree to a PLO evacuation of West Beirut to various Arab countries, including Syria, which would be monitored by a multinational peacekeeping force of American, French, and Italian troops. In addition, the United States guaranteed the safety of the Palestinians living in the refugee camps in and around Beirut.

The U.S. Marines in the multinational force left Lebanon September 10, after the PLO evacuation was completed. On September 14, Lebanon's president-elect, Bashir Gemayel, was assassinated, and his brother Amin was nominated to take his place. In apparent retaliation during the following days, Phalange militiamen massacred hundreds of Palestinian civilians in the Shatila and Sabra refugee camps in Beirut. The violence prompted Reagan to send a contingent of twelve hundred marines back into Lebanon September 29 as part of a multinational peacekeeping force. Some members of Congress criticized the president's action as an evasion of the requirements of the 1973 War Powers Resolution, since he had refused to seek congressional approval for the deployment of troops in Lebanon. The War Powers Resolution proscribed the use of U.S. forces in hostile situations for more than ninety days without congressional authorization.

Reagan's Peace Initiative. In 1982 Reagan tried to revitalize the Arab-Israeli peace process that began at Camp David in 1978. However, Reagan's Middle East peace initiative, launched in a televised speech September 1, made little headway. Reagan said the United States would support self-government for Palestinians on the West Bank of the Jordan River and in the Gaza Strip in association with Jordan, but not in an independent state or under Israeli sovereignty. He also called upon Israel to "freeze" further Jewish settlement in the West Bank and Gaza as a prelude to resuming negotiations under the 1978 Camp David accords. He added, however, that Israel could not be expected to pull back totally from the occupied territories.

The president pledged U.S. support for the Camp David plan for an interim agreement to provide self-government for the Palestinians in the West Bank and Gaza for five years while Egypt, Israel, Jordan, and the United States negotiated the ultimate status of the territories. "The final status of these lands must, of course, be reached through the give and take of negotiations," Reagan said. "But it is the firm view of the United States that self-government by the Palestinians of the West Bank and Gaza in association with Jordan offers the best chance for a durable, just and lasting peace."

Reagan said the U.S. position was based on the principle "that the Arab-Israeli conflict should be resolved through negotiations involving an exchange of territory for peace," as set out in United Nations Security Council Resolution 242 in 1967. Reagan ruled out the possibility of PLO participation in the negotiations. This continued the long-standing U.S. policy of refusing to recognize or deal with the PLO until that organization repudiated violence and terrorism, accepted Israel's right to exist, and declared its support for UN Resolutions 242 and 338. Israel promptly rejected the Reagan plan. Jordan's King Hussein initially gave it cautious support and opened talks with PLO chairman Arafat. Hussein failed, however, to secure permission from the PLO to negotiate on behalf of West Bank Palestinians, and by April 1983, when the Palestine National Council meeting in Algiers rejected the plan, Hussein backed away from further involvement.

Lebanon Linkage. The Reagan administration linked its initiative to a resolution of the Lebanese crisis. It viewed the possible resolution of the Lebanese situation as a first step in a broader Middle East peace. Fears grew in Congress, however, that the United States was getting too deeply involved in Lebanon and the lives of marines stationed in that country were in danger. That concern was confirmed when the U.S. embassy in Beirut was the target on April 18, 1983, of a bomb attack that killed sixty-three persons, including seventeen Americans.

The Reagan administration was intent on reducing Syrian influence in Lebanon and moving peace negotiations forward. To achieve these goals, U.S. officials sought an agreement between Lebanon and Israel. A long and difficult series of negotiations, involving top Israeli, Lebanese, and American officials, produced an agreement that in the end came to naught. The agreement, signed in Lebanon and Israel on May 17, 1983, was not called a treaty because the Lebanese were concerned about Arab reaction. Moreover, formal diplomatic relations were not to be established immediately. The agreement did, however, provide for an end to the state of war that had formally existed since 1948, a buffer security zone in south Lebanon to protect Israel, and absorption into the regular Lebanese army of the pro-Israeli militia, led by Sa'ad Haddad, that operated in southern Lebanon. It also ensured Israeli air superiority and established in both countries semi-diplomatic missions that would have immunity privileges. Last, the agreement provided for negotiations to reestablish normal relations between the nations.

The United States, in a separate letter to Israel, promised to guarantee the agreement, acknowledged Israel's right to retaliate against attacks from Lebanese territory, and assured the Israelis that they did not have to withdraw until Syria and the PLO pulled out. The pact had a very short life. Even though it was signed by both parties and the Israeli Knesset ratified it, the Lebanese parliament delayed action. The Syrians, who were never part of the negotiations and who saw their influence in Lebanon being undercut, refused to accept the agreement, which rendered it meaningless. Without a withdrawal by Syria and the PLO, the Israelis would not withdraw. Under increasing Syrian pressure, Gemayel's government abrogated the accord.

U.S. policy in Lebanon continued to focus on preserving Amin Gemayel's government, which was being opposed with increasing hostility from forces within Lebanon. Reagan's limited use of U.S. air and naval power to support Gemayel in late 1983 and early 1984, however, drew criticism from Congress. It also undermined what little legitimacy the United States had left with the Lebanese people—it was supporting a government that was without legitimacy except among the Maronite segment of the population. The Gemayel government was too closely linked with Israel, with the siege of Beirut, and with the atrocities committed in Sabra and Shatila to have legitimacy among any other confessional group. U.S. air strikes and naval bombardments against Syrian and Lebanese Shiite forces appeared only to increase Lebanon's chaos, further endanger U.S. peacekeepers, and undermine the status of the United States as a Middle East mediator. On October 23, 1983, 241 U.S. Marine and Navy personnel were killed in Beirut when a suicide truck-bomb crashed into their barracks. Lawmakers and the public pressured the administration to withdraw the marines from Beirut and end U.S. military involvement in Lebanon. That withdrawal, announced on February 7, 1984, concluded the U.S. policy of trying to support Gemayel's teetering government. Syrian domination of Lebanese affairs became nearly complete.

Bouts with Terrorism.   Ronald Reagan entered office in 1981 just as the American hostages were being released by Iran. Reagan had vowed his administration would give no quarter to terrorists, but during 1985 and 1986 a wave of Middle East violence against the United States and other Western nations dominated headlines, pressuring the Reagan administration to back up with action its hard-line rhetoric. On June 14, 1985, Arab gunmen hijacked Trans World Airways Flight 847

from Athens to Rome with 153 people aboard. The hijackers forced the pilot to fly to Beirut, where one American was killed and thirty-nine Americans were held hostage. The hijackers and their Shiite supporters demanded, among other things, that Israel release some 700 Shiite prisoners it was holding. Over the following two weeks of the crisis U.S. officials avoided both negotiating with the terrorists and publicly pressuring Israel to release the prisoners. Nevertheless, it appeared at one point as though U.S. officials were privately pushing Israel in that direction. The American hostages were freed at the end of the month, and Israel began releasing its prisoners. Israeli officials, however, pointedly noted they had intended to release the Shiites prior to the hijacking.

A second hijacking in 1985 caused even wider international ripples. On October 14 gunmen identified as being members of the Palestinian Liberation Front (PLF), a faction of the PLO, seized the Italian passenger liner *Achille Lauro*. The gunmen surrendered to Egyptian authorities a few days later and released the hostages, but not before they killed an elderly, wheelchair-bound American passenger.

In accordance with its stern antiterrorist campaign, the United States sought to capture the hijackers. U.S. intelligence sources soon learned that the terrorists were on an Egyptian airliner heading toward Tunisia, where it was denied permission to land, and then to Athens. Under orders from President Reagan, U.S. F-14 fighters intercepted the Egyptian airliner and forced it to land in Sicily where Italian authorities took the hijackers into custody to await trial. Then, much to the United States' astonishment and anger, the Italians released Muhammad Abu'l Abbas, the leader of the PLF, who the Egyptians said acted as a mediator but the United States claimed was the mastermind of the hijacking.

Although Syria and Iran had been implicated in supporting terrorist activities, the Reagan administration focused its antiterrorism efforts on Libya. That nation was of less importance to U.S. strategic interests than Iran and did not have a major role in the Arab-Israeli peace process, as did

Syria. Moreover, the unpredictable political ideas of Libyan leader Col. Mu'ammar al-Qadhafi and Libya's aggression in Africa—Libya and Chad had a long-running border dispute that frequently escalated to violence—had alienated many Arab governments and caused the Soviets to keep their Libyan allies at arm's length. Military action against Libya, therefore, was likely to involve fewer risks than action against Iran or Syria.

In 1985 Abu Nidal, a Palestinian who had defected from the mainstream of the PLO, moved his base of operations from Syria to Libya. In December 1985, members of his group attacked the check-in counters of El Al airlines at the Rome and Vienna airports with automatic weapons and hand grenades. They killed eighteen persons and wounded more than one hundred. On January 7, 1986, Reagan announced there was "irrefutable evidence" that Libya had supported the Palestinian terrorists who carried out the attack. He ended economic activity between the United States and Libya and ordered American citizens to leave Libya. The next day he froze Libyan assets in the United States. The United States had little success, however, in persuading its European allies to enact similarly tough sanctions against Tripoli.

In March Reagan ordered the U.S. Navy to conduct maneuvers in the Gulf of Sidra off the coast of Libya in defiance of Qadhafi's declaration that the gulf was Libyan territorial waters. While it may be argued under international law that the gulf is in fact Libyan, the question has never been put in front of a lawmaking body, and the United States does not recognize the claim. During the maneuvers Libya fired antiaircraft missiles at U.S. planes. In response, U.S. planes bombed several Libyan ships and a Libyan missile installation.

The U.S. show of strength in the Mediterranean, however, did not deter further terrorist violence. On April 2, a bomb blew a hole in the side of a TWA jet over Greece, killing four people. On April 5, a bomb exploded in a Berlin discotheque frequented by U.S. military personnel. The blast killed two persons, including an American soldier, and wounded more than two hundred.

After intelligence indicated that Qadhafi played a role in the Berlin attack, Reagan ordered an air strike against Libya. On the night of April 14 U.S. F-111 bombers based in Britain and carrier planes in the Mediterranean staged a large-scale raid on Libya. The warplanes' targets included a naval academy, air bases, and Qadhafi's home and headquarters. The raid killed at least fifteen people, including Qadhafi's infant daughter, and injured sixty.

One U.S. F-111 bomber was shot down, and its two crewmen were killed. The attack was overwhelmingly supported by the American public and Congress. A *Washington Post*-ABC News poll showed 76 percent of Americans surveyed approved of the strike. The U.S. attack, however, did not receive the same approval overseas. The British government was the only European government to support the bombing, which was widely condemned in the Arab world as well. France had refused to allow U.S. bombers based in Britain to fly over its territory. Moscow canceled a scheduled visit to Washington by Foreign Minister Eduard Shevardnadze to protest the strike.

The raid did not end terrorist attacks against the United States. Indeed, on April 17 one American and two British hostages in Lebanon were found executed in retaliation for the attack, and the same day an Arab tried unsuccessfully to smuggle a bomb on board an Israeli airliner in London. Nevertheless, Libyan involvement in terrorism appeared to decline after the raid.

Iran-Contra Scandal.   In addition to bombings and hijackings, the Reagan administration had to contend with the kidnappings of Americans by Iranian-backed Shiite groups in Lebanon. During 1984 and 1985, nine Americans had been kidnapped there. Although a few had been released, the Shiite groups continuously held several Americans captive.

The administration was particularly concerned with the fate of William Buckley, the CIA station chief in Beirut, who was kidnapped in March 1984. Intelligence reports indicated that Buckley was being tortured to extract his knowledge of

U.S. antiterrorist operations. While not of the magnitude of the 1979 Iranian hostage crisis, the plight of Buckley and the other American hostages in Lebanon frustrated the Reagan administration and led it to seek their release through methods that conflicted with the administration's policy of not dealing with terrorists.

In 1985 the Reagan administration began considering secret arms sales to Iran through Israel as a way to win the release of U.S. hostages and open a dialogue with "moderate Iranians." Reagan authorized three shipments of U.S. antitank and antiaircraft missiles from Israeli stockpiles to Iran in the late summer and fall. The shipments coincided with the release of one U.S. hostage in September 1985.

On January 17, 1986, Reagan signed a secret finding authorizing a covert U.S. diplomatic initiative to Iran. The document identified three goals of the plan: "(1) establishing a more moderate government in Iran, (2) obtaining from them significant intelligence not otherwise obtainable, to determine the current Iranian Government's intentions with respect to its neighbors and with respect to terrorist acts, and (3) furthering the release of the American hostages held in Beirut and preventing additional terrorist acts by these groups." During 1986 U.S. representatives communicated with Iran through intermediaries and on one occasion traveled to Iran to seek the release of hostages in Lebanon. During these dealings the United States transferred (with Israel's assistance) additional arms and spare parts for military equipment to Iran. Although two American hostages were released during 1986, three more were kidnapped to take their place.

On November 3, *al-Shiraa,* a Beirut magazine, reported on the secret trip by U.S. representatives to Iran earlier in the year. This disclosure led to investigations in the United States that uncovered the Iranian initiative and forced Reagan to admit on November 13 that the United States had shipped arms to Iran. Although Reagan insisted that he had not traded arms for hostages, the initiative appeared to undercut his administration's policy of not negotiating with terrorists. Moreover,

critics charged that Reagan had undermined U.S. standing in the Persian Gulf region, where moderate Arab nations such as Saudi Arabia had been opposing Iran in its war with Iraq. The revelation that the world's leading antiterrorist had sent arms to a nation that had been implicated in terrorist activities weakened U.S. credibility and international determination to fight terrorism.

On November 25, the Iranian initiative was further complicated by the disclosure that National Security Council officials had used some of the proceeds from the arms sales to aid the Nicaraguan contra rebels, despite a U.S. law prohibiting such assistance. This revelation transformed what had been an embarrassing and contradictory policy into a full-fledged scandal. Although a number of his top-level aides were implicated, no conclusive evidence was found that Reagan himself had known of the diversion of funds to the contras.

In 1987, at the request of Kuwait, U.S. ships began escorting reflagged Kuwaiti vessels through the Persian Gulf. The Reagan administration hoped the naval escorts of ships threatened by Iranian air power in the continuing Iran-Iraq war would restore confidence in the United States among the Gulf states, put pressure on Iran to end the fighting, and ensure the flow of oil from the Gulf. The escorts brought U.S. ships and planes into direct conflict with Iranian forces on a number of occasions. U.S. naval forces destroyed several Iranian ships and oil platforms in retaliation for Iranian attacks and minings in the Gulf.

The U.S. presence, however, did lead to tragedy on July 3, 1988, when the USS *Vincennes* mistook an Iranian airliner for an attacking Iranian warplane and shot it down after the airliner failed to respond to several warnings. All 290 passengers and crew were killed.

Later in July, Reagan's high-risk policy in the Gulf was partially vindicated when Iran accepted a cease-fire in the eight-year war with Iraq. Although the U.S. naval presence in the Persian Gulf had not been the dominant factor in pushing Iran to end the war, the escorts had helped check Iranian aggression in the Gulf and reestablish some measure of U.S. credibility with the Gulf states. The cease-fire officially began on August 20, allowing the United States to reduce its naval presence in the Gulf.

Intifada and the Shultz Plan.   The Palestinian uprising in the West Bank and Gaza in December 1987 gave new impetus to U.S. peacemaking efforts in the Middle East. This uprising, known as the intifada, differed from previous violence in the occupied territories in that it pervaded all areas of the West Bank and Gaza and became a permanent feature of life there. Palestinian youths armed with stones daily confronted Israeli soldiers. *(Arab-Israeli Conflict, Chapter 2, p. 13)*

In response to the intifada, Secretary of State Shultz took up Middle East peacemaking with a new urgency in early 1988. He made several trips to the Middle East, where he shuttled between capitals promoting his plan to start Arab-Israeli negotiations. His plan called for talks between Israel and a joint Palestinian-Jordanian delegation. By the fall the two sides were to agree on arrangements for local elections that would give Palestinians in the occupied territories some autonomy over their affairs for a period of three years. By December the parties were to begin talking about what and how much occupied territory Israel would eventually relinquish. The plan also called for an international peace conference attended by all five permanent members of the UN Security Council, including the Soviet Union. Shultz's plan was not greeted enthusiastically by Israel's Likud government, which opposed the idea of giving up occupied territory.

In July King Hussein stunned the international community and dealt a blow to Shultz's peace proposal by renouncing Jordan's claims to the West Bank and relinquishing administrative responsibility for it to the PLO. Hussein's action virtually foreclosed Jordan's participation in the peace process, which many Israeli and U.S. leaders had regarded as essential for progress toward a settlement. With Hussein out of the picture and U.S. and Israeli elections approaching in the fall, Shultz's peacemaking efforts made no progress.

U.S.-PLO Dialogue.   In a 1975 memo to Israeli leaders, Secretary of State Henry Kissinger confirmed that the United States would not negotiate with the PLO until it renounced terrorism, acknowledged Israel's right to exist, and accepted UN Resolutions 242 and 338. Successive administrations abided by this approach to the PLO. Yasir Arafat and his organization refused to meet U.S. conditions, and the United States along with Israel rejected any participation by the PLO in Middle East negotiations.

In late 1988, however, Palestinians under occupation, the Soviet Union, Egypt, Jordan, and other moderate Arab states pushed Arafat to adopt a more moderate stance toward Israel and peace negotiations. The intifada had not only raised questions about the viability of the Israeli occupation of the West Bank and Gaza but also had increased international sympathy for the Palestinian cause. The PLO determined that it could best take advantage of the intifada by being less confrontational and searching for recognition of a new Palestinian state. Meanwhile, King Hussein's renunciation in July 1988 of Jordan's ties to the West Bank had caused the United States to take a more careful look at the prospect of negotiating with the PLO.

On November 15, 1988, in Algiers, the Palestine National Council (PNC) declared an independent Palestinian state. The PNC accepted UN Security Council Resolutions 242 and 338 but issued ambiguous statements about its willingness to recognize Israel and renounce terrorism. The Department of State rejected contentions by the PLO that it had satisfied U.S. conditions for a U.S.-PLO dialogue. Nevertheless, the PNC's statements led to a month of diplomatic activity in which the PLO inched its way toward meeting the U.S. conditions.

On November 26, progress toward a U.S.-PLO dialogue appeared to be scuttled when Shultz announced that he would deny Arafat a visa to enter the United States to address the United Nations. The General Assembly, however, voted overwhelmingly to hold a session in Geneva, Switzerland, so Arafat could address the body. In

Arafat's UN speech on December 13 he came closer than ever before to uttering the precise words that Shultz wanted to hear, but Shultz again rejected Arafat's statement as insufficient.

Then on December 14 Arafat held a hastily arranged press conference in which he "renounced" rather than just "condemned" terrorism, accepted UN Resolutions 242 and 338 without qualification, and affirmed "the right of all parties concerned in the Middle East conflict to exist in peace and security, including the states of Palestine, Israel and their neighbors." Four hours later Shultz announced that Arafat's words had finally satisfied U.S. conditions and that "the U.S. is prepared for a substantive dialogue with the PLO." Shultz instructed the U.S. ambassador in Tunisia to begin negotiations with representatives of the PLO.

Although the PLO and the United States made little progress in the first eight months of their negotiations, the talks significantly changed the Middle East peace process. They reaffirmed the position of the United States as the dominant outside peacemaker in the Middle East and made Palestinian nationalism more sensitive to American opinion. The meetings between Israel's closest ally and its most bitter enemy also put pressure on Israeli leaders to construct peace proposals of their own. In addition, the talks gave Arafat's Fatah branch of the PLO something to lose if it engaged in terrorist acts, since the dialogue was conditioned on a PLO renunciation of terrorism.

The Bush Administration (1989–1993)

Despite its early protests over Israel's use of American weapons and the opening of a dialogue with the PLO, a move the Israeli government vigorously protested, the Reagan administration strongly supported Israel. The election of George Bush, Reagan's two-term vice president, seemed to promise continuity in U.S.-Israeli relations and Washington's approach to achieving Middle East peace. It became evident early on, however, that Bush and his foreign policy team would be less patient with Israel than Reagan had been.

At two congressional appearances in March 1989, Secretary of State James A. Baker III said that Israel some day might have to negotiate with the PLO about the status of the occupied territories, an approach that the Israeli government had consistently rejected. Then in a May speech to the annual AIPAC convention, Baker said: "For Israel, now is the time to lay aside, once and for all, the unrealistic vision of a greater Israel. Israeli interests in the West Bank and Gaza—security and otherwise—can be accommodated in a [peace] settlement. Forswear annexation; stop settlement activity; allow [Arab] schools to reopen; reach out to the Palestinians as neighbors who deserve political rights."

Although Baker's comments came within a speech that was pro-Israeli and he was reiterating long-standing U.S. positions, his blunt tone angered Israeli leaders and caused staunch American supporters of Israel to worry that the Bush administration was trying to put more distance between itself and the Jewish state.

While increasing the pressure on Israel to negotiate, the Bush administration nevertheless maintained the traditional strong U.S. support of Israel at the United Nations. On June 9, the United States vetoed a UN Security Council resolution that denounced Israel for violating the human rights of Palestinians in the occupied territories. In addition, the Bush administration opposed efforts to grant the PLO the status of a state in UN organizations. When the PLO petitioned for membership in the World Health Organization (WHO), an affiliated agency of the United Nations, the United States threatened to withhold its contribution to the WHO as well as to any other international organization that admitted the PLO.

Shamir Election Plan. After a U.S.-Israeli summit in April 1989, Israeli prime minister Yitzhak Shamir feared that Bush might accept the long-standing Arab demand for an international peace conference, where Israel perceived itself at a disadvantage. As an alternative, Shamir advanced a plan to hold elections in the occupied territories to select local Palestinians who would represent their people in peace negotiations with Israel. Many Palestinian leaders as well as conservative Israelis had rejected the idea, but Bush backed it as the best option for advancing the peace process. Jordan's King Hussein gave a qualified endorsement to the proposal in April 1989.

On June 8, Ambassador Robert H. Pelletreau Jr., the U.S. envoy to Tunisia who was holding regular talks with the PLO in Tunis, urged the PLO to accept Shamir's election plan. The PLO refused to endorse the plan but indicated some interest in it. Administration officials had hinted that if the PLO accepted the Israeli election proposal, the United States would upgrade its dialogue with the PLO to higher-ranking officials.

Ariel Sharon, the leader of the right wing of Shamir's own Likud Party, however, opposed the plan and maneuvered to force Shamir to accept conditions that most observers believed would make it unacceptable to any Palestinian leader. On July 5, before a Likud Party convention, Shamir accepted the hard-line conditions of party conservatives, which stated that Arab residents of East Jerusalem could not vote in the elections or run for office; no elections would be held until the Palestinian uprising ended; Israel would not give up any territory and no Palestinian state would ever be established; and Israel would continue to build Jewish settlements in the occupied territories. Because a large faction of his party backed the riders, Shamir could not reject them without risking a no-confidence vote from his party. The Labor Party, the junior member of Israel's unity government, threatened to resign over the riders, but it did not do so, partly because the United States urged it to remain in the government.

The Bush administration responded to the Likud's move by warning that if the vote plan were crippled by unreasonable conditions, it might have to consider organizing an international conference to reinvigorate the Middle East peace process. Baker told reporters July 8, "Our calculus all along has been that if things totally bog down, if you can't make progress with this election proposal, then we would have to look a little bit more closely at the prospects for an international con-

ference. There is an awful lot of support for that out there from other countries. We have always said that an international conference, properly structured, at the right time, might be useful."

In response to the new Israeli conditions, PLO leader Arafat announced his organization would no longer consider supporting the Shamir plan.

In early September, nearly six months after Shamir had floated his plan, Egyptian president Hosni Mubarak offered a ten-point proposal to bring together Israeli and Palestinian negotiators in Cairo. Movement on Shamir's plan had halted, and Mubarak hoped to restart the process on a new track. After struggling with Mubarak's proposal for several weeks, the divided Israeli government rejected it on October 6 over the proposed rules for the composition of the Palestinian delegation.

Struggles with Lebanese Hostages. By 1989 pro-Iranian groups in Lebanon were holding eight Americans hostage. With a civil war raging, authority in the country had effectively fallen into the hands of the many private militias. Despite extensive efforts, no American hostages had been released since 1986, when it was disclosed that the Reagan administration had sent arms to Iran in the hope that Tehran would use its influence to have the hostages freed in Lebanon.

For some time, Iran had been indicating its desire to improve relations with the United States. Bush repeatedly made clear, however, that no improvements could be made until the hostages were released. Beginning in late April, several of the American hostages were released, with Bush making a point of publicly thanking Iran and Syria for their efforts.

On July 28, 1989, Israeli commandos abducted Shaykh Abd al-Obeid, a spiritual leader of the pro-Iranian Shiite Hizballah group that was holding several Americans and Israelis hostage in Lebanon. In response, a Shiite organization released a videotape that purported to show the hanging of Lt. Col. William R. Higgins, a U.S. Marine being held hostage in Lebanon.

U.S. investigators determined that the man in the video was Higgins, although they could not verify when he had been hanged. The Shiite group threatened to kill another hostage unless the Israelis released Obeid. The Israelis offered to trade Obeid and other Shiite prisoners for all Israeli and Western hostages being held by the Shiites. The Bush administration, while saying it would not make concessions to terrorists, explored ways to gain the release of the remaining U.S. hostages in Lebanon and welcomed an offer in August from the Iranian government to help secure their freedom.

Soviet Immigrants. For decades the United States had pressed the Soviets to allow Jews and other oppressed groups to emigrate freely. The few that were permitted to leave were automatically offered refugee status in the United States on the presumption that they had a "well-founded fear of persecution." Beginning in 1989, the trickle became a flood as the Soviet Union relaxed its emigration restrictions.

In response to the wave of immigrants and because of the internal changes in that country, the United States no longer admitted refugees from the Soviet Union without specific proof of persecution. On October 1, President Bush capped Soviet immigration at fifty thousand a year, redirecting much of the flood to Israel, which welcomed the immigrants with open arms. The same day, Israel announced that it did not have the resources to handle the huge influx and formally asked the United States for loan guarantees so that it could borrow money cheaply to build housing for the new arrivals.

By January 1990, immigration had accelerated to more than one thousand a week. Noting that a "big Israel" would be needed to handle the flood of immigrants, Shamir indicated that the refugees could be a factor in Israel's decisions regarding the status of the occupied territories. "This is the best thing that could happen to Israel," he declared.

In response to fears that Likud would use the influx to further settle the occupied territories, Shamir said, "The Government has no specific policy of directing immigrants to Judea, Samaria [the biblical names for the West Bank] and the

Gaza Strip, just as it is incapable of preventing immigrants from opting for living in those places. . . . Every immigrant is free to choose his place of residence as he pleases." Nevertheless, huge new settlements began to appear in the territories. Arab countries, the United States, and the Soviet Union became alarmed that the growth of the settlements might lock in the West Bank as a permanent part of Israel. King Hassan II of Morocco declared that "the nightmare of Soviet Jews' emigration to the occupied territories, haunting the Arab nation, is considered a catastrophe." Soviet leader Mikhail Gorbachev began to hint that the flow of refugees would be cut if they were being settled on the West Bank.

In February 1990, Moscow bowed to Arab pressure and—despite U.S. appeals—refused to allow direct flights from Moscow to Tel Aviv, which would have accelerated the flow even further. American Jewish groups feared that in the unstable Soviet Union, political forces might abruptly turn against the refugees and stop the flow at any time. Thus, they sought every means to move the immigrants out of the Soviet Union as fast as possible.

Stalled Diplomacy. On March 13, 1990, Israel's national unity government fell when Prime Minister Yitzhak Shamir dismissed Finance Minister Shimon Peres, head of the Labor Party, and the rest of the Labor Party ministers followed him out of the government. This left Shamir as head of a caretaker government until new elections could be held. The immediate cause of the collapse was U.S. efforts to restart the peace process.

Baker had worked with the PLO and Egypt for a year to arrive at a formula acceptable to all in order to choose a Palestinian negotiating team. He now had his formula. Baker had proposed that Israel allow one Palestinian with a second address in East Jerusalem to be on the negotiating team. Likud and Labor's disagreement over accepting this proposal led to the collapse. Earlier in the month, Bush had stated that "the foreign policy of the United States says that we do not believe there should be new settlements in the West Bank or in

East Jerusalem." Likud officials later said that accepting the Baker proposal in light of President Bush's statement could be seen as backing down from their stance that the status of Jerusalem is not negotiable.

On June 8, after elections in which Likud came out ahead of Labor by a razor-thin margin, Shamir announced the formation of a new government coalition of Likud and several small rightist parties, the most conservative government ever in Israel. Sharon, an outspoken advocate of expanded settlement in the occupied territories, was appointed housing minister, in charge of a massive program of building new housing for the refugees still pouring in. With Shamir one of the most moderate members of the government, few observers expected a serious return to the peace process.

On June 13, Shamir laid down new and more rigorous preconditions for Palestinian negotiators, prompting a furious rebuke from Baker. If that is going to be the Israeli approach, Baker stated, "there won't be any dialogue and there won't be any peace, and the United States of America can't make it happen." If the Israelis did not make a good-faith effort to restart the process, Baker said, then the United States would simply "disengage" from Middle East diplomacy and Shamir could "call us when you are serious about peace."

On June 20, President Bush announced the suspension of the eighteen-month-old U.S. dialogue with the PLO as a result of an attempted terrorist attack against Israel on May 30. Six speedboats carrying Palestinian guerrillas tried to attack a beach in Tel Aviv but were thwarted by Israeli forces. Although he distanced himself from the attack—for which the Lebanon-based Palestinian Liberation Front took responsibility—PLO chairman Arafat refused to condemn the attack, despite repeated U.S. prodding.

Pelletreau, the U.S. ambassador to Tunisia, who was conducting the talks, stated that the United States was operating under the assumption that Arafat spoke in the name of the PLO and its constituent groups and that it was the PLO's responsibility to exercise control over those groups. In the event of a terrorist action by one of its members,

Washington expected the PLO to publicly condemn the action and discipline those responsible. Despite the setback for the peace process, Bush felt that he had no choice but to break off the talks, given Arafat's weak response to the attack. Combined with the hard line taken by the new Israeli government, most observers felt that the peace process was essentially stopped. Neither side seemed able or willing to make the necessary gestures to break the deadlock. For emphasis, at the same time that Bush announced the end of talks with the PLO, he repeated Baker's statement that the Israelis should "call us" when they get serious about peace.

During 1990 the flow of immigrants increased to more than ten thousand a month, holding close to this level through 1991—even during the Gulf war. On June 24, as a result of further U.S. and Soviet pressure, the Israeli government stated that as a matter of policy it would not settle immigrants on the West Bank or Gaza Strip. Nevertheless, the settlements in the territories continued to grow.

On October 2, after a full year of hesitation, Baker announced that the United States had agreed to provide Israel with the requested housing loan guarantees as a result of private assurances that none of the aid would be used in the territories. Relations between the United States and Israel, which had steadily worsened since Bush's inauguration, warmed noticeably.

Persian Gulf War.   The invasion and occupation of oil-rich Kuwait by Iraq in August 1990 set in motion a crisis that would remain at the forefront of the international agenda for seven months. President Bush responded to the invasion by pulling together an international coalition authorized by the United Nations Security Council to oppose Iraq. Nearly forty nations contributed combat forces, transport assistance, medical teams, or financial aid to the joint effort to force Iraq from Kuwait. The Persian Gulf crisis was the first major test of the effectiveness of the UN Security Council to confront international aggression in the post–cold war era. *(The Persian Gulf, Chapter 4, p. 137)*

In his August 8 speech announcing the first deployment of U.S. forces in Saudi Arabia, Bush declared that the U.S. would stand behind four principles in its campaign against Iraq: the unconditional withdrawal of Iraq from Kuwait; restoration of the Kuwaiti monarchy; stability in the Persian Gulf; and protection of U.S. citizens abroad. Bush and Secretary of State Baker directed a major diplomatic initiative aimed at Security Council adoption of a resolution to authorize the use of force against Iraq if it did not withdraw from Kuwait. The campaign culminated in the Security Council's adoption on November 29 of Resolution 678, which set January 15 as the deadline for Iraq to pull out of Kuwait. After that, the resolution authorized member states to use "all necessary means" to enforce previous UN resolutions demanding the withdrawal.

Congress supported the president's actions from the start of the crisis, but at times lawmakers were wary. They generally endorsed Bush's economic embargo against Iraq and his deployment of hundreds of thousands of troops to Saudi Arabia to ward off a possible Iraqi invasion of that country. Many members, however, opposed an early resort to force, hoping instead that the pain of severe economic sanctions would force Iraq to abandon Kuwait.

Most Americans backed Bush's initial deployments of troops to Saudi Arabia. As the crisis continued, however, public support for Bush's strategy weakened as fears of a recession and a long stalemate in the desert increased. A *New York Times*/CBS News public opinion poll taken October 8–10 showed that 57 percent of Americans supported the president's Gulf policies, as compared with 75 percent in early August.

War Decision.   Many journalists, politicians, and scholars who followed the administration's policy explanations commented that Bush had failed to make a coherent case for the need to use force if Iraq refused to withdraw from Kuwait. The difficulty the Bush administration was having in explaining its actions stemmed partly from the nature of the Iraqi threat and partly from the administration's haphazard presentation of the motivations behind its policy.

Saddam Hussein's invasion of Kuwait certainly did not threaten American shores. Instead, it threatened U.S. interests overseas, the international economy, and principles of international law. No single reason for going to war against Iraq was compelling by itself. The Iraqi invasion required citizens to weigh a complex balance sheet of variables for and against the use of force, instead of responding to a ringing cry to arms in the interest of national defense. Moreover, for Americans who saw Iraq as a threat but had doubts about the wisdom of war, continuing to enforce severe economic sanctions against Iraq offered a compromise option through which a person could oppose both Saddam's acts and the launching of what might be a bloody war in the desert.

During the crisis the Bush administration expanded on the reasons the president cited in his August 8 speech for his strong response to Iraq's invasion of Kuwait. Often the justifications were moral. Bush announced that the United States would not stand for Iraq's brutal aggression against Kuwait. The administration cited Iraq's duplicity before the invasion; Kuwait's peaceful history; reports of atrocities by Iraqi troops; and Iraqi efforts to depopulate Kuwait, strip it of its valuables, and annex it to Iraq. Bush stressed that the Iraqi invasion was an opportunity to establish a "new world order" in which collective action would deter and combat aggression and uphold international law. In mid-November growing concerns among Americans about the economy led the Bush administration to emphasize the importance of liberating Kuwait to the economic health of the nation. Baker said November 13 that the administration policy in the Gulf was motivated by economic concerns: "If you want to sum it up in one word, it's jobs. Because an economic recession worldwide, caused by the control of one nation—one dictator, if you will—of the West's economic lifeline [oil], will result in the loss of jobs for American citizens."

Similarly, when public opinion polls in late November showed that Americans were more concerned about Iraq's potential for developing nuclear weapons than any other aspect of the Gulf crisis, administration officials focused on the Iraqi nuclear threat. Bush aides noted that Iraq's aggressive nuclear research program could succeed in developing rudimentary nuclear weapons within several years. Some experts disputed that Iraq could build nuclear weapons that quickly, but the prospect of a nuclear-armed Iraq some time in the future was a potent argument for going to war against Iraq.

The deployment of large numbers of U.S. forces in Saudi Arabia also triggered a constitutional debate on the division of war powers between the executive and legislative branches in the United States. Most lawmakers asserted that because the responsibility to declare war rested with Congress, the president did not have the power to launch a military offensive against Iraq without prior congressional approval—unless Iraq attacked U.S. forces. The administration disputed this assertion, claiming that the president's role as commander in chief empowered him to order offensive actions against Iraq.

The president, however, promised to consult closely with Congress with regard to his Gulf policy. In January 1991, when war became likely and Bush appeared to have enough votes in Congress to win approval for the war option, he sought to unite the government and the country behind his policies by asking Congress to authorize an attack against Iraq if one became necessary in his judgment. The request satisfied most members of Congress that the president had not usurped their war-making role.

In early January last-ditch diplomatic efforts to persuade Iraq to withdraw failed. As the U.S.-led coalition prepared for war, Congress debated resolutions authorizing the president to use force to expel Iraq from Kuwait. The debate concluded January 12 with the adoption of identical resolutions (S.J. Res 2, H.J. Res 77) authorizing Bush "to use United States armed forces" to end Iraq's "illegal occupation of, and brutal aggression against, Kuwait." The Senate voted 52-47 for approval; the House vote was 250-183.

Once the UN deadline had passed, Bush acted swiftly. On January 16, he ordered coalition forces to begin a sustained bombing campaign against Iraq. On February 24, after thirty-eight straight days of bombing, the allies launched a ground offensive into Kuwait and Iraq that overwhelmed Iraqi defenders with surprising ease. On February 27, Bush announced a cease-fire and declared Kuwait liberated.

Aftermath of the War.   By most measures the U.S.-led coalition's war against Iraq was enormously successful. Kuwait was liberated and the legitimate Kuwaiti government was restored to power; coalition forces sustained fewer casualties than almost anyone predicted; Iraq's offensive military potential and nuclear weapons research facilities suffered serious setbacks; the wave of terrorism that Saddam had threatened to loose upon his enemies had not appeared; and the international community had demonstrated that it could collectively respond to aggression.

The victory was less complete than it might otherwise have been, however, because Saddam Hussein managed to retain power despite the ravages his leadership had brought to his country. His repression of dissent, frequent purges of the military and his Baath Party, and efforts to prevent anyone from accumulating too much authority had blocked the emergence of rival centers of power in Baghdad that could lead a coup against him. Though toppling Saddam had never been a stated purpose of the coalition military effort, his continued belligerence toward his own people and the international community created perceptions that President Bush had stopped the war too soon.

The Bush administration and the United Nations settled into the task of containing a weakened but still dangerous Iraq. As of the fall of 1999 the United Nations continued to maintain stringent, U.S.-backed economic sanctions against Iraq, and its inspectors engaged in a long-running struggle to force Saddam to reveal and relinquish the elements of his massive effort to develop nuclear, chemical, and biological weapons.

Even in defeat, Saddam managed to create headaches for the United States and the international community by refusing to cooperate fully with nuclear weapons inspectors sent to Iraq under the terms of the cease-fire agreement. Iraq's conventional military strength had been sharply reduced by the war, but policy makers worried that if Iraq acquired a nuclear weapon it could again menace the region. Inspectors determined that Iraq's program to develop nuclear bombs was far more extensive and advanced than the Bush administration or independent experts had predicted.

Iraqi Rebellions.   Soon after the cease-fire with the U.S.-led coalition forces was declared, Iraq was torn by civil violence. Realizing that much of the Iraqi military's best equipment and some of its best units had been destroyed, Kurdish resistance fighters in northern Iraq and Shiite Muslim rebels in southern Iraq began waging open warfare against Iraqi troops loyal to Saddam. With the war for Kuwait over, Saddam Hussein ordered what was left of his military to put down the rebellions.

During the Persian Gulf War, Bush had repeatedly said that he would welcome the overthrow of Saddam. Many commentators noted that his statements may have contributed to the confidence of Iraqi rebels that the United States would come to their aid. During the postwar insurrections, however, Bush emphasized that he had never promised to intervene in Iraq's internal affairs. "We're not going to get sucked into this by sending precious American lives into this battle," Bush said April 4. "We have fulfilled our obligations."

When the Iraqi army brutally turned back the Kurdish and Shiite rebellions, however, large numbers of Kurd and Shiite refugees were placed in peril. The Bush administration took limited measures designed to prevent disaster, including authorizing food and supply drops to refugees hiding in the mountainous border regions, providing financial aid to assist refugees, and warning Iraq that interference with refugee relief efforts would not be tolerated. Democratic critics in Congress, some of whom had originally opposed going to war, urged Bush to take more

effective steps to protect the Kurds, including banning Iraqi armed helicopter flights. The anti-Iraq coalition had prohibited any use of Iraqi combat airplanes since the end of the Gulf war, but it had not banned flights by armed helicopters.

Bowing to the necessities of a human tragedy, Bush announced on April 16 that U.S., British, and French forces would go back into Iraq to aid the Kurdish refugees, setting up tent cities and assisting the refugees in moving to them.

The deployment of an estimated sixteen thousand U.S., British, and French troops in the resettlement operation risked Bush's commitment to avoid interference in Iraq's internal affairs. Bush justified the deployment saying, "I think the humanitarian concern . . . is so overwhelming that there will be a lot of understanding about this." Iraq was not understanding, calling the plan interference in its internal affairs.

In late April the United States broadened the scope of its relief efforts, providing direct aid for the first time to an estimated 1 million people who had fled from southern Iraq into neighboring Iran. Allied forces also greatly expanded the size of a security zone established for hundreds of thousands of Kurdish refugees. The allies, encountering no resistance from Iraqi forces, created a safe haven for the refugees that encompassed more than 1,800 square miles in northern Iraq. Nonetheless, this did not allay Kurdish fears of reprisals from Hussein's government.

Throughout the period, Congress supported Bush's plans to aid the Kurdish refugees, approving nearly three quarters of a billion dollars to pay for the massive aid effort.

Toward a Peace Agreement.   The U.S.-led coalition's victory over Iraq produced a situation quite different from that called for by the Iraqi-dominated Arab summit of the previous summer. Instead of having its role in the Middle East limited, as the summit wished, the United States emerged from the Gulf crisis with its prestige and influence greatly strengthened, improving the climate for diplomatic achievement. The Bush administration recognized that it now had an opportunity to advance the Arab-Israeli peace process and other U.S. goals.

The U.S. position also had improved because of the continuing disintegration of the Soviet Union. Moscow was increasingly turning inward to address its domestic political and economic crises. Since its withdrawal from Afghanistan, completed in 1989, it had shown much less interest in an assertive role abroad. Soviet allies in the Middle East, especially Syria, could no longer expect financial or diplomatic backing from their patron. The United States was the only remaining superpower. By the end of 1991 the Soviet Union had completely dissolved. Its main successor state was not in a position to project military or financial influence into the Middle East.

Within weeks after the war, Baker began the first of numerous shuttle trips to Middle East capitals, hoping to achieve consensus on a Middle East peace conference. Baker chose not to press the U.S. advantage by demanding that Israel and the Arab states attend, but rather sought to create an atmosphere where real progress could be made. Yet, in two trips to the region, he found little support for the conference among Middle East nations, particularly in Israel and Syria. Outside of the region, however, support had begun to develop. Soviet foreign minister Aleksandr Bessmertnykh announced his government's willingness to co-sponsor a conference. The European Community also expressed its interest in attending.

Baker's first breakthrough came with the announcement on May 10 that the Gulf Cooperation Council—which represents Saudi Arabia, Kuwait, Bahrain, Qatar, the United Arab Emirates, and Oman—was willing to send an observer to a peace conference between Israel and its neighbors. The real turning point for the conference, however, came with the announcement by Hafiz al-Asad on July 18 that Syria would participate, although a number of issues remained regarding the conference format. Within days, Lebanon and Jordan followed suit—Palestinian willingness to participate had never been in question since they had few other options—and Baker found himself with a full deck of Arab participants. Only Israel's Yitzhak Shamir still refused to commit.

For Shamir, Syria's acceptance created a serious dilemma. Rejecting the conference could well cause irreparable damage to Israel's already sagging relationship with the United States, putting at risk the $3 billion in annual aid Israel received. Attending the conference, however, might cause his fragile right-wing coalition government to collapse.

The Conference Format.   While setting up the conference Baker became bogged down, not in the substance of what the participants would discuss but in the procedural issues and the format. Syria had insisted that any talks be held in the framework of an international conference, with the participation of the United Nations, the United States, and the Soviet Union. This would blur the fact that Syria was doing what it had always refused to do in the past—sitting down at a table with Israel.

Israel rejected such a format, instead calling for the conference to be no more than a one-day ceremonial affair without UN participation, before proceeding to direct bilateral talks with each of its neighbors. It also rejected Soviet participation until the Soviet Union consented to reestablish the diplomatic ties it had cut off in 1967. From the Israeli view, Palestinians could participate only as part of the Jordanian delegation. Allowing a separate Palestinian delegation might imply that Israel was amenable to the formation of a Palestinian state—something the Shamir government absolutely opposed.

The Syrians ultimately accepted a procedural compromise that was largely on the Israeli terms. The full conference would break up after a day of ceremonial speeches into three bilateral negotiations: Israel-Lebanon, Israel-Syria, and Israel-Jordan/Palestinians. On the question of reconvening, Syrian foreign minister Faruq al-Sharaa blurred this concession by noting that "our interpretation is that a conference in practice does not finish its plenary session until it fulfills its objective. That is peace. It can adjourn, but it does not finish until it fulfills its objective." The UN would be represented at the full conference by a single observer who would not be permitted to speak.

Shamir Agrees to Attend.   On July 23, still suspicious that the Syrian concessions were not genuine, Shamir gave Baker a tentative yes to attending the talks, with the condition that he be allowed a veto over the list of Palestinians with whom Israel would negotiate. Shamir was adamant that no PLO member or Palestinian from East Jerusalem be allowed to participate; since Israel had annexed the area, its residents lived in Israel proper, not the territories. This was especially problematic because much of the Palestinian leadership within the territories lived in East Jerusalem. Nevertheless, with some fine-tuning of the Palestinian delegation still to be worked out, the Israeli cabinet voted on August 4 to attend the proposed conference.

On October 18, the United States and the Soviet Union issued formal invitations to a conference to be held October 30, 1991, in Madrid. The opening session would last three days and include only ceremonies and speeches. Then, in mid-November, multilateral talks would open for all governments in the region to discuss topics such as arms control, water rights, and the environment.

The same day invitations were issued, Israel and the Soviet Union announced the resumption of full diplomatic relations. Consular ties had been established in 1987 and relations had slowly crept forward from that time. Nevertheless, Israel had long refused to allow the Soviets a role in Middle East peace making until diplomatic formalities were fully restored. The Palestinian team ultimately was composed according to Israeli specifications, mostly of medical persons, writers, and academics from the territories with no formal links to the PLO. They would be formally part of the Jordanian delegation. To Israel's frustration, however, a second team of Palestinian "advisers" with close PLO ties also showed up in Madrid to coordinate with the primary delegation, and in fact the PLO leadership in Tunis had selected the Palestinian members of the joint delegation.

Peace Negotiations.   On October 30, 1991, the Madrid conference opened as scheduled with speeches by the two sponsors, Presidents Bush and Gorbachev. The following day, representatives of each delegation spoke. The rhetoric, on the whole, was inflammatory—sinking at times to the level of name-calling—with little to indicate that the sides were in a mood to compromise. Despite invitations and counter-invitations to do so, no one walked out of the conference. The opening session was formally completed on November 1. The delegates went home on November 4 with no agreement on where—or if—the talks would resume.

Despite the harsh tone of the conference, most observers were upbeat in their views. One commentator used the metaphor of the talking dog to explain the significance of the conference: It's not what he says that counts, the amazing thing is that the dog speaks at all. The fact that such implacable enemies had even sat down and listened to speeches together mattered. On November 22, the United States issued invitations to the participants to continue the peace talks in Washington as a compromise location on December 4. However, because the invitations were issued on the eve of a meeting between Bush and Shamir, the Israelis perceived the timing as a snub. They bitterly complained that they had been effectively ordered to show up in Washington on the prescribed day. In response, they proposed that the direct talks be delayed five days, then be moved quickly to a site in or near the Middle East.

When December 4 arrived, all of the Arab delegates were in Washington, but the Israeli delegates did not arrive until five days later, as promised. Opposition parties in Israel heaped scorn on Likud for this behavior.

Finally, on December 10, the negotiators were ready to sit down and begin one-on-one talks. The Palestinians insisted, however, on breaking away from the Jordanian delegation and meeting separately with the Israelis. Until this issue was resolved, neither delegation would enter the meeting room. After a week spent in a Department of State corridor discussing the ground rules, the talks adjourned December 18.

In mid-January 1992 the talks resumed. Although the participants finally had reached the meeting rooms, they spent much of their time talking past one another with little result. In the three months since Madrid, what little initial enthusiasm there had been for the talks seemed to have dissipated. By prior agreement, no U.S. official was present in the room for any of the talks. Baker had insisted from the start that he had no intention of forcing an American solution on the parties; they would have to hammer one out on their own. His strategy, however, seemed to be producing few results.

Israeli intransigence was in part the result of the shaky political ground under the Shamir government. When the topic of interim Palestinian self-rule came up in the talks, it caused two small right-wing parties to announce their departure from the government on January 19, leaving Shamir without a majority in the parliament. Bowing to the inevitable, Shamir scheduled early elections for June 23, staying on until then as the head of a caretaker government. Shamir's political weakness relieved the U.S. pressure for concessions until after the elections. Any chances for a breakthrough in the bilateral talks were effectively put on hold until June.

On January 28–29, the first session of regional multilateral talks took place in Moscow. Although separate from the bilateral talks, they originally had been intended to take place in mid-November. Most observers expected little from the Moscow talks, but at least they threw no new snares into the peace process. Other Arab states from the Persian Gulf and the Maghrib also took part in the talks on economic cooperation, water sharing, refugees, the environment, arms control, and other regional concerns. Syria and Lebanon declined to attend, arguing that such matters should not be discussed with Israel until after diplomatic normalization had taken place.

In late February and April two more rounds of bilateral talks took place in Washington. These rounds achieved little, but the United States had insisted on them, fearing a gap of too many months would stall the "momentum" of the talks.

In May the five sets of multilateral talks that had opened in Moscow in January (refugees, environment, water, arms control, and economic development) met in five different capitals with more than twenty participants. Israel boycotted the refugee talks, complaining that the participation of Palestinians from outside the territories violated the agreement worked out in Madrid.

Israeli Elections and U.S. Ties. With Baker's frustration at Likud intransigence, and Shamir's complaints that U.S. pressure to stop building settlements was interference in Israeli affairs, U.S.-Israeli ties had sunk to nearly historic lows. Once Israeli elections were announced, Bush and Baker made little secret of their anger at Shamir and their hopes for a Labor victory. They were confident that with Labor's more flexible approach to territorial compromise more could be achieved at the peace negotiations.

Bush's sharpest weapon against Shamir was the long-delayed loan guarantees. On March 17, Bush effectively buried them and placed the blame on the Shamir government, declaring, "We're simply not going to shift and change the foreign policy of this country." The loss of the loan guarantees was a blow to the Israeli economy, but it alarmed Israelis more as an indication that Shamir had allowed something to go seriously wrong in Israel's strategic relationship with the United States, which had rarely denied Israel anything it asked for. This was certainly a factor in the sweeping electoral victory of Yitzhak Rabin and the Labor Party on June 23. Also, Israelis had grown tired of the Likud vision of a "Greater Israel" and were no longer willing to pay the price in blood and resources. Another significant factor in Likud's defeat, besides blame for the loss of the loan guarantees, was an awareness that long-standing ties with the United States were not to be taken for granted.

With the new government in place, U.S.-Israeli tensions eased immediately. Within days of his election, Rabin began to dramatically scale back settlement activity in the occupied territories and moderate the harsh statements of the Likud government. Even Hanan Ashrawi, one of the Palestinian negotiators, noted that there had been a "shift of tone" from Israel. However, Rabin refused to tie his hands by categorically stopping new building, declaring that he would continue to build "security" settlements but not "political" settlements, although the difference was never clear. Nevertheless, Baker reciprocated by hinting that the loan guarantees might now be possible and telling Israel's Arab negotiating partners that with this new compromise on settlements by Israel, it was time for them to show some flexibility.

On August 10 at Bush's family retreat at Kennebunkport, Maine, Bush and Rabin announced that they had reached agreement on terms for the U.S. loan guarantees and that another round of the peace negotiations would open in Washington on August 24. Rabin indicated his hopes that the new round would continue for a full month and begin to include discussions of the terms for Palestinian autonomy, leading to some future "territorial compromises."

As was hoped, the August 24 round did last a full month, with nearly all of the talk on substantive issues. Procedural questions, which had tied previous rounds in knots, were quickly resolved by the new Israeli negotiating team, which had shown up with a concrete thirty-three-page proposal for establishing Palestinian autonomy. Nevertheless, despite substantial progress, no breakthrough was achieved. Another short round of negotiations was squeezed into late October, but with U.S. elections and the looming defeat of George Bush overshadowing everything else, little was accomplished.

The Clinton Administration (1993–2001)

With the election of Bill Clinton to the presidency, many observers feared for the future of the peace process. Clinton was far more sympathetic to Israel than Bush had been, and it was unclear whether the Arabs would find him a credible mediator. Baker's Middle East team would soon leave the Department of State, delaying talks while the new administration filled vacancies and formed policy, despite Clinton's early insistence that there would be no delay.

Recognizing that almost nothing had been achieved in more than a year of talks, Clinton's secretary of state, Warren M. Christopher, sought to change the U.S. role from mediator to active participant. He could not persuade the two sides to adopt a U.S.-proposed statement of principles. Meeting in late June 1993, they still showed little interest in Christopher's proposals.

Declaration of Principles and Jordanian-Israeli Peace. In mid-August, reports began to appear in the Arab press about PLO and Israeli officials meeting secretly, bypassing the stalled official negotiations in Washington. On August 29, the reports were confirmed by announcements that Israeli foreign minister Shimon Peres and Mahmoud Abbas of the PLO had been meeting secretly in Oslo, Norway, with the assistance of Norwegian foreign minister Johan Jorgen Holst, and had reached rough agreement on mutual recognition and establishment of Palestinian autonomy in Gaza and Jericho within six months, with other areas to be added later. After an interim period of five years, the final status of the territories would be determined.

The sudden turnaround caught almost everyone by surprise. Hard-liners on both sides began to complain. Israeli settlers declared that they would shoot Palestinian policemen. Hamas supporters called Arafat a traitor for agreeing to start with such a tiny piece of land and without clear guarantees for the withdrawal of Israeli forces. Clinton and Christopher, also caught off guard, promised their support and invited the sides to Washington for a formal signing ceremony.

Official talks resumed in Washington on August 31, although they were effectively superseded by negotiations continuing in Norway. Members of the Palestinian team complained that they had not been informed of the Norwegian negotiations. On September 1, Jordanian officials hinted that they would be ready to sign a peace agreement with Israel once it inked a deal with the Palestinians. Although technically at war with Israel since 1967, Jordan had formally relinquished its claims to the West Bank in 1988. Its remaining disputes with Israel were minimal, involving only a few small slivers of borderland.

Whereas most Arab leaders moved to support the plan, Syria continued to voice its suspicions. President Hafiz al-Asad did not personally condemn the agreement, but he allowed the Palestinian movements based in Damascus to attack it, making clear where he stood.

On September 13, 1993, at a sun-drenched ceremony on the White House lawn, Israeli prime minister Yitzhak Rabin and PLO chairman Yasir Arafat, veterans of numerous Arab-Israeli wars, shook hands, and their foreign ministers signed the Declaration of Principles on Interim Self-Government Arrangements, the first ever agreement between Israel and the PLO, recognizing each other and agreeing on the outlines of a plan to end their long conflict. Although the agreement specified that the Israeli withdrawal from some occupied territory would begin on December 17, many of the details remained to be worked out.

Many analysts have speculated on the reasons why Israel and the PLO were finally able to come together. Although U.S. pressure for negotiations had brought the parties together, it did not bring about a settlement. On the Palestinian side, Arafat feared being forced out. The PLO had alienated its wealthy Arab backers with its support of Iraq's Saddam Hussein, and the rise of Hamas in the territories challenged its popularity among Palestinians. Without a dramatic move, Arafat might soon have found himself marginalized. The secrecy of the talks allowed Arafat to negotiate without the pressures from radical elements in the PLO. Rabin, for his part, had come to power promising peace and yet had presided over worsening violence and stalled talks. Failure to deliver an agreement with at least one of Israel's enemies would have sooner or later threatened his government's mandate. Also, the intifada had made Israel realize that it could no longer control the occupied territories indefinitely under the system in place.

The Clinton administration remained committed to expanding the Middle East peace process, though it generally steered away from issues related to implementation of the Israeli-Palestinian agreement. With certain elements of Clinton's foreign policy being sharply criticized by Republicans and commentators, the administration viewed the Middle East as a bright spot. Christopher sought to build on this hope through shuttle diplomacy between Syria and Israel, and Clinton lent the prestige of his office to the effort by meeting with Syria's Asad on January 16, 1994, in Geneva. By the fall of 1994, however, an agreement had not been reached. Should the Syrians and Israelis agree on a staged Israeli withdrawal from the Golan Heights, Clinton was expected to station U.S. troops in the area as part of an international peacekeeping mission.

The Clinton administration also pledged financial aid to the Palestinian Authority (PA), the quasi-governmental entity established to administer the areas evacuated by the Israelis. In 1993 it promised $500 million over five years for the development of Gaza, Jericho, and any additional areas coming under Palestinian autonomy. Congress, however, would have to appropriate the money. Half of the amount would be in the form of loans, the other half in grants. The United States also continued talks with the PLO. Like other donors, the United States had considered placing conditions on its aid to the Palestinian Authority to help ensure democratization and the efficient use of funds for development purposes.

Jordan and Israel finally reached an agreement in July 1994. Once again, although the accord had been negotiated without U.S. involvement, Washington played host to the formal signing ceremony. On July 25, King Hussein and Prime Minister Rabin signed the Washington Declaration at the White House, ending the state of war between their two countries. That ceremony was followed on October 26 by the signing of a formal peace treaty between Jordan and Israel on their border. President Clinton attended the signing.

Containment of Iraq and Iran.   Threats from Iraq and Iran continued to pose a challenge for the United States. Although Iraq remained severely weakened from the Gulf war and still besieged by the UN embargo, Saddam Hussein remained in power. In early October 1994, Hussein demonstrated that he could still command the world's attention: He deployed Republican Guard troops close to the Kuwaiti border, leading Clinton to respond by deploying 36,000 U.S. troops to the Gulf region. The Iraqis then pulled back. The Iraqi maneuver, part of an apparent plan to pressure the United Nations to lift sanctions, actually weakened support in the international community for an early lifting of sanctions.

Under the Clinton administration's policy of dual containment, Iran was regarded as a threat at least as great as Iraq, and probably greater. The United States sought to slow the development of Iranian military technology and weapons of mass destruction by lobbying nations to tighten controls on technology and weapons going to Iran. The United States also opposed World Bank loans for Iran and rescheduling of bilateral Iranian debt. Nevertheless, the United States had not precluded exploratory talks with Tehran, even as it used diplomacy to weaken Iran.

Trouble at Home, Trouble Abroad. Midterm congressional elections in November 1994 stunned Democrats, as Republicans captured the House and Senate for the first time in more than forty years. Moreover, the GOP majority in the House was strongly conservative, aggressive, and disinclined to work with Clinton's Democratic administration. Although the GOP focused primarily on domestic issues, such as tax cuts, an increasing strain of isolationism could be seen in the foreign policy outlook of important Hill leaders. The president's position was damaged further by slowly unfolding campaign finance and sex scandals, which hardened Republican resolve not to work with Clinton on any issues, foreign or domestic.

A crisis had been brewing in Eastern Europe since 1991 involving the ethnoreligious problems of the Balkan states of the former Yugoslavia, but the Clinton administration largely had left the issue to the European community. By 1994 it had become obvious that the European powers alone could not solve the conflict, and the brutal war

between Bosnian Muslims, Catholic Croats, and Orthodox Christian Serbs was taking a huge toll on the civilian population of the region. Refugees from the fighting were overwhelming European humanitarian assistance. The United States was drawn into the effort to mediate the conflict. In the Muslim world, the United States had been criticized for years because of upholding an arms embargo against the Bosnians, a policy that many Muslims believed was based on religious racism. By summer 1995, the fighting in Bosnia was entering a new stage, so the United States began preparing an intensive diplomatic push for a solution. The combatants and a joint U.S.-European negotiating team convened at Dayton, Ohio, and worked out an agreement in November 1995.

On November 4, three days after the Dayton negotiations got under way, Israeli prime minister Yitzhak Rabin was assassinated while leaving a political rally in Tel Aviv's main square. His assassin, Yigal Amir, was a right-wing Israeli vehemently opposed to the peace process. Foreign minister Shimon Peres became acting prime minister, overseeing a caretaker government until elections could be held. A spate of terrorist incidents immediately before polling for a new government in Israel appeared to influence the election, in which Israeli voters by a margin of less than 1 percent elected Benjamin Netanyahu, Likud leader and a hard-line opponent of the peace process.

Terrorism became the focus of U.S. policy in the Middle East in 1996 following a series of incidents in Tel Aviv and Jerusalem. President Clinton called on the Palestinian Authority in the West Bank and Gaza to detain individuals responsible for attacks but blamed most incidents in the Palestinian territories and Lebanon on Iran, which he accused of providing funding, weapons, training, and ideological support to Islamist groups in the region.

Americans voted to elect Clinton to a second term in November 1996 despite scandals and acrimonious relations with the Republican Congress. Through 1997 the Clinton administration tried to maintain some momentum in the Arab-Israeli peace process but was increasingly frustrated by the hard-line Israeli stance on security and land-for-peace issues. By 1998 the Arab states were taking a wait-and-see attitude toward the peace process. Efforts by Clinton officials to restart stalled Israeli-Syrian and Israeli-Lebanese bilateral tracks proved wholly unsuccessful.

In October 1998, the administration convened a conference at the Wye River Plantation in Maryland, with the goal of getting PLO chairman Arafat and Israeli prime minister Netanyahu to discuss implementing land, security, and economic issues to which the Israelis and Palestinians had already agreed. The Wye River talks were acrimonious and nearly ended in stalemate, but Clinton was determined to get the peace process back on track. He personally involved himself in the negotiations, reprising President Carter's role in the negotiations that led to the Camp David Accords. His secretary of state, Madeleine Albright, was also present for the negotiations. It took the arrival of King Hussein of Jordan, however, to move the parties toward agreement. The king was at the time receiving treatment for cancer at the Mayo Clinic in Rochester, Minnesota, but left his hospital bed to attend the conference at Clinton's invitation. The Wye River Memorandum, signed October 23, 1998, at the White House, laid ground rules for further land transfers in the West Bank, the opening of the Gaza airport, and cooperative security arrangements. It also set a deadline of May 4, 1999, for the conclusion of permanent status negotiations for the West Bank and Gaza.

Although the Wye gathering was an important event in the administration's Middle Eastern efforts, the United States spent much of 1997 and 1998 working on other foreign policy fronts, particularly UN reform and Iraq. Continuing pressure from congressional conservatives to alter U.S. relations with the United Nations forced Clinton officials to push the international body to reform its procedures toward more efficiency and better responsiveness to crises. They asserted that the United States did not want to always act alone, placing U.S. troops in danger, to help settle international disputes. The United Nations pointed to

the hypocrisy of the U.S. position, because no nation owed the organization more money in back dues than did the United States. Congress continued to refuse to appropriate funds to pay the arrears.

In 1997 and 1998 the United States focused its attention in the Middle East on Iraq's increasingly adamant refusal to comply with UN weapons inspectors, which threatened the humanitarian oil-for-food program in that country and sparked a renewed U.S. and British bombing effort that drew strong criticism, even from U.S. Arab allies. A low-profile campaign of aerial attacks on Iraqi sites continued without much attention until late 1999, when France began to make an issue of them. Even that did not stop Britain and the United States from carrying out what was essentially low-grade warfare against Iraq. *(The Persian Gulf, Chapter 4, p. 137)*

The United States repeatedly charged Iraq with withholding humanitarian aid from its own population in order to score public relations points, and by 1999 rumors had surfaced that some humanitarian aid supplies were being resold on the black markets of neighboring states.

Camp David and Taba Talks. President Clinton was determined to bring about an Israeli-Palestinian agreement before he left office. To that end, he invited Israeli prime minister Ehud Barak and PLO chairman Arafat to Camp David in an attempt to broker a final settlement. Barak, who had defeated Netanyahu in a fractious election in 1999, was a former chief of staff of the Israel Defense Forces and a protégé of the late prime minister Yitzhak Rabin. He had, however, been slipping in public opinion polls and in support in the Knesset and was desperately in need of a dramatic breakthrough to boost his prospects. Arafat was not enthusiastic about the summit, arguing that the Palestinians needed more time to prepare, but Clinton pressured him to attend.

The three leaders spent two weeks, from July 11 to July 25, 2000, sequestered at Camp David. Barak brought what he termed a final peace plan, featuring a sovereign Palestinian state based on the return of 92 percent of the West Bank (by Israeli calculations), all of Gaza, and some parts of East Jerusalem. The plan also called for Israel's annexation of Jewish settlements in East Jerusalem, an Israeli presence at Palestinian border crossings, and Israeli control of West Bank air space. Refugees would be allowed only a truncated right of return, to the new Palestinian state not to former Palestinian land in Israel. Arafat refused to agree to Barak's suggestions despite Clinton's attempts to persuade him.

Following the failure to reach agreement at Camp David, many people in Israel and the United States, following the lead of Barak and Clinton, laid the blame on Arafat, charging that the Israeli offer at Camp David was the "most generous" ever made—a Palestinian state in Gaza and most of the West bank with its capital at East Jerusalem, the removal of many Israeli settlements in the West Bank, and joint administration of the Temple Mount/Haram al-Sharif in East Jerusalem. Arafat was accused of starting the al-Aqsa intifada that erupted later, in September, and of sustaining it so that he would not have to agree to a settlement.

Not surprisingly, the account by Palestinians and other observers differed dramatically from Clinton's and Barak's. They contended that Barak's offer did not address all the disagreements over the territories to be returned, the precise status of Jerusalem, and Israeli settlements in the West Bank. Barak, they claimed, came to Camp David with a final and nonnegotiable plan that he demanded Arafat sign on to. That plan, they pointed out, would essentially divide the West Bank into three areas separated by Israeli settlements, prohibiting Palestinians' movement. In addition, it did not provide full sovereignty over the Arab areas of East Jerusalem or satisfy Palestinian demands regarding the right of return of Palestinian refugees. The intifada, they said, was a spontaneous rebellion flowing from long pent-up frustration over Israel's continuing occupation and confiscation of Palestinian land and, in the immediate sense, from the provocative visit of Ariel Sharon, the hard-line leader of the Israeli opposition party Likud, to the Temple Mount/Haram al-Sharif.

Despite the post-summit spin, Palestinian and Israeli negotiators met on several occasions in August and September 2000, and on December 23, 2000, President Clinton offered his own plan. It would create a sovereign Palestinian state in Gaza and 97 percent of the West Bank, give Israel sovereignty in East Jerusalem over Jewish areas and give Palestine sovereignty for Arab areas, reassure Israeli security concerns by insisting that the Palestinian state be demilitarized and allow Israeli early warning stations to remain in the West Bank. It also offered compromises on Palestinian refugees. As a result, Israeli and Palestinian negotiators met at Egypt's Taba resort January 21–27, 2001. Using the Clinton plan as a starting point, the talks came close to achieving an agreement but were suspended until after the Israeli elections, following Barak's resignation, which he had submitted on December 10 in order to seek a new mandate.

In the meantime, clashes and violence between Israelis and Palestinians strained the atmosphere for peace. Israel had responded quite forcefully to the Palestinian protests surrounding Sharon's visit to the Haram al-Sharif. When two Israeli soldiers were killed in Ramallah on October 12, the IDF used helicopter gunships to attack Palestinian Authority offices. Former U.S. senator George Mitchell was appointed by the administration in October to head a commission to investigate the violence.

The Likud Party won national elections in early 2001. As a result, Ariel Sharon became prime minister. Instead of resuming talks, Sharon declared the Camp David process "null and void" and asserted Israeli sovereignty over all of Jerusalem. He also said he would accept a Palestinian state on 42 percent of the West Bank. Prospects for peace receded, and the Palestinian intifada dragged on, becoming increasingly violent. Israeli tactics became increasingly repressive. Actions against settlers and Israeli troops by such underground groups as the Tanzim and the al-Aqsa Martyrs Brigade, both loosely associated with Fatah, the dominant faction in the PLO, and the suicide bombings carried out largely by Hamas and Islamic Jihad were met by Israeli occupation of Palestinian towns, the destruction of homes of suspected attackers and of Palestinian Authority infrastructure, and the arrest or "targeted killing" (assassination) of Palestinians believed to be involved as leaders in perpetrating attacks.

Other Relations. U.S. relations with the rest of the Middle East under the Clinton administration were mainly untroubled. Close economic and political ties marked relations with Saudi Arabia and the other Gulf Cooperation Council states. The United States expressed support for the Algerian government during its civil war with Islamic extremists. Relations with Syria, never very good, continued to be frosty, particularly as efforts to achieve an Israeli-Syrian peace remained at an impasse. Clinton met with Syrian president Asad in March 2000 in an apparent attempt to convince him to allow Israel to retain part of the Golan in a peace deal. Asad rejected the measure, reiterating his long-expressed demand for a return to the 1967 prewar border. The Clinton administration continued to seek to tighten sanctions on Iraq after the 1998 air strikes but with little effect.

The George W. Bush Administration (2001–)

The attacks of September 11, 2001, are undoubtedly the determining factor in the course of U.S. Middle East policy under the administration of George W. Bush. As a presidential candidate on the campaign trail, Bush appeared wary of internationalism and multilateralism and such endeavors as nation building and peacekeeping. As a result of al-Qaida's strike on the United States, Bush in 2005 found himself involved in three nation-building exercises and having issued proclamations of a U.S. foreign policy determined to hold nations accountable and to bring democracy to the four corners of the earth in conjunction with a global "war on terror."

The al-Aqsa Intifada and Israeli-Palestinian Relations. Having watched the active efforts of President Clinton fail to achieve a breakthrough in the long-running Arab-Israeli conflict, the initial policy of the George W. Bush administration

seemed to be one of keeping a distance from it. Ultimately, however, its hand was forced by the conflict's violence.

The Bush administration continued the U.S. policy of strong support for Israel. Financial assistance to Israel has averaged about $3 billion annually since 1985. Although ties between the Sharon government and the Bush administration were close, and Bush appeared to support Sharon's hard-line approach to the Palestinian Authority, the administration's decision not to appoint a special envoy to the region represented a clear reluctance to become overly involved.

As the al-Aqsa intifada wore on, and Israelis and Palestinians became increasingly bitter, negotiations essentially ended for a time after Prime Minister Sharon refused to deal with Arafat, and the Israeli army, having launched a major incursion into the occupied territories, confined Arafat to Palestinian Authority headquarters in Ramallah. Nevertheless, the United States made several attempts to restart negotiations.

The September 11 attacks led Bush to turn his attention again to the peace process. In part, U.S. relations with the Palestinian Authority were soured by Washington's tendency to view Hamas and Islamic Jihad as terrorist groups in the same camp as al-Qaida. Bush followed Sharon's lead in refusing to deal with the PA until it reined in these groups. On June 24, 2002, Bush said that the United States would support the creation of a Palestinian state once Palestinians had selected a new leadership "not compromised by terror" and steps toward democracy were introduced.

Arafat, relenting to pressure and deciding against further isolation, appointed Mahmoud Abbas as prime minister on March 7, 2003. Sharon and Abbas both made conciliatory gestures. With the appointment of Abbas as prime minister, in April 2003 the Bush administration made public the so-called road map, a three-phase, three-year peace plan developed by the Quartet—the European Union, Russia, the United Nations, and the United States. The Palestinians accepted it, and Israel accepted it in principle, with changes. Bush met with Abbas, Sharon, and

Al-Qaida

Al-Qaida shocked the United States, and indeed the world, with its attack of September 11, 2001. Osama bin Laden, the organization's founder, is one of many sons of a successful Saudi Arabian contractor of Yemeni origin and one of thousands of Muslim volunteers who fought the Soviet Union in Afghanistan between its 1979 invasion and 1988 withdrawal. These so-called Arab Afghans, who traveled to Afghanistan to join the fight, returned to their homelands radicalized by their experiences and conversion to a worldview of an Islamic world under threat from nonbelievers.

Bin Laden began organizing and gathering followers on his return to Saudi Arabia. He and Abd al-Aziz Azzam, a Palestinian religious theorist, agreed that the organization they had established in Afghanistan should carry on. Thus evolved al-Qaida (meaning the base, or foundation). The creation of a corps of Islamist volunteers to fight non-Muslims wherever they threatened Islamic lands and to overthrow Islamic governments perceived as being corrupt and anti-Islamic were two of al-Qaida's principal goals.

After Azzam's assassination in 1989, bin Laden became the unquestioned head of al-Qaida, with prominent roles also played by two Egyptians— blind cleric Umar Abd al-Rahman (whose followers in Egyptian Islamic Jihad assassinated President Anwar al-Sadat in 1981) and Ayman al-Zawahiri (another key figure in Islamic Jihad who facilitated its merger into al-Qaida).

With bin Laden's ideology growing more extremist and recruiting more followers, the Saudi government stripped bin Laden of his Saudi nationality in 1994, but by then he had already found refuge in a sympathetic Sudan, then dominated by an Islamist movement. When he continued to build his network, establish alliances with like-minded groups, and attract even more followers, international pressure forced Sudan to expel him. Afghanistan's Taliban regime invited him to settle there, where he took up residence and established training camps in terrorism and guerrilla warfare for al-Qaida members.

In 1998 bin Laden and Zawahiri issued a *fatwa*, declaring that because the United States had declared war on God and his messenger, Muslims should, as part of their duty, carry out attacks on Americans where possible. The organization had struck U.S. targets beginning in 1993 with the bombing of the World Trade Center in New York. They killed six people and wounded hundreds. Umar Abd al-Rahman, a key figure in the attack, was arrested and imprisoned for his role. Al-Qaida subsequently carried out the bombings of the U.S. embassies in Kenya and Tanzania in 1998, in which

King Abdallah II of Jordan in Aqaba in June 2003 to discuss the plan. Efforts to improve the situation on the ground inevitably failed, and neither side proved willing or able to implement even the first phase of the road map. *(Arab-Israeli Conflict, Chapter 2, p. 13)*

Faced with domestic opposition to his hard-line policies, Sharon announced plans to withdraw Israeli forces and settlements from Gaza and a few West Bank settlements and asserted that the separation barrier that Israel had begun to build on and around the West Bank would be continued. In April 2004, Bush announced his support for Sharon's disengagement plan, and at the same time stated that it was unrealistic to expect a return to the 1949 armistice borders, meaning that Israel should be allowed to retain some areas of the occupied territories, and that the Palestinian refugees should not expect fulfillment of the right of return. The Palestinians were troubled by what appeared to be a break in U.S. policy calling for the two sides in the conflict to reach mutual decisions on such issues.

After Arafat's death in November 2004, Abbas succeeded him as head of the Palestine Liberation Organization and easily won election as president of the Palestinian Authority on January 9, 2005. Sharon and Abbas subsequently declared their several hundred people died. The organization was also implicated in the killing of U.S. servicemen in Saudi Arabia and Somalia. In October 2000, the group exploded a bomb next to the USS *Cole,* in the port of Aden, Yemen, killing seventeen American sailors.

Planning and preparation for the September 11 attacks began long in advance. The first participants in the plot arrived in California in early 2000; others arrived later, bringing the total to six, and were scattered around the country. Most of these six enrolled in flight training schools, with some expressing particular interest in flying large commercial aircraft. bin Laden and al-Qaida then prepared a "muscle" group whose job would be to seize control of the various aircraft so that the first six could pilot them into the targets. There were in all nineteen hijackers who participated in the attacks.

The presence of fifteen Saudis among the nineteen has been ascribed to either the preponderance of Saudi recruits in al-Qaida's ranks or a deliberate attempt by bin Laden to harm relations between the United States and Saudi Arabia. The tactical leader of the plot was an Egyptian, Mohammed Atta. A French citizen of Moroccan origin, Zacarias Moussaoui, was suspected of being a potential twentieth hijacker, but he was in U.S. custody on September 11.

Early on the morning of September 11, 2001, five of the group boarded an American Airlines plane in Boston bound for Los Angeles. Shortly afterwards and a few gates away, another four boarded a United

Airlines plane, also bound for Los Angeles. Meanwhile, five more boarded an American Airlines flight departing Washington for Los Angeles. The last four boarded a United Airlines flight in Newark also headed for Los Angeles. Transcontinental flights carry a maximum amount of fuel.

Shortly after the planes took off, the muscle groups used box cutters to take control of the planes, and the other hijackers took command of the cockpits. They flew the two airplanes that had taken off from Boston into the World Trade Center, one into each of the two towers, both of which collapsed, killing more than 2,000 people. The Washington aircraft crashed into one side of the Pentagon outside Washington, killing more than two hundred people. The Newark aircraft crashed in the Pennsylvania countryside after passengers rushed the hijackers and prevented them from reaching their target, variously believed to be either the U.S. Capitol or the White House. The toll from the multiple attacks reached 3,126 dead, many of them New York police and firefighters killed when the World Trade Center towers collapsed in the midst of their rescue efforts.

Within a few days, the George W. Bush administration created the Homeland Security Council. After wrangling between the executive and legislative branches, the council evolved into the Department of Homeland Security and was charged with immigration, border control, transportation security, and other similar tasks.

intentions to end Israeli-Palestinian violence, entering into an informal truce.

As secretary of state in Bush's second term, Condoleezza Rice visited Israel and the Palestinian territories a month after Abbas's election, and she appointed Lt. Gen. William Ward as her Middle East security coordinator. She, however, was pointedly absent from a summit of Sharon, Abbas, King Abdallah II of Jordan, and President Hosni Mubarak of Egypt on February 8, 2005, declaring that the involved parties, and not the United States, should take responsibility for the peace process. On February 21, President Bush stated that Palestinian democracy was a necessary prerequisite for establishing a Palestinian state.

On a Sharon visit to Crawford, Texas, in April 2005, Bush pushed the Israeli leader to adhere to the road map and gained his agreement to dismantle "illegal" settlement outposts in the West Bank. Although Sharon indicated his commitment to the creation of a Palestinian state after the elimination of Palestinian attacks, he also emphasized that the status of major settlements was not negotiable. President Bush appeared again to indicate that he did not oppose retention of some settlements by Israel.

Earlier assertions by some administration officials that the overthrow of Saddam Hussein in Iraq would enable progress on the Israeli-Palestinian front had not been proven true in mid-2005.

September 11, 2001. After President Bush returned to Washington on the evening of September 11, 2001, he announced in an address to the nation, "We will make no distinction between the terrorists who committed these acts and those who harbor them." Before the day ended, Bush convened a "war council," announcing that it was time for the country to defend itself. It was agreed that anyone supporting al-Qaida should be the focus, so the Taliban regime in Afghanistan became a primary target. The administration approached Pakistan and secured agreement from it to end all support to the Taliban and assist the United States in eliminating al-Qaida. The United States delivered an ultimatum to the Taliban to hand over Bin Laden and shut down all al-Qaida camps or face attack. There was some discussion in the administration of acting against Iraq, but it was quickly dropped. Instead, plans began for a ground invasion of Afghanistan and the formation of a coalition of countries to fight terror wherever it occurred.

On September 20, Bush addressed the country before a joint session of Congress and accused al-Qaida not only of the September 11 attacks but also of the attacks on the U.S. embassies in 1998 and on the USS *Cole* in 2000. Asserting that a U.S. goal was to attack terrorists everywhere, as well as their supporters, he declared, "The Taliban must act, and act immediately . . . to hand over the terrorists, or they will share in their fate." He added, "Every nation, in every region, now has a decision to make: either you are with us, or you are with the terrorists."

In the following days, the military completed a plan for attacking Afghanistan codenamed Operation Enduring Freedom. U.S. forces moved into the region, including Uzbekistan and Pakistan, which border Afghanistan. On October 7, the next phase of the operation began, involving CIA and Special Forces working with Afghan opposition groups to strike at key Taliban and al-Qaida targets. A few weeks later, more intensive operations got under way, including the use of ground troops alongside Afghan opposition militias. The city of Mazar-i Sharif in northern Afghanistan was cap-tured on November 7, and the Taliban evacuated the capital, Kabul, four days later. By early December, all of Afghanistan's major cities had fallen, and on December 22, Hamid Karzai, a Pashtuni leader from Kandahar and former deputy foreign minister, was installed as the chairman of an interim administration for the country.

Efforts to find and eliminate remaining pockets of al-Qaida continued. In December, the United States used Afghan allies to fight al-Qaida forces in the Tora Bora cave complex. Muhammad Atif, al-Qaida's military commander and principal planner of the September 11 attacks, was killed in an air strike. In March 2002, a three-week battle raged with al-Qaida fighters in the mountainous Shah-i Kot region. As a result of the fighting, remaining al-Qaida members fled to the border region with Pakistan and across the border into adjacent tribal areas. Among those fleeing were the principal leaders, Osama bin Laden and Ayman al-Zawahiri, who remained at large through mid-2005 and periodically issued videos and audio recordings from their hiding places, threatening their enemies and exhorting their sympathizers to carry on the fight.

This phase of the Bush administration's "war on terror" had two prominent consequences: the establishment of a new government in Afghanistan and the capture of numerous non-Afghans accused of membership in or having connections to al-Qaida. Karzai, after heading the interim administration, was elected president of Afghanistan on October 9, 2004. The government's direct control of Afghan territory was limited largely to the areas around Kabul and Kandahar in the south, while the tribal leaders who had opposed the Taliban and cooperated with the United States operated mostly autonomously elsewhere in the country. Elements of the Taliban also remained active. U.S. forces are still stationed in Afghanistan and have been joined by a NATO peacekeeping force, the International Security Assistance Force (ISAF). In April 2005, President Karzai stated that his government would like to establish a formal security arrangement with the United States that would include permanent U.S. military bases.

The United States denied prisoner-of-war status to the approximately 700 captives from the Afghan campaign, choosing instead to declare them "enemy combatants," and transport them to a U.S. military base at Guantanamo Bay, Cuba, while holding others at Bagram Air Base in Afghanistan and on Diego Garcia Island in the Indian Ocean. Nearly a quarter of the detainees were believed to be Saudi. U.S. authorities interrogated the men in secret, without access to attorneys and the possibility of trial in special military tribunals. Some were "rendered," or transferred informally, to allied countries for further interrogation. On Guantanamo, the United States held them in a specially built prison known as Camp Delta, which replaced a wire-cage setup known as Camp X-Ray. By early 2005, none of the detainees had been convicted of an offense; a few had been released to their home countries, including Britain, France, Kuwait, and Saudi Arabia.

The revelation in April 2004 that American soldiers had abused prisoners in the Abu Ghraib prison in Baghdad redirected the spotlight onto the situation of the Guantanamo prisoners. In subsequent months, it came to light that some of the severe interrogation techniques used in Iraq had been practiced on prisoners at Guantanamo and in Afghanistan. Most of the prisoners at Abu Ghraib and Camp Bucca prisons in Iraq were suspected of criminal activity, not terrorism.

Criticism of the Bush administration's detention practices was initially most vocal in the human rights and legal communities, which charged it with denying prisoners basic human and civil rights and acting in violation of the Geneva Conventions, of which the United States is a signatory. With the revelation of abuses at the various detention facilities, the chorus of criticism broadened. In mid-2005, several members of Congress opened debate on whether it was time to close Guantanamo because of the harm it had done and likely will continue to do to the image of the United States abroad and its role, alleged by some, in contributing to anti-American sentiment.

The Neo-Conservatives and Iraq. Among the political appointees in the Bush administration were a number of so-called neo-conservatives, or "neo-cons." Many of the original neo-cons had once been liberals, but then decided to leave the Democratic Party in the 1960s. They differed from traditional conservatives in promoting an activist agenda for social change in such areas as welfare reform and ending affirmative action. More recent neo-cons are more likely to be Republicans advocating a foreign policy employing the aggressive use of force to defend and expand U.S. national interests and reshape the world to the United States' benefit. In a unipolar world, this means that alliances are less important than the application of force and power. Neo-cons view international institutions, such as the United Nations, with suspicion, because they put limits on U.S. action. They also defend the use of U.S. power to advance the spread of democracy throughout the world, and in the Middle East in particular.

Bush administration neo-cons were concentrated in the Pentagon, which assumed a more central and broader role in U.S. foreign policy than in any previous administration. The neo-con ranks were generally said to include Deputy Secretary of Defense Paul Wolfowitz, Undersecretary of Defense for Policy Douglas Feith, the head of the Defense Advisory Board Richard Perle, and Lewis "Scooter" Libby, chief of staff to Vice President Richard Cheney. Another neo-con, Elliott Abrams, was subsequently given the Middle East desk on the National Security Council. Although not regarded as neo-cons, Cheney, Secretary of Defense Donald Rumsfeld, and Undersecretary of State for Arms Control and International Security John Bolton agreed with many of the same views. In 1992, during Cheney's tenure as secretary of defense, Wolfowitz and Libby drafted a Defense Planning Guidance that advocated a strategy of preemptive attacks and a rise in defense spending to make the U.S. unchallengeable.

In the Bush administration, Secretary of State Colin Powell and his deputy, Richard Armitage, provided an unequal balance as the realists, holding that U.S. interests were best served by coordination with allies and friends and that military power should be used only when necessary to defend vital U.S. interests. National Security Adviser Condoleezza Rice was characterized as a pragmatist who saw her job as relaying information to the president and arbitrating differences of opinion.

The neo-con influence on Middle Eastern affairs dates back to a 1996 advisory paper for Israeli prime minister Benjamin Netanyahu in 1996 written by Perle and Feith. The paper, "A Clean Break: A New Strategy for Securing the Realm," called for rejection of the Oslo process and advocated a U.S.-Israeli condominium for dominating the Middle East through their combined military power. At the top of the list sat the removal of Saddam Hussein. Even before George W. Bush first took office, the neo-cons were arguing that the first priority of the United States in the Middle East should be removing Saddam Hussein. After the inauguration, the administration chose to leave Israeli-Palestinian matters on the back burner and turn its attention to the possibility of regime change in Iraq, arguing that the disappearance of Hussein's regime would make the Palestinians more malleable at the negotiating table.

After the attacks of September 11, the advice of the neo-cons was translated into U.S. policy. Planning began for a war on Iraq in addition to the campaign in Afghanistan. Wolfowitz became a principal architect of the Iraq War. After months of hinting at military action and a failed attempt to secure a UN Security Council resolution authorizing action against Iraq, the United States and its allies (principally Britain) launched an attack on Iraq on March 19, 2003. It took only a few weeks to topple Hussein's Baathist regime, but the chaos and determined resistance to the U.S. presence soon ended any ideas of a quick withdrawal. Instead, the United States was forced to maintain more than 100,000 troops in Iraq while creating a civilian authority to administer the country and eventually transfer sovereignty to Iraqis. The Department of Defense handled postwar Iraq policy and planning for the administration, while extensive planning by the Department of State for postwar reconstruction went ignored. Following the war, the influence of the neo-cons could be seen also in the sharp words the administration aimed at Syria and talk of striking Iranian nuclear facilities.

Iraq: Exit Strategy.   With the seemingly inexorable cost of the U.S. presence in Iraq, in terms of casualties and financial drain, many people began to raise the question of an exit strategy. Some commentators called for an immediate exit, contending that the occupation was doomed to failure, that the absence of weapons of mass destruction proved the invasion to have been a mistake, and that Americans and Iraqis would benefit from U.S. withdrawal. Some estimated that the United States would be obliged to remain in Iraq for at least ten years. The Bush administration steered clear of providing a timetable but continued to pledge that U.S. forces would remain as long as they were needed. In the meantime, the heavy demands of the deployment produced considerable strain on U.S. military capabilities overall. Military personnel were kept in uniform beyond their enlistment periods and increasing numbers of National Guardsmen and Ready Reserves were called up to help share the burden on extended and repeat tours of duty to Iraq and Afghanistan. By June 2005, more than 1,700 U.S. military personnel had lost their lives in Iraq and more than 12,000 had been wounded.

On the military side, the United States managed to persuade twenty-nine nations to contribute 28,000 personnel to Iraq after major conflict. A year after the war, eleven of these countries had withdrawn all or most of their troops. Spain withdrew its troops in the aftermath of the al-Qaida-inspired Madrid bombing in May 2004, and Italy already had indicated that it would reduce its numbers before the accidental U.S. shooting in March 2005 of an Italian journalist just freed from her kidnappers. The Netherlands, Poland, and Ukraine also began withdrawing troops in 2005. *(See the box "Military Contributions of Select Countries for the 2003 Iraq War and Postwar Presence," p. 161.)*

The Bush administration made some effort after the war to reach out to countries that had opposed the war, such as France, Germany, and Russia. At the United Nations, the administration supported UN Security Council Resolution 1483 (May 6, 2003), providing for a UN special representative to coordinate activities of UN personnel in Iraq and calling on nations to contribute forces to provide security. Resolution 1500 (August 13, 2003) legitimized the establishment of the Interim Governing Council, while Resolution 1511 (October 16, 2003) authorized a "multinational force under unified command," that is, U.S. command. This did not encourage countries to volunteer troops, because they still retained perceptions of a U.S. monopoly on decision making. NATO provided training for Iraqi security forces and logistical support but shied away from sending peacekeeping troops because of opposition from some of its European members.

Relations with Saudi Arabia. Saudi Arabia has been one of the United States' closest allies in the Arab world for more than sixty years. Since British withdrawal from the Gulf in 1971, and particularly since the emergence of the Islamic Republic of Iran in 1979, Washington's security support and extensive armaments and training provided to the kingdom have been the focal point of its Gulf security architecture. A major reason why the United States went to war with Iraq in 1991 was to prevent an Iraqi invasion of Saudi Arabia's massive oilfields. Although oil is the strongest link between the two countries—Saudi Arabia is the world's largest oil exporter, intermittently the largest source of U.S. crude oil imports, and the most powerful voice in the Organization of Petroleum Exporting Countries—the United States has relied upon Saudi political assistance in the Arab world, played a leading role in Saudi development, been one of the kingdom's principal trading partners, and host to thousands of Saudi students.

There have always been strains in the relationship, however. To Saudi frustration, U.S. ties to Israel have always taken precedence. U.S. popular opinion of Saudi Arabia has been largely negative because of its strict segregation of women, human rights abuses, and perceptions of "rich oil shaykhs" gouging the American consumer. September 11 multiplied these strains. Not only was Osama bin Laden of Saudi origin, but so were fifteen of the nineteen hijackers. Furthermore, it was alleged that prominent Saudis had provided funding to al-Qaida, whether knowingly or not, that the kingdom had promoted its austere Wahhabi version of Islam in Muslim communities around the world, and that its textbooks had preached hatred of non-Muslims.

Saudi Arabia's leaders also faced strong domestic opposition to its close relationship with the United States. Since the Persian Gulf War of 1991, Saudi Arabia had provided military facilities and basing for U.S. troops and operations in the region. As Islamist pressure grew, most people in the Gulf objected to U.S. support for Israel, and Washington increasingly seemed likely to launch an attack on Saddam Hussein, the presence of U.S. forces in the kingdom became increasingly problematic. Even bin Laden railed against the presence of "infidel" soldiers in the homeland of Islam. As a consequence, the United States situated the regional headquarters of the U.S. Central Command—which includes the Middle East and Central Asia in its sphere of responsibility—at al-Udayd in Qatar prior to the Iraq War. Washington also shifted its center of air operations for the Middle East from Prince Sultan Air Base near Riyadh to al-Udayd in late April 2003. Despite their problems, the Saudi and U.S. governments remained committed to continued cooperation. There is some concern that frequent attacks from the local al-Qaida organization might challenge the survival of the regime.

Outlook

The start of the second term of the Bush administration recorded significant personnel changes. Colin Powell resigned as secretary of state and was replaced by national security adviser Condoleezza Rice. Stephen Hadley, Rice's former deputy on the National Security Council, replaced

Arms Transfers

In recent years, the United States has been the largest seller of arms in the world. During the period 2000–2003, it had $35.8 billion in arms transfer agreements with developing countries, the largest market for international arms transfers. This amount represented 46.8 percent of all such agreements. Russia ranked second during the same period, with more than $21 billion (27.5 percent of the total) in agreements.

The Middle East had long been the largest recipient of arms in the developing world, accounting for $34.1 billion (44 percent) in arms transfer agreements during 1996–1999. During 2000–2003, however, it ranked second, behind Asia, with $24.6 billion (37 percent) in agreements. Given the close political and security ties between the United States and the Gulf Cooperation Council states, it is not surprising that U.S. sales accounted for an overwhelming 75.6 percent ($18.6 billion) of arms agreements in the Middle East during 2000–2003. Russian sales accounted for 8.1 percent ($2 billion).

During the period 1996–2003, France's 12.6 percent ($7.4 billion) in arms transfers was second to the United States', which led the market with 59.5 percent ($34.9 billion). The downturn in total arms transfer agreements to the Middle East from $34.1 billion during 1996–1999 to $24.6 billion during 2000–2003 reflected the final phases and deliveries of arms ordered in the aftermath of the 1991 Persian Gulf War, as well as budgetary crises in many of the Gulf states caused by low oil prices.

Significant agreements signed by the United States in 2003 with Middle Eastern countries included a co-production program with Egypt involving 125 M1A1 Abrams Main Battle Tank kits for $790 million; a number of light infantry vehicles (LAWS) with Saudi Arabia for $316 million; an AH-64D Apache Longbow helicopter with Israel; two Reconnaissance Systems with Oman; and six C-130E aircraft with Pakistan.

During the period 1996–2003, the United Arab Emirates (UAE) concluded $15.7 billion in arms transfer agreements totaling 10.4 percent of the value of all developing world agreements. China ranked first for the period 2000–2003, dropping the UAE to second place. Arms transfer agreements for the Gulf states during 2000–2003 were $400 million for Bahrain, $500 million for Iran, $200 million for Iraq, $2.2 billion for Kuwait, $1.2 billion for Oman, none for Qatar, $3.4 billion for Saudi Arabia, and $8.1 billion for the UAE. Saudi Arabia ranked seventh among developing world countries, and Kuwait ranked tenth.

During 2000–2003, Saudi Arabia received $23.9 billion in arms deliveries ($16.6 billion from Britain, France, Germany, and Italy; $6.3 billion from the United States; and $1 billion from other sources); Egypt received $5.4 billion in deliveries ($4.8 billion from the United States); Israel received $3.2 billion ($2.9 billion from the United States); the UAE received $2.6 billion ($1.9 billion from Britain, France, Germany, and Italy); Kuwait received $2.1 billion ($1.1 billion from the United States); and Iran received $600 million ($200 million from Russia). The value of U.S. arms deliveries to Saudi Arabia was considerably less than they had been for the period 1996–1999, when they totaled $16.6 billion. Arms deliveries to Saudi Arabia during 1996–2003 constituted 32.4 percent of the developing world's total.

Note: All figures in 2004 U.S. dollars.

Source: Richard F. Grimmett, "Conventional Arms Transfers to Developing Nations, 1996–2003," U.S. Library of Congress, Congressional Research Service, Report RL32547, August 26, 2004.

her at NSC. John Negroponte, the U.S. ambassador to Iraq who had replaced CPA administrator Paul Bremer, was recalled to Washington to assume the new position of director of national intelligence. Zalmay Khalilzad, a naturalized Afghan who had been serving as ambassador to Afghanistan, was named to replace Negroponte. Bush nominated Paul Wolfowitz as head of the World Bank and John Bolton as U.S. ambassador to the United Nations.

Little change was expected in U.S. Middle East policy. The United States remained committed to the peace process and to continued strong support for Israel. In early 2005, the Bush administration began speaking openly about the establishment of a Palestinian state while chiding Israel about its settlement policy. There were indications that the Bush administration might assume a more active role in the negotiating process.

States of Concern. Two years after the Iraq War, the insurgency raged on, tying down more than 100,000 U.S. troops and draining the U.S. Treasury of billions of dollars every month. Despite growing public concern over mounting American deaths, many observers were of the opinion that a U.S. presence would be required in Iraq for as long as a decade. The United States and Iran remained at loggerheads: the U.S. continued to impose trade sanctions on Iran and grow increasingly concerned over signs that Iran was seeking to build nuclear weapons.

Syria represents another regional concern. After lauding Syria for its cooperation in the "war on terror," following the end of the Iraq War the Bush administration charged Syria with providing refuge for former Iraqi officials and failing to take adequate steps to prevent the infiltration of Islamist insurgents into Iraq. Matters reached a head when former Lebanese prime minister Rafiq al-Hariri was assassinated in Beirut on February 14, 2005. The United States accused Syria of being behind the assassination and welcomed the large Lebanese demonstrations demanding that Syria evacuate its military and intelligence contingents from Lebanon, where they remained although the Lebanese civil war had been brought to an end more than a decade prior. Under mounting international and Lebanese pressure, Syria, to great surprise, subsequently withdrew the last of its troops in April 2005, though it is suspected that elements of its intelligence apparatus remained. The Bush administration continued to put pressure on Damascus concerning its border with Iraq and over Lebanon after its withdrawal. In spring 2005, the two countries had cut military and intelligence cooperation, with relations having reached the low level of "diplomatic contact."

The United States has long been concerned about Mu'ammar al-Qadhafi's government in Libya. Its apprehensions centered on Libya's ties to radical Palestinian groups and the Irish Republican Army and its support of terrorist activities—most notably its apparent orchestration of the bombing of a Pan Am Flight 103 over Lockerbie, Scotland. The George W. Bush administration opposed Libya's efforts to acquire weapons of mass destruction, and on December 19, 2003, following a long period of negotiations with Britain and the United States, Libya announced its intention to terminate all such efforts.

Military Presence in the Region. There were few signs that the United States intended to reduce its large military presence in the Persian Gulf region in the near future. While the level of troops might be gradually reduced in Iraq as security improves there, such a measure remained outside the realm of possibility in mid-2005, and the question of permanent U.S. bases in Iraq remained a matter of conjecture. An arrangement for the long-term U.S. use of Iraqi military facilities was hinted at for several years after the Iraq War. The nature of such an arrangement, however, would depend on termination of the postwar insurgency and negotiations with a permanent Iraqi government.

The U.S. military established the regional command center for the U.S. Central Command in Qatar prior to the Iraq War, and the United States continued to make use of al-Udayd base and another Qatari base at al-Sayliyah. It also maintained a sizeable military presence in Kuwait, particularly as Kuwait provided the gateway to move personnel, equipment, and supplies into Iraq. The U.S. Navy's Fifth Fleet is based out of Bahrain and use is made of facilities and prepositioned equipment in Saudi Arabia, the United Arab Emirates, and Oman. There were also signs that a return to use of Yemeni facilities might be a possibility.

War on Terror. The September 11 attacks abruptly forced the Bush administration to refocus much of its attention from domestic matters to foreign policy. Bush set the tone of his new foreign policy when he declared a global "war on terror" and urged allies and the "civilized world" to join in the campaign, warning that those who were not with the United States on this matter would be regarded as against it.

The "National Security Strategy of the United States of America" released on September 17, 2002, articulates the Bush administration's view of the world and the role it wants the United States to play in it. This document promises that the United States will "champion aspirations for human dignity; strengthen alliances to defeat global terrorism and work to prevent attacks against us and our friends; work with others to defuse regional conflicts; prevent our enemies from threatening us, our allies, and our friends, with weapons of mass destruction; ignite a new era of global economic growth through free markets and free trade; expand the circle of development by opening societies and building the infrastructure of democracy; develop agendas for cooperative action with other main centers of global power; and transform the United States' national security institutions to meet the challenges and opportunities of the twenty-first century."

Perhaps the most controversial aspect of the policy statement was the emphasis on the right to preemptive action. Noting that deterrence had been an effective defense against the use of weapons of mass destruction during the cold war, the document contended that the risk it now confronted was rogue states and terrorists who saw weapons of mass destruction as weapons of choice. Therefore,

To forestall or prevent such hostile acts by our adversaries, the United States will, if necessary, act preemptively. The United States will not use force in all cases to preempt emerging threats, nor should nations use preemption as a pretext for aggression. Yet in an age where the enemies of civilization openly and actively seek the world's most destructive technologies, the United States cannot remain idle while dangers gather.

It also declared, "While the United States will constantly strive to enlist the support of the international community, we will not hesitate to act alone, if necessary, to exercise our right of self-defense by acting preemptively against . . . terrorists, to prevent them from doing harm against our people and our country." This strategy underpinned U.S. policy toward Iraq and the decision to go to war despite widespread opposition. It also seemed to rest behind the administration's stream of strong words to Syria and Iran regarding those countries' support for Iraqi factions and Iran's pursuit of a nuclear weapons capability.

Democratization. The Bush administration took office asserting that one of its principal goals in the Middle East was to advance the prospects for democracy. The overthrow of Saddam Hussein and the introduction of a democratic government in Iraq was to be the opening move in regional transformation. While previous U.S. administrations had proclaimed democratization as a goal, the Bush administration was willing to use military means and threats to force reluctant regimes to reform.

The administration created the Middle East Partnership Initiative to fund programs that advanced change and then launched the Broader Middle East and North Africa Initiative to establish a forum for discussing and advocating democratic reforms. Arab governments resisted U.S. pressure as interference, and Arab intellectuals expressed their concerns that too rapid change as advocated by the United States would destabilize societies and lead to chaos. Critics of the administration pointed out that the United States was urging change and reform on those governments it did not like while maintaining close ties with repressive governments, such as Saudi Arabia and Pakistan, that were vital to the U.S. economy and regional security concerns.

Another major obstacle to the success of the United States as a force for positive change in the Middle East was the widespread hostility of most of the region's peoples toward it. The 2003 war against Iraq aroused strong opposition in most of the world, especially in Arab nations. A public opinion poll in six Arab states friendly to the United States registered that only 4 to 13 percent of respondents had a favorable opinion of the United States. Arab satellite television channels, including al-Jazeera (Qatar), al-Arabiya (UAE), and Abu Dhabi Television, regularly broadcast news and video of the violence in Iraq, the Abu Ghraib abuses, and Israeli actions against the Palestinians, which many Arabs believe has received the approval of the United States. Large numbers of Iraqis indicated that while they were glad to see the overthrow of Saddam Hussein, they were less than happy with the United States as an occupier of their country. Rather than seeing the United States as an agent of democratization in the region, many Middle Easterners see it as an intruder with its own agenda and a negative foreign policy.

CHAPTER **4**

THE PERSIAN GULF

The Persian Gulf is a strategically important body of water, around which and beneath is located about two-thirds of the world's oil deposits. It is fed by the two great rivers of antiquity—the Euphrates and the Tigris—and empties into the Arabian Sea through the Strait of Hormuz. Bahrain, Iran, Iraq, Kuwait, Oman, Qatar, Saudi Arabia, and the United Arab Emirates ring the Gulf with a combined population of more than 130 million people. Iran, the only non-Arab country on the Gulf, has more than 68 million people—more than all of its Gulf neighbors combined.

The Gulf nations are the primary source of oil for much of the world, producing millions of barrels each day. Much of the petroleum is loaded onto supertankers at vast terminals in the Gulf before being carried to the Indian Ocean through the narrow Strait of Hormuz. Although recent efforts throughout the region to build pipelines have reduced the Gulf nations' dependence on tanker shipments through the strait, the threat of disruption to the region's oil flow—from wars and other forms of unrest—remains an international and local concern.

The 1973 Saudi-led Arab oil embargo revealed how much a disruption of Persian Gulf oil could affect the world's economy. The embargo, a response to the Arab-Israeli war that year, halted oil shipments from most Gulf states to the United States and reduced supplies to much of the rest of the world, contributing significantly to a worldwide recession. Petroleum prices skyrocketed from less than $3 a barrel in early 1973 to about $11 a barrel in 1974. *(See Middle Eastern Oil and Gas, Chapter 5, p. 179)*

Another spurt in prices began in 1979 and again rocked the world's economy. Three events that year raised fears in Washington and the capitals of other major industrialized nations that the Persian Gulf oil supply was vulnerable to disruption. In February, Iranian revolutionaries deposed the shah and established an Islamist republic under the leadership of Ayatollah Ruhollah Khomeini. Later, in November, Iranian students seized the U.S. embassy in Tehran and took American diplomats hostage, confirming the hostility of the new government toward the West, the United States in particular. In December, the Soviet Union launched an invasion of nearby Afghanistan to prop up the pro-Soviet government there.

Although most analysts discounted the possibility of a Soviet military move beyond Afghanistan, the Soviet invasion and the upheaval in Iran prompted President Jimmy Carter to declare in his State of the Union address on January 23, 1980, "[A]n attempt by any outside force to gain control of the Persian Gulf region will be regarded as an assault on the vital interests of the United States of America, and such an assault will be repelled by any means necessary, including military force." The statement, which came to be known as the Carter Doctrine, reinforced perceptions that events in the Persian Gulf region were of vital importance to the United States and the rest of the world.

Whereas the 1970s demonstrated the significance of the Gulf region, the 1980s and 1990s underscored its vulnerability. In September 1980, Iraq launched a military offensive against Iran

that turned into an eight-year war of attrition. The Iran-Iraq War left hundreds of thousands dead, disrupted oil tanker traffic in the Gulf, and led the United States to provide naval escorts for oil tankers using Kuwaiti ports. In the mid-1980s, plummeting oil prices severely damaged the economies of the Gulf states, all of which depended to some degree on oil.

Despite these shocks, the Gulf states and their governments survived. The Iran-Iraq War ended in a stalemate in 1988. The revolutionary fervor associated with Iran did not lead to the overthrow of any Gulf government, the Soviets began withdrawing from Afghanistan in 1988, and oil prices recovered in the late 1980s as world oil consumption began to increase. Peace in the region, however, remained elusive. On August 2, 1990, Iraq invaded and occupied Kuwait, setting in motion an international crisis that ended only when Iraq suffered a military

In 2003 the United States led a coalition of forces in toppling Saddam Hussein's Baathist regime in Iraq and establishing control over the country. The ease with which the coalition forces won the war was followed, however, by years of insurgency and suicide attacks that resulted in many thousands of civilian and military deaths. The election of an interim Iraqi government in January 2005 marked only a middle point in the transition to a new era for Iraq.

With the downfall of the Baathist regime and resultant domestic chaos in Iraq, Iran is viewed by many in Washington as the principal threat to security in the Persian Gulf region. With its large population, proximity to the narrow Strait of Hormuz, and past inclination to support antigovernment activities abroad, Iran has the capacity to destabilize governments. A new leadership in the late 1990s hinted that Iran might improve its relations with the West. Moderate cleric Mohammad Khatami, elected president of Iran in May 1997, worked to reestablish relations with European and Gulf states that had withered during the cloistered twenty years of conservative rule following the Islamic revolution of 1979.

By the end of the decade, however, the thaw had not extended to relations with the U.S. government; the U.S. State Department continued to declare Iran a sponsor of terrorism. Prospects for further moderation in Iranian domestic and foreign policy grew dim with the inability of Khatami, even after a second term in office, to diminish the power of clerical hard-liners in Tehran. In 2002 the George W. Bush administration declared Iran, along with Iraq and North Korea, a member of an "axis of evil" and charged Tehran with seeking to acquire a nuclear weapons capability.

Some observers despair whether the Persian Gulf region will witness a stable peace. Ethnic conflicts, volatile personalities, territorial disputes, longstanding enmities, and the high financial stakes associated with oil wealth seem to ensure that the Gulf will remain an international hot spot. In the early 2000s the government of Saudi Arabia battled homegrown Islamic extremists, while across its border, the Iraqi insurgency gained strength. Such a view, however, overlooks the continued prosperity and development in six of the Gulf's eight littoral states.

Yet some positive developments have emerged from the war-torn years of the last several decades. The attention focused on the nuclear weapons programs in the region has made it more difficult for nations there to build a nuclear capacity. The collapse of the Soviet Union removed a potential threat to the security of the Gulf region, and movement in the Arab-Israeli peace process seemed to begin to diminish the usefulness of anti-Israeli sentiment as a rallying point for political ideologies.

The Iran-Iraq Rivalry

The disputes that led to the Iran-Iraq War in 1980 are rooted in historic, territorial, and ideological differences. Some analysts trace their enmity to the sixteenth century, when the Ottoman Sunni–Persian Shiite struggles began. Others assert that it began even earlier, in the seventh century, with the Arab invasion of Persia and the Persians' subsequent defeat at Qadissiya.

Origins of Conflict

Despite the longstanding rivalry between Iran and Iraq, their relations during the late 1970s seemed to be improving. Then, the Iranian Revolution in 1979, overthrowing Shah Mohammad Reza Pahlavi, reopened two historically contentious issues that eventually led to war: which country would control the Shatt al-Arab waterway (the 120-mile confluence of the Tigris and Euphrates Rivers that discharges into the Gulf) and how much influence each country would exercise over the Persian Gulf region in general and the minorities in each other's country.

In the early 1970s, Iran's support of the Iraqi Kurds' fight for independence from the Iraqi government complicated relations. The Kurds, who make up 20 percent of Iraq's population and predominate in the isolated mountains of the north, obtained arms from Iran and asylum when necessary. Iraq, in turn, backed religious and secular opponents of the Iranian shah and gave financial and military assistance to Iran's Arab, Baluchi, and Kurdish secessionist movements. Iranian-Iraqi relations reached a low point in 1974, when Iran, with U.S. and Israeli encouragement, began to increase aid to Iraq's Kurds. The combination of border clashes and support for rebel and dissident groups in each other's country brought Iran and Iraq close to open warfare.

By March 1975, however, tensions had begun to ease. Iraq believed it was imperative to avoid a full-scale war with Iran and to attempt to consolidate domestic power by putting an end to Iranian subversive activities. To accomplish these objectives, the shah of Iran and Saddam Hussein (then vice president of the Revolutionary Command Council) met at a session of the Organization of Petroleum Exporting Countries (OPEC) in Algiers. Assisted by the mediation efforts of the president of Algeria, the two leaders issued a joint communique on March 6, 1975, reaffirming the 1913 Constantinople Protocol land boundaries but defining the thalweg line as the new frontier on the Shatt al-Arab. (A thalweg line is the middle of the main navigable channel of a waterway that serves as a boundary between states.) Iran and Iraq signed a treaty on June 13, 1975, with three additional protocols on international borders and good neighborly relations. Each party also agreed to refrain from assisting insurgents in the other's country.

The Algiers treaty ushered in a period of friendly relations welcomed by Iran, Iraq, and neighboring Saudi Arabia, but Iraq was scorned by some of the more radical Arab states—Syria and South Yemen—for relinquishing Arab territory, and, in Iraq itself, the treaty conflicted with the Arab nationalist ideology of the Baath Party. In retrospect, it is clear that Iraqi leaders had no intention of accepting the agreement indefinitely, as they argued it had been made under duress. When Iraq became strong enough, it planned to reassert its authority over the Shatt al-Arab.

Relations between Iraq and the shah's regime remained stable throughout the late 1970s. In July 1977, the two states signed six bilateral agreements covering trade, cultural relations, agriculture and fishing, railway linkages, freedom of movement for Iranians visiting Shiite Muslim holy places in Iraq, and coordination of activities concerning the movement of "subversive elements." In October 1978, the Iraqi government complied with the shah's request to evict Ayatollah Khomeini from Najaf, where he had been in exile since 1964, when he was forced to leave Iran.

Post-Iranian Revolution

The Iraqi government initially welcomed the Iranian Revolution of February 1979. Iran broke unofficial relations with Israel, left the Western-dominated Central Treaty Organization, and announced that it would no longer police the Gulf. Iraq, favoring these changes, hoped the new government in Tehran would turn inward and address domestic concerns, leaving the Gulf open to Iraqi influence.

By mid-1979, Iranian-Iraqi relations had changed dramatically. Iranian clerics had renewed Iran's claims to Bahrain and urged Shiite communities in the Gulf to rebel against their ruling regimes. Shiites demonstrated in Bahrain, Kuwait, and Saudi Arabia. In Iraq, dozens of Shiites were reportedly arrested in Najaf for planning demonstrations; several were executed. In response, Saddam warned Iran, "Iraq's capabilities can be used against any side which tries to violate the sovereignty of Kuwait or Bahrain or harm their people or land." In October, Iraq broke diplomatic relations with Iran, branding the revolution as "non-Islamic."

In April 1980, several incidents further chilled the environment. On April 1, an Iranian threw a hand grenade at Iraqi deputy premier Tariq Aziz, wounding him. On April 6, Iraq cabled the United Nations to demand that Iran withdraw from the disputed islands of Abu Musa and the Greater and Lesser Tunbs. In response, Iran placed its border troops on alert. Harsh verbal attacks followed. Khomeini called on the people of Iraq to bring down their government: "Wake up and topple this corrupt regime in your Islamic country before it is too late." Saddam responded: "Anyone who tries to put his hand on Iraq will have his hand cut off." An attack on the Iranian embassy in London by Arabs from the Iranian province of Khuzistan was widely believed to have been instigated by Iraq.

The confrontation between Iran and Iraq had now gone far beyond a dispute over the river boundary of the Shatt al-Arab. The pan-Islamic ideology of the Khomeini revolution to unite all Muslims, despite ethnic or cultural divisions, directly opposed the pan-Arab ideology of the Baathist government in Baghdad. Despite the absence of a significant upheaval among Iraq's Shiites, the presence of a hostile Iranian government preaching a radical Islam and aggressively challenging Iraqi interests in the Persian Gulf disconcerted the regime in Baghdad. Even if Iran did not pose an immediate danger, its large population—about three times the size of Iraq's—made it a significant long-term military threat, and its revolutionary activities and intransigence on territorial issues ran counter to Iraq's regional ambitions. Given these considerations, Iraq began preparing for war in the summer of 1980.

The Iran-Iraq War, 1980–1988

For eight years the Iran-Iraq War threatened the stability and security of the Persian Gulf region. The conflict, which began in 1980, turned into the longest war in recent Middle Eastern history. An estimated 1 million people died in it, and its cost ran into the hundreds of billions of dollars.

Each adversary possessed distinct advantages. Iraq had a more advanced arsenal of weaponry and about five times as many combat aircraft as Iran. Iran, isolated internationally, found it difficult to purchase advanced weapons and spare parts for its prewar arsenal. Iraq also enjoyed the support of most of the Arab world, including Saudi Arabia and Kuwait, which underwrote the Iraqi war effort with assistance totaling billions of dollars. By contrast, Iran's supporters in the Middle East were limited to Algeria, Libya, and

Syria. Iran, however, had more people and greater territorial depth to aid in defensive efforts. In addition, many of the country's young fighters viewed the war as a religious crusade and generally were more motivated than Iraqi troops through much of the war.

Neither side, however, was able to translate its advantages into victory. Iran accepted a UN ceasefire after Iraq made battlefield gains in 1988, and the war came to an end with both combatants in possession of about the same amount of territory with which they had started. Yet the war devastated both societies and produced some of the most brutal tactics of the twentieth century, including rocket attacks on city centers, "human wave" assaults against fortified positions, and the use of chemical weapons.

Iraq Attacks

In mid-1980, with Iran's central authority apparently disintegrating, Iraq saw an ideal opportunity to end Iranian interference in the Gulf and to turn the clock back to the favorable border situation it had enjoyed until 1975. On September 17, amid escalating border clashes, Iraq terminated the 1975 treaty and claimed exclusive sovereignty over the entire Shatt al-Arab. September 22 saw Iraqi forces push across the Iranian border east of Baghdad. Other Iraqi troops crossed the Shatt al-Arab and attacked key cities and oil installations in the province of Khuzistan (also called *Arabistan* and claimed by Iraq because most of its people are Arab and Sunni). Iraq's strategy was to destroy Iran's oil sources, refineries, and transportation routes and thus debilitate the Iranian regime. Within a month, Iraq occupied an area within Khuzistan of almost 3,500 square miles. Meanwhile, Iranian jets knocked out the principal Iraqi oil installations at Kirkuk and Baghdad.

The Tide Turns

Despite initial success on the battlefield, Iraq failed to achieve its ultimate objective: the fall of Khomeini's regime. In fact, the war seemed to create a surge of Iranian patriotism; it was an issue around which the government could rally nationalist and religious fervor. It also gave the Khomeini government an excuse to suppress dissent.

By November, the Iranians had stopped the enemy offensive and were engaging the Iraqis in a war of attrition inside Iran. In the face of high casualties, the Iraqi government expressed its willingness to negotiate, provided Iran acknowledge Iraq's sovereignty over the Shatt al-Arab and pledge nonintervention in Iraq's affairs. Iran, however, rejected international appeals for mediation. Khomeini stated repeatedly that Iran would fight the war until it was won. His goal, he said, was "to establish an Islamic government in Iraq and to destroy the Iraqi regime in the same way as we destroyed the shah." In late summer 1981, Iranian forces launched heavy counterattacks designed to drive the Iraqis from Iranian territory. By April 1982, Iranian forces had recaptured the Khuzistan cities of Abadan, Dezful, and Khorramshahr. The Iraqi government decided to withdraw from the remaining Iranian territories under its control.

Iran now planned to cut off southern Iraq from Baghdad, thereby splitting Iraqi forces and creating conditions under which the large Iraqi Shiite population in the south could be induced to unite with Iran. In July 1982, Iranian troops entered Iraqi territory near Basra, just across the Shatt al-Arab. Iraqi resistance stiffened, however, and blunted the Iranian offensive.

In the fall, Iran continued attacks in the territory east of Baghdad and penetrated three miles into Iraqi territory. A large-scale Iranian offensive continued into the winter and spring of 1983. The apparent goal was to cut off Basra, Iraq's second largest city and its main port on the Gulf. An Iranian offensive in February 1983, described as the "decisive and last," failed. Of the some hundred thousand Iranian soldiers involved—many of whom attacked Iraqi lines in human waves—thousands were killed or wounded. Another major offensive, in April, netted Iran about twelve miles of Iraqi territory after bloody hand-to-hand fighting. Throughout

the fighting, Iraq's Shiite population generally remained loyal to the regime of Saddam Hussein.

During summer 1983, Iraq embarked on a deliberate plan to internationalize the war, and to a degree it succeeded. The French sold Iraq Exocet missiles, and the Soviets increased arms sales to Baghdad. Member states of the Gulf Cooperation Council (GCC), especially Kuwait and Saudi Arabia, increased their financial support of Iraq. Meanwhile, the United Nations passed resolutions that were tougher on the Iranians than on the Iraqis. Iraq's success stemmed primarily from a worldwide fear of an Iranian victory.

Fierce fighting continued into spring 1984. Iraq claimed that it had crushed Iranian offensives involving as many as 400,000 troops, while Iran and the United States accused Iraq of using chemical weapons in violation of the 1925 Geneva agreement outlawing such weapons. The United States also accused Iran of throwing untrained units of teenagers against Iraqi lines to wear down the enemy before attacking with regular army units.

Attacks on Tankers and Cities

In May 1984, the war entered a new and more dangerous stage. Iraq began striking at tankers sailing within a fifty-mile radius of the Iranian port of Kharg Island. Baghdad justified escalating the conflict by asserting that its Gulf ports had been unusable since the beginning of the war because of shelling, while Iranian ports remained open to export oil that provided revenue to finance Iran's war effort.

The Arab Gulf states vehemently protested the Iraqi strikes against the tankers. The Arab League also condemned Iraq, and the UN Security Council adopted a similar resolution of disapproval. Despite protests, the tanker attacks continued through September 1985; by then seventy-seven ships—mostly commercial vessels not involved in the war—had been attacked in the Gulf by either Iran or Iraq.

Although Iran and Iraq both had occasionally bombed the other's cities during the first four and a half years of the war, neither had launched intensive bombing campaigns against civilians. That changed in March 1985, when Iraq began systematically attacking Iranian population centers in an attempt to force Iran to accept a negotiated settlement. The Iraqis believed that such a campaign provided the best chance of ending the conflict on their terms. Iran countered with surface-to-surface missile strikes on Iraqi cities, but with a limited supply of missiles, it inflicted much less devastation on Iraqi cities than Iraqi missiles and planes were inflicting on Tehran and other Iranian cities.

Iranian Offensives

After fighting to a stalemate during much of 1985, Iranian forces launched a daring attack across the Shatt al-Arab in February 1986 that resulted in their capturing the Iraqi port city of Faw. The attack contrasted with previous Iranian offensives in that it was a well-planned military assault that relied on deception and mobility rather than on frontal assaults by poorly trained and ill-equipped Revolutionary Guards (volunteers known for their loyalty to Khomeini and their religious fervor). Although the attack led many observers in the Arab world and the West to predict an Iranian victory, all subsequent Iranian offensives failed.

In December 1986, Iran launched a major offensive against the Iraqi city of Basra. The attack had been planned for a year and publicized as the final blow that would topple the Baathist regime. After two months of human wave assaults, however, Iran had failed to take any significant territory and had suffered huge losses of men and equipment, as well as seriously damaged capabilities and morale. A UN-appointed team of observers disclosed that Iraq had used chemical weapons on a large scale against the Iranian attackers. Iran also had employed such weapons, but on a smaller scale.

In late spring 1988, the Iraqi army, supported by heavy air cover, began dislodging the weakened Iranian forces from their positions. For several months, the Iraqis won major victories on the battlefield as Iranian forces retreated. In July, facing a bleak political, military, and economic situation, Iranian leaders accepted UN Security Council Resolution 598, which called for a cease-fire. On August 20, 1988, the cease-fire went into effect.

The Persian Gulf Crisis, 1990–1991

During 1989 and early 1990, the Persian Gulf region commanded less of the world's attention than it had in recent years. Compared with the monumental changes taking place in Germany with its reunification and the collapse of the Soviet Union and of communism in Eastern Europe, events in the Persian Gulf seemed less central to world affairs than they had in the past. The region also appeared less turbulent. The Iran-Iraq War had ended in 1988 with an inconclusive but stable cease-fire, and after the death of Ayatollah Khomeini in 1989, Iran's leaders moderated their efforts to export Islamic revolution and concentrated instead on domestic reconstruction.

On August 2, 1990, any illusions that the Persian Gulf region had become more stable or predictable were shattered when Iraqi troops moved into neighboring Kuwait. The Iraqi invasion and annexation of Kuwait set in motion a crisis that would remain at the forefront of the international agenda for more than seven months.

The most widely felt consequence of the crisis was the dramatic rise in the price of oil. After the invasion and imposition of an international economic embargo against Iraq, oil prices skyrocketed as Iraqi and Kuwaiti oil disappeared from the market and fears rose that war would damage Saudi oil facilities. The price increases affected nations everywhere, but developing economies dependent on oil were especially hard hit.

Three factors distinguished the Iraqi invasion of Kuwait as an act to which the international community felt it must respond. First, Kuwait's importance to the international economy was far greater than its small size implied; it possessed the fourth largest oil reserves in the world. If Saddam Hussein could add Kuwait's oil resources to

Iraq's—which would total about 20 percent of known world reserves—and use his superior military strength to influence Saudi Arabia and the smaller Gulf oil states into supporting Iraq's positions in OPEC, he could dominate oil production and pricing policies. Oil prices still would have been tied to supply and demand, but Hussein would have been in a position to push prices up, thereby straining the world economy. Second, given its efforts to acquire nuclear weapons and its existing stocks of conventional, chemical, and biological weapons, Iraq constituted a long-term military threat to the entire Middle East and perhaps beyond. Third, Iraq's government had demonstrated an appetite for military conquest and a capacity for brutality. Since 1980 Iraq had invaded Iran, employed chemical weapons against Iranian soldiers and ballistic missiles against Iranian citizens, and used poison gas against its own Kurdish population.

Because much of the Arab world and the international community during the 1980s considered Iraq to be a counterweight to a more threatening Iran, world reaction to Iraqi behavior had been restrained. The invasion of Kuwait, however, changed that perception, and a multinational coalition felt compelled to destroy Iraq's offensive military capacity. The war left unanswered, however, many political and economic questions about the Gulf region. By forcing Middle Eastern countries to choose sides in an expanding conflict, Iraq's actions inflamed regional problems seemingly unrelated to the invasion.

Iraqi Invasion and Occupation

Iraq's attack on Kuwait grew out of Iraqi economic problems produced by the Iran-Iraq War, though during the course of Iraq's occupation Saddam Hussein would offer a number of other justifications, including rectifying historical wrongs and pan-Arabism.

The war with Iran had left Iraq $80 billion in debt, almost half of it owed to Saudi Arabia, Kuwait, and other Gulf states. Iraqi leaders believed that debts to Arab nations related to the war with Iran should be forgiven. They reasoned that Iraq had served as a shield against Iran, which threatened all Arabs, especially those on the Persian Gulf. During the eight years of war, Iraq had paid a steep price—hundreds of thousands of Iraqis had been killed or maimed, and the country was left with few funds for reconstruction, despite its huge oil reserves. Given these circumstances, Hussein regarded the refusal of his Arab brethren to forgive Iraq's debts an injustice.

During spring and summer 1990, Kuwait became the focus of Iraqi resentment against its Arab creditors. In addition to refusing to write off Iraqi war debts, Kuwait was exceeding its oil production quota set by OPEC, contributing to low oil prices and thereby hurting Iraqi reconstruction efforts that could be financed only by oil revenues. Iraq blamed quota violators—specifically, Kuwait and the United Arab Emirates—for the depressed prices. To the Iraqis, their overproduction amounted to economic warfare that threatened Iraq's security and prosperity.

Iraq also accused Kuwait of pumping $2.4 billion in oil that rightfully belonged to Iraq from the Rumaila oil field, only a small part of which lies under Kuwaiti territory. These charges alarmed Arab leaders, who feared that Iraq was not bluffing about its intention to force changes in the oil production policies of Kuwait and the United Arab Emirates. Their fears were well founded.

Although Kuwait's oil-production policies contributed to the Iraqi regime's posture toward Kuwait, it is likely that even if Kuwait had cut oil production, written off Iraqi debts, and compensated Iraq for oil taken from the Rumaila oil field, the Baghdad regime would have found another pretext to invade. The invasion was more than a response to oil production policies; it was an attempt to fix Iraq's severe economic problems and to obtain funding for continued expansion of Iraqi military capabilities by seizing Kuwait's immense wealth. The invasion also was intended to improve Iraq's access to the Persian Gulf and to redraw colonial borders, to which Iraq had long objected. Iraq had challenged Kuwait's claim to independence in 1961, citing old Ottoman records. In 1990

Iraq annexed Kuwait, "reclaiming" it and designating it the nineteenth province.

Stories of Iraqi atrocities compounded international outrage at Iraq's aggression. Refugees described torture and summary executions of Kuwaiti citizens and widespread looting by Iraqi troops. The behavior of Iraqi troops and commanders indicated a deep-seated resentment among many Iraqis of Kuwait's wealth. The occupation, investigations later revealed, was indeed bloody and destructive; much of the damage done had no strategic or military purpose. Iraq also sought to depopulate Kuwait and replace its citizens with Iraqis. By October 1991, intelligence reports estimated that only 240,000 of Kuwait's 600,000 citizens remained in the country.

The U.S. and Saudi Response

The Iraqi invasion caught the world off guard, including the administration of President George Bush and the U.S. intelligence community. Although the massing of Iraqi forces on the Kuwait border had concerned U.S. leaders, few officials or analysts believed Saddam Hussein would be audacious enough to invade. In fact, at a meeting Hussein held with U.S. ambassador April Glaspie in July, the Iraqi leader had interpreted statements she made in response to his assertions about Kuwait as signaling U.S. acquiescence to an invasion.

In the days after the invasion, President Bush's primary concern was deterring an Iraqi attack on Saudi Arabia, whose massive oil reserves were (and remain) vital to the world's economy. An Iraqi move against them or the Saudi government would force the United States to take military action, almost regardless of the circumstances or the relative strength of U.S. and Iraqi troops in the region at the time. To that end, Bush pressed the Saudi government to allow American soldiers to be stationed in the country. Although the Saudis maintained a close relationship with the United States, from whom most of their military equipment was purchased, they had never sought and rarely consented to a U.S. military presence within their

borders. In fact, because of U.S. support for Israel, most Arab countries were wary of accommodating U.S. troops. The presence of a large non-Islamic army in Saudi Arabia could expose the Saudi government, as the guardian of the Islamic holy places in Mecca and Medina, to criticism that it was allowing the holy places to be defiled.

In the early days of August, however, Saudi officials considered the threat from Iraq much greater than any damage incurred by the U.S. military taking up positions on Saudi soil. After August 6, when U.S. defense secretary Richard Cheney showed King Fahd satellite intelligence of Iraqi missiles pointed at Saudi Arabia and Iraqi forces massing near the Saudi border, the king threw his lot in with the United States. U.S. forces began arriving in Saudi Arabia the next day.

During the initial stages of the deployment, Iraqi forces in Kuwait and southern Iraq greatly outnumbered U.S. forces and their Saudi allies. By the end of the third week in August, however, the threat of an Iraqi offensive had diminished as the United States, Britain, and several other nations assembled formidable air and naval forces in the Gulf region. Meanwhile, the United States continued its deployments of ground forces. They were joined in August by troops from Britain, Egypt, France, Morocco, Pakistan, Syria, and other countries.

The Multinational Coalition

The coalition arrayed against Iraq was clearly U.S.-led. No other Western nation possessed a larger or better equipped military force. In coordinating the military effort to drive Iraqi forces from Kuwait, defend Saudi Arabia, and enforce UN sanctions, the Bush administration succeeded in building a broad multinational coalition that proved to be enduring and resilient. More than two dozen nations contributed combat forces, and other nations provided medical teams, transport assistance, or financial aid.

Egypt, Saudi Arabia, and Syria were the most important Arab members of the coalition. Egyptian president Hosni Mubarak led Arab opposition to the invasion and occupation. By January 1991, Egypt had deployed 30,000 troops in the Gulf. Syria had long denounced U.S. patronage of Israel, and the United States had declared Syria a supporter of international terrorism, but both temporarily set aside their differences to pursue their common interest of forcing an Iraqi withdrawal. Syrian president Hafiz al-Asad sent 19,000 troops to Saudi Arabia. Combat forces from the Arab states of Bahrain, Kuwait, Morocco, Oman, Qatar, and the United Arab Emirates also participated in the coalition under Saudi command. The Bush administration placed a high value on the continuing participation of the Arab members of the coalition. The presence in Saudi Arabia of troops from a variety of Arab countries weakened Iraqi claims that the United States and its Western allies were waging a war of aggression against Arab nations and peoples.

Throughout the Gulf crisis, Britain proved to be the staunchest Western ally of the United States. It contributed 35,000 troops—the largest Western contingent in the multinational force next to that of the United States—and it provided unswerving support for U.S. initiatives. The British also felt some responsibility for Kuwait, which had been under British protection until it received full independence in 1961.

France also made a sizable contribution to the coalition in supplying 17,000 troops. Italy and Canada provided warplanes, and many other Western nations sent combat ships to the region. Pakistan and Bangladesh each sent several thousand troops to Saudi Arabia, and Turkey maintained an imposing military presence on Iraq's northern border that guarded against an Iraqi attack and forced Iraq to keep several divisions near that border.

The Soviet Union declined to send significant forces—it did have ships in the Gulf—and sometimes pursued its own agenda during the crisis. Moscow, however, backed the United States in every important vote in the UN Security Council, including the votes imposing a total economic embargo against Iraq and authorizing coalition forces to go to war.

The Japanese government provided financial assistance instead of troops, pledging by early 1991 almost $11 billion to the United States and $3 billion to Middle Eastern nations. Germany also chose to make a financial contribution rather than send military forces. It pledged $2 billion to the Gulf effort on September 15 and later increased its total contribution to almost $8 billion, $6.5 billion of which would go to the United States. The biggest financial contributors to the military effort, however, were Saudi Arabia and Kuwait, both of which pledged more than $16 billion. All the major donors delivered on their pledges, which totaled $54 billion.

UN Sanctions

In tandem with the U.S. military effort to defend Saudi Arabia, the Bush administration launched a diplomatic campaign to create an anti-Iraq consensus within the international community. It directed the campaign from the UN Security Council.

On August 2, the day Iraq invaded Kuwait, the Security Council met in emergency session and unanimously passed Resolution 660, which condemned the invasion and called for an immediate Iraqi withdrawal. Four days later, the Security Council passed Resolution 661, which established an almost total embargo on all Iraqi imports and exports, with exceptions for humanitarian shipments of medicine and some food. Iraq was particularly vulnerable to a complete economic embargo, because it depended almost completely on oil exports for foreign earnings, and it imported about 75 percent of its food. Iraq was able to export oil only through the Persian Gulf sea route and through pipelines running across Saudi Arabia to the Red Sea and across Turkey to the Mediterranean. The embargo closed all three avenues of export, depriving Iraq of hard currency earnings.

Resolution 661 called on UN member states only to observe the embargo, and it provided no explicit authorization of a military blockade to enforce the sanctions. The United States insisted, however, that it had the right to use military force to prevent circumvention of the embargo. On August 16, U.S. naval forces in the Persian Gulf began interdicting ships carrying cargo to or from Iraq. Britain concurred in this judgment, but the other three permanent members of the UN Security Council—China, France, and the Soviet Union—asserted that a new resolution was required to authorize military force to prevent leakage through the embargo.

On August 25, after much lobbying by the United States, the Security Council passed Resolution 665, specifically authorizing the use of force to ensure compliance with the embargo against Iraq. Any commerce between Iraq and the rest of the world would have to occur over land. While circumvention of the embargo by traders operating out of Jordan (and to a lesser extent Turkey and Iran) would help keep Iraq supplied with food and certain other goods, the embargo crippled the Iraqi economy. The UN blockade succeeded in halting almost all of Iraq's exports and, by some estimates, 90 percent of its imports.

Arab Politics

The Iraqi invasion of Kuwait forced Arab governments to choose sides in a conflict that was fraught with dangers for the individual countries of the Middle East and the region as a whole. Saudi Arabia felt directly and immediately threatened by Iraqi forces and was therefore willing to join the United States in opposing Baghdad.

Almost every Arab state regarded Iraq's annexation of Kuwait as unlawful. Fourteen of twenty-one Arab League nations condemned the invasion the day after it happened. Like Kuwait's borders, the boundaries of most Middle East countries were created arbitrarily by Western colonial powers, generally following World War I. Saddam Hussein's argument that his invasion of Kuwait was merely an effort to redress past colonial injustices threatened to set the precedent that all Middle East boundaries could be subject to reinterpretation.

Arab leaders also understood that Hussein's ambitions might place their own regimes in jeopardy. They were initially hesitant, however, to abandon the myth of Arab unity or to take a position that could place them on the side of a Western military intervention against a fraternal Arab state, especially one with menacing military strength. After a week of indecision in the Arab world, President Mubarak of Egypt called an emergency meeting of the Arab League in Cairo on August 10. The meeting, Mubarak explained, would attempt to find an "Arab solution" to the crisis in an effort to avert outside intervention. Iraq, however, refused to make any concessions. Its delegation to the Cairo summit even asserted that Baghdad's August 8 annexation of Kuwait gave it the right to control Kuwait's seat at the meeting. The summit ended with Bahrain, Djibouti, Egypt, Kuwait, Lebanon, Morocco, Oman, Qatar, Saudi Arabia, Somalia, Syria, and the United Arab Emirates—twelve of the twenty-one Arab League members—voting that Arab troops be sent to Saudi Arabia to defend it against Iraq. The Arab forces would operate under Saudi command, distinct from whatever Western contingents might also be deployed. Iraq, Libya, and the Palestine Liberation Organization (PLO) voted against the measure. Jordan, Mauritania, and Sudan voted for it "with reservations." Algeria and Yemen abstained, and Tunisia did not attend the meeting.

Arab governments made their decision according to their own perceived self-interests, not according to their feelings toward Kuwait or their desire to preserve Arab unity. The wealthy Gulf states had the most to fear from Iraq, so they followed Saudi Arabia's leadership and joined with the West in opposing Iraq. Egypt received extensive financial aid from the United States and traditionally had been an Iraqi rival for Arab leadership. President Asad of Syria joined the coalition despite longstanding differences with the United States because of his personal enmity toward Saddam Hussein and his ambition that Damascus eclipse Baghdad as a power center in the Arab world; an Iraqi defeat represented for him a tantalizing prospect. Asad also was eager to improve relations with the wealthy Gulf states, which he saw as alternative sources of funding to replace dwindling Soviet financial support.

By contrast, the poorer Arab nations tended to side with Iraq or declare their neutrality. As the leader of a militarily powerful Arab nation confronting the oil-rich Gulf Arabs, Israel, and the West, Saddam Hussein appealed to poorer segments of the Arab population. Jordanians and Palestinians, in particular, rallied to support him, but pro-Iraq demonstrations also were common in Algeria, Lebanon, Libya, Sudan, Tunisia, and Yemen. Demonstrations of support for Iraq also were reported in some nations whose governments joined the coalition, including Egypt, Morocco, and Syria.

The Iraqi invasion and the willingness of Arab governments to pursue their own interests, even if it meant aligning with the West, demonstrated that pan-Arabism did not reflect Arab world realities. Although Arab states share common linguistic, religious, historical, and cultural roots and have sought to limit outside influence in the Middle East, they have, since the fragmentation of the Ottoman Empire after World War I, evolved into independent nations with widely different needs and objectives. The twenty-one members of the Arab League, an organization founded in 1945 on pan-Arabist principles, were divided by their ties to foreign powers, sectarian and ethnic compositions, levels of wealth, and other factors. Yet despite the obvious limits of pan-Arabism, the concept retained strong appeal among poorer Arabs who had seen their individual countries dominated by Western powers and threatened militarily by Israel and Iran. Pan-Arabism held hope of increasing Arab military strength, achieving economic independence from the West, and distributing oil wealth more equally among the Arab people. Saddam Hussein sought to capitalize on pan-Arabist romanticism by portraying his invasion of Kuwait as a first step toward a broader Arab union to restore the Arab world's glorious past.

Saddam's march into Kuwait and his stand against the West reinforced longstanding Arab resentments and frustrations. For Arabs with bitter memories of the colonial past, his confrontation with a coalition that included Britain, France, the United States, and other Western nations signaled a new beginning of Arab independence. For Arabs frustrated by military defeats at the hands of Israel, the apparent might of Iraq's army proved that Arab states were not always doomed to military inferiority. For poverty-stricken Arabs, the sight of Kuwait's elite being transformed from wealthy oil barons with extravagant lifestyles into refugees on the run was satisfying. When Saddam Hussein promised an equal distribution of oil wealth among the Arab people, the poor saw him as a modern-day Robin Hood whose brutal means were justified by his goals. He also was compared with Saladin, the twelfth-century Muslim military leader who defeated European crusaders and liberated Jerusalem.

Toward War in the Gulf

Once U.S. and allied military deployments in Saudi Arabia removed the threat of an Iraqi offensive against Saudi Arabia and its oil fields, the Bush administration had to decide on a strategy for dealing with Iraq's occupation of Kuwait. Most Americans and members of Congress agreed that Iraq should be opposed and Saudi Arabia should be protected, but public support for U.S. military action was less certain.

On November 8, 1990, two days after midterm congressional elections in the United States, President Bush announced plans to reinforce the 230,000 U.S. troops already in the Gulf participating in what was called Operation Desert Shield. The massive military buildup in Saudi Arabia reflected a change in the president's strategy, appearing to reject the long-term approach of relying on economic sanctions to force an Iraqi withdrawal. In announcing the deployments on November 8, Bush explained that the additional forces being sent to Saudi Arabia were intended to "insure that the coalition has an adequate offensive military option should that be necessary to achieve our common goals." Bush believed that his best option for forcing Iraq out of Kuwait peacefully would be to present Baghdad with a coalition force capable of inflicting terrible damage on Iraqi forces. Bush also believed that until such a coalition force was in place, the threat of attack was not credible. His high-stakes escalation increased the pressure on Iraq to withdraw, but it also greatly heightened the likelihood of war if it did not.

Several factors probably figured heavily in Bush administration decision making. First, Saddam Hussein was widely viewed as a ruthless dictator willing to sacrifice whatever lives necessary for his purposes, but also as someone who would act in self-interest and not risk destruction of his armies, on which he depended for personal power and prestige. Second, the fragile anti-Iraq coalition included Arab governments that might be weakened or toppled by popular unrest among their poorer populations. Third, and perhaps the most important factor, an Iraqi withdrawal from Kuwait might be almost as undesirable as a war, because it would leave intact Iraq's military and nuclear research facilities and chemical and biological weapons industries. Even if the international community maintained restrictions on sales of arms and military technologies to Iraq, Baghdad already possessed armed power vastly superior to that of its neighbors. Bush noted consequently that if Iraq withdrew, an international peacekeeping force would be needed on the ground, and U.S. Persian Gulf naval forces would need to be strengthened.

Western officials also feared that Iraq, after withdrawing, might pursue other aggressive policies, particularly against Israel, and that Israel might attack first to prevent Iraq from further developing advanced missiles and nuclear weapons. The Bush administration thus regarded peace based on an Iraqi withdrawal to be nearly as dangerous as a war. The official U.S. policy objectives continued to be the ouster of Iraq from Kuwait through economic sanctions and the threat of military force, but implicit in Bush's willingness to make the military threat was an underlying belief that war might be the wiser option.

UN Deadline

After announcing the new military deployments to Saudi Arabia, the Bush administration began to pursue a UN Security Council resolution for use of force against Iraq. On November 29, the UN Security Council voted 12-2 (with Yemen and Cuba dissenting) to implicitly authorize coalition nations to use force to expel Iraq from Kuwait. Security Council Resolution 678, however, allowed for a month and a half of diplomacy by authorizing force only after January 15. Diplomats would have forty-seven days to persuade Iraq to withdraw peacefully or to construct a compromise.

Diplomatic efforts came to a climax on January 9, 1991, when U.S. secretary of state James A. Baker III met with Iraqi foreign minister Tariq Aziz in Geneva. The negotiations began amid general pessimism that neither the Americans nor the Iraqis would make the compromises necessary to avoid war. After six and a half hours, Baker and Aziz emerged from their meeting and reported that neither side had budged from its original position. On January 12, both houses of Congress voted to empower the president to use force to drive Iraq from Kuwait. The vote was 250-183 in the House and 52-47 in the Senate. Bush had claimed the authority as commander in chief to order an attack against Iraq regardless of congressional action, but the vote strengthened his domestic position. Most members of Congress who had voted against authorizing war accepted the decision of the body and closed ranks behind the president. The coalition would go to war unless Iraq took steps to withdraw from Kuwait by January 15.

Persian Gulf War, 1991

On the morning of Tuesday, January 15, 1991, President Bush signed an executive order authorizing an aerial offensive against Iraq that would begin the following night unless a diplomatic breakthrough occurred before the deadline passed at midnight eastern standard time. The following afternoon, Secretary of Defense Cheney ordered Gen. H. Norman Schwarzkopf, the U.S. commander in Saudi Arabia, to launch the attack. The coalition's strategy was to wage an opening, extended air campaign against strategic targets in

Iraq and Kuwait. Coalition military leaders felt confident that they could quickly establish air supremacy over the badly outmatched Iraqi air force, using their warplanes to methodically destroy Iraq's military machine and soften its defenses before launching a ground offensive.

The world learned that the air campaign had begun at 2:35 A.M. Saudi time, on January 17, when journalists in Baghdad reported thunderous explosions amidst a torrent of antiaircraft fire. British, Kuwaiti, Saudi, and U.S. warplanes participated in the first wave of bombings. French and Italian aircraft soon joined them. The coalition had assembled more than two thousand planes in the Persian Gulf theater. Coalition air forces would average about two thousand sorties (one round-trip mission by one plane) per day during Operation Desert Storm.

Early on January 18, the Iraqis struck back by launching a salvo of Scud missiles armed with conventional high-explosive warheads at Israel. The eight Scuds injured more than a dozen people in and around the cities of Tel Aviv and Haifa but killed no one. Later in the day the Iraqis launched another Scud missile at Saudi Arabia, but a U.S. Patriot antimissile missile intercepted and destroyed it before it reached the ground. During the coming weeks, Iraq would fire dozens of Scuds at Israel and Saudi Arabia. Because of their small payloads and inaccuracy, the Scuds were of negligible strategic value; Iraq could not use them to destroy coalition military targets. They did, however, demonstrate to the Iraqi people and Iraq's supporters that the Iraqi military could strike back in some fashion against the coalition. More important, Saddam hoped the missile attacks against Israel would draw the Jewish state into the war.

Restraining Israel

Israel's military reputation in the Middle East is based on its consistent retaliation for attacks against it and on its superior technology. In launching missiles against Israel, Saddam counted on its leaders behaving as they had in the past. If Israel retaliated,

Arab members of the coalition would be in the uncomfortable position of fighting on the same side as Israel. Even if Arabs remained in the coalition, Israeli participation in the war would increase sympathy for Iraq in the Arab world.

After the initial Scud attacks, some cabinet members and citizens pressured the Israeli leadership to strike back, but most understood that by staying out of the war, they could help the coalition quickly destroy Iraq's military, and they could count on substantial political benefits and financial aid at war's end.

The Bush administration vigorously pressed the Israeli government to stay on the sidelines. Bush promised Israeli leaders that mobile Scud missile batteries in western Iraq would be a top-priority target of coalition pilots, and he dispatched Patriot antimissile batteries and their U.S. crews to Israel. This deployment represented the first stationing of U.S. combat forces in Israel. The Israeli government made it clear, however, that U.S. troops would remain only as long as it took to train Israeli units to operate the batteries.

The Air Campaign

The air campaign was an unqualified success given the minimal number of aircraft lost by the coalition and the destruction inflicted on the Iraqi military, defense industries, and weapons research facilities. In a January 23 briefing, Gen. Colin Powell, chairman of the U.S. Joint Chiefs of Staff, declared that the coalition had achieved air superiority. Indeed, Iraqi warplanes had been so ineffective that in late January the Iraqi leadership sent more than a hundred of its best planes to the safety of airfields in Iran. The few Iraqi warplanes that had challenged coalition aircraft or had attempted to penetrate air defenses in Saudi Arabia and the Persian Gulf had been shot down. Meanwhile, allied air attacks destroyed many of Iraq's hardened aircraft shelters, and presumably the warplanes concealed inside them. Yet despite the destruction it inflicted on Iraq, the coalition air war had not forced an Iraqi capitulation, nor had it triggered an internal Iraqi uprising against the

Baathist regime. If coalition forces were going to reclaim Kuwait, they would have to do it on the ground.

The Ground War

The international community feared the beginning of the ground campaign almost as much as it had feared the opening of hostilities. The Iraqi army, estimated at approximately 540,000, appeared to be much more formidable than the Iraqi air force. Commentators pointed out that many Iraqi soldiers had gained extensive experience during the eight-year Iran-Iraq War, while most coalition forces would be seeing combat for the first time; they had the advantage of defending heavily fortified positions; and they would almost certainly use their stocks of chemical weapons as they had done effectively during the conflict with Iran.

As noted above, the official goal of the coalition offensive against Iraq had been the liberation of Kuwait, but President Bush and other coalition leaders hoped to destroy Saddam Hussein's army in the process. The coalition battle plan, therefore, sought not only to drive Iraqi forces from Kuwait, but also to cut off and destroy retreating Iraqi units. In a January 23 briefing, General Powell had declared bluntly, "Our strategy to go after this army is very, very simple. First, we're going to cut it off, and then we're going to kill it."

As the ground war approached and Iraqi losses from the air campaign mounted, Baghdad showed interest in a negotiated settlement. The Iraqi regime announced on February 15 that it was willing to withdraw from Kuwait, but it attached numerous conditions to the offer, which Bush and the other coalition leaders rejected.

Iraqi officials then turned for mediation assistance to the Soviet Union, their longtime patron, which had been urging them since August to withdraw peacefully. President Mikhail Gorbachev presented a withdrawal plan to Iraqi foreign minister Aziz on February 18. Bush, who had been informed of the proposal, told Gorbachev the following day that it was inadequate.

Increasingly confident that a coalition ground campaign would be successful, Bush moved to head off further Iraqi peace proposals, which he feared could divide the coalition by offering terms that would come close to but ultimately fall short of meeting all coalition demands. On February 22, he announced that Iraq had until noon eastern standard time on February 23 to begin a withdrawal and accept "publicly and authoritatively" all coalition requirements for a cease-fire. The conditions appeared designed to allow Hussein no room to save face if he accepted them; they mandated a swift and humiliating retreat that the Bush administration hoped would disgrace Hussein in the eyes of his supporters in Iraq and the Arab world. Reports that Iraqi troops had begun committing systematic atrocities in Kuwait and setting Kuwaiti oil wells ablaze stiffened coalition resolve to go to war immediately if Iraq rejected Bush's terms. When the February 23 deadline passed without signs of an Iraqi withdrawal, Bush ordered the offensive to proceed.

A Hundred Hours

At 4:00 A.M. Saudi time on February 24, the coalition launched a ground offensive. The assault would last one hundred hours. The huge British, French, and U.S. force to the west penetrated deep into Iraq at a blitzkrieg pace. With the Iraqi army collapsing, Hussein delivered a radio speech on February 26 announcing an Iraqi withdrawal from Kuwait. He maintained a defiant tone, however, suggesting that the Iraqi retreat was a strategic withdrawal and telling Iraqis, "Kuwait is part of your country and was carved from it in the past." Most Iraqi forces were already engaged in a disorganized retreat by the time of the broadcast, and of those, almost all surrendered without a fight. Because coalition troops suffered only very light casualties, domestic public opinion strongly favored pressing the advantage to ensure that Saddam would not soon be able to threaten his neighbors.

U.S. Marines and Arab coalition troops entered Kuwait City on February 27 after fighting several pitched battles on the outskirts of the city. Once in, they found that all but a few stranded Iraqis had fled the capital the previous day. At 9:00 P.M. EST on February 27, President Bush declared in a televised address, "Kuwait is liberated. Iraq's army is defeated. Our military objectives are met." He announced that coalition forces would cease offensive operations three hours later at midnight EST (8:00 A.M. February 28 in the battle zone).

According to Lt. Gen. Sir Peter de la Billiere, the commander of British forces in Saudi Arabia, coalition casualty levels were "the smallest number for the size of the campaign in the history of warfare." Of the 125 Americans killed in combat during the entire six-week war, 28 were killed by a single Iraqi Scud missile that struck a barracks in Dhahran, Saudi Arabia, on February 25. Indeed, the total number of American soldiers killed in action was less than the 202 killed in accidents related to operations in the Middle East since August 2, 1990. Analysts attributed the low levels to the war weariness of Iraqi troops, the technological superiority of coalition weapons, the lack of Iraqi air cover, and an efficient U.S. battle plan.

Containing Iraq

Although Iraq was humiliated and its offensive military capacity weakened by the war, the government of Saddam Hussein remained in power through the 1990s. The Iraqi leader continued to denounce the West and its Persian Gulf allies and to resist full implementation of the cease-fire agreements ending the war.

The United Nations Special Commission on Iraq (UNSCOM), created after the war, was charged with identifying and destroying Iraq's weapons of mass destruction (WMD), its scientific development programs related to these weapons, and its ballistic missiles. After completing its task, UNSCOM was to establish a comprehensive monitoring system to prevent programs related to WMD from again moving forward.

Until late 1993, Iraq cooperated only minimally with UNSCOM inspectors. Baghdad denied them access to many key sites, hid nuclear equipment, and refused to destroy the weapons facilities they found. On January 13, 1993, U.S.-led coalition forces conducted a coordinated air strike in response to repeated Iraqi incursions into Kuwait and Iraq's refusal to allow seventy UNSCOM inspectors to reenter Iraq after the Christmas holidays.

On June 26, 1993, President Bill Clinton ordered a missile attack against intelligence service headquarters in Baghdad in response to evidence that Iraq had been behind a plot to assassinate former president Bush during a visit to Kuwait earlier in the year. The attack also came on the heels of an UNSCOM report five days earlier citing Iraq's lack of cooperation.

Meanwhile, the international embargo was taking a toll. Even though the embargo provided for humanitarian exceptions of food and medicine, disease rates and the price of food rose dramatically, and basic consumer goods became scarce. The June missile attack dismayed many Iraqis, who had hoped that the embargo would soon be lifted and that the Clinton administration would be inclined to take a softer line than had the Bush administration.

On November 26, 1993, responding to deteriorating conditions, Iraq formally agreed to abide by UN Security Council Resolution 715 requiring it to provide a full inventory of its assets related to weapons of mass destruction. This decision opened the way for UNSCOM inspectors to begin a more unobstructed campaign to establish positive verification of the elements of Iraq's weapons infrastructure.

In July 1994, UNSCOM announced that all known banned weapons had been destroyed, although the commission had not been able to verify that certain parts of Iraq's weapons programs were eliminated. The long-term monitoring program was almost in place to monitor more than 150 research, industrial, and military sites via remote cameras, unannounced inspections, and overflights.

Regardless, the United States and Britain had deep reservations about lifting the embargo.

Washington cited Saddam Hussein's implacable hostility, repression of minorities, and failure to account for missing Kuwaitis. Underlying these concerns was the fear that renewed Iraqi oil sales would produce the revenue needed to rebuild Iraq's military and carry forward a covert nuclear weapons program. Indeed, even if the Iraqis cooperated with the UNSCOM inspection regime, inspectors admitted it would not be foolproof. Moreover, if inspectors did uncover violations, the United States and its coalition partners would likely have difficulty reaching a consensus on reinstating effective sanctions or taking military action.

Iraq's deployment of Republican Guard divisions in a threatening posture near Kuwait in October 1994 bolstered the U.S. arguments against lifting the embargo. The Iraqis withdrew after Clinton dispatched 36,000 U.S. troops to the region.

From 1995 to 1998 Iraq continued to confound Western inspection efforts, fighting what Middle East analyst Tony Cordesman called the "war of the sanctions." Under UN Resolution 687, UNSCOM and the International Atomic Energy Agency (IAEA) had the right to look for and dismantle weapons of mass destruction and long-range missiles. Article 22 of the resolution restricted Iraqi oil exports until UNSCOM and the IAEA certified that Iraq had no long-range missiles and weapons of mass destruction and did not possess the capacity to manufacture them. Resolution 687 also required Iraq to fully disclose all information about its weapons of mass destruction programs, but it consistently frustrated the efforts of UNSCOM weapons inspectors by blocking access to suspected weapons sites. Iraq would deny entry to the inspectors for days or weeks and then relent as the pressure built for a military response from the United States and Britain.

The sanctions deprived Iraq of approximately $20 billion annually in oil revenues. Their human toll was devastating, totaling 1.4 million lives. Iraqi children were five times more likely to die under the sanctions regime than they were before it. (A UN-Iraqi survey released in 1999 showed that the mortality rate for children under five years of age had risen from 56 per 1,000 before economic sanctions to 131 per 1,000. Infant mortality increased from 47 per 1,000 to 108 per 1,000 during the same time frame.) Although Saddam Hussein sought sympathy from the world community by, among other things, holding mass funerals for children who allegedly died from malnutrition and other ailments stemming from sanctions, he had been accused in the past of depriving children and other vulnerable members of society in order to finance his presidential palaces. Even after the United Nations allowed Iraq to sell oil to raise revenue for humanitarian aid, the Iraqi government failed to distribute all of the food, medicine, and medical supplies that came into the country.

Iraqi attempts to break free of the sanctions yoke also included an effort creating fissures within the UN Security Council and between the countries of the Operation Desert Storm coalition. To a certain degree, the strategy was successful: China, France, and Russia were sympathetic to lifting the sanctions. Britain and the United States, however, advocated leaving them in place until Iraq fully complied with weapons inspections. This state of affairs lasted until late 1998, when Iraq pushed too far and Britain and the United States responded with a four-day air attack.

Postwar Tensions

In January 1995, Saddam had achieved an "electoral victory," taking 99.96 percent of the vote in a referendum in which he was the only candidate. The election came just days after UNSCOM announced that Iraq had disclosed information about its chemical weapons program that it had denied since 1991. In the months that followed, UNSCOM announced that Iraq had failed to account for a substantial amount of material that could be used to manufacture biological armaments and that it had uncovered evidence that Iraq had imported substances on which to grow toxins. Then, after four years of consistently denying a biological weapons program, Iraq admitted in July 1995 that it had made anthrax and botulism. In July

Iraq also acknowledged for the first time that it possessed stockpiles of germ warfare agents.

Further admissions came after Saddam Hussein's son-in-law, Lt. Gen. Hussein Kamel Hassan al-Majid, former minister of industry and director of military industrialization, defected to Jordan in August. Kamel's brother, Lt. Col. Saddam Kamel Hassan al-Majid, head of Saddam Hussein's security force, joined him in exile. Iraq then disclosed information about weapons of mass destruction before UNSCOM found out about them from Kamel. In late 1995, UNSCOM denounced Iraq for being uncooperative and for misleading the inspectors, declaring that its work would continue for the foreseeable future.

In addition to concealing or only selectively providing critical information about weapons of mass destruction, Iraq found other ways to thwart the efforts of the international community, especially the United States. In March 1995, Iraq imprisoned two Americans for allegedly illegally crossing the border from Kuwait. William Barloon and David Daliberti were freed four months later, after U.S. congressional representative Bill Richardson of New Mexico visited Baghdad to appeal for their release.

Iraq's ultimate goal, however, was to end UN sanctions. In April 1995, the Iraqi Revolutionary Command Council rejected a UN Security Council resolution that would have provided humanitarian relief for Iraqis, who by all accounts were suffering under the sanctions. The proposed "oil-for-food" deal would allow Iraq to sell $2 billion in oil every six months to fund the purchase of food and medicine. Iraq asserted that the program was only a ruse that allowed the UN to avoid lifting the full range of sanctions.

In May 1996, however, Iraq accepted the oil-for-food deal on the United Nations' terms. Under the agreement, to be renewed every six months, Iraq would spend the $2 billion "increments" as follows: 30 percent for war reparations, 5 percent for UN activities in Iraq, and another portion to fund aid to the Kurdish population, with the United Nations controlling distribution of supplies in those areas. The remainder would target Iraqi needs.

The oil-for-food deal did not presage the lifting of sanctions. In March, the United Nations renewed sanctions because of Iraq's failure to surrender weapons and materials of mass destruction and for developing such systems. That same month Iraq again prevented weapons inspectors from entering and searching facilities. Iraq would typically end its resistance only after the UN Security Council reiterated that sanctions would remain in place until UNSCOM could verify that Baghdad was not engaged in the development of these weapons.

During the spring and early summer, Iraq followed the familiar pattern of denying access to its military facilities, but in August it tried a new tack by deploying forces inside the Kurdish "safe haven," drawn at the 36th parallel in northern Iraq. Approximately 30,000 troops invaded Irbil in alliance with forces from the Kurdistan Democratic Party (KDP), one of two major Kurdish factions (the other being the Patriotic Union of Kurdistan, or PUK).

The United States responded to the Irbil invasion by increasing the number of its troops in the region to 30,000 and launching two missile attacks on Iraqi military and command positions in southern Iraq. After firing one missile at U.S. planes monitoring the northern "no-fly" zone (created in 1992 to protect the Kurdish minority in the area), Iraq backed down, saying it would no longer resist allied patrols.

In January 1997, the United Nations resumed the "oil for food" program, after having suspended it when Iraqi troops moved into the Kurdish safe haven five months earlier. In June, UNSCOM reported that Iraq had been conducting research on long-range ballistic missiles. UNSCOM chairman Rolf Ekeus also cited Iraq's failure to give the commission an accurate assessment of its chemical and biological warfare efforts. Ekeus complained of "arrogance" and "nonchalance on the Iraqi side." He also warned that Iraq was trying to produce "sanctions fatigue" among members of the UN Security Council.

On June 21, the Security Council unanimously adopted Resolution 1115, condemning Iraq's recalcitrance on inspections and threatening to impose new penalties if it did not begin to cooperate with UNSCOM. During the summer, Iraq stridently spurned inspection teams in more than a dozen incidents. On three occasions it blocked UNSCOM from investigating military facilities. In other instances it shot at UNSCOM helicopters and used planes to disrupt inspection flights.

The standoff continued into the fall, with Iraq blocking or delaying five inspections in September. Yet despite Iraqi resistance to inspections, the UNSCOM efforts did bear fruit, and the UN reported progress in eliminating weapons outlined in resolutions passed at the end of the Gulf war in 1991. For example, Iraq possessed fewer than a dozen missiles with a range of more than three hundred miles. In addition, UNSCOM had destroyed 690 tons of chemical warfare agents and more than 3,200 tons of material that could be used to produce the agents. These gains, however, were achieved in an often hostile environment.

UNSCOM, unsatisfied with its progress, in October reported its concerns about the veracity of Iraq's disclosures about its long-range missile and chemical and biological weapons programs. Iraq was suspected of possessing nerve gas as well as enough growth agent to produce substantial quantities of anthrax. Later that month, Iraq chafed at the presence of Americans on the UN weapons inspection teams, because it thought the United States was biased toward continuing the sanctions regime and was taking advantage of its UNSCOM participation to spy on Iraq. Baghdad also demanded that a timetable be set to end sanctions, which had been in place for seven years.

Opposition to American inspectors became a leitmotif in fall 1997. Divisions also began to deepen within the UN Security Council. The United States chose not to press for new sanctions because of opposition from France and Russia. In fact, France wanted to resume oil and trade relations with Iraq, which, in combination with Iran, possessed almost 21 percent of the world's proven oil reserves. Russia wanted to ease sanctions so the Iraqis could use oil revenue to begin repaying

the billions of dollars it owed for defense equipment purchased during the Soviet era.

By November the sanctions standoff had grown extraordinarily tense. When Iraq announced that U.S. inspectors would be barred from the UN weapons inspection team, the United Nations sent a delegation of diplomats to meet with Iraqi officials. Their efforts failed to produce a solution, and U.S. inspectors were forced to leave the country on November 13.

In response, Britain and the United States increased their military presence in the region. President Clinton ordered a second U.S. aircraft carrier into the Persian Gulf, and Kuwait and Bahrain allowed the deployment of fighter planes on their territory. The tension eased after Russia intervened, promising that it would support lifting economic sanctions against Iraq so long as the country adhered to UN weapons sanctions. UNSCOM inspectors returned to Iraq on November 21.

Two days later, however, Iraq refused UNSCOM access to presidential palace sites. UNSCOM claimed that Iraq routinely destroyed evidence of weapons of mass destruction and hid weapons in palaces around the country. Iraq then castigated UNSCOM chief Richard Butler, who had taken over from Ekeus in July, for being unobjective and inaccurate. A mid-December meeting between Butler, Iraqi foreign minister Aziz, and representatives from Britain, France, and Russia produced no results.

The 1998 Crisis

The standoff continued into the new year. A UN inspection team led by former marine Scott Ritter left Iraq on January 16, 1998, after being stymied by Iraqi authorities for three straight days. On January 27, President Clinton admonished Saddam Hussein to comply with sanctions inspections. The United States again threatened military consequences—air strikes—if Iraq did not provide UNSCOM unfettered access to suspected weapons sites.

In late January, Secretary of State Madeleine Albright began a tour of European capitals to bolster support for the U.S. position against Iraq. One of the most important stops on Albright's diplomatic mission was a visit with French foreign minister Hubert Vedrine in Paris. France advocated a diplomatic solution to the standoff. France insisted that it wanted to remove Saddam from power but thought that air strikes would backfire, killing Iraqi civilians and fomenting anti-Western sentiment in the Arab world. Two other members of the Security Council, China and Russia, also opposed the use of military force. Russia even warned of a world war if the United States commenced military action.

Also by this time, Arab countries that had allied with the United States in the war were beginning to drift out of the alliance. Egypt announced its opposition to air strikes, and Saudi Arabia and Turkey refused to let the United States use its air bases for attacks against Iraq. Bahrain imposed a similar ban. Only Kuwait, the victim of Iraq's invasion in August 1990, remained wedded to the aggressive posture against Iraq promoted by Britain and the United States.

In the midst of all the tension, UN secretary-general Kofi Annan proposed raising the ceiling on Iraqi oil sales to $5.25 billion every six months to finance the purchase of food and medicine for civilians. Annan said the new limit, permitted under UN Resolution 1153, was needed to avoid a humanitarian disaster. Observers had been reporting for months that the Iraqi economy was in a shambles and that acute and chronic malnutrition was widespread.

Even with the higher ceiling on oil sales, which allowed Iraq to export nearly the same amount of oil as it did before the Gulf war, it could not earn the full $10.5 billion annually. The war had destroyed 75 percent of the oil infrastructure, and experts estimated that Iraq would not reach full production capacity until early 2000. Under sanctions, Iraq could function as the eighth largest oil exporter in the world, but it still chafed at UN restrictions that dictated how its oil revenues could be spent.

Although the United States agreed in principle to raising the oil sales limit, it continued to pressure

Iraq to comply with UN weapons inspections. If the United States humored Iraq's recalcitrance, Saddam Hussein would "conclude that the international community has lost its will. He then will conclude that he can go right on and do more to rebuild an arsenal of devastating destruction," Clinton said.

Clinton also sought to build domestic support for the U.S. stand against Iraq. One tactic, however, backfired. On February 18, Albright, Secretary of Defense William Cohen, and national security adviser Samuel "Sandy" Berger traveled to Ohio State University to address a large student forum on the situation in Iraq. In a scene reminiscent of Vietnam-era protests, students shouted down the principals as CNN broadcast live to a worldwide audience estimated at 200 million.

Two days later, with tension at its height, Secretary-General Annan traveled to Baghdad to meet with Iraqi officials. Meanwhile, the United States continued to plan military air strikes and advised Americans to leave Iraq. On February 23, Annan and Iraqi foreign minister Aziz announced a deal that would allow the United Nations to resume weapons inspections with unfettered access to suspected weapons sites. A separate group of diplomats, appointed by Annan in consultation with UNSCOM and the International Atomic Energy Agency, would inspect the presidential palaces. No deadline was set for the conclusion of the inspection regime; it would continue until it had destroyed Iraq's chemical, biological, and nuclear weapons programs. In return, UNSCOM pledged to respect Iraq's national security, sovereignty, and dignity.

The Security Council approved the Annan-Aziz agreement on March 2. In its resolution, the council stated that Iraq's failure to adhere to the framework would result in "the severest consequences." The document, however, did not stipulate that the consequences would necessarily include air strikes. Inspection teams returned to Iraq and were granted access to many "sensitive" sites on March 23. The United Nations conducted its first inspection of a presidential palace in seven years on March 26. In April UNSCOM head Butler reported to the Security Council that "virtually no progress" had been made in verifying Iraqi disarmament since October. Thus a key condition for lifting sanctions remained unfulfilled.

Iraq largely complied with the Annan-Aziz agreement for several months, until its frustration with sanctions came to a head again in August. Iraq continued to complain that the UNSCOM teams contained too many British and U.S. representatives. Negotiations in early August to accelerate weapons inspections collapsed. On August 5, Iraq said it would end cooperation with UN inspectors and insisted on a restructuring of the disarmament commission. Butler, fed up with Iraqi intransigence, called it "going around the same track again and again."

In late August, Scott Ritter, head of UNSCOM's Concealment Investigations Unit, resigned, accusing the United Nations of caving to Iraq. In testimony before the Senate Foreign Relations and Armed Services Committees, Ritter delivered a critical appraisal of the U.S. and UN efforts to rein in Iraq. Baghdad could build chemical and biological weapons within six months of the conclusion of UNSCOM inspections, he said. In later testimony he noted that Iraq possessed components for three nuclear weapons but lacked fissile material.

Iraq, citing comments made by Ritter, claimed in early fall that UNSCOM was a vehicle for U.S. and Israeli spying and called for a special investigation into its activities. Iraq remained adamant in its refusal to allow UNSCOM inspections until a firm timetable was established for ending the eight-year sanctions regime. Tensions escalated further in late October, when Iraq declared that it would end all cooperation with UNSCOM. Listing the conditions for resuming cooperation, Iraq demanded that Butler be fired and that the sanctions regime be lifted. In early November, Butler deemed the latest crisis the worst in the ongoing Iraq saga. His team could no longer conduct meaningful inspections.

As Iraqi recalcitrance grew stronger, Secretary Cohen toured the region to build support for possible military action against Iraq. He was rebuffed, however, by Saudi Arabia, which refused to let the United States launch attacks from its air bases. Meanwhile, France urged Iraq to back down and resume cooperation with UNSCOM. Failure to do so would result in isolation, the French told Iraqi leaders. The Security Council passed a resolution deeming Iraq's actions a "flagrant violation" of the Gulf war cease-fire agreement and calling on Baghdad to begin cooperating immediately and unconditionally with UNSCOM and the IAEA.

The crisis ended when Present Clinton, on November 14, ordered an air strike against Iraq. At the same moment, Iraq agreed to let UN arms inspections resume and pledged unconditional access to UNSCOM. After the terms of the agreement had been clarified, Clinton aborted the strike. In a speech to the nation, Clinton said that Iraq must give inspectors "unfettered access to monitor and inspect all sites they choose" and "must not interfere with the independence . . . of the weapons inspectors." Two days later, Clinton demanded that Iraq live up to its promise to cooperate with weapons inspectors. "The burden of compliance is where it has always been, with Iraq," he said. "Our forces remain strong and ready if he does not."

That warning foreshadowed military action that would take place less than a month later and end the UNSCOM effort. Despite the November 14 agreement, questions remained regarding biological and chemical material possessed by Iraq. The Iraqi government, however, continued to hinder UN arms inspectors. On November 20, it refused to turn over information about its chemical, biological, missile and nuclear programs. On December 10, it denied UNSCOM access to the offices of the ruling Baath Party and blocked several other inspection efforts. "Iraq did not provide the full cooperation it promised on November 14, 1998. Iraq initiated new forms of restrictions upon the commission's activities," Butler wrote in a December 15 report to Annan.

That report represented the last straw for Clinton. On December 16, acknowledging that

Iraq had made it impossible for weapons inspectors to do their work, Butler withdrew all UNSCOM staff from Iraq. That evening Britain and the United States launched the first substantial military strike on Iraq since the Gulf war.

Dubbed Operation Desert Fox, the bombing campaign proceeded without the endorsement of the UN Security Council. In raids launched from bases in Bahrain, Kuwait, and Oman, Britain and the United States targeted Iraq's military and security infrastructure, including antiaircraft defenses, Saddam's elite forces, and facilities suspected of producing weapons of mass destruction.

The military campaign occurred at a politically sensitive moment for President Clinton. On December 19, 1998, the House of Representatives would impeach him on charges related to a sex scandal involving White House intern Monica Lewinsky. As members were casting historic votes calling for the president's removal from office, U.S. bombers were flying over Iraq trying to destroy Saddam's war-making capability.

Although some members of Congress had voiced concern about the purpose and timing of the air strikes and whether President Clinton had approved Operation Desert Fox to distract attention from the impeachment proceedings, on December 17, the House by a 417-5 vote approved a resolution backing U.S. actions and calling for the removal of Saddam Hussein and the establishment of a democratic government in Iraq. Overseas, however, Russia and China denounced Operation Desert Fox, and Russia recalled its ambassador from Washington in protest.

Operation Desert Fox ended on December 19, 1998, without decisive results. The United States claimed that Iraq's military strength had been substantially degraded and that internal stability in Iraq had been weakened. The Department of Defense asserted that Iraq's missile program had been set back a year by the bombing. The air strikes, however, effectively ended the UNSCOM inspections. Iraq called for an end to sanctions and refused to allow inspectors into the country after

Desert Fox. Russia and France wanted to restructure UNSCOM and change its mission, splitting with the United States, which urged returning UNSCOM to its original mandate.

Aftermath of the 1998 Crisis

Shortly after Operation Desert Fox, Iraq began to defy the no-flight zones established to protect the Kurdish population in the north and the Shiite Muslims in the south. Britain and the United States responded by conducting a low-grade war, the longest since Operation Desert Storm. Rather than responding only to attacks, allied pilots were allowed to strike any part of the Iraqi air defense system—surface-to-air missile sites, antiaircraft artillery, radar towers, and command and control centers. The attacks were deliberately carried out with little publicity, in part to minimize Arab protests. Many Arab Gulf states had wearied of the Iraq sanctions and were reluctant to endorse military strikes. Qatar's foreign minister, Shaykh Jassim bin Hamad Al Thani, called for a halt to military actions against Iraq in a March 1999 meeting with Secretary Cohen. Some Gulf neighbors even sought to strengthen ties with Iraq. During the course of 1998, Iran, Lebanon, Qatar, Syria, Saudi Arabia, Turkey, and the United Arab Emirates entered into trade agreements, agreed to diplomatic recognition, and provided humanitarian assistance with Iraq.

In addition to minimizing the Arab reaction, Britain and the United States had kept military action after Operation Desert Fox as quiet as possible to avoid deepening fissures on the Security Council, where China, France, and Russia favored lifting the sanctions on Iraq. The bombing campaign showed up mostly in brief news reports in newspapers and received little television coverage. The strategy was largely successful; it continued without high-profile protest from Arab countries or the Security Council until France in mid-August 1999 publicly criticized the bombings. Despite French and other objections, Britain and the United States would continue air strikes into 2003.

In this war of attrition, the United States attempted not only to damage Iraq's air defenses but also to undermine Saddam Hussein's authority. The "containment plus" strategy aimed to isolate and topple him while protecting Middle Eastern oil reserves, reinforcing regional stability, and containing the spread of weapons of mass destruction.

Early in November 1998, the United States had declared the overthrow of the Baathist government a primary goal. That same month, Congress had passed the Iraqi Liberation Act, authorizing the administration to provide $97 million in military aid to dissident Iraqi groups. In May 1999, the U.S. government announced that it would use part of the funding to provide exile groups computers, broadcasting equipment, and training in civil administration and public diplomacy. The United States also would help the anti-Saddam groups establish offices in London, New York, and possibly the Middle East.

This new strategy produced some controversy. Most Republicans in Congress advocated regime change in Iraq, but Gen. Anthony Zinni, head of U.S. forces in the Persian Gulf, warned against removing Saddam Hussein. In congressional testimony in spring 1999, Zinni questioned the viability of ousting Saddam and cautioned that a "disintegrated, fragmented" Iraq may be even more dangerous to its neighbors and U.S. interests.

An internal overthrow of Hussein was a politically more palatable option for the United States than one imposed from outside. Few Arab countries would support his removal if forced by the West. Although Hussein appeared firmly in control in the first half of 1999, a few signs of unrest emerged. In mid-February, a leading Shiite Muslim cleric, Ayatollah Muhammad Sadiq al-Sadr, and two of his sons were assassinated, sparking demonstrations— and Iraqi government retribution—in the Shiite south. In a rare public acknowledgment of unrest, Iraqi officials confirmed that riots had erupted in the impoverished Basra region. In April it was reported that Hussein's family was riven by a feud and that the patriarch lived in constant fear of assassination.

The end of UNSCOM's mission left many questions unanswered about Iraq. UNSCOM had been instrumental in dismantling Iraq's nuclear facilities, destroying tons of chemical and biological weapons agents, and eradicating scores of missiles and warheads. Yet UNSCOM left Iraq without accounting for tons of precursors for nerve gas and biological agents, hundreds of munitions, and many missiles and warheads.

The Iraq War, 2003

From the beginning of the George W. Bush administration, a small group of officials, notably Vice President Richard Cheney and senior officials in the Department of Defense, had pressed for a campaign against Iraq and its presumed weapons of mass destruction. Official administration policy, however, centered around other possibilities of introducing regime change in Iraq short of war. The events of September 11, however, completely changed that equation, as President Bush envisioned his "global war on terror" as including action against Saddam Hussein. The war plan signed by Bush after the attacks not only authorized an invasion of Afghanistan and operations against al-Qaida, but also authorized the development of plans for an invasion of Iraq. Only a few officials were privy to this knowledge, and by the time the rest of the government became aware of the directive, planning for war was well advanced.

The administration devised to sell the war to the American people by claiming that Hussein remained a threat to Iraq's neighbors and to the United States because he continued to secretly develop weapons of mass destruction and supported terrorism. It also asserted that Hussein had ties to al-Qaida and put forth the idea that he might provide WMD to terrorists. After coming up against opposition to taking unilateral action against Iraq, the administration decided to work through the United Nations to keep pressure on the Iraqi government. In a speech on September 13, 2002, to the UN General Assembly, Bush called on nations to act to confront the "grave and gathering danger" posed by Iraq. On November 8, the Security Council passed Resolution 1441, calling on Iraq to disarm its WMD and cooperate with UN inspections. Later that month, the United Nations Monitoring, Verification, and Inspection Commission (UNMOVIC), a team of some 100 inspectors created to replace UNSCOM in 1999, was dispatched to Iraq to continue the task of disarming Iraq of its chemical and biological weapons and prohibited missiles, while the UN's Iraq Nuclear Verification Office searched for nuclear weapons.

On December 7, as required by Resolution 1441, Iraq submitted a 12,000-page dossier detailing its weapons programs and denying that it possessed WMD. The report was met with skepticism in the United States and London, and U.S. claims that it had intelligence to the contrary. UNMOVIC chief Hans Blix asserted after examining the report that there was little new in it, and that there were holes in it, which led the United States to declare Iraq in "material breach" of UN resolutions. Although it seemed certain by the end of 2002 that the United States and its allies intended to go to war against Iraq, the timing of the attack remained unclear. Bush repeatedly denied that a decision had been made, and diplomatic efforts to gain support from European allies continued. While these activities delayed the onset of hostilities, avoidance of fighting during an extremely hot Iraqi summer provided reason not to delay for too long.

By early January 2003, there were about 75,000 U.S. military personnel in the Gulf; their numbers would double by mid-February. An aircraft carrier was already in the Gulf and another was in the Mediterranean with another two carriers on their way to the region. Bomber aircraft were deployed to regional air bases. On the eve of the war, the U.S. presence in the region consisted of some 380,000 military personnel, while Britain deployed some 47,000 troops, Australia 2,000, and Poland 200. Ground forces included the 3rd Infantry Division, the 101st Airborne Division, the 7th Cavalry Regiment, and the 1st Marine Expeditionary Force, as well as troops from three other army divisions. The U.S. Navy deployed three aircraft carrier battle groups while the U.S. Air Force provided some fifteen air wings and operated strategic bombers from bases on Diego Garcia Island in the Indian Ocean and elsewhere in Europe, the Middle East, and the United States.

Bush, under pressure—including from Britain, to seek a Security Council resolution explicitly authorizing the use of force against Iraq on the grounds that it was in violation of UN resolutions on its WMD programs—sent Secretary of State Colin Powell to the United Nations on February 5 to present the administration's case. Powell told the assembly, "The United States will not and cannot run [the risk of Iraq using WMD] on the American people. Leaving Saddam Hussein in possession of weapons of mass destruction for a few more months or years is not an option, not in a post–September 11th world." Although Powell's presentation seemed to make the case that Iraq was in breach of Resolution 1441, his argument that Hussein might use biological weapons against the United States imminently and his attempt to link Hussein with al-Qaida were less convincing. He disclosed that Abu Musab al-Zarqawi, a Jordanian who had fought in Afghanistan and was linked to the murder of a U.S. diplomat in Jordan, was believed to be in Iraq. Zarqawi, however, was apparently involved with Ansar al-Islam, an extremist group based in Kurdish territory outside the control of Hussein and the autonomous Kurdish authorities.

On February 12, 2003, UNMOVIC announced the discovery of Samoud 2 missiles with ranges exceeding those mandated in Gulf war cease-fire arrangements. A few days later, on February 14, Blix delivered an inspection report citing improved Iraqi cooperation with the inspections—a shift from his characterization in a previous report issued on January 27—and challenging some of the evidence Powell presented in his UN presentation. An interim report delivered March 1 was read by proponents of war as well as by opponents as bolstering their position, as it cited criticisms of Iraqi cooperation with the inspections but also spoke of having made progress. A Blix assessment on March 7 expressed similar ambivalence.

Military Contributions of Select Countries for the 2003 Iraq War and Postwar Presence

Albania—70 troops; commando company deployed in Iraq since June 2003

Australia—2,000 troops at time of war; Special Forces, attack aircraft squadron, naval frigate, cargo aircraft and reconnaissance detachments, air traffic controllers, security force to protect Australian government personnel in Iraq, and personnel in the Iraq Survey Group; 850 troops in 2004

Azerbaijan—150 troops; peacekeeping infantry company arrived after the war; numbers expected to increase in 2005

Bulgaria—450 troops

Czech Republic—110 troops

Denmark—520 troops; coastal submarine and frigate in the Persian Gulf, surgical team in Jordan, infantry battalion in Iraq after the war, including a mine-clearing and explosives disposal unit

Dominican Republic—forces withdrawn in 2004

El Salvador—380 troops

Estonia—43 troops

Fiji—150 troops[a]

Georgia—160 troops; commando battalion; troops to be increased to 900 in 2005

Honduras—forces withdrawn in 2004

Hungary—300 troops; forces withdrawn in 2004–2005

Italy—3,120 troops; amphibious battalion, infantry, military police, combat engineers; withdrawing forces in 2005

Japan—750 troops

Kazakhstan—27 troops

Latvia—120 troops

Lithuania—105 troops; infantry, medical, and logistical personnel

Macedonia—28 troops

Moldova—12 troops; forces withdrawn in 2005

Mongolia—140 troops

NATO—300 troops; trainers provided after the war

Netherlands—1,400 troops; withdrawing forces in 2005

New Zealand—forces withdrawn

Nicaragua—forces withdrawn in 2004

Norway—10 troops; staff officers; most forces withdrawn

Philippines—forces withdrawn

Poland—200 troops during war; special operations, armored division; 1,700 troops before withdrawing in 2005

Portugal—110 troops; military police; forces withdrawn in 2005

Romania—700 troops

Singapore—33 troops; most forces withdrawn

Slovakia—105 troops

Slovenia—5 troops; police instructors in Jordan

South Korea—2,800 troops

Spain—forces withdrawn in 2004

Thailand—engineers; forces withdrawn

Tonga—45 troops; peacekeeping contingent of Royal Marines; forces withdrawn in 2004

Ukraine—1,650 troops; peacekeeping infantry brigade

United Kingdom—47,000 troops in theater at time of war; fourteen warships and eight auxiliary ships, commando brigade, helicopter air groups, armored division, air assault brigade, logistics brigade, composite air force squadrons; 12,000 troops in 2004–2005

United States—340,000 troops in theater at time of war; mechanized infantry, airborne division, cavalry regiment, marine expeditionary force, five naval aircraft carrier battle groups, 15 air force wings; 145,000 troops in 2005

Notes: All numbers of forces in Iraq and theater are approximate and are as of November 2004 except where otherwise stated.

[a] Forces contributed to the United Nations Assistance Mission in Iraq (UNAMI).

Sources: U.S. Central Command, "International Contributions to the War on Terrorism," http://www.centcom.mil/Operations/Coalition/joint.htm; http://www.globalsecurity.org/military/ops/iraq_orbat_coalition.htm; Jeremy M. Sharp, "Post-War Iraq: A Table and Chronology of Contributions," Library of Congress, Congressional Research Service, Report RL32105, November 5, 2004; Steve Bowman, "Iraq: U.S. Military Operations and Costs," Library of Congress, Congressional Research Service, Report RL3270, November 20, 2004.

The United States and Britain—facing opposition from China, France, and Russia and calls for more time for inspections—finally decided not to introduce a resolution authorizing an attack. On March 17, 2003, Bush issued an ultimatum that Hussein step down within forty-eight hours or risk being attacked. Hostilities began on March 19 with air strikes on targets around Baghdad where intelligence had indicated Hussein or other senior Iraqi officials might be. The potential opportunity to kill Hussein is thought to have advanced the date of the assault slightly. These initial strikes, although failing in their objective, constituted the opening salvos of the war. Operation Desert Storm in 1991 had pursued a strategy of softening targets with massive air strikes for several weeks before beginning the ground offensive. In contrast, Operation Iraqi Freedom in 2003 employed simultaneous air and ground offensives.

In the first phase of the attack, coalition aircraft hit radar, communications, and command and control sites in southern Iraq. U.S. and British forces launched cruise missiles and aircraft strikes against military targets, Baghdad, and Basra. The coalition troops planned to move rapidly across Iraq from the Kuwaiti border toward Baghdad, bypassing urban centers while taking care to secure oil installations and port facilities. At the same time, U.S., British, and Australian Special Forces would begin operations inside Iraq, directing fire at targets, disabling airfields and WMD sites, and providing assistance to Kurds in the north and Shiites in the south. They would also be active in the western desert, trying to identify Scud sites, from which Iraq would launch missiles toward Kuwait in the early stages of the fighting.

The massed U.S. and British troops moved across the Kuwait-Iraq border and first encountered Iraqi defensive forces on the afternoon of March 20 and later surrounded the Iraqi port at Umm Qasr. Special Forces raided oil terminals in the Gulf and captured the Faw Peninsula, while another prong of attack was launched from Jordan into western Iraq to capture air bases.

The attacking forces lost little time in moving quickly toward Basra and Baghdad and were soon fighting Iraqi defenders around Basra and Nasiriya. Sandstorms on March 25 and 26 hampered operations, but U.S. forces maneuvered around Nasiriya and crossed the Euphrates River. Meanwhile, British troops tightened their control of Basra's perimeter. Air sorties, often numbering more than a thousand a day, continued against targets in Baghdad and elsewhere.

By March 28, mines in the waters around the port of Umm Qasr had been cleared, enabling humanitarian supplies to be brought ashore. On the same day, coalition forces captured a key Basra oil refinery, and U.S. troops engaged the Iraqi Republican Guards near Karbala. The following day, an Iraqi missile landed near a Kuwaiti shopping mall, and the first suicide bombing was carried out against coalition forces when a taxi exploded near Najaf, killing four American soldiers. By March 30, American forces had leapfrogged over Iraqi defensive positions and were approaching the region around Baghdad, where they called in heavy air strikes against Baghdad targets.

The next day, U.S. forces swept around Karbala and Kut to reach positions only thirty miles from Baghdad. After delays caused by Turkey's refusal to allow the coalition to use its military facilities, another wing of the assault belatedly opened in northern Iraq. The base of Ansar al-Islam in the north had been attacked in the first few days of the war. U.S. forces surrounded Saddam International Airport on the outskirts of Baghdad on April 3 and took it after twelve hours of fighting. On April 5, a raiding party swept through central Baghdad from the west to the airport while British forces attempted to enter Basra. The first fighters of the Free Iraqi Forces, led by Ahmad Chalabi, head of the Iraqi National Congress (INC), were airlifted into the Nasiriya area on April 6, in an apparent attempt by the Pentagon to provide them more legitimacy in the postwar construction of a new Iraqi government.

In the following days, U.S. forces tightened their control on Baghdad. An attack on Baghdad's

Palestine Hotel, well known as the headquarters for many journalists, occurred on April 8. Two journalists were killed, and a journalist for al-Jazeera, the Qatari satellite television channel, died when U.S. aircraft bombed his office. The collapse of Iraqi defenses produced widespread looting throughout Baghdad, including of the National Library and the National Museum, which coalition units had failed to guard.

By April 10–11, U.S. forces had entered Kirkuk and Mosul in the north and secured surrounding oil fields. Iraqi military resistance faded away in the ensuing days, and the regime's leadership, including Saddam Hussein and his sons, disappeared. The U.S. military issued a deck of fifty-five playing cards with the photographs and names of Hussein, his two sons, and the most wanted of their associates. On April 14, coalition forces completed their capture of the last Iraqi-held town, Hussein's hometown of Tikrit. They then turned their attention to halting looting, restoring public services, and searching for leading officials of the former regime.

During the next months, coalition forces steadily pursued leading Baathist figures. Deputy Prime Minister Tariq Aziz was captured soon after the war. Saddam Hussein's sons Uday and Qusay were killed by U.S. Special Forces in a firefight at a villa in Mosul on July 22, 2003. On December 13, 2003, forces captured Saddam Hussein as he hid in a hole at a farm, apparently betrayed by a member of his family. Two years after the war, forty of the fifty-five Iraqi officials on the Department of Defense playing cards had been captured, and two more were confirmed dead.

Postwar Developments

In planning for the war, on January 20, 2003, Bush had issued an executive order creating the Office of Reconstruction and Humanitarian Assistance (ORHA) to bridge the gap between the occupation and the establishment of a new, sovereign Iraqi state. Bush's order placed the ORHA under the control of the Department of Defense. Its head, Lt. Gen. Ret. Jay Garner, on

April 21, led a staff of about 200 U.S. government personnel to Iraq to serve as advisers and administrators in coordinating humanitarian assistance, initiating economic reconstruction, and establishing a framework for a successor Iraqi government while U.S. forces continued to search for WMD, purge the Baathist leadership, and rebuild Iraq's oil industry.

Even before the ORHA team entered Iraq, Garner met with about 100 Iraqis representing various ethnic and sectarian communities; a larger group of about 250 gathered in Baghdad on April 26 with the goal of convening a larger assembly that would create an interim Iraqi administration. Divisions among the Iraqis had already surfaced.

The Bush administration apparently grew dissatisfied with Garner's attempts at cobbling together a transitional regime, so on May 6, 2003, Bush named L. Paul Bremer III as his special envoy and civil administrator of Iraq. Creation of the Coalition Provisional Authority (CPA) that Bremer would head became public knowledge a few days later. Secretary of Defense Donald Rumsfeld designated Bremer CPA administrator on May 11. Garner left Iraq at the beginning of June, and the ORHA disappeared from the scene without formal announcement.

The Department of Defense ran the CPA through the secretary of the army, although Britain participated in it. British diplomat Jeremy Greenstock was appointed deputy to Bremer. The CPA's stated task was to restore security and stability, revamp national institutions leading to a new democratic regime, and facilitate reconstruction and development. In October 2003, the U.S. government created the Iraq Stabilization Group, headed by national security adviser Condoleezza Rice, and charged it with coordinating interagency support for the CPA. The Bush administration, particularly the senior officials in the Department of Defense, were heavily criticized for making little use of an extensive planning project on Iraq's future carried out by the Department of State.

UN Security Council Resolution 1511, approved by all 15 members, on October 17, 2003, legitimized the role of the CPA. In furtherance of the political aspect of its task, on July 13, 2003, the CPA established the Iraqi Governing Council (IGC) as an advisory body with a membership of twenty-five seats distributed between major Sunni Arab, Shiite, and Kurdish groups. In September, the IGC appointed a twenty-five-member cabinet that reflected the council's factional and ethnic complexion. It also began "de-Baathification" of the government and created a war crimes tribunal to try Saddam Hussein and other senior officials.

The factionalism of Iraqi politics soon emerged as a major impediment to the creation of a new sovereign Iraqi government. The IGC's work was hampered by perceptions of its being dominated by exile groups, who were seen as being out of touch with Iraq, having spent decades outside the country. Prominent among the groups was a coalition of exiles and Kurds (and later embracing some Shiite Islamist groups) founded in 1992 as the Iraqi National Congress. The two major Kurdish organizations, the Kurdistan Democratic Party and the Patriotic Union of Kurdistan, were INC members. The INC proclaimed its adherence to human rights, democracy, federalism, and compliance with UN Security Council resolutions on Iraq, thus securing the support of the U.S. government. There were questions, however, about the congress's reliability. Its leader, Ahmad Chalabi, a secular Shiite, had spent many years in exile and had been convicted in absentia in Jordan of banking fraud. Support for the INC was divided in Washington, with Vice President Cheney and the Department of Defense giving full backing to the INC, while the Department of State and the Central Intelligence Agency voiced doubts about its potential support within Iraq. In addition, questions surrounded the INC's use of money allocated to it by Congress. Nonetheless, Chalabi was selected to sit on the Iraqi Governing Council.

The Iraqi National Accord (INA), another exile group created in the aftermath of Iraq's 1990 invasion of Kuwait, consisted largely of defectors from the Baath Party and security organs in Iraq. Its head, Iyad Allawi, was a former Baathist and a secular Shiite, unlike most of the INA's membership, which was Sunni. Allawi also was chosen as

a member of the Iraqi Governing Council. Sharif Ali bin Hussein, a first cousin of the last Iraqi king, who was killed in 1958, headed the Movement for Constitutional Monarchy, another Sunni group. Although part of the INC, the movement had only marginal support.

The Kurdish Democratic Party was founded by Mullah Mustafa Barzani in 1961 as a guerrilla organization to fight for autonomy from Baghdad. After his death, leadership passed to his son Massoud Barzani. The Patriotic Union of Kurdistan split off from the KDP in 1965 under the leadership of Jalal Talabani. The groups became bitter rivals, even after they agreed in 1992 to share power in Kurdistan. As it became clearer that the United States would attack Iraq, the two groups reconciled. Barzani and Talabani were appointed to the IGC.

Although Iraq's Shiites constitute as much as two-thirds of the country's population, their political influence was not corresponsive. They suffered from Baath dominance, factionalization within their ranks, and differing degrees of secularization between rural and urban Shiites. Al-Dawa is the oldest Shiite political organization in Iraq, founded by Ayatollah Muhammad Baqir al-Sadr. It was particularly active in attacking the Baathist regime after Iran's 1979 Islamic revolution, and the government was vicious in its exhaustive crackdown. It began to fragment with some members establishing a branch in Iran and others founding Lebanon's Hizballah. One group carried out attacks on Western embassies in Kuwait and attempted to assassinate that country's amir in the 1980s. Its leader, Ibrahim al-Jaafari, and several other members joined the IGC.

The Supreme Council for Islamic Revolution in Iraq (SCIRI), an overtly political Shiite grouping, was founded by Muhammad Baqir al-Hakim, who was forced to seek refuge in Tehran in 1982 when al-Dawa began to suffer repression by the Iraqi regime. Said to be close to hard-line Iranian elements, SCIRI formed a large militia based in Iran. This provided the forces for the Badr Brigade, which infiltrated into Iraq during the 2003 war. Tension between the United States and SCIRI appeared early, as Washington suspected the brigade of being a front for Iranian intrigues, and SCIRI opposed the U.S. occupation and argued for the quick establishment of an interim Iraqi government. After an initial standoff at the close of the war, the United States and SCIRI began to coexist, with SCRI accepting representation on the IGC. Hakim was killed by a car bomb in Najaf on August 29, 2003. His brother Abd al-Aziz al-Hakim succeeded him as SCIRI leader. There are also other smaller Shiite groups.

Grand Ayatollah Ali al-Sistani is the most respected Shiite figure in Iraq. He is Iranian but has resided in the holy city of Najaf for decades. Primarily a theologian, Sistani entered the political arena only reluctantly and indirectly. After the end of the war, Sistani opposed a continued U.S. presence in the country and proclaimed the necessity of a quick establishment of an elected Iraqi government.

Muqtada al-Sadr, a member of the Shiite religious establishment, is Sistani's polar opposite. Following the assassination of his father, Ayatollah Muhammad Sadiq al-Sadr, by the Iraqi government in 1999, Muqtada al-Sadr went underground to establish opposition networks in Kufa, Najaf, and Baghdad's slums, particularly the sprawling Saddam City. Only in his early thirties and relatively junior in clerical rank, Sadr is regarded as a radical and militant political figure. It is assumed that he was responsible for the killing of U.S.-backed Ayatollah Abd al-Majid al-Khoei in Najaf soon after the fall of the Baathist government in an apparent attempt to destroy his rivals. Sadr opposed Sistani as being too quiescent and Chalabi as too corrupt. His followers took control of Saddam City after Baghdad's liberation and renamed it Sadr City; they are strong in other Shiite cities as well. Sadr refused to join the IGC and created the Mahdi Army to oppose the military occupation. He led the army in an uprising after U.S. authorities closed his newspaper, *al-Hawza,* in April 2004, and over the summer U.S. forces fought the army in various cities, notably in Najaf. Fighting erupted again in August after a cease-fire broke

down, and hostilities ended only after Ayatollah Sistani returned from medical treatment abroad and brokered a truce in which the Mahdi Army evacuated the shrine of Imam Ali.

Most of these factions and social divisions were necessarily replicated in the IGC, which consisted of thirteen Shiites (including Islamists and secularists), five Sunni Arabs, five Kurds, the head of the Assyrian Democratic Movement (Christian), and a Turkoman. Three of the members were women. The group decided to elect its president on a rotating basis to serve for one month. One president was killed by a car bomb in Baghdad on May 17, 2004. The council proved to be less active than anticipated.

Persistent Insurgence

The idea promoted by some members of the Bush administration and its supporters that the fall of the Baathist regime and the "liberation" of Iraq by coalition forces would immediately translate into a welcoming population, rapid and exhaustive reconstruction, and the creation of a model democratic system quickly proved false. Even as the war wound down, the lack of sufficient coalition troops to fully occupy Iraq allowed various Shiite groups to move into the vacuum and take control of a number of cities. The strong organization of some of these groups, combined with the Shiites forming an overwhelming majority, for the first time made Shiites a formidable force in Iraqi politics.

Instead of the termination of formal hostilities resulting in calm and order, guerrillas and suicide bombers set their sights on coalition forces. These elements were believed to be an array of groups with widely varying goals but a common cause. Many of the regime's senior figures had disappeared during the fighting and subsequently seemed to be directing underground guerrilla attacks. The preponderance of attacks appeared to have been orchestrated by Iraqi Sunni Arabs, who constitute as much as 90 percent of the insurgents. Although some were committed Baathists, others were likely a mixture of nationalists, Islamists, and even criminals. Because Bremer had dissolved the

Iraqi armed forces within weeks of his arrival in May 2003, it was assumed that former soldiers were well represented among those carrying out the attacks. The intense battle to assert coalition control over Fallujah turned increasing numbers of Sunnis against the occupation.

Foreign Islamist extremists joined the fight in Iraq in the same way they had rallied to fight the Soviets in Afghanistan, but their numbers were not thought to be more than a thousand. The most prominent among them was Abu Musab al-Zarqawi, who formally declared his allegiance to Osama bin Laden and al-Qaida in 2004. He headed the organization calling itself al-Qaida in Iraq. The Army of Ansar al-Sunnah, an offshoot of Ansar al-Islam, also carried out attacks against coalition forces.

As U.S. and other military targets began to better protect themselves, the insurgents increasingly focused on Iraqis. Infighting between Iraqi political factions added to the deteriorating situation, highlighted by a number of bombings of Shiite mosques and funerals. Coalition efforts to train a new Iraqi army and national guard were only partly successful in combating the insurgency.

One of the opening acts in the burgeoning climate of violence was the assassination of Ayatollah Abd al-Majid Khoei in Najaf on April 10, 2003, at the instigation of a rival Shiite group. On August 19, suicide bombers blew up UN headquarters in Baghdad, killing Vieira de Mello, the head of mission, and about two dozen other UN personnel, forcing the organization to abandon Iraq. Ten days later, the head of SCIRI, Ayatollah Muhammad Baqir al-Hakim became one of a hundred victims of a truck bomb in Najaf. On October 26, a rocket hit the Rashid Hotel in Baghdad, killing a U.S. military officer and wounding eighteen people; the presumed target, visiting U.S. deputy secretary of defense Paul Wolfowitz, narrowly escaped injury. The first U.S. civilian deaths occurred on March 9, 2004, when Iraqi policemen outside Baghdad killed two CPA officials and their Iraqi translator. Suicide bombers launched attacks at American-manned checkpoints. A U.S. Chinook helicopter and a Blackhawk helicopter were shot

down within five days of each other in November 2003, killing twenty-four. The number of U.S. casualties grew with the passage of almost every month.

Between May and September 2003, more than 700 Iraqi security personnel were killed, and their numbers grew worse later in the year. Forty-nine Iraqi army recruits traveling in three minibuses were ambushed on October 23; all of them died. On November 7, insurgents attacked a police station in Hadithah and executed twenty-one policemen. Leading police officers were assassinated throughout Iraq. On December 3, sixteen Shiite police officers were killed in Baghdad on the same day that fourteen people died in a car bomb attack on a Shiite mosque elsewhere in the city. Several police stations and checkpoints in the vicinity of Tikrit and Baghdad were attacked on December 28, resulting in the deaths of some sixty policemen. The same day saw an ambush of Iraqi national guard troops near Baquba, several car bombs in Baghdad, an attack on a joint U.S.-Iraqi patrol in Mosul, and the detonation of a bomb near Samarra.

Although tighter security resulted in a decreased frequency of attacks on U.S. positions, it did not prevent them. On December 13–14, suicide bombers struck on consecutive days at the entrance to Baghdad's Green Zone, the heavily fortified area housing the U.S. civilian administration and senior figures in the Iraqi interim government. A week later, another suicide bomber launched an attack on the mess tent at a U.S. base near Mosul, killing twenty-two U.S. and Iraqi soldiers and wounding another seventy-two.

Fallujah, just west of Baghdad, had always been a headache for Iraq's rulers, first for British occupiers in the early twentieth century and then for successive Iraqi governments. When U.S. troops accidentally killed ten Iraqi policemen in the city on September 12, 2003, residents vowed revenge. In the following months, the city's population swelled with anti-American fighters, including criminals and Islamist extremists, many of the latter arriving from outside Iraq. In a particularly gruesome incident, four American contractors were killed and their bodies mutilated on March 9, 2004. Two months later, on April 5, marines besieged the city, while several Iraqi battalions refused to take part. Iraqi politicians finally persuaded the Americans to end the siege on April 30, promising that Iraqi troops would take control. In October, the United States launched an assault to regain control of the city of Samarra. U.S. and Iraqi military forces began an all-out assault on Fallujah on November 8. Artillery pounded the city before ground troops entered and took control; much of Fallujah had been turned to rubble by the time the Iraqi prime minister declared it "liberated" on November 13. Some fifty-one U.S. servicemen and an estimated 1,200 insurgents were killed during the offensive. At the same time, insurgents took advantage of the attention focused on Fallujah to briefly seize control of Mosul in the north.

The atmosphere was further poisoned following the release of photographs in late April 2004 showing American soldiers mistreating and humiliating Iraqi prisoners at the Abu Ghraib prison in Baghdad. Although the United States charged seven low-ranking soldiers with the abuses, there were suspicions that more had been involved, that superior officers had been negligent in exercising control over prison staff, and that the Abu Ghraib abuses were part of a systematic culture of abuse practiced by U.S. forces at Guantanamo Bay in Cuba, in Afghanistan, and in undisclosed locations where the CIA interrogated terror suspects.

Over the months, attacks against Iraqi civilians increased in frequency and deadliness, with incident fatalities exceeding one and two dozen on repeated occasions. The kidnapping and videotaping of executions of foreigners, including Arabs, Asians, and Westerners, added a disturbing element to the violence. Rashes of kidnappings of Iraqis for ransom were also reported. The explosion of five bombs in Baghdad and Karbala on March 2, 2004, marred Ashura ceremonies being held for the first time in decades. (Ashura is the holiest time in the Shiite calendar.) Some 270 people died, and nearly 600 were wounded. A pattern emerged of multiple attacks deliberately targeting Shiites, designed presumably by Islamist extremists trying to create divisions between the Sunni and Shiite communities.

A steady stream of assassinations, car bombings, and detonations of IEDs (improvised explosive devices) continued through the first months of 2005. January 30, the day of elections for the new National Assembly, was marked by the death of 44 people in insurgent attacks, and a suicide car bomb in Hillah, south of Baghdad, resulted in at least 127 deaths and more then 150 wounded in what was the worst toll to date. Suicide bombers hit mosques in Mosul and Baghdad on March 10, and U.S. and Iraqi Special Forces killed a number of insurgents in a raid on their base near Tikrit on March 23.

The toll of U.S. personnel killed in Iraq hit 1,000 in September 2004. By early June 2005, that figure had swollen to 1,700 killed and 13,000 wounded. The toll for Iraqi security forces and civilians was far higher. While the U.S. government provided no estimates of Iraq fatalities, a private Western group, www.iraqbodycount.net, using corroborated press accounts, estimated that between 17,300 and 19,800 civilians had been killed by early April 2005. An article in the *Lancet,* a British medical journal, caused a stir in October 2004 by estimating that about 100,000 Iraqi civilians had died since the Iraq war began in March 2003, basing its reckoning on a survey conducted across most of Iraq.

The Hunt for WMD

As noted, the detection and destruction of Iraq's WMD capabilities was a primary focus of the sanctions regime imposed on Iraq from 1991 to 2003. From 1991 to 1998, the principal effort was carried out by UNSCOM's team of 70 to 80 inspectors who searched for potential WMD sites in Iraq and monitored and verified the destruction of WMD materials that they found. The International Atomic Energy Administration's Iraq Action Team complemented these inspectors. The Iraqi regime continually hampered their efforts, and when Baghdad finally refused them access in late 1998, the United States and Britain began low-grade-war air strikes. UNMOVIC's team worked in Iraq from November 2002 until being withdrawn in March 2003 on the eve of war. During this same time period, the UN's Iraq Nuclear Verification Office searched for nuclear weapons.

One of the principal arguments of the Bush administration and its coalition allies, notably Britain, for waging war against Iraq was that the Hussein government had not complied with UN resolutions regarding the total elimination of Iraq's WMD and that it was actively preventing inspectors from inventorying stocks and capability. As a consequence, it was widely believed and declared certainly by the U.S. and British governments that Iraq still possessed WMD and was likely to use them against its enemies. The containment program established after the 1991 Gulf war, it was contended, had broken down, making it imperative that the Hussein government be toppled to eliminate the threat. During and immediately after the 2003 war, the United States established several military and civilian task forces to find and destroy Iraq's remaining WMD capabilities. The task was subsequently taken over by the Iraq Survey Group (ISG), a multinational team of more than 1,000 sponsored by Australia, Britain, and the United States and coordinated by former UN inspector David Kay.

The inspectors did not uncover significant WMD or materials. Kay presented the findings in an interim report of the ISG on October 2, 2003. Iraq's nuclear program consisted of remnants, and apparently no attempts had been made to restart it. Its chemical weapons capability seemed to have been effectively eliminated by military actions and UN inspections considerably prior to the 2003 war. Although the status of biological weapons was more uncertain, the available evidence pointed to the abandonment of active production in the 1990s while maintaining the technical capability to restart it. Only the missile program remained truly active. The inspectors found that Iraq had continued to develop long-range missiles

outside the limits imposed by the United Nations. Furthermore, the inspectors found no evidence of cooperation between Iraq and al-Qaida or of any transfer of Iraqi WMD materials to terrorist organizations. The final report of the ISG, released on September 30, 2004, noted,

ISG assesses that Saddam clearly intended to reconstitute long-range delivery systems and that the systems potentially were for WMD. . . . [The] Iraq Survey Group discovered further evidence of the maturity and significance of the pre-1991 Iraqi Nuclear Program but found that Iraq's ability to reconstitute a nuclear weapons program progressively decayed after that date. . . . Saddam never abandoned his intentions to resume a [chemical weapons] effort when sanctions were lifted and conditions were judged favorable. . . . In spite of exhaustive investigation, ISG found no evidence that Iraq possessed, or was developing [biological weapons] agent production systems mounted on road vehicles or railway wagons.

As for the association and assistance of Saddam Hussein to terrorist groups—the administration's other argument for going to war—although evidence existed of contacts between Hussein's regime and al-Qaida, the 9/11 Commission reported, "But to date we have seen no evidence that these or the earlier contacts ever developed into a collaborative operational relationship. Nor have we seen evidence indicating that Iraq cooperated with al Qaeda in developing or carrying out any attacks against the United States."

Democratization

In the "The National Security Strategy of the United States of America," issued by the White House in September 2002, President Bush made the promotion of democracy throughout the world an explicit U.S. foreign policy goal: "We will actively work to bring the hope of democracy, development, free markets, and free trade to every corner of the world." He singled out the Palestinian territories in this regard, stating, "America stands committed to an independent and democratic Palestine, living beside Israel in peace and security."

One of the Bush administration's arguments in justifying an attack on Iraq was that it would bring freedom to Iraqis and lead to the creation of a democratic system there. It was also argued that the war with Iraq would provoke a democratic revolution across the Middle East, as well as serve as a necessary first step in advancing peace between Israel and the Palestinians. In support of its goals, in late 2002 the administration established within the State Department the Middle East Partnership Initiative, an aid program to help foster democratic trends in the region by providing economic, educational, and civil society assistance.

Bush returned to the freedom and democracy theme in a November 2003 speech to the National Endowment for Democracy in which he noted that "60 years of Western nations excusing and accommodating the lack of freedom in the Middle East did nothing to make us safe, because in the long run stability cannot be purchased at the expense of liberty." In February 2004, plans to assist development and reforms throughout the "Greater Middle East" were leaked to the press. These plans, formulated as an agenda for discussion at a forthcoming Group of Eight (G8) conference of industrialized nations, caused a stir throughout the Arab world, to which they were primarily directed. In part, Arab governments objected because they had not been consulted, but the plans were also regarded as yet another example of unwelcome U.S. government interference in the region. In response, some Arab governments announced reform initiatives, and a conference on democratization was held in Yemen. The initiative was also discussed at an Arab League summit.

The G8 summit in June 2004 approved the Broader Middle East and North Africa Initiative (BMENA) and set in motion the machinery to formulate and discuss programs in development and education to advance the cause. As a consequence, foreign and finance ministers of regional countries, officials from G8 nations, and representatives of business and advocacy groups participated in the Forum for the Future in Morocco in December 2004. Discussion during the meetings was heated, with Arab officials charging that the main obstacle to reform was the continued Arab-Israeli conflict and other participants charging that too much emphasis was being placed on economic liberalization and not enough on political reform. Among the points agreed upon was an acceptance of channels for civil society groups to discuss reform with their governments and the creation of a fund to provide technical support and financial assistance to small private enterprises. Another meeting of the forum was scheduled for November 2005 in Bahrain.

As noted, after the 2003 invasion, the Coalition Provisional Authority took de facto control of Iraq and appointed the interim Iraqi Governing Council. The CPA's handover of sovereignty to a temporary Iraqi government in June 2004 under the Transitional Administrative Law stipulated that elections for a provisional government be held no later than the end of January 2005. The elected government would then write a constitution for the country and organize elections in late 2005 for a permanent, democratic government. The success of the January 30, 2005, elections—despite skepticism in some quarters, threats of disruption by insurgents, and a partial boycott by Sunni Arabs—was hailed by the Bush administration as vindication of its Iraq policy.

In the following months, administration supporters pointed to the election of a new Palestinian leader, partial elections for municipal councils in Saudi Arabia, popular protests in Lebanon against the Syrian presence there, and protests against government inefficiency and corruption in Egypt as examples of a democratic spillover effect from Iraq. Detractors pointed out that the election of a new Palestinian leader was because of the death of Yasir Arafat (who had been elected himself), that Saudi Arabia had been pursuing its own agenda of reform in its own slow way for more than a decade, and that the Lebanese protests were provoked by the assassination of popular former prime minister Rafiq al-Hariri and were countered by other protests in support of Syria's role in Lebanese affairs. It appears that more time will be needed before one can effectively assess the impact of the U.S. government and developments in Iraq on fostering democracy in the Arab world and "Greater Middle East."

Islamic Extremism and Terrorism

Like any religion, Islam has its extremists, although they certainly do not represent the beliefs of the great majority of Muslims. Considerable attention has been given in recent years to Islamic extremism, not least because of the acts of one group, al-Qaida, in perpetrating the September 11 attacks, as well as others before and after. The roots of Islamic extremism in its modern form can be traced to the late nineteenth and early twentieth centuries as a reaction to the increased presence and influence of Western powers in Islamic lands. One strand of Muslim reformers held that the Islamic world should accept Western innovations in technology and organization while reemphasizing the role and requirements of Islam and Islamic society and polity. This strand has continued to resonate among many moderate Muslims. Another strand advocated rejection of the West as a destructive influence and sought to return Islamic society to the principles of the golden age of the Prophet Muhammad and his companions. Adherents of this strand are generally called *salafis* (*salaf* means the "ancestors," that is, the original or early Muslims). *(See Fifteen Centuries of Islam, Chapter 6, p. 195)*

The Muslim Brotherhood, founded in Egypt in 1928, is one of the earliest overtly political Islamist movements. Its unyielding stance and acts of violence, including the assassination of an Egyptian prime minister, provoked an extensive crackdown and the jailing or exile of many of its members. A number of these found work as bureaucrats or teachers in Saudi Arabia and the other Gulf states, thus spreading their version of radical Islam. Other groups subsequently appeared in Egypt, influenced by the brotherhood although organizationally distinct. One of these, al-Jihad (or Islamic Jihad), assassinated Egyptian president Anwar al-Sadat in 1981.

Al-Dawa ("the call to Islam") perhaps represents the earliest Islamic movement to appear in the Gulf, organizing in Iraq in the late 1950s. Al-Dawa is a Shiite organization, unlike the Sunni Muslim Brotherhood, and its violent opposition to successive secularized Iraqi regimes resulted in severe repression and the death or flight abroad of many of its members. Al-Dawa resurfaced in Iraq after the 2003 Iraq War. Its leader, Ibrahim al-Jaafari, was chosen as prime minister in 2005.

Iranian Revolution and Its Export

It is not surprising that Shiite activism took root in Iraq, because it is the home to Najaf and Karbala—the two holiest cities in Shiite Islam. When Iran expelled Ayatollah Ruhollah Khomeini in 1964 for his opposition to the shah's rule, he found refuge in the seminary city of Najaf and remained there until the shah pressured Baghdad to deport him to France in 1978. From there, Khomeini took leadership of an emerging Islamic revolution, and in 1979 he returned to Iran as the country's top political and religious figure.

The creation of the Islamic Republic of Iran marked the beginning of a new form of Islamic extremism. The successful proponents of the revolution in Iran set as their goal the export of Islamic revolution throughout the Islamic world. Their neighbors in the Gulf represented their primary targets, particularly the monarchies. In the tense atmosphere of the revolution, the Sunni populations of the Gulf monarchies began to doubt the loyalty of their Shiite minorities. Sunnis were the majority population in the monarchies, with the exception of Bahrain. The Saudi government forcibly repressed demonstrations in the Shiite towns of the country's Eastern Province in 1979–1980. Bahrain, which had witnessed organized opposition (involving Sunnis and Shiites) to its government for most of the twentieth century, accused Iran of providing training and weapons to Bahraini Shiites to overthrow the regime. Even in Kuwait, extremist members of the Shiite community apparently detonated several bombs.

After the conclusion of the Iran-Iraq War in 1988, Khomeini's death in 1989, and the emergence of more moderate figures in the Iranian government—epitomized by the election of Ali Akbar Hashemi Rafsanjani as president—the

Iranian threat to its Gulf neighbors became muted. The 1996 bombing against U.S. military personnel at Khobar Towers in Saudi Arabia was widely ascribed to Saudi Hizballah with help from Iran. As no conclusive evidence has emerged about the perpetrators, others with equal plausibility claimed that it had been an al-Qaida operation.

Al-Qaida in the Gulf

Al-Qaida's top leader, Osama bin Laden, was born in Jiddah, Saudi Arabia, and went from there to fight with other *mujahidin* (holy warriors) in Afghanistan in the 1980s. Between his return to Saudi Arabia and subsequent transfer to Sudan, bin Laden began organizing and recruiting followers for his extremist version of Islam. Many of these have been Saudis, partly because of bin Laden's Saudi background and others perhaps partly because of the formative influence of hardline Wahhabis in the kingdom.

Wahhabism (or more properly, Unitarianism or, as some adherents prefer at present, Salafism) is a particularly ascetic and conservative movement within Sunni Islam; it is not a separate sect. It predominates in Saudi Arabia and Qatar and traditionally was found in only a few other Gulf states. As practiced in Saudi Arabia, it forbids alcohol or the veneration of ancestors or saints, adheres to the strict segregation of men and women, and employs "religious police" to enforce acceptable public behavior and the closing of all shops and offices during the five daily prayers.

Saudi Arabia regards itself as the protector of Islam, because the birthplace of Muhammad and the two holiest cities in Islam are located on its territory. When oil income began to flow into the country in large amounts in the 1970s and 1980s, Saudi Arabia sought to extend its religious influence abroad, donating mosques and Qurans to Muslim communities around the world. In addition, it sought to persuade these communities to embrace Wahhabi thought and practices.

This influence left its mark notably in Pakistan, where conservative Islamic scholars began to propagate a very extreme view of Islamic tenets in *madrasas* (religious schools). Among their students were Afghans in exile from the Soviet invasion. Known as Taliban (students), these followers returned to Afghanistan to take control of the country and enforce their extreme religious views on its people. In the late 1990s, the Taliban welcomed Osama bin Laden and al-Qaida to take up residence in Afghanistan.

Al-Qaida is not a true representation of Wahhabism, as its ideological/theological development derives equally from other salafi or extremist views propounded in non-Wahhabi thinking, such as that of the Muslim Brotherhood and the Egyptian al-Jihad. These ideological currents focus on the need for a defensive *jihad* against the encroaching West. The term *jihad* has as many meanings as "crusade" in English. It can mean "holy war," a campaign to do good, or simply personal striving to become a better person. Mujahidin, Muslim extremists who believe in jihad as holy war, are often called "jihadists" in English.

While many members of al-Qaida, including the majority of the September 11 hijackers, have been Saudi, the network was quiescent inside Saudi Arabia until fairly recently. Angered by the excesses of some of the Saudi royal family and by the Saudi government's perceived deviation from al-Qaida's vision of Islam, as well as by the presence of "infidel" U.S. troops on holy soil, since early 2003 as many as several thousand jihadists have carried out a terror campaign in the kingdom, targeting housing compounds and government buildings; they also attacked the U.S. consulate in Jiddah. Al-Qaida in the Arabian Peninsula has also killed or kidnapped foreigners in the kingdom.

The Saudi government reacted forcefully, with its security forces fighting numerous battles with the extremists. By early 2005, most of the group's leaders had been killed, and it appeared to have lost much of its strength. The group may, however, have expanded its operations to neighboring states: There were violent confrontations with security forces in Kuwait in January 2005, and a suicide bombing shook Qatar in March 2005.

Afghanistan

The Republic of Afghanistan is a landlocked country, slightly smaller than Texas, at the nexus of Central Asia and South Asia. It is bordered to the north by Turkmenistan, Uzbekistan, and Tajikistan, to the west by Iran, and to the south and east by Pakistan. A strip of land running through the Hindu Kush provides a short border of fifty miles with China. The country's population was estimated in 2004 at 28 million. Kabul is its capital, and other major cities are Kandahar in the south, Mazar-i Sharif in the north, Herat in the west, and Jalalabad in the east. Afghanistan is highly diverse ethnically, Pashtunis comprising some 40 percent of its population and Tajiks more than a quarter. There are also Aimaks, Baluchis, Hazaras, Turkmen, and Uzbeks represented in smaller proportions. The great majority of Afghans are Muslim, some 80 percent of whom are Sunnis with less than 20 percent Shiite (mainly among the Hazara centered around Herat).

Afghanistan's strategic location has often subjected it to invasion. Few invading armies have, however, achieved success because of the country's rugged and inhospitable terrain and the vulnerability of the required long lines of communication and support. The Soviet Union intervened militarily in 1979 at the invitation of the leaders of a leftist coup. Soviet forces, however, sustained heavy losses from an Islamist opposition, the *mujahidin,* many of whom were volunteers from Arab countries. The Soviets were forced to withdraw in 1989, and the Marxist regime in Kabul collapsed in 1992. Infighting among the leaders (or so-called warlords) of the various ethnic groups and the continued resistance of the mujahidin prevented the establishment of a stable government to replace the toppled regime.

The emergence of the Taliban—Afghan Islamic students who had studied in Pakistan and been influenced there by the hard-line Islamist Jamiat-ul-Ulema-e-Islam (Assembly of Islamic Clergy)—altered the political landscape in subsequent years. Several thousand Taliban seized control of Kandahar in November 1994. After several years of fighting among the Taliban, the warlords, and elements of the mujahidin, the Taliban succeeded in capturing Kabul and extending their control over most of the country, with the exception of the northeast, which was held by the Northern Alliance, comprised mainly of

Islamic Extremists in Iraq

Prior to the 2003 war, Islamic extremists in Iraq were limited to Ansar al-Sunnah. During the occupation following the war, Abu Musab al-Zarqawi emerged as the most proficient and best-known Islamic extremist attacking U.S. forces and Iraqi allies. While the Bush administration has declared the invasion and occupation of Iraq to be part of its "war on terror," its critics contend that it has actually benefited terrorism by creating more recruits among the many Arabs and Muslims who oppose U.S. actions against and in Iraq.

Although Islamic extremists are probably only a minority of insurgents in Iraq, they are thought to comprise most if not all of the suicide bombers who have hit U.S. and Iraqi targets. As in the case of al-Qaida, numerous Saudis, Yemenis, and other nationalities are believed to be among their ranks. They infiltrate into Iraq through its porous borders with Saudi Arabia and Syria and view the struggle in Iraq as part of the defensive jihad against Western domination of the Islamic homeland. Their Sunni background probably has facilitated an alliance with Sunni Arab nationalists and loyalists of Saddam Hussein. As noted, a number of suicide attacks were carried out against Shiite targets.

Iran, Pakistan, and the "Islamic Bomb"

Although the George W. Bush administration did not materially alter the Clinton administration's policy of containing Iran, it was demonstrably concerned about Iran's presumed pursuit of a nuclear

THE PERSIAN GULF 173

Tajiks and Uzbeks. The Taliban proceeded to impose their harsh version of Islam on the territories they controlled.

In 1998 the Taliban gave refuge to Osama bin Laden and his al-Qaida organization, which established training camps in Afghanistan for mujahidin dedicated to fighting what were perceived as corrupt Islamic governments and the West's campaign to control the Islamic world. People from a number of countries were indoctrinated and trained in these camps and tasked with carrying out such acts as the bombing of the U.S. embassies in Kenya and Tanzania in 1998, the bombing of the USS *Cole* in a Yemeni harbor in 2000, and the suicide hijackings on September 11, 2001.

The Taliban rejected Saudi Arabia, UN, and U.S. efforts to hand over bin Laden or at least expel him from Afghanistan. Immediately after September 11, President George W. Bush demanded that bin Laden be turned over to the United States, and when the Taliban refused, launched military actions, Operation Enduring Freedom, on October 7, 2001, against Taliban and al-Qaida targets. With forces of the Northern Alliance doing most of the fighting, supported by U.S. air cover and bombings, the Taliban were forced to withdraw from Mazar-i Sharif and from Kabul in early November. After a period of confusion and intense negotiations, a UN-sponsored conference in December appointed Hamid Karzai, a relatively obscure former deputy foreign minister who enjoyed U.S. backing, as the head of an interim administration. In 2004 Afghanistan adopted a new constitution, and Karzai was elected president.

Meanwhile, a joint U.S. and Northern Alliance effort continued to roust al-Qaida from their hiding places. An intense battle for the Tora Bora caves in March 2002 forced the remaining al-Qaida fighters to retreat to the border region with Pakistan, where they went into hiding.

The new central government faced numerous economic and security issues. Despite continued searches and fighting, Osama bin Laden and Ayman al-Zawahiri, the number two figure in al-Qaida, remained at large through early 2005, as did Taliban leader Mullah Omar. The Taliban continued to strike at Afghan and U.S. targets from their hiding places.

Karzai's support comes mainly from fellow Pashtunis, and his direct control over the country is largely restricted to Pashtuni areas around Kabul and Kandahar. Although formally committed to the central government, the warlords remained largely autonomous.

weapons capability. Even before the administration took office, Condoleezza Rice, soon to be named national security adviser to the president, warned, "Iran's tactics have posed real problems for U.S. security. It has tried to destabilize moderate Arab states. Iran has also supported terrorism. . . . Iranian weaponry increasingly threatens Israel directly." As evidence of Iranian support of terrorism, the U.S. government cited in particular Iranian assistance to Hizballah in Lebanon and to Hamas and Islamic Jihad in the Palestinian territories and accused Tehran of providing sanctuary to al-Qaida members fleeing Afghanistan. It also faulted Iran for opposing Israeli-Palestinian peace efforts.

The administration's view of Iran had hardened by early 2002 as more reports of nuclear-related activity emerged from Iran, and Tehran was alleged to have sent arms to the Palestinian Authority. President Bush, in his January 2002 State of the Union Address, designated Iran a member of his "axis of evil," along with Iraq and North Korea. Suggestions began to circulate on how regime change might be achieved in Iran, and attempts were made to persuade the United Nations that sanctions should be implemented. Iran's tacit cooperation with the United States during the ouster of the Taliban in Afghanistan and its further cooperation during the Iraq War did little to moderate the Bush administration's animosity toward the Tehran regime. The administration appeared to have reached the conclusion that Iranian president Mohammad Khatami and his supporters did not have, and would not be able to obtain, sufficient power to moderate Iranian policies. As a result, only regime change could neutralize the perceived threat from Iran.

Pakistan

The Islamic Republic of Pakistan was created in 1947 by the partition of British India into the heavily Hindu Republic of India and a new entity in Pakistan intended to serve as a home to most of India's Muslim population. Until 1971 Pakistan consisted of two noncontiguous parts: dominant West Pakistan and more populous East Pakistan. During the 1971 Indian-Pakistani war, East Pakistan, with Indian assistance, broke away and formed the independent state of Bangladesh.

Since then Pakistan has consisted of four provinces. Sind, in the southeast and along the Arabian Sea, is the most populous region and contains Pakistan's largest city, Karachi. The Punjab, to the northeast of Sind and contiguous to India, is the second most populous province. Its main city is Lahore, and it also contains the Pakistani capital, Islamabad. Baluchistan, east of Sind and bordering on the Arabian Sea and Iran, is heavily tribal and only fitfully governed by the central government. The North West Frontier Province, inhabited by Pashtunis closely tied to the Pashtuni population of neighboring Afghanistan, contains many areas outside the central government's control.

Muhajirs, Muslims from elsewhere in India who migrated to Pakistan at the time of independence and their descendants, form a contentious fifth element in the volatile mix of often-fractious Sindis, Punjabis, Baluchis, and Pashtunis. Most of Pakistan's estimated population of 160 million is Sunni Muslim, but some 20 percent are Shiites, and 3 percent are Christian and Hindu. Urdu is the official language, but because most Pakistanis speak other languages at home, English also serves as a lingua franca.

Pakistan's military has ousted elected civilian governments and taken control more than once. In 1999 Prime Minister Mohammad Nawaz Sharif attempted to fire army chief of staff General Pervez Musharraf while the latter was out of the country. When Musharraf attempted to return, Sharif ordered that his airplane be denied permission to land. Musharraf supporters in the army thereupon seized the airport and arrested the prime minister and his cabinet. Musharraf proclaimed himself "chief executive of Pakistan" and later dismissed the country's president and assumed that office.

The country's political difficulties derive from internal disturbances and its intense rivalry with India. The two countries fought wars in 1947–48, 1965, and 1971, and skirmishes still occur over the disputed province of Kashmir, divided between the two countries at the time of independence. Pakistan's fear of India's military superiority and its pursuit of nuclear capability prodded Pakistan to begin its own nuclear research program. In 1998, after Pakistan test-fired its first surface-to-surface missile, the hard-line Hindu nationalist Bharatiya Janata Party, which had just won election in India, exploded several nuclear devises. This prompted Pakistan to quickly set off its own. International economic sanctions were subsequently imposed on both countries.

Pakistan traditionally had been aligned with China, whereas India has aligned with the Soviet Union. The dispatch of Soviet troops to Afghanistan in 1979 alarmed Islamabad. Worried by continued instability after the Soviet withdrawal in 1989, Inter-Services Intelligence, Pakistan's intelligence agency, supported the newly emergent Taliban movement of Afghan students who had studied in radical Islamist schools in Pakistan's North West Frontier Province. With covert Pakistani assistance, the Taliban assumed control of most of the important areas of Afghanistan in the mid-1990s.

However, the September 11 attacks on the United States forced Pakistan's government to give unreserved support to the United States in its intervention against the Taliban and al-Qaida. While the Musharraf government has wholeheartedly backed the subsequent Afghan government of President Hamid Karzai and provided military assistance in operations against the Taliban and al-Qaida, elements of those groups have found refuge in the wild Pushtun border areas of the North West Frontier Province outside Islamabad's control.

Under President Bush, the United States has continued to prevent arms sales and technology to Iran. With the renewal of the Iran-Libya Sanctions Act (ILSA) in August 2001, it continued to ban U.S. purchases of Iranian oil and prohibit U.S. companies from investing in Iran. In the first month or two after Bush began his second term, the possibility that the United States or Israel would use military force to destroy Iranian nuclear facilities was taken quite seriously.

Iran has consistently maintained that its nuclear research is restricted to civilian use and that the construction of a nuclear facility at Natanz, near Bushehr on the Gulf coast, is only intended to establish a reactor to produce energy, using fuel obtained from and to be returned to Russia. Despite persistent Iranian denials of any intention of building nuclear weapons, commentators suggested that Tehran might be tempted to make the effort because of its overriding security concerns. The presence of U.S. troops on either side of Iran—in Afghanistan and Iraq—undoubtedly jangled the nerves of the Iranian regime. In addition, Iran had to consider that Pakistan, its neighbor to the southeast, already had nuclear bombs.

The International Atomic Energy Agency imposed an October 2003 deadline for Iran to fully disclose its nuclear activities. As the deadline approached, Britain, France, and Germany reached an agreement with Tehran: Iran agreed to suspend uranium enrichment activities and to cooperate with the IAEA's requirements to provide details of its nuclear activity; in return, the European states promised that Iran would be allowed to import nuclear technology for peaceful uses. In December 2003, Iran signed the Additional Protocol to the Nuclear Non-Proliferation Treaty, binding it to accept no-notice inspections. The Europeans contended that negotiation and compromise would create a more amenable Iranian stance. The IAEA subsequently reported that Iran had violated some of its agreements.

Pakistan's nuclear intentions have been a concern for several decades, as it was well known that its desire to acquire a nuclear weapons capability largely resulted from its long and intense rivalry with India. The country's nuclear program began after the 1971 Indo-Pakistani War and made considerable progress under the leadership of Abdul Qadeer "A.Q." Khan, the founder of Pakistan's nuclear weapons program, with help mainly from China. When India exploded several nuclear devices on May 11, 1998, Pakistan responded by speeding the testing for its own bomb, exploding several devices May 28–30, 1998.

In addition to creating fears that an India-Pakistan war might escalate into nuclear attacks, Pakistan's possession of a nuclear capability raises two other concerns: Some observers regard Pakistan as the possessor of an "Islamic bomb," that is, Pakistan could use its nuclear weapons to protect other Islamic states, and it could transfer technology and perhaps fuels to other Islamic states. It has been speculated that Saudi Arabia has sought Pakistani assistance in developing a bomb to deploy on Chinese missiles that it purchased in 1988, but no evidence thus far supports this thesis.

Perhaps more troubling is the discovery in early 2004 that Abdul Qadeer Khan had sold nuclear technology and designs to Iran, Libya, and North Korea. Although it was stressed that Khan had acted on his own behalf and that the Pakistani government had had no knowledge of the transactions, the revelations reinforced suspicions that central authority control over such weapons might be easily compromised. In addition, there remains concern that Pakistan is an inherently unstable country with a deeply fractured population, considerable internal violence, and a history of support for al-Qaida in some sectors.

Gulf Cooperation Council

In February 1981, Bahrain, Kuwait, Oman, Qatar, Saudi Arabia, and the United Arab Emirates founded the Gulf Cooperation Council (GCC) to strengthen regional security and improve economic, political, and military cooperation. The council holds an annual summit of heads of state in December, as well as occasional summits at other times of the year, and a conference of foreign ministers meets four times a year. The Saudi capital of Riyadh hosts the council's permanent secretariat.

The GCC faces significant changes as it deals with political transitions, uncertain relations with a new Iraq, rapprochement with Iran, and a shifting oil market. Political transitions in the Persian Gulf vary, ranging from succession challenges within royal families to moves toward democracy. In Bahrain, a collection of thirty-five islands covering 260 square miles, the Shiite majority has long agitated for equal political and economic rights and is seeking to reestablish a national assembly to replace the appointed Consultative Council established after the Gulf war. The country, troubled by political unrest for several years, faced another crisis in March 1999, when Amir Isa bin Al Khalifa died of a heart attack. He was succeeded by his son, Hamad bin Isa Al Khalifa. Amir Hamad took a number of steps to diffuse the tensions of the late 1990s and revised the constitution to establish a new, partly elected parliament. Bahrain's Shiites, however, contend that he has failed to deliver on all his promises. Unlike most Bahrainis, who are Shiite, the ruling family is Sunni, which is a source of tension.

In Saudi Arabia, King Fahd has played a decreasing role in governing the country since suffering a stroke in 1995. His brother, Crown Prince Abdallah ibn Abd al-Aziz, has served as Saudi Arabia's de facto leader, but the future of Saudi leadership is uncertain. Fahd and Abdallah are both in their eighties. Under the kingdom's unwritten rules of succession, each of the forty-four sons of their father, King Abd al-Aziz Al Saud, has a claim to the throne, and many of them are still alive. If leadership is not passed down to a new generation, there is a chance that Saudi Arabia's future will rest in the hands of a series of geriatric kings.

Some GCC countries are experimenting with holding on to power by giving more of it away. Several have begun to introduce aspects of democracy and to extend political rights to women. In March 1999, Qatar held an election in which women for the first time could vote and run for seats in the twenty-nine-member municipal affairs council. Women took advantage of their empowerment by

contending in six races. Moreover, 10,000 of the 23,000 registered voters in the election were women. In a society that circumscribes women's freedom, however, even this development retained vestiges of the past. Men and women stood in separate lines and voted at separate ballot boxes. The vote, which was seen as a test run for parliamentary elections in 2006, produced a turnout above 90 percent. In subsequent municipal elections, held in March 2003, a Qatari woman won election for the first time.

In Oman, 2003 elections for the consultative council were open to the entire adult population. Two women were once again elected. The Kuwaiti National Assembly in May 2005 voted to enfranchise women, who will cast their first votes in legislative elections scheduled for 2007. Also in 2005, the Kuwaiti government appointed its first female cabinet minister when it gave Massuma al-Mubarak the portfolios for planning and administrative development. Two women were also appointed to municipal councils.

Saudi Arabia expanded its appointed consultative council to 150 members in 2005. While there was discussion of including women among the council's all-male members, this seems unlikely to happen in the near future. When the government made public its plans for elections in 2005 for seats on municipal councils, several women announced their candidacies. For months, uncertainty surrounded whether they would be allowed to run, but ultimately, they were barred from doing so, and all women were prohibited from voting. The possibility of granting more rights to women continues to attract attention, however. After the government began issuing women their own identity cards, there was some agitation to permit them to drive. The government, fighting a conservative trend in the country, took no action. Women must wear veils in public, and they are barred from studying journalism, engineering, or law. Women comprise 50 percent of the student population, but only 5.5 percent of the workforce. More than 80 percent of the women who work are teachers or in health care.

For GCC countries, one of their most prominent external issues is how to handle a diplomatically revived Iran. The May 1997 election of Mohammad Khatami, a political moderate, appeared to have ushered in a new era for Iran. After the Islamic revolution of 1979, Iran's leaders were mostly cloistered, but the peripatetic Khatami operated differently. He traveled throughout the Middle East and Europe during the spring of 1999 in an effort to strengthen Iran's relationships with its Arab neighbors and to increase Iran's acceptance in the world community. A visit he made to Saudi Arabia was the first by an Iranian leader since 1979.

That visit, however, created a fissure in the GCC, which was formed in part as protection against Iran. The Iranian-Saudi rapprochement drew a particularly strong negative reaction from the United Arab Emirates, which continues to be embroiled with Tehran in a dispute over three tiny islands in the Persian Gulf that Iran claimed on the eve of UAE independence in 1971. The UAE wants the matter settled in the World Court, but Iran has constantly balked. Gulf states generally remain wary of attempts by Tehran to export Islamic revolution.

Khatemi's visit to Saudi Arabia helped to forge unity among Gulf oil producers, whose budgets and economies in the late 1990s were hurting because of weakening world oil prices. By 2004–2005, a number of global factors had combined to push oil prices to record levels, and Gulf production, not pricing, began to feel pressure. Although OPEC raised members' production quotas, most were already operating at full capacity. Only Saudi Arabia was able to pick up some of the slack, increasing production to nearly 10 million barrels a day and announcing that it would expand its spare capacity as soon as possible. With prices above $50 by early 2005, the Gulf oil-producing states saw their budgets going back in the black. Saudi Arabia reversed eighteen consecutive years of budget deficits. The country's high rate of population growth, however, meant that growing expenditures quickly neutralized increases in income.

The GCC has tried over the years to foster economic cooperation to reduce tariffs and other barriers to trade between members. Steps are being taken to finalize a common market among the six members with the free movement of citizens, capital, and labor among them. A major role of the GCC is to enhance members' security. A joint military command oversees GCC defense activities and has conducted a series of joint military maneuvers—the first ever among Arab states when they began—to test coordination of the Western equipment and command systems of the six member states. These exercises were a visible symbol of the GCC working toward diminishing needs and pretexts for outside intervention. Plans for the establishment of an integrated GCC force—beyond the symbolic Peninsula Shield Force stationed in Saudi Arabia near the Iraqi border—have never gotten off the ground.

Long before the Iraqi invasion of Kuwait, analysts pronounced the GCC joint defense system incapable of halting an attack by a major regional power. The Gulf states' small populations, diversity of weapons systems, and divergent domestic interests have impeded mutual defense efforts despite major outlays in military spending. The United Arab Emirates ranked as the top weapons buyer in the developing world during the period 1996–2003 with $15.7 billion in purchases, while Saudi Arabia ranked sixth with $9.4 billion in purchases. The alliance's continuing vulnerability is perhaps why Gulf states have granted U.S. naval forces greater access to their port facilities. In addition, U.S. enforcement of the no-fly zones over Iraq were based out of Saudi Arabia, and Qatar provided the regional headquarters of U.S. forces during the 2003 Iraq War. Bahrain hosts the permanent U.S. naval headquarters in the Gulf, and the United Arab Emirates is a frequent port of call.

Yet, Gulf Arabs remain suspicious that the United States will some day move to dominate them, perhaps in response to a global energy crisis. The regimes of the Gulf also fear that accommodating the United States may make them vulnerable to attacks from Islamic extremists. For the moment, however, GCC countries have no alternative but to accept a strong U.S. military presence in the region.

CHAPTER 5

MIDDLE EASTERN OIL AND GAS

The modern history of the Middle East is inextricably intertwined with petroleum. Oil and gas resources are the economic lifeblood of a number of nations in the region. In 1971 oil-importing nations paid about $2 a barrel for petroleum produced by the eleven-member Organization of the Petroleum Exporting Countries (OPEC), an intergovernmental organization created in September 1960 by Iran, Iraq, Kuwait, Saudi Arabia, and Venezuela to coordinate and unify their national petroleum policies.

By 1981 the price of OPEC oil had jumped to about $35 a barrel, largely as a result of oil-price shocks in 1973–1974 and 1979–1980. This 1,700 percent increase fundamentally changed the rules that had governed international economic and political relationships. The effects of that change were still being felt worldwide at the beginning of the twenty-first century. Although the late 1990s witnessed a precipitous drop in oil prices, by late 2004 prices had risen again, holding steady above $50 a barrel for an extended period of time. Experience with such fluctuations made the international community more accustomed to such changes, but price volatility nonetheless remains a rallying cry for U.S. politicians who advocate for less dependence on foreign oil sources. At the beginning of 2005, many analysts speculated that prices might remain at elevated levels for years.

The role of natural gas in the Middle Eastern economies is growing exponentially. The vast gas reserves of Qatar and Iran, improvements in technology that make getting gas to markets feasible and more economical, and the burgeoning demand for natural gas in Europe, Asia, and the United States point toward the potential for substantial increases in export revenues.

In the last few years, China has accounted for approximately 40 percent of world oil demand, and its economic growth is expected to continue to increase its energy consumption. In the United States and Europe, demand for natural gas as a cleaner burning fuel for generating electricity is steadily increasing. The current state of Middle Eastern natural resources and the outlook concerning global supply and demand will remain critically important worldwide.

History

During the first half of the twentieth century, the Middle Eastern oil-producing nations played a role subservient to the major international oil companies contracted to develop their oil fields. Concessions granted by Arab rulers gave foreign oil companies a free hand in exploiting their oil reserves. Such agreements required that the companies pay only a nominal royalty, an average of twenty-one cents a barrel, to the oil-producing country. In return, the oil companies were exempted from taxes in the producing nations and independently set production and pricing policy.

The oil-producing countries found these arrangements satisfying prior to World War II, when demand was low, prices were fluctuating or dropping, and prospects for discovering large quantities of oil were uncertain. During and after World War II, however, inflation reduced the purchasing power of the fixed royalties paid to the producing nations. In other words, their share of the value of the oil produced declined.

Venezuela became one of the first countries to challenge these arrangements, when in 1945 the government demanded and received an even split in oil profits with the companies. In subsequent years, Middle Eastern oil-producing nations, which had been receiving royalties of 12.5 percent of profits, adopted the Venezuelan model. By the early 1950s, all the oil producers had negotiated 50-50 agreements. Between 1948 and 1960, these contracts increased the revenues of Middle East producers almost tenfold, to nearly $1.4 billion.

The entry into the oil-production business of a number of new, independent companies in the 1950s put downward pressure on prices. The American firms of Esso (now Exxon), Gulf, Mobil, Socal (the predecessor to Chevron), and Texaco along with Royal Dutch Shell and British Petroleum—the corporations that controlled the world oil market—found themselves confronted by smaller, more aggressive companies eager to produce at high levels. These so-called Seven Sisters had in the past reduced overseas production when the world oil market became saturated, thus preventing a drop in price.

The independents, among them Amoco, Getty, and Occidental, made it more difficult for the major companies to control prices. The smaller businesses set their prices lower than the majors' for gasoline and other oil products, upsetting the established market structure. Their actions forced the larger companies to cut posted prices (the asking price) in addition to matching the lower market prices (the price at which the oil sells). As a result, producing nations experienced reductions in their royalty and tax incomes. The lower prices for foreign oil also led to an increased U.S. dependence on it and to a direct negative impact on domestic U.S. oil production. In an effort to protect U.S. oil companies, President Eisenhower imposed mandatory oil import quotas in 1959.

Concerned about these developments, Iraq called a meeting of oil-producing governments to discuss the situation. Iran, Kuwait, Saudi Arabia,

and Venezuela responded quickly and agreed that action should be taken. The participants at the Baghdad Conference, held September 10–14, 1959, agreed to establish OPEC, with the initial goal of returning oil prices to their earlier levels and obtaining the right to consult with oil companies on future pricing decisions.

The oil companies made no further cuts in posted prices. Instead, the U.S. government helped ensure that producer-nation revenues increased without forcing companies to raise their price. It did so using an expansive interpretation of the foreign tax credit that lowered the taxes oil companies paid to the U.S. government, thereby offsetting the extra taxes they paid to producer governments. Some critics charged that such treatment amounted to a subsidy for foreign oil production.

A Unified OPEC

During the 1960s, Abu Dhabi (whose membership later was transferred to the United Arab Emirates), Algeria, Indonesia, Libya, and Qatar joined OPEC. In 1975 the roster again expanded with the addition of Ecuador, Gabon, and Nigeria (the first two of which dropped out in the 1990s). This last expansion brought OPEC's membership to thirteen.

OPEC proved successful in preventing further cuts in posted prices for oil, but it failed during the early 1960s to restore prices to their earlier levels or to agree on a formula to limit output among its members. Moreover, throughout the 1960s, the producing states increasingly criticized the 50-50 split on oil profits that had become standard. In the later half of the decade, OPEC began consequently to agitate for higher revenues.

In June 1968, OPEC issued a declaration of principles asserting the right of member nations to control world oil production and prices. It also agreed on a minimum taxation rate of 55 percent of profits, more uniform pricing practices, a general increase in posted prices in all member countries, elimination of excessively high earnings for the operators, and the renegotiation of contract provisions that granted the oil companies excessive earnings. Also in 1968, a dozen Middle Eastern nations

World Crude Oil Production and Petroleum Consumption

CRUDE OIL PRODUCTION			PETROLEUM CONSUMPTION		
Country	Thousands of Barrels per Day	Percentage	Country	Thousands of Barrels per Day	Percentage
Saudi Arabia[a]	9,100	12.6	United States	20,520	24.9
Russia	8,805	12.1	Other Non-OECD[b]	13,220	16.0
United States	5,430	7.5	Other Asia	8,250	10.0
Iran[a]	4,001	5.5	Other OECD Europe	7,270	8.8
China	3,485	4.8	China	6,630	8.0
Mexico	3,383	4.7	Japan	5,440	6.6
Norway	2,973	4.1	Former Soviet Union	4,160	5.0
Venezuela[a]	2,556	3.5	Germany	2,670	3.2
Nigeria[a]	2,508	3.5	Canada	2,290	2.8
United Arab Emirates[a]	2,478	3.4	Korea, South	2,140	2.6
Canada	2,398	3.3	Mexico	2,040	2.5
Kuwait[a]	2,375	3.3	France	2,040	2.5
Iraq[a]	2,011	2.8	Italy	1,880	2.3
United Kingdom	1,845	2.5	United Kingdom	1,860	2.3
Algeria[a]	1,676	2.3	Australia and New Zealand	1,050	1.3
Libya[a]	1,515	2.1			
Brazil	1,477	2.0	World Total	82,550	
Indonesia[a]	1,113	1.5			
Angola	1,052	1.5			
Qatar[a]	817	1.1			
Malaysia	755	1.0			
Oman	751	1.0			
Argentina	691	1.0			
India	683	0.9			
Egypt	594	0.8			
Colombia	529	0.7			
World Total	72,477				

Notes: Figures are preliminary totals for 2004.

a. Member of the Organization of Petroleum Exporting Countries (OPEC)
b. Organisation for Economic Co-operation and Development

Source: Energy Information Administration, *International Petroleum Monthly,* 2004, tables 4.1a, 4.1b, 4.1c, and 4.6, http://www.eia.gov/ipm.

established the Organization of Arab Petroleum Exporting Countries (OAPEC). Established to promote distinctly Arab oil interests, OAPEC included the non-OPEC nations of Bahrain, Egypt, and Syria as well as OPEC Arab states.

Price fluctuations resulting from political events in producer nations and the devaluation of the U.S. dollar produced continuing uncertainty and continuous demands from producer nations for increases to the posted price of crude oil. The international oil companies largely conceded, increasing prices by nearly 12 percent over the course of a few years.

The OPEC countries also were increasing their power at the expense of the oil companies on another front. Algeria, Iraq, Iran, and Libya nationalized their petroleum sectors in the early 1970s. In December 1972, Kuwait, Qatar, Saudi Arabia, and the United Arab Emirates, which sought a more orderly transfer of control, reached a participation agreement with various oil companies that was intended to gradually increase state control over the oil industry from an initial 25 percent in 1972 to 51 percent in 1982. By the mid-1970s, however, producing countries had gained either full control or majority state participation in the oil companies' operations in the Middle East, although management for the most part remained in the hands of westerners. Thus the share of

Middle Eastern oil owned and controlled by the international oil companies declined sharply. In 1972 the companies had an equity interest in 92 percent of the oil leaving the Middle East. By 1982 their portion was less than 7 percent.

In October 1973, OPEC convened a meeting with the oil companies to discuss a substantial price increase. At the same time, Egypt and Syria attacked Israel. The ensuing war served to strengthen the OPEC representatives' resolve to raise prices. When OPEC and the oil companies proved unable to reach agreement on an increase, OPEC unilaterally set the posted oil price at $5.12 a barrel, up from $3 a barrel. At the same time, OAPEC decided to cut production by 5 percent each month until Israel withdrew from the Arab territories that it had occupied since the 1967 war and agreed to respect the rights of Palestinians. Saudi Arabia stiffened the sanction, announcing that it would cut oil production by 10 percent and end all shipments to the United States if Washington failed to modify its pro-Israel policy.

On October 19, President Nixon asked Congress for $2.2 billion in emergency military aid for Israel. Libya announced an embargo that same day. On October 20, Saudi Arabia reduced production by 25 percent and halted supplies to the United States. Within a couple of days, most other Arab producers had joined in cutting production and boycotting sales to the United States.

Fears of inadequate supplies caused prices to skyrocket, making the once-shocking OPEC price of $5.12 a barrel seem reasonable. With renewed confidence, OPEC met again in December and announced a new posted price of $11.65 a barrel. The industrialized world, by now painfully aware of its dependence on a dozen once-obscure countries, paid the cartel's price. The quadrupling of world oil prices led to a worldwide recession in 1974–1975 that most economists at the time labeled the worst since the Great Depression of the 1930s.

Effects of the Arab Oil Embargo

The Arab states implemented their boycott systematically, dividing countries into categories. These included nations considered to be friends of Israel, namely, the United States and the Netherlands. They exempted certain other nations, including France and Spain. The countries designated as nonexempt could purchase what oil remained after the exempt nations had met their needs. With the 1973 embargo, Arab nations asserted a new role in the global market, emerging as a significant power in the international economy. They produced 37 percent of the oil consumed by the noncommunist world. In contrast, U.S. production had been falling since about 1970. The United States had no excess oil capacity.

Consuming nations quickly felt the effects of the Arab nations' cut in monthly petroleum production. To cope with the shortage, they introduced various measures, including rationing, restricting gasoline purchases to odd or even days, banning driving on Sundays, lowering speed limits, implementing prudent climate control in public buildings, and using alternative fuels.

Estimates vary, but the oil embargo is thought to have shorted the United States about 2 million barrels a day. A 1974 Federal Energy Administration report estimates that the five-month embargo cost half a million U.S. jobs and led to a decrease in the gross national product of between $10 billion and $20 billion. Some Arab oil, reportedly from Iraq and Libya, leaked through the embargo. The United States began withholding data on its oil imports in October 1974 to prevent these leaks from being plugged.

The embargo proved to be immensely effective as a political tool. European and Japanese leaders expressed concern over the Israeli occupation and urged a settlement based on earlier cease-fire lines. Both were rewarded with OAPEC exemptions from the 5 percent cut in oil production for December 1973 and January 1974 and benefited from a 10 percent oil production increase.

Secretary of State Henry Kissinger engaged in extensive shuttle diplomacy to mediate a settlement between Israel and Egypt. His efforts did not go unrecognized, as Egyptian president Anwar Sadat noted the "evolution" in U.S. policy toward the Middle East in January 1974.

OAPEC announced the end of the embargo against the United States on March 18, 1974. Libya and Syria, however, refused to formally end the boycott until later in the year.

Post-Embargo Prices

After the embargo ended, oil-consuming nations hoped and even expected that OPEC would disintegrate. The oil producers moved cautiously, however, displaying considerable acumen. Saudi Arabia exerted significant influence over the organization through the mid-to-late 1970s, using its huge productive capacity unilaterally to shape the world oil market. Although some OPEC nations—namely, Algeria, Iraq, and Libya—were eager to increase prices and their revenues, the influence of Saudi Arabia and the inability of the nations actually to implement required changes made such a move impractical at the time.

With inflation shrinking national revenues, however, prices eventually had to be increased to reflect the reduced value of the dollar, the currency in which oil transactions are generally conducted. The position of those OPEC members pushing for higher prices was enhanced in late 1978, when oil field work stoppages and other political disruptions in Iran led to production cuts, and Western economies continued to grow vigorously. The price lull thus came to an end.

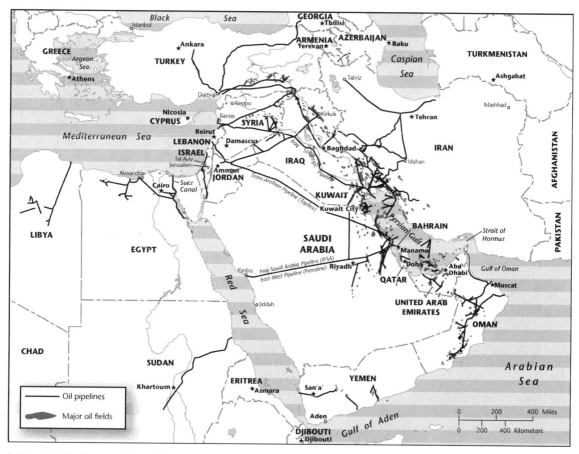

Major Middle Eastern Oil Fields and Pipelines

The Market Takes Over

In December 1978, OPEC agreed to end the eighteen-month freeze on prices. Oil ministers established a schedule for price increases, but by March 1979, the market had superseded their schedule. Prices reached $14.54 a barrel, an increase of 14.5 percent in three months, largely because of the substantial drop in Iranian production resulting from the overthrow of the shah and imposition of an Islamic republic under Ayatollah Ruhollah Khomeini.

Strong demand produced a tight global oil market and exposed again the vulnerability of importers, including the United States. The outbreak of the Iran-Iraq War in 1980 exacerbated importing nations' fears over Middle Eastern oil supplies. OPEC oil ministers ratified the market price of oil in June 1979. Saudi Arabia, along with the United Arab Emirates (UAE) and Qatar, increased prices to $18 a barrel, but other members raised their prices to $20 a barrel.

Increasing prices and concerns over supply led many industrial nations to pursue alternative energy supplies and promote conservation. By the early 1980s, efforts in industrial nations to reduce their dependence on OPEC oil were showing significant results. The amount of electricity generated by nuclear energy increased by 33 percent between 1982 and 1984. Some nations, including Japan, tried to diversify their energy supply by importing liquefied natural gas. The Japanese increased their natural gas usage by 31 percent between 1983 and 1984. Most nations, though not the United States, increased gasoline taxes to cut petroleum consumption. At the same time, support continued for already extensive mass transportation networks. In addition, a number of nations began to exploit newly discovered oil-production areas. Britain and Norway, for example, began to reap the benefits of oil discovered in the North Sea before the embargo.

During the next three years, prices continued to climb, reaching $41 a barrel in 1981, as OPEC members openly and often bitterly disagreed over pricing structures and production levels. Saudi Arabia repeatedly urged restraint on the upward march of prices. When they remained high, U.S. demand decreased, and Saudi Arabia was forced to decrease its production to help prop up the price.

At the same time, world oil production continued to decline. From a peak of 62.5 million barrels per day (bpd) in 1979, it dropped in each of the following four years: to 59.5 million bpd in 1980, 55.9 million in 1981, 53.5 million in 1982, and 53 million in 1983. By 1984, with the world beginning to recover from the effects of recession, it increased to an average of 54.1 million bpd. Further recovery was slow in coming, with production reaching only about 56.1 million bpd by 1987.

Weak demand compelled OPEC to agree for the first time on production quotas, in March 1983, introducing a collective production ceiling of 17.5 million barrels per day and sharply reducing prices. The key grade of OPEC crude, Saudi light, fell from $34 a barrel to $29 a barrel.

For about fifteen months these arrangements helped maintain a rough balance in the world market. As economic activity picked up in oil-importing countries, energy consumption increased in the first half of 1984. Economic growth slipped in the second half, however, and oil consumption again fell, aided by warm winter weather. Further downward pressure on prices resulted from some OPEC members exceeding their quotas and secretly engaging in price discounting.

The quotas turned out to be too loose, so in October 1984 the oil ministers of six OPEC members, along with Mexico and Egypt, agreed in principle to restrict production by a further 1.5 million bpd to defend the $29 a barrel price of Saudi light. The official price of Saudi light remained at $29 a barrel until the beginning of 1985, when the Saudis dropped it to $28.

By early 1985, OPEC production had fallen 57 percent from pre-embargo levels. OPEC was producing only about 46 percent of its maximum sustainable capacity, and of this amount the greatest declines had been absorbed by its Middle Eastern members. They produced only 41 percent of the amount they otherwise could, while allowing non-Arab members to produce at 65 percent of their capacity.

Prices Plummet

By May 1985, Saudi production had fallen to a twenty-year low of 2.5 million bpd. It declined even further during the summer. Meanwhile, the Saudi government was running a budget deficit of at least 46 billion rials, or more than 27 percent of revenues. An ambitious domestic development program depended on the use of gas produced with oil. With oil production so low, gas production became inadequate to meet the development program's requirements. Tired of bearing the burden of holding down production while other OPEC members cheated on their quotas, in late 1985 Saudi Arabia announced that it would no longer take up the slack between supply and demand by producing well below its quota. It thereafter began to sell the additional quantities up to its quota limit at market rather than official prices.

The results of the Saudi initiative were dramatic. The world's largest oil producer increased sales by underpricing oil in an already glutted market. Demand was flat. After peaking around $35 per barrel in 1981, world crude prices eased toward $28 over the next five years. By January 1986, prices had fallen below the psychological threshold of $20 a barrel—a ten-year low.

Although the Saudis intended their policy to garner a larger market share for OPEC as well as for itself, it was not an OPEC policy. Some OPEC nations, such as Kuwait and the UAE, still holding cash reserves and feeling the same pressures as Saudi Arabia, seemed to support the market-share strategy. Meanwhile, some of the poorer OPEC nations—Algeria, Indonesia, Iran, Libya, Nigeria, and Venezuela—starved for cash or burdened with debt, resisted it.

OPEC's inability to reach consensus caused oil markets to continue their downward pricing slide through the spring and summer of 1986, finally settling in the $10–$12 range. Action by OPEC finally halted the long price slide, when at a meeting in early August 1986, members reached an agreement to cut combined output to 16.8 million bpd, about 4 million barrels less than they had been pumping earlier in the summer.

The price drop brought serious revenue losses in the near term for most OPEC producers. Estimates have them losing $50 billion in 1986 in their efforts to reassert market influence. The inability to further endure such revenue losses forced OPEC to stop its market-share offensive. At the same time, in response to lower prices, consumption started to inch up for the first time since 1979.

As oil prices and sales volumes declined, OPEC members reduced their imports of goods and services, but not fast enough to prevent a $15 billion collective trade deficit. Although members' deficits represented relatively minor offsets against the cumulative surplus of nearly $400 billion earned over the previous decade, they were growing.

After prices hit bottom in August 1986, they gradually recovered during the fall. OPEC members renewed their production control agreement in December, and shortly after the beginning of 1987, the world price leveled off near $18 a barrel.

A suspension in political antagonisms between Saudi Arabia and Iran helped to alleviate overproduction, but despite this shift toward production quotas, in August 1987 OPEC was still producing 20 percent more oil than the quotas allowed. This cheating affected, albeit less significantly, the stability of prices, which additionally was offset by a drop of about 15 percent in the value of the dollar in the same year.

Petroleum Industry Investments

OPEC nations adapted to the emergence of an increasingly open and volatile oil market in the 1980s in a number of ways beyond competing for sales. Multibillion-dollar barter deals, usually oil-for-arms swaps, became common. OPEC producers also increasingly worked to acquire new positions "downstream," in the refining and distribution sectors of the petroleum industry. While low prices for crude hurt the producers who pumped it from the ground, they helped refiners by widening their profit margins. It was a lesson not lost on OPEC that during and after the price crash of 1986, earnings stayed healthy and even grew for the oil companies. The major corporations profited because they were "vertically integrated," meaning that they were involved in every step of the supply process, from exploration and production to petrochemicals to retail gasoline stations.

OPEC members began to hedge against price uncertainty by moving downstream as well. The most prominent example of downstream reintegration was Saudi Arabia's June 1988 acquisition for $1.2 billion of 50 percent ownership of three Texaco refineries in the United States as well as marketing access to 11,420 gasoline stations in twenty-three states. Some Americans and Europeans felt uneasy about such investments by Middle Eastern oil states, but at the same time the deals appeared to promise greater security for consuming nations.

The OPEC Roller Coaster

Although many observers expected the resolution of the Iran-Iraq War in July 1988 to boost oil prices, disputes between the two nations over appropriate production quotas hindered any increase. Instead, Saudia Arabia continued to produce well above its quota, once again pushing prices down around $10. After Iran and Iraq reached an agreement in November 1988, oil prices rose immediately and stayed in the $18–$22 range for the first six months of 1989. Prices rose again in late 1989 as a result of unexpectedly cold weather and falling output from oil fields in the collapsing Soviet Union, the fate of which created an Eastern European market for OPEC oil. Prices jumped so fast in late 1989 that OPEC raised its production quota by about 3 million bpd, to 22 million bpd.

In April 1990, crude prices went into a nosedive following reports that OPEC's production continued to climb, reaching its highest level since 1981. Prices had fallen about $3 by late March and were threatening to sink below $18. OPEC output exceeded 24 million bpd in March, well above the ceiling of 22.1 million barrels it had set for itself in November 1989.

In May 1990, OPEC announced commitments from major producers to cut production a further 1.445 million barrels, the bulk of which was to be borne by Kuwait, Saudi Arabia, and the UAE. The announced cuts were not enough to persuade the market that supply and demand would be brought back into balance, so prices continued to slip.

The Persian Gulf Crisis and War

By the end of June 1990, the price of oil hovered around the $14 range. On June 26, Iraq issued a chilling warning to Kuwait to curtail its overproduction. On July 12, two weeks in advance of the regular mid-year OPEC meeting, Saudi Arabia boosted sagging oil markets by announcing that it would temporarily and unilaterally cut production. A few days later, on July 17, Iraqi president Saddam Hussein publicly threatened to use force against other Arab OPEC nations unless they curbed overproduction. Hussein charged that the policies of the overproducing nations were "inspired by America to undermine Arab interests and security." Shortly thereafter, Iraq accused Kuwait of several transgressions unrelated to oil pricing, in particular that Kuwait had been drilling for oil and deploying troops on Iraqi territory. By July 23, Western intelligence sources reported Iraq massing tens of thousands of troops near its border with Kuwait.

The troop deployments and diplomatic friction offered an inauspicious backdrop for the opening of the July OPEC meeting. Despite significant doubt that Iraq would carry out its threats, it nonetheless got virtually everything it wanted at the meeting: The thirteen oil ministers signed an agreement raising their target price from $18 to $21 a barrel, and to achieve that price they agreed to a new production ceiling of 22.5 million bpd, which was higher than the previous ceiling but below the amount members actually pumped.

Oil and Aggression

Despite meeting apparent success at the OPEC summit, Iraq invaded Kuwait on August 2, 1990. The geopolitics of Middle Eastern oil played a major part in motivating Iraq. At the same time, it is possible to overemphasize the role of oil, which is important primarily because of the economic, political, and military power it represents. Hussein may have seen oil simply as a means to an end.

The price-versus-production dispute of 1990 was, if not a pretext for the invasion, a surface manifestation of much deeper tensions. The issue of price-versus-production had provoked dissension among OPEC nations throughout most of OPEC's three-decade history. Even in 1990 the issue was a legitimate question of strategic philosophy. The positions of various OPEC nations tended to reflect their particular circumstances as well as market conditions. During much of the 1980s, Saudi Arabia and other nations had argued against pushing the price of oil too far. Too high a price encouraged conservation by consuming nations, brought more non-OPEC production on line, reduced OPEC's market share and economic leverage, raised supply, and eventually drove prices down again. Hard lessons of the previous two decades indicated that price stability was in the best interest of producers as well as consumers.

Iraq's treasury suffered from far more than the price of oil. Iraq owed Kuwait and other Gulf states some $30 billion that they had lent to Iraq in support of its war against Iran. Hussein had demanded before invading Kuwait that it forgive these debts, in part arguing that Iraq had fought Iran in the interest of protecting not only itself, but other Arab states from the export of Iran's Islamic revolution. Iraq also needed money to finance an expensive arms buildup underway since 1988.

The Rumaila oil field represented another point of contention between Iraq and Kuwait. This crescent-shaped reservoir, nearly two miles deep and fifty miles long, was thought to be one of the world's biggest fields, possibly several times larger than that at Prudhoe Bay, Alaska. The Iraq-Kuwait border bisected it, with more of it believed to be under Iraq. When Iraq refused to negotiate a deal for sharing the oil, Kuwait began pumping without an agreement. Before the Iran-Iraq War, Iraq had pumped intensively from its side of the reservoir. During the war, however, Iraq mined the field to keep it out of Iranian hands and was not able to match the rate at which Kuwait depleted the pool. Iraq considered Kuwait to be "stealing" its oil.

The broader geopolitical context ultimately made oil important to Iraq, as Hussein attempted to use oil prices as a club in his bid for leadership and power in the Arab world. Iraq's invasion brought a jump in the price of oil, as commodity markets reacted to expected decreases in production and heightened uncertainty, which were confirmed when the United Nations imposed a trade embargo on Iraq, effectively removing Iraq's 3 million bpd from the market. Kuwait's production, almost 2 million bpd, also was lost. By mid-August, the price of oil had reached the $27 range and was rising. Increased production by other OPEC members helped to temporarily decrease prices.

Despite the belief of many analysts that supplies were adequate for the immediate future, war speculation pushed the price to $31 by mid-September. Price volatility continued through the fall, with prices reaching as high as $40 on rumors of war. The high prices of 1990 naturally produced increased revenue for OPEC members. OPEC nations exported about $160 billion worth of oil, bringing in some 42 percent more revenue than in 1989.

After an initial brief rise after the start of the allied bombing campaign on January 16, 1991, oil prices went into a steep decline. Energy traders reacted on the assumption that the rapid neutralization of the Iraqi air force had removed most of the danger to Saudi oil facilities. General stability in the oil market belied the predictions of some veteran oil traders that war would cause oil prices to jump above $50 a barrel.

With the start of the ground war, President George H.W. Bush kept a promise to release a million barrels a day from the U.S. Strategic

Petroleum Reserve. His commitment was originally intended to dampen the upward volatility of oil prices, but with the price having already tumbled, the move only added to the downward pressure on prices. They remained well below $20 even after the February 28 cease-fire.

OPEC ministers held their first postwar meeting on March 11 in Geneva. The most pressing item on the agenda was bolstering the price of oil, or at least keeping it from sagging further, which could only be achieved by reining in production. Worldwide, oil production in 1990 reached its highest level in eleven years, while consumption dropped for the first time in thirteen years. At the meeting, OPEC decided to cut production by about 1 million bpd, about 5 percent, to support a $21 target price.

Oil from Kuwait was slow to return to the market. By early May, only 10 percent of Kuwait's burning wells had been extinguished. Not only was Kuwait's considerable output of refined product off the market, but the nation had to import gasoline and other fuels for domestic consumption. Kuwait finally announced in July that it would resume exporting crude oil. At the time, it could export only about 140,000 bpd, but that increased steadily to almost 600,000 by the end of the year.

Worries about a shortage of oil on the world market receded after the war ended. Even with the absence of Iraqi and Kuwaiti oil, more than enough oil to meet world demand found its way onto the market. OPEC took no significant action to adjust supply or price. By the end of June, OPEC members collectively had pumped more than the official production ceiling of 22.6 million bpd. Their elevated production continued through the year, making 1991 production OPEC's highest in more than a decade.

The Post–Gulf War Era

In the years after the Gulf War, debate continued within OPEC with regard to appropriate production ceilings. Saudi Arabia repeatedly sought to increase its production quotas in an effort to increase its market share. Iran regularly argued the necessity of more drastic production cuts. The continued disagreements forced prices on a downward trend, as the international perception was that OPEC lacked self-discipline.

January 1993 brought new military tensions between Iraq and the United States and its allies over Iraq's failure to comply fully with UN Security Council resolutions. Oil prices remained almost unchanged, although war jitters normally raise prices. Price stagnation was a sign that the fundamental forces affecting the market were tending to push prices downward.

Also in January, Saudi Arabia surprised the world petroleum market with a call for OPEC production cuts of at least a million barrels a day. The proposal seemed to be a reversal in basic Saudi policy; oil prices rose strongly on the news. The increased prices did not, however, last long, as Algeria, Iraq, and Kuwait dissented from the proposed plan. This disunity sent prices downward, as traders again doubted OPEC's ability to enforce discipline. By May 1993, OPEC nations were pumping 600,000 bpd more than the new ceiling of 23.6 million.

Disagreement between OPEC members continued throughout 1994 and 1995 as world oil prices continued to slide. Attempts to impose additional production cuts proved unsuccessful, so OPEC retained its existing quotas through the summer of 1995.

Most of the 1990s went by with Iraq's oil production curtailed by economic sanctions imposed in the wake of the Gulf War. The volume of oil removed from production as well as the length of its absence significantly affected the Middle East's oil picture.

In January 1996, after the United Nations offered to allow Iraq $2 billion worth of oil exports rather than $1.6 billion, Iraq signaled its willingness to begin negotiating over the terms of the proposed oil-for-food program. In May, the United States, United Nations, and Iraq reached an agreement for Iraq to sell $2 billion worth of oil every 180 days at market price. After some delay, oil began flowing in an appreciable quantity in December 1996, and Iraq began exporting limited amounts of oil to generate revenue to purchase food and medicines. The flow amounted to about 500,000 barrels a day, one-eighth of Iraq's estimated capacity of 4 million bpd. By late 1998, Iraq was producing, under UN restrictions, about 2.4 million bpd, of which 1.8 million bpd was being exported.

As the 1990s came to a close, OPEC attempted to regain control of the market through occasional production cuts and production increases. Nonetheless, the price of oil remained volatile, bottoming out under $10 a barrel in late 1998. OPEC still had not reestablished an effective grip on world markets. Market prices continued to jump and skid on the slightest rumor of what OPEC might do. At the same time, forces stronger than OPEC were at work on the market, including the Asian economic crisis, which significantly lessened demand for oil and the ability of Asian nations to pay for it. Oil prices appeared to be in recovery in March 1999, when OPEC and non-OPEC countries agreed to production cuts of more than 2 million bpd.

Caspian Sea Petroleum

Since the breakup of the Soviet Union in 1991, the abundant reserves of oil and gas in the Caspian Sea region have had significant, if indirect, influence on the economics and politics of Middle Eastern oil. Iran, although considered a Middle Eastern state, is among the oil nations bordering the Caspian Sea, along with Azerbaijan, Kazakhstan, Russia, Turkmenistan, and Uzbekistan.

With proven reserves estimated to be as large as those of the United States or under the North Sea, the Caspian region had been a major source of oil for the Soviet Union but had remained virtually closed to world markets. Moreover, Caspian oil and gas resources were comparatively undeveloped. Their distance from markets and the limited infrastructure for processing and transport restricted their availability. During the 1990s, multinational oil companies signed agreements worth tens of billions of dollars with Caspian nations to develop their oil and gas resources.

A key issue was where to route the pipelines that would bring Caspian oil and gas to world markets. Existing lines had been routed to carry oil and gas via Russia to other parts of the Soviet Union, although some of these lines ended at the Russian Black Sea port of Novorossisk, from which tankers could carry it through the Bosporus to the Mediterranean. That route came with political and environmental problems. In September 1998, twelve nations signed the Baku Declaration, agreeing to develop a transport corridor from Europe—across the Black Sea, Caucasus, and Caspian Sea—to Central Asia, positioning the corridor close to Asian markets with good long-term growth prospects. One of several possible outlets for Caspian oil is through Iran to the Persian Gulf and Turkey, but sanctions instituted by the United States in 1995–1996 against companies doing business with Iran have made this alternative untenable.

One of the most important effects of petroleum development in the Caspian region on Middle Eastern oil nations might ultimately be to depress the world price of oil by adding supply not balanced by demand. Such an impact would be years into the future if it ever develops. Analysts expect that development of Caspian resources will take decades to complete, and maritime boundary disputes among the states bordering the Caspian Sea continue to pose an obstacle to full development of the area's oil and gas resources. In any event, Caspian reserves will operate independently from Middle Eastern oil and gas.

Oil in the Twenty-First Century

In the early 2000s, the world oil market was in recovery. Increased global demand, cooperation between OPEC and non-OPEC producers, improved quota discipline on the part of OPEC members, and political developments in the Middle East all played a role in reinvigorating the petroleum sector. This recovery continued despite increasing calls for U.S. independence from Middle Eastern sources of energy in light of the September 11 attacks and the U.S.-led war in Iraq.

Estimated Crude Oil and Natural Gas Reserves of Select Countries

Region/Country	Crude Oil[a]		Natural Gas[b]	
	Reserves	Percentage	Reserves	Percentage
North America	41.45	3.9	268.85	4.0
Canada	4.96		59.07	
Mexico	14.60		20.74	
United States	21.89		189.04	
Central and South America	75.16	7.2	240.94	3.5
Argentina	2.67		21.63	
Bolivia	0.46		27.62	
Brazil	10.60		8.66	
Trinidad and Tobago	0.76		19.13	
Venezuela	52.45		149.21	
Western Europe	16.38	1.6	170.05	2.5
Germany	0.26		7.66	
Italy	0.49		4.77	
Netherlands	0.05		55.10	
Norway	9.40		74.73	
United Kingdom	4.30		21.75	
Eastern Europe and Former Soviet Union	89.01	8.5	2,693.23	39.6
Poland	0.28		6.23	
Romania	0.47		5.01	
Russia	65.39		2,340.50	
Other Former Soviet Republics	22.34		336.33	
Middle East	686.34	65.3	2,539.65	37.3
Iran	105.00		935.00	
Iraq	115.00		112.60	
Kuwait	99.38		56.60	
Oman	5.70		31.00	
Qatar	27.35		913.40	
Saudi Arabia	261.78		238.50	
Syria	2.40		18.00	
United Arab Emirates	66.23		204.05	
Yemen	2.85		17.00	
Africa	104.64	10.0	443.20	6.5
Algeria	14.00		171.50	
Angola	8.80		4.00	
Egypt	3.61		7.13	
Equatorial Guinea	1.28		3.40	
Gabon	2.29		3.43	
Libya	30.50		46.00	
Nigeria	33.00		180.00	
Asia and Oceania	37.70	3.6	449.91	6.6
Australia	3.95		142.90	
China	15.51		47.91	
India	4.00		14.58	
Indonesia	5.50		67.65	
Malaysia	3.06		57.61	
Pakistan	0.29		28.17	
Vietnam	2.28		7.20	
World Total	1,050.69		6,805.83	

Notes: Estimates are as of January 1, 2004. Sums of components may not equal totals because of rounding.

a. Billions of barrels
b. Trillion cubic feet
Source: Adapted from Energy Information Administration, *International Energy Annual, 2003,*
http://www.eia.doe.gov/pub/international/iea2003/table81.xls. See the Web site for additional sources and notes on estimates.

In October 2004, oil reached $55.17 per barrel, the highest closing price then on record, only to be surpassed in March 2005 at $56.10 per barrel. In the intervening months, oil prices remained above $50 a barrel, with most analysts believing that prices would remain at elevated levels for some time. In March 2005, the chief executive officer of the Kuwait Petroleum Corp. asserted that oil prices would never again dip below $40 per barrel. OPEC again agreed to raise production in an effort to curb prices, despite the strong disagreement by several members.

Global oil demand continued to rise, leading the International Energy Agency (IEA) to repeatedly modify its estimates upward. Its predictions for 2005 put demand at 84.3 million bpd, up from 80 million bpd in November 2003 and 77 million in 2002. The IEA estimated that global oil demand will rise to 92 million bpd by 2010 and to 110 million bpd by 2020. The U.S. Energy Information Administration (EIA) similarly projects that world energy demand will increase by 54 percent by 2025, with demand for oil reaching 121 million bpd in 2025. The United States and developing nations in Asia, primarily China and India, are expected to experience the largest growth. In developing nations, oil consumption is expected to increase for all end uses, including residential, commercial, industrial, and electric power generation. Such increases will require incremental production of more than 44 million bpd over current levels.

With their majority position in OPEC, Middle Eastern nations undoubtedly stand to gain a greater market share of increasing demand as a result of declining non-OPEC reserves. Indeed, in 2002 Middle Eastern producers represented five of the top ten oil exporters, a trend that likely will continue given their proven reserves.

Moreover, the cost of producing a barrel of oil in the Persian Gulf (before royalties or taxes) is estimated at about $2. Oil from most other regions is considerably more expensive to extract because of higher production and exploration costs. Major declines in world oil prices are consequently more harmful to oil producers outside the Middle East,

and significant increases in oil prices benefit Middle Eastern producing nations the most.

Middle Eastern oil nations enjoy another advantage in that their proven reserves are high in relation to their rate of production–roughly ten times higher in the Persian Gulf than in the United States. Their excess production capacity gives them market power.

On the supply side of the equation, the EIA put the Middle East's proven oil reserves, as of January 2004, at 726.8 billion barrels, which accounts for approximately 60 percent of all reserves. The EIA had also predicted, under a normal pricing scenario, a rapid increase in Middle Eastern production, from 20.5 million bpd in 2001 to 42.1 million bdp in 2025, which would account for approximately 35 percent of world consumption. Under a high-price scenario, Middle Eastern production would taper off to approximately 29.9 million bpd in 2025 because of decreased demand as a result of price.

For years there has been an underlying assumption, certainly by many Americans, that Middle Eastern oil reserves are so vast that exhausting them was not a possibility. In recent years, however, the concept of "peak oil" has been receiving significant industry attention.

"Peak oil" refers to the point at which the world's finite supply of oil begins to decline. M. King Hubbert, an American geophysicist, first coined the term in 1956, and the concept is appropriately called Hubbert's Peak. Hubbert accurately predicted 1970 as the point at which U.S. oil supplies would peak. Well-respected analysts and industry participants are today questioning quite seriously whether the world oil supply is approaching Hubbert's Peak or in fact may have already reached it. A 2005 study commissioned by the U.S. Department of Energy specifically focused on analyzing viable technologies to mitigate the expected oil shortages associated with the impending peaking of world oil production.

A May 2004 *New York Times* article heightened concerns about the peaking of global oil supplies in implying that Saudi oil fields were in decline and that the kingdom likely would be unable to expand its production capacity much beyond current production levels. Some analysts speculate that excessive, aggressive drilling by the Saudis could have inflicted substantial damage to some of its most productive wells, thereby reducing their productivity. Although Saudi officials emphatically denied the article's assertions in a published rebuttal, more experts are of the thinking that Saudi fields may quickly decline.

A number of energy analysts take the position that if the world currently is experiencing peak oil or is going to experience it in the near future, it will be a critical, devastating event—the largest energy crisis in world history. When discussing the adequacy and sustainability of global supplies, it is not uncommon for a few individuals to warn of dire consequences should the world run out of fossil fuel. What made predictions remarkable in 2004 and 2005, however, was the number and consistency of industry experts stating that the peak will occur in ten years or less. Such an event should spark widespread recognition that oil supplies are, in fact, limited, meaning that oil prices likely would remain quite high, well above the $55 high of October 2004.

Although it is not immediately clear whether these predictions will play out in the near term, if they do, energy-importing nations will face severe economic crisis as their most important fuel source becomes drastically reduced.

Natural Gas

Natural gas is the fastest growing global source of primary energy. The EIA predicts that from 2001 to 2025, natural gas consumption will rise by 67 percent, to 151 trillion cubic feet (Tcf). The Middle East's natural gas reserves are estimated between 2,000 and 2,500 Tcf, or between 35 and 40 percent of the world's reserves. Qatar alone holds approximately 900 Tcf. Despite these significant reserves, natural gas has always been the lesser-favored commodity of Middle Eastern nations because of the sizeable capital investment required and the economic difficulty in getting the gas to consuming markets.

One of the critical factors leading to the increase in demand for natural gas is the growing importance of it to the electricity-generating sector in the industrialized world. Natural gas is the preferred option for new power generation, because it is more efficient and environmentally friendly compared to other fossil fuels. Among industrialized nations, natural gas's share of total power generation is projected to grow from 20 percent in 2001 to 30 percent in 2025.

In the United States, domestic gas production remains relatively flat, while the marginal costs of domestic production continue to increase, causing a fundamental shift in long-term gas prices. The EIA estimates that domestic natural gas production will increase more slowly than consumption, rising to 20.5 trillion cubic feet (Tcf) in 2010 and

U.S. Energy Consumption by Source, 1997–2004 (in Trillion Btu)

Year	Coal	Natural Gas	Petroleum	Nuclear Electric Power	Hydroelectric Power	Geothermal	Solar and Wind	Renewables	Total Consumption
1997	21,445	23,328	36,266	6,597	3,640	325	104	7,075	94,727
1998	21,656	22,936	36,934	7,068	3,297	328	101	6,561	95,146
1999	21,623	23,010	37,960	7,610	3,268	331	115	6,599	96,774
2000	22,580	23,916	38,404	7,862	2,811	317	123	6,158	98,905
2001	21,914	22,906	38,333	8,033	2,242	311	135	5,328	96,380
2002	21,904	23,628	38,401	8,143	2,689	328	170	5,835	97,788
2003	22,321	23,069	39,047	7,959	2,825	339	178	6,082	98,223
2004	22,390	23,096	40,130	8,232	2,725	340	206	6,116	99,763

Source: Energy Information Administration, *Monthly Energy Review,* May 2005, http://www.eia.doe.gov/emeu/mer/contents.html.

21.9 Tcf in 2025. The combination of higher natural gas prices, rising natural gas demand, and lower liquefied natural gas (LNG) production and transportation costs is setting the stage for increased LNG trade in the years ahead. Estimates are that worldwide LNG trade will increase 35 percent by 2020. The EIA projects that in the United States natural gas imports will more than double over the next twenty years. Almost all the projected increase is expected to come from LNG, requiring a nearly twenty-eight-fold increase in LNG imports compared to those in 2002.

LNG is natural gas, primarily methane, that has been cooled to its liquid state, which is reached at $-260°F$ ($162.2°C$). Liquefying natural gas reduces the volume it occupies by more than 600 times, making it practical for storage and transportation via large ocean-going vessels. LNG in its liquid state is not flammable or explosive. The continental United States currently has four LNG receipt terminals, where LNG vessels discharge their cargo for storage, regasification into natural gas, and ultimately transportation on the interstate pipeline grid. With natural gas prices and U.S. industrial demand expected to continue to rise, more than fifty new LNG terminals have been proposed for North America, with the bulk of them concentrated around the Gulf of Mexico. Analysts agree that ultimately four to ten new terminals are likely to be constructed, coupled with expansions of the four existing facilities. The first of the new terminals is scheduled to come on line in 2007–2008.

Much of the LNG that will be imported into the United States will come from Middle Eastern nations, including Algeria, Egypt, and Qatar. A number of international oil companies have agreements with Qatar to develop its massive gas reserves and operate liquefaction facilities. Because the LNG supply chain is so capital intensive—requiring upwards of $4 billion for exploration, liquefaction, shipping, regasification at the import terminal, and transportation via pipelines—many of the oil majors are involved in all aspects of the LNG supply chain, from the production end to constructing their own receiving regasification terminal.

Although still not as critically important as oil, natural gas represents an alternative source of revenue to petroleum for several Middle Eastern nations, and given the projected substantial increases in demand in the United States and abroad, it will be a profitable undertaking for LNG-exporting nations.

Outlook

The U.S.-led war against Iraq reinforced the geopolitical importance of Middle Eastern oil reserves. Despite claims by the George W. Bush administration justifying the war on Iraqi connections between Saddam Hussein and Osama bin Laden and Iraq's weapons program, attacking Iraq was probably partially motivated by the fact that the United States considers Middle Eastern oil

Share of U.S. Oil Consumption Supplied by Imports, 1997–2003 (Millions of Barrels per Day)

Year	Total Consumption	Total Imports	Percentage Imported	Imports from OPEC Countries	Percentage of Total Consumption Imported from OPEC
1997	18.62	10.16	54.6	4.57	24.5
1998	18.92	10.71	56.6	4.91	26.0
1999	19.52	10.85	55.6	4.95	25.4
2000	19.70	11.49	58.3	5.20	26.4
2001	19.65	11.87	60.4	5.53	28.1
2002	19.76	11.53	58.3	4.61	23.3
2003	N/A	12.25	N/A	5.18	N/A

N/A not available

Source: Energy Information Administration, *Annual Energy Review, 2003* (Washington, D.C.: Department of Energy, September 2004), tables 5.1, 5.4, 11.10.

vital to its national security and economic interests. The large number of U.S. troops detailed to
protecting the Iraqi oil infrastructure appear to
confirm this.

As U.S. oil production continues to decline, the
United States and many other nations sorely need
access to Middle Eastern oil and gas. U.S. reliance
on foreign oil imports, and now natural gas
imports, likely will continue to increase. Threats to
energy security seem less identifiable, and perhaps
less manageable, if indeed the forces of al-Qaida
and other terrorist organizations are targeting critical energy infrastructure as a means of inflicting
economic harm.

Although Saudi Arabia has had a vested interest
in helping to maintain the economic health of a
good customer—the United States—hostility in
some quarters toward the United States has made
and continues to make the relationship fraught
with challenges and perils for the Saudis. The presence of U.S. troops on Saudi soil—the birthplace
of Islam—had become a rallying cry for Islamist
opponents of the Saudi government. Al-Qaida and
other groups attacked Saudi and American targets
in the kingdom, killing scores of people, and consistently railed against the government. Some saw
in the U.S. invasion of Iraq acknowledgment of the
need to tamp down the threat to the Saudis. Shortly
after the invasion, in 2003 the United States withdrew its forces from Saudi Arabia and announced
plans to build "enduring" bases—later changed to
"contingency operating bases"—in Iraq.

Saudi Arabia's market-share offensives and the
apparent eagerness of some OPEC members to
increase their individual market shares at the
expense of other members illustrate the fundamental and persistent debate spanning all four
decades of the organization's history. OPEC has
long been divided into two competing camps: the
price moderates, typified by Saudi Arabia, advocating for stable prices but often greater production, and the price hawks, such as Libya, pushing
for a higher price regardless of market conditions.
This division has often made it difficult for OPEC
to operate as an effective cartel.

Fluctuating prices and repeated efforts to reign
in or cheat on production quotas demonstrate a
loss of some OPEC control over oil prices as
market forces realign supply and demand. On
occasion the cartel demonstrates market leverage,
when its members summon the self-discipline and
collective resolve to rein in production. Although
Saudi Arabia has consistently dominated OPEC
and the world market, there is no guarantee that
this situation will continue, especially if Saudi
reserves have peaked.

By the early 2000s, several events promised to
significantly change the world energy markets: the
more complete integration of countries like China
and Russia into the international economy as oil
and gas exporters or importers and the reintroduc-
tion of Libya into the global market after the
lifting of UN and U.S. sanctions.

The global importance of the Middle Eastern oil
states remains unquestioned. For 2002, the five
Gulf countries with the largest reserves—Iran, Iraq,
Kuwait, Saudi Arabia, and the UAE—potentially
supplied 60 percent of the oil in world trading.
Record high oil prices in late 2004 and early 2005
greatly increased revenues for Middle Eastern producers. The enormous petroleum and gas reserves
under Middle Eastern nations and the significant
cost advantages these countries enjoy in extracting
oil and gas leave little doubt that they will continue
to influence the world's oil and gas supply and
demand for many years to come.

CHAPTER **6**

FIFTEEN CENTURIES OF ISLAM

God is most great! I testify that there is no god but Allah. I testify that Muhammad is the messenger of Allah." Five times a day, Muslims hear Islam's credo calling them to pray. For fifteen centuries, Islam has shaped peoples and nations of a mosaic of races, languages, regions, and cultures. Today, some 1.3 billion people in Africa, the Americas, Asia, Europe, and the Middle East profess faith in Islam.

Unity and Diversity

Although as a catchall term *Islam* identifies an underlying unity among a people of faith, it fails to convey the substantial differences among the many sects, nations, and cultures of that religion. The Islamic world is no more monolithic or homogeneous than the world of Christianity. From an anthropological perspective, vast differences distinguish Muslim Uzbeks of Central Asia, Muslim Berbers from North Africa, Muslim Sumatrans from South Asia, and Muslim Fulanis from Nigeria. The geographic dispersion of the fifty-six or so Muslim countries has naturally produced different societies. The cultural and historical development of Indonesia, for example, is quite distinct from that of Morocco. In the Middle East, Egypt, Iran, Saudi Arabia, and Turkey are all Muslim countries, but they have little else in common.

The varying ideological commitments of governments in predominantly Muslim countries highlight the sometimes overlooked diverse nature of politics in the Muslim world. Take, for example, the conservative monarchy of Saudi Arabia, the Islamic fundamentalism of Iran, the military-led Islamic Republic of Pakistan, the secular socialism of the Baathist regime of Syria, the official state secularism of Turkey, and the "limited democracies" of Malaysia and Indonesia. Such ideological diversity has sometimes promoted interstate conflict and tension. Moreover, divergent ideologies within Islamic nations have at times threatened to destabilize governments. On the theological level, Muslims also differ over interpretations of the Quran and the teachings of the Prophet Muhammad. As with other religions, Islam's various sects and offshoots differ in terms of doctrine, political views, and tolerance of others.

Despite Islam's diversity, one should not overemphasize the differences and ignore the factors that unite Muslims worldwide. Islamic ideals and precepts provide the most important element of religious and cultural continuity and tradition in most Muslim countries today. Although it remains largely an ideal, the notion of "the community of Islam" (*ummah*) holds the majority of Muslims together in an informal transnational allegiance. With the formation of the Organization of the Islamic Conference (OIC) in 1972, this bond assumed a more formal, institutional shape.

A way of life as well as a religion, Islam provides Muslims with a powerful frame of reference. On the conscious and subconscious levels, Islam shapes and informs Muslims' identity, habits, and attitudes. This common religious identity, heritage, and tradition have been reinforced by most

Muslim nations' shared experience of having been dominated and exploited by European colonial powers.

In spite of the ascendance of nationalism as the principal basis of political identity in modern times, in many Muslim countries the line between national and religious identity is blurred. The two identities often overlap, so that to Indonesians, Iranians, Pakistanis, and Saudis, for example, national identity is largely synonymous with affiliation to Islam. The constitutions of many predominantly Muslim nations expressly declare Islam to be the official religion. In these countries, Islam is more than a faith: It is a centuries-old system of values, norms, and beliefs that permeates all aspects of social, political, and cultural life.

Islam and the West

In the past, the image of Islam in the West tended to be one of something totally foreign, exotic, and sometimes sinister. Many Muslims today feel that this stereotypic image still prevails, only with images of desert "sheikhs" and harems replaced by that of religious extremists and terrorists. The latter perspective was exacerbated exponentially by al-Qaida's attack on the World Trade Center and the Pentagon in 2001 and others that followed, such as in Bali in 2002 and in Madrid in 2004.

Of all the world's religions, Islam is closest theologically and politically to Christianity. Yet perhaps because of this closeness and the consequent threat Islam represented as a theological and political rival, from the medieval era and into the modern era, Christian Europe often denigrated and ridiculed Islam and its founder, the Prophet Muhammad. Works by Carlyle, Dante, Voltaire, and other influential European writers, thinkers, theologians, and Orientalists attacked the Quran or Muhammad, shaping the attitudes of generations of westerners.

Western hostility toward Islam results not so much from theological differences as from history, politics, and geography. The Arab armies that carried the faith forward across distant horizons to new frontiers overran Spain, Sicily, and parts of Eastern Europe and ruled them for centuries. They crossed the Pyrenees and raided France as far as Nîmes. The armies of the last Islamic empire, the Ottoman Turks, twice stood at the gates of Vienna but ultimately failed to occupy it.

Alarmed by Islam's conquests, the nations of the West embarked on the Crusades between the eleventh and thirteenth centuries in an attempt to retake the Holy Land. These four campaigns further deepened the hostility between the followers of the two religions, reinforcing mutual suspicions and insecurities.

Literature and folk culture perpetuated the legacy of alienation germinated by Islamic conquests and Western counterconquests. Later, during the nineteenth and twentieth centuries, Western industrialization and military strength spearheaded European colonialism and Western hegemony in much of the Middle East. In the process, Muslims came to feel victimized and dehumanized, their national identities suppressed and their cultural heritage and contributions to civilization denigrated.

Recent decades have witnessed a significant revival of Islamic sentiment. The overthrow of the shah of Iran in 1979 and the rise to power of Ayatollah Ruhollah Khomeini symbolized this revival and its rejection of Western colonialism and lifestyles. The Islamic resurgence, in turn, renewed historically rooted fears in the West of the specter of "Islam on the march." Events such as the Iranian Revolution of 1978–1979, the U.S. embassy hostage crisis of 1979–1981, and the assassination of Egyptian president Anwar al-Sadat by Islamic radicals in 1981 stirred embers of concern in the West that had never fully died. The subsequent proliferation of Muslim extremist groups, kidnappings and attacks by such groups, and Western intervention and policies in the Middle East did little to douse the mutual suspicions and misperceptions on both sides.

The grievances of mainstream and extremist groups vary from one country context to another, but a core of grievances resonates with many in the Muslim world. Among the more prominent are the Palestinian-Israeli conflict and the belief that the United States has been biased diplomatically, politically, and economically in its support of Israel; U.S. military and economic support for authoritarian Muslim regimes; a double standard in the United States' promotion of democracy and human rights that in the past often excluded the Middle East and broader Muslim world and today appears to be hypocritical in light of revelations about activities in Iraq and at Guantanamo Bay, Cuba; sanctions against Iraq after the Gulf War that had a devastating impact on the Iraqi people (but not its leadership); the George W. Bush administration's war on terror whose trajectory is often seen as a war against Islam and the Muslim world in a neocolonial attempt to reshape the Middle East and Muslim worlds. The current hostility and anti-Americanism show few signs of subsiding.

Arabia: Birthplace of the Muslim Community

Arabia, the homeland of Islam, was situated between two great empires in the seventh century. The eastern Roman emperors of Byzantium (330 B.C.E.–1453 C.E.) controlled the Roman provinces of the Middle East, while farther east the Sassanids of Persia (205–641 C.E.) led a rival empire in Mesopotamia and areas of present-day Iran. The Byzantines ruled a diverse collection of cultures and peoples, including Arabs, Egyptians, Greeks, Palestinians, Phoenicians, Jews, and Syrians. The Arabs, a Semitic people originally from the hinterlands and shores of Arabia (present-day Saudi Arabia), had fanned out into the Middle East and established several communities and states.

During the seventh century, Arabia was home to socially ordered sedentary peoples who populated towns and oases and had contacts beyond the peninsula. The camel had revolutionized settled and nomadic life there by joining city and desert in a well-integrated regional system and by linking Arabia with other areas—particularly with the prosperous states of the Mediterranean— through trade.

The demands and prosperity of the Byzantine and Roman worlds, especially their growing appetite for spices, incense, and silk, provided a powerful impetus for trade between India and Africa and the Mediterranean world. Trade was conducted over two major routes—one across the Persian Gulf and the other through the Fertile Crescent (Iraq, Jordan, Palestine, Lebanon, and Syria). Wars between the Byzantines and the Sassanids, however, made these routes increasingly risky. In time, traders shifted to routes along the Red Sea through the rugged western part of Arabia known as the Hijaz. Soon, caravans began carrying goods from Yemen by way of the Hijaz to Syria and the Mediterranean.

The booming caravan trade worked to the advantage of one particular Arabian settlement: Mecca, which was destined to become the region's largest city and the most important trading center on the peninsula. Mecca sits in a long, rocky valley among bare, mountainous hills, some forty miles inland from the Red Sea. Fed by a permanent spring, it grew as a settlement around a revered local shrine called the Kaaba (literally, cube). The Kaaba houses a black stone, a meteorite, that was held sacred by the Bedouins of the desert, the townsfolk of Mecca, and nearby settlements. Muslim tradition has it that the archangel Gabriel brought the black stone to Earth and delivered it to Abraham and his son Ismail. Ismail, from whom Meccans claim descent, is considered the progenitor of all Arabs. According to tradition, Ismail encased the black stone in the Kaaba, which then became a pilgrimage site. Over time, however, pagan practices distorted its significance.

By the sixth century, when Muhammad was born, the enterprising Meccan merchants had developed into a powerful mercantile oligarchy not unlike the Italian mercantile republics of the Middle Ages. The prosperity of Mecca gave added prominence and power to the Quraysh, the major tribe in the city and part of the ruling aristocracy. The Quraysh consisted of several clans and families, including the Banu Hashim family, from whom Jordan's Hashimite dynasty claims descent. It was into this family that Muhammad was born.

The Prophet Muhammad

Very little is known about the early life of Muhammad. No biography of him was written until a century after his death. His date of birth generally is given as 570 C.E.. Muhammad's father, Abdullah, probably died before he was born, and his mother died when he was about six. His grandfather became his guardian and protector, and when his grandfather died, an uncle took custody of him. Without inheritance from his father, the young Muhammad had to fend for himself. He did so by working as a caravan trader. His efficiency and honesty eventually caught the eye of a wealthy and influential widow, Khadija, who was many years his senior and made him her business agent. They eventually married and had many children, but only four girls lived to maturity.

The Mecca in which Muhammad grew to manhood was the center of Arabia's polytheistic religion, attracting tribal pilgrims from all over the Arabian Peninsula. Meccans at that time generally were pagan, although as a center of trade, Mecca had come into contact with Christianity, Judaism, and some Christian heretical and gnostic sects. In addition, some Jewish and Christian tribes lived in Arabia. Zoroastrianism, a monotheistic religion practiced by Persians, also was known to some Meccans. Like most people in Arabia, Meccans believed in a creator God, or High God, that remained remote, with access gained only through intercessors, such as the tribal gods and goddesses, whose 360 idols came to be installed in the Kaaba.

Muhammad's Revelations.   In time, Muhammad became deeply troubled by the low moral standards of Meccan society. He is said to have retreated on occasion to secluded places to think and meditate. According to a seventh-century biographer, Muhammad experienced his first revelation in a cave in 610, when he was around forty years of age. The angel Gabriel commanded him to read a message sent from God stating that man was a creature of God and subservient to him. Muhammad, who was likely illiterate, is said to have memorized the message and repeated it to his wife and his close friends. Additional revelations followed his first, on and off for some twenty-two years. These revelations, which mark the birth of Islam, became the text of the Quran and established Muhammad's role as the Prophet and Messenger of God. Muhammad slowly began to attract followers. Most Meccans, however, spurned his teachings and ridiculed his claims of being a prophet. They were outraged particularly by his audacious denunciation of Mecca's paganism and his condemnation of the Kaaba, which provided Mecca its position of prestige and eminence in Arabia and which enjoyed the protection and sponsorship of the Meccan aristocracy.

The First Islamic Community.   Meccan leaders' disdain for Muhammad turned into hostility when they became aware of his growing appeal and the implications of his teachings. His message clearly threatened the established order and jeopardized the city's income from trade and pilgrimage. To avoid persecution, in 622 Muhammad secretly fled with some seventy of his followers for Yathrib, a city to the north. The flight from Mecca—called the Hegira—and the creation of the first Muslim community marks the beginning of the Islamic calendar.

Yathrib, later renamed Medina, the "city" of the Prophet, welcomed Muhammad in the hope that he would help alleviate serious divisions and civil problems caused by a large influx of outsiders—mostly Yemenis and Bedouins—and internal feuds among rival groups and clans. In this first test of the nascent religion, Muhammad achieved success. With Medina as a base, Muhammad set out to conquer Mecca. He succeeded in 630, after years of intermittent warfare. Entering Mecca in triumph, Muhammad proceeded to the Kaaba, where he destroyed the idols of paganism and reconsecrated the Kaaba, which subsequently became the holiest shrine of Islam.

The Islamic commonwealth then began to emerge and take shape through raids and conquests, common among the tribes of Arabia, and diplomatic missions, negotiations, treaties, and alliances with other tribes. Arab Muslims in

Muhammad's lifetime carried their religion to many parts of Arabia, but the Prophet did not live long enough to see its spectacular expansion. When Muhammad died in 632, only two years after seizing Mecca and making it the center of Islam, he bequeathed to his followers not only a religion, but a sociopolitical system and an ideology. His followers assumed the task of propagating that ideology and carrying it beyond the confines of Arabia.

Islam after Muhammad

With, as Muslims believe, Muhammad being God's last prophet on Earth, no one could succeed him. Some provision had to be adopted, however, for filling Muhammad's other roles as political and military leader of the community. The issue of succession produced a major schism in Islam that endures to this day. Some of Muhammad's followers claimed that the mantle of leadership should pass within the Prophet's family to his cousin and son-in-law Ali. They argued that Muhammad had made this designation. Proponents of this view evolved into the Shiite branch of Islam around 656. Most Muslims, however, opposed this position and preferred instead to rely on tribal tradition, in which tribal elders choose a leader according to the prestige and power of his family or position in the tribal system. Supporters of this view formed the Sunni tradition in Islam. ("The Branches and Sufis of Islam," box, p. 200)

Muhammad's Early Successors. Muhammad's trusted lieutenants passed over Ali and chose Abu Bakr (632–634), one of their own, as the Prophet's successor. Abu Bakr is thought to be the first convert to Islam outside Muhammad's immediate family. He was also the father of Aisha, Muhammad's last wife. Abu Bakr thus became the first of the four Rashidun ("rightly guided") *caliphs*—a term derived from Abu Bakr's title as successor to the Prophet—who promoted the expansion of Islam. Abu Bakr's first goal was to Islamize the rest of the Arabian Peninsula and exert control over it. His brilliant military commander, Khalid ibn al-Walid, conquered eastern and southern Arabia, subduing even tribes that had renounced their allegiance after Muhammad's death. With Islam secure in Arabia, Khalid and other generals conquered the Sassanids in what is now Iraq, wrested Syria from the Byzantines, and opened all of Palestine to the Muslims.

Abu Bakr was succeeded as caliph by Umar ibn al-Khattab (634–644), whom Muslims sometimes call the second founder of Islam. During his ten-year reign, he consolidated the theocratic foundations of Islam and conquered new lands. Islamic forces overran Persia, central Asia, western India, and Egypt, all bastions of great empires and early civilizations. Economic considerations as much as religious zeal drove this expansion. Under Umar, the territories of the Middle East were unified into a single, great empire for the first time in thirteen centuries, since the age of Alexander the Great.

Uthman ibn Affan (644–656) succeeded Umar as the third of the Rashidun caliphs. Like his two predecessors, Uthman had been a companion of Muhammad, but unlike them, he belonged to a powerful family, the Umayyad. Uthman drew from his family to appoint some of his senior aides as governors and generals. His most significant and historically important appointment was that of his dynamic and able cousin Muawiyah ibn Abi Sufyan as governor of Damascus. Muawiyah soon became the ruler of all Syria.

Uthman's weak leadership and his penchant for appointing Umayyads to high office angered other Muslims, including those who considered themselves keepers and protectors of Muhammad's legacy. In 656 a group of rebels murdered Uthman, outraged by his nepotism and deviation from the path set by Muhammad. The assassination set off a civil war that lasted until 661.

Muhammad's cousin and son-in-law Ali ibn Abi Talib finally assumed the caliphate (656–661), chosen to succeed Uthman. Some powerful and influential Muslims, however, opposed Ali, accusing him of condoning the murder of Uthman.

The Umayyad Islamic Empire. After Ali's ascension, an unstable period ensued in which

The Branches and Sufis of Islam

About 85 percent of all Muslims are Sunni, while approximately 15 percent are Shiite. The schism within Islam occurred following the death of the Prophet Muhammad in the seventh century when Muslims could not agree on a successor.

When Muhammad died in 632, his cousin and son-in-law Ali ibn Abi Talib claimed to be the Prophet's successor. Believing that Muhammad had not designated Ali as such, most of Muhammad's followers rallied around Abu Bakr—reputed to be the first person outside the Prophet's immediate family to convert to Islam—and selected him the first of the four Rashidun ("rightly guided") caliphs, or "successors" to the Prophet. Abu Bakr thus became the leader of the Muslim community, though not as a prophet, because Muslims believe Muhammad to be the last prophet of God.

Ali was rebuffed two more times, as Muslims selected Umar ibn al-Khattab and Uthman ibn Affan as the second and third caliphs. In 656 the caliphate finally passed to Ali. Muawiyah ibn Abi Sufyan, the governor of Syria, and other members of the powerful Umayyad tribe refused, however, to recognize Ali's authority. Ali ruled from Kufah, in Iraq, but his reign was marked by strife and dissension.

The Shiites—"partisans of Ali"—take their name from the Arabic *shiah,* meaning "followers" or "party." The party, or shiah, of Ali emerged during a civil war from 656 to 661. The first war between Muslims erupted when Ali's army engaged Muawiyah's forces. Ali had been accused by his adversaries of having condoned the murder of his predecessor, Uthman, a member of the Umayyad family. The issue was submitted to arbitration, but nevertheless, in 661 a Muslim rebel assassinated Ali. Hasan, Ali's eldest son, succeeded his father as caliph but shortly thereafter was challenged by Muawiyah. Hasan abdicated, and Muawiyah was proclaimed the caliph, with his capital in Damascus.

Muawiyah designated his son, Yazid, as his successor. Hasan's younger brother, the popular and charismatic Hussein, rose against Yazid only to be routed and slain with his army at Karbala, in Iraq, in 680. The martyrdom of Hussein became a defining moment for Shiism. His death is commemorated annually on the tenth day (*ashura*) of Muharram, the first month of the Muslim lunar calendar. Shiite communities reenact the tragedy in a passion play that includes expressions of sorrow, remorse, and self-mortification (beating of the breast and self-flagellation) to make them one with Hussein's suffering and death. The martyrdom of Hussein has become a paradigm for the Shiite struggle against

Muhammad's widow, Aisha, and then Muawiyah, the ruler of Syria, challenged Ali for control of the Islamic movement. Ali was assassinated by some of his opponents in 661, and Muawiyah (661–680) seized the caliphate that year. Damascus became the center of the Umayyads (661–750) and their Arab empire. Shiites regard the caliphs, in particular Muawiyah, as a usurper and believe Ali's son Hussein to be Ali's rightful successor.

In contrast to the Sunni caliph, who was selected by community leaders as a political, not religious, leader of the community, the Shiites believe that leadership of the Muslim community belongs to the imam, a direct descendant of Muhammad who serves in a religious as well as a politico-military capacity. Although the imam is not a prophet, he is nevertheless considered to be divinely inspired, infallible, sinless, and the final and authoritative interpreter of God's will as formulated in Islamic law.

The Umayyad dynasty lasted from 661 to 750 and ushered in a new wave of conquests that complemented the breathtaking expansion achieved by the Rashidun caliphs. The Muslim empire extended its hegemony to the fringes of India and China, overran North Africa, and in 717 pushed across the Strait of Gibraltar. The occupation of Spain by the Muslims—who were called Moors—lasted until 1492. During the Umayyad dynasty, Muhammad's followers gained control of an tyranny, oppression, and injustice. It featured prominently in the Iranian Revolution.

The political dispute that gave rise to Shiism was later reinforced by doctrinal differences between Shiites and Sunnis. The Shiites replaced the caliphate with an imamate and declared a hereditary line of succession from Muhammad's family and descendants through twelve imams, beginning with Ali, his cousin and son-in-law. In contrast to the Sunni caliph, the Shiite imam, or leader, is believed to be religiously inspired (though not a prophet) and sinless.

There are three major branches of Shiism: the Zaydis, Ismailis (a major branch is led by the Aga Khan) and Ithna Asharis (Twelvers, who take their name from the number of imams that they recognize as legitimate successors of the Prophet). The Twelvers comprise the largest Shiite branch. Muhammad al-Muntazar, the twelfth imam, reportedly disappeared under mysterious circumstances in 878. Twelvers do not believe that he "died," but that he "disappeared" or went into hiding to avoid persecution by Sunnis. Also called The Expected One, the twelfth imam is a messianic figure who is to reappear to complete the mission of God on Earth.

Twelver Shiism is the state religion of Iran, which has a majority Shiite population. Among the larger Arab states—Iran is non-Arab—only Iraq, where the sect originated, is predominantly Shiite. The majority of Bahrain's population is Shiite, while the ruling family is Sunni. The other Arab nations are mostly Sunni, with the exception of Lebanon, which has a significant and growing plurality Shiite population.

In the eighth century, Sufism developed as a mystical reform movement in response to the growing materialism and wealth of Muslim society that accompanied the expansion and growing power of the Islamic Empire. The term *Sufi* derives from *suf*, the Arabic word for "wool," because the first Sufis wore coarse woolen garments. Although many early Muslims believed that strict adherence to Islamic law and rituals would suffice to counter the excesses of imperial lifestyles and luxuries, Sufis found emphasis on laws and duties spiritually lacking. Instead, they emphasized the "interior" path, seeking through discipline of body and mind and devotional love the direct and personal experience of God.

Sufi orders played an important role in the spread of Islam through missionary activities. Their tendency to adopt and adapt to local non-Islamic customs and practices, and their strong devotional and emotional character, helped them to become a popular mass movement. Sufism has had and continues to exert great influence within the Muslim world and in the West.

empire that surpassed in size that of Alexander the Great.

It was during the height of this period that the newly conquered peoples—including the Syrians, Egyptians, and Berbers—became Arabized and Islamized, adopting the faith, culture, and language of the Arabs. The Berbers retained certain local attributes, such as a native dialect, and the Persians, Turks, and some Indian groups adopted the Arabic alphabet and script but retained their own language. The Arabs themselves were exposed to a process of acculturation as the new faith acquired millions of converts among non-Arab peoples. As a result, the Arab character of Islam became diluted.

A combination of powerful trends finally brought about the demise of the Umayyad Empire. The most decisive were the growing decadence of the Umayyad court in Damascus, the Shiites' persistent opposition to the Umayyad dynasty, the constant feuding among the Sunni tribes of Arabia, and the emergence of rebellious and alienated forces in Iraq and in a region of Iran known as Khurasan, both erstwhile centers of great power that resented their subordinate status under the Umayyads.

The Abbasid Islamic Empire. Around 740, the Abbasids, led by Abu al-Abbas, a descendant of an uncle of Muhammad, emerged as the major opposition group to Umayyad rule. They became the main rallying point of all anti-Umayyad forces, especially the non-Arab Muslims of Khurasan. In 747 the Abbasids, led by Abu al-Abbas, openly revolted. They defeated the Umayyads within three years.

The Abbasids ruthlessly pursued the Umayyad rulers. Only a few escaped, among them Abd al-Rahman, who fled to Spain, where he established the Umayyad caliphate of Cordoba. The Umayyads at Cordoba were threatened by internal factionalism, Berber invasions from North Africa, and resistance by Christians in the north of Spain. The regime survived these challenges, however, and went on to prosper under subsequent Berber/Arab dynasties that arose in North Africa. Moorish power in Spain came to an end in 1492 with the capture of the last Islamic stronghold at Granada by the Christian forces of King Ferdinand and Queen Isabella.

The emergence of the Abbasid Empire (750–1258), with its capital in Baghdad, ushered in profound changes. Non-Arab Muslims achieved greater prominence and influence than ever before. The Abbasids extended the Islamic empire to Mediterranean ports in southern France and Italy and took control of Sicily and Sardinia and, in the east, part of present-day Turkey and India.

The imperial munificence and wealth of the Baghdad court far outstripped its Umayyad predecessor in Damascus and was immortalized in the tales of *The Arabian Nights*. The arts flourished, and a great cultural movement flowered along the banks of the Tigris and Euphrates Rivers. The works of the ancient Greeks, Romans, Persians, and Hindus in philosophy, medicine, astronomy, mathematics, and science were translated into Arabic and became part of Islamic culture. A whole generation of Arab and Arabized Muslim scholars left their imprint on Western civilization.

The Abbasids leaned heavily on Persian administrators and Turkish soldiers to run their burgeoning empire, which extended almost from the borders of China to the Pyrenees. The influence of the Persians and Turks grew until the caliphs themselves became little more than figureheads of the new administrative elite.

As the power of the caliphs diminished, they became easy prey for their governors and generals, who proceeded to carve out their own principalities. Numerous little dynasties and states ultimately sprouted within the Abbasid Empire, rendering it an empty shell ruled by caliphs appointed or deposed at will by Turkish soldiers or Persian administrators. In Spain, Morocco, Tunisia, Egypt, Syria, Persia, and other areas, new, self-styled caliphates and sultanates emerged, maintaining a semblance of allegiance to the caliph in Baghdad. By the year 1000, self-proclaimed and independent caliphs in Cairo and in Cordoba rivaled the Abbasid caliph in Baghdad.

The Abbasid dynasty continued through the eleventh century, when a group of Turks, called Seljuks, conquered Baghdad and won recognition from the Arab caliph there. The Seljuk rulers captured most of Anatolia (Turkey) from the Byzantines, triggering the chain of events that culminated in the Crusades.

The Ottoman Empire.   The final blow to the Abbasid Empire came in 1258, when Mongols overran Baghdad. As the Middle Ages drew to a close, Muslim power shifted decisively to Anatolia, where a small Turkish tribe led by Osman began to accumulate power and territory at the expense of the Byzantine Empire. By 1453 the Ottomans, as they are called in English, had captured Byzantium. The Ottoman Turks changed the name of Constantinople to Istanbul, which became their capital.

The greatest of the Ottoman sultans, Suleiman the Magnificent (1520–1566), extended the frontiers of the empire to include the Middle East and North Africa as well as most of present-day Hungary and southeastern Europe. In India, another Turkish dynasty, the Moguls, established an Islamic empire that reached its height between 1556 and 1658. It was during that era that the Taj Mahal was built at Agra.

The Ottoman Empire began to break up even before the European powers emerged in the nineteenth century as the new masters of the international order. The "sick man of Europe," as tottering

Ottoman rule was labeled at the turn of the century, was finally defeated in World War I. The victors partitioned its territories. The remnants of the empire were centered in Turkish-populated Anatolia, which became the Turkish Republic in 1923 under the leadership of Mustafa Kemal (Atatürk).

Foundations of Islamic Faith and Practice

Islam incorporates spiritual and temporal aspects of life into a social and religious system that seeks to regulate a believer's relationship to God and relations with people. Its precepts and tenets, though clearly the product of a particular society and historical period, are considered to be good for all people and all times and, therefore, unalterable.

Islam in Arabic means "submission"—to obey, follow, and implement the will of God. A Muslim is one who submits. The root for the word *Islam* also means "peace," the peace that comes from following God's will. An uncompromising assertion of monotheism—the unity, uniqueness, and sovereignty of "Allah," the Arabic word for God—is the central theme of the Islamic faith. Muslims accordingly reject the Christian doctrine of the Trinity but do consider Jesus a prophet. The affirmation of the oneness of God is linked symbolically to another fundamental tenet, namely, that Muhammad is the messenger of God and that he is the last prophet. These two affirmations constitute the *shahadah*, or confession of faith.

The Sources of Islam

Faith, practice, and doctrine and law in Sunni Islam have four sources (usul al-fiqh): the Quran (revelation), Sunnah (as preserved in the Hadith) (example of the prophet), consensus (*ijma*), and inference by analogy.

The Quran. The Quran (literally, "reading or recitation") is the primary source of Islamic teachings and doctrine. Considered the word of God, it is thus divine, eternal, and immutable. Muslims believe that the Quran is a replica of an archetype in heaven. Because the Quran was revealed to Muhammad in Arabic, Muslims are prohibited from using it liturgically in any other language.

The Quran consists of 114 chapters of varying lengths that Muslims believe were revealed to Muhammad piecemeal over a period of about twenty-two years by the archangel Gabriel. The various utterances in the Quran initially were memorized or written on parchment, leather, palm leaves, stone tablets, and other objects. They remained scattered for a period, only pieced together and collected into a standard text well after Muhammad's death. The first canonized version appeared under the caliph Uthman in the seventh century.

Islam has no unifying priestly or clerical caste and no centralized body. Muhammad has no divine attributes; he simply is considered God's messenger. Thus the Quran possesses an overwhelming spiritual importance in Muslims' lives. The Quran is the very word of God, the final and complete revelation. Its spiritual content and the majesty of its prose exercise a powerful hold for its adherents. The Quran is a work of such beauty to Muslims that it sometimes transports them into a state of spiritual and aesthetic elation when they hear its verses, which are chanted or intoned, accentuating the rhythmic cadence and elegance of the text. The mutually reinforcing link between the linguistic and the spiritual importance of the Quran, especially to native Arabic speakers, underlies Muslims' deep belief in the inimitability of the holy book.

Some in the West, including Orientalists of the past, referred to Islam as Mohammedanism. The Christian paradigm of naming the religion after Muhammad as they named Christianity for Christ is misleading. The Quran, not Muhammad, is the cornerstone of Islam. Unlike Christ, Muhammad is not God. His attributes remain those of a man who is a prophet and messenger of God. The Quran identifies Muhammad's status clearly when it commands, "Obey God and his prophet." In Islamic tradition, Muhammad is the model, the exemplar of the ideal Muslim, the "living Quran" who is to be obeyed and emulated. Veneration of Muhammad is reflected in the phrase that always follows mention of his name, "God's Blessings and Peace be upon him," but Muslims do not worship him.

The Sunnah and Hadith.   The Quran contains a variety of devotional regulations and rules for everyday living and for personal matters such as marriage, divorce, inheritance, and contracts. Like the testaments of other religions, however, the Quran is not comprehensive. It does not address a number of problems, especially those resulting from the growth of the community of Islam after Muhammad's death and the establishment of modern secular states. Thus Muslims have sought guidance in the "prophetic practice," or Sunnah. The Sunnah of the Prophet refers to his words and actions or attitude toward the actions of others. They are preserved in the Hadith, narrative stories or traditions. In modern usage, the two words, *sunnah* and *hadith*, are often used interchangeably.

Codification of the Hadith did not begin until the second half of the second Islamic century (767–795), and it was not completed until the third (869–896), during the reign of the Abbasid dynasty. Because the sources of what Muhammad said and did derive from oral testimonies and reports handed down from one generation to another, they in many ways reflect the social history of the early Muslim community. During this process, however, a great deal of distortion and even spurious attributions to Muhammad slipped into the record. Sifting through the mass of oral history and traditions that accumulated after Muhammad's death, Islamic scholars in the Abbasid era faced a formidable task of verification and compilation. Their efforts eventually resulted in six authoritative collections or compilations, the so-called Six Books.

Consensus.   The third source of Islamic doctrine is consensus of the community. In fact, however, it has come to be equated with the consensus of leading Muslim religious scholars (*ulama*), the interpreters of Islamic doctrine. When the Muslim community faces an issue for which the Quran or the Hadith and Sunnah have no provision, scholars may study the matter to determine how to deal with it.

Inference by Analogy.   Inference by analogy is the fourth source of Islamic doctrine. It is a deductive rather than inductive process. Where no clear text is found in the Quran or Hadith concerning an issue, judges and scholars devise a solution based on principles or solutions inferred from the previous three sources. Inference by analogy corresponds to the use of precedents in the Anglo-Saxon legal tradition.

The Five Pillars of Islam

The Quran enjoins Muslims to follow the straight path of God. The four doctrinal sources above provide the basis for Islamic law, the ideal blueprint, system, or path for Muslim life. The development of Islamic law was and is an attempt to delineate that path, those obligations that determine and define the identity and way of life of Islam and Muslims. The most essential elements are the Five Pillars of Islam.

I. The Confession of Faith.   The confession is an oral declaration: "I testify that there is no God but Allah; I testify that Muhammad is God's messenger." Implicit in this testimony is the commitment to belief in one true God (monotheism) and affirmation that God's revelation (the Quran) through the Prophet Muhammad is true. To proclaim this declaration of faith is to become a Muslim.

II. Prayer or Worship.   Muslims must meet several conditions before they can pray: They must be Muslim, decently attired, physically clean, and face Mecca. A Muslim prays five times daily: at daybreak, noon, afternoon, sunset, and evening. Successively standing, kneeling (prostrating), and touching their foreheads to the ground, Muslims repeat ritual prayers drawn from the Quran, always beginning with the declaration, "God is most great." Muslims can perform daily prayers anywhere.

Many carry a prayer rug with them. On Friday at noon, the Muslim equivalent of the Sabbath, Muslims gather at mosques for community prayer.

III. Alms. The giving of alms, like the tithe in Christianity, is obligatory for Muslims. Alms are a wealth tax, not an income tax, to be given to the poor or to an institution that supports the Muslim community.

IV. Fasting during Ramadan. Ramadan, the ninth month in the lunar Islamic calendar, is the month in which the Prophet Muhammad customarily retreated to fast and pray and in which the Quran was first revealed to him. In memory of the Prophet's practice and in honor of Allah's revelation, Muslims are required to fast from sunrise to sunset and to pray and perform charitable works for the month. Not even water is to be consumed during the fast. Sexual activity and smoking are also forbidden during fasting. Because Ramadan follows the phases of the moon, it may occur during any of the four seasons. The sick, the elderly, travelers, pregnant women, and nursing mothers are traditionally exempt from the rites of fasting during Ramadan.

In many countries, when the traditional cannon is fired to signal the breaking of the fast at sunset, Ramadan usually takes on a festive character in which families and friends gather around tables, for breakfast (the breaking of the fast, an *iftar*), laden with traditional dishes. The month culminates in the colorful three-day holiday of 'Id al-Fitr, one of the most important Muslim holidays. It is a festive occasion, like Christmas, during which families and friends gather to celebrate and exchange gifts.

V. Pilgrimage. The twelfth and last month of the Islamic calendar is the season of *al-hajj*, the ritual pilgrimage to Mecca, the holiest city of Islam, where Muslims reenact some the earliest sacred stories of the faith. Muslim males and females of sound body and mind are required to journey to Mecca at least once in a lifetime. *("Al-Hajj: The Pilgrimage to Mecca," box, p. 206)*

Articles of Faith

Muslims accept the following five articles of faith.

Belief in God Muslims are believers in one God. They pride themselves for being the only true (absolute) monotheists.

Belief in Spirits: Angels, Jinn, and the Devil. The Quranic universe consists of three realms—heaven, Earth, and hell—in which there are two types of beings—humans and spirits. All are called to obedience to God. Spirits include angels, jinn, and devils. Angels are created from light, are immortal and sexless, and serve as the link between God and human beings. They are guardians, recorders, and messengers from God who transmit his message to human beings by communicating with prophets. Thus, for example, the angel Gabriel is believed to have communicated the revelation of the Quran to Muhammad. Jinn, beings created by fire, exist between angels and humans and can be either good or bad. Although invisible by nature, jinn can assume visible form. Like human beings, they are to be rewarded or punished in the afterlife. Jinn are often portrayed as magical beings, such as the genies in the story of Aladdin and his lamp. Devils are fallen angels or jinn that tempt human beings, who are torn between the forces of good and evil. Satan (Shaytan, or Iblis), leader of the devils, represents evil, which is defined as disobedience to God. His refusal to prostrate himself before Adam upon God's command caused his fall.

Because God breathed his spirit into Adam, the first human being, all humans enjoy a special status as God's representatives on Earth. The Quran teaches that God gave Earth to human beings as a trust so that they can implement his will. Although Muslims believe in the Fall of Adam and Eve in the Garden of Eden, in contrast to Christianity there is no doctrine of inherited, original sin. The punishment of Adam and Eve stems from their personal act of disobedience to God. Each person is held responsible for his or her

Al-Hajj: The Pilgrimage to Mecca

Once a year, Mecca—Islam's holiest city—becomes a teeming microcosm of the Islamic world, as Muslims of every race and color converge on it from all corners of the globe to perform the rites of *al-hajj* (pilgrimage). There in Mecca's Sacred Mosque, some 2 million believers come together around the Kaaba, the shrine rising majestically in the middle of the mosque's large open court.

The Kaaba

The hajj is the Fifth Pillar of Islam. In pre-Islamic Arabia, tribesmen trekked to the Kaaba at least once a year to worship the idols it housed. With the advent of Islam, Muhammad destroyed the idols and reconsecrated the Kaaba as Islam's holiest shrine, restoring it, according to Muslims, to the house of God built by the Prophet Abraham and his son Ismail.

Today, the cube-like stone structure of the Kaaba stands forty-nine feet high and is shrouded by the *kiswah,* a brocaded black cloth made anew each year and adorned with quotations from the Quran. The focal point of the Kaaba is the Black Stone, a piece of rock twelve inches in diameter set in silver and mounted in the east corner of the holy shrine. Muslims believe the archangel Gabriel delivered this sacred rock to Ismail. It is said to be the only remaining relic from the original house of God built by Abraham and Ismail.

A Holy Ritual

All Muslims who are physically and financially able to do so are required to perform the hajj at least once in their lifetime. To devout Muslims, the hajj represents the crowning event of their lives. During the pilgrimage, they ritually remember and reenact a sacred past and rededicate themselves to God and to their faith.

The formal pilgrimage lasts only ten days, beginning on the first day of Dhul-Hijjah (the month of Hajj), the twelfth and last month of the Muslim lunar calendar. In another sense, for the individual pilgrim, the pilgrimage begins when a Muslim leaves home for Mecca and does not end until he or she returns. During the entire period, the pilgrim is considered to be in a dedicated state, participating in a holy ritual.

Before entering the sacred territory around Mecca, Muslims must be in a state of *ihram* (consecration), symbolized by a seamless two piece white garment worn by men. Women wear their customary modest dress and can be unveiled. Unlike the men, however, women must keep their heads covered. The state of ihram also requires that Muslims refrain from cutting their nails or hair,

own actions. Human beings are mortal because of the human condition, not because of sin or the Fall. The Fall also demonstrates God's mercy and repentance, returning to the straight path of God. The Quran does not emphasize shame, disgrace, or guilt, but the ongoing human struggle—or *jihad*—to do what is right and just.

Belief in God's Messengers or Prophets. Prophets are inspired by God to communicate his will to mankind. The Quran speaks of a line of prophets beginning with Adam and ending with Muhammad. These include Abraham and Moses of the Hebrew Bible and Jesus and John the Baptist of the New Testament.

Belief in God's Books. Islam acknowledges that God's revelations are found in the Torah, the Psalms, the Gospel, and the Quran: "We sent Jesus, the son of Mary, confirming the Torah that had come before him: We sent him the Gospel in which is guidance and light, and confirmation of the Torah that had come before him, a guidance and an admonition to those who fear God" (Quran 5:46). Christians and Jews are "people of the book," those having received a divine scripture, hunting, wearing jewelry, or engaging in sexual relations.

As the pilgrims approach Mecca, they shout, "I am here, O Lord, I am here!" When they enter Mecca, their first obligation is to go to the Kaaba. The crowds of pilgrims move counterclockwise around it seven times. This circumambulation, like prayer, symbolizes the believer's entry into the divine presence. In the days that follow, pilgrims participate in a variety of ritual actions and ceremonies symbolizing key religious events. They walk and sometimes run seven times along a quarter-mile corridor of the Grand Mosque to commemorate Hagar's frantic search in the desert for water for her son Ismail. The pilgrims drink water from the well, called Zamzam (meaning "bubbling"), inside the Grand Mosque, where Muslims believe God provided water for the mother and son.

In the final days of the hajj, pilgrims proceed four miles east of Mecca to the village of Mina, where they rest before moving on the next day to the Plain of Arafat for the ritual prayers of "standing" from noon to sunset. More than 2 million people have been known to assemble on the vast, empty plain where Muhammad prayed and delivered his farewell sermon before he died.

On the return trip to Mina, pilgrims stop for the night at Muzdalifah. There they collect pebbles for the ritual stoning of Satan's three pillars, located in Mina and representing evil and temptation. Pilgrims symbolically reject the devil, the source of all evil, by throwing stones at three pillars that stand at the site where Satan met Abraham and Ismail and tempted them to disobey God as Abraham prepared to sacrifice his son in obedience to God's command.

Feast and Sacrifice

On the tenth and last day, pilgrims celebrate 'Id al-Adha (festival of sacrifice) by slaughtering an animal. This ritual, marking the end of the pilgrimage season, recalls Abraham offering his son Ismail as a sacrifice, but Ismail then being delivered when the archangel Gabriel brings a ram to kill instead. (The biblical version of the same story has Abraham offering his son Isaac in sacrifice.) While the pilgrims celebrate 'Id al-Adha at Mina, Muslims worldwide are gathering for similar celebrations in their homes and towns. 'Id al-Adha is the highest holy day of the Islamic calendar.

With the completion of the sacrifice ceremonies, the pilgrimage is considered completed, although many pilgrims return to the Kaaba for prayers or visit the Prophet's tomb in Medina before returning home. Many Muslims go to Mecca at other times during the year as well to perform *umrah* (visit), the lesser pilgrimage that includes a visit to the Kaaba, the circumambulation, and walking between Safa and Marwah seven times.

Muslims who complete the pilgrimage have earned the honorific "hajji."

and Muslims are to respect their places of worship, law codes, schools, and property. Muslims believe that over time, the texts of the Torah and Gospel were corrupted or distorted through outside or foreign religious and cultural influences. They contend that only the Quran is perfectly preserved intact and is the final, complete revelation from God.

Belief in the Day of Judgment. In the Quran, Hadith, and Sunnah, believers are constantly enjoined to conduct their lives with awareness that they will ultimately confront the day of God's judgment. For this reason, they must be attentive to Allah's commands, submit themselves to them, and act with compassion and justice toward others. According to Islamic doctrine, at the end of the world, on a day of resurrection, all humans will be revived and stand before God for judgment. The righteous believer will live eternally in paradise, a green, well-watered place of ease and comfort. Believers guilty of evil will serve a certain time in hell, most often described as fire, before being restored to paradise. Eternity in hell is reserved for nonbelievers, those who deny or reject God. Martyrs in the cause of Islam are believed to go directly to paradise.

Islamic Law

The concept of Islamic law (*sharia*) embraces all aspects of human life and endeavor, private and public, civil and criminal. Sharia is divided into two broad categories: worship and social transactions or relations. Thus, the law deals with prayer, fasting, and almsgiving as well as commercial activities, property, marriage, divorce, inheritance, personal conduct, hygiene, and diet. It sets forth penalties for crimes and offenses. Islamic law also covers political concerns, such as war and peace, relations among states, and treaties. In most modern Islamic nations, although the legal system may acknowledge the sharia as a source of law, state law is primarily inspired by or based upon Western models. A few Muslim countries, notably Saudi Arabia, maintain that the sharia is the sole source of law and still apply penalties such as stoning or beheading for adultery and amputation for theft.

Sunni Schools of Thought. Islamic law was compiled by scholars and jurists during the first three centuries of Islam—the seventh, eighth, and ninth centuries of the Christian era—according to Sunni Islam, on the basis of the four sources or roots of jurisprudence: the Quran, the Sunnah and Hadith, consensus, and inference by analogy. Although early jurists freely interpreted the law (*ijtihad*, individual interpretation), using reason and drawing on local customs, the desire to limit the latitude of jurists and restrict them more so to using sacred texts as the basis for interpretation led to an emphasis on reasoning by analogy. Where no clear sacred text could be invoked, jurists were expected to seek analogous situations in the Quran or Sunnah upon which they would base their legal reasoning in addressing new problems or issues. Concern for justice led to the development of subsidiary legal principles by some schools of law. Among the more prominent principles are equity,

which permits exceptions to strict, or literal, legal reasoning, and public interest or human welfare, which gives judges flexibility in arriving at just and equitable decisions.

In Sunni Islam, four major schools (or interpretations) of law have survived: the Hanafi, the Maliki, the Shafi'i, and the Hanbali. The Hanafi is the official school in most of the Middle East, except in the Arabian Peninsula and Iran. It also predominates in Afghanistan, Pakistan, Turkey, and among Muslims in India. Developed in Iraq and named after the prominent Islamic scholar Abu Hanafi, a Persian by origin, the Hanafi emphasizes the role of reason and independent legal opinion in the development of Islamic doctrine and law. It is considered the most liberal and adaptable of the four schools and has the most followers.

The oldest school, the Maliki, developed in Medina. It emphasizes the Sunnah and Hadith and the opinions of Medinan scholars, who were thought to retain the best memory and thus knowledge of the state and society that existed during the lifetime of Muhammad. Today, it is followed widely in North Africa and West Africa, but has few adherents elsewhere in the Islamic world.

The Shafi'i, considered the most legally rigorous of the four schools, originated from an attempt to reconcile the Maliki and Hanafi schools, but instead became a third school of legal doctrine. It remains influential in East Africa, Egypt, Yemen, and Indonesia and other parts of Southeast Asia.

The Hanbali, the most conservative of the four schools, rejects all sources of Islamic law except the Quran and the Sunnah and Hadith and emphasizes imitation of (Arabian) society during the lifetime of Muhammad. Today, it is the official school of law in Saudi Arabia and Qatar.

On the whole, each school accepts the other three as orthodox expressions of Sunni Islamic doctrine.

Shiite School of Thought. Shiites follow their own school of thought, the Jaafari school, which differs from the four Sunni schools in its interpretations of Islam. In addition to the prophetic traditions, Shiites include among the source of Islamic law collections of the traditions of Ali—who they believe was the first legitimate successor or leader (imam)—and of other divinely inspired imams, descendants of Muhammad through Ali, whom they regard as supreme religious authorities and legal interpreters. Despite the schism over the role and importance of Ali, the similarities between Sunnis and Shiites are far greater than their differences, and neither denies the Islamic character of the other.

Sharia and Fiqh

Critical to understanding the nature of Islamic law and its potential for change is the distinction between sharia—the divine law, which is to be found in sacred texts, the Quran, and traditions of the Prophet—and *fiqh,* the human interpretation and application of the sharia. Although there is a tendency to use the term *sharia* simply to mean Islamic law, in fact sharia refers to divinely revealed principles and values. Fiqh—understanding or human interpretation—refers to the corpus or body of laws developed by jurists that thus are the product of divine principles and human interpretation. This helps explain the diversity among the schools of law and their legal doctrines and lays the groundwork for the ongoing reinterpretation of Islam and legal reform.

The diverse geographic, social, historical, and cultural contexts in which jurists wrote and still write also account for differences in Islamic law. Many conservative ulama today continue to equate God's divinely revealed law (sharia) with legal manuals developed by early law schools. Reformers, however, call for changes in laws that are the products of social custom and human reasoning, arguing that duties and obligations to God (worship) are unchanging but that social obligations to one's fellow human beings reflect changing circumstances. They reclaim the right of ijtihad (independent reasoning) to reinterpret Islam to meet modern social needs.

Impact of Modernization

Like other entities emerging from colonial rule or discarding the old order, modern Muslim nation-states borrowed heavily from the West to build political and social institutions and run increasingly complex societies. Nationalism—a secular, nineteenth-century European ideology—was adopted worldwide by peoples whose identity and impulses had long been suppressed by foreign rule and control. Once these peoples achieved independence in the post–World War II era, their ruling elites, many of whom were educated in the West, turned to Western ideas as a model for nation building. To a large extent, the legacy of their former rulers predetermined their choice of European-style administrative, legal, and educational models. These systems were too deeply entrenched to dismantle, and moreover, they worked.

In the late nineteenth and early twentieth centuries, Western influence had begun to accelerate the process of modernization in Muslim societies well before the emergence of independent nations in the Middle East. From the West came industrialization, urbanization, technology, commercialization, constitutionalism, and other powerful forces of change. The economic and political benefits of these methods and ideas heightened expectations and aspirations in the Muslim world, motivating the political elites that stepped into power in the mid-twentieth century to continue the process of modernization.

This acculturation gradually led to the dismantling of the old order. There were, however, limits to this process directly related to the role of Islam in society. Given the powerful mix of politics and religion in the Middle East, where religious doctrine, cultural and behavioral patterns, and political values intersect at various levels of daily life, borrowing from the West often required or was legitimated by some degree of religious sanction.

Turkey, the only Muslim country to formally institute a secular system, in the 1920s, represents the exception to this proposition. At the other end of the spectrum, Saudi Arabia based its government and social system on an Islamic model. In other Muslim states, countries where the ruler and the majority of the population were Muslim, political elites could not ignore Islam and its role in society. Thus, officials sought to justify their actions in Islamic terms and to relate modern political concepts to their countries' Islamic heritage.

Working primarily through official religious organizations long accustomed to accommodating the ruling elite and sanctioning the established order, secular officials modified and reinterpreted legal and theological aspects of Islamic doctrine. In doing so, they drew on the historical precedent of Islamic scholars and jurists who had adapted Islamic doctrine to current conditions. They rationalized that Islamic law should not be taken literally as a fixed repository of commandments and prohibitions, but as a model to be emulated.

The process in which governments and their elites imposed reform from above by modifying or reinterpreting Islamic doctrine was not easy. In countries as diverse as Egypt and Pakistan, traditionalists contended that Islamic doctrine—immutable and sacred—provides an ideal and coherent model for society superior to that found in the West. The ulama in particular challenged the "Islamic credentials," the religious authority, training, expertise, and competence of reformers. Consequently, they viewed departures from that ideal model as religiously heretical (*bida,* innovation or an unwarranted departure from sacred tradition) and socially dangerous, threatening faith and the fabric of society. This approach was popular not only among many of the ulama, as guardians of Islamic traditions, but also was often supported by professionals, merchants and shopkeepers, small landowners and peasants in the countryside, and other groups that felt alienated or threatened economically by modernization.

Because governing elites had to take into account these deep-seated Islamic impulses—and they themselves wished to preserve at least the essence of their traditions—they sought to reconcile traditional values and secularism. This desire resulted in a set of compromises that produced systems incorporating elements of traditionalism, modernism, secularism, socialism, and other political ideas. Not all regimes in the Muslim world subscribed to this amalgam, but most did.

Economic dislocations compounded the strains in the traditional fabric of Islamic society. On the one hand, the pressures of modernization widened the gap between the rich minority and the poor majority, further impoverished the peasantry, and created a class of urban poor leading squalid lives in congested cities. On the other hand, sudden and enormous increases in wealth from oil revenues in some hitherto underdeveloped societies created acute problems, as the pressures of rapid development began to unravel the old order and clash head-on with the forces of traditionalism.

Many of the systems that eventually emerged in the Middle East lacked an essential ingredient of most successful Western societies: citizen participation. The governing groups usually failed or proved unwilling to create the mechanisms and institutions necessary to allow their people to participate in decision making. Colonial domination simply dissolved into native variations of repression or authoritarianism, regardless of the socialist, progressive, or democratic labels attached to them. Although these modern economic and governing systems sought to use Islamic symbols of identification, and most religious establishments sanctioned them, they failed to gain grass-roots support and popular mandates. Popular responses to the modernizing experiences buffeting Middle East societies took primarily political forms, but with an Islamic hue.

Islam Today

By the late 1960s and early 1970s, many parts of the Islamic world experienced an Islamic revival, or reassertion of Islam in private and public life. In some Islamic countries, Muslim activists or Islamists, often popularly called fundamentalists, challenged the legitimacy of regimes, calling for an Islamic state and society. In others, Muslims advocated emphasizing Islam in the political and social structures of the nation, making it a principal factor in public life.

Resurgence

Political Islam is rooted in a contemporary religious resurgence affecting personal and public life.

On the one hand, many Muslims have become more religiously observant, taking care to pray, fast, and dress according to Islamic precepts. On the other, Islam has also reemerged as an alternative ideology to the perceived failures of more secular forms of nationalism, capitalism, and socialism. Islamic symbols, rhetoric, actors, and organizations have become major sources of legitimacy and mobilization, informing political and social activism. Governments and Islamic movements spanning the religious and political spectrums from moderate to extremist have appealed to Islam to enhance their legitimacy and to mobilize popular support.

The Iranian Revolution in the late 1970s and early 1980s illustrates the potential dramatic impact of Islam on political developments, though the case of Iran is unique and should not be seen as representative of what is likely to occur elsewhere in the Middle East. In this instance, an Islamic government replaced a modernizing but repressive regime. Shiite *mullahs* (scholars) in Iran had traditionally played a political role, unlike their counterparts in Sunni Muslim countries. When the shah of Iran, Mohammad Reza Pahlavi, outlawed political opposition, dissidents among the Western-educated middle class, shopkeepers, and various leftist groups joined the only existing pocket of organized resistance—the religious community. A regime led by clergy under Ayatollah Ruhollah Khomeini took power in 1979 after bringing down one of the strongest and heavily Western-supported dynasties in the Middle East. The emergence of theocratic rule in Iran signaled and symbolized the contemporary Islamic revival and its potential impact on Muslim politics.

The causes of Islam's resurgence are religio-cultural, political, and socioeconomic. More often than not, faith and politics have been intertwined causes or catalysts. Such issues of political and social injustice as authoritarianism, repression, unemployment, inadequate housing and social services, maldistribution of wealth, and corruption have combined with a desire to regain religio-cultural identity and values in the face of westernization and secularization.

A series of crises and failures beginning in the late 1960s discredited many regimes and the Western-inspired paradigms of modernizing elites, triggering a politics of protest and a quest for identity and greater authenticity. The result was the positing of an "Islamic alternative" by governments and movements that has taken many forms—mainstream and extremists, government and opposition, clerical and lay. Among the earliest and more visible crises and "failures" that proved to be catalytic in the rise of political Islam are the following: the 1967 Arab-Israeli war, in which Israel decisively defeated the combined Arab armies of Egypt, Syria, and Jordan, occupied the Golan, the Sinai Peninsula, the West Bank, Gaza, and East Jerusalem, transforming the liberation of Jerusalem and Palestine into a transnational Islamic issue; the Pakistan-Bangladesh civil war of 1971–72, heralding the failure of Muslim nationalism; the Lebanese civil war from 1975 to 1990, stemming from sectarianism and failed government and resulting in the popularity and growth of extremist groups; the Iranian Revolution of 1978–79, a pivotal event of long-term global significance for the Muslim world and the West; and the economic failures in the late 1980s and 1990s of governments in Algeria, Egypt, Iran, Jordan, and Turkey, leading to calls for greater political participation and democratization.

While Iran initially offered the most visible and sustained critique of the West, embodying moderate as well as more extremist or rejectionist anti-Westernism, the failures of the West as an ally and of its development models and fear of its cultural penetration became pervasive themes of the Islamic resurgence. Many Muslims blame the ills of their societies on the excessive influence of and political, economic, military, and sociocultural dependence upon the West. Modernization as a process of progressive westernization and secularization came to be regarded as a form of neocolonialism exported by the West and imposed by local elites, undermining religious and cultural identity and values and replacing them with imported foreign values and models of development.

Islamist Movements

The history of Islam is replete with attempts to reaffirm Islamic ideals or resurrect the past in the face of internal crises or external challenges. Such revivalist movements are a common feature of Christian and Jewish histories as well. The eighteenth and nineteenth centuries, during which European power and hegemony reached its zenith in the Middle East, produced a number of Islamic movements: the Mahdi in the Sudan, Wahhabi in Saudi Arabia, Sanusi in Libya, and the Islamic modernist movements inspired by Jamal al-Din al-Afghani and Muhammad Abduh in the Middle East and Ahmad Khan and Muhammad Iqbal in South Asia. Some of these movements were forward looking in that they advocated a rejuvenated and purified Islam while encouraging assimilation of the political organization and technical advances introduced by European colonial administrations.

Moderate and extremist Islamic movements and organizations proliferated in the last decades of the twentieth century, becoming major actors and agents of change. They established modern political and social organizations and embraced modern means—the media, audio- and videotapes, faxes, and the Internet—to disseminate their messages. The majority functioned within civil society as social and political activists. They built schools, hospitals, clinics, and banks; they offered inexpensive legal and social services and led political and professional associations of doctors, lawyers, engineers, and teachers. At the same time, a minority of extremists waged a war of violence threatening the stability and security of many regimes and making its presence felt in Europe and the United States through sensational attacks.

The landscape of the Muslim world since the late twentieth century reveals the emergence of new Islamic republics in Iran, Sudan, and Afghanistan, a proliferation of Islamic movements that function as major political and social actors within existing systems, and the confrontational politics of radical and violent extremists. In contrast to the 1980s, when political Islam was simply equated with revolutionary Iran or clandestine groups with names like Islamic Jihad or the Army of God, in the 1990s and today it is part of the electoral process in the Middle East and wider Islamic world, made visible through representatives in the form of prime ministers, cabinet officers, Speakers of national assemblies, parliamentarians, and mayors in places as diverse as Bangladesh, Egypt, Indonesia, Iran, Israel/Palestine, Jordan, Kuwait, Lebanon, Malaysia, Pakistan, Sudan, Turkey, and Yemen. At the same time, Islamic extremism and terrorism have metastasized beyond national and regional boundaries into a global threat.

The Islamic revival or resurgence has been the major expression of Muslims' disenchantment with political leadership and ideological alternatives over the past few decades. For most Muslims, regardless of where they live, Islam remains the most genuine expression of their inherited cultural tradition. Any search for social and political recovery among the peoples of an Islamic society must include an assertion of its values and traditions.

The Globalization and "Hijacking" of Jihad

In the late twentieth century and into the early twenty-first century, the word *jihad* attained global currency. On the one hand, jihad's primary Quranic religious and spiritual aspects—the "struggle" or effort to follow God's path, to lead a good life—remained central to Muslim spirituality. On the other hand, the concept of jihad became more widespread and diverse in application, used by resistance movements, liberation movements, as well as extremist and terrorist organizations alike to legitimate, recruit, and motivate their followers. The *mujahidin* and Taliban in Afghanistan and Muslims in Bosnia, Chechnya, Kashmir, Kosovo, the southern Philippines, and Uzbekistan cast their armed struggles as jihads. Hizballah, Hamas (the Islamic Resistance Movement), and Islamic Jihad Palestine have characterized war and opposition against Israel as jihad. Al-Qaida (The Base), through leader Osama bin Laden, claims to be waging a global jihad against corrupt Muslim governments and the West.

In short, the term *jihad* has become comprehensive. Resistance and liberation struggles and militant jihads, holy and unholy wars, are all declared to be jihads. Jihad is waged at home not only against unjust rulers in the Muslim world but also against a broad spectrum of civilians and sometimes against military personnel. Jihad's scope abroad became chillingly clear in the attacks of September 11, 2001, that targeted the U.S. government and struck the symbols of U.S. economic and military power, killing thousands of civilians in the process.

The actions of bin Laden and others who attack civilian populations go beyond classical Islam's criteria for a jihad, which is considered just. They reject Islamic law's regulations regarding the goals and means of a valid jihad: violence must be proportional, meaning that only the amount of force necessary to repel the enemy should be used; civilians should not be targeted; jihad must be declared by a ruler or head of state. Today, religious and lay individuals and groups seize the right to declare and legitimate unholy wars by hijacking the name of Islam and recognizing no limits but their own.

Islamic scholars and religious leaders across the Muslim world—including the Islamic Research Council at al-Azhar University, regarded by many as the highest moral authority in Islam—have made strong, authoritative declarations against bin Laden's initiatives. In November 2001, the al-Azhar council released the following statement: "Islam provides clear rules and ethical norms that forbid the killing of non-combatants, as well as women, children, and the elderly, and also forbids the pursuit of the enemy in defeat, the execution of those who surrender, the infliction of harm on prisoners of war, and the destruction of property that is not being used in the hostilities."

The September 11 attacks are a watershed in the history of political Islam and of the world, signaling the extent to which Muslim extremists have become a global threat, in particular bin Laden and al-Qaida. The seemingly devout, well-educated son of a prominent Saudi family, bin Laden had fought against the Soviets in Afghanistan, a struggle that allied him with a cause supported by Pakistan, Saudi Arabia, the United States, and many other countries. After the war, he became radicalized by the U.S.-led coalition in the 1991 Persian Gulf War to oust Iraqi forces from Kuwait and the presence and increased influence of the United States in the Gulf. An ardent critic of U.S. foreign policy toward the Muslim world, bin Laden denounced U.S. support for Israel, sanctions against Iraq that resulted in the deaths of hundreds of thousands of civilians, and the substantial U.S. military and economic presence and involvement in Saudi Arabia, which he considered the "new Crusades." Bin Laden's message appealed to the feelings of many in the Arab and Muslim world. To his list of complaints were added other populist causes involving Muslims in Bosnia, Chechnya, Kosovo, and Kashmir.

Bin Laden is regarded as the "godfather" of global terrorism and a major funder of extremist groups. His involvement is suspected in the bombing of the World Trade Center in 1993, the killing of eighteen American soldiers in Somalia in 1993, bombings in Riyadh in 1995 and in Dhahran in 1996, the killing of fifty-eight tourists at Luxor, Egypt, in 1997. In February 1998, bin Laden and other militant leaders announced the creation of a transnational coalition of extremist groups, The Islamic Front for Jihad against Jews and Crusaders. Al-Qaida carried out the U.S. embassy bombings in Tanzania and Kenya in 1998 that killed 263 people and injured more than 5,000 and the attack against the USS *Cole* that killed seventeen American sailors.

Bin Laden and al-Qaida represent a new, international brand of militancy associated with the Afghan Arabs, men from the Arab and Muslim worlds who travelled to Afghanistan to fight alongside the mujahidin against the Soviets. This militancy is reflected in the growth of extremism and acts of terrorism in Central Asia, South Asia, and Southeast Asia, where it has often been referred to as Wahhabism because of its reported Saudi financial backing. Proponents and practitioners of this militancy are informed by bipolar vision that sees the modern world in mutually exclusive, black and white categories—the world of belief and unbelief, the land of Islam and of warfare, the forces of good against the forces of evil. Those who are not with them, whether Muslim or non-Muslim, are the enemy and are to be fought and destroyed in a war with no limits, no proportionality of goal or means. The extremists have attempted to legitimate their acts of violence and terror by "hijacking" Islam's norms and values concerning good governance, social justice, and the requirement to defend Islam when under siege.

The Democracy Debate

A diversity of harmonious as well as strident voices can be heard in ongoing discussions and debates about political participation and democratization. Secularist Muslims argue for secular forms of democracy involving the separation of religion and the state. Rejectionists maintain that Islam has its own forms of governance and that it is incompatible with democracy. Moderates and militant Muslims, from King Fahd to radical Islamists, hold this position. Accommodationists believe that traditional concepts and institutions—consultation (*shura*), consensus, reinterpretation—can be utilized to develop forms of popular political participation and democratization acceptable by Islam.

In the late 1980s and early 1990s, the economic failures of governments and the euphoria that accompanied the fall of communism in the Soviet Union and Eastern Europe led to an opening of political systems and elections. During that time, a "quiet revolution" took shape, with Islamists emerging as mainstream political actors. Their popularity derived from their creation and support of social institutions and services, such as schools, clinics, and publishing houses. Islamist political parties and candidates thus could present themselves as effective alternatives to the establishment. Religion-oriented candidates were elected as mayors and parliamentarians in countries as diverse as Bahrain, Egypt, Indonesia, Kuwait, Lebanon, Malaysia, Morocco, Pakistan, and Turkey. They

served in cabinet-level positions and as Speakers of national assemblies, presidents, prime ministers, and deputy prime ministers in Indonesia, Malaysia, Pakistan, and Turkey. To the surprise of many, Islamist candidates in Egypt, Jordan, and Tunisia emerged as the leading opposition. In Algeria, after sweeping municipal elections and the first round of parliamentary elections, the Islamic Salvation Front (FIS) seemed poised to take power through ballots rather than bullets. Islamists subsequently proved successful in elections in Kuwait and Yemen. In Turkey, the prime minister, members of parliament, and mayors of major cities are Islamists.

The continued importance and diversity of mainstream Islamic movements and the forces of democratization were evident in electoral politics in 2001 post–September 11. In Morocco, Islamic candidates and Muslim parties increased their influence threefold; in Pakistan such influence increased tenfold. In Bahrain, Islamic candidates won 19 of 40 parliamentary seats, and in a stunning victory, Turkey's Justice and Development (AK) Party assumed power.

The AK Party's victory in Turkey is remarkable in that it won a parliamentary majority in a Muslim country long regarded as a symbol of secularism in the Middle East. Its example shows that the realities of politics can lead Islamists to learn from experience and adapt if necessary. Though its roots are Islamist—with key founders from the former Welfare and Virtue parties—the AK Party chose to create a more inclusive pluralistic organization. The AK-led Turkish government not only responded successfully to domestic issues, such as economic development, but also proved successful internationally, working with Europe, the United States, and others in the international community while upholding Turkey's independence.

The overthrow of Saddam Hussein and postwar reconstruction in Iraq offer a striking example of the continued role of religion and democratization in Middle Eastern politics. U.S. postwar policies were seriously hampered by the failure of the George W. Bush administration to anticipate the emergence of Shiite Islam as a major political force. The administration was unprepared to respond to Shiite religious leaders and parties and was caught off guard by the sharply contrasting roles and orientations of Ayatollah Ali al-Sistani and the militant cleric Muqtada al-Sadr. A secular bias overestimated the secular character of Iraq and thus underestimated the significance of Shiite Islam, the multiple layers and breadth of Shiite identity (which spans a broad spectrum of orientations from religious to secular), the diversity and influence of Shiite leaders and groups, and the extent to which Islam and the role of Islamic law would be a serious constitutional challenge that could not simply be dismissed or avoided.

The acceptance of pluralism and tolerance is a major issue raised by the examples of many religious and secular governments and movements in the Middle East and broader Muslim world. The record of Islamic governments in Afghanistan under the Taliban, Iran, Pakistan, and Sudan underscores the failures of political Islam. Attempts to limit or silence political and religious opposition, to restrict women's rights, to separate women and men in public, to enforce veiling and to restrict women's public roles remain serious concerns among many constituencies, including Western governments and human rights organizations in the West and in the Muslim world among others. The issue of authoritarianism and repression cuts across the political and ideological spectrum of Muslim politics. The track record of non-Islamist governments (Algeria, Tunisia, Egypt, and Syria) as well as Islamist governments (Iran, Sudan, Afghanistan) in the Muslim world demonstrates a refusal whatever the ideological orientation to tolerate opposition. For example, in Tunisia, despite a pledge to open up the political system after seizing power in a coup, President Zine al-Abidin Ben Ali crushed al-Nahda, his Islamist opposition, after their impressive performance in parliamentary elections in 1988. He subsequently won national elections in 1999 with 99.94 percent of the vote and in 2004 with 95 percent of the ballots. The issue of political participation and democratization in Muslim societies is not primarily one of religion but of politics and power. Failure to strengthen civil society and support the values and culture of political participation contributes to the danger of religious authoritarianism as well as secular authoritarianism.

Whose Islam? What Islam?

Islam's entry into politics has raised questions about Islam itself and about Islamic governance. Most can be encapsulated by two questions: Whose Islam? What Islam?

Whose Islam touches on who is to interpret and implement Islam? Should it be rulers, the vast majority of whom are unelected kings, military leaders, or former members of the military (such as the House of Saud in Saudi Arabia, Mu'ammar Qadhafi in Libya, Umar al-Bashir in Sudan); the ulama or religious elite (as in Iran); or elected prime ministers and national assemblies (as in Bahrain, Indonesia, Kuwait, Pakistan, Malaysia, and Turkey).

The ulama were historically the advisers to rulers, acting as guardians of religion who enjoyed royal patronage. In contrast to the mullahs of Iran, the vast majority of ulama today do not seek to rule; rather, they see themselves as the primary interpreters of Islam and thus a necessary part of any process of Islamization. In the twentieth century, Islamic modernists, intellectuals, and activists began to challenge the ulamas' prerogative as Islamic scholars and leaders. As critics, they note that Islam knows no clergy, so no one can deny others the right to speak in the name of Islam; that the classical Islamic educations of many ulama do not prepare them to respond creatively and effectively to modern realities; and that the notion of scholar (*alim*, pl. ulama) or expert must be broadened today to include other areas of expertise, such as economics, medicine, and biochemistry. The vast majority of activist Islamic political and social movements and leaders have been established and led by laity and groups such as the Muslim Brotherhoods of Egypt, Kuwait, Jordan, and Sudan, Ennahda (Renaissance) in Tunisia, and the Jamaat-i-Islami (Islamic Party) in South Asia. The call in recent years for greater political participation and democratization, with its implied empowerment

Islam in the United States

An estimated 5 million to 6 million Muslims live in the United States, and their numbers are growing along with Americans' interest in Islam. In fact, Islam appears poised to overtake Judaism as the second-largest religion in the country. Christianity remains the largest.

Every major and minor ethnic group and sect that practices Islam is represented in the U.S. population. Because of a hundred years of Muslim immigration, the American Muslim community, like almost every ethnic and religious community in the United States, has strong roots. In addition, an indigenous American Muslim community, generally discrete from the immigrant communities, has been growing since the early years of the twentieth century, particularly among African Americans. Together, these Muslim communities comprise 2 percent of the U.S. population.

Religious solidarity among Muslims in the United States is nominal. Like Christians and other religious groups, Muslims have tended to perpetuate their sectarian and national distinctions, seldom mixing, even after migrating to the same country.

With the growth of the Islamic community in the United States, various Muslim leaders inevitably set out to organize and create organizations to aid fellow Muslims in practicing their faith. Today, mosques and Islamic centers dot the landscape of cities and towns across the country, transmitting the religious and cultural values and teachings of Islam.

Muslims have also established such groups as the Muslim Students Association of the United States and Canada, the Muslim Public Affairs Council, the Council for Arab-Islamic Relations, and think tanks. Islamic bookstores serving local and mail order customers have mushroomed in many metropolitan areas and on the Internet.

Although most Muslims in the United States are first- or second-generation immigrants, indigenous African American Muslims constitute a significant minority of the American Muslim community. There have been several movements, the most notable being the Moorish Science Temple, established by Timothy Drew (Noble Drew Ali) in New Jersey in 1913, and the Nation of Islam, founded by Wallace Fard (W. Fard Muhammad) in Detroit in 1930. The latter group was the most influential, growing significantly in size and importance throughout the 1950s and 1960s under the charismatic leadership of Elijah Muhammad, and his deputy, Malcolm X (Malcolm Little). Both groups had a strong black nationalist component.

Malcolm X made the pilgrimage to Mecca in 1964 and from his experience there came to the conclusion that the black separatist doctrines of Elijah

of elected national assemblies, further challenges the traditional authority of the political and religious establishments alike.

The second question—What Islam?—questions whether the process of Islamization of state and society should be one of restoration or reformation. Some call for an Islamic state based upon the reimplementation of classical formulations of Islamic laws. Others argue the need to reinterpret and reformulate law in light of the new realities of contemporary society. Several historical facts are important to remember: although the period of Muhammad and the Medinan state remain the ideal paradigm, historically a single, detailed model of an Islamic state has never existed; Islamic law is the product of divine prescriptions and human interpretations conditioned by social contexts; and contemporary Islamic activists have generated their own interpretations or paradigms that are themselves human constructions based upon sacred texts. The contrasting visions and interpretations of conservatives, fundamentalists, and liberal reformers can be seen among Iran's reform-minded intellectuals and leaders, such as Mohammad Khatami and Abdol Karim Soroush, and militant hardliners, such as those who follow Ayatollah Ali Khamenei of Iran, and in Afghanistan's interpretation of Islam under the

Muhammad's movement represented only a dim approximation of Islam. He broke with the movement shortly thereafter and was assassinated the following year. Malcolm X's commitment to mainstream Sunni Islam, despite his death, led to a split in the Nation of Islam movement.

Wallace D. Muhammad (Warith Deen Muhammad), the son of Elijah Muhammad who took over the movement in 1975 following the death of his father, guided the movement toward more orthodox Sunni Islam and renamed the movement the American Muslim Mission. A more militant faction under the leadership of Louis Farrakhan broke away from Wallace Muhammad in 1978 and established the Nation of Islam in an effort to remain loyal to the memory of the militant teachings of Elijah Muhammad. Farrakhan has often attracted negative publicity for himself and his organization because of expressions of anti-Semitic and racist views as well as pointed criticism of U.S. policy-making. Other members of his organization, however, have drawn favorable publicity through their community activism in drug- and crime-infested neighborhoods in several cities. In recent years, Farrakhan has claimed that he and his movement have abandoned their racist and separatist positions and are now within mainstream Islam, part of the larger community of Muslims in the United States.

The February 1993 bombing of the World Trade Center in New York and the attacks of September 11, 2001, reflected a mood of militant Islamic radicalism found in various parts of the Muslim world. Most American Muslims condemned these attacks, calling them un-Islamic and emphasizing that the actions of those involved were not indicative of the attitudes and contributions of the Muslim community in this country. Many did, however, see a connection between the September 11 attacks and U.S. policies in the Middle East.

September 11 proved not only to be a watershed in global security and international relations, it also represented a turning point for many Muslims in the United States. Although President George W. Bush and others were careful to distinguish between the religion of Islam and religious extremists, many political commentators and militant Christian leaders did not. The attacks against the World Trade Center and the Pentagon raised disturbing questions in many American minds about the nature of Islam itself: Was it a religion of peace or a peculiarly violent religion? Can Muslims in America be loyal citizens? Many feared that anti-terrorism legislation, such as the USA PATRIOT Act and secret evidence provisions, were being used not simply to monitor and apprehend terrorists, but to target Muslims indiscriminately. Muslims experienced racial profiling, increased incidents of discrimination in the work place, arrest, and deportation. Hate crimes against Muslims increased sharply.

Taliban or Saudi Arabia's Wahhabi ideology regarding the relationship of Islam to state and society versus that of Turkey's ruling AK Party of Prime Minister Recep Tayyip Erdogan.

The Struggle in Islam

Islam, like all religious traditions, is an ideal that has taken many forms historically and is capable of multiple levels of discourse conditioned by reason or human interpretation and historical and social contexts. For example, much of the debate over the relationship of Islam to women's rights must be seen in terms not only of religion but also, as in other religions, of patriarchy. The status and role of Muslim women in law and society was defined in a patriarchal past by a male religious elite, the ulama, the interpreters of religion.

As in the past, today there continue to be multiple interpretations, or perhaps more accurately reinterpretations, of Islam. Although some Muslims tend to equate their preferred interpretation of Islam with the sacred, the line between the divine and human, revelation and reason, is often blurred and subject to debate. Part of the struggle of Islam today is between the competing voices and visions of an extremist minority, as represented by Osama bin Laden and al-Qaida, and the vast majority of mainstream Muslims whose voices include political leaders, such as Turkish prime minister Erdogan and Malaysian prime minister Abdullah Badawi; religious leaders, such as Mufti Ali Gomaa of Egypt; and leading intellectuals, including Tunisia's Rached Ghannoushi of Tunisia, Leith Chebelial of Lebanon, and Ayatollah Ali Montazeri of Iran. Although the extremists grab the bulk of the headlines and threaten Islamic as well as Western societies, the latter, like believers worldwide, pursue the normal everyday goals of the majority of humankind.

Islam is in the midst of reexamination, reformation, and revitalization. For decades, quietly, persistently, and effectively, a group of reform-minded Muslims have articulated a progressive, constructive Islamic framework in response to the realities of Muslim societies. As intellectual activists, these academics, lawyers, physicians, journalists, and religious scholars represent voices of reform from North Africa to Southeast Asia. They respond to the realities of diverse Muslim societies, the challenges of authoritarian regimes and secular elites, the dangers of religious extremism, and the dead weight of well-meaning but often intransigent conservative religious scholars and leaders.

Contemporary reformers share a common commitment and framework for Islamic intellectual and moral revitalization and reform. They seek to identify and build upon a common ground of shared beliefs and values and engage in interreligious and intercivilizational dialogue. Many advocate change through the peaceful cultural and educational transformation of society, advocate gender equality and full citizenship rights for non-Muslims, and denounce the use of violence by militants. They call for government reforms to address political, social, and economic grievances. Many critique Western political or cultural hegemony. At the same time, the visions and ideologies of reformers often differ substantially, as their ideas and activities are conditioned by and respond to differing cultural and political contexts and reflect diverse interpretations of religious texts and history.

In addition, reformers struggle today against powerful forces that include conservative religious establishments with medieval paradigms and political elites who perceive reformers as a threat to the established order. The lessons of the Protestant Reformation, the Catholic Counter-Reformation, and more recently Vatican II demonstrate that religious reformations take time and are often fraught with conflict and danger.

The magnitude and diversity of the role of Islam in Muslim politics today is exemplified by bin Laden and al-Qaida, the wars and constitutional debates in Afghanistan and Iraq, the continued significance of Hizballah and Hamas, and the significant role that Islamists play in society and democratization efforts. The political and economic realities in the Middle East—from authoritarian and repressive regimes, failing economies, and calls for greater democratization and rule of law to the growth of extremist movements—will continue for some time to challenge governments and policymakers in the Muslim world and the West.

PART TWO

COUNTRY PROFILES

CHAPTER 7

EGYPT

Geography, history, and culture underlie Egypt's traditional preeminence in the Arab world. Egypt is centrally situated among the Arab nations, which stretch westward across North Africa to the Atlantic and eastward through the Fertile Crescent and the Arabian Peninsula. Egypt is also, by far, the most populous Arab country, though size alone does not account for the influence it has long exerted among its neighbors.

Modern Egypt has left an indelible imprint on the politics of individual Arab nations and on the Middle East as a whole. The 1952 coup, in which Colonel Gamal Abdel Nasser and his colleagues seized power and broke with colonial rule, transformed Egyptian society and resonated throughout the Arab world. Nasser became chief Arab spokesman and influenced at least two generations of Arab political leaders. He was the model for military leaders who came to power through coups in North Yemen (1962), Sudan (1969), and Libya (1969). During Nasser's years in power, his calls for pan-Arabism and socialism echoed all over the Arab world and influenced developing nations around the globe.

Upon Nasser's death in 1970, his successor, Anwar al-Sadat, exercised Egypt's leadership in another way. After several years of military confrontation and a major war with Israel, Sadat courted capitalism, curbed Egypt's ties to the Soviet Union, sought American aid and friendship, and boldly made peace with Israel. For this last act, he made Egypt a pariah among Arab nations and incurred the wrath of radical Islamists. The Arab League expelled Egypt and imposed political and economic sanctions against it.

Sadat's assassination in 1981 elevated Hosni Mubarak to the presidency. Unlike his two predecessors, the charismatic Nasser and the flamboyant Sadat, Mubarak is cautious—some have said plodding. He managed, however, to return Egypt to the good graces of its Arab neighbors without reneging on its treaty with Israel or weakening ties with the United States. Beginning in 1988 he gradually assumed a leadership role among Arab nations—just as had Nasser and Sadat at the height of their power.

After being shunned for nearly a decade for signing the 1979 peace treaty with Israel, Egypt returned once again to the political center of the Arab world. Mubarak led the Arab nations opposed to Iraq's invasion of Kuwait in 1990, and Egyptian troops helped expel Iraqi forces from Kuwait during the ensuing war. Egypt's diplomatic backing also contributed to the historic agreement between the Palestine Liberation Organization and Israel in September 1993, and Egypt continues to support the peace process.

Inspired by changing political dynamics in the Middle East, in 2004–2005 Egyptians began to vocally demand that the Mubarak government open the political system to allow for greater participation. After the establishment of a "national dialogue" on reform, the National Assembly responded by passing a constitutional amendment allowing for multicandidate presidential elections, the first political concession of consequence in years. Although the amendment appeared to open

Key Facts on Egypt

Area: 386,660 square miles (1,001,450 square
  kilometers)
Capital: Cairo
Population: 77,505,756 (2005)
Religion: Muslim (mostly Sunni), 94 percent;
  Coptic Christian and others, 6 percent
Ethnic Groups: Eastern Hamitic (Egyptians,
  Bedouins, and Berbers), 99 percent; Armenian,
  Greek, other European, Nubian (primarily
  Italian and French), 1 percent
Official Language: Arabic; English and French
  widely spoken by upper and middle classes
Type of Government: Republic
GDP: $316.3 billion; $4,200 per capita (2004)

Source: Central Intelligence Agency, *CIA World Factbook,*
2005.

the system while at the same time keeping it
firmly closed, the government's response to criticism and protests raised the opposition's hope of
securing additional reforms. Meanwhile, the
Egyptian economy continued to struggle under
mounds of debt, the legendary inefficiency of the
state bureaucracy, and corruption. The Egyptian
government faces a number of political and economic challenges that it must deal with while
under pressure from domestic opponents clamoring for reform as well as pressures from abroad,
primarily from the U.S. administration of George
W. Bush and its call for democratization across the
region.

Geography

Although Egypt has a land area of 386,660
square miles, roughly equal to the combined size
of Texas and New Mexico, most of the country is
desert. Less than 3 percent of the land is arable,
and it is being diminished by uncontrolled urbanization, soil salinization, and desertification. In a
country where rainfall is only an inch or two a
year, nearly all of the food that Egypt grows

comes from the acreage within reach of irrigation
from the Nile.

The Nile—the world's longest river—runs the
length of Egypt, rising in the mountains of interior
Africa and flowing northward to the Mediterranean. In Egypt, the Nile is no wider than nine
miles until it branches into tributaries north of
Cairo and widens into a delta. From the air, the
Nile River Valley appears as a green ribbon
bisecting brown desert for the 500 miles between
Cairo and the Aswan High Dam. Lake Nasser,
formed by the dam and extending 185 miles
southward and some 62 miles into the Sudan, is
hemmed in by geologic formations that make irrigation extremely difficult along its edges.

After the Aswan High Dam started controlling
the release of irrigation water, Egypt put millions
of additional acres into cultivation, increasing its
total by a third. Such gains in farm production,
however, could not keep pace with Egypt's rapid
population growth. In addition, an unintended side
effect of the Aswan High Dam was to deprive
farmlands of soil-enriching silt that floodwaters
leave behind. The fertility of the soil has consequently been depleted, necessitating the use of
commercial fertilizers that Egypt can barely
afford and the production of export commodities
that are highly sensitive to world trade prices.

The Western (or Libyan) Desert, running the
length of Egypt west of the Nile, comprises about
two-thirds of the country. It is a low plateau punctuated by depressions and basins, some of which
form oases, and the Great Sand Sea.

The Eastern (or Arabian) Desert, a sloping
plateau that evolves into dry, barren hills, stretches
eastward from the Nile to the Red Sea. There, and in
the plateau- and mountain-strewn Sinai Peninsula
across the Suez Canal and Red Sea, habitation is
confined chiefly to a few seaside villages and resort
communities and Bedouin communities.

Problems in a Crowded Land

Overpopulation is the source of many of
Egypt's intransigent internal problems and a
compounding factor for others. In 1998 Egypt

had a population of 66 million people and was adding 1 million additional mouths to feed every ten months. By 2005 the population had reached an estimated 77.5 million. The country, which once fed itself, now must import more than half of its food.

Ninety-nine percent of Egypt's population is concentrated along the Nile valley and in the delta, creating some of the highest population densities on Earth. About one-fourth of Egyptians live in and around Cairo, the capital, making it the largest and possibly the fastest-growing metropolis in Africa and the Middle East. Their number overwhelms basic municipal services, causes massive traffic congestion, and results in housing shortages so severe that makeshift quarters litter the urban landscape. Untold thousands live in the city's ancient cemeteries, while others make do in shacks perched atop high-rise buildings in downtown Cairo. The city has spread outward into the desert as far as the famous pyramids at Giza, twenty miles west of the Nile, and up and down the river, removing thousands of valuable acres from cultivation.

The government advocates birth control, and Muslim authorities in Egypt have said that it does not violate Islamic doctrine, but birth control is said to be practiced almost exclusively in the cities, where middle-class Egyptians find they cannot adequately support large families. Egyptian officials say rural peasants *(fellahin)* believe each family needs five or six children to assure the parents' security in old age. Migratory patterns in Egypt indicate that when the children come of age, many leave their family's small plots—a legacy of Nasser's breakup of great estates into small units for the peasants—and go to already crowded cities seeking jobs.

Unemployment and underemployment are pervasive. The government estimated unemployment to be at 10 percent in 2004, but some observers believe it is probably twice as high. Per capita income is approximately $4,200 (up from less than $2,000 in the early 1990s), but half of the population remains illiterate. For educated Egyptians, the government is the employer of last resort.

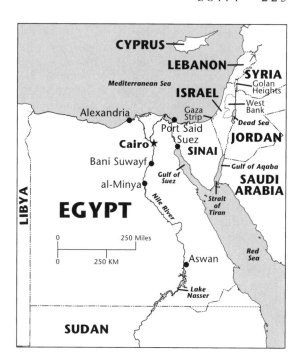

Since the end of the Nasser era in 1970, the government has guaranteed all qualifying students a free education through college and then a job until retirement. Out of the large university system, thousands upon thousands of graduates have marched directly into low-paying jobs in already bloated bureaucracies. These days, however, graduates may wait eleven years to obtain a government job, and then only to be assigned to an isolated village. The dominance of the public sector is widely recognized as hampering growth, and it certainly cannot provide the number of jobs necessary for Egypt's ever-increasing population.

History

Unlike the many Arab states that are the product of political unification in this century, Egypt has existed as a nation-state since ancient times. The Egyptian people claim a civilization continuously recorded for more than five thousand years that at various times attained great cultural heights.

Egypt's lack of natural barriers has always made it vulnerable to invasion. The Hyksos, Nubians, Ethiopians, Persians, Greeks, Romans, Arabs, French, Turks, and British were among the invaders of the lower Nile valley. From 525 B.C.E., when the last pharaoh fell to Persian invaders, until the 1952 Free Officers coup, foreigners ruled or controlled Egypt. The advent of Islam in the seventh century changed Egyptian life permanently. By the tenth century, Cairo had become a center of Islamic scholarship. The mosque of al-Azhar, which became al-Azhar University, remains one of the preeminent centers of Islamic learning and exerts a strong influence on Egyptian political life.

Ottoman rule of Egypt, which began in 1517 and would last some four and a half centuries, was interrupted in 1798 by the invasion of Napoleon, who dominated Egypt until 1801. Many scholars mark the beginning of modern Egyptian history with the Napoleonic invasion. The French brought with them liberal ideas, the printing press, and a lively interest in modern science and in Egypt's glorious but half-forgotten past.

The last dynasty to rule Egypt emerged following the French evacuation. Muhammad Ali, appointed by the Ottoman sultan in 1805, ruled Egypt until 1849. Seizing control of the Egyptian state, Muhammad Ali imported European ideas and technology. During his autocratic reign, he transformed the country, building canals and other transport systems, introducing cotton cultivation, fostering education, and bringing scholars from Europe to Egypt. Through skill, daring, and intrigue, he gained virtual independence in Egypt from his nominal overlord, the sultan in Constantinople.

Although French engineers under the direction of Napoleon carried out the first survey for the Suez Canal, Said, one of Muhammad Ali's successors, granted the concession to the French entrepreneur Ferdinand de Lesseps for construction of the canal. The canal opened in 1869, dramatically shortening the sea route from Europe to Asia.

In 1882 Britain sent troops into Egypt to protect its extensive financial holdings, including partial ownership (with France) of the Suez. Six years later, Ismail, the Egyptian khedive (a ruler under the sovereignty of the Ottoman Empire), faced bankruptcy and sold his shares in the canal to the British. Through the khedives, whom they kept in office, the British gained indirect political control of Egypt. In 1914, at the outbreak of World War I, Britain declared Egypt a protectorate, ending the legal fiction that Ottoman sovereignty still prevailed. By the end of the war, the Wafd al-Misri (Egyptian Delegation), a new organization, had emerged as the focus of Egyptian nationalist sentiment. Led by educated, upper-class Egyptians, the Wafd favored complete Egyptian independence as a republic. In 1922, however, Britain granted Egypt nominal independence, declaring it a monarchy and placing Fuad, a compliant khedive, on the throne.

Fuad reached a new agreement with Great Britain in 1936, leading to the termination of the British military occupation. British troops remained along the Suez Canal, however, and London continued to exercise influence over internal Egyptian affairs. During World War II, Egypt became a base of operations for Great Britain and its allies. Nevertheless, disputes between the British and the Egyptians continued, as did disagreements between King Farouk, who had succeeded his father, Fuad, in 1936, and the Wafd over the direction of the country.

In 1945 Egypt joined other Arab states in establishing the Arab League. Three years later, King Farouk sent Egyptian troops to fight in the first Arab-Israeli war. The Arab armies were stunned by the Israelis, who they imagined would be overcome within a matter of days. Egypt and the new state of Israel signed an armistice in February 1949, and Gaza—a small parcel of land along the Mediterranean coast—came under Egyptian administration. *(Major Middle Eastern Wars, Chapter 1, p. 6–7)*

Blame for the poor showing of the Egyptian army fell on the government, which was guilty of corrupt military procurement and incompetent leadership. The Muslim Brotherhood, or Ikhwan, founded in 1928 in Egypt and intent on ridding Egypt of the British, became openly active and was banned in 1948 after engaging in violent attacks against the government and the British. In 1950 the Wafd finally rose to power, pursuing an anti-British line. Anti-Western rioting broke out in Cairo in January 1952, and the political situation became increasingly volatile.

The Nasser Era

On July 23, 1952, a group of young military men calling themselves the Free Officers brought about the abdication of King Farouk in favor of his infant son, Fuad II, and ended decades of de facto British rule in a bloodless coup. The officers established the Revolutionary Command Council through which they governed. Their putsch, initially staged with the goal of "cleaning up" the army and the state, soon developed into a genuine political, cultural, and economic revolution.

The heterogeneous group of coup plotters included Islamist sympathizers as well as leftists. Land reform became their first domestic policy initiative. In September 1952, the new regime began breaking up large landholdings in an attempt to destroy the economic and political grip of wealthy, absentee foreign and Egyptian owners. Minimum-wage decrees and reduced working hours followed. Muhammad Naguib, a more senior member of the Free Officers, served briefly as the president of the newly proclaimed Republic of Egypt in 1953 and again in 1954, but he was essentially a figurehead recruited by the younger Free Officers to lend them credibility. After a power struggle, Col. Gamal Abdel Nasser emerged as the regime's strongman and president, articulating the pent-up frustrations of poor Egyptians and winning their hearts as no other ruler had done.

Nasser's Foreign Policy, 1955–1961

The new regime at first declared that it favored neither East nor West, but by the mid-1950s Nasser's course of nonalignment and anti-imperialism brought him into direct conflict with the West. Nasser played a prominent role in the 1955 conference of nonaligned nations in Ban-

dung, Indonesia, and was granted equal international status with leaders such as Josip Broz Tito of Yugoslavia, Jawaharlal Nehru of India, and Chou En-lai (Zhou Enlai) of China. That year, in response to the reluctance of Western nations to sell Egypt arms without conditions attached, Nasser agreed to purchase weapons from Czechoslovakia. Many Arabs approved of the deal—the first Soviet-bloc arms sale to an Arab nation—viewing it as a step away from traditional Western domination. U.S. secretary of state John Foster Dulles, however, viewed it as a step by Egypt toward the communist world despite Nasser's professed aversion to communism and his banning of the Egyptian Communist Party.

Moreover, Nasser opposed Dulles's attempts to build an anticommunist alliance in the Middle East. On July 19, 1956, Dulles played his trump card against Nasser by announcing that the United States planned to withdraw financial support for the Aswan High Dam, the centerpiece of Nasser's economic planning. Seven days later, Nasser seized the British- and French-owned Suez Canal Company and applied the canal's revenues toward the dam project.

Egypt promised to pay off the stockholders, but Britain and France were not of the mind to let Cairo control the waterway, Europe's lifeline to the petroleum of the Middle East. After months of secret negotiations among Britain, France, and Israel—whose ships were barred from the canal—Israeli forces launched an attack on Egypt across the Sinai Peninsula in October 1956. Britain and France, on the pretext of securing the safety of the canal, seized it by force. Under pressure from the United States, the Soviet Union, and the United Nations, however, they were forced to withdraw, as was Israel. President Dwight Eisenhower was furious that Britain and France, U.S. allies, had acted without consulting him, and he denied them much-needed support. By March 1957 a peace-keeping force, the United Nations Emergency Force, was deployed on the Egyptian side of the 1948 Egyptian-Israeli armistice line.

The U.S. stand during the Suez crisis improved its relations with Nasser only slightly and only briefly. For Nasser it was a sweet victory. He had thumbed his nose at the West and gotten away with it. The outcome confirmed Egyptian control of the canal. In addition, when Nasser gained Soviet support for his Aswan Dam project in 1958, he effectively sent the message to the West that he did not need to depend on it and that Western nations could not take the Arab states for granted. The Soviets soon assumed an important position in Egyptian foreign policy and became Egypt's major weapons supplier.

In 1958 Syrian rulers asked Nasser to head a union of Egypt and Syria. Nasser, who had long espoused Arab unity, found it difficult to say no, even though he was wary of the project. He agreed, but only on the condition that the union be complete. Syrian political parties were abolished, Cairo became the capital of the new United Arab Republic (UAR), and a new political party, the National Union, was created. North Yemen later joined the republic in a federative manner, with the UAR and Yemen called the United Arab States. The union fared badly, however, and was dissolved when Syrian anti-unionists seized control of the Damascus government in 1961. In Egypt, the Arab Socialist Union (ASU), a new Nasser creation, replaced the National Union.

Nasser's Foreign Policy, 1961–1970

In contrast to the period from 1955 to 1961, which saw the rise of Nasser's influence in the Arab world and the achievement of personal successes, the years from 1961 to his death in 1970 were marked by a series of policy failures, notably Egyptian involvement in the North Yemeni civil war and the Arab defeat in the June 1967 Arab-Israeli war. In 1962 Nasser responded to a call from officers in the North Yemeni army who had overthrown the ruling Hamid al-Din family. Nasser agreed to send troops to bolster the new government against royalist forces that were backed by Saudi aid and threatened the survival of the republican government. With as many as eighty thousand Egyptian soldiers engaged in the fighting, the Yemeni war became a drain on the

Egyptian treasury. Nasser's efforts to control the Yemeni republicans and the brutal measures Egyptian forces used against royalist villages in Yemen tarnished Egypt's image.

Perhaps the most damaging consequence of Egypt's involvement in the Yemeni civil war was its effect on Egyptian defenses. When the 1967 Arab-Israeli war erupted, Nasser's best troops were tied down far from home. The June war, a turning point in regional relations, evolved from increasing tensions between Israel and its Arab neighbors. In November 1966, Israel had destroyed a village in the West Bank (controlled by Jordan) in retaliation for Palestinian guerrilla raids, and in April 1967 Israeli and Syrian air forces had skirmished. Nasser engaged in a series of threatening steps short of war, in part egged on by Arab leaders challenging his pan-Arab credentials. He asked the United Nations to remove some of its peacekeeping troops from the Sinai, closed the Strait of Tiran to Israeli shipping, and signed a mutual defense treaty with Jordan.

Israel launched a surprise attack on Egypt, Jordan, Syria, and Iraq on the morning of June 5. During the first hours of the attack, Israel virtually destroyed the air forces of the four Arab states as they sat on the ground. Without air support, the Arab armies were devastated, and by the time a cease-fire went into effect on June 11, the Israelis had taken the eastern sector of Jerusalem and all of the West Bank from Jordan, seized the Golan from Syria, and pushed the Egyptians out of Gaza and the whole of the Sinai Peninsula, all the way to the Suez Canal.

The Egyptians were again humiliated, as in 1948. Nasser publicly blamed himself for the defeat, implicitly agreeing with the verdict of history that the war had resulted from his miscalculated brinkmanship. He had provoked Israel in the belief that the United States would prevent the Jewish state from going to war and that the Soviet Union would come to his rescue if war did ensue.

The effects of the defeat reverberated. Nasser resigned as president, but a massive outpouring of support persuaded him to remain in office. He then withdrew Egyptian troops from Yemen, purged the top echelons of the army, and reorganized the government. Perhaps most important, Nasser's foreign policy objectives shifted. The quarrel with Israel was no longer only a matter of securing Palestinian rights. The return of the Sinai—approximately one-seventh of Egypt's land area—became a top Egyptian priority. Toward this end, and despite opposition from many Arabs, including the Syrian government and the Palestine Liberation Organization, Nasser accepted UN Security Council Resolution 242, which, among other things, recognizes the territorial rights of all states in the area (including Israel).

Nasser died in September 1970 of a massive heart attack. Following his death, tens of thousands of Egyptians took to the streets, passionately mourning the man who, more than any other single figure in modern Egyptian history, had confirmed Egypt's preeminent position in the Arab world. He had been an authoritarian leader, intolerant of dissent from any quarter. He had failed to provide any genuine institutions of political participation. He had presided over the most disastrous military defeat in modern regional history. His economic policies had not produced prosperity. Yet, Nasser changed the life of the average Egyptian, and the Egyptian masses loved him in a way that Western political leaders never understood.

Egypt under Sadat

As first vice president, Anwar al-Sadat succeeded Nasser. It was whispered that he had remained in government—one of only two of the original Free Officers still in power—because he was never a political threat to Nasser. Few would have guessed that he would become a daring and powerful leader. It was widely presumed that stronger rivals would soon divest him of power. Sadat, however, proved to be shrewd, outmaneuvering his rivals, emerging from Nasser's shadow, and transforming Middle Eastern politics. He set his primary goals as regaining Egyptian territory lost to Israel and improving the country's standard of living. He achieved the first goal, but not the second.

Sadat's Foreign Policy

Disillusioned with Nasser's Soviet connection, Sadat had grown confident enough by mid-1972 to expel thousands of Soviet military advisers and civilian technicians—though without breaking diplomatic relations with Moscow—and offer Washington an olive branch. According to Alfred Leroy Atherton Jr., ambassador to Cairo from 1979 to 1983, the Nixon administration was preoccupied with its reelection campaign and the Vietnam War, so did not respond promptly or fully to Sadat's overtures. Sadat, unable to draw upon U.S. diplomatic clout to assist in the return of the Sinai, decided on war.

Egyptian forces, better prepared than in 1967 and this time with surprise on their side, crossed the Suez Canal on October 6, 1973, and advanced deep into the Sinai while Syrian forces attacked in the east. By the time a UN-arranged cease-fire took effect on October 22, an Israeli counterattack had retaken most of the ground, and in one area Israel held both sides of the canal. The final position of the armies, however, was less important than Israel's initial rout.

The war had a tremendous effect on Sadat's image in Egypt. Once viewed as a colorless Nasser "yes-man," Sadat became Hero of the Crossing (of the canal), an epithet he treasured. The display of Arab solidarity during the war, when the oil-producing Arabs implemented an oil embargo against Western nations that supported Israel, provided a great boost to Sadat's standing in the Arab world.

Sadat finally had Washington's attention. Secretary of State Henry Kissinger began shuttle diplomacy between Jerusalem and Cairo to work on a peace settlement. His efforts led to the first of two disengagement agreements between Egypt and Israel, on January 18, 1974, that went beyond the original cease-fire. That year, Egypt and the United States restored diplomatic relations, which Nasser had severed after the 1967 war. In addition,

Nixon became the first president to visit Egypt since Franklin D. Roosevelt went there in November 1943, during World War II. U.S. aid, cut during the Nasser years, resumed. The U.S. Navy helped clear the Suez Canal of wartime wreckage, permitting its reopening in 1975.

Sadat, clearly cultivating a closer relationship with the United States, envisioned it as a "full partner" in Egypt's drive for peace and prosperity. He came increasingly to view the United States as the key to resolving the Arab-Israeli conflict. Although Sadat was often disappointed in the United States, his trust in successive administrations did not diminish publicly. When U.S.-mediated negotiations with the Israelis bore no fruit, he proposed going to Jerusalem to talk directly with them about settling their conflict.

Sadat's November 1977 trip to Jerusalem set in motion a chain of events that ultimately led to the Camp David Accords. President Jimmy Carter later prevailed upon Sadat and Israeli prime minister Menachem Begin to meet at Camp David, the presidential retreat in Maryland, for twelve days in September 1978. There they hammered out two documents, A Framework for Peace in the Middle East and A Framework for the Conclusion of a Peace Treaty between Israel and Egypt. On March 26, 1979, they returned to the United States to sign the treaty in a White House ceremony.

The peace with Israel cost Sadat and Egypt their standing in the Arab world. Most Arab leaders and peoples saw Sadat's agreement with Israel as a betrayal. Five days after the treaty signing, the Arab League expelled Egypt and instituted an economic boycott against it. Of the twenty-one remaining league members, all but Oman, Somalia, and Sudan severed relations. In May 1979, the forty-three-member Organization of the Islamic Conference also expelled Egypt. Similarly, it was cast from the Organization of Arab Petroleum Exporting Countries.

Sadat's Domestic Policy

Sadat trained his sights on Western capitalism in an effort to improve Egypt's economic condition, introducing his open-door economic policy (infitah) in 1971. At first disguising it as a mere widening of Nasser's socialism, he set out to lure foreign investment and build a job-creating entrepreneurial class. His new policies served, however, to create a class of much-resented nouveau riche without invigorating the nation's sluggish economy. Few jobs or piasters—the small change of Egyptian currency—trickled down to the workers. Average income remained below $500 a year. Part of Nasser's social contract included government-subsidized food, housing, public transportation, and electricity. In January 1977, under budget-cutting pressures from foreign creditors, Sadat reduced food subsidies and touched off weeks of rioting.

In political matters, Sadat loosened some of the tighter restrictions on political dissent that he had inherited from Nasser, and in 1975 he permitted four ideological groups, or platforms, to organize within the rubric of the Arab Socialist Union. The following year they received permission to operate as political parties. The center-left Egyptian Arab Socialist Organization became the government party, and in 1978 it was reorganized as the National Democratic Party (NDP), serving as a vehicle of autocratic control. The center-right platform became the Socialist Labor Party (SLP) and consisted of moderate Islamists, including the Muslim Brotherhood, whose leaders had been freed from prison along with other dissidents in 1973.

Another party, the National Progressive Unionist Grouping, comprised a coalition of small leftist groups and perhaps formed a counterweight to the SLP. Sadat's brother-in-law led the SLP, which Sadat outlawed in 1981 after deciding that its Islamist tendencies had grown too strong. The Liberal Party spun off from the ASU right and drew most of its support from Islamists who felt that the Muslim Brotherhood had been compromised by its membership in the SLP. Sadat's political liberalization ended when the political groups outside his direct control, principally Nasserites on the left and Islamists on the right, began to criticize his peacemaking with Israel.

Sadat cracked down on dissidents, most dramatically in September 1981, when he abruptly jailed fifteen hundred foes.

Death came for Sadat on October 6, 1981, as he reviewed a military parade on the anniversary of the canal crossing. Soldiers belonging to al-Jihad, a radical Islamic faction, assassinated him, not in order to take over the government, but because they regarded Sadat as a traitor to Egypt, the Arab world, and Islam. His murder surprised Egyptians less than it did westerners, who remembered him as initiating peace with Israel, a corecipient (with Begin) of the 1978 Nobel Peace Prize, and the man who moved Egypt out of the Soviet orbit of influence. To fellow Arabs, Sadat's difficulties with Islamists and other dissidents had become increasingly clear, erasing much of the popularity he enjoyed in the heady days following the October 1973 war. There was no outpouring of grief in Egypt for Sadat as there had been for Nasser. Three former U.S. presidents—Richard Nixon, Gerald R. Ford, and Jimmy Carter—attended his funeral, but no Arab head of state publicly mourned the Egyptian president.

Mubarak and Return to the Fold

Hosni Mubarak, trying to steer a middle course in all matters, foreign and domestic, did not embrace the Egyptian "partnership" with the United States with Sadat's fervor. He recognized, however, the economic and military necessity of U.S. assistance, and U.S. officials generally gave him high marks for trying to keep irritants in the relationship from magnifying.

Mubarak continued to promote the central tenet of Sadat's notion of peace with Israel—that the treaty means the end of military hostilities and the establishment of a proper relationship—but its promotion often resulted in a "cold peace" beset by problems. Israel's unilateral annexation of the Golan in 1981 and its invasion of Lebanon in June 1982, both of which Mubarak criticized, did not help build stronger relations. The Lebanese invasion in particular put Egypt in an awkward position because it confirmed to foes of the Egyptian-Israeli

treaty that Israel could act with impunity since it no longer had to consider a military attack from Egypt. For Mubarak, the invasion came just as Egyptian-Israeli relations seemed to be stabilizing. Egypt was still savoring the sweetest fruit of the treaty: On April 25, 1982, Israel had returned the remaining section of the Sinai that it had occupied since the 1967 war—except for Taba, a tiny strip of beach where the Israelis had built a resort hotel. (After a seven-year dispute, Israel relinquished Taba on March 15, 1989.)

In September 1982, Mubarak recalled Egypt's ambassador from Israel to protest the massacre of Palestinians by Lebanese Christians in the Sabra and Shatila refugee camps outside Beirut, which were guarded by Israeli soldiers. The ambassador later returned to his post, but the relationship was further jolted by three shooting incidents in Cairo between 1984 and 1986 that left five Israeli diplomats dead and one wounded and several other incidents over the years, including one in October 1990 that left nineteen Palestinians dead near the al-Aqsa mosque, the third-holiest Islamic shrine, on the Haram al-Sharif.

From a "cold peace" the Egyptian-Israeli relationship has sometimes deteriorated into an "angry peace." The massive immigration of Jews from the Soviet Union, and especially their settlement on the Israeli-occupied West Bank, became a contentious issue in the early 1990s. Despite deep-rooted mistrust, the two countries continue to uphold the peace and maintain bilateral ties based on solid national interests.

Reconciliation with Arab Nations

A pivotal event on Egypt's road to reconciliation with its Arab neighbors took place in November 1987. At that time, sixteen Arab League heads of state met in the Jordanian capital of Amman and issued a surprisingly strongly worded resolution attacking Iran for its "procrastination in accepting" a cease-fire proposal in what was then its seven-year war with Iraq. Jordan's King Hussein, the conference host, used the occasion to ask the participants—in the interest of

Arab unity—to drop the league's ban on formal relations between its member countries and Egypt. They answered his appeal by declaring that a renewal of relations with Egypt would be considered "a sovereign matter to be decided by each state in accordance with its constitution and laws; and is not within the jurisdiction of the Arab League." Most Arab nations felt compelled to close ranks against Iran and the potentially subversive Islamic radicalism that it was attempting to export. In short, they needed Egypt, by far the strongest Arab country, as a counterweight to Iran.

Jordan had already renewed relations with Cairo, and by the end of 1989 all Arab League members had done likewise. The next step would be readmission to the Arab League. On May 23, 1989, after a ten-year absence, Egypt took its seat at an Arab League summit, in Casablanca, where Mubarak was accorded the honor of making the opening address. Only weeks before the meeting, the Organization of Arab Petroleum Exporting Countries had readmitted Egypt, which had already reentered the Organization of the Islamic Conference in 1984. To promote regional economic cooperation, Egypt, together with Iraq, Jordan, and Yemen, founded the Arab Cooperation Council in 1989. In March 1991, the Arab League transferred its headquarters back to its original location in Cairo, finalizing Egypt's return to the Arab fold.

Mubarak, meanwhile, had become a leading supporter of the PLO and its chairman, Yasir Arafat. "There is no war without Egypt, and there is no peace without Egypt," Arafat said in December 1988 on one of his frequent visits to Cairo. His very presence symbolized Egypt's new harmony with the Palestinian leadership, which in 1981 had applauded Sadat's assassination. In this new era of buried hatchets, Mubarak joined with Arafat and Arafat's old nemesis, King Hussein, in pushing for an international conference to negotiate the Palestinians' demand for statehood.

In late 1988 Mubarak implored Arafat to satisfy the U.S. government's conditions for holding talks with the PLO. In November 1988, the Palestine National Council met in Algiers. It formally declared Palestinian independence and implicitly recognized Israel's right to exist, but U.S. secretary of state George P. Shultz demanded that Arafat explicitly renounce terrorism, accept UN Security Council Resolution 242, and recognize Israel's sovereignty.

After much prodding by Mubarak and a few false starts, Arafat on December 14 uttered the precise words that Shultz wanted to hear. Within hours, the secretary of state said U.S. talks with the PLO could begin. According to diplomatic sources in Cairo, Mubarak was one of several Arab and West European leaders who urged Shultz and President Ronald Reagan to accept Arafat's words as genuine.

Throughout the 1990s, Egypt acted as a leading participant in the peace process with Israel, serving as a mediator and interlocutor between the PLO and Israel in the wake of the Oslo Accords of 1993. This relationship became increasingly complex after the acrimony generated toward Arafat by the United States and Israel after the breakdown of the Camp David talks in July 2000 and Israel's employment of overwhelming military might during the second Palestinian uprising that began in September 2000. These events, combined with Ariel Sharon heading the Israeli government, created discord so severe that Egypt withdrew its ambassador from Israel.

In 2004 Egypt reengaged in efforts to bring Palestinians and Israelis back to the negotiating table. After the death of PLO chairman Arafat, the Egyptian government openly supported the efforts of his successor, Mahmoud Abbas, to resume peace talks and quickly improved its relations with Israel, pledging to return its ambassador.

The Persian Gulf and Iraq Wars

The Iraqi invasion and occupation of Kuwait in August 1990 created a dilemma for Mubarak and Egypt: Opposing Iraq would put Egypt on one side of an intra-Arab conflict, just as it was solidifying relations with its fellow Arab states; failing to oppose the invasion, however, would invite further aggression by Iraqi president Saddam Hussein, poison relations with the wealthy Arab states in the

Gulf, and weaken Egypt's crucial ties to the United States. Under these circumstances, Mubarak chose to lead the Arab military and diplomatic effort against Iraq.

On August 10, eight days after the invasion, Mubarak hosted a meeting of the Arab League in Cairo, out of which came a decision by the league to oppose Saddam Hussein and send troops to help defend Saudi Arabia against any possible Iraqi attack. The first Egyptian troops began to land in Saudi Arabia the next day. Egypt would ultimately send four hundred tanks and thirty thousand troops to Saudi Arabia, the largest contingent of any Arab nation.

The opposition of Egyptian Islamists to Egypt's participation in the anti-Iraq coalition was largely drowned out by a government campaign to win popular support by highlighting the brutality of the Iraqi occupation. Egyptian-Iraqi ties had already been strained by widespread reports of sometimes-violent discrimination against Egyptians working in Iraq.

Mubarak's anti-Iraq position during the 1990–1991 Persian Gulf crisis and war, and his success in persuading other Arab countries to participate in the multinational force, earned him the gratitude of the United States and the Gulf countries. The participation of Egypt and other Arab nations undercut Saddam Hussein's claims that his invasion of Kuwait was a blow against U.S. imperialism and advanced the Palestinian cause. Mubarak also held Egypt solidly in the coalition when it appeared that Israel might enter the war against Iraq. U.S. leaders worried that if Israel retaliated against Iraqi missile attacks, Arab nations would withdraw from the coalition rather than fight on the same side as their old enemy. In the end, the United States prevailed on Israel not to attack.

Egypt expected to reap major economic benefits for its role in the coalition against Iraq. Military cooperation between Egypt and the United States continued on an expanded basis after the war, and the United States promised Egypt preferential treatment in receiving sophisticated military equipment being withdrawn from bases in Europe.

The United States also rewarded Egypt by forgiving a $7 billion debt for arms purchased in the 1970s and by rescheduling its remaining debts. Saudi Arabia wrote off outstanding Egyptian debts of $4 billion. By early 1991 Egypt's debt had been reduced from more than $50 billion to $36 billion. Nevertheless, Egypt claimed to have lost as much as $20 billion in revenue during the war, as the Gulf crisis weakened several pillars of the Egyptian economy. Egyptian oil revenues went up temporarily, but those gains were more than offset by the depression in Egypt's tourism industry brought on by fears of traveling in the Middle East, the loss of remittances from the half a million Egyptian expatriate workers who fled the Gulf region, and the dwindling of Suez Canal revenues as fewer commercial ships chose to sail in Middle Eastern waters.

In March 1991, the Damascus Declaration was signed, providing that Egypt and Syria join Gulf Cooperation Council (GCC) countries in a new Gulf security arrangement—"the GCC plus two." Saudi Arabia's reluctance to station a non-Gulf Arab force in the area on an open-ended basis and its preference instead to rely on Western forces resulted in Mubarak's withdrawing Egyptian troops from the Gulf after the war. At the same time, the GCC countries, suffering their own financial difficulties, cut back on their aid commitments to Egypt. Egyptian expectations for increased contracts, assistance, and cooperative ventures from the Gulf states for its efforts went largely unfulfilled. The Damascus Declaration essentially had become a dead letter.

The transformation of U.S. Middle East policy after the attacks of September 11, 2001, put Egypt in an awkward position. The Mubarak government initially sought to portray its long battle with al-Gamaat al-Islamiyya (Islamic Group) and other radical Islamist groups as part of the U.S.-led global "war on terror" and thus as justification for a continuing state of emergency and other restrictions on political life. (The second-in-command of al-Qaida, Ayman al-Zawahiri, is an Egyptian doctor who had headed Egyptian Islamic Jihad and has long been wanted for prosecution in Egypt.)

As the United States shifted toward a confrontation with Iraq and began to advocate greater human rights and democratization throughout the Arab world, the longstanding but always somewhat fragile relations between Cairo and Washington deteriorated somewhat. Mubarak and other Egyptian leaders openly accused the United States of meddling in their internal affairs and insisted that they were committed to democratization, but in their own way and at their own pace, and not according to a U.S.-imposed model.

During the Iraq War initiated by the United States in March 2003, Egypt maintained its distance from U.S. policy, in contrast to its open support of the coalition forces in 1991. Mubarak openly criticized the war on a number of occasions but did not interfere with the U.S. military's use of the Suez Canal.

Government and Politics

With a characteristic touch of self-deprecatory humor, Egyptians are fond of recalling King Farouk's last words to the rebellious officers who sent him into exile: "Your task will be difficult. It is not easy to govern Egypt." Since the time of the pharaohs, successful rulers of Egypt have learned to play one set of potential foes against another. The fact that Mubarak has never named a vice president has inspired observers to think that he exerts more political leverage by leaving the office open than by choosing among leading contenders. The absence of a designated successor, however, has raised troubling questions about Egypt's political stability. Mubarak has regularly denied any intention of having his son Gamal succeed him, although Gamal has become political secretary of the ruling NDP and has sought to reform the party from within and commit it to economic reforms. He also maintains a high profile in the official media.

Mona Makram Ebeid, a professor of political science at the American University in Cairo and a member of the opposition al-Ghad Party, speaks of "Egypt's continued experiment with democracy—we can't yet call it democracy." The press, while not completely controlled by the government, is still restricted by repressive libel, censorship, and publication permit laws. In December 1988, the very month the Egyptian novelist Naguib Mahfouz was awarded the Nobel Prize in literature, religious authorities blocked a newspaper serialization of one of his books on the grounds that it was "destructive of Islamic values and defamatory to Islamic prophets." In 1980 Egypt had amended its 1971 constitution to stipulate that Islamic law, *sharia,* is *the* rather than *a* principal source for legislation and the legal system. The governmental structure is, however, essentially that of a Western parliamentary system.

Executive power is vested in the president. Until amendment of the constitution in 2005, the legislature, the People's Assembly, nominated a presidential candidate, who was then approved for six-year terms by popular referendum. In 1993 the ruling National Democratic Party nominated Mubarak for a third term, and he garnered 94.9 percent of the more than 15 million votes cast. The opposition parties refused to back the president's nomination, arguing that the people should directly elect the president from a choice of candidates instead of approving the assembly's chosen candidate by referendum. In the referendum of September 26, 1999, Mubarak won a fourth term with 93.8 percent of the vote.

The 2005 elections marked the first time that multiple candidates could stand for elections. The promise of presidential elections being competitive was considerably dampened, however, with the actual adoption of the constitutional amendment concerning the change in procedure: it barred parties established for less than five years from running candidates (thus apparently blocking the al-Ghad Party); it required that a party's candidates be members of the party's political bureau (thus blocking the Labor Party from running Muslim Brotherhood candidates); and it placed virtually unachievable requirements on independent candidates, requiring a large number of endorsements by members of both houses of parliament or local councils, bodies overwhelmingly dominated by the ruling party.

The president may appoint vice presidents, in addition to government ministers and all other officials. The chief executive is also supreme commander of the armed forces and may rule by decree when granted emergency powers by the People's Assembly, which Mubarak has done since Sadat's assassination. In addition, the NDP, Mubarak's party, holds 94 percent of the seats in the People's Assembly and commands the patronage system and the broadcast media.

A prime minister heads the cabinet, but in the strong presidential system, the prime minister is essentially a technocrat, sometimes offered up as a scapegoat for failed policies, but more often basically serving as the chairman of the board of the ministers, rather than as an executive. For example, Ahmad al-Nazif, the prime ministerial nominee in 2004, had a technocratic background, not a political one. The president nominates the prime minister, who serves at the president's will, not that of the parliament.

Although democratic in structure, Egypt's government is authoritarian in practice, as was demonstrated by the 1990 and 1995 parliamentary elections. In 1990 the electoral districts were determined six weeks before the elections. The ruling NDP won 348 of the 444 directly elected seats (compared with 346 in the 1987 general election) in a poll characterized by low voter turnout. The official estimate of 44.9 percent voter turnout was thought to be inflated. Four of the NDP's main opposition groups—the New Wafd, the Socialist Labor Party, the Liberal Party, and the banned but officially tolerated Muslim Brotherhood—boycotted the elections to protest the government's refusal to repeal the emergency regulations or allow election supervision by the judiciary rather than by the Ministry of Interior.

In 1995 there was almost no semblance of a fair electoral process. NDP candidates padded voter registers and otherwise encouraged voter fraud; government officials harassed opposition candidates before the elections and physically interfered with their right to vote on election day; supervisors stuffed ballot boxes or allowed polling stations to be ransacked; some ballot boxes disappeared while in the custody of the police, in transit to counting centers. Just prior to election day,

Hosni Mubarak

more than one thousand opposition-party campaign workers and supporters, almost all members of the Muslim Brotherhood, were arrested. Many of the detainees had been scheduled to observe the polling process as a check on government-appointed monitors. Serious irregularities were charged in the counting process. Finally, Egypt's highest court investigated complaints about the elections and recommended that the election of more than two hundred members of parliament (nearly half the membership) be voided. The People's Assembly, however, declined to act on the recommendation.

The 2000 parliamentary elections were also controversial. The NDP won about 85 percent of the seats, but in many cases, independents or NDP challengers who nonetheless were supporters of the government defeated its preferred candidates. The opposition parties slightly increased their representation, while a number of members of the Muslim Brotherhood entered parliament as independents.

Egypt's modern political party system is a creation of the Sadat era, although most of the parties that emerged in the 1970s and 1980s were reincarnations of pre-1952 parties. The main opposition party in the Sadat era, the New Wafd, was led by members or descendants of the upper and middle classes, which opposed British rule. The New Wafd may be the only opposition with the prospect of wide popular support. The party consists of Copts, Nasserites, Islamists, former army officers, socialists, and liberal businessmen championing the advancement of the private sector. The original Wafd, the Wafd al-Misri, was the majority party between 1922, when Egypt was accorded nominal independence, and the 1952 revolution. When Nasser came to power, he abolished it. The successor party formed in 1978, at Sadat's behest, during a period of mild political liberalization. The New Wafd remains an influential, if rather conservative, opposition party, with a vigorous newspaper, but its political strength has waned somewhat.

Among the other legalized political groups is the increasingly Islamist Socialist Labor Party, abolished by Sadat in 1981 only to be resurrected by Mubarak in 1982 as a loyal opposition after it supported him for president. By forming a coalition with the Liberal Party and opening its ranks to the Muslim Brotherhood—which is forbidden its own party—the SLP became the main parliamentary opposition in the 1987 elections. It was barred, however, from running in 2000 polling; Muslim Brotherhood members went on to be elected as independents instead. At the far left sits the splinter National Progressive Unionist Grouping, composed mostly of well-known Marxists and Nasserites. The political influence of the party's intellectuals is disproportionate to the size of its following. The People's (Umma) Party, a tiny organization with a strong religious orientation, has little popular support or political significance.

A serious impediment to political party development—and, indeed, to civil society—is a 1960s-era law stating that all private voluntary organizations must be registered with and approved by the Ministry of Social Affairs. This law has been amended under Mubarak to make official status as a nongovernmental organization difficult to achieve, thereby limiting the formation of human rights and other social watchdog groups. Regardless, other parties have gradually emerged. A Nasserite Party has been legalized, though it remains somewhat marginal. Intellectuals identifying themselves as Nasserites remain influential in many areas. In 2004, after several aborted efforts, the government finally legalized the liberal reformist al-Ghad (Tomorrow) Party.

The Muslim Brotherhood, widely believed to be the most influential Islamist movement because of its extensive network of mosques, schools, hospitals, and other social activities, is technically illegal, though brotherhood members sit in the People's Assembly as independents or members of other parties. The Wasat (Center) Party, a modern, centrist Islamist party of younger members of the brotherhood, continues to be denied licensing by the government's Parties Committee.

Although the Muslim Brotherhood is the strongest voice of the diffuse Islamic movement in Egypt, observers of Egyptian politics disagree on whether it represents the movement's main thrust. Since its founding in 1928, the brotherhood has been the embodiment of Egyptian opposition to a secular, Westernized society. Militant spin-offs have attempted to achieve their objectives by violence. Nasser, the target of an assassination attempt, suppressed the brotherhood. Partly rehabilitated by Sadat, the brotherhood emerged under Mubarak as a political and economic force during the 1980s.

The army, though not actively involved in party politics, is a major player in Egyptian society. All of Egypt's post-1952 leaders—Naguib, Nasser, Sadat, and Mubarak—have so far been military officers. Sadat separated the army from politics but gave it enormous perquisites and benefits, including control of a significant sector of the country's industrial base. Although in theory restricted to defending the country from foreign threats, while the Ministry of Interior handles internal policing, the army in 1986 answered the government's call to quell a mutiny in suburban Cairo by 20,000 conscripts of the Central Security Force who were angered by their low pay and bad living conditions. Similarly, after attacks by Islamists on tourists at Luxor in 1997, the government deployed the army to provide additional security.

Religion and Society

Nasser and Sadat both tried to enlist Islamic backing for their governments, although without permitting Muslim factions to achieve any real degree of influence. In speeches, Nasser sometimes appealed to Islamic history and culture and Islamic socialism, even as he followed a secular model of modernization.

About 94 percent of Egyptians are Muslims, and almost all of them are of the majority Sunni branch. Coptic Christians account for most non-Muslims in Egypt and in actual numbers are the largest non-Muslim minority in any Arab country. Official estimates cite Copts as 4 to 6 percent of the Egyptian population, but unofficial figures range from 14 to 19 percent. Copts are abundantly represented in the middle and professional classes, though many live in villages and are poor farmers. In addition to the Copts, other Christians and the tiny remnant of a once-large Jewish population continue to live in Egypt.

Egypt's Copts embraced Christianity in the first century but broke with its orthodoxy in the fifth century over a theological issue: they accepted the divinity of Christ but rejected the doctrine then accepted by the rest of Christendom that Christ was also fully human. The Coptic Church survived not only its break with the mainstream of Christianity but also the Islamic conquest of Egypt in the seventh century. Nevertheless, over the centuries it has suffered several persecutions at the hands of the country's Muslim majority.

Nasser attempted to improve Coptic-Muslim relations by integrating Egyptian society and by forcing members of the two faiths to live together in the same neighborhoods. The experiment seemed only to increase tensions between the two groups. By the 1970s, as Islamic resurgence became more widespread and demands grew for the government to implement Islamic law, several Coptic-Muslim clashes occurred. In Sadat's crackdown on dissidents shortly before his assassination, he dismissed his critics from their posts in the mosques and banished Coptic pope Shenuda from Cairo for inciting Coptic-Muslim strife. Moreover, Sadat banned publications issued by Coptic associations and by the Muslim Brotherhood. Only after Mubarak became president did hostilities between the government and the Copts begin to subside. In 1985 the government allowed Pope Shenuda to return to Egypt, and in 2003 Mubarak recognized Coptic Christmas (January 6) as a national holiday.

Despite the relative tolerance of Egyptian Muslims, the Islamic revival of the 1980s and 1990s proved troubling to the Coptic-Muslim relationship. Copts perceived demands for the complete implementation of Islamic law as a direct threat to their political, economic, and social status, as well as to their physical well-being. Attacks on Christians represented not only manifestations of chronic sectarian tension, but were also part of an Islamist strategy to undermine the Mubarak government.

By the mid-1980s clashes between security forces and Islamic militants were increasing. In December 1988, violent battles erupted between police and Muslim extremists in Cairo's Ayn Shams neighborhood, resulting in several deaths and hundreds of arrests. The following April, the government cracked down on what Interior Minister Zaki al-Badr called "extremist groups fueling religious strife." After more Muslim clashes with police, this time in the town of al-Fayyum, southwest of Cairo, authorities attributed the violence to al-Jihad and arrested fifteen hundred people.

Determined to keep militants in prison or under close surveillance, the government arrested an estimated ten thousand Islamists during 1989, including the spiritual leader of al-Jihad, Shaykh Umar Abd al-Rahman, who was later tried and convicted for his involvement in the 1993 bombing of the World Trade Center in New York.

The number of Islamic groups in Egypt is estimated at between thirty and sixty, ranging from the large, mainstream Muslim Brotherhood, to the medium-sized and violent al-Jihad, to the small, militant, and clandestine Gamaat al-Islamiyya, an offshoot of the politically and spiritually influential Muslim Brotherhood. Al-Jihad claimed responsibility for several assassination attempts on political figures, police officials, intellectuals, and tourists in the mid- and late 1990s. Although the more militant groups draw their support from the lower middle classes, especially in the deprived areas of Upper Egypt and the slums of Cairo, the membership of Gamaat al-Islamiyya is composed of a cross-section of society, the common thread being a desire to turn Egypt from a secular state into one based on Islamic religious law and principles.

Critics claim that the Islamists lack the resources, unity of purpose, and leadership to be a serious threat to the government. Their strengths, however, seem to be their ability to channel widespread discontent into popular support and their organizational skills, which they initially demonstrated during the devastating Cairo earthquake of 1992. Islamic-controlled professional societies quickly provided food, shelter, and emergency medical care to survivors, many of whom were injured by the collapse of substandard housing. The government was criticized for its slow response to the disaster, and its corruption was blamed for the shoddy construction of buildings.

Although Mubarak often attempted to meet some of the Islamists' demands, in response to a wave of attacks on foreign tourists during the 1990s that seriously damaged Egypt's economy, he oversaw an unprecedented security crackdown. The People's Assembly passed antiterrorist legislation in July 1992 introducing the death penalty for members of terrorist groups and three-day detentions for suspects. In 1993 the government shifted all terrorism cases to the military courts, regardless of whether the accused belonged to the military. These courts have proven more willing than their civilian counterparts to issue death sentences, and there is no appeals process. International and domestic human rights organizations have condemned reported torture and beatings by government security police and have been harassed themselves by the government.

On November 17, 1997, following a lull in Islamist violence, six armed men attacked a tourist site in Luxor, near the Valley of the Kings, killing fifty-eight foreigners and four Egyptians. The attack resulted in the cancellation of thousands of trips to Egypt, despite government and tourism industry efforts to reassure potential visitors and attract them with free tourist visas and discounted hotel rates and airline and train tickets. It is estimated that Egypt lost $500 million in tourism revenue after the Luxor attack.

In recent years, several imprisoned Gamaat al-Islamiyya figures have proclaimed a cease-fire, and there have been no major anti-government attacks in Egypt proper since the Valley of the Kings incident. In 2004 bombs exploded at a tourist hotel and beach camp in the Sinai, but these appeared to be linked to al-Qaida or other international groups and apparently targeted Israeli tourists. In early April 2005, a group calling itself the al-Ezz Islamic Brigades claimed responsibility for a suicide bomb that exploded in Cairo's Khan al-Khalili suq, killing and injuring several tourists and Egyptians. Later that month, a man exploded a bomb near the Egyptian Museum, killing himself and injuring seven; his fiancee and sister opened fire on a tourist bus before killing themselves. Whether these incidents are politically motivated or reflect a broader social unrest remains uncertain. The government laid the blame on a single family group, but the incidents nonetheless raised security concerns in the capital for the first time in years.

By the end of the 1990s, secularists appeared to be receiving less sympathy from the government, as Mubarak quietly attempted to ameliorate religious dissent by allowing for greater incorporation of Islamic principles into the political system. He also courted Islamists in an attempt to co-opt the moderates among them and isolate the radicals. At times he tried to steer a middle course between Islamic and secularist demands by, for example, allowing previously banned opposition and religious newspapers to circulate (though retaining the tool of censorship), but refusing to overturn some controversial court decisions, such as a 1985 ruling abolishing 1979 women's rights laws.

Economy

Egypt's exhausted economy and the political challenges arising from economic reform are of potential peril to the Mubarak government. The country continues to suffocate under enormous foreign debts from loans secured in the early 1980s. At that time, oil commanded high prices in the world market, and Egypt was cashing in on new fields along the Red Sea and the return of older ones from Israel in the Sinai. In addition, the petroleum industry provided jobs for as many as 4 million Egyptians in other Arab countries. The Suez Canal's reopening in 1975 restored another important source of revenue.

Oil prices plummeted in 1986, however, affecting not only the government's royalties but also the amount of money Egyptians remitted from abroad. Many Egyptians in the Persian Gulf lost their jobs. Moreover, sporadic political violence in the Middle East weakened the tourist trade. Even during the "good years," the early 1980s, the government incurred annual budget deficits. Large international banks eagerly extended credit. More and more of the debt incurred during that period came due in the late 1980s.

In return for the government's pledge to stimulate production and exports, the IMF and Western creditor nations agreed in May 1987 to let Egypt reschedule $8 billion of its $44 billion in foreign debt on generous repayment terms. For its part, Egypt moved to satisfy the IMF demand by devaluing its currency 60 percent to make exports cheaper in foreign markets and thus increase demand, even though Egyptian officials complained that devaluation increased the price of consumer goods and fueled inflation.

Chronic budget deficits have perpetuated Egypt's dependence on foreign aid. U.S. aid accounts for almost half of the economic assistance that Egypt receives from all foreign sources. The rest comes chiefly from international lending institutions, such as the IMF and the World Bank, and the governments of Western Europe and Japan. Since the Camp David Accords, Egypt has received about $45 billion in aid from Washington; only Israel has received more. That assistance, military and economic in various forms, has been averaging about $3 billion a year for Israel and $2.2 billion for Egypt, in line with an unwritten policy in Washington that Egypt will be given a somewhat smaller amount than Israel. Although both countries had received U.S. aid before signing their peace treaty, the amount of aid increased dramatically afterward.

Aid to Egypt (but not to Israel) is explicitly conditioned on its continued observance of the Camp David agreements and, as stipulated in the early 1990s, its pursuit of economic reforms. In 1999 Egypt received $1.3 billion in military aid from the United States and $775 million in nonmilitary aid, a decrease of $40 million from recent years' allocations; the decrease came wholly from the nonmilitary aid package and reflected the belief in the U.S. Congress that spending on foreign aid should be reduced. It also mirrored a drop in U.S. aid to Israel resulting from political tensions between Tel Aviv and Washington. In 2003 U.S. military aid to Egypt again totaled $1.3 billion, with economic assistance at $615 million. U.S. non-military assistance to Cairo annually averages $815 million.

Increasingly under pressure from the United States and the IMF to reform Egypt's economy, Mubarak gradually continued Sadat's conversion from a centrally controlled economy to a market economy more open to private enterprise and foreign investment. The IMF's demands included unifying the exchange rate (effectively raising prices), eliminating state subsidies on consumer goods, reforming tax collection, and reducing imports. The dilemma for Mubarak's government has been in maintaining the delicate balance between the conflicting demands of foreign creditors and the masses of Egyptians living at or below the poverty line. Memories of past food riots remain strong, and Mubarak wants no recurrence.

In 1991 Mubarak signed on to a comprehensive structural adjustment program under the aegis of the IMF and the World Bank. The IMF agreed to provide $372 million in assistance over a period of eighteen months to support Egyptian reforms. The IMF agreement paved the way for the Paris Club of Western creditors to reschedule a $10 billion debt and cancel another $10 billion debt over a three-year period.

By October 1998, Egyptian implementation of its IMF program had met with impressive results. Budget deficits, long a serious handicap to government economic activity, had been reduced to manageable levels. Foreign currency reserves had increased, and privatization had begun taking hold in the banking sector. In other sectors, privatization was also well under way, with approximately one-third of a planned 314 state-owned enterprises having been shifted to the private sector. Inflation was being held to a reasonable 4 percent per year. These moves, along with legislative and bureaucratic reforms aimed at making Egypt more attractive to foreign investment, were a positive contrast to the country's political climate.

Egypt continues to face serious economic problems despite its structural adjustment program. The decline in tourism after the September 11 attacks and the U.S. invasion and occupation of Iraq crippled a valuable source of revenue for a time; tourism was reported to have rebounded strongly by late 2004. Unemployment the same year, however, was estimated at 25 percent, and growth in gross domestic product hovered in the 2–3 percent range during 2001–2003. The pound suffered a sharp drop in value in 2004 after its overvaluation led the Central Bank to float it. Foreign investment in 2003 declined to a twenty-year low and is not expected to vastly improve without economic reforms beyond some implemented in 2004 involving corporate taxes, customs, energy subsidies, and privatization. As a result of some of

these measures, the deficit rose 1.9 percent to 8 percent of GDP.

Outlook

With the support of 4 million bureaucrats and a half-million-man army, the government of Hosni Mubarak does not likely face an imminent political death. The corrosive effects of ossified political structures, a struggling economy, endemic corruption, and Islamist violence are, however, aspects of the regime's vulnerability.

Mubarak has stated that his priority is the "preservation of the security and stability of the homeland." Egypt is currently stable by virtue of a successful internal security crackdown against a number of armed opposition groups. Less violent measures have been used to quell other dissenting voices, including those of moderate Islamists, the press, and secular intellectuals. Egypt jails house thousands of political prisoners. Security clearly takes precedence over democratization and political reforms, although in the long term the government's actions may create as much instability as they have prevented.

The government argues that it cannot make concessions to the opposition while under attack by radical Islamist groups, although the relative absence of major Islamist violence in Egypt for several years challenges the assertion that the government must keep a tight lid on to control terrorism. Rather, instead of addressing Islamist and reformist criticisms, with which most Egyptians agree, the government alienates the masses with its harsh repression of its critics. An instability wrought by a violent struggle between Islamists and the government terrifies ordinary Egyptians, who fear the hand of the state as much as they fear any religious extremism.

The relationship of the state and the people appeared to have changed somewhat in the wake of such events as the Iraqi elections and the Lebanese response to the assassination of former prime minister Rafiq al-Hariri in 2005, and U.S. criticisms of the Egyptian government offered encouragement to democratic reformers. Mubarak's concession of allowing multiple candidates in the 2005 presidential elections opened the floor to new demands, with the Muslim Brotherhood and other non-party groups seeking legalization and the right to contest elections. A genuine shift in public opinion is evident in that in the run up to elections in 2005, the movement demonstrating for more openness and political participation adopted the word *kifaya* (enough)—which the Lebanese used in demanding a Syrian withdrawal. For the Egyptians it means that Mubarak has served long enough.

Egypt and the United States remain allies, and U.S. assistance continues to be of vital importance. Tensions did, however, develop in the relationship in the late 1990s and into the early 2000s. For example, Cairo broke with Washington in expressing its belief that sanctions against Iraq should be lifted, and the United States' unconditional support of Israel remains a controversial issue, as does current U.S. involvement in Iraq.

The United States has a great strategic interest in Egypt and is concerned about a perceived lack of vision in Cairo for addressing persistent problems. Although the United States applauded Egypt's improvements in its economic condition in the 1990s and remained assertive regarding its human rights situation, the administration of Bill Clinton brought minimal pressure to bear on the government to make substantive political reforms. The U.S. attitude changed after September 11, 2001.

The George W. Bush administration's call for greater democracy in the Middle East has on several occasions been directed specifically at the Egyptian government; it openly criticized Egypt's human rights record. The two trials and imprisonment of sociologist Saad Eddin Ibrahim—a dual national with U.S. citizenship accused of accepting foreign money and tarnishing Egypt's image—sparked considerable criticism in the United States, as did the imprisonment in 2005 of al-Ghad Party leader Ayman Nour for allegedly forging names on licensing petitions for his party. The government, in response, accused the United States of meddling in Egypt's internal affairs and even categorized some domestic reformers as U.S. "agents."

Despite Egypt's many problems and rising voices of dissent, in mid-2005 the NDP remained firmly in control, and President Mubarak—though officially unannounced as a presidential candidate—appeared poised for a fifth six-year term in office.

CHAPTER 8

IRAN

More than twenty-five years after the revolution that drove Shah Mohammad Reza Pahlavi from his throne, the Islamic Republic of Iran continues to survive, defying predictions by many analysts that its government would collapse from internal contradictions, be defeated by Iraq in the war between the two countries that lasted from 1980 to 1988, or be replaced by a new secular revolution. The Iranian government still faces the enormous task of reinvigorating a struggling economy and overcoming the country's lingering international isolation in the face of strong opposition from religious conservatives.

Under the Iranian political system the president's ability to implement change is seriously circumscribed. The preeminent position in the power structure is that of supreme leader, or *faqih,* who sits at the top of a group of clerics that parallels the government, which is headed by the president, and oversees the most important elements of power. Although the Iranian people elected a moderate, Mohammad Khatami, as president in the 1997 and 2001 elections, the conservative religious establishment opposed many of his policies, highlighting the political and social tensions at work in Iran. That Iranians twice selected Khatami as a reformist candidate clearly illustrates their desire for a change in the status quo. Mahmoud Ahmadinejad, a conservative, emerged to succeed Khatami in June 2005 after a runoff election held amid charges of vote rigging by the establishment. The clerics have demonstrated little desire to relinquish any of their power, so it is unlikely that any type of radical reform lies ahead in Iran's immediate future.

Overreliance on oil revenues in a volatile international market remains a major structural weakness of the Iranian economy. Since 2003 high world oil prices have allowed Iran to avoid deep social and economic crises that could gravely affect national stability. Although the government is attempting to diversify and shift some resources to the private sector, it has made little headway against the resistance of the conservative clerics. To secure access to international financial capital, Iran has intensified overtures to Western countries and to its Gulf neighbors, but with only limited success. Despite some progress in changing external perceptions of Iran, the country has had difficulty shedding its hostile, subversive image, particularly given foreign uncertainties about Iran's internal political dynamics. Tehran's reported attempts to obtain a nuclear weapons capability, perceived support for international terrorism, and implacable hostility toward the Untied States, Israel, and Palestinian-Israeli peace efforts all contribute to Iran's image problem.

Iran's Islamic revolution has atrophied, giving rise to an intense power struggle among the ruling clerical elite, an increase in Iranian nationalism, and a growing demand for social, political and economic reforms. Consolidation and maintenance of the ruling clerical elites' power and resolving the country's myriad problems drives day-to-day politics.

Geography

Iran lies on a plateau that is four thousand feet high and almost entirely surrounded by mountains.

Key Facts on Iran

Area: 636,293 square miles (1,648,000 square kilometers)

Capital: Tehran

Population: 69,018,924 (2004)

Religion: Shiite Muslim, 89 percent; Sunni Muslim, 9 percent; Jews, Bahais, Zoroastrians, and Christians, 2 percent

Ethnic Groups: Persian, 51 percent; Azeri, 24 percent; Gilaki and Mazandarani, 8 percent; Kurd, 7 percent; Arab, 3 percent; Lur, 2 percent; Baloch, 2 percent; Turkmen 2 percent; other, 1 percent

Official Language: Persian and Persian dialects, 58 percent; Turkic and Turkic dialects, 26 percent; Kurdish, 9 percent; Luri, 2 percent; Balochi, 1 percent; Arabic, 1 percent; Turkish, 1 percent; other 2 percent

Type of Government: Theocratic republic

GDP: $478.2 billion; $7,000 per capita (2003)

Source: Central Intelligence Agency, *CIA World Factbook,* 2004.

Vast deserts form equally impenetrable barriers. These conditions restrict internal movement by land and have contributed to the development of numerous ethnically and linguistically distinct groups within the country.

Iran is bounded by the Caspian Sea, Armenia, Azerbaijan, and Turkmenistan to the north, Iraq and Turkey to the west, the Persian Gulf and the Gulf of Oman to the south, and Afghanistan and Pakistan to the east. The Zagros Mountains, which stretch southeastward from the junction of the borders with Azerbaijan, Turkey, and Iraq, cover much of western Iran and then extend eastward, fronting the Arabian Sea and extending into Baluchistan in the southwest. With few primary roads, the villages in Baluchistan have remained isolated. Transportation networks are only slightly better on the eastern edge of the Zagros range in central Iran.

Mountains and deserts also separate people living in northern and eastern Iran. The Elburz Mountains, which run along the southern shores of the Caspian Sea, form a rugged barrier north of Tehran. High humidity and rainfall have created fertile, green fields along the Caspian Sea. Two uninhabited deserts, the Dasht-e-Lut and the Dasht-e-Kavir, cover much of eastern and central Iran, isolating the settlements along the borders with Afghanistan and Pakistan.

Iran suffers from occasional but severe earthquakes. In June 1990, more than 40,000 people were reported killed and more than 60,000 injured in an earthquake that struck the northwestern part of the country. Two earthquakes during the first half of 1997 each killed several thousand people. In December 2003, an earthquake at Bam killed nearly 50,000 and injured additional thousands. Iran's climate is one of extremes, ranging from scorching hot summers with high humidity to subfreezing winters with heavy snowfall in the northwest. Annual rainfall averages about fifty inches in the western mountains and along the Caspian littoral, but less than an inch in the central plateau.

Demography

Farsi, the language of Iran's dominant ethnic group, the Persians, is the first language of 58 percent of Iran's estimated 69 million people. Turkic and Turkic dialects are spoken by about 26 percent of Iranians, while Kurdish is the language of approximately 9 percent. Most Persians are urban dwellers, although they also occupy fertile mountain valleys in the central and northern portions of the country. Persians comprise the bulk of the upper class, occupy the most important bureaucratic positions, and dominate the ranks of the economic elite. Since 1502 all the rulers of Iran have been Persians. Azeri represent another 24 percent of the population. Gilaki and Mazandarani number about 8 percent, while Kurds comprise 7 percent. The remaining 10 percent of the population consists of Arabs, Baloch, Lurs, and Turkmen.

Because of Iran's geographic barriers, many Iranians historically have had a greater allegiance to their local ethnic group than to the nation. This has changed somewhat during the past twenty-five years, as a new sense of Iranian nationalism has taken hold. The Kurds, numbering more than 4 million, are the second largest ethnic group. Most live in northwestern Iran along the Iraqi and Turkish borders. Kurds are generally Sunni Muslims, and their social organization is tribal. In northern Iran, Turkic-speaking ethnic groups that entered the area around the eleventh century predominate. Like the Kurds, they are tribally organized, and some are semi-nomadic; they have resisted all efforts by the Persians to control them. The tribes, found around Mashhad, are isolated from the capital by the Dasht-e-Kavir. The largest Turkic ethnic group is the Azerbaijani/Azeri, who live in northwestern Iran between the Caspian Sea and the Turkish and Azerbaijan borders. The rugged terrain of the area has enabled the Azerbaijani to maintain their distance from Tehran. Even so, prominent Azeri hold key government and clerical positions. The Bakhtiari and the Lurs, distant relatives of the Kurds, inhabit the remote mountain areas in the southeast. Sixty percent of these people are nomadic.

The Baluch and the Arabs living in Iran take great pride in their ancestry; their tribal loyalties are far stronger than any national ties. The Baluch, the poorest and least integrated of all Iranians, remain isolated from the rest of the nation by the deserts of the east. Although the Iranian Baluch are nationalists, they do have much in common with their fellow Baluch who live in the vast desert of southwest Pakistan. More than half a million Iraqi refugees, most of whom fled Iraq during the 1991 civil war, have largely returned home following the collapse of the Iraqi regime in 2002–2003. Some 2 to 3 million Afghan refugees fled to Iran during Afghanistan's twenty-five years of turmoil. Most refugees returned to Afghanistan following the U.S. invasion in pursuit of al-Qaida and to overthrow the Taliban in the wake of the September 2001 attacks on the United States.

Shiism

Islam is the most powerful unifying force in Iran. Although Shiites are the majority religious

community in Iran, and Shiism is closely identified with Iran, Shiism's origins are not Iranian. Rather, they are Arab. During the mid-seventh century, following the death of the Prophet Muhammad, a schism developed over leadership of the Islamic community. Muslims split into Sunnis (the majority in the Middle East) and Shiites (89 percent of Iran's population). Sunni Muslims held that succession should flow to the most able leader of the Islamic community, whereas Shiites maintained that only a descendant of the Prophet could be the rightful leader. The Shiites accordingly considered Ali, a cousin who had married the Prophet's daughter, the rightful successor, or imam. In addition to being a political leader, the imam must also be a spiritual leader who can interpret the meaning of the Quran and *sharia,* Islamic law.

In 661 rivals of Ali assassinated him. His supporters, calling themselves Shiat Ali, or the partisans of Ali, revolted against the Sunnis but were defeated in 680 at Karbala, in Iraq. Their leader, Hussein, Ali's youngest son, was executed. Large numbers of Shiites fled to Iran. Proselytizing increased their numbers, until they became the majority in Iran under the Safavids during the sixteenth century.

Shiite Muslims believe there are seven pillars of faith. In addition to the first five pillars, which they share with the Sunnis—confession of faith, prayer, alms giving, fasting during Ramadan, and the pilgrimage to Mecca—the Shiites add *jihad,* the struggle to protect Islamic lands, beliefs, and institutions, and the requirement to do good works and avoid evil thoughts, words, and deeds.

Of the several Shiite sects, the Twelve Imams, or Twelvers, is dominant in Iran. The principal belief of Twelver Shiites is that spiritual and temporal leadership of the Muslim community, in the person of the imam, passed from the Prophet Muhammad to Ali, the first imam, and continued on to eleven of Ali's direct male descendants. The twelfth, and final, imam is believed to have gone into hiding because of Sunni persecution and will reappear as the Mahdi, or messiah, on the day of divine judgment. *(Fifteen Centuries of Islam, Chapter 5, p. 195)*

The *ulama,* or religious authorities, have played a prominent role in the development of Islamic scholarly and legal traditions. The highest religious authority is vested in the *mujtahids,* scholars who by their religious studies and virtuous lives act as leaders of the Shiite community and interpret the faith as it applies to daily life. Prominent Shiite mujtahids with near-total authority over the community are accorded the title of *ayatollah.* Qom is the center of religious intellectual live and learning for Iranian Shiites, while Mashhad, in the northeast, is the center of Shiite pilgrimage in the country because of the presence of the burial shrine of the Imam Reza, the only direct descendant of Muhammad to be buried in Iran.

History

Iran is the modern manifestation of at least twenty-five centuries of continuous civilization, and according to the Old Testament, ancient Persia existed as a civilization even before that. In the sixth century B.C.E., however, Cyrus the Great established the Persian Empire, which his grandson Darius extended to the Nile Valley and almost to Asia Minor through his conquest of Babylonia and Egypt. The empire gradually shrank because of Greek and Roman conquests and internal decay. By the seventh century C.E. it was beset by Arab invaders, who brought with them Islam and foreign rule. Through the eighth and ninth centuries, the Persians gradually regained autonomy as the Islamic Empire became increasingly decentralized, but Islam remained.

Modern Iranian history begins with nationalist protests in 1905 that pressured the ruler of Iran, Mohammad Ali Shah, into establishing a parliament and allowing the introduction of a constitution in 1906. He was forced to abdicate a few years later, in 1908, after he repudiated the constitution. His son Ahmad replaced him. World War I interrupted the sporadic growth of constitutionalism in Iran, but today's democratic expression can trace its intellectual roots to the constitutional movement of 1905–1911.

In 1901 the Iranians had granted William D'Arcy, an Australian, a concession to search for oil. The discovery of oil in Iran in 1908 intensified a developing British-Russian rivalry over Iran. On the eve of World War II, Britain purchased 51 percent of D'Arcy's company, the Anglo-Persian Oil Company (renamed the Anglo-Iranian Oil Company in 1935).

Although Iran officially remained neutral during World War I, the importance of oil to Britain—Persian oil fueled the British fleet during World War I—and Russia's desire to secure its southern flank resulted in British and Russian soldiers invading and occupying Iran. In 1919 Iran concluded a trade agreement with Britain that formally affirmed Iranian independence but in fact established a British protectorate over the country. After the 1917 Bolshevik Revolution and Iran's recognition of the Soviet Union, Moscow's new communist government renounced the imperialistic policies of the tsars toward Iran and withdrew the Russian troops that remained there.

A second revolutionary movement, directed largely by foreigners, was initiated in 1921 by Reza Shah, an Iranian military leader and the founder of the Pahlavi dynasty. In 1925 he was placed on the throne and implemented major domestic programs, including the establishment of a modern education system and the construction of roads and a trans-Iranian railroad. In 1935 Reza Shah changed Persia's traditional name to Iran. During World War II, Iran's close relations with Germany led, in 1941, to another occupation by the British and Soviets; the latter saw Iran as a key supply route from the West to the Soviet Union. The two powers forced Reza Shah to abdicate in favor of his son, Mohammad Reza. After the war, the Soviet Union helped Azeri and Kurds in their unsuccessful bid to establish separatist regimes in northern Iran. The effort failed after strong protests from the United States led the Soviets to withdraw their forces.

Post–World War II

Western influence in Iran's postwar affairs antagonized the country's political right and left. Deteriorating economic conditions only exacerbated the domestic political climate. Dissatisfaction with the shah, who had tried to accommodate foreign oil interests, led in April 1951 to the election of Mohammad Mossadeq, the leader of the rightist National Front, as prime minister. In May, with the support of the Iranian nationalist movement, Mossadeq nationalized Iran's oil industry. Iran, however, did not have the technical resources to operate the facilities without foreign help, so its production fell. Amid growing national discontent, Mossadeq took repressive measures to protect his power. He dissolved the Majlis in the summer of 1953 and tried to take full control of the government. Mohammad Reza was forced to flee the country in August. Within days, however, shah loyalists in the military, with the backing of the U.S. Central Intelligence Agency, defeated military units controlled by Mossadeq, and the shah returned to power.

With Mossadeq imprisoned and the effectiveness of his National Front allies in parliament greatly reduced, the shah consolidated his power by smashing the communist Tudeh Party and purging its members from the army's lower ranks. The shah rewarded his supporters in the officer corps and sought improved relations with the nationalist-minded clerical authorities. Although Iran's oil industry remained nationalized, the shah negotiated a deal with foreign oil companies under which they managed oil operations for a substantial profit.

In 1961, amid a resurgence of the National Front, the shah announced the White Revolution, an ambitious plan to stimulate economic growth and social development. The plan was a response to increasing criticism of government corruption and the privileges enjoyed by the regime and its supporters. It promoted women's suffrage, literacy, health, the sale of state-owned factories, and profit sharing for workers. The cornerstone of the revolution, however, was land reform. The landed classes, with allies among the Shiite clergy, incited violent demonstrations in June 1963 to protest the threat to their holdings. The shah crushed their dissent. Afterward, he instituted reforms to mollify moderates and used repression to silence all others, especially the clergy.

The shah then used the nation's oil riches to turn Iran into a regional power. He spent billions of dollars on sophisticated military equipment from the United States, with whom he developed close relations and which considered him a bulwark against communism. Following the 1973 Arab-Israeli war and the Arab oil embargo imposed on Israel's supporters, Iran's oil revenues soared. Before October 1973, its oil revenues totaled $2.5 billion a year. By 1979 annual oil revenues had grown to $19.1 billion.

Islamic Revolution

Iran's political upheaval in 1979 was a thoroughly modern revolution that unleashed social forces whose potential for change is now the driving force for democratization. At its heart, this revolution was cultural, fueled by the overwhelming sense among Iranians that they were losing control of their values, traditions, and identity to an alien and hostile West.

In February 1979, after months of civil violence, a broad-based, grassroots revolution led by Ayatollah Ruhollah Khomeini ended the thirty-seven-year reign of the shah. The revolution was long in coming; social, economic, and religious pressures had been building within the country for several decades. Khomeini's followers mark the start of the revolution with the riots in 1963 in response to the land reform program.

During the 1960s and 1970s, sentiment against the government grew in nearly every segment of Iranian society. Middle-class Iranians who opposed the government found allies in the religious hierarchy. The clerics were incensed not only by the secularization of the education system, which they viewed as a direct assault on their position within society, but also by the law giving women the right to vote and the Family Protection Law, which allowed women to disobey Islamic teaching and divorce their husbands. The shah further alienated many Iranians by brutally suppressing dissent and by bringing in foreigners, especially Americans, to support his programs and provide technical skills. The monarchy increasingly became an anti-Islamic symbol.

By relying on non-Muslim foreigners and by reducing the traditional influence of the ulama on government policy, the shah disrupted the balance that had existed between religious and secular authority in Iran. The urban poor came to oppose the shah mostly on moral grounds, seeing his attempts to westernize Iranian society as attacks on revered Islamic institutions. The clerics and the poor were joined in their opposition to the shah by modernist groups. Islamic modernists, such as the Marxist Mujaheddin-e-Khalq, opposed him for his capitalist economic policies. Progressive religious and secular intellectuals wanted a modernized Iran without a monarchy. Secular modernist groups, such as the Fedayin-e-Khalq and the Tudeh Party, both longtime opponents of the shah, were joined by the professional middle class, which viewed the shah's highly centralized control over the political and economic process as the greatest obstacle to their advancement. The opposition found its leader in Khomeini, who had been exiled to Iraq in 1964 for leading demonstrations against the shah. Khomeini believed that the political role of the clerics was to provide moral guidance to secular forces, who would manage the technical aspects of

the state. Such statements left modernists with the mistaken impression that they would run the government once the shah had been defeated.

After mass demonstrations in 1976 against the shah's switch from the Islamic calendar to one based on the coronation of Cyrus the Great, relative quiet descended for a time. Sporadic protests took place, however, in response to the repressive activities of SAVAK, the shah's hated intelligence service. Some protests escalated into large-scale riots after a 1978 government-inspired article in the Tehran newspaper *Etelaat* impugned Khomeini's character and accused him of conspiring with communists against the shah. In January 1978 in Qom, a religious center dominated by the nation's Shiite clergy, Khomeini supporters protested the article. During the march, army troops fired into the crowd. The victims of this shooting were the first of an estimated 10,000 people killed that year during rioting. Demonstrators protested against the shootings, and the shah's forces put down the riots with increasing fervor. The government closed the universities in June, creating greater support for the demonstrators among students. From exile in Iraq, Khomeini encouraged the demonstrations. The Iraqi government, concerned with maintaining good relations with Iran, expelled Khomeini, who moved to France in October 1978.

In November, Iranian workers staged strikes in solidarity with the anti-shah demonstrators. The most important were those called by workers in the petroleum industry, whose walkout soon produced a fuel shortage, seriously damaging the economy. On the eve of the revolution, the shah imposed price controls to curb inflation. While enforcing them, the government closed nearly 250,000 small shops. This move alienated the merchant class, many of whom were jailed or excessively fined for "profiteering."

Once the breadth of the opposition became apparent, the shah made several last-ditch efforts to appease his opponents. Among them, he granted amnesty to Khomeini. The demonstrations and strikes continued. Soon even civil servants refused to report to work. The shah then offered to step down as head of the government, although not as shah. He appointed Shapour Bakhtiar as premier. Bakhtiar, a member of the National Front who had always opposed the shah, accepted the appointment and moved quickly to placate the opposition. He promised to disband SAVAK, proclaimed that no more Iranian oil would be sold to Israel or South Africa, turned over the Israeli embassy to the Palestine Liberation Organization, and openly criticized U.S. policies supported by the shah. These efforts, however, came too late. Bakhtiar was denounced by his own party for accepting the premiership. Rioting continued.

With the end near, the shah flew to Egypt on January 16, 1979, never to return to his country. Two weeks later, on February 1, Khomeini returned triumphantly to Iran. His supporters overthrew Bakhtiar's government on February 11. Bakhtiar fled to France, and Mehdi Bazargan replaced him as premier. The Islamic Republic of Iran was declared on April 1, 1979.

Consolidation of Power

After the fall of the shah, Iran's internal security apparatus collapsed, and bands of armed youth calling themselves Revolutionary Guards, or the Pasdaran, ran amok, attacking anyone associated with the former government. Thousands of self-appointed committees *(komitehs)* exercised civil authority by taking it upon themselves to stamp passports, distribute food, set prices for goods, and police the streets, mostly without state supervision. The Revolutionary Council—a group of about a dozen clerics, military leaders, and political figures close to Khomeini—was soon created to provide central direction and to oversee policy during the establishment of the new revolutionary government.

In this atmosphere, a struggle for power ensued between the Shiite clerics and secular nationalists. Although these two groups had cooperated in overthrowing the shah, they had different goals. The clerics and their Islamic Republican Party (IRP) sought the establishment of a conservative society based on Shiite tenets and dominated by religious leaders. The secular nationalist groups sought a secular government, envisioned an advisory role for religious leaders, and were generally more receptive to foreign ties and influence.

The clerics had several advantages over the secular nationalists, however. First, the secular nationalists were a broad group of organizations, including the Tudeh Party, the Fedayin-e-Khalq, and the National Front, without common goals or a united leadership like that of the IRP. Second, the clerics had the support of Khomeini, who commanded enormous respect among many segments of the Iranian population. When competing for support, the clerics were able to tap into the deep religious convictions of many Iranian citizens.

Khomeini led a revolution that was and remains plural in construction and united only in its enmity toward its common foe, the shah and his "master," the United States. The revolution was as much defined in opposition to the United States as it was to the shah. Nationalists, religious zealots, and the Left all had reason to distrust and dislike the United States. Designating it as the "Great Satan" had enormous resonance within the Iranian body politic and remains today a mainstay of the clerical regime's rhetorical anti-American campaign.

From 1979 to 1983, the clerics, led by Khomeini, used political maneuvering, propaganda, and terror to sweep their secular rivals aside. The liberal intelligentsia, represented by President Abolhassan Bani-Sadr, who had been elected with 75 percent of the vote in January 1980, were gradually removed from positions of power. Bani-Sadr's presidency was crippled by the war that began on September 22, 1980, when Iraqi forces invaded. After Khomeini withdrew his support of Bani-Sadr, the Majlis declared him politically incompetent. Khomeini removed him in 1981. Bani-Sadr fled the country in July. With him was Massoud Rajavi, leader of the Mujaheddin-e-Khalq. France granted the two men asylum.

One week after Bani-Sadr and Rajavi were forced into exile, the Mujaheddin bombed IRP headquarters, killing seventy-four of the nation's political elite, including the founder of the IRP, Ayatollah Mohammad Beheshti. The Mujaheddin espoused Islamic Marxism, arguing for a divinely integrated classless society with nationalization of major industries and banks. The Mujaheddin's views on the direction of the revolution were not irreconcilable with the clerics' views, but the IRP was unwilling to share power with anyone.

In retaliation for the bombing, Khomeini turned the full force of the Revolutionary Guards against the Mujaheddin, and by the end of 1982 they were forced underground. Amnesty International estimated that between 4,500 and 6,000 Mujaheddin were killed by Revolutionary Guards; thousands were imprisoned.

Khomeini's regime also suppressed the Tudeh Party and the Fedayin-e-Khalq. The Revolutionary Guards' treatment of the Fedayin-e-Khalq was so harsh that in December 1982 Khomeini publicly criticized the komitehs for their excesses. In 1983 Khomeini's government banned the Tudeh Party and jailed more than a thousand of its members.

Throughout this period of consolidation, during which the clerics and their supporters eliminated the secular nationalists and other opponents, the military remained loyal to the revolution. Numerous officers owed their positions to Khomeini's regime, and rank-and-file soldiers demonstrated intense loyalty to Khomeini. The military also was probably reluctant to confront the disorganized but ubiquitous Revolutionary Guards, whose zeal and propensity for violence was intimidating, even to the armed forces.

U.S. Embassy Hostage Crisis

On November 4, 1979, a group of students took sixty-six Americans hostage at the U.S. embassy. Within a few days, thirteen hostages were released. The students soon received the support of Ayatollah Khomeini and most of the government, and the event would become of central importance to the Iranian power struggle.

The hostage crisis lasted for 444 days, that is, until January 21, 1981, when Iran released the diplomats as Jimmy Carter left office and Ronald Reagan assumed the presidency. Iran's hard-line, anti-Western clerics used the episode to weaken the position of moderates in the government. The

hard-liners justified the continued holding of the hostages by pointing to the diplomatic, military, and economic measures taken by the Carter administration to obtain their release and the admission of the shah into the United States for medical treatment as evidence of U.S. malevolence. In addition, the publication of documents captured by the students who took over the embassy revealed U.S. intelligence activities in Iran that confirmed the suspicions of many Iranians that the United States was interfering in their internal affairs. In this atmosphere, Iranian moderates previously connected with U.S. officials became suspect, while extremists in Tehran gained credibility. Moreover, the refusal of some moderate Iranian leaders to actively support the hostage taking made them more vulnerable to the machinations of the hard-liners.

Within the context of the revolution, the hostage taking allowed the hard-liners to take control of the revolution. The United States publicized the event out of all proportion to its inherent significance by personalizing and moralizing, by threatening and posturing, and by being seen as attacking Iran in the fatally flawed hostage rescue attempt of April 1980. The failed mission greatly enhanced Khomeini's credibility and stature and helped solidify the legitimacy of the revolution in the minds of Iranians.

Government Structure

The constitution drafted in 1979 centers Iran's government around the concept of the *velayat-e-faqih,* rule by a single spiritual leader charged with the guardianship of the community of believers. The *faqih,* or supreme leader, is an expert in religious jurisprudence whose authority and piety permit him to render binding interpretations of religious laws and principles, and under the constitution he is granted ultimate authority in all matters of government and social policy. In addition, he appoints the heads of the military, the security forces, the judiciary, and the broadcasting services. In 1979 Khomeini asserted that "there is not a single topic of human life for which Islam has not provided instruction and established norms." According to this principle, the clergy, with their superior knowledge of Islamic law, are the best qualified to rule the community of believers. Khomeini's concept of the velayat-e-faqih, incorporated into the constitution, provided him with the doctrinal basis for Iran's theocratic government.

Iran's constitution, approved by the Assembly of Experts in November 1979, is full of contradictions that reflect the extraordinary range of political forces in the Iranian Revolution. The first contradiction arises from Islamic legalist and non-Islamic secular elements over the provision that Shiite laws and rule by Islamist jurists offer all solutions to all problems. The second contradiction flows from democratic and anti-democratic elements, which arise from the notion of the sovereignty of the people as opposed to the sovereignty of the faqih. In essence, these basic contradictions between the legalist, Islamist elements and the democratic, secular proponents are the basic underpinnings of the political tensions that pervade Iran today. Ayatollah Ali Khamenei, Khomeini's successor as supreme leader, clearly does not have the same religious credential or status to be faqih as Khomeini. He was, however, deemed the most acceptable candidate to all clerical parties. As a result, the dual nature of Iran's governmental structure became more pronounced.

Iran's parallel power structures are paramount to the clerical regime's stability as well as the persistent tensions that prevail. This construct consists of a number of loosely connected and competitive formal and informal power centers. The formal centers are represented by the constitution and governmental regulations and are evident in state institutions and offices. The informal centers include religious-political organizations, revolutionary foundations, and paramilitary organizations aligned with various factions of Iran's clerical leadership.

The president, as the chief executive, is elected for a four-year term and can be reelected for a second term. Although he holds responsibility for the day-to-day running of the government, he does not determine basic domestic or foreign policy nor does he command the armed forces or the security apparatus. This authority resides in the hands of the supreme leader, as provided in the constitution, who is the most powerful political and religious figure in the country.

The formal power structure also includes a series of major institutions that are the heart and soul of the regime: the supreme leader and his office, the president, the Assembly of Experts, the Expediency Council, the Majlis, the Council of Ministers, the Council of Guardians, the judiciary, state media and the commanders of the armed forces (the Iranian Revolutionary Guard Corps [IRGC], the regular military), and the police and other security services.

Several of the councils are unique to revolutionary Iran. The Assembly of Experts—an elected body of seventy to eighty eminent Islamic scholars—has responsibility for such matters of state as revising the constitution and selecting a successor to the faqih. The twelve-member Council of Guardians screens and modifies all legislation from the Majlis before passing it on to the faqih for his approval. Laws that do not meet the council's Islamic standards are sent back to the parliament, often in a modified form with the expectation that they will be passed and resubmitted as returned. The Council of Guardians also screens presidential candidates to ensure that they possess the proper Islamic credentials. The faqih and the Majlis select the members of the council.

A duality characterizes the top leadership positions, as evident in the president and the supreme leader, and pervades all formal government organizations. The parliament vies with the Council of Guardians, and the regular armed forces stand in competition with the Iranian Revolutionary Guard Corps. This duality results in a high degree of inefficiency and incoherence in the county's domestic and foreign policies.

The informal power structure consists of four major groupings that include many of the same personalities found in the formal structure, but who in this guise operate independently of the formal structure. The first and most important of these consists of the so-called patriarchs, the most powerful of the clerics in the executive, legislative, and judicial branches as well as in the other formal centers of power. A second group includes the most senior nonclerical government bureaucrats and administrators. The third group provides the power base for the regime—members of revolutionary organizations, the "bonyads" (religious foundations), the IRGC, the Basij paramilitary militia, religious security elements, and the media. The fourth grouping contains formerly influential personalities and groups positioned between the regime and civil society whose goal is peaceful systemic reform from within.

Further complicating the picture, a leadership composed of Islamic, revolutionary Shiite clerics and laity controls all the formal and informal power centers. Expressed simply, two ideological factions represent the main left-right, conservative-reformist orientations. In reality, however, such a simplistic representation does not adequately reflect the broad range of Iranian political forces. Because these centers assume quite divergent positions on different political issues it is impossible to categorize them merely by calling them moderate or radical, conservative or extremist, and so on. A more accurate representation is how Iranians refer to them: the Islamic left, the new left, the traditionalist right, and the modernist right.

Political parties in post-revolutionary Iran were banned, but identifiable factions among the ruling clerics and their patronage networks exist. These factions express political views, hold meetings, and organize parliamentary caucuses, but they are less formal than political parties and do not provide an opportunity for grassroots membership. The Islamic Republican Party was Iran's dominant political party until its dissolution in 1987. Iran now has a variety of parties and groups that perform political activities, pressure groups, as well as entities with an ideological perspective, and others more akin to professional organizations. Among the more prominent of the conservative groups are the Ansar-e Hizballah, the Students Following the Line of the Imam, the Tehran Militant Clergy

Association, the Islamic Coalition Party, and the Islamic Engineers Society. The Organization for Strengthening Unity is an active pro-reform group. Opposition groups include the Freedom Movement of Iran, the National Front, Marz-e Po Gohar, as well as various ethnic and monarchist organizations.

Iran-Iraq War, 1980–1988

The apparent weakness of Iran's political center encouraged Iraq to attack Iran in September 1980. Much of the dispute between the two countries centered around sovereignty over the Shatt al-Arab waterway between the two countries, but the more likely cause was the covert desire of both countries to overthrow the other's government. Iraq's president, Saddam Hussein, expected that the chaos in Tehran would result in a quick victory. Instead of collapsing, however, the Iranian government responded with surprising speed, mobilizing what was left of the shah's army, and rallied behind their leader, Ayatollah Khomeini, repelling the Iraqi invaders in 1982. Waves of untrained young men, some of them unarmed, threw themselves into the conflict and halted the Iraqis' advance. *(For discussion of the war, see The Persian Gulf, Chapter 4, p. 137, and Iraq profile, p. 267)*

Iran and Iraq both carried out a program of demonization of the other to such an extent that the sense of national identity strengthened on both sides. Iran's calculation that the Shiite majority in southern Iraq would rally to its cause and Iraq's conviction that the Arab citizens in Khuzistan would welcome the Iraqi army as their liberators were both wrong. Indeed, the war helped Iran's revolutionary government consolidate power and distracted attention from pressing social and economic problems.

Iranian counterattacks in late 1981 and 1982 forced the Iraqi army to retreat. In June 1982, Iraq began to seek peace. Iraqi president Saddam Hussein withdrew his troops into Iraq and unilaterally called a cease-fire. Regardless, in July, Khomeini ordered a major attack across the border toward Basra. Iranian forces, weakened by purges of officers and shortages of equipment, were unable to sustain the offensive. The assault failed, and the war deteriorated into a brutal standoff with the two armies lodged inside Iraqi territory.

During the war, both countries attacked the oil facilities of the other as well as neutral tankers in the Persian Gulf. Iranian attacks succeeded in substantially reducing Iraqi exports early in the war, although the construction of pipelines restored Iraqi export capacity by 1987. Iraqi attacks in 1984 and 1985 on Iranian refineries, oil tankers doing business with Iran, and Kharg Island, Iran's principal Gulf oil terminal, sharply reduced Iranian oil revenues. In 1983 Iran had earned $21.7 billion from its petroleum exports, but by 1985 revenues had fallen to $15.9 billion. In 1986 a worldwide collapse of oil prices limited Iran's oil export earnings to just $7.3 billion.

The loss of oil revenue further weakened an economy already suffering from poor management by inexperienced clerics and the resource drain caused by the war. In addition to economic strains, the war brought Iran increasing international isolation. Its stated goal of exporting its revolution to neighboring states and its attacks on ships in the Gulf pushed Arab nations, with the exception of Libya, Syria, and the People's Democratic Republic of Yemen, to back Iraq financially and diplomatically. Saudi Arabia and Kuwait provided billions of dollars to the Iraqi war effort, and the Gulf states formed the Gulf Cooperation Council (GCC) to coordinate their defenses. It also was the first example of the United States and the Soviet Union being on the same side of an issue, with both favoring Iraq. *(Gulf Cooperation Council, p. 175)*

During the war, a covert attempt by the Reagan administration to use arms sales to Iran to improve U.S. relations with Iranian moderates and obtain the release of American hostages held in Lebanon by pro-Iranian groups caused a scandal in the United States. Not only had the plan contradicted Reagan's policies of not negotiating with terrorists and not selling arms to Iran, but investigations disclosed that administration officials had also used proceeds from the arms sales to illegally fund contra rebels in Nicaragua. In an effort to repair its image among Gulf states and head off growing Soviet involvement in the region, the United States, at the behest of the Kuwaiti government, began escorting reflagged Kuwaiti oil tankers through the Persian Gulf. These U.S. naval escorts clashed with Iranian forces on several occasions and increased Iranians' sense of encirclement.

Iranian morale was reduced further by Iraqi air and missile attacks on Iran's largest cities, Iraq's use of chemical weapons on the battlefield (and especially in Halabja, at the time held by Iran, where about 5,000 Iraqi Kurds were massacred), and the failure of major offenses in 1986 and 1987 to breach Iraqi defenses around Basra. In early 1988, Iraqi forces began pushing the Iranians back toward their border. By July, the Iraqis had recaptured virtually all of their territory occupied by Iran and appeared poised to achieve significant territorial gains across the border.

Faced with this prospect, Khomeini agreed to UN Resolution 598 in July 1988, providing for a cease-fire, despite his earlier vow to fight until Saddam Hussein had been driven from power. The cease-fire went into effect in August 1988. The war resulted in the deaths of hundreds of thousands of Iranians and left the nation financially bankrupt. When the war ended, neither side had achieved its war aims. Each felt outside powers had cheated it of victory. Iraq did not bring down Iran's revolutionary government, and Iran did not foment revolution in Iraq. The leaders of both countries remained in power, and their troops, with minor exceptions, were within their own borders.

After Khomeini

On June 6, 1989, Ayatollah Khomeini was laid to rest amidst a chaotic display of national grief. Hundreds of thousands of mourners showed up at the War Martyrs' Cemetery in Tehran, and thousands pressed through elaborate barriers at the burial site, trying to touch Khomeini's body. The crowd overwhelmed security personnel, and mourners grabbed at the corpse, causing it to fall from its wooden litter. Soldiers fought to retrieve the body as helicopters scattered the crowd. The body was airlifted, and officials were forced to delay the burial for six hours. For years Khomeini had defied premature predictions of death, while Western observers speculated on the type of government that would emerge upon his departure.

In March 1989, the eighty-nine-year-old Khomeini had forced Ayatollah Hussein Ali Montazeri to resign as his designated heir. The resignation of Montazeri, considered a moderate on social and economic issues, appeared to indicate that radical factions opposed to the expansion of private enterprise and a greater opening to the West were well-positioned to maintain power after Khomeini's death. Montazeri's ouster confused the issue of succession, increasing the possibility of a bitter power struggle for the office of supreme leader.

While the crowds at Khomeini's burial reinforced Western perceptions of an out-of-control Iran, the country's leadership was defying Western speculation about a power struggle by effecting an apparently smooth and peaceful transition of power. Within twenty-four hours of Khomeini's death, the Assembly of Experts had chosen outgoing president Ali Khamenei, a compromise candidate, to succeed Khomeini as supreme leader. In August, Ali Akbar Hashemi Rafsanjani, Speaker of the Majlis, was overwhelmingly elected president. Rafsanjani had repeatedly stated his intention to give priority to reinvigorating the economy. Iranian voters approved the elimination of the post of prime minister, thus strengthening the executive power of the president. Despite the smooth transition, Khomeini's death created a vacuum in Iranian politics. Neither Rafsanjani nor Khamenei commanded the reverence and respect of Khomeini, who served as the final arbiter of all leadership disputes.

To the outside world, the government appeared as a solid and unyielding front, but internally pragmatists and radicals were deeply divided over objectives. Rafsanjani understood that Iranians were tired of the privations of war and revolution. Without marked improvement in living standards,

the possibility existed that large segments of society would turn against the government. These circumstances trapped Rafsanjani between the urgent need to implement reforms to reinvigorate the economy and the continuing power of conservative clerics. Measures likely to improve the economy, including the involvement of foreign capital and selective privatization, were also likely to draw the fire of radicals.

As a result, Rafsanjani adopted a policy of gradual change. In an attempt to revive the economy, he put forth a five-year development plan that allocated a large share of national resources to economic reconstruction and allowed for modest economic openings to the West. This spending and a decline in oil prices, however, put Iran deeper in debt. The economy was squeezed by the requirements of servicing the nation's external debt, and austerity measures raised the specter of popular discontent. Growing disillusionment among the lower classes became evident with increasing incidents of protests in early 1990, mass riots protesting the removal of squatter settlements in 1992, and protests against the lifting of housing subsidies in 1993 in several cities.

The death of Khomeini brought a modest liberalization of government controls over social and cultural practices, including dress and information technology, but beginning in 1992 Khamenei and a conservative Majlis instituted a cultural crackdown. Mohammad Khatami, who had been culture minister since 1982, was sacked in 1992, and satellite television antennas were banned. Internal security forces were granted wider latitude to suppress government opponents. As supreme leader, Khamenei frequently railed against Western influences in the media and the arts.

Despite economic and social hardships and widespread frustration, no viable political alternative appeared to exist to Rafsanjani's government. Rafsanjani maintained a good working relationship with Khamenei, although the former's technocratic approach was sometimes at odds with the supreme leader's stated positions. Rafsanjani was elected for a second four-year term in June 1993 with just 63.2 percent of the vote, down from 94.5

percent in the 1989 election. Voter turnout by an apathetic electorate was just 55 percent.

The Persian Gulf War, 1991

Despite the cease-fire that brought about the end of the Iran-Iraq War in 1988, no resolution of outstanding issues between Iran and Iraq seemed forthcoming. In early 1990, however, the two countries agreed to resume negotiations in the Soviet Union, but talks were overtaken by events, as Iraq invaded Kuwait on August 2, 1990. Iran condemned the invasion and offered to defend other Gulf countries.

Shortly thereafter, Iraqi leader Saddam Hussein, seeking to prevent the possibility of fighting a two-front war, capitulated to Iranian terms for a resolution of their dispute. On August 15, 1990, he offered to return Iranian territory still occupied by Iraq and to recognize Iranian control of the eastern half of the Shatt al-Arab waterway. Iran accepted. On August 18, Iraqi troops began withdrawing from Iranian territory. The two countries also began the exchange of an estimated 80,000 prisoners of war. On September 10, they agreed to reestablish diplomatic relations.

The Iranian government recognized that it stood to gain from the crisis created by the Iraqi invasion. Iraq would be weakened militarily, while Iran could appeal to people throughout the Middle East who were uncomfortable with Iraq's aggression and the Western presence in the multinational force assembled to counter the Iraqi occupation. On January 17, 1991, the coalition began its air campaign against Iraq, pitting Iran's two most recent and hated antagonists, Iraq and the United States, against one another in a war that promised to destroy much of Iraq's military might while increasing opposition to the United States in some parts of the Middle East.

Despite Iran's declared neutrality in the conflict, Iranian interests were threatened by Iraq's annexation of Kuwait. An Iraq bolstered by the oil reserves of Kuwait and in possession of an excellent port and a wide outlet to the Persian Gulf would be in a position to launch another war against Iran, or at least undercut Iranian influence and ambitions in the Persian Gulf region. Iran therefore pledged its cooperation with the UN embargo against Iraq. Throughout the crisis, Iran presented itself as a responsible mediator that denounced all military aggression and foreign military deployments in the region.

Soon after the war began, Iran agreed to receive Iraqi aircraft that Baghdad wished to shelter from allied air attacks. A total of 137 Iraqi warplanes, many of them among Iraq's best, were flown to Iranian airfields. Iran assured the coalition that it would not return the aircraft until the end of fighting. After coalition forces drove the Iraqis from Kuwait and destroyed a large part of Iraq's military power, Iran adopted a harder line toward Baghdad: Tehran informed Iraq that it intended to keep its warplanes, thereby substantially boosting the strength of the Iranian air force. In addition, Iran began supporting a Shiite rebellion in southern Iraq, providing rebels sanctuary in Iranian territory and supplying them with weapons and supplies. Iran also provided weapons to Kurdish groups in northern Iraq, who had had close relations with Iran in the past.

Iran-Iraq relations deteriorated after the Iraqi government suppressed the Shiite rebellion Iraq countered by resuming support for the military activities of the largest Iranian dissident groups, the Mujaheddin-e-Khalq and the Kurdish Democratic Party.

The 1997 Elections

With Rafsanjani's presidency limited to two terms under the constitution, the 1997 presidential election was to be a test of the popularity of the ruling clerics and their policies. The Council of Guardians approved only 4 of 238 applicants to run for the office. During the election, the religious establishment made clear that it supported Ali Akbar Nateq-Nouri, Speaker of the Majlis. Ayatollah Khamenei maintained an officially neutral stance, but his statements left little doubt that he favored Nateq-Nouri.

Nateq-Nouri's principal challenger was Mohammad Khatami, who had solid Islamic credentials. Having studied at Qom, Khatami, like

Rafsanjani and Nateq-Nouri, held the religious rank of *hojatolislam,* a step below ayatollah. As cultural minister from 1982 to 1992, however, Khatami had gained a reputation as a moderate inclined toward greater permissiveness in the areas under his control, which included books, newspapers, and films, and which resulted in his ouster from that office by the conservative-dominated Majlis. In 1997 he was the choice of technocrats and left-leaning clerics. His approval as a candidate by the Council of Guardians reflected the Islamic leadership's desire to produce a large turnout by giving the people a real choice.

Although Nateq-Nouri appeared to be the favorite to win, his endorsement by the religious establishment backfired, as many Iranians flocked to Khatami's camp out of resentment toward the ruling elite's efforts to ensure Nateq-Nouri's election. Also, during the campaign, Khatami called for expanded civil liberties and the rule of law, greater cultural and political participation by women, and improved relations with Europe and the Arab Gulf states. It was a message enthusiastically received, particularly by women and young people. University students and recent graduates, with their prospects limited by a stagnant economy, saw Khatami's campaign as an opportunity for change.

Although Khatami was an attractive candidate with a positive message and an appealingly unassuming demeanor, his victory cannot be attributed to electoral skill alone. By giving Khatami almost 70 percent of the vote over a more prominent rival, Iranians signaled their discontent with the direction of the Islamic Republic. The election drew 91 percent of eligible voters to the polls. The clerics remained in control of the most important levers of power, but their security was shaken, though not so much by Khatami as by the clear displeasure of a sizable majority of the Iranian people.

The 2001 Elections

Khatami's reelection in June 2001 surprised many observers. Voter turnout was so large that the polls remained open an additional two hours. Khatami received more than 21 million of the nearly 28 million votes cast, a larger mandate than he had received in 1997. The percentage exceeded that of former presidents Khamenei or Rafsanjani in their second term reelections in 1985 and 1993, respectively. Khatami had been expected to gain a reduced percentage of the vote based on voter dissatisfaction. The two preceding years of his presidency had been marred by a sharp rise in the closure of newspapers and other media, an increased number of arrests for political activities, and controversies over the serial killing of intellectuals. He appeared unable to control the military, the revolutionary institutions, or the judiciary. He had problems with a truculent parliament. He had also failed to improve the economy, despite a sharp rise in oil prices, as well as cope with rampant unemployment and inflation. All these problems seemed to indicate an erosion of presidential and personal power.

Khatami, however, did have certain advantages. Foremost, he retained public trust. Large numbers of Iranians saw him as the leader who spoke truthfully about the country's problems and of his limited powers to deal with them. He had brought a degree of transparency to office previously lacking. Voters perceived his trying to reform society and open political space. He reached out to youth and women; he encouraged the movement for democracy and pluralism; he argued for a strengthened civil society and the rule of law as the rule of law was being systematically undermined by elements in the security forces and the judiciary. Women and youth were instrumental in both of Khatami's victories. No Iranian leader since the establishment of the Islamic republic in 1979 had so vigorously addressed their needs, nor did other candidates have Khatami's charisma or broad base of support. With his plea for a "Dialogue Among Civilizations," Khatami seemed to project a vision of an Iran seeking to break from its international isolation. The Council of Guardians and the judiciary would have preferred that he not run, but he bowed to pressure from his supporters and the public not to abandon the reformist causes he had championed.

Opposing candidates received only 7 million votes. Ali Shamkhani, Khatami's defense minister and an Iranian Arab from Khuzistan province, was thought by the right wing to be capable of siphoning votes away from Khatami. Abdollah Jasbi, the chancellor of Azad University, targeted the youth vote by promising to eliminate the university entrance examination and provide free access to higher education. Ahmad Tavakoli, a former labor minister, another conservative candidate, emphasized ridding the country of corruption and poverty, and returning to the austerity of the first years of the revolution. Ali Fallahian, a former intelligence minister, ran on a seemingly middle-of-the-road platform, but he apparently wanted to exonerate himself of the unsavory actions by the intelligence service during his tenure as minister.

More than 815 candidates, including 45 women, applied for consideration to run for the presidency. The Council of Guardians approved only ten of them. In contrast to the 1997 election, the conservative establishment did not support a single candidate as it had Nateq-Nouri previously. Campaigning was limited to the three weeks before the election.

The Economy

Pre-revolutionary Iran's economic development had advanced rapidly. Traditionally an agricultural society, by the 1970s Iran had achieved significant industrialization and economic modernization. The pace of growth, however, had slowed appreciably by 1978. Since the revolution, increased government involvement in the economy has further stunted growth. Persistent economic crises remain the nightmare of successive governments.

Iran's economy is marked by a bloated, inefficient state sector, overreliance on the oil sector, and statist policies that create major distortions throughout society. The state controls most economic activity. The private sector is typically small scale, consisting mainly of farming, private trading, and service ventures. Khatami tried during his two terms as president to accelerate the market reform plans of former president Rafsanjani but with only limited success. The untold story of Iran, however, is one of economic decline: a steady deterioration of a nation that once boasted a per capita income equal to Spain's, pumped 6 million barrels of oil a day, and nurtured a vibrant middle class. Today's Iran has a real per capita income one-third pre-revolution levels, oil production is two-thirds of what it was then, and the middle class is being squeezed by chronically high inflation, widespread unemployment, and debilitating wage stagnation.

The country's rugged terrain conceals large deposits of oil, the country's most important natural resource. Most of Iran's fields are located in the southwest corner of the country in a 350-mile corridor beginning north of Dezful and running southeast almost to Bushehr. There are also sizeable offshore fields in the Persian Gulf. Iran's proven oil reserves are estimated at more than 105 billion barrels, or nearly 10 percent of the world's total. Iranian officials contended in mid-2004 that proven reserves were actually 132 billion barrels following discoveries in two fields in Khuzestan and the Gulf. Only Saudi Arabia and Iraq have larger proven reserves. Iran also has the world's second largest natural gas reserves (behind Russia), with some 935 trillion cubic feet. About 62 percent of Iran's natural gas fields have not been developed, meaning the country has huge potential for gas development.

Despite these riches, Iran's economy struggled during much of the 1990s and early 2000s because of a combination of low oil prices, high debt, lack of foreign investment, stalled efforts at privatization, high unemployment, and restrictions on information technology. (The Internet is now making significant inroads in society.) With sufficient investment, it is widely believed that Iran could significantly increase its crude oil production capacity, but for now production has leveled out at a daily rate of 3.9 million barrels per day.

President Khatami, like President Rafsanjani before him, promised to devote much of his attention to the economy. Despite some minor reforms, little fundamental change had occurred as of mid-2005. Although Khatami urged more diversification of the economy, many of his government's most prominent economic initiatives focused on further development of the petroleum sector. His government sought to boost production through exploration for new fields and modernization of equipment. It also attempted to expand oil earnings and meet domestic demand by investing in refining and petrochemical production.

Iran hopes to capitalize on its almost unlimited, natural gas potential with a sharp increase in gas exports. It is negotiating new gas pipeline arrangements with most of its neighbors and bringing several pipelines to completion. A long-delayed pipeline with Turkey was finally inaugurated in January 2002, but the flow only resumed permanently in early 2005. Iran plans to export about 300 billion cubic feet per year for European markets by 2007 via the Turkey pipeline. In March 2002, Greece agreed to extend Iran's gas pipeline with Turkey. China agreed in 2005 to a $100 billion, twenty-five-year contract to import liquid natural gas, as well as construction of a refinery in China. India and Iran signed an understanding in 1993 on an overland pipeline, but regional political and security concerns have delayed progress. In February 2002, however, Iran and Pakistan signed a memorandum of understanding on a pre-feasibility study for a possible 1,600-mile gas pipeline from southern Iran to southeastern Pakistan with an extension to India. A recent thaw in India-Pakistan relations has given this pipeline new impetus. In January 2005, India signed a deal for delivery of 7.5 million tons of liquefied natural gas per year beginning in 2009–2010.

Iran has failed to develop major exportable products outside the energy sector. Exports of oil, natural gas, and other petroleum products account for 80 to 90 percent of export earnings and 40 to 50 percent of the government budget. Iran's lack of exportable manufactured goods is reflected in the fact that pistachios, carpets, and fruits rank behind petroleum and related products as leading exports.

Iran's economy also has been held back by a lack of experienced governmental and technical experts capable of implementing an economic reform policy; political squabbling between the conservative and reformist factions has also been a major impediment. The revolution produced a brain drain of many of Iran's most experienced administrators and technocrats, and repressive regime policies since have sustained the effect. Often, ministerial nominees and other officials have been chosen according to their religious standing rather than their governmental experience. Further, the conservatives are strongly allied to the powerful merchant class, the *bazaaris,* who hold a near monopoly on the purchase and distribution of most goods. The bazaaris generally have opposed efforts to strengthen the domestic manufacturing sector.

The bonyads, or religious foundations, act as an enormous drain on the economy. These government-associated Islamic charities and businesses control between a quarter and a half of the nation's real gross domestic product. Bonyads originally were created to serve as legitimate charitable organizations to meet the needs of the 1980s war survivors and their families and to fund the office of the supreme leader. They continue these functions, but have also become off-budget, non-accountable mechanisms for enriching the senior clerics and their families. Khatami proposed bringing the bonyads under governmental control and supervision in both of his five-year plans, but to no avail.

In late 2004, Iran's external debt stood at $11.9 billion, and its short-term debt at an additional $12 billion. Its ability to service this debt depends largely on international oil prices. It was forced to negotiate a debt restructuring with foreign creditors, especially France, Germany, Italy, and Japan, when oil prices fell in 1998. Iran's oil earnings dropped from $15.7 billion in 1997 to $10.2 billion in 1998. An improvement in oil prices in March 1999 decreased the possibility of a default, but servicing the debt continued to be a drain on the budget. Dramatically higher oil revenues since the late-1990s have not allowed Iran to lower its budget deficits. These remain a chronic problem because of large-scale subsidies of about $12 billion annually on foodstuffs, gasoline, and other necessities. The official estimate of unemployment was 12 percent in 2004, but foreign observers concede that it may be as low as 16 percent, but more probably it could actually be as high as 30 percent.

Adoption of decisive economic policies has proved nearly impossible, because the regime is divided over how much private sector and foreign involvement to permit. Hard-liners have argued that any foreign involvement would undermine Iranian independence and that opening the economy to domestic private enterprise could erode Islamic values and weaken the control of religious leaders. In mid-September 1999, however, Khatami announced plans to privatize several major industries. His plan, to be implemented over a five-year period ending in 2004, and extended in his second five-year plan, called for privatization of the communications, post, railway, and tobacco industries. If carried out, about 30 percent of the economy would be in private hands, compared with an estimated 10 to 15 percent in 1999. Khatami's second five-year plan called for more intensified attention to investment, cleaning up rampant corruption, providing for more transparency and closer accountability for the bonyads. Iran's debt, however, has made it difficult for the government to fund major projects without foreign participation. In addition, U.S. sanctions, many of which date back to the 1979–1980 hostage crisis, have discouraged some foreign investors from risking capital in Iran.

Foreign Affairs

The Khomeini revolutionary regime initiated stark changes from the foreign policy pursued by the shah, particularly in reversing the country's orientation toward the West. Since the revolution, Iran's only significant regional ally has been Syria, but during the last years of the Rafsanjani presidency and during Khatami's tenure, Iran made significant strides in improving relations with its Persian Gulf neighbors, particularly Saudi Arabia. Cordial relations exist with China, India, Russia, and North Korea.

Tehran's "Islamic foreign policy" emphasizes maintaining vehement anti-U.S. and anti-Israel stances; eliminating outside influence in the region; supporting Muslim political movements abroad; and greatly increasing diplomatic contacts with developing countries. Despite this broad outline, Iran's foreign relations are frequently confused and contradictory due to its oscillation between pragmatic and ideological concerns. Since the revolution, Iran's foreign relations have been tumultuous. The West and Iran's neighbors remain suspicious of Tehran's intentions, though the election of Khatami and his government's attempts to put a kinder face on Iran created some foreign policy openings. Foreign leaders were anxious to reward Khatami with agreements that might bolster his position against hard-line clerics.

Iran's current relations with its Arab neighbors were shaped by the revolution and the Iran-Iraq War. The Iranian leadership's desire to export its revolution to other states made Iran a primary security threat to the Gulf nations. As noted earlier, in response to Iran's threat to export revolution and its attacks on Gulf shipping during its war with Iraq, Jordan, Kuwait, and Saudi Arabia openly supported Iraq financially and militarily. An Iranian-backed plot to overthrow the Bahraini government in 1981, Iran's support of Shiites who bombed Western embassies in Kuwait in 1983, and riots in 1987 by Iranian pilgrims in Mecca that left 402 people dead were among the most troubling instances of Iranian subversion and agitation. The underlying causes of the GCC countries' suspicion of Iran involved ongoing territorial disputes, its arms buildup, its support for extraterritorial Islamist groups, the long rivalry of the Gulf Arabs and Persians, and Iranian claims of Persian Gulf hegemony.

The 1990–1991 Persian Gulf crisis and war and the lingering threat from Iraq did have the positive effect of Persian Gulf states seeking better relations with Iran. During the crisis, Iran normalized relations with Egypt, Jordan, Tunisia, and the Arabian Peninsula states. It reestablished diplomatic ties with Saudi Arabia on March 26,

1991, and subsequently Iranian pilgrims were able to participate in the 1991 hajj. Domestically, these were controversial measures, as radical members of the Majlis opposed normalization of relations with Egypt, Jordan, and Saudi Arabia because of their history of cooperation with the West.

Khatami made improved relations with Saudi Arabia and the smaller Gulf states a high priority. Iran favors using stricter OPEC oil-production quotas to elevate prices, and it needs Saudi cooperation to achieve this goal. Both nations supported a March 1999 OPEC agreement to cut output. In May 1999, Khatami became the first Iranian leader to visit Saudi Arabia since the 1979 revolution. He addressed King Fahd as Iran's "good friend," a departure from the condemnation that Iran routinely directed at the king during the Khomeini years. No longer does Iran favor the export of its revolution, though some remain suspicious of it, nor does it contend as vigorously with Saudi Arabia for primacy in the Islamic world. Iran applauded the Saudi boycott of the 1996 Middle East–North Africa Economic Summit. These two key Persian Gulf states also signed a security pact in April 2001. Private Saudi investors have indicated they could invest in Iran's petrochemical sector, but so far this has been limited. Another factor in the relationship has been the sometimes-strained relations between the United States and Saudi Arabia. Khatami's efforts also yielded restored relations with Bahrain, which had accused Iran in 1996 of attempting to overthrow its government. A lingering crisis from the shah's reign with the Untied Arab Emirates over the sovereignty of the Gulf islands of Abu Musa and the two Tunb Islands continues to keep Gulf states' relations with Iran less cordial than they would be absent this issue.

Bilateral relations between Iran and Syria intensified in 2004 and 2005, as each believed that it was being increasingly challenged by the United States. Syria perhaps felt the heat more so, with its being forced out of Lebanon in early 2005 and with U.S. allegations of its harboring Iraq Baathists and assisting the insurgency in Iraq. Syria and Iran had for many years cooperated in funneling arms and money to anti-Israeli groups in Lebanon while Israel occupied the southern part of that country. The Rafsanjani government condemned the September 1993 accord between Israel and the Palestine Liberation Organization, calling it treason. The United States has continued to accuse Iran of working to subvert the peace process through its active support of groups such as Hamas, Hizballah, and Palestinian Islamic Jihad. Khatami issued statements renouncing terrorism as a foreign policy tool but continued to maintain that armed Arab groups were waging a legitimate fight against an illegal Israeli presence in Palestine and southern Lebanon. A rapprochement between Israel and its Arab neighbors would deprive Iran of one of the main issues through which it exercises influence in the Arab world. Tehran contends that it will honor any agreement the Palestinians arrive at with Israel.

In Central Asia, the dramatic dissolution of the Soviet Union after August 1991 opened the possibility of a new sphere of Iranian influence. Iran, Saudi Arabia, and Turkey vied for influence in the newly independent Muslim republics. Although well positioned geopolitically, Iran was at a disadvantage linguistically and religiously, because Central Asians are predominately Sunni Muslims. Lacking the economic resources to pursue any large-scale ambitions, Iran has thus far sought to enhance its position through bilateral economic and cultural ties.

Iran also has contended with instability on its eastern border. In 1998 it accused the Afghan Taliban of killing nine (Shiite) Iranian diplomats in the northern part of the country. The Taliban, Sunni Muslims who sought to establish a radical Islamic theocracy in Afghanistan, had fundamental theological differences with Iran. These tensions led to an Iranian buildup of troops near the Afghan border in August and September 1998 and calls by Khatami for international cooperation in containing the Taliban. Cool heads prevailed in Tehran, and a military clash was avoided. In 1998 Iran along with China, Pakistan, the United States, and Russia formed the Six-Plus-Two group on Afghanistan, with the aim of finding ways to deal with the Taliban and al-Qaida's presence in Afghanistan. In the aftermath of the September 11, 2001, attacks, the United States launched the military action codenamed Operation Enduring Freedom to topple the Taliban in Kabul and flush out al-Qaida. Iran was helpful to the United States military, but was especially useful in the Bonn process that forged a political solution for Afghanistan.

India has become a key Iranian ally, with the two states announcing a strategic partnership in 2003. Iran in the early 1990s had looked to India as a way to escape international isolation and deflect a variety of regional challenges. Both countries now see their relationship as a move toward cementing an Iranian-Indian-Central Asian trade and transit nexus. Pakistan hopes to neutralize Iranian ties with India by proposing an Iran-Pakistan-India gas pipeline.

Even before the U.S.-led invasion in 2003 to overthrow Saddam Hussein, Iraq posed a perplexing question for Iran. Iran's Iraq policy had become one of widespread but diversified involvement that sought to secure fundamental Iranian goals. These included preserving Iraq's territorial integrity; avoiding a descent into chaos or civil war; promoting a Shiite-dominated, friendly and non-threatening regime in Baghdad; maintaining ties and influence with a wide range of Iraqi actors; and keeping the United States pre-occupied. Iran's imperative today is that Iraq not emerge as a threat, but most importantly, not become a genuinely democratic model or a Shiite-dominated state that vies with Iran for supremacy in the Shiite world. In sum, Tehran seeks to prevent Iraq's complete stabilization by a policy of "managed chaos" while hedging its bets by building ties with a wide array of key Iraqi actors. As a result, Iran hopes to maintain influence regardless of how the Iraqi political situation evolves.

Iran remains for the United States one of the world's premier outlaw states. President George W. Bush in his State of the Union address in January 2002 included Iran as a member of his so-called axis of evil, along with Iraq and North Korea. During the Clinton administration, U.S. foreign policy toward Iran had focused on containment, even as U.S. leaders declared Iraq to be the greatest threat to Gulf security. Clinton routinely opposed Iranian attempts to obtain international loans and tried to persuade allied nations to limit their trade with Iran, particularly trade involving dual-use technology that could be used militarily. The 1996 Iran-Libya Sanctions Act (ILSA) prohibits investments of more than $40 million by U.S. firms and their subsidiaries in the development of Iranian energy projects. In 1997, however, the Clinton administration acquiesced to the construction of a major natural gas pipeline from Turkmenistan to Turkey that will traverse northern Iran. Tehran complains bitterly that its efforts to moderate its policies have not led the United States to soften its anti-Iranian policies.

Although among Western nations the United States has continued to draw the hardest line against Iran, even Washington at times has signaled some interest in improving relations. In September 1998, President Clinton said, "There is no inherent clash between Islam and America. Americans respect and honor Islam." The statement was seen as significant given that Khatami spoke to the General Assembly two hours later. In December 1998, the United States deleted Iran from its list of major drug-producing nations based on evidence that poppy cultivation in Iran had been cut drastically. In April 1999, the Clinton administration issued a decision allowing U.S. companies to sell food and medicine to Iran in some circumstances.

The George W. Bush administration in its first four years dealt little with Iran except for tacit cooperation during the wars in Afghanistan and Iraq and in regard to its overarching goal of denying Iran nuclear weapons. In March 2005, citing the threat Iran posed to U.S. national interests, President Bush extended for another year sanctions originally imposed in 1995 by Clinton. In July 2001, ILSA was renewed for five more years. The United States has additionally imposed sanctions on Russian and Chinese companies for engaging in the prohibited transfer of nuclear-related technology to Iran. Just as the Iranian leadership has been highly ambivalent in setting a U.S. policy, so too Bush has not developed a coherent policy for dealing with Iran, though its rhetoric has been strong on the issues of terrorism and nuclear proliferation.

Support for Terrorism

The capture of the U.S. embassy in 1979 followed by the 444-day hostage crisis, with the explicit acquiescence of the government, set the tone of Iranian relations with the United States (and many other countries), and it resonates to this day. To the United States, the incident represents a quintessential act of state-sponsored terrorism.

In the years after the revolution, Iranian militants, with or without official state support, attempted to export the revolution by stirring up radical Islamist discontent in Bahrain, Saudi Arabia, and other Gulf states. A botched assassination attempt on senior Iraqi officials was one of the catalysts that persuaded Saddam Hussein to invade Iran in 1980. Iran's ambassador to Syria in the early 1980s provided financial and organizational support for the creation of Hizballah. Iranian officials still take pride in its support of Hizballah as a national resistance organization but deny having operational control over its decision making.

Iran routinely assassinated "enemies of the state" in Europe until mid-1994. Later assassinations focused primarily on members of the Mujahedeen-e-Khalq, but these too have ceased in recent years. Reports of Iranian ties or even an alliance with al-Qaida and the reported presence in Iran of its cadre are unproven. Iran has, however, been linked to the June 1996 bombing of the U.S. military barracks at al-Khobar in Saudi Arabia in which nineteen U.S. service personnel were killed.

Since the first Khatami election, direct government involvement in terrorist activities seems to have given way to proxy support of non-Iranian organizations. One possible reason is that prior acts had caused immeasurable harm to Iran's broader national interests. Iran does, however,

sponsor on a nearly annual basis a conference in Tehran to which key radical groups are invited. This gathering provides political or rhetorical support for the armed Palestinian groups and other entities engaged against Israel, and it also includes training, planning, and financial activities.

In September 1998, Khatami had sought to heal a major rift between Iran and the West by declaring, "We should consider the Salman Rushdie matter completely finished." Rushdie is the author of *The Satanic Verses,* a novel considered by much of the Islamic world to be blasphemous, because it contains an irreverent portrayal of a character resembling Muhammad and insinuates that the Quran might not be the word of Allah. On February 14, 1989, Ayatollah Khomeini had called on Muslims to assassinate Rushdie. The West denounced the order, and Britain and the other eleven nations of the European Economic Community recalled diplomats from Tehran in protest. The Rushdie incident left West European nations wary of moving too quickly to expand economic contacts with Iran. Despite Khatami's pronouncement, a foundation associated with militant clerics in Iran continues to reiterate its offer of $2.5 million for the killing of Rushdie.

The Nuclear Equation

Iran has been interested in obtaining a nuclear capability since the days of the shah. To that end, it has carried out research since the 1960s centered on a research reactor supplied by the United States that began operation in 1967. It had an extensive nuclear energy program underway by the mid-1970s, with a goal of producing roughly 23,000 megawatts of electrical power from a series of power stations within twenty years. The government obtained supplies through contracts with dealers in Europe and the United States. A subsidiary of Siemens of Germany agreed to build two 1,200 megawatt reactors at Bushehr, and a French company was to provide two additional 900 megawatt reactors. In 1974 Iran reportedly invested $1 billion in a French uranium enrichment plant owned by a European consortium.

Iran's indigenous nuclear fuel cycle work included plans for a new nuclear research center and the exploration of uranium mining and ore processing.

The 1979 revolution brought most of this work to a halt for several years. The war with Iraq consumed valuable resources and damaged Iran's existing nuclear infrastructure. The two reactors under construction at Bushehr were bombed several times, after which Siemens abandoned the project. The government revived the nuclear program in the late 1980s during Rafsanjani's presidency. By the early 1990s, with assistance from China, Pakistan, and Russia, progress was being made. China signed two nuclear cooperation protocols in 1985 and 1990. In 1995 Iran concluded a cooperation agreement with Russia to complete the construction of the light-water reactor at Bushehr and possibly to supply a uranium enrichment plant. Pressure from the United States precluded delivery of the plant.

Iran used Bushehr as a cover to obtain other sensitive materials. Throughout the 1990s, companies and government entities in China and Russia continued to work with Iran, despite occasional pledges from their governments to curtail nuclear assistance. During this period, Pakistan provided nuclear enrichment technology through the black market network operated by the nuclear scientist Abdul Qadeer "A.Q." Khan. In early 2005, it was revealed that Ukraine had supplied Iran with the KH-55 nuclear-capable cruise missile in 2001.

Global interest in Iran's nuclear program greatly heightened in summer 2002, with the disclosure of two previously secret nuclear sites. Iran seemed to have built or was building everything it needed to produce enriched uranium, which can fuel nuclear weapons and reactors. Since March 2003, following additional revelations that Iran had concealed nuclear work, the IAEA has been investigating Iran's nuclear history and the extent of its nuclear program.

Iran continues to assert that its nuclear program is benign, legal, and authorized by its being a non-nuclear weapon state signatory of the Nuclear Non-Proliferation Treaty (NPT): The NPT guarantees its members the right "to develop nuclear

Mahmoud Ahmadinejad

energy for peaceful purposes." Tehran maintains it is pursuing its nuclear energy program for when its petroleum resources decline. The United States vehemently rejects this contention, arguing that Iran has no need for nuclear energy and that its civilian energy program only serves to camouflage a nuclear weapons effort. Bowing to intense international pressure, Iran signed the Additional Protocol to the NPT in December 2003. Russia publicly continues to support the Iranian program to complete the Bushehr reactor and has signed multiyear agreements for additional cooperation.

For several years now, the IAEA and Britain, France, and Germany—on behalf of the European Union—have sought ways to ameliorate growing concerns about the Iranian nuclear program. The European approach—which in 2004 involved offering assistance with civilian nuclear technology provided Iran halted its uranium enrichment programs—at times appeared to offer some hope of reducing tensions surrounding Iranian activities, but the situation became increasingly urgent as revelations emerged in 2004 and 2005 about the scope of Iran's work on uranium enrichment and disregard for the NPT. Iran seems well on its way to attaining all the elements needed to produce fissile materials through plutonium or uranium enrichment. Analysts' best guess is Iran could produce its first nuclear weapon within two to three years.

Outlook

Radical-conservatives have been ascendant in Iran since local elections held in February 2003 and the controversial parliamentary elections of 2004, for which the Council of Guardians disqualified thousands of would-be candidates, including a considerable number of reformists. Mohammad Khatami's inability to make any appreciable inroads during his eight years in office coupled with the disarray in the conservative and reformist camps have left Iran badly fragmented. The conservatives achieved electoral victory through bureaucratic infighting, use of organized violence, intimidation, assassination of prominent intellectuals, jailing of leading reformers, and election manipulation. The conservatives can be expected to again employ such tactics in order to maintain their grip on power, while at the same time making enough concessions in the social and economic spheres to keep dissent at the lowest possible level. Another development, and an ominous one, has been the deliberate growing prominence of the IRGC in securing control of many levers of power and an intrusive role in the economic life of the country.

The conservatives' strong positioning does not mean that the reform movement has been a total failure or portend its disappearance. Some observers believe that Iran is ripe for a counterrevolution, especially since the uproar surrounding the February 2004 parliamentary elections. In a country accustomed to autocracy and despotism, Khatami widened Iran's democratic horizons and broadened social goals. Even under inhospitable conditions, there was a relaxation by the "moral"

police, and cultural and social policies were loosened. The media thrived, despite regime repression, and Internet activity burgeoned.

Although Iran is often viewed as a monolithic, totalitarian police state, it is a complex, pluralistic, dynamic nation in transition. Moderates espouse reform and democratization while confronting authoritarian clerical conservatives. In essence, Iranian society seeks secularization, has become highly nationalistic, and chafes under the sanctimonious piety of the hard-line theocratic establishment. Although the conservatives hold ultimate power, they realize that they can only apply repressive measures up to a point and therefore must exercise caution, permitting relaxation of some of the social and economic restrictions that have produced stagnation, political malaise, and widespread apathy. All sides to the debate in Iran recognize the carefully nuanced and delicate balancing act in play. The resurgent conservatives believe they have the answers for Iran's ills, and with the firm grip they hold on political power and the security apparatus, they hope to make inroads in resolving them. No one is willing to challenge the conservative regime with violence. The bloodletting during the revolution and the war with Iraq seem to have been enough.

The theocratic regime apparently intends to embark upon an Iranian form of the "China" model: offer economic growth, increased employment opportunities, and more limited social freedoms in exchange for continued control of the political sphere. Such an approach buys the ruling clerics, by permitting them to retain their grasp on power while continuing to reap the financial benefits of their control of the economy. Real economic reform would undermine regime stability and expose the serious deficiencies of the regime. This is to be avoided at all costs. Thus Iran is hardly ready for an economic resurgence. The extreme hard-line conservatives show little interest in genuine economic reform, instead preferring a form of crony capitalism that expends state resources on political patronage of key constituents. The more modest approach of creating limited employment opportunities and producing minor economic growth could prove successful in forestalling unrest.

Iran's political landscape will likely remain highly fragmented and somewhat schizophrenic. Despite all the failures of the reform movement and Khatami's disappointing legacy, the "genie" of democratization and reform is out of the bottle. One of the most important effects of Khatami's tenure was the spread of the language of democracy. Political discourse talks in terms of universal suffrage as the true basis of governmental legitimacy. This shift among the Iranian polity is the subject of an intense debate that will not be snuffed out by conservative political domination. The harsh realities of political life in Iran would seem to have little relationship to talk about democracy, liberalization, and political legitimacy, yet it flourishes. The award of the Nobel Peace Prize for 2003 to an Iranian woman, Shirin Ebadi, provided a major psychological boost for large numbers of Iranians.

Existing divisions in society will remain, but they will be blurred over time as Iran grapples with its myriad internal problems. On the one side are those who defend the Islamic democracy and on the other are those who espouse democratic aspirations and seek a new political vibrancy. It is likely that in post-Khatami Iran, civil society will service political gridlock and factionalism, as new channels for social networking and representation other than the Islamic government and its institutions emerge.

Iran's leaders not only confront economic crisis, but also a population in which youth comprise 65 percent of the population. Unemployment and inflation will remain rampant, fueling an ongoing poverty crisis in which a living wage is difficult to attain. The expectations of the population will remain dangerously largely unmet. At the same time, Iran's long-term economic problems create considerable leverage for the rest of the world. Iran needs expanded commercial ties with Europe, Japan, and the United States, but without a full-scale rapprochement with Washington it cannot make economic progress. Although concerted international pressures will continue to be applied to restrain Iranian nuclear program, there is a decided unity among the Iranians to proceed. Ambiguity about the full scope of the program appears to be Tehran's policy.

Iran is suspicious and anxious about U.S. intentions toward it and the region. When Tehran looks around its neighborhood, it sees Iran surrounded by U.S. political and military might. A newly elected government in Baghdad, possibly aligned with Washington, and the Karzai government and U.S.-driven political process in Afghanistan are alarming. A large U.S. naval force sits in the Persian Gulf, and U.S. troops occupy or have access to military bases in adjacent Arabian Peninsula states. Azerbaijan seeks stronger ties with the United States, as the U.S. military presence grows in a few Central Asian nations. Pakistan is becoming a strategic U.S. ally. These developments fuel the Tehran regime's paranoia about encirclement and U.S.-Israeli designs. Thus, Iran is likely to remain highly anxious and prickly to deal with and probably unwilling to compromise in any meaningful manner on its nuclear program.

CHAPTER **9**

IRAQ

More than two years after a U.S.-led invasion overthrew Saddam Hussein's Baathist regime, Iraq remained a virtual battleground, headed by an interim government relying on some 130,000 U.S. troops for security and to bring to heel an increasingly sophisticated and deadly insurgency. The work of the new government, to write a new constitution and prepare for elections for a permanent government, was overshadowed by almost daily news of suicide bombings against Iraqi civilians, officials, and security personnel as well as U.S. troops. The situation did not lend itself to credible speculation as to when an Iraqi government would be able to stand on its own.

Iraq had previously been the center of international attention during the Persian Gulf crisis of 1990–1991. The international community viewed Iraq's invasion of Kuwait as a grave threat to the world's oil supply and a brutal attack against a defenseless neighbor. The United States led a multinational force to expel Iraqi forces from Kuwait, and the resulting war devastated Iraq and left it a pariah among the countries of the world. The United Nations continued to enforce an economic embargo against Iraq for more than a decade after the war ended, and Britain and the United States regularly attacked Iraqi antiaircraft and related facilities responding to their patrolling of no-fly zones established after the war.

Despite the deprivation and suffering created by the war and embargo, Iraqi president Saddam Hussein maintained a tight grip on power. His ruthlessness and political acumen enabled him to thwart assorted coup attempts and ethnic upheavals. Into the early 2000s, he succeeded in building a cult of personality and presenting himself as the only leader capable of holding Iraq together. After his overthrow, he went into hiding. U.S. forces captured him in December 2003 hiding out near his hometown of Tikrit. The Iraqi government planned to prosecute him for war crimes.

In post–Saddam Hussein Iraq, the Shiite population appeared poised to acquire political power reflective of its majority status. A Shiite, Ibrahim al-Jaafari, was prime minister, and Shiites comprised the majority of the interim legislature. The Kurds too were prominently represented, notably by Kurdish leader Jalal Talabani, who held the position of president. The Sunnis, who had been called on by some of their leaders to boycott the legislative elections held for seats in the interim government, decided in spring 2005 that they wanted a voice in rebuilding Iraq after all, so accommodations were made to bring more of them into the drafting of a new constitution.

According to polls, most Iraqis were relieved to have the yoke of Saddam Hussein removed, but by mid-2005 they had grown weary and frustrated by the lack of personal security during the ongoing presence of foreign troops. It did not appear that Iraqi security forces would be ready to shoulder the burden in the immediate future. The Bush administration would not provide a timetable or any indication of when it expected to be able to withdraw substantial numbers of troops.

Key Facts on Iraq

Area: 168,754 square miles (437, 072 square kilometers)

Capital: Baghdad

Population: 25,374,691 (2004)

Ethnic Groups: Arab, 75–80 percent; Kurdish, 15–20 percent; Turkoman, Assyrian, or other, 5 percent

Religion: Muslim, 97 percent (Shiite, 60–65 percent; Sunni, 32–37 percent); Christian or other, 3 percent

Official Languages: Arabic, Kurdish (official in Kurdish regions), Assyrian, Armenian

Type of Government: Undetermined

GDP: $37.92 billion; $1,500 per capita (2003)

Source: Central Intelligence Agency, *CIA World Factbook,* 2004.

Geography

Iraq is located at the northern end of the Persian Gulf. The country's only access to the high seas is a thirty-mile coastline with two major ports: Umm Qasr on the Gulf itself and Basra, an inland port city at the confluence of the Tigris and Euphrates Rivers, where a 120-mile waterway called Shatt al-Arab is located. A vast alluvial plain stretches from Basra to Baghdad between the Tigris and Euphrates; this largely fertile area is interlaced with irrigation canals and small lakes and provides a home for most Iraqis. To the east and north of Shatt al-Arab lies 6,000 square miles of marshland that extends into Iran. The Syrian Desert, west of the Euphrates, continues into Jordan and Saudi Arabia. The Iraqi highlands cover the region between the cities of Mosul and Kirkuk and north to the Turkish and Iranian borders; beginning as undulating hills, the land rises to mountains as high as 12,000 feet. Rainfall in this area, unlike that for most of the country, is sufficient to support agriculture.

Iraq's most valuable national resource is oil, with reserves estimated at 112 billion barrels, a quantity second only to that of Saudi Arabia. The largest and most productive fields are located around the northern cities of Mosul and Kirkuk, with smaller fields around Basra in the south. In 1979, the year before the start of the war with Iran, Iraq produced nearly 3.5 million barrels per day (bpd). Although the war destroyed much of its oil industry, in 1989 Iraq's petroleum export earnings reached $11.8 billion, third among the members of the Organization of the Petroleum Exporting Countries (OPEC).

Before the Iran-Iraq War, most of Iraq's oil was transported through pipelines to two oil terminals at Khor al-Amaya and Mina al-Bakr on the Persian Gulf where it was loaded onto tankers. Iranian attacks against these offshore terminals and other Iraqi oil facilities early in the war, however, severely reduced oil exports. In addition, Syria, in support of Iran's war effort, reached an agreement with the government of Iran in 1982 to shut down the Banias line, a pipeline running from Iraq through Syrian territory to the Mediterranean Sea. These losses prompted Baghdad to launch an ambitious pipeline construction program to avoid future Iranian attacks, circumvent the Syrian blockade, and expand the capacity of other pipelines. (Oil pipeline map, p. 183)

The international embargo against Iraq, in place since August 1990, initially limited Iraqi oil exports to approximately 80,000 bpd, most of which went to neighboring Jordan as part of a trade arrangement approved by the United Nations. In December 1996, the UN Security Council approved Resolution 986, which allowed Iraq to sell $2 billion of oil every six months in order to purchase food and medicine. A UN committee oversaw and approved all transactions under the so-called oil-for-food program. In 1998 the UN Security Council passed Resolution 1153 allowing Iraq to export oil worth up to $5.26 billion every six months. By 1999 Iraqi oil exports had reached 2 million bpd.

Iraq possesses other rich natural resources, including natural gas, produced at the Kirkuk fields and used domestically for power stations, and limestone, which gives Iraq the capacity to export limited quantities of cement, salt, and gypsum. Iraq's potential for agricultural production is greater than that of most nations in the Middle East, but the country must import stone, metallic ore, timber, and other resources.

Demography

Once known as *Mesopotamia,* or "the land between rivers," Iraq served as a frontier province for the Persian, Greek, Roman, Arab, Mongol, and Ottoman empires. The Arab invasion in the seventh century brought Islam and the Arabic language to Iraq. No invader ever succeeded in completely conquering the region, however, and as each empire fell it left a cultural residue that survived succeeding invasions. Historically the nation's religious, communal, ethnic, and linguistic groupings have had a tendency to identify with their own parochial communities rather than with the central governing authority.

During Ottoman rule, which lasted from the sixteenth century until World War I, provincial councils granted religious communities, or *millets,* representation and self-governance in communal matters. A weak or intermittent government allowed these groups to survive as coherent, nearly autonomous entities, often in conflict with the central government and with each other.

Of Iraq's estimated 25 million citizens, approximately 75 to 80 percent are Arabs and 15 to 20 percent are Kurds, with the remaining 5 percent a combination of Armenians, Assyrians, Turkomans, Yazidis, and Sabeans. Approximately 70 percent of the population lives in urban areas around the cities of Baghdad, Basra, and Mosul. Arabic is the dominant language, especially in the valley between the Tigris and Euphrates from Basra to Mosul and the western steppe. Muslims comprise 97 percent of Iraq's population, and 60 to 65 percent of them are Shiites; the remaining 3 percent of the population is Christian, Yazidi, Jewish, and other faiths. In the seventh century, a dispute over leadership of the Muslim community split the faith into two camps, Sunni and Shiite. Shiism, which began in Iraq, endorsed the succession of Ali,

cousin and grandson of the Prophet Muhammad. Najaf and Karbala, the two holiest Shiite cities where many martyrs are buried, are located in central Iraq. They attract large numbers of Shiite pilgrims from Iran, which also has a Shiite majority, and from other Muslim countries.

Iraq's approximately 3.3 million Kurds live in the mountains of the northern and eastern sections of the country, specifically in the governorates of Irbil, Dohuk, and Sulaymaniya. The vast majority of the Kurds are Sunni Muslims who maintain their own distinct language and cultural traditions and identify with the broader Kurdish population in Turkey, Iran, and Syria.

History

In the nineteenth century, imperial Great Britain sought protection for trade routes from India and, after 1903, for the Baghdad Railroad. In 1912, while Iraq was still under Ottoman domination, British, Dutch, and German entrepreneurs obtained a concession to explore for oil in the vicinity of Basra. Two years later, the Ottoman Empire allied with Germany in World War I, and the British dispatched an expeditionary force to Iraq to maintain control. In 1920 the Treaty of

Sevres placed Iraq and Palestine under British mandate and Syria under the French. The following year Britain established a constitutional monarchy in Iraq and placed at its head Faisal ibn Hussein (Faisal I), a Meccan Hashimite prince who held legitimacy as a ruler as a descendant of the Prophet Muhammad. Iraq became independent in 1932, but British influence over the ruling elite continued for nearly three decades.

The concept of nation was alien to most Iraqis, who identified more readily with ancient local orientations. The process of fragmentation began almost as soon as the constitutional monarchy. The Kurds revolted against the central government between 1922 and 1924. The death of King Faisal I in 1933 ushered in a period of political instability that undermined the nation-building process. The first of many coups occurred in 1936, led by army officers who opposed the British and advocated socialism. These officers were in turn deposed in 1939 by pro-British and economically conservative officers who placed King Faisal's four-year-old grandson, Faisal II, on the throne. This last group controlled Iraq until 1958.

During and after World War II, anti-imperialist sentiments grew. Opposition groups demanded the reduction of British influence in the country, the liberalization of politics, and land reform. On July 14, 1958, a group known as the Free Officers, led by Brig. Gen. Abd al-Karim al-Qasim, overthrew the Hashimite monarchy. Revolutionaries killed King Faisal II, members of his family, and others associated with his regime. The new government rejected the pro-Western orientation of the monarchy and embarked on a nonaligned course. The assertive nationalism of Iraq's revolution caused concern among the United States, Great Britain, and other Western powers during the era of cold war confrontation.

The new Iraqi republic established relations with communist nations and began purchasing military equipment from the Soviet Union. In March 1959, Iraq officially withdrew from the British-dominated Baghdad Pact, which it had joined in 1955 with Great Britain, Iran, Pakistan, and Turkey. The pact, a source of great political controversy in Iraq, had been promoted by U.S. president Dwight D. Eisenhower as a means to counter Soviet influence in the region. When Iraq withdrew, the organization moved its headquarters to Ankara, Turkey, and changed its name to the Central Treaty Organization.

Iraq's domestic policies also changed dramatically under the Qasim government. Land reform laws were enacted and the political system liberalized. Segments of Iraqi society that previously had been denied access to the political process began to press parochial demands on the central government. As a result, ancient local enmities became a factor in national politics. In March 1959, army officers from Mosul tried but failed to overthrow the Qasim regime, and in 1961 Kurdish groups launched an armed rebellion against the government. On July 25 of that year Qasim laid claim to a newly independent Kuwait; Great Britain dispatched troops to Kuwait in order to thwart any Iraqi aggression.

Out of this political milieu emerged the group that would eventually dominate Iraqi politics. A pan-Arab faction opposed to the narrow nationalist policies of the Qasim government formed the Arab Socialist Resurrection Party, better known as the Baath Party. In October 1959, members of the Baath, including a young Saddam Hussein, attempted to assassinate Qasim. Aided by sympathetic members of Iraq's officer corps, the Baath Party did seize power in February 1963, only to fall nine months later as the result of a coup engineered by a group of officers led by Col. Abd al-Salam Arif. Arif died in a plane crash the next year, and his brother, Abd al-Rahman Arif, assumed the presidency. The "republican" governments of the brothers generally favored an Arab nationalist foreign policy.

A coup in July 1968 brought the Baath Party back to power. Maj. Gen. Ahmad Hassan al-Bakr, a key figure in the 1958 and 1963 coups, assumed the presidency and set a harsh authoritarian tone for his regime. A former president, two former prime ministers, numerous high-ranking officers, and prominent members of the Shiite Muslim and Kurdish communities were executed in a purge of alleged U.S., Israeli, and imperialist spies.

The real power in the new government, however, rested with Saddam Hussein, Bakr's second in command. A long-time Baath Party activist and organizer, Hussein consolidated his power through a vast and intrusive security apparatus; over time, none dared question his initiatives. As vice president, he played a key role in the government's major achievements of the 1970s: an autonomy agreement with Iraqi Kurds in 1970; the nationalization of the Iraq Petroleum Company and a military and economic cooperation treaty with the Soviet Union in 1972; and the Algiers Agreement with Iran in 1975, which ended Iranian support for Iraqi Kurds battling the Baghdad government in return for moving the boundary between the two countries from the Iranian bank of the Shatt al-Arab to the middle of the main navigable channel.

In July 1979, Saddam Hussein moved Bakr aside and took full control of the Iraqi state. The new president sought to eliminate all rivals within the Baath Party and the military. In addition, members of the Iraqi Communist Party and Islamic opposition groups faced harassment and persecution. In order to thwart any challenge from Islamist quarters, Hussein ordered the execution in April 1980 of Ayatollah Muhammad Baqir al-Sadr, a prominent Shiite cleric, as part of a massive crackdown. The regime allowed no dissenting voices.

Iran-Iraq War

The war with Iran overshadowed all other issues in Iraq from September 22, 1980, when Iraq attacked Iran, until July 18, 1988, when Iran agreed to a cease-fire. By waging war against Iran, Saddam Hussein sought to regain total control over the Shatt al-Arab and expand Iraq's power in both the Gulf and the Arab world. He also aimed to destabilize—if not topple—the vulnerable government in Iran; eighteen months after the 1979 revolution, individuals and groups were still fighting for influence and the military was in disarray following purges of officers who had supported the shah.

A year after the war began, however, it became obvious that the Iraqi government had miscalculated. Initial success quickly turned to failure as a combination of poor strategy and bad tactical execution brought the invasion to a halt. By June 1982, Iran had driven the Iraqi army back to its own border. Hussein announced a unilateral cease-fire and expressed a willingness to negotiate through the Saudi Arabian government and other potential mediators. Iran ignored the proposals, and in July 1982 it launched an attack across the border toward Basra. The Iraqi army halted the offensive, but the war degenerated into a bloody stalemate on Iraqi territory.

In the first years of the war, Iraq had few international supporters. The Baath Party's repressive treatment of communists and the greater geopolitical importance the Soviet Union placed on Iran led Moscow to suspend the delivery of weapons to Baghdad. Soon after the war began, Libya, North Korea, and Syria began supplying Iran with Soviet military equipment, apparently with Moscow's blessings; Israel, too, secretly supplied Iran with military spare parts. The conservative Arab nations on the Persian Gulf initially hedged their support for Iraq out of concern that Iran, in its revolutionary zeal, might retaliate against them. At first, France was the only Western nation to support Iraq's war effort.

As the war dragged on, however, and as Iran's foreign policy became more aggressive, many Arab states and some nations in the West began to support Iraq actively in order to contain the export of Iran's revolution. Jordan, Kuwait, and Saudi Arabia expedited the transport of consumer goods through their ports to compensate for closed Iraqi port facilities. Moreover, Kuwait, Saudi Arabia, and other Gulf states extended Iraq tens of billions of dollars in aid and interest-free loans. To compensate for Iraq's loss of oil revenues, Kuwait and Saudi Arabia agreed to sell 300,000 barrels a day of their own oil to Iraq's customers, with the understanding that Iraq would pay it back at some future date. The Soviet Union resumed arms shipments to Iraq in 1983.

Fearing the consequences of an Iranian victory, Western governments and most Arab nations continued supporting Iraq despite internal repression by Hussein's regime, Iraqi attacks on neutral ships doing business with Iran, and Iraqi air strikes against Iranian cities and poison gas attacks against Iranian troops. In part because of the war, Iraq and the United States restored diplomatic relations on November 26, 1984. (Iraq had severed ties with the United States during the June 1967 War because of its support for Israel.) However, in 1986 the U.S.-Iraqi relationship suffered as a result of the disclosure that the administration of President Ronald Reagan had sold arms to Iran in an effort to build contacts among Iranian moderates and win the release of U.S. citizens held hostage in Lebanon by Iranian-backed forces. Iraq also accused the United States of providing it with false intelligence information.

In May 1987, an Iraqi jet fired a missile at the USS *Stark,* killing thirty-seven crew members. The United States accepted Iraq's explanation that the attack was an accident. The relationship between the two wary nations improved that summer, when the United States began naval patrols in the Persian Gulf to halt Iranian attacks on Kuwaiti ships, but became strained once more in 1988 when the Reagan administration vigorously condemned Iraq for using chemical weapons against Kurdish rebels and civilians.

After several Iranian offensives in 1986 and 1987 failed to capture Basra, Iraqi forces pushed the exhausted Iranians back across the border in the spring and summer of 1988, causing Iran finally to accept a cease-fire. Although the war ended with Iraqi victories that allowed Saddam Hussein to claim success, the eight-year conflict had left hundreds of thousands of Iraqis dead while achieving none of his goals. Moreover, it had seriously damaged Iraq's economy by drastically reducing oil exports and requiring huge expenditures on defense. To pay for the war, Iraq had gone into debt and liberally injected new currency into its economy. The resulting inflation reduced the value of the Iraqi dinar and squeezed most workers, who had to be content with prewar salaries. Iraq needed a period of economic recovery during which it could pump and sell oil reserves at capacity to rebuild the country.

Persian Gulf Crisis and War

Iraqi society was exhausted from the war with Iran, and the nation's debts totaled a staggering $80 billion. As the leader of the nation that had turned back the Iranian threat, Saddam Hussein felt that Arab and Western powers were indebted to him and should forgive Iraq's wartime debts. During the first half of 1990, Hussein and his lieutenants believed that Kuwait and the United Arab Emirates were cheating on oil production quotas; in their view, these two countries' high output was keeping prices low and thus reducing Iraq's sorely needed oil revenues. On August 2, 1990, Iraqi forces drove into Kuwait and occupied the country after facing minimal resistance. Dredging up an old historical claim, Hussein declared Kuwait to be Iraq's "nineteenth province" and announced Iraq's intention to annex it, and its oil wealth, permanently. The United States and its allies, including Saudi Arabia and the Persian Gulf states, moved quickly to contain the Iraqi threat and prevent Baghdad from gaining control over 20 percent of the world's oil reserves. Within a few weeks, tens of thousands of foreign troops were deployed to defend Saudi Arabia and its oil fields from any potential Iraqi military thrust. By the end of the year, more than half a million troops had reached the Gulf region and were preparing to expel Iraq from Kuwait.

U.S. policy toward Iraq focused on persuading its government—and Saddam Hussein in particular—that the United States and its allies were serious about waging war and that, if war began, Iraq would lose. U.S. policymakers thought that Saddam's instinct for survival would lead him to withdraw from Kuwait if he believed he and his army would face a crushing defeat. If he refused to pull out, they reasoned, it was because he grossly overestimated his army's capabilities or believed that the United States was bluffing.

Evidence suggests that Hussein was not convinced that the United States would attack Iraq, especially if the war were likely to be a long one. According to the Iraqi transcript of a July 25, 1990, meeting in Baghdad between him and U.S. ambassador April Glaspie, Hussein remarked, "Yours is a society which cannot accept 10,000 dead in one battle." Arab, European, and U.S. diplomats who had dealt with Hussein in the past had reported that U.S. conduct of the Vietnam War had greatly influenced his opinions about the United States. His strategy seemed to be to present Washington with the prospect of an extremely bloody war by heavily fortifying Kuwait. If U.S. leaders perceived that coalition casualties would be high, they would be unlikely to order an attack; if the coalition did attack, Hussein hoped that by inflicting heavy casualties, Iraqi forces might cause U.S. public backing for the war to erode, as it had during Vietnam, thus forcing the administration of President George Bush to seek a negotiated peace on terms favorable to Iraq.

It is also possible that Hussein accepted the fact of the impending war with the U.S.-led coalition and hoped to manufacture political victory out of military defeat, as did one of his heroes, President Gamal Abdel Nasser of Egypt in the 1956 Suez crisis and June 1967 War with Israel. By taking on Israel, Nasser had raised his prestige in the Arab world. Similarly, Hussein's confrontation with a coalition made up of the United States, former European colonial powers, wealthy Arab Gulf states, and others already had made him the most popular leader in many areas of the Arab world. If his forces could give the coalition a good fight and strike a few blows against Israel, Hussein would become a legend among dispossessed Arabs frustrated by Arab military weakness and passivity. Through military defeat, Hussein, like Nasser, could solidify his reputation as the only Arab leader willing to go to war to defend Arab rights and interests. In the process, he could weaken the pro-Western Arab regimes that had sided with the international coalition.

The theory that Saddam Hussein invited war is supported by his half-hearted efforts to avoid it.

During the crisis, Arab and Western officials put forward numerous diplomatic plans designed to allow the Iraqis to save face. Hussein and his diplomats did not seize any of them with sufficient vigor or flexibility to achieve a negotiated settlement. He even rebuffed two last-minute diplomatic initiatives by the French and by UN Secretary General Javier Pérez de Cuéllar, when a positive response could have yielded substantial propaganda benefits.

Air and Ground Campaign

The war that began on January 17, 1991, proved to be a disaster for Iraq. Before invading Iraq and Kuwait with ground forces, coalition aircraft carried out a thirty-seven-day aerial and sea-based bombing campaign that severely damaged Iraq's military industries and civilian infrastructure. Iraq was virtually helpless against the high-tech assault of Western aircraft. Rather than see the Iraqi air force destroyed, Hussein sent more than one hundred warplanes to Iran, which impounded them.

When the ground attack began on February 24, Hussein's vaunted army collapsed. Tens of thousands of Iraqi troops surrendered without firing a shot, and entire Iraqi tank units were obliterated by the coalition assault. In addition, the Arab nations that had joined the U.S.-led effort remained firmly in the coalition despite Iraq's conventional missile attacks against Israel. Hussein was celebrated in the occupied territories and in Palestinian refugee camps, but the magnitude of his army's defeat and the brutality of the Iraqi forces that had occupied Kuwait limited his appeal in most of the Arab world.

One hundred hours after the ground attack began President Bush ordered a cease-fire. Iraq signed agreements to abide by a series of UN Security Council resolutions that established its postwar conduct. The international embargo that had been imposed shortly after the invasion of Kuwait remained in force.

Ethnic Rebellion

Following Iraq's defeat and sensing a weakened Saddam Hussein, the Kurdish minority in northern

Iraq and the Shiites in the south rebelled against the regime in Baghdad. U.S. president Bush called upon the Iraqi people and military to overthrow their leader. Early in the fighting, in March 1991, it appeared that the rebellions might pose a danger to the regime, but despite the vast amount of military equipment lost during the Gulf war, Hussein still had enough military muscle in reserve to squelch his enemies.

The two rebel movements had a long history of grievances with the ruling regime. Since the collapse of the monarchy, Iraq had been ruled by Arab Sunnis, which contributed to the frustration and political alienation of Iraq's Kurdish and Shiite citizens. The Shiites posed the most complex political problems for Hussein's regime; they were, and remain, a generally less affluent majority whose political and military advancement has been limited. Over time, the wretched living conditions in most Shiite villages prompted a massive urbanization of the poorest and least educated of their numbers, which gave rise to sprawling urban slums.

Antiregime protests had taken an increasingly religious turn under Baath rule, and the Iranian revolution of 1979 radicalized existing Shiite political movements. Islamic opposition parties flourished in Iraq, especially around the Shiite holy cities of Najaf and Karbala, traditional centers of religious scholarship and activism. Some of these parties, such as the Supreme Council for the Islamic Revolution in Iraq (SCIRI) and al-Dawa, continued to challenge the Baath hold on power.

The Kurds, with significant populations in Iran and Turkey and smaller numbers in Syria and the Soviet Union, generally maintain a separate, salient identity. Their society was once tribal in organization but has become increasingly urbanized. After five major conflicts and nearly a decade of intermittent guerrilla warfare from 1961 to 1970, a stalemate ensued, with Kurdish forces occupying the highlands and the Iraqi army holding the valleys. By 1974 Kurdish forces had become better equipped and more numerous—an estimated 100,000 strong. They occupied favorable terrain and proved themselves to be excellent mountain fighters. War broke out again in 1975, but this time a reequipped and retrained Iraqi army soon gained the upper hand, driving Kurdish forces to the Iranian border. The shah of Iran supplied military equipment to the Iraqi Kurds for a time, but he was unwilling to use his armed forces against Iraq on their behalf. When the shah signed the Algiers Agreement and vowed to end Iranian support of the Kurds in 1975, they were forced to capitulate. Many were imprisoned, and more than 200 of their leaders were executed. Thousands fled to Iran to escape further suppression by Baghdad.

Relations between Baghdad and Tehran deteriorated when Ayatollah Ruhollah Khomeini deposed the shah in 1979. Iraqi and Iranian forces skirmished along the borders, and the Iraqi military battled resurgent Kurdish guerrillas. The war between Iran and Iraq that began in 1980 prevented Hussein's regime from focusing its armed might against the Kurds; soon after the cease-fire was concluded in summer 1988, however, Baghdad initiated a military campaign, Anfal ("spoils"), to break the Kurdish resistance. The campaign drew international condemnation, in part because the army used poison gas against Kurdish villages and camps in northern Iraq. Thousands of Kurds fled into Turkey.

The 1991 rebellions had divergent goals. The Iraqi Kurdistan Front, a coalition of the two largest Kurdish parties, wanted to establish an independent Kurdish state in northern Iraq. The Shiites, however, hoped to overthrow Hussein and establish a Shiite-led government in Baghdad. Although less organized than the Kurds, the Shiites did receive support from Iran.

Hussein's success at crushing the Kurdish and Shiite rebellions led Washington to take steps to protect these two groups. It established "no-fly" zones, patrolled by U.S. and British warplanes, into which no Iraqi aircraft could enter. The Kurds received substantial U.S. humanitarian aid, totaling more than a half billion dollars; the Shiites received more modest humanitarian assistance.

Containment and Confrontation

Although Iraq did not repudiate the UN Security Council resolutions by which it had agreed to abide after the Persian Gulf War, it resisted implementing them. UN Security Council Resolution 687, adopted on April 3, 1991, linked the lifting of economic sanctions to the government's compliance with the UN Special Commission (UNSCOM), which was charged with documenting, monitoring, and eliminating Iraq's nuclear, chemical, biological, and ballistic missile weapons programs. Baghdad resisted UNSCOM's inspections and its overall efforts to prevent Iraq from rebuilding its weapons programs, which prompted the UN Security Council to continue the international embargo against Iraq.

The United States periodically employed military force to give teeth to its containment policy toward Iraq. For example, U.S. warplanes attacked the country on January 13, 1993, after Iraqi provocations toward Kuwait. Five months later, U.S. president Bill Clinton ordered missile strikes against the Iraqi intelligence service headquarters in Baghdad after evidence surfaced that Iraq was responsible for a foiled assassination plot against former president Bush during his visit to Kuwait earlier in the year. In October 1994, Clinton ordered 36,000 U.S. troops, as well as aircraft carriers and additional air force squadrons, to Kuwait and Saudi Arabia in response to Iraqi troop movements on the Kuwaiti border. Although Hussein backed down and recognized Iraq's long-disputed border with Kuwait, the cycle of crisis and confrontation continued.

Shortly after the war, several Iraqi opponents of Saddam Hussein sought to close ranks against the regime, some at the behest of the Bush administration. The Iraqi National Congress (INC), formed in 1992 and based in Iraqi Kurdistan, brought together representatives of many of the established opposition groups, including the Kurdistan Democratic Party (KDP), the Patriotic Union of Kurdistan (PUK), and the Supreme Council for the Islamic Revolution in Iraq. In August 1995, Hussein Kamel Hassan al-Majid, former minister of industry and director of military industrialization and Saddam Hussein's son-in-law, defected to Jordan. His flight from Iraq signaled the possible fraying of the president's inner circle. Although Majid and his

brother returned to Iraq to meet their deaths in January of the next year, many analysts thought the regime in Baghdad might be in its final days. Reports of Saddam Hussein's demise, however, proved premature.

On August 31, 1996, Hussein's military forces captured Irbil and delivered a major blow to Iraqi opposition forces there. Prior to the strike, the KDP and PUK had been at odds over sharing political power and revenues acquired from trade to Turkey through Iraqi Kurdistan. The KDP claimed that Iran was providing support for the PUK, so KDP leader Massoud Barzani invited Hussein to come to his aid. Hussein's quick hit broke Iraqi National Congress operations in Irbil and sent a signal that he could, and would, use military force against those who opposed his regime. Washington responded by bombing antiaircraft sites in southern Iraq.

The Iraqi regime also benefited from "sanctions fatigue" among Arab countries and members of the UN Security Council. Although few Arabs had any illusions regarding Saddam Hussein's tyranny, many questioned whether the toll that sanctions had taken on the Iraqi people was worth the price, especially since Hussein and his clan seemed to be prospering. Within the Security Council, China, France, and Russia preferred policies and initiatives that offered sanctions relief once Iraq complied with its disarmament obligations. In March 1997, U.S. secretary of state Madeleine Albright clarified U.S. policy: the United States would work to keep sanctions in place as long as Saddam Hussein ruled Iraq.

During a period of increasing tensions between the Iraqi government and UNSCOM inspectors over access to so-called sensitive or presidential sites, on October 29, 1997, Iraqi deputy prime minister Tariq Aziz announced that Baghdad would no longer allow the United States to participate in the inspection teams inside Iraq. The Iraqi position on cooperation with UNSCOM hardened, and Baghdad again called for the immediate lifting of sanctions. The crisis carried into 1998 as the United States threatened military action to force Iraqi compliance with UNSCOM inspections. Iraq again backed down, this time by signing a memorandum of understanding with UN secretary-general Kofi Annan on February 23, 1998. Many hoped that Annan's intervention would allow UNSCOM inspectors to complete their work with the cooperation of Iraqi officials.

The lesson of the crisis of 1997–1998 for Hussein and his government was that confrontation, not cooperation, offered Iraq the best means of lifting sanctions and ending the weapons inspections. Despite the memorandum of understanding, Iraqi officials showed little good faith in working with UNSCOM inspectors. On August 5, 1998, the government of Iraq again ended cooperation with UNSCOM inspectors and demanded a timetable for lifting the economic embargo. On October 31, Baghdad terminated all cooperation with UNSCOM after the Security Council refused to support initiatives favorable to Iraq regarding a "comprehensive review" of the sanctions issue. The United States again threatened military action, and Baghdad again backed down. On November 14, following a last-minute Iraqi agreement to cooperate with UNSCOM, President Clinton called back U.S. warplanes en route to bomb Iraq.

U.S. policy toward Iraq further toughened in response to Saddam Hussein's machinations and provocations. On October 31, 1998, President Clinton signed the Iraq Liberation Act into law, calling on the United States to take active measures to bring about a change of regime in Iraq. To this end, the United States intensified its efforts to unify the Iraqi opposition. The application of military force became a regular part of the new, hardline U.S. policy toward Iraq. On December 16, President Clinton ordered a four-day bombardment after UNSCOM executive chair Richard Butler submitted a scathing report to the United Nations regarding Iraqi noncompliance with UN weapons inspectors. U.S. warplanes hammered targets associated with Saddam's military, security, and intelligence services. In the months after Operation Desert Fox, as it came to be known, U.S. and British warplanes regularly bombed antiaircraft and related sites in northern and southern Iraq in what many consider a low-grade war against Hussein's government.

The U.S. campaign appeared to shake, at least temporarily, the Iraqi president's hold on power. In January 1999, he lashed out, calling for the overthrow of those Arab governments that did not oppose U.S. air strikes on Iraq. That same month, Ayatollah Sadiq al-Sadr, a leading Shiite cleric, was killed in southern Iraq, presumably by government assassins. The Iraqi government took additional measures to deal with the growing challenges from antiregime forces in northern and southern Iraq. While dissent from within and confrontation abroad were nothing new to Hussein, his regime appeared increasingly isolated at home and in the international arena.

Economy and Society

More than two decades of dictatorship, war, and sanctions have taken a heavy toll on Iraq's economy and society. Iraqi GNP fell by more than half, from $38 billion in 1989 to close to $17 billion in 1992, with GNP per capita falling from $2,160 to $907 over the same period. The fiscal policies the Iraqi government used to deal with the loss of oil export earnings contributed to hyperinflation and increases in the prices of basic goods and services. The lack of foreign exchange meant a reduction in imports, causing the price of such goods, including food and medicine, to rise disproportionately relative to the purchasing power of Iraqi households.

The UN sanctions hit Iraq's sanitation and health systems especially hard. The breakdown of Iraq's electrical power system contributed to chronic problems for its sewage and water treatment plants. Poorly functioning sanitation systems, unsafe drinking water, and inadequate diets resulted in chronic malnutrition and a proliferation of diseases among Iraqi children. According to a Fourth Freedom Forum report, between 1991 and 1998 the mortality rate for children under five years of age rose dramatically, calculated as a minimum of 100,00 excessive deaths to a maximum of 227,000. (Of these, one-fourth were thought to be war-related.) The sanctions led to social ills, including a rise in crime and in the number of street children, uncommon in Iraqi society prior to

1990. Many professionals and educated citizens were forced to find unskilled employment in order to make ends meet, and scores in the professional classes sought exit permits to escape the deprivations of life under sanctions.

Imports of food and medicine allowed under the UN oil-for-food program improved the plight of some Iraqis. Basic caloric intake increased as food became more readily available, especially in those areas under the control of the Kurdish regional government—a political coalition of the PUK and KDF established after the Gulf war and protected in part by U.S. no-fly zones. Subsequent UN Security Council resolutions also allowed Iraq to import the machinery and spare parts necessary to rebuild its infrastructure, especially its oil facilities and electrical, sanitation, and water treatment plants.

The Iraq War and Occupation

Frustration marked the last years of the Clinton administration's dealings with Saddam Hussein as he resisted UN resolutions on the disarmament of Iraq's weapons of mass destruction. Sanctions remained in force, and the United States and Britain continued to maintain the no-fly zones in the southern and northern sections of the country. Still, the perception was that sanctions were ineffective. The idea of regime change gained favor in Washington circles, and assistance began to flow to select Iraqi exile groups.

Some members of the George W. Bush administration that took office in January 2001 had long advocated removing Hussein by force, but their thinking did not become policy until after the attacks of September 11, 2001. Although the immediate response to that operation was to go after the Taliban and al-Qaida in Afghanistan, planning for an invasion of Iraq accelerated. Throughout 2002, the Bush administration publicly hammered away at Hussein—accusing him of developing weapons of mass destruction, having links to al-Qaida, and posing a threat to Iraq's neighbors and to the United States—in making a case to justify going to war. By the beginning of 2003, the only question seemed to be when the war would begin. Although Washington failed to secure a final UN Security Council resolution authorizing action against Iraq, on March 19, 2003, U.S. aircraft opened the war on Iraq with strikes on targets that intelligence sources had identified as the possible locations of Hussein and his inner circle. *(For details on the war and its aftermath, see The Persian Gulf, Chapter 4, p. 137)*

It took little more than a month for coalition forces, led by the United States and Britain, to fight their way through Iraq and take the main cities. Major figures in the Baathist regime fled but were captured or killed within a year. Coalition forces found Saddam Hussein in December 2003. Although active hostilities ended by April 14, the coalition faced growing problems in restoring public services and suppressing an increasing level of anticoalition violence carried out by Hussein loyalists, Sunni Arab Iraqi nationalists, opportunists and criminals, and Islamist extremists from Iraq and other countries. Scattered anticoalition attacks gradually escalated into a full-scale insurgency. As coalition military targets became hardened against attack, the insurgents turned their attention to Iraqi targets. The Iraqi police and the Shiite community suffered disproportionate numbers of casualties. After the city of Fallujah, west of Baghdad, fell to the control of insurgents, combined U.S. and Iraqi forces fought their way into the city in November 2004. The battle of Fallujah further turned Sunni Arabs against the United States and the Iraqi interim government.

Toward Sovereignty

In early 2003, the Bush administration created the Coalition Provisional Authority (CPA), run out of the U.S. Department of Defense, to oversee the transfer of authority back to Iraqis after the invasion. It in turn, established the Iraqi Governing Council (IGC), an appointed body charged with working with the CPA on the handover of sovereignty. The United Nations blessed the arrangement in Security Council Resolution 1511.

Ibrahim al-Jaafari

The drafting of the Transition Administrative Law (TAL) to serve as an interim constitution would be key to facilitating the return of sovereignty. On November 15, 2003, the plan was announced to complete the TAL by February 28, 2004, transfer sovereignty on June 30, 2004, and hold direct elections (rather than a system of caucuses as originally preferred by the United States) for a national assembly. Adnan Pachachi, a prominent Sunni exile, returned to head a team of Iraqi and U.S. legal specialists who worked from late 2003 into early 2004 drafting the TAL. The IGC approved it on March 8, 2004.

The TAL provided for a strong prime minister and vested some supervisory and veto power in a three-person presidential council. It also stipulated that elections for a transitional national assembly would be held no later than January 31, 2005; the assembly would then have until August 15, 2005, to draft a permanent constitution, which should be put to a referendum by October 15, 2005. Elections for a permanent government would take place by December 15, 2005, with the government taking office no later than December 31, 2005.

Iraq suffered from numerous problems—poverty, high unemployment, a violent insurgency, inconsistent security forces, and persistent factional infighting—and the CPA had only begun to address them when it announced its intention to hand over power to an interim Iraqi government on June 30, 2004. Nevertheless, the Bush administration felt the consequences of delaying the process too adverse. On June 1, the Iraqi Governing Council dissolved itself immediately following the surprise announcement that an interim government had been sworn in. The creation of the government ended a struggle among the CPA, IGC, and UN envoy Lakhdar Brahimi over who would head it. The IGC's choice of Ghazi al-Yawar, a businessman from the large Shammar tribe who had been in exile in Saudi Arabia, became president, while Iyad Allawi, a Shiite returned from exile and head of the Iraqi National Accord, accepted the prime ministership. To avert an anticipated uptick in violence on the date set for the official transfer of authority, the CPA secretly relinquished power to their interim government two days early, on June 28, to the interim government.

Toward a Constitution and Permanent Government

With an interim government in place, the United States and the new Iraqi leadership turned to elections for the new 275-seat National Assembly on January 30, 2005. Elections were to be held at the same time for governing councils in the eighteen governorates as well as in the autonomous Kurdish areas for a 111-seat Kurdish National Council.

The United Iraqi Alliance emerged as the overwhelming favorite. The coalition of sixteen largely Shiite parties was dominated by the Supreme Council for the Islamic Revolution in Iraq and its leader, Abd al-Aziz al-Hakim, and received the endorsement of Ayatollah Ali al-Sistani, Iraq's most widely respected senior cleric. A number of alliance members were followers of the rebel Shiite leader Muqtada al-Sadr. Other groups in the running included the Iraqi List, a coalition of six parties headed by interim prime minister Allawi; the Kurdistan Alliance, comprising the two major Kurdish parties—the Kurdistan Democratic Party and the Patriotic Union of Kurdistan—along with some Assyrian and Chaldean Christians; and some communist and monarchical groups.

One of the United Iraqi Alliance candidates was the prominent exile Ahmad Chalabi. His organization, the Iraqi National Congress, had received support from the U.S. government for providing intelligence on Iraq, and speculation abounded during the war that the Pentagon would push Chalabi to take leadership of the interim government. Chalabi, however, had little support within Iraq, having spent decades living outside of the country; in addition, a Jordanian court had convicted him of embezzlement in absentia. On May 20, 2004, Iraqi police backed by U.S. forces raided INC headquarters in Baghdad amid allegations that Chalabi had passed classified information to Iran. In August an Iraqi judge issued a warrant for Chalabi's arrest on counterfeiting charges, which were later dropped. He won a seat in the new National Assembly in January 2005 and continued to play a role in Iraqi politics.

Despite fears that insurgents would cause major disruptions, the elections went off relatively smoothly. To no surprise, Shiite candidates won a majority of the seats. The United Iraqi Alliance garnered 48 percent of the vote, followed by the Kurdistan Alliance, with 26 percent. The Iraqi List finished third, with 14 percent. None of the other lists obtained more than 2 percent. A large number of Sunni Arabs failed to vote, most likely because they were intimidated by insurgent threats or because they heeded Sunni leaders' calls to boycott the elections. Some Sunni leaders had requested that the elections be postponed for six months for fear that large numbers of people would not be able to vote because of the poor security situation. There were also calls to boycott the elections to protest U.S. actions in Fallujah and the ongoing occupation.

The National Assembly was created to serve as the country's parliament until the approval of a new constitution and subsequent elections. It was also expected to reach a security agreement and a status of forces agreement for the operation of foreign forces in Iraq, because the CPA had not concluded a formal accord before it disbanded in June 2004. More immediate problems, however, ensued during the opening sessions in February and March.

The political wrangling that began over the largely ceremonial position of Speaker intensified with differing opinions on such key matters as control of oil revenues, the adoption of personal status law, and the role of Islam in Iraqi politics. On April 3, 2005, Hajim al-Hasani, a prominent Sunni Arab and industry minister in the interim government, was eventually appointed Speaker. His appointment broke the deadlock over the formation of the new government, leading to the selection of a three-person presidential council. Two days later, the assembly voted to elect Jalal Talabani, head of the Patriotic Union of Kurdistan, as president. At the same time, Adil Abd al-Mahdi, a prominent Sunni, and Ghazi al-Yawar, a Sunni, were elected vice presidents. The presidential council soon thereafter named Ibrahim al-Jaafari, leader of the Shiite al-Dawa, as prime minister.

Outlook

The Iraq government formed in 2005 must confront a number of important and potentially divisive issues. Among them is the growing compartmentalization of Iraq into three separate Kurdish, Shiite, and Sunni Arab regions. Although the Kurdish north has not declared itself independent, it expects to continue to exercise a high degree of autonomy and to have veto authority over any major changes that might affect it. Kurdish leaders have been adamant that Kirkuk, an oil-producing city, be recognized as Kurdish, and many Arab residents resettled in and around Kirkuk by the Baathist regime have been forced out.

Dealing with the continuing insurgency ranked as a high priority for the interim government, particularly as the increasing balance of attacks in early and mid-2005 occurred against Iraqi police, political figures, and citizens. While a few kidnappings of foreigners received attention around the world, the far more numerous kidnappings of Iraqis for ransom did not.

Effective reconstruction of the Iraqi army, national guard, and police forces proceeded at a painfully slow pace. The disbanding of the Iraqi army by the CPA meant that new security forces had to be created from scratch; officers were carefully vetted for their allegiance to the former regime. Only about 4,000 troops, instead of a projected 27,000, had been recruited by early 2005. The Iraqi national guard had approximately 40,000 recruits on hand or trained out of a projected 62,000. In addition, the quality of the forces and their effectiveness as demonstrated during the insurgency remained questionable. It did not help matters that the insurgents frequently targeted security personnel and recruits for their perceived collaboration with the U.S.-led coalition. The role that private militias might play in the new Iraq remained unresolved. Although the occupying forces regarded Muqtada al-Sadr's Mahdi Army as marginal, it continued to show force in several Iraqi cities. Given that the government might prove incapable of disarming the militias, officials considered finding a way to co-opt them within the state structure.

The continuing presence of coalition troops, especially U.S. forces, created a thorny situation. One of the first priorities of the interim government was to negotiate a status of forces agreement with the United States and to define the role of the U.S. embassy vis-à-vis the emerging government. This presented itself as no easy task given the wide divergence of opinion among Iraqis— ranging from those who supported the U.S. presence and benefited from it to those who violently opposed it—and the centrality of a stable Iraq to the Bush administration's foreign policy.

Paralleling this concern was the U.S.-led effort to internationalize the burden of reconstruction and state building. After the invasion, Washington sought to engage the United Nations to provide legitimacy and expertise for the emerging government. The United States also attempted to find donors willing to provide financial contributions. Some eighty countries participated in a donors conference held in Madrid October 23–24, 2003, and promised to add $13 billion to the U.S. pledge of $20 billion. These figures, however, fell well short of the target amount of $56 billion that the World Bank and the United Nations declared necessary for the following four years. The United

States also went in search of countries willing to help share responsibility for security, as a number of coalition partners began to withdraw their troops.

There is little doubt that Iraq's economic recovery will be long and difficult. Attacks on oil pipelines meant a continued reliance on international assistance, as Iraq could not use oil revenues to finance reconstruction. In addition to the physical destruction of infrastructure and to the casualties of war, unemployment soared; in late 2003, it was estimated that as many as 70 percent of adult males were unemployed. It took many months to restore electricity and other utilities. Food distribution, sanitation, health care, education, and transportation became pressing issues. Outside aid remained slow in coming, despite international pledges. Even U.S. government assistance was held up by bureaucratic procedures: a year and a half after the war, only $1 billion of the $20 billion earmarked for Iraqi reconstruction had been spent. State subsidies for gasoline and electricity ran at least $10 billion a year. Most Iraqis were dependent on the Public Distribution System, the successor to the UN oil-for-food program, which added a financial burden of about $4 billion a year to the government and destroyed the market for local production as a result of the bulk purchase of wheat and other grains from abroad.

The nature and extent of Iran's influence in postwar Iraq has thus far been relatively low-key. Iranian concerns primarily revolve around the status and welfare of its Shiite co-religionists in Iraq and of Najaf and Karbala. Tehran, however, was and will remain concerned about the shape of the new Iraqi regime, given historical relations with Iraq. In addition, Iran feels itself being squeezed by a hostile United States, which created a new pro-U.S. government in Afghanistan on Iran's eastern border, stationed some 150,000 troops adjacent to Iran's western border, kept ships in the Gulf, and accessed bases around the Gulf. While Iran supported and armed anti-Hussein groups before the war and assisted their entry into Iraq during the 2003 war, it appeared to be content in the aftermath to keep a low profile, providing discreet assistance to Shiite parties while maintaining its distance.

The most pressing and fundamental task of the interim government is the formulation of a new permanent constitution. Although the Transition Administrative Law specified that the first draft of the constitution had to be completed by August 15, 2005, there were reasons to believe that agreement would not be reached by that date. This was due in part to the nature of the TAL, a document cobbled together in negotiations between the Coalition Provisional Authority, the Iraqi Governing Council, and various factions. Although only a majority of Iraqi voters are required to approve a new constitution, the stipulation that at least one-third of the voters in sixteen out of eighteen Iraqi provinces endorse it made the approval process more complicated. This provision, originally conceived to provide the Kurdish provinces with a veto over the constitution, also provided a veto for the minority Sunni Arab central provinces. Provisions allow for a possible extension of the TAL if a constitution is not approved as originally scheduled.

The drafting of the constitution must take into consideration key areas of disagreement over the federal nature of Iraq, the type of government (a presidential system or a parliamentary system with a strong prime minister), and the nature and extent of personal freedoms. The role of Islam, particularly the degree to which the constitution and laws should rely on sharia (Islamic law), is a potential minefield.

The interim government also grappled with growing corruption in the ranks of officials, as it potentially threatens the regime's legitimacy and credibility. At the same time, it was aware that its credibility depended on its ability to restore functioning utilities and to create employment opportunities for the hard-pressed population.

CHAPTER 10

ISRAEL

Hostile relations with neighboring Arab states have been the central feature of Israel's political, economic, and social condition since its founding in 1948. Treaties signed with Egypt (in 1979) and Jordan (in 1994) and an uneasy engagement with the Palestinians since 1991 have established Israel's place among the nations in the region, yet the Jewish state is yet to know a time of total peace. It has fought five wars against the Arabs—in 1948, 1956, 1967, 1973, and 1982—and openly battled Palestinians in the West Bank, Gaza Strip, and Jerusalem during uprisings from 1988 to 1991 and from 2000 to 2005. By early 2005, the initial signs appeared of an Israeli-Palestinian cease-fire, a rapprochement with the possibility of reinvigorating diplomatic efforts to address Israel's continuing occupation of Palestinian territories conquered in June 1967.

None of the participants are predicting a quick settlement of such long-contentious disputes as Palestinian control of the West Bank and other areas in which Palestinians have historically lived, return of the Golan to Syria, or the status of Jerusalem. Israeli leaders of different political stripes agree, however, that the potentially greater threat posed by Iran is a powerful incentive to move beyond the deadlocks of the Arab-Israeli dispute.

Moreover, Israel faces substantial internal challenges. Public resentment continues to grow concerning the privileges and state subsidies accorded the growing Orthodox population. Israeli leaders also must deal with the long-simmering antagonisms between its Ashkenazi and Sephardic populations, the two primary groups that hail from the West and from the Mediterranean region and the East, respectively. Although both are Jewish, economic disparities between the two groups divide them. Additionally, Israel confronts the challenge of striking a balance between the sometimes-conflicting objectives of continuing as a Jewish state specifically created to be just that and its desire to be a modern democratic nation with an Arab minority approaching 25 percent.

The overriding necessity of surviving in a region with enemies on three sides has to an extent kept Israel's domestic tensions at a relatively low level. Since early in its history, Israel made a point of building and maintaining the most potent fighting force in the Middle East and of keeping Arab states and the Palestinians in check through a strategy of deterrence based on its military strength. It also developed an officially unacknowledged nuclear weapons capability with delivery systems. Since the June 1967 War, Israel has positioned itself as a staunch U.S. ally.

Ruling the 2 million Palestinians residing in the West Bank, Gaza, Golan, and East Jerusalem—the territories seized by Israel during the June 1967 War—did not prove to be too costly for the Israeli public or its leaders until December 1987, when the intifada, or uprising, began. The costs of occupation that emerged as a consequence of the rebellion forced Israel to seriously consider a means of ending its control over the Palestinians while at the same time preserving its security and other national interests.

Key Facts on Israel

Area: 8,019 square miles (20,770 square kilometers)

Capital: Israel declares Jerusalem its capital, but this designation is not recognized internationally. Tel Aviv is the diplomatic capital.

Population: 6,276,883 (includes Israelis in the occupied territories) (2005)

Religious/Ethnic Groups: Jewish, 80 percent; non-Jewish 20 percent (Muslim, 80 percent; Christian, 10 percent; Druze, 10 percent) (2003)

Official Language: Hebrew; Arabic used officially for Arab minority; English widely spoken

Type of Government: parliamentary democracy

GDP: $129 billion; $20,800 per capita (2004)

Sources: Central Intelligence Agency, *CIA World Factbook,* 2005, and Department of State, *International Religious Freedom Report,* 2003.

After the 1992 election victory of Yitzhak Rabin and his Labor Party, Israel began a more concerted diplomatic effort to construct a compromise with the Palestinians and neighboring Arab states. In the early 1990s, the collapse of the Soviet Union, a financial patron and arms supplier of some Arab states, and the decisive defeat of Iraq during the 1991 Persian Gulf War strengthened Israel's negotiating position. With encouragement from Washington, a diplomatic process ensued with the Palestine Liberation Organization (PLO), and subsequently Jordan, that produced peace agreements and initiated the transfer of limited powers of self-rule to the Palestinians in the occupied territories.

After the initial handover of some occupied areas to Palestinian control, Israeli leaders and PLO representatives—now empowered as ministers and leaders of the nascent Palestinian Authority (PA), the governing entity established to oversee Gaza and Jericho in May 1994—continued their diplomatic efforts to establish Palestinian self-rule in other areas of the West Bank and Gaza.

After the second Palestinian uprising, or al-Aqsa intifada, Israeli prime minister Ariel Sharon promoted a "disengagement plan" that promised to permanently remove most if not all Israeli military forces and all 7,000 settlers from Gaza by the end of 2005. The ultimate territorial extent of Palestinian rule, the powers of the Palestinian Authority, the status of the 250,000 Israeli settlers living in the West Bank and 200,000 others residing in parts of East Jerusalem, and the future of Jerusalem and of Palestinian refugees residing outside Palestine are among the myriad issues that remain to be resolved.

Geography

Israel is a small country, about the size of New Jersey, created on the former territory of Palestine. It sits between the Mediterranean Sea and a crescent of Arab nations: Lebanon to the north, Syria to the northeast, Jordan and the West Bank (the latter with pockets of PA rule) to the east, and Egypt and the Gaza Strip (also with PA rule) to the southwest. Despite its small size, Israel contains three disparate geographical regions: the coastal plain, the most populous region, situated in the east and running from Haifa in the north to Tel Aviv in the south; the Galilee, a hilly and lush region in the north dominated by the Sea of Galilee; and the Negev Desert, located in the south and lacking material and natural resources.

With the exception of the Negev, which is hot and dry throughout the year, most of the country enjoys a temperate climate. Water is an important commodity in Israel because of the small amount of rainfall: twenty-eight inches annually in the north, nineteen to twenty-one inches in the central regions, and only one to eight inches in the Negev. Large investments have been made on desalinization, irrigation, and water conservation projects, and water has featured prominently in Israel's disputes with Jordan, Syria, and the Palestinians on the West Bank.

Almost totally devoid of natural resources of any commercial value, Israel in its early years concentrated on agricultural production. Today, however, chemical manufacturing, diamond cutting and polishing, and the development of high-technology products with commercial and military applications have surpassed agriculture as the most important areas of Israel's economy. One out of every four Israeli workers is employed directly or indirectly by the arms industry. Even the kibbutzim, the socialist agricultural cooperatives that were the most prominent and literal expression of the Jews' "return to the land," now earn more of their income through manufacturing and land development than from agricultural production.

The government owns and manages 77 percent of the country's area, and as a matter of policy, it never sells land. The Jewish National Fund, an organization established in 1897 for the purchase and management of land for Jews, owns 8 percent of the country's land, including a considerable amount transferred directly from the government; it manages another 8 percent on behalf of the government. The fund's statute prohibits the sale or lease of land to non-Jews, although exceptions sometimes are made. A ruling in early 2005 by Israeli attorney general Menachem Mazuz has called this discriminatory practice into question. Foreigners are allowed to freely purchase or lease land in the remaining 7 percent of Israel.

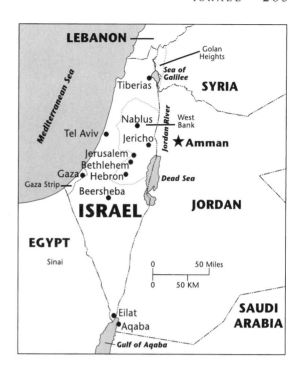

Demography

Creation of the State of Israel in 1948 resulted in cataclysmic demographic changes. During the 1940s, more than half a million Palestinian Arabs fled Arab-Jewish fighting over control of Palestine or were expelled by Jewish (and later Israeli) forces, ensuring an overwhelming Jewish majority of approximately 85 percent in the newly created state. Israel is unique as a state in that it was specifically constituted for Jews: Jews everywhere are automatically entitled to Israeli citizenship.

In 1948 some 100,000 Jewish refugees and Holocaust survivors languishing in European "displaced persons" camps immigrated to Israel. The next year saw an even more massive influx of Jewish immigrants, including 250,000 from Libya, Poland, Romania, and Turkey, and almost 50,000

from Yemen alone. From May 1950 to December 1951, Israel organized the emigration of 113,000 Jews from Iraq. As a result of this influx, by 1951 Israel's Jewish population, at 650,000 in 1948, had more than doubled, to 1.4 million. The most recent wave of large-scale immigration began in the early 1990s and consisted of almost 1 million Jews from the former Soviet Union, mainly from Russia. Highly educated and ambitious, tens of thousands of these immigrants continue to arrive in Israel every year. A much smaller number of Jews also have recently emigrated from Ethiopia. Although Israel is a nation created by immigrants primarily from Europe, Israelis originate from more than a hundred countries. Among Israel's Jewish population today, 57 percent are native born, 24 percent hail from Europe and the Western Hemisphere, and 19 percent were born in Asia or Africa. Those of Western origin are called Ashkenazim. Jews from Eastern lands and the Mediterranean region, including Greece, Iraq, Morocco, Spain, and Turkey, are called Sephardim. The Sephardim and their native offspring now make up 60 percent of

Israel's Jewish population. Arabs comprise approximately 18 percent of the total population.

Much has been made of antagonisms between the Ashkenazim and Sephardim. These animosities and differences are as much the product of the economic gulf dividing the two communities as any cultural dissimilarities. The Ashkenazim are Israel's founders, the original Zionist "pioneers" and ideologues; political Zionism is a European creed, calling for the ingathering of the Jews. The institutions of the state—the Knesset (parliament) and, most significant, the army—are Ashkenazi creations to which the Sephardic majority came late and the Arab minority hardly at all. Israeli society in its early days was predominantly European and reflected the traditions of Ashkenazi Jews.

Israel's leadership welcomed the waves of Sephardic immigrants in the 1950s, but many of them, largely poor and illiterate, were forced to live in shantytowns far from the established Jewish settlements along the coastal plain, breeding resentment toward the better-off Ashkenazim. Further complicating relations, the Ashkenazim viewed their co-religionists from Yemen and Iraq with disdain and not a little chauvinism. To Ashkenazi eyes, the key to Sephardim integration into Israeli life relied on their adoption of the dominant Ashkenazi culture. Such assimilation proved impossible for the Sephardim, who possessed a varied and vibrant heritage of their own. In addition, their comparatively large families, lack of education, and meager financial resources put them at additional disadvantage.

The disparities dividing the two communities persist. In educational and economic achievement and political representation, the Sephardic majority still suffer from the structural barriers erected in previous generations. In times of recession, the poor Jewish residents of the inner city and development towns, along with Israeli Arabs, particularly feel the brunt of retrenchment and cutbacks in state services.

Israeli society also suffers from religious divisions. All issues of religious identification, marriage, birth certification, and divorce are the province of the religious establishment, which, while supported by the state, exercises this authority relatively independently. Many citizens, however, object to the Orthodox religious authorities' exclusive control over marriage, divorce, and burial. Their powers in these areas also extend to non-Orthodox Jews. The Orthodox refuse to recognize marriages or conversions to Judaism performed in Israel by Conservative or Reform rabbis. A large number of Jews who wish to be married in secular or non-Orthodox religious ceremonies do so abroad. The Interior Ministry recognizes such marriages although the Orthodox do not. The role of the Orthodox in personal matters has been a source of sharp division within Israeli society, particularly in recent years, as thousands of Jewish immigrants from the former Soviet Union and Ethiopia have brought with them family members not recognized as Jewish by Orthodox authorities.

The government provides proportionally greater financial support to institutions in the Jewish sector compared with those in the non-Jewish—Muslim, Christian, and Druze—sector. For example, only 2 percent of the budget for the Religious Affairs Ministry goes to the non-Jewish sector, despite Muslims, Christians, and Druze constituting 20 percent of the population.

Israel's Arab minority are ostensibly full citizens of the state—they carry Israeli passports, they vote, and Arab politicians hold seats in the Knesset—but as a community they suffer state-supported economic and political discrimination as non-Jews in a Jewish state. Such discrimination is written into law and is apparent in economic development and government assistance. The Israeli government does not provide its Arab citizens with the same quality of education, housing, employment, and social services as it does Jews, and in addition, government spending is proportionally far lower in predominantly Arab areas than in Jewish areas. Israeli Arab organizations have challenged the government's Master Plan for the Northern Areas of Israel on the grounds that it is discriminatory. The plan lists among its priorities increasing the Galilee's Jewish population and preventing the territorial contiguity of Arab villages and towns.

Israeli Arabs, relative to their numbers, are underrepresented in the student bodies and faculties of most universities and in the higher-level professional and business ranks. Well-educated Arabs are often unable to find jobs commensurate with their level of education. Arabs holding doctoral degrees confront the greatest problems in this regard. A small number of Israeli Arabs have risen to responsible positions in the civil service, but generally only in the Arab departments of government ministries. The government allocates only very limited resources to enforcing landmark legislation from 1995 prohibiting discrimination in employment, and local officials and representatives of quasi-national institutions have obstructed implementation of a High Court ruling asserting the right of Arabs to purchase state lands.

Israel in practice forbids its Arab citizens to work in companies with defense contracts or in security-related fields; it also excludes them from compulsory military service. The Israeli Druze and Circassian communities are, however, subject to the military draft, and although some have refused to serve, the overwhelming majority accept service willingly. Some Bedouin and other Arab citizens not subject to the draft serve voluntarily. Citizens excluded from the draft have less access than other Israelis to social and economic benefits, because military service is sometimes a prerequisite or provides advantages in obtaining housing, homeowner subsidies, and government or security-related industrial employment. In an exception to the rule, the social security child allowances are equal for parents (including Arabs) who do not serve in the military or attend a yeshiva (a Jewish seminary) and those who have done so.

Government and Religion

Israel has a parliamentary form of government with a prime minister and a president. The prime minister is head of government and is responsible for maintaining a ruling coalition and for running the government. The powers of the president, as head of state, are quite limited. From 1996 until the election of Ariel Sharon in 2001, the prime minister was popularly elected. The prime minister is now once again selected by the party having won the most seats in parliamentary elections. The Knesset, Israel's unicameral parliament, consists of 120 members. To form a government, the prime minister must assemble a majority of at least 61 members from the various and disparate parties represented in the Knesset.

Israel's method of proportional representation all but guarantees a faction-ridden parliament and successions of coalition governments. Never in Israel's short history has a single party commanded a Knesset majority and thus ruled as a single bloc. Unlike members of the U.S. Congress or British Parliament, Israel's legislators do not stand for election as representatives from a geographic district. Rather, their primary allegiance belongs to their party. Candidates selected by the party apparatus run on a single slate, and the electorate casts votes for a party rather than for a particular candidate.

The percentage of votes a party receives determines the number of seats allocated to it. To qualify for a Knesset seat, a party must garner at least 1 percent of the votes cast. The total number of votes for all eligible parties is then divided by 120 to determine the minimum number of votes required for each seat. Each party is given the largest number of seats possible. Any seats not distributed in this fashion are awarded to those parties with the largest number of remaining votes. If any seats still remain unassigned, they are given to the parties with the largest number of seats.

Economy

Israel's economic development has been shaped by its isolation from the markets of neighboring countries, its lack of natural resources, and its extraordinary expenditures on defense.

Israel has an advanced industrial economy, and its citizens enjoy a high standard of living, with a 2004 per capita income of $19,800. Unemployment rose to 10.7 percent in 2004 but was substantially higher, sometimes double the national average, in the country's peripheral regions and among low-skilled workers. In recent years, an increase in income inequality has accompanied rapid economic growth. The long-standing gap in levels of income between Jewish and non-Jewish citizens continues, and regional income disparities also appear to be growing. Heavy reliance on foreign workers, principally from Asia and Eastern Europe, is a source of economic as well as social problems. Such workers—about 11.8 percent of the labor force in 2003—generally find employment in the agriculture and the construction sectors.

Beginning in the early 1990s, the Israeli economy experienced a profound transformation. Buoyed by a political rapprochement with Jordan and Egypt, the beginnings of an agreement with the Palestinians, and the substantial increase in population from the former Soviet Union, the Israeli economy averaged growth of 6 to 7 percent in the first half of the decade. Israel's economic managers have found success in reorienting the economy away from the traditional low-tech and heavy-industry sectors into services and the production of products for high-tech industries. Gross foreign direct investment rose from 0.7 percent of GDP in 1990 to 3 percent of GDP in 2002.

Israel's economic transformation from socialism to dynamic entrepreneurial capitalism is an impressive, if underacknowledged, international success story. The government-instituted economic reforms and policies created a global high-tech powerhouse in the industries of semiconductors, computer software, telecommunications, and biomedical equipment. Net foreign investment rose sharply, from $505 million in 1992 to some $3.4 billion in 1997. The U.S.-Israel Free Trade Agreement contributed greatly to an expansion of bilateral trade to $18 billion in 2002. Israel has concluded free trade area agreements with four other countries, the European Free Trade Area (EFTA), and the European Union.

As rapprochement with the Arab world stalled in the mid-1990s, so too did Israel's prospects for economic integration that was supposed to boost regional demand for Israeli products and services. The outbreak of the al-Aqsa intifada in September 2000 and the failure of efforts to reach a final status agreement with the Palestinians and Syrian severely depressed economic prospects. Economic growth slowed substantially beginning in the latter part of the 1990s, decreasing from 7.1 percent in 1995 to 1.9 percent in 1997, before increasing by 4.3 percent in 2004. Israel remains well positioned to compete in the knowledge-intensive industries of the twenty-first century, and its economy has the potential to grow at some 4 to 5 percent per year.

Israel's proportion of scientists, engineers, and other skilled personnel in the labor force is high by international standards, and Israeli companies are rapidly developing experience in the business aspect of transforming technology into marketable products and services. Further, the ongoing structural transformation of the economy, especially its shift from traditional to higher-value goods and services, should add to Israel's growth potential in the near future.

Israel receives an annual grant of approximately $2.7 billion from the United States—making it the single largest recipient of U.S. foreign aid—and approximately $500 million in grants from the world Jewish community. In 2003 it spent 7.3 percent of almost $110 billion in GDP on defense. Israel has invested a large portion of its national wealth in creating an arms industry, primarily to ensure a reliable source of supply. Since the 1970s, however, the maintenance and expansion of a defense industry producing top-of-the-line weapon systems for the Israel Defense Forces (IDF) required Israel to join the international competition for foreign arms sales. Israel is today one of the world's leading arms exporters. Its military-industrial complex and diamond-cutting sector now dominate industrial production and export sales, a significant change from the era when citrus and agricultural products were the country's most significant earners of foreign currency and its most popular international symbols.

History

Since the Roman destruction of Jerusalem's Second Temple in 70 C.E., the return to Zion has been a leitmotif of the Jewish people. In the mid-nineteenth century, the confluence of political emancipation, race-based theories of nationalism, and state-sponsored anti-Semitism throughout Europe created the conditions for an organized effort to establish Jewish sovereignty in Palestine. Early Zionist thinkers argued that the immutability of anti-Semitism and the "otherness" of Jews in nations that were created as expressions of non-Jewish cultural or racial purity and pride required that Jews too create their own nation. Such proponents included Moshe Hess, an associate of Karl Marx and author of *Rome and Jerusalem,* the first Zionist tract; Leo Pinsker, who in 1882 at the outset of the Russian pogroms wrote *Autoemancipation*; and Theodor Herzl, author of the seminal *Jewish State.*

Creating a Jewish State

From 1882 to 1914, more than 2.5 million Jews emigrated from Eastern Europe, the heart of Ashkenazi Jewry, with the overwhelming majority relocating to countries in the West. Only small numbers of ideologically committed Jews, Zionists, immigrated to Palestine, where they established a variety of communal and capitalistic agricultural settlements. Herzl, to gain popular support for his idea of a Jewish state, convened the First Zionist Congress in Basel, Switzerland, in 1897. The World Zionist Organization was established at this conference as part of a program whose stated goal was "to create for the Jewish people a home in Palestine secured by public law." While Herzl and his successors tried to win diplomatic recognition for a Zionist enterprise from the European and Ottoman powers, from 1910 onward the exponents of "practical Zionism," notably Chaim Weizmann, worked to create a new reality in Palestine by fostering Jewish settlement that would be difficult to uproot.

The exigencies of World War I prompted Britain on November 2, 1917, to issue the Balfour Declaration, which promised British support for "the establishment in Palestine of a national home for the Jewish people." The statement was designed to gain Jewish support for the British

war effort and to help ensure British control over Palestine should the shaky Ottoman Empire collapse. Britain, however, conditioned its support for a Jewish national home on the understanding that "nothing shall be done which may prejudice the civil and religious rights of existing non-Jewish communities in Palestine" who comprised the majority of the population. This policy established the contradictory impulses that would affect British actions toward Palestine until the declaration of Israel.

With the defeat of the Ottoman Empire in World War I, Britain and France collaborated to divide its Middle Eastern holdings. Palestine was placed under mandatory authority, a new form of colonial supervision. In 1920 the League of Nations legitimated the British mandate in Palestine. Although the yishuv, the growing Jewish community in Palestine, viewed the mandate as an opportunity to expand Jewish control there, Palestinian Arabs, the majority of the population, saw British rule as a further obstacle to independence, which had been granted or promised to Egypt, Iraq, Lebanon, and Syria. The yishuv therefore adopted a strategy of cooperation with the British authorities and under their protection constructed the administrative, economic, and military building blocks for Jewish sovereignty. Palestinian Arab efforts failed to halt or slow Jewish immigration and takeover of their land. Organized around factional clan-based groupings, and not having the ear of the British authorities, as did the Zionists, Palestinian Arabs could neither hold on to their patrimony nor attain independence.

In 1947, overextended and exhausted from trying to meet the conflicting nationalist demands of the Jewish and Arab populations of Palestine, Britain announced that it would terminate its mandate and withdraw on May 15, 1948. The fledgling United Nations came to be entrusted with the problem of determining the successor regime to the mandate. On November 29, 1947, the UN General Assembly proposed the partition of Palestine into separate Arab and Jewish states and the internationalization of Jerusalem. The Zionist leadership supported the UN decision and prepared for statehood.

Leaders of the Palestinian Arabs and the Arab League, the federation of Arab states formed in 1944, rejected partition on principle.

The succeeding months brought scattered warfare between Palestinian and Jewish irregulars throughout Palestine. On May 14, 1948, David Ben-Gurion, the head of the Zionist Executive, the leadership body of the yishuv, declared the establishment of the State of Israel and became the country's first prime minister and defense minister. From May until January 1949, armies from Egypt, Iraq, Jordan, Lebanon, and Syria fought unsuccessfully to abort Israeli statehood. Although the warring parties eventually signed armistice agreements, they failed to fix permanent boundaries or to establish a contractual peace.

Arab-Israeli Wars

The issues left unresolved after the first Arab-Israeli war, from 1948 to 1949, remained a source of constant confrontation in succeeding decades. On four subsequent occasions—1956, 1967, 1973, and 1982—this endemic conflict erupted into full-scale military hostilities.

In October 1956, Israel launched an invasion of the Sinai Peninsula aimed at toppling Egyptian leader Gamal Abdel Nasser, opening the port of Eilat to maritime commerce, and neutralizing Palestinian guerrilla attacks from Gaza. Israel launched the attack in coordination with the British and French, who saw their regional interests, including control of the Suez Canal, threatened by Nasser's regime. The invasion succeeded in opening Eilat to international commerce, but it also boosted rather than deflated Nasser's prestige. Under strong U.S. pressure, Israel was ultimately forced to withdraw to the pre-invasion boundaries. *(See Chapter 2 for more on the 1956 Suez crisis and war.)*

In June 1967, Israel launched an attack against Egypt and Syria. In the ensuing days, the Israeli armed forces captured the Syrian Golan, Jordanian-controlled West Bank (including East Jerusalem), Egyptian-administered Gaza, and Egypt's Sinai Peninsula. Israel thus gained control of what had

been mandatory Palestine. The argument was then made to hold on to these lands, because the addition of territory on three fronts gave Israel the "strategic depth" needed to defend its borders.

In the absence of diplomatic progress after the 1967 war, Egypt and Syria launched a coordinated offensive on October 6, 1973, with the limited objectives of recovering the territories they had lost in June 1967. Their attack took Israel by surprise. In the Sinai, Egypt breached Israel's Bar-Lev Line, strongly fortified positions along the east bank of the Suez Canal, while on the Golan, Syrian advanced early in the fighting. Within days, however, the tide turned and Israel gained the military advantage. In negotiations following a cease-fire, Israel and Syria signed a disengagement agreement. Egyptian-Israeli talks resulted in an interim agreement on the Sinai.

In June 1982, Israel invaded Lebanon in an attempt to destroy the political and military power of the PLO, which had successfully frustrated Israeli efforts at attaining Palestinian acquiescence to permanent Israeli rule in the occupied territories; Israel had annexed the Golan in 1981 (but the measure was not recognized internationally). Israel also wanted to establish a new political order in Lebanon based on the rule of the Christian Phalange Party led by Bashir Gemayel. The Israelis aimed additionally to humiliate Syria and end its historical influence over Lebanese affairs. Although the Israeli military dominated the battlefield and destroyed Syrian air defenses in its 1982 invasion of Lebanon, the war failed to achieve its objectives. Instead, the invasion contributed in 1983 to the ignominious end of Menachem Begin's long tenure.

Politics and National Security

The victory of Menachem Begin's Likud Party in 1977 had been a political earthquake. For the first time in Israel's history, the Labor Party—the political embodiment of Israel's state-building generation—was removed from power. The Likud's platform expressed no ambiguity in its view that the West Bank—"Judea and Samaria" in

Likud's vocabulary—was an inseparable part of the Land of Israel, promised by God to the Jewish people. It replaced the Labor alignment's security rationale for remaining permanently in the occupied territories with one based upon divine right.

Unfettered by Labor's desire to maintain a negotiating posture that did not rule out some degree of withdrawal from the territories as part of a future peace agreement, Likud embarked on an ambitious settlement drive throughout the West Bank and Gaza, expanding the areas that Labor had marked for eventual annexation. Likud's settlement program attempted to create a new reality of more than 100 Jewish settlements and hundreds of thousands of Jewish settlers in the territories. Likud's leaders believed that such a settlement program would subvert any attempt to trade territory for peace as outlined in UN Security Council Resolutions 242 and 338, adopted after the 1967 and 1973 wars.

Worsening economic conditions, highlighted by a November 1980 announcement of an annual inflation rate of 200 percent, set the stage for Israel's 1981 election contest. Labor fielded a team headed by Shimon Peres, party leader since 1977, and Yitzhak Rabin, a former prime minister and perennial challenger to Peres's leadership. Labor and Likud each won forty-eight seats in Knesset balloting. The preference of the religious parties for Likud led to a coalition government headed by Begin and marked Labor's second consecutive defeat.

The 1984 elections took place against the backdrop of military quagmire in Lebanon and growing economic problems. Begin—stunned by the death of his wife and traumatized by Israel's troubles in Lebanon and its failure to end the PLO's political challenge to Israeli hegemony in the occupied territories—resigned the premiership in August 1983. His successor, Yitzhak Shamir, a veteran of the Jewish underground in Palestine and the Mossad, the Israeli intelligence agency, was initially viewed as a caretaker whose tenure would not disrupt the ambitions of Likud's second generation, which included Moshe Arens, David Levy, and Ariel Sharon. In the months following

his appointment, Shamir wrestled with rapidly rising inflation and dwindling foreign currency reserves, a crisis in Israel's Lebanon policy that portended a controversial, indefinite occupation of parts of that country, and incipient challenges to his leadership by the Likud's young guard.

The 1984 elections resulted in a national unity coalition government unique in Israeli history. The willingness of Israel's two major political blocs to rule together suggested that the issues separating them were more apparent than real. There had been one unity government previously, formed in the months before the June 1967 War and under Labor's leadership. The 1984 coalition agreement, however, called for an unprecedented rotation of the premiership between Shamir and Labor Party leader Peres. Each man would serve as prime minister for two years while the other would serve as foreign minister. Both major parties would be awarded an equal number of cabinet portfolios.

It was widely believed that such a two-headed government amounted to a prescription for disaster, but it confounded expectations. It tamed inflation without a significant increase in unemployment or decrease in purchasing power, postponing if not solving the country's economic problems. It effected a partial withdrawal of Israeli forces from Lebanon, leaving troops to occupy only a strip of southern Lebanese territory.

Colonization efforts in the occupied territories continued uninterrupted, albeit at a slower pace, during the stewardship of Peres as well as Shamir. Labor's Rabin managed policy in the occupied territories during the government's entire four-year tenure. It was during his tenure as defense minister that a new chapter was written on Israel's "iron fist" policy, a series of tough, repressive measures against the Palestinians under occupation. Attempting to quell growing Palestinian resistance to Israeli efforts to further entrench the occupation, Rabin resurrected the deportation and administrative detention of Palestinians, two measures that had fallen into relative disuse during the Begin era.

The national unity government established after the 1984 elections served a full four-year term, and the 1988 elections became in large measure a public referendum on the record of this political accommodation. The election, conducted against the background of the Palestinian intifada and a poor economy, confirmed popular support for the hard-line policies the unity government employed against the uprising. Labor, led by Peres, won thirty-nine Knesset seats, as did Shamir's Likud. The U.S. decision to begin a "substantive dialogue" with the PLO in December 1988, after PLO chairman Yasir Arafat renounced terrorism, contributed to the decision of Labor and Likud to reestablish a national unity government.

The new government, however, unlike its predecessor, would function under the unchallenged leadership of the Likud. The terms of this power-sharing agreement made Shamir prime minister for the entirety of the government. Labor's Rabin remained in the post of defense minister, the second-most-powerful position in Israel. Peres accepted the finance portfolio, a measure of his eclipse as a political force.

Intifada

The intifada erupted after the deaths of four Palestinian day laborers from the Gaza Strip in the second week of December 1987. As the van in which they sat waited at a military checkpoint, an Israeli in a truck struck it. Their funerals attracted thousands of demonstrators whose protests evolved into years of organized Palestinian resistance to lift the occupation. *(Also see Arab-Israeli Conflict, Chapter 2, p. 13.)*

Confrontations between Palestinians of all ages and the Israeli military and Jewish settlers became a constant feature of life in the occupied territories. Almost five hundred Palestinians and approximately twenty-five Israelis were killed within two years, undermining the assumption that Israel could indefinitely maintain its occupation of Palestinian lands. By 1993, the year Israel and the PLO signed the Declaration of Principles recognizing each other's legitimacy, the Israeli Information Center for Human Rights in the Occupied Territories reported that since the outbreak of the intifada 1,067 Palestinians had been killed by Israeli soldiers, 54 Israeli soldiers had been killed by Palestinians, 67 Palestinians had been killed by Israeli civilians, and 97 civilians had been killed by Palestinians.

Israel's response to the Palestinian protests, which involved the sustained participation of all sectors of the Palestinian community, was grounded in its long-standing determination to crush any opposition to Israeli rule. Thus, Israel ignored Palestinian political demands—halting the Israeli policies of de facto annexation and generating negotiations. Instead, Defense Minister Rabin stated on January 21, 1988, that Israeli policy would be one of "force, might, and blows." By the end of February, 80 Palestinians had been killed and 650 wounded in confrontations generally pitting stone-throwing Palestinians against Israeli soldiers armed with M-16s. The U.S.-based Physicians for Human Rights issued a report charging the Israeli government with implementing "an essentially uncontrolled epidemic of violence by soldiers and police in the West Bank and Gaza Strip, on a scale and degree of severity that poses the most serious medical, ethical, and legal problems." In January 1989, Amnesty International charged that the methods Israel employed in its unsuccessful effort to end the uprising "show that the Israeli government is apparently not willing to enforce international human rights standards." As television broadcast around the world the display of Israel's overwhelming force against the Palestinians, international sympathy began to flow toward the Palestinians.

The political program of the uprising had always linked the allegiance of Palestinians in the occupied territories to the leadership of the PLO. The decision of the Palestine National Council to recognize Israel and endorse UN Resolutions 242 and 338 in November 1988, almost one year into the intifada, was seen as a victory for Palestinians under occupation who had long urged the PLO to adopt a realistic diplomatic posture toward Israel.

The intifada proved to be a vital component in the PLO's diplomatic effort toward winning Israeli withdrawal from the occupied territories and the realization of a Palestinian state in the West Bank and Gaza Strip with East Jerusalem as its capital.

It convinced Israeli leaders that a new framework had to be created that would permit them to retain strategic control of the West Bank and Gaza Strip without the burdens of ruling a Palestinian population hostile to continued occupation. Despite the creation of the Palestinian Authority in 1994, however, Israel continued to exercise wide-ranging control over the movements and activities of Palestinians under nominal PA rule. These restrictions were expanded considerably during the course of the al-Aqsa intifada, imposing unprecedented hardship on Palestinian social, economic, and national political life.

Persian Gulf Crisis

On the eve of August 2, 1990, Iraqi president Saddam Hussein ordered Iraqi troops to invade Kuwait. Thus began an occupation that would unite most of the international community, including much of the Arab world, in a coalition against Iraq. *(The Persian Gulf, Chapter 4, p. 137)*

Hussein linked the Arab-Israeli conflict to Iraq's invasion, offering a mutual withdrawal whereby Iraqi forces would leave Kuwait when Israeli forces withdrew from the West Bank and Gaza. His offer was rejected. After the U.S.-led coalition began a massive air assault on Iraq on January 17, 1991, Iraq targeted Israel with conventional Scud missiles in an attempt to undermine the Arab coalition arrayed against him. The Iraqis fired thirty-nine Scuds at Israel between January 17 and February 24, 1991. Although the missiles killed few Israelis, more than 200 injuries were reported, hundreds of homes and apartments were damaged by falling debris, and thousands deserted metropolitan Tel Aviv in search of temporary safe haven in peripheral areas.

Israel had prepared an array of military options in case of an Iraqi attack, ranging from a commando raid into western Iraq to destroy Scud launchers to Iraq's nuclear destruction. Despite intense internal pressure, Prime Minister Shamir refrained from attacking Iraq as long as it did not employ nonconventional weapons—chemical, biological, or nuclear agents—against Israel. This policy was actively encouraged by the United States, anxious to keep the Arab countries in the coalition from bolting, as it was thought they might balk at fighting on the side of Israel against another Arab country. For this show of restraint, the United States generously rewarded Israel after the war. In 1991, in addition to the annual $3 billion in military and economic support packages, the United States provided Israel an additional $3 billion for expenses incurred during the war.

The United States, anxious to forestall another Middle East conflict in which the prospect of the use of nonconventional weapons loomed large, took the lead in arranging an international peace conference that convened in October 1991 in Madrid, Spain, with the Soviet Union as cosponsor. After opening ceremonies, separate, bilateral, and later multilateral discussions were held between Israel and Jordan (and Palestinians), Lebanon, and Syria without formal U.S. mediation. Although arrangements in Madrid allowed Israel to uphold its refusal to negotiate directly with the PLO, it became obvious that the Palestinian contingent of the joint Jordanian-Palestinian negotiating team made decisions only after consulting with the PLO leadership based in Tunis.

1992 Elections

Israel held elections in June 1992 in the aftermath of the Gulf crisis and amid the sporadic, albeit unsettling, violence of the intifada. Also, the Shamir government's provocative diplomatic and economic support for settlement expansion throughout the West Bank began to have a profoundly negative impact on U.S.-Israeli relations. The administration of President George Bush had objected to the Israeli failure to honestly apprise the United States of its settlement policies and therefore refused to approve $10 billion in loan guarantees that Israel had requested to help settle the influx of new immigrants from the former Soviet Union.

Rabin, Labor's prime ministerial candidate, differentiated between settlements built for political purposes and those necessary for security. Shamir, meanwhile, continued to pledge that "not one inch" of the occupied territories would be ceded to the Palestinians. For a great many Israelis, however, Shamir's intransigence and its effect on relations with the United States, coupled with the intifada, proved enough to sway swing voters into trying something new.

Although Likud won a majority of Jewish votes, Labor garnered five additional seats, while Likud lost eight. The smaller parties made the most impressive gains. To secure a majority and form a ruling government, Labor joined with leftist parties, including two Arab parties. For the first time in Israeli history, the ruling party was in the unusual, and vulnerable, position of relying on Arab seats to form a government.

Shamir had led Likud to its worst electoral showing since the mid-1960s. It won only thirty-two seats, the same number, ironically, as Labor had won when it ceded power to Menachem Begin's ascendant Likud in 1977. Rabin ran on the message that he could be trusted with safeguarding Israeli security and with leading the country out of economic stagnation and rising unemployment. This strategy resulted in the most personalized, nonideological Labor campaign ever, with Rabin running a U.S.-style presidential operation that all but excluded from public view the other, largely dovish politicians on Labor's list. As a result, Labor's improvement over its 1988 showing came wholly at Likud's expense, and it provided a margin of victory that enabled Rabin to form a government without the religious parties or Likud. Also by ousting Shamir, Israeli voters sent a strong message to the PLO leadership. Chairman Arafat observed that "it was the results of the Israeli election that made a deal first seem possible."

Palestinian-Israeli Peace Accords

Notwithstanding Rabin's victory, Palestinian-Israeli talks—held under the auspices of the 1991 Madrid conference—remained stalemated. Looking for another negotiating vehicle, Israel and the PLO opened secret discussions in Norway in February 1993. After numerous meetings by lower-level officials, Israeli foreign minister Shimon Peres met with senior PLO members to propose a Palestinian self-rule agreement. During the course of fourteen rounds of talks, which came to be called Oslo I, the parties agreed that Israel would withdraw from parts of the Gaza Strip and from the West Bank city of Jericho and transfer selected administrative responsibilities to the Palestinians. The final status of the territories, Jerusalem, Israeli settlements, and other issues would be determined during a five-year interim period.

With the White House as a dramatic backdrop, Rabin and Arafat exchanged letters of mutual recognition on September 13, 1993, and embarked upon a contentious diplomatic effort to find a successor regime to thirty years of Israeli occupation of the West Bank, Gaza, and East Jerusalem and to respond to the long-standing Palestinian demand for self-determination.

The signatures by the government of Israel and the PLO on the Declaration of Principles on Interim Self-Government Arrangements were a landmark in the history of the Israeli-Palestinian conflict. Following up on this initiative on May 4, 1994, the Palestinians and Israelis concluded an agreement in Cairo for the implementation of the Declaration of Principles. On that date, the interim period formally began. Soon after the Cairo agreement, in Gaza the Israeli army completed withdrawals and a redeployment of troops, leaving forces in the areas surrounding sixteen Israeli settlements occupied by approximately 4,000 settlers.

On September 28, 1995, in Washington, D.C., the Rabin government and the PLO signed the Israeli-Palestinian Interim Agreement on the West Bank and Gaza Strip, commonly referred to as Oslo II. This accord detailed the mechanisms for, and the limitation of, the extension of Palestinian self-rule to additional, significant portions of the West Bank. The main feature of the agreement was the provision for the division of the West Bank into three areas, each with varying degrees of Israeli and Palestinian responsibility:

- Area A: the seven major Palestinian towns—Bethlehem, Hebron, Jenin, Qalqilya, Nablus, Ramallah, and Tulkarm—where Palestinians would have complete authority for civilian security and administration.

- Area B: other Palestinian population centers (except for some refugee camps), where Israel would retain "overriding security responsibility" while Palestinians would handle administrative control.
- Area C: all Israeli settlements, military bases and areas, and territories proclaimed "state lands," where Israel would remain the sole authority.

Oslo II provided for the partial redeployment of the Israeli army, allowing the newly created Palestinian Authority to assume its civil and security responsibilities according to the schedule provided for in the agreement. The Israeli army began withdrawing from Jenin on November 13, 1995, followed by Tulkarm on December 10, Nablus and other villages in the Tulkarm area on December 11, Qalqilya on December 17, Bethlehem on December 21, and finally Ramallah on December 28. Hebron was left as the last of the West Bank towns from which Israeli soldiers were to redeploy under Oslo II in order to allow time to work out security issues arising from the presence of 450 Israeli settlers in the city center.

The Hebron protocol was concluded by the government of the Likud Party's Benjamin Netanyahu (elected in 1996) and the Palestinian Authority on January 15, 1997. Under its provisions, the city was divided into two parts: Israel retained full security control over the settlement enclaves in downtown Hebron and the Kiryat Arba settlement, just outside the city, and the surrounding area for the movement of the settlers and the army; the Palestinian Authority was made responsible for security for the rest of Hebron, although this responsibility would remain closely monitored by Israeli authorities.

On October 23, 1998, the Netanyahu government and the PLO agreed in the Wye River Memorandum to a revised timetable for the phased implementation of the first and second of three "further redeployments" of Israeli military forces outlined in the Oslo II accords signed in September 1995 but never implemented. The first redeployment was initially

scheduled to begin in October 1996. The third redeployment was to have been completed, according to the Oslo II timetable, by October 1997. The Wye memorandum makes no mention of a date for this third redeployment. At the end of the redeployments agreed to, Israel would still be in full security control of 82 percent of the West Bank and Gaza, of which 59 to 60 percent would also fall under full Israeli administrative control.

Stage one of the Wye redeployments was completed in November 1998, but then the Israeli cabinet decided the following month to postpone indefinitely any additional redeployments. Further redeployments would have to wait for Israeli elections, which occurred in spring 1999 and had Ehud Barak of the One Israel Party defeating Netanyahu. In late August 1999, Israeli and Palestinian negotiators meeting in Egypt worked out new details for implementing the Wye agreement. The major points of contention involved a timetable for Israeli troop withdrawals from the West Bank and the release of Palestinians held in Israeli jails for "security" offenses other than the murder of Israeli citizens. The agreement marked an important step back onto the path toward final status talks after a year of stalemate.

The agreement signed on September 4, 1999, in Sharm al-Shaykh, Egypt, reaffirmed Israel's commitment, first made by Prime Minister Netanyahu almost a year earlier, to reduce the area of the West Bank under exclusive Israeli control from 72 percent to 59 percent. Unlike the original Wye agreement, however, this agreement included a commitment to conclude a Framework Agreement on Permanent Status issues (or FAPS) by February 13, 2000, and a comprehensive final status agreement by September 2000.

Israel implemented the second stage of its West Bank redeployment in January 2000, when it transferred 2 percent of Area B to PA-controlled Area A and 3 percent of Israeli-controlled Area C to Area B. By mid-February, Area A represented 12.1 percent of the West Bank; Area B, 26.9 percent; and Area C, 61 percent. The transfer of 5.1 percent of Area B and 1 percent of Area C to full Palestinian control (Area A) was implemented on

March 21, 2000, leaving the Palestinian Authority with nominal security and civil control over 17.2 percent of the West Bank (Area A) and civil control over an additional 23.8 percent (Area B).

As tensions between Israel and the PLO eased during the 1990s, Israel's international standing improved somewhat. Early in 1994, the Vatican established full diplomatic relations with Israel, ushering in an era of unprecedented goodwill between the Catholic Church and Judaism. As the prospect of a quick transition to Palestinian sovereignty receded, however, Israel's budding relations with the Arab world and allies, including Turkey, suffered. The regional economic conferences languished, and the tenor of public diplomacy slackened. Nevertheless, Israel maintained limited (open and surreptitious) economic ties with the Arab world. Total trade measured in the hundreds of millions of dollars in the wake of an increasingly ineffective primary boycott promoted by the Arab League.

Jordanian-Israeli Agreement

In July 1994, Israel followed up its agreement with the Palestinians by signing the Washington Declaration, a pact with Jordan to end their forty-six-year state of war. Israel and Jordan had been at a de facto peace since the end of the June 1967 War. The PLO's agreement with Israel opened the way for King Hussein to conclude a formal peace with Israel.

The Washington Declaration led to intense negotiations that produced an Israeli-Jordanian peace treaty on October 26, 1994. The pact established broad economic cooperation between Israel and Jordan and provided for a formal exchange of ambassadors. It also formalized Jordan's pledge not to allow a third party to use its territory as a staging area for attacks on Israel and Israel's recognition of Jordan's privileged position in matters of Jerusalem's Islamic heritage.

The Rabin Assassination

Prime Minister Rabin's narrow ruling coalition and steady, if incremental, progress with the PLO

had sparked a settler campaign against the government beginning in mid-summer 1995. Its main instigators were drawn from settlers to the right of the settlement movement's mainstream as represented by the settler council YESHA. The Zu Aretzenu (This Is Our Land) movement, one of whose members filed a charge of treason against Rabin, led the settler opposition to the government's conciliation with the Palestinians.

Their strategy complemented that of the more traditional settler leadership, which was enmeshed in coordinating increased security measures with the Israeli army in anticipation of the latter's redeployment from parts of the West Bank. Unlike these deliberations, the actions of Zu Aretzenu—stopping traffic along Israel's highways or charging up West Bank hilltops to establish ersatz settlements—garnered headlines and mobilized large numbers of Rabin's rightist opponents. Prominent among them were settlers, for whom the Oslo process marked the beginning of the end of Jewish control over the West Bank, and religious Jews, who believed that the Oslo agreements were yet another sign of Israel's debasement as a Jewish state. In summer 1995, what was once the rightist fringe within the settler movement emerged as its most vibrant force.

The campaign against the government included an increasingly vitriolic assault on Rabin as well as Peres, who were vilified in public demonstrations. Rabin was portrayed as a Nazi. Government ministers were physically harassed, and Rabin's car was vandalized by rightists who boasted that if they could get to his car, they could also get to the prime minister.

The Likud, led by Benjamin Netanyahu, was content to lend its aura of respectability to many of these incidents, some of which occurred, without condemnation, during rallies addressed by Likud Party officials. Netanyahu saw political advantage in the increasingly poisonous atmosphere that attended public discussion about Rabin's policies toward the Palestinians.

Within the government there were two views on the meaning of the growing virulence of the campaign to delegitimize government policy. Most viewed it as a dangerous but containable challenge to Israel's political tradition, whose history had been punctuated by extreme rhetorical condemnation of opponents, as during the war in Lebanon in the early 1980s. Demonstrators and right-wing leaders tended to be handled leniently by Israel's legal and security systems. Right-wing movements like those associated with the late Meir Kahane, although formally banned, persisted in barely changed forms and even increased their activities.

This forbearance of settler challenges was deeply rooted in the Rabin government and, indeed, in Israel's political tradition. Throughout its tenure, the Rabin government refrained from directly challenging the settlers, even after the killing of thirty-one Palestinians in Hebron by a settler in February 1994 and in the face of growing extremist sentiments during 1995. This forbearance made it difficult to convince Rabin and other leaders to take full measure of the transformation occurring among his more extreme opponents. One minister, Benjamin Ben Eliezer, was lucky to escape unhurt from a mob. Rabin, however, like most Israelis, continued to view the extremists as essentially a political rather than a security or legal problem.

Through the Oslo process, Rabin attempted to build an Israeli policy for the West Bank's future on what he rightly considered to be a broad national consensus: leaving the Israeli army in strategic control of the occupied territories and the settlers, despite their apocalyptic visions, with an unprecedented measure of protections aimed at securing their future. For his efforts he paid with his life, as he was assassinated by a right-wing Israeli Jewish extremist in November 1995. Rabin was succeeded by Peres, who during his short tenure proved unable to move forward with the Palestinians or negotiations with Syria.

The 1996 and 1999 Elections

Benjamin Netanyahu was the first Israeli prime minister selected directly by the electorate. In the 1996 elections, in a radical political departure from past Israeli leaders, Netanyahu received a mandate independent of his party.

Netanyahu was born and bred in the Herut Party, the ideological heart of the Likud. His support for the main tenets of the party was second nature: Israel's right to rule over Greater Israel (from the Mediterranean to the Jordan River), the right of the Jewish people to settle throughout this area, and a relationship with the Arab world based upon Israel's superior military power.

In a speech in August 1997, Netanyahu declared his support for an Israeli policy based on realpolitik of the sort practiced by Israel's first prime minister, David Ben-Gurion. Netanyahu made known his intention to establish restraints on the "adventurism" of Israel's neighbors through pursuit of a "clear military advantage," contrasting his vision with the "Rose Garden dreams" of Rabin and Peres, whose appearance at the White House ceremony with Arafat in September 1993 became a symbol of the era that Netanyahu was determined to repudiate.

"The type of peace that is possible in the Middle East," Netanyahu declared, "is a peace based on power." Where Rabin and Peres were prepared to move beyond this static notion by exploiting Israeli power to make far-reaching agreements with former enemies, Netanyahu appeared content to return to the less imaginative formulations of Israel's founding generation.

Netanyahu also did not share the basic strategic view of Syria adopted by Rabin and Peres. For them, a resolution of the dispute with Syria was a necessary prerequisite for establishing an effective politico-military response to the nonconventional threats in Iraq and Iran. Failure to reach an accommodation with Damascus, therefore, had consequences. Netanyahu, like Shamir, who was forced by the Bush administration to sit with the Syrians at the Madrid peace conference, did not believe that it mattered if peace with Damascus failed to materialize.

Rabin and Peres viewed Arafat and the Palestinian Authority as "strategic partners," a relationship that became the cornerstone upon which the Oslo edifice was to be constructed. Netanyahu acknowledged support for Oslo, but even in the final months of his abbreviated tenure, he had yet to decide whether he favored a strategic partnership with Arafat. The achievement signified by the Wye memorandum and his subsequent decision to abort its implementation reflected this indecision. Netanyahu's government fell in late 1998, in part as a consequence of the disaffection among the Israeli religious and settler movements toward his policies, most notably the Wye memorandum, and also as a consequence of widespread unhappiness with his operating style.

The One Israel movement—which included Labor, Gesher, and the moderate religious Meiman parties—came into existence under the leadership of Ehud Barak in March 1999. The dynamics of the contest between Barak, a former minister and IDF chief of staff, and Netanyahu began to change in Barak's favor when he announced his intention to withdraw all Israeli forces from Lebanon if elected. Barak won the May 17 contest for prime minister with 56.08 percent of the votes cast. One Israel won 26 Knesset seats, while the Likud's representation fell from 32 seats to 19. The ultra-Orthodox Shas Party increased its representation from 10 seats to 17. The newly elected Knesset contained an unprecedented fifteen factions. Nevertheless, the coalition established under Barak's leadership could count not only upon its seventy-five members, but also upon an additional ten members representing Arab parties.

Barak's victory was widely viewed as first and foremost a repudiation of Netanyahu himself, rather than of his policies, especially those relating to the Palestinian question. In the domestic arena, Barak pledged to heal social rifts between the secular and religious communities that emerged as potent political and social issues and which were exacerbated during the election campaign. Labor and Likud both lost considerable numbers of seats in the Knesset, together commanding fewer than 50 of the parliament's 120 seats. Perhaps the biggest political surprise was the extraordinary success of Shas, which draws its constituency from the ranks of Israel's poorer, Sephardic majority. Shas almost doubled its seats, from 10 to 17 mandates, emerging as the Knesset's third largest party.

Barak always viewed the Oslo process with a far greater degree of skepticism than most of his colleagues in the Labor Party. As interior minister in Rabin's cabinet, Barak abstained in the Knesset vote on the Oslo II accords held barely one month before Rabin's assassination in October 1995. His primary concerns related to the accord's security provisions, which he thought too lax, and its timetable, which he believed would place too much territory in Palestinian hands before final status talks commenced and which, he argued, should be extended.

Barak entered office prepared to countenance the creation of an independent Palestinian state. Indeed, he viewed some form of Palestinian self-determination as an essential Israeli interest if Israel hoped to maintain its existing political institutions and Jewish majority. He was also determined to enforce a more permanent exclusion from Israel of Palestinians from the occupied territories. Yet unlike all of his predecessors, Barak believed that he could win Palestinian acceptance of a final status agreement that would legitimize long-standing Israeli territorial, strategic, and settlement objectives and formally end all Palestinian claims against Israel.

Withdrawal from Lebanon

As Barak had promised during the election campaign, on July 15, 1999, he announced that he would propose a unilateral withdrawal from Lebanon within one year if no peace accord had been reached with Syria over the Golan. On March 5, 2000, the Israeli cabinet unanimously endorsed Barak's proposed withdrawal from southern Lebanon by early July. The implosion of Israel's local surrogate force—the South Lebanon Army—required Israel to accelerate this timetable, moving the withdrawal to May.

The withdrawal marked a clear change in the strategy that Israel had pursued since its initial occupation of Lebanese territory in the late 1970s. Some 900 Israelis had died there since 1978. The forces of Hizballah had lost 1,276 fighters since it began resistance operations in 1982, and many more Palestinians, Lebanese civilians, and others also lost their lives in years of endemic conflict.

Israel's withdrawal left unresolved the territorial issue of the approximately ten-square-mile enclave called Shab'a Farms, which lies at the southern edge of the Lebanese-Syrian border and remains occupied by Israel, which captured it from Syria in June 1967.

Camp David, 2000

At the Israeli-Palestinian talks at Camp David in July 2000, Prime Minister Barak put his indelible mark on the diplomacy begun in Madrid. Notwithstanding the failure to reach agreement, Barak established himself as the first Israeli prime minister prepared to directly engage Palestinian nationalism on the range of issues critical to resolving the contest between them.

At Camp David, Barak transformed the domestic Israeli debate on Jerusalem, even if he failed to satisfy minimal Palestinian demands. He acknowledged that Israeli claims to East Jerusalem were not absolute and that some measure of Palestinian control, and perhaps even sovereignty, could be accommodated.

Barak was committed to winning Palestinian, Arab, and international acceptance of Israeli sovereignty over the Old City's Temple Mount/Haram al-Sharif as well as much, if not all, of East Jerusalem. While demonstrating at Camp David a degree of innovation unmatched by any of his predecessors, he was determined to ensure Israel's strategic control over the West Bank and Gaza Strip, including their airspace, borders, and transport routes to and from settlements, necessarily including the settlement "bypass roads," whose construction, with U.S. support and financing, was a central feature of the physical transformation of the West Bank during the Oslo period.

The dynamic established by U.S. diplomacy at Camp David was characterized by a postponement of Palestinian sovereignty and the implementation of the third and final Israeli redeployment established in the Oslo II accords; Barak's

increasing political isolation at home; a growing Palestinian crisis of confidence in U.S. mediation and Israeli intentions; Israeli and U.S. exasperation with the lack of Palestinian readiness for concessions that they both demanded; Washington's internalization of Israeli views of what was required for a deal; and finally, the Clinton administration's inability to wield U.S. power in order to produce an agreement. Barak—who at Camp David and in the last days of his tenure at talks in Taba, Egypt, in early 2001, engaged Israel for the first time in serious negotiations with Palestinian representatives on an agreed division of historical Palestine—also distinguished himself as the only prime minister of the Oslo period who did not originate the redeployment of Israeli forces from occupied territory.

2001 Elections

In late May 1999, Ariel Sharon became chairman of the Likud Party. He was initially viewed as an interim leader of a defeated and demoralized party. In November 2000, however, Barak, who had lost his parliamentary majority on the eve of the Camp David talks, announced that he would resign in order to seek a renewed mandate.

Elections for the premiership between Barak and Sharon were scheduled for February 2001. The Knesset voted against its own dissolution and thus avoided an early general election. Sharon, who campaigned on a platform promising victory over the Palestinian intifada, crushed his opponent, taking an overwhelming 62 percent of votes cast. The unity government that Sharon formed was the largest in Israel's history, representing a broad spectrum of left, right, center, and religious parties.

Negotiations with the Palestinians in 2000 had established options for Israeli withdrawal ranging from 80 to 96 percent of the West Bank, including security zones. Sharon was not, however, a party to this view. Nevertheless, he was one of the first Israeli leaders to publicly acknowledge the inevitability of Palestinian statehood in part of the occupied territories, and as foreign minister in

Ariel Sharon

will require the evacuation of some settlements, sacrificed in the face of Palestinian resistance in order to establish the minimal territorial conditions for the creation of a weak Palestinian state.

Sharon's leadership has been especially important in the creation of what former prime minister Rabin derisively termed "political settlements," those sparsely populated outposts that dot the West Bank central highlands running in a north-south line between Jenin and Jerusalem. These settlements, whose number has increased during the Netanyahu, Barak, and Sharon years, were conceived by Sharon to explicitly forestall the creation of a territorially viable Palestinian entity and to serve the tactical security function of dispersing the Israeli military throughout the entire region.

The Oslo process accommodated these settlements as well as the larger outposts—Ma'ale Adumim, the Etzion bloc, Ariel—historically favored by much of Israel's ruling establishment. The map created by the Oslo II accord in September 1995 and modified in the March 2000 redeployment is almost a mirror image of Sharon's "cantonization" plan, which envisaged the creation of noncontiguous Palestinian cantons in the West Bank and Gaza Strip surrounded by Israeli settlements and roads.

As a minister under Netanyahu, Sharon endeavored to establish an agreed-upon basis for the creation of a Palestinian state, albeit one subject in both its territorial and sovereign dimensions to Israeli territorial and security demands. Sharon's formula, however, was consistent with the Oslo process crafted by Rabin, with its focus upon interim agreements and a postponement of final status agreements.

Sharon's notion of the territorial dimensions of the state of Palestine includes the 41 percent of the West Bank now classified as Areas A (17.2 percent) and B (23.8 percent) and all of Gaza. While he does not come close to meeting minimal Palestinian demands for a final status agreement, Sharon also does not require the kind of Palestinian concessions—first among which is an explicit agreement to "end the conflict"—unsuccessfully demanded by Barak.

the government of Benjamin Netanyahu had held extensive discussions with top Palestinian officials.

Sharon is a pragmatic expansionist who views Israeli settlement in the West Bank, East Jerusalem, and the Golan as less an ideological imperative than a security asset. Sharon has always been confident that the management of the lives and politics of Palestinians in the occupied territories could be married to a strategy of expanding Israeli settlement and strategic military control throughout these areas.

Sharon's pragmatism is today expressed in a willingness to acknowledge that a policy intended to secure Israel's hold on the occupied territories

2003 Elections

On November 5, 2002, Sharon informed President Moshe Katzav that he was resigning, thereby bringing down the government. In elections held January 28, 2003, the Likud won 29.4 percent of the vote and forty seats in the Knesset, enabling Sharon to remain prime minister. Israel thus elected Sharon to a second term, an expression of public support not bestowed on an Israeli prime minister since Menachem Begin. Labor, lead by retired general Amram Mitzna, won only 14.5 percent of the vote and nineteen seats in the Knesset.

Unable to persuade Labor into a coalition, Sharon looked to the smaller parties to create a new government. His new cabinet comprised members of Likud, Shinui (the centrist party that had made an impact in the election campaign with its strident opposition to the ultra-Orthodox parties), the National Religious Party, the National Union, and Israel B'Aliyah, led by Natan Sharansky. Sharon's disengagement plan for Gaza forced his estrangement from his right-wing coalition partners, leading in late 2004 to Labor's entry into the coalition.

Continuing Occupation and Settlement

The eruption of the al-Aqsa intifada and Israel's response to it literally changed the landscape of the occupied territories, introducing yet another dimension to the already complicated situation.

The al-Aqsa Intifada

On September 28, 2000, Ariel Sharon, before his election as prime minister, had led a group of Likud lawmakers in a visit to the Haram al-Sharif, or Temple Mount, an area sacred to Jews as the site of the former Temple and to Muslims as the site of the Dome of the Rock and al-Aqsa mosques. After Sharon and his entourage left, Palestinians engaged with the estimated 1,000 or so Israeli riot police deployed around the al-Aqsa compound for Sharon's visit. The police fired rubber bullets and tear gas at the Palestinian protesters, injuring twenty-four of them. Disturbances spread throughout East Jerusalem and to Ramallah in the West Bank. The next day, when Palestinians emerging from prayers on the compound threw stones at Israeli police officers, the Israeli forces stormed the compound, shooting live ammunition and rubber bullets.

The al-Aqsa intifada rapidly escalated into the most sustained revolt by Palestinians in the West Bank and Gaza since the beginning of the occupation in 1967. In Israel, debate still rages about the extent to which this violent rebellion against the occupation represented a considered Palestinian strategy. Among Palestinians, the perception remains that it was largely spontaneous, driven more by the enormous frustration of their people than by any strategic decision by the Palestinian leadership. The energy sustaining the four-year uprising derived in large measure from Palestinian frustration with Israel and their own leadership at the lack of any improvement in their situation despite the seven-year-old Oslo peace process.

The massive growth of Israeli settlements in the occupied territories during the Oslo interim period played a critical factor in souring Palestinian attitudes. While Sharon's demonstration of Israeli sovereignty over the Muslim holy sites provided the catalyst for the intifada, Israel's settlement policy had fostered the tensions that erupted into violence. Between 1993 and 2000, Israel's settler population had grown from 116,400 to 194,300 (excluding the 180,000 settlers in East Jerusalem). Settlers resided in 145 "official" settlements and 55 unofficial "outposts," both of which are illegal under international law. The settlements, strategically scattered throughout the West Bank and Gaza, blocked any contiguous or urban development for and between the 700 Palestinian localities in the territories.

The intifada inaugurated a new era in relations between the Israelis and Palestinians characterized by violent confrontations throughout the occupied territories, including in East Jerusalem. Settlement areas and the military installations protecting them became the principal flash points, sparking increasingly draconian restrictions imposed by the

IDF on Palestinian movement throughout the occupied territories.

Israel's military operations in the West Bank in April 2002 and the associated decimation of the Palestinian security apparatus were a consequence of the requirement to protect settlements against irregular Palestinian militants and to preserve a normal everyday existence for the almost 400,000 Israelis who live across the Green Line and the millions residing in Israel whose daily lives were transformed by Palestinian attacks.

The Sharon government dismissed Arafat and the institutions he represented—the PLO and the Palestinian Authority—as no longer being diplomatic or security partners. Israel under Sharon exercised a policy characterized by Israel's direct exercise of security responsibilities everywhere in the occupied territories, a dramatic transformation from the Oslo decade. Arafat's death in late 2004, Sharon's plan to withdraw from the Gaza Strip, and mutual exhaustion after four years of warfare led in February 2005 to Mahmoud Abbas, Arafat's successor, declaring an end to the intifada, leading to expectations of a change in Israeli policy and military deployments in the West Bank.

Separation and Disengagement

In the midst of the al-Aqsa intifada and in part as a result of it, Israel began construction of a separation barrier in the West Bank and along the Green Line. Work on it is proceeding approximately along a line—with the prominent exception of the route in and around East Jerusalem—suggested by Barak at Taba that includes West Bank lands that Israel had hoped to annex as part of an agreement with the PLO. Today's project, however, is not part of a final status agreement that includes Israel's evacuation of settlements, but rather represents the imposition of a security concept by the public upon reluctant military and political officials who initially questioned its utility and cost effectiveness. *(See Chapter 2, map, p. 76)*

Israel began building a fence around the Gaza Strip in 1993 to stop Palestinian infiltrators from entering Israel. In early 1995, Prime Minister

Rabin called for the separation of Palestinians and Israelis and established a committee within his cabinet to pursue the goal of separating the Palestinians in the occupied territories from Israel, a goal supported by Netanyahu and Barak. The construction of the West Bank barrier, however, did not begin until the Sharon administration.

The barrier's construction has been subject to international condemnation, including a ruling by the International Court at The Hague in mid-2004. Palestinians, who often demonstrate against the construction, have condemned it as a unilateral action that prejudices the prospect of an agreed upon resolution of their conflict. The structure affects some Palestinians by blocking or restricting access to lands and separates them from vital health and educational services. Petitions filed in Israeli courts by Palestinians and by Israelis have succeeded in delaying the barrier's construction and in effecting locally significant but marginal changes in its trajectory.

On January 30, 2002, Sharon's cabinet approved the "Wrapping Greater Jerusalem" scheme, a concept for ensuring Israeli and settlement security in the metropolitan Jerusalem region. Significant parts of the West Bank define its territorial perimeter, including the settlements of Givat Ze'ev in the north, Ma'ale Adumim to the outskirts of Jericho in the east, and the Etzion bloc to the south.

As a consequence of Israelis' support for separation, the territorial division of historical Palestine has entered its most decisive stage since Israel's occupation of the West Bank and Gaza Strip in June 1967. In a variety of roles over the last generation, Sharon has labored to undermine an Israeli withdrawal to the June 1967 lines. He has masterminded the settlement map that is the template of the "separation zone"—popularly known as the "fence" or the "wall"—that is fast dividing the occupied territories between Israel and an ersatz Palestine—the "state with provisional borders" whose creation is called for in the road map endorsed by President George W. Bush in 2003.

In Jerusalem, the Palestinian city emerging from this vision will be a series of disjointed communities disrupted by expanding Israeli settlement and linked, if at all, by an aging road network interrupted by checkpoint bottlenecks. Palestinian East Jerusalem is largely sandwiched between Israeli West Jerusalem, to which access is infrequently unreliable but complicated, and its Arab hinterland in the West Bank, which is blocked by a physical barrier. In 2004 Prime Minister Sharon made the unprecedented decision to end Israel's military and civilian occupation of the Gaza Strip and to evacuate four West Bank settlements. The plan's central strategic objective is to remove Gaza's 1.3 million Palestinians from the sphere of Israel's internationally recognized responsibility by ending the military occupation of Gaza that began in June 1967 while continuing to exercise control over the entry and exit of people and goods. No similar objective is intended even for the areas of the West Bank from which Israel plans to redeploy.

In the case of the West Bank, the plan claims to create "territorial contiguity" for Palestinians in the region around the town of Jenin, where Israel will evacuate four settlements. This area will, however, continue to be surrounded by Israeli-controlled checkpoints. Israel's territorial objective for the remainder of the West Bank, in contrast, is defined as "transportation contiguity," that is, connecting separate Palestinian enclaves by bridges, tunnels, and crossing points, all of which will continue to be controlled by Israeli forces.

Sharon's idea marks a turning point in the history of Israeli occupation policy. Most significant, Gaza (but not the West Bank) has joined the Sinai and Golan as areas where Israel is prepared to endorse evacuation of settlements and military withdrawal as a means of enhancing Israeli security.

Settlements

Despite Israel's recognition of the PLO, the Declaration of Principles, and the creation of a system in which Israel and the PLO have become partners to a negotiated solution of their conflict and created an environment far different from that which historically has characterized Israeli-Palestinian and Israeli-Arab relations, Israeli settlements continue to be valued by Israeli leaders as a preferred means of establishing physical and demographic obstacles to an Israeli retreat from the territories captured in June 1967. When the map of a final territorial settlement between Israel and the Palestinians is drawn, it will be the settlement "facts" created since 1967 that determine the extent of Israel's territorial demands.

Israeli settlements have been built at more than 250 sites seized by civilian and military bodies representing the government of Israel as well as by Israeli civilians empowered by Israel to undertake such activity. All civilian settlement in the occupied territories is considered illegal under international law.

By the end of 2004, Israel had established approximately 200 settlement areas in the West Bank with a civilian population of 250,000; in East Jerusalem, approximately 190,000 Israelis were in residence; in Gaza, 7,000 settlers lived in 17 settlements; and on the Golan, 18,500 settlers resided in 33 settlements. In sum, some 500,000 Israelis resided in the settlement communities established since 1967 in the West Bank, East Jerusalem, Gaza, and the Golan.

Israeli Settler Population in the West Bank and Gaza, Select Years, 1972–2004

	West Bank	Gaza	Total
2004	250,000	7,000	257,000
2003	218,800	7,500	226,300
2002	207,900	7,300	215,100
2001	196,700	6,900	203,600
2000	187,600	6,700	194,300
1999	174,000	6,300	180,300
1998	163,300	6,100	169,400
1997	154,400	5,700	160,100
1996	142,700	5,600	148,300
1995	127,900	5,000	138,500
1994	122,700	5,100	127,800
1993	111,600	4,800	116,400
1992	101,100	4,300	105,400
1991	90,300	3,800	94,100
1990	78,600	3,300	81,900
1989	69,800	3,000	72,800
1985	44,100	1,900	46,000
1983	22,800	900	23,700
1972	800	700	1,500

Source: Statistical Analysis of Israel, 1992, 1994, 1995, 1997–2002, 2004, table 2.7.

The expansion of Israel's civilian settlement infrastructure throughout the occupied territories was a consistent aspect of Israeli policy in the latter years of the Oslo period and the two terms of the Sharon government. During this time, the settler population increased from 180,000 to 250,000 in the West Bank. The issue of 42 "outposts" established in the West Bank during the Netanyahu era contributed to a loss of Palestinian confidence in Israel's intentions. As prime minister, Barak decided in October 1999 to maintain most of these settlements. At the end of June 2004, there were 96 so-called outposts in the West Bank. Forty-four of these sites were established prior to the Israeli elections of February 2001, leaving 52 that were built after the elections, including 51 constructed after March 2001.

During 2003, housing expansion in Israeli settlements continued at an unprecedented pace, increasing at a rate higher than anywhere in Israel. Compared to 2002, there was a 35 percent increase in housing starts in the settlements, excluding those in East Jerusalem and the Golan, at a time when Israel's national housing market continued to shrink. There were 1,849 construction starts in West Bank and Gaza Strip settlements in 2003 compared to 1,369 during 2002. More than one out of every fifteen Israeli dwellings begun in 2003 was located in West Bank or Gaza settlements. When settlement neighborhoods in East Jerusalem are included, the percentage increases to one in every ten. Construction starts nationally declined by 8 percent in 2003. Only 29,670 dwellings were begun that year, the lowest number since before the onset of the large-scale immigration from the Soviet Union that began in 1989. Most settlement expansion continues to occur in the larger settlements around Jerusalem and in those within easy commuting distance of the Mediterranean coast. Significant construction proceeds, however, in many settlements with populations of less than 5,000 and continues to grow at two to three times the national average.

In East Jerusalem, settlement activity has continued at a more measured pace. Despite decades of intensive settlement that brought almost 200,000 Israelis to settle in East Jerusalem, and policies designed to hamper Palestinian growth, the percentage of Palestinians in the city rose from 25.8 percent in 1967 to 32.6 percent in 2002.

Outlook

Notwithstanding the severe economic costs of the intifada, Israel's economic transformation has made it the most prosperous and dominant country in the Middle East. Nevertheless, this transformation has increased the gap between rich and poor and made the reduction of economic inequality into a politically potent issue. Israelis must confront this issue along with others that have bedeviled their country since before its creation.

The government must address, perhaps as never before, the rising tide of public antipathy against the privileges and state subsidies accorded the growing population of Orthodox Jews. One of the most emotive issues is the exemption from national military service that many religious young men receive. Another is the system of state-supported religious education run virtually without state direction by politically affiliated religious institutions. These issues are by-products of the more fundamental tension that has always existed in Israel between its increasingly conflicting objectives of simultaneously maintaining its Jewish and democratic aspirations.

Israel's current leadership is anxious to create a framework for relations with its Arab neighbors that cements its role as the dominant military force in the Middle East. The coming years will be important ones for the adoption of a framework for Palestinian political sovereignty in parts of the West Bank and Gaza that will provide Palestinians with a politically viable state. Within this context, Israel of course brings to the table its own military, security, and settlement objectives.

Along the road to a Palestinian-Israeli peace, the two parties must decide the fate of Jerusalem. All Israeli leaders have stated that Jerusalem must remain under the control of Israel. Ariel Sharon adheres to this line while his government constructs a barrier that leaves tens of thousands of the city's Palestinian residents outside its perimeter. Palestinians also make claim to the city as their rightful capital. Deciding the fate of Jerusalem, a holy city for Muslims, Jews, and Christians worldwide, will undoubtedly test the diplomatic creativity of all concerned.

If Israel can maintain a good-faith effort in the peace process, it stands to benefit from increased trade and investment as the international financial community looks to the region for high-growth markets. Access to and use of freshwater resources will continue to take a high priority in discussions with neighboring states.

Israel's peace with Jordan was especially encouraging to many Israelis because it was achieved in an atmosphere of friendship. What they have found discouraging, however, is that like the 1979 treaty with Egypt—which in practice has resulted in a "cold peace" of minimal cooperation—the treaty with Jordan has failed to generate broad economic dividends and demonstrate to other Arabs the potential economic advantages of making peace with Israel.

The Israeli-Syrian Track

Ehud Barak, during the first year of his abbreviated tenure, directed the focus of his diplomatic efforts on reaching an agreement with Syria. In December 1999 in Washington, D.C., President Bill Clinton inaugurated peace talks between Israel and Syria. The central issue of these and subsequent discussions in January 2000 was the question of Barak's stance toward the 1994 "Rabin deposit"—a commitment given by the late prime minister to the United States that Israel was in principle prepared to withdraw to the June 1967 border with Syria if Israel's concerns regarding security and normalization were met.

Clinton and Asad met at the former's invitation in Geneva, Switzerland, on March 20, 2000. Asad arrived with a large delegation, assuming that Clinton would bring an assurance from Barak that he was ready to recognize the June 4, 1967, line as the border between the two countries. When it became clear that Barak continued to insist on a permanent Israeli presence east of this line, the talks ended, in failure.

The on again, off again nature of formal talks between Israel and Syria raises legitimate questions about the successful outcome of efforts to arrange a peace between these long bitter enemies. What is not in dispute, however, is the degree to which Israel has reassessed long-held views of its territorial and settlement requirements on the Golan, a transformation in elite military and strategic concepts, if not in public attitudes.

Although such views have enabled Israeli prime ministers since Rabin to conclude that Israel's strategic interests in the twenty-first century will be better served by a contractual peace with Syria and without Golan settlements, there is little evidence that Prime Minister Sharon shares this view. At the least, Sharon's government felt no pressure to move on the Syrian front. Hafiz al-Asad died in 2000 and was succeeded by his son Bashar al-Asad. Although the new president expressed a willingness to negotiate with Israel, an unenthusiastic Sharon government determined that he was politically too weak to be in a position to make a deal.

Security Issues

Prime Minister Barak, in a speech marking the fall 1999 opening of the Knesset, reaffirmed his intention to maintain Israel's strategic deterrent capability even in peacetime, for whatever geographical or time range required. Israel boasts sophisticated and wide-ranging strategic deterrents founded upon the reach and power of its air force and its arsenal of undeclared nuclear weapons. The latter have a variety of specialized uses and can be delivered by land-based and sea-based missiles as well as by airplane.

The basic elements of Israel's nuclear capability—the Dimona nuclear plant, which has been manufacturing plutonium for almost four decades, the quantity, deployment, and type of Israel's nuclear weapons, and the doctrine regulating their use—remain the state's deepest secrets.

The current view of Israeli strategists is that the main threat facing Israel will not be a Palestinian state on the West Bank and in Gaza, nor a surprise attack across the Golan plateau by Syria. Rather it is the possession of nuclear weapons by the leaders of Iran.

On September 14, 2000, Israel successfully tested its Arrow antiballistic missile system over the Mediterranean. For the first time, the Arrow successfully targeted an incoming projectile simulating a Scud missile, locked on it, and destroyed it. Israel's conventional and nuclear deterrent capabilities have convinced most of its Arab enemies of the necessity of ending their military confrontation with the Jewish state. These capabilities, in Israel's view, permit it an unprecedented degree of flexibility in recasting its territorial requirements, enabling it to withdraw from the Sinai, Golan, Gaza, and parts of the West Bank. The diplomatic arrangements fashioned to accommodate these withdrawals form the foundation of a strategic partnership with the United States, whose principal aim is to establish the diplomatic, political, and military framework for Israel's continuing strategic superiority throughout the region.

In general, Israel and the United States have maintained good ties since Israel's creation in 1948, when the United States was the first country to grant Israel de facto recognition. Although no issue has challenged the essential comity of interests upon which U.S.-Israeli relations are based, there have been occasions when the two nations have clashed over goals, actions, and priorities. Israeli collaboration with Britain and France in attacking Egypt in 1956 is the most notable instance of such conflict. More recent examples include the arrest of the convicted spy Jonathan Pollard, who passed U.S. secrets to Israel; the inauguration of the U.S. dialogue with the PLO; contention over the loan guarantees for settling new immigrants; and calls during the administrations of both George Bush and Bill Clinton for a "time out" in settlement expansion and disputes over Israel's weapons and technology sales to China.

The relationship between Bush and Sharon continued this tradition of amity, marred only by a short-lived tension in the weeks after the September 11 attacks, when Israel feared a U.S. attempt to mollify its Arab and Islamic critics at Israel's expense. Washington's perception of its interests in the Middle East, the strong support of American Jews for Israel, and the support they are able to garner for Israel in the political arena would appear to ensure that Israel and the United States will remain close, regardless of who is in power in either nation.

CHAPTER **11**

JORDAN

Jordan, formerly Transjordan, has faced many challenges since its founding in the aftermath of World War I. It is a small and poor state surrounded by regionally powerful neighbors. Most of the attention and aid that Jordan has received since 1948 result from the country's pivotal position in the Arab-Israeli conflict. King Hussein, who ruled the West Bank and East Jerusalem from his ascension in 1953 until the territories' capture by Israel in the 1967 war, was viewed by many as one of the most important players in the Arab-Israeli conflict. Jordan has a majority Palestinian population, and Hussein struggled to preserve its integrity and his leadership.

For thirty-five years, Hussein weathered any number of Arab-Israeli and inter-Arab conflicts before removing himself from the heart of the Arab-Israeli dispute by relinquishing all claims to the Israeli-occupied West Bank in July 1988. This decision allowed him to devote greater attention to the internal problems of his kingdom. Hussein's popularity proved vital in helping him survive the crisis posed by Iraq's August 1990 invasion and occupation of Kuwait. Jordan had close economic ties to Iraq, and although the king repeatedly voiced his opposition to Iraq's annexation of Kuwait, he also resisted supporting the U.S.-led multinational coalition that marshaled forces to oust the Iraqi army from Kuwait. This stance isolated Jordan and led to much economic pain, as the international community withdrew aid to and restricted trade with Jordan. The king's position, however, greatly reinforced his popularity at home.

Movement in the Arab-Israeli peace process during the early 1990s repaired Jordan's status in the West, since many there saw the king as an indispensable participant in negotiations. The agreement between the Palestine Liberation Organization (PLO) and Israel reached in September 1993 opened the way for a comprehensive Jordanian-Israeli peace treaty, signed in October 1994. Jordan's opening toward Israel, however, ran parallel with a gradual withdrawal of political liberties on the domestic front, a process dating roughly to 1993 and lasting until Hussein's death in February 1999.

The challenges before Hussein's son and successor King Abdallah II at the outset of his rule were manifold. These included a regional "peace process" that by 1999 hardly deserved such a label, a poor state of economic and political liberties, Abdallah's inexperience in power politics. After ascending the Hashimite throne, however, the young king, a career military officer, quickly stamped his mark on Jordan. In his first years, he concentrated on pushing through wide-ranging economic and administrative reforms, concomitantly bringing into the political elite a pool of younger, business-oriented individuals in tune with his policy priorities. Abdallah faced internal demonstrations following his hesitant stance during the al-Aqsa intifada in the early 2000s and concerning the U.S.-led war on Iraq that began in March 2003 and which he supported, at least indirectly. Abdallah has thus far managed the issues that have confronted him, but he and Jordan must

Key Facts on Jordan

Area: 34,445 square miles (91,971 square kilometers)
Capital: Amman
Population: 5,759,732 (2005)
Religion: Sunni Muslim, 92 percent; Christian, 6 percent; others, 2 percent
Ethnic Groups: Arab, 98 percent; Circassian, 1 percent; Armenian, 1 percent
Official Language: Arabic; English widely spoken by upper and middle classes
Type of Government: Constitutional monarchy
GDP: $25.5 billion; $4,500 per capita (2004)

Source: Central Intelligence Agency, *CIA World Factbook,* 2005.

continue to perform a balancing act in the heart of a turbulent Middle East.

Geography

Jordan is bounded to the north by Syria, to the east by Iraq and Saudi Arabia, to the south by Saudi Arabia, and to the west by Israel and the Israeli-occupied and Palestinian-administered areas of the West Bank. Aqaba, Jordan's only port, located on the Gulf of Aqaba, sits on a narrow crescent of coastline between Israel and Saudi Arabia. The kingdom is about the size of Indiana, but less than 10 percent of the land is arable. Virtually all the rest is steppe or desert, suitable for nomadic grazing and periodic pasturage. A small, forested region in the northwest near Ajlun covers about 1 percent of Jordan's territory.

The Jordan River Valley and Wadi al-Araba (officially Wadi al-Jayb) are an extension of the Great Rift that begins in East Africa and continues up the Red Sea into Jordan. The Jordan River, which rises in Lebanon and Syria, descends from an elevation of 9,842 feet to Earth's deepest land-surface depression at the Dead Sea, some 1,400 feet below sea level. The East Bank of the Jordan River rises precipitously to form a sharp escarp-

ment cut by numerous valleys and gorges. From the top of the plateau, extremely arid land, receiving less than twelve inches of rain a year, extends to the east as part of the Great Syrian Desert. The land near the East Bank tributaries of the Jordan River is the only area that receives sufficient rainfall for intensive cultivation.

Jordan's main crops are fruits and vegetables. Although Jordanians grow various other crops, the country must import foodstuffs to meet its needs. Jordan has developed several light industries and prosperous phosphate mining operations in the Dead Sea area. Many of the banks and commercial enterprises that fled Beirut during the Lebanese civil war relocated to Amman, the capital of Jordan, attracted by the country's economic stability and active governmental support.

Demography

In 2004 Jordan had a population of approximately 5.7 million. Ethnically, 98 percent of the population is Arab, and Arabic is the official language. English is widely spoken and understood. About 94 percent of the population are Muslim, nearly all of them Sunni; most non-Muslim Jordanians are Christians. Jordanian authorities proudly boast of almost 90 percent literacy, which highlights the government's emphasis on education and the degree to which education is viewed as a key to social mobility.

Hashimite leadership in Jordan is in part built on the political support of Bedouin tribes that comprise only 6 to 8 percent of the population. Abdallah ibn Hussein, Abdallah I, who became amir of Transjordan in 1921, developed a special relationship with these groups during the early 1920s. His grandson King Hussein strengthened and institutionalized it. The Bedouin constitute the core of Jordan's army, a major source of power for the monarchy. Abdallah II, like his father and grandfather, has a personal interest in the welfare of these tribesmen.

Originally a martial, desert people, the Bedouin of today are more sedentary. Although their political influence has diminished somewhat, they still occupy key positions in the military and remain largely committed to the Hashimite regime, notwithstanding the 2002 riots in the southern tribal town of Ma`an resulting from a mixture of socio-economic deprivation and political marginalization.

An estimated 70 percent of Jordan's population is ethnic Palestinian. Many of the Palestinians who arrived in Jordan during the late 1940s and early 1950s were better educated than the native population, so they tended to prosper economically. Palestinians who settled in Jordan during the 1960s, however, brought with them considerably fewer skills and resources. Many of them simply moved from refugee settlements on the West Bank to similar ones on the East Bank, while others were displaced from their homes west of the Jordan by the 1967 Arab-Israeli war.

The problem of absorbing hundreds of thousands of displaced persons, coupled with the more traditional and conservative orientation of the East Bank's social and political milieu, led to mutual suspicion and distrust between indigenous Jordanians and Palestinians. Palestinian support for military action against Israel resulted in numerous confrontations with Jordan's leadership, the most serious and potentially catastrophic occurring in September 1970, Black September, when the Palestine Liberation Organization (PLO) challenged Hussein's political leadership. After quelling the Palestinian rebellion, thereby preserving Hashimite rule, Hussein made a concerted effort to integrate more Palestinians into the mainstream of Jordanian society, thus enhancing his kingdom's political stability. King Abdallah II has an advantage over his late father vis-à-vis his Palestinian constituency: his politically involved wife Rania is a Palestinian from the West Bank town of Tulkarm.

Following the sharp rise in oil prices in 1973, as many as 400,000 Jordanians—many of them Palestinians with Jordanian passports—moved to live and work outside the country. Many of them remitted a portion of their income to family members in Jordan. Remittances totaled an estimated $1.3 billion a year in the mid-1980s, but they fell sharply later in the decade and were nearly wiped

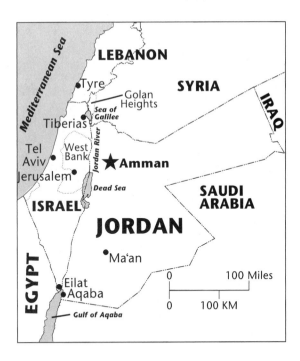

out during the 1990–1991 Persian Gulf crisis and war, when (according to government estimates) as many as 300,000 expatriate workers were forced to return to Jordan. Their return meant not only a loss of funds, but also increased domestic unemployment and strains on the resources of the Jordanian state.

History

The Old Testament recounts the settlement of present-day Jordan by Ammon, Edom, Gilead, Joshua, and Moab. Others, such as the Nabataeans, Greeks, Romans, Arabs, and European crusaders, held sway at various times until the Ottoman Empire extended its domination over much of the Arabian Peninsula and Transjordan in the early 1500s. The British and their Arab allies in 1918 ousted the Ottomans from Palestine and Transjordan, and by mid-1919 the last British forces had withdrawn from Damascus, the regional power center.

The Arabs who sided with the Allies during World War I had done so with the expectation that the victorious Europeans would champion Arab independence at the conclusion of hostilities. Following a congress of Syrian, East Bank Jordanian, and Lebanese notables, Amir Faisal of Hijaz was appointed king of the region. At the 1920 League of Nations conference at San Remo, however, the French secured a mandate over Lebanon and Syria and went on to remove Faisal from power in July of that year. At the same conference, in accord with secret agreements made during World War I, the British received mandates for Iraq, Palestine, and Transjordan. By 1921 the British had come to an understanding with their erstwhile allies, the Hashimites of the Hijaz: Faisal would renounce his claims to Syria and become king of Iraq, and his brother Abdallah would rule Transjordan. In May 1923, Britain recognized Transjordan within its established, informal parameters with Abdallah as its ruler.

Abdallah sought to meld the disparate Bedouin tribes into a cohesive group capable of maintaining Arab rule in the face of increasing Western encroachment. To maintain his position, Abdallah accepted financial assistance from Britain and agreed to its guidance on financial and foreign affairs. It was during this period that the fabled Arab Legion—with British officers leading Bedouin troops—was established as the cornerstone of the regime. The British mandate over Transjordan ended on May 22, 1946. Three days later, Abdallah was proclaimed king of the newly independent state of Transjordan.

The British relinquished their mandate over Palestine on May 14, 1948, and Zionists proclaimed the state of Israel the next day. Transjordan joined its Arab neighbors in attacking the new Jewish state, and when the fighting ended in 1949, Transjordanian forces controlled central and eastern Palestine, the West Bank, and East Jerusalem. In April 1949, the government in Amman announced that Transjordan would henceforth be known as Jordan, following Abdallah's annexation of the West Bank and East Jerusalem. The parliament approved the unification in April 1950. Nearly a half million Palestinian Arabs who

had fled the fighting could not return to their homes in Palestine and had therefore to remain as refugees in Jordan.

Abdallah conducted a number of talks with the Israelis in an attempt to resolve some of the Arab grievances against Israel. On July 20, 1951, however, a Palestinian angry about the king's opposition to Palestinian nationalist aspirations assassinated him. Abdallah's eldest son, Talal, was proclaimed his successor on September 5, 1951, but mental illness led to his forced abdication in favor of a regency for Talal's eldest son, Hussein. The new king, studying at Sandhurst Military Academy in Britain, returned to be crowned king on his eighteenth birthday, May 2, 1953.

The next two decades proved to be difficult for the young monarch. In 1955 and 1956 anti-Western, pro-Egyptian sentiments—sparked by the Suez crisis and Palestinian bitterness at the creation of Israel—made Jordan's ties to Britain a political liability. In 1956 Britain, along with Israel and France, attacked Egypt after the government in Cairo nationalized the Suez Canal. Arab support for Egypt ran high. To calm the situation, Hussein relieved the British commander of the Arab Legion, Gen. John Glubb (popularly known during his twenty years of service in Jordan as Glubb Pasha), and renounced Jordan's mutual defense pact with Britain. Hussein also refused to join the pro-Western Baghdad Pact, even though he had been involved in its creation. Hashimite rule in Jordan under Hussein barely survived a military plot uncovered in 1957 and a number of assassination attempts, including an effort by the Egyptian air force to down his plane. Hussein managed to remain in power because the army continued to back him in his efforts to curb domestic unrest and foreign meddling.

In 1958 a socialist, populist backlash against Arab regimes with close ties to Western powers came to a head: Egypt and Syria united in February to form the United Arab Republic. In July Lebanon descended into a civil war between nationalist and pro-Syrian socialist elements. Saudi Arabia, with the support of the West, was trying to form a counterweight to pan-Arabism, fearing its potential destabilizing effects. It was in this environment that Hussein struggled to maintain his throne and his nation's independence.

To withstand the forces arrayed against him, Hussein sought to form a union with his uncle, King Faisal of Iraq. The Iraqi revolution and the killing of Faisal in July 1958, however, destroyed that avenue. In addition, the revolution emboldened anti-Hashimite elements in Jordan to defy the king and his government. Fearing a concerted anti-Hashimite campaign directed by charismatic Egyptian president Gamal Abdel Nasser, whose calls for Arab unity widely appealed among Arabs throughout the region, Hussein requested British and U.S. assistance. In response, the British stationed troops in Jordan from July 17 to November 2, 1958, and the United States greatly increased its economic assistance to the kingdom.

In the years immediately following the successful defense of his crown, Hussein kept a low profile in inter-Arab politics as he tried to ameliorate domestic tensions. The more-or-less tolerable state of nonbelligerence between Jordan and Israel was broken on June 5, 1967, by Israel's surprise attack against its Arab neighbors. During the first few hours of the war, Israeli warplanes destroyed almost in their entirety the air forces of Egypt, Jordan, and Syria, leaving Jordan's forces vulnerable to air attack and with almost no chance at stopping the Israeli advance. After a spirited defense of East Jerusalem, Jordanian units were forced to withdraw completely from the West Bank with sizable casualties and loss of equipment.

Civil War

After the 1967 war, guerrillas of the Palestinian resistance movement expanded their organizational and recruitment activities in Egypt, Jordan, and Syria and used these countries as bases for assaults against Israel. Their attacks on Israeli targets captured the imagination of the Arab world. In particular, Palestinian refugees and expatriates saw in these fighters hope for regaining their homeland from Israeli control. Hashimite claims

to the West Bank had never been supported by most Palestinians or Arab states, and the military debacle in 1967 destroyed any lingering Palestinian hope that the Jordanian government could facilitate the return of their land.

In the immediate aftermath of the war, Hussein permitted Palestinian guerrillas to organize and strike at Israel from Jordanian territory in the hope that he would gain some degree of influence over their operations. By 1970 these hopes were dashed as the PLO sought to establish its political dominance within the Palestinian community there.

By September 1970, tensions had escalated into a full-scale civil war. The Popular Front for the Liberation of Palestine ostensibly triggered the war by hijacking three commercial U.S., British, and Swiss airplanes, holding 400 passengers hostage on a deserted airstrip in Jordan. Hussein viewed the hijacking and standoff as the beginning of a power struggle for control of the country. In an attempt to save his throne, he decided to pit his army against the Palestinian resistance movement.

Intense fighting erupted between the Jordanian army and the PLO in Amman and in a string of villages and towns near the Syrian border. Syrian armored units, camouflaged to look like PLO units, charged across the Jordanian border on September 20, 1970, in support of the rebellion against the monarchy. They were prompted not only because of longstanding animosity between Damascus and Amman, but also because the establishment of a Palestinian-controlled state in Jordan would allow Syria to support Palestinian anti-Israeli activities without having to provide physically for PLO guerrillas on its soil.

The United States provided public moral support to Jordan, increased its naval presence in the eastern Mediterranean, and offered Israeli military assistance to expel the Syrians. After consultations with Washington, Hussein decided to deploy his small air force against the invading Syrians. Syrian air force commander Hafiz al-Asad, noting Israel's mobilization along the Jordanian and Syrian borders, decided not to support the Syrian tanks with air cover, thereby allowing Jordanian air power to pummel the nearly defenseless tanks as they retreated into Syria. The lightly armed PLO guerrilla forces were no match for the artillery, tanks, and aircraft of the Jordanian army.

Foreign ministers of surrounding Arab states met in Cairo on September 22, 1970, to try to resolve the conflict. King Hussein and PLO chairman Yasir Arafat signed an agreement calling for substantial concessions by the Palestinians, but tensions remained. In July 1971, the Jordanian army crushed the last PLO positions in the pine forest above the northwestern Jordanian village of Ajlun. Although Hussein preserved Hashimite rule in Jordan, his regime was forced to bear an onerous political burden: the PLO's revenge. The first casualty was Jordan's prime minister, Wasfi al-Tal, who was assassinated in Cairo in November 1971.

Regional Politics

Jordan's marginal involvement in the October 1973 War, launched by Egypt and Syria against Israel on the Jewish holy day of Yom Kippur, did nothing to enhance its standing among other Arab countries. Hussein entered the war well into its final stages, and when he did, he only sent armored units to fight on the Syrian Golan. The border between Israel and Jordan remained quiet during the entire war.

In October 1974, the objections of King Hussein notwithstanding, Arab leaders meeting in Rabat officially recognized the PLO as the sole legitimate representative of the Palestinian people. Hussein argued that the PLO would never be able to wrest Palestine from the Israelis militarily or to effect a political settlement, but he grudgingly acquiesced to the Rabat decision. At the same time, however, being ever cautious, Hussein maintained his options by strengthening his contacts with the Palestinian community in the West Bank, cooperating more with the Syrians, and intimating that he remained open to discussions with Israel on a wide range of issues. Hussein considered the actions of the Rabat summit to be a direct challenge to his rule over the West Bank and a seeming endorsement of the parastatal behavior of the PLO in

Jordan that had led to Black September. At the same conference, the Arab states agreed to pledge financial support to the so-called frontline states in the fight against Israel and to the PLO, now headquartered in Lebanon.

The civil war that began in Lebanon in 1975 gave Jordan an opportunity to decrease its political isolation. Catalyzed by Syria's increasing involvement in Lebanon, which included opposition to the Palestinian leadership, the Arab consensus on the PLO's preeminence in Palestinian matters came unglued, thereby increasing Hussein's maneuvering room. Beginning in 1977 he and Arafat fashioned an uneasy reconciliation. *(See the Syria profile, p. 403)*

Also in 1977, Egyptian president Anwar al-Sadat visited Jerusalem, and two years later Egypt and Israel signed the Camp David Accords, after which the Arab League voted to eject Egypt. The agreement visualized a role for Jordan in a future settlement of the Palestinian issue, raising considerable skepticism in Amman. To Hussein, Sadat seemed to be opting out of the struggle for Palestinian national rights and bypassing the truly difficult issues—the political nature of the Palestinian entity on the West Bank and Gaza, the level of Israel's official presence there, and the future of Jerusalem. Hussein believed that if Egypt, with the support of the United States at Camp David, could not coax a viable compromise out of the Israelis, then he had little chance of doing so. Hussein feared the role envisaged for Jordan by Camp David a recipe for disaster. Without the outline of a settlement in sight that addressed most of the issues critical to the Palestinians, Hussein resolved not to move too far ahead of the Arab consensus on the matter. Assertions by influential members of the Israeli Likud Party that Jordan was a Palestinian state angered King Hussein.

From late 1982, when Israel forced the PLO out of Lebanon in a military invasion, until early 1986, King Hussein sought to co-opt or subordinate Chairman Arafat by discussing with him the formation of a joint Palestinian-Jordanian position vis-à-vis Israel and, possibly, a negotiating team. Arafat, politically weakened in the wake of the

PLO defeat in Lebanon, agreed in February 1985 to an accord for political coordination with Hussein, although the details remained unclear. Hussein worked to obtain PLO acceptance of UN Security Council Resolution 242, but Arafat, whose leadership had been rendered tenuous by radical elements within the organization, refused. In February 1986, Hussein severed his dialogue with the PLO, and his relations with the organization returned to a state of coolness.

Unsuccessful in his negotiations with Arafat and stung by the refusal of the U.S. Congress in 1985 to sell mobile air defense missiles, F-16s, and Stinger missiles to Jordan—because of the failure of his attempts to negotiate with Israel, efforts quashed by President Ronald Reagan— Hussein focused his attention on relations with other Arab states. The ongoing Iran-Iraq War and attending attacks on shipping in the Persian Gulf by both combatants had pushed the Palestinian issue lower on the agenda of Arab states and the international community. Hussein worked hard to achieve reconciliation among the Arabs, especially to gain acceptance of Egypt's return to the Arab fold. Although focusing primarily on Arab relations, he quietly made efforts aimed at cultivating a moderate, non-PLO leadership on the West Bank, including the announcement of an ambitious $1.3 billion West Bank development plan in mid-1986.

In April 1987, Hussein secretly met with Israeli Labor Party leader Shimon Peres in London and reached an agreement to work toward a five-power international peace conference. The attempt at advancing negotiations foundered, however, when Peres failed to secure the Israeli cabinet's support for the initiative.

By late 1985, Jordan's relations with Egypt, Iraq, and Saudi Arabia were good, and its relations with Syria—which had been hostile because of Jordanian support of Iraq and Syria's support of Iran during the Iran-Iraq War—had begun to improve slightly. The high point of Hussein's diplomatic efforts in the Arab world came in November 1987, when he hosted an Arab League summit in Amman. Through relentless diplomacy, Hussein secured agreement on two contentious issues. First, Syria agreed to support a resolution condemning Iran for holding Iraqi territory and for failing to accept a UN-sponsored cease-fire. Second, although Syria did not believe that Egypt should rejoin the Arab League, Syrian president Hafiz al-Asad agreed to a resolution explicitly permitting Arab League states to restore diplomatic relations with Cairo.

The intifada, the popular Palestinian uprising on the West Bank and Gaza that began in December 1987, transformed Jordan's diplomatic position and brought with it serious domestic consequences as well. Unlike the concerns of other Arab countries abutting Israel, Jordan's unease regarding the Palestinian issue represented more than a foreign policy issue, as Hussein feared that the uprising could spill over and encourage the Palestinians on the East Bank to rebel, despite their having become more or less integrated into the Jordanian polity since Black September. Moreover, the intifada threatened to diminish Hussein's role in the Middle East peace process relative to the PLO, which, although it had not started and did not control the uprising, still commanded the allegiance of most West Bank and Gaza Palestinians. Hussein hoped to prevent a ripple effect by relying on international efforts to jump start the peace process.

The United States and moderate factions in Israel remained committed to a key role for Jordan in the peace process and the outcome of any Arab-Israeli negotiations. In March 1988, U.S. secretary of state George P. Shultz proposed a multistep, two-track negotiating process. The first track would be multilateral, consisting of an international advisory committee to the second track, which would consist of direct, bilateral talks between Israel and a joint Jordanian-Palestinian negotiating team, mediated by the United States. Hussein could not agree to the proposals, however, because they went beyond the Arab consensus on the conflict. He nevertheless remained cordial to U.S. attempts to restart negotiations, knowing that he would be a key player in any such effort.

Arafat, meanwhile, took advantage of the uprising to strengthen his leadership. In June 1988, the PLO chairman succeeded in assembling an extraordinary conference of the Arab League at which the heads of state—with the exception of Egypt, which was yet to be readmitted—gave their full attention to the Palestinian issue. The Jordanian king could not prevent the summit from adopting Arafat's proposal to provide the PLO full financial control over support going to the Palestinians in the occupied territories. Arafat then suggested that as leader of the PLO, he should be the sole legal representative of Palestinians everywhere. The summit did not adopt this position, but the Palestine National Council affirmed it in November 1988.

Renunciation of West Bank Claims

In response to the above events, and perhaps hoping to insulate his kingdom from the intifada, on July 31, 1988, King Hussein formally renounced all Jordanian legal and administrative claims to the West Bank and called on the PLO to take responsibility for the Palestinians in the occupied territory. He dissolved the Jordanian parliament, half of whose members represented the West Bank, ordered Jordanian passports held by West Bank Palestinians to be changed into two-year travel documents, and eliminated salaries to West Bank residents whom Jordan paid to administer the territory but who had not been able to perform their jobs since 1967 because of the Israeli occupation.

The new Jordanian policy profoundly altered the situation in the Middle East. Pressure grew on the PLO to act like a government-in-exile, and by the end of 1988 the PLO proclaimed the independence of Palestine (which King Hussein recognized immediately), accepted UN Security Council Resolution 242, recognized the existence of Israel in a formula acceptable to the United States, and began a formal dialogue with Washington.

The king's announcement displeased the United States and moderate Israeli leaders, who had long hoped to avoid the establishment of a Palestinian state by implementing some kind of arrangement with Jordan. Although both had viewed Hussein as the Arab leader around whom a solution to the Arab-Israeli conflict could most

likely be constructed, neither had given him much support in his efforts to maintain leadership of the West Bank. The United States had provided Jordan with considerable economic assistance over the years, but recent U.S. administrations had found Congress mistrustful of Jordan, an attitude exemplified by its unwillingness to sell King Hussein weapons that he regarded as essential.

A Brief Political Opening

Hussein's renunciation of claims to the West Bank resulted in a decrease in Jordanian influence regionally, but the decision also freed Hussein to devote more attention to pressing internal problems caused by the kingdom's dire economic circumstances. The collapse of oil prices in the second half of the 1980s had sparked a regionwide economic crisis, and in 1988–1989 Jordan found itself on the verge of bankruptcy. As a consequence, Hussein called in the International Monetary Fund (IMF) to implement a comprehensive debt-rescheduling agreement, which included the freezing of state-sector salaries and the cutting of subsidies for basic commodities. A 30 percent increase in fuel prices triggered demonstrations throughout the country, starting in the south, in April 1989. In turn, Hussein announced the establishment of a new National Assembly, to be chosen openly from and by citizens on the East Bank, to which the frontiers of Jordan were now clearly limited. The elections, which took place in November 1989, were the first held in Jordan since the 1967 war.

A notable feature of the new eighty-person assembly was the election of thirty-two moderate Islamist candidates. Campaigning under the slogan "Islam is the solution," the Islamists, with the principal goal of reviving Islamic law in Jordan, emerged as the largest bloc—with 40 percent of the seats—but they did not control the assembly. Reacting pragmatically rather than ideologically to their newfound political strength, the Islamists tended to support the king's policies, despite disagreement with some of them, including disengagement from the West Bank.

The king also exhibited his commitment to increased political liberalization in his April 1990 appointment of a 60-member royal commission for the purpose of drafting a national charter to legalize political parties—banned since 1957—and regulate Jordanian political life. In January 1991, Hussein accepted the draft of the commission's work, and in June the national charter was formally ratified and implemented. Perhaps the highlight of the charter is its assertion of a social contract between the monarchy and its politically active subjects. Where political opposition in Jordan historically had expressed itself by questioning the legitimacy of the monarchy, the charter provided for the expression of all political views in return for the stated allegiance of any recognized political party to the institution of the monarchy. In short, the charter sought to channel political opposition away from the king, yet it enabled him to continue to play the decisive role in Jordanian politics.

The Gulf Crisis

Iraq's August 1990 invasion of Kuwait created a dilemma for King Hussein. During the Iran-Iraq War, Iraq had become highly dependent on Jordan as a transit route for materiel and other goods, which were shipped via the port of Aqaba. Meanwhile, Jordan had become highly dependent on Iraq, which supplied it with more than 90 percent of its petroleum requirements and nearly 50 percent of its international trade. Many Jordanian businesses profited from and were dependent on the brisk trade in goods and services between Iraq and the outside world. In addition, King Hussein favored a strong Iraq as guarantor of Jordanian national security in the event of a serious conflict with Israel or even with Syria.

The Jordanian monarchy also had close ties with Egypt, Saudi Arabia, the smaller Arab Gulf states, and the principal Western powers—the United States and other countries that coalesced to oppose the Iraqi invasion of Kuwait. King Hussein was quick to condemn the Iraqi aggression and worked to reverse it diplomatically. At the same time, however, he opposed the U.S.-led coalition's

commitment to resolve the crisis by force, if necessary. The economic embargo imposed on Iraq harmed Jordan perhaps to a greater extent than it hurt the more self-sufficient Iraq.

Caught in a difficult situation, Jordan pursued a policy of neutrality. In the king's view, he chose a principled stance, but in the eyes of most members of the anti-Iraq coalition, his policy was tantamount to supporting Saddam Hussein. Indeed, during the Persian Gulf crisis, Jordan experienced near-complete international isolation. Fortunately for King Hussein, despite the economic hardships that flowed from general adherence to the economic embargo, the loss of aid from members of the anti-Iraq coalition, and a large influx of refugees from Iraq and Kuwait, most sectors of the Jordanian population looked favorably upon his policy, pushing his popularity to new heights.

On the downside, Jordan suffered serious consequences as a result of the crisis. Severe shortages ensued, so the government imposed rationing of basic commodities, such as rice, sugar, and powdered milk. The rapid decline in international trade threw the country almost immediately into an economic recession from which it was difficult to emerge after the conflict ended. The sudden influx of nearly 300,000 expatriate workers from Iraq and Kuwait increased the size of Jordan's resident population by almost 8 percent in a matter of weeks. This additional population compounded the country's unemployment problem and represented a loss in worker remittances, which had amounted to $623 million in 1989.

Lost, too, was the economic aid that Jordan had received from Saudi Arabia and the small, oil-rich Arab Gulf states, who were less than pleased with Jordan's stance. Some estimates placed Jordan's economic losses from the Gulf crisis as high as $2 billion (and even higher when the loss is projected over subsequent years).

The Peace Process and the Israeli-Jordanian Treaty

Although Jordanian relations with the Arab Gulf states improved only slowly following the

Persian Gulf crisis and war, relations with the United States and other Western countries improved rapidly. The vital role required of Jordan in the U.S.- and Soviet-sponsored postwar Arab-Israeli peace initiative allowed Jordan to escape some of its isolation. By July 1991, the United States had restored $35 million in economic aid frozen during the crisis, and following Jordan's participation in the first round of Arab-Israeli talks held in Madrid in October 1991, it extended a further $22 million in military assistance.

The participation of Jordan made it possible for Palestinian representation in the negotiations as part of a joint Jordanian-Palestinian delegation. Had the arrangement been otherwise, Israel indicated that it would refuse to join the process. Once talks began, however, Jordanian members of the delegation assiduously avoided addressing questions related to the occupied territories, referring them to the Palestinian members of the contingent who spoke for themselves rather than as an element of a joint delegation. It soon became clear that the Palestinian delegation was negotiating separately from the Jordanian contingent and was coordinating its positions with PLO headquarters in Tunis. The PLO therefore had a de facto place at the table, despite Israel's commitment never to negotiate with it.

Such a development arose also because of a general agreement that a Jordanian-Palestinian confederation—not an independent Palestinian state—would be the farthest-reaching outcome of the process. In June 1992 in Israel, however, the Labor Party took control of the government from the Likud Party. Soon thereafter the new Israeli government, led by Prime Minister Yitzhak Rabin, opened a secret, direct dialogue with the PLO that ultimately culminated in mutual recognition and the formal signing of the Declaration of Principles in Washington on September 13, 1993.

The Israeli-PLO agreement caught King Hussein, and all other parties involved in the peace process, by surprise, but he quickly endorsed it. Hussein then authorized the signing and publication of the Jordanian-Israeli agenda for an eventual settlement that had been worked out in the bilateral negotiations stemming from the Madrid summit. Others in Jordan, particularly Islamist members of parliament and some leftists, denounced the Israeli-PLO agreement and also opposed the Israeli-Jordanian agenda. The status of the Palestinian majority in Jordan following a comprehensive Arab-Israeli settlement became an issue of concern that the king sought to ameliorate by assurances that all Jordanians, whatever their origins, had a place in his kingdom.

With the PLO heavily engaged with Israel in a peace process, Jordan had plenty of political cover to pursue its own agreement with Israel. Jordanian-Israeli enmities were far less extreme than those between Israel and the Palestinians and Israel and Syria. Since the 1967 war, Jordan and Israel had not engaged in significant combat. Moreover, the Israeli leadership and King Hussein had already established a working relationship behind the scenes, and Hussein had long been the Israeli government's preferred negotiating partner.

In the wake of Israeli redeployments from the Gaza Strip and Jericho in late spring 1994, Jordan and Israel moved quickly on bilateral negotiations. On July 25, King Hussein and Prime Minister Rabin arrived in Washington for the ceremonial signing of an agreement between their two countries. The Washington Declaration was not a full-scale peace treaty, but an agreement ending the forty-six-year state of war between the two countries and providing for further negotiations on a range of issues leading toward a comprehensive agreement. The two sides signed a wide-ranging peace treaty on October 26, 1994, providing for an exchange of ambassadors and broad cooperation in trade, tourism, water allocation, transportation, communications, environmental protection, and border arrangements. Both governments pledged not to allow third parties to use their territory for attacks against the other, and Israel recognized Jordan's role as a guardian of Islamic holy places in Jerusalem. Both leaders hoped their new relationship would translate into trade and other economic benefits that would build a strong constituency for peace among the people of their nations.

Hussein's Era Closes

An anticipated "peace dividend" did not materialize for Jordan to the extent that it was hoped, despite debt forgiveness and financial support from Western donors as well as some growth in the tourism sector. By 1996 it had become evident that Jordanian trade with Israel and the Palestinian territories would not increase substantially. A number of bureaucratic issues led to delays in various bilateral and trilateral cooperation projects. The Jordanian public, skeptical from the start, became increasingly frustrated with the reality and impact of the peace treaty.

In general, King Hussein's economic policies during much of the 1990s resembled a balancing act between external necessities and domestic considerations: The structural adjustment programs dictated by the IMF and the World Bank were partially implemented, as was the introduction of a general sales tax in 1994. Its main rate was reduced, however, from 10 percent in the original proposals to 7 percent, thereby taking into account the potential detrimental impact on the poor and the ensuing likelihood of widespread protests. In the arena of public sector reform, Hussein proved his understanding of the paternalistic state as a provider of jobs and money in exchange for loyalty from its citizens. He adamantly refused to agree to even small-scale dismissals from public enterprises and the bureaucracy. At the end of Hussein's rule and after a decade of reforms under the auspices of the Bretton Woods institutions, the Jordanian economy still displayed many features of the rentier era of the 1970s and 1980s.

Jordan's opening toward Israel and its partial economic reforms paralleled a gradual political shift away from liberalization on the domestic front, a process that began roughly with the parliamentary elections of 1993. A newly implemented electoral law favored rural and tribal areas and thereby limited the ability of the urban-based Islamists to garner votes and win seats in the Chamber of Deputies. Although running (unsuccessfully) in the 1993 ballot, the Islamic Action Front (IAF)—by far the strongest opposition party—chose to boycott the next parliamentary elections in 1997. The Press and Publications Law, enacted during the negotiations with Israel in 1994 and amended in 1997, represented another indicator of the gradual withdrawal of previously granted political liberties. It imposed stiff fines or jail time on newspaper publishers, editors, and reporters whom the government perceived to be errant. The law led to self-censorship on the part of the media and drew criticism from numerous international and domestic observers.

Toward the end of the 1990s, King Hussein's health overshadowed political developments in the country. Diagnosed in June 1998 with lymphatic cancer, Hussein underwent six months of treatment at the Mayo Clinic in Rochester, Minnesota. During his time abroad, his brother Crown Prince Hassan acted as regent. Hussein returned home in January 1999 and was greeted by hundreds of thousands of well-wishers. Speculation about the succession came to the fore when the king, in an interview with CNN on the day after his return, failed to give his unqualified support to Hassan as crown prince. Following the publication of a letter from Hussein to Hassan (released by the palace to the Jordanian press), it became apparent that Hussein had taken exception to rumors spread by Hassan's supporters as well as to certain of Hassan's actions during his stay in the United States. Never one to be outmaneuvered, the king had returned home to remind everyone that he was still in charge, and that they could not yet count him out.

A week later, Hussein named his eldest son, Abdallah, the new crown prince. The ceremony was held at Amman's military airport just prior to Hussein's departure to the United States for further treatment. The treatment proved unsuccessful, and the king returned home to Amman on February 4, 1999. He passed away three days later at the age of sixty-three, plunging the nation into mourning. Hussein had ruled Jordan for forty-six years, making him the longest-ruling leader in the Middle East and the second longest in the world. Some observers considered the king's role in domestic and regional politics to be so paramount that they equated Hussein as a person with Jordan as a state.

Abdallah's Succession

Hussein's large legacy and various unresolved domestic and regional political issues rendered King Abdallah II's succession a difficult undertaking. The challenges he faced in February 1999 ranged from a tense regional situation, including a moribund peace process, to a distressed national economy and lack of political experience. Abdallah's position was further complicated by the short notice of his succession, which left him neither the chance nor the time to develop a degree of personal and charismatic legitimacy, which his father had enjoyed for several decades. In short, he had not been prepared for his new task.

Despite these constraints at the outset, Abdallah quickly consolidated his position as uncontested at the top of the Hashimite regime. His gradual personnel changes among the political elite became

King Abdallah II

particularly obvious in 2000, when he managed to ease out two influential old guard figures, Prime Minister Abd al-Rauf al-Rawabdah and the head of the General Intelligence Department, Samih Battikhi, and replace them with less-opinionated and more loyal politicians. In December 1999, Abdallah had created the Economic Consultative Council (ECC), which served as a stepping-stone for primarily young, Western-educated, and business-oriented individuals. Some former members of the ECC subsequently became influential ministers, among them Finance Minister Bassam Awadallah, Government Performance Minister Salah al-Bashir, and Khalid Touqan, minister of education, higher education, and scientific research. Overall, King Abdallah maintained control over Jordan's intricate elite dynamics by constantly reshuffling a pool of loyal politicians.

Abdallah's partial inclusion of businessmen among the elite represented a corollary of his policy priorities. From the beginning of his reign, the king focused tangibly on economic and administrative reforms with the goal of integrating Jordan into the world economy. Major reform projects included Jordan's accession to the World Trade Organization (WTO) in January 2000, the establishment of a Special Economic Zone at the port of Aqaba in January 2001, and the creation of a number of Qualifying Industrial Zones (QIZ), which offer duty- and quota-free access to U.S. markets for products managed by "qualifying" enterprises. (The most important criterion requires a Jordanian and Israeli share of the value added.)

The young king's early decisions rewarded him with good standing abroad, above all among the Western donors, on whom Jordan still relies heavily. Despite all Abdallah's reforming zeal, it became obvious that decisions about reforms and their implementation typically stopped at the point where they might hurt an important domestic power base, as with large-scale dismissals in the bloated and inefficient public enterprises or the state bureaucracy. Abdallah's reluctance to privatize fully indicates that his economic reforms are still very much subject to the political logic of regime maintenance.

Current Regional Issues

King Abdallah's early foreign policy moves reflected his focus on domestic economic reforms. In April 1999 on his first tour abroad, Abdallah visited Saudi Arabia to improve Jordan's previously strained ties with the world's largest oil exporter. He also managed rapprochements with the smaller Gulf states, including Kuwait, with which a slow process of normalization began, representing quite a feat after the total breakdown of bilateral relations during the Iraqi occupation.

Jordan's relations with Syria also improved markedly. With the leadership changes that had taken place in both countries—the Syrian succession of President Bashar al-Asad took place in June 2000—the decades-long "cold peace" that had characterized Jordanian-Syrian relations was easily overcome. A shared interest in increased cooperation led to a far-reaching bilateral trade agreement in 2001, and the two states initiated the joint al-Wihdah dam project on the Yarmuk River. Abdallah concluded similar bilateral and multilateral agreements with Egypt, Morocco, Tunisia, and Yemen. Jordan's relations with the region's non-Arab states—Iran and Turkey—also improved.

In expanding regional ties, Abdallah sought to diversify Jordan's partners, above all in the fields of trade cooperation, and with regard to the Gulf states, a subsidized oil supply. At the same time, relying on a plurality of partners offered more policy options and flexibility in times of crisis: Jordan would not, for instance, be dependent on a sole regional ally, as it had been on Iraq for oil in the late 1990s and on the United States for security. The more potential allies the small and weak Hashimite kingdom could count on, the more likely it would be successful in walking the tightrope so characteristic of its foreign policy.

Reliable partnerships with external powers seemed an obvious necessary condition for the success of Abdallah's balancing act. The young king therefore moved to deepen Jordan's relations with the United States, the European Union (above all France, Germany, and Great Britain),

and Japan, its most important donor states. Jordan's relations with the United States, in particular, intensified, as embodied in the bilateral free trade agreement that went into force in December 2001 and involved a gradual dismantling of tariffs and other trade barriers over a ten-year period. The agreement, Washington's successful lobbying of the Paris Club to approve a fresh round of debt rescheduling in July 2002, and annual U.S. military and economic aid in return for a pro-Western stance in regional affairs underscored the strong ties between Washington and Amman.

The nature of the U.S.-Jordanian relationship became particularly evident in the context of the U.S.-led war on Iraq that began in March 2003. During summer 2002, Abdallah tried to persuade the Bush administration not to attack its eastern neighbor, as a war would seriously threaten the intra-regional balance of power and likely produce unpredictable consequences. An invasion also would endanger Jordan's supply of subsidized Iraqi oil. When it became clear, however, that the U.S. government had every intention of attacking Iraq and oust the regime of Saddam Hussein, the Jordanian king jumped on the bandwagon: The Jordanian government allowed the United States to use two air force bases in the eastern desert and station hundreds of soldiers on its territory. The two states also participated in joint military maneuvers in August and October 2002. In turn, the Hashimite kingdom received $1.1 billion in U.S. aid, which was officially declared as compensation for its war-related losses. This assistance comprised approximately one-third of Jordan's annual income in 2003.

Abdallah and the government denied supporting the war, as they were rather uneasy about the potentially harsh reaction of the political opposition and of large parts of the Jordanian population. Popular antiwar and pro-Iraq demonstrations were allowed, but only if flanked by a heavy police force and the pervasive intelligence service.

The Israeli-Palestinian conflict did not figure prominently in Jordanian policy during Abdallah's first one and a half years on the Hashimite throne. Only with the beginning of the al-Aqsa intifada in the Palestinian territories in September 2000 did the issue gain a prominent spot on his foreign policy agenda. As was the case during Hussein's era, King Abdallah tried on the role of mediator, along with Egyptian president Hosni Mubarak and, since 2002, Saudi crown prince Abdallah. He also urged the U.S. administration forward in its vital role as facilitator in the conflict. Abdallah strongly supported the so-called road map, the three-step peace plan put forth in April 2003 and supported by the European Union, the United Nations, the United States, and the Russian Federation. (Jordan's foreign minister at the time, Marwan al-Muashir, was nicknamed "Mr. Roadmap" because of his strong commitment to the initiative.)

With the lack of progress and the escalation of violence during the Palestinian rebellion, however, the Hashimite regime came under heavy pressure from the Jordanian public. Particularly vocal was the "anti-normalization front," a loose network of members of professional associations as well as parts of the Islamic Action Front, which called for severing relations with Israel and abrogating the 1994 treaty. Their critique was primarily directed against Israeli prime minister Ariel Sharon, in office since February 2001, who is loathed in Jordan for his attacks against the Palestinians and for his claim, made in the 1980s and repeated afterwards, that Jordan would make a natural home for the Palestinians.

Current Domestic Issues

All in all, political opposition in Jordan continues to be dominated by the professional associations of engineers, lawyers, doctors, teachers, and writers. Political parties do not play a decisive role. In 2005 there were thirty parties in Jordan, but with an estimated 9,000 members between them, most represented little more than status symbols for their respective leaders. Only the moderate Islamists of the IAF have any serious claim to being a fully constituted, ideologically based party.

The withdrawal of previously granted political liberties, a process that began under King Hussein in 1993, continued under Abdallah. Most prominent in this regard was the postponement of parliamentary elections initially scheduled for November 2001, based on the four-year election cycle. Before the end of the third legislative period in summer 2001, the king dissolved parliament, citing the tense political situation between Israel and the Palestinian Authority. Abdallah governed subsequently by royal decrees and during the next two years issued some 200 "temporary laws" that officially involved security concerns but de facto curbed political freedoms. The post–September 11 "war on terror" facilitated this trend, as the regime used it to mount a major clampdown on radical Islamists. Political freedoms suffered another blow when in August 2002 the king postponed parliamentary elections for a second time, again citing regional instability. Fear that the IAF would gain influence is a more likely reason for the postponement.

When legislative elections finally took place in June 2003, a few months after public shock and anger over the war on Iraq had somewhat subsided, the old electoral law ensured a landslide victory for pro-regime candidates. The system clearly privileged rural and tribal areas over the largely Palestinian-dominated cities. To win a parliamentary seat representing Amman, for instance, required about 52,255 votes. The required number of votes to represent the southern tribal regime stronghold of Karak was more than eight times lower, at about 6,000 votes. In an expanded Chamber of Deputies—with 110 parliamentarians, including six women as per a newly established quota—only 17 IAF candidates plus a handful of moderate Islamists gained seats, leaving an absolute two-thirds majority to pro-regime individuals.

Outlook

Jordan's geographic location between the regional hot spots of Israel/Palestine and Iraq, in addition to its military and economic weaknesses, necessitates that its government constantly perform a balancing act. Foreign policy under King Abdallah II thus far remains reactive and largely dependent on external influences. Jordan's special relationship with the United States, in particular, will ensure essential external support in the foreseeable future. Despite the obvious difficulties in walking a fine line between bigger and more powerful neighbors, such a position might also be considered an asset for the Hashimite regime in that it can continue to capitalize on its role as a reliable Western ally in the strategic Middle East.

It is therefore unlikely that the United States will pressure Abdallah to liberalize Jordan's authoritarian polity in any substantial way, as this would decisively strengthen moderate Islamists, many of whom share an anti-Western and anti-U.S. agenda. From this perspective, it is easy to understand the lack of criticism when the regime delayed parliamentary elections from 2001 to 2003 as well as of its attempt in January 2005 to muzzle the professional associations, which remain the strongest opposition in the country.

King Abdallah's projects for political reform are also unlikely to encounter strong external criticism even though they serve primarily to perpetuate the current system, albeit with a more liberal facade: His plan for a new electoral law, ratified as it stands, would only bring about cosmetic changes, as pro-regime gerrymandering would continue. His decentralization initiative, once implemented, might merely produce an additional layer of red tape rather than render the state apparatus more efficient. Abdallah's proposal for a merger of the thirty smaller parties into three larger parties, representing the left, center, and right of the political spectrum, is no more than wishful thinking when one takes into account the fact that tribalism is likely to remain the predominant aspect of political allegiance in Jordan.

All in all, the Hashimite regime under King Abdallah remains fundamentally stable, and no signs in the short term point to a change in that status. In the midterm, however, two major internal challenges could threaten the political status quo. Despite Abdallah's push for economic reforms, Jordan's foreign debt in 2004 stood at $7.5 billion, while the unemployment rate approached 25 percent. Almost one-fifth of the population lived below the poverty line. Add to these figures Jordan's annual demographic growth rate of roughly 3 percent, and it becomes obvious that job creation, particularly among the young, and poverty alleviation will be among the major politico-economic tasks facing Abdallah in the years ahead.

A second and related challenge concerns the politicization of competing identities in Jordan. In recent years, protests by Palestinian Jordanians (such as those in the refugee camp of al-Wihdat near Amman in 2004), the riots in the tribal town of Ma'an in 2002, and intense public discussions about Jordanian nationalism suggest that the unresolved matter of political identities may become more of an issue in the future. Of particular concern for Abdallah will be his relationship with the East Bank tribes, one of the most important and longstanding bases of the Hashimite regime. The tribes have criticized the modernist king for his neglect of traditional customs that, allegedly, have led to their economic and political marginalization in recent years. Thus, in the realms of foreign, domestic, and economic policies, King Abdallah II must perform balancing acts between multiple and competing interests in order to preserve Hashimite dominance of Jordanian politics.

CHAPTER **12**

KUWAIT

The central event in Kuwait's modern history is the August 1990 invasion of the country by Iraq. During a seven-month occupation, Iraqi forces inflicted horrendous suffering on the Kuwaiti population, destroyed the country's infrastructure, stole or pillaged public and private property, and ignited more than 700 oil wells. An international military campaign led by the United States ejected the Iraqis and restored Kuwaiti sovereignty, but the invasion and occupation laid to waste the fundamental assumptions on which Kuwait based its security policy.

Sitting atop some of the richest oil deposits in the world, Kuwait possesses almost unrivaled natural wealth. Profits from oil have enabled the government to establish generous cradle-to-grave benefits for Kuwaiti citizens, though declining oil prices in 1998 and the cost of reconstruction following the Persian Gulf War strained the government's finances and lowered per capita income. The rise in oil prices in 2004–2005 enabled the government to restore fiscal balance and assured the Kuwaiti budget of a handsome surplus in oil revenues. The rise in oil income was great enough to allow the government to increase the salaries of public servants in spring 2005.

Although Kuwait is the first Gulf monarchy with a freely elected parliament, voting rights and political participation remain restricted to a narrow group of Kuwaitis. On May 16, 2005, after six years of placing obstacles in the way of granting women the right to vote, the Kuwaiti National Assembly finally approved a measure enfranchising them and allowing women to run as candidates for parliament.

Geography and Demography

Kuwait—meaning "little fortress"—lies at the head of the Persian Gulf, bordering Iraq and Saudi Arabia and facing Iran across the gulf. Roughly the size of New Jersey, Kuwait covers 6,880 square miles, including ten offshore islands, the main ones being Bubiyan, Warba, and Failaka. Kuwait's terrain is mainly flat desert with a few oases. Summer temperatures often reach well into the hundreds, with frequent dust and sand storms. Winters are mild. Because rainfall is so infrequent, most drinking water is provided by distilling seawater from the Shatt al-Arab waterway, which runs into the Persian Gulf. With only 0.4 percent of the land arable, agriculture is extremely limited. As a result, Kuwait imports nearly all of its food.

In 2004 the population of Kuwait was estimated at 2.3 million, with some 966,000 of those being citizens. The rest are primarily foreign workers from other Arab countries, South Asia, and the West. Indigenous Kuwaitis are primarily descendants of Arabian tribes. Kuwaiti citizenship is highly restricted even for families that have lived in the country for generations. The group on the lowest wrung of the social ladder is the *bidun* (meaning "without documents"), stateless Arabs from Iraq, Jordan, and Syria who lived in Kuwait prior to 1965 but who failed to qualify for citizenship. Who obtains citizenship rests on the discretion of the interior minister (and ultimately the approval of the Council of Ministers). On the whole, few foreigners have been able to obtain Kuwaiti nationality. The government grants citizenship to some

Key Facts on Kuwait

Area: 6,880 square miles (17,820 square kilometers)

Capital: Kuwait City

Population: 2,335,648, of which 1,291,354 are nonnationals (2005)

Religion: Muslim, 85 percent; Christian, Hindu, Parsi, and other, 15 percent

Ethnic Groups: Kuwaiti, 43 percent; other Arab, 35 percent; South Asian, 9 percent; Iranian, 4 percent; other, 9 percent

Official Language: Arabic; English widely spoken

Type of Government: nominal constitutional monarchy

GDP: $48 billion; $21,300 per capita (2004)

Source: Central Intelligence Agency, *CIA World Factbook,* 2005.

5,000 biduns each year. The number of stateless residents is estimated at 100,000.

Eighty-five percent of Kuwaiti residents are Muslim. The other 15 percent consist of non-Muslim foreign workers. The ruling Al Sabah family and more than half of Kuwait's Muslims are Sunnis; the remaining Muslims are Shiites. Kuwaiti law prohibits non-Muslim public worship but is tolerant of such private worship. Non-Muslims cannot become Kuwaiti citizens.

By the 1960s, oil wealth had transformed Kuwait into the ultimate welfare state. Kuwaiti citizens enjoyed unparalleled access to subsidized social services and virtually free housing. They paid no income tax. The government guaranteed all citizens a job, an education, health care, and retirement benefits. (The government employs about 90 percent of all citizens.) The state also provided cash gifts to defray the costs of weddings and funerals. Electricity and water charges were negligible, and petroleum products were provided at deep discounts. Even domestic telephone calls were free. Until the mid-1980s, Kuwaitis enjoyed per capita incomes that ranked among the top five in the

world. Per capita income remains quite high, estimated in 2004 to be $21,300. Although citizens are entitled to a wide range of free services, the benefits offered immigrant workers are limited, leading to hostility between the minority native Kuwaiti population and the majority immigrant population.

Kuwait relies heavily on foreigners to fill positions in its workforce. Large numbers of expatriate Arabs were drawn to Kuwait by employment opportunities in the oil industry and the service sector supported by the country's oil wealth. Fears of internal unrest and terrorism related to radical Islamist ideologies and the Palestinians' struggle for statehood prompted the government to work quietly toward changing the workforce from one dominated by Arabs and Iranians to one that relied more on workers from India, Pakistan, and other parts of Asia. In 1987 the government announced a five-year plan aimed at reducing the number of Arab and Iranian expatriates working in the country, but the plan ultimately had little effect on their overall numbers.

The 1991 Persian Gulf War allowed the government to attempt once more to take assertive steps toward reducing the expatriate population. Many of the Palestinians who remained in Kuwait were deported on the grounds that they had collaborated with the Iraqi occupiers. Kuwait also induced large numbers of non-Palestinian Arabs, particularly Jordanians, Yemenis, and Sudanese, to leave. Just before the Iraqi invasion, Kuwait's population was estimated at 2.14 million people. By mid-1992, it had decreased to just 1.3 million, in part because the devastation of the war led many Kuwaitis to remain abroad. As reconstruction progressed during the 1990s, however, most citizens returned. Many noncitizens who had fled also returned, although they remained largely ineligible for government services and compensatory benefits. By 1994 the numbers of expatriates in Kuwait had rebounded and then began to rise.

History

Kuwait's modern history begins with the founding of Kuwait City in the early eighteenth century by members of the Anaiza tribe, the first settlers, who arrived from the Najd (central Arabia). The Al Sabah dynasty dates from 1756, when Kuwaiti settlers decided to appoint a shaykh, an Al Sabah, to administer their affairs, provide for their security, and represent them in dealings with the Ottoman Empire. Although Kuwait remained independent of the Ottomans, the Al Sabahs recognized Ottoman influence and interests in the region and paid financial tribute to the empire. The Kenaat are another prominent family (from the Basra region of Iraq) who settled Kuwait, along with a few notable families of southwestern Persian (Iranian) origin.

During the latter half of the nineteenth century, Kuwait looked to Britain as a counterbalance to Ottoman dominance in the region and for protection from raiding Wahhabi tribes of central Arabia. In return, Kuwait recognized British trading rights in the Persian Gulf. In 1899 Shaykh Mubarak Al Sabah signed an agreement with Great Britain effectively establishing Kuwait as a British protectorate.

This arrangement, under which Britain controlled Kuwait's foreign affairs and security, lasted until 1961. The British intervened on Kuwait's behalf at three critical junctures. In 1899 they prevented an Ottoman invasion. In 1920 they repelled attacks from Wahhabi tribesmen, though Kuwait nevertheless lost some 40 percent of its territory to the expanding Saudi kingdom. The 1922 Treaty of Uqair settled this conflict and established a neutral zone south of Kuwait. In 1961, shortly after Kuwait gained independence and established a constitutional monarchy, Iraq claimed sovereignty over its territory based on old Ottoman records. When Baghdad threatened to invade, Kuwait asked for and received British military assistance, deterring an Iraqi invasion. An Arab League peacekeeping force representing Jordan, Saudi Arabia, Sudan, and the United Arab Republic arrived in September 1961 to replace the British. In 1963 Kuwait was admitted to the Arab League and the United Nations. Iraq recognized Kuwait's independence in 1963.

Kuwait predicated its regional foreign policy during the 1960s, 1970s, and early 1980s on its commitment to Arab causes and nonalignment in inter-Arab disputes. Because of the country's

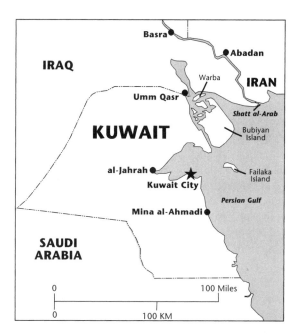

small size and location, Kuwaiti leaders did not believe its security could be achieved solely through a strong defense. They sought consequently to ensure Kuwait's security by maintaining an accommodating posture toward its neighbors. It also supported mainstream Arab goals—such as Palestinian rights, Yemeni unity, and Lebanon's integrity—with political backing and generous financial assistance. Kuwait's oil wealth—which allowed it to use checkbook diplomacy to co-opt critics and reward friends and allies—made the country an influential player in the Arab world despite its small size. Through the Kuwait Development Fund, the government also distributed millions to developing countries.

During the 1967 Arab-Israeli war, Kuwait declared its support for the Arab combatants and contributed significantly to the reconstruction of Egypt, Jordan, and Syria. Kuwaiti forces stationed along the Suez Canal during the 1973 Arab-Israeli war took part in the fighting, and Kuwait provided substantial financial aid to the Arab states involved in the conflict. Kuwait also played a major role in convening the Organization of Arab Petroleum Exporting Countries (OAPEC) to develop a policy for the use of Arab oil as a weapon to pressure

Western countries, particularly the United States, into forcing an Israeli withdrawal from occupied Arab lands. Kuwait joined other countries in increasing the posted price of crude petroleum by 70 percent and participated in the embargo on petroleum shipments to the United States. At the Arab summit held in Baghdad in November 1978, Kuwait pressed for unanimity in condemning the Egyptian-Israeli peace agreement and supported sanctions against Egypt.

Along with Bahrain, Oman, Qatar, Saudi Arabia, and the United Arab Emirates, Kuwait became a founding member of the Gulf Cooperation Council (GCC) in 1981. In the hostile climate created by the Iran-Iraq War, the oil-producing Gulf countries

Jabir al-Ahmad Al Sabah

hoped that economic integration and political coordination would increase their security.

Government and Politics

Kuwait, as a hereditary constitutional monarchy, is ruled by an amir who hails from one of two branches of the Al Sabah family. The current amir, Shaykh Jabir al-Ahmad Al Sabah, succeeded his cousin to the throne on December 31, 1977. Shaykh Mubarak Al Sabah, who ruled Kuwait from 1896 until 1915, had two sons, Jabir and Salim. The succession of the monarchy alternates between the descendants of Jabir and those of Salim. According to the Kuwaiti constitution, the crown prince, the heir apparent, is designated by an amiri order. The National Assembly then signifies its approval by a majority vote. The second-most-powerful position, crown prince and prime minister, goes to the side of the family not occupying the post of amir. The amir appoints the Council of Ministers, or cabinet, which is headed by the prime minister. Al Sabah family members hold the major cabinet positions, including the key portfolios of foreign affairs, defense, and interior. Legislative authority is vested in a fifty-member National Assembly.

Domestic politics in Kuwait is driven by four points of conflict: among the members of the ruling family along dynastic lines; between the old established merchant families and the ruling family; between the regime and those advocating change in the political order, which is to say nationalists, Islamists, and secular politicians; and between upper-class male Kuwaiti citizens and the nonenfranchised population. Political parties are banned, although increasingly well organized caucuses *(diwaniyya)* comprising tribal constituencies, Arab nationalists, and Islamists have existed since the early 1980s. The Kuwaiti press has enjoyed relative freedom since the Persian Gulf War. In February 2005, a group of Islamists announced the formation of the Islamic Umma (Islamic Nation) Party, a symbolic measure, as Kuwaiti law does not allow political parties.

The amir has suspended the National Assembly three times—from 1976 to 1981, from 1986 to

1992, and in 1999—because of its criticism of the regime, particularly regarding corruption and economic policy. Before the Iraqi invasion, many Kuwaitis had been unhappy with the form and substance of Al Sabah rule. The family had occasionally allowed citizens to dabble with various constitutional and parliamentary reforms, but the changes never endured. Many of the Kuwaitis who survived Iraqi atrocities felt empowered to demand change. With the royal family in exile, the invasion provided fertile ground for a resistance movement to organize and gain strength and purpose. As a result, a new willingness to challenge the old order evolved.

This assertiveness expressed itself in the National Assembly, for which elections were held in 1992, 1996, 1997, and 1999. The assembly began to exert significant influence after its reinstatement following the war and is known for its lively debate. Kuwait is the only Gulf country with an assembly elected entirely by popular vote.

On May 4, 1999, the amir dissolved the National Assembly and scheduled new elections for July 3. Although government supporters held a majority in the body, cooperation between members of parliament and the government's fifteen cabinet members had been disintegrating for months. Legislators launched weekly attacks against the government, accusing it of corruption, questioning basic economic policies, and holding no-confidence votes. The gridlock was felt outside the government, as the Kuwaiti stock market slumped and arms purchases were delayed because of charges of contract fraud.

Also in May, the amir took advantage of his dissolution of parliament to issue roughly sixty edicts. Most pertained to economic and budgetary policy, but the one that gained the most attention was his declaration that Kuwaiti women be granted the right to vote and to run for office beginning with elections scheduled for 2003. Although Kuwaiti women held prominent positions in business, diplomacy, and the oil industry, they were excluded from politics. The amir's edict concerning them became the centerpiece of the July elections.

The outcome of the elections revealed sharp disagreement among Kuwaiti men on the issue of women's rights. Only 113,000 men met the requirements necessary to vote in the elections: They had to be literate, at least twenty-one years old, and able to trace their Kuwaiti ancestry several generations; members of the military police were excluded from the franchise. Islamist and tribal candidates, who generally opposed greater political participation for women, won twenty of the fifty seats, but liberal candidates in favor of women's suffrage increased their numbers from four to fourteen. The other sixteen seats were won by independent and pro-government candidates, who saw their numbers shrink.

The parliament cannot amend an edict of the amir, but it does have the power to approve or reject it by a majority vote of its members and ministers voting together. (Kuwait's fifteen government ministers are ex-officio members of the assembly.) Immediately after the elections, it was unclear whether forces in favor of women's suffrage could muster the thirty-three votes necessary to approve the amir's edict. Some of the more liberal members of parliament who favored women's suffrage were also among the foremost advocates of government reform. Even as they approved of the substance of the edict, they challenged the right of the amir to issue such an edict, arguing that the constitution limited the use of edicts to emergencies. In 2000, when the National Assembly finally took up the issue, it rejected women's suffrage. That same year, the conservatively oriented assembly passed a law requiring certain private universities to segregate students by gender. By September 2001, gender segregation extended to the national university.

On July 5, 2003, liberals sustained heavy losses in National Assembly elections, handing control of parliament to conservative Islamists and pro-government elements. The results shocked the liberals, who had been quite vocal in demanding political reforms. Nevertheless, after the elections, the amir responded by meeting one of their most urgent demands—separating the posts of crown prince and prime minister. On July 13, 2003,

Shaykh Sabah al-Jabir Al Sabah, the former foreign minister, was appointed prime minister, and Shaykh Saad al-Abdallah al-Salim Al Sabah continued in the position of crown prince. This change subjected the prime minister to questioning by the National Assembly. The right of interpellation, which had caused tensions over the years, gives deputies the authority to question ministers on matters falling within their competence.

In February 2005, the issue of women's suffrage again made the headlines when the government submitted another proposal to parliament granting women the right to vote. Under pressure from Kuwaiti liberals, women, and the government, in May 2005 the parliament approved the measure by a 35-23 vote. Also in May, Massuma al-Mubark became the first woman appointed to the cabinet. She holds the portfolios for planning and administrative development. In addition, two women received appointments to municipal councils.

Oil and the Economy

Before the development of the oil industry, Kuwait's economy was based on fishing, trading, and pearling. The Anglo-Persian Oil Company (now British Petroleum) and the Gulf Oil Corporation discovered oil in Kuwait in 1938. They capped the wells at the onset of World War II, but further development was delayed until 1948. By 1956 Kuwait had become the largest oil producer in the Middle East. The government bought out British Petroleum and Gulf Oil in March 1975, thereby becoming the first Arab petroleum-producing nation to achieve complete control of its output.

Kuwait's oil exports in 2003 were an estimated 2 million barrels a day, resulting in revenues that totaled $29.41 billion. Natural gas production reached some 293 billion cubic feet in 2002. Kuwait possesses almost 10 percent of the world's proven petroleum reserves. With an estimated 93 billion barrels, Kuwait's reserves as of 2003 were the fourth highest, after only Iran, Iraq, and Saudi Arabia. The nation also has large natural gas deposits at approximately 56 trillion cubic feet.

The Kuwaiti constitution declares all natural resources to be the property of the state. Oil sales provide 75 percent of government income. In addition to funding a comprehensive social benefits package for Kuwaiti citizens, Kuwait's oil revenues were also used to create the Reserve Fund for Future Generations, which held approximately $65 billion as of late 2003 and is intended to provide for Kuwaiti society after the country's oil resources are exhausted.

Kuwait saw its oil export revenue decline by about 33 percent in 1998 because of a collapse in oil prices. In 1997 Kuwait earned about $11.8 billion from oil exports, compared with $7.9 billion in 1998. Oil prices rebounded in 1999 to nearly 1997 levels. Nevertheless, reducing the country's dependence on the sale of oil has been a government priority for more than two decades. In doing so, it established small petrochemical and fertilizer industries to help offset declines in income during slumps. It also made substantial overseas investments through the Kuwait Investment Office to help cushion the blow of low oil prices. Regardless, oil continues to account for more than 90 percent of Kuwait's export earnings and almost half of its gross domestic product. About 60 percent of Kuwaiti oil is sold to Asian and European countries.

From August 1990 until July 1991, during the Iraqi occupation and its aftermath, the Kuwaiti government depended solely on its income from international financial investments and profits from Kuwait Petroleum International, which operates Kuwaiti petroleum companies in Europe and Asia. The government's funding efforts during the crisis and war drained Kuwait's investments, decreasing them from $100 billion to $40 billion.

The occupying Iraqi forces severely damaged the country's oil-producing facilities, sabotaging an estimated 800 of 950 oil wells and setting aflame 723. The cost of repairing the wells and extinguishing the fires, combined with losses in oil revenue, was estimated at more than $40 billion. Rehabilitation of the petroleum sector became the government's highest economic priority and one that it has since successfully completed.

Budget deficits persisted during the 1990s as a result of low oil prices, lingering reconstruction and defense costs, and the Kuwaiti leadership's reticence to reduce benefits for citizens. The government ran deficits of more than $5 billion in 1997 and more than $6 billion in 1998. In an effort to reverse this trend, the government began considering plans to significantly expand its oil production capacity, which stood at about 2.4 billion barrels per day in 1998. In 1999 the government floated a controversial proposal to allow foreign oil companies to help develop fields in the north. As of mid-2005, however, an agreement had yet to be reached with an oil company, but talks continued.

Insecurity and the Iran-Iraq War

Fearing the spread of radical Islamic fundamentalism, especially if Iran emerged victorious from its conflict with Iraq, Kuwait backed Iraq financially throughout the eight-year Iran-Iraq War from 1980 to 1988. Kuwait also allowed Iraq access to Kuwaiti ports, enabling the flow of Iraqi petroleum exports to continue. It, however, refused Iraqi requests for access to the strategic islands of Bubiyan and Warba.

In retaliation for Kuwait's support of Iraq, Iran targeted Kuwaiti territory and shipping, attacking merchant ships and seizing cargo en route to and from the country. It bombed Kuwaiti oil installations near the Iraqi border in September 1981. Five people died and sixty-one were wounded when six bombs exploded in Kuwait City in December 1983, increasing concern about Kuwaiti security. Al-Jihad al-Islamiyya (Islamic Holy War), a militant Shiite organization with acknowledged connections to Iran, claimed responsibility for the attack and another in 1984.

The fear of domestic unrest among Kuwait's Shiites led the government to deport more than 600 Iranian workers in 1984. In December of that year, tensions rose when hijackers of a Kuwaiti airliner forced the plane to land in Tehran and demanded the release of seventeen Shiites imprisoned for the 1983 bombings. The hijackers were overwhelmed after killing two Americans. In April 1988, another hijacking of a Kuwaiti airliner, with the same goal of a prisoner release, failed and resulted in the death of two Kuwaitis.

In May 1985, an Iraqi member of the banned organization al-Dawa al-Islamiyya (Call of Islam) attempted to assassinate Amir Jabir al-Ahmad by driving a car bomb into a royal procession. Other violent incidents during the remainder of 1985 and 1986 included explosions at Kuwait's main export refinery and deadly bombings in Kuwait City. Security became an obsession. The government deported some 27,000 expatriates, many of them Iranians, and the National Assembly unanimously approved the death penalty for people committing terrorist acts resulting in the loss of life.

After Iranian forces began attacking Kuwaiti shipping, Kuwait sought outside protection, in December 1986, for its oil tankers. After the Soviet Union offered protection, the United States agreed to Kuwait's request in an attempt to head off growing Soviet influence in the Persian Gulf. In May 1987, eleven Kuwaiti tankers were reregistered and provided protection by U.S. naval forces. Kuwaiti tankers also sailed under the flags of Liberia, the Soviet Union, and the United Kingdom. Within days, a reflagged tanker hit a mine. The United States and Saudi Arabia helped in clearing other mines, and in August, after initially refusing, France and Great Britain sent minesweeping vessels to the Gulf, as did Belgium, Italy, and the Netherlands in September. Following the August 20, 1988, cease-fire between Iran and Iraq, the naval escorts were gradually discontinued.

The Iraqi Invasion, Occupation, and War

The UN-sponsored cease-fire between Iran and Iraq held the promise of stability for an exhausted region. After years of war and recession, Kuwait's economy began to improve. In its drive for market share to increase oil revenues, Kuwait in 1987 began consistently ignoring OPEC production quotas. Iraq's economy, on the other hand, emerged from the war with Iran exhausted and on the verge of crisis. Kuwait expected repayment for the equivalent of $16 billion in cash and oil sales that it had provided during the war. Meanwhile, Iraq considered relief from the massive debts that it had accumulated during the war the minimum contribution that Iraq's sacrifices merited in defense of the Arab world against the threat of revolutionary Iran.

In July 1990, Iraqi president Saddam Hussein accused unspecified countries of petroleum overproduction in violation of quotas, which had been fixed at a May 1990 OPEC meeting. He also accused Kuwait of stealing $2.4 billion worth of oil reserves from the Rumaila oil field, which straddles their undemarcated border; he demanded border modifications and the leasing of Bubiyan Island. Iraqi foreign minister Tariq Aziz in addition insisted that Kuwait cancel Iraq's war debt, compensate it for lost revenue incurred during its war with Iran and as a result of Kuwait's overproduction, and provide $10 billion in emergency aid. Iraq also sought redress through the Arab League.

Iraqi and Kuwaiti representatives met in Saudi Arabia on August 1 in an attempt to resolve the conflict, but the talks collapsed. Saddam Hussein, seeing an opportunity to seize the vast financial and petroleum resources of Kuwait, gambled that the international community would not intervene if he used military force. On August 2, 1990, 100,000 Iraqi troops invaded Kuwait. Kuwaiti forces numbered 20,000. Amir Jabir al-Ahmad and the royal family fled to Saudi Arabia, along with some 300,000 Kuwaiti citizens; many others were already abroad on holiday. Only one in four Kuwaitis remained in the country, together with the bidun and Palestinian populations who had few options for resettlement.

In the days leading up to the attack, Kuwaiti military officials had pressed the government to allow them to call a military alert. The regime, however, believed that such a move would only give Iraq a pretext for invasion. As a result, when the assault began, at least three-fourths of Kuwait's armed forces personnel were on leave or away from their posts.

Iraq formally annexed Kuwait on August 8 and declared it the nineteenth province of Iraq on August 28. From the first day of the occupation, Iraqi troops plundered, burned, and ransacked the country. They also kidnapped, tortured, raped, and assassinated Kuwaiti citizens and foreigners. What they could not steal they destroyed in a seemingly deliberate effort to efface all traces of Kuwaiti culture. Kuwaiti resistance groups inflicted persistent, if minor, damage on Iraqi forces.

The Kuwaiti government-in-exile, headquartered in Taif, Saudi Arabia, used the Kuwait Investment Office in London as a national treasury to pay the living expenses of Kuwaiti citizens stranded abroad. On October 13, the Al Sabahs held a national convention in Taif attended by a thousand delegates. The gathering was designed to present a united front against Iraq, counter Iraq's popular appeal with the Arab and Muslim masses, demonstrate the legitimacy of Al Sabah rule, and accommodate U.S. and Arab wishes to see a more democratic Kuwait worthy of the international efforts being made for its liberation. The opposition members of the dissolved National Assembly used the event to extract concessions for democratic reforms. Determined to present a strong national front, the Al Sabahs agreed to "consolidate democracy under the 1962 constitution" after liberation and to hold new elections. The Al Sabahs also acted to solidify the support of regional powers, giving $2.5 billion to anti-Iraq coalition members Egypt and Turkey and forgiving Egypt's huge debt.

On January 17, 1991, the UN-backed, U.S.-led multinational force launched the military campaign to drive Iraqi forces from Kuwait. After an intense aerial bombardment of Iraq that lasted more than a month, ground forces entered Kuwait on February 24. Within three days, Iraqi troops had fled the country.

The amir returned to a devastated Kuwait on March 14. Most government buildings and harbor facilities had been destroyed or damaged; during the war, Iraqi forces had released oil into the Gulf, causing considerable harm to desalination facilities and the fishing industry. The enormous structural and environmental damage left the country scarred.

Repatriation of the national population became a high priority. The government initiated a program to register all resident non-Kuwaiti nationals and prohibited the return of non-Kuwaitis until labor requirements could be calculated. The government exploited the invasion's displacement of expatriates by restricting the number of non-Kuwaiti residents to less than 50 percent of the pre-crisis total. The Palestinian population—paying the price for the Palestine Liberation Organization (PLO) having sided with Iraq—declined from a high of 400,000 to no more than 40,000 after the occupation. Scores of Palestinians complained of abuse and discrimination. Human rights groups alleged that security forces and random gangs had tortured as many as 2,000 Palestinians suspected of collaboration. After the death of PLO chairman Yasir Arafat in late 2004, Kuwait reestablished relations with the PLO and announced the lifting of restrictions imposed on Palestinians seeking to work in Kuwait.

Foreign Policy and Defense

The Iraqi invasion and the victory by the U.S.-led coalition resulted in a dramatic shift in Kuwaiti foreign policy from one of neutrality to one of overt dependence on the United States (as well as on France and Britain) for military protection. The reflagging of Kuwaiti tankers in 1987 had established a cooperative relationship between the United States and Kuwait, but after the Iran-Iraq War, Kuwait had downplayed its ties to Washington to avoid charges of being too close to an outside power. Kuwait had also sought to diversify its arms purchases and improve relations with the Soviet Union and other European and Arab states. Even as Iraq had become increasingly aggressive in 1989, Kuwait had not wanted to align itself openly with the West.

After the Persian Gulf War, however, Kuwait came to regard the United States as its ultimate defender. In September 1991, Kuwait and the United States signed a defense agreement that provided for the stockpiling of U.S. military equipment in Kuwait, U.S. access to Kuwaiti ports and airports, and joint training exercises and equipment purchases. The Kuwaiti government also paid $50 million for the construction of a new U.S. embassy.

Kuwait pays the United States about $350 million per year to offset the cost of joint exercises and other U.S. military efforts in the country. U.S. ground troops are not permanently stationed in Kuwait, but there are usually ground units training there. Since 1994 the United States has prepositioned enough military equipment in Kuwait to outfit a brigade; troops can be rushed there to access the equipment in case of hostilities. U.S. Air Force personnel enforcing the postwar "no-fly" zone in southern Iraq were stationed in Kuwait, and the government accommodated U.S. military buildups during periods of tension with Iraq in the postwar period.

After the end of the Persian Gulf War, the Kuwaiti government attempted to rebuild and strengthen its military so that it could at least slow any future Iraqi advance long enough for U.S. and international forces to arrive. To this end, Kuwait purchased large numbers of tanks, artillery, fighter aircraft, and antitank helicopters from the United States. It also purchased Patriot antimissile units to down short-range missiles launched from Iraq or Iran. Kuwait's purchases of sophisticated military equipment bolstered its firepower, while U.S. training improved the Kuwaiti military's professionalism. To complicate an attack from Iraq, Kuwait also fortified its border with a ditch and twelve-foot-high barrier.

Kuwait's sense of betrayal by Arab nations that sided with Iraq during the war runs deep. Kuwait had been a major contributor of foreign aid to Jordan and Yemen as well as to the PLO, but after the war Kuwait discontinued financial assistance to them because of their support of Iraq. It continued to direct its foreign aid toward those Arab countries that had contributed to the anti-Iraq coalition, especially Egypt, Morocco, and Syria. Despite its break with the Jordanian and PLO leaderships, however, Kuwait welcomed the agreement between Israel and the PLO in September 1993. The government had traditionally approached the Arab-Israeli conflict within the context of consensus among Gulf states, but it became the first country, after Egypt, to relax its economic boycott of Israel.

In 2000 relations between Kuwait and Yemen, Jordan, and the Palestinian Authority began to improve. This development came after Jordan, Yemen, and the Palestinians strongly condemned the Iraqi occupation of Kuwait. In 2004 the Kuwaiti government lifted the restrictions it had imposed on the employment of Palestinians during the postwar period.

Toward the end of 2002 and the beginning of 2003, the threat of a U.S-led invasion of Iraq began increasingly to look like a real possibility. The Kuwaiti government supported international voices calling on Saddam Hussein to resign and leave Iraq, after he was accused of failing to cooperate in revealing an alleged secret program to produce weapons of mass destruction. It also supported the massive military build up on its territory of British, U.S., and other coalition forces in preparation for military intervention to remove Hussein from power. No Kuwaiti military forces participated in the invasion of Iraq that started on March 19, 2003, and ended some four weeks later with the toppling of Hussein's Baathist regime.

The Kuwaiti government welcomed Hussein's removal and was one of the first countries to provide Iraq with humanitarian assistance. The fall of the Iraqi government aroused the interest of Kuwaiti businessmen and investors, who saw an opportunity not only to make money but also to help rebuild the country. Their interest was short-lived, however, as the rise of an insurgency in Iraq and the deterioration of the security situation made working and investing there unattractive prospects.

A small percentage of Kuwaitis did not welcome the presence of U.S. troops in their country, the use of Kuwaiti territory to invade Iraq, or the support of the Kuwaiti government for U.S. military operations against Iraqi insurgents following the official end of combat. Their dissent came to light when Kuwaiti Islamist activists and imams began criticizing the government. In January and February 2005, the government announced the discovery of terrorist cells and weapons caches. The cells, alleged to have ties to the al-Qaida network, were composed of Kuwaitis and Saudis planning acts of sabotage inside Kuwait as well as sending fighters to battle alongside insurgents inside Iraq. Confrontations with Kuwaiti authorities left a few people dead and the government vowing to crack down on such groups.

In 2004 the Kuwaiti government took official steps to ease residual tensions with Iraq. It recognized the interim government installed on June 1, 2004, and the two countries announced the reestablishment of diplomatic relations. Iraqi prime minister Iyad Allawi visited Kuwait at the end of July 2004, followed thereafter by President Ghazi al-Yawar. In response to Iraqi demands that Kuwait reduce or forgive its huge debt and reparations, the Kuwaitis promised to study the matter. Despite great efforts, the new Iraqi government and the U.S. and coalition forces did not find any of the 600 Kuwaitis forced from their homes by the Iraqi army as it retreated in 1991. All parties now assume that these missing persons are likely dead. The bodies of a few missing Kuwaitis were found in mass graves in Iraq.

Outlook

Kuwait's post–Gulf War reconstruction program was swift and successful. The economy, however, was not so easy to fix. The regime has had to weigh the political risks of ending subsidies and other assistance that Kuwaitis had come to expect against the risks of economic problems caused by high budget deficits. Despite a reduction in the number of non-Kuwaitis receiving social services, the government is likely to increase user fees and reduce the subsidy of services, as it did in 1985, when it allowed domestic energy prices to rise and imposed user fees on some goods and services that previously had been free.

It is clear that the solution to the deficit will come at a price. While the fundamental problems of Kuwait's state-dominated economy are long-standing and officially acknowledged by the ruling family, there is little consensus about how to resolve them. In this budgetary environment, Kuwait will continue to seek ways to expand its oil-production capacity. Its economic situation appears to be improving, as revenues from oil increased substantially in 2004 and 2005 when oil prices rose sharply on the international market. As a result, the 2003–2004 budget registered a surplus of $54.4 billion. In a first for Kuwait, at the beginning of 2005, the government allowed three foreign banks to open branches in the country. In 2004 the government allowed private owners to buy some state-owned gas stations, and privatization continues in other areas as well, including the sale of Kuwait Airways, the national carrier.

Relations between Kuwait and Iraq should steadily improve, with substantial Kuwaiti investment in Iraq when the security situation improves. Being a small country, Kuwait realizes that it must maintain balance in its relations with its much larger neighbors, mainly Saudi Arabia and Iran.

Kuwaiti citizens traumatized by the brutalities of the Iraqi occupation can no longer be placated by public services alone. Their heightened political consciousness has focused greater attention on Kuwait's international investments and the country's security and defense. The National Assembly is self-confident and confrontational in exposing corruption and demanding greater accountability from the government. Kuwaiti women receiving the vote should revolutionize politics in Kuwait. Not only will it place in doubt the results of the first election in which they vote, but the grounds for denying the vote and citizenship to other members of Kuwaiti society have been weakened.

CHAPTER 13

LEBANON

The assassination of former prime minister Rafiq al-Hariri in the streets of Beirut on February 14, 2005, changed the political map of Lebanon. After initially reviving memories of fifteen years of devastating civil war, the attack quickly elicited a response from the Lebanese that evolved into the "Beirut Spring," with mass demonstrations—and strong international backing—demanding that Syria, believed responsible for the assassination, end its twenty-nine year occupation of Lebanon. To the surprise of all, within three months of Hariri's death, Syria had withdrawn the last of its troops.

By 1990 Lebanon's civil war had burned itself out without solving any of the internal identity issues that had rendered the country vulnerable to manipulation and penetration at the hands of its two feuding neighbors, Syria and Israel. For fifteen years, Syria had been Lebanon's undisputed suzerain, anointing presidents and prime ministers while exploiting the gradual resurrection of Lebanon's once vibrant economy. Syria's decision in August 2004 to dictate the extension of Lebanese president Emile Lahoud's term may have appeared to be business as usual, but something had changed. Prime Minister Hariri voiced his disagreement and then resigned. The UN Security Council adopted a resolution demanding the withdrawal from Lebanon of all foreign forces and the disarming of all militias, a gesture clearly aimed at Syria and its ally, Hizballah. Lahoud's term was extended nonetheless (by a constitutional amendment), and Hariri was murdered.

The political trajectory of Lebanon is far from certain. How will the Lebanese political system respond with the Syrian presence removed from the equation? In a political system based on confessionalism—institutionalized sectarianism—most of Lebanon's Christians, Sunni Muslims, and Druze seem to count themselves among those joyful about the Syrian departure. Yet the country's largest and poorest sect—heavily represented in Lebanon's armed forces and with a militia of its own—was ambivalent. In June 2005, anti-Syrian forces led by Saad al-Hariri, the son of the former prime minister, won the majority of seats in the first legislative elections held after the Syrian withdrawal. Perhaps the key question now facing Lebanon is whether it will be necessary to discard confessionalism and create a true nation in order to unify the population in restoring the country's independence.

Geography

Lebanon is a small country of 4,015 square miles—smaller than the state of Connecticut—located on the eastern edge of the Mediterranean Sea. From north to south it has a maximum length of 135 miles, and its average width from west to east is less than 35 miles. It shares a 200-mile internationally recognized border with Syria to the north and east. To the south the border with Israel corresponds in part with the "line of withdrawal" (also known as the "blue line") demarcated by the United Nations in 2000 to confirm the full evacuation of Israeli military forces from southern

Key Facts on Lebanon

Area: 4,015 square miles (10,400 square kilometers)

Capital: Beirut

Population: 3,777,218 (2004)

Religion: Muslim, 59.7 percent; Christian, 39 percent; other, 1.3 percent

Ethnic Groups: Arab, 95 percent; Armenian, 4 percent; other, 1 percent

Official Language: Arabic; French, Armenian, and English widely spoken

Type of Government: Republic

GDP: $17.82 billion; $4,800 per capita (2003)

Source: Central Intelligence Agency, *CIA World Factbook,* 2004. There are no reliable statistics available on the demographics of Lebanon. The last census was conducted in 1932.

Lebanon. The line of withdrawal actually has two distinct components: a line that approximates the Palestine-Lebanon boundary demarcated in 1922 and reconfirmed by the 1949 Israel-Lebanon armistice; and the line between Lebanon and the Israeli-occupied Golan. Neither component of the line of withdrawal enjoys the status of a universally recognized international boundary.

Lebanon's only two neighbors, Syria and Israel, have a history of mutual hostility, and each has exploited the underlying diversity and disunity of Lebanon in pursuit of its own strategic advantage. Both countries are far stronger than even a politically unified Lebanon could be, and both have vested security interests in Lebanon's foreign and domestic policies. Over the years, the nation's governments have been forced to balance competing pressures related to the Arab-Israeli conflict; that fine line is manifested in the government's claim that the withdrawal of Israeli forces from Lebanon in 2000 was not complete, that "occupation" was ongoing, and that continued "resistance" by Hizballah (the Party of God) was justified.

Lebanon's compact land area is divided into four distinct, longitudinal parallel geographical regions: (1) a narrow coastal plain that runs the full length of the Mediterranean coast, where the major port cities of Tripoli, Beirut, Sidon, and Tyre are located; (2) a coastal mountain range, known as Mount Lebanon, where the country's principal non–Sunni Muslim religious communities of Maronite Christians, Druze, and Shiite Muslims have their roots; (3) the fertile, grain-producing Bekaa Valley, which varies from five to eight miles in width; and (4) a lower, interior mountain range called the Anti-Lebanon, through which runs the border with Syria. Each of these regions has a different climate, soil, water supply, density of settlement, lifestyle, and history.

In the Mount Lebanon range, deep valleys divide the mountains into a number of distinct districts that give the Jbaylis, Kisrawanis, Metnis, Shufis, and other Lebanese living in them a strong sense of local identity that competes with a broader national identity. Most Lebanese define themselves by their town, city, district, or region, as well by their clan and religious community.

The climate of the country's coastal plain, where more than half the population lives, is typically Mediterranean—hot and humid with little rain during the nine-month summer, and quite rainy but with almost no snow during the three-month winter. The climate of coastal Lebanon contrasts sharply with the climate of the mountains, where heavy snows fall in the winter, the summers remain cool and invigorating, and the four seasons are distinct.

Economy

Aside from its largely self-subsistent agricultural base, Lebanon is poor in natural resources. As a result, its modern economic structure developed around trade, banking, and tourism. Before the civil war, two-thirds of the country's gross national product was based on these service industries. The routing of most Middle Eastern trade with the West through the port of Beirut gradually transformed that city into the region's main commercial and financial entrepôt. Sidon and Tripoli, the sites of two major oil pipeline terminals and refining facilities, also profited.

Lebanon's economic growth, boosted by enterprise and a laissez-faire approach to government interference, was spectacular but uneven. Although Beirut became a glittering center of international trade, some parts of Lebanon, such as the Shiite-dominated southern regions and the northern Bekaa Valley, remained largely underdeveloped. The attraction of Beirut to the less fortunate led to the haphazard development of housing, which deteriorated into massive slums, particularly in the southern suburbs. There, large numbers of rural poor, especially Shiite Muslims and Palestinian refugees, settled to seek work in the city.

The civil war pummeled the Lebanese economy. The commercial center of Beirut—where most of Lebanon's banks, hotels, and international businesses were located—was almost totally destroyed in the early years of the war and is only now beginning to be rebuilt. Nevertheless, some Lebanese entrepreneurs, businessmen, and traders continued to function through a number of militia-controlled "illegal" ports that sprang up along the coast. Israel's 1982 invasion and the chaos that followed only exacerbated Lebanon's economic deterioration.

Economic policy under post–civil war governments succeeded in restoring economic growth and stabilizing Lebanon's currency. Development was uneven, however, favoring the tourism and service sectors to the detriment of agriculture and industry. Although governments took pains to restore the downtown area of Beirut and repair Lebanon's many hotels and tourist facilities, they did little to supply low-income housing. Moreover, reconstruction was financed primarily through debt. The Hariri government was shadowed by accusations of corruption, and Lebanon's public debt exceeds 185 percent of gross domestic product. In November 2002, Lebanon submitted a comprehensive financing program to the Paris II Donors Conference, attracting pledges totaling $4.4 billion to retire or replace maturing debt.

Demography

Historically, Lebanon has been a haven for religious, ethnic, and political minorities. Canaanite (Phoenician) in biblical times and largely Christianized prior to the rise of Islam, Lebanon became a country in which Christian and Muslim minorities could maintain a relatively autonomous communal existence. This was particularly true in the Mount Lebanon region, around which the historical development of the country turned. In general, Lebanon's northern region was occupied by Maronite Christians, its central portion by the Druze, and its southern tip by Shiites. Fiercely independent, these communities in the Mount Lebanon region have alternately banded together to resist external control and battled one another to keep any one group from becoming dominant.

The major cities along the coast—Tripoli, Beirut, and Sidon—developed apart from Mount Lebanon for centuries and were eventually populated by

Sunni Muslims. The few Christians who lived in these towns were usually Greek Orthodox. Only in the mid-nineteenth century did large numbers of Maronites, Druze, and Shiites begin to settle along the coast, and then primarily in Beirut. Tyre, the main coastal city in southern Lebanon, has long been inhabited principally by Shiites.

The Bekaa Valley and its neighboring Anti-Lebanon mountains historically served as arenas of contest between the prevailing powers in Mount Lebanon and the Syrian interior. Nevertheless, the Bekaa is characterized by sectarian diversity: in the north, Shiites; in the central valley, Sunnis, Greek Orthodox, and Greek Catholics (that is, Greek Orthodox who adhered to Rome in the late eighteenth century); and in the south, Druze.

A 1932 census placed the ratio of Christians to Muslims at six to five: Maronites were the largest group, at 30 percent of the population, while Sunnis composed the next largest group at 20 percent. Representation in the Lebanese political system would be based on these figures.

By 1975 lower birthrates and higher rates of emigration among the more prosperous Christian communities, combined with higher birthrates and lower emigration rates among the more disadvantaged Muslim and Druze communities, had greatly altered the country's demographic composition. Tens of thousands of deaths during the civil war and massive emigration in response to new eruptions of violence further altered the country's demography. In 2004 Lebanon had an estimated population of about 3.8 million, roughly 95 percent of which was Arab. Reliable figures as to the sectarian breakdown of the population do not exist (Lebanon's last census was taken in 1932), but some estimates of this politically sensitive demographic situation reflect a Muslim majority of up to 70 percent. Some argue that overseas Lebanese (presumably predominantly Christian) should be counted. Complicating Lebanon's demographic situation is the fact that tens of thousands of Palestinian refugees fled to Lebanon following the 1948 Arab-Israeli war and the civil strife in Jordan in 1970. Although 182,000 Palestinians were officially registered in Lebanon in December 1971,

estimates of their numbers during the 1980s were as high as 350,000. In 2004 the Palestinian population was estimated at 400,000.

The Ottoman Period, 1516–1918

The Ottoman Turks incorporated Mount Lebanon into their vast empire with their conquest of Syria in 1516. Nevertheless, for most of the Ottoman period it remained an autonomous political entity under the rule of an indigenous amir who recognized the sovereignty of the Ottoman sultan. The amirs were Druze, but they governed on behalf of all the inhabitants of the mountain. Lebanese local autonomy lasted for several centuries but began to weaken during the first half of the nineteenth century. Locally, by that time, the Maronite Christian population had expanded, moving from their traditional region in northern Lebanon into the predominantly Druze central areas, which led to incidents of interconfessional violence. The character of the Ottoman Empire was also changing, with Constantinople in 1826 embarking on a policy of political centralization that some Lebanese viewed as a threat to their autonomy.

Although the European powers had traded in Lebanon for centuries, only in the nineteenth century did they begin to seek out indigenous political actors with whom to form alliances. When established, these relationships were couched in terms of "protection": in return for preferential access to markets and political decision making, the Europeans would advocate and "protect" the interests of their client community at the Ottoman court. Faced with the centralization policies of the Ottoman government, the Maronites viewed French protection as the best guarantee of political autonomy. Thus, the French formed a relationship with the Maronite Christians, the Russians with the Orthodox Christians, and the British with the Druze and, to a lesser extent, the Sunnis. Following disturbing interconfessional unrest in 1860, these relationships allowed the European powers to control Mount Lebanon to the virtual exclusion of the Ottoman Empire.

After nearly thirty years of mounting unrest and the spread of sectarian conflict, an international commission headquartered in Beirut was established to resolve the crisis. Its members represented the five principal European powers—Austria, France, Great Britain, Prussia, and Russia—plus the Ottoman government. The regime imposed on Lebanon by the commission did not resolve conflicting sectarian interests, but it did restore general order and security. The six-power international treaty of June 9, 1861, served as a kind of constitution for Mount Lebanon for the next fifty years, making the governor, or *mutasarrif,* of Lebanon an Ottoman appointee. French and Maronite concerns were met by a provision that the governor be a non-Lebanese Ottoman Christian acceptable to the European powers. The treaty also created a twelve-member central administrative council with representatives from the principal religious communities in the country. The council had the authority to assess taxes, manage the budget, and give advice on issues submitted to it by the governor. As time passed, the Ottoman-appointed governor became more of a figurehead, and the authority of the central administrative council increased.

Significant social and economic development took place between 1860 and 1914. Roads and railroads opened up Lebanon and the Syrian interior to international commerce. Beirut began to flourish as a commercial center and to attract many immigrants from the countryside, gradually transforming the traditional, largely Sunni town into a thriving multisectarian and cosmopolitan city. Some refer to this period as the Arab Renaissance in learning and culture.

By the end of the nineteenth century, Lebanon had emerged as one of the most tranquil, prosperous, and highly developed regions of the Ottoman Empire. Many Maronite and Druze peasants acquired real estate and became prosperous landowners. In the coastal cities of Tripoli, Beirut, and Sidon, trading families rose to positions of great wealth.

These economic developments led to the emergence of a strong sense of Lebanese identity among the people of Mount Lebanon, especially among the Maronites. The Maronites tended to perceive themselves as the vanguard of progress in the country, partly because of their closer links with the West, particularly France. Even more important was Lebanese leadership of the Arab nationalist movement against Ottoman rule. The despotic policies of Sultan Abdul Hamid (1876–1909) and of the Young Turk regime (1909–1918) that deposed him led Christians and Muslims throughout Syria, Lebanon, and Palestine to organize into clandestine political opposition groups.

French Mandate, 1918–1943

Since the mid-nineteenth century, France had considered itself the protector of the Maronites, a relationship that facilitated Maronite ecclesiastical union with Rome. Prior to World War I, France had used the Maronites as a compradore class to facilitate its trade in Syria. With the division of the Ottoman Empire following the war, the League of Nations granted France a mandate in 1920 to oversee the political development of Syria and Lebanon. Its first action was to expand the frontiers of Ottoman Mount Lebanon to make the territory more economically and demographically viable. The additional areas included the major coastal towns, the Bekaa Valley and portions of the Anti-Lebanon mountains, and territories to the north and south of Mount Lebanon itself. This territorial revision added new populations of Sunni and Shiite Muslims to the demographic mix of "Grand Liban," or Greater Lebanon. Because in the nineteenth century the Maronite Christian community had become a virtual French client, expansion of Lebanon's demographic base enabled Maronite political leaders to exert more power. They cultivated the allegiance of more politically passive groups, especially the Sunni Muslim community of coastal Lebanon, as a means of dominating the Druze and Shiites, who fiercely resented Maronite control of the new state.

The most significant problem of the French mandate era was conflict between the Maronite

Christians on Mount Lebanon, who generally supported the concept of an independent Lebanon, and the Sunnis on the coast, who favored reincorporation with Syria of those regions that France had annexed to Mount Lebanon in 1920. The conflict continued until an alliance between the two was formed during the course of World War II.

On May 26, 1926, an elected Lebanese representative council adopted a constitution that transformed the expanded Lebanon into the Lebanese Republic, although France retained overall control. Despite the fact that the constitution was adopted under French mandate and would be amended many times by successive governments, it has remained a fundamental document outlining the organization of the Lebanese government and defining its powers. The document provided for equitable representation of the various sectarian communities, but it did not establish a fixed ratio for confessional representation, nor did it reserve specific government positions for members of different communities. Constitutional amendments in 1927 and 1929 transformed the original bicameral legislature into a unicameral body and extended the three-year renewable term of the president to a six-year nonrenewable tenure. Members of parliament were to be popularly elected from established electoral districts. The president would be elected by the parliament rather than by popular vote—a provision that would later provide for a degree of stability in turbulent times. For example, although the 1972 parliament, the term of which was to end in 1976, served until 1992 without re-election, presidential elections were held in 1976, 1982, and 1989.

The French administered Lebanon through the interwar period and into World War II. A domestic Lebanese political alliance between Maronites and Sunnis favoring independence formed in the late 1930s and gained momentum following the Allied occupation of the country and the removal of the Vichy-appointed high commissioner by Great Britain and the United States in 1941. The Lebanese Republic proclaimed its independence in 1941, although Free French officials continued their administration until 1943. In 1943 new constitutional procedures were instituted based on sectarianism.

As noted earlier, a national census in 1932 had determined that the ratio of Christians to Muslims was six to five. The census defined the Maronite and the Sunni Muslim communities as the two largest sectarian groups—30 percent and 20 percent of the population, respectively—and on this basis agreement was reached that the president of Lebanon would be a Maronite and the prime minister a Sunni. The agreement, the National Covenant of 1943, remained the formula, however obsolete and flawed, upon which the Lebanese government was structured until 1989.

The formula proved fragile from the start because it represented an agreement between the political leaders of only two of Lebanon's many sectarian communities. It also reinforced the notion that sectarian affiliation was politically significant, thereby hindering the development of national unity. The main weakness of the covenant, however, was its rigidity and inability to anticipate socioeconomic and demographic changes. Its implicit assumption of Maronite-Sunni collaboration in governing Lebanon was also flawed. Despite these fundamental problems, the formula worked to a reasonable degree for more than thirty years, in part because the Lebanese feared the consequences of its failure. In 1943 Bishara al-Khoury, the Maronite leader of the Lebanese independence movement, was elected the first president of the newly independent Lebanon. He immediately named his Sunni Muslim partner, Riyad al-Solh, as his first prime minister.

Lebanese Politics, 1943–1975

Lebanon's most profound political crises occurred at the time of presidential elections in 1952, 1958, 1976, 1982, and 1989, although there have been countless subplots in the drama of Lebanese politics. After Lebanon gained independence in 1943, its strong presidency proved to be the principal stabilizing element in an otherwise chaotic political environment. In general, a consensus prevailed that no one party or power should dominate and thus destabilize the delicate political status quo established in 1943. In 1975 this consensus was breached, and more than fifteen years passed before a degree of order could be reestablished in the country.

Lebanese politics from 1943 to 1975 was based almost exclusively on family networks and patron-client relationships among the country's dominant political figures and less central actors. All of the major sectarian communities produced leading families that dominated the country's politics: the Khourys, Eddes, Chamouns, Chehabs, Franjiyyahs, and Gemayels among the Maronites; the Solhs, Salams, Yafis, and Karamis among the Sunnis; the Jumblatts and Arslans among the Druze; and the Asads and Hamadahs among the Shiites. Closely associated with the leading families was another tier of families counted among the Lebanese "aristocracy" but who had not yet attained a position of dominance. Through a combination of wealth and political influence, these families built powerful patron-client relationships in the mountain districts and urban quarters that served as the principal base of their national political influence. Political parties tended to be the creations of prominent families, which thus controlled voting blocs in parliament. Political status generally passed from father to son, and with certain exceptions, members of the families that dominated Lebanon at the time of independence remained key political figures into the early 1990s.

Lebanon's first two presidents, Bishara al-Khoury and Camille Chamoun, governed effectively during their first years in office (1943–1952 and 1952–1958, respectively). However, both ran into political opposition over charges that they were trying to influence parliamentary elections with the aim of securing a parliament amenable to changing the constitution to extend their terms in office. These power struggles highlighted the interconfessional as well as the intraconfessional difficulties in Lebanese politics.

When parliament did extend Khoury's term, Chamoun, his protégé, turned against him.

Chamoun, Kataib Party leader Pierre Gemayel, Progressive Socialist Party leader Kamal Jumblatt, and others in 1952 formed an alliance known as the Socialist Front, which called for an end to sectarianism and the corruption and favoritism they accused the regime of fostering. In the summer of 1952 the Socialist Front organized a countrywide general strike to force Khoury to resign. Following Khoury's capitulation, the Lebanese parliament on September 23 elected Chamoun president.

Like his predecessor, Chamoun governed effectively during the first years of his term. The crisis that brewed during the latter half of his presidency varied in a number of important ways from Khoury's. Khoury had based his power on a strong alliance with a Sunni Muslim prime minister, whereas Chamoun sought to dominate the Muslim community by changing prime ministers regularly and playing Sunni politicians against each other as well as weakening the political strength of his Maronite rivals. To boost his own popularity, Chamoun presented himself as a populist leader of all Lebanese citizens.

Chamoun's tactics to guarantee his political ascendancy were undermined by the marked regional instability that coincided with the end of his term. In February 1958, Egypt and Syria merged to form the United Arab Republic (UAR), a move supported by many Lebanese Muslims, who favored Lebanon's joining the union. This debate over joining the union highlighted the conflicted nature of Lebanese identity. If Lebanon was an Arab country, it should seek union with Egypt and Syria; on the other hand, if perceived as a haven for Maronites seeking autonomy in a world of Muslims, Lebanon should not join. Hence, Chamoun's ploy to augment his personal power at the expense of both Muslims and Christians was further fueled by a political union largely favored by Muslims and opposed by Christians.

In 1957 Chamoun, like Khoury in 1947, was accused of fraudulently influencing parliamentary elections and of seeking a constitutional amendment that would enable him to be reelected. Unable to resist effectively through constitutional procedures, his opponents turned to violence and terrorism following the vote. In contrast with 1952, when Chamoun joined with Maronite and Druze politicians to protest Khoury's effort to extend his term, in 1957 the conflict had a much stronger sectarian tone, since Chamoun had come to dominate Christian politics to prevent the appearance of a rival Maronite candidate. In addition, at a time when Chamoun was perceived as undermining the Muslim role in Lebanese politics, Gamal Abdel Nasser's appeal was strong. As a Christian, however, Chamoun believed that growing pan-Arab sentiment in Lebanon, inflamed and supported by Egyptian influence, threatened Lebanon's independence.

In May 1958, violence erupted in Lebanon after the assassination of an anti-Chamoun journalist; a full revolt broke out in the countryside. The government charged that pan-Arab forces in Syria were smuggling arms and munitions into the country in an attempt to overthrow the government and ordered the military, under Gen. Fuad Chehab, to crush the revolt. General Chehab refused, maintaining that the role of the military was not to become embroiled in domestic politics but to defend the nation from external threats.

On July 14, Nasserists staged a bloody coup in Iraq. President Chamoun, fearing not only for the independence of Lebanon but also for his life, invoked the Eisenhower Doctrine and, over strong Muslim opposition, requested military intervention by the United States in order to fend off any chance of a pan-Arab coup in Lebanon. In January 1957, the U.S. Congress had approved the Eisenhower Doctrine, a resolution declaring that "if the President determines the necessity . . . [the United States] is prepared to use armed forces to assist . . . any nation or groups of nations requesting assistance against armed aggression from any country controlled by international communism."

On July 15, the first of nearly fifteen thousand U.S. Marines landed on a Beirut beach. The marines' presence stabilized the country and allowed a U.S.-mediated compromise to be implemented between Chamoun and his opponents.

Chamoun finished out his term of office in September 1958 and was succeeded by General Chehab, who had won the support of Lebanon's Sunni Muslim leaders by refusing to deploy the army against them earlier in the year. The last of the marines withdrew in late October.

Chehab's presidency marked a turning point for Lebanon. Domestically, Chehab consolidated his power (and mended fences) by drawing into the government both pro- and anti-Chamoun politicians, by strengthening Maronite-Sunni ties, and by concerning himself with the development of infrastructure in previously neglected regions of the country. His foreign policy was neutralist, walking a line between his Arab neighbors and the West. He also worked to maintain the image that he was above the hurly-burly of Lebanese day-to-day politics, a strategy that gained him many adherents among the populace. By no means was he disconnected from goings-on in the country, however. Chehab relied on the military intelligence office, the Deuxième Bureau, to monitor and report on domestic political developments, injecting a note of authoritarianism into an otherwise democratic system.

In 1964 Chehab, after encountering opposition to the extension of his presidency, supported Charles Helou's bid to become his successor. Helou was elected president, but he had no base of power other than the Chehabist-controlled parliament and government, and he lacked the political authority to govern effectively. Lebanon's descent into political polarization following the 1967 Arab-Israeli war appears to have been inevitable, considering the circumstances. It was at this time that the PLO emerged as an autonomous political and military force in the region; Lebanon was important to the PLO because of its border with Israel and its concentration of Palestinian refugees—about 10 percent of Lebanon's total population. Maronite politicians sought an approach that would enable Lebanon to support the Palestinian cause yet keep a lid on the armed activities of the PLO in Lebanon. Muslim politicians, however, also seeking to reflect the will of their constituencies, generally supported the PLO and its activities. The PLO and its cause became divisive political issues that ultimately provoked Lebanon's civil war.

The Civil War, 1975–1990

Although it was sparked by a specific event—the April 13, 1975, attack by unknown gunmen on Maronite worshipers at a Sunday church service in the Beirut suburb of Ayn Rummaneh—the Lebanese civil war had deeper causes. The polarization of the Lebanese public over government policy toward the PLO could be seen as early as December 1968, when an Israeli commando raid on Beirut International Airport destroyed thirteen Lebanese civilian aircraft. Undertaken in retaliation for airplane hijackings and commando raids by the PLO, the Israeli attack paralyzed the Lebanese government and radicalized public opinion.

Further Israeli attacks in southern Lebanon in response to PLO guerrilla operations there led to the collapse of the Lebanese government in May 1969; Prime Minister Rashid Karami resigned rather than sanction military actions against the PLO. Unable to form a new cabinet with another Sunni prime minister, President Helou resolved the crisis by acceding to an Egyptian-sponsored agreement in November 1969 in Cairo that confined the PLO armed presence to certain localities in the south.

Meanwhile, the Syrian Socialist Nationalist Party (SSNP), the Lebanese Communist Party (LCP), the Lebanese branch of the Syrian Baath Party, and other new parties, often closely affiliated with the PLO, attracted more and more adherents during the late 1960s. Many of these organizations were disillusioned with established Muslim politicians who used their influence to protect the PLO but at the same time failed to support it actively. The result was the formation of the multiparty Lebanese National Movement (LNM) in 1969, led by Kamal Jumblatt, who since 1949 had organized his own political followers into the Progressive Socialist Party (PSP).

In the August 1970 presidential elections, Sulayman Franjiyyah, a Maronite politician from Zghorta in northern Mount Lebanon, defeated his Chehabist rival, Elias Sarkis. Franjiyyah's election was generally perceived as a victory for those who sought to crush the PLO's growing strength in Lebanon. The parliamentary vote electing him, however, had been only 50 to 49, and the decisive vote had been cast by LNM leader Jumblatt, who in siding with Franjiyyah was really voting against continued Chehabist control of the government. Owing his election at least partly to the LNM, Franjiyyah began his presidency as a radical reformer, seeking to co-opt the LNM's opposition by trying to implement needed changes in government administration. Entrenched political interests, however, stymied the reforms, and he soon abandoned the effort. After 1972 Franjiyyah's rule was increasingly based on personal control of the government bureaucracy and defense of the established political system. The LNM, angered by this reversal of policy, tried to mobilize public opinion against the government.

Following the defeat of the PLO in Jordan in 1970–1971, Lebanon became the last center of armed Palestinian resistance against Israel. Israeli retaliatory raids against Palestinian guerrilla bases located in Lebanese border towns and villages produced a steady exodus of Shiite Muslims from the south to Beirut. Shantytowns sprang up, usually in and around the long-established Palestinian refugee camps that ringed Beirut. Rampant inflation during the early 1970s, partly due to the growing flow of Arab oil money into Lebanon's thriving banking sector and to the absence of controls over the country's freewheeling economy, accentuated the gap between rich and poor and increasingly infused the political conflict in Lebanon with the issue of class. At this time, Amal, a populist Shiite organization, was established with the goal of obtaining a larger role for the Shiite community in the Lebanese system.

The 1972 parliamentary elections provided the LNM an opportunity to elect antiestablishment candidates, but the outcome demonstrated the traditional leaders' powerful hold over the electoral process. To those who sought radical transformation in Lebanon, revolutionary violence seemed the only available route. Lebanon was fracturing into increasingly smaller class- and confession-based ideological groups.

In April 1973, Israeli commandos raided the heart of Beirut, killing three PLO leaders. The LNM organized mass demonstrations against the government to protest its passivity in the face of Israeli aggression. President Franjiyyah and other Maronite leaders, however, decided that the government could delay no longer in moving against the PLO. Heavy fighting on May 2 between the army and PLO fighters in the Burj al-Barajina refugee camp quickly spread to other parts of the country, but the government's actions provoked powerful opposition. Maronite leaders, as yet unprepared to carry on alone the fight against the PLO, had to back down. A May 18, 1973, settlement signed at Melkart basically reaffirmed the provisions of the Cairo Agreement of 1969, but it did not resolve the fundamental issue that had provoked the fighting; further showdowns were inevitable. In the months that followed, Maronite leaders, the parties of the LNM, and the PLO intensified recruitment efforts and searched worldwide for the arms and funds necessary to meet the challenge that awaited them.

The civil war that finally erupted in April 1975 was not so much a conflict between Christians and Muslims, as widely reported in the Western press, as a battle between the militias of the dominant Maronite leaders of the established political order and the various militias of the LNM, whose leaders sought to overthrow the traditional political system. Indeed, the vast majority of Lebanese were victims rather than active participants in the conflict. The fighting continued only because of the army's political incapacity to intervene. The established Muslim politicians refused to countenance army intervention so long as the conflict remained a fundamentally domestic one, but the army did intervene when the PLO, which at first had held back from the fighting, entered the fray in late 1975 to shore up the sagging fortunes of the LNM militiamen in Beirut's hotel district. The army thus became an enemy of the joint PLO-LNM forces and a tacit ally of the Maronite mili-

tias. Sensing impending victory, the Maronites undertook a massive destruction and depopulation campaign against Palestinian and Shiite refugee camps on the east side of Beirut. This action brought the PLO fully into the conflict and prompted retaliatory attacks against strategically located Maronite towns in areas otherwise controlled by the PLO-LNM forces. As these campaigns continued during January 1976, morale within Lebanon's multiconfessional army could not be sustained. By early February the army had totally collapsed, and many of its soldiers took sides with one or another of the fighting militias. Lebanon plunged into full-scale civil war.

Syrian Intervention

Unlike 1958, when U.S. intervention played a role in stabilizing Lebanon, in 1975 Lebanon's president had no relatively disinterested external party to turn to for help in stemming the political chaos. To Lebanese nationalists, particularly Maronites, independence primarily meant independence from Syria. Yet in 1975–1976 only Syria had the vital interest in the outcome of the crisis to expend the political, military, and financial resources necessary to bring it under control. Syria was, no doubt, interested in expanding its sphere of influence into Lebanon. It was strategically important to Damascus that Lebanon not become either a base or a corridor for an Israeli invasion of Syria. Moreover, the Syrians had never been completely reconciled to the French-imposed division between it and Lebanon.

Prior to 1975 Syria had strongly supported the PLO and the LNM in Lebanon. By late March 1976, a PLO-LNM victory seemed imminent. Syrian president Hafiz al-Asad became convinced that such a victory would lead to Israeli intervention—an action that he sought to preempt. At the same time, Lebanon's Maronite leaders and their Muslim political colleagues feared the possible results of a PLO-LNM victory. Consequently, Asad began to seek, and the Maronite leaders began to accept, the principle of a primary role for neighboring Syria in resolving the Lebanese conflict.

Syrian forces dispatched to Lebanon in March 1976, at Maronite request, defended the presidential palace in Baabda, provided security for the presidential elections held in May, and in June forcibly restored the pre-April 1975 political balance. Fighting, primarily between Syrian and PLO-LNM forces, continued throughout the summer, and the better-trained Syrian units gradually managed to achieve strategic superiority. In October representatives of the various warring parties concluded a generally accepted cease-fire agreement in Riyadh, Saudi Arabia.

At an Arab League summit in Cairo on October 25, 1976, member states ratified the Riyadh Agreement, a key provision of which was the establishment of the Arab Deterrent Force (ADF) to provide security throughout Lebanon while a process of national reconciliation was undertaken. Placed technically under the authority of newly elected Lebanese president Elias Sarkis, the ADF was to be composed of units from several Arab countries. It was tacitly understood, however, that Syrian elements would form the main body of the force. By this means, Syria's role in Lebanon gained legitimacy. As various units from other Arab countries were recalled in the months that followed, the ADF became a completely Syrian force, albeit supported and at least partially financed by the Arab League. Syrian intervention temporarily restored order to most of the country, but with fundamental problems left unresolved, the peace was short-lived. Conflict and violence, often in the form of terrorist bombings and attacks, soon returned to dominate Lebanese political life.

Although Syria intervened on behalf of Lebanon's Maronite leaders against the PLO and LNM, it did not put an end to PLO activity in Lebanon. Indeed, the Riyadh Agreement specifically affirmed the 1969 Cairo Agreement. The terms of the Cairo Agreement, however, had never been fully accepted by the Maronite leadership. Thus, the honeymoon between Syria and Maronite leaders—grouped together as the Lebanese Front—was brief. In May 1977, only days after Menachem Begin was elected prime minister of Israel, the front issued a statement declaring that the Cairo Agreement was null and void and that the Maronite militias would remain armed as long as the PLO did.

During the earlier period of the civil war, Maronite leaders had entered into covert arms deals with Israel's Labor government. With the coming to power of Begin, who openly supported the Lebanese Front, Maronite leaders dared to challenge Syria directly with assurances of Israeli support, making confrontation between Syria and the Maronite militias inevitable.

Under the terms of the Riyadh Agreement, PLO fighters returned to southern Lebanon in spite of warnings by Israel that it would not tolerate a resumption of commando activity in the region. As the PLO returned, Israel responded by arming and helping to organize a local, predominately Christian militia commanded by Maj. Saad Haddad, a renegade Lebanese officer who sought to counter and contain PLO and LNM expansion into the border area.

After Syrian forces entered Lebanon in 1976, Israel announced the existence of an undefined "red line" somewhere in southern Lebanon, beyond which it would not tolerate Syrian troops. The line was generally considered to be in the vicinity of the Litani River. Syria never seriously challenged this Israeli position, and southern Lebanon, historically one of Lebanon's most neglected and underdeveloped areas, became a virtual no-man's land to which neither Lebanese, Syrian, nor even Israeli authority extended. Bloody conflict among the supporters of Saad Haddad, the PLO, the LNM militias, and the predominately Shiite population that lived in the area poisoned the political atmosphere elsewhere in Lebanon, where every group in the south had its supporters.

Syria's conservatism in dealing with security problems also contributed to tensions. Syria sought to mediate agreements among Lebanon's various militias and political parties, but it did not seriously try to disarm them even though it was authorized to do so by the Riyadh Agreement. As a result, Lebanon continued to live on the edge of violence and renewed civil war. Syria's policy for containing conflict was to move in with sufficient strength to crush violence when it erupted. Such a policy, although it produced respect, also produced resentment, and it did little to halt the growing number of terrorist acts of various militias. As a result of Syria's tolerating every group but supporting none, most Lebanese increasingly perceived Syria as serving no particular interest except its own.

Disenchantment with the PLO also grew during the late 1970s, especially among Lebanon's southern Shiites, who previously had seen themselves as sharing a common plight with the Palestinians. Three events in 1978 and early 1979 helped rally support for the Amal organization: Israel's invasion of southern Lebanon in March 1978, the unexplained disappearance of Amal leader Musa Sadr while on a visit to Libya in September, and the Shiite revolution in Iran in 1979. The escalating conflict in the south between the Shiite Muslim population and the PLO laid the basis for the Shiites' initial popular reception of Israeli armed forces during their 1982 invasion. The sectarian solidarity of the community, however, also laid the basis for the ultimate failure of Israeli policy in Lebanon.

Israeli Invasions of 1978 and 1982

Israel's invasions of southern Lebanon in March 1978 and June 1982, although allegedly provoked by Palestinian terrorist incidents, were aimed at achieving broader policy goals. The principal result of the 1978 invasion was the clearing of an area several kilometers wide along Israel's northern frontier to serve as a "security zone" under the control of Major Haddad's Free Lebanon Militia (FLM). The inability of the FLM to achieve this mission on its own was the chief factor leading to Israel's military intervention.

In spite of the operation's success, PLO groups continued to find ways to cross the frontier and to conduct attacks in northern Israel. The creation of the United Nations Interim Force in Lebanon (UNIFIL) on March 20, 1978, and the subsequent deployment of some 6,000 soldiers in the south

curbed the incursions. However, UNIFIL did not deploy in the Israeli self-declared "security zone" because of Israeli opposition and its own inability to control Palestinian movements in the south. Moreover, various PLO groups acquired long-range artillery and rocket launchers capable of firing over the heads of both UNIFIL and the FLM. This development led Begin's government to try to devise new strategies for dealing with the threat to northern Israel.

Events in Lebanon in 1980–1981 had a significant effect on how the 1982 invasion was carried out. The Maronite militias, except for that of former president Franjiyyah, joined under the leadership of Bashir Gemayel, son of Maronite Kataib Party leader Pierre Gemayel. This made Bashir the principal Maronite wielding military power and thus a viable presidential candidate in the 1982 elections. For him to be elected, however, Syrian opposition to his candidacy had to be overcome. Militantly opposed to the PLO and Syrian presence in Lebanon, Bashir favored decisive action to end the cycle of violence. Like the Israelis, Amal followers, and a growing number of ordinary Lebanese citizens, Bashir attributed the violence largely to the PLO's continued presence. Increasingly isolated, the PLO found it advantageous on July 24, 1981, to enter into a cease-fire agreement with Israel that had been negotiated by U.S. special envoy Philip Habib. The isolation of the PLO also cleared the way for Israel to launch a full-scale invasion of Lebanon in June 1982 targeted at the PLO. *(Arab-Israeli Conflict, Chapter 2, p. 13)*

As a result of the 1982 invasion and subsequent U.S.-brokered negotiations, the PLO was formally expelled from Beirut and southern Lebanon in August. Lebanon's Maronite leaders understandably interpreted this as a victory for their cause and particularly for Bashir Gemayel, who was duly elected president. However, Bashir was assassinated before he could take office, and his brother Amin was elected to the presidency. The continuing occupation of Lebanon by both Israeli and Syrian forces transformed the domestic conflict into a regional one in which

Lebanon remained the principal arena of death and destruction.

U.S. Involvement, 1982–1984

In August 1982, the United States, France, Italy, and the United Kingdom dispatched a 5,000-member multinational peacekeeping force to Beirut to bolster the confidence of the Lebanese government and to assist in the evacuation of the PLO. At the same time, U.S. diplomats sought to broker agreements that would lead to the full withdrawal of Syrian and Israeli forces, provide for the security of Israel's northern border, and strengthen the Lebanese government's authority. Unresolved conflict between Syria and Israel in other areas, especially regarding the status of the Golan Heights, which Israel had effectively annexed in December 1981, made even indirect negotiations between these two countries impossible.

After receiving assurances from Syria that it would leave Lebanon if Israel unconditionally withdrew, the United States sought to mediate a withdrawal agreement between Israel and Lebanon. On May 17, 1983, representatives of Israel, Lebanon, and the United States initialed an agreement containing guarantees that Israel would withdraw completely from Lebanon in return for Lebanese political, economic, and military concessions that Israel considered necessary for the security of its northern frontier. After initialing the document, however, Israel tied full implementation to a similar commitment by Syria to withdraw its forces from Lebanon.

Syria asserted that its forces would not withdraw unless the agreement was abrogated. Damascus objected to the agreement's establishment of security zones in southern Lebanon and a joint Lebanese-Israeli committee that would hold authority over matters of security within the zones. These and other provisions were perceived by Syria as, in effect, partitioning the country into zones of Israeli and Syrian influence and increasing the Israeli threat to Syria.

The agreement was also rejected by most Lebanese political factions, which came together as the National Salvation Front to resist it. Moreover, Syrian forces, from their strategically dominant position in the hills overlooking Beirut, supported Lebanese groups opposing the agreement and intimidated the Maronite community with shellfire and threats. Meanwhile, the high cost of sustaining the Israeli occupation, the increasingly heavy Israeli casualties from Lebanese resistance, and the September 1982 massacres at the Sabra and Shatila refugee camps, in which hundreds of Palestinians were killed by Maronite militiamen on the watch of the Israeli army, had begun to erode support at home for Israel's involvement in Lebanon.

Militia groups virtually crushed by Israel's invasion in 1982 regrouped with Syrian support during the summer of 1983. Events climaxed in September 1983 when Israel undertook a partial, unilateral withdrawal from its forward positions along the Beirut-Damascus highway to more defensible positions below the Awali River north of Sidon. Fighting erupted throughout the Shuf region in central Lebanon between Druze militias supported by PLO and Shiite elements on the one hand, and the Lebanese armed forces and Maronite militia forces on the other. Druze forces prevailed, causing a mass flight of Maronite Christians from villages in the region. Walid Jumblatt, who had become the Druze leader after pro-Syrian forces assassinated his father, Kamal, in March 1977, was able to consolidate his authority throughout the Shuf. The Lebanese army succeeded in maintaining control over militias in West Beirut.

On October 23, 1983, suicide bombings of the U.S. Marine and French barracks in Beirut killed 241 American and 58 French servicemen. This attack and an earlier bombing of the U.S. embassy in Beirut on April 18, 1983, which had killed sixty-three, diminished U.S. public support for a military role in Lebanon.

Following the collapse of Lebanese government authority in West Beirut in early February 1984, the United States announced its decision to withdraw its contingent from the multinational force. The last U.S. Marines were evacuated in

March; Italy, Britain, and France also withdrew their forces during early 1984.

Revived Syrian Hegemony

With the departure of Western troops, Syria reemerged as the dominant external power influencing affairs in Lebanon. President Amin Gemayel moved to restore relations with Damascus, and on March 5, 1984, the Lebanese government announced its abrogation of the May 17, 1983, agreement with Israel. Following further discussions between Syrian representatives and Lebanese political leaders, a government of "national unity" was formed in April, and a security plan aimed at restoring government authority throughout the country was agreed upon. Implementation of the plan proved impossible, however, because of sectarian conflict, particularly over the continuing Israeli occupation of southern Lebanon. Shiite, Druze, and other militia groups there refused to disarm while Israeli troops still occupied the region. Attacks against Israeli forces escalated.

Turmoil in Southern Lebanon

With the disintegration of its policy objectives in Lebanon, Israel in the spring of 1985 began a graduated, unilateral withdrawal. As it did so, however, it left in place an expanded self-declared "security zone" under the control of a surrogate militia, the South Lebanon Army (SLA), commanded by retired Lebanese general Antoine Lahd. The zone—controlled ultimately by Israel, which armed, funded, and advised the SLA—provoked continuing resistance on the part of the mainly Shiite inhabitants of southern Lebanon. Shiite resistance to the SLA was split into two rival factions. The first, more closely linked with Syria, was Amal, which sought to control the PLO in Lebanon and thus remove any pretext for Israel to remain in the country. In May 1985, Amal's efforts to control PLO activities by maintaining a siege around Palestinian refugee camps in Beirut and southern Lebanon erupted into open warfare.

The "camp wars" continued until January 1988, when Amal leader Nabih Berri lifted the siege following the outbreak of the Palestinian *intifada* in the Israeli-occupied West Bank and Gaza Strip.

Amal's rival, the Shiite Hizballah movement, received inspiration and support from Iran. Unlike Amal, which sought a stronger Shiite role in Lebanon's multisectarian political system, the partisans of Hizballah favored the transformation of Lebanon into a fully Islamic state. In addition, they preferred to collaborate with Palestinian guerrillas in their struggle against Israel. Amal-Hizballah differences occasionally led to intra-Shiite conflict and violence.

One tactic used, in most cases by Hizballah, was the taking of Western hostages. Beginning in early 1984, soon after the withdrawal of the U.S. Marines, isolated kidnappings of Americans and later British, French, Saudi, West German, and even South Korean nationals began. Among other motives, the kidnappers sought to win the release of Shiite prisoners held in Israeli, Kuwaiti, and Western jails and to enhance their influence in local Lebanese and regional affairs. The kidnappings greatly reduced the Western presence in Lebanon and consequently the ability of Western nations to exert influence in that country or to react forcibly because of the potential danger to the hostages. Israel's efforts to contain Shiite and Palestinian guerrilla activity in southern Lebanon through commando raids, air strikes, artillery shelling, and the capture of guerrilla leaders only intensified the region's turmoil and provoked retaliation, including airline hijackings and further kidnappings.

Tripartite Agreement

Efforts by the Gemayel government to reconcile with Syria in 1984 prompted elements of the Maronite Christian Lebanese Forces militia in northern Lebanon to revolt against central government authority in early 1985. The Lebanese Forces regarded Gemayel's accommodation toward Damascus as evidence that the government was caving in to Syrian efforts to establish hegemony.

Syria, in December 1985, working with Sunni prime minister Rashid Karami but not with President Gemayel, managed to forge a "tripartite agreement" among Elie Hobeika, representing a counterfaction of the Lebanese Forces; Druze leader Jumblatt; and Amal leader Berri. The agreement was aimed at reaching a compromise settlement of the Lebanese conflict centered around the principal militias rather than the traditional politicians. To be implemented, it required that Hobeika and Berri assert control over the more radical factions of their respective communities. Despite increased Syrian support, neither proved able to do so, and fierce intra-Maronite and intra-Shiite conflict erupted during the spring and summer of 1986.

The continued deterioration of the security situation throughout the country finally led Syria in August 1986 to reintroduce some 700 troops into Beirut. In February 1987, President Asad increased his commitment by sending into Lebanon an additional 7,000 troops, supported by tanks and heavy artillery. With the reimposition of Syrian military control in West Beirut and central Lebanon, Damascus began slow but deliberate efforts to strengthen Amal at the expense of Hizballah and PLO elements remaining in Beirut and southern Lebanon. Syrian leaders, however, were careful to avoid jeopardizing relations with Iran, whose alliance with Syria against Iraq took priority over any heavy-handed effort to crush the Hizballah movement entirely. Anti-Syrian resistance grew, symbolized by the emergence during 1987 of the Lebanese Liberation Front, which assassinated Syrian officials and soldiers in Lebanon. Nevertheless, Syrian influence in Lebanon by the summer of 1988 was sufficiently strong to have a decisive bearing on Lebanese presidential elections, which were mandated by the constitution to occur before September 23.

Syrian-Maronite Conflict

In the pre-election period, the Syrians made clear that they would veto Samir Geagea, the commander of the Lebanese Forces, as a presidential candidate. The U.S. government sought to intercede and develop a compromise candidate. Initial negotiations centered on Michel Aoun, the commander of the Lebanese army, as a candidate acceptable to the Lebanese Forces, Syria, and the United States. However, on August 16, two days prior to the election, Sulayman Franjiyyah, the seventy-eight-year-old former president and Syrian stalwart, declared his candidacy. The Syrians opted to support Franjiyyah, who was utterly unacceptable to the Lebanese Forces.

The parliament, in order to elect a president, required a quorum of fifty-three deputies. Only thirty-five deputies convened, so the session was adjourned. The Lebanese Forces had forcibly prevented the attendance of fifteen deputies. The coming days were marked by renewed violence. On August 23, Muslim deputies jointly declared that they would boycott a second ballot attempt unless an agreement was reached on a new political system that would grant greater powers to the Muslim communities. A second ballot was nonetheless called for September 22, the last day of Gemayel's term.

The election was a topic of intense interest in the U.S. government. A number of U.S. officials visited Beirut and Damascus, including Secretary of State George P. Shultz. Assistant Secretary of State Richard Murphy traveled to Damascus in mid-September and attempted to negotiate for a compromise candidate, Michel Daher. This tactic backfired, and Christians accused Murphy of imposing a pro-Syrian candidate. Christian leaders quoted Murphy as having told them that if they did not support the election of Daher, the U.S. government would leave them to the Syrians. The Daher candidacy was rejected. The second ballot was no more successful than the first.

Just before midnight on September 22, President Gemayel appointed the commander of the Lebanese armed forces, Michel Aoun, as acting prime minister to preside over an interim military government until elections could be held. When the government of prime minister Selim al-Hoss refused to step down and recognize the Aoun government, Lebanon found itself with two acting governments, one (al-Hoss's) recognized as legitimate by Syria and its Muslim allies, and the other (Aoun's) recognized by the Lebanese Forces and most of the Maronite community.

To counter Syrian efforts to dictate the outcome of the election, the Lebanese Forces found a willing ally in Iraqi president Saddam Hussein, who, having achieved a cease-fire in his war with Iran in August 1988, welcomed a way to retaliate against Syria for having supported Iran. Iraqi arms began reaching Lebanon in October.

Efforts by the Arab League in late January 1989 to mediate the impasse led Aoun in mid-February to assert the authority of his government and armed forces over the various independent militias. Aoun ordered the army to take over militia headquarters and barracks in the greater Beirut area and to bring all illegal militia-controlled ports under the control of the army. He began with the Lebanese Forces, which at first resisted in a series of bloody clashes, but as this operation proved successful, he extended the order in early March to include illegal ports controlled by the Druze and Muslim militias. After Aoun attempted to impose a naval blockade, the Druze and Muslim militias countered by shelling Maronite areas. Aoun considered the attacks inspired by Syria, so he responded to Druze and Muslim shelling by targeting Syrian military positions, although many of these were located in heavily populated residential areas of Beirut. At the same time, he sought to appeal to increasingly widespread anti-Syrian sentiment in all sectors of the Lebanese population by calling for a general uprising against Syrian control and occupation.

Iraqi support of Aoun, and reportedly support from Israel as well, virtually guaranteed that Syria would strongly resist Aoun's efforts to weaken its position in Lebanon. Because Aoun could not expect to dislodge the Syrian occupation by force alone, he hoped for international intervention and mediation on behalf of continued Lebanese sovereignty and independence. Arab League efforts in late April resulted in a cease-fire agreement, and Aoun lifted his blockade of Druze and Muslim ports. Continued efforts by Aoun and the

Lebanese Forces, however, to receive military supplies through ports along the Maronite portion of the coast prompted Syria to shell the ports and to blockade ships serving them. Continued retaliatory shelling by Aoun's army and the Lebanese Forces against Syrian military positions made the cease-fire agreement a dead letter and the summer of 1989 one of the bloodiest and most violent seasons in Lebanon's fifteen-year conflict. Ironically, the summer of 1989 proved to be the catalyst for at least a partial settlement of the conflict.

The Taif Accord

General Aoun failed to see that with the rapid deterioration of communism in eastern Europe and the former Soviet Union, the West's interest in Lebanon was declining. Syrian involvement in the Lebanese conflict could no longer be cast as a cold war move by a pro-Soviet state to consolidate its influence in Lebanon at the West's expense. Indeed, both the United States and the Soviet Union, seeking to stay out of the Lebanese quagmire, lent support to a Saudi-sponsored effort by the Arab League to mediate the conflict of 1989.

On September 30, 1989, the Saudi government convened a summit of the Lebanese parliament in Taif, Saudi Arabia. Sixty-two of the seventy-one living deputies of the original ninety-nine-member parliament that had been elected in 1972 were present for the opening session. For more than three weeks the deputies contentiously debated the text of a national reconciliation charter drafted by a committee of the Arab League and coordinated with Syria. Finally, mindful that the continued legitimacy of the Lebanese government was in their hands, fifty-eight of the assembled deputies on October 22 signed an amended charter that became known as the Taif Accord.

By no means a revolutionary document, the Taif agreement made only minor alterations to the traditional, confessional Lebanese political system. The composition of the parliament, which had been fixed at a ratio of six Christian to five Muslim deputies, was restructured 50:50. To ensure that no sect would lose seats because of this change, the size of the chamber was increased from 99 to 108 deputies. (On the occasion of the first post-Taif elections in 1992, this number was increased to 128.) In addition, the deputies agreed that the whole confessional system would be reviewed with the aim of abolishing it some time in the future. The powers of the Sunni prime minister and his cabinet were significantly enhanced at the expense of the Maronite president. Most significantly, however, the agreement, every provision of which had been cleared by Damascus, tasked "Syrian forces" with assisting "the forces of the legitimate Lebanese government to extend the authority of the Lebanese state within a period not exceeding two years." Following the two-year period, the Lebanese government, newly reestablished under Syrian supervision, would negotiate with Syria the terms for the withdrawal of the latter's armed forces.

The terms of the Taif agreement, therefore, more fully legitimized the Syrian presence in Lebanon. This outcome was quite the opposite of what General Aoun had desired, and he vowed to resist implementation. Syria moved quickly, however, convening the Lebanese parliament on November 4 to elect René Muawwad as the new president of Lebanon. Swift international recognition of the Muawwad government, including recognition by the United States, should have communicated to Aoun his isolation, but buoyed by significant popular support, he continued his resistance and refused to vacate the presidential palace. Syria demonstrated its control of the situation when, after the car-bomb assassination of Muawwad eighteen days following his election, it supervised yet another election on November 24 in which Elias Hrawi was chosen to replace Muawwad.

Second Lebanese Republic

Despite a number of threats, Syria and the Hrawi government failed to move forcibly against Aoun, concentrating instead on institutionalizing the reforms adopted in the Taif Accord. Meanwhile, intense conflict erupted in early 1990 between Aoun and Geagea, who had decided to accept the Taif agreement and work with the Hrawi government.

While Aoun continued to hold on, the Lebanese parliament in August 1990 passed amendments to the constitution that formally incorporated the compromises reached at Taif. Aoun violently rejected the changes and called for the overthrow of Hrawi. Despite Aoun's threat, Hrawi formally approved the amendments, making them law on September 21. By thus limiting his own powers, Hrawi also proclaimed the establishment of the Second Lebanese Republic.

The coup de grace for Aoun came two weeks later, on October 13, when a combined force of Syrian and Lebanese armed forces moved against him. The attack was facilitated by the Persian Gulf crisis provoked by Iraq's invasion of Kuwait in August. Syria's decision to join the U.S.-led coalition against Iraq had resulted in much improved U.S.-Syrian relations. That Syria had a green light to move against Aoun without fear of provoking a serious Western reaction was apparent when Israeli aircraft failed to challenge Syrian planes bombing Aoun's positions. By the end of the day, Aoun had taken refuge in the French embassy after ordering his men to follow the orders of Gen. Emile Lahoud, the legitimate armed forces commander of the Hrawi government.

Consolidation of State Authority

With the collapse of the resistance posed by Aoun, relative calm settled over much of Lebanon, as the Lebanese reconciled themselves to the inevitability of the new order mandated by the Taif Accord and enforced by Syria. Most Lebanese were weary of fighting and grudgingly recognized the dominance of Syria. They also regarded the Taif agreement as having addressed at least some of the root causes of the Lebanese conflict, namely the perceived inequity of the old political system.

The Hrawi government negotiated agreements with the various militias to redeploy from Beirut, to place their weapons in storage, and to return to civilian occupations. Increasingly, in early 1991, Lebanese armed forces took over militia checkpoints and sought to extend the state's authority beyond the outskirts of Beirut. In early February, taking advantage of renewed conflict in southern Lebanon between the PLO and Israel and the SLA, elements of the Lebanese army began deploying toward the area. Despite the army's success in confining the PLO within the refugee camps, Israel remained skeptical of Lebanon's ability to guarantee the security of its border and refused to withdraw support from the SLA or to allow the army to deploy into the so-called security zone.

By April 1991, all the militias, except Hizballah in the south, had agreed to disarm; Lebanese troops deployed throughout most of the country; citizens increasingly felt free to move about; new construction and reconstruction was getting under way; and commercial life was beginning to regain momentum.

At this stage Syria and Lebanon took steps to approve the Treaty of Brotherhood, Cooperation, and Coordination, which was signed by presidents Hrawi and Asad in Damascus on May 22, 1991. Requiring total cooperation and coordination between the two governments, including in defense and foreign affairs, the treaty formally affirmed Syria's recognition of Lebanese sovereignty and independence. Despite this affirmation, the treaty contains a clause nullifying all Lebanese laws conflicting with the treaty. As the dominant partner in the alliance, Syria expected Lebanon to coordinate its decision making with Damascus.

In early June the Lebanese president, prime minister, and Speaker of parliament collectively appointed forty new deputies to the parliament. These included thirty-one to fill seats that had become vacant since the last election in 1972 and nine to fill seats created by the Taif agreement. The decision to appoint rather than elect these deputies proved controversial, as most of the deputies chosen were pro-Syrian. The new chamber's term of office was to be four years, but in 1992 the government reversed its position and held general parliamentary elections.

Yet another manifestation of increasing Lebanese government authority was the agreement by the PLO to close its military operations in

Lebanon and to ship its heavy weapons out of the country. Although anti-Arafat Palestinian groups remained intact, their activities were sharply circumscribed in Lebanon, as they were in Syria. The virtual shutdown of PLO military activities in Lebanon coincided with the surprise announcement in July 1991 by Syrian president Asad of his agreement to accept a joint U.S.-Soviet invitation to enter negotiations with Israel. Lebanon followed Syria's lead, and it too sent a delegation to the Madrid summit, which opened on October 30. The Lebanese played a peripheral role in the series of multilateral negotiations in Washington that followed the initial summit, as the agendas of Israel, Jordan, Syria, and the Palestinians all took precedence.

Occupation of Southern Lebanon

Fighting in southern Lebanon flared up dramatically in 1991, following the government's increasingly successful consolidation of authority throughout most of the rest of the country. The government in Beirut, unable to deploy into the southern Israeli-controlled area, did not press Hizballah to disarm as it did other militias. As a result, Hizballah continued to conduct attacks against SLA positions and Israeli troops, inviting Israeli retaliatory operations. In response to Israeli operations, Hizballah forces occasionally were able to fire Katyusha rockets or conduct military operations across the border into Israel. Such actions invited massive Israeli retaliation, including heavy bombing and shelling of Shiite positions and villages in the south in February 1992 and July 1993. The Israelis, however, proved unable to stop Hizballah operations. Hizballah activities only reinforced the view of Israeli policy makers that they had no alternative to occupying the territory in order to protect their northern border.

In April 1996 Israel launched seventeen days of intense air raids over southern Lebanon in an effort to eliminate Hizballah bases, from which fighters had been attacking Israeli patrols and intermittently firing on towns in northern Galilee.

The raids caused hundreds of thousands of civilians to flee north to Beirut. One of the attacks, observed by an unmanned Israeli air force "drone," shelled the UN refugee camp at Qana, killing 107 civilians. This action further soured relations between Israel and the Arab world and drew strong criticism from many sectors within Israeli society. These events led to a U.S.-mediated "April Understanding" aimed at limiting the scope of Hizballah-Israeli violence and provoked increased sentiment within Israel in favor of withdrawing from southern Lebanon.

Israeli forces unilaterally withdrew from Lebanese territory in May 2000, four months after the collapse of Israeli-Syrian peace talks that, had they been successfully concluded, would have provided for a coordinated evacuation and follow-on border security measures. The United Nations moved quickly to confirm the completeness of Israel's withdrawal by demarcating a "line of withdrawal" from the Mediterranean Sea to the slopes of Mount Hermon. Syria saw the unilateral nature of the evacuation as an Israeli attempt to solidify its occupation of the Golan Heights.

In order to maintain its strategic advantage, Syria prevailed upon the Lebanese government and Hizballah to lay claim to a lightly populated, 25-square-kilometer stretch of the Israeli-occupied Golan Heights adjacent to Lebanon known as Shab'a Farms. Claims of Lebanese citizens to property in the area were advanced in support of the argument that the territory lay within Lebanon. The United Nations, however, ruled that the area was part of the Golan, a finding substantiated by official Lebanese, Syrian, and UN maps. Regardless, the claim has provided Hizballah with a justification to continue its ongoing "resistance" to Israeli "occupation." Sporadic low-level attacks on Israeli military personnel in the area are met with Israeli artillery and overflights, which in turn provoke Hizballah antiaircraft fire that occasionally rains metal fragments down on Israeli border towns. For the most part, however, Hizballah—while providing service to Syria through its defense of the disputed territory—has been scrupulous about maintaining calm along the

1949 armistice sector of the line of withdrawal. Whereas the foothills of Mount Hermon are lightly populated on both sides of the blue line, Hizballah's constituents reside in large numbers elsewhere along the line. The party has been careful to spare these constituents from ongoing violence and possible dislocation.

1992 Parliamentary Elections

Perhaps the most dramatic development in post–civil war Lebanon was the parliamentary elections of August–September 1992. The last elections had been held in 1972, and the deputies elected at that time had maintained limited powers. During the presidential crisis of 1988–1989, the parliament remained the only source of government legitimacy. In 1992, with about one-third of its members dead and many more advancing in years, the parliament could not claim to be an accurate reflection of the Lebanese electorate. The appointment of forty deputies in the summer of 1991 to fill empty seats could not restore this fading legitimacy. Thus the electoral process organized in 1992 was a major step toward reinvigorating the Lebanese government.

Even so, the elections proved controversial, and many in the Maronite community boycotted them, seeking to cast doubt on the legitimacy of what they perceived as a Syrian-rigged process. Nevertheless, turnout was high in parts of the country, and the process appeared to be conducted with reasonable fairness within the limitations of Syrian hegemony. Finally, even the Maronite-inhabited Kisrawan Province returned deputies in a late special election held in October. The election brought many new faces to the parliament. Many of the militias, including Hizballah, that had fought for recognition during Lebanon's long era of anarchy and violence, now found themselves represented by deputies. The elections raised hopes that Lebanese politics might be moving away from the battlefield and into the parliament.

Another outcome of the 1992 elections was the selection of a new parliamentary Speaker,

Nabih Berri, and the appointment of billionaire Rafiq al-Hariri to the post of prime minister on October 22, 1993. Hariri's personal fortune came to play a major role in the reconstruction of Lebanon, despite the conflict of interest generated by his political office. He provided the start-up funds for the Council for Development and Reconstruction, the government agency responsible for rebuilding the country's infrastructure and answerable to the prime minister. Under the powers of his office as granted by Taif, Hariri also controlled numerous committees and ministries whose budgets were drawn up and implemented without parliamentary oversight. Moreover, the governor of the Central Bank and the director of Solidere, the private firm overseeing the reconstruction of Beirut's downtown, were old associates of Hariri. In short, Hariri wielded immense power, in both the public and private spheres of Lebanese political life.

The Speaker was granted expanded powers under the Taif Accord. The Speaker, a Shiite, has financial control over the Committee for the South, without further oversight. Berri, an adept politician, built for himself a national constituency composed of Muslims and Christians, including former bitter enemies. He also skillfully managed the parliament, weakening and slowing passage of pro-Syrian legislation and thus acting as a check on the powers of the Council of Ministers and the prime minister.

Politics since 1995

On October 11, 1995, Lebanon's parliament extended the Hrawi presidency for another three years, acting in accordance with the wishes of the Syrian government. The ease of the extension was in marked contrast to the numerous failed attempts to extend the presidential term since President Khoury sought to do so in 1952, attempts that were accompanied by civil disorder.

Lebanon held five rounds of parliamentary elections in August and September 1996 amid charges of election and voter fraud. The election returned the Speaker to parliament, as well as all of the major politicians from the previous administration. Hariri became a member of parliament for the first time. Government and pro-government candidates gained seats, leaving a diminished opposition and further cementing Syria's ability to conduct its affairs in Lebanon unchallenged.

May and June 1998 saw the first municipal elections held in Lebanon in thirty-five years. The polling reversed a trend toward state centralization of power. The last such elections had been held in 1963, and since that time, local governments had been run by aging mayors and council members or by government appointees. Politicians from many of the traditional political families of Lebanon were reelected, but this did not necessarily indicate their support for (or by) the government in Beirut and Damascus.

In October 1998, the Lebanese parliament elected a new president, General Emile Lahoud, to replace Hrawi, whose extended term had come to an end. Lahoud was sworn into office in November, at which time Prime Minister Hariri, in a surprise announcement, resigned his office. Lahoud subsequently asked veteran politician Selim al-Hoss, who had led the government in opposition to Aoun in 1989–1990, to form a new government.

Parliamentary elections in August and September 2000 swept Hariri back into office, much to the disappointment of his archrival, President Lahoud. In June 2001, Syria completed a pullout of its troops from Beirut, and on March 3, 2002, Syrian president Bashar al-Asad visited Lebanon and met with President Lahoud. One year later, Syria reportedly withdrew some 4,000 soldiers from Lebanon in an attempt to reduce internal Lebanese resentment over the ongoing presence of its forces.

Yet Syrian-Lebanese tensions increased dramatically in August 2004, when Damascus pressured Hariri into offering a constitutional amendment that would extend President Lahoud's term of office. Hariri did as ordered: Lahoud's term was extended, and on October 20, 2004, Hariri resigned, dissolved his cabinet, and announced that he would not try to form a new government. President Lahoud appointed Omar Karami as prime minister the next day. More than a month earlier, the United States and France, in response to Syria's involvement in the extension of Lahoud's term, had persuaded the UN Security Council to adopt Resolution 1559, calling for the withdrawal of foreign troops from Lebanon and the disarmament of all militias—a clear allusion to Syria and its ally, Hizballah. The Syrian government reportedly held Hariri responsible for the resolution's passage.

On February 14, 2005, Hariri was killed in a massive explosion that tore through his motorcade in downtown Beirut. Syria and Syrian-controlled Lebanese security and intelligence services were widely believed to have orchestrated the attack. There followed a series of often large and daily anti-Syrian demonstrations in Beirut. After two weeks of anti-Syrian protests, Prime Minister Omar Karami resigned, on February 28. A few days later, he was called on to form another government. On March 9, 2005, Hizballah organized a pro-Syrian demonstration of several hundred thousand people, which provoked an even larger anti-Syrian rally on March 14, attracting an estimated 1 million participants.

Meanwhile, Karami attempted to form a national unity government, but the opposition refused to join. He then tried assembling a pro-Syrian cabinet, but that effort succumbed to disagreements over seats. After seven weeks of trying, he gave up, and Najib Mikati, a moderate pro-Syrian legislator who had served as public works and transport minister under Hariri, got the nod to form a government, whose main task would be to prepare for parliamentary elections scheduled for May and June.

Hariri's assassination removed from the scene the one person widely viewed as able to organize a coherent opposition to Syrian suzerainty in Lebanon. International pressure, led by the United States, France, and the United Nations, seemed to be the critical factor behind the April 2, 2005, announcement by a UN envoy that Syria planned to remove all of its soldiers and intelligence personnel from Lebanon by the end of the month. Most observers remained skeptical, but in late April 2005 the last Syrian troops left the

Najib Mikati

country. The United Nations verified the military withdrawal in May. It remained unclear whether all Syrian intelligence had departed as well.

Outlook

Syria's decision in August 2004 to compel the extension of President Emile Lahoud's term provoked Lebanon's first domestic political crisis since the end of the civil war and brought to the fore fundamental questions concerning the country's identity and future. Although the public response to Hariri's assassination greatly accelerated the departure of Syrian soldiers and intelligence officers from the country, anti-Syrian popular sentiment alone is an insufficient basis for domestic tranquility, economic prosperity, and peaceful relations with powerful neighbors.

The National Covenant on which Lebanese independence was based did not create a nation. Lebanon's Christian leaders agreed to break free from France, and Muslim leaders agreed to oppose political union with Syria, but they nonetheless maintained a sectarian political system derived from the Ottoman Empire. Although the Taif Accord of 1989 held out the prospect of a new form of government, in fact it changed little, especially in the minds of Lebanese. At the same time that many Lebanese favored an end to Syrian suzerainty, they continued to define themselves through a multiplicity of identities. Indeed, sect continues to trump citizenship. A nonsectarian sense of Lebanese nationalism remains elusive.

The absence of nonsectarian nationalism did not prevent Lebanon from prospering in the 1950s and 1960s, despite periodic bouts of political instability. Yet Lebanon's long-standing internal divisions inevitably drew the country into the vortex of the Arab-Israeli conflict after the June 1967 War. The absence of a shared national destiny exposed the Lebanese government to the manipulations of outsiders, who themselves were manipulated by Lebanese actors. The result was civil war and Syrian suzerainty.

Lebanon's future, therefore, depends on two separate but related factors: Arab-Israeli relations and the evolution of internal Lebanese identities. Peace between Israel and its neighbors could solve two fundamental problems for Lebanon: the status of 400,000 Palestinian refugees currently residing within its borders and an unsettled frontier with Israel, which permits a powerful Lebanese political party—Hizballah—to maintain an armed militia under the guise of continued resistance. Developments with respect to the identity issue will dictate whether internal political consensus on the fundamentals of governance and legitimacy can transcend anti-Syrian sentiment, which itself is far from universal.

Although many Lebanese will wish to avoid it, a debate about sectarianism—political confessionalism—seems inevitable. The Shiites—the community in Lebanon that has traditionally been at the end of the line in terms of political and economic privilege—seems now to be the largest in terms of numbers. Having gained politically from Syria's suzerain status, will this community now uphold a system under which its votes may count for less than the votes of others? For the sake of unification and nation building, will Lebanon's traditionally privileged make substantial political and economic concessions to the Shiites? For example, will the country move in the direction of "one man, one vote" or will internal divisions be exacerbated as the initial excitement over Syria's withdrawal dies down, threatening civil conflict and perhaps providing a pretext for future Syrian continued intervention in Lebanon's internal affairs?

Syrian control, while implemented with corrupt brutality and incompetence, advanced the political fortunes of Lebanon's Shiites while preserving the appearances of Lebanon's founding compromise, including the "first among equals" status of Lebanon's Christians, led by the Maronites. Can the Lebanese people achieve a legitimate and sustainable internal political consensus on their own or will Syrian suzerainty be sustained even without a single Syrian soldier in Lebanon? Interestingly, in recent years, Syria had extended its influence mainly through parts of the Maronite establishment, such as President Lahoud, and through the main Shiite parties, Amal and Hizballah. Syria's withdrawal, therefore, provides a challenge to these groups: Will they do Syria's bidding, and be perceived as an instrument of an outside power, or will they break with Syria and attempt to increase their strength domestically. Much will depend on the prospects for peace in the region, the political stability of Syria itself, and the ability of Lebanese to produce national leaders of the caliber of the murdered Rafiq al-Hariri.

CHAPTER **14**

LIBYA

In the late 1990s, Libya launched an effort to break free from six years of international sanctions and end its relative isolation from the rest of the world. The United Nations, United States, and other members of the global community responded with step-by-step measures intended to reward Libyan behavior and take advantage of the possibilities for resumed economic ties and security cooperation. This period also saw halting economic reforms intended to deal with popular discontent and to attract outside investment and other business opportunities. Political reforms were even more tentative and met with resistance from Libyan vested interests whose influence had grown relative to the rest of Libyan society during the preceding decades of ideological turmoil. Reformers emerged, but they met with determined opposition by those who had benefited from regime favoritism doled out according to tribal identity and loyalty to the shifting dogma of longtime leader Mu'ammar al-Qadhafi.

The new directions in Libyan foreign policy, economic reforms, and especially steps toward political reforms reflected Qadhafi's highly personal, unpredictable, and dominant leadership. Clearly dissatisfied with Libya's isolation and lack of international influence, Qadhafi shifted dramatically from identification with the Arab and Muslim worlds to espousing Libya's role in Africa as being the country's primary international vocation. He then demonstrated pragmatism and vision by initiating openings to the United States and key European governments, foreswearing support for terrorism and efforts to obtain weapons of mass destruction. Qadhafi vacillated on the domestic front between encouraging reforms but opposing the development of institutions outside his firm control. By 2005 the pace of change had accelerated, but its duration remained uncertain.

For more than thirty-five years, Libya's neighbors and much of the Western world were skeptical of the Libyan government's intentions. The September 1969 coup d'etat that replaced King Idris I with a government headed by Qadhafi ushered in dramatic social and political transformations. By most standards, what transpired can only be described as a revolution. The nation went from a loose collection of relatively conservative Arab societies to a sometimes inscrutable blend of dictatorship, pan-Arabism, militarism, socialism, and militancy in foreign affairs. As head of state, Qadhafi functioned not only as political leader, but also as chief ideologist.

During more than three decades in power, Qadhafi periodically has enjoyed considerable popularity. At times, however, he mismanaged Libya's huge oil profits, and failed to efficiently use income from oil exports to lift the lower classes of society, but he also effected improvements in the country's infrastructure and overall standard of living. During the most recent decade, Libya entered a deepening economic and social malaise marked by high unemployment and education and health systems falling increasingly behind many countries with much lower per capita incomes.

Despite rhetoric to the contrary, Qadhafi has never risked allowing the type of open political process necessary for earning a popular mandate.

Key Facts on Libya

Area: 679,359 square miles (1,759,540 square kilometers)

Capital: Tripoli

Population: 5,765,563 (2005)

Religion: Sunni Muslim, 97 percent

Ethnic Groups: Berber and Libyan Arab, 97 percent; Greeks, Maltese, Italians, Egyptians, Pakistanis, Turks, Indians, sub-Saharan Africans, Tuareg, Tunisians, 3 percent

Official Language: Arabic; Italian, and English widely spoken in major cities

Type of Government: Jamahiriya (state of the masses)–in theory, governance by the populace through local councils in reality, control by dictatorship

GDP: $37.48 billion; $6,700 per capita (2004)

Source: Central Intelligence Agency, *CIA World Factbook,* 2005.

Qadhafi's political power ultimately rests on a combination of state distribution of income and benefits, domestic repression, control of the military, and tribal politics.

Geography and Demography

Libya lies in the center of the North African coast of the Mediterranean Sea. It is bounded by Egypt to the east, Sudan to the southeast, Tunisia and Algeria to the west, and Niger and Chad to the south. Except for a few areas bordering Tunisia and Egypt, Libyan territories adjacent to neighboring countries are inhabited sparsely, if at all.

With an area of 679,359 square miles—about two-and-a-half times the size of Texas—Libya is the fourth-largest country in Africa. Most of its territory is desert. More than 90 percent of its people live on less than 10 percent of the land, primarily inhabiting the fertile areas along the 1,100-mile Mediterranean coastline. This coastal strip experiences a typically Mediterranean climate of warm summers, mild winters, and scant rainfall,

but most of Libya has arid, desert weather with little or no rainfall and no permanent rivers. There are two small areas of hills and mountains in the northeast and northwest regions and another zone of hills and mountains in the Sahara in the south and southwest.

Libya is divided into three regions with distinct histories. Tripolitania—about 16 percent of the nation's land area—extends from the center of the Libyan coast westward to Tunisia and is linked culturally with the Maghrib, historically the areas of Algeria, Morocco, Mauritania, and Tunisia. Directly to the south of Tripolitania lies the desert region of Fezzan, which constitutes some 33 percent of the nation. Cyrenaica, the entire eastern region from the Mediterranean south to the border with Chad, comprises 51 percent of Libya's land area. The culture of this region is more closely associated with the Arab states to the East than with the Maghrib.

Libya's population was estimated in 2005 to be around 5.8 million. With only about eight people per square mile, Libya ranks as one of the most sparsely populated nations in Africa. Because of the country's small population, the government encourages a high birth rate. The population growth rate is almost 2.4 percent. Experts question many of Libya's economic and social statistics, such as the suspiciously precise life expectancy figures of 74.29 years for males and 78.82 years for females.

About 97 percent of Libyans are Arabic-speaking Sunni Muslims who are ethnically Arab and Berber. The rest are Tuareg (Muslim nomads of the central and western Sahara), black Africans, or the dwindling members of various foreign communities of long-standing residence, primarily Greeks and Maltese). An estimated 1.6 million foreign workers and business people also reside in Libya on a temporary basis.

The Arabic dialect in Tripolitania and Fezzan is similar to that of the other Maghrib nations' to the west, while the Arab dialect prevalent in Cyrenaica is closer to that of Egypt. Although urbanization increases steadily, nomadic and semi-nomadic Bedouins continue to roam the desert and adjacent areas. Qadhafi is from one such tribe.

History

In contrast to the comparatively small modern nation-state of Libya, the term *Libya* was used historically—particularly by the Greeks—to denote most of North Africa. Unlike Egypt, for example, Libya had no history as an identifiable nation before achieving independence in 1951. Rather, its history is that of several regions, groups, and tribes out of which the modern state of Libya was formed. Even after Libya attained unity and independence, many of its people continued to identify with their region—Cyrenaica, Fezzan, or Tripolitania.

The coastal area of Libya appears to have been inhabited since Neolithic times. Although the origin of the indigenous Berbers remains unconfirmed, some scholars believe that they migrated from southwestern Asia beginning around 3000 B.C.E. The coast was over the years the site of Phoenician, Greek, and Roman settlements.

The most important event in Libya's history was the introduction of Islam in the middle of the seventh century. Slightly more than a decade after the death of the Prophet Muhammad in 632, Arab Muslim armies took control of Cyrenaica and overcame fierce resistance from the Berbers in Tripolitania. By 663 the Muslims controlled Fezzan, and by 715 Andalusia, in present-day Spain, also had come under Arab Islamic rule. North Africa, like most of the great Arabo-Islamic empire, was governed by caliphs—successors of the Prophet Muhammad—ruling first from Damascus and later from Baghdad and then from Cairo. After a brief period of Spanish rule from 1510 to 1551, the Ottomans established their authority in Tripolitania, at least nominally, and by the end of the sixteenth century they had brought even Fezzan under their rule.

Early in the eighteenth century, a local Turkish officer, Ahmad Karamanli, established an Ottoman-supported dynasty in Tripolitania that extended into parts of Cyrenaica. European merchants feared the corsairs supported by the rulers in Tripoli, and in 1799 the United States, like many European nations, paid tribute to Tripoli to prevent attacks against its vessels. When in 1801 the United States

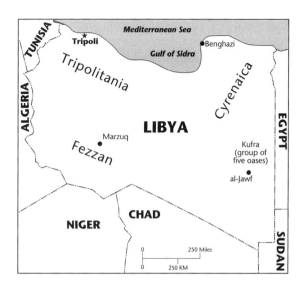

failed to meet in a timely manner Tripoli's demand for an increase in payments, the U.S. consulate was attacked and the consul expelled. Peace came only after a small-scale naval war.

After the Napoleonic Wars ended in 1815, European naval forces undertook a successful campaign to destroy Tripoli's corsairs and end the payment of tribute. Denied their principal source of revenue, Tripoli's rulers attempted to impose taxes on their people, leading to rebellion and civil war. Fearing that the weakness of Tripolitania would invite expansion by the French, who had already established colonial rule over Algiers and Tunis to the west, the Ottomans ended these internal power struggles in 1835 by reestablishing direct rule in Tripoli. They exercised limited control over the more inaccessible parts of Cyrenaica and Fezzan, but in the coastal areas, where they retained full control, their rule was repressive, corrupt, and unpopular.

Also during the nineteenth century, a Muslim religious sect began to change the lives of the people of Cyrenaica. Muhammad bin Ali al-Sanusi, a native of what is now Algeria, settled in Cyrenaica in the 1840s and attracted Bedouins and town dwellers to a new approach to Islam that combined the mysticism of Sufism and the rationalism of orthodox Sunnism. Tribal adherents venerated him. His descendants increased the following of what became known as the Sanusi order, and by the beginning of the twentieth century it claimed the allegiance of virtually all the Cyrenaican Bedouins as well as followers in Egypt, the Sudan, and even Arabia.

Italy was a latecomer to the European colonial rivalry in the Middle East and Africa, but by 1912 it had wrested what is now Libya from the weakened Ottoman Empire. The Italian government had great difficulty subduing its new domain but managed to maintain control despite heavy losses inflicted on Italian troops in Libya's hinterland by Sanusi followers.

By 1916 leadership of the Sanusis rested in the hands of young Muhammad Idris al-Sanusi, who would become King Idris of Libya. Although Italy recognized Idris as amir (ruler) of the Cyrenaican hinterland and granted him substantial autonomy over his realm, the victorious allies of World War I recognized Italian sovereignty over Libya as a whole. Conflicting personalities and tribal affiliations badly divided the nationalists in Tripolitania who wanted independence from Italy. In 1922, to construct a united front against the Italians, the nationalists offered Idris the title of amir of Tripolitania and thus the leadership of their region. Idris did not aspire to authority in Tripolitania, where he had few followers, but he accepted the role regardless. This situation did not sit well with the Italians, who by then viewed Idris as a threat to their control. In late 1922, Idris fled to Egypt, where he continued to guide his followers from exile.

Following Benito Mussolini's accession to power as Italian prime minister in 1922, Italy again attempted to subjugate its Libyan possessions. After a brutal campaign, by 1931 it had succeeded against strong resistance from Libyan nationalists. More than a hundred thousand Italian colonists settled in Libya during the 1930s, and in 1939 Italy formally annexed Libya. Most leaders of the Sanusi sect remained in exile.

World War II provided Libyan nationalists with the opportunity to oust the Italians by cooperating with Britain. They hoped that the British would support Libyan independence after the war was won. Despite serious disagreements between the nationalists from Cyrenaica and Tripolitania, the two regions agreed to accept the leadership of Idris and to provide volunteers to the British forces. The Libyan Arab Force fought alongside the Allies under British command until they drove the Axis powers out of Libya in February 1943.

From 1943 until 1951, the British administered Cyrenaica and Tripolitania, while the French controlled Fezzan. Although the Libyan people enthusiastically welcomed Idris from exile and the British allowed him to form an independent Sanusi emirate in Cyrenaica, the European powers were slow to reach a consensus on how to administer the former Italian colonies.

United as a single entity only since 1939, Cyrenaica and Tripolitania had their social and political differences. Tripolitanians demanded a republic, while Cyrenaicans—fearing domination by the larger and more sophisticated Tripolitanian population—called for a Sanusi monarchy. Fezzan, with a tribal society like that of Cyrenaica, had its own leading family. In addition, the three regions collectively appeared to face a profoundly unpromising economic future, as Libya possessed no known natural resources and depended heavily on external aid.

The United Nations adopted a resolution calling for the establishment of an independent, unified Libyan state by the beginning of 1952. An international council that included Libyans from each of the three regions was set up to assist in establishing a government. The National Constituent Assembly began deliberations in late 1950 and, despite some dissent, decided on a federal system with Idris as monarch. On December 24, 1951, King Idris I formally declared Libya an independent country.

Despite the existence of a legislature, the king held most of the power. The three regions occasionally challenged the central government's authority, and when political parties showed signs of dissent, Idris banned them. His eighteen-year reign was, however, generally stable. He led conservatively and established close ties with Britain and the United States, to which he granted the use of military bases in exchange for economic assistance.

Under Idris, Libya enjoyed particularly good relations with other conservative Arab and African nations, such as Saudi Arabia and Ethiopia, and Libya remained somewhat removed from the Arab-Israeli conflict. The discovery of large oil reserves in 1959 and an active role by U.S. and other foreign oil companies gradually improved the Libyan economy.

Libya's low literacy rate and rising prosperity resulting from oil revenues might have enabled Idris to insulate his country from external conflicts and upheavals if it had not been for two factors. First, the growing influence of Egypt's Nasser permeated Libya, as Egyptian broadcasts carried his speeches throughout the Arab world. Second, the June 1967 Arab-Israeli war, and the attendant humiliation of the Arab nations, galvanized Libyans to action as it did Arabs elsewhere. Workers and the young began rallying to the call of Arab nationalism.

Idris ultimately failed to create a Libyan nation united around the institution of the monarchy. After nearly two decades in power, Tripolitanians still mistrusted him. Support for the monarchy eroded as Libyans in urban areas grew disillusioned with Idris's failure to broadly spread the benefits of the country's oil income among the population. Although Idris supported subsidies to the "frontline" Arab states of Egypt and Jordan, he generally continued to pursue policies that favored the West at a time when anti-Western sentiments were growing more pronounced throughout the Arab world. On September 1, 1969, with Idris and many other senior government officials out of the country, army units in Tripoli and Benghazi seized power. Although their numbers were initially small, the mostly young coup plotters met little resistance. In the coming years, they transformed Libya's government and radically altered Libya's foreign and domestic policies.

Enter Qadhafi

Although the names of the twelve members of the Revolutionary Command Council who seized power remained secret until the following year, a week after the coup, one of the RCC members,

Mu'ammar al-Qadhafi

Capt. Mu'ammar al-Qadhafi, was promoted to colonel and named commander in chief. He was only twenty-seven years old and in the coming years and decades would become the dominant political and ideological force in Libyan politics. His Bedouin background, his education in Islamic schools, and his adolescence during the height of anti-imperialism and Nasserism all influenced his thinking.

The new government championed Arab unity, the Palestinian cause, and an Arab-Islamic style of socialism. From the beginning, Qadhafi and the Free Officers, the group of young reformist military men who carried out the coup, looked to Nasser's Egypt as a model. Qadhafi had been profoundly affected by what he had heard on broadcasts of Radio Cairo, which he listened to growing up during the height of Nasser's influence. The slogans promoting socialism and Arab unity, the nomenclature—for example, the Free Officers, the Revolutionary Command Council—and the organizations—the Arab Socialist Union political party—all reflected Qadhafi's hero worship of Nasser. By 1969 Nasser had tempered his political objectives in light of prevailing political realities and defeats, but Qadhafi remained committed to pursuing the goals his new government espoused.

The new regime sought to allay the concerns of foreign allies of the deposed king by declaring that Libya would adhere to its treaty obligations. Despite such assurances, relations with the United States and Britain rapidly deteriorated. The regime declared a national holiday in June 1970 on the day that the United States completed its evacuation of Wheelus Air Force Base. The United States had hoped that this step, which followed lengthy negotiations, would refocus relations on mutually beneficial commercial activity and set the stage for continuing security cooperation on a new basis. In the mid-1970s, however, Qadhafi began to move closer to the Soviet Union and its allies, the most prominent aspect of their relations being arms transfer agreements. Despite this relationship, Qadhafi consistently denounced communism as a form of atheism and never permitted the establishment of a communist or any other nongovernmental party.

In 1972 and 1974 Qadhafi disappeared from public view. On both occasions, however, he retained the post of commander in chief of the armed forces. These "retreats" do not appear to have resulted in a diminution of his power. Analysts believe that during these brief withdrawals from politics, Qadhafi devoted himself to political reflection and the formulation of ideology. In 1973, after his first retreat, he introduced a "cultural revolution." Castigating the Libyan people for their lack of revolutionary fervor, Qadhafi ordered the annulment of all pre-1969 laws and the repression of communism, capitalism, any manifestation of atheism, and the Muslim Brotherhood. He rejected all "non-Islamic thinking" and established "people's committees" throughout the country and at every level of government. He

declared that this program marked the beginning of a return to the true Islamic heritage of decision making by consultation.

In 1975, after his second retreat, Qadhafi dissolved the Arab Socialist Union and replaced it with "people's congresses," large gatherings of Libyans that were to operate, in Qadhafi's view, as manifestations of direct democracy. These gatherings are close in concept to the town meetings in parts of New England. At a people's congress, individuals are in theory free to express their views openly, but in practice these meetings often tend to be little more than rallies to back government policy. When a controversial local issue, such as public health facilities, appears on the agenda, participation increases and debate can be lively. The system becomes less representative of popular views as it moves toward the national level.

During his 1974 retreat, Qadhafi had assembled his political philosophy into the Green Book. Part one, "The Solution of the Problem of Democracy," was published in 1976. Part two, "The Solution of the Economic Problem—Socialism," followed in 1978. In part one he declares that representation is an inherently undemocratic concept. He explicitly rejects parliaments, referendums, majoritarian electoral systems, and multiparty and single-party systems. In part two, Qadhafi proclaims his belief that every man has the right to a house, an income, and a vehicle. While mandating rights to private ownership of one house (and no more), Qadhafi urges the abolition of business and encourages the takeover of certain business establishments by people's committees. Qadhafi's fundamental thesis, which he calls the Third Universal Theory, rejects capitalism and communism and claims to establish in Libya direct democracy. This he put forth in 1980 in part three of the Green Book, "The Social Basis of the Third Universal Theory."

In March 1977, the Libyan constitution was amended and the country's name changed to the Socialist People's Libyan Arab Jamahiriya. *Jamahiriya* is an invented word meaning roughly "state of the masses." The constitution designates the unicameral General People's Congress (GPC) the main organ of government, though it holds little power. Despite Qadhafi's condemnation of representation, congresses at lower levels send representatives to the General People's Congress.

The implementation of Qadhafi's ideas has sometimes wrought havoc with daily life in Libya. One plan, in the late 1980s, called for moving the capital and scattering government ministries around the nation. Other actions in the interest of Qadhafi's utopian notions of equality—such as the abolition of retail trade and rental housing, the seizure of bank accounts and businesses, the destruction of land tenure records, and a proposal for the abolition of money—severely damaged the economy. Repressive government tactics constrained daily life for most Libyans. Hundreds of Libyans reportedly were executed during the most repressive periods of Qadhafi's rule, and the government continues to hold political prisoners. Political parties remain banned, and there is no legal mechanism for political activity other than that controlled by the government.

Although there has been virtually no movement toward political reforms, the opposite holds true in the economic sphere. In March 2003, the GPC adopted legislation intended to initiate a course of economic liberalization. In June 2003, Qadhafi called for the abolition of public sector institutions that had failed to deal with the country's economic problems. Under his guidance, the GPC named Shukri Ghanim as the Libyan equivalent of prime minister, albeit a weak one. Ghanim, a well-regarded economist and an exponent of privatization and liberal economic reforms, gathered around him a team of technocrats that included Abdallah Badri, whom Ghanim appointed to head the state-owned National Oil Corporation (NOC) with a mandate to bring U.S. companies back to Libya. The Ghanim government also accepted the expertise of the International Monetary Fund to assist in the liberalization process. By 2004 the government was drafting plans to privatize 360 state companies. Such moves inevitably gave rise to opponents among the ranks of the entrenched bureaucracy and their ideologically socialist allies. The latter include senior officials of the GPC who attacked Ghanim's proposals in acrimo-

nious debate at the January 2005 GPC, arguing that they were protectors of the revolutionary heritage of Libya. Some ideologues, such as GPC assistant secretary Ahmad Ibrahim, have the authority of past statements and writings of Qadhafi to justify their opposition to the reforms. Ghanim has the task of persuading the GPC to pass laws, approve regulations, and set up institutions to implement the reforms. In fact, Qadhafi was probably ambivalent about the reforms, but nonetheless convinced of their practical necessity. The delicacy of the government's task is indicated by its use of the euphemism "extension of popular ownership" to describe privatization.

Oil and the Libyan Economy

Petroleum production dominates Libya's economic life, accounting for 25 percent of its gross domestic product and 95 percent of its export earnings. Libya has about 36 billion barrels of proven oil reserves, the eleventh largest in the world. Of nations outside the Persian Gulf region, only Mexico, Russia, and Venezuela have more.

After oil was discovered in Algeria in the early 1950s, exploration began in Libya under the rule of King Idris. The first oil was found in 1957 in western Fezzan, and the first major strike followed in 1959 in Cyrenaica. Libya joined the Organization of Petroleum Exporting Countries (OPEC) in 1962. Although Libya possesses dozens of major and minor oil fields, including some offshore, the major strikes of the late 1950s and early 1960s occurred in Sirtica, an arid zone in the center of the coastal area; this remains the source of most of the country's oil exports. Unlike other Middle Eastern oil-producing states that granted rights to a single company or a consortium of a few companies to develop their oil, Libya encouraged foreign competition in exploration. It gave concessions to numerous petroleum companies in Britain, the United States, and West Germany among others. This policy vaulted Libya into the top ranks of oil producers in a relatively short period.

After Qadhafi came to power, Libyan oil policy became more assertive and increasingly intertwined with political objectives. Soon efforts were under way to "Libyanize" employment in the industry, increase posted oil prices, establish government control over the rate of oil production, and increase government ownership of the oil companies. Within a year, Libya managed to break the solid front of the foreign oil companies and greatly increase its take from their production. This set a precedent that led other oil-producing countries to follow suit. In September 1973, Libya nationalized 51 percent of the local assets of all the foreign oil companies operating in the country, and six months later it completely nationalized the Libyan holdings of three U.S. corporations. It then embarked on a policy of joint production instead of simply granting concessions to foreign concerns.

The National Oil Corporation and its subsidiaries now take credit for more than two-thirds of Libya's annual production, a figure that will increase given the pattern of recent joint production contracts. The remaining production is retained by foreign oil companies, primarily European, though they now face competition from U.S. firms.

Beginning in the 1970s, Libyan joint production contracts failed to provide adequate incentives to stimulate investment and new exploration that might reverse the decline of Libya's proven oil reserves. The less attractive terms for the companies combined with lower oilfield investments also slashed Libyan production from its high of 3.3 million barrels a day in 1970 to only 1.5 million in 1975. In the mid-1970s, Libyan production began to recover as continental European firms moved in to replace the Americans and the British, but combined Libyan and foreign investment in exploration and field maintenance remained inadequate.

Throughout the Libyan oil industry's ups and downs, European countries continued to view it as an important energy source. Several factors have made Libyan oil particularly marketable. First, Libyan light crude has a low sulfur content, which makes it more attractive for engine use because it burns more cleanly and produces less air pollution. Second, because of its proximity to the Mediterranean coast, most Libyan oil can be piped directly from wells to tankers. Third, the proximity of Libya and major European oil-importing nations lowers transport costs. The high gasoline yield of Libyan crude makes the United States a potential customer, but U.S. sanctions prohibited the import of Libyan oil until recently.

With roughly 75 percent of the government budget dependent on oil revenues, Libya finds itself vulnerable when oil prices fluctuate widely. The sharp decline in world oil prices in 1998 cut Libya's oil earnings by about 33 percent. The government and the people adapted to the decreased revenues, but not without a significant decline in the quality of life and rise in political discontent. Outside economists estimate unemployment to be at 25 to 30 percent. The higher oil prices of 2003 and 2004 offered some relief, and oil revenues were forecast to exceed $19 billion dollars in 2005.

The UN sanctions imposed on Libya in 1992 and 1993 exacerbated the economic problems caused by falling oil prices. A ban on airline flights to Libya discouraged foreign investment and forced Libyans seeking to fly abroad to travel long distances to airports in Egypt, Malta, or Tunisia. A ban on the sale of oil equipment set back the government's plan to add value to its oil by developing its refining capacity. The lifting of sanctions in the early 2000s revived this sector. Already able to refine oil in excess of its domestic energy requirements, Libya seeks to become a major supplier of refined products to European consumers.

The end of sanctions also brought U.S. oil companies back to Libya after decades of watching from the sidelines as European companies replaced U.S. leadership in the sector. The Occidental Oil Company and the Oasis consortium of Conoco, Marathon, and Amerada Hess retained legal claims on old production areas, and Libya partially accommodated them. In August 2004, the government offered substantial new acreage for exploration, and U.S. companies emerged as successful bidders on eleven of the fifteen sites. European and other non-U.S. companies are expected to be more competitive in future rounds.

Like many other countries dependent on oil, Libya reacted to low oil prices by attempting to diversify its economy. Libya has 52 trillion cubic feet of natural gas reserves, the twentieth largest. Experts believe actual gas reserves to be much larger. The government has sought to build an infrastructure that will allow for a greater use of natural gas in the domestic economy, thereby freeing up more of its high-quality oil for export. Gas exports to European markets are increasing rapidly, and the Mediterranean is no longer a barrier requiring costly liquification before export, as a pipeline from the Libyan coast to Sicily came online in October 2004 with other trans-Mediterranean pipeline projects in the development or planning stages.

In addition to oil and natural gas, Libya counts among its mineral resources large iron deposits, salt beds, and construction materials, including gypsum, limestone, cement rock, and building stone. With the exceptions of cement rock and gypsum, these nonpetroleum resources have only begun to be exploited. In the manufacturing sector, Libya has focused on developing its petrochemical, steel, and aluminum industries. Although only 1 percent of Libyan territory is arable, the government has emphasized the development of an agricultural sector, which employs 20 percent of the workforce. Libyan farmers raise wheat and barley as well as such traditional Mediterranean crops as dates, olives, grapes, and citrus fruits.

The government has invested in a $30 billion complex of pipelines, known as the Great Man-Made River Project, to pipe water from aquifers in the Sahara to irrigate farmland on the Mediterranean coast as well as to improve the water supply to populated areas. This five-stage undertaking began in 1983. Tripoli and Benghazi, as well as other cities and agricultural areas, already benefit from it. Now in stage three, the network of pipelines continues to expand. Given environmental concerns and the limitations of Libyan agriculture, it is questionable whether the project will yield the economic benefits necessary to justify its cost. The significance of such an ambitious project must, however, be measured in non-economic ways as well. It has helped politically by binding disparate parts of Libya's vast land area and building a sense of national purpose.

The resumption of airline traffic to and from Libya may reinvigorate the country's tourism industry, which not surprisingly stagnated under the UN sanctions. Libya has excellent Mediterranean beaches and some of the most notable Roman ruins in North Africa. As the site of heavy fighting during World War II, Libya also could promote itself to World War II buffs and veterans and their families seeking to visit graves and battle sites. At this point in time, however, inadequate hotels and other tourism infrastructure are impediments to the revitalization of this sector.

Foreign Policy Issues

Qadhafi has not been content simply to rule. As noted, he has also formulated a novel philosophy of government that he has tried to implement. He has also tested the waters at making himself a major international actor, but the inconsistencies in his foreign policies, his frequent antagonism toward neighboring countries, his support for radical, fringe groups and his inability to rally Arab or African support for his more extreme positions have consistently undercut his efforts at leadership beyond Libya's borders. For nearly three decades, the defining characteristics of Qadhafi's foreign policy were hostility toward the West and Israel, Arab unity schemes, and the exertion of Libyan influence over its neighbors. Pursuit of these objectives tended to isolate Libya on the international stage, but in the late 1990s, Qadhafi shifted course: He began to focus on Africa rather than on the Arab world, he ended his support of Palestinian rejectionists, and he extended feelers for better relations with Western Europe and rapprochement with the United States.

Qadhafi's penchant for Arab mergers displayed itself shortly after he assumed power. In 1969 Libya proposed a union with Egypt, Sudan, and Syria. They formed a nominal federation in 1971, but in practice the four nations continued to operate independently. Libya also pursued unsuccessful mergers at various times with Algeria,

Chad, Tunisia, Malta, and Morocco. Most of these negotiations ended in acrimony. Qadhafi has supported rebel factions or coup attempts against sitting governments in Chad, Morocco, Sudan, Tunisia, and Mauritania and in West Africa. Such actions, and Libya's arsenal of Soviet weaponry, made its neighbors highly suspicious of Tripoli's intent and undercut its attempts to join with other nations. Libyan forces intervened in Chad in 1973, 1980, 1983, and 1987. Twice in 1987, Chadian forces, equipped and supported by France and the United States, routed invading Libyan troops. These adventures resulted in growing foreign disenchantment with Libya and embarrassment at home.

Beyond merger attempts, Qadhafi sought a leading role in Arab politics by taking a hard line toward Israel. Libya provided funds, bases, and training to the most militant Palestinian groups and denounced the Egyptian peace overtures to the Israelis that resulted in the 1979 Camp David Accords. Libya remained hostile toward Egypt until 1989, when the two countries repaired relations after Egypt gained readmission to the Arab League. In 1993 Libya was one of the few countries to voice outright opposition to the Israeli-Palestinian Oslo agreements, putting it at odds with most other Arab states. In the late 1990s, however, Libya established relations with the Palestinian Authority, ceased operating as a safe haven for Palestinian rejectionists, and downplayed its hostility toward Israel.

Libyan financial (and sometimes logistical) support of terrorism during the 1980s exacerbated its already strained relationship with the United States. In late December 1985, gunmen attacked travelers waiting at El Al ticket counters at Rome and Vienna airports, killing twenty people, including five Americans. Evidence suggested that the Palestinian group headed by Abu Nidal (Sabri al-Banna), who had close ties to Libya, had carried out the operations. On January 7, 1986, President Ronald Reagan banned all U.S. trade with Libya and directed U.S. nationals to leave the country. The following day, he froze Libyan government assets in the United States.

On April 14, 1986, Reagan ordered an air strike against Libya after communications intercepts led U.S. officials to believe that the Libyan government had played a role in the bombing of a West Berlin nightclub earlier that month. The U.S. raid destroyed several military targets and killed dozens of Libyan military personnel and civilians, including Qadhafi's infant daughter. These developments left Qadhafi increasingly isolated. Although Arab governments verbally supported Libya in its military confrontations with the United States, they nevertheless maintained a strategic, diplomatic distance. A few years later, the collapse of the Soviet Union, Libya's wary patron and supplier of arms, brought further isolation from the global community and increased the danger to Libya of maintaining a radical foreign policy.

On December 21, 1988, Pan Am Flight 103 exploded over Lockerbie, Scotland, killing the 259 people on board in addition to 11 people on the ground. After an extensive investigation, the United States and Scotland indicted two Libyan nationals, Abd al-Baset Ali al-Megrahi and Al-Amin Khalifah Fhimah, whom they identified as Libyan intelligence agents. French authorities announced that the two men also were suspects in the bombing of a French jet over Niger in 1989 that killed 171 people.

Libya's refusal to hand over the men for trial in Scotland led the UN Security Council in April 1992 to adopt resolutions calling for their extradition and for sanctions against Libya. The sanctions banned military sales to Libya and prohibited airline traffic from taking off or landing there. In November 1993, the United Nations stiffened the sanctions by banning the sale of oil equipment and freezing Libya's foreign assets.

The financial cushion provided by oil reserves saved the Libyan economy from total devastation. Libyans continued to enjoy the highest per capita income—estimated at $6,700 in 1998—of any nation on the African continent, but the combined effect of falling oil prices in 1998 and the gradual erosion of funds caused by the sanctions increased unemployment and inflation as well as Libyans' sense of isolation.

For several years, the Libyan government sought without success to have the United Nations lift the sanctions, but the sharp drop in oil prices in 1998 gave this goal more urgency. Libya therefore sought a face-saving way to relinquish the two bombing suspects, while simultaneously improving relations with neighboring nations to relieve its isolation. As early as 1992, Libya made secret overtures to resume a dialogue with the United States. After initial rebuffs, the Clinton administration and the British government decided to engage Libya in discreet, high-level talks beginning in 1999.

In August 1998, Libya had agreed in principle to relinquish the Lockerbie suspects for trial in the Netherlands under Scottish law. Diplomatic intervention by South African president Nelson Mandela helped pave the way for a final agreement. The suspects were delivered to UN representatives in April 1999. The United Nations immediately suspended the sanctions as an interim step pending full Libyan cooperation with the trial, compensation of the victims' families, acknowledgment of responsibility, and declarations of intent to end any involvement in terrorist activities, as required by the UN resolution. In January 2001, the Scottish court acquitted Fhimah but found Megrahi guilty. Megrahi lost his appeal and began serving a life sentence in March 2002.

In August 2003, following prolonged negotiations with lawyers for the families of Pan Am 103 victims, Libya agreed to pay $2.7 billion in compensation, or $10 million per victim. By other terms of the agreement, Libya would release the funds in three tranches, dependent upon the permanent end to UN sanctions, the lifting of U.S. unilateral sanctions, and the removal of Libya from the Department of State's list of state sponsors of terrorism. In parallel negotiations, U.S. and British diplomats elicited formal Libyan statements satisfying other conditions for the end of UN sanctions in September 2003. Normalization of bilateral relations with most states (though not the United States) followed fairly rapidly.

The United States had asserted since March 1990 that Libya was attempting to build a concealed chemical weapons production capability. For more than a decade, Libya publicly denied the charge, claiming that all its chemical research was devoted to developing a domestic chemical industry. In secret talks with the United States and Britain, however, Libya indicated as early as 1999 that it was prepared to put the matter of chemical weapons on the table. In doing so, the government hoped that it would gain U.S. and British support for ending the UN sanctions. The United States, however, declined to discuss weapons-related matters until Libya had further progressed on the various terrorism issues tied to UN sanctions. Finally satisfied that Libya would meet the criteria for ending the UN sanctions, the United States made clear that improvement in bilateral relations would depend on dealing with the weapons issue.

A delicate series of backstage diplomatic maneuvers in 2003 brought dramatic progress. In March 2003, Qadhafi's son Saif al-Islam al-Qadhafi told British officials that his father was ready to dispel the question of chemical weapons. Britain, the United States, and Libya then worked out the details in secret. After the interception of a ship transporting nuclear material to Libya, the matter of nuclear weapons precursors was added to the agenda. In December 2003, Muhammad Chalgam, the Libyan equivalent of foreign minister, publicly announced that the Libyan government would disclose and end all of its unconventional weapons programs. In a brief television appearance, Qadhafi expressed public support for this "wise and courageous step." U.S. president George W. Bush and British prime minister Tony Blair praised the decision and indicated that they would work for Libya's international rehabilitation. Arms control teams from the United Kingdom, the United States, and the International Atomic Energy Agency have since conducted inspections in Libya, destroyed chemical weapons, and removed supplies that could be used to build nuclear weapons.

Britain had quickly normalized relations after Libya extradited the Lockerie suspects in 1999, and Prime Minister Blair visited Libya and met with Qadhafi. Other Western European leaders have made similar gestures. The United States moved more slowly, but its direction was clear. The two countries opened offices in each other's capital in 2004. That same year, the United States lifted restrictions on American travel to Libya and ended most economic sanctions. Libya remains on the Department of State's list of state sponsors of terrorism, a designation that imposes sanctions on dual use and civil aviation equipment. In early 2005, diplomatic relations were still below the full ambassadorial level, and lack of visa issuance in Washington and Tripoli remained a major obstacle to travel by Libyans as well as Americans.

Libya's relations with Arab countries have deteriorated in recent years. Libyan disenchantment with Arab nationalism and collective diplomacy intensified during the period of UN sanctions, which Arab governments generally observed. Libyan relations have been difficult with several Arab states, but they reached a new low with Saudi Arabia after an exchange of insults between Qadhafi and Saudi crown prince Abdallah at an Arab League meeting in March 2003. The Saudis subsequently arrested alleged Libyan intelligence officers promoting the assassination of Abdallah. In a parallel development, the United States arrested a Muslim American activist who was convicted in July 2004 for participating in the plot and who reportedly linked it directly to Qadhafi.

African countries have proven to be somewhat more receptive to Libyan efforts at improving relations, but the record is mixed. In June 1999, Qadhafi proposed the formation of a "United States of Africa." He backed the idea with Libyan checkbook diplomacy in the form of economic aid and selective military transfers. Most African governments remain wary, but a less ambitious African Union officially came into being in July 2002 with Libyan promises of support.

Outlook

The suspension of UN sanctions in 1999 and their formal end in 2003 marked key psychological turning points for Libya and its people. The rapid improvement of relations with European nations and the cautious but promising steps

regarding the United States have also encouraged Libyans to believe that they are once again welcome participants in the global community. Higher oil prices in recent years and the considerable commercial interest that international firms are expressing in Libya have enhanced optimism.

Although Western European governments observed the UN sanctions, they proved far less inclined to demonize the Libyan government than was the United States. The economies of Libya and a number of European countries, in particular Italy, are complementary. Libya's emotional empathy with Africa, the Arab world, and Muslim countries in general is not matched by the high degree of mutual economic interests it shares with Europe. In the historical long view, the Mediterranean basin has often been a region with strong cultural and economic ties.

U.S. interests in Libya are more political in nature than economic. Although certain U.S. companies may benefit greatly from improved U.S.-Libyan relations, the U.S. government has a strategic concern that Libyan energy resources be integrated into the global economy and that Libyan wealth be used in constructive ways. The events of September 11, 2001, injected a new and promising element into what had been a slow moving and secretive dialogue. Qadhafi was among the first Muslim and Arab leaders to express public sympathy for the United States. Through intelligence channels, the two governments exchanged information on radical Islamist groups that might threaten either of them. On the international stage, the United States needed to demonstrate that alternatives existed to the measures used against the governments of Afghanistan and Iraq. The example of Libya provided a safer and less costly paradigm for dealing with states on the U.S. terrorism list or thought to be seeking weapons of mass destruction. Libya was both, and the two governments took initiatives that turned this potential into reality.

On the domestic front, Qadhafi faces a potential threat from conspiracies within the military by officers who share the discontent of civilian technocrats over the failure of his political system to satisfy the economic and social needs of the Libyan people. Dissident forces and rivals attempted coups during the 1980s and 1990s, but so far Qadhafi appears to have mastered the skills necessary to detect and preempt any plots by officers who might try to repeat his success of 1969.

Radical Islamist groups may, however, pose a threat greater than that from the military. Although Islam has always had a place in Qadhafi's philosophy, his governance has generally been secular. Devout Muslims resent some of his policies, and he was one of the first Muslim leaders to identify Osama bin Laden and al-Qaida as a threat. In 1995 Libyan nationals associated with bin Laden in Afghanistan formed the Libyan Islamic Fighting Group, which is committed to Qadhafi's overthrow. In December 2004, the United States designated the group as a terrorist organization, indicating that the global "war on terror" might directly benefit the Libyan government.

Maintaining internal stability will depend in great part on oil production and the use of oil revenues to improve the lives of Libyan citizens. It seems probable that Libyan oil and gas revenues will increase dramatically in decades to come. What is less certain is whether internal economic reforms will take hold. The bloated public bureaucracy opposes them, as do the ideologues spawned by Qadhafi's revolutionary theories of decades past. For now, at least, Qadhafi seems prepared to support the reformers at the helm of the current government.

Qadhafi faces no obvious rival and is still not old by the standards of Arab world leadership. Clear rules for succession to his role as head of state do not exist, and Qadhafi's role as charismatic leader of the revolution would probably disappear with his passing from the scene. All of his sons and one daughter who shows an interest in politics have mixed reputations, but some reform-minded business elements are placing their hopes in Saif al-Islam al-Qadhafi. Although he holds no formal position, he often speaks in public, including at international forums, such as at the Davos economic summit in January 2005.

Mu'ammar al-Qadhafi has demonstrated for more than thirty years that he has the political skill necessary to remain in power. Nevertheless, an assassination or coup, by Islamists or military officers, remains a real possibility. In a closed society such as Libya's, there is often little warning that change is afoot. If Qadhafi is removed against his will, the event is likely to be as much of a surprise as was Qadhafi's seizure of power in 1969. Even more surprising would be changes as revolutionary as what Libya has witnessed during the three decades of his rule.

CHAPTER **15**

PERSIAN GULF STATES

A few decades ago, the desert shaykhdoms on the Persian Gulf were remote and generally unassuming, populated mostly by nomadic pastoralists, pearl harvesters, subsistence farmers, and fishermen. Bahrain, Oman, Qatar, and what was to become the United Arab Emirates (UAE) were barely known by the outside world. That, however, was before the dramatic increase in demand for oil in the early 1970s, coupled with price hikes caused by the Arab oil embargo of 1973–1974. Since then the oil-producing Persian Gulf states have become significant forces in the world economy, with Abu Dhabi—one of the seven shaykhdoms composing the UAE—and Qatar enjoying per capita incomes exceeding those of many Western industrialized nations. Gulf oil revenues have produced substantial funds for domestic development projects and investments overseas.

The oil glut of the mid-1980s, however, sent prices plummeting and cut the Gulf states' revenues from petroleum. As a result, their leaders were forced to reduce spending for social services, construction, economic development, and defense. Although oil was still their main source of income, and oil prices recovered somewhat in the late 1980s, the Gulf states continued their efforts to diversify their economies as a hedge against price fluctuations and in preparation for the future depletion of reserves. The Gulf countries also worked to reduce the central role that public expenditures play in their economies. To this end, they attempted to reduce red tape, establish free-trade zones, and set up stock exchanges

to encourage private investment and expand trade. In the late 1990s, with real oil prices at their lowest since 1973, pressures to diversify their economies further increased dramatically. The rise in oil prices in the early 2000s helped to balance current budgets and reduce debts but did not solve many of the basic economic problems.

At the beginning of the twenty-first century, the Gulf states faced other, often related domestic challenges including dependence on foreign labor, rapid population growth, and attendant education and infrastructure issues. In the UAE and Qatar, expatriates outnumber nationals by 80 percent or more; in Bahrain and Oman, they make up one-third and one-fourth of the population, respectively. Of the four states, Qatar's population growth rate is slightly more than 4 percent, one of the highest in the world, while the UAE's growth rate is more than 7 percent, mostly through immigration. The basic infrastructures of all four countries are racing to keep up with increasing demand. Problems in the education sector are, however, especially worrying; domestic institutions are not turning out graduates with the training and skills demanded by employers, leading to greater national unemployment and hampering efforts to nationalize workforces. These long-term problems are threatening the lifestyle and conservative nature of these states' populations and perhaps even their political stability.

In foreign policy, the Gulf states are dependent to varying degrees on Saudi Arabia for guidance and the United States for security, yet all are determined to maintain as much independence as possible. After the Iran-Iraq War broke out, Bahrain, Kuwait, Oman, Qatar, Saudi Arabia, and the UAE were finally able to carry through plans to establish the Gulf Cooperation Council (GCC) in 1981. The organization's purpose is to enhance regional security and prosperity through greater military, economic, and political coordination. Geopolitical developments in the region have, however, challenged the efficacy of the council in security terms, slowing moves toward economic integration because of the discrepancies in size between Saudi Arabia on the one hand and the other five states on the other.

BAHRAIN

Area: 257 square miles (665 square kilometers)
Capital: Manama
Population: 677,886, of whom 235,108 are expatriates (2004)
Religion: Muslim: Shiite Muslim, 70 percent; Sunni Muslim, 30 percent
Ethnic Groups: Bahraini, 63 percent; Asian, 19 percent; other Arab, 10 percent; Iranian, 8 percent
Official language: Arabic; Farsi, Urdu, and English widely spoken
Type of Government: Constitutional hereditary monarchy
GDP: $11.29 billion; $16,900 per capita (2003)

Source: Central Intelligence Agency, *CIA World Factbook,* 2004.

Bahrain, the smallest of the Persian Gulf states, was the first Gulf state to export oil, in the 1930s. Its early establishment of the foundations for a modern, industrialized economy enabled it to become a regional banking and service center during the oil boom of the 1970s. The British military presence in Bahrain until 1971 made Bahrain International Airport the first major airline hub in the region. It was also one of the first Gulf states to develop an educated citizenry: a number of Bahrainis filled important positions in the lower Gulf states in the early stages of development.

During the 1980s, Bahrain faced a number of challenges to its political and economic stability. Soon after Ayatollah Ruhollah Khomeini became

the head of the new Islamic Republic of Iran in 1979, some factions in Tehran tried to incite Bahrain's Shiites to carry out a similar fundamentalist revolution. The depression of the oil market in the mid-1980s further aggravated social tensions and complicated the government's development plans. With rapidly diminishing oil resources, Bahrain became more dependent on its Gulf neighbors, especially Saudi Arabia, to whom it looked to finance the state's continued development.

Although the threat of Islamic revolution diminished greatly over the next decade, the Bahraini regime continued to face the twin challenges of a politically disenfranchised Shiite majority and a domestic economy destined to become the first in the Gulf to enter the post-petroleum era. The 1990s saw another period of overt political opposition, as had occurred at various times throughout the twentieth century. On this occasion the dissidence was concentrated among the Shiites, dissatisfied with their political and economic situation, and there were a number of violent incidents.

In 1999 Amir Isa bin Salman Al Khalifa died, after having ruled Bahrain since 1960, and was succeeded by his son Hamad, who reached an accommodation with the political opposition and brought an end to the unrest. He established a partly elected parliament, but the Shiites boycotted the elections because they felt their new ruler had not carried through on his promises. In 2001 Hamad declared himself king and his country a kingdom.

Geography

Bahrain, meaning "two seas," is an archipelago of about thirty-five islands, six of which are inhabited. Al-Bahrain, the largest island and the location of the capital, Manama, is also the country's namesake. Situated in the Persian Gulf, Bahrain lies between the Saudi Arabian coast and the Qatari Peninsula. Its total land mass is one-fifth the size of Rhode Island.

Al-Muharraq, connected to Manama by several causeways, is the second principal island and the location of Bahrain's international airport.

Bahrain's climate is hot and humid most of the year, with daytime temperatures often exceeding 100 degrees Fahrenheit in the summer. Oil and gas are the country's only significant natural resources. Pearling, a traditional industry, has virtually ceased. In the 1930s the local pearling industry withered under strong competition from Japanese cultured pearls. Today profitability and environmental factors, as well as lack of interest, make revival of pearling unlikely.

Demography

Nearly all Bahrainis are Muslims. Bahrain has a higher proportion of native citizens to resident aliens than many other Gulf countries. Immigrant residents, slightly more than one-third of the total population of about 675,000, are primarily non-Arab Asians from India, Iran, and Pakistan. Bahrain is the only Gulf country besides Iran and Iraq in which Shiite Muslims outnumber Sunnis. Approximately 75 percent of Bahrain's population is Shiite, but the ruling Al Khalifa family and its allies are Sunni. As in Iraq before 2003, Shiites do not hold wealth and power in proportion to their numbers. There are also a few Christian and Jewish Bahrainis. Arabic is the official language, and English is widely used, but Farsi is often spoken among Iranian-descended Bahrainis.

History

Bahrain was the site of the ancient civilization of Dilmun, which flourished as a trading center from 2000 to 1800 B.C.E. Portugal captured the strategically important islands from local Arab tribes in 1521 and ruled them until 1602. Arab and Persian forces then alternately controlled the islands until the Arabian Utub tribe expelled the Persians in 1783. The members of the Al Khalifa family established themselves as shaykhs in 1782 and have ruled ever since. They also claimed suzerainty over neighboring Qatar until 1868, when at the request of Qatari notables Britain intervened against Bahraini claims and acquired for itself a larger role in Qatari affairs.

British interest in the Persian Gulf had developed in the early nineteenth century, as London sought safe passage for its ships to India, Iraq, and Iran. By 1820 Britain had established hegemony over the Bahraini islands, taking over responsibility for defense and foreign affairs.

British interference in Bahraini domestic affairs was minimal. After World War II, Britain moved its political resident (like a regional ambassador) from Iran to Bahrain. In 1968 Britain announced its intention to end its treaty obligations to the Persian Gulf shaykhdoms by 1971. Bahrain then joined Qatar and the Trucial States—now called the United Arab Emirates—in negotiations aimed at forming a confederation. Plans for a union failed, and in 1971 Bahrain became an independent state.

Current Issues

Bahrain is officially a constitutional monarchy under the dynastic rule of the Al Khalifa family. Amir Isa bin Salman Al Khalifa, who ascended to the throne on November 2, 1961, at the age of twenty-eight, suffered a fatal heart attack on March 6, 1999, and was succeeded by his son, Shaykh Hamad bin Isa Al Khalifa, age forty-nine. During his reign, Isa bin Salman ruled through an appointed cabinet, and members of the Al Khalifa family held all major ministerial posts (law prohibits political parties). The traditional administrative system of *majlis,* whereby residents directly present petitions to the amir, remains, and a forty-member Majlis al-Shura (consultative council) existed through the 1990s but held no legislative authority. A partially elected parliament was created in 2002 with somewhat more power.

Bahrain's modest petroleum reserves provided steadily decreasing revenues in the 1980s and 1990s. By the end of 2004, its oil production had fallen to a miniscule 38,000 barrels per day and the country relied mainly on its major oil refinery to export refined oil products; much of the crude oil supplied to the refinery came from Saudi Arabia. These forecasts compelled Bahrain to intensify its efforts to diversify its economy. Bahrain expanded its petroleum refining and aluminum smelting industries and developed a ship repair center. Bahraini leaders also put considerable effort into developing the emirate as an international financial center, replacing the void created by Beirut's destruction during Lebanon's protracted civil war of the 1970s and 1980s, but it faces stiff competition in this endeavor from Dubai.

Bahrain established a relatively stable environment for offshore banking services largely by exempting financial institutions from regulation or taxation. As a result, more than a hundred international banks have offices in Bahrain. At the height of the oil boom in the late 1970s, Bahrain succeeded in becoming the region's financial and banking capital, surpassing Hong Kong in total assets. A number of factors, however, have since stymied Bahrain's progress in this arena: the collapse of world oil prices in the mid-1980s; defaults on loans to lesser-developed countries; and Iraq's 1990 invasion of Kuwait, which scared away investors. The resulting decline in revenues severely depressed Bahrain's economy and forced cuts in government spending.

Tensions created by the economic slowdown raised the specter of discontent among the politically disenfranchised in Bahrain. Of principal concern to the Al Khalifa regime has been domestic unrest among the emirate's Shiite population. A cleavage has existed always between the dominant Sunnis and the larger but powerless Shiites, compounded by differences between the ruling elite and the rest of the population. Although Bahrain's history for more than a century has been punctuated by periodic outbreaks of political unrest, the Iranian Revolution of 1979 added to Sunni-Shiite sectarian tensions in the emirate. In 1981 security officials uncovered a conspiracy that was alleged to be an abortive coup plot, thought to be inspired by Iran, which provided guerrilla training for seventy-three convicted members of the Islamic Front for the Liberation of Bahrain. In February 1984, an arms cache discovered in a Shiite section was attributed to Iran. Another plot to overthrow the government was discovered in 1985, and a plan to sabotage

Bahrain's major petroleum refinery was disclosed in December 1987. By the mid-1980s, however, the level of support among Bahraini Shiites for the Iranian government diminished, as most became disenchanted with the direction of Iran's revolution and the Iran-Iraq War.

Despite this change, the Shiites continued to express basic grievances with the Al Khalifa regime. Unemployment among Shiites remained high, Shiite villages received fewer services than Sunni villages, and Shiites were underrepresented in higher levels of the government and were not allowed to join the army or security forces. Shiite unrest broke out in 1994 and continued into 1999, with a situation characterized by scattered acts of violence and repressive countermeasures by security forces, calmed only after Shaykh Hamad's moves to release political prisoners and allow exiles—including Sunnis and radicals—to return to Bahrain.

Furthermore, the example of Kuwait's democracy movement after the country's liberation from Iraqi occupation in 1991 did not go unnoticed in Bahrain. In an attempt to preempt calls for more open and participatory political processes, the royal family expressed support for more democracy in the emirate. In December 1992, Shaykh Isa announced plans to form a thirty-member consultative council. Composed of appointed members, its role was to have been solely advisory, without any real power to enact legislation or challenge decisions made by the royal family. Although hardly a democratic innovation, the council's creation was nevertheless the first move toward broadening political participation since 1973, when an initial national assembly was elected, only to be dissolved two years later. Three major dissident political organizations—the Islamic Front for the Liberation of Bahrain, the Bahrain National Liberation Movement, and the Popular Front—rejected the proposed council on the ground that it did not respond to popular sentiment. In its place, a larger, forty-member (but no more powerful) Majlis al-Shura was appointed by the amir in October 1996.

Amir Hamad responded to popular demands for liberalization by unveiling a national charter—overwhelmingly approved in a public referendum—that incorporated the promise of a new parliament. Details of the proposed parliament were not made public, however, until after the referendum. The principal opposition groups, including the Shiite al-Wefaq Society and the mixed Sunni-Shiite National Democratic Action Society, boycotted the 2002 elections because the appointed upper chamber would be equal in size to the elected lower chamber and the Speaker of the upper chamber would have the deciding vote in case of a tie. The momentum of political change seemingly stalled from this point.

The Bahraini regime is equally concerned with issues of regional security. Because of the country's small size and important strategic position, it is particularly vulnerable to instability in the Gulf and depends heavily on collective defense arrangements. In 1981 Bahrain joined with Saudi Arabia and four other Gulf states to form the Gulf Cooperation Council (GCC), an organization with common economic, social, and cultural characteristics but heavily focused on collective security. In 1984 Bahrain received funds from the GCC for improvement of its defenses. By the end of the 1991 Persian Gulf War, Bahrain had bought four F-16s from the United States and begun constructing an air base. Bahrain has an onshore facility for U.S. forces, and there is a large U.S. naval presence in the country, dating from World War II. Bahrain also provided facilities for the U.S.-led campaign against Iraq in 2003.

Relations between Bahrain and Qatar were strained for many years over a border dispute with regard to the Hawar Islands and the Fasht al-Dibal and Jaradah shoals, located between the two countries. Although uninhabited, these lands have potential for oil and gas exploration and therefore are of extreme importance to both countries, each of which faces dwindling reserves. A World Court ruling in 2001 settled the dispute by awarding the Hawar Islands to Bahrain and splitting ownership of the shoals. The two countries subsequently announced plans to build a causeway to connect the two countries.

Outlook

Bahrain managed to escape the Iran-Iraq War, the invasion of Kuwait, and the U.S.-led occupation of Iraq relatively unscathed, but it remains vulnerable to the geopolitical aspirations of its more powerful neighbors. It will become increasingly dependent on its income from peripheral industries servicing better-endowed Gulf countries as its oil reserves dwindle. Joint industrial projects undertaken by the GCC will become more important to Bahrain's prosperity. It currently receives 100 percent of the profits from Saudi Arabia's offshore Abu Saafa oil field, illustrating Bahrain's already close ties—both economic and political—to the kingdom.

Although the Bahraini banking industry scaled back in the mid-1980s because of declining oil revenues and competition from Kuwaiti, Saudi, and UAE banks, Bahrain is still a preferred location for business in the region because of its first-rate communications, permissive banking laws, tolerance of Western social customs, and time zone, which allows investors to trade with Tokyo and Singapore in the morning and London and New York in the afternoon. Bahrain in 1992 became the first country in the Gulf to allow 100 percent foreign-owned businesses to operate in the country without local sponsorship.

Despite its efforts to diversify economically, Bahrain will remain highly vulnerable to the uncertainties of the oil market and instability in the region. Future downturns in oil prices could jeopardize Bahrain's extensive industrial projects and expanding financial markets. A resumption of hostilities in the Gulf could threaten the Bahraini economy by destroying international business confidence and placing the country's security at risk.

With Shiites in the majority, Bahrain must continue to keep close watch over political and religious developments in Iran. Tehran maintained an eighteenth-century territorial claim to Bahrain until 1971, and some politicians continue to urge that Iran regain control of the island state. With fewer rights and riches than the minority Sunnis who hold power, the Shiites remain an unpredictable force in

Bahraini politics and are likely to demand greater political and economic equality.

Another potential source of domestic instability is Bahrain's young educated class, who may press for white-collar jobs, personal freedom, and political participation if the Al Khalifa regime does not move forward with political reforms. With unemployment unofficially estimated at 25 percent or more in the early 2000s, and government spending still curtailed by years of low oil prices, the potential for unrest was restrained only by the potential of a renewed emphasis on a strong internal security apparatus. This, in turn, could damage Bahrain in the long term because of its potential to undermine the confidence of the very foreign investors it needs to attract.

OMAN

Area: 82,030 square miles (212,460 square kilometers)
Capital: Muscat
Population: 2,903,165 (2005)
Religion: Muslim, 75 percent from the Ibadhi sect
Ethnic Groups: Arab, Baluchi, South Asian (Indian, Pakistani, Sri Lankan, Bangladeshi), African
Official language: Arabic; English, Baluchi, Urdu, and Indian dialects also spoken
Type of Government: Monarchy
GDP: $36.7 billion; $13,100 per capita (2005)

Source: Central Intelligence Agency, *CIA World Factbook,* 2004.

During the past thirty-five years, the sultanate of Oman has experienced perhaps the most dramatic social and economic progress of any Middle Eastern nation. Formerly known as the Sultanate of Muscat and Oman, the country changed its name in 1970 after the current sultan, Qaboos bin Said, gained power. Before the reign of Sultan Qaboos, Oman was notable as perhaps the most isolated nation in the Middle East. Surrounded by sea and desert, its previous ruler had rejected virtually all outside influences. The palace coup that brought Sultan Qaboos to power ushered in an era of devel-

opment during which Oman used its oil revenues to increase living standards, build a modern infrastructure, and establish social services for the populace. In 1970 Oman had just 3 schools, 2 hospitals, and 6 miles of paved road; by 2003 it had 1,022 schools, 49 hospitals, 199 health centers, and more than 12,400 miles of paved road.

Oman has pursued an independent foreign policy based on close cooperation with the West, especially the United States. A reliable U.S. ally in the Persian Gulf, Oman was the only Gulf nation that endorsed the 1978 Camp David accords and refused to sever relations with Egypt because of its peace with Israel. Since 1980, when Oman signed a defense agreement with the United States, it has become increasingly enmeshed in U.S. strategic plans for projecting force in the region. Oman was a valuable ally of the multinational coalition during the 1990–1991 Persian Gulf crisis and war and opened its military facilities to U.S. use during the 2003 war in Iraq.

Geography

Oman stretches for one thousand miles, from the mouth of the Persian Gulf around the southeast coast of the Arabian Peninsula to a southwestern border with Yemen. The country has four distinct regions: the Musandam Peninsula, a small, noncontiguous province that juts into the Persian Gulf at the strategic Strait of Hormuz; the Batinah, a fertile and prosperous coastal plain that lies northwest of Muscat, the capital; the expansive Inner Oman, which is located between Jabal al-Akhdar (Green Mountain), where peaks reach 9,900 feet, and the desert of the Rub al-Khali (Empty Quarter); and the Dhofar region, which stretches along the southern coast to Yemen. The remainder of Oman's territory is largely barren, flat desert. During much of the year Oman's desert climate is hot and exceptionally humid along the coast. The coastal area of Dhofar, however, is more tropical, with less extreme temperatures. The southern mountains of Dhofar receive monsoon summer rains that support the local mountain population of cattle, goat, and camel herders and draw tourists from elsewhere in the Gulf to Dhofar's capital of Salalah.

Demography

Oman's second census, taken in 2003, showed the population stood at slightly more than 2.3 million people. About one-third of all Omanis live in the central hill region of Inner Oman; the most densely populated area is the Batinah plain, where another third of Oman's people live. Over a quarter of the total population is in the Muscat metropolitan area. The Dhofar region has approximately 215,000 inhabitants. The al-Shihuh is the predominant tribe in the Musandam Peninsula and numbers about twenty thousand.

About one-half of Omanis, including the royal family, are Ibadhi Muslims, a small sect that believes in a nonhereditary imam, who is a combination of religious and temporal ruler. The rest of the Omanis are mostly Sunni, although Shiites account for as much as 5 percent of the population. The rapid growth in expatriate labor in Oman has slowed but still numbers 560,000 workers and their families, most of whom come from Bangladesh, India, Pakistan, and Sri Lanka.

History

Oman's early history is obscure. Converted to Islam in the seventh century C.E., many native Omanis embraced Ibadhism, which traces its roots to the Kharijite movement, an early Islamic offshoot. Europe's influence arrived in 1507, when Portugal seized much of the Omani coastline. Seventeenth-century Portuguese fortifications still stand in and around Muscat on the Omani coast. The Portuguese were ousted in 1650, as an Omani renaissance began. Elected Ibadhi imams of the central hill region and hereditary sultans situated in Muscat became the political leaders of the region. Oman remained independent after 1650, except for a brief period of Persian rule from 1741 to 1744. Ahmad bin Said defeated the Persians and shortly thereafter founded the Al Bu Said dynasty, which remains in power today. Divisions between inhabitants of the coast and interior were

exacerbated in 1786, when the capital moved from al-Rustaq to coastal Muscat. The Muscat rulers were responsible for extending Oman's control to Zanzibar (near Tanzania) and other East African coastal areas, Bahrain in the Gulf, and part of the Makran coast (present-day Pakistan). By the early nineteenth century, Omani power was unchallenged in southern Arabia and East Africa.

Oman's regional power began to decline during the latter half of the nineteenth century, however, when it was forced to relinquish control of its East African colonies. In 1958 Oman sold its last colonial possession, Gwadur, to Pakistan for 3 million pounds.

Around the beginning of the twentieth century a movement began in the interior to restore the traditional Ibadhi imamate, and by 1920 it had gained autonomy from the sultans. The attempts in the 1950s by Sultan Said bin Taimur to extend his control over the interior resulted in scattered opposition, but by 1959 Sultan Said was firmly in charge of the entire country, and the last imam had fled to Saudi Arabia.

The government of Sultan Said was, in its day, regarded as one of the most traditional and conservative in the Arab world. Slavery still existed and Sultan Said refused to allow social and economic development until he began receiving oil revenues in the late 1960s. Even then, development seemed to move far too slowly for most Omanis. His situation was complicated in the southern province of Dhofar, which Sultan Said regarded as his personal estate. A small rebellion beginning in 1962 escalated into a major revolt: Marxists eventually secured leadership of the insurgency, newly independent South Yemen provided logistical support and the Soviet Union arms and advisers, and Sultan Said was forced to turn to Britain for military assistance.

Sultan Said was overthrown by his son Qaboos in a 1970 palace coup, and the new sultan immediately embarked on a program of development throughout the country and a policy of gaining the trust of the Dhofari population. Soviet assistance to the rebels was countered by additional British and new Iranian assistance to the Sultan. Sustained offensives in the rugged mountains broke the back of the rebellion, and many rebels surrendered and were placed in militias to defend their tribal territory. In December 1975, Sultan Qaboos declared complete victory.

Relations with leftist South Yemen remained strained in the following years, and the two countries nearly went to war in the early 1980s. Thanks to mediation by other Arab states, however, the two countries established diplomatic relations in October 1982 and eventually signed a border agreement.

Current Issues

Oman is an absolute monarchy dominated by the sultan, who legislates by decree. No parliament exists, but a basic law was promulgated in 1996. The sultan acts as prime minister as well as foreign and defense minister. In 1980 the sultan established a consultative council (al-Majlis al-Istishari lil-Dawla), which was transformed into an indirectly elected council (Majlis al-Shura) in 1991. At present, the council's eighty-two members are freely elected men and women made up mostly of government officials, merchants, business leaders, and tribal leaders from various regions. Chaired by the sultan, the council has no legislative powers. Nevertheless, it performs a valuable advisory function, oversees the operations of social services ministries, and has been seen as a vehicle through which Omanis might begin to participate in government.

Sultan Qaboos is noted for his strong leanings toward the West. Some of his closest advisers have been Britons and other Arabs who have encouraged Oman's Western orientation. A 1980 defense agreement with Oman, renewed every five years, grants the United States access to Omani military installations, emergency landing rights, and the authority to preposition military hardware at Omani storage facilities. After the Iraqi invasion of Kuwait in 1990, the first U.S. soldiers sent to Saudi Arabia used military equipment that had been prepositioned in Oman, and the facilities were utilized again during the 2003 Iraq War.

An Omani military base in the Musandam and near the Strait of Hormuz, to which the United

States has access, is a valuable listening post for monitoring activity in Iran and was a strategic point from which the United States coordinated logistical operations in support of Operation Desert Storm. Oman also sent combat troops to fight Iraq under Saudi command in Desert Storm. It did not participate in the 2003 war. A founding member of the Gulf Cooperation Council, Oman has been an advocate of an integrated GCC defense force. As its close ties with the United States and Britain indicate, however, Oman has recognized that without Western assistance the GCC cannot ensure the security of its members from attacks by the region's larger states.

Despite its close ties to the West, Oman has pursued an independent foreign policy. The sultan has been known to go to great lengths to demonstrate neutrality in inter-Arab and regional disputes. For example, in 1988 Oman and Syria agreed to establish formal relations at a time when Syria's involvement in Lebanon was a source of frustration for Washington and its Arab allies. Oman maintained relations with Iran throughout the Iran-Iraq War, again breaking ranks with most other Arab states, and enjoyed correct relations with Saddam Hussein's Iraq throughout the sanctions period between 1991 and 2003. In 1987 the Omanis established diplomatic relations with the Soviet Union at the ambassadorial level, following the example of Kuwait and the United Arab Emirates. Official relations with the Soviet Union helped pave the way for improved relations with South Yemen, a Soviet ally and longtime regional rival. Saudi Arabia and Oman settled a long dispute over their common borders in 1990, and a border settlement was reached in 1992 with the Republic of Yemen, created by the merger of North and South Yemen. Some border issues occasionally crop up, however, between Oman and Saudi Arabia.

Throughout its recent history, Oman's economy has been largely dependent on the oil industry, which provides the government with most of its revenues. In 2003, 80 percent of Oman's total export revenue of $11.5 billion came from the petroleum industry. Compared with those of other Gulf states, Oman's oil fields are difficult to access, which restricts its capacity to pump, and its reserves are only of moderate size, slightly in excess of 5 billion barrels. Oil production dropped steadily from 956,000 barrels per day in 2001 to an expected 750,000 barrels per day in 2005. Barring advances in technology or discoveries of new deposits, Oman's reserves are expected to be depleted within a decade or two.

Oman is not a member of the Organization of Petroleum Exporting Countries (OPEC) or the Organization of Arab Petroleum Exporting Countries, but it tends to honor OPEC's quota system. Yet even Oman's freedom from OPEC could not insulate its economy from the volatile oil prices of the late 1980s. As a result, spiraling prices led to falling government revenues and budget slashing. Numerous development projects and military purchases were delayed or discontinued, and the government devalued the Omani riyal. By 1990 the Central Bank of Oman was forced to introduce a bond program to finance the country's budget deficit. The subsequent rise in prices in the early 2000s was only partially effective in correcting the state's financial deficits due to the decline in oil exports. Oman's per capita income in 2004 was estimated at $8,000, lowest in the GCC.

Oman has made a concerted effort, especially since 1989, to diversify its economy. The government has sought to reduce budgetary expenses by privatization of utilities and communications. Oman was the first country in the Gulf to develop a privately owned electricity grid. Fortunately, Oman's picturesque mountains and coastline are ripe for tourism. The government has eased restrictions on visas for tourists and businesses to encourage foreigners to visit. Although taking time to develop, this sector is growing. Oman received 1.2 million foreign visitors in 2002, with some 700,000 coming from neighboring GCC states. Many regional tourists visit Dhofar during the relatively cool summer monsoon season.

The possibilities for developing fishing, agriculture, and mining are better in Oman than in the rest of the region. Fishing and farming are still the occupation of much of Oman's population. Miners have identified gold and chromite resources, and the sultanate has turned to the private sector to develop them. To encourage investment, the Muscat stock exchange opened in 1990, and trade volumes initially exceeded expectations. Nevertheless, Oman has not lodged its hopes in becoming a center of international commerce, like Bahrain. Omani leaders have instead sought to develop long-term investment projects.

The most significant economic developments for Oman in recent years have been in the industrial sector, where it has established joint ventures and the Oman Oil Company has been involved in a number of overseas projects. To exploit its large reserves of natural gas, the sultanate built a two-train plant for liquefied natural gas (LNG) exports in 2000 and began work in 2005 on a third train. Customers are located primarily in East Asia, although some LNG is exported to Europe and the United States. The sultanate established a large container port in Salalah to tap the regional transshipment trade and made joint agreements in early 2005 to build an aluminum smelter as well as the country's second oil refinery in Sohar, the main town of the Batinah coast. In addition, Oman has focused on strengthening its economic ties with India. Both countries are investigating major joint ventures, including the construction of new refineries and a fertilizer plant. Of Western nations, Britain is the most heavily involved in the Omani economy.

Outlook

The sultanate enjoys broad popular support, and the public generally approves of its foreign and domestic policies. No significant political opposition or abuse of human rights exists. A number of people were, however, arrested in 1994 as alleged Islamists, and early 2005 saw the arrest of another group. As Oman's development continues, the sultan will have to meet the growing expectations of his increasingly well-educated population. A perpetually high population growth rate has produced a growing problem of unemployment. If Oman's long-term growth or the state's paternal distribution of wealth is disturbed, perhaps the sultan's staunch commitment to the principle of monarchical rule, with little popular representation, will become less acceptable to Omanis.

Oman's major concern is how best to diversify its economy beyond the petroleum sector. Thus far, Oman's efforts in this regard have proved partially successful, in part because its reliance on oil was never as dramatic and absolute as that of its neighbors. However, with an educated middle class growing rapidly, meeting rising expectations with an expanding economy will be the principal domestic challenge. To this end, the sultan has implemented policies to nationalize the workforce and adjust the educational system to meet private-sector business demands. The economy remains dependent on government spending despite the government's efforts to encourage private-sector development. Without an heir, Sultan Qaboos (unmarried and sixty-five years old in 2005) has left the form of Oman's future government open to speculation, although the basic law stipulates that a family council will decide on a successor, and if the council is unable to do so, the state's defense council will.

QATAR

Area: 4,247 square miles (11,437 square kilometers)
Capital: Doha
Population: 840,290 (2004)
Religion: Muslim, 95 percent, mostly Wahhabi Sunni
Ethnic Groups: Arab, 40 percent; Pakistani, 18 percent; Indian, 18 percent; Iranian, 10 percent; other, 14 percent
Official language: Arabic; English is widely spoken
Type of Government: Traditional monarchy
GDP: $17.54 billion; $21,500 per capita (2003)

Source: Central Intelligence Agency, *CIA World Factbook,* 2004.

Qatar has gone through a profound social transformation since oil production began there in 1947. Before then, Qatar (KAH-tar) was one of the poorest and least developed countries of eastern Arabia. The economy depended heavily on fishing and pearling. Petroleum production and export rapidly converted a nomadic population into a mostly urban and settled people, with one of the highest per capita incomes in the world.

The ruling Al Thani family is one of the largest ruling families in the region, numbering in the thousands. It is divided into three main branches, each quite independent of the other: the Bani Hamad, Bani Ali, and Bani Khalid. The current amir, Shaykh Hamad bin Khalifa Al Thani, comes from the Bani Hamad branch, whose members dominate all important government functions, including the major ministries—interior, defense, and foreign affairs.

Qatar, like all the Gulf states, felt the economic recession and instability that rocked the region in the 1980s. Although its shipping was endangered during the Iran-Iraq War, Qatar was not seriously challenged during that decade by foreign intrigue or domestic unrest. During the 1990s, Qatar pursued an independent foreign policy that emphasized accommodation with its three large neighbors: Iran, Iraq, and Saudi Arabia. Qatari leaders attracted controversy by speaking out against the economic embargo of Iraq after its invasion of Kuwait, making overtures to Israel, and signing a defense cooperation agreement with the United States. Shaykh Hamad has not been afraid of making waves amongst his neighbors, however: he has confronted Saudi Arabia over border issues, fought against Bahraini claims to disputed territory, and established the al-Jazeera satellite television channel that angered many Arab countries and the United States by its provocative stance on sensitive issues.

Geography

Qatar occupies a thumb-shaped desert peninsula, about the size of Connecticut, that stretches north into the Persian Gulf. In the south it borders the United Arab Emirates and Saudi Arabia. The peninsula is a low, flat, barren plain, consisting mostly of sand-covered limestone. The climate is hot and humid. On the west coast is the Dukhan anticline, a chain of hills beneath which lie some 2.2 billion barrels of crude oil. Qatar's total reserves are estimated at 3.7 billion barrels. The offshore North Field, shared with Iran, is one of the world's largest concentrations of natural gas not associated with oil. Its share provides most of Qatar's total known reserves of 500 trillion cubic feet of natural gas, the third largest in the world.

Demography

Qatari society constituted one of the most ethnically homogeneous communities among the Gulf states until petroleum production began in the late 1940s. Today, foreign workers—principally from India, Iran, and Pakistan—constitute the overwhelming majority of Qatar's workforce; expatriates, including Arabs from neighboring states, represent at least 74 percent of the population. Detailed rules govern their entrance into the country and their political rights. Although laws restrict the industrial and commercial activities of non-Qataris, foreign workers are usually content to forgo civil and political rights in exchange for the high wages they earn.

Qatari society is staunchly religious and conservative. Most Qataris adhere to the Wahhabi school of Sunni Islam. Approximately 16 percent of the population, including expatriates, is Shiite. More than 80 percent of all of Qatar's inhabitants reside near the capital city of Doha. The government provides free education and medical services to all its citizens.

History

Qatar formerly was dominated by Bahrain's ruling Al Khalifa family, which regarded Qatar as an errant province. Rising to prominence in the nineteenth century, the Al Thani family established its own dynasty in Qatar, gaining independence and legitimacy through successive agreements with Britain. At the request of leading Qatari families, Britain in 1868 opposed the Bahraini claim in exchange for a larger British role in Qatar's affairs.

The British-Qatari relationship was interrupted in 1872 when the Ottoman Turks established a garrison in Qatar. After the Ottomans evacuated the peninsula at the beginning of World War I, however, the Al Thani dynasty entered into treaty obligations with Britain, and Qatar formally became a British-protected state in 1916; a 1934 treaty gave Britain a more extensive role in Qatari affairs. World War II delayed exploitation of oil discovered in 1940. During the 1950s and 1960s, gradually increasing oil revenues brought prosperity, rapid immigration, and social change.

From 1947 to 1960 Qatar was led by Amir Ali, who abdicated in favor of his son Ahmad. Qatar declared its independence on September 1, 1971, after attempts to form a union with neighboring Gulf emirates Bahrain and the Trucial States failed. Later that year British forces completed their withdrawal from the region. Amir Ahmad's profligate and venal rule ended in a 1972 bloodless coup led by his cousin, Khalifa bin Hamad Al Thani, who should have succeeded originally instead of Ahmad. In June 1995, Khalifa was overthrown by his son Hamad, the current amir. Khalifa and one of his other sons were accused of attempting a failed February 1996 counter-coup. Khalifa and Hamad reportedly later resolved their differences, and Khalifa receives a monthly stipend from the royal coffers.

Current Issues

Amir Hamad holds absolute authority to enact all laws, to appoint ministers, and to name his heir. No popularly elected governmental body yet exists. Amir Hamad rules under the guidance of Islamic law, but he is also aware of his (mostly younger) subjects' desire for democratic reforms. He seeks a family consensus on major decisions. The Qatari throne is hereditary within the Al Thani family, but it is not automatically passed from father to son. Amir Hamad named his son, Shaykh Jasim bin Hamad, as heir apparent, per tradition, but in 2003 he changed his mind and named another son, Shaykh Tamim bin Hamad, as his new successor.

The amir's rule is constrained by rival families and by the conservative religious establishment. The Al Atiyyah family continuously vies with the Al Thani for predominance within Qatar's economy and the armed forces, and one of the family served in the early 2000s as the GCC's secretary general. Other family clans, such as al-Misnad (the wife of the amir comes from this family), al-Mani`, and al-Manna`i, are prominent in business and the government.

Before Amir Hamad's accession, political change was minimal. The advisory council, established in 1972, was expanded to thirty members in 1975 to represent more educated elements of the population. Subsequent years saw muted agitation for more participation. In May 1992, for example, fifty-four prominent Qataris presented Amir Khalifa with a petition demanding parliamentary elections, a written constitution, and greater personal and political freedoms, at personal cost: some were called in for questioning; others had their passports confiscated.

Amir Hamad, however, has set a number of reforms in train. Elections for a central municipal council were held in 1999. Women were granted suffrage and ran as candidates, despite the objections of the more conservative segments of society. The second elections for the municipal council in 2003 saw a female candidate elected—the first woman to hold an elective office in the Gulf.

Soon after his accession, Amir Hamad announced plans for a new constitution and a partly elected parliament. A draft constitution was completed in late 2002 and then submitted to a popular referendum on April 29, 2003, in which it was overwhelmingly approved. The constitution provides for a forty-five-member Majlis al-Shura, or parliament, thirty of whom are to be elected and the remaining fifteen appointed by the amir. The parliament would have the right to question cabinet ministers, enact legislation, and vote on the national budget. Although elections had been expected in 2004, they had not taken place by early 2005.

The development of modern Qatari society has historically depended upon revenues generated by the emirate's principal export, petroleum. Oil accounts for about 70 percent of Qatar's state income. As a result, the Qatari economy suffered when oil prices fell in the latter half of the 1980s; by the end of the decade, government revenues were half the level they had been in the mid-1980s, and the GDP was approximately $15,000 per capita, which was less than half of the 1981 per capita GDP of $36,000. One response was to increase oil production in defiance of OPEC quotas, in large part to help finance natural gas development. Another drop in oil prices in the late 1990s forced Qatar to cut its budget and borrow money through bonds. The subsequent rise in oil prices in the following years allowed the country to balance its budget in 1999 and begin to repay debts that totaled more than $13 billion in 2000. By 2003, with income streaming in from its natural gas ventures and sharply increased oil prices, Qatar's per capita income had risen to about $30,000.

The government has focused its economic diversification effort on development of its North Field project, designed to exploit Qatar's large offshore natural gas resources. In 1987 the government began construction of offshore production facilities linked to the mainland by submerged pipelines. The North Field is a valuable source of energy for Qatar's cement, steel, and petrochemical industries, but, even more important, it is a major source of export income and will continue to be for the next hundred years. The first liquefied natural gas (LNG) exports—to Japan—began on December 23, 1996. By 2003 Qatar's massive investment in gas had begun to pay off. A $12 billion deal was signed with ExxonMobil that year for supplying the United States with LNG. New deals signed with Shell and Total in early 2005, worth $10 billion, would expand Qatar's gas production from 19 million tons per year to 77 million tons, making Qatar potentially the world's largest producer. Closer to home, the Dolphin Project was established to supply the nearby United Arab Emirates with natural gas via an underwater pipeline.

Qatar joined the Gulf Cooperation Council in 1981 and supported Iraq throughout the Iran-Iraq War. In 1982 Qatar signed a bilateral defense agreement with Saudi Arabia; it generally follows the kingdom's lead in policy matters. However, border disputes in 1992 between the two countries complicated otherwise good relations. The dispute resulted from Qatari accusations that Saudi troops were attacking border posts at al-Khafus in an attempt to redefine the border. With a rift opening in Gulf regional security, Egyptian president Hosni Mubarak mediated a successful compromise that led to demarcation. A final border agreement was signed in 2001. Saudi-Qatari relations continued to be tense, however, particularly because of criticism of the kingdom by the Qatari satellite television channel al-Jazeera.

Qatar also was engaged in long-running border disputes with its other neighbor, Bahrain. In April 1986, Qatar raided the island of Fasht al-Dibal, which had been reclaimed from a coral reef by the Bahraini government. Qatari forces seized twenty-nine foreign workers who were building a Bahraini coast guard station on the island. The dispute was resolved when the two countries agreed to destroy the island and submit future disputes to international arbitration. In addition to Fasht al-Dibal, Qatar and Bahrain each claim the town of Zubara, on the mainland of Qatar, and the Hawar Islands off the coast of Qatar. More complications arose in 1996, when Bahrain declared its intent to build a causeway to Hawar; in response, Qatar vowed to destroy any such structure. Matters reached a head when Bahrain boycotted the annual GCC summit in protest. However, the two countries opened bilateral talks in 1999 and accepted a World Court ruling in March 2001 that the Hawar Islands belonged to Bahrain and Zubara to Qatar. The two countries have since moved forward with plans to build a causeway between Bahrain and Qatar.

Although Qatar remains strongly pro-Western, its relationship with the United States was strained in March 1988 when Washington learned that Qatar had secretly acquired thirteen U.S.-made Stinger antiaircraft missiles. After Qatar refused to disclose the source of the missiles, the U.S. Senate voted to prohibit weapon sales to Qatar. Later in 1988 Qatar became the fourth Gulf state to establish diplomatic relations with the People's Republic of China and the Soviet Union.

As did most of its neighbors, Qatar strengthened its ties to the United States in the wake of Iraq's 1990 invasion of Kuwait. Qatari troops played a major role in the first land battle of the war near the town of al-Khafji, where a large Iraqi unit penetrated Saudi territory before being repelled by coalition forces. In March 1991, Qatar joined the other Gulf states in endorsing an arrangement with the United States to ensure the security of the region through a multinational peacekeeping force, U.S. naval deployments, and joint maneuvers. In June 1993, Qatar signed a bilateral defense cooperation agreement with the United States. Nevertheless, Qatar has pursued good relations with Iran and Iraq since the Gulf war. Qatar signed a major trade pact with Iran in 1993, and it sent an ambassador back to Baghdad shortly after the war.

When Saudi Arabia expressed concerns about the domestic effect of the large U.S. military presence on its soil, the Qataris offered use of a military facility at al-Udayd air base outside Doha that subsequently served as the regional command center of the U.S. Central Command during the 2003 Iraq war, as well as the press headquarters for the campaign.

Qatar's al-Jazeera satellite television channel has managed to ruffle the feathers of most of its neighbors by its frank reporting and open discussion of sensitive issues. It was also characterized by members of the George W. Bush administration as being anti-American because of its reporting from Afghanistan and Iraq. Qatar has also gained international notice by mounting prominent sporting events, including car rallies, tennis matches, and golf tournaments. Doha also hosted the 2000 Organization of the Islamic Conference summit and the most recent negotiations of the World Trade Organization in 2001, which continue under the name of the Doha Round.

Outlook

Because of the fluctuating nature of oil prices, Qatar will have to continue to diversify its economy in order to maintain its high standard of living and contented population, but its economic future remains promising. In the short term, the country's oil reserves are required to support its conservative economic path, and the development of the North Field natural gas project provides a cushion in times of low oil revenues and will offer continued prosperity in the post-oil era. Still, as a small state, Qatar has interests that are tied closely to the fortunes of OPEC and the regional security provided by the GCC. One potential threat to Qatar's future economic prospects is an Iranian claim to a substantial portion of the North Field gas reservoir, which lies partially under Iranian territorial waters.

Although calls for radical changes or greater participation in the government are muted, they no doubt contribute to the frustrations of an educated population. Despite the rapid pace of development, Qatari society has been unable to absorb the thousands of secondary school and college graduates who enter the workforce each year. At the same time, few Qataris are able or willing to fill the technical and manual labor jobs that are critical to the economy. Such inconsistencies in the labor market are likely to cause increasing frustration among Qatar's native population, while making it more difficult for the government to reduce the number of foreign workers, who appear content to reap the benefits of Qatar's oil economy despite the constraints placed upon them.

If the ruling family can maintain revenues and foreign workers remain quiescent, the threat to the political status quo will remain minimal. Amir Hamad's minor democratic reforms provided some outlet for potential disaffection. The route to political change, however, will more likely involve the amir's health, although the succession seems clearly defined. In 1997 Amir Hamad underwent a kidney transplant, and in early 1999 he was reported to be quite ill with complications from diabetes. Since then, however, his health seems to have been stable.

UNITED ARAB EMIRATES (UAE)

Area: 29,182 square miles (82,880 square kilometers)
Capital: Abu Dhabi
Population: 2,523,915, including 1,606,079 expatriates (2004)
Religion: Muslim, 96 percent; Christian, Hindu, and others, 4 percent
Ethnic Groups: Emirati, 19 percent; other Arab and Iranian, 23 percent; South Asian, 50 percent: other expatriates (includes Westerners and East Asians), 8 percent (1982)
Official language: Arabic; Persian, English, Hindi, and Urdu also spoken
Type of Government: Federation with specified powers delegated to the UAE federal government and other powers reserved to member emirates
GDP: $57.7 billion; $23,200 per capita (2003)

Source: Central Intelligence Agency, *CIA World Factbook,* 2004.

The United Arab Emirates (UAE), formerly known as the Trucial States, is the only federation of states in the Middle East. In December 1971, six disparate emirates ruled by individual tribal shaykhs merged to create a federal framework within which they could preserve their local autonomy and also avoid being dominated by their two larger neighbors, Saudi Arabia and Iran. The original members of the UAE were Abu Dhabi, Ajman, Dubai, al-Fujairah, Sharjah, and Umm al-Qaiwain. Ras al-Khaimah joined in February 1972.

Commercial development of petroleum resources, which began in the early 1960s, stimulated population growth and development in the emirates. The combined population of the emirates increased from 180,000 in 1968 to more than 1million by 1980 and to 4 million by 2003, largely because of immigration. Development among the emirates proceeded unevenly, however, as the smaller emirates that lacked oil were left almost untouched by petroleum riches.

Inequalities persist in size, population, development, and wealth. Abu Dhabi and Dubai stand out among the emirates because of Abu Dhabi's vast oil revenues, Dubai's role as an entrepôt, and both states' relatively large populations and expansive territories. Most of the UAE's population lives in Abu Dhabi, Dubai, and Sharjah, a latecomer to oil production. Ajman, with one hundred square miles, and adjacent Umm al-Qaiwain, with only sixty thousand inhabitants, are the smallest emirates. All the shaykhdoms fiercely compete with each other for development funds and projects, often at the expense of federal unity and economic planning. Because of the absence of a strong centralized government, duplication of facilities such as international airports and harbors is common throughout the country.

Geography

The UAE extends for 746 miles along the southern rim of the Persian Gulf, where six of the emirates are located. Al-Fujairah faces the Gulf of Oman, a part of the Arabian Sea. Sharjah has additional, noncontiguous territory along the coast with al-Fujairah. About the size of South Carolina, the UAE has approximately 29,000 square miles of mostly barren, flat land. Temperatures sometimes soar to 125 degrees Fahrenheit. Its southern border with Saudi Arabia merges into the great, virtually uninhabited wasteland of the Rub al-Khali (Empty Quarter). In the east, along the Omani border, lie the Western Hajar Mountains.

The UAE's major natural resources are oil and natural gas. The UAE is OPEC's fourth largest producer. Its proven published reserves in 2000 were estimated at 98 billion barrels of petroleum, 94 percent of which is located in Abu Dhabi. Abu Dhabi also possesses most of the UAE's more than 200 trillion cubic feet of natural gas reserves. The UAE earned a record $29.5 billion from oil revenues in 2004. As a result, per capita income rose to nearly $20,000, despite a population growth rate of 7 to 8 percent.

The Seven Emirates

Abu Dhabi, the largest, most populous, and most influential of the seven emirates, is the federal capital. With the advent of petroleum production, Abu Dhabi became a classic example of a traditional society transformed almost overnight by newfound, tremendous wealth. As the UAE's largest oil producer, Abu Dhabi has proven reserves of 92 billion barrels and accounts for more than 60 percent of the federation's gross national product. Abu Dhabi also contributes 60 percent of the UAE federal budget.

Dubai, a distant second to Abu Dhabi in oil riches, has a long tradition of entrepôt trading. Dubai boasts one of the Gulf's most important deepwater ports, Jabal Ali, the largest man-made port in the world. Recently, this port has become a major re-exporting center, free trade zone, and assembly center for goods destined for Iran, Oman, and elsewhere in the Gulf. Dubai also has sought to increase tourism through a number of megaprojects, among them holding the Dubai Shopping Festival during the pleasant winters, the world's tallest building and most expensive hotel, tripling the size of its busy airport, expanding Dubai's Emirates Airlines, and constructing several huge residential and hotel complexes on islands built on reclaimed land.

After Sharjah began modest oil production in 1974, it joined Abu Dhabi and Dubai to form an elite group of oil producers within the federation. Comparatively large and fertile, Ras al-Khaimah possesses only minor offshore oil reserves, which were discovered in 1983 and which have yet to be developed commercially. Al-Fujairah, Ajman, and Umm al-Qaiwain are subordinate to the wealthier emirates and rely on their largess for development programs and to ease the gap in economic and social disparities. Some of the emirates have turned to the creation of new universities—including the American Universities of Dubai and Sharjah—to increase their income.

Demography

Indigenous inhabitants of the seven emirates account for less than 20 percent of the federation's 2.5 million people. Most of the immigrant residents are Indians, Pakistanis, and Iranians; most of the expatriate Arab residents are Egyptians, Jordanians, Omanis, Palestinians, and Yemenis. More than 90 percent of the labor force is foreign. The country is overwhelmingly Sunni, with about 16 percent following the Shiite branch of Islam. Hindus and Christians live among the foreign communities; few are granted citizenship rights. Bedouins, making up 5 to 10 percent of the population, live around oases and are slowly settling in towns or migrating to urban areas.

History

The Qawasim family was the dominant Arab power along the lower Gulf coast during the early nineteenth century. The British, regarding the Qawasims as pirates because of their aggressive tactics at sea in defense of their territory, destroyed their headquarters at Ras al-Khaimah. To secure the lower Gulf for safe passage, Britain negotiated a peace treaty in 1820 with the local shaykhs. They signed with Britain a "perpetual maritime truce" in 1853, thus becoming known as the "Trucial States," and an exclusive agreement in 1892 that gave Britain control over the Trucial States' foreign policy.

Britain supported Abu Dhabi in a 1950s dispute with Saudi Arabia over the Buraimi oasis and other territories in the south. The oasis is now shared by Abu Dhabi and Oman. The border between the UAE and Saudi Arabia remains contested, and minor boundary differences still persist between the UAE and Oman. After Britain announced in 1968 its intention to withdraw from the Gulf by the end of 1971, Qatar, Bahrain, and the Trucial States initiated plans to form a confederation. Qatar and Bahrain, however, decided in favor of independent sovereign status.

On December 2, 1971, the UAE proclaimed its independence and immediately entered into a treaty of friendship with Britain. Originally only six emirates signed the act of confederation, but two months later Ras al-Khaimah joined. Shaykh Zayed bin Sultan Al Nahayan, the ruler of Abu Dhabi, served as the UAE's only president until his death in November 2004; he was succeeded by his eldest son Khalifah bin Zayed as both ruler of Abu Dhabi and president of the UAE. The president heads the highest body in the country, the Supreme Council of the Union (SCU), which is composed of the rulers of the federation's seven member states. The SCU is responsible for the election of the president and vice president, for general federal policy, for the ratification of federal laws, and for appointing the legislative body. Abu Dhabi and Dubai have veto power over all federal matters. The ruler of Dubai serves as the UAE's vice president. The forty-member Federal National Council functions primarily as a consultative assembly and forum for debate. Its members are chosen by each amir.

The government of the UAE is based on a provisional constitution promulgated in 1971, which is renewed at five-year intervals. The establishment of a permanent constitution has been delayed by the reluctance of individual emirates to relinquish their autonomy, particularly in the areas of natural resources and defense. Contributions to the federal budget have also been a source of dispute, as Abu Dhabi has become increasingly reluctant to continue contributing more than 80 percent of the total budget.

Family rivalries also have influenced interemirate politics. In June 1987, Abd al-Aziz al-Qasimi, the older brother of Shaykh Sultan al-Qasimi of Sharjah, tried to replace his younger brother as ruler of the emirate. Abu Dhabi favored Abd al-Aziz in the power struggle, while Dubai supported Shaykh Sultan. After days of uncertainty, the other members of the GCC stepped in to help negotiate a compromise in which Shaykh Sultan retained power and Abd al-Aziz eventually took up residence in Abu Dhabi.

Current Issues

The economy of the UAE has historically been sensitive to the world oil market. Because of the oil glut in 1982, the government began running budget deficits for the first time in its history; a number of development projects were postponed, canceled, or scaled back. When oil prices collapsed in 1986—oil revenues fell 40 percent below those of 1984—the emirates suffered a dramatic decline in gross national product. The rebound of oil prices in the early 2000s permitted the UAE to balance its federal budget for the first time in twenty years. Budget figures, however, do not include returns on the approximately $250 billion in foreign assets held by the emirates. To maintain a surplus in their balance of payments, the emirates placed greater emphasis on economic diversification through the development of industry and trade. In 1993 the UAE began constructing a multimillion-dollar facility to produce steel for the domestic and export markets. In addition, the UAE has aggressively pursued developing its natural gas fields with Japanese partners.

The emirates were thrust into the international spotlight in 1991 with the collapse of the Bank of Credit and Commerce International (BCCI). Seventy-seven percent owned by Abu Dhabi's Shaykh Zayed, the bank was shut down after auditors in England and other countries disclosed fraud, improper loans, and deceptive accounting, and accused the bank of catering to drug dealers, arms merchants, and dictators. Abu Dhabi contended it was a victim also, losing nearly $6 billion of the $10 billion the bank lost worldwide from its closure. Two years after the bank collapsed, the UAE indicted thirteen BCCI officers on criminal and forgery charges. In the early 2000s, the emirates' loose banking regulations permitted al-Qaida and other terrorist groups to launder money, particularly through the use of the *hawwalah* system—money given to a broker in the emirates can then be retrieved from the broker's counterpart in another country with just a slip of paper or a telephone call. The UAE responded in January 2002 with new regulations to control financial transfers.

In foreign policy, the federation has tried to pursue a strategy of balance. In October 1984, it opened diplomatic relations with China. In November 1985, it became the third Gulf government to establish ties with the Soviet Union. In regional affairs, the federation attempted to steer a neutral course during the Iran-Iraq War. The UAE joined other Arab Gulf states in forming the Gulf

Cooperation Council in 1981, and in 1982 it entered into a bilateral defense agreement with Saudi Arabia. The UAE has maintained stable relations with Iran, which in the mid-1980s permitted Shaykh Zayed to play a mediating role as the Iran-Iraq War escalated. The UAE is also close to the United States, recognizing that it is the ultimate security guarantor in the region. In 1990 the UAE joined the 1990 Persian Gulf War coalition, though in the late 1990s Shaykh Zayed called for lifting sanctions against Iraq and criticized U.S. support of Israel. The country later permitted the United States and Britain, with whom ties remain particularly close, to make use of its military facilities during the 2003 Iraq War.

In spite of the UAE's relatively good rapport with Iran, the two countries have an unresolved dispute over the islands of Abu Musa and the Greater and Lesser Tunbs. In 1971 the shah of Iran sent a small force to claim the islands but agreed with the UAE to cede administrative control and split offshore oil revenues. In September 1992, Iran claimed full sovereignty and expelled UAE forces and inhabitants from the islands. Since 1992 Iran has further developed the islands and fortified them militarily. Negotiations are currently at a standstill, and the issue continues to strain Iranian-UAE relations.

Outlook

Whereas Bahrain, Kuwait, Saudi Arabia, and Yemen have confronted domestic calls to broaden political participation, no such pressure appears to be rising in the UAE. The ruling families' generous, albeit paternalistic, political tradition seems to satisfy most of the UAE's citizens. The UAE's principal political concern is its heavy reliance on foreign labor. Although the federal government has stepped up efforts to "nationalize" employment, the small size of the country's native labor force and its strong commitment to industrial development have given the federation no option but to retain a large number of foreign workers. The expatriates have thus far remained relatively quiescent.

Political succession was resolved smoothly in late 2004, when Shaykh Khalifa succeeded his father, Shaykh Zayed, as amir of Abu Dhabi and president of the UAE. Shaykh Khalifa quickly named his half-brother Muhammad as his heir apparent instead of his son. A similar situation exists in Dubai, where Shaykh Maktum is both ruler and vice president of the UAE but his brother Muhammad is heir apparent and essentially runs the emirate. The succession issue has also been a problem in Ras al-Khaimah, where the aging ruler abruptly replaced his eldest son as heir apparent by another son in 2004 amidst considerable controversy.

Like other oil-producing states, the UAE felt the pinch of slumping oil prices in the late 1990s. Declining revenues led to adjustments in some of the federation's development projects. The trend in the early 1990s was for increased oil production and refining capacity, but these projects have since taken a back seat to new petrochemical endeavors. The government decided that, in the long term, the increased value added in downstream projects would be more beneficial to the economy as a whole. The country's gas resources are being aggressively developed, for export as well as domestic consumption, and plans are well underway for a natural gas pipeline from Qatar to provide for the growing needs of Dubai and Sharjah.

Another effect of low and fluctuating oil prices has been a greater push to privatize certain sectors of the economy, such as utilities, and to increase the employment rate of nationals in the private sector. All of these are long-term issues that the UAE, like the rest of the region, will be dealing with for many years to come. In the meantime, Dubai, with its oil supplies dwindling, looks to continue to exploit its market position through Jabal Ali, the free-trade zone, in which companies can operate without paying taxes yet enjoy access to cheap oil and other economic incentives. Situated close to Iran, Jabal Ali stands to cash in on Iran's reentry into the international economy and become the center of the nonpetroleum industry for the UAE.

In foreign affairs, the UAE is likely to continue to maintain close ties with the other conservative, pro-Western GCC states, while seeking to develop a balanced relationship with Iran and to support the new regime in Iraq. The UAE is in the unfortunate position of being the trip wire vis-à-vis Iran's foreign policy posturing. It must engage Iran diplomatically and economically to strike a balance of strength and friendship to protect its territory and natural resources. In the coming years, the UAE may be forced to accept Iranian "settlements" regarding the islands over which they dispute in order to avoid a larger confrontation.

CHAPTER 16

SAUDI ARABIA

The September 11, 2001, attacks on the United States marked a turning point for the Kingdom of Saudi Arabia in its foreign relations with the United States and, most critically, in regard to its own internal political and economic life. Fifteen of the suicide bombers were Saudi citizens. Osama bin Laden, an exiled Saudi, continues to threaten Saudi Arabia, asserting that the kingdom's loose alliance with the United States and its allowing westerners in the kingdom are antithetical to Islam. Bombings and other attacks on Saudi soil, including one on the U.S. consulate in Jiddah in December 2004, highlight the kingdom's vulnerability. Conservative religious leaders who see Islam undermined by the "waywardness" of westernization and the ruling family continue to demand reform.

During the buildup to the U.S.-led invasion of Iraq, the internal political challenges facing the kingdom led the U.S. to move the regional headquarters of the U.S. Central Command to Qatar. After September 11 and with the war in Iraq, it appears that yet another new regional order is emerging, as Saudi Arabia turns its focus on domestic internal stability and greater independence from Western influence.

Saudi Arabia significantly benefited from increasing oil prices in the early 2000s. Coupled with increased production, the rise in prices resulted in substantial increases in oil export revenues. Although still under pressure to control spending, the government is utilizing its budget surplus to pay down public debt and to increase spending on education and security. Saudi Arabia

has pursued membership in the World Trade Organization (WTO, or its predecessor, the General Agreement on Tariffs and Trade [GATT]) for more than ten years, but disagreements remain as to the kingdom's willingness to increase market access to foreign goods and services and the timeline by which it must comply with WTO obligations. In late 2004, the kingdom announced its intention to accelerate its accession to the WTO.

Geography and People

The Kingdom of Saudi Arabia extends over four-fifths of the Arabian Peninsula. Approximately 760,000 square miles, or about one-third the size of the continental United States, the kingdom stretches from the Gulf of Aqaba and the Red Sea in the west to the Persian Gulf in the east. It borders Jordan, Iraq, Kuwait, Bahrain, Qatar, the United Arab Emirates (UAE), Oman, and the Republic of Yemen. Parts of the boundaries with the UAE and with Yemen remain undefined. Saudi Arabia faces Iran across the Persian Gulf and Egypt, the Sudan, and Eritrea across the Red Sea.

Geographically, the country can be divided into regions characterized by distinctive terrain: coasts, sand deserts, plateaus, escarpments, and mountains. Along the eastern shore of the Red Sea, a narrow plain running the length of the coastline called the Tihama rises gradually from the sea to mountain ranges of 4,000 to 7,000 feet. Adjoining the Red Sea is the Hijaz, the location of the Islamic holy cities of Mecca and Medina. South of the Hijaz, the rugged coastal

Key Facts on Saudi Arabia

Area: 756,981 square miles (1,960,582 square kilometers)

Capital: Riyadh; diplomatic capital located at Jiddah

Population: 25,795,938; includes 5,576,076 nonnationals (2004)

Religion: 95 percent Sunni Muslim, 5 percent Shiite Muslim

Ethnic Groups: Arab, 90 percent; Afro-Asian, 10 percent

Official Language: Arabic

Type of Government: Monarchy

GDP: $287.8 billion; $11,800 per capita (2003)

Source: Central Intelligence Agency, *CIA World Factbook,* 2004.

highland of the Asir has peaks rising more than 9,000 feet. East of the mountainous coast is the central rocky plateau called the Najd, the birthplace of Saudi Arabia and the location of the capital, Riyadh. The Syrian desert in the north extends southward into the 22,000 square miles of the reddish al-Nufud desert. A narrow strip of desert known as al-Dahna separates the Najd from eastern Arabia and arcs downward toward one of the largest sand deserts in the world, the Rub al-Khali, or Empty Quarter, which measures more than 250,000 square miles and is about the size of Texas. The Eastern Province, sloping toward the sandy coast along the Persian Gulf, contains Saudi Arabia's rich oil fields and al-Hasa, the world's largest oasis.

Saudi Arabia has no permanent rivers or bodies of water; it is incredibly dry. Rainfall is erratic and averages about two to four inches per year, except in the mountainous Asir region, which often has torrential downpours and flash floods and averages twenty inches of annual rainfall. The Rub al-Khali may receive no rain for as long as ten years. Rainfall, ground water, desalinated seawater, and scarce surface water supply the country's growing needs.

The kingdom has invested more than $20 billion in desalination projects and is currently the largest producer of desalinated water in the world. During the Persian Gulf War, Iraq engineered an intentional oil spill that fouled much of Saudi Arabia's Persian Gulf shoreline, resulting in serious consequences for the ecosystem, desalination plants, and fishing industry.

Heat is intense during the summer months, frequently exceeding 120 degrees Fahrenheit in some areas, and coastal humidity is excessive. Snow and ice are rare in winter, although temperatures sometimes drop below freezing in the central and northern regions. Strong winds called the *shamal* frequently whip up dust and sandstorms along the eastern coast.

Almost all Saudis can trace their lineage either from the Qahtan or Adnan, the ancestral, indigenous Arabian tribes. The remaining minorities—mostly Africans, Indians, Indonesians, Iranians, and Turks—tend to be the descendants of pilgrims to Mecca who settled in the Hijaz region.

The population of Saudi Arabia is about 25.8 million according to 2004 estimates, which includes more than 5.5 million resident foreigners. The annual population growth rate is approximately 2.4 percent. Nearly 40 percent of the population is under the age of fifteen. Literacy is approximately 78 percent for the nation. Much of the population is concentrated in the commercial city of Jiddah on the Red Sea, the holy cities of Mecca and Medina, the resort town of Taif, the capital city of Riyadh, and the major industrial and petrochemical centers on the Persian Gulf, including the Dammam-Hofuf complex. As a result of rapid urban and economic growth, more than 96 percent of the once heavily nomadic Saudi population now is settled, with some cities and oases having population densities exceeding 2,600 people per square mile.

About 95 percent of all Saudis are Sunni Muslims adhering to the strict Wahhabi interpretation of Islam; the remainder are Shiite Muslims. Many Shiites, indigenous to the oil-rich Eastern Province, consider themselves oppressed and are viewed with apprehension by the government because of their suspected sympathy to predominately Shiite Iran.

The government relies on recruited foreign workers to augment Saudi Arabia's limited labor supply. Westerners have filled many upper-level managerial and executive positions, while the balance of the labor force comprises mainly Bahrainis, Egyptians, Filipinos, Indians, Jordanians, Pakistanis, and Yemenis. Saudis make up only 10 percent of the private sector workforce. The presence of foreigners, however, has long been viewed as a threat to the country's traditional Islamic society. The government frequently has declared its intention to curtail the influx of workers, but several factors have hampered its ability to do so. For example, despite the increasing number of female university graduates, social constraints limit women's employment to more traditional fields. Foreign laborers often fill the low-skilled, low-paying occupations that Saudis will not accept.

History

Arabian history, while traceable to extremely early civilizations, is generally the account of small urban settlements subsisting mainly on trade and living in the midst of nomadic tribes that survived by raising livestock and raiding. Arabia remained largely unsettled until the peninsula came under the suzerainty of the Ottoman sultans of Istanbul in the early sixteenth century. At the same time, European merchant adventurers began exploring the Persian Gulf. The Portuguese arrived first, followed by the British, Dutch, and French. By the nineteenth century, Great Britain had become the dominant European power in the region.

Meanwhile, the Najd was the scene of a religious upheaval. The puritanical and reforming Wahhabi movement launched by Muhammad ibn Abd al-Wahhab in the eighteenth century called for a return to the belief of the absolute oneness of God, a monotheistic concept. His unitarian message was unwelcome among the Arabian tribes, and he was driven to seek refuge among the Al Sauds, the ruling family in the Najd settlement of

Diriyya, who were willing to support him. In 1744 the Wahhab and Al Saud families sealed a pact dedicated to the preservation and propagation of pure Islam.

This union provided the Al Saud with a clearly defined religious message that became the basis of their political authority. Bent on destroying the hold of the Ottoman occupiers, the Wahhabi movement had spread by 1800 to Ottoman territories, including Mecca and Medina in the Hijaz, much of modern day Oman, and parts of Yemen. This era is commonly known as the first Saudi state. In 1816 the Ottoman sultan called upon Muhammad Ali, his viceroy of Egypt, to drive out the Wahhabis. His son, Ibrahim Pasha, finally completed the task, laying waste to Diriyya in 1818, driving the Al Sauds into exile.

Several years later, Turki ibn Abdallah Al Saud captured Riyadh and restored the Al Saud dynasty with the second Saudi state, which flourished until 1865. By 1871, however, the Ottomans had recaptured eastern Arabia, during which time the power of the Rashid family, based in Hail, northeast of Riyadh, grew at the expense of its rival, the Al Sauds. The Rashids ruled much of Arabia during the late 1800s, and in 1891 the Al Saud family fled the Najd and took refuge in Kuwait.

In 1902 Abd al-Aziz, a member of the deposed Al Saud family, returned to the Najd from exile in Kuwait to regain the family's former domain. In a legendary battle, Abd al-Aziz captured Riyadh, expelled the Rashidi dynasty, and proclaimed himself ruler of the Najd. His loyal Wahhabi Bedouin forces, known as the Ikhwan, or brethren, abandoned their nomadic lifestyle for agricultural settlements in remote desert areas in order to spread the Wahhabi doctrine.

By 1913 Abd al-Aziz's armies had driven the Ottomans from the al-Hasa coast of the Persian Gulf (now the Eastern Province of Saudi Arabia), a move that led to closer contact with the British. During World War I, Abd al-Aziz expanded his domain to encompass the northern regions then held by the Rashidi tribes loyal to the Turks. He signed a treaty with the British in 1915 that recognized him as the independent ruler of Najd and Its Dependencies under a British protectorate. In 1920 and in 1926 Abd al-Aziz signed treaties with the Idrisi, a semi-independent people in the Asir in southwestern Arabia just north of Yemen, giving him suzerainty over the Idrisi's territories.

Abd al-Aziz realized the final step in his unification of the Arabian Peninsula in 1926, when he ousted his chief rival, Hashimite leader Sharif Hussein (King Hussein of Jordan's great-grandfather) from the Hijaz. Abd al-Aziz, a traditional Arab clan leader, now had to consider the varied constituencies that his expanding realm encompassed, from the cosmopolitan Hijazis to his fervent Ikhwan Bedouin followers.

As the only truly independent Arab leader after World War I, Abd al-Aziz began to play a wider role in Arab politics. His adoption of Western technologies and the increasing presence of non-Muslim foreigners in the country were not acceptable to the Ikhwan. Defying the authority of Abd al-Aziz, the Ikhwan launched attacks against Saudi tribes in 1929 and pushed beyond the borders established after World War I into Iraq. With British support, Abd al-Aziz put down the Ikhwan rebellion. The short civil war ended in 1930, when British forces captured the rebel leaders in Kuwait and delivered them to Abd al-Aziz. On September 24, 1932, Abd al-Aziz unified the Hijaz and the Najd and Its Dependencies as the Kingdom of Saudi Arabia.

During World War II, Abd al-Aziz took a neutral stance, but his preference for the Allied cause was apparent. Recognizing the importance of the country's oil and its strategic geographic location, U.S. president Franklin D. Roosevelt declared in 1943 that the defense of Saudi Arabia was of vital interest to the United States and dispatched the first U.S. military mission to the kingdom. Roosevelt and Abd al-Aziz sealed this alliance in 1945, when they met aboard the USS *Quincy* in the Suez Canal. Abd al-Aziz nominally declared war on Germany in 1945, a move that ensured Saudi Arabia's charter membership in the United Nations and made it eligible for U.S. lend-lease aid. That same year, Abd al-Aziz was instrumental in the formation of the Arab League.

Post–World War II Developments

Abd al-Aziz died in November 1953 at the age of seventy-one and was succeeded by the oldest of his thirty-four surviving sons, Crown Prince Saud. Faisal, another of Abd al-Aziz's sons, became the crown prince and prime minister. King Saud's incompetent leadership and profligate spending, which had a detrimental effect on the country's development, led to growing dissatisfaction by more liberal princes and the foreign-educated sons of the rising middle class.

Relationships with its Arab neighbors and domestic politics also tested the growing nation. In 1961 Saudi Arabia responded to newly independent Kuwait's request for assistance in deterring Iraqi expansionist threats by sending troops. Brigadier General Abd al-Karim al-Qasim had recently overthrown the Hashimite monarchy in Iraq and sought territorial rights over Kuwait. (Iraq first claimed Kuwait in the 1930s.) Saudi troops remained in Kuwait until 1972. Hostility between Saudi leaders and Egyptian president Gamal Abdel Nasser dominated Saudi-Egyptian relations during Nasser's tenure from 1954 to 1970. Nasser's foreign policy encouraged revolutionary attitudes in Arab countries and irritated royal regimes. The merger of Syria and Egypt in 1958 into the United Arab Republic shocked the Saudis. Tensions flared in 1962 and continued through the remainder of the decade, when Egypt and Saudi Arabia backed opposing sides in the Yemeni civil war.

An alleged conspiracy by King Saud to assassinate Nasser led senior members of the Al Saud family to pressure the king to relinquish power to Crown Prince Faisal. On March 24, 1958, Faisal assumed executive powers of foreign and internal affairs, but Saud remained king. By means of an austerity program, Faisal balanced the budget and improved the country's fiscal health, but his cuts in royal subsidies incensed Saud and drove him to reassume the post of prime minister. After almost a decade of external and internal pressure to depose Saud, the *ulama,* or religious scholars, supported by the royal family, issued a *fatwa,*or religious decree, on November 2, 1964, deposing Saud and declaring Faisal king.

King Faisal reorganized the Central Planning Organization to develop priorities for economic development and invested oil revenues to stimulate growth. Education was emphasized as crucial to development, with annual expenditures for education increasing to about 10 percent of the kingdom's budget.

Between 1952 and 1962 the United States maintained an air base at Dhahran on the Persian Gulf. (The arrangement was not renewed in 1961 due partly to Saudi Arabia's opposition to U.S. support of Israel.) The United States became an important ally to Saudi Arabia during the cold war. Both King Saud and King Faisal warned against communist influence in Arab and Muslim countries. Saudi opposition to communism became evident at the time of the establishment of the People's Republic of South Yemen in 1967, later renamed the People's Democratic Republic of Yemen (PDRY), which was created after the British withdrew from the Aden Protectorate. The kingdom had no diplomatic relations with South Yemen until 1976, actively provided rebellious tribal elements within South Yemen with arms and ammunition, and engaged in several rather serious border clashes with it over their undelimited frontier.

In other regional matters, Saudi Arabia supported the Arab cause in the June 1967 War against Israel. At the Khartoum Conference in August of that year, Saudi Arabia agreed to contribute $140 million to rebuild the economies of those countries involved in the war.

Political and economic developments during the 1970s catapulted Saudi Arabia to the forefront of world politics. Despite good relations with the United States, heightened regional pressures for a resolution to the Arab-Israeli conflict caused King Faisal to use oil as a political weapon against Israel and the United States. When the Arab-Israeli war of October 1973 erupted and the United States continued its support of Israel despite repeated warnings of an embargo, Saudi Arabia led a movement by the Arab oil-producing countries to exert pressure on the United States by reducing oil exports. The kingdom joined with ten other oil-producing Arab nations in cutting by 5 percent each month the amount of oil sold to the United States and other Western countries. On October 18, Saudi Arabia independently cut oil production by 10 percent to bring direct pressure on the United States. Two days later, after President Richard Nixon unveiled plans for additional U.S. aid to Israel, Riyadh announced a total halt in oil exports to the United States. Members of the Organization of Arab Petroleum Exporting Countries (OAPEC) joined the embargo.

The embargo triggered serious discussions in the United States about using military force to keep the oil flowing, but force was not used to resolve the crisis. At a meeting in Vienna on March 18, 1974, Saudi Arabia agreed to lift the five-month-old embargo, and Abu Dhabi, Algeria, Bahrain, Egypt, Kuwait, and Qatar followed suit; only Organization of Arab Petroleum Exporting Countries (OAPEC) members Libya and Iraq dissented. The tripling of oil prices after 1973 vastly increased the revenues available to the Saudi government for domestic programs.

Discovery of Oil

Oil discoveries around the Persian Gulf in the 1920s suggested that the peninsula might also contain petroleum deposits. In 1933 Saudi Arabia granted to Standard Oil of California (later Chevron) an exclusive sixty-six-year concession to explore for, produce, and eventually export Saudi Arabia's oil under the operating name Arabian-American Oil Company (Aramco). The liberal terms of the grant reflected Abd al-Aziz's need for funds, his low estimate of oil's potential in the global arena, and his weak bargaining position. The terms of the original agreement were modified in 1938, with substantially higher payments to the Saudi government, after oil was discovered in the kingdom. Other U.S. oil companies acquired shares in Aramco, and by 1948 Standard Oil of California, Standard Oil of New Jersey (later Exxon), and Texaco each owned 30 percent of the company, and Mobil Oil owned 10 percent.

Saudi Arabia marked 1950 with two momentous events: the completion of a 753-mile oil pipeline by Aramco subsidiary Trans-Arabian Pipeline Company (Tapline) across Jordan, Syria, and Lebanon to the Mediterranean Sea, and the signing of a 50-50 profit-sharing agreement with Aramco, thereby greatly increasing the government's revenues. Other oil-rich Middle East nations would later negotiate similar terms.

In 1962 Saudi Arabia created the General Petroleum and Mineral Organization (Petromin) to increase state participation in the petroleum and gas industries. The 1960s and 1970s saw a spectacular expansion of petroleum output in response to rising world demand. Production increased from 1.3 million barrels per day (bpd) in 1960 to 8.5 million bpd in 1984. Increased output was accompanied by rising prices; petroleum revenues rose from $1.2 billion in 1970 to $22.6 billion in 1974.

Convinced that the strength or weakness of Western economies had a major effect on its own fortunes, Saudi Arabia emerged after the events of 1973–1974 as a pro-Western influence in the Organization of the Petroleum Exporting Countries (OPEC), using its high potential output to hold down petroleum prices. The shortfall in petroleum output in early 1979 caused by the revolution in Iran was filled by Saudi Arabia's increased output from below 8.5 million bpd to

10 million bpd. Nevertheless, prices increased sharply in response to the West's fear of shortages. Saudi production was raised again in 1980 to compensate for lost output due to the Iran-Iraq War.

In 1980 the Saudi government made payments to Aramco's parent companies to attain total ownership of Aramco, a process that began in 1973 with the oil crisis. In 1988 Aramco became the Saudi Arabian Oil Company (Saudi Aramco), an entirely Saudi-owned enterprise with responsibility for all domestic exploration and development. A 1990 acquisition of a South Korean oil-refining company established Saudi Aramco as the world's largest petroleum-producing company, a position that it still holds today.

Saudi Arabia's oil pricing policy has predominantly focused on three factors: maintaining moderate oil prices to ensure the long-term use of crude oil as a major energy source; developing sufficient excess capacity to stabilize oil markets and maintain the kingdom's importance to the West; and generating adequate oil revenues to further economic development and prevent fundamental changes to its political system. Additionally, Saudi Arabia's pricing policy often has been used to compensate for other OPEC members' failure to abide by cartel quotas, which has brought Saudi Arabia into conflict with its fellow members since OPEC's founding in 1960. As the nation with the largest oil reserves in the world (nearly 26 percent of known reserves), Saudi Arabia is undeniably positioned to influence the organization's pricing and production policies. It has the capacity to pump more than 10 million bpd. Indeed, in the aftermath of the 1991 Gulf war, Saudi Arabia emerged as the unchallenged leader within OPEC. (*Middle Eastern Oil and Gas, Chapter 5, p. 179*)

During the 1970s and early 1980s, the Saudi position was that excessive price hikes would reduce world oil consumption and encourage investment in alternative sources of energy—two developments that would lower OPEC's long-term income. To force other OPEC members to reduce their prices, the Saudis pumped 10 million bpd in the spring of 1981 and vowed to continue until other countries lowered their prices.

Saudi Arabia in other instances has cut its production to prevent poorer OPEC countries—those that rely almost exclusively on oil income—from bearing the burden of low prices. In October 1984, Saudi Arabia agreed to become OPEC's "swing producer," cutting its own production to keep prices and production levels as high as possible for other OPEC nations. At the time, the Saudi economy could afford the reduction because of a cash surplus of more than $100 billion.

By mid-1985, however, the kingdom's economic situation had deteriorated. Saudi production dropped sharply and its oil revenues declined rapidly. Under significant domestic pressure, King Fahd, who ascended the throne in 1982, decided to abandon the kingdom's role as swing producer and to substantially increase production. The government's intention was to force the price of oil to decline in an effort to discipline OPEC members and coerce non-OPEC countries into limiting their production, thereby enabling Saudi Arabia to regain what it considered its fair share of the market.

The strategy resulted in a collapse of oil prices during the first half of 1986. As Saudi Arabia increased its production to 5.7 million bpd, other OPEC members refused to rein in their production to accommodate the extra Saudi output. The corresponding oil glut led prices to tumble to below $10 a barrel, which was about one-third the level of the early 1980s. As a result, despite increased production, the Saudi oil industry was generating only a fraction of the previous year's revenue. In desperation, the kingdom abandoned its "fair-share" policy in October and dismissed longtime oil minister Ahmad Zaki Yamani, who had designed the plan.

During the late 1980s, Saudi Arabia sought to maintain an $18 benchmark price, but its strategy proved largely unsuccessful due to overproduction by Kuwait and the UAE. It was not until Iraq invaded Kuwait in 1990 that prices, driven by panic buying, rebounded to around $40 per barrel. In the absence of Kuwaiti and Iraqi oil, Saudi Arabia increased its production to pick up the slack.

After the Gulf war, oil production was again market driven, which meant that the continued recession in consuming countries decreased total demand for oil. At the September 1993 OPEC meeting, in response to falling oil prices, Saudi Arabia again signaled its willingness to temper its drive for market share in the interest of price stability. Indeed, OPEC supply grew at a minimal rate from 1993 through 1997. Coupled with the rapid growth of the Asian economies and their increase in demand for oil, this minimal increase in supply led in 1996 and 1997 to higher prices averaging $20 per barrel, and thus increased revenues for Saudi Arabia and other oil-producing countries.

As the growth in Asia precipitated a greater demand for oil, however, OPEC members were too slow to adjust their output. When they finally agreed to raise their production quotas in November 1997 by 2.5 million bpd, a 9.5 percent increase, it was too late. Asian demand, which had accounted for 80 percent of the annual growth in world oil demand from 1990 to 1997, had already begun to shrink as Asian economies crashed. As a result, the market was glutted.

The reentry of Iraq into the world oil market through the United Nation's oil-for-food program compounded the problem. In November 1997, OPEC increased Iraq's quota by 9.5 percent, which matched its UN export allowance. In 1998, however, the United Nations more than doubled Iraq's allowable export value, at a time when the per barrel price of oil had declined sharply. Iraq increased its production, reaching the technical maximum of its production capacity without even approaching the export ceiling established by the UN. In this way, Iraq significantly contributed to the huge oversupply of oil and low price.

At a November 1998 OPEC meeting, the countries failed to agree on substantial cuts in crude oil output. This led to a bottoming-out of world oil prices at under $10 per barrel, a twelve-year low. By the end of 1998, oil prices had fallen 30 percent compared with December 1997, and analysts speculated that the price increases in 1999 would be minimal, settling somewhere between $10 and

$15 per barrel. By mid-September 1999, however, the average price of $15.11 per barrel had already exceeded that range.

Estimates in late 2004 indicate that the petroleum sector accounts for approximately 75 percent of budget revenues for the kingdom, between 40 and 45 percent of its gross domestic product (GDP), and 90 percent of its export earnings. The country's oil export revenues exceeded $100 billion in 2004, up from $77 billion in 2003. The kingdom produced around 10.4 billion barrels per day in 2004, which was a substantial increase from the 8.5 billion barrels per day in 2003. Moreover, recent estimates indicate that the kingdom's oil reserves could reach 461 billion barrels within the next few years, more than one-third of the world's conventional oil reserves. Revenues for 2005 and likely 2006 are expected to be similarly strong as oil prices have been consistently more than $50 per barrel in recent months and are expected to remain high for the foreseeable future. Although the Saudi government has made several references regarding the potential partial privatization of the oil industry, no significant movement in this direction has occurred.

The Persian Gulf War and Its Aftermath

Saudi Arabia has traditionally pursued two primary foreign policy objectives: regional security and Islamic solidarity. Fearing aggression and externally supported subversion as threats to its security, Saudi Arabia has worked to maintain stability in the region surrounding the Arabian Peninsula. Iraq and Iran, its more populous and powerful neighbors, have been particular security concerns. The Iraqi invasion of Kuwait on August 2, 1990, took Saudi Arabia and the world by surprise. Fearing that Saddam Hussein planned to seize the Eastern Province's oil fields and installations, King Fahd abandoned the illusion of Arab solidarity and discreet diplomacy. He requested the deployment of U.S troops on Saudi soil to defend its territory, in contravention to long-standing policy to keep U.S. forces "over the horizon" on naval platforms in the Arabian Sea.

Saudi concerns regarding the U.S. commitment to the security relationship were dissolved by the United States' dispatch of more than 400,000 troops to defend the kingdom against aggression during the 1991 war.

From mid-August 1990 to the outbreak of hostilities on January 16, 1991, Arab states attempted to mediate a solution, but the United States, and increasingly King Fahd, would settle for nothing less than Iraq's full compliance with UN Security Council Resolution 660, which called for Iraq's complete and unconditional withdrawal from Kuwait.

The invasion of Kuwait demonstrated the vulnerability of Saudi Arabia despite the billions it had invested in arms purchases. The need to bring in foreign forces to defend the kingdom sparked widespread domestic criticism of the government's failure to construct a viable military deterrent to regional threats. In response, King Fahd promised a major expansion of the armed forces, including a doubling of the army's size and the creation of a reserve system.

Saudi Arabian oil revenues have provided the country with the means to administer a generous and extensive aid program throughout the Islamic world, yet this aid failed to ensure the loyalty in the Gulf crisis of several principal beneficiaries—Iraq, Jordan, Yemen, and the Palestine Liberation Organization (PLO). The Gulf war split the Arab world into two: those countries that supported the U.S.-led coalition and those that were neutral or opposed to it. Saudi retribution against the Arab nations that supported Iraq was swift and severe: Oil supplies and the $400 million in annual aid to Jordan ceased. Funding to the PLO—$6 million monthly since 1989—also stopped. Thousands of Palestinians were expelled from the kingdom. Yemen's neutral stand, as well as its continuing claims on Saudi territory, led to a suspension of its annual $400 million subsidy and to the immediate expulsion of more than 800,000 Yemenis from Saudi Arabia. Meanwhile, Saudi Arabia expanded aid programs to its allies from the Gulf crisis: Syria received between $1.5 billion and $2.5 billion for its participation in the multinational force. Egypt was extended massive debt relief and promises of future financial aid and labor contracts.

Although President Clinton greatly downsized U.S. defense spending in his first six years in office, officials in his administration regarded arms sales to the Saudis as crucial for maintaining jobs for U.S. arms makers. To ensure that the Saudis would be able to afford the pending purchases of $30 billion in weapons and $6 billion in commercial airliners, the United States allowed the Saudis to buy on credit what they once bought with cash. Saudi Arabia, however, remained unwilling to institutionalize defense relations with the United States because of criticism from Arab countries.

Government and Politics

Saudi Arabia is ruled as an absolute monarchy, headed by the king and a crown prince who is chosen as the heir apparent. The Quran, the holy book of Islam and the basis of *sharia,* or Islamic law, serves as the constitution. Major decisions are usually made by consensus among senior princes of the Al Saud clan, in close consultation with the ulama. Since 1953 the Council of Ministers, appointed by the king, has advised Saudi rulers on policy and on the administration of the country's growing bureaucracy. Not all of Saudi Arabia's estimated 4,000 princes play a major role in the government, but at least a few hundred do. The Al Saud family always has been careful to cultivate its bonds with the two other influential families in the country, the Sudayris and the Al Shaykh, who backed the Al Sauds' campaign from 1750 to 1926 for control of most of the Arabian Peninsula.

In 1975 King Faisal was assassinated by a disaffected member of the royal family. Crown Prince Khalid then became king, reviving a period of more collective family rule. One of the most significant events during King Khalid's reign was the seizure of the holy mosque in Mecca by Muslim radicals in 1979. This attempt to incite people against the monarchy was quashed, although not without significant loss of life.

King Fahd ibn Abd al-Aziz

In 1982 at the age of sixty, King Fahd ascended the throne after the death of his half-brother King Khalid, who died at age sixty-nine. Fahd's half-brother Abdallah, the commander of the National Guard since 1962, became crown prince and first deputy prime minister. Sultan, second deputy prime minister and minister of defense and aviation since 1962, became second in the line of succession.

Fahd had served in top government posts for nearly three decades before taking the throne. He was appointed the first minister of education in 1953, and during King Faisal's reign he served as minister of the interior. As crown prince under the ailing King Khalid, Fahd was the chief spokesman for the kingdom and a major architect of Saudi economic and foreign policies. After becoming king, Fahd played an important mediating role in inter-Arab conflicts. His visit to Egypt in March 1989 marked the end of Egypt's isolation because of its signing of the 1979 Camp David Accords. In October 1989, acting with Algeria and Morocco,

Fahd convened the Lebanese National Assembly in Taif to develop a peace initiative for war-torn Lebanon.

Speculation continues about Fahd's ailing health and his leadership abilities. He has been insulated from daily Saudi life and his subjects since 1996. As a result, Crown Prince Abdallah has essentially served as the regent, although he has not been officially designated as such. In this respect, Abdallah has occupied the role that Fahd once played for King Khalid, often speaking for the country, traveling abroad, and dealing with foreign policy issues.

Abdallah is perceived to be more in tune than Fahd had been with the tribal and Bedouin ways of life that buttress the foundation of Saudi Arabia. Nonetheless, he has hinted that when he becomes king, he might lift the ban on women driving. Another sign of his intentions might be reflected in his meeting with U.S. oil executives in September 1998 to discuss limited privatization of the oil industry, a radical change from the policy of his predecessors.

The close association of the Al Sauds with the ulama has provided the family with its primary source of religious legitimacy. In exchange for the recognition of their political influence, the ulama provide tacit or public approval, when requested, on potentially controversial policies. The Gulf war reestablished the ulama as central figures in the Saudi political process. Fahd's decision to permit non-Muslims to be stationed in the kingdom to protect the territory needed special legitimacy, which the ulama eventually provided. Not all the religious establishment was in agreement on the issue, however, thus creating divisions and leading to the fomenting of dissident groups.

In February and May 1991, Fahd was urged by two petitions from a group of conservative clerics to bring the kingdom's policies into closer accord with the sharia. The growing assertiveness of Islamic conservatives in the debate about the future of the country contrasted with the position of liberal intellectuals and businessmen. In April 1991, they too petitioned the king, but they urged the institution of national and municipal councils and the curbing of the *muttawin,* or religious police, who patrol towns and cities apprehending blasphemers, persons consuming alcohol, and others breaking Islamic law.

In response to domestic unrest following the 1991 Gulf war and pressure for democratization from Saudi Arabia's Western allies, Fahd published three decrees on March 1, 1992. In these Fahd established a Basic Law defining the Saudi system of government, promised to create and appoint within six months a Majlis al-Shura, or Consultative Council, and issued new regulations covering municipal administration. These decrees represented key elements of reforms promised but unimplemented for thirty years.

The Basic Law is the closest Saudi Arabia has come to having a formal constitution. In accordance with the sharia, it codifies for the first time the direction of economic and judicial principles, social welfare and education programs, and the process of succession. In August 1993, Fahd named the sixty members of the Majlis al-Shura to positions that can be renewed, plus an appointed chairman, deputy chairman, and secretary general. The council has played an advisory role to the Council of Ministers and the king, but it does not have legislative powers. In July 1997, membership of the Majlis al-Shura was expanded from 60 to 90 members, and in May 2001, it was expanded again to 120 members.

In September 1993, the memberships of new councils for provincial administration in the kingdom's thirteen regions were also announced. In February 2005, Saudi Arabia held its first elections ever, for half the members of the Riyadh municipal council. Similar municipal elections will take place across the country throughout 2005. Women were not eligible to vote in the elections.

Legislation in Saudi Arabia is enacted by royal decree and must follow the tenets of the Quran as well as the Hadith and Sunnah, the chronicled sayings and traditions of the Prophet Muhammad. Judges appointed by the ulama head a system of religious courts. The king serves as the highest court of appeal and has the right to issue pardons. Alcohol is forbidden, the sexes are segregated, and sharia penalties are applied for criminal acts. Political parties, labor unions, professional associations, and non-Islamic religious ceremonies are banned. The media exercise self-censorship.

For more than sixty years the Saudi citizenry has accepted the rule of the royal family with little resistance. Abdallah's succession to Fahd has been endorsed by the royal family and much of the citizenry. The issue of succession is bound to become much less clear after Abdallah, however. Unless Saudi Arabia can figure out a way to skip generations to the grandsons of Abd al-Aziz, the country will be facing a long line of very old kings, as there are currently twenty-five surviving sons of the founder of Saudi Arabia.

Nevertheless, self-preservation has forced the monarchy to strive to maintain wide popular support by relying on its Islamic legitimacy and by dramatically increasing government services. The Saudi government provides free education, medicine, and health care services to all citizens, as well as pensions to widows, orphans, elderly adults, and people with permanent disabilities. Assistance is given to victims of natural disasters and persons who are temporarily disabled. In the past the government also supplied interest-free loans for home mortgages, small businesses, and construction and agricultural development projects. All of these services are provided without taxing the population. The huge increase in oil prices over the last couple of years has given the kingdom a sizeable budget surplus, which likely will allow the country to continue many of its social programs and subsidies, and has eliminated the need for the kingdom to consider imposition of an income tax, which the government is reluctant to pursue.

Islamic Unrest

In November 1979, an extremist group laid siege to the mosque in Mecca, raising the specter of militant Islamic revolt. The armed insurgents were mostly Saudis, with some Kuwaitis, Sudanese, Yemenis, and students recruited from Medina University. Although many in the Muslim world supported in principle the group's attacks on alleged Saudi royal family corruption, they were outraged by the violation of Islam's sanctuary by guns and bloodshed. For two weeks the rebels held the mosque until army, national guard, and police units received the approval of the nation's top religious leaders to storm the site. One hundred three insurgents and 127 Saudi troops were killed. Afterward, enforcement of sharia penalties increased.

The 1979 Iranian revolution initially sparked unrest among the Shiites of the Gulf. Successive attempts to disrupt the hajj, the annual pilgrimage of Muslims to Mecca, and turn it into a political demonstration against Saudi Arabia were thwarted by authorities until July 1987, when Iranian pilgrims clashed with Saudi security forces. Some of the 100,000 Iranians present demonstrated around the Kaaba, Islam's holiest shrine, sparking violent riots that resulted in the deaths of 402 people, including 275 Iranians. In the following days, mass demonstrations took place in Tehran. The Saudi embassy was sacked, and Iranian leaders vowed to avenge the pilgrims' deaths by overthrowing the Saudi ruling family. Shortly afterward, two powerful explosions were reported at Saudi oil installations in the Eastern Province. The explosions were widely believed to be acts of sabotage by Shiite workers with connections to Iran.

The Saudis responded to the disturbances during the hajj by creating national quotas for all pilgrims based on a formula of one pilgrim per one thousand citizens. Iran announced that it would boycott the 1988 hajj. In July 1989, on the anniversary of the 1987 riots, two bombs exploded in Mecca, killing one person and injuring sixteen others. The worst tragedy of any pilgrimage occurred, however, in a July 1990 accident, when 1,426 pilgrims suffocated or were trampled to death in a tunnel near the pilgrimage sites, giving the Iranian government another opportunity to declare that the Saudi rulers were not fit to administer Islam's holy cities.

The Saudi regime responded to these threats to its Islamic credentials by expanding the influence of religious authorities in affairs of state and calling more frequently upon religious leaders to sanction government actions. In 1986, to de-emphasize his monarchical status and enhance his

Islamic legitimacy, King Fahd dropped the honorific "His Majesty" and adopted the title "Custodian of the Two Holy Mosques" (that is, those in Mecca and Medina).

To stem the tide of unrest by the minority Shiite Muslims in the oil-rich Eastern Province, the government bolstered its security forces and accelerated government-funded development in relatively deprived areas. The regime also broadened the social and religious rights of the Shiites. The combination of money and repression, however, did not eliminate the appeal of the Islamist movement in Saudi Arabia, which has become the main vehicle for the expression of discontent.

The Islamist movement is growing in popularity among young Shiites and Sunnis alike. Opposition clerics and other Islamists have distributed audiotapes and literature that harshly criticize the Saudi regime for its close relationship with the West, its extravagance, its failure to provide for the defense of the country, and its failure to implement an even more rigorous standard of Islamic law. Although many Saudis do not identify with them, the Islamists have become the focus of opposition by including mainstream concerns about security, finances, and political participation in their attacks on the regime.

Osama bin Laden is alleged in some quarters to be behind the 1996 attack on the U.S. military installation in al-Khobar, which killed nineteen Americans. He is wanted by the U.S. government in connection with the bombings of the U.S. embassies in Nairobi, Kenya, and Dar es Salaam, Tanzania, in 1998, as well as for his role in the attacks of September 11, 2001. Islamists are also thought to be behind the December 2004 bombing of the U.S. consulate in Jiddah and attacks on other infrastructure in Saudi Arabia in 2003. Undoubtedly, radical Islamic elements will continue to threaten the stability of the kingdom as they seek to harm foreign interests as well as the royal family's authority in Saudi Arabia.

The Economy

The production of crude petroleum and petroleum products dominates the Saudi economy.

In 1962 Crown Prince Faisal announced his program for using the kingdom's ever-increasing oil revenues to modernize the country's agricultural, industrial, and infrastructure bases. Since 1970 the development of the Saudi economy has been outlined in a series of five-year plans. Each of these plans has focused on different means by which the kingdom can transform its relatively undeveloped, oil-based economy into a modern industrial state while at the same time maintaining Saudi Arabia's Islamic values and traditions. Efforts have centered on increasing defense, education, and urban development spending; maintaining a balanced budget; developing of critical transportation and communications infrastructure; developing of downstream petroleum industries; and increasing agricultural production. The elements of the plans have often been based on current circumstances. For example, the fifth five-year development plan (1990–1995) allocated about 34 percent of total expenditures to defense because of the Gulf war and the ongoing threat Iraq posed to Saudi Arabia. Much of the increase in defense funding went toward a major upgrade of weapons systems. Although the kingdom has not always achieved the goals outlined in these plans and the oil sector still accounts for nearly 40 percent of the kingdom's GDP, it nonetheless has progressed beyond being a petroleum-only economy. In 1999 King Fahd issued a decree establishing the eleven-member Supreme Economic Council in an effort to centralize and control the economic affairs of the Kingdom.

More recently, fluctuations in oil revenues have had a similarly fluctuating effect on the economy. For example, despite incredible oil wealth, the Saudi government ran a hefty budget deficit in the late 1990s. By 1998 the deficit had grown to $12.27 billion, an increase equivalent to nearly 10 percent of the country's GDP. Because of the more than 30 percent reduction in oil revenues in 1998, Saudi Arabia's budget for 1999 promoted more austere measures, with a 12.6 percent cut in government spending, including major cuts in transportation, communications, and social welfare spending.

Saudi Arabia also faces problems with a high unemployment rate of approximately 14 percent. Coupled with a very high population growth rate of 2.4 percent, there is an ever-increasing need for government spending, which is acceptable when oil export revenues are high, but more difficult when global demand for oil is low.

The banking industry has had a positive effect on the Saudi economy. The banking system has a solid net foreign interbank surplus, and Saudi banks are highly capitalized by international standards. Many industry analysts noted with cautious optimism Saudi Arabia's announcement that it would allow an international bank, Germany's Deutsche Bank AG, to begin independent operations in the kingdom. Its operations will be limited to investment banking activities, and it will not engage in retail banking. In June 2003, the government enacted the Capital Market Law, which is intended to help restructure the kingdom's capital market in order to broaden its base, attract new foreign investment, and provide a regulatory structure.

In the spring of 1998, the government corporatized the telecommunications industry as a precursor to full privatization. The Saudi Telecommunications Company completed successful partial privatization in January 2003. The phased opening of the telecom sector has been aimed at encouraging private investment in networks and telecom services initially, followed by mobile telephone services in 2004 and fixed lines in 2008. The electricity industry has undergone a similar process. Tariffs were increased, a move that was intended to limit the subsidies that have been provided to consumers, and as a result electricity companies have sustained huge losses. Not surprisingly, these tariff increases were met with major opposition, and the government was forced to scale back its proposal.

On January 1, 1999, Saudi Arabia officially launched the Internet within its borders. With an estimated 1.5 million users in 2003, the Internet has provided additional market opportunities for telecommunications providers. As of 2003, there were twenty-two Internet service providers (ISPs) and nearly 16,000 internet hosts. As always, the monarchy has maintained substantial restrictions on access due to potentially objectionable materials available on the Internet.

A recent major development in Saudi trade was the launch of a Gulf Cooperation Council (GCC) customs union in 2003. The council expected to establish a monetary union by the end of 2005 and a common currency in 2010. To achieve the objectives of the union between the six GCC states, Saudi Arabia—the only non-WTO member of the GCC—has already lowered its customs tariffs from 12 percent to the union's agreed upon level of 5 percent.

National Security

Saudi Arabia's vast oil wealth makes it an inviting prize for a potential aggressor. Until the Gulf war it had avoided a security alliance with the United States because of the fear of Western influences, differences over the Arab-Israeli conflict, and the discontent such an alliance could create among conservative Muslims. The Saudis sought to ensure their security through high-tech arms purchases and through regional security arrangements, even as they maintained a close but "over the horizon" relationship with the United States. The instability in the Gulf caused by the rise of Ayatollah Ruhollah Khomeini and the Iranian Islamic revolution in 1979, as well as the outbreak of the Iran-Iraq War in 1980, provided Saudi Arabia and smaller Persian Gulf countries the impetus to form an alliance. The Saudis were the driving force behind the creation of the Gulf Cooperation Council (GCC) in 1981, which also includes Bahrain, Kuwait, Oman, Qatar, and the UAE. The GCC was devised to promote economic cooperation and collective security. The Gulf war, however, later proved that the GCC was not up to the task of ensuring its members' security.

Perhaps the most pressing problem confronting the Saudis during the 1980s was the Iran-Iraq War. Although the Saudis were highly suspicious of the Iraqis, the potential threat from Iran was sufficient to induce them to support Iraq throughout the eight-year war, providing Baghdad with $25.7 billion in aid, according to Saudi officials. *(The Persian Gulf, Chapter 4, p. 137)*

As attacks on tankers escalated during the war in 1984, the kingdom appeared to be on the verge of becoming involved directly. On June 4, Iranian F-4 fighter planes flew over Saudi territorial waters, presumably seeking naval targets. They were intercepted by Saudi F-15s and shot down. Despite the threatened disruption of tanker traffic in the Gulf during the latter half of the war, the Saudis resisted U.S. intervention to safeguard the region. Concerned about Arab reaction abroad and anti-American sentiment at home, Saudi Arabia refused to give the United States access to military facilities on its territory. Yet the Saudis did countenance the U.S. decision to escort reflagged Kuwaiti tankers in the Gulf in June 1987, when the United States provided essential cooperation in clearing mines and extending surveillance operations to the area.

Fearing a widening of the conflict, Saudi Arabia and its GCC allies supported diplomatic efforts to bring sanctions against Iran if it refused to halt the war. In November 1987, Saudi Arabia joined the other members of the Arab League in unanimously condemning Iran for prolonging the war, deploring its occupation of Iraqi territory, and urging it to accept without preconditions UN Security Council Resolution 598, which called for an end to the hostilities.

Saudi Arabia came close to a confrontation with Iran again in 1987, following the July 31 clashes between Iranian pilgrims and Saudi security forces in Mecca. As the level of hostility rose between Riyadh and Tehran, Iranian leaders threatened armed retaliation for the deaths of the pilgrims. The tense situation culminated in a Saudi decision in April 1988 to sever diplomatic relations with Iran. Tehran's moves toward normalization of relations with Western countries, its neutrality during the Gulf war, and Riyadh's concerns about postwar Iraq led to a reestablishment of diplomatic relations with Iran in 1991.

The dramatic breakup of the Soviet Union, its withdrawal from Afghanistan, and its support during the Gulf war facilitated a change in attitude by Saudi policymakers. Formal relations were restored with the Soviet Union in 1990 (and also with China) after a hiatus of about fifty years. Saudi Arabia has extended some financial assistance to the six predominately Muslim Central Asian republics of the former Soviet Union, and its relations with Iran continue to improve.

In March 1990, Saudi Arabia signed a treaty with the Sultanate of Oman delimiting their common border, and in July 2000, Saudi Arabia and Yemen signed a treaty resolving their significant, intense boundary dispute. Although relations between Saudi Arabia and Yemen fluctuate, as a general matter the resolution of the boundary dispute has helped normalize relations between the two nations, despite the resistance of several nomadic groups to the boundary demarcation. In the summer of 2000, Saudi Arabia also resolved its maritime boundary with Kuwait, ceding sovereignty over the two disputed islands to Kuwait. The government also has resolved its border issues with the UAE, although the exact alignment of the boundary is unknown because the treaty has not been made public.

Since 2001 Saudi national security has been focused on domestic elements of dissent. Ongoing attacks in the kingdom on major infrastructure, including the diplomatic and petroleum sectors, have sharpened the monarchy's efforts to control extreme religious elements within the kingdom that seek to damage the monarchy because of its perceived acquiescence to Western nations, specifically the United States. As a result, and in an effort to cooperate with the United States, Saudi Arabia has launched raids within the kingdom seeking to root out terrorist elements.

Relations with the United States

Since the 1940s, Saudi Arabia has had a close strategic alliance with the United States, despite U.S. support for Israel. The commitment of President Harry S. Truman to Abd al-Aziz Al Saud to support the territorial integrity and political independence of Saudi Arabia became the basis for the 1951 mutual defense assistance agreement, under which the United States provided military equipment and training for the Saudi armed forces. The

U.S.-Saudi security relationship was an outgrowth of Saudi Arabia's preoccupation with regime stability and regional security. The U.S. interest in Saudi Arabia was to ensure U.S. access to Saudi oil resources and preserve the kingdom as a bulwark against the encroachment of communism.

The United States has increasingly relied on Saudi Arabia as its major strategic ally in the Gulf since the fall of the shah of Iran in 1979. During the early 1980s, Saudi cooperation was considered critical to the Reagan administration's "strategic consensus" policy that sought to mobilize the anticommunist states of the Middle East to counter threats of Soviet advancement in the region. Maintaining that the Soviet Union, and not the Arab-Israeli conflict, was the main threat to regional security and oil supplies to the West, the White House supported the sale of sophisticated military equipment to the Saudis, often over Israel's objections. Saudi suspicions of Soviet intentions in the Middle East were intensified by the close relationship between Moscow and South Yemen and, most dramatically, by the Soviet invasion of Afghanistan in 1979. Throughout the nine-year occupation, Saudi Arabia financed the rebels fighting against the Soviets.

Washington also sought Saudi assistance in dealing with the Palestinian issue. In 1983, when President Ronald Reagan called for a partial Israeli withdrawal from the occupied territories and self-rule for West Bank Palestinians, he asked the Saudis to pressure the PLO to allow Jordan's King Hussein to speak for the Palestinians.

In the mid-1980s, Saudi Arabia and the United States found that their common interest in containing the spread of Iranian revolutionary activity and securing free shipping in the Gulf provided additional areas for cooperation. In 1986 Washington finally delivered the sophisticated airborne warning and control system (AWACS) aircraft, early-warning surveillance planes, that the Saudis had purchased in 1981. Later Riyadh provided essential aid to the U.S. naval convoys that began escorting reflagged Kuwaiti tankers through the Gulf in June 1987 during the Iran-Iraq War. Nevertheless, as noted earlier, Riyadh refused to allow U.S. access to its military facilities.

Differences over the Arab-Israeli conflict continue to strain relations between Washington and Riyadh. The kingdom's reluctance to pressure its Arab neighbors toward a peace settlement has frustrated some American leaders. U.S. support for Israel has led to restrictions on U.S. military sales to Saudi Arabia and has reduced the willingness of Saudi leaders to support U.S. policies in the region.

In early 1987, congressional opposition to supplying sophisticated weapons to an Arab country forced the Reagan administration to withdraw its proposal to sell the Saudis Stinger missiles, F-15 planes, and Maverick antitank missiles. In frustration, the Saudis vastly increased their purchase of weapons from the United Kingdom, ultimately leading the British to displace the Americans as the main supplier of arms to Saudi Arabia.

In March 1988, the disclosure that Riyadh had secretly purchased an unspecified number of CSS-2 medium-range missiles from China led to a diplomatic confrontation between Washington and Riyadh. The missiles had a range of 2,600 kilometers and were capable of carrying nuclear weapons. Washington was stunned that the Saudis had acquired the missiles and had kept the deal hidden for more than two years.

Throughout the 1990s, Saudi Arabia and the United States nonetheless managed to maintain a strong, albeit complex, relationship. In President Clinton's first year in office, the administration approved $13.4 billion in arms transfers (gifts and sales) to Saudi Arabia, Kuwait, Singapore, and Indonesia. As Iraq continued to threaten the international order, the United States maintained a presence in the Gulf and continually reassured Saudi Arabia of its support.

Although many observers expected the U.S.-Saudi relationship to solidify under President George W. Bush as a result of close ties between the Bush and Al Saud families, the relationship instead has been strained since September 11, 2001. This is the result of a combination of factors, including that fifteen of the September 11 hijackers were Saudi citizens and the kingdom's concerns about internal political threats from dissidents within its own borders. The Saudi government restricted the use of bases in Saudi Arabia during the U.S. wars in Afghanistan in 2001 and Iraq in 2003, a move that many U.S. politicians loudly denounced. By September 2003, all U.S. combat forces had been withdrawn from the kingdom and repositioned in Qatar.

Outlook

The attacks of September 11 and the ensuing U.S.-led war in Iraq clearly prompted a shift in Saudi Arabian foreign policy and forced the kingdom to focus more of its attention on internal dissidents and political and religious unrest. During the 1970s and 1980s, the Saudi royal family generated broad popular support with the help of prominent clerics and an unstated social bargain: the monarchy would use Saudi Arabia's immense oil wealth to provide Saudi citizens with a good living in return for tolerance of rule by the monarchy. Although recent increased revenues from high oil prices and an increase in production will allow the kingdom to continue many of its social programs and subsidies, the nation's demonstrated vulnerability to terrorist attacks makes clear that social programs and subsidies may not be enough to ensure stability.

Budget deficits from the late 1990s have been replaced with significant budget surpluses in recent years. The kingdom should continue its limited privatization efforts to secure additional foreign investment. Saudi Arabia will continue to be the driving force of OPEC, as it can influence oil production and pricing.

Security will remain the top priority for the kingdom. Saudi Arabia has spent billions of dollars enhancing its national and regional security by comprehensively upgrading its defense systems. In another respect, the withdrawal of U.S. troops from the kingdom is intended to provide security, by eliminating one of the critical factors cited by Osama bin Laden in his attacks against the monarchy. Statements by al-Qaida, however, indicate that this action alone is unlikely to halt the attacks on the kingdom.

Saudi Arabia undoubtedly will face significant political and economic challenges in the years ahead. As the situation in postwar Iraq continues to evolve and the Saudi government increases its efforts to combat internal terrorism, the monarchy will have to balance its actions between national security and self-preservation.

CHAPTER 17

SYRIA

Syria faces many challenges in the coming decades. Its young president, Bashar al-Asad, inherited from his father, Hafiz al-Asad, a closed and stagnant state and a set of foreign policy orientations difficult to maintain post–September 11. The former president, who died in June 2000, maintained political stability for more than two decades by ruling with an autocratic hand.

Syria's period of relative calm under Hafiz al-Asad followed more than two decades of intense political turmoil. Between 1946, when French soldiers withdrew and Syria became independent, and 1970, when Asad seized power, Syria experienced more than a dozen attempted and successful coups, including three in 1949 alone. Under Asad's leadership, Syria not only achieved domestic stability but also took a leading role in regional politics. These achievements, however, came at a price of limited political participation and abundant evidence of human rights violations.

Hafiz al-Asad, having won a February 1999 national referendum that gave him a fifth seven-year term as president, remained until his death firmly in control of Syria's destiny. The biggest challenge for Syria remains the nature of the regime. Despite modest political liberalization and releases of political prisoners in the late 1990s, the government remains highly centralized and authoritarian, buttressed by extensive domestic security forces. The government of Hafiz al-Asad never tolerated opposition. Bashar al-Asad has promised Syrians reform but "within continuity." Although reforms were highlighted at a Baath Party congress in June 2005, Syrians and

observers remained skeptical that much will change. Asad's initial attempts at reform met with opposition from the entrenched old guard and were scaled back. Five years after assuming the presidency, Bashar al-Asad continues to struggle with constructing coherent policies. To many observers, Syrian insistence on extending the term of the pro-Syrian Lebanese president in 2004 and the likelihood that Syria was involved in the assassination of former Lebanese prime minister Rafiq al-Hariri exemplify Asad's inexperience. With the consequent withdrawal of Syrian forces from Lebanon following massive protests by the Lebanese and international pressures, Asad may be able to focus on consolidating his power at home and distinguishing his tenure from his father's rule.

Geography and Demography

Syria is located at the eastern end of the Mediterranean Sea and shares borders with Turkey to the north, Iraq to the east, Jordan to the south, Israel to the southwest, and Lebanon to the west. It has a land area of 71,498 square miles, including the 500 square miles of the Golan Heights occupied since 1967 by Israel, which in 1981 unilaterally annexed it.

Syria is geographically divided into an inland plateau in the east and a much smaller coastal zone in which two mountain ranges enclose fertile lowland. A chain of low mountains crosses the inland plateau diagonally, extending from the mountainous Jabal Druze area in the southwest

Key Facts on Syria

Area: 71,498 square miles, including about 500 square miles occupied by Israel (185,180 square kilometers)

Capital: Damascus

Population: 18,448,752; includes 40,000 people living in the Israeli-occupied Golan Heights (2005)

Religion: Sunni Muslim, 74 percent; Alawite, Druze, and other Muslim sects, 16 percent; Christian,10 percent; tiny Jewish communities in Aleppo, Damascus, and al-Qamishli

Ethnic Groups: Arab, 90.3 percent Kurds, Armenians, and others, 9.7 percent

Official Language: Arabic; Kurdish, Armenian, French, Circassian, and English also spoken

Type of Government: nominal republic, but in reality authoritarian with domination by the Baath Party

GDP: $60.44 billion; $3,400 per capita (2004)

Source: Figures from Central Intelligence Agency, *CIA World Factbook,* 2005.

The coastal zone receives fairly plentiful rainfall, as the mountain ranges catch precipitation blown in from the Mediterranean. The barren desert regions of the southeast receive little rain. The 75 percent of the country that lies between these two regions has a semiarid climate.

Other than arable land, Syria's most important natural resources are low-grade phosphate deposits and small amounts of natural asphalt, rock salt, and construction materials, including sand, stone, gravel, and gypsum. Oil and gas production has provided the Syrian economy with a small but important boost since the 1970s. Syria's oil and gas deposits are quite small by regional standards and were late in being exploited. Oil was first discovered in 1956, but production began only in 1968. Larger fields were found in 1984. Syria also profited from two petroleum pipelines that cross its territory, transporting petroleum products to the Mediterranean from the oil-producing states bordering the Persian Gulf. *(See map, Chapter 5, p. 183)*

In Syria, as in neighboring Lebanon, demography has played a powerful role in shaping the country's political development. Syrians are mostly Arab (at least 90 percent) and Sunni Muslim (at least 74 percent). Ethnic minorities include Kurds (5 to 7 percent), Armenians (approximately 3 percent), and even smaller numbers of Assyrians, Circassians, and Turkomans. Religious minorities include several Islamic sects—the two most important being the Alawites and the Druze—as well as Greek Orthodox Christians, various other Christian sects, and a small number of Jews.

Political and national identification in Syria often overlaps with religious and ethnic affiliations. Because no single indigenous power was ever been able to control all of Greater Syria, and the Ottoman Empire did not try to forge a nonsectarian identity among its citizens, people in the area tended to identify closely with their city or region. This tendency left its mark on the modern nation of Syria, where religious and ethnic differences are often promoted as political identities, and identification with the tribe and sect may, in fact, supersede loyalty to the nation.

corner of the country to the Euphrates River, which flows diagonally from the mountains of Turkey across Syria to Iraq. South of these mountains, along the eastern portion of the Syrian-Jordanian border and the southern portion of the Syrian-Iraqi border, sits the Hamad desert region. The largest fertile area of Syria is known as Jazirah "island," which is northeast of the Euphrates and where modest amounts of oil also have been discovered. Syria's largest cities have histories as traditional centers of trade: Latakia, a major port, sits on the coastal plain, while Aleppo, Damascus, Hama, and Homs lie in fertile river plains.

About 50 percent of Syria's land is arable, but only about 31 percent is under cultivation. Syria is one of the few nations of the Middle East that still has unexploited arable land. Most of Syria's water is supplied by its rivers—80 percent from the Euphrates alone—and underground reservoirs.

Geography has also served as a fragmenting influence: Having two distinctive zones—the coastal plain and the interior plateau—separated by mountains and lacking navigable rivers reinforced Syrians' historical identification with their region and group. Discrimination on sectarian and ethnic grounds further forged sectarian and ethnic identification.

Although Alawites comprise less than 15 percent of the population, they represent a majority in the coastal province of Latakia; they are mostly poor farmers. Druze, who make up some 3 percent of the population and who have not accepted converts since the eleventh century, reside primarily in Jabal Druze, in the southwest corner of the country, the Golan Heights, and Damascus. Traditionally denied political influence by the Sunni majority and lacking means of advancement other than free military training during the French mandate, the Alawites and Druze flocked to the armed forces and to the secular Baath Party. When the Baath Party rose to power in the 1960s, the Alawites, who dominated the secret Baathist military apparatus within the Syrian army, gained disproportionate political influence. The Asad regimes have been Alawite-based, with the most sensitive posts in government and the army occupied by members of the sect.

The Alawite and Druze sects are offshoots of Shiite Islam, but their theologies diverge so sharply from mainstream Sunnism and Shiism that they are considered heretical by most Sunnis and Shiites. This has compounded the government's difficulties in dealing with Sunni fundamentalism.

Early History

The modern nation of Syria did not come into existence until the twentieth century, although the "notion" of Syria, or al-Sham in Arabic, has been in existence since at least the time of the Prophet Muhammad. The name *Syria,* used first by the Greeks, historically denoted the region at the eastern end of the Mediterranean lying between Egypt and Asia Minor. This larger region, generally called Greater Syria to distinguish it from the

nation-state that bears the name today, includes the present-day countries of Israel, Jordan, Lebanon, Syria, and the Palestinian territories and may also include Cyprus according to some experts. Greater Syria, located at the crossroads of three continents, possesses a rich and long history. It was an arena of conflict for centuries, serving as an invasion route for numerous armies and the battleground of neighboring empires. Waves of migration and invasion in ancient times and ever-changing religious and political leaders made Greater Syria a mosaic of ethnic and religious groups, which were often in conflict.

Damascus, one of the oldest continuously inhabited cities in the world, may have been settled as early as 2500 B.C.E. Over the centuries, it came to be dominated at one time or another by the Aramaean, Assyrian, Babylonian, Persian, Greek, Roman, Nabataean, Byzantine, and Ottoman civilizations. In 636 C.E. Damascus came under Muslim rule and rose to its peak of power as the capital of the Umayyad Empire, which stretched from India to Spain, lasting from 661 to 750.

After the decline of the Umayyads, Greater Syria became the prey of powerful neighboring states and empires in Anatolia, Egypt, and Mesopotamia. Religious conflict is an integral part of the history of the area. The Fatimid rulers of Egypt did much to spread Islam in Greater Syria, often by force. When the Christian crusaders arrived in the area to fight the Muslims, some local Christian groups provided aid, while others fought alongside Muslim armies. The support by segments of the local Christian communities for the European invaders created bonds between some Levantine and European Christians and may have led to animosity between Muslim and Christian inhabitants of Greater Syria. Damascus served as a provincial capital of the Mamluk Empire from 1260 until 1516, when the Ottoman Turks gained control of the region over which they would rule for four hundred years.

The Ottoman Empire was extraordinarily heterogeneous and included most of the lands of the eastern and southern Mediterranean coast. The Ottoman system permitted substantial autonomy not only for provincial governors but also for different religious groups as long as they paid their taxes to the Ottoman government. The system allowed each recognized religious community, or *millet,* to observe its own personal status laws and perform certain civil functions. Furthermore, the Ottoman government recognized the religious leaders of each sect as representatives of the sect, blurring political and sectarian divisions. The Ottomans' approach to governing thus accentuated the localism and communal separatism of Syria's assorted groups, perpetuating their identity with their own city or region rather than with a larger political entity.

By the nineteenth century, the Ottoman Empire had weakened, and European nations began to develop direct ties with minority groups in Greater Syria: the French with the Catholics, especially the Maronites of Mount Lebanon (the mountains near the coast of what is now Lebanon); the Russians with the Orthodox; and the British with the Protestants and the Druze.

Shortly after the turn of the twentieth century, Ottoman authorities, fearing the growth of Arab nationalism, clamped down on Greater Syria. Ottoman repression did not, however, succeed in quelling the Arab independence movement. Many

Syrians supported Sharif Hussein, also known as Hussein ibn Ali, the leader of Mecca in the Arabian Peninsula, in his efforts to achieve full Arab independence from Ottoman control. Hussein and Arab nationalists throughout the area believed that the British would back the establishment of independent Arab states in the eastern Mediterranean after the end of World War I in return for Arab military support against the Turks. In 1918 Faisal, Hussein's son, gained control of Damascus, taking advantage of international uncertainty and local popular Arab nationalist enthusiasm. By the end of the war and the Ottomans' collapse, an Arab administration was already functioning in Damascus and in the interior areas of what is now Syria. The British controlled Palestine, and the French controlled the Syrian coastal areas.

The victorious Europeans made conflicting promises concerning the future of the region. In 1915 Britain had assured Hussein that independent Arab entities would be established in parts of the former Ottoman Empire. This assertion was, however, contradicted on at least two accounts: The Sykes-Picot Agreement of 1916 between Britain and France—kept secret until 1917, when it was disclosed by the revolutionary communist government of Russia—divided Greater Syria between the British and French. Shortly thereafter, the 1917 Balfour Declaration promised British support for the establishment of a Jewish homeland in Palestine.

Although Syrian and Arab nationalists called in 1919 for an independent nation with Faisal as king, the 1920 San Remo Conference of the victorious allies placed the area that is now Syria and Lebanon under French control. French troops entered Damascus, and in 1922 the League of Nations formally recognized France's mandate over the area. The French ruled oppressively and divisively. They split the mandated area into regions that roughly corresponded to religious and ethnic groupings to discourage unified opposition to their rule. They also intended to create minisectarian states. Against the wishes of local non-Maronite inhabitants, the French enlarged Mount Lebanon—the heart of the Maronite Christian community, a group with strong historic ties to France—by adding to it the coastal cities and the Bekaa Valley to the east. This had the effect of increasing the area dominated by Maronites, but at the same time it diluted Maronite strength in the region, because it added Druze from the mountains and Muslims from the adjacent lands. Other areas of the mandate were also administered by the local dominant groups: Latakia by Alawites, Alexandretta by Turks, Jabal Druze by the Druze, and Aleppo and Damascus by Sunni Muslims.

France held negotiations with local Arab nationalists throughout the late 1920s, as European nations and inhabitants of the French mandate pressured France to discuss the future independence of the area. A major point of disagreement concerned the links between Mount Lebanon, Jabal Druze, Alexandretta, and the rest of the region. Arab nationalists insisted that the entire area under French control become independent as one nation, whereas the French were intent on protecting the autonomy of certain minority groups, especially the Maronites of Mount Lebanon. France further alienated local nationalists when it granted the area around Alexandretta—Iskandarun, known also as the Hatay province—to Turkey in 1939.

Syria finally achieved independence during World War II. When the Free French took control of Syria from Vichy government representatives in 1941, they promised independence in order to gain local support. They granted de jure independence in late 1941, and an elected government under President Shukri al-Kuwatly took power in 1943, the same year that neighboring Lebanon achieved independence. The last French soldiers were not, however, withdrawn until 1946, and even then only reluctantly.

Syrian Independence

Political instability and party factionalism characterized the first twenty-five years of Syrian independence, earning Syria the reputation as the Arab state most prone to military coups. Col. Husni al-Za'im, army chief of staff, overthrew the civilian government of President Kuwatly in March 1949 in a bloodless coup. Syria's poor military showing in the 1948 Arab-Israeli War, bickering among the members of the civilian government, and a weak economy prompted the insurrection. It is now known that the U.S. Central Intelligence Agency was behind this coup, which marked the beginning of more than twenty years of instability and military involvement in political affairs. The military's involvement gave minority groups disproportionately represented in the army greater power than the majority Sunnis and politicized the army, with harmful effects to its combat capability and credibility.

Syria's first military regime was toppled only four and a half months after taking power by another military grouping, which was itself overthrown in December 1949. The new regime, led by Lt. Col. Adib al-Shishakli, seemed relatively liberal during its first two years in power: A constitution was enacted in 1950, and a parliament was elected that permitted free speech, within limits. Rising opposition triggered repressive measures beginning in late 1951, however, and these steps resulted in February 1954 in Shishakli's overthrow, which led in turn to elections and other political transformations.

The next four years of democratic government saw frequent cabinet changes and the rapid growth of political parties, some with strong ideological bases, the most important of which was the Arab Socialist Resurrection Party, or the Baath Party. The Baath resulted from the merger in 1953 of two political groups with distinctive ideological objectives. From one group, led by Hama-based Akram al-Hawrani, the Baathists inherited a socialist orientation, although they explicitly rejected Marxism. From the other group, led by Sorbonne-educated Michel Aflaq and Salah al-Din al-Bitar, they inherited an emphasis on Arab unity and nationalism. Although the party recognized a connection between Arabism and Islam, the party was not based on Islamic solidarity. Baathism developed some appeal in other Arab countries, especially among teachers and army officers, and ultimately came to be the ruling ideology in Iraq as well. The Baath, working for the ultimate goal of Arab unity, could not, ironically, unite its two branches in Syria and Iraq, resulting in a factional split that became a divisive element in Syrian-Iraqi relations for many years.

The Syrian Baathists worked assiduously to build party support within the army, because democratic struggle was too cumbersome and its fruits too uncertain. The secular ideology of the party attracted many young officers of minority religious groups who feared Sunni political domination. Two other parties with strong ideological orientations, the Syrian Communist Party and the Syrian Social National Party, also sought to increase their power between 1954 and 1958. The Baathists gained representation in the cabinet for the first time in 1956 and soon began to accrue power disproportionate to their numbers.

By late 1957, the Baathists feared that the Communist Party was overtaking them in their efforts to control policy in Damascus. (U.S. officials exaggerated the communists' appeal at the time.) The appeal of the political Left in Syria grew not only because of the ineptitude of the democratic (albeit precarious) governments, but also because of the wave of anti-Westernism sweeping the Arab world in the late 1940s and 1950s. The creation of Israel in 1948 and the 1956 Suez crisis and war had accelerated opposition to the West. Egyptian president Gamal Abdel Nasser's appeals for Arab nationalism offered the Baathists an opportunity to salvage their faltering domestic position: They asked Nasser to establish a Syrian-Egyptian union.

Nasser had cracked down on communists in Egypt and could be expected to do the same in Syria if he agreed to a union. Although the Baathists knew that their own party would be restricted as well, they favored a union because they believed it would eliminate the threat from the far Left. Baathist officials miscalculated, however, when they assumed that they could control Nasser. In fact, the reverse occurred, with tragic results for the future of the party. Although Nasser was initially reluctant to form a union, because he never trusted the Baathist leaders and was nervous about ruling an unstable Syria, the United Arab Republic (UAR) was announced in February 1958.

The three-and-one-half-year union with Egypt proved to be unpleasant for Syrian politicians and were even more so for Syria's Baathist leaders. Nasser insisted on a complete merger, not a federation, so the much smaller Syrian nation was subsumed in the union. The religious leaders, landowners, and wealthy businesspeople comprising Syria's traditional political elite strongly opposed the union, and the Baathists soon came to regret the arrangement. In 1961 Nasser began to emphasize socialism, and Syria suffered a drought and an economic downturn. More important, Syria was being ruled by a heavy hand from Cairo, and the most senior positions in the Syrian government were held by individuals loyal to the Nasserist military intelligence apparatus. The head of Egyptian intelligence in Damascus was the strongest man in the country, while Baathist leaders held official positions but enjoyed no power. The Baath, ultimately, was forced to dissolve itself.

The union experience caused friction between Egypt and Syria and weakened, rather than strengthened, the bonds of Arab solidarity. Disaffected Syrian officers stationed in Egypt, many hailing from Druze, Ismaili, and Alawite backgrounds, began to form secret organizations. In this context, and amid the complaints of Syrian merchants unhappy with the scope and pace of socialist nationalizations, the coup of September 1961 brought to power in Damascus traditional political figures who immediately implemented Syria's secession from the union.

The September coup ushered in another period of confusion and instability in Syrian politics. Government succeeded government, and popular discontent grew as traditional Sunni politicians inside and outside the military proved incapable of providing stable leadership. In March 1963, the Baath Party, having regrouped and recovered from the forced experience of self-dissolution, reassumed power following yet another coup. Elements of the party have ruled Syria since. The party itself became an arena of political conflict, with civilian and military factions jockeying for power. This came to an end in 1970, when Hafiz al-Asad took control.

The Asad Dynasty

In July 1963, the Baathist regime had violently suppressed an attempted coup by Nasserist officers, marking a change in the relatively peaceful pattern of coups in Syria up to that point. Lt. Gen. Amin al-Hafiz became president and ruled for the next two and one-half years. In February 1966, a coup by Alawite officers, who had begun to organize in Cairo during the UAR, ushered in a period of civilian Baathist rule, although Gen. Salah Jadid was clearly the final arbiter of Syrian politics. Between 1966 and 1970, tension grew between the more radical wing of the Baath Party and the more pragmatic (military) wing. The militant leaders of the party, under Jadid, were ardent supporters of pan-Arabism and a people's liberation war on behalf of the Palestinians, while the military group led by air force lieutenant general Hafiz al-Asad, a forty-year-old Alawite, represented a more cautious approach and a less aggressive policy toward other Arab countries. In November 1970, Asad seized power in a bloodless coup.

During his first five years in office, Asad consolidated power domestically and strengthened ties abroad. Syria began to gradually emerge from the isolation created by years of domestic instability and militant foreign policy. Although Asad was careful to place loyal Alawite officers in key positions, especially in intelligence and the army, he also broadened the base of his regime by bringing various leftist elements into the government and reserving the prime ministership for a Sunni. As early as 1973, Sunnis demonstrated against the regime, but objections to the political domination of the Sunni majority by an Alawite minority did not become politically significant until the latter part of the 1970s, perhaps because most Syrians were relieved by the stability of the new regime and the relatively liberalized political atmosphere that Asad established during his early years in power. Most Syrians were simply exhausted after the turmoil of the 1960s, especially in the wake of the 1967 defeat by Israel.

The foreign policy of Asad's first five years brought improved relations with the Soviet Union, after some strain in late 1970; renewed diplomatic relations with several Western nations, including Great Britain in 1973 and the United States and West Germany in 1974; and friendly relations with most of the Arab states. Asad's cooperation with the Arabs reached its peak in the close coordination with Egypt that led to the October 1973 Arab-Israeli war. Despite Syria's failure to retake the Golan Heights, many Syrians regarded the war as a success because their troops performed well during the fighting and achieved some successes in the early phase, before the United States began its massive effort to bolster Israel's position.

In the mid-1970s, serious domestic and foreign problems began to plague Asad's regime. Political dissent, especially from disaffected Sunnis, became more violent, and Syria became politically and militarily entrenched in the Lebanese civil war.

Involvement in Lebanon

The involvement of Syrian troops after 1976 in the Lebanese civil war complicated every aspect of Syria's foreign policy. Syrian troops would eventually support virtually every faction in the Lebanese war at one time or another.

Since the beginning of Baathist domination in Syria in 1963, the concepts of Syrian nationalism and Arab nationalism have conflicted. Baathist ideology gives high priority to Arab nationalism. Although Asad's coup represented the victory of the less radical, more pragmatic wing of the party, Syria remained committed to the concept of Arab unity. The Palestinian conflict with Israel lies at the heart of Arab nationalism, and Syrian commitment to Arab nationalism therefore entailed strong support of the PLO. Syria's intervention in Lebanon highlighted the contradiction between these two threads of Syrian foreign policy and vastly complicated Asad's desire to maintain good relations with fellow Arab leaders and to play a leading role in the Arab world.

Syrian objectives in Lebanon are rooted in the history of Syria and Lebanon before their independence. As noted, in the 1920s the French added areas with Muslim majorities to the predominantly

Bashar al-Asad

Maronite Christian Mount Lebanon region, which was ruled separately from other parts of the mandate. Syrian nationalists viewed French policy as an unjustified division of one national entity, and Syrian governments never openly accepted the legitimacy of a separate Lebanon. Despite the close ties between the two states, Syria resisted establishing diplomatic relations with Lebanon, although migration, trade, and other forms of contact with it have continued throughout Syria's history. Some of the minority groups that make up the fractured Lebanese polity are also found in Syria.

Given these connections and the fragility of Lebanese governments, Syria had always sought to influence events in Lebanon. In the first half of the twentieth century and later, some Syrians even advocated annexing the country outright. Some Lebanese agreed, but Asad never desired such an outcome. Annexation of Lebanon, with its quarreling factions and bitter religious and political differences, might have destabilized Syria, dragging it into an unwanted confrontation with Israel, who Syrians feared would attempt to manipulate events there.

Asad's objective in Lebanon appears to have been the creation of a peaceful, compliant, and prosperous state with a weak, politically moderate central government dependent on Syria for its survival, a goal he had substantially, and juridically, achieved by 1990. It became important for the Syrian regime to exercise ultimate control over the Lebanese government to prevent Lebanon from being used as a base against Syrian national interests. Asad's intervention was motivated primarily by his desire to contain the PLO in order to avoid the radicalization of the country and the provocation of Israel. At the same time, however, Syria did not wish to permit Israel to insulate Lebanon from the responsibilities of the Arab-Israeli conflict.

After the war in 1970 between the Jordanian government and the Palestinians in Jordan, most PLO troops were displaced to Lebanon, the one Arab state adjacent to Israel where they could operate without being threatened by a strong government. The arrival of PLO troops upset the fragile balance of the Lebanese political system, and in April 1975 their presence served as a catalyst for civil war, the product of internal sectarian, socioeconomic, and political tensions and conflicts. The Lebanese people, divided along sectarian and ideological lines, disagreed over whether the Lebanese government should support PLO military activity from Lebanese territory. Furthermore, Maronite-oriented, right-wing militias had formed in the 1960s to prevent the redistribution of power and the reorientation of Lebanese foreign policy. At first Syria played a constructive role, receiving praise from other Arab states as well as the United States and France for its attempts to reconcile the warring factions.

By mid-1976, however, an alliance of the PLO and the Lebanese Left appeared on the verge of triumph over the conservative Christian Maronites and their allies. The prospect of a radical government in Beirut and a PLO unresponsive to Syrian control prompted Asad to send troops into Lebanon in June 1976 to prevent the collapse of the Maronite coalition. With the aid of Syrian forces, the Maronites, who through their political leadership had invited the Syrian forces, were able to stave off defeat, and the leftist-PLO coalition was forced to retreat.

Some Arab states, appalled at the sight of Syrian troops attacking the PLO and participating in Maronite assaults on Palestinian refugee camps, broke ties with Syria. By the end of 1976, a temporary halt in the fighting had been brokered, and Syria attained political and military supremacy in Lebanon. Saudi Arabia helped mediate a compromise under which an Arab peacekeeping force would patrol Lebanon to prevent violence, with the Syrian forces already present comprising the majority of the peacekeepers. Saudi Arabia and other Arab oil producers agreed to pay for most of the expenses incurred in maintaining Syria's troops in Lebanon.

This compromise allowed Syrian rapprochement with some of its Arab critics. The surprise 1977 visit of Egyptian president Anwar al-Sadat to Israel caused Arab governments angry with Egypt to reaffirm relations with Syria, which helped lead Arab opposition to Sadat's version of peace. Relations between Syria and the Lebanese Maronites cooled, as Asad improved relations with the PLO, the Lebanese Left, and other anti-Israeli (and anti-Sadat) forces in the Arab world. Although Asad had agreed to a U.S.-sponsored disengagement agreement with Israel in May 1974, he opposed Sadat's growing rapprochement with the United States as well as his willingness to accept a separate peace with Israel. Like other Arab states, Syria insisted on a comprehensive solution that would not leave any Arab lands under occupation.

Fearful of the new direction in Syrian policy, the Maronite-oriented militias under Bashir Gemayel by 1978 had begun to turn to Israel for aid, a circumstance Asad found threatening. Arab collective strength was further weakened by Iraqi president Saddam Hussein's 1980 declaration of war on Iran, a move that Asad interpreted as the withdrawal of yet another important Arab state from the collective struggle against Israel. As a result, Asad felt cornered in the region and became even more determined to control affairs in Lebanon.

When Israel invaded Lebanon in June 1982, Syrian forces in the Bekaa Valley suffered serious losses but refrained from engaging the Israeli forces in all-out confrontations. Asad had preached for years that Syria would not be dragged into an unwanted confrontation with Israel, which would have the upper hand. Although the Soviet Union quickly replaced Syrian weapons and military equipment lost during brief fighting, the damage to Syrian military prestige was substantial and underlined Syria's inability to use military means to reverse Israel's annexation of the Golan Heights. Asad's foreign policy problems were compounded by political dissent at home, which he violently suppressed. The opposition movement comprised a variety of leftist and Islamic-oriented groups and organizations, but only the Islamist opposition posed a serious threat.

Asad surprisingly rebounded from the lackluster performance of his troops in Lebanon in 1982. Taking advantage of the growing anti-Israeli mood in Lebanon following the invasion and growing opposition to the pro-U.S. regime of President Amin Gemayel, Asad supported a coalition of Lebanese and Palestinian forces working to drive Israeli and U.S. forces out of the country. By 1985 the powerless Gemayel government had abandoned a 1983 U.S.-brokered accord with Israel that Asad and the Lebanese opposition had rejected; the U.S. marines sent to Lebanon as part of an international peacekeeping force had withdrawn in disarray following the bombing of their barracks in October 1983; and Israel had withdrawn the bulk of its forces from Lebanon, leaving some units to occupy a self-declared "security zone" in the south on one-tenth of Lebanon's territory.

This resurgence of Syrian military and political power in Lebanon was soon, however, challenged, as Syrian forces again found themselves in conflict with the PLO and with pro-Iranian segments of the Shiite community. In early 1987, Syria increased its military contingent in Lebanon, in response to internecine warfare in West Beirut, and took over the Muslim section of the city. In early 1988, Syria tried to force the PLO out of Beirut by having Amal, the Shiite militia allied with Damascus, lay siege to the refugee camps where the PLO held sway. After three years of bloody fighting, Amal partially lifted the siege, and the PLO moved to the predominantly Sunni town of Sidon, on the southern coast of Lebanon. Although Syria controlled a small faction within the PLO, Arafat remained the ultimate power broker among the Palestinians in Lebanon. Bitterness tainted relations between the PLO and Asad and between pro-Iranian and pro-Syrian factions within the Shiite community.

Syria's conflict with the most important Maronite militia, the Lebanese Forces, was more straightforward. For Asad, the Lebanese Forces were reactionary, pro-Israeli diehards who stood in the way of his domination of internal Lebanese affairs. The Lebanese Forces regarded Asad as a relentless enemy who wanted to take over Lebanon and destroy Maronite hegemony in the country. In summer 1988, the Syrians failed in their attempt to force the rump Lebanese parliament to select as president the pro-Syrian Maronite and former president Sulayman Franjiyyah. They failed again in September to have elected another pro-Syrian Maronite, Michel Daher.

The deadlock ended with President Gemayel stepping down at the end of his term and naming Gen. Michel Aoun, the Christian commander of the armed forces, as head of government. Syria and those parties and personalities allied with it refused to accept Aoun's appointment and viewed Gemayel's last prime minister, Selim al-Hoss, as the official head of government. In early 1989, Aoun, after attempting to unify the Christian militias by ruthless force, challenged the Syrians directly by calling for the evacuation of all foreign forces and by bombarding Syrian-dominated West Beirut. He struck an alliance with the Iraqi regime

of Saddam Hussein, and the PLO smuggled arms to his movement. In response the Syrians bombarded Christian sections of Beirut and areas outside the capital.

Aoun, strengthened by Iraq's material assistance, resisted fiercely. Aoun and Asad—along with the many militias—made the spring and summer of 1989 perhaps one of the worst periods in Lebanon's fifteen years of civil war and violence. Although Aoun knew that he could not defeat the Syrians, he hoped that the situation would provoke international outrage over Syria's heavy-handed role and prompt foreign intervention leading to a Syrian withdrawal. He miscalculated, failing to grasp that with the decline of the Soviet Union, Western nations no longer viewed a consolidation of Syrian control in Lebanon as an advance for Soviet influence. Indeed, the Soviet Union and the United States, both desirous of avoiding involvement in the conflict, blessed a Saudi-sponsored Arab League initiative during 1989 to resolve the conflict at the regional level. In Taif, Saudi Arabia, in October 1989, the Saudi government convened a sufficient number of deputies from the Lebanese parliament to form a quorum and took the lead in mediating a settlement of the Lebanese crisis.

The October 22, 1989, Taif Accord, which was closely coordinated with Syria, recognized the existence of a special relationship between Syria and Lebanon. It prescribed that a reformed Lebanese government reconstituted under Syrian tutelage should negotiate the final withdrawal of Syrian forces. The agreement also redistributed political power in an attempt to bring about parity and equality in sectarian representation. Cornered, Aoun continued to resist the Syrian presence and the Taif agreement, which authorized Syria to oversee new presidential elections as a prelude to undertaking the further reforms agreed upon at Taif.

Meanwhile, Asad began reconstituting central authority in Lebanon, overseeing the election of René Muawwad as president in November 1989 and of Elias Hrawi three weeks later, after the car-bomb assassination of Muawwad, probably by forces loyal to Aoun. Syria's success marginalized Aoun, who fell to a combined force of Syrian and Lebanese soldiers in October 1990.

Asad's final move against Aoun coincided with the buildup of U.S.-led Western forces in Saudi Arabia to dislodge the Iraqi military from Kuwait. Courted by the United States, which wanted the broadest possible coalition against Iraqi president Saddam Hussein, Asad offered forces for the effort, cemented relations with other members of the coalition (especially Saudi Arabia), and got tacit acquiescence for a forcible resolution of affairs in Lebanon. This acquiescence was apparent when Syrian aircraft launched raids on Aoun's positions on the morning of October 13, 1990, and Israeli aircraft did not rise to meet them. By the end of the day, Aoun had fled to the French embassy in Beirut. He later moved to France. Further resistance to Syrian hegemony in Lebanon collapsed.

The death of Hafiz al-Asad changed the nature of Syrian involvement in Lebanon, as the taboo against opposition to Syrian authority began to crumble. In June 2001, a year after assuming office, Bashar al-Asad ordered the withdrawal of Syrian troops from Beirut in the wake of Lebanese criticism of the ongoing Syrian presence.

In 2004 rumblings began to be heard in Lebanon after the extension of the term of pro-Syrian president Emile Lahoud at the behest of Damascus and the continued presence of Syrian troops despite the withdrawal of Israeli forces from the south. Rejection of Syrian influence gained momentum when Druze leader Walid Jumblatt unexpectedly shifted course, declaring an alliance with the opposition and calling for the redeployment of Syrian forces to the Bekaa, a measure that was supposed to have taken place in 1992 according to the Taif agreement. The opposition also called for an end to the heavy-handed intervention in Lebanese affairs by the Syrian intelligence apparatus.

Asad attempted to improve relations by withdrawing some troops (and some intelligence services) from central Lebanon in late 2004. Syrian-Lebanese relations took a dramatic turn in February 2005 with the bombing assassination of former Lebanese prime minister Rafiq al-Hariri in Beirut. Hariri, a former Syrian ally, had recently joined the chorus calling for a Syrian withdrawal, and his killing was widely viewed as a message from Syria to its most vocal opponents.

The assassination galvanized the Lebanese as nothing had in recent memory, bringing them together daily in large demonstrations and rallies. Damascus continued to enjoy support among some Lebanese groups, particularly in the Shiite community, but a precarious alliance of Christian and Druze elements (plus Sunni deputies loyal to the deceased prime minister) prominently expressed Lebanese demands for a withdrawal. France, the United States, and the United Nations pressed the case internationally.

Syria, atypically, could not muster the support of other Arabs to overcome its international isolation. When the Saudi government publicly called for the withdrawal of Syrian troops, Asad knew that he must comply. In a speech delivered to the parliament in March 2005, he conceded that Syrian forces in Lebanon had "made mistakes" and that he would withdraw them to the Bekaa, as per the Taif agreement.

Despite widespread expectations that Asad would manage to somehow stop short of a full military evacuation, to much surprise, the last Syrian troops left Lebanon at the end of April 2005—a little more than two months after the Hariri assassination and twenty-nine years after intervening during the civil war. The United Nations certified the withdrawal in late May 2005. Opinions varied over whether the Asad regime had completely dismantled its intelligence apparatus in the country.

Even with the troop withdrawal, it is not a foregone conclusion that Syria will lose all influence in Lebanon. It still has supporters among the Lebanese, and deep divisions and conflicts ensure the continuation of some degree of Syrian influence.

The Syrian Economy

A significant turnaround in the Syrian economy accompanied Hafiz al-Asad's Lebanon policy. In part, this change arose from reforms Asad began to adopt in the mid-1980s. Because of the decline and then collapse of socialist regimes in Eastern Europe, Asad inaugurated a gradual economic liberalization program aimed at reversing some of the socialist policies that had prevailed since the Baath took power in 1963. Many observers of economic change in Syria have focused on Law Ten, promulgated in May 1991 and aimed at encouraging private investment. By late 1992, more than 735 private ventures valued at nearly $2 billion had been established.

The deadening effect of a large bureaucracy had contributed to an economic and foreign exchange crisis. Furthermore, Asad's foreign policies had alienated some potential Arab and non-Arab foreign aid providers. Centralized economic planning had suppressed agricultural production as well as industrial development. In response, Asad reduced consumer subsidies, devalued the national currency, relaxed central control of agriculture, and granted greater freedom for individuals and private companies to participate in international trade. By 1989 Syria had achieved a balance-of-trade surplus of $1.2 billion, the first such surplus in more than thirty years.

Some of this surplus derived from earnings on a commodity relatively new to Syria—oil. By the late 1980s, Syria was beginning to benefit from new, light high-quality crude oil discovered in the northeastern part of the country in 1984. Although Syria's oil deposits are only a fraction of the size of those of the oil-rich Arab states, the discovery freed Syria from having to expend foreign exchange earnings on oil imports. By 1993 production had reached more than 500,000 barrels a day, about half of which was exported, with estimated earnings of more than $2 billion for the year.

Asad's strategic shift in late 1990, when he sided with the Western alliance against Iraq, also had a positive economic dimension. Following the conflict, the Gulf states collectively pledged $10 billion in development funds for those Arab countries that had supported the victorious alliance. Although they subsequently reduced this figure, by 1993 Syria reportedly had received $1.5 billion for investment in its economic infrastructure.

As a result of these developments, Syria experienced significant economic growth in the early 1990s. As is often the case in developing countries, in Syria growth in the private sector increased income differentials. Although shops filled with goods that previously had been unavailable, only a small fraction of the population could afford to buy them. As many as 65 percent of all Syrians were estimated to have fallen below the poverty line. Many such people were public sector workers and landless peasants—historically important bases of support for the Baath.

A population growth rate of 3.4 percent compounded Syria's rising poverty. Moreover, nearly 60 percent of Syrians were under the age of twenty, making the population nonproductive economically and placing heavy demands on the state for education, health care, and future employment. In the 1990s, Syria also contended with a huge foreign debt left over from the 1980s.

A recession at the end of the 1990s wiped out the modest prosperity of the mid-1990s. In the early 2000s, Syria's economy continued to expand at a slow rate of growth. According to U.S. government statistics, Syria's gross domestic product rose by a slight increase to 2.3 percent in 2004. No reliable unemployment figures are available, but the government reported unemployment at 10 percent in 2002, while unofficial estimates cited a figure of 20 percent.

Funding from Gulf nations decreased as those states increased defense expenditures to prepare against possible instability and for military action after the attacks of September 11, 2001, and the U.S.-led wars in Afghanistan and Iraq. The 2003 invasion and occupation of Iraq additionally caused some disruption within the Syrian economy and also resulted in the stoppage of subsidized oil from Iraq. Syria's own oil production is thought to have leveled off at some 500,000 barrels per day, though it may increase if new concessions lead to new discoveries and foreign investment in the petroleum industry. A new natural gas facility was opened in 2000.

In an attempt to improve Syria's economic fortunes, President Asad flew to Russia in January 2005 and obtained forgiveness for some three-fourths of the debt—an estimated $10 billion to $13 billion—that Syria owed the former Soviet Union.

The Asad government has been inconsistent in its pace and implementation of economic reforms. In 2001 it legalized private banking, and in 2003 it approved three private banks. The government also removed a number of import-export restrictions, liberalized the investment law, and reworked tax regulations, in part to satisfy the requirements of an association agreement negotiated with the European Union in 2004 for economic (and political) cooperation.

Bringing corruption and the system of patronage under control will be necessary to the successful implementation of any long-lasting economic reform. Bashar al-Asad pledged to fight corruption, but he has faced and will likely continue to face opposition to such efforts by those who benefited under the old regime.

Subtle Political Change

Hafiz al-Asad did not match his more liberal economic policies in the 1990s with even a commensurate degree of political liberalization. His regime remained highly centralized and authoritarian, based on the extensive deployment of security and intelligence forces throughout the country and on the promotion of a cult of personality. Nevertheless, Asad did try to adapt to changing circumstances with a subtle shift in political strategy. Gradually, he moved from a reliance on his traditional base of support—the rural and urban working classes—to a closer relationship with the emerging Damascene mercantile class, the principal beneficiary of the new, liberal economic policies.

This change was apparent in the electoral process that returned Asad to office as president in December 1991 and again in 1999 with (on both occasions) 99.98 percent of the vote. In the run-up to the 1999 election, the Baath Party played virtually no role. Instead, Asad presented himself as a populist candidate representing Syrians, rather than as the heroic leader of an ideological vanguard party representing the interests of the

oppressed in society. He promoted mass demonstrations by people from within and outside the party and rallied the support of professional associations.

In the parliamentary elections that preceded those for the presidency, Asad similarly diminished the stature of the Baath Party by declining to convene a congress prior to the election and by reserving 80 of the 250 seats in the Peoples' Assembly for nonparty independents. Although the electoral process remained structured so that the party controlled by Asad would maintain control of the chamber, the fairly open and unprecedented competition for the 80 nonparty seats added a new democratic dimension to Syrian political life. The elections brought to prominence a number of people who ran on a platform of eliminating corruption from the government and bureaucracy. The new deputies constituted a bloc that not only benefited from Asad's changed economic policies but also constituted a potential lobby for further changes. Their minority status, however, guaranteed that in the short run their influence would be limited. The regime also tolerated some parliamentary and media criticism of the government, though never of itself or of Asad.

Bashar al-Asad has thus far been cautious in moves toward political liberalization. Because of the high degree of political instability that had plagued Syria before Hafiz al-Asad took power, some analysts speculated that the country would fall into chaos after his passing. Contrary to such concerns, however, the transition from father to son transpired rather smoothly.

The new president was immediately faced with trying to strike a balance between placating the old guard—the longtime close allies of his father who were likely to resist political liberalization—and the Syrian populace, who it was said, hoped that the younger Asad would usher in a new era of openness and relaxation. Asad quickly moved to staff key positions with his own people—a relatively young generation of technocrats referred to as the "new guard"—while being careful not to make enemies of the old guard, who would fight any actions that might diminish their hold on power.

Asad allowed some privatization of the press and education, though with tight controls from above. Syrians felt emboldened enough to speak out in public forums against the government and to sign petitions calling for more openness and political participation. The Internet served as another vehicle for expressing dissent. This short period of optimism—the Damascus spring—lasted from summer 2000 to spring 2001, when in the face of public pressure for more reform, the state retreated. Several key would-be reformers were arrested on trumped-up charges, some as recently as April 2005.

In March 2004, violence between Kurds and Arabs in the northeastern part of the country caught the government off guard. It began in Qamishli when clashes erupted at a soccer match between supporters of opposing teams, one of which was largely Kurdish, and security forces moved in, killing at least 36 people. Rioting and protests soon spread to other areas of the country, evolving into a general expression of Kurdish dissatisfaction with their lack of civil and political rights. Thousands were arrested over the course of several weeks. A short time later, Asad publicly stated his intent to address some of the Kurds' grievances, such as citizenship for Syria's estimated 150,000 Kurds who have been denied the right since the mid-1960s.

Although rumblings of dissent and debate continue, the Syrian opposition—consisting mainly of leftists and nationalists, the Kurdish minority, and the outlawed Muslim Brotherhood—remains fragmented and incapable of speaking with a strong voice. The government continues to forbid political parties based on sectarianism.

Joining the Peace Process

In July 1991, Hafiz al-Asad surprised the international community by responding positively to the joint U.S.-Soviet invitation requesting Israel and its Arab neighbors to convene negotiations in Madrid aimed at resolving the Arab-Israeli conflict. Syria's participation in the coalition that defeated Iraq in the 1991 Persian Gulf War and its agreement to hold talks with Israel marked a significant departure for Syrian foreign policy.

Syrian goals in the Arab-Israeli conflict had long been twofold: to lend support to the Palestinian cause and, since the June 1967 War, to recover the Golan Heights from Israel. In pursuit of these goals, Asad, since 1973, had held steadfastly to three key policy positions: that any Arab-Israeli negotiation should take place under UN sponsorship, whereby Soviet and developing world support could be expected to buttress the Arab negotiating position; that only a joint Arab delegation representing a common position should negotiate directly with Israel; and that Israel should withdraw from the territories it occupied in 1967, as demanded in UN Security Council Resolutions 242 and 338, as a precondition for the start of negotiations.

Meanwhile, conscious that these conditions were unacceptable to Israel, Asad pursued a policy of achieving "strategic parity" with the Jewish state in an effort to develop a position of relative strength from which to possibly negotiate. As Syria worked to improve its military strength through its relationship with the Soviet Union, however, its diplomatic position weakened. Syria's controversial and often unpopular policies toward the PLO and Lebanon, its support of Iran in the Iran-Iraq War, and its deepening reliance on the Soviet Union undercut its position in the Arab world and isolated the regime in the region, especially as Saddam Hussein, Asad's bitter enemy, emerged as a regional power broker in the 1980s.

By 1990 the efficacy of the military track had sharply declined because of the impending collapse of the Soviet Union. Meanwhile, Iraq's invasion of Kuwait in August gave Syria an alternative approach. Syria's participation in the anti-Iraq coalition led to a renewed alliance with Egypt and Saudi Arabia and to much improved relations with the United States and other Western countries. Asad could now consider achieving by diplomatic means those same objectives that he had failed to attain by military means.

In agreeing to attend the Madrid peace conference in 1991, Asad compromised significantly on a number of issues—namely, that the talks be held under UN auspices and that Israel withdraw from the Golan Heights as a precondition for negotiations. The Syrian position that the Arabs should negotiate as one delegation was finessed by an agreement among various Arab parties—Jordan, Lebanon, Syria, and the PLO (although Israel did not yet recognize a role for the PLO)—to coordinate their positions between each round of the Arab-Israeli talks. On other key issues—that the Palestinians should achieve their "legitimate national rights" and that Israel should withdraw entirely from the Golan Heights—Asad remained adamant.

By late summer 1993, eleven Arab-Israeli negotiating sessions deriving from Madrid had been held in Washington, and the formula of bilateral talks between Israel and its Arab neighbors, long detested by the Syrian government, had prevailed. The control Syria exercised over the Lebanese negotiating team boosted Syria's negotiating stance. The participants made little progress on substantive issues, but some observers had predicted a breakthrough between Israel and Syria. Israel, now led by Prime Minister Yitzhak Rabin, indicated that compromise on the Golan Heights was possible, and Asad made it known that a "liberated" Golan could remain demilitarized.

In late August, it was announced that secret PLO-Israeli talks had culminated in an agreement to be signed in Washington on September 13, 1993. This Gaza and "Jericho First" agreement could not be, and was not, condemned outright by Syria. Asad did, however, criticize the PLO for failing to coordinate its moves with other members of the Arab negotiating group and also expressed skepticism concerning the wisdom of an agreement that would divert attention from the issues of the Golan Heights and south Lebanon. Indeed, from Syria's perspective, the agreement derailed the joint Arab negotiating process in which it was the key player. It weakened Asad's ability to obtain through negotiation a return of the Golan Heights on his terms. Syrian spokesmen continued to announce, however, their government's commitment to an eventual, comprehensive settlement of the Arab-Israeli conflict.

During 1994 Syria and Israel engaged in sporadic but serious negotiations through the shuttle diplomacy of U.S. secretary of state Warren Christopher. The conclusion in July of an agreement ending the state of war between Jordan and Israel left Syria as the last major frontline Arab nation in a state of war with Israel. Asad and Rabin recognized that it would be in their best mutual interests to conclude an agreement, so both offered genuine proposals for resolving the Golan Heights issue. Israel reportedly agreed, in principle, to a phased withdrawal from the Golan in conjunction with an internationally guaranteed demilitarization of the area. Rabin's assassination in 1995 and the election of the right-wing government of Benjamin Netanyahu brought the process to a standstill.

Ehud Barak, Netanyahu's successor in 1999, took a different path, pursuing the Syria track, some argued, to the point of ignoring Israeli relations with the Palestinians. Asad—thinking Barak was willing to make a deal, picking up where he and Rabin left off—agreed to meet President Bill Clinton in Geneva in 2000 to discuss an Israeli withdrawal from the Golan. Clinton attended hoping to urge Asad to accept Israeli retention of some Syrian lands, specifically Lake Tiberias, its shoreline, and a road around it. Asad reiterated his long-held position of a complete withdrawal to the 1967 borders.

Bashar al-Asad has affirmed on several occasions his willingness to enter into negotiations with Israel but refuses to begin from scratch, as the Israelis had indicated was their preference. Asad instead wants negotiations to build on the past progress made between the administration of his father and that of the Rabin government. His father, of course, had been in a much stronger position given his domestic consolidation of power, while Bashar continues to work to consolidate his power.

While publicly expressing a willingness to negotiate with Syria, the Israeli government did not seem much interested in actual talks, believing Syria's new president too weak to deliver a deal. Meanwhile, Israel under Prime Minister Ariel

Sharon pressured Syria on other matters, sometimes through the United States and at other times directly. In the run-up to the U.S.-led invasion of Iraq, Israel accused Damascus of hiding Iraqi chemical and biological weapons and missiles. Syria refuted the charges, and no definitive evidence has emerged to the contrary.

Israel also threatened to bomb sites inside Syria if the government allowed Palestinian factions to operate from Damascus, and the Syrian government consequently put pressure on the PLO and other Palestinian factions to cease their military as well as media activities in the country. Syrian action followed an Israeli air strike near Ayn al-Sahib, north of Damascus, in October 2003 on what Israel claimed was a training camp used by Hamas and Islamic Jihad, the latter of which earlier had claimed responsibility for a suicide attack that killed nineteen people. Syria charged that the attack was on a civilian area, and the Popular Front for the Liberation of Palestine claimed that the facility was one of its bases but that it had been abandoned years prior. Reports noted that locals used the area for social activities. Islamic Jihad denied that it trained in Syria.

U.S. Pressures

Although Syria managed to escape its regional isolation of the 1980s and ally itself with Egypt and Saudi Arabia, the two Arab countries that dominated regional politics following the 1991 Persian Gulf War, the stalemate of the peace process left the regime frustrated and unable to capitalize on its new ties with the United States. The government of Hafiz al-Asad had hoped in part by cultivating closer relations with the West to gain concessions from Israel.

The 2003 U.S. invasion of Iraq significantly altered U.S.-Syrian relations. After the attacks of September 11, Damascus received praise from the United States for agreeing to exchange information on terrorism and cooperating in the interrogation of terror suspects. Syrian actions appeared to indicate that it shared an interest in combating al-Qaida, though not necessarily that it supported or

agreed with U.S. policy in the region. Relations took a turn for the worse as the United States geared up to overthrow Saddam Hussein, and Syria opposed the plan to invade Iraq.

The Syrian government feared that the United States had designs to invade Syria as well, as U.S. officials ratcheted up their rhetoric during and after the invasion. U.S. officials in 2002 listed Syria as part of the so-called axis of evil and referred to it as a rogue state, which many interpreted as an implicit threat of "regime change." Undersecretary of State John Bolton also accused Damascus of attempting to develop weapons of mass destruction, which Damascus denied, and the administration continued to complain that Syria aided and abetted Hizballah in Lebanon and harbored radical Palestinians set on committing acts of violence against Israel.

The rise of the Iraqi insurgency and the challenges that the U.S. military faced in Iraq diminished Syrian fears, but they did not reduce U.S. economic and political pressures. Syria did not publicly support the insurgency, but the United States accused it of failing to seal its borders to infiltrators joining the resistance and of allowing pro–Saddam Hussein Baathists and alleged terrorists to operate from its territory.

To put pressure on Syria, in December 2003 Congress passed the Syria Accountability Act, which had been introduced initially in 2002 and the administration had tried to squelch. This time President George W. Bush signed the legislation threatening to impose economic and political sanctions while attempting to distance himself from it by indicating that he might waive implementation of some of its provisions on national security grounds. The measure called for Syria to halt all support to terrorists, withdraw its troops from Lebanon, cease development and procurement of weapons of mass destruction and long-range ballistic missiles, and prevent insurgents and weapons from entering Iraq across its border.

Bush announced the imposition of sanctions in May 2004, calling Syria a threat to the United States and accusing it of supporting terrorism, impeding the stabilization and reconstruction of

Iraq, continuing to occupy Lebanon, and pursuing weapons of mass destruction. He banned flights between the United States and Syria, froze some Syrian assets held in the United States, and halted non-humanitarian exports to Syria.

In September 2004, following the Syrian demand to extend the term of President Lahoud, the United States and France introduced Security Council Resolution 1559, which called for free and fair presidential elections in Lebanon, disarmament of all militias in the country, and the withdrawal of all foreign forces. France's role in the resolution particularly surprised the Syrian government.

The regime shortly thereafter redeployed troops from the outskirts of Beirut and assumed a lower profile in an attempt to escape additional sanctions. It also cooperated at least partially with U.S. forces to prevent insurgents from crossing into Iraq.

Following the Hariri assassination, U.S.-Syrian relations reached a new low, with the United States withdrawing its ambassador indefinitely in February 2005. A few months later, in May, the Bush administration stepped up its rhetoric, accusing Syria of not doing enough to prevent infiltration into Iraq. Shortly thereafter, Syria announced that it had halted all military and intelligence cooperation with Washington. The two nations remained, however, in "diplomatic contact."

Outlook

Syria is not the complete master of its own destiny, given the context of the larger, turbulent region in which it sits. Its influence and role in the Middle East historically has ebbed and flowed in reaction to events and developments in the area. There is little reason to doubt that the future will be any different.

Much in Syria, however, will depend on the type of regime Bashar al-Asad creates. Although he proved himself to be skillful at building a power base among the youth of a rejuvenated Baath Party, a task he accomplished while being groomed for the presidency, his ability to control the powerful military-intelligence apparatus remains in doubt.

In appointing new faces, he retired or otherwise removed scores of top political and security officials and hundreds of military personnel, but it is not clear that he actually rules Syria by himself. His brother-in-law and his brother Mahir play important roles in the regime, but some of the old guard continue to be influential.

Speculation continues concerning the pace of political and economic reforms the government will allow and their extent. Reforms under the new regime proceeded in fits and starts until ultimately being squelched. After dashing Syrians' initial high hopes, Asad appointed Muhammad Naki al-Utari as prime minister in October 2003 and later promised a new round of reforms to be announced in mid-2005. In its first few years the regime reportedly released around 600 political prisoners and granted amnesty to some 100 dissidents, but many more were reported to remain in jail. In 2005 reform-minded Syrians complained of ongoing harassment and arrest of vocal opposition members. With a high birth rate and the majority of the population under twenty years of age, pressures are likely to increase on the system as demands on state resources grow.

Bashar al-Asad has repeatedly expressed his willingness to reach a settlement with Israel, but talks appear unlikely in the immediate future with the increase in U.S. pressure on Syria following its invasion of Iraq and Israeli perceptions that a deal is not possible because of the weakness of the Syrian regime. Assuming negotiations do resume at some point, Asad cannot compromise too much on what Syrians see as the key issues—the Golan Heights and the legitimate rights of the Palestinians—without jeopardizing his legitimacy.

U.S. pressure on Syria will likely continue, especially concerning matters related to alleged Syrian assistance to the insurgency in Iraq. To counter the United States, Asad is hoping that Russia will emerge as a sponsor or as a major actor in the Middle East. In February 2005, Russia announced its intention to sell Syria anti-aircraft defense missile systems.

In late May 2005, Syria test-fired three Scud missiles, one of which broke up and fell as debris over Turkey. The operation was the first Syrian missile test since 2001. Observers speculated that the Syrians timed the test to coincide with Lebanese parliamentary elections and as a show of defiance toward the United States and United Nations.

The Asad government is also working to improve relations with neighboring Turkey and the European Union. In 1998, under Turkish pressure, Syria expelled from Lebanese territory Abdallah Ocalan, the leader of the Kurdish Workers' Party, and after decades of cool relations, in January 2004 Bashar al-Asad became the first Syrian leader to visit Turkey. Syria is dependent on water from the Euphrates River, which originates in Turkey, and needs to work with Turkey on irrigation and water-sharing issues. If the association agreement with the European Union is signed and ratified, Syria can expect not only economic co-operation, but also financial and technical assistance.

CHAPTER **18**

YEMEN

In the early 2000s, the stability of unified Yemen, formerly North Yemen (the Yemen Arab Republic, YAR) and South Yemen (the People's Democratic Republic of Yemen, PDRY), appears no longer to be in question. Rather, Yemen faces the daunting tasks of shoring up a struggling economy, developing stronger relations with its Middle Eastern neighbors, and juggling its society's empathy with al-Qaida with its desire to garner favor from the United States as a means of encouraging investment.

After the suicide attack on the USS *Cole* in the port of Aden in 2000, Yemen experienced considerable uncertainty as the United States began to take notice of al-Qaida's presence in Yemen. The Yemeni government's decision to support the Bush administration's "war on terror" allowed the country to receive much-needed U.S. assistance. Yemen likely will continue to cooperate with U.S. efforts to combat terrorism as it struggles to further advance its economic development and to acquire more foreign investment.

Yemen continues to promote economic restructuring programs to strengthen its international standing. It has made some progress politically, holding more open parliamentary elections and creating a bicameral legislature. The submission of its territorial dispute with Eritrea to international arbitration and the resolution of its disputed boundary with Saudi Arabia have improved Yemen's image vis-à-vis its geographic neighbors.

Geography

With a total area of 203,849 square miles, Yemen is approximately twice the size of the state of Wyoming. It occupies the southwestern corner of the Arabian Peninsula, bordered by the Red Sea to the west, the Arabian Sea to the south, Oman to the east, and Saudi Arabia to the north and northeast. It also controls the small, strategic Perim Island in the Bab al-Mandab Strait and the much larger island of Socotra in the Gulf of Aden. Yemen's once poorly defined borders had, over the years, led to armed conflict with its neighbors as well as between the YAR and PDRY.

The country is divided roughly into four ecosystems: a semidesert coastal plain called the Tihamah, which stretches along the Red Sea coast and extends inland for about forty miles; a chain of highlands and mountains in the interior; the edges of the vast, sandy desert known for being one of the least hospitable places on Earth, the Empty Quarter, or Rub al-Khali; and the Wadi Hadramawt, the fertile valley in the eastern part of the former South Yemen.

The mix of heat and humidity makes the coast uncomfortable, and in the interior summer temperatures soar to around 130 degrees Fahrenheit. Although only 6 percent of the country's land is considered arable, abundant rainfall makes the interior highlands of the north one of the most important agricultural areas on the Arabian Peninsula. In the southern region, only scant and irregular rains fall from the tail end of the Indian monsoons, severely

Key Facts on Yemen

Area: 203,849 square miles (527,970 square kilometers)

Capital: San'a'

Population: 20,727,063 (2005)

Religion: Muslim; small numbers of Christians, Hindus, and Jews

Ethnic Groups: predominantly Arab; some Afro-Arabs, Europeans, and South Asians

Official Language: Arabic

Type of Government: republic

GDP: $16.25 billion; $800 per capita (2004)

Source: Central Intelligence Agency, *CIA World Factbook,* 2005.

limiting agriculture and forcing southern Yemen to subsist heavily on fishing and nomadic herding.

San'a', the capital of the former YAR, is Yemen's largest city and now serves as the capital of the republic. Aden, once one of the busiest and most significant ports in the world, was the capital of the former PDRY and is now the economic and commercial capital of unified Yemen.

Demography

Yemen's population is estimated at close to 21 million, according to 2005 figures, making it the second most populous nation on the Arabian Peninsula, after Saudi Arabia. Its population is growing rapidly, at a rate of 3.45 percent annually. Arabic is spoken nearly everywhere, although some people in the extreme eastern part of the country continue to speak a pre-Arabic dialect.

Ethnically, Yemenis pride themselves on being primarily Qahtani, or southern Arabs, those with the most ancient roots, as opposed to Adnani, or northern Arabs. Most of the population is Muslim, and in the former North Yemen the Muslims fall into two principal groups of almost equal size: the Zaydis, a Shiite sect predominantly in the northern mountain areas, and the Shafi'is, a Sunni sect located primarily in the south and along the coastal plain. The Zaydi-Shafi'i division has plagued Yemen throughout its history and continues to be a major obstacle to the country's political stability and development. The political and military dominance of the Zaydis have sustained the tension between the two groups. Historically, Yemen had a significant Jewish minority, tracing its roots back to biblical times, that was fully integrated into Yemeni society. A majority of the Jews have since emigrated to Israel, and as a result, the Yemeni Jewish culture has largely disappeared.

The most important demographic element in Yemen is the tribe. In the north, tribes remain the dominant social structure and play a pivotal role in contemporary politics. In the south, in the former PDRY, despite efforts by the ruling communists to dismantle the tribal establishment, the tribes reemerged with the collapse of communism and once again are the dominant political and social force.

Life expectancy in Yemen is about sixty-one years, and the illiteracy rate is approximately 50 percent. Education and health services, confined to Yemen's urban centers, are woefully inadequate. Malnutrition and poverty are rampant in the hinterlands of the south, where the lack of basic services and facilities, small and dispersed communities, and rugged terrain have hindered development. Yemen's infant mortality rate is 6.3 percent, one of the highest in the world.

Yemen's human resources are greatly underdeveloped. More than half of the workforce is engaged in agriculture. Less than one-fourth of the population is occupied in services, construction, industry, and commerce. Many of the remaining workers provide unskilled labor to the labor-poor, capital-rich countries of the Arabian Peninsula, such as Saudi Arabia and the United Arab Emirates. The wages paid to these workers have provided a steady capital inflow that, along with foreign aid, has been vital to the country's economic stability.

History

The territory of Yemen, known to the ancient Arabs as al-Yaman, was once divided into kingdoms and enclaves of various sizes. Strategically poised at the junction of major trading routes between Africa and India and endowed with an abundance of fertile land, Yemen's ancient kingdoms grew prosperous and powerful. Among Yemen's centers of civilization was the fabled Kingdom of Saba, ruled by the Queen of Sheba of biblical fame.

Around 1000 B.C.E., the Kingdom of Saba was a great trading state with a major agricultural base supported by a sophisticated system of irrigation, at the heart of which was the large Marib dam. In the north of Yemen, the Kingdom of the Mineans arose, coexisting with Saba and maintaining trading colonies as far away as Syria. During the first century B.C.E., the Kingdom of Himyar was established, reaching its greatest extent and power in the fifth century C.E. Christian and Jewish kings were among its leaders.

The growth of the Roman Empire was largely responsible for the decline of pre-Islamic civilization in Yemen. New trade routes established by Europeans bypassed the old caravan trails, and the Yemeni frankincense trade died, as Christian Romans did not use the resins in their funeral rituals as had pagans. By the sixth century C.E., the Marib dam had collapsed, symbolizing the political disintegration in southern Arabia that helped pave the way for the followers of Islam, who captured Yemen in 631 C.E.

When members of the Shiite sect split from the mainstream Sunnis in what is today Iran and Iraq, large numbers of persecuted Shiites fled, during the eighth and ninth centuries, to the highlands of northern Yemen. Claiming descent from the Prophet Muhammad, one of their leaders proclaimed himself imam and in about 897 C.E. established the Rassid dynasty, which espoused Zaydism. The Rassid dynasty produced 111 imams before it was uprooted in the 1962 revolution.

In the sixteenth century, the Ottoman Turks captured the Yemeni plains and the port of Aden, but a young Zaydi imam led a successful resistance, forcing the Ottomans to conclude a truce and eventually leave Yemen in 1636. One of his successors unified the mountains and plains into a single state extending to Aden, with the northern

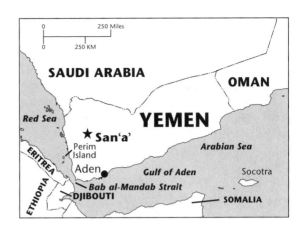

city of San'a' as its capital, but war and chaos soon returned to Yemen. In 1728 the sultan of the southern province broke from the Zaydi regime, thus creating the division between north and south that prevailed until 1990.

The Ottoman sultan in Constantinople continued to claim suzerainty over all of Yemen, but his control was tenuous. The Turkish administration of Yemen officially came to an end after the Ottomans' defeat in World War I. The Zaydi imam Yahya Hamid al-Din was left in control of the coastal areas of the north that were evacuated by the Turks. He subsequently tried to consolidate his control over all of northern Yemen, but his efforts were opposed by the British and their local protégés in the south and by the Saudis in the north. The 1934 Saudi-Yemeni Treaty of Taif temporarily settled one war between Yemen and Saudi Arabia. It was a humiliating defeat for Imam Yahya, but through the benevolence of the Saudi king, he remained in control of much of northern Yemen.

In the early 1900s, the port of Aden gradually became a major international fueling and bunkering station between Europe, South Asia, and the Far East, due to the building of the Suez Canal and the development of large steamships in the nineteenth century. In 1937 the British made Aden a crown colony and divided the hinterland sultanates in the south into the Western and Eastern Aden Protectorates; the Aden colony itself remained a separate entity. The British further developed the port facilities in Aden in the 1950s and built an oil refinery there. Consequently, Aden became the dominant economic center in southern Arabia—a densely populated urban area with a rapidly growing working class.

Imam Yahya, whose isolationism and despotism had alienated a large number of Yemenis, was assassinated in a coup in 1948. His son, Ahmad, succeeded him. Growing nationalism among the Arab countries after World War II, exemplified by the rise of Egypt's Gamal Abdel Nasser as a pan-Arab leader, as well as improving communications and the emergence of Arab oil wealth, forced Ahmad to abandon the isolationist policies of his father. He joined Egypt and Syria's ill-fated United Arab Republic in 1958 and sought aid from communist and capitalist nations alike.

The Yemeni Republics

Repressive domestic policies instated by Ahmad, coupled with Egyptian instigation, touched off a coup on September 26, 1962, that led to the establishment of the Yemen Arab Republic in the north, with San'a' as its capital. This coup put an end to the Rassid dynasty, one of the oldest and most enduring in history.

In southern Yemen, which was still under British colonial rule, the coup was a great inspiration to underground groups agitating for political freedom. This rise in nationalism, combined with severe urban problems in congested Aden, created instability in the south. The British, hoping to withdraw gracefully from the area while also protecting their interests, persuaded the sultans in the Western and Eastern Aden Protectorates to join Aden in 1963 in forming the Federation of South Arabia, which was to be the nucleus of a future independent state.

Arab opponents of the British plan mounted a campaign of sabotage, bombings, and armed resistance. Britain, failing to persuade the various factions to agree on a constitutional design for a new, independent state, announced early in 1966 that it would withdraw its military forces from Aden and southern Arabia by the end of 1968.

(Britain had signed a treaty in 1959 guaranteeing full independence to the region by 1968.)

London's announcement turned the anti-British campaign into one of interfactional competition. The National Front for the Liberation of South Yemen (or the National Liberation Front, NLF), backed by the British-trained south Arabian army, emerged as the victor among the various factions, and on November 30, 1967, Aden and southern Arabia became an independent state under the name of the People's Republic of Southern Yemen, later changed to the People's Democratic Republic of Yemen. Relations between Aden and San'a' would, over the ensuing years, be soured by political and ideological differences, despite intermittent mutual advocacy of Yemeni reunification.

Yemen Arab Republic, North Yemen

Civil war raged in North Yemen for eight years after the establishment of the Yemen Arab Republic in 1962. The last imam, Muhammad al-Badr, Imam Ahmad's son, fled San'a' after the coup and mustered support among tribal royalists to wage war against the new republican government. Aid from Saudi Arabia and Jordan helped sustain his resistance movement. In response, the new president, Col. Abdullah al-Sallal, turned to Egypt's Nasser, who sent a large military force to support the new republic.

Hostilities between Badr and the republic continued. Meanwhile, fighting broke out among the republican leaders themselves, primarily about the future role of Egypt in Yemen. President Sallal was removed from office. Moderate republicans, led by Gen. Hasan al-Amri, seized power and pushed back a serious monarchist offensive against San'a'. After the withdrawal of Egyptian forces in late 1967, Saudi Arabia began reducing its commitment to the royalists, and in 1970 it recognized the YAR after the monarchists agreed to drop their claims and cooperate with the republican regime.

In the early 1970s, the formation of a three-person republican council headed by Abd al-Rahman al-Iryani seemed to bring about stability.

During that period, Saudi Arabia became a major provider of foreign aid, perhaps to forestall greater Soviet aid to San'a' and to counter the growing Marxist orientation of the PDRY to the south. Relations between the two Yemens deteriorated and flared into sporadic border fighting, pushing the YAR closer to Saudi Arabia.

In 1976 Col. Ibrahim al-Hamdi ousted the civilian government of Iryani and set out to heal old factional and religious wounds. Though a popular leader, Hamdi was assassinated in 1977, possibly because he had planned to visit Aden. His successor, Ahmad al-Ghashmi, was assassinated in 1978. Lt. Col. Ali Abdullah Salih then took over and has remained in power ever since. Under Salih's rule, the YAR was beset by turmoil, much of it resulting from tensions between the two Yemens that erupted in 1979 in a border war. In March 1979, the YAR and PDRY announced plans for a merger. Although the unification failed to materialize, Salih's government sought to reassure Saudi Arabia and the United States that it was not abandoning its traditional policy of nonalignment and that its proposed merger with the PDRY did not mean the emergence of a Soviet-oriented alliance.

In the 1980s, the major threat to the Salih government came from the National Democratic Front (NDF), a coalition of opponents engaged in political and military action against the government and backed by the PDRY. Despite significant early NDF victories and occupation of much of the southern part of the YAR, Salih turned the situation around through military action and reached an astute political compromise with PDRY leader Ali Nasser Muhammad in May 1982. Muhammad agreed to halt support for the NDF in return for amnesty for and political incorporation of NDF elements. This agreement led to a gradual normalization of the situation in the YAR and strengthened Muhammad against his hard-line opponents in Aden, who wanted to support NDF military operations vigorously.

With the discovery of oil in the early to mid-1980s, Salih was able to finance the building of schools, hospitals, and better roads and to dispense other jobs and services that increased his government's presence. The advancement of significant infrastructure helped neutralize rebellious tribes, especially in the north, where inhabitants had always been more loyal to local clan leaders than to central authorities.

In 1988 Salih permitted elections to establish a long-promised consultative assembly. In the voting, 1.2 million Yemenis chose 1,200 delegates to the assembly, which is not authorized to initiate legislation, only to amend or critique it. One of its first official acts was to name Salih head of state de jure.

People's Democratic Republic of Yemen, South Yemen

At its independence in 1967, the People's Republic of Southern Yemen had a strong socialist orientation. The ruling party, the National Front for the Liberation of South Yemen, preached "scientific socialism" with a Marxist flavor. Its first president, NLF leader Qahtan al-Sha'bi, sought closer ties with the Soviet Union and China as well as with the more radical Arab regimes. Saudi Arabia joined the YAR in opposing the south's Marxist regime and backed opposition efforts there.

Sha'bi's orientation was not radical enough for some elements of the NLF. In 1969 he was overthrown by a group led by Salim Rubayyi' Ali, and in 1970 the new regime renamed the country the People's Democratic Republic of Yemen. The regime took extreme steps, including repression and exile, to break traditional patterns of tribalism and religion and to eliminate vestiges of the bourgeoisie and familial elites.

Ali had a powerful rival in Abd al-Fattah Ismail, secretary general of the NLF (renamed the National Front). Ali was considered a Maoist with pro-China sympathies, whereas Ismail was thought of as a pragmatic Marxist loyal to Moscow. In June 1978, Ismail seized power and executed Ali. He reorganized the National Front into the Yemeni Socialist Party (YSP), became chairman of the Presidium of the People's Supreme Assembly, and named Ali Nasser Muhammad as prime minister. In October 1979, Ismail signed a friendship and cooperation treaty with the Soviet Union.

Ismail, however, was unable to hold on to power. In April 1980, he relinquished his posts as presidium chairman and YSP secretary general. The party indicated that he had resigned because of poor health, but it appeared that Ismail had lost a power struggle, in part because of his foreign policy positions. The YSP Central Committee named Ali Nasser Muhammad to take his place. Ismail had intended to further cement ties with the Soviet Union and Eastern Europe, and on this point he was in agreement with Muhammad. The latter, however, also wanted to improve relations with Saudi Arabia and other Gulf countries to end the PDRY's isolation in the Arab world, secure new sources of foreign aid, and facilitate union between the two Yemens. Muhammad began his tenure with visits to the Soviet Union and Saudi Arabia, the YAR, and other neighboring countries. He signed agreements on economic and technical cooperation with the Soviets and in late 1980 agreed to a friendship and cooperation treaty with East Germany.

Overall, Muhammad's regime pursued a more moderate path than had Ismail's, cultivating economic ties with the West, achieving political reconciliation with the YAR and Oman, and moderating as many tribal rivalries as possible. In the fall of 1985, however, Ismail precipitated a power struggle. Concerned about his own maintenance of power, Muhammad called a meeting of Ismail's advisers and staff in January 1986 in the parliament. Once those unfavorable to Muhammad had gathered, Muhammad's bodyguards entered the chambers and opened fire, killing dozens and setting off a brief, violent civil war that resulted in Muhammad being driven from the country. It is believed that Ismail, who disappeared during the fighting, died of wounds received in the shootout.

Haidar Abu Bakr al-Attas, the prime minister in Muhammad's government who happened to be out of the country during the conflict, returned to Aden on January 25 and was named provisional president. In October 1986, he was elected president for a full term. His government also followed a local brand of "pragmatic Marxism," pursued a close relationship with the Soviet Union, discussed unification with the YAR, and supported mainstream Arab causes. Aden restored diplomatic relations with Egypt in 1988 and considered reestablishing ties with the United States.

Unification of the Yemens

The YAR and PDRY pursued independent destinies in a climate of mutual suspicion throughout much of the 1980s. In the second half of the decade, however, fundamental changes in the global and regional geopolitical map set the stage for Yemeni unification. Most observers trace the beginning of the unification process to the spring of 1988, when presidents from both countries met to reduce tensions at their common border, create an economic buffer zone for joint investment, and

Ali Abdullah Salih

revive discussions regarding unification. In 1989 the YAR initiated a series of talks with the PDRY aimed at fulfilling this goal.

The crumbling of the Soviet Union in the early 1990s and its inability to provide economic and military aid, coupled with regional instability in the wake of the Iran-Iraq war, led the PDRY to decide that unification with the YAR was in its best interest. The PDRY's economy sagged under the government's socialist principles. After the country became independent, industrial production declined, the once-famous port of Aden lay in disrepair, and workers' remittances from the oil-rich Gulf states provided half of the government's annual budget. Due in part to substandard Soviet technology, the PDRY's oil sector, which had the potential to lift the country economically, was in shambles. Only in 1989 did it begin exporting oil in significant quantities.

The YAR's leadership had equally compelling reasons for considering unification. Salih saw merger as a means of increasing the power and influence of his country as well as procuring his place in history as the broker of Yemeni unification. By incorporating the PDRY, Salih would have control over more land and loyalties unfettered by tribal allegiances.

In the final unification agreement, the two countries divided the ministerial positions, although local bureaucracies in the north and south remained intact, and Salih retained his position as head of state. The two economies were generally left to function as they had previously, and the militaries exchanged senior staff but left most rank-and-file personnel unintegrated.

Soon after its union in May 1990, the new Republic of Yemen fell under a plague of internal political violence and tribal warfare. Yemen's internal instability was compounded by Iraq's invasion of Kuwait in August 1990. Yemen expressed sympathy for Iraq and condemned the involvement of Western forces in what it considered an Arab problem. By doing so, it offended its wealthy Gulf neighbors. Saudi Arabia expelled nearly 1 million Yemeni workers, whose remittances were crucial to Yemen's economy. Unemployment and poverty

rose in 1991. Popular frustration and disillusionment with the new government, bloated and inefficient because of unification, mounted. Riots occurred throughout 1992, caused by a devalued currency and a rising cost of living. Because of these developments, high-level officials of nearly every political persuasion were the objects of assassination attempts or harassment.

On April 27, 1993, Yemen held its first free, multiparty elections. Thousands of candidates competed for 301 seats in the parliament. Before election day, the ruling coalition, headed by President Salih, and the YSP, the party of power in the former YAR, traded accusations over buying votes, inflating the electoral register, and unfair use of the media. The government deployed more than 35,000 troops on the streets of San'a' to keep order on election day.

With a large and peaceful turnout, Salih's party, the General People's Congress (GPC), won a plurality of the parliamentary seats. International observers declared the vote fair, and several opposition parties won seats in the legislature—a step toward multiparty democracy virtually unprecedented in the Gulf region. Salih formed a coalition with the Yemeni Alliance for Reform, a party with strong Islamic influences, despite promises to diversify the government beyond the traditional Islamic parties. Ali Salem Baydh, leader of the YSP, became vice president. Rivalries within the government, based on the old north-south division, remained alive. In August 1993, Baydh boycotted the five-person Presidential Council and returned to Aden, accusing Salih of refusing to integrate the military and hiding oil revenues. Baydh subsequently charged Salih and his followers with responsibility for the assassination of key YSP officials and supporters.

Throughout 1993 and the early part of 1994, frequent skirmishes broke out between the military divisions of the north and south. On May 5, 1994, when Salih fired Baydh as vice president, essentially in absentia, armed conflict erupted. Baydh declared a separate government on May 21 and led a southern rebellion against Salih. He established a presidential council and a rump parliament to lead the "Democratic Republic of Yemen." The larger northern army invaded the south and drove toward Aden and the oil port of Mukalla, 300 miles to the east. International mediation efforts failed. The northern forces dealt a crushing defeat to the southern army, capturing Aden and Mukalla in early July, as southern fighters abandoned the cities or melded into the populace. The civil war lasted less than two months but devastated Yemen's economy and caused more than $11 million in infrastructure damage.

Post–Civil War Yemen

Because most Yemenis supported unification despite tribal and religious differences, there was widespread relief when the fighting ended, and President Salih emerged from the civil war a stronger leader. Thousands of southerners returned to Yemen under a general amnesty, and some southern leaders engaged the San'a' government in discussions on recovering from the war. In October 1994, the GPC and Islah, an Islamist reform party, formed a new coalition government. With the YSP ineffective after the war, Islah adopted the role of the opposition, frequently challenging the majority GPC.

In April 1997, Yemen held its first parliamentary elections since the civil war. The GPC won decisively, while Islah won a small minority. In the first direct presidential elections, President Salih won a five-year term in September 1999. In 2000 a constitutional amendment extended Salih's term by two years, moving the next presidential election to 2006.

Another constitutional amendment, passed in February 2001, created a bicameral legislature consisting of the Shura, a council with 111 seats appointed by the president, and a House of Representatives with 301 popularly elected members. Multiparty parliamentary elections held in April 2003 were deemed free and fair by international observers. The GPC won more than two-thirds of the seats, and two women were elected.

Tribal unrest continues to pose difficulties. Yemeni tribes frequently kidnap Western tourists and oil workers in an effort to wrest concessions from the government for basic social services, such as roads and schools. Although the tribes generally treat their captives with respect, providing them with the traditional Arab hospitality, several Western hostages have been killed by their captors.

Having damaged relations with its Gulf Arab neighbors by supporting Iraq in 1990 and 1991, San'a' has made efforts to improve relations with them. In 1995 after several violent border disputes with Saudi Arabia, the two countries signed a memorandum of understanding, pledging cooperation to resolve their outstanding boundary issues. In 2000 Yemen and Saudi Arabia signed a treaty delimiting their land and resolving maritime boundary disputes. Across the Red Sea, Yemen similarly resolved its dispute with Eritrea over the sovereignty of the Hanish Islands and maritime delimitation through arbitration by a five-judge panel.

In December 1996, Yemen made a formal request for membership in the Gulf Cooperation Council (GCC), which includes Bahrain, Kuwait, Oman, Qatar, Saudi Arabia, and the United Arab Emirates. Although the request was denied, the GCC's consideration of the request marked a significant shift in relations on the Arabian Peninsula. In early 2005, Yemen revived its effort to join the GCC. President Salih ordered elements of his government to accelerate the harmonization of Yemeni economic legislation with legislation in the GCC states. It is expected that Yemen will be permitted to join certain GCC working groups, although not as a full member.

Yemen also has actively tried to improve its relations with the West. On October 12, 2000, suicide bombers attacked the USS Cole, which was docked in the port of Aden, killing seventeen U.S. sailors and wounding thirty-seven others. Yemen immediately offered all available assistance to the United States and received significant praise for its cooperation. After the September 11, 2001, attacks, President Salih announced his support for the Bush administration's war on terror, receiving aid from the United States as a result of this pledge. The government has launched occasional raids and attacks against al-Qaida's presence in Yemen, as well as allowing the United States to carry out preemptive operations there against the organization and its supporters. The growing links between the Yemeni and U.S. militaries are not insignificant. In 2003 Yemen received $1.9 million in foreign military financing from the United States and approximately $14 million in 2004.

Economy

Prior to unification, the YAR and PDRY had relied on a combination of workers' remittances, coffee exports, a thriving fishing industry, and foreign assistance to supplement their revenues from oil and gas exports. During the oil booms of the 1970s and 1980s, the exodus of Yemen's workers to other parts of the Gulf made it difficult for Yemen to develop its own agricultural and industrial bases. The civil war of the 1990s had a disastrous effect on Yemen, prodding the government toward a course of economic rehabilitation.

Because of its low level of industrial and agricultural output, Yemen today is dependent on revenues from its oil sector for virtually all of its essential needs. Estimates of Yemen's total oil reserves are 4 billion barrels. Yemen's oil production in 2003 reached 420,000 barrels a day, and in 2003 oil exports accounted for $3.7 billion and comprised about 70 percent of the government's revenue. Although the 1994 civil war threatened the substantial Western investment in Yemeni oil facilities, today Hunt Oil Company and Canadian Occidental Petroleum have increased production in their respective fields of Marib-Jawf and Masila.

In addition, Yemen has approximately 17 trillion cubic feet of proven natural gas reserves. ExxonMobil, Hunt Oil, Total (France), and Yukong (South Korea) are partners in the development of a significant liquefied natural gas facility that will liquefy the gas and ship via ocean vessels to markets in Asia and the United States. The project is a $3.5 billion investment over twenty-five years.

In 1995 San'a' announced an aggressive scheme to rebuild and redevelop the port of Aden.

The aim of the new Yemen Free Zone and Public Authority is to restore Aden's port as the region's primary container hub on shipping routes from Europe to Asia. To this end, the first phase, a container terminal, began operations in March 1999. Other projects include upgrading the Aden airport, constructing a new oil-fired power plant, developing land for export-oriented industries, and building a $65 million trade center.

With unification, the Republic of Yemen agreed to assume the international obligations of both the YAR and PDRY, saddling the unified nation with a combined official debt of approximately $7 billion. Both the YAR and PDRY had depended on foreign aid to a large extent, which made them prey to international political and economic fluctuations.

In April 1995, worsening economic conditions prompted the government to adopt an aggressive economic recovery plan. The primary objectives were to secure control of the rapidly increasing budget deficit, reinforce the value of the riyal, initiate privatization of many state-run sectors, and encourage national, Arab, and foreign investment by providing better facilities for investors.

Since the plan's inception, Yemen has attracted hundreds of millions of dollars in foreign aid and investment from the International Monetary Fund (IMF) and World Bank, the United States, the European Union, and Japan. Yemen brought its rampant inflation under control, decreasing it from more than 55 percent in 1995 to less than 6 percent in 1997, and it stabilized its exchange rate. Even though Yemen experienced a sharp rise in its budget deficit because of low oil prices and decreased demand in the late 1990s, it continued its strident efforts to control spending and cut subsidies. Significantly higher oil prices in late 2004 and early 2005 likely will have a positive impact on Yemen's revenues and budget deficit.

In May 1998, the United States agreed to a $17 million debt forgiveness program, and in October 2002 international donors provided a further $2.3 billion in economic assistance. Moreover, Yemen has continued to adhere to the International Monetary Fund's structural adjustment program. The World Bank has twenty-two active projects in

Yemen, including some focusing on improving governance, efficient use of scarce water resources, and education.

Despite some successes, Yemen still struggles in certain respects. It was chosen as one of eight nations by the United Nations Development Program to participate in the Millennium Development Goals program to promote human development as the key to sustaining economic and social progress. Thus far, Yemen has failed to reach its goal of sustained growth in GDP of 5.6 percent. In addition, a 2005 government report found that the shortfall between required and actual investment will reach $29 billion by 2015.

Yemen's economy has been hampered over the years by the widespread social habit of chewing *qat*. Men and women of all social classes chew the mildly narcotic leaves of the qat shrub daily, which induces lethargy. Qat also has affected northern Yemen's agricultural industry, since the qat bush is easy to grow, tolerates frequent cropping, and provides instant cash returns. As a result, many fields that previously grew edible and exportable crops have been converted into qat fields, transforming Yemen into an import-dependent country. Government efforts to discourage qat production have largely foundered.

Foreign tourism in Yemen has picked up and looks to be a significant, albeit small, element of the country's revenue. The government has been focusing development efforts on the Red Sea coast to try to attract tourists.

Outlook

Yemen's future does not appear as bleak as it has in the past. Its ongoing support of the U.S.-led war on terror has provided it with much-needed foreign investment and has increased confidence in the Yemeni government and economy. Its oil and gas revenues continue to provide the foundation for the nation's economy and are experiencing an upswing because of rising and high oil prices.

Yemen still faces numerous challenges. Its population growth rate is high, and its economy lacks the diversification required to effect a major change in the average living standard of its citizens. The best prospect for improvement lies in developing long-term sustainable industries that utilize Yemen's large labor sector and crucial geographic location, which in turn will promote Yemen's economy abroad, in terms of both international aid and investment.

By conducting relatively free and fair national elections, Yemen has proved itself an innovator among the countries of the Arabian Peninsula. It has set a positive example of moving toward a free and democratic society much faster than Kuwait and Saudi Arabia, whose populations have been clamoring for similar commitments to pluralism and democracy from their leadership. Yemen's 2006 presidential elections must continue on this same path to demonstrate to the international community that the country is committed to democratic principles.

Yemen will probably never rid itself of tribal dissent, because it is deeply rooted in the long history of al-Yaman. However, through continued implementation of economic reforms, Yemen can marginalize the extreme tribal elements and their often destructive activities—including kidnapping and destruction of oil pipelines—and can avert potential tensions with its neighbors and Western nations. This will allow Yemen to develop its oil and gas sectors and take advantage of its labor force and strategic geographic location.

APPENDIX

CHRONOLOGY OF MAJOR EVENTS, 1900–1944

CHRONOLOGY OF EVENTS, 1945–2005

BIBLIOGRAPHY

CHRONOLOGY OF MAJOR EVENTS, 1900–1944

The following chronology cites major Middle Eastern events from 1900 through 1944. A more detailed chronology follows this section covering 1945 through March 30, 2005.

1900. Russia lends Persia funds to secure Russian commercial and political influence throughout the region.

1901. Fifth Zionist Congress begins collections for the Jewish National Fund to purchase land in Palestine. May, Iran grants William D'Arcy a concession to search for oil.

1902. First Aswan Dam opens, greatly expanding irrigation and food production in Egypt. Ibn Saud makes successful raid on Riyadh against Ottoman forces.

1903. August 22, Zionist Congress opens at Basel, Switzerland.

1904. April, Anglo-French Entente Cordiale ends contest for control of Egypt.

1905. Death of Muhammad Abduh, leader of Egyptian Islamic modernist movement opposed to foreigners and imperialist occupation. December, prominent Iranian business and religious leaders protest shah's corruption and demand "House of Justice" for safe expression of views opposing the government.

1906. May 13, Sinai Peninsula officially becomes part of Egypt after the British force the Ottomans to withdraw from Taba. December, Iranian revolution erupts in response to British and Russian intervention and local corruption; shah is forced to grant constitution.

1907. January 4, Muzaffar Ali Shah, Persian monarch, dies. August 31, Anglo-Russian agreement divides Iranian territory into separate spheres of influence.

1908. May 26, first major oil strike in Iran is made at Masjed Soleyman. July, Muhammad Ali Shah is forced to abdicate in Iran. July 21, after uniting under Committee of Union and Progress, Young Turk movements demand the sultan's immediate restoration of Ottoman constitution.

1909. Anglo-Persian Oil Company is formed to exploit the D'Arcy concession in Iran. April, Ottoman counterrevolt quashes the Ottoman Third Army and deposes Abd al-Hamid II.

1910. February 10, Premier Boutros Ghali of Egypt is assassinated.

1911. The Italian army invades Libya and defeats the Ottoman forces. Lord Herbert Kitchener takes power in Egypt.

1912. Ottomans cede Libya to Italy. Ibn Saud establishes his army of Ikhwan (brethren) from Wahhabi soldiery.

1913. January, Committee of Union and Progress takes direct control of Ottoman government. June, Arab Congress convenes in Paris supporting an Ottoman government in which every nation under its rule would have equal rights and obligations.

1914. August, Ottomans enter World War I on the side of Germany. November, British declare war on the Ottomans, annex Cyprus, and land troops in lower Iraq. December 18, British declare protectorate over Egypt.

1915. February, Ottoman forces attack the Suez Canal. April 25, allied troops mount an amphibious operation at Gallipoli designed to knock the Ottoman Empire out of the war by seizing Istanbul, the imperial capital; the British fail to capture the Dardanelles. November 16, Sir Henry MacMahon promises Hussein ibn Ali, the amir of Mecca, that Britain will support Arab independence if the Hashimites rebel against Ottoman rule.

1916. Arab revolt against Turks begins; British appoint T. E. Lawrence as political and liaison officer to Faisal's (Hussein's son's) army. May, Britain, France, and Russia conclude the Sykes-Picot Agreement outlining the future division of Ottoman lands. July 19, second Ottoman campaign against the Suez begins. December 15, British recognize Hussein as king only of Hijaz.

1917. November 2, Britain issues Balfour Declaration calling for "support of the establishment in Palestine of a national home for the Jewish people." December 9, Turks surrender Jerusalem to Gen. Edmund Allenby.

1918. June, Amir Faisal ibn Hussein and Zionist leader Chaim Weizmann meet in Transjordan to discuss future cooperation between the Arab and Jewish national movements. October, British and Arabs capture Damascus, then Aleppo.

1919. March, Egyptians rebel against British after the deportation of nationalist leader Saad Zaghlul. June, King-Crane commission, appointed by Paris peace conference, arrives in Syria to determine wishes of the population concerning the future of Palestine and Syria. August, proposed Anglo-Persian treaty stirs national opposition in Iran and is never ratified by Persian Majlis (parliament).

1920. March, Syrian National Congress proclaims Faisal king of Syria and Palestine. April 24, through League of Nations' San Remo Agreement, Britain is awarded mandates over Iraq and Palestine, and France over Syria and Lebanon. July, French forces evict Faisal from the throne in Damascus, and Faisal's brother Abdullah is offered the throne in Baghdad, causing large-scale riots in Palestine and Iraq. August, French high commissioner creates Greater (modern) Lebanon in an attempt to utilize religious differences, particularly between Christians and Muslims, to ease the task of French administration.

1921. February, Reza Khan seizes power in Iran. March, organized by the British under Winston Churchill, the Cairo Conference names Faisal ibn Hussein king of Iraq and Abdullah ibn Hussein amir of Transjordan (which was carved out of Palestine).

1922. February 28, Britain unilaterally terminates its rule over Egypt while retaining control over communications vital to the empire, foreign interests, the Sudan, and minority rights in a policy known as the Four Reserved Points. March, Fuad takes title of king of Egypt. July 22, Council of the League of Nations confirms mandate allocations made to Britain and France two years earlier. October 10, Anglo-Iraqi treaty signed. November, Mustafa Kemal abolishes the Ottoman sultanate.

1923. April, Egypt drafts constitution and holds elections. May 15, Britain recognizes Transjordan as a self-governing state. October, Kemal officially proclaims Turkish republic and begins his fifteen years as president.

1924. Ibn Saud takes Hijaz from Hashimites. March, Kemal abolishes the caliphate. November, Sir Lee Stack, governor general of Sudan, is murdered in Egypt.

1925. April, Hebrew University in Jerusalem opens. December 12, Iranian Majlis approves Reza Khan's establishment of Pahlavi dynasty; he becomes Reza Shah Pahlavi.

1926. January 8, Ibn Saud is proclaimed king of the Hijaz. May 26, Lebanese constitution adopted.

1927. May, British recognize Ibn Saud as king of the Najd and Hijaz.

1928. April, Turkey is declared a secular state and adopts the Latin alphabet.

1929. August, prolonged Arab-Jewish riots spring from conflict over claims that the Jews were seeking control of the Temple Mount; the riots eventually lead to a pro-Arab turn in British policies.

1930. October 20, Britain issues Passfield White Paper, limiting Jewish immigration to "economic absorptive capacity" and restricting land sales to Jews.

1931. February, responding to Jewish criticism of Passfield White Paper, Prime Minister Ramsay MacDonald sends letter assuring Chaim Weizmann that Britain will promote a national Jewish home in Palestine in accordance with its mandate.

1932. June 1, oil is discovered in Bahrain. September 24, Ibn Saud issues royal decree unifying the kingdoms of Hijaz and Najd into Saudi Arabia. October 3, Britain grants Iraq independence but retains military bases and oil interests.

1933. August, Assyrian uprising in Iraq suppressed. September 8, King Faisal of Iraq dies.

1934. Kuwait grants first oil concession, for seventy-four years, to the Kuwait Oil Company.

1935. March, Iran becomes the official name for Persia. October, Italians invade Ethiopia.

1936. April-October, Arab general strike is mounted in Palestine. July, Montreux Convention gives Turkey control of Straits of Dardanelles.

1937. Sadabad Treaty is concluded among Afghanistan, Iran, Iraq, and Turkey, implicitly designed to block Soviet expansion. July, Peel commission calls for partition of Palestine.

1938. Oil discovered at al-Burqan, just south of Kuwait City. Saudi Arabian oil exports begin. November, Woodhead commission declares partition plan for Palestine unworkable.

1939. February, Anglo-Arab Conference on Palestine held in London. May 17, British publish white paper limiting Jewish immigration into Palestine. September, most independent Middle East countries declare their neutrality as World War II begins.

1940. September 12, Italian forces in Libya invade Egypt. November 25, French freighter *Patria,* holding 1,800 illegal Jewish immigrants who were prevented from entering Palestine by British authorities, explodes and sinks in Haifa harbor.

1941. June, a nationalist coup d'etat in Iraq, led by military commanders sympathetic to Germany, prompts Britain to invade the Baghdad and Basra areas, then occupy Syria and Lebanon. August 26, British and Soviet forces invade Iran. September 16, Reza Shah is forced to abdicate in favor of his son, Mohammad Reza Pahlavi.

1942. January, Britain and the Soviet Union sign treaty guaranteeing Iranian independence and securing vital communications between Soviet and Allied forces in the Middle East. February, British force King Farouk to appoint pro-Allied cabinet. May, Zionists issue Biltmore Program. July, Allies halt German advance in Egypt. October 23, Allied forces begin decisive assault against German lines at El Alamein in Egypt.

1943. November, Lebanon declares its independence; its Christians and Muslims adopt their "National Pact." December, Syrian state absorbs Jabal Druze.

1944. February 3, the Arabian-American Oil Company (Aramco) announces plans to build a refinery in Saudi Arabia. October 8, Syria, Transjordan, Iraq, Lebanon, and Egypt sign a protocol providing for establishment of the Arab League. November 6, the Jewish Stern Gang assassinates Lord Moyne, the British resident minister in the Middle East.

CHRONOLOGY OF EVENTS, 1945–2005

The following chronology cites major Middle Eastern events from 1945 through March 30, 2005.

1945

REGIONAL AFFAIRS

March 22. Arab League Established. The Arab League is founded in Cairo. Members are Egypt, Iraq, Lebanon, Saudi Arabia, Syria, and Transjordan.

ARAB-JEWISH CONFLICT

August 16. Truman on Palestine. President Harry S. Truman calls for free settlement of Palestine by Jews to the point consistent with the maintenance of civil peace.

November 13. Committee of Inquiry Created. President Truman in Washington and British foreign secretary Ernest Bevin in London agree to create the Anglo-American Committee of Inquiry to examine the problems of European Jews and Palestine.

December 12. Congress on Palestine. The Senate Foreign Relations Committee approves, 17 to 1, a resolution urging U.S. aid in opening Palestine to Jews and in building a "democratic commonwealth."

1946

ARAB-JEWISH CONFLICT

March 2. Arab League on Palestine. The Arab League asks the Anglo-American Committee of Inquiry to support an Arab Palestinian state and says the league will oppose creation of a Jewish state in Palestine.

April 30. Recommendations on Palestine. The Anglo-American Committee of Inquiry recommends the immediate admission of one hundred thousand Jews into Palestine and continuation of the British mandate pending establishment of a United Nations trusteeship. The Arab League protests.

July 25. Tripartite Partition Recommended. The Anglo-American Committee of Inquiry in London pro-

poses a tripartite partition of Palestine into Jewish-, Arab-, and British-controlled districts.

October 4. Truman Backs Jewish State. On the Jewish holiday of Yom Kippur, President Truman makes public a message sent to Great Britain expressing support for the Zionist plan to create a "viable Jewish state" in part of Palestine.

IRAN

February 25. Soviets to Keep Troops in Iran. Moscow tells Tehran it will retain some troops in Iran after the March 2 deadline for foreign troop withdrawal set by the 1942 Anglo-Soviet-Iranian treaty.

March 5. Truman Protests Troops in Iran. The United States protests Soviet retention of troops in Iran. President Truman warns Moscow that U.S. forces will be sent to Iran if the Soviets do not withdraw.

April 5. Soviet Troops Leave Iran. The Soviet Union and Iran reach agreement on a Soviet troop withdrawal. Soviet forces leave Iran May 6.

TRANSJORDAN

March 22. Transjordan Mandate Ends. Great Britain and Transjordan sign a treaty ending the British mandate in that country.

1947

ARAB-JEWISH CONFLICT

February 14. Conference Fails. The London conference on Palestine attended by Arab delegates and Zionist observers closes after a two-and-a-half-week session without an agreement on a plan for Palestine. The conference is informed of Great Britain's decision to refer the Palestine question to the United Nations.

April 28. UN Session on Palestine Opens. The UN General Assembly opens a special session to study the Palestine question. The UN Special Committee on Palestine (UNSCOP) is established May 13.

August 31. Committee Backs Palestine Division. The UN Special Committee on Palestine issues a majority report recommending Palestine be divided into two separate Arab and Jewish states by September 1, 1949, with Jerusalem and vicinity maintained as an international zone under permanent UN trusteeship. Zionist leaders approve the majority plan of UNSCOP; the Arab Higher Committee denounces the plan and threatens military action. The British cabinet accepts the UNSCOP majority report on September 20.

October 9. Military Preparations. The Arab League recommends member nations station troops along Palestine's borders to prepare for action if British troops evacuate. The league pledges December 8 to help Palestinian Arabs resist any move to partition Palestine.

October 11. U.S. Endorses Partition. The U.S. representative to UNSCOP endorses the proposal to partition Palestine. The Soviet Union endorses the plan October 13.

November 29. UN Votes for Partition. The UN General Assembly votes, 33 to 13, with 10 abstentions, to partition Palestine into separate, independent Jewish and Arab states, effective October 1, 1948, with the enclave of Jerusalem to be administered by the UN Trusteeship Council. Arab members denounce the decision and walk out.

December 5. Arms Embargo. The United States embargoes arms shipments to the Middle East because of fighting and violent disorders that followed the UN decision.

1948

REGIONAL AFFAIRS

September 17. UN Mediator Assassinated. UN mediator Count Folke Bernadotte is assassinated, allegedly by Jewish terrorists; Ralph Bunche is named to succeed him.

ARAB-ISRAELI CONFLICT

March 19. U.S. Urges Suspension of Plan. The United States proposes to the UN Security Council suspension of the plan to partition Palestine and urges a special General Assembly session to restudy the issue.

April 1. Council Adopts Resolution. The UN Security Council adopts a U.S. resolution calling for a truce and a special session of the General Assembly to reconsider the Palestine question.

May 13. Arab League Proclaims War. The Arab League proclaims the existence of a state of war between league members and Palestinian Jews.

May 14. Israel Proclaimed. The state of Israel is proclaimed in the afternoon. Israel comes into existence when the proclamation goes into effect at midnight. The British mandate for Palestine ends as the British high commissioner sails from Haifa.

May 15. U.S. Recognizes Israel; Arabs Invade. President Truman recognizes Israel at 12:11 a.m. (6:11 p.m.

in Washington), eleven minutes after its independence. Simultaneously, five Arab states—Transjordan, Egypt, Iraq, Syria, and Lebanon—invade Israel. Egyptian planes bomb Tel Aviv. The Soviet Union recognizes Israel May 17.

September 20. Arab Government Announced. The Arab League announces establishment of an Arab government for Palestine—a move denounced by Transjordan and Iraq as amounting to recognition of Palestine's partition.

December 11. New UN Commission. The UN General Assembly sets up a new Palestine Conciliation Commission.

ISRAEL

May 25. Israel Asks for Loan. Israel's president, Chaim Weizmann, visits President Truman and appeals for a $90 million to $100 million loan to arm Israel and assist immigration. Truman says May 27 that Israel's loan application should be sent to the World Bank and the U.S. Export-Import Bank.

1949

ARAB-ISRAELI CONFLICT

January 6. Cease-Fire Announced. Israel and Egypt agree to a final cease-fire on all fronts, to begin January 7. Israel withdraws its troops from Egypt January 10.

February 1. Israel Incorporates Jerusalem. Ending its military governorship of Jerusalem, Israel formally incorporates the city as part of the new state.

March 11. Transjordan-Israel Cease-Fire. Transjordan and Israel sign a "complete and enduring" cease-fire agreement, to be binding even if they fail to reach agreement on other points.

March 21. UN Palestine Commission Meets. The first meeting of the UN Palestine Conciliation Commission to settle the question of Arab refugees opens in Beirut, Lebanon.

April 28. Israel Blocks Return of Refugees. The Israeli government rejects a proposal to allow Arab refugees to return to their homes inside Israel's borders.

July 20. Syria and Israel Sign Armistice. Syria and Israel sign an armistice agreement setting up demilitarized zones and calling for both countries to keep their forces behind the frontiers.

July 27. Mediator Says War Has Ended. UN Middle East mediator Ralph Bunche reports that "the military phase of the Palestine conflict is ended."

September 13. UN Drafts Jerusalem Proposal. The UN Palestine Conciliation Commission issues a draft statute whereby the United Nations would control Jerusalem, neither Israel nor the Arab states could have government offices there, and neither would control the city except for local administration of areas where their citizens lived. Holy places would be under permanent international supervision. Israel rejects the statute November 15.

December 16. Jerusalem to Become Capital. Israeli prime minister David Ben-Gurion announces that Jerusalem will become the country's capital January 1, 1950. Transfer of government offices from Tel Aviv to Jerusalem's New City is already under way.

EGYPT

March 7. Suez Canal Agreement. Egypt signs an agreement with the British-owned Suez Canal Company calling for 80 to 90 percent of the company's jobs to be held by Egyptians and for Egypt to receive 7 percent of its profits.

ISRAEL

January 25. First Israeli Election. In the first Israeli election, Prime Minister David Ben-Gurion's Labor Party wins the largest number of seats in the Knesset.

January 31. U.S. Extends Full Recognition. The United States extends full diplomatic recognition to Israel and Transjordan following a flurry of diplomatic activity during which a number of Western nations, including France and Great Britain, recognize Israel.

May 11. Israel Admitted to UN. Israel is admitted to the United Nations by a vote of 36 to 12 in the General Assembly. Great Britain abstains from voting. Six Arab delegates walk out to protest the vote.

JORDAN

April 26. Transjordan to Be Called Jordan. The government of Transjordan changes the name of the country to the Hashimite Kingdom of Jordan, or Jordan for short.

April 26. Syria Closes Jordanian Border. In response to Jordan's statement on April 7 that a "greater" Jordan may evolve, Syria closes its Jordanian border and warns against attempts to annex its territory.

1950

ARAB-ISRAELI CONFLICT

April 1. Israel Rejects Arab League Terms. The Arab League Council votes to expel any member making a separate peace with Israel. Israel April 13 rejects Arab League peace negotiation terms, which include a return to 1947 UN partition boundaries. The Arab League secretary condemns Anglo-American policy in the Middle East April 20 and urges Arab states to turn to Moscow.

EGYPT

November 21. Britain Refuses to Leave Canal. In response to Egyptian demands for Great Britain's immediate withdrawal from the Suez Canal Zone, British foreign secretary Bevin tells Parliament that British troops will remain in Egypt until the 1936 Anglo-Egyptian treaty is altered "by mutual consent."

ISRAEL

March 9. Turkey, Iran Recognize Israel. Turkey becomes the first Muslim state to recognize Israel. Iran recognizes Israel March 15.

April 27. Full Israeli Recognition. Great Britain changes its recognition of Israel from de facto to full.

JORDAN

April 24. Jordan Annexes Eastern Palestine. Jordan formally annexes Jordan-occupied eastern Palestine, including the Old City of Jerusalem. Great Britain recognizes the Jordan-Palestine merger April 27.

1951

ARAB-ISRAELI CONFLICT

May 18. UN Protests Israeli Project. The UN Security Council adopts a resolution calling on Israel to halt the Huleh border zone drainage project that has set off boundary clashes between Israel and Syria. Criticizing Israeli aerial attacks on Syria, the resolution denounces the use of force by both countries to settle their differences. Israel halts work on the drainage project June 6.

September 1. Egypt Urged to End Blockade. The UN Security Council calls on Egypt to end its three-year-old blockade of the Suez Canal to ships carrying cargoes bound for Israel. Egypt refuses September 2 to comply until Israel obeys previous UN resolutions dealing with the partition of Palestine, repatriation and compensation of Arab refugees, and internationalization of Jerusalem.

September 13. UN Conference Opens. The UN Palestine Conciliation Conference with Israeli and Arab delegates opens in Paris.

September 21. Israel Willing to Sign Pacts. Israel agrees to sign nonaggression pacts with each of its four Arab neighbors but warns that peace negotiations should not continue if Arabs will not meet in the same room with Israeli delegates. Israel offers to compensate Arab refugees and to make contributions to their resettlement in Arab countries, but it is unwilling to accept repatriation of the refugees in Israel.

November 21. UN Commission Ends Efforts. Citing the "rigid positions" on both sides, the UN Palestine Conciliation Commission ends mediation efforts between Israel and the Arab states.

EGYPT

October 8. Egypt Announces Canal Aims. Egypt announces plans to expel British troops from the Suez Canal. The next day, Great Britain declares it will not vacate the Suez Canal.

October 16. British and Egyptians Fight. Tension builds in the Suez Canal Zone as eight persons are killed and seventy-four wounded during fighting between

British troops and Egyptian rioters. A three-day state of emergency is proclaimed throughout Egypt.

IRAN

March 7. Iranian Premier Assassinated. Gen. Ali Razmara, Iranian premier since June 26, 1950, is assassinated by a group favoring the nationalization of Iran's oil industry. He is succeeded March 11 by Hussein Ala, a strongly pro-Western official who had served as a former ambassador to the United States.

April 28. Iran Nationalizes Oil Company. The Iranian parliament votes unanimously to sanction government expropriation of the British-owned Anglo-Iranian Oil Company. With favorable Senate action April 30, the oil nationalization bill becomes law.

July 24. Britain and Iran to Negotiate. Secret plans for Iranian-British negotiations over nationalization of the Anglo-Iranian Oil Company are sent to London after formulation during eight days of talks between Iranian officials and W. Averell Harriman, a U.S. envoy sent to Iran by President Truman. Great Britain and Iran formally agree August 2 to begin negotiations aimed at settling the dispute.

September 25. Iran Expels British Oil Workers. Iran orders the last British oil technicians to leave the country by October 4. Great Britain's remaining three hundred oil employees depart October 3.

JORDAN

July 20. King Abdallah Assassinated. Jordan's King Abdallah is assassinated, reportedly by a member of a faction opposing his annexation of parts of Palestine. The king's son, Prince Talal, is crowned king September 6 in Amman.

LIBYA AND NORTH AFRICA

December 24. Libya Gains Independence. The Federation of Libya, an Arab kingdom created with the endorsement of the United Nations, becomes independent. By agreement, Great Britain and the United States will retain their military bases in the country.

SYRIA

December 2. Coup in Syria. Following a bloodless military coup in Syria, the army chief of staff, Col. Adib al-Shishakli, becomes president, after the resignation of President Hashim Atassi. Col. Fawzi Silo is appointed premier December 3.

1952

EGYPT

January 18. Egyptians Fight British Troops. British troops and Egyptian guerrillas battle for four hours at Port Said. British troops disarm Egyptian police in

Ismailia January 25. Fighting breaks out, killing forty-two persons. Martial law is imposed January 26 in Egypt following widespread rioting and burning in Cairo. Extensive damage to American, British, and French property is estimated at more than $10 million.

May 3. Britain Offers to Withdraw Troops. Great Britain, proposing a solution to the dispute with Egypt over the Suez Canal and the Sudan, offers to evacuate British troops from the base in the Suez Canal, but it denies recognition of Egyptian king Farouk as ruler of the Sudan until the Sudanese people are consulted.

July 23. Farouk Abdicates. King Farouk flees Egypt following a military coup that empowers Maher Pasha as premier. Farouk abdicates July 26 and goes into exile in Italy. The king's infant son, King Fuad II, is proclaimed ruler of Egypt and the Sudan by the cabinet.

IRAN

August 11. Mossadeq Given Dictatorial Power. The Iranian Senate grants full dictatorial powers to Mohammad Mossadeq, the prime minister and leader of the National Front. The chamber of deputies had approved the dictatorial powers August 3.

October 7. Iran Severs Ties with Britain. Mossadeq demands $1 billion from Great Britain before talks can resume on the question of nationalizing the Anglo-Iranian Oil Company. Iran severs diplomatic ties with Great Britain October 22 after London's rejection October 14 of Iran's demand.

ISRAEL

November 7. Israeli President Weizmann Dies. Israel's first president, Chaim Weizmann, dies. The Israeli Knesset names Isaac Ben-Zvi to succeed him.

JORDAN

August 11. Hussein Crowned King. Declaring that King Talal, suffering from mental disorders, is unfit to rule, the Jordanian parliament proclaims Crown Prince Hussein the new king.

LEBANON

September 18. Lebanese President Resigns. Ending a nine-year rule, Lebanon's president Bishara al-Khoury resigns in the face of general strikes to protest political corruption. The parliament elects foreign minister Camille Chamoun president September 23.

1953

IRAN

August 16. Shah Flees to Iraq. The shah of Iran seeks sanctuary in Iraq after his unsuccessful attempt to dismiss Mossadeq.

August 19. Iranian Royalists Oust Mossadeq. A revolt by Iranian royalists and troops loyal to the shah ousts Mossadeq. Announcing plans to return to Iran, the shah names Maj. Gen. Gazollah Zahedi as premier. The shah returns August 22.

December 21. Court Convicts Mossadeq. An Iranian military court convicts former premier Mossadeq of attempted rebellion. Instead of the death penalty, the court imposes a three-year solitary confinement sentence after the shah requests clemency.

IRAQ

May 2. Iraq Crowns King Faisal II. King Faisal II of Iraq is crowned on his eighteenth birthday, thus ending the regency of his uncle, Amir Abdallah.

1954

ARAB-ISRAELI CONFLICT

November 2. Jordan Protests River Diversion. Jordan summons the ambassadors of Great Britain, France, and the United States to ask their governments to halt Israel's unilateral diversion of the Jordan River.

EGYPT

April 18. Nasser Named Premier. Col. Gamal Abdel Nasser, a leader of Egypt's revolt against King Farouk, replaces Mohammed Naguib as premier of the government. Naguib retains the largely ceremonial post of president.

July 27. Egypt and Britain Sign Agreement. Egypt and Great Britain sign an agreement ending the dispute over the Suez Canal. Great Britain will remove its forces from the area within twenty months, but it will retain the right to use the canal base in the event of aggression against an Arab state or Turkey.

November 14. Naguib Deposed. Egypt's ruling military junta deposes President Mohammed Naguib. Gamal Abdel Nasser, who has held most executive power since he became premier April 18, is named president.

SYRIA

February 26. Syrian President Ousted. A Syrian army revolt ousts president Shishakli. Former president Hashim Atassi succeeds him February 28.

1955

REGIONAL AFFAIRS

February 24. Iraq and Turkey Sign Baghdad Pact. Iraq signs a mutual defense treaty (the Baghdad Pact) with Turkey despite Egyptian protests. Great Britain joins the Baghdad Pact April 4, and Pakistan joins September 23.

October 20. Egypt and Syria Sign Agreement. Egypt and Syria sign a mutual defense treaty, triggering Israeli requests for an Israeli-American security pact.

November 3. Iran Joins Baghdad Pact. Iran joins Baghdad Pact despite Soviet warning October 12 that such a move by Iran would be "incompatible" with peace in the Middle East.

November 22. New Baghdad Pact Organization. The five Baghdad Pact countries announce the establishment of a permanent political, military, and economic organization, the Middle East Treaty Organization, to be based in Baghdad. Members are Great Britain, Iran, Iraq, Pakistan, and Turkey.

1956

REGIONAL AFFAIRS

March 3. Jordan Grants Bases to Britain. Agreeing to honor the 1948 treaty of friendship with Great Britain, Jordan announces it will grant Great Britain bases in Jordan.

April 18. U.S. Joins Baghdad Pact Committee. The United States, which has not joined the Baghdad Pact in deference to Israel, becomes a full member of the pact's Economic Committee. The next day the United States agrees to set up a military liaison office at the headquarters of the Baghdad Pact.

November 9. Iraq Breaks Ties with French. Iraq breaks off ties with France and announces it will boycott any future meeting of the Baghdad Pact attended by Great Britain.

ARAB-ISRAELI CONFLICT

March 10. Jordan Launches Raids. Ending a two-year period of relative quiet on their border, Jordan stages raids on Israel.

October 29. Israel Attacks Egypt. After secretly conspiring with Great Britain and France to strike a coordinated blow against Egypt, Israel attacks Egyptian forces in the Sinai. The Israeli attack is intended to provide the British and French with a justification for using military force to seize the Suez Canal. Israeli troops drive to within twenty-five miles of the Suez Canal on the first day of fighting. Israel claims the attack was designed to eliminate Egyptian commando bases in the Sinai that had been used to stage raids against Israel.

October 30. British-French Ultimatum. Great Britain and France warn that troops will be sent to the Suez unless Egyptian and Israeli troops cease fighting and withdraw ten miles from the canal. Israel accepts on condition that Egypt also agrees; Egyptian president Nasser rejects the ultimatum. British and French forces on Cyprus are readied for an attack on Egypt. American president Dwight D. Eisenhower appeals to the allies to refrain from military intervention. Great Britain and France veto a U.S.-sponsored UN Security Council resolution calling for a halt to all military action in the area and an Israeli withdrawal.

October 31. British-French Air Attacks. British and French aircraft attack Egypt as Israel continues its drive in the Sinai. Israel reaches the banks of the Suez Canal before withdrawing to the ten-mile limit demanded by the British-French ultimatum. Israeli forces continue operations in the Sinai and the Gaza Strip, which is captured November 3.

EGYPT

June 13. Britain Ends Occupation of Canal. Great Britain turns over full responsibility for the defense of the Suez Canal to Egypt. On June 18 London declares its occupation of the canal ended.

June 24. Nasser Becomes President of Egypt. After an uncontested election, Gamal Abdel Nasser becomes Egypt's first elected president, having received 99 percent of the vote.

July 20. U.S. Refuses Egypt Aswan Dam Loan. Following disputes over funding for the Aswan Dam, the United States refuses to lend Egypt funds for the project, and Great Britain withdraws its offer to supplement the American loan.

July 27. Nasser Nationalizes Suez Canal. Nasser nationalizes the Suez Canal and imposes martial law in retaliation for American and British withdrawal of support for the financing of the Aswan Dam. Income from the canal will be used to build the dam. The British government freezes assets of Egypt and the Suez Canal held in Great Britain July 28.

August 16. Suez Crisis Meeting. In London, twenty-two nations open a conference on the Suez Canal crisis. Eighteen nations agree August 23 to ask Egypt to negotiate for international operation of the Suez Canal. On August 28 Nasser agrees to meet with a five-nation delegation.

September 21. Suez Conference Concludes. The Suez conference in London concludes with a draft plan for a Suez Canal Users' Association. The following day, Great Britain issues invitations to eighteen nations for another conference on the Suez Canal situation.

October 8. Canal Proposal Rejected. Egypt and the Soviet Union reject proposals for international supervision of the Suez Canal.

November 1. Egypt Breaks Ties. Egypt breaks off diplomatic relations with Great Britain and France and seizes their property in Egypt as bombing of military targets continues. Jordan also severs ties with France and tells Great Britain that it will no longer be allowed to use ground or air bases in Jordan for further attacks on Egypt. Great Britain and France reject the UN's call for a cease-fire.

November 5. British and French Troops Attack. British and French paratroopers enter the fight against Egypt; allied commandos are landed by sea November 6. The Soviet Union warns that it is prepared to use force "including rockets" to restore Mideast peace. The Soviets call for joint Soviet-American action against "aggressors," a proposal the United States rejects as "unthinkable."

November 6. Cease-Fire. British and French troops capture the Egyptian city of Port Said. Under heavy U.S. pressure, France and Great Britain agree to a cease-fire in Egypt at midnight.

November 7. UN Calls for Withdrawal. The UN General Assembly calls on Great Britain, France, and Israel to withdraw their forces from Egypt. The UN also decides to send a peacekeeping force to the area. The French and British governments say they welcome creation of the peacekeeping force and will withdraw. President Eisenhower in a personal note to Prime Minister Ben-Gurion says Israeli rejection of the UN appeal would "impair friendly cooperation between our two countries." Israel agrees November 8 to withdraw from the Sinai.

November 10. Volunteer Force Threatened. The Soviet Union calls for the withdrawal of British, French, and Israeli troops from Egypt and warns that Soviet volunteers will be allowed to join Egyptian forces unless the withdrawal takes place. On November 14 President Eisenhower says the United States would oppose any such Soviet intervention.

November 15. UN Force Arrives in Egypt. The UN Emergency Force lands in Egypt. UN troops begin monitoring the truce at positions near Port Said November 20.

November 21. Withdrawal from Egypt Begins. British, French, and Israeli troop withdrawals from Egypt begin. Eisenhower, according to sources, is reported to have sent private messages to the British and French governments urging complete troop withdrawal from the area. The last British and French troops leave Egypt December 22.

ISRAEL

January 30. Israel Appeals for Arms. Israel urges the United States and Great Britain to allow it to buy arms. Secretary of State John Foster Dulles, not excluding "the possibility of arms sales to Israel," suggests February 6 that Israel look for security in the United Nations and the 1950 Anglo-American-French Three-Power agreement.

May 9. U.S. Rejects Arms Sales to Israel. Dulles states that the United States will refrain from selling arms to Israel because it fears confrontation in the Middle East.

1957

REGIONAL AFFAIRS

January 5. Eisenhower Doctrine Announced. President Eisenhower addresses a joint session of Congress to urge support for a declaration, dubbed the Eisenhower Doctrine, calling for American action to counter communist actions in the Middle East. Turkey, Pakistan, Iran, and Iraq, the four Muslim nations of the Baghdad Pact, endorse the doctrine January 21. Saudi Arabian king Saud states his approval during a meeting in Washington with Eisenhower February 6.

March 22. U.S. Joins Military Committee. The United States announces it will join the Military Committee of the Baghdad Pact.

September 5. U.S. Announces Arms Shipments. The United States announces plans to send arms to Jordan, Lebanon, Turkey, and Iraq. Affirming his doctrine on the Middle East, President Eisenhower says September 7 that the United States will take action to protect pro-West Middle East countries if Syria threatens them.

EGYPT

January 4. Suez Canal Opens. The Suez Canal opens halfway, for medium-sized ships.

January 15. Nasser Begins "Egyptianization." Egyptian president Nasser undertakes an "Egyptianization" process whereby only natural Egyptian citizens may hold shares of Egyptian-based companies. British and French banks and insurance companies are nationalized.

March 1. Israelis Withdraw from Gaza. Israel agrees to withdraw its troops from the Gaza Strip and the Gulf of Aqaba on "assumptions" that the UN Emergency Force will administer Gaza until a peace settlement is reached and that free navigation of the gulf will continue. The last Israeli forces withdraw from Egyptian territory March 7.

March 14. Egyptian Administrators to Gaza. In violation of UN resolutions, Egypt sends civil administrators into Gaza and on March 15 announces that Israel would not be permitted to use the Suez Canal. Saudi Arabia halts Israeli use of the Gulf of Aqaba March 15.

JORDAN

March 13. Jordan and Britain End Alliance. Jordan and Great Britain cancel their 1948 treaty of alliance. British troops are to withdraw from Jordan within six months.

April 24. United States Backs Jordan. As internal political turmoil continues in Jordan, a U.S. statement, authorized by President Eisenhower and Secretary of State Dulles, warns that the United States regards "the independence and integrity of Jordan as vital." On April 25 the United States orders the Sixth Fleet into the eastern Mediterranean. The United States extends $10 million in military supplies and services June 29.

May 5. Hussein Defeats Leftists. King Hussein announces that the government's battle against leftist elements in Jordan has succeeded.

June 10. Jordanian-Egyptian Rift. A rift arises in Jordanian-Egyptian relations as Jordan charges that an Egyptian military attache is plotting against Jordanian officials. His recall is requested. Egypt complies.

PERSIAN GULF STATES

July 19. British Troops Clash with Rebels. British-led forces step in to suppress a tribal revolt in Muscat and Oman on the Arabian Peninsula. On July 24 British planes attack military targets controlled by rebel tribesmen in Oman after the rebels refuse to heed a British warning. British troops withdraw from Oman August 20, following rebel recognition August 1 of the sultan of Oman's authority.

SYRIA

August 13. Syria Ousts American Diplomats. Following Syrian accusations of U.S. efforts to overthrow that government, Syria ousts three American embassy officials. On August 14 the United States expels Syrian diplomats.

November 12. Shah Seeks Bahrain. The shah of Iran instructs his cabinet to present a bill to parliament to bring Bahrain, a British oil protectorate, under Iranian jurisdiction.

1958

REGIONAL AFFAIRS

January 30. Dulles Affirms U.S. Commitment. Secretary of State Dulles, addressing the Baghdad Pact countries meeting in Ankara, Turkey, tells the delegates that the Eisenhower Doctrine commits the United States to the Mideast as effectively as would membership in the Baghdad Pact.

August 13. Eisenhower Peace Plan. President Eisenhower presents the UN General Assembly with a "framework of a plan of peace" in the Middle East. It includes provisions for a UN peacekeeping force in the region and for an "Arab development institution on a regional basis, governed by the Arab states themselves."

EGYPT

February 1. Egypt and Syria Form UAR. Egypt and Syria merge into the United Arab Republic (UAR). Citizens of the two countries approve the merger, nearly unanimously, in plebiscites February 21. Yemen agrees to federation with the UAR February 11.

IRAQ

July 14. Coup in Iraq. Revolutionaries seize Baghdad, overthrow the Iraqi government, kill King Faisal and Premier Nuri Said, and proclaim a republic. Brig. Gen. Abd al-Karim al-Qasim is named premier. In reaction to the coup, King Hussein of Jordan announces his assumption of power as head of the Arab Federation of Iraq and Jordan. Hussein and Lebanese president Chamoun each appeal for U.S. military assistance because of the Iraqi coup. Martial law is declared in Iraq July 15.

July 19. UAR-Iraqi Pact. The UAR and the new Iraqi regime sign a mutual defense treaty. Jordan severs relations with the UAR July 20 because of its recognition of the new Iraqi regime. Iraq and the UAR set up committees July 24 to enhance cooperation between member countries in political, economic, military, and educational fields.

August 2. Jordan and Iraq Split. Iraq says it has not renounced the Baghdad Pact, nor will it buy arms from the Soviet Union at this time. Jordan announces the formal dismemberment of the Arab federation of Jordan and Iraq, in light of the new regime in Iraq. The United States recognizes the new Iraqi government.

JORDAN

February 14. Iraq and Jordan Form Federation. Iraq and Jordan form the Arab Federation, with Iraq's King Faisal II serving as head of the two-state federal union. King Hussein retains sovereignty in Jordan. The federation is approved February 17 by the Iraqi parliament and by the Jordanian parliament February 18.

July 17. British Troops to Jordan. British paratroopers land in Jordan at the request of King Hussein.

LEBANON

May 24. UN Debates Lebanon. The UN Security Council meets to discuss Lebanon's complaint that the UAR has incited antigovernment rioting.

June 11. UN Troops to Lebanon. The UN Security Council votes 10-0 to send UN observers to Lebanon to guard against the smuggling of arms or troops into that country.

July 15. U.S. Troops to Lebanon. President Eisenhower dispatches five thousand U.S. Marines to Lebanon. He asserts that the troops will protect American lives and help defend Lebanon's sovereignty and independence. At a meeting of the UN Security Council, the United States says its troops will remain in Lebanon until UN forces can guarantee Lebanon's "continued independence."

July 31. Chehab Elected President. Gen. Fuad Chehab, sympathetic to the Lebanese rebels, is elected president of Lebanon by parliament over the strong objections of premier Said.

August 13. U.S. Troops Depart. U.S. forces begin withdrawing from Lebanon August 12 to demonstrate to the UN that the United States was not trying to build up its forces in that country. The last U.S. troops leave Lebanon October 25.

August 21. UN Urges Early Withdrawal. The UN General Assembly unanimously adopts an Arab resolution calling on Secretary General Dag Hammarskjöld to take the necessary steps to restore order in Jordan and Lebanon and thereby "facilitate the early withdrawal" of foreign troops. In the next few days, tension in the Mideast appears to lessen.

September 22. Karami Becomes Premier. Lebanon's pro-Western cabinet resigns. Rashid Karami, a rebel leader, becomes premier September 24. The United States September 27 assures Karami of continued U.S. support.

LIBYA AND NORTH AFRICA

July 19. British Land in Libya. British commandos land in Libya in support of the government when rumors surface of an Egyptian plan to overthrow it.

PERSIAN GULF STATES

March 24. Faisal Receives Power. King Saud of Saudi Arabia transfers some of his absolute power to his brother, Crown Prince Faisal. Faisal is granted full power to lay down the state's internal, external, and financial policies and to oversee their implementation.

1959

REGIONAL AFFAIRS

March 5. Mutual Defense Pacts Signed. Iran signs a bilateral defense treaty with the United States despite Soviet protests. Turkey and Pakistan also sign mutual defense treaties with the United States that are described by the Eisenhower administration as extensions of its policy to resist Soviet expansion into the Middle East.

August 18. Baghdad Pact Renamed CENTO. With the departure of Iraq from the Baghdad Pact, the organization is renamed the Central Treaty Organization (CENTO), with Great Britain, Iran, Pakistan, and Turkey remaining as members. The United States supports the organization and participates in certain committees, but it is not an official member.

September 4. UAR-Saudi Arabia Talks. After four days of talks, UAR president Nasser and King Saud of Saudi Arabia agree to resume relations with Great Britain and to seek to end communist penetration in Iraq.

December 1. Britain and UAR Reestablish Ties. Great Britain and the UAR reestablish diplomatic relations after a three-year break.

EGYPT

January 17. Suez Pact Signed. Egypt and Great Britain sign the British-Egyptian Suez Pact, which resolves their two-year dispute generated by the Suez crisis in 1956. The agreement contains provisions requiring the British release of frozen Egyptian assets in Great Britain and Egyptian payments for British property it had nationalized.

March 20. Nasser Attacks Soviet Interference. UAR president Nasser denounces Soviet interference in Arab affairs and protests Soviet premier Nikita Khrushchev's remark the day before that Nasser's hostility toward Iraq was "hot-headed." Nasser on March 11 had accused Iraq and foreign communist agents of attempting to divide the Arab world.

IRAQ

March 24. Iraq Leaves Baghdad Pact. Iraq withdraws from the Baghdad Pact, which is left with four members—Great Britain, Iran, Pakistan and Turkey. The United States announces June 1 the termination of U.S.-Iraqi military assistance agreements.

July 13. Upheaval in Iraq. Communist demonstrations in Kirkuk, an Iraqi oil center, nearly erupt into civil war. After the Iraqi army bombs the rebels, the government regains control.

1960

EGYPT

January 18. Soviet Support for Dam. The UAR announces that the Soviet Union will finance the second stage of the Aswan Dam.

February 11. Nasser Threatens Israel. Jordanian foreign minister Musa Nasir says the Arab states are "completely united" on a "declaration of war" against Israel if Israel attempts to divert the Jordan River to irrigate the Negev Desert.

April 8. Suez Canal Seizures. UN Secretary General Hammarskjöld protests UAR seizure of ships carrying Israeli supplies and products through the Suez Canal.

IRAN

July 23. Iran Recognizes Israel. Iran announces recognition of Israel. The new diplomatic ties cause the UAR to break relations with Iran July 27 and impose an economic boycott of Iran July 28.

JORDAN

November 17. Jordan and Iraq to Restore Ties. Jordan and Iraq agree to resume diplomatic ties in December. Relations had been cut off in July 1958, following the Iraqi revolution.

PERSIAN GULF STATES

September 15. OPEC Established. At the end of a five-day conference in Baghdad, representatives of Iran, Iraq, Kuwait, Saudi Arabia, and Venezuela agree to form the Organization of the Petroleum Exporting Countries (OPEC). The permanent organization is intended to help member nations unify their oil policies. Other oil exporting nations may join if all the charter members approve.

December 21. Prince Faisal Resigns. Prince Faisal resigns as Saudi Arabian premier, returning complete control of the government to his brother, King Saud. Saud had relinquished executive power to Faisal early in 1958.

1961

EGYPT

December 26. Nasser Ends Union with Yemen. UAR president Nasser dissolves his country's union with Yemen, formed in 1958, thus reducing the United Arab Republic to only the state of Egypt.

PERSIAN GULF STATES

March 16. U.S.-Saudi Pact Expires. It is disclosed that a U.S.-Saudi Arabian pact of 1957, which called for the setting up of a U.S. military base at Dhahran, will not be renewed. On April 11 King Saud explains that the decision was partially due to American aid to Israel.

June 19. Kuwait Gains Independence. Great Britain grants independence to Kuwait and signs a treaty with the new nation assuring British protection if requested. Kuwaiti shaykh Abdallah al-Salim Al Sabah says June 26 he will fight to maintain Kuwait's independence after Iraq claims that Kuwait is an "integral part" of Iraq.

July 20. Kuwait Joins Arab League. The Arab League unanimously admits Kuwait to membership. Iraq walks out of the meeting, accusing the league of aiding "British imperialism." British protective forces in Kuwait are replaced September 19 by Arab League troops sent to ensure Kuwait's sovereignty against Iraqi claims.

SYRIA

September 29. Syria Breaks with UAR. Following a coup September 28 by dissident Syrian army units, the revolutionary command sets up a civilian government for Syria and announces independence from the UAR. Jordan and Turkey recognize the new Syrian government. President Nasser announces October 1 in Cairo that the UAR has broken ties with Jordan and Turkey for their recognition of the new Syrian government. Syria is reseated at the United Nations October 13, regaining the seat it gave up when it merged with the UAR. The new Syrian government is recognized by the Soviet Union October 7 and by the United States October 10.

1962

PERSIAN GULF STATES

August 29. Saudi-Jordanian Agreement. Saudi Arabia's King Saud and Jordan's King Hussein agree to merge military troops and economic policies.

September 26. Military Revolt in Yemen. Yemen's Imam Badr, only days after assuming power, is driven from San'a' (the capital) in a military revolt led by Col. Abdallah al-Sallal. Al-Sallal received political support from UAR president Nasser, who later sent Egyptian military forces to Yemen.

November 6. Saudis Break Ties with UAR. Saudi Arabia breaks off diplomatic ties with the UAR following charges that UAR planes bombed Saudi Arabian villages near the Yemen border.

SYRIA

March 28. Syrian Army Ousts Government. Syrian army leaders oust the new Syrian government, which was elected after the break with Egypt in the fall of 1961. The Syrian army leaders declare their intentions to work closely with Egypt and Iraq.

April 13. Syrian President Returns to Office. Syrian president Nazem al-Kodsi, ousted by an army coup March 28, returns to office. Kodsi tells Syrians April 14 that he will seek a union of "liberated Arab states, beginning with Egypt."

1963

ARAB-ISRAELI CONFLICT

August 21. Arab League Meets. The Arab League meets to consider a unified stance in support of Syria against Israel as fighting breaks out near the Sea of Galilee. Iraqi forces are placed "at the disposal of" Syria. UAR troops are on alert for possible support of Syria. Israel and Syria agree to a UN-mediated cease-fire August 23.

August 25. Israel, Jordan Clash. Israeli and Jordanian troops clash in Jerusalem before UN truce observers persuade both sides to agree to a cease-fire.

EGYPT

April 10. Federation Plan Outlined. UAR prime minister Aly Sabry outlines plans for a new federation of the UAR, Syria, and Iraq. Later it is announced that the federation proposal will be submitted to national plebiscites to be held September 27, 1963. Street demonstrations break out in Jordan April 20 in support of Jordan's joining the new UAR federation.

July 22. Nasser Renounces Unification. UAR president Nasser renounces an agreement to unite Egypt, Syria, and Iraq and denounces the Syrian Baath Party.

IRAQ

February 8. Iraqi Coup. The Iraqi air force overthrows the government of Premier Qasim. He is killed by a firing squad. A Nasserite and conspirator in the coup, Col. Abd al-Salam Arif, is appointed provisional president.

November 18. Iraqi Coup. Iraq's President Arif announces that his forces have overthrown the civilian Baathist government. Arif becomes president and chief of staff of the army. The new government announces November 21 that it will seek to fulfill the April agreement between Iraq, Syria, and Egypt on the formation of a union and offers November 22 to settle differences with the Kurds.

PERSIAN GULF STATES

May 21. UAR Troops Remain in Yemen. In violation of an agreement reached in April, UAR president Nasser declares that UAR troops will not leave Yemen until royalist factions have been put down.

SYRIA

March 8. Syrian Coup. A coup by pro-Nasser and Baath Party followers ousts the Syrian government. The UAR and Iraq governments threaten war if other nations interfere in the Syrian revolt.

March 12. Syrian Premier Advocates Federation. Syria's new premier, Salah al-Bitar, voices hopes of a federation of Syria, Iraq, and Egypt under one president.

November 12. Syrian Premier Resigns. Syrian premier al-Bitar resigns and a new Syrian government is set up with Maj. Gen. Amin al-Hafiz as president of the Revolutionary Council.

1964

ARAB-ISRAELI CONFLICT

April 14. Hussein-Johnson Talks. In talks with President Lyndon B. Johnson in Washington, Jordan's King Hussein stands firm on Arab intentions to dam two tributaries of the Jordan River and block Israel's plans to divert the Jordan for irrigation purposes.

September 11. Arab Heads Urge Water Projects. After seven days of talks, chiefs of state of thirteen Arab nations issue a final communique urging immediate Arab efforts on water projects to cut off the Jordan River from Israel and thwart its plans to dam the Jordan for irrigation.

IRAQ

February 10. Iraqi-Kurdish Cease-Fire. Iraq's president Arif announces a cease-fire agreement with Iraqi Kurds, apparently concluding the Kurds' struggle for autonomy within Iraq.

May 3. Iraqi Constitution Backs Union. Arif introduces a new provisional constitution May 3 that has as its main goal the union of Iraq with the UAR. The two countries sign an agreement May 26 providing for joint command of their troops in time of war.

LIBYA AND NORTH AFRICA

August 22. United States, Britain to Leave Bases. Libyan premier Mahmud Mutasser announces that both the United States and Great Britain have agreed to give up their military bases in Libya.

PERSIAN GULF STATES

March 28. Faisal Gains Power. King Saud of Saudi Arabia turns over his powers to his half-brother Crown Prince Faisal. Faisal's maneuverings to gain power were backed by a council composed of members of the royal family and religious and tribal leaders who recommended that Saud be deposed. Instead, the council accepts the recommendation of Prince Faisal to retain Saud as a figurehead monarch.

November 2. Prince Faisal Crowned. The Saudi Arabian cabinet and consultative counsel proclaim Crown Prince Faisal the king of Saudi Arabia, thus dethroning King Saud.

1965

ARAB-ISRAELI CONFLICT

January 12. Israel's Allies Warned. After four days of talks in Cairo, the premiers of thirteen Arab nations issue a communique saying they will take joint action against nations henceforth recognizing Israel or aiding in her "aggressive military efforts." The statement is regarded as directed primarily at West Germany, which had shipped arms to Israel the previous month.

February 17. U.S. Approval Disclosed. The State Department acknowledges that the United States had secretly approved the West German-Israeli military aid agreement that sent U.S.-made tanks to Israel in December 1964.

April 21. Tunisian Peace Proposal. Tunisian president Habib Bourguiba criticizes Arab policy toward Israel and proposes broad terms to end the Arab-Israeli conflict. He calls for opening direct negotiations between Israel and the Palestinian Arabs on the basis of the 1947 United Nations plan for partition of Palestine into Jewish and Arab states and for cession of one-third of Israel's territory for a Palestine Arab nation. Israel rejects Bourguiba's plan April 25. The UAR rejects the proposal April 27 and "strongly denounces the issuance of such a proposal from the head of an Arab state."

May 12. Israeli-West German Ties Established. Israel and West Germany establish full diplomatic relations. The UAR breaks diplomatic ties with West Germany. Nine other Arab states later also break ties with Bonn.

EGYPT

February 24. Ulbricht Promises Aid to UAR. After East German leader Walter Ulbricht arrives in Cairo despite West German protests, West Germany suspends its economic assistance to the UAR and cancels its program of guarantees for private investment there. During his seven-day visit, Ulbricht agrees to provide the UAR with $100 million in economic aid.

March 16. Nasser Reelected. UAR president Nasser is elected to another six-year term.

IRAN

January 26. Iranian Premier Dies of Wounds. Premier Hassan Ali Mansour of Iran dies of gunshot wounds inflicted by a student January 21.

PERSIAN GULF STATES

August 24. Agreement on Yemen. Saudi Arabia's King Faisal and UAR president Nasser sign an agreement aimed at stopping the fighting in Yemen. The accord calls for an immediate halt to hostilities, for Saudi Arabia to end military aid to the royalists, and for the UAR to withdraw its troop support of the revolutionary republicans. Representatives of the opposing factions had agreed August 13 to end the three-year civil war.

November 24. Kuwaiti Emir Dies. Kuwait's amir Al Sabah dies and his younger brother Sabah al-Salim Al Sabah is proclaimed the new ruler.

SYRIA

January 3. Syria Nationalizes Industries. Syria nationalizes, in whole or part, 107 principal industries, reportedly to stem the flow of capital from the country.

March 4. Syria Nationalizes Oil Companies. Syria nationalizes nine oil companies: six Syrian, two U.S. affiliates, and one joint British-Dutch company.

August 23. Syrian Legislature Formed. The Arab Socialist Baath Party in Syria establishes a National Council (legislature) to consolidate the party's political control. The new provisional legislature reelects Amin al-Hafiz as chairman of the Presidency Council, September 2.

1966

IRAQ

April 13. Iraqi President Killed. Iraqi president Abd al-Salam Arif dies in a helicopter crash. Maj. Gen. Abd al-Rahman Arif is elected April 16 by a joint session of the cabinet and the national defense council to succeed his brother as president.

ISRAEL

May 19. U.S. Sells Jets to Israel. It is reported in Washington that the United States agreed in February to sell several tactical jet bombers to Israel.

JORDAN

May 25. Hussein Begins Dam Construction. King Hussein lays the first stone of Jordan's Mokheiba Dam. The dam is part of an Arab effort to divert the Jordan River from Israel.

November 29. Hussein Accuses Soviets. Jordan's King Hussein charges the Soviet Union with fomenting tension in the Middle East following a week of antigovernment demonstrations and riots.

December 7. Syria Calls for Hussein's Ouster. Syrian chief of state Nureddin Atassi calls on Jordanians and Palestine Arabs to overthrow Jordan's King Hussein and offers them arms.

SYRIA

February 25. Coup in Syria. Following a coup February 23 by left wings of the military and of the Baath party, Syria announces that the military junta in power has named Nureddin Atassi chief of state. Atassi had been ousted from office by a coup in December 1965.

November 4. Syria-UAR Treaty. Syria and the UAR sign a mutual defense treaty that provides for joint command of their armed forces.

1967

ARAB-ISRAELI CONFLICT

May 15. Military Alert. The UAR alerts its military forces because of mounting tension with Israel. Syria also announces that its military forces are ready for action.

May 19. UN Peacekeepers Withdraw. The UN Emergency Force in the Middle East ends its patrols in the Gaza Strip and at Sharm al-Shaykh at the mouth of the Gulf of Aqaba at the request of the UAR, ending a ten-year commitment to peacekeeping in that area. The UAR declares May 20 that a state of emergency exists along the Gaza Strip.

May 22. UAR Blockades Israel. The UAR closes the Strait of Tiran at the entrance to the Gulf of Aqaba to Israeli ships and to ships carrying strategic cargo bound for Israel. The United States and Israel each issue strong warnings May 23 against the UAR's blockade. U.S. president Johnson orders the Sixth Fleet toward the eastern Mediterranean. Reports on May 24 disclose Egypt has mined the Strait of Tiran. Egyptian and Israeli troops skirmish in the Gaza Strip, May 29.

June 5. Six-Day War Begins. Israeli warplanes carry out early morning surprise attacks that almost entirely destroy the air forces of Egypt, Syria, and Jordan. Israeli troops drive deep into the Sinai and engage Arab troops in Jerusalem on the first day of fighting. The UN Security Council calls for an immediate cease-fire in the Middle East.

June 6-7. Arab Responses. In response to the Israeli attack, the UAR, Syria, Iraq, Sudan, Algeria, and Yemen sever diplomatic relations with the United States; Kuwait and Iraq cut off oil supplies to the United States and Great Britain; and the UAR closes the Suez Canal, charging that U.S. and British planes are aiding Israel. The United States strongly rejects the charges.

June 7. Israelis Capture Territory. In a sweeping seizure of territory, Israel breaks the blockade of the Gulf of Aqaba and takes over the Old City of Jerusalem, Bethlehem in Jordan, the Sinai Peninsula between the Negev Desert and the Suez Canal, and the Gaza Strip. Israel announces it will accept the UN cease-fire resolution if the Arab states do. The cease-fire is accepted by Jordan June 7. The UAR accepts the cease-fire June 8.

June 8. U.S. Ship Attacked. Israeli planes erroneously attack the U.S. Navy vessel *Liberty* in the Mediterranean, killing at least thirty-four. Israel apologizes and later pays the United States $3 million for the families of the dead sailors.

June 9. Nasser's Resignation Refused. Claiming sole responsibility for Egypt's defeat by Israel, President Nasser resigns. The National Assembly rejects his resignation.

June 10. Soviets Cut Ties with Israel. The Soviet Union severs diplomatic ties with Israel, pledging assistance to Arab states if Israel refuses to withdraw from conquered territory.

June 10. Israel Captures Golan Heights. Israeli air attacks force the Syrian army to withdraw from the strategic Golan Heights on the sixth day of the war. Israel and Syria sign a cease-fire agreement that goes into effect that evening, bringing the war to an end.

June 12. Israel Refuses to Withdraw. Israel announces that it will not withdraw to the 1949 armistice boundaries and calls for direct negotiations between Israel and Arab nations.

June 19. Johnson Peace Plan. President Johnson, in a nationally televised speech, sets forth five points for peace in the Middle East: right of each country's national existence, fair and just treatment of Arab refugees, freedom of innocent maritime passage, limitation of arms buildup, and guaranteed territorial integrity for each Middle East country. Meanwhile at the UN, Soviet premier Aleksei N. Kosygin calls for the condemnation of Israel, the withdrawal of Israeli forces from occupied Arab lands, and Israeli reparations to Syria, Jordan, and the UAR for damages incurred during the war.

June 23. Glassboro Summit. Johnson and Soviet premier Kosygin meet for five and one-half hours at Glassboro State College in New Jersey to discuss the Middle East, Vietnam, and arms control. They meet again for more than four hours June 25, but later Johnson says that "no agreement is readily in sight on the Middle East crisis." Kosygin, at a televised news conference, says the first step to peace in the Middle East is Israel's withdrawal to 1949 armistice lines.

June 28. Jerusalem Unified under Israelis. Israel proclaims the merger of all of Jerusalem under Israeli rule. The action ends the de facto division of the city that had existed since the 1948 Arab-Israeli war and defies demands from other countries that the city be internationalized.

July 4. Suez Cease-Fire. UN Secretary General U Thant asks Israel and the UAR to accept UN supervision of the cease-fire in the Suez Canal Zone. The UAR agrees July 10, and Israel accepts July 11.

July 17. Israeli Conditions for Talks. Israel tells the UN General Assembly that the Arab states must recognize Israel's "statehood, sovereignty, and international rights" before peace talks can begin.

September 1. Nonmilitary Means Endorsed. Arab heads of state, meeting in Khartoum, agree to seek a non-military solution to the tensions with Israel.

September 24. Israel Announces Settlements. Israel announces it will move settlers into occupied Syria and the captured Jordanian sector of Jerusalem. The United States expresses its "disappointment" with that decision September 26.

September 27. Israeli Proposals. Israeli foreign minister Abba Eban suggests economic cooperation between Israel, Lebanon, and Jordan, the demilitarization of the Sinai, and the establishment of a "universal status" for the "holy places" of Jerusalem.

October 22. Israel Announces Pipeline. Israel announces plans to build an oil pipeline between Eilat on the Gulf of Aqaba and Ashdod on the Mediterranean to circumvent the Suez Canal.

November 5. Hussein Ready to Recognize Israel. Jordan's King Hussein tells an American television audience that his country is ready to recognize Israel's right to exist.

November 22. Resolution 242 Adopted. The UN Security Council unanimously adopts a British proposal (Resolution 242) for bringing peace to the Middle East. Under the plan, Israel would withdraw from conquered territory, each country would agree to recognize the territory of the other states, and free navigation through international waterways would be ensured.

November 23. Nasser on Israel. UAR president Nasser says he will continue to deny Israeli ships passage through the Suez Canal and that Israeli withdrawal from occupied lands is not open to negotiation.

IRAN

February 19. Iran Buys Soviet Arms. Iran and the Soviet Union sign an agreement whereby Iran will purchase $110 million in arms and supplies.

JORDAN

May 23. Jordan Closes Syrian Embassy. Following the explosion of a bomb on the Jordan-Syria border, Jordan orders the closing of the Syrian embassy and the departure of Syria's ambassador to Jordan.

May 30. Jordan-UAR Pact. Jordan and the UAR sign a mutual defense pact.

PERSIAN GULF STATES

April 20. Iraq and Kuwait Battle. Iraq and Kuwait call home their ambassadors as fighting erupts along their common border.

November 28. South Yemen Independence. Great Britain declares the independence of South Arabia, which is renamed the People's Republic of South Yemen. British troops complete their evacuation of Aden November 29. The country had been a British colony

since 1839. The new government announces the dismissal of all remaining British military and administrative officers February 27, 1968.

1968

ARAB-ISRAELI CONFLICT

February 15. Israel and Jordan Battle. Significant fighting between Jordan and Israel erupts along their common border. U.S. embassies in both states successfully negotiate a cease-fire after eight hours of fighting. The next day, Jordan's King Hussein calls for an end to attacks originating within Jordan against Israel because, he says, such raids prompt Israeli retaliation.

April 10. Support for Palestinians. UAR president Nasser says his country is "fully prepared to support and arm the Palestine resistance movement" in its fight against Israel. Iraq April 13 announces the formation of a committee to raise funds for the Arab guerrillas.

July 5. Israel Rejects UN Force. Israel rejects plans for a UN peacekeeping force in the Israeli-occupied Sinai Peninsula, endorsed the day before by the UAR. Israeli leaders again call for direct negotiations on a peace settlement with Arab states.

July 10. Palestine National Council Meets. The Palestine National Council holds its first meeting, in Cairo.

August 11. UAR Proposals. Easing its position on a Middle East settlement, the UAR says it will agree to a demilitarization of the Sinai, lift demands for the return of Arab refugees to their homeland, accept internationalization of the Gaza Strip, and grant passage through the Suez Canal to Israeli cargoes on non-Israeli ships and passage through the Strait of Tiran to Israeli vessels.

October 8. Israeli Peace Plan. Israeli foreign minister Eban offers a nine-point peace plan at the United Nations. The proposal calls for Israeli withdrawal from occupied territory following the establishment of "permanent" boundaries between the Arab states and Israel. The UAR rejects the plan October 9 but agrees October 10 to accept a UN timetable for implementing UN Security Council Resolution 242.

December 2. Jordan and Israel Battle. Jordanian and Israeli troops clash in heavy fighting. After a predawn Jordanian artillery attack December 3, Israeli jets strike Jordanian targets.

December 26. Israeli Jet Attacked. Two Arabs attack an Israeli passenger jet at the Athens airport, setting it afire. In retaliation, an Israeli task force December 28 attacks the Beirut International Airport, destroying several airplanes.

IRAQ

July 17. Iraqi Coup. The fourth coup in ten years deposes Iraq's government. Ahmad Hassan al-Bakr is named president and premier July 31.

1969

ARAB-ISRAELI CONFLICT

February 2. Nasser Interview. Newsweek magazine publishes an exclusive interview with UAR president Nasser, who suggests a five-point peace plan for the Middle East: "a declaration of non-belligerence; the recognition of the right of each country to live in peace; the territorial integrity of all countries in the Middle East, including Israel, within recognized and secure borders; freedom of navigation on international waterways; a just solution to the Palestinian refugee problem." Israel rejects Nasser's plan February 4.

April 10. Hussein Peace Plan. In Washington for talks with President Richard Nixon, Jordan's King Hussein addresses the National Press Club and sets forth a six-point peace plan that he says has the approval of UAR president Nasser. Similar to UN Resolution 242, the plan is contingent upon Israeli withdrawal from occupied lands. Israel rejects the plan the following day as propaganda.

April 22. Israeli-Egyptian Conflict. UN Secretary General U Thant says that Israel and Egypt are engaged in "a virtual state of active war" and declares that the UN cease-fire has become "totally ineffective in the Suez Canal sector." The UAR April 23 repudiates the UN cease-fire.

July 20. Israeli Air Attacks. After two weeks of sporadic fighting along the Suez Canal, Israeli jets attack UAR ground installations for the first time since the June 1967 war.

August 3. Israel to Keep Territory. Israel announces that to protect its security it will retain the Golan Heights, the Gaza Strip, and part of the Sinai Peninsula.

August 21. Al-Aqsa Mosque Fire. A fire damages the al-Aqsa mosque in Jerusalem, one of Islam's holiest shrines. Israeli authorities arrest Michael Rohan, an Australian tourist, and charge him with arson. Arabs in the occupied territories discount the arrest and hold a general strike August 23 to protest Israel's failure to prevent the fire. The same day UAR president Nasser charges Israel with responsibility for the fire and calls for an all-out war with Israel to restore Arab control over Jerusalem and its holy sites. The mosque reopens September 19 after repairs are completed. Rohan pleads guilty at his arson trial in Israel October 7.

August 31. TWA Hijacking. Arab hijackers blow up a TWA airliner after diverting it to Damascus following takeoff from Rome. The hijackers demand imprisonment of all the Israeli passengers, but Syria releases all but six Israelis August 30. Those six are held hostage for the release of Syrian prisoners of war in Israel.

December 9. U.S. Peace Proposal. Secretary of State William Rogers discloses a previously secret U.S. proposal for Middle East peace, including a provision for Israel's withdrawal from occupied lands in exchange for a binding peace treaty signed by the Arabs. Israeli premier Golda Meir says December 12 that the plan is an attempt by the United States to "moralize."

ISRAEL

February 26. Eshkol Dies. Prime Minister Levi Eshkol of Israel dies following a heart attack. Foreign Minister Golda Meir accepts election as leader of the Labor Party March 7 and thereby becomes premier, succeeding Eshkol.

LIBYA AND NORTH AFRICA

September 1. Idris Overthrown. Libya's King Idris is overthrown by a revolutionary council. The council, on September 2, says it will honor existing agreements with oil companies. Mu'ammar al-Qadhafi, head of the Revolutionary Command Council, emerges as leader of the regime.

October 28. Libya Orders U.S. Withdrawal. The new military regime in Libya notifies the United States that Wheelus Air Force Base, near Tripoli, must be evacuated by December 24, 1970. The United States formally relinquishes the base on June 11, 1970.

PERSIAN GULF STATES

October 22. Gulf Federation Established. The nine-nation Federation of Persian Gulf Emirates is established with Zayed bin Sultan Al Nahayan of Abu Dhabi as president.

1970

ARAB-ISRAELI CONFLICT

January 21. Arabs and Israelis Battle. Israel, launching its largest ground operation since June 1967, captures the Egyptian island of Shadwan at the entrance of the Gulf of Suez. The heaviest fighting between Israel and Syria since the June 1967 war breaks out in the Golan Heights February 2.

May 9. Israeli Warning. Responding to an apparent infusion of Soviet troops and antiaircraft missiles into Egypt, Israel warns that the installation of Soviet SAM-3 missiles along the Suez Canal will not be permitted. It threatens to attack Soviet planes if they interfere with Israeli attacks on Egyptian bases.

June 24. Soviets Flying Combat Missions. Foreign intelligence reports received in Washington indicate that Soviet pilots have taken over the air defense of Egypt against Israel and are flying combat missions south of the Suez Canal.

June 25. Cease-Fire Proposal. Secretary of State Rogers tells a news conference in Washington of a broad-based diplomatic effort to encourage Arab and Israeli representatives "to stop shooting and start talking" under UN supervision. The heart of the proposal is a ninety-day cease-fire tied to withdrawal of Israeli forces from territory occupied during the June 1967 war. Israeli prime minister Meir rejects the plan June 29.

July 23. UAR Accepts Cease-Fire. The UAR accepts a U.S. proposal calling for a ninety-day cease-fire in the Middle East. Jordan accepts the proposal July 26. One of the terms of the cease-fire requires Jordan to control guerrilla activities organized within its borders. Yasir Arafat, head of the Palestine Liberation Organization (PLO), rejects a cease-fire and all other compromise solutions to the conflict with Israel July 31.

August 4. Israel Accepts Cease-Fire. Israel formally accepts the Middle East cease-fire. Prime Minister Meir tells the Israeli parliament that she agreed to accept the proposal after receiving assurances of military and political support from U.S. president Nixon. The cease-fire goes into effect August 7.

September 6. PFLP Hijackings. Members of the Popular Front for the Liberation of Palestine (PFLP), a member organization of the PLO, succeed in three of four attempts to hijack commercial jets. A Pan Am 747 is forced to land in Cairo, passengers are disembarked, and the plane is blown up. A Swissair jet and a TWA jet are forced to land at a desert airstrip in Jordan controlled by the PFLP. The use of the Jordanian airstrip is regarded as a direct challenge to King Hussein's authority by the Palestinian hijackers. The next day, the PFLP releases nearly half of the passengers from the planes brought down in the desert. It demands the release of Arab guerrillas held in Israel and Western Europe in exchange for the remaining hostages. The seizure of a fourth plane, an Israeli passenger jet bound from Amsterdam to New York, was thwarted by security guards aboard the aircraft.

September 9. Hijacking Continues. Members of the PFLP seize a fifth plane, a British BOAC jet, and hijack it to Jordan to join the two other planes in the desert. Hostages total nearly three hundred. The PFLP releases all but fifty-four of its hostages September 12 and blows up the three empty airplanes. Great Britain announces it will release an Arab commando seized in an aborted hijack effort September 6.

September 18. Meir-Nixon Meeting. Israel's prime minister Meir meets with President Nixon in Washington and says Israel will not participate in the UN peace talks until Egypt removes new missile installations along the Suez Canal.

September 29. Hostages Released. Palestinian commandos release the last hostages held since several planes were hijacked earlier in the month. Forty-eight others had been released September 25. Switzerland announces that a total of nineteen Arabs will be released by Great Britain, West Germany, Switzerland, and Israel.

EGYPT

September 28. Nasser Dies. UAR president Gamal Abdel Nasser, 52, dies of a heart attack. Anwar al-Sadat

is sworn in as UAR president October 17, following an October 15 election in which he receives 90 percent of the vote.

JORDAN

September 1. Hussein Escapes Assassination. The motorcade of Jordan's King Hussein is fired upon by unidentified gunmen in Amman. The assailants escape and the king is not injured. The attack follows several days of hostilities between Jordanian army troops and Palestinian guerrillas and causes the fighting to intensify.

September 16. Hussein Proclaims Martial Law. King Hussein proclaims martial law in Jordan and installs a military government in response to continued fighting between his army and Palestinian guerrillas. The move precipitates open civil war between Jordanian troops and Palestinian forces. Thousands of military and civilian casualties are reported during the following weeks. In Amman, where the fighting is heaviest, the government enforces an around-the-clock curfew that leaves many residents without food or water. President Nixon indicates September 17 that the United States would intervene if the Jordanian government were threatened by outside powers.

September 19. Jordanian Civil War. A Syrian column enters northern Jordan September 19 in support of the Palestinian guerrillas. With Syrian help, the guerrillas gain control of much of northern Jordan by September 21. U.S. forces in the Mediterranean are reinforced September 20 in preparation for a possible intervention. The U.S. government reports September 22 that the Soviet Union has said it has asked Syria to withdraw its forces from Jordan. Jordanian tanks and planes push Syrian tanks out of northern Jordan September 23.

September 25. Cease-Fire. The Jordanian government and the leaders of the Palestinian guerrillas agree to a cease-fire. Sporadic fighting continues in Amman, but the cease-fire effectively ends fighting between major units. King Hussein appoints a new civilian-military government to replace the military government appointed September 16.

September 27. Jordanian-Palestinian Pact. A fourteen-point agreement is signed in Cairo by Arab heads of state—including Jordan's King Hussein and PLO leader Yasir Arafat—to end hostilities in Jordan. The agreement calls for King Hussein to remain on the throne, but for a three-member committee, headed by Tunisian premier Ladgham, to supervise the government until conditions are normalized. Arab leaders also pledge to support the Palestinian struggle against Israel.

LIBYA AND NORTH AFRICA

January 16. Qadhafi Becomes Premier. Mu'ammar al-Qadhafi, leader of the Revolutionary Command Council, becomes premier and defense minister of Libya, succeeding Mahmoud Soliman al-Maghreby.

July 5. Libya Nationalizes Oil Distributors. Libya's Revolutionary Command Council announces nationalization of that country's four oil-distributing companies.

PERSIAN GULF STATES

April 14. Yemen War Ends. The civil war in Yemen between republican and royalist forces ends. Saudi Arabia signs an agreement with the republican regime, pledging to discontinue supplying arms and funds to royalist rebels, which it has done since the outbreak of hostilities in 1962.

SYRIA

November 13. Syrian Coup. Syrian president and premier Nureddin Atassi is reported to have been placed under house arrest. "Provisional leadership" will guide the government until a national congress can elect permanent leaders.

1971

ARAB-ISRAELI CONFLICT

March 12. Israeli Position. Golda Meir, stating Israel's position on a Middle East settlement, calls for demilitarization of the Sinai, Israeli possession of Jerusalem, and Israeli retention of Sharm al-Shaykh, Israel's sole land link with East Africa and Asia.

October 4. U.S. Peace Plan. Secretary of State Rogers presents a detailed account of the U.S. position on the Middle East. He calls on Israel and Egypt to agree to open the Suez Canal as a first step toward peace in the area. Egypt rejects the proposal October 6, lacking assurances of Israeli withdrawal from Arab lands.

EGYPT

January 15. Aswan Dam Dedicated. UAR president Sadat and Soviet president Nikolai V. Podgornyi dedicate the Aswan Dam.

April 17. Federation Agreement Signed. Egypt, Libya, and Syria sign an agreement to form the Federation of Arab Republics. Plebiscites will be held September 1 in the three countries to gain popular approval for the union.

May 27. UAR-Soviet Treaty. Sadat and Podgornyi sign a fifteen-year treaty of friendship and cooperation. The UAR and the Soviet Union issue a joint communique July 4, declaring that the Suez Canal will be opened only after Israel withdraws all of its forces from Arab territory.

September 2. Citizens Favor Federation. Citizens of Egypt, Libya, and Syria vote almost unanimously in favor of the proposed Federation of Arab Republics that is intended to provide a solid front against Israel.

October 4. Sadat Chosen Federation President. Egyptian president Sadat is selected as the first president of the Federation of Arab Republics.

IRAN

November 30. Iranians Occupy Islands. Iranian troops occupy the Iraqi territory of Abu Musa, Greater Tunb, and Lesser Tunb, all in Persian Gulf waters near the Strait of Hormuz. Iraq severs relations with Iran and Great Britain as a result.

JORDAN

April 3. Fighting in Jordan Continues. Amid continued Palestinian guerrilla activity in Jordan, King Hussein says the guerrillas must remove their weapons from Amman within two days. The commandos have said they will stay in Amman and continue their fight to overthrow Hussein and to use Jordan as a base for operations against Israel.

November 28. Wasfi al-Tal Assassinated. Jordanian premier Wasfi al-Tal is assassinated while visiting Cairo. Ahmad al-Lawzi succeeds him as premier November 29. The Jordanian government December 17 formally charges the Palestinian group Fatah with responsibility for the slaying.

PERSIAN GULF STATES

December 2. UAE Proclaims Independence. The United Arab Emirates proclaims its independence. Zayed bin Sultan Al Nahayan of Abu Dhabi is named president of the union, which consists of six Persian Gulf shaykhdoms. Ras al-Khaimah later becomes the seventh shaykhdom to join the union.

SYRIA

March 13. Asad Becomes President. Premier Hafiz al-Asad is proclaimed president of Syria.

August 12. Syria-Jordan Rift. Syria breaks off diplomatic relations with Jordan following clashes on their common border.

1972

ARAB-ISRAELI CONFLICT

May 8. Hijacked Jet Rescued. Four Palestinians, later identified as members of the Black September organization, seize a Belgian airliner after leaving Vienna en route to Tel Aviv. Israeli troops break into the plane at Lod Airport in Tel Aviv May 9, killing two of four Palestinian commandos and rescuing all ninety passengers and ten crew members.

May 30. Lod Airport Massacre. Three Japanese attack the Lod International Airport near Tel Aviv with hand grenades and automatic weapons. They kill twenty-six people and wound at least seventy-five others. Two of the three are killed and the third is captured. The Popular Front for the Liberation of Palestine headquartered in Beirut says it recruited the killers and takes responsibility for the attack.

September 5. Olympic Hostage Crisis. Eight Arab commandos of the Black September organization seize a building housing the Israeli team at the Olympic Games in Munich, West Germany. Two Israelis are killed immediately, and nine are taken hostage. After day-long negotiations, the Arabs and their hostages are flown by helicopter to a Munich airport, where West German police engage the Arabs in a gun battle. All nine of the Israeli hostages, five of the Arabs, and one West German police officer are killed. The remaining three Arabs are wounded and captured. In response Israel September 8 launches the most extensive air raids on Arab guerrilla bases in Syria and Lebanon since the June 1967 war.

September 19. Israeli Diplomat Killed. A letter bomb, believed to have been sent by the Black September organization, explodes in the Israeli embassy in London, killing the Israeli agricultural counselor. Similar incidents in the next two days are blamed on the Black September group.

October 15. Israel Launches Attack. Israel, launching its first unprovoked attack on Palestinian guerrilla bases in Syria and Lebanon, says "we are no longer waiting for them to hit first."

October 29. Hijacking of West German Plane. Two Arab guerrillas of the Black September organization hijack a West German airliner, forcing the release of three commandos held in the September 5 murder of eleven Israeli athletes at the Olympic Games. Israel protests the German action, calling it "capitulation to terrorists."

EGYPT

July 18. Sadat Expels Soviets. Egyptian president Sadat orders all Soviet military advisers out of his country and places all Soviet bases and equipment under Egyptian control. Sadat says July 24 during a four-hour speech that the Soviet Union's "excessive caution" as an ally led him to his decision.

IRAQ

June 1. Iraq Petroleum Nationalized. Iraq nationalizes the Iraq Petroleum Company, owned jointly by American, British, French, and Dutch oil companies. The company produces 10 percent of Middle East oil.

JORDAN

March 15. Hussein Plan. King Hussein unveils his plan to make Jordan a federated state comprising two autonomous regions on the East and West Bank of the Jordan River. Hussein proposes Jerusalem as the capital of the West Bank, or Palestine, region. Israel, the same day, denounces the plan. The Federation of Arab Republics denounces the plan March 18 and calls on all Arab governments to similarly reject it. Egypt severs diplomatic relations with Jordan April 6, criticizing Hussein's proposal.

November 27. Hussein Confirms Coup Attempt. King Hussein confirms reports of an aborted coup to overthrow him, planned by Libyan leader Qadhafi, PLO leader Arafat, and other Palestinians.

LIBYA AND NORTH AFRICA

August 2. Libyan-Egyptian Unity. Libyan leader Qadhafi and Egyptian president Sadat jointly declare their intention to establish "unified political leadership."

September 18. Unification Progress. Sadat and Qadhafi, taking a step toward unification, agree to make Cairo the capital of their projected unified state, to popularly elect one president, and to allow one political party.

PERSIAN GULF STATES

October 28. Yemen Accord. Ending several weeks of heavy fighting, Yemen and South Yemen sign an accord in Cairo calling for their merger.

SYRIA

September 13. Soviet-Syrian Agreement. Syria and the Soviet Union agree to security arrangements. The Soviets will improve naval facilities in two Syrian ports for Soviet use and Syria will receive jet fighters and air defense missiles.

1973

ARAB-ISRAELI CONFLICT

February 21. Israel Downs Airliner. A Libyan passenger airliner, reportedly failing to heed Israeli instructions to land after straying over Israeli-occupied Sinai, is fired upon and crashes, killing 106 persons. Israel assumes no responsibility for the crash and instead blames the airline pilot for not landing and Cairo air controllers for misguidance.

July 20. Japan Air Lines Hijacking. Arab and Japanese hijackers seize a Japan Air Lines jet and demand the release of a Japanese man serving a life sentence for taking part in the May 1972 massacre of twenty-six persons at the Tel Aviv airport. The hijackers blow up the plane July 24 at Libya's Benghazi airport after the passengers and crew are evacuated. The hijackers are arrested by Libyan officials.

August 5. Athens Attack. Two Black September guerrillas kill three persons and wound another fifty-five after firing machine guns and hurling grenades in the Athens airport.

August 11. Israelis Divert Plane. Israel forces a Middle East Airlines jet, flying over Lebanon, to land in Israel. Israel announces it diverted the wrong plane in its search for the leader of the Popular Front for the Liberation of Palestine, the group held responsible by Israel for the slayings in the Athens airport.

October 6. Arab-Israeli War Begins. War breaks out on the Jewish holy day of Yom Kippur. Egyptian forces cross the Suez Canal and establish a bridgehead on the Israeli-held eastern bank. Syria attacks Israeli positions in the Golan Heights. UN observers report that the Egyptian and Syrian armies initiated the hostilities.

October 7. Fighting Continues. Israeli forces counterattack in the Sinai and on the Golan Heights. Fierce fighting leaves hundreds of Arab and Israeli soldiers dead. Iraq nationalizes the American-owned Mobil Oil and Exxon Corporations in retaliation for U.S. support of Israel.

October 8. Arab Support. Tunisia, the Sudan, and Iraq pledge support of Egyptian and Syrian forces battling Israel.

October 10. Israeli Retreat. Israel acknowledges it has abandoned its Bar-Lev defense line near the Suez Canal. The Egyptian offensive has forced the Israelis to withdraw about ten miles from the canal. Israel also says its forces in the Golan Heights have turned back the Syrian advance and have crossed the 1967 cease-fire line.

October 12. Israelis Advance in Syria. Israeli forces advance to within eighteen miles of Damascus.

October 13. Jordan, Saudi Arabia Join Fight. Jordan announces it will join Egypt and Syria in the war against Israel. Saudi Arabian troops also participate after urging by Egyptian president Sadat. The same day, Israel claims to have nearly eliminated an Iraqi division in Syria.

October 15. U.S. Resupply Effort. The United States announces it is resupplying Israel with military equipment to counterbalance a "massive airlift" to Egypt by the Soviet Union. In the Sinai, Israeli detachments cross to the western bank of the canal and establish a bridgehead while the main Egyptian and Israeli forces continue to fight on the eastern side of the canal.

October 17. Sadat Proposes Cease-Fire. Egypt's president Sadat, in an open letter to President Nixon, proposes an immediate cease-fire on the condition that Israel withdraw to pre-1967 boundaries. The same day, foreign ministers of four Arab states meet in Washington with President Nixon and Secretary of State Henry Kissinger to present a similar peace proposal. Meanwhile, a major battle erupts between Egyptian and Israeli tank units on both sides of the Suez Canal.

October 20. Kissinger-Brezhnev Talks. Kissinger arrives in Moscow for talks with communist party chief Leonid I. Brezhnev on restoring peace to the Middle East.

October 21. UN Cease-Fire Resolution. The United States and the Soviet Union present a joint resolution to the UN Security Council calling for a cease-fire in the Middle East and Israeli withdrawal from lands occupied since the 1967 war. The proposal, known as Resolution 338, was formulated during Kissinger's trip to Moscow. It is adopted by the Security Council early October 22.

That day a cease-fire takes effect on the Egyptian-Israeli front, but fighting continues nonetheless. Jordan accepts the U.S.-Soviet cease-fire proposal. Iraq and the Palestine Liberation Organization reject it.

October 23. Egyptian III Corps Cut Off. Egypt and Israel accuse each other of cease-fire violations as heavy fighting resumes on the canal front. Israeli forces on the canal's western bank push south to cut off both the city of Suez and the twenty-thousand-troop Egyptian III Corps on the eastern bank. The UN Security Council votes to reaffirm the Middle East cease-fire, asks Egypt and Israel to return to the cease-fire line established the day before, and asks that UN observers be stationed along the Israeli-Egyptian cease-fire line.

October 24. Sadat Appeal. Sadat appeals for the United States and the Soviet Union to send troops to supervise the cease-fire. The White House announces it will not send forces.

October 25. U.S. Military Alert. President Nixon orders a worldwide U.S. military alert as tension mounts over whether the Soviet Union may intervene in the Middle East crisis. Kissinger says there are "ambiguous" indications of that action. To avert a U.S.-Soviet confrontation, the UN Security Council votes to establish an emergency supervisory force to observe the cease-fire. The force would exclude troops from the permanent Security Council members, particularly the United States and the Soviet Union.

October 27. Egypt and Israel to Talk. The United States announces that Egypt and Israel have agreed to negotiate directly on implementing the cease-fire.

October 28. Egyptian III Corps Receives Supplies. The trapped Egyptian III Corps receives food, water, and medical supplies after Israel agrees to allow a supply convoy to pass through Israeli lines. It is reported that Israel yielded following U.S. warnings that the Soviet Union threatened to rescue the troops. Israeli sources concede that on October 23 their units drove to the port of Adabiya to isolate the III Corps.

October 29. Syria Accepts Cease-Fire. Syrian president Asad says Syria has accepted the cease-fire after receiving Soviet guarantees of Israel's withdrawal from all occupied territory and recognition of Palestinian rights.

October 31. Meir in Washington. Israel's prime minister Golda Meir arrives in Washington for talks with President Nixon on her country's concern over U.S. pressure to make concessions. The same day, Egypt's Sadat warns that his country will take up the fight again if Israel does not withdraw to the cease-fire lines of October 22, 1973. Meir says November 1 that she has been assured of continued U.S. support.

November 11. Cease-Fire Signed. Israel and Egypt sign a cease-fire accord, drawn up by Kissinger and Sadat. The six-point plan calls for both sides to observe the cease-fire; immediate discussions on returning to the October 22 cease-fire lines; immediate food and medical supplies for Suez City; immediate nonmilitary supplies to the stranded Egyptian III Corps on the eastern bank of the Suez Canal; replacement of Israeli troops along the Suez by UN forces; and exchange of all prisoners of war. The cease-fire is the first important document signed by the two parties since the 1949 armistice agreement. The first planeloads of Egyptian and Israeli POWs are exchanged November 15.

December 21. Geneva Conference. The first Arab-Israeli peace conference opens in Geneva. Israel, Egypt, Jordan, the United States, the Soviet Union, and the United Nations are represented. Syria boycotts the conference.

EGYPT

August 29. Libya, Egypt Pursue Gradual Unity. Libyan leader Qadhafi and Egyptian president Sadat announce the "birth of a new unified Arab state" and a gradual approach to unification of their countries. Egypt had insisted on gradual unification instead of completion of the union by September 1, 1973, as originally agreed.

November 7. United States, Egypt Agree to Restore Ties. After talks between Kissinger and Sadat, it is announced that Egypt and the United States will resume diplomatic relations. Ties are resumed February 28, 1974.

ISRAEL

December 31. Israeli Election. Israel holds general elections, resulting in a loss of parliamentary seats for Prime Minister Meir's Labor-led coalition. A governmental crisis begins that extends into the spring of 1974 as Meir seeks unsuccessfully to form a government.

PERSIAN GULF STATES

October 18. Arab Oil Strategy. Saudi Arabia announces a 10 percent cut in oil production and pledges to cut off all oil shipments to the United States if it continues to support Israel. The day before, OPEC ministers meeting in Kuwait agreed to reduce oil production by 5 percent each month until Israel withdraws from the occupied territories and agrees to respect the rights of the Palestinians.

October 19. Nixon Asks for Aid to Israel. President Nixon asks Congress to appropriate $2.2 billion for emergency military aid for Israel. Libya cuts off all oil exports to the United States and raises the price of oil from $4.90 to $8.92 per barrel. Saudi Arabia halts oil exports to the United States October 20.

October 21. Arab Oil Embargo. Kuwait, Qatar, Bahrain, and Dubai announce suspension of all oil exports to the United States, theoretically marking the total cutoff of all oil from Arab states to the United States.

November 18. Arabs Cancel Output Cut. The Organization of Arab Petroleum Exporting Countries (OAPEC) cancels its 5 percent output cut slated for December in a conciliatory gesture to most West European nations. The embargo against the Netherlands and the United States continues because of their pro-Israel stance. Saudi Arabia threatens November 22 to cut oil production by 80 percent if the United States retaliates for Arab oil cuts or embargoes.

December 25. Oil Production Increase. The Saudi Arabian oil minister, speaking for the OAPEC countries, announces the cancellation of a further 5 percent oil production cut and instead discloses a 10 percent production increase. The U.S. oil embargo will continue, however.

1974

REGIONAL AFFAIRS

June 12–18. Nixon Middle East Tour. During a Middle East tour, President Nixon signs a friendship accord with Egypt's Sadat June 14. The United States promises Egypt nuclear technology for peaceful purposes. In Damascus June 16, Syria's president Asad and Nixon restore full U.S.-Syrian diplomatic relations that were broken in the 1967 war. In Israel June 17 Nixon says the United States and Israel will cooperate in nuclear energy and the United States will supply nuclear fuel "under agreed safeguards."

ARAB-ISRAELI CONFLICT

January 17. Suez Disengagement. Secretary of State Kissinger's "shuttle diplomacy" results in announcement of accords on Suez disengagement. The accords are signed January 18. The chief provisions are that Israel is to abandon its western bank bridgehead and withdraw on the eastern bank about twenty miles from the canal, Egypt is to keep a limited force on the eastern bank, a UN truce force is to patrol the buffer zone between the two, and the pullback is to be completed in forty days. Sadat says he will press Syria to open talks with Israel. Israeli forces begin the Suez pullback January 25. By January 28 the withdrawal lifts the siege of the city of Suez and ends the isolation of the Egyptian III Corps.

April 29. Kissinger Diplomacy. Meeting in Geneva, Kissinger and Soviet foreign minister Andrei Gromyko pledge U.S.-Soviet cooperation in seeking a troop separation accord on the Syrian-Israeli front. The next day Kissinger in Cairo begins a month-long quest to end the Golan Heights confrontation.

May 15. Maalot Crisis. In a schoolhouse battle at the Israeli town of Maalot, sixteen teenagers are killed and seventy are wounded after three Arab guerrillas seize the school and demand the release of twenty-three prisoners held by Israel. The Arabs are slain when Israeli soldiers attack the school. Israel initiates a week-long series of raids May 16 in reply to the Maalot tragedy. Planes and gunboats hit Palestinian camps and hideouts in Lebanon, killing at least sixty-one persons.

May 29. Israeli-Syrian Disengagement. Syria and Israel agree on a disengagement. The accords, achieved by Kissinger in his latest round of "shuttle diplomacy," are signed in Geneva May 31. Israel and Syria accept a separation of forces, a UN-policed buffer zone, and a gradual reduction of forces. Israel returns 382 Arab prisoners June 6 to Syria, which hands over 56 Israeli POWs. Israeli withdrawal from the buffer zone is completed June 23.

EGYPT

February 28. United States, Egypt Renew Ties. The United States and Egypt renew full diplomatic relations after a seven-year break. President Sadat announces he has invited President Nixon to visit Egypt.

March 4. Israel Completes Pullback. Israel completes its Suez front pullback, restoring to Egypt control of both banks of the canal for the first time since the 1967 war.

ISRAEL

March 10. Israeli Cabinet Formed. A nine-week political crisis ends in Israel with the formation of a new cabinet, including Moshe Dayan as defense minister. He had wanted the right-wing Likud Party included in the coalition, a move rejected by Prime Minister Meir.

April 10. Meir Resigns as Prime Minister. Golda Meir quits the Israel premiership in an intraparty squabble over where to put the blame for military shortcomings in the October war.

April 23. Rabin Asked to Form Government. Labor Party leader Yitzhak Rabin is asked to form a new Israeli government by President Ephraim Katzir.

November 20. UNESCO Cuts Off Aid to Israel. The United Nations Educational, Scientific, and Cultural Organization (UNESCO) votes 64-27 in Paris to cut off annual financial aid to Israel because of its "persistence in altering the historical features of Jerusalem."

December 1. Katzir on Atomic Weapons. Israeli president Ephraim Katzir says Israel has the capacity to produce atomic weapons and will do so if needed.

LIBYA AND NORTH AFRICA

August 7. Sadat-Qadhafi Dispute. Egyptian president Sadat blames Libyan president Qadhafi for plots against Sadat and for the recall of Libya's Mirage jets loaned to Egypt.

December 31. Libyan Embargo Ends. The *Times* (London) reports Libya has quietly ended its fourteen-month oil embargo against the United States.

PALESTINIAN AFFAIRS

October 14. PLO Invited to UN Debate. The UN General Assembly overwhelmingly passes a resolution inviting the PLO to take part in its debate on the Palestine question. Israel denounces the UN vote October 15.

October 28. Rabat Summit. The twenty Arab League heads of state in a summit meeting at Rabat, Morocco, unanimously recognize the PLO as the "sole legitimate representative of the Palestinian people on any liberated Palestinian territory." Jordan's King Hussein announces he will honor the PLO's claim to negotiate for the West Bank.

November 4. Hussein on West Bank. King Hussein says Jordan will rewrite its constitution to exclude the West Bank from Jordan and that it is "totally inconceivable" that Jordan and a Palestinian state could form a federation.

November 13. Arafat at UN. Addressing the UN General Assembly, Yasir Arafat says the PLO's goal is "one democratic [Palestinian] state where Christian, Jew, and Muslim live in justice, equality, and fraternity." In rebuttal, Israeli delegate Yosef Tekoah asserts the Arafat proposal would mean the destruction of Israel and its replacement by an Arab state.

November 22. UN Resolution on the PLO. The UN General Assembly approves a resolution recognizing the right of the Palestinian people to independence and sovereignty and giving the PLO observer status at the UN.

PERSIAN GULF STATES

March 18. Arabs Lift Oil Embargo. After a joint meeting in Vienna, Saudi Arabia, Algeria, Egypt, Kuwait, Abu Dhabi, Bahrain, and Qatar lift a five-month oil embargo against the United States. Libya and Syria refuse to join in the decision.

1975

REGIONAL

January 2. Kissinger Interview. In a *Business Week* interview, Kissinger warns that the United States might use force in the Middle East "to prevent the strangulation of the industrialized world" by Arab oil producers. His remarks arouse angry world reaction.

ARAB-ISRAELI CONFLICT

January 6. Lebanon Charges Israeli Aggression. At the UN, Lebanon charges Israel with 423 acts of aggression in the past month. These include border crossings made by Israel to wipe out guerrilla forces in southern Lebanon.

February 18. Shah Offers Oil to Israel. The shah of Iran says he will send additional oil to Israel if Israel cedes the Rudais oil fields to Egypt in a general peace settlement. His offer comes after a meeting with Kissinger, who visited several Middle East countries seeking "a framework for new negotiations."

February 21. UN Commission Condemns Israel. The UN Commission on Human Rights adopts resolutions condemning Israel for carrying out the "deliberate destruction" of Quenitra, a Syrian city in the Golan Heights, and for "desecrating" Muslim and Christian shrines.

March 5. Palestinians Seize Hotel. Eighteen persons, including six non-Israeli tourists, are slain when eight Palestinian guerrillas seize a shorefront hotel in Tel Aviv. Israeli troops kill seven attackers and capture the other.

March 22. Kissinger Suspends Peace Efforts. Kissinger suspends his efforts to draw Israel and Egypt into new accords, calling the breakdown "a sad day for America."

June 2. Ford-Sadat Meeting. U.S. president Gerald R. Ford holds a two-day conference with Egyptian president Sadat in Salzburg, Austria. During the parley, Israel orders a partial withdrawal of its forces in the Sinai in response to a reopening of the Suez Canal. Sadat cautiously hails the Israeli gesture as a step toward peace.

August 21. Shuttle Diplomacy. Kissinger arrives in Israel to begin a new round of shuttle diplomacy. His arrival sparks nationwide demonstrations by Israelis who dislike his brand of diplomacy and are skeptical of agreements with the Arabs. At Tel Aviv airport, Kissinger says that "the gap in negotiations has been substantially narrowed by concessions on both sides."

August 28. Progress on Sinai Accord. A senior official with the Kissinger party in Jerusalem says implementation of a new Sinai agreement hinges on approval by Congress of the use of American civilian technicians to man Sinai monitoring posts.

September 1. Sinai Pact Concluded. In separate ceremonies in Jerusalem and Alexandria, Israeli and Egyptian leaders initial a new Sinai pact. Israel withdraws from Sinai mountain passes and returns the Rudais oil fields to Egypt in return for modest Egyptian political concessions. Kissinger initials provisions for stationing U.S. technicians in the Sinai. President Ford asks that Congress approve the new U.S. Middle East role. Egyptian and Israeli representatives sign the agreement in Geneva September 4. Syria calls the Sinai pact "strange and shameful," while Zuhayr Muhsin of the PLO calls Sadat a "traitor and conspirator" for signing the accord.

October 28. Sadat Urges U.S.-PLO Dialogue. Sadat urges Washington to open a dialogue with the PLO, while Egypt and the United States sign four economic and cultural exchange agreements.

November 10. UN Resolution on Zionism. The UN General Assembly adopts a resolution defining Zionism as "a form of racism or racial discrimination" on a 72-35 vote with thirty-two abstentions and three absences. U.S. ambassador Daniel Patrick Moynihan says, "The United States . . . does not acknowledge, it will not abide by, it

will never acquiesce in this infamous act." A second resolution recognizes Palestinians' right to self-determination and to attend any UN Middle East negotiation. The Israeli Knesset rejects the UN resolution on Zionism and indicates Israel will not participate in the Geneva talks if the PLO is invited.

December 4. PLO Invited to UN Debate. After Israeli jets attack Palestinian refugee camps in Lebanon, killing seventy-four persons, the UN Security Council votes 9-3 with three abstentions to invite the PLO to participate in debate about the air attacks. The PLO is granted the speaking privileges of a member nation.

December 5. General Assembly Resolution. The UN General Assembly by an 84-17 vote with twenty-seven abstentions adopts a resolution condemning Israel's occupation of Arab territories and calling upon all states to refrain from aiding Israel.

EGYPT

June 5. Suez Canal Reopens. The Suez Canal reopens after an eight-year closure to commercial shipping. President Sadat leads a ceremonial convoy of ships through the waterway to mark the opening.

ISRAEL

January 23. Israelis Buy Missiles. The Pentagon announces the Israeli purchase of two hundred Lance missiles, to be armed with conventional warheads but capable of carrying nuclear ones. Israel also asks for $2 billion in U.S. military and economic aid.

KURDISH AFFAIRS

March 5. Iran-Iraq Agreement. Iraq and Iran agree to end their long-standing dispute over frontiers, navigational claims, and Iranian supply of the Kurdish rebellion in northern Iraq. Two days later Baghdad launches a major military offensive against the Kurds, who seek total autonomy.

March 22. Kurdish Rebellion Fails. The Kurdish rebellion collapses in Iraq. Rebel leader Mustafa Barzani flees to Iran.

LEBANON

May 28. Karami Becomes Premier. Rashid Karami is appointed Lebanese premier, promising to end the bloody Christian-Muslim strife over the Palestinian refugee question. Karami replaces Rashid al-Solh, who resigned under criticism of his handling of riots in April.

July 1. Beirut Truce. After ten days of fighting in Beirut, during which at least 280 persons are killed, a truce is proclaimed. Premier Rashid Karami forms a "rescue cabinet," which includes all major Muslim and Christian groups except the warring Muslim Progressive Socialists and Christian Phalangists.

PERSIAN GULF STATES

March 25. Faisal Assassinated. King Faisal of Saudi Arabia is shot to death by his nephew, Prince Faisal ibn Musaed. Crown Prince Khalid becomes king. Prince Fahd is named heir apparent. The royal family claims the assassin is deranged and acted alone. Prince Faisal is beheaded June 18.

1976

ARAB-ISAELI CONFLICT

January 12. Security Council Vote. The UN Security Council opens its Middle East debate by voting 11-1 with three abstentions to allow the PLO to participate with the speaking rights of a member.

January 28. Rabin Visits Washington. Prime Minister Rabin rules out any negotiations with the PLO in an address to a joint meeting of the U.S. Congress. Rabin and President Ford end talks January 29, reportedly with the understanding that the United States will promote the convening of the Geneva conference without the PLO.

February 13. UN Human Rights Commission Vote. The UN Commission on Human Rights votes 23-1 with eight abstentions for a resolution accusing Israel of having committed "war crimes" in the occupied Arab territories. The United States casts the lone "no" vote.

February 22. Sinai Accord Implemented. The final step in the previous September's Sinai accord is carried out, with UN personnel turning over the final eighty-nine square miles in Sinai to Egyptian forces.

March 23. U.S. Position on Settlements. U.S. ambassador to the UN William Scranton tells the Security Council the United States considers the presence of Israeli settlements in the occupied territories to be "an obstacle to the success of the negotiations for a just and final peace."

March 25. Security Council Vote. The Security Council votes 14-1, with the United States vetoing the action, to deplore Israel's efforts to change the status of Jerusalem, to call on Israel to refrain from measures harming the inhabitants of the occupied territories, and to call for an end to Israeli settlements in the occupied territories.

April 18. Israeli West Bank Demonstration. About thirty thousand Israelis march for two days through the West Bank under the leadership of Gush Emunim. Arab counterdemonstrations in Nablus and Ramallah are broken up. Prime Minister Yitzhak Rabin tours Jordan Valley settlements April 20 and assures the settlers in new villages that they are "here to stay for a long time."

June 27. Entebbe Hijacking. A jetliner on its way from Tel Aviv to Paris is hijacked in Athens and taken to Entebbe airport in Uganda the following day. Israeli commandos raid the airport July 4, freeing the 103 passengers held hostage.

November 11. Security Council on Settlements. The UN Security Council, in a consensus statement, deplores the establishment of Israeli settlements in occupied Arab territories and declares "invalid" Israel's annexation of eastern Jerusalem.

November 24. UN Supports Palestinian Rights. The UN General Assembly approves 90-16, with thirty abstentions, the report of the Committee on the Inalienable Rights of the Palestinian People proclaiming the right of Palestinian Arab refugees to establish their own state and reclaim former properties in Israel.

EGYPT

September 17. Sadat Elected to Second Term. President Sadat of Egypt receives over 99 percent approval for a second six-year term as president. He is sworn into office October 16.

ISRAEL

March 14. Israeli Nuclear Capacity. Senior CIA officials estimate Israel has ten to twenty nuclear weapons "ready and available for use." Israel says April 5 that it is not a nuclear power and will not be the first to introduce nuclear weapons into the Middle East conflict.

December 19. Israeli Elections Called. Prime Minister Yitzhak Rabin ousts the National Religious Party from his coalition government five days after the NRP abstained on a vote of no-confidence in the Knesset. Rabin resigns December 20 and new elections are called.

LEBANON

March 13. Franjiyyah Refuses to Resign. Lebanese president Sulayman Franjiyyah is presented with a petition signed by two-thirds of parliament asking him to resign, but he refuses.

May 8. Sarkis Elected President. Elias Sarkis is elected president of Lebanon. Backers of Raymond Edde boycott the election, protesting interference by Syria.

May 31. Syrians Advance into Lebanon. Syrian troops numbering five thousand begin advancing into Lebanon's Akkar Valley in the north. Large numbers of additional Syrian troops enter Lebanon a week later to help control the Lebanese crisis.

June 16. U.S. Diplomats Killed. U.S. ambassador Francis Meloy and economic counselor Robert Waring are shot to death on their way to a meeting with President Sarkis in Beirut. The State Department strongly urges June 19 that all American citizens leave Lebanon. The United States evacuates 263 Americans and foreign nationals from Lebanon by sea with the help of the PLO.

June 21. Arab Peacekeepers Arrive in Lebanon. About a thousand Syrian and Libyan troops, the vanguard of an Arab League peacekeeping force, arrive in Lebanon.

July 16. Beirut Embassy Closes. The U.S. embassy in Beirut announces closure of all consular services and urges all Americans to leave Lebanon. The United States evacuates 308 more American and foreign nationals from Beirut July 27, again with the PLO helping provide security.

September 23. Sarkis Inaugurated. Elias Sarkis is inaugurated as president of Lebanon before sixty-seven members of the National Assembly.

October 18. Riyadh Peace Plan. Arab leaders of Saudi Arabia, Kuwait, Syria, Egypt, Lebanon, and the PLO, meeting in Riyadh, sign a Lebanon peace plan calling for a cease-fire and a thirty-thousand-troop peacekeeping force under the command of Lebanese president Sarkis. In Cairo October 25, all members of the Arab League, except Iraq and Libya, approve the Riyadh agreement.

PALESTINIAN AFFAIRS

September 6. PLO Admitted to Arab League. The PLO is unanimously granted full voting membership in the Arab League.

September 28. Arafat Appeals for Help. With his PLO units in Lebanon under attack from Syrian troops, Yasir Arafat sends an urgent appeal to all Arab heads of state asking for immediate intervention to prevent Syria from "liquidating the Palestinian resistance."

1977

ARAB-ISRAELI CONFLICT

April 4. Sadat Visits Washington. Egyptian president Sadat visits Washington and tells President Carter that the Palestinian question is the "core and crux" of the Arab-Israeli dispute. U.S. officials report April 8 that Sadat said Egyptian-Israeli relations could be normalized within five years.

June 17. U.S. Peace Plan. U.S. vice president Walter F. Mondale delivers a major speech on the Middle East that outlines the Carter administration's views and emphasizes a three-point peace plan: a return to approximately the 1967 borders, creation of a Palestinian homeland probably linked to Jordan, and establishment of complete peace and normal relations between the countries in the area.

July 13. Assassination Threat. A spokesman for the Palestinian "rejection front" threatens with assassination any Arab leader who signs a peace agreement with Israel.

July 13. Sadat on Egyptian-Israeli Relations. President Sadat, speaking to members of the U.S. Congress, expresses Egypt's willingness to establish diplomatic and trade relations with Israel within five years of signing a peace agreement.

July 20. Carter and Begin Meet. Israel's prime minister Menachem Begin visits Washington and confers with President Carter, who after their meeting states, "I believe that we've laid the groundwork now that will lead to the Geneva Conference in October." At a news conference telecast live to Israel from Washington, Begin discloses his "peace plan," which is loudly criticized by all Arab parties.

August 1. Sadat Proposes Pre-Geneva Meeting. Secretary of State Cyrus Vance confers with President Sadat in Cairo to push resumption of the Geneva Peace Conference on the Middle East. Sadat proposes a pre-Geneva meeting of Egyptian and Israeli foreign ministers. Prime minister Begin endorses Sadat's proposal August 3.

August 17. New West Bank Settlements. The Israeli government approves plans for three new settlements in the West Bank. In an August 23 news conference, President Carter reiterates the administration's position that Israel's plan for new settlements in the West Bank is "illegal" and "an unnecessary obstacle to peace."

August 25–26. PLO Denounces U.S. Efforts. The Central Council of the PLO meets in Damascus, Syria, and denounces U.S. peace efforts in the Middle East. The PLO underscores its objection to Resolution 242 as the basis for a settlement, calling for an agreement that recognizes the Palestinian people's right to independence and sovereignty.

September 18. Documents on Liberty *Attack.* The American Palestine Committee releases CIA documents suggesting Israel deliberately attacked the U.S. Navy ship *Liberty* during the 1967 Arab-Israeli war. Thirty-four Americans died in the attack. A CIA spokesman calls the documents "unevaluated information."

September 19. Israeli Peace Proposal. Israeli foreign minister Moshe Dayan submits his country's proposal for a Middle East peace agreement during White House talks with President Carter and U.S. officials. The proposal contains provisions for internal autonomy and self-government for Arabs in the occupied West Bank.

September 25. Israel Endorses U.S. Plan. Israel accepts U.S. plan for reconvening the Geneva peace conference. The plan calls for a unified Arab delegation, including Palestinians, at the talks. Egypt, Syria, and Jordan also approve the plan but reject Israel's conditions limiting Palestinian participation.

November 9. Sadat Willing to Go to Israel. In a major speech, Egyptian president Sadat urges an all-out effort to reconvene the peace talks in Geneva. He says, "I am ready to go to the Israeli Parliament itself to discuss [peace]."

November 11. Begin Welcomes Sadat Proposal. Israeli prime minister Begin is receptive to a visit from President Sadat and states, "I, for my part, will, of course, come to your capital, Cairo, for the same purpose: no more wars—peace, a real peace and forever."

November 15. Begin Invites Sadat. Begin extends a formal invitation to President Sadat to address the Israeli Knesset, at the same time offering an informal invitation to other Arab leaders to come to Israel for diplomatic discussions.

November 17. Sadat Accepts Invitation. Sadat accepts the invitation of the Begin government. Egyptian foreign minister Ismail Fahmy resigns in apparent disagreement over Sadat's decision to go to Israel.

November 19. Sadat in Israel. Sadat arrives in Israel, the first Arab leader to visit that nation since it was established in 1948. In a historic address to the Israeli Knesset in Jerusalem November 20, he says that "we welcome you among us with all security and safety." Sadat and Begin hold a joint news conference November 21 and express their desire for peace and the hope that the Geneva peace conference will reconvene soon. At Sadat's departure Begin calls his visit "a great moral achievement."

November 22. Sadat Visit Reaction. The Egyptian delegate to the UN walks out on a speech by the Syrian delegate after the Syrian called Sadat's visit to Israel "a stab in the back of the Arab people." The European Community adopts a resolution praising Sadat's visit and "his courageous initiative."

November 26. Cairo Conference Invitation. Sadat invites all parties in the Middle East conflict to a pre-Geneva preparatory meeting in Cairo to resolve procedural differences. The United States and Israel announce they will accept, but Syria, Lebanon, Jordan, and the Soviet Union reject Sadat's offer.

December 5. Egypt Splits with Arab Nations. Egypt severs diplomatic relations with Syria, Iraq, Libya, Algeria, and South Yemen, citing attempts by the hard-line Arab states to disrupt Sadat's recent peace efforts. The action follows conclusion of a December 2 meeting in Tripoli, Libya, where the Arab states declared a new "front for resistance and opposition" to thwart Egypt's peace initiatives. Egypt also closes several Soviet and Soviet-bloc cultural centers and consulates in Cairo because of Moscow's endorsement of the Tripoli Declaration.

December 14. Cairo Conference. The Cairo conference to discuss procedures for reconvening the Geneva peace talks opens. Representatives from Egypt, Israel, the United States, and the United Nations participate.

December 25. Begin and Sadat Meet. Begin and Sadat hold a summit in Ismailia, Egypt, to draft guidelines for establishing peace in the Middle East. Talks conclude with no substantive agreement on any major issue.

EGYPT

January 18. Egyptian Demonstrations. Thousands of Egyptian workers demonstrate against price rises. President Sadat cancels the price increases January 19. At least sixty-five persons are reported killed in clashes with police. Sadat bans demonstrations and strikes January 26. In a February 10 referendum on Sadat's decree outlawing demonstrations and strikes, 99 percent vote to approve, according to the government. About four hundred students demonstrate in Cairo February 12 against the new law banning such protests.

October 26. Egypt Suspends Soviet Payment. Egypt announces it will suspend payment on its $4 billion military debt to the Soviet Union because of Moscow's refusal to continue arms sales to Egypt.

IRAN

August 2. Carter Suspends Iran AWACS Sale. The Carter administration announces the suspension of the proposed sale to Iran of seven Airborne Warning and Control Systems (AWACS) planes because of congressional opposition to the deal.

ISRAEL

February 22. Rabin Wins Labor Nomination. By a vote of 1,445 to 1,404 the Israeli Labor Party selects Yitzhak Rabin over Shimon Peres as its candidate for prime minister. In exchange for a real peace agreement, the Israeli Labor Party platform adopted February 25 calls for return of some West Bank territory to Jordan.

March 15. Rabin Bank Account Disclosed. The Israeli newspaper *Ha'aretz* reports that Prime Minister Rabin's wife has an illegal bank account in Washington.

April 7. Rabin Withdraws. Prime Minister Rabin withdraws from the top spot on the Israeli Labor Party ticket with elections only six weeks away. Shimon Peres is selected to replace him April 10. Rabin's wife, Leah Rabin, pleads guilty to maintaining an illegal bank account April 17 and is fined $27,000. Rabin is fined $1,500 for his role in maintaining the illegal account.

May 12. Carter on Middle East. President Carter pledges "special treatment" for Israel in regard to arms requests and coproduction of advanced U.S. weaponry.

May 17. Likud Victory. Menachem Begin's right-wing Likud Party unexpectedly wins a plurality in the Israeli election. President Katzir officially asks Begin June 7 to form Israel's next government.

May 20. Rabin Admission. Prime Minister Rabin admits that he maintained an illegal Washington bank account with his wife.

May 25. Dayan Accepts Foreign Ministership. Moshe Dayan agrees to serve in a Begin government as foreign minister. He resigns from the Labor Party May 27 because of the furor over his acceptance.

June 21. Begin Becomes Prime Minister. Begin officially becomes prime minister of Israel after winning a 63-53 vote of confidence in the new Knesset. Begin delivers his first major speech as prime minister June 23. He announces that Israel will not "under any circumstances" relinquish the West Bank or allow the creation of a Palestinian state west of the Jordan River.

JORDAN

March 9. Arafat, Hussein Meet. In Cairo, Yasir Arafat and King Hussein meet publicly for the first time since "Black September" in 1970.

LEBANON

March 16. Jumblatt Assassinated. Leftist leader Kamal Jumblatt is assassinated near Beirut.

September 26. Cease-Fire in Southern Lebanon. Heavy fighting ends in southern Lebanon as a U.S.-arranged cease-fire goes into effect. Key elements of the truce include withdrawal of Palestinian guerrillas six miles from the Israeli border and their replacement with Lebanese troops.

October 5. Lebanese Fighting Resumes. The U.S.-arranged cease-fire in southern Lebanon breaks down as serious fighting resumes between Christian and Palestinian forces.

November 6. Arafat Rejects Lebanon Pullout. PLO leader Arafat says Palestinian guerrilla forces will not pull out of southern Lebanon in accordance with the U.S.-arranged truce agreement.

November 9. Israelis Bomb Guerrillas. Israeli jets bomb Palestinian guerrilla enclaves in southern Lebanon. The Lebanese government reports that more than a hundred people are killed.

LIBYA AND NORTH AFRICA

April 16. Egypt Accuses Libya. Egypt delivers to the Arab League a note accusing Libya of plotting against the Sudan, seizing portions of Chad, and harboring "international criminals." Moscow accuses Egypt April 27 of attempting to provoke armed clashes between Egypt and Libya. Libya reportedly plans to expel some of the approximately two hundred thousand Egyptians working in Libya.

PALESTINIAN AFFAIRS

March 12. Palestine National Council Opens. The Palestine National Council opens in Cairo and President Sadat pledges that Egypt "will not cede a single inch of Arab land."

March 16. Carter Endorses Idea of Homeland. At a Clinton, Massachusetts, town meeting President Jimmy Carter endorses the idea of a Palestinian "homeland," the first American president to do so.

July 22. PLO Joins ECOSOC. The PLO becomes the first nonstate to have full membership in any UN body when it is accepted as a member of the Economic Commission for Western Asia of the UN Economic and Social Council.

1978

ARAB-ISRAELI CONFLICT

January 4. Hammani Killed. Said Hammani, chief representative of the PLO in Great Britain, is killed in London by an unknown assassin. Hammani had strained relations with other PLO representatives because of his moderate stance on coexistence with Israel and his opposition to terrorism.

January 18. Sadat Recalls Delegation. Meetings in Jerusalem of the Israeli-Egyptian Political Committee

end abruptly following Egypt's recall of its delegation. Egyptian president Sadat blames the breakdown on Israel's "aim at deadlocking the situation and submitting partial solutions."

July 5. Egyptian Peace Plan. Egypt formally announces its plan for peace in the Middle East. Under the proposal Israel will withdraw from occupied territories over a five-year period and the Arab residents of the West Bank and Gaza Strip "will be able to determine their own future." The Israeli cabinet rejects the Egyptian peace plan July 9.

July 22. Sadat Criticizes Begin. In a political rally speech, Sadat calls Prime Minister Begin an "obstacle" to peace.

August 8. Camp David Talks Announced. U.S. authorities announce that Sadat and Begin will meet with President Carter in September at Camp David, Maryland, to explore ways to resolve the Middle East deadlock.

September 5–17. Camp David Accords. President Carter, Begin, and Sadat hold peace talks at Camp David, Maryland. On September 17 they sign two historic documents: "A Framework for Peace in the Middle East" and a "Framework for the Conclusion of a Peace Treaty Between Israel and Egypt." The Egyptian cabinet unanimously approves the Camp David agreements September 19. The Israeli cabinet approves the accords September 24. The Israeli Knesset gives its approval September 28 by an 84-19 vote.

February 3. Sadat in United States, Europe. Sadat visits the United States to press his plans for peace in the Middle East and to seek American arms assistance. Sadat leaves the United States for Europe February 9 to continue his campaign for peace.

February 14. Middle East Arms Package. The Carter administration announces a $4.8 billion arms package for Egypt, Saudi Arabia, and Israel that will include advanced warplanes. Secretary of State Vance says February 24 that the sale must be a "package deal." The administration plans to void the deal if Congress tries to veto any part of it.

March 4. Begin 242 Interpretation. Begin informs President Carter that his government does not interpret UN Security Council Resolution 242 as saying that Israel is obligated to withdraw from the occupied West Bank and Gaza Strip. Carter reiterates the U.S. position that the resolution mandates an Israeli withdrawal "from all three fronts."

March 14. Israel Occupies Lebanese Territory. Israel launches an all-out attack on Palestinian bases in Lebanon in retaliation for a raid March 11 that killed thirty Israeli civilians. Israeli troops occupy a six-mile-deep "security belt" on Lebanese territory along the Israeli border. Egyptian, Syrian, and Lebanese leaders denounce Israel's actions in southern Lebanon March 15. Israel declares a unilateral truce in southern Lebanon

March 21, and UN troops move into the region to enforce the cease-fire. Israel begins a two-phase withdrawal from its positions in southern Lebanon April 11. The withdrawal is completed June 13.

March 23. Begin-Carter Talks. President Carter and Prime Minister Begin conclude two days of talks in Washington after failing to reach agreement on any of the major points blocking progress in the Middle East peace negotiations.

April 1. Rally in Israel. An estimated twenty-five thousand Israelis rally in Tel Aviv, calling on Begin to soften his stance on relinquishing Israeli-occupied territory in the West Bank and Gaza Strip.

September 24. Arabs Break Egyptian Ties. Syria, Algeria, South Yemen, Libya, and the PLO break off all political and economic relations with Egypt because of the Camp David Accords.

October 12–21. Draft Treaty Negotiations. Negotiations on a U.S. draft treaty between representatives of Egypt and Israel are held in Washington. President Carter intervenes to head off a breakdown in the talks after Israel announces its delegation will be called home for consultations. As a result, Israeli and Egyptian negotiators reach agreement on main elements of a peace treaty.

October 25. Cabinet Acts on Draft Treaty. The Israeli cabinet approves the draft treaty "in principle" but adds amendments drafted by Prime Minister Begin dealing with linkage between the treaty and the future of the West Bank and the Gaza Strip. The cabinet submits the treaty to the Knesset for approval.

October 27. Nobel Prize Announced. The Norwegian Nobel Prize Committee announces that the 1978 Peace Prize will be awarded to Sadat and Begin for their contributions to peace in the Middle East. The prizes are awarded December 10.

November 2–5. Arab Meeting. Arab nations, minus Egypt and six other moderate nations, meet in Baghdad and vow to impose an economic and political boycott on Egypt if Sadat signs a separate treaty with Israel. Sadat refuses to meet with a delegation from the Baghdad summit November 4.

November 12. Peace Negotiations Continue. U.S. secretary of state Cyrus Vance and Israeli foreign minister Moshe Dayan reach a tentative agreement on a new formula for satisfying Egypt's concerns about the Palestinian issue. Vance presents the latest U.S. compromise plan to Begin. Administration officials say President Carter gave no secret guarantees or commitments to Sadat on the West Bank, Gaza, or Jerusalem. The Israeli cabinet, meeting without Begin, Dayan, or Defense Minister Ezer Weizman, rejects Egypt's demands for linking a treaty to a timetable for transferring power to the Palestinians.

November 21. Israeli Cabinet Vote. The Israeli cabinet votes 15-2 to accept a U.S.-proposed draft of a peace treaty that contains a generalized commitment to negotiate toward a settlement on the West Bank and the Gaza Strip. But the cabinet rejects Egypt's demands that a treaty be linked to a timetable for Palestinian autonomy. Egypt announces the recall of its chief negotiator from Washington in an apparent expression of displeasure.

December 12. U.S. Treaty Proposal. Sadat accepts U.S.-proposed side letters aimed at resolving the outstanding issues blocking conclusion of a peace treaty. Prime Minister Begin, however, raises strong objections November 13 to proposed treaty side letters: one explaining Egypt's legal commitment to other Arab nations and a second letter that sets a "target" date, rather than a timetable, for talks on Palestinian self-rule.

December 15. Cabinet Backs Begin. The Israeli cabinet backs Begin's rejection of the latest draft. Begin says Egypt bears "total responsibility" for the failure of negotiators to settle on a treaty by the December 17 deadline. President Carter says the decision on future negotiations "is primarily in the hands now of the Israeli cabinet."

EGYPT

February 18. Sebai Killed; Hostages Taken. In a hotel lobby in Nicosia, Cyprus, two Palestinian gunmen assassinate Youssef el-Sebai, an Egyptian newspaper editor and confidant of Anwar al-Sadat. After killing Sebai, the men seize thirty hostages and demand safe conduct to the Larnaca airport. Seventy-four Egyptian commandos land at the airport February 19 with orders to free the hostages, who are now being held aboard a Cypriot jet by the two Palestinians. Cypriot national guard troops intercept the commandos, and fifteen Egyptians are killed in an exchange of gunfire. Following the fighting the Palestinians release their hostages and surrender. Egypt cuts diplomatic ties with Cyprus February 22 in anger over the attack by Cypriot troops on Egyptian commandos.

February 27. Egypt Action on Palestinians. Egypt announces it is revoking special privileges granted to the thirty thousand Palestinians living in Egypt because of the assassination of Youssef el-Sebai by two Palestinians in Cyprus.

IRAN

September 8. Iranian Demonstrations. Hundreds of Iranian demonstrators are killed when government troops open fire during an antigovernment march in Tehran. In a September 10 White House statement President Carter assures the shah of Iran of continued U.S. support for his regime.

October 31. Iranian Oil Strike; Martial Law. Forty thousand Iranian petroleum workers go on strike in the largest single antigovernment move to date. The strike drastically reduces Iranian oil production and exports.

The shah of Iran imposes martial law November 6 in an effort to quell violent antigovernment riots that have shaken the country since January. By November 13 government pressure has caused most oil workers to return to their jobs.

December 4. Iranian Oil Strike. Thousands of antigovernment workers renew their strike in Iran, reducing oil output by 30 percent.

December 11. Isfahan Riot; Oil Strike. Fifty Iranians die and five hundred are wounded in an antigovernment riot in Isfahan, Iran's second largest city. The United States begins evacuating American dependents. Seventy percent of Iran's petroleum workers stay off the job December 12 in response to exiled Muslim leader Ayatollah Khomeini's calls for continuance of the strike. Oil production there drops to near-record lows. Widespread antigovernment demonstrations in Iran December 14–21 result in hundreds of deaths and injuries.

December 29. Shah Appoints Bakhtiar. The shah of Iran appoints Shapour Bakhtiar, a member of the opposition National Front, to head a new civilian government. The shah had earlier established a military government in an attempt to bring the uprising against the monarchy under control.

LEBANON

July 1. Syrians, Christian Militia Battle. Syrian troops of the Arab League peacekeeping force in Lebanon attack Christian militia in Beirut. At least two hundred people are killed in the worst fighting since the 1975–1976 civil war.

August 13. Explosion in Beirut. Two hundred people die in an explosion that levels a nine-story building in Beirut. The building housed the headquarters of the pro-Iraqi Palestine Liberation Front and the rival Fatah faction of the PLO.

September 28. Lebanese Crisis. President Carter calls for an international conference to end the hostilities between Muslims and Christians in Lebanon. Syria declares a unilateral cease-fire in Beirut October 7 after a week of heavy fighting with Christian militia forces.

PERSIAN GULF STATES

June 24. Assassination in North Yemen. North Yemen president Ahmad al-Ghashni is slain in San'a'. He is succeeded by Lt. Col. Ali Abdallah Salih.

June 26. Ali Deposed in South Yemen. South Yemen president Salim Rubayyi' Ali is deposed and executed in Aden. Ali, a Maoist with pro-China sympathies, is replaced by 'Abd al-Fattah Isma'il, who has close ties to Moscow.

December 17. OPEC Price Increases. OPEC ends an eighteen-month price freeze by adopting a phased-in increase plan that would raise crude oil prices 14.5 percent by October 1, 1979.

SYRIA

January 11. Soviet-Syrian Arms Deal. Syria and the Soviet Union sign an arms deal under which Damascus will begin receiving shipments of Soviet planes, tanks, and advanced air-defense missiles.

1979

ARAB-ISRAELI CONFLICT

March 1–4. Carter-Begin Talks. Prime Minister Begin arrives in Washington for new talks with President Carter. In a strongly worded statement, Begin says the Egyptian-Israeli talks are "in a state of deep crisis." Carter and Begin fail to make progress toward resolving remaining issues. Carter announces March 4 he will fly to Egypt and Israel in the hope of breaking the impasse blocking a peace treaty between the two nations.

March 8. Carter in the Middle East. President Carter arrives in Cairo March 8 for talks with President Sadat, who says Egypt and Israel are "on the verge of an agreement." Carter travels to Jerusalem March 10 where he meets with Begin and members of the Israeli cabinet.

March 13. Cairo Airport Announcement. Before returning to the United States from Israel, President Carter flies to Cairo for a final meeting with Sadat. In a dramatic announcement at the Cairo airport Carter says Sadat has approved all outstanding points of a proposed treaty. Carter says Begin has agreed to submit to his cabinet "the few remaining issues" that Israel has yet to endorse. In Jerusalem, Begin says that if the Knesset rejects the compromise, his "government will have to resign."

March 14. Cabinet Approves Proposals. The Israeli cabinet approves the compromise proposals by a 15-0 vote, making approval of the entire treaty by the Knesset likely. Carter returns to the United States and tells congressional leaders of his plans to provide an additional $4 billion in aid to Egypt and Israel over three years.

March 15. Egyptian Cabinet Approves Treaty. The Egyptian cabinet votes unanimously to approve the peace treaty.

March 19–21. Israel Approves Treaty. The Israeli cabinet approves the treaty by a 15-2 vote. On March 21, after two days of debate, the Israeli Knesset votes 95-18 in favor of the treaty.

March 26. Begin and Sadat Sign Treaty. Begin and Sadat sign the peace treaty at a White House ceremony witnessed by President Carter. The treaty formally ends the state of war between Egypt and Israel.

March 31. Arabs Isolate Egypt. In response to the Israeli-Egyptian peace treaty, the foreign ministers of eighteen Arab League countries and a PLO representative vote to impose a total economic boycott on Egypt and exclude it from the league. The ministers also announce the immediate withdrawal of their ambassadors from

Cairo and recommend that all Arab League members break diplomatic ties with Egypt within one month.

April 10. Egyptian Assembly Ratifies Pact. The Egyptian People's Assembly (parliament) ratifies the Egyptian-Israeli pact. The treaty is also overwhelmingly approved in a nationwide Egyptian referendum April 19.

April 22–27. Arabs Break Egypt Ties. Kuwait, Saudi Arabia, Morocco, and Tunisia sever diplomatic relations with Egypt, bringing to fifteen the number of Arab states that have cut ties with Cairo.

April 25. Ratification Documents Exchanged. The Egyptian-Israeli peace treaty formally goes into effect as the two nations exchange ratification documents. Israeli and Egyptian military officers begin talks April 29 on the details of Israel's withdrawal from the Sinai.

May 9. Egypt Expelled. Egypt is expelled from the forty-three-member Conference of Islamic States during a five-day meeting in Fez, Morocco, because of its peace treaty with Israel.

May 25. Israel Begins Withdrawal. Israel begins withdrawing from the Sinai Peninsula and returns El Arish, capital of the Sinai, to Egypt in accordance with the peace treaty. Both countries open talks in Beersheba on granting Palestinian autonomy in the West Bank.

May 27. Border Opened Early. Egypt and Israel announce the opening of borders between the two countries, agreeing not to wait until January 1980 as planned.

June 11. Begin on Territories Policy. Begin defends Israel's right to establish settlements in the West Bank and Gaza Strip. He pledges to implement the autonomy plan for residents of the occupied territories as agreed to in the September 1978 Camp David Accords.

June 20. Court Blocks Israeli Settlement. The Israeli Supreme Court, in response to a suit by Arab landowners, orders a halt to work on the controversial West Bank settlement of Elon Moreh. Arabs in the West Bank city of Nablus continue riots and demonstrations protesting the settlement.

June 24. Weizman Removed as Negotiator. Israeli defense minister Ezer Weizman is removed from the team negotiating with Egypt and the United States on Arab self-rule in the West Bank and Gaza. Weizman had earlier opposed establishment of the Israeli Elon Moreh settlement near Nablus.

July 6–24. Israeli Attacks. Israeli jet fighters and ground troops attack Palestinian guerrillas in southern Lebanon. The heaviest raids occur July 22 when Israeli planes bomb a twenty-one-mile stretch south of Beirut, killing approximately twenty persons and wounding fifty, according to Beirut radio.

July 16. Saddam Hussein Named President. Iraqi president Ahmad Hassan al-Bakr resigns, naming Gen. Saddam Hussein as his successor.

July 24. UN Peacekeeping Plan. The UN Security Council allows the term of the United Nations Emergency Force (UNEF), which separated Egyptian and Israeli forces in the Sinai, to expire. The council agrees to a U.S.-Soviet plan to use an expanded United Nations Truce Supervision Organization (UNTSO) force in the area to monitor the Israeli withdrawal.

August 15. Young Resigns. Andrew Young resigns as U.S. ambassador to the United Nations because of his unauthorized contacts with the PLO.

September 16. Israel Rescinds Law. Despite opposition from the United States and Egypt, Israel lifts the 1967 law preventing Israeli citizens and businesses from buying Arab-owned land in the occupied West Bank and Gaza Strip.

September 19. Monitoring Agreement Reached. After two days of negotiations U.S., Egyptian, and Israeli officials reach a tentative agreement for monitoring the Israeli-Egyptian peace pact in the Sinai.

September 24. Syrian-Israeli Air Battles. Syrian warplanes challenge Israeli fighters over southern Lebanon. Israel claims its pilots downed four Syrian MiG-21 fighters. Syria acknowledges the losses but claims that Israel also lost two jets.

October 21. Dayan Resigns. Moshe Dayan resigns as foreign minister of Israel. He reportedly favored a more moderate stand on the Palestinian autonomy question than other leaders in the Begin government.

October 22. Court Bans Israeli Settlement. The Israeli Supreme Court bans the controversial settlement of Elon Moreh, near Nablus on the West Bank.

EGYPT

June 21. Khalil Sworn In. Prime Minister Mustafa Khalil and his cabinet are sworn into office in Cairo. President Sadat's National Democratic Party won a large majority in parliamentary elections held June 7 and 14, the first multiparty elections since the 1952 revolution in Egypt.

IRAN

January 6. New Iranian Government. The shah of Iran officially installs a new civilian government headed by Shapour Bakhtiar. A crowd of one hundred thousand Iranians demonstrates in a rally denouncing the new government. The shah announces he will temporarily leave the country soon. A nine-member regency council is formed January 13 in Iran to carry out the duties of the shah after he leaves.

January 16. Shah Leaves Iran. Shah Mohammad Reza Pahlavi leaves Iran for a "vacation" abroad. Foreign observers agree the monarch will probably remain in permanent exile, ending his thirty-seven-year rule. Exiled religious leader Ayatollah Khomeini, from his home near Paris, hails the shah's departure, calling it "the first step" toward ending the reign of the Pahlavi dynasty.

January 26. Khomeini's Return Blocked. Khomeini plans to return to Iran from Paris, then postpones his trip after Iranian officials close the nation's airports. Iranian army troops open fire on a crowd of demonstrators in Tehran, killing more than sixty people. The United States orders the evacuation of all dependents and nonessential American officials from Iran.

February 1. Khomeini Returns. Khomeini returns to Iran after fifteen years in exile and threatens to arrest Bakhtiar if he does not resign. Speaking to a crowd of his followers, Khomeini says, "The parliament and the government are illegal. I will appoint a government with the support of the Iranian people." In the first step of a plan to establish an Islamic republic in Iran, Khomeini appoints Mehdi Bazargan February 5 to head a proposed "provisional government."

February 11. Bakhtiar Overthrown. Armed revolutionaries and army sympathizers overthrow the Bakhtiar government. A provisional government formed by religious leader Khomeini takes power.

February 14. U.S. Embassy Occupied. Leftist guerrillas storm the U.S. embassy in Tehran and hold more than a hundred employees hostage. The embassy personnel are later freed by armed supporters of Khomeini.

February 18. Arafat in Tehran. In Tehran, PLO leader Arafat meets with Khomeini and Bazargan. Arafat says the Iranian revolution "turned upside down" the balance of forces in the Middle East. The new Iranian government executes the former head of the Iranian secret police and three former army generals.

April 1. Khomeini Proclaims Republic. After Iranian voters approve the formation of an Islamic republic in a national referendum during the previous two days, Khomeini proclaims the establishment of the regime calling it "the first day of a government of God."

August 12–14. Tehran Riots. Supporters and foes of Khomeini clash in Tehran in the most serious rioting since the overthrow of the shah in February.

October 24. Shah Has Surgery in New York. Shah Mohammad Reza Pahlavi, who arrived in New York for surgery two days earlier, has his gallbladder and several gallstones removed at New York Hospital–Cornell Medical Center. Doctors report November 5 that the shah will receive radiation therapy for cancer.

November 4. Hostage Crisis Begins. Demanding the return of the shah, Iranian students seize the U.S. embassy in Tehran and take sixty-six Americans hostage. On November 6 Khomeini accepts the resignation of Bazargan, who opposes the hostage taking, and orders the Revolutionary Council to run the country.

November 9. Carter Responses. In response to the hostage crisis President Carter blocks delivery of $300 million in military equipment and spare parts to Iran. The next day he orders the deportation of Iranian students residing illegally in the United States.

November 11. Iranians Attack Beirut Embassy. About fifty Iranian students break into the grounds of the U.S. embassy in Beirut. They lower the American flag and burn it before the crowd is dispersed by Syrian troops.

November 12. Additional U.S. Sanctions. The Carter administration suspends Iranian oil imports. Iran had cut oil deliveries to the United States, Great Britain, and Japan by 5 percent retroactive to October 1. President Carter issues an executive order November 14 freezing Iranian assets in the United States. The freeze affects an estimated $8 billion, according to the U.S. Treasury.

November 19–20. Some Hostages Freed. Iranians free thirteen American hostages—five women and eight black men.

December 4. Security Council on Hostages. The UN Security Council unanimously adopts a resolution calling for the release of the hostages in Tehran.

December 15. Shah Goes to Panama. The shah flies to Panama after his treatment for cancer in New York.

LEBANON

April 18. Christians Declare Strip Independent. Leaders of the Christian militia in southern Lebanon declare a six-mile-wide strip of land there "independent" of Beirut's control. Militiamen say the "independent area" will return to Lebanese control only after all Palestinian and Syrian troops have left Lebanon.

May 16. Lebanese Premier Resigns. Lebanese president Elias Sarkis accepts the resignation of Premier Selim al-Hoss and his ministers in an effort to resolve disunity between warring Christian and Muslim factions.

LIBYA AND NORTH AFRICA

December 2. U.S. Embassy Attacked. Two thousand Libyans attack the U.S. embassy in Tripoli. The demonstrators heavily damage the building, but no Americans are injured.

December 6. Libya Pressures PLO. Libyan troops surround the PLO office in Tripoli as part of an effort to induce the organization to adopt a more radical stance toward Israel. Libyan leader Qadhafi accuses the PLO of accommodation with Israel on the question of Palestinian autonomy and expels the top PLO official in Libya December 9.

December 22. Libya Cuts Ties with PLO. Libya severs relations with the PLO. Qadhafi questions PLO leader Arafat's commitment to the Palestinian cause.

PERSIAN GULF STATES

June 28. OPEC Meeting. At the end of a three-day meeting in Geneva, OPEC ministers agree to raise the average price of oil 16 percent, making the price hike for the first six months of 1979 more than 50 percent.

July 15. Carter Energy Plan. In a nationally televised address, President Carter presents a six-point energy package designed to reduce U.S. dependence on foreign oil.

October 25. South Yemen–Soviet Pact. Representatives of the Soviet Union and South Yemen sign a twenty-year friendship pact in Moscow.

November 20. Grand Mosque Seized. Three hundred armed Islamic militants seize control of the Grand Mosque in Mecca. Iranian radio broadcasts accuse the United States and Israel of involvement in the takeover of Islam's most sacred shrine. These rumors precipitate an attack on the U.S. embassy in Pakistan in which two Americans are killed. Pakistani troops help embassy staff escape.

December 4. Saudis Gain Control of Mosque. Saudi troops regain full control of the Grand Mosque in Mecca from Islamic militants who seized it November 20. Nearly 130 people are killed during the fighting, including 60 Saudi troops and many civilian hostages.

December 17–20. OPEC Abandons Pricing System. At a meeting in Caracas, Venezuela, OPEC ministers abandon their collective pricing system, causing oil prices to soar. Prices for a barrel of oil range from Saudi Arabia's $24 to Libya's $30.

SYRIA

September 1. Latakia Riots. The Syrian government sends fourteen hundred troops to the port of Latakia to quell rioting by members of the Alawite Muslim sect.

1980

ARAB-ISRAELI CONFLICT

January 26. Border Opened. Ceremonies mark the formal opening of the Egyptian-Israeli border. The day before, Israel completed its withdrawal from two-thirds of the Sinai.

February 26. Ambassadors Exchanged. Egypt and Israel exchange ambassadors in another step toward normalization of diplomatic relations.

March 1. U.S. Reversal on Settlements Vote. The UN Security Council unanimously adopts a resolution calling on Israel to dismantle its West Bank and Gaza Strip settlements. On March 3 President Carter disavows U.S. chief delegate Donald McHenry's vote for the resolution and explains that the action "does not represent a change in our position regarding Israeli settlements . . . nor regarding the status of Jerusalem." On March 4 Secretary of State Cyrus Vance accepts responsibility for the communications failure.

June 22. Jerusalem Move. The Israeli government announces the transfer of Prime Minister Begin's office and the cabinet's conference room from West Jerusalem to East Jerusalem. On June 30 the UN Security Council votes against Israeli actions to make the whole of Jerusalem the capital of Israel.

July 30. Knesset Reaffirms Jerusalem Claim. The Israeli Knesset adopts a law reaffirming its claim to all of Jerusalem. Egypt protests the move August 3 by asking for a temporary suspension of talks on Palestinian autonomy. Egyptian president Sadat informs Israeli prime minister Begin in a letter August 9 that Egypt regards the new law and the establishment of additional Israeli settlements in the occupied territories as obstacles to the resumption of the talks.

August 20. Security Council Jerusalem Vote. The UN Security Council adopts, 14-0, a resolution condemning Israel's claim to all of Jerusalem. The United States abstains.

IRAN

January 13. Iran Resolution Vetoed. A U.S.-proposed UN Security Council resolution urging economic sanctions against Iran is vetoed by the Soviet Union. Moscow justifies its vote by saying that sanctions would have "dealt a blow to the Iranian revolution."

January 23. Carter Doctrine. In his State of the Union address, President Carter warns that "an attempt by any outside force to gain control of the Persian Gulf region will be regarded as an assault on the vital interests of the United States of America, and such an assault will be repelled by any means necessary, including military force." This statement comes to be known as the "Carter Doctrine" and is aimed primarily at the Soviet Union.

January 28. Bani-Sadr Elected President. Abolhassan Bani-Sadr, a former foreign minister, is elected president of Iran.

January 29. Canadians Aid U.S. Personnel. Canada announces that six Americans from the U.S. embassy in Tehran, who had been secretly sheltered by Canadian embassy personnel since the November takeover, were flown out of Iran January 28.

February 11. Conditions for Hostage Release. Bani-Sadr sets conditions for the hostages' release: the United States must acknowledge "past crimes," promise not to interfere in Iran's internal affairs, and recognize Iran's right to extradite the former shah and take control of his fortune.

March 24. Shah Given Asylum in Egypt. The former shah of Iran flies from Panama to Egypt, where he is offered permanent asylum.

April 7. Carter Breaks Ties with Iran. President Carter severs diplomatic relations with Iran. All Iranian diplomatic employees still in the United States are ordered to leave by April 8. Carter imposes an embargo on American exports, except food and medicine, to Iran.

April 8. Khomeini Calls for Saddam's Ouster. Iran's Ayatollah Khomeini appeals to the Iraqi army and people to overthrow the government of President Saddam Hussein. Baghdad permits armed Iranian exiles to organize against Khomeini's government.

April 17. More U.S. Actions against Iran. President Carter bans all imports from Iran and prohibits travel there by American citizens. U.S. military equipment previously purchased by Iran and impounded after the embassy takeover is made available for sale to other nations. Carter also asks Congress to use frozen Iranian assets to pay reparations to the hostages.

April 25. Rescue Mission Fails. A hostage rescue mission undertaken by a U.S. commando team is aborted in the Iranian desert because of equipment failure. Eight Americans are killed in a helicopter-airplane accident that occurs as the rescue team is about to leave the area. Secretary of State Vance resigns in protest against the rescue mission April 28. The Senate confirms Vance's successor, Sen. Edmund S. Muskie, D-Maine, May 7.

May 5. London Hostage Crisis. British commandos storm the Iranian embassy in London and free nineteen persons held hostage since April 30 by Arab Iranians. Two hostages reportedly were killed before the attack. The kidnappers had demanded that the Iranian government release ninety-one prisoners being held in Iran's Arab-speaking Khuzistan province and grant the province greater autonomy.

July 11. Hostage Released. Iran releases hostage Richard I. Queen, a vice consul, because of an illness later diagnosed as multiple sclerosis.

July 27. Shah Dies. The deposed shah of Iran dies in Cairo of cancer.

September 12. Khomeini's Release Terms. Khomeini sets terms for release of the hostages: the United States must relinquish the property and assets of the shah, cancel all financial claims against Iran, release Iran's frozen assets, and promise not to interfere in Iran's internal affairs.

December 28. U.S. Hostage Proposal. The United States proposes a three-stage process for the return of the hostages. If the Iranians release the hostages, the United States would simultaneously transfer $2.5 billion of Iranian assets on deposit with the Federal Reserve to an escrow account in Bonn or London, unblock approximately $3 billion of the estimated $4.8 billion in Iranian assets held by American banks abroad, and establish an international claims commission to decide the disposition of Iran's remaining assets. The proposal is delivered by Algerian intermediaries to the Iranians on January 3, 1981.

IRAN-IRAQ WAR

September 17. Iran-Iraq Border Clashes. Iraqi president Saddam Hussein declares a 1975 border agreement with Iran void. Frontier clashes between the two countries intensify.

September 22. Iran-Iraq War. The Iran-Iraq dispute escalates into full-scale war. Both sides bomb oil fields.

Iraq invades Iran and threatens to block the strategic Strait of Hormuz. President Carter says an oil cutoff from Iran and Iraq poses no current danger of shortages for the United States, but he warns that "a total suspension of oil exports from the other nations who ship through the Persian Gulf would create a serious threat to the world's supplies." The United States and the Soviet Union pledge neutrality in the conflict September 23. The UN Security Council unanimously approves a resolution September 28 calling on Iran and Iraq to "refrain immediately from the further use of force." Iraq conditionally accepts the UN resolution September 29, but Iran rejects it October 1.

LEBANON

July 7–8. Fighting in Lebanon. The Phalangist Party emerges as the dominant Christian armed force in Lebanon after decisively defeating National Liberal Party forces in and around Beirut. Fighting kills an estimated 320 people.

PERSIAN GULF STATES

June 9–10. OPEC Sets $32 Base Price. OPEC ministers in Algiers set a $32-a-barrel base price for crude oil and a ceiling price of $37. Saudi Arabia and the United Arab Emirates call the base price excessive and vote against it.

September 4. Saudis Complete Takeover. The Saudi government completes its takeover of assets of the Arabian-American Oil Company (Aramco), which accounts for about 97 percent of Saudi oil output.

October 5. Yamani on Oil Production. Saudi Arabia's oil minister, Shaykh Ahmad Zaki Yamani, says major Persian Gulf oil producers will step up oil exports to offset losses caused by the Iran-Iraq war.

SYRIA

September 10. Merger Agreement. Libya and Syria sign an agreement to merge the two countries into a unified Arab state. The proclamation announcing the merger urges other Arab states to join the union.

October 8. Soviet-Syrian Pact. Representatives of the Soviet Union and Syria sign a twenty-year friendship pact in Moscow.

December 16–18. Syria and Libya Slow Merger. Syria and Libya disagree on details of their proposed merger at talks in Benghazi, Libya. The countries decide instead to establish a "revolutionary leadership for unionist action until the time the merger is fulfilled."

YEMEN

April 23. South Yemen President Resigns. 'Abd al-Fattah Isma'il resigns as president of South Yemen and secretary general of the ruling Yemeni Socialist Party. His premier, Ali Nasser Muhammad, replaces him.

1981

ARAB-ISRAELI CONFLICT

March 24. Asad to Permit PLO Bases. Syrian president Asad says he will permit PLO guerrillas to use his country's territory to mount attacks against Israel. Asad criticizes King Hussein's refusal to let the PLO establish bases in Jordan.

June 4. Sadat-Begin Meeting. Egyptian president Sadat and Israeli prime minister Begin, meeting at Sharm al-Shaykh in the Israeli-occupied part of the Sinai, hold their first high-level meeting since January 1980. Talks focus on the situation in Lebanon. Sadat supports the withdrawal of Syrian forces but criticizes Israel's attacks on PLO bases in Lebanon.

June 7. Israel Bombs Iraqi Reactor. Israeli warplanes bomb and destroy the Osirak nuclear reactor near Baghdad, Iraq. The United States, the Soviet Union, and other foreign nations, including France—which sold the Osirak reactor to Iraq—condemn the raid. At a news conference June 9 Israeli prime minister Begin rejects international criticism and defends the attack as an action meant to prevent another Holocaust. The United States suspends delivery June 10 of four F-16 fighters ordered by Israel. On June 11, however, President Reagan tells Israeli ambassador Ephraim Evron that despite U.S. opposition to the raid, no "fundamental reevaluation" of the U.S.-Israeli relationship is planned.

July 10–16. Israeli Raids. The Israeli air force bombs Palestinian positions in southern Lebanon, killing about 50 people. Deaths caused by Israeli bombings total 160 since January 1981.

July 24. Israeli-PLO Cease-Fire. Israel and the PLO endorse separate cease-fire agreements to end the fighting along the Lebanese-Israeli border. The agreement had been mediated by Saudi Arabia and the United States.

August 3. Israeli-Egyptian Agreement. Israel and Egypt sign an agreement establishing a twenty-five-hundred-member international peacekeeping force in the Sinai by April 25, 1982, the day Israel is to complete its withdrawal from the peninsula.

August 7. Saudi Peace Plan. Saudi prince Fahd offers an eight-point peace plan that recognizes Israel's right to exist. Israeli prime minister Begin rejects the plan while PLO leader Yasir Arafat states August 16 that it could lead to peace.

August 11. Reagan Holds Back More Fighters. The Reagan administration suspends the delivery of four more F-16 and two F-15 fighter planes to Israel. Resumption of deliveries is said to depend on the success of the June 24 cease-fire between Israel and the PLO. The delivery ban is lifted August 17.

October 29. Reagan on Saudi Plan. In remarks to reporters President Reagan indicates that the Saudi peace plan announced in August was a significant step toward Middle East peace because it "recognized Israel as a nation to be negotiated with." Previously the administration had dismissed the plan. Reagan's comments stir new interest in the eight-point plan. Israel, however, denounces it and expresses regret over Reagan's statements. The State Department says October 30 that the administration does not support all provisions of the plan and remains committed to the Camp David peace process, which was not mentioned by the Saudi proposal.

November 30. U.S.-Israeli Strategic Pact. The United States and Israel sign a strategic memorandum of understanding in Washington that establishes joint measures to meet threats in the Middle East "caused by the Soviet Union or Soviet-controlled forces from outside the region." The agreement does not provide for joint U.S.-Israeli maneuvers or pledge the United States to aid Israel if the Jewish state is attacked.

December 14. Israel Annexes Golan Heights. The Israeli Knesset passes a bill supported by Prime Minister Begin that annexes the strategically important Golan Heights. The United States immediately denounces the annexation.

December 18. U.S. Suspends Agreement. The United States suspends the strategic pact concluded with Israel November 30 in response to Israel's surprise annexation of the Golan Heights.

EGYPT

September 15. Egypt Expels Soviets. Egypt expels Soviet ambassador Vladimir Polyakov, six embassy aides, and two Soviet correspondents accused of fomenting religious unrest.

October 6. Sadat Assassinated. Men in military uniform assassinate Egyptian president Sadat as he watches a military parade commemorating the 1973 war with Israel. Vice President Hosni Mubarak assumes control of the armed forces and reaffirms Egypt's commitment to the Camp David Accords and other international treaties. Sadat is buried with full military honors October 10. Former U.S. presidents Nixon, Ford, and Carter, Israeli prime minister Begin, and other leaders from more than eighty nations attend the funeral. President Reagan and Vice President George Bush stay away for security reasons.

October 13. Mubarak Elected. Vice President Mubarak, the National Democratic Party candidate, is elected president of Egypt.

IRAN

January 15. Hostage Agreement Close. Behzad Nabavi, the chief Iranian negotiator in the American hostage crisis, says Iran is close to agreement with the United States on releasing the hostages but demands the transfer of frozen Iranian assets.

January 18. Hostage Agreement Announced. Iranian negotiator Nabavi announces that the United States and Iran have "reached agreement on resolving the issue of the hostages."

January 19. Hostage Release Delayed. Shortly before 5:00 a.m., President Carter announces resolution of the hostage crisis. When Iranian negotiator Nabavi objects to an appendix to the agreement dealing with Iran's ability to recover assets, the hostages' release is delayed.

January 20. Hostages Released, Reagan Sworn In. Iranian and American negotiators in Algiers agree on the disputed appendix. Soon afterward the United States transfers $8 billion in frozen assets to the Bank of England. The hostages board two Algerian planes at 12:25 p.m. (EST), minutes after Ronald Reagan succeeds Jimmy Carter as president of the United States. The Algerian government notifies the Algerian central bank when the planes clear Iranian air space. The bank then notifies the Bank of England that it may transfer assets to Iran.

February 18. Reagan to Observe Agreement. The Reagan administration formally announces that it will observe the terms of the hostage agreement with Iran negotiated by the Carter administration.

June 22. Bani-Sadr Dismissed. Khomeini dismisses Abolhassan Bani-Sadr as president of Iran.

July 5. Bani-Sadr Verdict. Iran's revolutionary court calls for the execution of former president Bani-Sadr, who is hiding in the Kurdistan region under the protection of Kurdish tribes.

July 29. France Grants Asylum to Bani-Sadr. Bani-Sadr receives asylum in France.

August 30. Bombing in Tehran. A bomb explosion in the prime ministry building in Tehran kills Iranian president Mohammed Ali Rajai and Premier Mohammed Jad Bahonar.

ISRAEL

June 30. Likud Wins Narrow Victory. The Likud Party led by Menachem Begin wins 48 seats in the 120-member Israeli Knesset and is expected to take the lead in forming a coalition government. The rival Labor Party wins 47 seats.

August 5. Begin Establishes Government. Begin wins approval for his four-party coalition government of 61 seats in a vote of confidence in Israel's 120-seat Knesset.

LEBANON

April 2. Fighting in Lebanon. Lebanese Christian militia and Syrian troops clash in Beirut. Thirty-seven persons are killed. Lebanese president Elias Sarkis issues a cease-fire order April 8.

April 28. Israel Joins Battle in Lebanon. For the first time, Israel intervenes in fighting between Syrian and Lebanese Christian militia forces near Beirut. Israeli jets shoot down two Syrian helicopters. The Israeli government says that it "cannot acquiesce in the attempt of the Syrians to conquer Lebanon and liquidate the Christians in that country."

April 29. Syria Installs Missiles. Syria moves SAM-6 surface-to-air missiles into Lebanon's Bekaa Valley April 29 in response to the Israeli attack the day before. The move precipitates a diplomatic crisis. Israel demands that the missiles be removed and contends that the Syrian action violates an agreement concluded with Syria in 1976 that such missiles would not be introduced in Lebanon. Syria contends that the missiles are necessary to defend against Israeli air attacks.

May 7–13. Habib Diplomatic Efforts. U.S. special envoy Philip Habib shuttles among Beirut, Damascus, and Jerusalem seeking a settlement to the Israeli-Syrian missile dispute. Syrian forces fire at Israeli reconnaissance planes over Lebanon May 12. The Syrians claim they downed one Israeli jet.

May 14. Missile Crisis Deepens. Syrian missiles down an Israeli reconnaissance drone over Lebanon's Bekaa Valley. Israel confirms the incident. This is the first time Israel acknowledges the loss of an Israeli aircraft since the Syrians moved missiles into Lebanon in late April. Israel acknowledges the loss of two more drones by May 25. Begin demands May 21 that Syria remove not only those missiles in Lebanon but also those on Syrian territory near Lebanon.

June 30. Syria Lifts Siege of Christians. Syria agrees to lift its three-month siege of the Lebanese city of Zahle, where a Christian militia force had been holding out. The Syrian action is seen as a first step toward resolving the Lebanese missile crisis.

July 17. Downtown Beirut Bombed. After a week of Israeli air raids against Palestinian positions in southern Lebanon, Israeli jets attack the headquarters of the PLO in downtown Beirut. Bombs falling on the heavily populated area kill three hundred persons, mostly Lebanese civilians. The United States on July 20 indefinitely suspends delivery of six F-16s to Israel but declines to link the action to the July 17 Israeli bombing raid.

LIBYA AND NORTH AFRICA

January 6. Libya, Chad Merge. At the end of a four-day visit to Libya by Chadian president Goukouni Oueddei, Libya announces a merger with Chad and the opening of the Chad-Libya border. France condemns the agreement, saying that the merger defies an earlier international agreement that scheduled free elections in Chad in 1982 to decide that country's future.

May 6. U.S. Closes Libyan Mission. The United States orders Libya to close its diplomatic mission in Washington because of Libya's support for terrorism and its sanctioning of assassination attempts on Libyans living abroad.

August 19. Libyan Jets Downed. Two U.S. Navy F-14 jets down two attacking Soviet-built Libyan SU-22s about sixty miles from the Libyan coast in the northern part of the Gulf of Sidra. The confrontation occurs during U.S. naval maneuvers. Libya claims the Gulf of Sidra as part of its territorial waters, but the United States regards it as international waters.

PERSIAN GULF STATES

March 6. Saudi Arms Sale. The Reagan administration announces plans to sell Saudi Arabia air-to-air missiles and fuel tanks that would enhance the combat capability of its F-15 jet fighters. Israel and some members of Congress object to the sale.

April 19. Yamani Disclosure on Oil Glut. Saudi oil minister Yamani on "Meet the Press" confirms that Saudis engineered the current oil glut and pledges that his country will maintain its record production levels until other OPEC members agree to a long-term price strategy.

April 21. AWACS Sale Announced. The Reagan administration announces a massive arms sale package for Saudi Arabia, including five controversial AWACS radar defense planes. Israel vigorously protests the sale. Saudi oil minister Yamani says Israel, not the Soviet Union, is the chief danger to his country. On April 26 Reagan delays submitting the arms package for congressional approval until later in the year.

May 26. OPEC Meeting. Meeting in Geneva, OPEC ministers freeze oil prices between $36 and $41 per barrel and cut oil production by a minimum of 10 percent. Iran and Iraq are exempted from the new production levels. Saudi Arabia opts to maintain its high production (10.3 million barrels a day) and keep its crude oil prices at $32 a barrel. The Saudis resist pressure to increase their price of oil or lower production in a continuing effort to win support for a unified OPEC price strategy.

August 24. AWACS Sale Announced. The Reagan administration formally notifies Congress of its plan to sell Saudi Arabia five sophisticated Airborne Warning and Control System (AWACS) planes. The sale had originally been announced April 21, 1981.

October 28. Senate Approves AWACS Sale. After President Reagan certifies to the U.S. Senate that the Saudi government agreed not to use AWACS against Israel, the Senate approves the AWACS sale, 52–48. The House opposed the deal by an overwhelming margin, but by law a majority of both chambers had to vote against the arms sale to block it.

1982

ARAB-ISRAELI CONFLICT

January 20. U.S. Vetoes Resolution. The United States vetoes a UN Security Council resolution calling for punishment of Israel for annexing the Golan Heights.

February 28. Israeli Conditions for Visit. The Israeli government says Egypt's president Mubarak will not be invited to Israel if he refuses to visit Jerusalem. Prime Minister Begin vows March 2 not to go to Egypt until Mubarak agrees to visit Jerusalem. Mubarak postpones his scheduled trip to Israel March 15.

April 11. Dome of the Rock Shooting. Alan Harry Goodman, an American-born Israeli soldier, kills two Arabs and wounds many in a shooting spree at the Dome of the Rock Mosque in Jerusalem.

April 25. Israel Returns Territory. Israel returns the final portions of the Sinai Peninsula to Egypt under the terms of the 1979 peace treaty. Mubarak commends Israel's "enthusiasm for peace" April 26.

June 3. Attempted Assassination. Shlomo Argov, the Israeli ambassador to Great Britain, is shot and severely wounded in London. Israel accuses the PLO of responsibility.

September 9. Fez Summit Peace Plan. The Arab League summit in Fez, Morocco, announces an eight-point plan calling for an Israeli withdrawal to pre-1967 borders, the creation of a Palestinian state, and UN guarantees of peace among "all states of the region." U.S. secretary of state George Shultz sees a chance for a "breakthrough" in light of the Arab League proposal, but Israel rejects the plan.

September 15. Arafat Meets Pope. PLO leader Yasir Arafat meets with Pope John Paul II at the Vatican. Israel condemns the meeting.

December 21. Hussein, Reagan Meet. Jordan's King Hussein meets with President Reagan in Washington and expresses sympathy for Reagan's peace initiative, but he says Jordan will not represent Palestinians in peace negotiations with Israel unless the PLO and other Arab states approve of such an arrangement.

EGYPT

April 15. Sadat's Killers Executed. Five Muslim militants convicted of assassinating President Sadat are executed in Egypt.

IRAN-IRAQ WAR

March 22. Iranian Offensive. Iran launches a major spring offensive that forces Iraqi troops to retreat from long-held positions inside Iran.

May 26. Israeli Arms to Iran. Israeli defense minister Ariel Sharon confirms that Israel has supplied Iran with arms in its war with Iraq.

ISRAEL

March 23. No-Confidence Vote. Prime Minister Begin submits his government's resignation after three motions of no confidence in the Israeli Knesset result in 58–58 votes. The tie votes do not require the government to resign, and Begin agrees to remain in office after the cabinet rejects his resignation, 12-6. The no-confidence votes are a response by the opposition parties to the government's handling of disorder on the West Bank, where Israeli troops had engaged protesters in violent clashes.

LEBANON

January 19. Begin on Lebanon. Prime Minister Begin, reacting to U.S. speculation, assures Washington that Israel will not attack Lebanon unless provoked by Palestinian guerrillas or Syria.

June 6. Israel Invades Lebanon. Israel launches a three-pronged armored assault across the Lebanese border supported by air strikes. Israeli forces penetrate all the way to Sidon, thirty miles north of the border, on the first day of the invasion. Begin informs President Reagan that the purpose of the assault is to establish a twenty-five-mile security zone in southern Lebanon that will ensure the security of northern Israeli towns from Palestinian artillery attacks. The UN Security Council unanimously calls on Israel to withdraw from Lebanon.

June 7. Reaction to Invasion. The Reagan administration refuses to condemn the Israeli invasion of Lebanon but says "Israel will have to withdraw its forces from Lebanon, and the Palestinians will have to stop using Lebanon as a launching pad for attacks on Israel."

June 9. Syrian Missiles Destroyed. In a massive air battle, Israeli pilots destroy Syrian surface-to-air missiles in Lebanon's Bekaa Valley. Israel claims that Syria lost twenty-two planes while all ninety of Israel's jets returned unharmed. Syria admits losing sixteen planes but claims that nineteen Israeli jets were downed. Israeli forces advance to within sight of Beirut.

June 10. Israel Threatens Beirut. Israeli warplanes repeatedly bomb targets in and around Beirut and drop leaflets warning Syrians to evacuate the city in advance of an Israeli assault upon it. The Reagan administration reportedly warns Israel against trying to capture the city.

June 11. Israeli-Syrian Cease-Fire. Israel declares a unilateral cease-fire that is quickly joined by Syria. Israel and the PLO announce a cease-fire June 12 that breaks down the following day.

June 13. Israel Sets Conditions for Pullout. Israeli leaders tell U.S. envoy Philip Habib that they would withdraw from Lebanon if Syrian forces left the country and a demilitarized zone were created in southern Lebanon that would be patrolled by an international peacekeeping force not controlled by the UN.

June 14. Egypt Suspends Talks. Egypt suspends autonomy talks with Israel because of Israel's invasion of Lebanon. Israeli forces cut off West Beirut, trapping PLO leaders.

June 21. Begin Meets with Reagan. Begin and Reagan, meeting in Washington, agree that all foreign forces should be removed from Lebanon. In comments after the meeting Reagan emphasizes the common long-term interests of the United States and Israel and says that Israel "must not be subjected to violence from the north."

June 24. U.S. Closes Embassy. The United States closes its embassy in Lebanon. The U.S. Sixth Fleet evacuates hundreds of Americans, Europeans, and Lebanese from the country. Israel June 25 begins its heaviest bombing of Beirut since June 6. It announces June 26 that it is observing a cease-fire.

June 27. Israeli Peace Plan. Israel promises to guarantee safe passage to Syria to Palestinians in Lebanon who lay down their weapons. Israel says it would then open negotiations on establishing the territorial integrity of Lebanon and achieving the withdrawal of all foreign forces from that country. PLO leader Yasir Arafat agrees in principle to accept the Israeli proposal.

July 6. Reagan Offers U.S. Forces. President Reagan agrees to contribute a small contingent of U.S. Marines to a multinational peacekeeping force that would oversee the withdrawal of PLO forces from West Beirut.

July 9. Syria Rejects Plan. Syria says that it will not allow PLO forces to be evacuated to Syria. The Syrian rejection prompts weeks of international negotiations on how and where to evacuate the PLO.

July 16. U.S. Stops Sale of Shells to Israel. The United States suspends further sales of cluster artillery shells to Israel pending review of their use in Lebanon. Israel asserts July 18 that it did not violate the agreement governing their use. President Reagan bans the sale of the shells indefinitely July 27.

July 22. Cease-Fire Broken. Israeli jets attack Palestinian and Syrian forces in Lebanon in retaliation for alleged violations of a ten-day-old cease-fire. The cease-fire is restored July 28 after several days of fighting and Israeli bombing raids.

August 4. Israel Enters West Beirut. Under cover of heavy artillery fire, Israeli armored units enter West Beirut.

August 6. PLO Agrees to U.S.-Mediated Plan. The PLO agrees to all major points of a U.S. plan for PLO withdrawal from Beirut. Syria and several other Arab countries agree to accept PLO fighters.

August 9. U.S. Presents Plan to Israel. The United States formally presents Israel with a plan calling for the evacuation of the PLO from Beirut with the aid of UN forces. Israel accepts the plan in principle August 10 but insists on the departure of PLO forces before UN troops arrive.

August 12. Israeli Bombing Raids. Israeli jets bomb Beirut for eleven hours. President Reagan telephones Begin to express U.S. "outrage" and demand an end to the attacks. Israel's cabinet votes to stop the bombing, and Begin calls Reagan to announce that a "complete" cease-fire has been ordered.

August 15. Israel Accepts Peacekeeping Force. Israel accepts U.S. envoy Philip Habib's plan for deploying an international peacekeeping force in Beirut. Lebanon approves the plan August 25.

August 19. PLO Withdrawal Pact Concluded. The Israeli cabinet unanimously accepts a U.S. plan that provides for the withdrawal of PLO forces from Lebanon. The Lebanese government and the PLO had approved the pact the day before. President Reagan orders eight hundred Marines to participate in the peacekeeping force overseeing the withdrawal. The Marines arrive in Lebanon August 25.

August 21. PLO Withdrawal Begins. French paratroopers arrive in Lebanon to participate in the international peacekeeping force. The first group of 397 PLO guerrillas then departs Lebanon for Cyprus, beginning the two-week pullout. Yasir Arafat leaves Beirut for Greece August 30.

August 23. Bashir Gemayel Elected. Bashir Gemayel, Christian Phalangist leader, is elected president of Lebanon.

September 1. Reagan Peace Plan. President Reagan, in a major address, presents his "initiative" for peace in the Middle East. It calls for "self-government by the Palestinians of the West Bank and Gaza in association with Jordan," a "freeze" on Israeli settlements in the occupied territories, and an "undivided" Jerusalem with final status to be decided in negotiations. The Israeli cabinet unanimously rejects the plan September 2.

September 1. PLO Withdrawal Completed. The last of fifteen thousand PLO and Syrian troops leave Beirut. Lebanese forces take full control of the city the following day.

September 14. Gemayel Assassinated. Lebanese president-elect Bashir Gemayel is killed by a bomb blast at Phalange Party headquarters in East Beirut.

September 15. Israelis Occupy West Beirut. Israeli troops and tanks reenter West Beirut in a move the Israeli government describes as a "police action." Israeli leaders contend the presence of Israeli troops is necessary to keep order after the assassination of Bashir Gemayel.

September 18. Sabra and Shatila Massacre. Reports emerge of the massacre of hundreds of Palestinian civilians in the Sabra and Shatila refugee camps outside Beirut by Lebanese Christian militiamen permitted into the area by Israeli authorities September 15–18. President Reagan expresses "outrage and revulsion" and demands an immediate Israeli withdrawal from West Beirut. Israeli Labor Party leader Shimon Peres September 19 calls for the resignation of Prime Minister Begin and Defense Minister Ariel Sharon.

September 20. Peacekeepers Requested. Lebanese leaders request the return of an international peacekeeping force to Beirut. Italy, France, and the United States agree to again provide troops, but Reagan stipulates that Israel must give permission and pull back its forces in the area. Israel agrees September 21.

September 20. Amin Gemayel Elected. Amin Gemayel is elected president of Lebanon to succeed his slain brother Bashir. He is sworn in September 23 for a six-year term.

September 22. Sharon Disclosure. Defense Minister Ariel Sharon acknowledges that Israel coordinated the entry of the Lebanese Phalangist forces into the refugee camps where the massacre occurred. Sharon says Israeli military commanders had emphasized to their Phalangist counterparts that the refugee camp operation was to be directed only at "terrorists."

September 26. Begin Requests Commission. Begin requests the establishment of a judicial commission of inquiry to investigate Israel's role in the Beirut massacre. The panel is established September 28.

November 8. Begin Testifies. Begin tells the commission investigating the September Beirut massacre that he was not aware of the army's plan to send Lebanese militiamen into the refugee camps where the killings took place.

November 29. Peacekeeping Force Expanded. Lebanon requests an expansion of the international peacekeeping force. The United States agrees December 1 to double its troop strength in Lebanon.

December 28. Israeli-Lebanese Talks Begin. Negotiations between Lebanon and Israel begin in Khalde, Lebanon, on withdrawal of foreign forces from Lebanon.

PERSIAN GULF STATES

January 26. Gulf Council Founded. The Gulf Cooperation Council is founded in Riyadh. Defense ministers of Saudi Arabia, Kuwait, Bahrain, the United Arab Emirates, Qatar, and Oman agree on measures to promote their collective security.

June 13. Fahd Becomes King. King Khalid of Saudi Arabia dies of a heart attack and is succeeded by his half-brother, Crown Prince Fahd. Fahd chooses Prince Abdallah ibn Abd al-Aziz to be crown prince.

SYRIA

February 2. Syrian Uprising. An uprising by Muslim fundamentalist rebels in the Syrian city of Hama leads to heavy fighting between the rebels and Syrian troops. The two sides engage in artillery battles that destroy parts of the city. Reports from Damascus February 18 indicate that thousands of Syrians have died in the fighting and hundreds of rebels have been executed by Syrian troops who gradually gain control over the city. Syrian authorities admit for the first time February 22 that the Hama confrontation was a major uprising.

1983

ARAB-ISRAELI CONFLICT

January 17. Palestinian Groups Meet. Hard-line Palestinian factions meeting in Tripoli, Libya, reject the

Reagan plan and other peace proposals. They call for continued armed struggle against Israel. Their position is seen as a challenge to the authority of PLO leader Arafat.

March 21. Cabinet Announces New Settlements. The Israeli cabinet announces plans to build twenty-three additional Jewish settlements in the West Bank during the next two years.

ISRAEL

August 28. Begin to Resign. Menachem Begin announces his intention to resign as Israeli prime minister for personal reasons.

September 12. New Israeli Government. Six parties of Begin's governing coalition agree to form a new government under Foreign Minister Yitzhak Shamir. Shamir's government wins the Knesset's endorsement October 10.

LEBANON

February 8. Commission Findings. The Israeli commission of inquiry investigating the September 1982 massacre near Beirut recommends the dismissal of several officers for neglect of duty, including Defense Minister Ariel Sharon. The cabinet accepts the commission's findings February 11. Sharon resigns the same day but accepts Begin's offer to remain in the government as a minister without portfolio. Former ambassador to the United States Moshe Arens is named to succeed Sharon as Israeli defense minister February 14.

February 15. Army Moves into East Beirut. Christian militia forces withdraw from East Beirut and are replaced by Lebanese regular army units.

March 31. Reagan Delays Shipment of F-16s. President Reagan says that the United States will not ship F-16 jets to Israel until it withdraws from Lebanon. The White House had delayed the delivery of seventy-five F-16s after the Israelis invaded Lebanon in June 1982.

April 18. Beirut Embassy Bombed. A car bomb attack partially destroys the U.S. embassy in Beirut, killing sixty-three persons and wounding more than a hundred. A pro-Iranian group, the Islamic Jihad, claims responsibility. President Reagan says the attack "will not deter us from our goals of peace in the region."

May 4. Israeli-Lebanese Pact. The Lebanese government accepts a U.S.-mediated draft agreement on withdrawal of Israeli troops from Lebanon. The accord calls for an end to the state of war between Israel and Lebanon, the withdrawal of Israeli troops in eight to twelve weeks if Syrian and PLO forces also leave, and limitations on the Lebanese military's presence near the Israeli border. The Israeli Knesset and the Lebanese parliament approve the pact May 16. Representatives of the two countries sign the agreement May 17. Syria rejects the agreement May 13 and closes land routes and communication channels between Beirut and Syrian-held areas of Lebanon May 17.

May 20. Reagan Ends Embargo. President Reagan lifts the ban on the sale of seventy-five F-16 fighters to Israel imposed after the invasion of Lebanon.

August 29. Fighting Spreads to Beirut. Two U.S. Marines are killed and fourteen wounded in Beirut as units of the Lebanese army and Muslim militia clash. Reagan September 1 orders two thousand Marines to be stationed in ships off Beirut in case troops in Lebanon should need to be reinforced. Four French peacekeepers are killed August 31.

September 3. Israeli Redeployment. Israeli troops begin redeploying from the Shuf Mountains south of Beirut to more defensible positions in southern Lebanon. Druze forces take control of the area after the Israeli pullout.

September 13. Marines to Return Fire. U.S. Marine peacekeeping forces are authorized to call in naval gunfire and air strikes to defend themselves against artillery attacks.

September 16–19. U.S. Begins Shelling. For the first time U.S. naval guns fire on targets in Syrian-controlled Lebanon. President Reagan defends the action as essential to the safety of American peacekeepers. French planes attack antigovernment positions east of Beirut in response to the shelling of the French peacekeeping headquarters.

September 25. Lebanese Cease-Fire. A cease-fire is announced between warring factions in Lebanon. The agreement takes effect September 26.

September 29. War Powers Compromise. Congress authorizes Marines to remain in Lebanon for eighteen more months. President Reagan indicates that he will sign the law.

October 23. U.S. Marine Barracks Bombed. A suicide truck-bomb attack on the barracks of U.S. peacekeeping forces in Beirut kills 241 Marines and Navy personnel. An almost simultaneous attack against the French compound kills fifty-eight. President Reagan condemns the attack and reaffirms the U.S. commitment to the peacekeeping effort.

November 4. Israeli Headquarters Bombed. The Israeli headquarters in Tyre, Lebanon, is destroyed by a suicide truck bomb. Sixty Israeli soldiers and Arab prisoners are killed. In retaliation, Israeli jets hit Palestinian positions in the mountains east of Beirut.

November 24. Prisoner Exchange. Israel trades forty-five hundred Palestinian and Lebanese guerrilla prisoners for six Israeli soldiers held by the PLO.

December 4. U.S. Air Strikes. U.S. planes attack Syrian positions in Lebanon in response to Syrian attacks on unarmed American reconnaissance planes December 3. Two U.S. planes are shot down; one pilot is killed and the other captured. The same day eight U.S. Marines are killed by artillery fire from Druze militia near Beirut.

LIBYA AND NORTH AFRICA

August 18. French Troops to Chad. Reacting to the massing of Libyan forces in northern Chad, Paris sends planes and 450 additional troops to Chad. The reinforcements build French troop strength in the country to two thousand. The French presence is credited with deterring further Libyan advances.

PALESTINIAN AFFAIRS

April 10. Sartawi Assassinated. Issam Sartawi, a close adviser to PLO leader Arafat and an advocate of mutual Israeli-PLO recognition, is assassinated in Lisbon, Portugal. The Fatah Revolutionary Council, a radical Palestinian faction, claims responsibility.

June 1. PLO Rebellion. More than twenty leading members of Arafat's Fatah wing of the PLO announce their support for an ongoing rebellion within the PLO against Arafat's leadership. Arafat supporters and Al Fatah rebels engage in heavy battles in Lebanon's Bekaa Valley. Arafat accuses Libyan leader Qadhafi June 7 of supporting the rebels.

June 24. Syria Expels Arafat. Syria's president Asad expels Arafat from Syria. The day before Arafat had accused Syria of aiding PLO rebels in their fight against Arafat. Syrian tanks had reportedly supported rebel PLO attacks on Arafat's forces in the Bekaa Valley during the previous week.

July 24. PLO Fighting. Heavy fighting breaks out in Lebanon between PLO rebels and Arafat loyalists, ending a three-week-old cease-fire. The rebels reportedly drive Arafat's forces from several positions in the Bekaa Valley.

November 3. PLO Rebels Attack Arafat Forces. Syrian-backed PLO rebels attack positions held by forces loyal to Arafat outside Tripoli, Lebanon.

November 16. Arafat Stronghold Captured. PLO rebels overrun the Beddawi refugee camp, a stronghold of forces loyal to Arafat. Arafat sets up headquarters in Tripoli and vows November 17 to "fight to the end."

November 23. PLO Cease-Fire. PLO factions in Damascus accept a Saudi-sponsored cease-fire to allow Arafat and his troops to evacuate Tripoli.

December 3. Evacuation Plan. UN Secretary General Javier Pérez de Cuéllar agrees to allow Arafat's PLO forces to evacuate Tripoli under the UN flag. The UN Security Council unanimously agrees to the plan.

December 9–19. Israeli Ships Shell PLO. Israeli gunboats continually shell PLO positions in Tripoli, forcing a delay in the evacuation of forces loyal to Arafat. The United States publicly urges Israel to allow the evacuation December 19.

December 20. Arafat Forces Evacuated. Greek ships flying UN flags evacuate Arafat and four thousand of his PLO troops from Tripoli. The convoy is escorted out of Tripoli harbor by French warships and sails for Tunis.

December 22. Arafat, Mubarak Meeting. Arafat meets in Cairo with Egyptian president Mubarak. They announce resumption of relations broken off after the signing of the Egyptian-Israeli peace treaty.

PERSIAN GULF STATES

March 14. OPEC Price Cut. OPEC members agree to establish national production quotas and cut their benchmark crude oil prices from $34 a barrel to $29 a barrel. The price cut, brought on by the developing world oil glut, is the first in OPEC's history.

1984

ARAB-ISRAELI CONFLICT

April 29. Jewish Attack Prevented. Israel says that it has uncovered a plot by a Jewish underground organization to blow up Arab buses. Twenty-one persons are arrested.

May 28. Bus Hijackers Beaten to Death. The Israeli Ministry of Defense admits that two of four bus hijackers killed April 13 were captured alive and beaten to death by police.

EGYPT

April 19. Egypt, Soviet Union Restore Ties. Egypt and the Soviet Union agree to restore diplomatic relations after a three-year break.

May 27. Egyptian Elections. President Mubarak's National Democratic party wins 73 percent of the popular vote and 391 of 448 contested parliamentary seats.

IRAN

December 4. Kuwaiti Airliner Hijacked. Four Arabs hijack a Kuwaiti jet carrying 161 people and divert it to Tehran. The hijackers demand the release of seventeen Arabs in Kuwaiti prisons for attacks on American and French missions. One American hostage is killed December 4 and another December 6. Iranian police storm the aircraft and free the hostages December 9. The United States December 11 accuses Iran of backing the hijackers and demands that they be extradited. Iran refuses the extradition request December 12 and says the hijackers will be tried in Iran.

IRAQ

November 26. United States, Iraq Establish Ties. The United States and Iraq resume diplomatic relations after a seventeen-year split.

IRAN-IRAQ WAR

February 27. Iraq Blockades Kharg Island. Iraq announces a blockade of the Iranian oil facilities on Kharg Island. Baghdad says the blockade will continue until Iran agrees to end the war.

March 5. United States Accuses Iraq. The United States accuses Iraq of using chemical weapons in its war against Iran. The Red Cross March 7 supports the U.S. claim after examining Iranian victims.

May 29. Stingers to Saudi Arabia. President Reagan authorizes the sale of four hundred Stinger antiaircraft missiles to Saudi Arabia in the face of increasing attacks on Persian Gulf shipping by Iran and Iraq. During the past weeks Iran had attacked Saudi and Kuwaiti tankers in retaliation for Iraq's attacks on Iranian ships. The sale did not require congressional approval because Reagan certified that U.S. national security demanded an immediate transfer of the weapons.

July 31. Red Sea Explosions. The pro-Iranian Islamic Jihad claims responsibility for numerous mine explosions that have damaged ships in the Red Sea during June. The United States, France, and Great Britain send minesweeping units to the Red Sea in August. Iran radio hails the explosions August 7, but Khomeini August 9 denounces the mining.

ISRAEL

July 23. Israeli Elections. In Israeli elections, the Labor Party wins 44 seats in the 120-seat Knesset. The Likud Party wins 41 seats. President Chaim Herzog asks Labor leader Shimon Peres August 5 to form a new government.

September 13. Coalition Government Formed. Peres and Likud Party head Yitzhak Shamir agree to form a coalition government in which they will exchange the posts of prime minister and defense minister in 1986 at the midpoint of the coalition's fifty-one-month term. Peres will serve as prime minister first. The Knesset approves the agreement September 14.

JORDAN

March 12. Jordanian Elections. For the first time since 1967, Jordan holds elections for vacancies in its sixty-member Council of Delegates.

September 25. Jordan to Establish Egypt Ties. Jordan announces it will reestablish diplomatic relations with Egypt. Of the seventeen Arab countries that broke ties with Egypt after Egypt signed the 1979 peace treaty with Israel, Jordan is the first to reestablish relations.

LEBANON

February 5. Government Resigns. Under pressure from Muslim factions, the Lebanese government of Amin Gemayel resigns. Gemayel himself remains president and calls for national reconciliation.

February 6. Muslim Militia Routs Army. After a week of heavy fighting, Muslim militia forces drive the Lebanese army from West Beirut.

February 7. Peacekeepers Withdraw. President Reagan orders U.S. peacekeeping troops to redeploy to ships off the Lebanese coast. Great Britain and Italy also announce they will withdraw their peacekeepers from Lebanon. The British pullout begins February 8; the Italians leave February 20. The U.S. redeployment begins February 21 and is completed February 26. Reagan reaffirms U.S. support for the Gemayel government February 22 and says the Marines will return to Beirut if necessary.

February 8. Naval Bombardment. In accordance with new rules of engagement that allow U.S. commanders to respond to artillery attacks on Beirut whether or not U.S. soldiers are threatened, the battleship *New Jersey* fires more than 250 one-ton shells into positions southeast of Beirut.

March 5. Lebanon Cancels Israeli Accord. The Lebanese government breaks the May 1983 troop withdrawal agreement with Israel. The move paves the way for reconciliation talks between warring Lebanese factions.

March 12. Reconciliation Talks. Lebanese president Gemayel opens talks in Lausanne, Switzerland, with leaders of factions fighting in Lebanon. The conference ends March 20 without agreement.

May 10. New Lebanese Cabinet Meets. A new unity cabinet that includes top Muslim and Christian leaders meets for the first time in Lebanon.

July 4–7. Lebanese Army in Beirut. A reconstituted Lebanese army assumes control of Beirut from militias and begins the destruction of the Green Line wall dividing Muslim and Christian sectors. An agreement approved by the Lebanese cabinet June 23 restructured the army to provide more equal representation between rival Muslim and Christian factions.

LIBYA AND NORTH AFRICA

April 17. Britain-Libya Embassy Incident. A hail of gunfire from inside the Libyan embassy in London kills a British policewoman and wounds ten Libyan exiles demonstrating outside. British police surround the embassy after the shooting and demand the right to search it. In response, Libyan troops surround the British embassy in Tripoli. London breaks diplomatic ties to Libya April 22. The Libyan government agrees April 24 to a mutual exchange of diplomats. British and Libyan diplomats return to their respective countries April 27.

September 25. Libyans, French Leave Chad. Libya and France begin a mutual troop withdrawal from Chad under a September 17 understanding.

PALESTINIAN AFFAIRS

February 22. Shultz Confirms PLO Contacts. U.S. secretary of state Shultz confirms a *New York Times* report of February 18 that the Reagan administration held secret talks with the PLO through an intermediary from August 1981 to May 1982.

SYRIA

January 3. Goodman Released. In response to a visit by the Rev. Jesse L. Jackson, Syria releases U.S. Navy Lt. Robert Goodman Jr., who had been captured when his plane was shot down December 3.

1985

ARAB-ISRAELI CONFLICT

February 22. Jordan-PLO Plan. Jordan makes public the text of a February 11 agreement on the Middle East peace process between King Hussein and Yasir Arafat. The plan calls for a total Israeli withdrawal from occupied territories, the right of self-determination for Palestinians within the context of a Jordan-Palestine confederation, and peace negotiations under UN auspices with the five permanent Security Council members and all parties to the conflict, including the PLO within a joint Palestinian-Jordanian delegation.

March 21. Reagan on the Middle East. In a televised news conference, President Reagan says the United States is willing to meet with a Jordanian-Palestinian delegation that does not include PLO members. Israeli prime minister Peres rejects the idea March 24.

April 30. U.S. Aid. The Reagan administration, responding to an urgent request from Peres, agrees to grant Israel $1.5 billion in additional economic aid. In keeping with U.S. policy, Egypt will receive $500 million in additional aid.

September 25. Palestinians Attack Yacht. Palestinian gunmen storm a small private yacht in Cyprus, killing three Israelis. Before surrendering to police, they demand the release of twenty Palestinians held by Israel.

October 1. Israel Bombs PLO Headquarters. Israeli planes destroy the PLO headquarters in Tunis in retaliation for the killing of three Israelis by Palestinians in Cyprus six days earlier. Leaders throughout the Arab world condemn the bombing, which kills more than seventy persons. The United States calls the attack "a legitimate response" to terrorism. On October 2, however, it revises its position, saying the attack was "understandable" but that it "cannot be condoned."

October 7. Achille Lauro Hijacking. Heavily armed gunmen hijack the Italian cruise ship *Achille Lauro* with more than four hundred people on board. They demand that Israel release fifty Palestinian prisoners. Arafat denies PLO involvement. Israeli officials say they have proof a wing of the PLO is behind the hijacking.

October 9. Hijackers Surrender. The four hijackers of the *Achille Lauro* surrender in Egypt after gaining assurances of safe passage to an undisclosed location. Italy later reports that Leon Klinghoffer, a wheelchair-bound New Yorker, is missing and is believed to have been slain and his body thrown overboard. Egypt later confirms the report.

October 10. Hijackers Intercepted. U.S. warplanes intercept an Egyptian plane carrying the hijackers of the *Achille Lauro* and force it to land in Sicily. An Italian public prosecutor October 11 charges the four Palestinians with murder and kidnapping. Egyptian president Mubarak October 12 condemns the U.S. interception of the hijackers and says the action has strained U.S.-Egyptian relations.

October 23. Abbas Implicated in Hijacking. One of the *Achille Lauro* hijackers reportedly tells Italian investigators that Muhammad Abu'l Abbas, leader of the Palestine National Front, was the mastermind behind the operation. Italy allowed Abbas to leave Italy October 21 despite American requests for his detention.

November 23. Egyptian Airliner Hijacked. Egyptair Flight 648 from Athens to Cairo is hijacked. The airplane is the same one intercepted October 10 while transporting the *Achille Lauro* hijackers out of Egypt. A hijacker and an Egyptian security agent are killed in a midair gun battle. Stray bullets pierce the fuselage, depressurizing the cabin and forcing the plane to land on Malta. There the hijackers release eleven female passengers and demand fuel. When their request is not granted, they begin shooting Israeli and American passengers and throwing them from the plane. Three of the five passengers who are shot do not receive fatal wounds.

November 24. Rescue Attempt. Egyptian special forces storm the hijacked Egyptair plane after dark. The hijackers shoot at the passengers and toss three incendiary grenades that set the cabin on fire. Fifty-nine of the original ninety-eight passengers and crew are killed. Only one hijacker survives. The hijackers are reported to be pro-Libyan followers of Mazen Sabry al-Banna, alias Abu Nidal, who heads a Palestinian group opposed to PLO chairman Arafat. Egyptian officials accuse Libya of backing the hijacking. Libya denies any involvement. Before the rescue attempt Egypt had declared a state of emergency along its border with Libya and had reinforced troops in western Egypt.

November 25. Hassan Agrees to Meet Peres. King Hassan II of Morocco agrees to meet Israel's prime minister Peres if Peres has serious proposals for Middle East peace. Peres says he would meet with the king. Israel declares November 26 that it will seek clarification of conflicting accounts of Hassan's offer to meet with Peres after Hassan is quoted as setting conditions on his purported invitation.

December 27. Airport Attacks. Palestinian gunmen attack travelers at El Al Israeli Airlines check-in counters in Rome and Vienna, killing 18 people and wounding 111. Four of the gunmen are killed and 3 wounded and captured. One identifies himself as a member of the Fatah Revolutionary Council, a renegade Palestinian group led by Abu Nidal. The PLO condemns the airport attacks.

IRAN

November 23. Montazeri Named Successor. The eighty-three-man Council of Experts formally designates Ayatollah Hussein Ali Montazeri as the eventual successor to Ayatollah Ruholla Khomeini as leader of Iran. Montazeri is said to be Khomeini's personal choice.

IRAN-IRAQ WAR

April 9. De Cuéllar Diplomatic Effort. After a three-day diplomatic tour of Iran and Iraq, UN Secretary General Javier Pérez de Cuéllar says the gap between Tehran and Baghdad is "as wide as ever." Iraqi officials tell de Cuéllar April 8 that they are ready to discuss a comprehensive settlement to the war, but Iran rejects any halt to the fighting until Iraqi president Saddam Hussein is ousted.

ISRAEL

July 1. Israeli Austerity Measures. Israel declares a state of economic emergency and announces new austerity measures. These include an 18.8 percent devaluation of the shekel, sharp cuts in government subsidies of basic commodities, and a three-month wage and price freeze.

November 21. Pollard Arrested. Jonathan Jay Pollard, a civilian employee of the U.S. Naval Intelligence Service in Suitland, Maryland, is arrested outside the Israeli embassy in Washington while attempting to seek political asylum. He is charged with selling classified information to Israel over the previous eighteen months. Pollard's wife, Anne Henderson-Pollard, is arrested November 22 and charged with unauthorized possession of classified U.S. documents. The Israeli government denies knowledge of the spy operation November 24 but says it will investigate the allegations.

December 1. Peres Apologizes. Prime Minister Peres apologizes to the United States for Israeli espionage exposed by the Pollard spy case. Peres says Israel will dismantle the unit involved if allegations are proven true.

JORDAN

September 27. Jordanian Arms Sale. President Reagan notifies Congress of his intention to sell Jordan between $1.5 billion and $1.9 billion in arms, including forty fighters, seventy-two Stinger missiles, and thirty-two Bradley fighting vehicles.

October 23. Jordan Arms Sale Postponed. Congressional opposition to the Reagan administration's proposed arms sale to Jordan prompts Reagan to delay the deal until March 1, unless Jordan and Israel begin "direct and meaningful" peace negotiations before then.

LEBANON

January 14. Israeli Withdrawal Plan. The Israeli cabinet endorses a three-stage plan to withdraw Israeli forces from Lebanon during the next six to nine months. Israel begins the initial phase of the pullout January 20. Israeli troops leave Sidon February 16.

February 14. Hostage Escapes. Jeremy Levin, an American journalist held almost a year in Lebanon, escapes and seeks help at a Syrian army post. The Syrians transport Levin to the U.S. embassy in Damascus. Middle East analysts speculate that Levin's captors allowed him to escape.

April 17. Lebanese Cabinet Resigns. After heavy fighting between rival Muslim militias in West Beirut, the one-year-old Lebanese unity cabinet resigns.

April 24. Israeli Withdrawal. The Israeli army begins withdrawing from eastern and central Lebanon as part of the second phase of the Israeli troop withdrawal. This phase is completed April 29.

June 10. Israeli Withdrawal Completed. The Israeli army completes its withdrawal from Lebanon.

June 11. Jordanian Airliner Hijacked. Shiite gunmen in Beirut hijack a Jordanian airliner carrying seventy-four passengers. The hijackers demand that all Palestinian guerrillas leave Lebanon. After forcing the pilot to fly to Cyprus and Sicily June 12, the hijackers order the plane back to Beirut, where they release the hostages and blow up the plane.

June 14. TWA Hijacking. Trans World Airlines Flight 847 carrying 153 passengers and crew, including 104 Americans, from Athens to Rome is hijacked and forced to land in Beirut, where 19 passengers are freed, mostly women and children. The plane then flies to Algiers, where 18 more passengers are released and the hijackers threaten to execute the remaining passengers unless Israel releases Muslim prisoners captured in Lebanon. The plane returns early June 15 to Beirut, where passenger Robert D. Stethem, a U.S. Navy diver, is shot and killed. The two or three hijackers claim to be members of the Islamic Jihad group. The jet is forced to return later that day to Algiers, where about 70 more passengers are released. The plane returns early June 16 to Beirut, where Amal militia leader Nabih Berri assumes negotiations on behalf of the hijackers. Several passengers with "Jewish sounding names" are removed from the plane but are kept hostage elsewhere. The remaining thirty passengers are removed June 17 but also are not freed. The pilot and two crew members remain hostage aboard the plane. Berri says the former passengers are being held "somewhere in Beirut." The Amal militia allows Western journalists to hold a news conference with the hostages June 20.

June 18. Reagan News Conference. President Reagan vows at a news conference that the United States would never give in to terrorists or ask any other government to do so. However, administration officials say June 20 that if the forty American hostages from TWA Flight 847 were freed, Israel would later release more than 700

Lebanese Muslim prisoners. Israel says June 23 that it will release thirty-one Shiite prisoners but that the move is "not linked whatsoever" to the demands of the hijackers. Amal says it has no plans to release the American hostages.

June 24. Hostage Negotiations Continue. Nabih Berri sets a new demand for release of the hijack victims: withdrawal of U.S. warships from positions near the Lebanese coast. The White House warns June 25 of economic and military reprisals against Lebanon unless the hostages are released in the "next few days." One hostage is released June 26.

June 30. Hostages Freed. Thirty-nine U.S. hostages from Flight 847 are freed and driven to Damascus. They arrive in West Germany July 1. The Syrian government reportedly was instrumental in negotiating their release. The Reagan administration made no direct concessions to the hijackers, but it assured Syria that Israel would release 735 Lebanese Muslim prisoners in stages soon after the Americans were freed. Israel releases 300 of the prisoners July 3.

September 14. Hostage Released. The Rev. Benjamin Weir, one of seven Americans held hostage in Lebanon by Shi'ite militia, is released after sixteen months in captivity. The Reagan administration confirms his release September 18.

December 28. Lebanese Pact Signed. Leaders of Lebanon's rival militia forces sign a pact in Syria to end fighting in Lebanon. The agreement has two sections, one containing a mechanism to end the civil war, the other describing a new political power-sharing arrangement between Christians and Muslims.

LIBYA AND NORTH AFRICA

April 12. Qadhafi Assassination Attempts. The *Washington Post* reports that conservative Libyan army officers recently made two attempts to assassinate Libyan leader Qadhafi and that he retaliated by executing as many as seventy-five officers.

PALESTINIAN AFFAIRS

May 19. Palestinians Battle Shiites. Heavy fighting breaks out between Palestinians living in refugee camps near Beirut and the Amal Shiite militia. Amal, aided by a Shiite brigade of the Lebanese army, establishes partial control over the camps by May 30. The Shiites are trying to prevent the PLO from reestablishing a presence in southern Lebanon that would invite Israeli reprisals. Members of PLO factions that fought each other in 1983 reportedly unite against the threat from the Shiites.

October 14. UN Withdraws Arafat Invitation. The UN General Assembly declines to invite Arafat to attend ceremonies marking the UN's fortieth anniversary after the United States threatens to boycott the ceremonies if he attends.

PERSIAN GULF STATES

May 25. Assassination Attempt. Kuwaiti amir Shaykh Jabir al-Ahmad Al Sabah narrowly escapes harm when a bomb-laden car rams his motorcade. The would-be assassin and three other people are killed by the blast.

July 25. OPEC Cuts Prices. At the end of a contentious four-day meeting, OPEC agrees to small price cuts. Iran, Libya, and Algeria vote against the measure. Saudi Arabia indicates July 31 that it is planning to double its production rate.

September 15. Saudi-British Arms Deal. Great Britain announces that Saudi Arabia will purchase between $3 billion and $4 billion worth of British combat aircraft, including forty-eight Tornado fighter bombers. The Saudis approached the British after being frustrated in their efforts to buy U.S. F-15 fighters. The sale is concluded September 26.

December 8. OPEC Meeting. OPEC oil ministers agree to abandon their official pricing structure in an effort to gain a larger share of the world's oil market. Although many OPEC members had been selling oil below OPEC prices, the formal announcement causes oil prices to drop 10 percent amidst predictions of an oil price war.

1986

ARAB-ISRAELI CONFLICT

February 19. Hussein Speech. In a televised speech Jordan's King Hussein declares that he is ending a year-long joint effort with the PLO to revitalize the Arab-Israeli peace process. He accuses Arafat of failing to cooperate by rejecting UN Security Council Resolutions 242 and 338, despite major U.S. diplomatic concessions secured by Jordan. Hussein nevertheless reaffirms his support of the 1974 Arab League designation of the PLO as the sole legitimate representative of the Palestinian people.

April 2. Explosion on TWA Jet. A bomb explodes on a Trans World Airlines passenger jet en route from Rome to Athens, killing four, all Americans, and injuring nine. The bodies are sucked out through a hole torn in the side of the plane. The flight lands safely in Athens. An anonymous caller in Beirut claims the group responsible is the Ezzedine Kassam unit of the Arab Revolutionary Cells, believed to be a faction associated with Abu Nidal.

June 8. Achille Lauro Report. An Italian report says the group that hijacked the *Achille Lauro* was selected and directed by Muhammad Abu'l Abbas and trained in one of his camps in Algeria.

July 10. Achille Lauro Hijackers Convicted. An Italian jury convicts eleven of the fifteen men charged with participating in the *Achille Lauro* hijacking. Three of the defendants receive sentences of between fifteen and thirty years. Muhammad Abu'l Abbas and two other fugitives—tried in absentia—are given life sentences for organizing the hijacking.

July 22. Peres Meets Hassan. Israeli prime minister Peres and Moroccan king Hassan II meet in Ifrane, Morocco. In reaction Syria breaks all diplomatic ties with Morocco. Other hard-line Arab countries and the PLO denounce the meeting as a betrayal of the Arab cause. Egypt's president Mubarak hails the talks as a "good initiative." Peres calls the meetings a success. Hassan stresses that Israel must accept the PLO and evacuate all of the occupied territories before a peace settlement can be achieved. Hassan resigns as chairman of the Arab League July 28 because of Arab criticism.

September 6. Istanbul Synagogue Attack. Two Arabs attack Jewish worshippers in an Istanbul synagogue with automatic weapons and grenades. Twenty-one Jews are killed. The assailants kill themselves after being trapped in the synagogue by police. Israeli trade minister Ariel Sharon causes a furor when he claims the attack was the result of Peres's peace initiatives. After refusing one retraction, Peres accepts Sharon's second letter of apology September 8.

September 11–12. Egyptian-Israeli Summit. In the first talks between leaders of Egypt and Israel in five years, President Mubarak meets with Peres in Alexandria, Egypt.

IRAN-CONTRA ARMS DEAL

May 25. Secret U.S. Mission to Tehran. Former U.S. national security adviser Robert McFarlane, National Security Council staff member Lt. Col. Oliver North, and several other American officials arrive in Tehran on a secret diplomatic mission aimed at freeing U.S. hostages in Lebanon. Their plane also carries a pallet of Hawk missile spare parts, which had been loaded in Israel. They meet officials in the Iranian prime minister's office. McFarlane demands May 27 that U.S. hostages in Lebanon be released the next day. On May 28 McFarlane is told the Iranians think they can get two hostages out now and the remaining two after delivery of the missile parts. McFarlane rejects the offer and the delegation leaves Tehran, but not before the Iranians take the missile parts from the aircraft. McFarlane reports May 29 directly to President Reagan on his trip to Tehran and suggests that the arms-for-hostages initiative be discontinued.

November 3. Magazine Reports McFarlane Visit. A pro-Syrian Beirut weekly magazine, *al-Shiraa,* discloses Robert McFarlane's secret trip to Tehran in May. The magazine says that the information was leaked through the office of Ayatollah Hussein Ali Montazeri, the designated heir to Iranian leader Khomeini. During a bill-signing ceremony, President Reagan tells reporters November 6 that stories about McFarlane traveling to Tehran have "no foundation."

November 13. Reagan's Speech. In a televised speech from the White House, President Reagan admits that his administration sent arms to Iran but says that the shipments were not ransom payments for hostages but were good-faith gestures intended to open a "dialogue" with moderates there. The president's speech is the first official acknowledgment that the United States directly shipped military equipment to Iran.

November 19. Reagan Press Conference. President Reagan says in a news conference that he has ruled out future arms sales to Iran. He insists that the covert operation was not a mistake. Reagan denies that Israel was involved in the Iran initiative, but after the press conference the White House issues a statement acknowledging that a third country was involved.

November 25. Diversion Disclosed. In a hastily called news conference, Reagan says that he had not been "fully informed" about the Iran arms deals. Attorney General Edwin Meese III discloses that members of the administration may have helped divert an estimated $10 million to $30 million from the Iran arms sales to support the Nicaraguan contra rebels. Reagan admits in a radio address December 6 that "mistakes were made" in the Iran initiative.

IRAN-IRAQ WAR

February 11. Iranians Capture Fao. Iranian forces capture Fao, an Iraqi oil port near Kuwait, in one of the most daring offensives in the five-and-a-half-year Iran-Iraq war.

ISRAEL

June 4. Pollard Pleads Guilty to Spying. Jonathan Jay Pollard pleads guilty to spying on the U.S. government for Israel. The Justice Department names four Israelis as unindicted conspirators. The guilty plea is part of an agreement to avoid a trial that might further strain U.S.-Israeli relations.

June 25. Shin Bet Affair. Avraham Shalom, the head of Shin Bet, Israel's internal security agency, resigns in exchange for immunity from prosecution. He had been accused of ordering and then covering up the killings of two Palestinian bus hijackers in 1984. Members of the Israeli Labor Party demand that Peres order a commission of inquiry to investigate the involvement of political leaders in the Shin Bet affair. Foreign minister Shamir opposes any further inquiry. A leading Labor Party minister calls for Shamir's resignation June 29. After a month of silence, Shamir July 3 denies approving the killings of the bus hijackers or the subsequent cover-up. The Israeli cabinet decides July 14 not to form a commission of inquiry. The attorney general then announces that he is ordering an investigation of the scandal. The Israeli Justice Ministry December 28 clears Shamir of any wrongdoing in the killings or the cover-up.

August 18. Soviet-Israeli Talks. Soviet and Israeli diplomats meet in Helsinki to discuss the establishment of consulates. The talks are the first formal diplomatic contact between the two countries in nineteen years.

October 5. Israeli Nuclear Arsenal Report. The *Sunday Times of London* reports that, according to former Israeli nuclear technician Mordechai Vanunu, Israel has been manufacturing nuclear weapons for twenty years at a secret underground factory near its Dimona nuclear research plant. Vanunu maintains that Israel had built between one hundred and two hundred atomic bombs and has the capability to produce thermonuclear weapons. Israel confirms November 9 that it has arrested Vanunu. He is charged with espionage November 28.

October 20. Shamir Becomes Prime Minister. Israeli leaders Shamir and Peres trade jobs in accordance with a power-sharing agreement concluded between the Likud and Labor Parties after the 1984 election. Shamir takes over as prime minister, while Peres becomes foreign minister.

JORDAN

January 31. Reagan Halts Jordan Arms Sales. President Reagan indefinitely postpones plans to sell $1.9 billion in U.S. arms to Jordan, because of overwhelming congressional opposition.

LEBANON

January 15. Christians Fight in Lebanon. Phalangist Party forces loyal to President Amin Gemayel defeat the Lebanese Forces militia, commanded by Elie Hobeika, in a two-day battle that leaves more than two hundred dead. Hobeika is captured and forced to resign as leader of the Lebanese Forces. His defeat collapses a December 1985 Syrian-brokered peace accord signed by Christian and Muslim militia leaders.

February 17. Israelis Raid Lebanon. Lebanese Muslim guerrillas capture two Israeli soldiers near the Israeli border in southern Lebanon. Israel launches a large-scale land, sea, and air operation to search for its men. In Beirut the Islamic Resistance Front claims responsibility February 18 for seizing the Israelis. An anonymous caller February 19 tells news services in Beirut that one Israeli soldier has already been executed.

April 17. Hostages Shot. One American hostage, Peter Kilburn, and two British hostages, Leigh Douglas and Philip Padfield, are found shot to death near Beirut. Two days earlier, Abu Nidal had warned that his forces would strike against the United States and countries that cooperated with it.

July 26. Jenco Released. The Rev. Lawrence Jenco, who had been kidnapped January 8, 1985, is released in Lebanon.

September 9. Kidnappings in Beirut. Frank Herbert Reed, the American director of the Lebanese International School in West Beirut, is kidnapped. Joseph J. Cicippio, acting comptroller at the American University of Beirut, is kidnapped September 12. American author and book salesman Edward Tracy is kidnapped October 21.

November 2. Jacobsen Released. Hostage David P. Jacobsen, who had been kidnapped May 28, 1985, is released in Beirut.

LIBYA AND NORTH AFRICA

January 7. U.S. Sanctions against Libya. President Reagan asserts there is "irrefutable evidence" of Libyan support for Abu Nidal, who is believed to be behind the December 27, 1985, airport attacks in Rome and Vienna. Reagan ends all trade and economic activity between the United States and Libya and calls for the 1,000 to 15,000 Americans working in Libya to leave the country. He signs an executive order January 8 freezing Libyan assets in the United States.

March 23–27. U.S. Mediterranean Maneuvers. The U.S. Navy's Sixth Fleet begins "freedom of navigation maneuvers" in the disputed Gulf of Sidra near Libya. Libya fires antiaircraft missiles at U.S. warplanes March 24, prompting U.S. air strikes against Libyan ships and a Libyan missile installation later that day. The U.S. fleet leaves the area March 27.

April 5. Bomb Explodes in Berlin Disco. A bomb explodes in a Berlin discotheque, killing an American soldier and a Turkish woman and injuring more than two hundred, including sixty-four Americans. The United States says it suspects Libyan participation. In a televised news conference April 9 Reagan says the United States will respond militarily if it finds evidence that Libya was involved in the bombing of the Berlin discotheque.

April 14. U.S. Attacks Libya. American planes attack targets in Libya, including the home and headquarters of Qadhafi, a naval academy, and air bases in Benghazi. A residential neighborhood in Tripoli is inadvertently hit. The raid kills at least fifteen people and injures sixty. Qadhafi's infant daughter is among the dead. One U.S. F-111 bomber is shot down and its two crewmen are killed. All Arab nations condemn the air strike, and most West European nations criticize the action.

December 11. Libyan Troops Attack Chad. Libya launches a major offensive against Chad. France and the United States send aid to Chad's government, but France says its troops in that country will not enter the battle unless Libyan forces cross the sixteenth parallel.

PERSIAN GULF STATES

March 11. Reagan Announces Saudi Arms Sale. The Reagan administration notifies Congress of its intention to sell $354 million in advanced missiles to Saudi Arabia because of concern over the escalation of the Iran-Iraq war. Delivery is scheduled for 1989.

May 7. Congress Rejects Saudi Arms Deal. The U.S. House of Representatives, in a 356-62 vote, adopts a resolution rejecting the $354 million arms deal with Saudi Arabia. The Senate had rejected the sale 73-22 May 5. President Reagan vetoes the resolution May 21.

June 5. Saudi Arms Deal Allowed. Thirty-four senators vote to approve Reagan's proposed arms sale to Saudi Arabia, sustaining Reagan's veto of a congressional resolution blocking the deal.

August 4. OPEC Agreement. The ministers of OPEC reach a unanimous tentative agreement on an Iranian proposal to limit oil production to bolster prices. The agreement aims to raise prices from below $12 to $15–$19 a barrel.

October 29. Yamani Dismissed. Saudi Arabia's King Fahd dismisses Ahmad Zaki Yamani from his post as Saudi oil minister.

YEMEN

January 13. Civil War in South Yemen. An attempt by president Ali Nasser Muhammad to have rival Politburo members assassinated precipitates a coup against his rule in South Yemen. Fierce battles between loyal government forces and supporters of the coup erupt in and around Aden. Both sides declare their allegiance to Moscow. British and Soviet ships evacuate thousands of foreigners. The rebel forces claim victory January 19. Prime Minister Haidar Abu Bakr al-Attas, who was out of the country when the fighting erupted, returns to Aden January 25 and is named provisional president in a Marxist coalition government. Ali Nasser Muhammad reportedly flees the country.

1987

ARAB-ISRAELI CONFLICT

January 13. Hamadai Arrested. West German authorities arrest Muhammad Ali Hamadai at the Frankfurt airport after they discover a powerful liquid explosive in his possession. Hamadai is one of four men indicted by the United States for the hijacking of a TWA jet in June 1985. The United States January 15 asks West Germany to extradite him.

February 27. Peres-Meguid Communique. After two days of meetings, Foreign Ministers Peres of Israel and Meguid of Egypt issue a joint communique calling for an international peace conference in 1987 that would lead to direct Arab-Israeli talks. Israel's prime minister Shamir denounces the communique at a March 1 cabinet meeting, and Peres does not press his plan.

IRAN-IRAQ WAR

May 17. Iraqi Missile Hits U.S. Ship. An Iraqi warplane fires a missile that seriously damages the U.S. frigate *Stark,* killing thirty-seven crew members and

wounding twenty-one others. The ship is struck eighty-five miles from its final destination of Bahrain in the Persian Gulf. The Iraqi government calls the attack an error.

July 20. UN Resolution 598. The UN Security Council unanimously adopts a resolution calling for a cease-fire between Iran and Iraq. The United States says it would support sanctions and an arms embargo against either nation if it refused to accept Resolution 598. Iraq accepts the resolution July 21, but Iran rejects it, declaring it will pursue its goal of toppling Saddam Hussein's regime.

October 26. United States Embargoes Iran. President Reagan orders the embargoing of all imports of Iranian products and prohibits the exportation of fourteen types of "militarily useful" items to Iran.

November 8–11. Arab Summit. At an emergency Arab League summit hosted by King Hussein in Amman, Arab leaders focus on the Iran-Iraq war while largely ignoring the Arab-Israeli conflict. Members unanimously condemn Iran's "aggression," express support for Iraq, and call on the international community to "adopt the necessary measures to make the Iranian regime respond to the peace calls." The league votes November 10 to allow members to reestablish relations with Egypt at their own discretion. Within six weeks nine Arab nations restore ties with Egypt.

ISRAEL

March 11. Israel Investigates Pollard Affair. Prime Minister Shamir appoints a commission in Israel to conduct an inquiry into the Pollard spy case. The commission May 26 criticizes the government's role in the affair but declares top Israeli officials innocent of involvement.

July 12. Soviets Arrive in Israel. The first Soviet consular delegation to visit Israel since the 1967 Six-Day War arrives in Tel Aviv.

LEBANON

January 20. Waite Disappears. Anglican church emissary Terry Waite, on his fifth mission to Lebanon to negotiate the release of hostages, is last seen on his way to a meeting with a Shiite group. Muslim militia officials January 30 confirm reports that he has been taken hostage.

January 24. Four Kidnapped in Lebanon. In the largest single kidnapping of American citizens in Beirut, men disguised as Lebanese police abduct three Americans and one Indian from the Beirut University campus. The three Americans are Alan Steen, Jesse Jonathan Turner, and Robert Polhill, all professors at the university. Mithileshwar Singh, chairman of the business school, is an Indian citizen who is a permanent resident of the United States.

February 15. Beirut Factions Battle. Heavy fighting in West Beirut between Shiite Amal militia forces and a Druze-led leftist coalition leaves three hundred dead.

Lebanese Muslim leaders request February 20 that Syria send troops to halt the fighting. Thousands of Syrian troops enter West Beirut February 22–23. Outbursts of factional fighting continue, but the Syrians gain control of the city.

May 4. Karami Resigns. Lebanese prime minister Rashid Karami announces his resignation, citing criticism of his leadership and the inability of Lebanon's divided cabinet to function. He agrees to serve until a successor is named.

June 1. Lebanese Prime Minister Killed. Rashid Karami, awaiting appointment of his successor as Lebanon's prime minister, is killed when a bomb explodes in his helicopter. No group takes responsibility for the assassination. Selim al-Hoss is appointed acting premier. Christians and Muslims mourn Karami's death and stage a general strike to observe his funeral.

August 18. Hostage Escapes. American journalist Charles Glass escapes from his captors in Beirut amid speculation that he was allowed to escape because of Syrian efforts to secure his release. He had been kidnapped June 17.

LIBYA AND NORTH AFRICA

March 27. Libyan Retreat. Libyan troops withdraw from Faya-Largeau, a strategic town in northern Chad, after Chadian battlefield victories imperil the Libyan stronghold. The withdrawal is seen as a major setback for Libyan leader Qadhafi's ambitions in Chad.

PALESTINIAN AFFAIRS

April 20–26. PLO Reunites. At a convention of the Palestine National Council in Algiers, Arafat is reelected head of the PLO. To gain the support of PLO radicals, Arafat pledges to adopt a harder line toward Israel. The meeting ends with a declaration of unity.

December 9. Palestinian Uprising—Intifada. Palestinians in the Gaza Strip confront Israeli soldiers with rocks and molotov cocktails in response to an accident involving an Israeli army truck the day before that killed four Arabs. Israeli soldiers kill one Palestinian, mortally wound another, and wound fifteen. The unrest spreads quickly to the West Bank. Israeli efforts to suppress protests in the occupied territories fail, as the sudden explosion of Palestinian anger turns into a sustained uprising that came to be known as the intifada. By December 18, Israeli soldiers kill at least seventeen Palestinians.

December 21. Palestinian General Strike. As the Palestinian death toll rises and protests continue, Palestinians residing in Israel hold a general strike in support of the uprising in the occupied territories.

December 22. Security Council Faults Israel. With the United States abstaining, the UN Security Council unanimously approves a resolution that "strongly deplores" Israel's handling of the Palestinian protests and its "excessive use of live ammunition." Israel announces December 25 that its troops have incarcerated nearly a thousand Palestinian suspects from the territories.

PERSIAN GULF STATES

March 23. U.S. Offers Tanker Protection. The United States offers to protect Kuwaiti oil tankers sailing in international waters in the Persian Gulf. Kuwait April 6 proposes reflagging some of its tankers as U.S. ships.

May 19. U.S.-Kuwaiti Agreement. The United States announces an agreement with Kuwait to reflag eleven Kuwaiti tankers that will receive U.S. naval protection while in the Persian Gulf.

June 11. Saudi Missile Sale Delayed. President Reagan announces that he is temporarily withdrawing a plan to sell sixteen hundred air-to-ground missiles to Saudi Arabia because of congressional opposition. Reagan cancels the missile sale October 8 as part of a compromise that allows $1 billion in other arms to be sold to Saudi Arabia.

July 22. Escorts Begin. American ships escort the first two Kuwaiti tankers to receive American protection into the Persian Gulf. The reflagged Kuwaiti tanker *Bridgeton* sustains minor damage after hitting an underwater mine July 24. Subsequently the United States and other Western nations send minesweeping equipment to the Persian Gulf.

July 31. Mecca Riots. Protests by thousands of Iranian pilgrims near the Grand Mosque in Mecca lead to a riot in which more than 400 people, including 275 Iranian pilgrims, are killed. The Saudi government claims its security forces did not fire on the crowd and that most of the victims were killed by a stampede of Iranian pilgrims near the Grand Mosque. Iran accuses Saudi Arabia of slaughtering Iranian pilgrims with automatic weapons. Iranian rioters sack the Saudi and Kuwaiti embassies in Tehran August 1.

August 29. Tanker War Resumes. Iraq attacks Iranian ships and oil installations, breaking a forty-five-day pause in the tanker war in the Persian Gulf. Iran responds with attacks against Arab tankers. By September 3 as many as twenty ships are damaged.

September 21. U.S. Actions in the Gulf. American helicopters disable an Iranian ship reportedly laying mines in the Persian Gulf.

October 16. U.S.-Flagged Tanker Attacked. The Kuwaiti tanker *Sea Isle City* is hit by an Iranian Silkworm missile while within Kuwait territorial waters, where Kuwait is responsible for defending the U.S.-flagged ships. The attack wounds eighteen crew members. In retaliation U.S. destroyers bombard an Iranian oil platform in the Persian Gulf. The oil platform served as a base for launching small boat attacks against Persian Gulf shipping.

1988

ARAB-ISRAELI CONFLICT

February 25. Shultz's Shuttle Diplomacy. U.S. secretary of state Shultz arrives in Israel to begin a week-long diplomatic offensive that includes stops in Jordan, Syria, and Egypt. Shultz is unable to garner much support among Middle East leaders for a U.S. peace initiative that calls for local elections to achieve limited Arab autonomy in the occupied territories.

April 16. Wazir Assassinated. Khalil Wazir (also known as Abu Jihad), the PLO's military chief and the second-ranking official of the PLO's Fatah faction, is killed in his home in Tunisia by a commando team presumed to have been sent by Israel. The Israeli government refuses to confirm or deny responsibility for the action.

September 29. Egypt Awarded Taba. An international arbitration panel awards Egypt control of the Sinai resort of Taba. The area was claimed by Egypt but had been occupied by Israel since the 1967 Six-Day War. The two countries agreed in 1986 to settle the dispute through binding arbitration. Egypt takes possession of Taba March 15, 1989.

IRAN-IRAQ WAR

February 29. War of the Cities. After Iraq bombs an Iranian oil refinery near Tehran February 27, Iran hits Baghdad with two long-range missiles. For the next several months the two sides fire missiles at each other's major cities almost daily, although Iraq launches many more missiles than Iran. These missile exchanges become known as the "war of the cities" and cause heavy damage and casualties.

April 18. Iraq Recaptures Fao. Iraq recaptures the Fao Peninsula from Iran in a surprise attack that began April 17.

July 18. Iran Accepts Cease-Fire. Iranian president Ali Khamenei accepts UN Security Council Resolution 598, which calls for a cease-fire in the eight-year Iran-Iraq war. Ayatollah Khomeini says July 19 that the decision to accept the cease-fire was "more deadly than taking poison." Iraq expresses skepticism about Iran's intentions and continues its attacks against Iranian positions. United Nations officials arrive in Tehran to negotiate a cease-fire July 23. Iraqi forces penetrate into Iran before ending offensive operations July 24. Iraq announces July 25 that it will withdraw from Iranian territory occupied during the previous week.

August 8. Cease-Fire. After two weeks of mediation, UN Secretary General Javier Pérez de Cuéllar announces a cease-fire agreement between Iran and Iraq that will go into effect August 20. The cease-fire begins on schedule as a 350-member UN peacekeeping force commences patrols along the Iran-Iraq border August 20. Talks on achieving a broader peace agreement begin August 25 in Geneva, but they stall the following day over Iraq's insistence that it control the entire Shatt al-Arab waterway. The negotiations recess September 13 without progress.

ISRAEL

November 1. Israeli Elections. The Likud Party claims victory after it wins thirty-nine parliament seats, compared with thirty-eight for the Labor Party. Likud's chances of leading a ruling coalition are increased by the strong showing of Israel's small, right-wing religious parties, which win a total of eighteen seats—six more than in 1984. Likud leader Yitzhak Shamir says November 2 that his party will be able to form a coalition with the religious parties. President Chaim Herzog November 14 asks Shamir to form a government.

December 19. Israeli Coalition Formed. Israel's Likud and Labor Parties agree to form a coalition government. Shamir is designated as prime minister for the duration of the government. The U.S.-PLO dialogue and the reluctance of either party to accept the right-wing religious parties as coalition partners led to the decision to form another unity government.

JORDAN

July 31. Jordan Renounces West Bank Claim. Jordan's King Hussein surrenders Jordan's claim to the West Bank in favor of the PLO and says he will cut all legal and administrative ties to the occupied territories. The move is seen as a blow to U.S. peace efforts, which had envisioned a major role for Jordan in settling the issue of the occupied territories. On August 4 Jordan says that it will stop paying the salaries of twenty-one thousand Palestinian civil servants on the West Bank.

KURDISH AFFAIRS

March 16. Iraqi Chemical Attack. The Iraqi army reportedly bombs the Kurdish town of Halabja in northeastern Iraq with chemical weapons after it is captured by the Iranian army. Iran claims that nearly five thousand Kurds died. Iran allows Western journalists to survey the destruction. A UN investigative team says April 26 that chemical weapons were used, but its report makes no conclusions about who used them.

August 30. Turkey Opens Borders to Kurds. Turkey officially opens its borders to tens of thousands of Iraqi Kurds fleeing Iraqi government attacks, which were designed to defeat Kurdish resistance groups and began July 30 after a de facto cease-fire had been achieved in the war with Iran. Since that time as many as one hundred thousand Iraqi Kurds are reported to have fled into Turkey. Many Kurdish refugees say Iraqi attacks have included the use of poison gas. The U.S. government says that intercepted Iraqi military communications and interviews with Kurds in Turkey have confirmed Iraq used chemical weapons.

LEBANON

February 17. American Officer Abducted. While serving as a UN observer in southern Lebanon, U.S. Marine Lt. Col. William R. Higgins is taken captive near Tyre. The Organization of the Oppressed on Earth, a shadowy Shiite movement with close ties to Hizballah, claims responsibility and charges Higgins with spying for the CIA.

May 6. Rival Shiite Militias Clash. Syrian-backed Amal troops battle Iranian-backed Hizballah forces in southern Lebanon and West Beirut. Fighting continues despite Iranian and Syrian officials' attempts to impose a cease-fire. Syria and Iran agree May 26 to a plan that sends Syrian troops into the area to restore order. Syrian deployments May 27–28 end the three-week battle, which has killed more than three hundred people.

September 22. Rival Governments Formed. After the Lebanese parliament fails to elect his successor, President Gemayel, whose term expires at midnight, appoints Gen. Michel Aoun, a Maronite Christian, as acting premier of a provisional military government. On September 23 Muslims refuse to recognize Aoun's government and form a rival government around Selim al-Hoss, who had been acting premier under Gemayel. Before Gemayel's term expired, the United States and Syria tried unsuccessfully to find a presidential candidate acceptable to all major factions.

LIBYA AND NORTH AFRICA

May 25. Qadhafi Recognizes Chad. Libyan leader Qadhafi announces that Libya will end its armed conflict with Chad and recognize the Chadian government of president Hissene Habra. The two countries formally restore diplomatic relations October 3.

December 21. Reagan on Libyan Plant. President Reagan says in a television interview that the United States and its allies are concerned about a chemical plant under construction in Rabta, Libya, which he maintains is capable of producing chemical weapons.

December 21. Lockerbie Crash. A Pan Am airliner breaks apart during a flight from London to New York and crashes in Lockerbie, Scotland. All 259 people aboard the jet and at least 11 people on the ground are killed. British investigators determine December 28 that a bomb caused the crash. No group claims responsibility for the bombing.

PALESTINIAN AFFAIRS

January 19. Israeli Policy Criticized. Israeli defense minister Rabin announces that Israeli forces will combat the Palestinian intifada with "force, might, and beatings" in an effort to reduce the number of Palestinians being killed. Thirty-eight Palestinians had been shot to death during the first six weeks of the uprising. The new tactic is criticized by Great Britain and the United States.

March 10–12. Arab Police Resign. After Palestinian leaders issue leaflets calling on Arab members of police forces in the occupied territories to quit or risk being considered collaborators with Israel, nearly half of the one thousand police officers in the territories resign.

June 7–9. Arab Summit on Uprising. In an emergency meeting in Algiers, members of the Arab League adopt a resolution to "support by all possible means" the Palestinian uprising, but they do not respond to PLO requests for a specific commitment of financial aid. The summit also declines to designate the PLO as the sole distributor of financial aid to the uprising.

June 29. PLO Office Closure Blocked. A U.S. District Court judge rules that the United States may not close the PLO's UN observer mission in New York City because such an action would violate U.S. obligations as the host country under the UN Charter. The Justice Department announces August 29 that it will not appeal the decision.

November 15. Palestinian State Declared. At the end of a four-day meeting in Algiers, the Palestine National Council (PNC) proclaims an independent Palestinian state in Gaza and the West Bank. On November 14 the PNC had voted to accept UN Security Council Resolutions 242 and 338, an action that implicitly recognized Israel's right to exist. The United States rejected the declaration of independence and said that the PNC's actions did not satisfy U.S. conditions for opening a dialogue with the PLO.

November 26. Arafat Denied Visa. Secretary of State Shultz denies PLO leader Arafat an entry visa into the United States to address a special session of the UN General Assembly. Shultz says he acted because the PLO has engaged in terrorism. The General Assembly December 2 votes 154-2 to move the meeting to Geneva so Arafat can speak.

December 6–7. Arafat Meets American Jews. The Swedish foreign minister and a delegation of five American Jews meet with Arafat in Stockholm to discuss Middle East peace. They issue a statement December 7 to clarify the positions taken by the PNC in November. The statement says the council recognized Israel "as a state in the region" and "declared its rejection and condemnation of terrorism in all its forms, including state terrorism."

December 13. Arafat Addresses UN in Geneva. Arafat calls on Israel to join peace talks and reiterates the PNC's acceptance of UN Resolutions 242 and 338 and rejection of terrorism.

December 14. U.S. Opens Dialogue with PLO. At a press conference in Geneva, Arafat explicitly renounces terrorism and accepts both Israel's right to exist and UN Resolutions 242 and 338. Hours later the United States announces that Arafat has finally met its conditions for opening a U.S.-PLO dialogue. The State Department instructs Ambassador Robert H. Pelletreau Jr. to begin the dialogue with PLO representatives in Tunisia.

PERSIAN GULF STATES

March 19. Saudis Purchase Chinese Missiles. Saudi Arabia confirms reports that it has purchased from China a number of CSS-2 ballistic missiles with a range of about sixteen hundred miles. The United States criticizes the sale but warns Israel against attempting to destroy the missiles in a preemptive strike. To ease U.S. concerns about the missiles, Saudi Arabia announces April 25 that it will sign the multinational Nuclear Nonproliferation Treaty concluded in 1968.

April 5. Kuwaiti Airliner Hijacked. Shiite hijackers seize a Kuwaiti airliner en route from Bangkok to Kuwait and force it to land in Mashad, Iran. They demand that Kuwait release seventeen Shiites convicted of bombings. Iran refuels the plane April 8 after the hijackers fire warning shots and throw a grenade from the plane. The jet then flies to Beirut but is prevented from landing by Lebanese air controllers and is diverted to Cyprus. There, two Kuwaiti passengers are killed before hijackers force the plane to fly to Algiers April 13. Algerian officials obtain the release of the remaining thirty-one hostages April 20 in return for guaranteeing the hijackers free passage out of the country.

April 14. Frigate Strikes Mine in Gulf. Ten U.S. sailors are wounded when the frigate *Samuel B. Roberts* strikes a mine in the Persian Gulf near Bahrain.

April 26. Saudi Arabia Breaks Iran Ties. The Saudi government breaks off diplomatic relations with Iran because of its actions regarding the 1987 riots in Mecca by Iranian pilgrims and its continuing attacks on Gulf shipping.

July 3. U.S. Downs Iranian Airliner. The American cruiser *Vincennes,* after a clash in the Persian Gulf with several Iranian gunboats, shoots down an Iranian passenger airliner, killing all 290 people aboard. The captain of the ship claims to have mistaken the airliner for an Iranian F-14 fighter. The ship warned the plane several times but received no response. President Reagan calls the incident "an understandable accident." Reagan announces July 11 that the United States will offer compensation to the victims' families.

July 8. Saudi-British Arms Deal. Great Britain announces that it has concluded an arms sale to Saudi Arabia worth $12 billion to $30 billion. The sale includes fifty advanced Tornado fighter planes. Saudi officials indicate that they sought the huge arms deal because of the difficulty of obtaining U.S. congressional approval to purchase American arms.

SYRIA

April 25. Arafat, Asad Meet. In Damascus, PLO chairman Arafat meets with Syrian president Asad for the first time since 1983.

1989

ARAB-ISRAELI CONFLICT

April 6. Shamir Election Plan. Israeli prime minister Shamir discusses a new election plan with President George Bush in Washington during a ten-day trip to the United States. Shamir's plan is similar to the formula for achieving Palestinian autonomy agreed upon in the Camp David Accords. Under the plan Palestinians would elect local representatives, who would then negotiate with Israel on establishing Palestinian autonomy in the occupied territories. Later the two sides would hold talks on a permanent peace. Bush expresses his support for the plan.

April 26. Palestinians Reject Shamir Plan. More than eighty local Palestinians representing East Jerusalem, the West Bank, and the Gaza Strip issue a statement rejecting Prime Minister Shamir's plan to hold elections in the occupied territories. The Palestinians call the plan "nothing more than a maneuver for the media to save Israel from its international isolation."

May 22. Baker on Territories. U.S. secretary of state Baker, speaking bluntly to the American Israel Public Affairs Committee in Washington, calls on Israel to renounce "the unrealistic vision of a greater Israel" that would incorporate the occupied territories. He says, "Israeli interests in the West Bank and Gaza—security and otherwise—can be accommodated in a settlement." Shamir rejects Baker's approach as "useless."

June 20. Shamir Heckled by Settlers. At the funeral of an Israeli stabbed to death in the West Bank, right-wing Jewish settlers shout down Shamir as he tries to deliver a eulogy. Later a few settlers try to assault him but are blocked by security officers. Many settlers in the crowd of about one thousand maintain that Shamir had not been tough enough with Palestinians in the occupied territories.

July 5. Shamir Accepts Hard-Line Conditions. Under pressure from the right wing of his Likud Party, Shamir accepts conditions on his West Bank and Gaza election plan in return for the party's endorsement of it. The conditions—which include the barring of Arab residents of East Jerusalem from participation, the postponement of any elections until the Palestinian uprising ends, and the continuation of Jewish settlements—appear to ensure that the plan would be unacceptable to Palestinians. On July 6 the PLO says that the move has ended further Palestinian consideration of the plan.

EGYPT

May 22. Egypt Rejoins Arab League. Arab leaders formally welcome Egypt back into the Arab League after a ten-year suspension resulting from Egypt's peace treaty with Israel.

December 27. Diplomatic Ties Restored. After a ten-year break, Egypt and Syria restore diplomatic ties. Syria severed relations in 1979 over Egypt's peace agreement with Israel.

IRAN

February 14. Khomeini Calls for Author's Death. Ayatollah Khomeini calls on Muslims everywhere to kill Indian-born British author Salman Rushdie for writing *The Satanic Verses.* Khomeini also urges the assassination of persons involved in publishing the novel. The book, which many Muslims considered blasphemous because of its irreverent portrayal of a character resembling Muhammad and its insinuation that the Quran might not be the word of God, had recently been protested in many Islamic nations.

February 20. Europeans Recall Diplomats. The twelve member states of the European Economic Community vote unanimously to recall their ambassadors from Tehran to protest Khomeini's call for Rushdie's death. West Germany announces February 22 that it is withdrawing an offer to guarantee credits for West German exporters doing business with Iran.

March 7. Iran Breaks British Ties. Iran breaks diplomatic relations with Great Britain after the British government refuses to denounce Rushdie and his novel *The Satanic Verses.*

March 28. Khomeini's Heir Resigns. Ayatollah Hussein Ali Montazeri, appointed heir of Iranian spiritual leader Ayatollah Khomeini, announces his resignation after Khomeini asks him to step down. Montazeri had recently come into disfavor for criticizing the regime's policies.

June 3. Khomeini Dies. Ayatollah Ruholla Khomeini, Iran's top spiritual and political leader, dies in a Tehran hospital, reportedly after suffering a heart attack earlier in the day. Iran's Council of Experts names President Ali Khamenei to replace Khomeini June 4. Khomeini had undergone surgery May 23 to stop internal bleeding.

August 17. Rafsanjani Inaugural. Iranian president Ali Akbar Hashemi Rafsanjani takes the oath of office in Tehran. In his inaugural address he criticizes the failures of the Islamic revolution and says that it is time to concentrate on the economic reconstruction of Iran.

November 6. Iranian Assets Unfrozen. The United States returns to Iran $567 million in Iranian assets that it had frozen in 1979.

IRAQ

December 7. Iraq Announces Satellite Rocket. Iraqi radio announces a successful test of a rocket capable of launching a satellite into space. The launch on December 5 made Iraq the first Arab country with satellite capabilities.

ISRAEL

December 31. Shamir Fires Minister. Prime Minister Shamir dismisses Science Minister Ezer Weizman for allegedly violating Israeli law prohibiting contacts with the PLO.

JORDAN

April 18. Riots in Jordan. Riots break out in Jordan over an increase in food prices. The government imposes tight security measures to stop the riots, but they continue until April 22. King Hussein, who had been in the United States, cancels a planned stop in Great Britain April 21 and returns to Jordan April 23. Hussein accepts the resignation of Prime Minister Zaid Samir al-Rifai April 24 and appoints an interim government that is to stay in power until elections can be held. Demonstrators had accused Rifai of economic mismanagement and corruption.

KURDISH AFFAIRS

January 11. Chemical Weapons Conference. A 149-nation conference in Paris condemns the use of chemical weapons but fails to single out any nation for violating the 1925 Geneva Protocol that prohibits their use. The outcome is seen as a victory for Iraq, which had recently been criticized for using chemical weapons against its Kurdish minority and Iranian troops.

LEBANON

January 30. Shiite Truce. After a month of fighting, the rival Amal and Hizballah Shiite Lebanese militias conclude a truce sponsored by Iran and Syria.

March 14. Conflict in Lebanon. The heaviest artillery exchange between Muslim and Christian forces in Lebanon in several years kills forty people. Afterwards Maronite Christian leader Michel Aoun declares "a campaign of liberation against the Syrian presence in this country." During the next several months the Lebanese army under his command carries on an artillery duel with Syrian forces and Muslim militias that devastates Beirut and the surrounding area.

March 21. Christians Isolated in Lebanon. Muslim militia and Syrian troops block all routes to Lebanon's Christian heartland, thereby imposing a blockade on the region controlled by forces under Aoun.

July 28. Israelis Abduct Hizballah Leader. Israeli commandos abduct Shaykh Abdul Karim Obeid, a spiritual leader of the pro-Iranian Shiite group Hizballah, from his home in southern Lebanon. Israel says Obeid was "arrested" because he had encouraged and helped plan kidnappings and terrorist attacks.

July 31. Shiite Group Claims It Killed Hostage. After Israeli authorities refuse to release Shaykh Obeid, the Organization of the Oppressed on Earth releases a videotape that it claims shows the hanging of U.S. Marine Corps Lt. Col. William Higgins, a hostage held in Lebanon since February 1988. President Bush condemns the "brutal murder" of Higgins but refrains from ordering military retaliation. Israeli officials acknowledge that they originally had hoped to trade Obeid for three Israeli hostages held in Lebanon. The Israelis widen their position on a hostage swap by offering to release all Shiite prisoners in Israel in exchange for the freedom of all Western hostages held by Shiite groups in Lebanon. The FBI says August 7 that its forensic experts determined it was likely that Higgins was the person in the videotape, but that he probably was already dead when the tape was made.

August 13. Syrian Ground Offensive. Syrian troops and their Muslim allies in Lebanon attack Christian positions with infantry and tanks. Fighting continues despite a call for a cease-fire by the UN Security Council on August 15. Since March, fighting in Lebanon had been confined almost exclusively to artillery barrages. The shelling had killed about seven hundred people, according to local police.

September 6. Beirut Embassy Evacuated. The skeleton staff of the U.S. embassy in Beirut evacuates to Cyprus in response to threats from the Lebanese army commander, General Aoun.

September 30. Taif Summit. The Saudi government hosts a summit of sixty-two members of the Lebanese parliament in Taif. During the following three weeks, the deputies debate a national reconciliation plan.

October 22. Taif Agreement Concluded. Fifty-eight members of Lebanon's parliament vote for the Taif Accord, a blueprint for national reconciliation that allows continuing Syrian influence. The agreement, which is formally signed on October 24, provides for equal Muslim and Christian representation in a new parliament, a Maronite Christian president, and a Muslim premier with enhanced authority. The agreement does not include an immediate withdrawal of Syrian troops. Christian army leader Gen. Michel Aoun vows to oppose it.

November 5. Muawwad Elected President. In accordance with the Taif agreement, René Muawwad is elected president of Lebanon by members of the Lebanese parliament meeting at an airbase in northern Lebanon. Muawwad, a Maronite Christian, is sworn in the same day. General Aoun denounces his election.

November 22. Muawwad Assassinated. Newly elected Lebanese president René Muawwad is assassinated by a bomb while traveling in a motorcade in Beirut. Twenty-three other people also are killed. On November 24 the Lebanese parliament elects Elias Hrawi president.

LIBYA AND NORTH AFRICA

January 4. Mediterranean Dogfight. Two U.S. Navy warplanes down two Libyan fighters in international waters near Libya. The United States contends that its pilots were on a routine training exercise and fired in self-defense.

October 16–17. Egyptian, Libyan Leaders Meet. In his first trip to Egypt in sixteen years, Libyan leader Qadhafi meets with Egyptian leader Mubarak. Meetings between the two also take place the next day in Libya, where they reach agreements related to agriculture, transportation, communications, and easing border restrictions.

PALESTINIAN AFFAIRS

January 2. Arafat Threat. During a radio broadcast, PLO leader Arafat reputedly threatens Arabs standing in the way of the Palestinian uprising. After U.S. officials January 4 characterize Arafat's remark as inconsistent with his renunciation of terrorism, the PLO insists that the remark had been taken out of context.

May 5. Rafsanjani Advocates Killings. Speaker Rafsanjani of the Iranian parliament urges Palestinians to kill Americans and other westerners in retaliation for Israel's handling of the uprising in the occupied territories. PLO leader Arafat May 7 denounces Rafsanjani's statement. Rafsanjani recants his call to kill westerners May 10, saying, "I really do not advise this and consider it a weak point."

May 12. UN Agency Defers PLO Application. The UN's World Health Organization defers until 1990 consideration of a PLO application for admission as a member state. The United States had vigorously opposed PLO admission and had threatened to withhold its contribution to any international organization granting the PLO membership.

PERSIAN GULF STATES

September 21. Kuwaitis Beheaded. Sixteen Kuwaiti Shiites are beheaded for planting bombs in Mecca during the heavily visited pilgrimage in July.

1990

ARAB-ISRAELI CONFLICT

January 19. Palestinian Leader Arrested. Faisal al-Husseini, a prominent Palestinian nationalist and a senior PLO agent, is arrested by Israeli police in the West Bank. He had been banned from entering the West Bank or the Gaza Strip for six months in December 1989.

February 4. Egyptian Bus Attacked. Nine Israelis are killed in Egypt when two masked gunmen attack their tour bus with automatic weapons and grenades. The bus had been en route from Ismailia to Cairo. The Islamic Jihad for the Liberation of Palestine claims responsibility the next day.

May 20. Israeli Gunman Kills Seven. An Israeli gunman opens fire on a group of Palestinian laborers south of Tel Aviv, killing seven. The incident touches off Palestinian riots throughout the Gaza Strip and the West Bank. Israeli troops and police kill fifteen Palestinians during the following two days of rioting. The gunman,

Ami Popper, had been discharged from the Israeli army in 1988 after he was determined to be unsuitable for military service.

May 25. UN Security Council Meets in Geneva. The UN Security Council meets in Geneva to hear PLO chairman Arafat. He pleads for protection of Palestinians in Israel in the aftermath of the slaying of seven Palestinians by a gunman in the Gaza Strip. The United States October 31 vetoes a resolution that would have sent an observation team to the occupied territories.

May 28–30. Arab League Summit. Members of the Arab League meet in Baghdad, Iraq, to discuss rapidly increasing tensions in the Middle East.

May 30. Palestinian Speedboat Attack Thwarted. Israeli forces capture two heavily armed speedboats bound for Israeli beaches and piloted by Palestinians. Israeli officials determine that they had intended to attack crowded Israeli beaches, hotels, and resorts. The Palestine Liberation Front, a PLO faction, claims responsibility. The incident strains the U.S.-PLO diplomatic dialogue.

June 20. U.S.-PLO Dialogue Suspended. Citing the failure of the PLO to condemn the attempted speedboat attack on Israeli beachfront targets, President George Bush suspends all diplomatic talks between the United States and the PLO.

October 8. Israeli Police Kill Palestinians. Israeli police respond with automatic weapons fire to an attack in Jerusalem by thousands of Palestinian stone throwers. Between nineteen and twenty-one Palestinians are reported killed.

October 9. U.S. Proposes Resolution. The United States proposes a UN Security Council resolution condemning Israel for the shootings in Jerusalem the day before, hoping to preempt efforts by other nations to propose a tougher resolution.

October 12. Resolution 672 Passes. The UN Security Council votes 15-0 in favor of a resolution drafted by the United States condemning Israel. The vote follows four days of furious diplomacy by U.S. officials to prevent a resolution supported by the PLO from being brought to a vote. Resolution 672 criticizes both the Israeli security police and the Palestinian rioters, but it "condemns especially the acts of violence" committed by the police. The resolution also provides for a fact-finding mission to be sent to Israel to investigate the Jerusalem clash. It is the first UN resolution condemning Israel that receives U.S. backing since 1982, when Israel invaded Lebanon. The Israeli cabinet votes unanimously October 14 not to cooperate with the UN investigative mission.

October 18. Arab League Defeats PLO Resolution. At a meeting in Tunis, the Arab League votes 11-10 to defeat a resolution written by the PLO condemning U.S. policy toward Palestinians. After the vote the PLO and its supporters in the Arab League walk out of the meeting in

symbolic protest. Later the Arab League passes a resolution condemning only Israel.

October 24. UN Casts Second Vote against Israel. The UN Security Council votes 15-0 to deplore Israel's refusal to accept a UN mission intended to investigate the October 8 killing of as many as twenty-one Palestinians by Israeli police. The United States joins in the vote after Shamir refuses Bush's personal request that Israel cooperate with the mission.

October 26. Israeli Commission Issues Report. An Israeli government commission concludes that Israeli police were justified in firing upon Arab rioters on the Haram al-Sharif/Temple Mount in Jerusalem October 8. The commission's report blames the violence on the Palestinian rioters and the political and religious leaders who it says incited them.

December 11. Bush, Shamir Meet. Bush and Shamir meet in Washington to repair damage done to the U.S.-Israeli relationship by Israel's policies toward the occupied territories and U.S. support for UN Security Council resolutions condemning Israel. After the meeting, Shamir says he received Bush's assurances that the United States would not support an international conference on the Arab-Israeli issue or other concessions to the Palestinians in return for an Iraqi pullout from Kuwait.

December 20. U.S. Joins Third Vote against Israel. The United States votes in favor of a UN Security Council resolution condemning Israeli treatment of Arabs in the occupied West Bank and Gaza Strip and calling for the secretary general to monitor the safety of Arabs there. The resolution, which referred to the occupied territories as "Palestinian territories," was introduced by nonaligned countries for the PLO.

December 31. Israeli Air Force Targets PLO. Israeli warplanes bomb a PLO stronghold in Lebanon, reportedly killing twelve members of Yasir Arafat's Fatah faction. It is the twenty-first time in 1990 that Israel has attacked targets in Lebanon.

IRAN

February 9. Rushdie Death Edict Renewed. Ayatollah Ali Khamenei, supreme Iranian religious leader, reaffirms a year-old edict calling for the death of British author Salman Rushdie. The edict urges Muslims to carry out this death sentence in retaliation for Rushdie's publication of *The Satanic Verses.*

June 21. Iranian Earthquake. An earthquake measuring 7.7 on the Richter scale shakes northern Iran, killing more than 35,000 and injuring hundreds of thousands. The United States offers humanitarian aid. President Rafsanjani indicates that Iran would accept aid from all countries except South Africa and Israel, including bitter enemies such as the United States and Iraq.

IRAN-IRAQ WAR

August 15. Saddam Hussein Offers Settlement to Iran. Faced with a growing coalition opposing his occupation of Kuwait, Saddam offers Iran a favorable peace settlement to the Iran-Iraq war. (The fighting had ended in August 1988 without a formal peace being concluded.) His proposal amounts to an acceptance of Iranian terms. He offers to return Iranian territory still occupied by Iraqi troops, recognize Iranian control of the eastern half of the Shatt al-Arab waterway, and begin a prisoner exchange. Iran accepts the proposal. Iraqi troops begin withdrawing from Iranian territory August 18 and complete their withdrawal August 21, according to Baghdad.

September 10. Iran, Iraq Agree to Restore Ties. After two days of talks in Tehran, Iraqi foreign minister Tariq Aziz and Iranian foreign minister Ali Akbar Velayati announce that their nations have agreed to restore diplomatic relations. Iran and Iraq open their embassies October 14 in Baghdad and Tehran.

IRAQ

January 30. Rights Groups Cite Iraq. Two human rights groups, Middle East Watch and Amnesty International, criticize the Iraqi government for human rights abuses ranging from deportation and political execution to violent and deadly campaigns to capture army deserters.

March 15. Iraq Executes Alleged Spy. Iraq executes as a spy an Iranian-born reporter for a British publication, despite British pleas for clemency. Farzad Bazoft was arrested in September 1989 after investigating the site of an explosion at an Iraqi military base.

March 28. A-Bomb Smuggling Ring Discovered. British customs agents arrest five people and seize a shipment of devices used to trigger nuclear weapons before they were loaded onto an Iraqi Airways flight. British and American agents had collaborated during an eighteen-month undercover operation that lead to the arrests. The smuggling plot had been fronted by a British company, Euromac Ltd.

April 2. Iraq Threatens Use of Chemical Weapons. Saddam Hussein threatens to use chemical weapons against Israel should Israel take any military action against Iraq.

ISRAEL

February 12. Sharon Resigns from Cabinet. Citing policy differences with Prime Minister Yitzhak Shamir, Trade and Industry Minister Ariel Sharon announces that he will resign. Sharon officially leaves the cabinet February 18.

March 15. Shamir Government Falls. Shamir loses a no-confidence vote in the Israeli Knesset 60-55. The vote sets in motion a leadership contest with both Shamir and Labor Party leader Shimon Peres trying to construct a coalition.

June 8. Shamir Forms Coalition. Shamir announces the formation of a governing coalition in Israel comprising the Likud Party and several small right-wing parties. The government is officially approved by the Knesset June 11.

LEBANON

April 22. Pohill Freed. American hostage Robert Pohill is freed by his Lebanese kidnappers after more than three years as a prisoner.

April 30. Second American Freed. American hostage Frank Reed is released in Beirut by the pro-Iranian Hizballah group. He had been held since 1986. President Bush thanks the Iranian government for its assistance, but he insists that the release was not part of a deal.

October 13. Aoun Abandons Struggle. Lebanese Christian leader Gen. Michel Aoun ends his fight against Syrian forces and the Lebanese government and takes refuge in the French embassy in Beirut following heavy Syrian-led attacks against his army. For more than two years, Aoun and his supporters had refused to submit to the rule of the Syrian-backed Lebanese government. Aoun's defeat is a blow to Iraq, which had provided the general's forces with weapons as a means of opposing Syrian goals in Lebanon and punishing President Asad for his support of Iran during the Iran-Iraq war.

PERSIAN GULF STATES

July 2. Pilgrims Killed in Mecca. When air conditioning fails in a pedestrian tunnel in Mecca, a stampede of pilgrims attempting to escape results in the death of 1,426 people.

July 17. Saddam Speech. Iraqi president Saddam Hussein accuses unnamed Gulf leaders of plotting with the United States to keep oil prices low through overproduction. He says in a speech marking Iraq's Revolution Day that artificially low oil prices have damaged the Iraqi economy, and he threatens to use force to stop noncompliance with production quotas. Observers agree that his accusation is aimed at Kuwait and the United Arab Emirates (UAE).

July 18. Iraqi Letter Names Kuwait, UAE. Iraq discloses the contents of a letter written by Iraqi foreign minister Aziz to the Arab League. The letter charges that Kuwait and the United Arab Emirates are part of an "imperialist-Zionist" conspiracy to hold down oil prices. The letter also charges Kuwait with pumping $2.4 billion worth of Iraqi oil out of the Rumaila oil field, a small part of which extends into Kuwait. Aziz says Iraq's Arab creditors should forgive the debt incurred by Iraq during the war with Iran.

July 25–27. OPEC Raises Target Price. The Organization of Petroleum Exporting Countries announces a $3 increase to $21 a barrel in OPEC's target price for oil. The increase is seen as a victory for Iraq.

August 29. OPEC to Increase Production. At a meeting in Vienna, ten of thirteen OPEC members support an increase in oil production to make up for the shortfall created by the Persian Gulf crisis. Saudi Arabia and Venezuela had previously increased their production in response to the crisis and had told other members that they would make up for the loss of Iraqi and Kuwaiti oil by themselves if necessary. Libya and Iraq boycott the meeting. Iran attends but opposes any production increase.

September 17. Saudi Arabia, USSR Restore Ties. Saudi Arabia and the Soviet Union announce that they will restore diplomatic relations, which had been severed since 1938.

PERSIAN GULF WAR

July 23. Iraq Deploys Troops on Border. Arab and U.S. officials report that Iraq is massing tens of thousands of troops on Kuwait's border. The United States discloses July 25 that Iraqi deployments have reached 100,000 troops.

July 24. U.S.-UAE Maneuvers. The United States announces that American ships and refueling planes are participating in joint maneuvers with forces from the United Arab Emirates. The maneuvers are intended to demonstrate U.S. commitment to defending friendly Gulf nations. The following day UAE officials deny that their country is holding special maneuvers with the United States, saying the two nations merely are engaging in routine training.

July 25. Mubarak Diplomacy. After four days of talks with Arab leaders in Egypt, Iraq, Saudi Arabia, and Kuwait, Egyptian president Hosni Mubarak announces that Iraq and Kuwait have agreed to discuss their differences in talks to be held in Jiddah, Saudi Arabia. Mubarak says Saddam Hussein has told him that Iraq has "no intention" of invading Kuwait.

July 25. Glaspie Meets Saddam. The American ambassador to Iraq, April Glaspie, meets with Hussein in Baghdad. She expresses concern about the massing of Iraqi forces on the Kuwaiti border but emphasizes that the United States wants better relations with Iraq. According to an Iraqi transcript of the meeting released in September, she tells him that the United States has "no opinion on the Arab-Arab conflicts, like your border disagreement with Kuwait." Saddam reportedly tells Glaspie that Iraq does not wish a confrontation with the United States and that Iraq's forces on the Kuwaiti frontier have not been deployed for the purpose of invasion.

August 2. Iraq Invades Kuwait. Iraqi forces massed on the border of Kuwait invade the shaykhdom and quickly seize control of most strategic locations. Kuwait's ruler, Shaykh Jabir al-Ahmad Al Sabah, flees to Saudi Arabia. Hussein claims Iraq was responding to appeals for help from Kuwaiti revolutionaries who had overthrown the government. By the end of the day, Iraqi troops are in firm control of the country, although isolated incidents of armed resistance by Kuwaitis continue. U.S. president George Bush denounces the invasion and imposes economic sanctions against Iraq. The governments of the United States, Great Britain, and France freeze Iraqi and Kuwaiti assets in their countries. The Soviet Union cuts off arms deliveries to Iraq. The UN Security Council votes 14-0 (with Yemen abstaining) to condemn the invasion and threatens to impose mandatory economic sanctions if Iraq does not withdraw immediately from Kuwait.

August 3. Aftermath of the Invasion. Russian foreign minister Eduard Shevardnadze and U.S. secretary of state James Baker issue a joint statement in Moscow condemning the Iraqi invasion of Kuwait and calling for an international arms embargo against Iraq. Fourteen of twenty-one Arab League members vote to condemn Iraq's "aggression." The European Community August 4 announces broad economic sanctions against Iraq, including an arms embargo, a freeze on Iraqi assets, and a ban on imports of Iraqi and Kuwaiti oil. Japan announces similar economic sanctions August 5.

August 6. UN Imposes Sanctions. The UN Security Council passes Resolution 661, imposing mandatory economic sanctions on Iraq. All members of the Security Council vote for the resolution except Yemen and Cuba, both of which abstained. The resolution calls on UN members to end all economic intercourse with Iraq, including trade. Food and medicine are exempted from the embargo "in strictly humanitarian circumstances."

August 6. Saudis Request U.S. Forces. Responding to an Iraqi buildup in southern Kuwait near the Saudi border, King Fahd ibn Abd al-Aziz of Saudi Arabia requests that U.S. forces be stationed in his country. The request follows a meeting between King Fahd and U.S. secretary of defense Dick Cheney, at which Cheney shows the king satellite photographs of the Iraqi troop buildup. That evening, Bush orders U.S. forces to Saudi Arabia. British prime minister Margaret Thatcher orders naval and air forces to Saudi Arabia August 8.

August 8. Iraq Annexes Kuwait. Despite a statement August 3 that it would withdraw its forces from Kuwait, Baghdad announces that it has annexed Kuwait. The UN Security Council August 9 votes 15-0 for a resolution declaring the annexation "null and void."

August 8. Bush Address. In a televised address from the White House, Bush says U.S. policy toward the Gulf crisis is based on "four simple principles": Iraq's unconditional and complete withdrawal from Kuwait, the restoration of Kuwait's legitimate government, Persian Gulf security and stability, and the protection of Americans abroad.

August 10. Arab League Votes to Commit Troops. At a closed meeting of the Arab League in Cairo, twelve Arab League members vote for a resolution backing Arab troop deployments to Saudi Arabia to oppose Iraq. Iraq, Libya, and the Palestinian Liberation Organization vote against the resolution. Jordan, Sudan, and Mauritania vote for it with reservations. Algeria and Yemen abstain, and Tunisia does not attend. The first Egyptian and Moroccan troops land in Saudi Arabia August 11. Syrian forces begin arriving August 14.

August 12. Saddam Hussein Links Iraqi Pullout to Israel. Hussein says Iraq might withdraw from Kuwait if Israel withdraws from "the Arab-occupied territories in Palestine, Syria, and Lebanon."

August 16. U.S. Begins Blockade. Responding to an order issued by President Bush August 12, U.S. naval forces begin forcibly "interdicting" ships headed to or from Iraq with commercial or military cargoes.

August 17. Iraq Places Hostages at Key Sites. The speaker of Iraq's parliament, Saadi Mahdi Saleh, says Iraq will house American and other Western citizens at important military and industrial installations. Baghdad announces August 20 that it has begun moving westerners to key facilities.

August 23. Japan Pledges $1 Billion. The Japanese government announces that it will provide $1 billion in aid to Arab governments hurt by the UN embargo of Iraq. The Japanese government had been criticized for not doing more to support the coalition effort.

August 24. Troops Surround Embassies in Kuwait. Iraqi troops surround several foreign embassies in Kuwait, including those of the United States, Great Britain, and France, which are operating with skeleton staffs. In an apparent effort to force the closure of the embassies without a confrontation that could lead to war, the troops begin cutting off the embassies' electricity and water. At least twenty-seven nations have kept their embassies in Kuwait open despite Iraqi demands that they be shut.

September 1. Hostages Begin Leaving Iraq. The first hostages released by Iraq, a group of sixty-eight Japanese women and children, leave Baghdad. In the days that follow, many other foreign women and children are allowed to leave.

September 6. Saudis, Kuwaitis Pledge Billions. The Saudi government pledges to contribute about $500 million a month to help defray the costs of the U.S. military deployments to Saudi Arabia. The Saudis also pledge $4 billion a year in financial aid to states whose economies have been damaged by the crisis. The Saudi contribution follows a meeting between Secretary of State Baker and King Fahd in Jiddah. Baker meets with the exiled amir of Kuwait September 7 in Taif, Saudi Arabia. The amir pledges $2.5 billion in 1990 to help pay for U.S. military operations in the Gulf region and another $2.5 billion to help struggling Middle East economies. The exiled Kuwaiti government says September 21 that it is prepared to provide even more aid in support of the effort to liberate its country.

September 14–15. Japan, Germany Announce Aid. Responding to international criticism, especially from the United States, the Japanese government announces that it will provide an additional $3 billion in aid to the Gulf effort (it had previously pledged $1 billion); $2 billion of this would be economic aid to Egypt, Jordan, and Turkey. The West German government announces a $2 billion aid package September 15.

September 20. Saudi Actions against Jordan. The Saudi government cuts off oil shipments to Jordan, citing Jordan's support for Iraq and its failure to pay for recent oil shipments.

September 23. Saddam Hussein Threatens Israel, Oil Fields. Hussein issues a statement threatening to attack Israel and the oil fields in Saudi Arabia and other Gulf states if Iraqis "are being strangled" by the UN economic embargo.

November 8. Bush Announces Deployments. Bush announces that he is ordering a huge increase in U.S. military forces in the Persian Gulf region.

November 29. Security Council Authorizes Force. The UN Security Council passes Resolution 678 by a 12-2 vote. It authorizes coalition forces in the Persian Gulf region to use "all necessary means" to expel Iraq from Kuwait if Iraq does not withdraw by January 15. Yemen and Cuba vote against the resolution. China (which, as a permanent member of the Security Council, could have vetoed the resolution) abstains. The resolution is the first UN authorization to wage war against a member nation since 1950, when the Security Council called on members to help defend South Korea against the North Korean invasion.

December 7. Kuwait Embassy to Be Evacuated. The State Department announces that all diplomatic personnel will be evacuated from the U.S. embassy in Kuwait after Americans who want to leave the country have gone.

December 13. Last Hostage Flight Leaves Iraq. The last U.S.-chartered flight carrying Americans and other westerners from Iraq departs for Frankfurt, Germany. Among the passengers are the five remaining members of the U.S. embassy staff in Kuwait, including Ambassador W. Nathaniel Howell III. Great Britain evacuated its embassy staff December 12.

YEMEN

May 22. Yemen Unites. North Yemen and South Yemen announce their merger into a unified state, the Republic of Yemen. Ali Abdallah Salih, the president of North Yemen, is president of the new republic.

1991

ARAB-ISRAELI CONFLICT

January 4. Security Council Condemns Israel. The United States joins with other Security Council members in condemning Israel for its treatment of the Palestinians.

The unanimous vote is a response to Israel's use of force during increasingly violent confrontations between Israeli security police and soldiers and Palestinian protesters. The Security Council resolution is the fourth condemning Israel since October.

March 7. Baker to the Middle East. Secretary of State Baker departs for a seven-day tour of Middle East capitals. He advocates a gradual, dual-track peace process under which Israel and the Arab states would take steps to moderate their positions toward one another, while Israel and the Palestinians engage in direct negotiations.

July 18. Madrid Peace Talks. Syria accepts a joint U.S.-Soviet invitation to a Middle East peace conference to be held in Madrid, Spain. Lebanon accepts July 20. After meeting with Baker July 21, Jordan's King Hussein pledges that his country will attend.

August 1. Shamir on Peace Conference. Prime Minister Yitzhak Shamir announces that Israel will attend the Madrid peace conference if the PLO is not given a role and Palestinians from East Jerusalem do not serve as delegates. Palestinian leaders denounce Shamir's restrictions August 2. The Israeli cabinet approves Shamir's policy August 4.

October 23. Parties Agree to Conference. The United States announces that Israel, Arab states, and a Palestinian delegation have agreed to attend a Middle East peace conference in Madrid.

October 30. Madrid Conference Opens. The Middle East peace conference opens in Madrid. Egypt, Lebanon, Jordan, Syria, Israel, and Palestinians from the occupied territories send delegations. U.S. and Soviet presidents Bush and Gorbachev address the conference on the first day. On October 31 Shamir calls for direct Arab-Israeli negotiations. Syria reiterates its position that a peace treaty cannot be concluded until Israel returns all the Arab land it has occupied by force. The conference concludes November 4.

December 10. Peace Talks Open. Arab-Israeli peace talks begin in Washington, D.C. The talks had been delayed since their planned December 4 starting date because the Israeli delegation had not arrived. The talks adjourn December 18 with little progress.

December 16. UN Overturns Resolution. The United Nations votes 111-25 with 13 abstentions and 17 votes uncast to overturn a 1975 resolution that equates Zionism with racism. No Arab nation votes in favor of the repeal, but several were absent, indicating a passive acceptance of it. The Soviet Union and East European nations vote in favor of the repeal.

IRAN

August 8. Former Iranian Premier Slain. Former Iranian premier Shapour Bakhtiar is found stabbed to death along with his secretary in his home outside Paris. Bakhtiar was premier in 1979 before being ousted by Islamic revolutionaries. The assassination is carried out by three Iranians. One suspect is arrested.

November 26. U.S. Compensates Iran. The United States agrees to pay the Iranian government $278 million for U.S.-Iranian arms agreements canceled after the 1979 Islamic revolution. Iran sought $11 billion, and U.S. officials put the value on the amount owed at $1 billion. U.S. officials deny any link between the compensation and negotiations for the release of hostages.

IRAQ

March 1. Civil Unrest in Iraq. Reports from refugees and other sources indicate Basra has degenerated into chaos, as mobs openly defy government authorities. On March 3 Shiite Muslim rebels claim to have taken control of the city. By March 5 fighting spreads to numerous other southern Iraqi cities. However, forces loyal to Saddam Hussein are effectively counterattacking Shiite rebels and disaffected Iraqi soldiers who had joined them. Leaders of the Kurdish resistance movement based in northern Iraq announce March 6 that they have begun a large-scale offensive against Iraqi government troops and have taken control of many areas.

March 13. Iraqi Uprising Continues. For the first time since the Iraqi uprising began, the regime of Saddam admits its troops are engaged in a war with rebel groups. Kurdish resistance leaders claim to be in control of most of the Kurdish region of Iraq. Several sources report large Shiite demonstrations in Baghdad. At the end of a three-day conference in Beirut, leaders of twenty-three Iraqi opposition groups appeal for outside assistance and announce they will cooperate to topple the Iraqi regime.

March 16. Saddam Promises Reforms. In a televised speech, Saddam appeals for the support of Iraqis by promising democratic reforms as soon as the antigovernment rebellions have been put down. The reforms are to include a multiparty system and a referendum on a new constitution. He claims that the insurrection in the south was the work of foreigners and traitors and that it has been broken. He admits that fighting continues in the north.

June 28. Iraq Blocks Arms Inspectors. Iraqi soldiers fire shots into the air to prevent UN arms inspectors from examining equipment believed to be used in the manufacture of weapons-grade uranium. The incident follows a week of obstruction by Iraqi authorities to prevent UN inspectors from visiting suspect facilities. After negotiations with Iraqi officials fail to break the deadlock, the UN team leaves Iraq July 3.

July 8. Iraq Discloses Atomic Research. Iraq releases a report detailing an extensive nuclear development program, but it claims the program was not aimed at producing nuclear weapons. A UN inspection team is shown a secret nuclear research facility July 9. However, the five permanent members of the UN Security Council announce July 12 that Iraq must fully disclose its nuclear program or face renewed military action.

August 15. Iraq Oil Sale Plan Approved. The UN Security Council votes 13-1 to allow Iraq to sell $1.6 billion of oil to obtain funds for importing food and medicine pending a review of Iraqi needs. The funds would go into an escrow account to be used by the UN to buy and distribute the food and medicine directly to the Iraqi people. The Iraqi government rejects the conditions and refuses to cooperate with the plan. The Security Council formally passes the proposal September 19.

ISRAEL

September 6. Bush Asks for Delay of Loan Guarantees. After the Shamir government requests $10 billion in loan guarantees from the United States to help settle Russian Jewish immigrants, U.S. president George Bush asks Congress to delay consideration of the request until 1992. Israel claims the loan guarantees are necessary to finance the settlement of hundreds of thousands of Jewish immigrants from the Soviet Union. Bush says the guarantees could upset delicate negotiations aimed at constructing an Arab-Israeli peace conference.

KURDISH AFFAIRS

March 31. Kurdish Insurgency Collapses. After weeks of fierce fighting, Iraqi troops overcome Kurdish fighters in northern Iraq, causing up to a million Kurds to flee to mountains along Iraq's borders with Turkey and Iran. A week earlier, Iraqi troops had put down the largest elements of the Shiite insurgency in southern Iraq.

April 17. Kurdish Zone Established. American, British, and French forces arrive in Iraq to secure a "safe zone" for Kurds in the northern part of the country. American troops begin building camps for the refugees April 21.

April 24. Saddam Says Kurds Can Return. After talks with Kurdish leaders, Saddam Hussein issues a guarantee of safety to all Kurds who wish to return to their homes in Iraq. Most Kurds remain skeptical, but the presence of nearby U.S. troops causes many to return to their homes.

May 13. UN Takes Over Kurd Relief Effort. The United States transfers control of Kurdish refugee camps to the United Nations. Allied forces complete their withdrawal from northern Iraq July 15.

LEBANON

May 22. Lebanese-Syrian Accord. President Hafiz al-Asad of Syria and President Hrawi of Lebanon sign a "Treaty of Brotherhood, Cooperation, and Coordination."

August 8–11. Two Hostages in Lebanon Are Released. The Islamic Jihad releases John McCarthy, a British journalist, on August 8, and the Revolutionary Justice Organization releases Edward A. Tracy, a book salesman. Tracy had been missing since 1986.

August 29. Lebanese General Exiled. Gen. Michel Aoun, a rebel Christian military leader, leaves Lebanon for exile in France. He and two aides were granted political asylum at the French embassy.

September 16. Syria-Lebanon Security Pact. Lebanon and Syria sign a pact providing that both countries will suppress any military or political activities within their country that could be harmful or damaging to the other nation. A clause gives each country the right to arrest and prosecute criminals in the other country.

October 21. Prisoners Released. The Islamic Jihad releases Jesse Turner, an American University professor held captive since 1987. Fifteen Lebanese prisoners who were being held in the Israeli security zone in southern Lebanon were released the same day in an apparent link to Turner's release.

November 18. Hostages Released in Lebanon. The Islamic Jihad releases Church of England envoy Terry Waite, who had been held hostage in Lebanon since 1987, and American Thomas Sutherland, who had been held since 1985.

December 4. Last U.S. Hostages Freed. Terry Anderson, the last American hostage in Lebanon, is freed by his captors. He had been kidnapped in March 1985. Two other American hostages, Joseph Cicippio and Alann Steen, were released December 2 and 3, respectively. They had been held since January 1987.

December 22–27. Hostages' Remains Found in Lebanon. The body of Marine Lt. Col. William R. Higgins was found on a street in Beirut on December 22. He was kidnapped in February 1988 and was reportedly hanged in 1989. The remains of William F. Buckley, former Beirut bureau chief for the CIA, were found on a roadside in south Beirut. The Islamic Jihad kidnapped him in March of 1984 and reportedly executed him in 1985.

LIBYA AND NORTH AFRICA

November 14. Libyans Linked to Attacks. The U.S. Justice Department indicts two Libyan operatives in the December 21, 1988, bombing of Pan American Airlines Flight 103 over Lockerbie, Scotland, which killed 270 people. A U.S. State Department spokesman asserts that the Libyan government was involved.

PALESTINIAN AFFAIRS

January 14. PLO Officials Assassinated. Two high-ranking PLO officials of the mainline Fatah faction headed by Yasir Arafat are assassinated in Tunis by one of their bodyguards. The PLO initially blames Israel, which denies any involvement in the slayings. The assassin is subsequently revealed to have had ties with a rival faction of the PLO headed by Abu Nidal.

PERSIAN GULF STATES

March 9. Kuwait Leader Promises a Parliament. During a meeting with Secretary of State Baker, Prince Sa'ad Abdallah al-Salim Al Sabah, Kuwait's prime minister, tells reporters the Kuwaiti government will soon reinstitute the Kuwaiti parliament that had been dissolved in 1986.

March 14. Amir Returns to Kuwait. Shaykh Jabir returns to Kuwait for the first time since the Iraqi invasion of his nation. His return coincides with statements of concern by U.S. officials about the deportation from Kuwait of Palestinians and other Arabs suspected of collaborating with Iraqi troops. Many of the deported Palestinians charge that they were tortured by Kuwaiti police or vigilantes.

June 2. Kuwaiti Elections Announced. The amir of Kuwait announces that long-awaited parliamentary elections will be held in October 1992.

September 4. U.S.-Kuwait Security Pact. A ten-year security pact is concluded that allows the United States to conduct military exercises and stockpile equipment in Kuwait.

November 6. Kuwaiti Oil Fires Extinguished. The last of the more than seven hundred Kuwaiti oil wells set on fire by Iraqi forces is capped. The total cost of the operation is estimated at $1.5 billion.

PERSIAN GULF WAR

January 2. NATO Sends Jets to Turkey. The North Atlantic Treaty Organization (NATO) announces that it will send forty-two warplanes to alliance member Turkey to strengthen the 100,000 Turkish troops on the Iraqi frontier. Among the NATO warplanes are eighteen German jets. During January, Turkey reinforces its border with an additional 80,000 troops. Iraq reportedly has 120,000 troops facing Turkey in northern Iraq.

January 12. Congress Authorizes Force. Following three days of intense debate, the U.S. Congress votes to give President George Bush the authority to wage war against Iraq. The Senate passes the measure 52-47 to approve the use of "all means necessary" to expel Iraq from Kuwait. The House passes it 250-183. Bush praises the action, saying it demonstrates U.S. resolve.

January 13. Pérez de Cuéllar Unsuccessful. UN Secretary General Javier Pérez de Cuéllar meets for two and a half hours with Saddam Hussein in Baghdad in a last-ditch effort to persuade him to withdraw his forces from Kuwait. Pérez de Cuéllar reports that Saddam is determined not to budge.

January 15. Bush Authorizes Attack. Bush signs executive order authorizing an attack on Iraq unless diplomatic progress is made.

January 16. Deadline Passes. At 8:00 a.m. in Saudi Arabia (12:00 midnight EST January 15) the deadline for Iraq to withdraw from Kuwait passes.

January 17. Coalition Forces Attack. At 12:50 a.m. in Saudi Arabia (4:50 p.m. EST January 16) the first wave of allied warplanes takes off from Saudi airfields on their way to targets in Iraq and Kuwait. In addition, cruise missiles are launched from American ships in the Persian Gulf and Red Sea. At 2:35 a.m. Western television reporters in Baghdad report that the city is under attack. A half hour later the White House announces that coalition forces have begun the process of liberating Kuwait.

January 18. Iraq Hits Israel with Scuds. At 2:15 a.m. (7:15 p.m. EST January 17) Iraq launches eight Scud missiles with conventional high explosive warheads at Tel Aviv and Haifa. Fifteen Israelis are injured, but no one is killed. Israel does not retaliate but officials say they may. Bush urges Israel not to retaliate.

January 19. Patriots Sent to Israel. After four more Scud missiles strike Israel, American Patriot antimissile missiles and their army crews arrive in the Jewish state. These forces are the first U.S. combat personnel ever deployed in Israel.

January 20. Iraq Displays Prisoners. Iraqi television broadcasts interviews with seven prisoners (three of whom are Americans) identified as coalition pilots. The prisoners, who denounce the war against Iraq, appear dazed and have bruises on their faces. The Iraqi government January 21 declares that captured pilots will be housed at strategic military and scientific sites that might be coalition bombing targets.

January 22. Scud Attack on Israel. An Iraqi Scud missile strikes a residential area in Tel Aviv, reportedly killing three people and wounding more than sixty. A Patriot missile had struck the incoming Scud but failed to destroy it.

January 22. Israel Requests Aid. During a meeting with Deputy Secretary of State Eagleburger, Israeli finance minister Yitzhak Modacai says that because of expenses related to the Persian Gulf crisis and the settlement of hundreds of thousands of Jewish immigrants from the Soviet Union, Israel needs $13 billion in additional aid from the United States.

January 23. Powell Briefing. At a Pentagon briefing, chairman of the Joint Chiefs of Staff Gen. Colin Powell claims that the coalition has achieved "air superiority." He also says that Iraq's nuclear reactors have been destroyed and no Iraqi warplane has attacked a coalition ground target.

January 24. Kaifu Proposes Aid. Japanese premier Toshiki Kaifu proposes that Japan contribute an additional $9 billion to the Persian Gulf War effort. Japan had already pledged $4 billion.

January 25. U.S. Accuses Iraq of Spilling Oil. The United States accuses Iraq of "environmental terrorism," saying that Iraq has created the largest oil spill in history by deliberately leaking oil into the Persian Gulf. On January 27 U.S. warplanes bomb parts of the complex, successfully cutting off the flow of oil into the sea. The spill, which covers an estimated 350 square miles, threatens Persian Gulf wildlife and desalinization plants in Saudi Arabia.

January 26. Iraqi Planes Flee to Iran. The Pentagon says at least twenty-four Iraqi planes have fled to the safety of Iran. On January 30 General Schwarzkopf says the number of Iraqi aircraft seeking shelter in Iran had risen to eighty-nine.

January 29. Battle of Khafji. In the first major ground engagement of the war, three Iraqi tank battalions cross the Saudi border and occupy the deserted town of Khafji. By the evening of January 31, however, Saudi, Qatari, and U.S. forces retake the town.

January 29. Germany Pledges More Aid. The German government pledges an additional $5.5 billion in aid for the Gulf war effort. Germany also announces that it is sending to Turkey new air defense systems and 580 troops to operate them.

January 29. Israel Arrests Nusseibeh. Israeli authorities arrest prominent West Bank Palestinian leader Sari Nusseibeh for allegedly providing Iraq information on the location of its Scud missile strikes in Israel. He is sentenced to six months of administrative detention without a trial. A judge later reduces his sentence to three months. Nusseibeh is among thousands of Palestinians detained by Israel during the Gulf war.

February 6. King Hussein Allies with Iraq. In a speech broadcast on Jordanian television, King Hussein abandons Jordan's officially neutral posture and states in unequivocal terms his country's new alliance with Iraq. He condemns the coalition's air campaign against Iraq and claims it is a war "against all Arabs and Muslims." He does not, however, offer Iraq any military aid.

February 13. Attack Kills Hundreds of Iraqis. More than four hundred civilians are killed when a U.S. Stealth F-117A bomber drops two laser-guided, one-ton bombs on a building housing an underground bomb shelter in Baghdad. Iraqi officials maintain the shelter was deliberately targeted, calling the raid "a well-planned crime."

February 15. Iraq Offers Conditional Withdrawal. Iraq's Revolutionary Command Council (a ruling body headed by Saddam Hussein) announces that it is prepared to withdraw Iraqi forces from Kuwait. Initial response from world leaders is optimistic, but hope fades as Iraq reveals numerous conditions for its withdrawal.

February 21. Iraq Backs Soviet Plan. Soviet officials announce that Iraq has agreed to withdraw unconditionally from Kuwait under the terms of a Soviet six-point plan. The White House announces Bush told Gorbachev that he had "serious concerns" about the plan.

February 22. Bush Sets Deadline. Bush announces that to end the war and avoid a ground offensive, Saddam Hussein must accept coalition terms "publicly and authoritatively" and Iraq must begin an unconditional withdrawal from Kuwait by noon EST February 23.

February 23. Iraq Ignores Ultimatum. Aziz issues a statement in Moscow reiterating his government's acceptance of the Soviet peace proposal. As Bush's deadline passes, however, Iraq makes no moves to withdraw from Kuwait. Bush declares that there is "no alternative to war."

February 24. Coalition Launches Ground War. At 4:00 a.m. Saudi time, eight hours after Bush's deadline passes, coalition ground forces launch a massive offensive against Iraqi defenses in Kuwait and Iraq. President Bush announces the offensive in a televised address delivered two hours later (10:00 p.m. EST February 23). Coalition troops quickly breach Iraqi fortifications on the Saudi-Kuwaiti border. Meanwhile a huge coalition force secretly deployed on the Saudi-Iraqi border to the west penetrates deep into Iraq against light opposition. Thousands of Iraqi troops surrender without a fight. By the end of the ground offensive an estimated sixty-three thousand Iraqis are taken prisoner.

February 25. Scud Hits U.S. Barracks. An Iraqi Scud missile strikes a U.S. Army reservist barracks in Dhahran, Saudi Arabia. Twenty-eight soldiers, including three women, are killed, and at least eighty-nine others are wounded.

February 25. U.S. Forces Reach Euphrates. American troops leading the assault into southern Iraq reach the Euphrates River valley late in the evening, severing the main escape route between Kuwait and Baghdad.

February 26. Iraqis Abandon Kuwait City. As coalition forces press toward Kuwait City, Iraqi troops abandon the capital, taking thousands of Kuwaitis with them as hostages. Coalition warplanes create a massive traffic jam of Iraqi vehicles on the road running north out of Kuwait City by destroying vehicles at the front and rear of the fleeing Iraqi convoy. For hours coalition pilots bomb the stalled convoy, destroying more than a thousand Iraqi vehicles. Kuwaiti resistance fighters take control of Kuwait City and begin hunting the few Iraqis who had stayed behind. From Saudi Arabia, the amir of Kuwait, Shaykh Jabir, declares that the country will remain under martial law for three months. Kuwaiti, Saudi, and U.S. troops march into the city in the early morning hours of February 27.

February 26. Saddam Announces Withdrawal. Saddam Hussein delivers a defiant speech over Baghdad radio announcing the withdrawal of Iraqi troops from Kuwait, although most Iraqi forces already are in full retreat. Bush angrily responds to Saddam's speech, saying that the war will continue because the announcement failed to meet the coalition's conditions for a cease-fire.

February 27. Tank Duel with the Republican Guard. American and British forces engage several divisions of Iraq's elite Republican Guard troops in a furious tank battle west of Basra. The clash is the largest tank battle since World War II. More than two hundred Iraqi tanks are destroyed without the loss of a single coalition tank.

February 27. Aziz Letter Accepts UN Resolutions. Aziz notifies the United Nations by letter that Iraq will accept the twelve Security Council resolutions related to Iraq's invasion of Kuwait.

February 27. Bush Announces a Cease-Fire. In a televised address delivered at 9:00 p.m. EST from the White House, Bush declares that the coalition's military objectives have been met and announces a cease-fire that will begin at 12:00 midnight EST (8:00 a.m. February 28 Saudi time). The ground war lasts exactly one hundred hours. Baghdad radio announces the cease-fire soon afterward. Bush also enumerates the conditions that Iraq must meet to achieve a permanent cease-fire.

February 28. Iraq Accepts Cease-Fire. The Iraqi government says it will accept a cease-fire and send military officers to meet with coalition commanders to arrange the specifics of the cease-fire. The White House announces that coalition troops will remain in Iraqi territory until Iraq complies fully with all terms of the cease-fire.

March 2. Cease-fire Broken. Unaware of a cease-fire, Iraqi tank units southwest of Basra fire upon U.S. forces. American helicopters and tanks attack the Iraqi forces, destroying sixty vehicles before the Iraqis surrender. No Americans are killed in the fight.

March 3. Iraqis Accept Allied Terms. General Schwarzkopf meets with high-ranking Iraqi military leaders near the southern Iraq town of Safwan. The Iraqis accept all allied terms for formally ending the Gulf war. The Iraqis promise to release promptly all prisoners of war and Kuwaiti civilians, provide locations of all mines, avoid further skirmishes, pay Kuwait for war damages, and comply with all UN resolutions pertaining to Iraq's invasion of Kuwait.

March 4–5. Iraq Frees Prisoners of War. Iraqi authorities, who claim to hold forty-five coalition prisoners of war, release ten on March 4 and the remaining thirty-five on March 5. A few coalition troops remain listed as missing in action, but U.S. officials say they believe Iraq has released all the prisoners of war they captured. Iraq begins freeing its Kuwaiti civilian hostages March 7.

March 5. Iraq Voids Annexation of Kuwait. Baghdad radio reports that the Iraqi government has voided its annexation of Kuwait and promised to return Kuwaiti assets seized during the occupation.

March 9. U.S. to Bomb Iraq if It Uses Poison Gas. The Bush administration announces that it will bomb Iraqi government forces if they use chemical weapons against Iraqi rebels. American officials say that U.S. intelligence had intercepted a March 7 communication from the Iraqi government to troops in the field directing them to initiate a chemical weapons attack against a specific rebel target.

March 10. Coalition Arabs Endorse Security Plan. Foreign ministers from Saudi Arabia, Egypt, Syria, Kuwait, Oman, Qatar, Bahrain, and the United Arab Emirates meet with U.S. secretary of state James Baker in Riyadh. They agree that a Persian Gulf security structure should include an Arab peacekeeping force consisting of troops from the eight Arab nations, an enhanced U.S. naval presence in the Persian Gulf, the storage of U.S. military equipment in Saudi Arabia, and frequent U.S.-Arab joint military maneuvers.

April 3. Iraq Resolution Passed. The UN Security Council adopts Resolution 687, which establishes a permanent cease-fire in the Persian Gulf War and sets conditions for a gradual lifting of international sanctions against Iraq. Baghdad accepts the terms April 6. They call for Iraq's renunciation of terrorism and its cooperation in the destruction of chemical, biological, and nuclear weapons facilities and ballistic missiles.

May 15. UN Team Begins Inspection. UN atomic energy experts begin inspecting Iraq's nuclear installations and chemical warfare facilities.

1992

ARAB-ISRAELI CONFLICT

January 6. Security Council Condemns Deportations. The UN Security Council votes unanimously to "strongly condemn" Israel for deporting twelve Palestinians from the occupied territories. The United States supports the resolution. Arab delegates to peace talks with Israel had boycotted the talks after Israel announced the deportations January 3. However, in response to the Security Council vote, the Arabs announce they will return to the talks, which resume January 13 in Washington, D.C.

January 28–28. Moscow Conference. Delegates from ten Arab states, Israel, and the European Community meet in Moscow at a conference cosponsored by Russia and the United States. The delegates discuss an array of regional issues. Syria, Lebanon, and the Palestinians boycott the conference.

February 16. Lebanese Shiite Leader Killed. Hizballah leader Shaykh Abbas al-Musawi is killed when Israeli helicopter gunships attack his motorcade in southern Lebanon. Musawi's family is also killed in the attack. Israeli defense minister Moshe Arens says Musawi was a terrorist. Hizballah guerrillas fire rockets into northern Israel in retaliation. The Israeli army conducts a raid into southern Lebanon February 20–21 aimed at stopping the rocket attacks. Despite denunciations of the Israeli assassination by Arab countries, it does not derail ongoing Arab-Israeli peace talks.

March 17. Israeli Embassy Destroyed. A car bomb destroys the Israeli embassy in Buenos Aires, killing twenty-eight. The Islamic Jihad claims responsibility, saying the bombing is in retaliation for the killing of Hizballah leader al-Musawi.

July 21. Rabin Travels to Cairo. In an effort to create momentum in Arab-Israeli peace negotiations, Prime Minister Yitzhak Rabin travels to Cairo for talks with President Hosni Mubarak. It is the first meeting between Israeli and Egyptian leaders since 1986.

September 9. Asad on Peace Treaty. In a speech to residents of the Golan Heights, Syria's president Hafiz al-Asad says publicly for the first time that he is willing to negotiate a peace treaty with Israel. Talks between Syria and Israel in Washington later in the month, however, make little progress.

December 17. Israel Deports 415 Palestinians. Israel deports to its security zone in southern Lebanon 415 Palestinians allegedly linked to militant Arab groups. The deportation follows the kidnapping on December 13 of an Israeli border policeman. His body is found December 15. The Lebanese government refuses to admit the deportees December 18, leaving them camped in the Israeli security zone. The UN Security Council unanimously condemns the deportations December 18.

IRAN

May 8. Rafsanjani Gains Majority. Supporters of President Ali Akbar Hashemi Rafsanjani gain a majority in Iran's parliament (Majlis) in the second stage of elections. The opening round had concluded April 10. The results are seen as an endorsement of Rafsanjani's plan for a more open economy.

IRAQ

February 26. Iraq Defiant on Missiles. Iraq refuses to meet a deadline for allowing UN arms experts to begin dismantling its ballistic missile manufacturing facilities and equipment. In response, the UN Security Council February 28 condemns Iraq and warns that Baghdad will face "serious consequences" if it does not comply with UN Security Council resolutions. The council gives Iraq until the week of March 9 to resolve the impasse. The United States rejects any linkage between Iraqi compliance and an easing of UN sanctions against Iraq.

March 11. Iraq Does Not Comply. The UN Security Council tells a visiting Iraqi delegation that Iraq is not in compliance with UN Security Council resolutions. The United States warns Iraq that unless it relents and allows UN arms inspectors to dismantle missile production facilities, it will face military action.

March 20. Iraq Accepts UN Inspections. UN officials announce that Iraq, after a month of defiance, has agreed to comply with UN Security Council demands for arms inspections and dismantling of its missile production facilities. Iraqi cooperation is communicated in a letter delivered to the Security Council March 19. Iraq states

its willingness to allow the destruction of all facilities and equipment identified by UN arms inspectors.

July 2. Alleged Iraqi Coup Attempt Thwarted. Reports surface of an unsuccessful coup attempt against Saddam Hussein by Republican Guard military units. Officers loyal to the Iraqi leader reportedly put down the rebellion, which Saddam follows with a purge of the military.

July 26. Iraq Yields to Inspectors. After three weeks of refusing to let UN inspectors examine a ministry building in Baghdad, Iraq relents after the United States issues threats of military action. However, the search, carried out July 28–29, turns up nothing related to the Iraqi nuclear arms program.

August 26. No-Fly Zone Established. The United States, Great Britain, and France establish a "no-fly" zone in southern Iraq for Iraqi aircraft. Under the plan, Iraqi planes and helicopters flying south of the 32d parallel will be targeted by coalition warplanes. The move comes in response to reports of increasing attacks and harsh repression by Iraqi government forces against Shiite Muslims in the region.

December 27. Iraqi Warplane Shot Down. A U.S. fighter downs an Iraqi jet after it violates the no-fly zone in southern Iraq.

ISRAEL

February 19. Rabin to Head Labor Party. The Israeli Labor Party elects Yitzhak Rabin as its leader in a primary election, replacing Shimon Peres.

February 24. Baker on Loan Guarantees. Secretary of State Baker tells the House Appropriations Subcommittee on Foreign Operations that Israel must halt construction of new settlements on the West Bank before the Bush administration will extend $10 billion in loan guarantees to Israel. The Israeli government, which had requested the guarantees in 1991, says it will not suspend settlement activity.

June 23. Labor Party Wins in Israel. The Labor Party wins a convincing victory in Israeli parliamentary elections. It secures forty-four seats, compared with the ruling Likud Party's thirty-two. The election results are expected to strengthen the Arab-Israeli peace process. Israeli president Chaim Herzog July 2 calls on Labor Party head Yitzhak Rabin to form a government.

July 13. Rabin Forms Government. The Israeli Knesset votes 67-53 to confirm Rabin as prime minister. The Labor Party had joined with several smaller parties to create a 62-vote ruling coalition in the 120-seat Knesset. In his inaugural address, Rabin states his commitment to advancing the Arab-Israeli peace process.

August 11. Israel to Get U.S. Loan Guarantees. After two days of talks between Rabin and President George Bush in Maine, Bush announces agreement on terms for U.S. provision of $10 billion in loan guarantees to Israel. Bush had withheld the guarantees during the previous year because Israel's former Likud government had refused to restrain new settlements in the occupied territories.

KURDISH AFFAIRS

May 19. Kurds Elect Legislature. Kurds in northern Iraq hold free elections to choose a legislature. The elections result in a virtual draw between the two main political parties, which agree to share power until a runoff election can be held.

LEBANON

May 6. Lebanese Cabinet Resigns. Lebanese prime minister Omar Karami and his cabinet resign in response to a national economic crisis and collapse of the Lebanese currency. The crisis had brought on rioting in several cities. President Elias Hrawi names Rashid al-Solh premier on May 13.

August 23. Lebanese Elections. Lebanon begins the opening round of its first parliamentary elections in twenty years. Many Christians boycott the elections, charging that Syria dominates the procedure. The elections conclude October 11.

October 22. Hariri Appointed Premier. Hrawi appoints Rafiq Hariri as premier. Hariri names his thirty-member cabinet on October 31.

LIBYA AND NORTH AFRICA

March 31. UN Threatens Libya with Sanctions. The UN Security Council votes for a resolution placing sanctions against Libya if it refuses to extradite two Libyans indicted for the bombings of Pan Am Flight 103 over Scotland in 1988 and UTA Flight 772 over Niger in 1989. The pair, who are suspected of being Libyan agents, had been indicted by the United States, Great Britain, and France. Resolution 748 gives Libya until April 15 to deliver the suspects. It calls on UN members to ban air travel and military sales to Libya if it does not meet the deadline.

April 15. UN Sanctions against Libya Take Effect. United Nations sanctions against Libya take effect after Libya fails to extradite the two suspects in the Lockerbie bombing.

PALESTINIAN AFFAIRS

April 8. Arafat Survives Crash. Yasir Arafat's plane is forced to crash land in southeastern Libya during a sandstorm. He is rescued by a search party a few hours afterward. Several weeks later on June 1 he undergoes surgery to remove a blood clot from his brain that is suspected to have resulted from a head injury sustained during the crash.

PERSIAN GULF STATES

March 1. King Fahd Announces Saudi Reforms. King Fahd of Saudi Arabia issues decrees establishing a sixty-one-member Consultative Council and outlining some protections for individual rights. The council would have the authority to suggest legislation and review national policy, though ultimate power would remain with the king and the ruling Saud family. The decrees are seen as a positive, but modest, step toward greater political participation.

September 11. F-15 Sale to Saudi Arabia. U.S. president Bush approves a $9 billion sale of seventy-two F-15 fighters to Saudi Arabia. The Israeli government objects to the sale but says it will not back a campaign in the U.S. Congress to defeat it.

October 5. Kuwait Elections. Parliamentary elections are held in Kuwait for the first time since 1985. Though political parties are illegal, candidates associated with opposition groups gain a solid majority in the fifty-member parliament.

SYRIA

April 27. Syria Lifts Ban on Travel by Jews. Syria ends its restrictions on travel by its small Jewish population. The policy change is seen as a goodwill gesture toward Israel and is expected to bring the emigration of many of Syria's forty-five hundred Jews.

1993

ARAB-ISRAELI CONFLICT

January 19. Israel to Allow PLO Contacts. The Israeli parliament repeals a law prohibiting contacts between Israeli citizens and members of the PLO. The move is seen as an attempt to invigorate the peace process and deflect criticism of Israel for the December 1992 deportation of 415 Palestinians. The repeal is passed 39-20 with more than half of Knesset members absent or not voting.

February 1. Israel Proposal on Deportees. Prime Minister Rabin says Israel will allow 100 of the 415 Palestinians deported in December to return to Israel immediately. The remaining deportees would be allowed to return within a year. The deportees denounce this approach, saying they will all remain where they are. The Israeli Supreme Court had ruled January 28 that the deportations were legal. The United States indicates that in light of the Israeli announcement, it will not support sanctions or other measures against Israel that might be proposed in the UN Security Council.

February 18–24. Christopher Tours Middle East. During a tour of the Middle East, U.S. secretary of state Warren Christopher tries to restart the stalled Arab-Israeli peace talks. Arab leaders continue to demand that Israel must first take back all the Palestinians deported in December 1992. After meeting with Russian foreign minister Andrei Kozyrev in Geneva February 25, Christopher invites Arab and Israeli delegations to resume peace talks in Washington in April. Palestinian leaders reject the U.S.-Russian invitation March 10.

March 30. Israel Seals Off Territories. Rabin says in a nationally televised speech that in response to a surge of Arab violence, Israel will seal off the occupied territories indefinitely.

April 21. Peace Talks to Resume. Arab negotiators announce that they will resume peace talks with Israel. The move follows the PLO's dropping of its condition that Israel immediately repatriate all the Palestinians it deported in December 1992. Israel states that it has no plans for further deportations and that it would repatriate some of the deportees immediately and review the cases of the rest. The deportees continue to reject partial repatriation. The negotiations are set to resume April 27 in Washington.

August 15. Israeli Announces Repatriation. Israel announces that leaders of the Palestinians deported in December 1992 have accepted a two-phased repatriation plan. About half of the deportees would return from southern Lebanon in September. The other half would return in December.

August 30. Oslo Peace Negotiations Breakthrough. Foreign Minister Shimon Peres discloses a draft statement of principles on an agreement to establish Palestinian self-rule over the Gaza Strip and the West Bank city of Jericho. The agreement had been negotiated at highly secret, direct Israeli-PLO talks held in Norway and Tunisia. The talks had taken place between April and August, while public negotiations with Arab delegations proceeded in Washington.

September 9. PLO, Israel Recognize Each Other. Yasir Arafat and Rabin exchange letters of mutual recognition. In the letters, the PLO recognizes Israel's right to exist and Israel recognizes the PLO as the sole legitimate representative of the Palestinian people.

September 13. Declaration of Principles Signed. At a White House ceremony, Peres and PLO negotiator Mahmoud Abbas sign a declaration of principles for establishing interim Palestinian self-rule in the Gaza Strip and Jericho. The agreement provides for the eventual extension of self-rule to the rest of the West Bank. As three thousand guests look on, Rabin and Arafat greet each other with a historic handshake.

October 6. Arafat and Rabin Meet in Cairo. Arafat and Rabin meet in Cairo to arrange negotiations on the details of Palestinian self-rule. They agree that a series of talks to be held in Cairo and Taba, Egypt, will begin October 13.

October 19. Israel Frees Palestinian Prisoners. Israel begins releasing about six hundred Palestinian prisoners from Israeli jails.

November 2. Israeli-PLO Negotiations Stall. Negotiators for the PLO suspend talks with Israel after reaching an impasse over issues related to Israeli West Bank settlements and the role of Israeli troops in the occupied territories.

December 13. Withdrawal Date Passes. The target date for the beginning of an Israeli withdrawal from Gaza and Jericho and the transfer of power to a Palestinian authority passes without an agreement on details. Street violence in Gaza between Palestinians and Israeli troops had escalated November 24 after Israeli forces killed a local Hamas leader. Security issues remain an obstacle in Israeli-PLO negotiations on self-rule.

IRAN

January 31. Rafsanjani on Rushdie. Iranian president Rafsanjani says that the late Ayatollah Khomeini's call for the death of author Salman Rushdie cannot be lifted.

June 11. Rafsanjani Reelected. Rafsanjani is elected to a second four-year term. Rafsanjani receives just 63 percent of the vote, compared with the 95 percent he received four years earlier.

IRAQ

January 13. Jets Bomb Iraq. American, British, and French warplanes strike Iraqi targets. The attacks are a response to Iraq's placement of antiaircraft missiles in the southern no-fly zone, Iraqi incursions into Kuwait, and the Iraqi government's refusal to cooperate with international weapons inspectors. About 110 planes are used in the attack, which focuses on destroying Iraq's antiaircraft missile installations in the south. Smaller coalition strikes against surviving Iraqi missile sites and other targets take place from January 17 through January 23. Iraq announces January 19 that it will not resist coalition air patrols over its territory.

June 26. U.S. Strikes Iraq. In response to evidence that Iraq sponsored an assassination plot against former U.S. president Bush when he visited Kuwait, the United States launches a cruise missile attack against the Iraqi intelligence service headquarters in Baghdad. Twenty-three cruise missiles are fired from U.S. warships in the Persian Gulf.

November 26. Iraq Accepts Resolution 715. Iraq agrees to abide by UN Security Council Resolution 715. The resolution mandates intrusive UN inspections to prevent Iraq from developing weapons of mass destruction. The move is seen as part of Iraq's campaign to build support for a lifting of the economic sanctions imposed against it since its 1990 invasion of Kuwait.

ISRAEL

March 25. Netanyahu Takes Over Likud. Benjamin Netanyahu is elected to replace retiring Yitzhak Shamir as leader of Israel's Likud Party. Netanyahu, age forty-three, was a deputy foreign minister in Shamir's government.

July 25. Israel Attacks Hizballah. Israel carries out intense air and artillery assaults in southern Lebanon in retaliation for rocket attacks by Hizballah guerrillas. Hizballah responds by firing more rockets into northern Israel. A U.S.-mediated cease-fire agreement goes into effect July 31, ending a week of Israeli attacks.

December 30. Israel and Vatican Establish Ties. Israel and the Vatican establish diplomatic relations at a ceremony in Jerusalem. Eighteen months of negotiations had preceded the agreement.

LIBYA AND NORTH AFRICA

April 8. Libya Sanctions Renewed. The UN Security Council votes to renew sanctions on Libya for its refusal to extradite the Lockerbie suspects. For lack of support, however, the United States drops its proposal to expand the sanctions to include an embargo of Libyan oil.

November 11. Sanctions on Libya Tightened. The UN Security Council votes to tighten economic sanctions on Libya for its refusal to extradite the Lockerbie suspects. The additional measures include a ban on the sale of oil industry equipment and the freezing of Libya's overseas assets.

PALESTINIAN AFFAIRS

October 1. Aid Pledged for Palestinians. A conference of forty-three nations meeting in Washington pledges $2 billion in aid for the new Palestinian entity. The United States pledges $500 million over five years.

PERSIAN GULF STATES

April 14–16. Bush Visits Kuwait. Former U.S. president Bush visits Kuwait as a private citizen. He is hailed as a national hero for his role in the liberation of Kuwait from Iraqi occupation. The Kuwaiti government announces April 27 that it had arrested a group of Iraqis who had plotted to assassinate Bush during his visit. FBI investigators assert May 19 that the Iraqi government was linked to the plot.

YEMEN

April 27. Yemen Election. The Republic of Yemen holds its first parliamentary elections since the unification of North Yemen and South Yemen in 1990.

1994

ARAB-ISRAELI CONFLICT

January 16. Asad on Peace Treaty. For the first time, President Asad publicly voices Syria's willingness to negotiate a peace treaty with Israel if Israel returns the Golan Heights. His comments follow a meeting with U.S. president Clinton in Geneva.

February 9. Cairo Document Signed. Foreign Minister Peres and Arafat sign the Cairo Document, which details security procedures related to the transfer of power to a Palestinian authority. The agreement removes the largest obstacle to implementation of Palestinian self-rule in Gaza and Jericho.

February 25. Hebron Massacre. Baruch Goldstein, a Jewish settler, opens fire with an assault rifle on praying Muslim worshippers in Hebron on the West Bank, killing twenty-nine. The attack takes place at the mosque of the Tomb of the Patriarchs, revered as the burial place of Abraham, Isaac, and Jacob. Goldstein, a reserve captain in the Israeli army who had immigrated from New York City, is killed by the crowd at the mosque. Palestinians riot and clash with security forces. Eleven more Palestinians and one Israeli are killed before the end of the day. Arab delegations break off peace talks with Israel in response to the violence.

February 28. Arafat Calls for International Troops. Arafat calls for an international peacekeeping force to ensure the safety of Palestinians in the occupied territories.

March 18. Talks to Resume. U.S. secretary of state Warren Christopher announces that Syria, Jordan, and Lebanon have agreed to resume talks with Israel. The move follows passage of a UN Security Council resolution condemning the Hebron massacre. The PLO consents to reopen talks with Israel March 31 after the two sides agree on terms allowing foreign monitors to be stationed in Hebron.

April 6. Car Bomb Kills Eight. A suicide car bombing destroys an Israeli bus in Afula, Israel, killing eight people and wounding more than forty others. Both Hamas and the smaller Islamic Jihad group claim responsibility for the blast, calling it retaliation for the Hebron killings in February.

April 12. PLO, Israel Agree on Prisoner Release. In Cairo, Israeli and PLO negotiators agree on terms for Israel's release of five thousand Palestinian prisoners and the PLO's establishment of a police authority in Palestinian-administered areas.

April 21. Rabin Golan Statement. Speaking in Jerusalem, Rabin says Israel would be willing to tear down settlements in the Golan Heights as part of a peace agreement with Syria.

May 4. Palestinian Self-Rule Pact Signed. Arafat and Rabin sign an agreement in Cairo implementing Palestinian self-rule in the Gaza Strip and Jericho. The agreement fulfills the intent of the Declaration of Principles signed in September 1993. It contains a detailed plan for establishing Palestinian civil authority over Gaza and Jericho.

May 13. Israelis Withdraw from Jericho and Gaza. Under the terms of the self-rule agreement, Israeli troops withdraw from Jericho and are replaced by Palestinian police. Israeli troops leave Gaza May 18.

May 21. Muslim Leader Abducted. Mustafa al-Dirani, a Lebanese Muslim guerrilla leader, is kidnapped from his home in the Bekaa Valley by Israeli forces. Israel says it hopes to gain information from Dirani regarding airman Ron Arad, missing since he was shot down in 1986.

June 26. Hebron Massacre Investigation. An investigative panel chaired by Israeli supreme court president Meir Shamgar clears the Israeli army of responsibility for the deaths of twenty-nine Palestinians killed at a mosque in Hebron in February. The report, however, criticizes security methods at the site and makes recommendations for preventing future tragedies. The Shamgar Commission concludes that Baruch Goldstein, the Jewish settler who committed the killings, acted alone.

July 17. Israeli and Palestinian Forces Exchange Fire. The first confrontation between Israeli troops and Palestinian police since Palestinian self-rule had been instituted occurs at a checkpoint in northern Gaza. The skirmish begins when Palestinian laborers throw stones at Israeli troops. The incident escalates into a day of riots that leaves two Palestinians dead and approximately one hundred injured.

July 18. Jordanian-Israeli Talks. Jordanian and Israeli peace negotiators meet in a tent straddling their border. It is the first time the delegations from the two nations have met publicly in their own region.

July 25. Washington Declaration Signed. Jordan's King Hussein and Rabin sign the Washington Declaration before several hundred guests at a White House ceremony. The document ends the state of war between the two countries and commits them to negotiate a comprehensive peace. Rabin and Hussein address a joint session of the U.S. Congress on July 26.

August 29. Palestinians Gain Authority Beyond Jericho. Israel and the PLO sign an agreement granting the Palestinian Authority (PA) administrative power over some economic, education, and social welfare functions throughout the West Bank.

September 8. Rabin States Position on Syria. Rabin offers a "very partial" Israeli withdrawal from the Golan Heights, to be accompanied by a three-year period of normal relations with Syria. A successful testing period would set the stage for a total Israeli withdrawal and an Israeli-Syrian peace treaty. Syria responds that a complete withdrawal should take place without a testing period.

October 9. Israeli Soldier Kidnapped. Palestinians abduct Cpl. Nahshon Waxman near Jerusalem. Hamas threatens to kill Waxman if Israel refuses to release two hundred Palestinian prisoners. When reports suggest during the following week that Waxman is being held in the Palestinian-controlled Gaza Strip, Rabin says he will hold Arafat responsible and suspend implementation of Palestinian self-rule in Gaza and Jericho if Arafat's government does not secure Waxman's release.

October 11. Hussein on Treaty. King Hussein announces that Jordan will sign a full peace treaty with Israel if remaining issues can be resolved. He says Jordan will not wait for Syria and Lebanon to make peace with Israel.

October 14. Nobel Peace Prize Announcement. Arafat, Rabin, and Peres are named recipients of the 1994 Nobel Peace Prize. The awards are presented December 10 in Oslo, Norway.

October 14. Israeli Soldier Killed. Three Hamas kidnappers and their Israeli hostage, Cpl. Nahshon Waxman, are killed when Israeli commandos assault a house on the West Bank where Waxman was being held. An Israeli commando also is killed in the raid. Israeli intelligence had discovered that Waxman was being held near where he had been kidnapped, rather than in the Gaza Strip as at first suspected.

October 17. Israel and Jordan Initial Draft Accord. Prime Ministers Rabin and Abd al-Salam al-Majali initial a draft Israeli-Jordanian peace treaty in Amman. The accord provides for full diplomatic relations and economic and security cooperation. Annexes to a final agreement remain to be negotiated, but a signing ceremony for a formal treaty is scheduled for October 26.

October 19. Tel Aviv Bus Attack. A member of the Hamas movement boards a bus in downtown Tel Aviv and detonates an explosive charge that kills him and twenty-one passengers. About fifty people are wounded. Hamas identifies the bomber as twenty-seven-year-old Salah Abdal Rahim Nazal Souwi. Israel seals its borders with the occupied territories in response to the Tel Aviv bombing.

October 26. Jordan-Israeli Peace Treaty Signed. Israel and Jordan sign a comprehensive peace treaty. The signing takes place in front of 4,500 guests at the border crossing between the two nations. The treaty is signed by Prime Ministers Rabin and Abd al-Salam al-Majali. U.S. President Clinton signs as a witness. The treaty normalizes relations between the two countries, settles land and water disputes, and provides for wide-ranging cooperation on economic and security issues.

November 8. Agreement to Bolster PA. In an effort to strengthen the Palestinian Authority against its Hamas rivals, the Israeli government and the PLO agree to speed the transfer of authority for some government functions throughout the West Bank to the Palestinian Authority. Israel also agrees to admit more Palestinian day laborers.

December 6. Arafat Pledges to Curb Terrorism. During a meeting with Secretary of State Christopher in Gaza, Arafat pledges to work to stop attacks against Israel by Palestinians. Israel says December 8 that if the Palestinian Authority is able to ensure the security of Israeli settlers, it will carry out a commitment to withdraw troops from Palestinian population centers.

EGYPT

September 5–13. Cairo Conference. Cairo hosts the third UN Conference on Population and Development.

IRAN

June 20. Bomb Kills Twenty-Five in Iran. A bomb at a crowded religious service in the Iranian city of Mashad kills twenty-five people gathered for a Shiite religious commemoration. An Iraqi-based opposition movement, the People's Mujahedeen (Mujaheddin-e khalq), initially claims responsibility, although a Paris office of the group condemns the attack.

IRAQ

April 14. U.S. Downs UN Helicopters. U.S. warplanes mistakenly shoot down two American helicopters on a UN mission over northern Iraq. Twenty-six UN representatives are killed, including fifteen Americans.

July 24. Saudis Sought Iraqi Nuclear Technology. The *Sunday Times* of London reports that the Saudi government allegedly gave Iraq $5 billion in exchange for information on Iraq's nuclear weapons program during the late 1980s. A high-ranking Saudi diplomat reportedly disclosed the deal while seeking asylum in the United States. The exchange ceased with the Iraqi invasion of Kuwait in August 1990.

October 8. Clinton Orders Buildup. U.S. president Clinton orders a U.S. military buildup in Saudi Arabia and the Persian Gulf region in response to an Iraqi buildup of troops in southern Iraq. About 20,000 Republican Guard troops had moved to positions near the Kuwaiti border. More than 36,000 U.S. troops are sent to the region, along with additional warplanes and several ships. Iraqi troops begin pulling back from the border October 11.

November 14. Iraq Sanctions Retained. The UN Security Council votes to retain its sanctions against Iraq. The move comes despite a November 10 declaration by Saddam Hussein that Iraq would recognize Kuwait's sovereignty and territorial integrity.

PALESTINIAN AFFAIRS

July 1. Arafat Returns to Gaza. Yasir Arafat returns to the Gaza Strip after twenty-seven years in exile. He is welcomed by thousands of Palestinian supporters. Arafat visits Jericho July 5, where he takes an oath of office as president of the Palestinian Authority.

November 18. Palestinian Police Fire on Militants. Palestinian police in the Gaza Strip for the first time fire upon Hamas demonstrators. The clash leads to a day of violence that leaves at least fifteen dead. Hamas leaders denounce the police for firing on fellow Palestinians. A truce goes into effect November 19.

November 30. Meeting of Donors Brings Aid. A meeting of twenty-two donor nations in Brussels produces an agreement to provide $200 million in immediate financial aid to the Palestinian Authority. The development aid is intended to solidify Palestinian support for the peace process.

YEMEN

July 7. Northern Yemen Captures Aden. Northern Yemeni forces capture the southern city of Aden, effectively ending a two-month civil war.

September 28. Yemen's Parliament Adopts New Constitution. Yemen passes a new constitution and announces that presidents will be elected by universal suffrage for a five-year term with the right to appoint their own vice presidents. The House of Representatives re-elects President Ali Abdallah Salih.

1995

REGIONAL AFFAIRS

February 8. World Trade Center Bombing Mastermind Arraigned. Ramzi Ahmad Yusuf, accused of being the mastermind of the bombing February 26, 1993, at the World Trade Center in New York City, is arraigned in New York and pleads not guilty to all charges. Yusuf had been arrested in Pakistan on February 7 and extradited to the United States the next day.

June 10. Iran and Iraq Agree to Investigate Prisoners of War. Iranian brigadier general Najafi announces that Iran and Iraq will exchange documentation on prisoners of war and establish committees to search for remains of soldiers considered missing in action during the Iran-Iraq war from 1980 to 1988. On September 9 Iranian and Iraqi officials meet to discuss identification of bodies. In October, the two countries exchange the bodies of fifteen Iranians and sixty-one Iraqis killed during the war.

October 31. Region Establishes Middle East Development Bank. Participants in the Middle East/North Africa Economic Summit in Amman, Jordan, announce the Middle East Development Bank to be capitalized at $5 billion and located in Cairo. Egypt, Israel, and the PLO had proposed its creation in January at a meeting with thirty-nine countries and financial institutions.

ARAB-ISRAELI CONFLICT

January 2. U.S. Citizen Convicted by Israel. An Israeli military court convicts Muhammad Salah, a U.S. citizen of Palestinian origin, of channeling funds to Hamas. He is sentenced to five years imprisonment.

January 9. Peres and Arafat Strike Agreements. At the Erez checkpoint, Israeli foreign minister Shimon Peres and PLO chairman Yasir Arafat meet. Peres agrees to allow: Israeli recognition of Palestinian passports, Palestinian vehicles to use Israeli roads, Palestinian men over fifty and students to cross between Gaza and Jericho, and cooperation in the construction of an industrial park in the West Bank.

January 16. Israel Grants Egypt Most-Favored-Nation Trading Status. Egyptian foreign ministry sources report that Israel has granted Egypt most-favored-nation trading status.

January 16. Israel and Jordan Reach Transportation Agreement. Israeli transportation ministry representative Otniel Schneller announces that Israel and Jordan have agreed to build rail lines from Haifa in Israel to Irbid in Jordan, from the Dead Sea to Aqaba and Eilat, and from al-Safi, Jordan, to the southern Dead Sea.

January 19. Arafat and Rabin Discuss Israeli Construction. Arafat and Israeli prime minister Yitzhak Rabin meet at the Erez checkpoint where Rabin agrees to halt approval of new settlements and monitor existing construction. He states that further land confiscations from Arabs would be for the purpose of road construction to circumvent Arab towns and to hasten Israeli military evacuations.

January 22. Car Bombs Explode in Bet Lid. Two car bombs explode in Bet Lid, Israel, killing nineteen people and wounding sixty-one. Islamic Jihad claims responsibility. As a result, Israel closes its borders with Gaza and the West Bank and suspends Israeli-Palestinian negotiations.

January 24. Clinton Freezes U.S. Assets of Alleged Terrorist Groups. U.S. president Clinton orders a freeze on U.S. assets of groups suspected of terrorist activities. Twelve organizations and eighteen individuals are affected, including Hamas, Islamic Jihad, Kach, Kahane Chai, and the Popular Front for the Liberation of Palestine.

January 30. Israel Turns Over Territory to Jordan. As part of the October 1994 Israeli-Jordanian peace treaty, Israel releases to Jordan 132 square miles of land located along the Arava Valley.

February 2. Egypt, Israel, Jordan, and the PLO Meet in Cairo. In Cairo, Arafat, Jordan's King Hussein, Egyptian president Mubarak, and Rabin meet to revive the peace process. They agree to talks on Palestinian elections, Israeli withdrawal from the West Bank, and Israeli settlements. They release a joint statement condemning violence, reiterating commitment to the peace process, calling for increased financial support of the Palestinian Authority, and supporting establishment of a regional development bank.

February 6. Israel and Jordan Sign Agriculture Accord. Israel and Jordan agree to cooperate on agricultural marketing, hygiene, research, and technology. On the same day, direct postal service begins between the two countries in accordance with the October 1994 treaty.

February 8. Details of Israeli "Separation" Plan Announced. Israeli police minister Shahal reveals that the "separation" plan, which the Israeli cabinet had instructed him to design in January, consists of patrol roads along the border with the West Bank, observation posts, patrols, and electronic surveillance. On February 27 the Palestinian-Israeli Economic Committee agrees that Israeli moves toward security "separation" will not interfere with Palestinian-Israeli economic cooperation.

March 9. Peres and Arafat Make Promises. At the Erez checkpoint, Arafat and Peres set a July 1, 1995, target date for agreements on Israeli military redeployment in the West Bank and Palestinian elections. Arafat promises to crack down on Islamists, and Peres vows to open safe transportation lines between Gaza and the West Bank and to allow 22,000 Palestinian laborers into Israel.

March 14. Syrian-Israeli Peace Talks to Resume. In Damascus, U.S. secretary of state Christopher meets with Syrian president Asad. Asad agrees to direct talks with Israel. Israeli officials later report that Asad has agreed with Christopher to establish low-level diplomatic relations with Israel before complete Israeli withdrawal from the Golan Heights.

March 16. PA Rejects Israeli Proposal on Gaza. The Palestinian Authority rejects Israel's proposal to establish a Palestinian state in Gaza and to postpone talks on the status of the West Bank for twenty years.

April 10. Jordan and Israel Exchange First Ambassadors. Marwan al-Muashir, Jordan's first ambassador to Israel, presents his credentials to the Israeli government, and Shimon Shamir, Israel's first ambassador to Jordan, presents his credentials to the Jordanian government.

April 26. Saudi Arabia Rescinds Demand. Saudi Arabia rescinds its March 1995 requirement that Israeli Arabs traveling to Mecca hold a Palestinian passport.

April 28. PA and Israel Agree on Aid. The Palestinian Authority and Israel agree to accept $60 million from international donors toward meeting the PA's $136-million budget gap.

May 8. PA to Acquire Control over Economic Sectors. In Cairo, Peres meets with the Palestinian Authority minister of planning and international cooperation, Nabil Shaath. The Palestinian Authority acquires jurisdiction over banking, energy, industry, labor, and securities in the West Bank. Israel agrees to increase work permits for Palestinians in Israel by five thousand, to a total of thirty-one thousand. The two sides also agree to establish a committee to examine Israeli land expropriations in East Jerusalem.

May 9. U.S. Official Advocates Embassy Transfer. U.S. senator Robert Dole introduces legislation in Congress calling for the transfer of the U.S. embassy from Tel Aviv to Jerusalem. Congress approves the bill on October 24 specifying the move will take place by 1999, but it includes a provision allowing the president to delay the move for national security reasons.

May 17. United States Vetoes UN Resolution. The United States vetoes a UN resolution to condemn as illegal the Israeli confiscation of Palestinian land in the West Bank near East Jerusalem. Meanwhile, in Amman, Jordan, sixty of the eighty members of the Jordanian parliament call for the suspension of the peace agreement with Israel to protest Israel's seizure of Palestinian land bordering East Jerusalem. On May 22 Israel suspends plans to confiscate 131 acres of land on the outskirts of East Jerusalem. The move avoided a no-confidence vote and caused cancellation of an Arab summit to discuss the land confiscations.

June 6. PA to Receive All Civilian Powers. Israeli negotiators agree to transfer all civilian powers to elected Palestinian authorities following Palestinian elections in Gaza and the West Bank.

June 21. Israel and PA Sign Communications Agreement. The Palestinian Authority and Israel sign an agreement that establishes a television station in Ramallah and a radio station in Gaza.

June 28. Syria and Israel Reach an Agreement. Israeli sources state that Israeli-Syrian talks in Washington have resulted in an agreement in principle that a Golan Heights settlement will include a demilitarized zone, a limited-militarized zone, an early-warning system, and confidence-building measures between members of the Israeli and Syrian armies.

July 20. Israel Arrests PA Suspects. Israeli police report they have arrested eleven Palestinians in Jerusalem suspected of conducting official Palestinian Authority security operations in Israel.

July 24. Suicide Bombing Near Tel Aviv. In Ramat Gan, near Tel Aviv, a suicide bomber detonates a bomb on a bus, killing himself and five others and wounding thirty-two. Israel responds by suspending negotiations with the Palestinians and blocking entry to Palestinian laborers from Gaza and the West Bank. Hamas claims responsibility. Negotiations resume on July 30, and Israel reopens its borders to male Palestinian workers over age thirty. Hizballah-Palestine claims responsibility for the bombing on August 1.

July 25. United States Arrests Hamas Leader. In New York City, U.S. immigration officials arrest Musa Muhammad Abu Marzuq, alleged leader of Hamas's political committee, on suspicion of raising funds to support terrorism. On July 31 Israel issues a warrant for the arrest of Marzuq. U.S. prosecutors in New York City announce, on August 9, that Hamas member Marzuq had raised funds, recruited, and organized terrorist activities for Hamas in Israel. On October 5 Israel formally requests that the United States extradite Marzuq to Israel.

July 31. Israeli Security Forces Evict Jewish Settlers. Israeli security forces evict Jewish settlers from a hilltop they have occupied near Efrat, south of Bethlehem, arresting 213. Security forces also seize radio transmission equipment, which the settlers had used to operate a radio program. Two hundred supporters of the settlers clash with police in Jerusalem on August 2. On August 13, Israeli forces remove more Jewish settlers from the hilltop.

August 21. Bomb Explodes in Jerusalem. A bomb explodes on a bus, killing five and wounding sixty. Hamas claims responsibility. Israel suspends talks with the PLO and seals its borders with Gaza and the West Bank. Despite violent clashes with right-wing Jewish groups following the explosion, Israel resumes talks with the Palestinians on August 22 in the southern city of Eilat.

September 8. Palestinian Homes Invaded by Jewish Extremists. In Halhul, in the West Bank, five men impersonating Israeli soldiers enter Palestinian homes and kill one Palestinian. The right-wing Jewish group Eyal claims responsibility.

September 10. Jewish Settlers Forcibly Enter Palestinian School. In Hebron, Jewish settlers enter a Muslim girls' school to remove a Palestinian flag. They clash with female students and teachers, hospitalizing the school's headmistress and four students. The conflict continues September 13 when Israeli security forces use tear gas to break up a fight between Jewish settlers and Palestinians defending the flag. Israeli forces also battle stone-throwing Palestinians protesting the recent activities and presence of Jewish settlers in Hebron.

September 18. Negotiators Reach Agreement in Taba. Israeli and Palestinian representatives agree that the Palestinian council will consist of eighty-two members; that Israel will withdraw from Palestinian population centers within one hundred days; that Palestinian elections will occur twenty-two days after the Israeli withdrawal; and that Israel will release five thousand Palestinian prisoners. They also agree on terms for distributing water.

September 28. Oslo II Agreement Signed in Washington. Arafat and Rabin sign the Taba Agreement, known as the "Oslo II" agreement, expanding Palestinian self-rule in the West Bank. Egyptian president Mubarak, Jordan's King Hussein, and U.S. president Clinton preside over the signing. One thousand Jewish settlers protest the accord in Hebron, while an unspecified number of Palestinians tear down fences protecting a road from the Jewish settlement in Hebron. The next day, settlers destroy Palestinian property during a march from the Tomb of the Patriarchs to their enclave in Beit Hadassah, Hebron.

October 10. West Bank Town Handed Over to the PA. As part of the Oslo II agreement, Israel releases some nine hundred Palestinians in its custody and hands over authority of the West Bank town of Salfit to the Palestinian Authority.

October 11. PA Gains Control of West Bank Towns. Israel relinquishes authority over the West Bank towns of Kharbata, Qabatiyya, and Yatta to the Palestinian Authority.

October 17. United States and PA Agree to Preferential Trade Agreement. U.S. trade representative Mickey Kantor announces that the United States has agreed to a preferential trade agreement with the Palestinian Authority. In return, the PA agrees to work toward lifting the Arab trade boycott of Israel.

October 26. Islamic Jihad Leader Killed. In Malta, unidentified assailants fatally shoot Fathi Shiqaqi, the leader of Islamic Jihad.

November 4. Yitzhak Rabin Assassinated. In Tel Aviv, Yigal Amir, an Israeli law student at Bar-Ilan University, fatally shoots Israeli prime minister Rabin after a pro–peace process rally. Foreign minister Peres becomes acting prime minister. On December 5 the Israeli district attorney formally charges Yigal Amir with the premeditated murder. Haggai Amir and Dror Adani are charged with conspiracy to kill Rabin.

November 13. PA Gains Control of Janin. In Janin, celebrations mark the evacuation of Israeli forces and the assumption of full control of the city by the Palestinian Authority.

December 9. PA Begins to Assume Control. The Palestinian Authority gains control of the West Bank town of Tulkarm. On December 12 Palestinians celebrate when Israeli forces withdraw from the city of Nablus and the Palestinian Authority takes over. The PA takes over Bethlehem on December 21 and Ramallah on December 27.

December 27. Syria and Israel Resume Negotiations. At the Wye Conference Center in Maryland, Israeli representative Uri Savir, Syrian ambassador to the United States Walid al-Mualim, and U.S. special envoy Stuart Ross meet to discuss an Israeli-Syrian peace agreement. On December 29 negotiations recess until January 3, 1996.

EGYPT

March 29. Two Executed for Attempted Murder. Two men are executed for the attempted murder of Nobel Laureate Najib Mahfuz. His killers had objected to the writer's advocacy of Arab-Israeli peace. Other Islamists continue to battle government forces, primarily in Upper Egypt.

April 13. Rector of al-Azhar University Sued. The Egyptian Organization for Human Rights reportedly sues Shaykh Ali Jad al-Haq, rector of al-Azhar University, because of a fatwa he published in October 1994 advocating female circumcision.

June 26. President Mubarak's Motorcade Attacked. In Addis Ababa, Ethiopia, President Mubarak's motorcade is attacked en route to a meeting of the Organization of African Unity. Mubarak, unharmed, blames the Sudan. On July 4, after Ethiopia captures several Egyptian perpetrators, the Egyptian Islamic Group claims responsibility.

August 25. Mubarak Offers Iraqi President Hussein Asylum. Mubarak offers Iraqi president Saddam Hussein asylum in Egypt in order to ensure the stability of Iraq. The day before, Egypt, Jordan, Kuwait, and Saudi Arabia agree to a U.S. diplomatic initiative to remove the Iraqi leader from power.

September 16. Muslim Brothers Tried. The trial of forty-nine Muslim Brotherhood members, charged with attempting to revive the organization, begins in the Supreme Military Court. Three thousand Cairo University students demonstrate against the trial on October 17.

October 1. Shaykh Umar Abd al-Rahman Found Guilty. In New York, a U.S. federal court finds Egyptian Shaykh Umar Abd al-Rahman and nine others guilty of conspiring to commit terrorist acts in the United States.

October 18. Police Crackdown on Islamists. In the southern governorate of al-Minya, police announce that a week-long series of raids has resulted in the arrest of 107 suspected Islamists and 1,367 nonpolitical criminals.

October 31. Police Arrest Muslim Brotherhood Leader. Sayf al-Islam Hasan Banna, son of Muslim Brotherhood founder Hasan al-Banna, is arrested.

November 8. Dutch and French Citizens Wounded. Unknown gunmen fire on a Dutch citizen and a French citizen near Luxor.

IRAN

February 1. Norway Withdraws Ambassador Indefinitely. Following a diplomatic dispute regarding the death sentence of author Salman Rushdie and the 1993 wounding of Rushdie's publisher, William Nygaard, Norway withdraws its ambassador and prohibits official visits and promotions of trade between the two countries. Norway later finds no connection between Iran and the shooting of Nygaard but recalls its ambassador July 3 because Iran refuses to rescind its death warrant on Salman Rushdie.

February 28. Iran Increases Troops. U.S. military officials state that Iran has increased its troops on islands in the Strait of Hormuz from 700 to 4,000 since October 1994 and has stationed antiaircraft and antiship missiles on the islands.

May 8. U.S. Trade Ban on Iran. The United States announces a ban on all trade between U.S. companies and Iran.

IRAQ

January 10. Iraq Retains Military Equipment. U.S. ambassador to the UN Madeleine Albright displays satellite photographs and intelligence reports that illustrate that Iraq still has more than nine thousand pieces of Kuwaiti military equipment, in violation of UN Resolutions 686 and 687.

January 19. Hussein and Son Survive Coup Attempt. The *Wall Street Journal* reports that Iraqi president Saddam Hussein and his son Udayy Saddam survived an assassination attempt in early January. On March 3 the younger Hussein is wounded in a coup attempt. Executions and arrests follow both incidents. A Kuwaiti source claims, May 1, that Saddam's son had been wounded in an ambush by an Iraqi opposition group.

March 13. U.S. Nationals Arrested. Two U.S. nationals working in Kuwait, William Barloon and David Daliberti, are arrested by Iraqi police when UN border guards mistake the Americans' vehicle for one belonging to the UN. Iraq sentences them to eight years imprisonment on March 25 and releases them on July 16.

April 14. UN Approves Oil Sales. The UN Security Council approves a plan to allow the Iraqi government to sell $2 billion of oil every 180 days, subject to review every 90 days. The revenue from the sales will subsidize humanitarian aid. Thirty percent will support Kuwaiti victims of the 1990 invasion. The government rejects the plan April 17.

June 14. Shiite and Government Forces Clash. Shiite Iraqi opposition sources in Damascus report that several Iraqi army units clashed with each other in Abu Ghrayb, west of Baghdad. Members of the al-Dulaymi tribe participate. Three hundred tribesmen are executed July 2, according to Kurdistan Democratic Party (KDP) radio.

July 11. Iraqi Sanctions Retained. During a UN Security Council meeting to review sanctions against Iraq, U.S. representative Madeleine Albright states that Iraq has enough biological weapons to kill tens of thousands of people. The UN Security Council retains the sanctions.

August 8. President Hussein's Sons-In-Law Defect. Minister of Industry and Minerals Lt. Gen. Hussein Kamel Hassan al-Majid and his brother, Lt. Col. Saddam Kamel al-Majid, defect to Jordan with an unspecified number of family members, including their wives, and military officers. Jordan's King Hussein grants all of them political asylum.

ISRAEL

February 8. Israeli Evacuations from Northern Iraq. Israeli officials reportedly evacuate one thousand people of "Jewish extraction" from northern Iraq via Turkey.

September 12. Israel Appoints Arab Ambassador. Israel sends Ali Adib Hasan Yahya to Finland as its first Arab Israeli ambassador.

November 21. Jonathan Pollard Granted Citizenship. The government grants Israeli citizenship to Jonathan Pollard, whom the United States convicted in 1987 of spying for Israel.

November 22. Shimon Peres Becomes Prime Minister. Following the assassination of Yitzhak Rabin, Shimon Peres is sworn in as prime minister of Israel.

JORDAN

January 21. Mubarak and Hussein Meet. For the first time since Egypt suspended diplomatic relations with Jordan in 1990, Egyptian president Mubarak meets with King Hussein in Aqaba, Jordan.

September 25. Debt to United States Canceled. Jordan and the United States sign an agreement that cancels Jordan's $400 million debt to the United States.

November 27. Foreign Workers Leave Country. Jordan's labor minister reports that nearly 30 percent of foreign workers left the country by the end of October because of government efforts to reduce the number of foreigners competing for low-wage jobs.

KURDISH AFFAIRS

March 20. Turkey Establishes Buffer Zone. Approximately 35,000 Turkish forces invade northern Iraq to crack down on the Iraqi-based Kurdish Workers' Party (PKK). On May 4 the Turkish defense minister announces that Turkish forces have been completely withdrawn from northern Iraq.

March 26. Kurds Evacuated by United Nations. The United Nations evacuates 1,000 Kurds from Zakho, Turkey, because of the Kurdish offensive in Iraq. Fearing Turkish Army soldiers, 177 Kurdish refugees force their way into a UN aid base in northern Iraq on March 28. The UN agrees to transport the refugees to safety.

April 12. Kurdish Parliament Established. In The Hague, sixty-six Kurdish delegates from Iran, Iraq, and Turkey establish a Kurdish parliament.

July 5. Turkish Forces Invade Iraq Again. Turkish officials report that their forces have attacked PKK bases in northern Iraq. Kurdistan Democratic Party (KDP) sources allege that Turkish soldiers had attacked eighteen villages and caused three thousand Kurds to flee by the end of the invasion, July 12.

August 11. KDP and PUK Officials Meet in Drogheda, Ireland. Under U.S. auspices, the KDP and Patriotic Union of Kurdistan (PUK) agree to a cease-fire of longstanding hostilities in northern Iraq. They agree to release each other's prisoners of war and continue peace talks.

September 15. PUK and KDP Representatives Meet. In Dublin, the PUK and KDP again meet to discuss an end to the conflict between the two groups. They convene again on October 9 in Tehran. Despite continuing third-party mediation, clashes continue.

LEBANON

February 1. Beirut Stock Exchange to Reopen. The Lebanese government allocates $1 million to finance the reopening of the stock exchange, which closed in 1983. The exchange opens on September 25.

February 8. Israel Blockades Port of Tyre. The Israeli navy blockades Tyre. On February 23 it extends the blockade of the Lebanese coast to Sidon. Approximately eighteen hundred Lebanese fishermen are without work until Israel lifts the blockade March 9.

March 14. Nationwide Strike. A nationwide strike halts official and business activity to protest the Israeli occupation of southern Lebanon.

May 21. New Government Forms. Lebanese prime minister Rafiq Hariri returns to office after resigning the day before. On May 25 President Elias Hrawi announces a new government.

June 24. Samir Geagea Sentenced. Five judges, one from each main religious community, sentence Samir Geagea, a leader of Christian forces during the civil war, to life imprisonment for killing Christian politician Danny Chamoun, his wife, and one of their children in 1990.

September 15. United States Eases Ban on Air Travel. A ten-year-old ban on air travel to Lebanon is eased to allow U.S. airlines to route passengers to Lebanon via a third country and airline.

October 19. Lebanese Constitution Amended. Parliament amends the constitution to allow President Elias Hrawi to extend his six-year term to nine years.

LIBYA AND NORTH AFRICA

March 29. State Airline to Transport Pilgrims. In defiance of a UN ban on Libyan flights, Libyan president Qadhafi says that he will use the state airline to transport pilgrims to Mecca and that he will leave the United Nations if he is prevented from doing so. On April 19 the UN Security Council eases its ban on Libyan air flights to allow Libyan pilgrims to make the hajj to Mecca. Two airplanes land in Jidda, Saudi Arabia. Egyptian airliners also fly pilgrims to Saudi Arabia on April 20.

March 31. UN Security Council Extends Sanctions. The UN Security Council extends sanctions against Libya because of its refusal to hand over two Libyans wanted for bombing Pan Am flight 103 in 1988. On May 23 the U.S. Federal Bureau of Investigation offers a $4-million reward for the apprehension of the two suspects.

September 3. Libya Expels Palestinians. To protest Israeli-Palestinian negotiations on extending Palestinian self-rule in the West Bank, Qadhafi expels thousands of Palestinians living in Libya. By mid-October most Palestinians stranded on the Egyptian-Libyan border are allowed to return to Libya while others travel to Gaza via Egypt.

September 10. Islamists Arrested. After government and Islamist forces clash in the Mediterranean coastal town of Benghazi on September 1 and 8, Libyan authorities arrest thirty-five hundred Islamic rebels.

PALESTINIAN AFFAIRS

January 21. PFLP Reveals Financial Woes. The Popular Front for the Liberation of Palestine (PFLP) reportedly disbands 30 percent of its fighters and stops payments to families who had lost members in PFLP service.

January 26. Jordan and the PLO Sign Accord. Jordanian and Palestine Liberation Organization (PLO) officials sign an accord that will turn over control of Muslim holy sites in Jerusalem to the PLO if it acquires authority over East Jerusalem. The agreement also stipulates that the Jordanian dinar will become the official currency in the territories of Palestinian self-rule.

February 13. Human Rights Watch Issues Report. The New York–based Human Rights Watch releases a report that accuses the Palestinian Authority of "political arrests, press censorship, and prisoner beating."

February 26. Arafat Cuts Back Police. PLO chairman Arafat terminates police recruitment and announces plans to fire two thousand police from its force of nine thousand. An agreement with Israel had limited the Palestinian Authority to six thousand officers.

March 24. U.S.-PLO Aid Agreement Announced. In Jericho, U.S. vice president Gore meets with Arafat and announces that $65 million in U.S. aid will be given to the Palestinian Authority. Gore says that products and produce from the PA-administered areas will enter the United States duty-free.

April 11. Splinter Groups Support PA. The Right Movement for Championing the Palestinian People's Sons splits from Hamas and declares support for the Palestinian Authority. The Palestinian National Democratic Grouping splits from the PFLP and allies with the PA.

April 12. PA Curtails Firearms. The Palestinian Authority orders the registration of all firearms by May 11. Palestinian police also arrest an unspecified number of Islamic Resistance Movement (Hamas) and Islamic Jihad supporters.

May 4. Palestine Telecommunications Company Planned. Palestinian Authority minister of planning and international cooperation Nabil Shaath announces that a telecommunications consortium, consisting of the al-Aqqad Development Group, the Arab Bank, and the Palestine Development and Investment Company, will establish the Palestine Telecommunications Company.

July 5. Morocco to Supervise Construction of Airport. Morocco and the Palestinian Authority sign an accord in which Morocco agrees to supervise construction of an airport in Gaza and to train Palestinians to be airport personnel.

July 9. PA Receives World Bank Grant. The World Bank extends a $20 million grant to the Palestinian Authority to improve health and education services.

July 27. United States Announces Grant to Palestinians. The United States agrees to grant the Palestinian Authority $40 million over the following five years for waste water and sewage projects.

November 15. Arafat Averts Assassination Attempt. Palestinian police report that they have arrested five men in Gaza, Libyans and Algerians, involved in a plot to assassinate PLO chairman Arafat.

December 6. Palestinians Can Travel under PA Passports. Passports issued by the Palestinian Authority become valid.

PERSIAN GULF STATES

January 26. Shiites Continue to Oppose Bahraini Government. The Islamic Front for the Liberation of Bahrain reports that twenty-seven hundred people have been arrested since demonstrations began on December 5, 1994. Others, they maintain, have been tortured to death in prison.

January 27. Qatar's Amir Ousted. Crown Prince Hamad bin Khalifa Al Thani deposes his father, Amir Shaykh Khalifa bin Hamad Al Thani. On July 11 he names himself prime minister and defense minister. He also announces formation of a new cabinet.

March 15. Bahrain and Oman Link Stock Exchanges. In the first such deal in the region, Bahrain and Oman link their stock exchanges.

March 21. Kuwait Upholds Iraqi Convictions. A court upholds death sentences for two Iraqis convicted of attempting to assassinate former U.S. president Bush in 1993. Four others convicted had their death sentences commuted to life imprisonment.

April 23. Saudis Protest in London. Five hundred people gather in front of Saudi Arabia's embassy in London to protest the arrest of three hundred religious scholars.

May 21. Kuwait Privatizes State-Owned Property. As part of its privatization drive, the government sells 15.5 percent of the Kuwait Commercial Markets Complex, a state-owned property management company.

June 14. Saudi Arabia Arrests Shiites. In the eastern region of Awamiyya, an unspecified number of Shiite residents are arrested while protesting confiscation of their land.

November 13. Car Bomb Explodes in Riyadh, Saudi Arabia. A car bomb explodes outside the headquarters of the Saudi National Guard, which also houses the U.S. military liaison office. The explosion kills seven, including five U.S. military personnel, and wounds up to sixty others. The next day, U.S. president Clinton dispatches agents from the FBI to aid in the investigations. By November 17 three Islamist groups have claimed responsibility.

December 12. Yemen and Saudi Arabia Clash. Saudi Arabian and Yemeni troops battle near the Omani, Saudi, and Yemeni border, resulting in an unspecified number of casualties.

SYRIA

December 15. Political Prisoners Released. Over a ten-day period, the Syrian government releases twelve hundred political prisoners with connections to the Muslim Brotherhood, which had battled government forces in the early 1980s.

YEMEN

March 15. Natural Gas Project Realized. Yemen signs a $6 billion agreement with Total, the French oil group, to establish a liquefied natural gas project.

December 15. Eritrean and Yemeni Soldiers Clash. Near the Red Sea Island of Greater Hanish, Eritrean and Yemeni soldiers engage one another for four days. On December 18, Eritrean forces capture Greater Hanish and 160 Yemeni soldiers, whom they release December 30.

1996

REGIONAL AFFAIRS

August 13. Oil Pipeline Reestablished. Turkey and Iran agree to increase trade and to reestablish an oil pipeline between their two countries to accommodate the UN-sanctioned Iraqi "oil for food" deal.

November 12. MENA Summit Held in Cairo. Egyptian president Mubarak hosts the Middle East/North Africa (MENA) Economic Summit. Israeli foreign minister Levy attends.

December 17. Claims against Iraq Settled. The UN Compensation Commission, charged with settling claims against Iraq for the 1990 Iraqi invasion of Kuwait, awards the Kuwait Oil Company $610 million for damage to seven hundred oil wells that had been wrecked by retreating Iraqi troops.

ARAB-ISRAELI CONFLICT

January 5. Yahya Ayyash Killed in Gaza. Yahya Ayyash, "The Engineer," dies from wounds sustained from a booby-trapped cellular phone. He was widely believed to have been responsible for Islamic Resistance Movement (Hamas) bombings in Israel.

January 27. Israel and Oman Reach Agreement. Israel and Oman sign an agreement providing for the establishment of offices in Muscat and Tel Aviv to represent their economic interests in each other's country.

February 13. Water Accord Signed. Israel, Jordan, and the Palestinian Authority sign an agreement on water management.

February 25. Bus Bombed in Downtown Jerusalem. A bomb explodes on a bus, killing twenty-three, including the bomber. Hamas claims responsibility and says that the attack was in retaliation for the January 5 murder of Yahya Ayyash. Israel halts talks with the Palestinian Authority and closes its borders with Gaza and the West Bank. The next day, Palestinian police arrest ninety Hamas members in connection with the bombing.

March 3. Second Bus Bombing in Jerusalem. Hamas claims responsibility when another bomb explodes on a bus, killing nineteen and wounding ten. Israeli prime minister Peres declares "war" on Hamas and orders the destruction of houses of families of the suicide bombers.

March 4. Bomb Explodes in Tel Aviv. A Hamas suicide bomber kills 12 people and wounds 126 others in a downtown shopping area. Israel suspends negotiations with the Syrians at the Wye Conference Center in Maryland, citing the recent bombings at home.

April 2. Israel and Qatar Strike Deal. Israel and Qatar agree to establish trade interest offices in each other's country. Qatar cancels the plan July 12.

April 7. Passenger Flights Begin. Direct passenger airline flights between Amman and Tel Aviv begin.

April 15. DFLP Leader Admitted to PA Areas. Israel agrees to admit Nayif Hawatima, the leader of the Democratic Front for the Liberation of Palestine (DFLP), into Palestinian-controlled areas for a meeting of the Palestinian National Council (PNC) on amendments to the PLO charter.

April 24. PNC Revokes Key Part of Charter. The PNC votes 504 to 54 (14 abstaining and 97 absent) to revoke those parts of the PLO charter that call for the destruction of Israel.

April 25. Palestinian Authorities Arrest Suspect. Palestinian police report that they have arrested Hamas member Adnan al-Ghul, number two on the Israeli list of people wanted in connection with recent anti-Israeli bombings.

May 8. Hamas Leader Extradited. In New York City, a court orders Hamas leader Musa Muhammad Abu Marzuq to be extradited to Israel, where he is wanted in connection with 1995 terrorism charges.

June 16. Netanyahu Declares Intentions. Israeli prime minister-elect Benjamin Netanyahu issues a directive stating that Israel will continue to negotiate with Syria and the Palestinian Authority but that Israel will retain sovereignty over the Golan Heights.

July 31. Plan for Palestinian State Disclosed. Yossi Beilin, an Israeli negotiator in the Israeli-Palestinian talks under former Israeli prime minister Peres, reveals that negotiators from the two sides have developed a plan for a Palestinian state that would have its capital in a suburb of Jerusalem.

August 2. Ban on New Construction Lifted. The Israeli cabinet lifts the previous administration's ban on new construction of Israeli settlements in Gaza and the West Bank.

August 22. Peres Meets with Arafat. In Gaza, Peres meets with Palestinian Authority president Arafat. Peres issues a statement urging the Netanyahu government to honor agreements with the PA and redeploy Israeli troops from Hebron.

August 29. Peaceful Protests Launched by PA. Ordered by Palestinian Authority president Arafat, Palestinians in Gaza, the West Bank, and East Jerusalem strike to protest resumption of Israeli settlement efforts. The next day between eight thousand and fifteen thousand Palestinians come to Jerusalem's al-Aqsa mosque for a protest prayer meeting called by Arafat.

September 15. Arab League Criticizes Israel. Meeting in Cairo, the Arab League passes a resolution criticizing Israel for failing to redeploy soldiers from areas of the Gaza Strip and the West Bank; not establishing safe passages between Palestinian areas; confiscating Palestinian land; and not releasing Palestinian prisoners.

September 24. Tunnel Opened under Temple Mount. In Jerusalem, Israeli authorities open the northern door of a tunnel under the retaining wall of the Haram al-Sharif/Temple Mount as an aid to tourist passage through the site. Over the next four days, Israeli security forces clash with Palestinians, protesting the move, throughout the West Bank, Gaza, and East Jerusalem. On September 29 U.S. president Clinton announces that Arafat and Netanyahu will attend a meeting in Washington in order to end the violence and restart negotiations.

October 9. King Hussein Voices Displeasure. Jordan's King Hussein states that Israel's unwillingness to fulfill the terms of the Oslo I and Oslo II agreements jeopardizes Israel's peace treaties with Egypt and Jordan.

October 20. Europe Desires Greater Role. In Damascus, French president Jacques Chirac meets with Syrian president Asad to discuss increasing Europe's role in the Arab-Israeli peace process. Israeli foreign minister David Levy issues a statement rejecting greater European participation.

October 27. Drilling in Golan Heights Approved. Netanyahu reportedly approves a plan for Israel's National Oil Company to drill for oil in the Golan Heights.

October 28. U.S. Special Envoy Returns Home. U.S. special envoy Dennis Ross leaves Israel for Washington because of lack of progress in Israeli-Palestinian talks, which stalled on the issue of Hebron.

November 22. PA to Document Israeli Abuse. Arafat announces that Palestinians will be given fifteen video cameras in order to document abuse by Israeli security forces.

November 26. Syria on Peace Talks. Syrian foreign minister Faruq al-Sharaa says that Syria will resume negotiations with Israel at the point where talks were suspended under the Peres government, and not start from scratch as the Netanyahu government prefers.

November 29. United States Moves on Saudi Boycott. The United States reportedly informs Saudi Arabia that it will block Saudi Arabia's admission to the World Trade Organization until Saudi Arabia drops its economic boycott of Israel.

December 1. Arab League Holds Emergency Session. In Cairo, the League of Arab States calls on Israel to stop expanding Jewish settlements and warns that the settlement policy will destroy the peace process. The league rejects a Syrian proposal for Arab states to suspend relations with Israel.

December 10. Israel to Revoke Residency Rights. The U.S. consul general in Jerusalem, Edward Abington, reveals that Israel plans to revoke residency rights of Palestinian-Americans living in Jerusalem unless they drop their U.S. citizenship.

December 13. Settlers Receive Subsidies. The Israeli cabinet approves subsidies for Jewish settlers in the West Bank, including special grants and lower income taxes.

December 16. Clinton Criticizes Israel. At a news conference, U.S. president Clinton states that Israel's settlement policy is an "obstacle to peace" and urges Israel not to act unilaterally in its policy.

EGYPT

January 17. Egyptian Shaykh Sentenced. A federal court in New York City sentences Egyptian Shaykh Umar Abd al-Rahman to life in prison for having planned a series of assassinations and bombings. Nine codefendants receive sentences ranging from twenty-five years to life in prison. Al-Sayyid Nusayr receives a life sentence for the murder of rabbi Meir Kahane in 1990.

January 23. Leader of the Muslim Brotherhood Dies. In Cairo, the leader of the Muslim Brotherhood since 1986, Hamid Abd al-Nasser, dies of natural causes. Mustafa Mashhur is elected to replace al-Nasser.

April 3. United States Implicates Sudan. During a UN Security Council debate over sanctions against the Sudan, U.S. ambassador Albright presents evidence that implicates the Sudan in the attempted assassination of Egyptian president Mubarak in 1995.

April 18. Greek Tourists Attacked in Cairo. The Islamic Group, intending to attack Israelis in retaliation for the April 1996 bombing of a UN camp in Lebanon, kills eighteen Greek tourists and wounds twenty-one others.

IRAN

February 22. The United States and Iran Reach Settlement. The United States and Iran agree to a $131.8 million settlement for the 1988 downing of Iran Air Flight 655 by the USS *Vincennes* in the Strait of Hormuz.

August 24. Iran Files Lawsuits. Arguing that recent U.S. legislation is a violation of the 1981 "Algiers Accord," Iran files lawsuits against the United States at the International Court at The Hague. The U.S. legislation had provided funds for covert anti-Iranian action and had established secondary sanctions against non-U.S. investment in Iran.

November 17. Woman Appointed Mayor. The first woman to hold a mayoral post under the Islamic Republic, Sadra Azam-Nuri, becomes mayor of the seventh district of Tehran.

December 7. Sunni Leader Dies in Kermanshah. The Iranian news service reports that Sunni leader Mullah Muhammad Rabi I has died of a heart attack in Kermanshah. Opposition reports state that Rabi I was killed by the government, inspiring several days of antigovernment riots in Kermanshah.

IRAQ

February 23. Saddam Hussein's Sons-in-Law Executed. Hussein Kamel Hassan al-Majid and Saddam Kamel al-Majid are divorced from their wives (daughters of the Iraqi president) and executed after returning from self-imposed exile in Jordan. On March 1 family members and supporters of Hussein Kamel Hassan al-Majid are executed.

March 27. UN Security Council Approves Monitoring System. The UN Security Council approves a monitoring system to check items imported into Iraq that have civilian and military uses. The United Nations banned the latter in 1991 when it imposed sanctions.

March 1. U.S. Organization Violates Travel Ban. Five members of the Chicago-based group Voices in the Wilderness deliver medicine to the Qadisiyya Children's Hospital in Baghdad, violating a U.S. travel ban on Iraq.

May 20. Oil-for-Food Deal Reached. The United Nations and Iraq reach agreement on a plan for Iraq to sell $1 billion worth of oil every ninety days. According to the agreement, more than half of the proceeds will purchase food and medicine; one third of the proceeds will go to compensate Kuwaitis for Iraq's 1990 invasion; and $150 million will be earmarked for Kurdish areas.

July 31. U.S. Vetoes UN Plan. The United States vetoes a UN plan to allow Iraq to sell $2 billion worth of oil in order to raise funds for humanitarian goods. After the United States agrees to another version of the plan, the UN secretary general suspends the deal on September 1 because of the deterioration of the situation in northern Iraq, where Kurdish and Iraqi Arab forces are in conflict.

August 31. Iraqi Government Forces Enter Kurdish Region. In order to counter Iranian support of the Patriotic Union of Kurdistan (PUK), government tanks and infantry units enter the Kurdish region of northern Iraq. Government troops capture the regional capital, Irbil, at the request of the Kurdistan Democratic Party (KDP). On September 4, U.S. officials state that Iraqi government troops have left Kurdish areas, with the exception of one mechanized unit and intelligence officials.

September 3. United States Extends No-Fly Zone. The United States fires two salvoes of cruise missiles at Iraqi air defense targets south of Baghdad and extends the existing no-fly zone from the 32d to the 33d parallel. An unnamed U.S. official reports, on October 14, that Iraq has completely rebuilt its air defense system despite U.S. threats of further bombings.

September 7. CIA Operation Uncovered. U.S. intelligence agents, who had been working on covert operations to overthrow Saddam Hussein, flee Iraq after their attempts to arm and train Iraqi opposition groups are discovered.

September 15. U.S. Relocates Employees. The United States begins relocating from Iraq to the United States employees of U.S. agencies and their families.

October 28. UNICEF Reports Child Deaths. Carol Bellamy, the director of UN Children's Emergency Fund (UNICEF), states that forty-five hundred children under five years of age die every month in Iraq because of hunger and disease associated with UN-imposed sanctions.

November 25. Final Oil-for-Food Agreement Reached. The United Nations announces that the final "oil-for-food" agreement has been reached with Iraq. According to the plan, Iraq can begin selling $2 billion worth of oil every six months, beginning December 10.

December 30. UN Security Council Censures Iraq. The UN Security Council censures Iraq for refusing to permit UN weapons inspectors to take weapons parts from the country for examination, citing this as a violation of Iraq's obligations under UN resolutions.

ISRAEL

March 27. Yigal Amir Convicted. A Tel Aviv court convicts Yigal Amir of killing Israeli former prime minister Rabin on November 4. He is sentenced to life imprisonment.

April 25. Labor Party Modifies Platform. The Labor Party drops a provision from its platform rejecting the establishment of a Palestinian state. Also removed is a plank stating that the Golan Heights is of essential strategic importance to Israel.

May 29. New Prime Minister Elected. Likud leader Benjamin Netanyahu wins the election for prime minister, defeating Prime Minister and Labor leader Peres, with 50.4 percent of the vote. In parliamentary elections, Likud wins 31 seats, and Labor wins 33 seats in the 120-seat house.

November 14. Ruling Permits Use of Force. The Supreme Court rules that security agencies can use force on prisoners to obtain information that might prevent loss of life or terrorist attacks.

JORDAN

August 16. Bread Prices Inspire Demonstrations. Beginning in the southern town of Karak and spreading to Man and Amman on August 17 and 18, demonstrators protest the end of government price subsidies for bread and call for the resignation of Prime Minister Abd al-Karim Kabariti. On November 12 King Hussein pardons all those who were involved in the demonstrations and riots.

December 27. Three Arrested for Attempted Assassination. Security forces arrest three members of the Democratic Front for the Liberation of Palestine (DFLP) for the attempted murder of Palestine National Council member Hamza Nazzal on December 25.

KURDISH AFFAIRS

March 22. Turkey Bans Mine-Clearing Equipment. Fearing use by the Kurdish Workers' Party (PKK), Turkey prevents delivery of mine-clearing equipment to the Kurdish areas of northern Iraq.

September 9. KDP Captures Sulaymaniyya. In the ongoing conflict between Patriotic Union of Kurdistan (PUK) and Kurdistan Democratic Party (KDP) forces in northern Iraq, the KDP takes Sulaymaniyya, the PUK's last major stronghold. With Iranian support, the PUK regains possession of Sulaymaniyya on October 14.

September 10. Iran Refuses, Grants Shelter. Iran refuses to open its borders to an estimated fifty thousand Kurds who have fled the fighting between KDP and PUK forces. On September 15 the Iranian interior ministry reports that it has accepted sixty thousand Kurdish refugees.

September 12. United States Welcomes Refugees. The United States announces that it will organize the safe passage of Kurds employed by U.S. agencies through KDP-controlled areas to Turkey and, then, to the United States.

September 26. KDP Announces Parliament. The KDP declares the establishment of a Kurdish government with a parliament in Irbil. Included in the authority are the Islamic Movement, the Kurdistan Communist Party (KCP), the Kurdistan Islamic Union, the Assyrian Democratic Movement, and an unnamed Turkomen party.

October 23. KDP and PUK Agree to Cease-Fire. In U.S.-brokered talks, the KDP and PUK agree to cease fighting. Negotiations continue in meetings in Ankara, Turkey, under the sponsorship of Britain, Turkey, and the United States. On November 16 the two parties meet to discuss a settlement at a meeting organized by the United States.

October 24. Turkey and Iran Attack PKK. An Istanbul-based newspaper reports that Turkish and Iranian forces carried out joint operations against PKK camps in Iran.

November 30. Turkey Bombs PKK. Turkish warplanes bomb suspected PKK bases in northern Iraq. Ground units then cross the border and clash with PKK forces.

December 27. France Withdraws from Operation Provide Comfort. Citing the limited degree of assistance provided by the air patrols over northern Iraq to the Kurds whom the operation was designed to protect, France announces that it will no longer participate in Operation Provide Comfort.

LEBANON

February 12. Israelis End Blockade. Beirut radio reports that Israeli naval forces have ended their blockade of the Lebanese coast south of Sidon, which had begun in February 1995.

March 13. Court Reverses Conviction. A court reverses the 1994 death sentences of two men convicted of killing U.S. ambassador Francis Meloy, another U.S. diplomat, and their Lebanese driver in 1976.

March 25. Suspects Ordered to Stand Trial. A military court overturns a 1993 lower-court ruling that applied an amnesty to fifteen suspects accused in the April 1983 bombing of the U.S. embassy in Beirut.

April 18. Israeli Forces Shell UN Camp. As part of intense, two-week clashes between Israeli and Hizballah forces in southern Lebanon, Israeli soldiers shell a UN peacekeeping camp in Qana, killing 107 and wounding 100 refugees who had taken shelter there.

August 21. Samir Geagea Charged with Assassination. Samir Geagea, a former leader of Christian militias, already serving two life sentences for murder, is charged with the June 1987 assassination of former prime minister Rashid Karami.

December 16. Lebanon to Receive Aid. Eight international organizations and twenty-nine countries, including the United States, award $2.2 billion to Lebanon.

LIBYA AND NORTH AFRICA

January 24. Louis Farrakhan Meets with Qadhafi. In Libya, U.S. Nation of Islam leader Louis Farrakhan meets with Libyan head of state Qadhafi to discuss mobilizing African Americans to influence U.S. elections. The U.S. Treasury Department does not allow Farrakhan to accept a $1 billion gift from Libya. Libya awards Farrakhan a $250,000 human rights prize.

March 9. Opposition Group Attempts Assassination. The London-based *al-Hayat* reports that the Islamic Militant Group (IMG) attempted to assassinate Qadhafi.

July 9. Stampede Kills Fifty People. A shoot-out between the bodyguards of Qadhafi's sons and unknown hecklers leads to a stampede during a soccer match in Tripoli.

September 1. Great Man-Made River Project Announced. At a celebration to recognize the 1969 overthrow of former Iraqi king Idris, Qadhafi inaugurates the Great Man-Made River, a $25 billion project to pump water from underground aquifers to coastal areas.

PALESTINIAN AFFAIRS

January 9. PA Receives Financial Pledge. A group of donors organized by the World Bank pledge $865 million to the Palestinian Authority.

February 12. Arafat Becomes PA President. Arafat is officially sworn in as president of the Palestinian Authority after winning 88 percent of votes cast on January 20 by 75 percent of eligible Palestinian voters.

April 21. Arrests Made in Assassination Attempt. Police announce that they have arrested seven Islamic Resistance Movement (Hamas) members involved in a plot to kill Arafat on April 28 in Gaza City.

May 2. Loan Agreement Reached. The World Bank and the Palestinian Authority agree to a $20 million loan for structural improvement projects, such as road construction.

July 1. PFLP and PLO Sever Relations. The Popular Front for the Liberation of Palestine (PFLP) ends its association with the Palestine Liberation Organization, citing opposition to the peace process.

October 23. Chirac Addresses Palestinian Council. In Ramallah, French president Chirac, the first head of state to address the Palestinian Council, expresses support for a Palestinian state and criticizes recent Israeli actions.

November 20. International Investors Back PA. In Paris, international investors, including the World Bank, meet with Palestinian Authority president Arafat and pledge $845 million in new investments in Palestinian areas.

December 16. Environment Authority Established. Arafat issues a decree establishing the Palestinian Environment Authority, to be based in Hebron.

PERSIAN GULF STATES

January 1. Saudi King Fahd Relinquishes Power. Citing a need to rest, King Fahd turns control of the government over to Crown Prince Abdallah. King Fahd resumes full control of the government February 22.

January 3. United Kingdom Deports Saudi Opposition Figure. Britain orders Saudi opposition leader Muhammad Masari, head of the Committee for the Defense of Legitimate Rights, to leave the country for the island of Dominica, in the Caribbean Sea. Masari appeals the order. On April 19 Britain grants him a four-year permit to remain in the country.

January 14. Bahraini Authorities Arrest Opposition Leader. Security forces in Bahrain arrest Shiite opposition leader Shaykh Abd al-Wahhab Hussein. On January 22, state television reports that authorities have arrested Shaykh Abd al-Amir al-Jamri and seven other Shiite opposition leaders who had supported antigovernment actions.

April 9. Citibank to Open Islamic Bank in Bahrain. The U.S. firm Citibank announces that it will open Citi-Islamic Investment Bank in July to conform to Islamic bans on paying and collecting interest.

June 5. Bahraini Oppositionists Give Statements. Alleged participants in a plot against the Bahraini regime give televised statements, saying that they had trained in Iran and Lebanon and had received instructions from Iranian officials.

June 25. Truck Bomb Explodes in Khobar, Saudi Arabia. Near Dhahran, a truck bomb, outside a base housing U.S. and European military personnel, kills nineteen U.S. airmen and wounds four hundred others. A September 16 Pentagon report acknowledges that U.S. military commanders had ignored intelligence reports that an attack was imminent. In December, after U.S.-Saudi disagreements on procedures for apprehending and prosecuting suspects, Saudi Arabia gives the United States information that places responsibility with Saudi Shiites, whose training in Lebanon had been funded by Iran.

September 23. Qatar Proceeds with Legal Action. The Ministry of Justice announces that the government will proceed with international legal action to recover $3.5 billion from the former amir of Qatar, Shaykh Khalifa bin Hamad Al Thani.

SYRIA

June 10. Bombs Rock Syrian Cities. A series of bomb blasts result in numerous arrests. One blast, on May 6 in Damascus, reportedly targets President Asad. Security forces arrest six hundred people in connection with that explosion.

December 31. Bomb Explodes on Bus. In Damascus, a bomb detonates on a bus, killing nine people and wounding forty-four others.

YEMEN

January 25. French Tourists Kidnapped. In retaliation for the imprisonment of a tribe member who had abducted a U.S. citizen in 1995, the Aslam kidnap seventeen French tourists. Four days later they release the tourists, and the next day they clash with government forces. On February 2 authorities arrest fourteen tribe members.

October 21. French Diplomat Abducted. In San‘a’ the Tayman tribesmen kidnaps a French diplomat, Serge Lefèvre, and release him October 26. Failing to win promises from the government for more job opportunities, they abduct Lefèvre again on October 27.

December 28. Dutch Tourists Captured. Radio Monte Carlo reports that members of the Bani Jabr tribe have kidnapped four Dutch tourists. Yemeni security forces and tribesmen battle, resulting in the deaths of three tribe members.

1997

REGIONAL AFFAIRS

January 2. Al-Hayat Receives Letter Bombs. In Washington, the Federal Bureau of Investigation (FBI) disarms six letter bombs sent to the Washington office of the London-based daily *al-Hayat.* The bombs were postmarked in Alexandria, Egypt, on December 21, 1996. On January 13 a letter bomb wounds two workers in *al-Hayat*'s London office, and two more letter bombs are discovered at the newspaper's New York office at the United Nations.

June 5. Syria and Iraq Open Crossings. Syria and Iraq reopen the Abu Kamal, Abu al-Shamal, and Tal Qujayt border crossings.

June 13. Egypt and Libya Announce Cooperation. Egypt and Libya agree to establish a free trade zone between their two countries. The two also agree to construct a joint airport.

August 13. Syria and Iraq Meet on Borders. Syrian foreign ministry officials begin talks in Baghdad on the demarcation of the borders between Iraq and Syria.

September 21. Arab States Vote to Defy Sanctions. In Cairo, the League of Arab States votes to defy UN sanctions by permitting planes from Libya to land on its members' soil.

November 18. MENA Conference Convenes in Doha, Qatar. The Middle East/North Africa Economic Conference adopts the Doha Declaration, signed by delegates from sixty-five participating countries, calling on Israel to trade land for peace and remove restrictive measures on the West Bank and Gaza.

December 3. Saudi Arabia Mediates Dispute. Egyptian president Mubarak flies to Riyadh to meet with Saudi officials who are attempting to solve a disagreement between Egypt and Qatar over accusations of Egyptian involvement in a 1996 coup attempt in Qatar.

December 11. OIC Summit Condemns Israel. In Tehran, the Organization of Islamic States (OIC) adopts a joint declaration condemning Israel's "state terrorism" and demanding that Israel stop building settlements. The statement also denounces violence committed in the name of Islam.

December 22. GCC Summit Ends in Communique. In Kuwait, leaders from Bahrain, Kuwait, Oman, Qatar, Saudi Arabia, and the UAE meet for the annual Gulf Cooperation Council (GCC) summit. Participants express GCC support for the UAE's claim to three Gulf islands occupied by Iran and reject Israeli policies toward the peace process. They also call on states not to harbor terrorists and ask Iraq to fulfill all UN Security Council resolutions.

December 31. Arab Free Trade Zone Announced. Arab League secretary general Ismat Abd al-Majid announces that implementation of the Arab free trade zone will begin on January 1, 1998, reducing customs fees and taxes by 10 percent annually on all Arab commodities exchanged among Arab countries.

ARAB-ISRAELI CONFLICT

January 1. Israeli Soldier Massacres Palestinians. In Hebron, Noam Friedman, an off-duty Israeli soldier, opens fire on a Palestinian market, wounding eleven Palestinians before Israeli soldiers disarm him.

January 14. Bedouin Homes Razed. In Jahalin, in the West Bank, Israeli forces bulldoze three Bedouin homes and evict their occupants to make room for the expansion of the Maale Adumim settlement. On January 27 Israeli authorities force the evacuation of the Jahalin Bedouin tribe from their homes near East Jerusalem. They are relocated to a site on the outskirts of the city.

January 17. Israelis Withdraw from Hebron. Ending months of diplomatic and violent conflict, Israeli forces redeploy from 80 percent of the city. Palestinian police enter Hebron and begin security patrols.

January 19. Arafat Addresses Hebron Public. For the first time since 1965, Palestinian Authority president

Arafat enters Hebron to address a crowd of approximately sixty thousand Palestinians.

February 26. Israelis to Build Housing Units in Har Homa. The Israeli government approves a plan to build a 6,500-unit housing settlement for Jews in Har Homa, known to Palestinians as Jabal Abu Ghunaym.

March 7. UN Condemns Har Homa Plan. The United States, a permanent member of the UN Security Council, vetoes a Security Council resolution that finds the Israeli plans to build at Har Homa "illegal and a major obstacle to peace."

March 9. King Hussein Criticizes Har Homa. Jordan's King Hussein writes a letter to Israeli prime minister Netanyahu in which he says, "I sense an intent to destroy all I worked for to build between our peoples and states."

March 13. Israeli School Girls Murdered. At a border area jointly controlled by Jordan and Israel, Ahmad Musa Daqamsa, a Jordanian border guard, kills seven and wounds six Israeli school girls on a field trip. On March 16 King Hussein, accompanied by Israeli prime minister Netanyahu, visits the families of the seven Israeli school girls whom Daqamsa killed. On July 19 Daqamsa receives a sentence of life imprisonment from a Jordanian military court.

March 18. Construction Begins on Har Homa. Construction begins on a Jewish housing project in Har Homa. The United States vetoes, on March 21, a UN Security Council resolution calling on Israel to stop construction.

March 24. Oman Disinvites Israelis. The Omani International Trade Company rejects Israeli applications to participate in its October trade conference, citing the breakdown of the peace process.

March 31. Arab States Renew Boycott. Meeting in Cairo, the League of Arab States reactivates the boycott of Israel and freezes relations with Israel because of Israeli construction at Har Homa.

April 25. UN Majority Votes against Israel. The UN General Assembly votes 134 to 3 (with 11 abstentions) for a resolution demanding that Israel stop housing construction at Har Homa and recommending that nations end support for Israeli settlements. Israel, Micronesia, and the United States vote against the resolution.

April 26. Egyptian Parties Call for Suspension of Relations. Six Egyptian political parties, including the Muslim Brotherhood and several secular parties, sign a document calling on Egypt to suspend normalization with Israel because of Israeli building at Har Homa. On May 23 Israeli television reports that Prime Minister Netanyahu had proposed to the Egyptian representative that Israel freeze construction.

April 30. Jordan to Accept Hamas Leader. The Jordanian government agrees to allow Islamic Resistance Movement (Hamas) leader Musa Muhammad Abu Marzuq, imprisoned in the United States since 1995, to

be deported to Jordan. Israel had decided to withdraw its request for his extradition to Israel on April 3.

June 4. Plan Revealed. Netanyahu reveals to select cabinet members his plan for a final settlement with the Palestinians. It calls for Israeli control of greater Jerusalem, the Jordan River, and settlements in the West Bank.

June 10. U.S. House Approves Embassy Transfer. The U.S. House of Representatives passes a resolution affirming Jerusalem as Israel's capital and allocating $100 million to move the U.S. embassy from Tel Aviv to Jerusalem.

June 28. Prophet Muhammad Depicted as a Pig. In Hebron, Israeli Tatiana Suskind is arrested for displaying posters that show the Prophet Muhammad as a pig. The posters inspire demonstrations in Hebron and Ramallah.

July 15. UN Censures Israel. The UN General Assembly votes 131 to 3 (with 14 abstentions) in favor of a resolution to censure Israel, calling for the cessation of construction at Har Homa.

July 28. Palestinians and Jordanians Counter Settlements. Businessmen from Jordan and the West Bank/Gaza launch a $60 million investment firm for the construction of houses and tourist projects in East Jerusalem to counter Israeli settlement plans.

July 30. Double Suicide Rocks West Jerusalem. A suicide bombing in the Mahane Yehuda market kills 13 people and wounds more than 150. A communique found outside the Red Cross offices in Ramallah declares the bombings to be the work of Hamas. On August 11 Israeli and Palestinian intelligence officers agree to work with the U.S. Central Intelligence Agency to identify the group responsible.

September 5. Israel Suspends Oslo Obligations. After three suicide bombers set off explosions on Ben Yehuda Street in West Jerusalem, Netanyahu suspends Israel's obligations under the Oslo accords, demanding Palestinian compliance with security cooperation.

September 10. Albright Visits Region. During her first official visit to the Middle East, U.S. secretary of state Albright meets with Israelis and Palestinians to discuss security and terrorism. Before she leaves, she announces that the two parties will meet in Washington and at the annual UN General Assembly meeting in New York.

September 15. Jewish Settlers Occupy Arab House. In the Ra's al-Amud neighborhood of East Jerusalem, Jewish settlers take over a house owned by U.S. businessman Irving Muskowitz and inhabited by an Arab family. Netanyahu condemns the move and allows Jewish religious students to replace the settlers as caretakers. Israeli peace activists and Palestinians demonstrate against the occupation and eviction.

September 25. Hamas Leader Nearly Assassinated. In Amman, two men carrying Canadian passports attack Khalid Mishal, political leader of Hamas, injecting a toxin in his left ear. The men are taken into Jordanian custody, and Israel provides the antidote for the poison.

October 1. Shaykh Ahmad Yasin Freed. Israel releases from prison the founder and spiritual leader of Hamas, Shaykh Ahmad Yasin. Israel flies him to Jordan.

October 6. Mossad Agents Return to Israel. After a helicopter flies Shaykh Yasin to Gaza from Jordan, another helicopter leaves Jordan for Israel with two Mossad agents linked by Jordan to the attempted assassination of Hamas political leader Mishal.

October 7. Shaykh Yasin Lists Conditions for Truce. From Gaza, Shaykh Yasin lays out conditions for a Hamas truce with Israel, including a full Israeli withdrawal from the West Bank and Gaza. On October 22 the shaykh vows to continue jihad (holy war) against Israel.

November 13. UN Again Censures Israel. The UN General Assembly votes 139 to 3 (with 13 abstentions) to condemn Israel's refusal to stop building housing units in East Jerusalem. The United States, Micronesia, and Israel vote against the resolution.

December 5. Plans for Israeli Security Unveiled. Israeli infrastructure minister Ariel Sharon announces detailed plans for future Israeli security zones that will form a ring around the West Bank, redrawing the demarcation lines of the 1995 Oslo Interim Agreement.

December 18. Laborers Allowed Overnight in Israel. For the first time in three years, Israel grants overnight permits to 4,600 Palestinian laborers from the Gaza Strip and to 350 laborers from the West Bank. Israeli authorities wish to reduce the number of people passing through the Erez Crossing each morning.

December 21. Netanyahu Claims the West Bank. At an international Likud Party convention, Israeli Netanyahu claims the West Bank up to the Jordan River, including Jewish settlements.

EGYPT

January 9. Canal Construction Inaugurated. President Mubarak launches construction of the first stage of the New Valley project, which will create a 150-mile-long canal west of Lake Nasser.

February 23. Martial Law Extended. The People's Assembly approves a presidential decree continuing martial law for three more years. The state of martial law allows detention without trial and extends the jurisdiction of military courts to civilian areas.

March 13. Coptic Village Attacked. In Naj Dawud, a mostly Coptic (Christian) village three hundred miles south of Cairo, the Islamic Group kills thirteen people and fires on a train south of the village, killing one person and wounding six.

July 2. Farmers Protest Law. Security forces use force to break up a demonstration by farmers, killing three people. The farmers disapprove of a new law that will end rent controls on agricultural land.

September 18. Tourists Attacked in Cairo. Unknown assailants attack a tourist bus with automatic weapons and gasoline bombs, killing ten people, nine of whom are German tourists. They injure twenty-four others and start a fire in Tahrir Square.

October 1. Clashes Erupt over New Law. The new "Land Lease" law, giving landlords the right to expel tenants from land they had been leasing since Nasser's land reforms, provokes deadly protests in Qina governorate and in the Nile Delta area.

October 22. Illegal Computer Software Seized. The *Financial Times* reports that Egyptian police have seized $18 million of illegal computer software. The Egyptian government had agreed to raid software pirates in return for a commitment from Microsoft that it would contract out production of Arabic versions of its software to Egyptian companies.

October 27. New Canal Opened. Mubarak opens a new canal, running under the Suez, to irrigate the Sinai Peninsula with water from the Nile River.

November 17. Massacre Occurs Near Luxor. Near the Temple of Hatshepsut, six gunmen from the Islamic Group kill an estimated seventy people, including sixty foreign tourists. Members of the Islamic Group claim that the attack is in retaliation for the U.S. imprisonment of Shaykh Umar Abd al-Rahman, founder of their group, who is in prison in the United States in connection with the 1993 World Trade Center bombing in New York City.

IRAN

April 10. German Ruling Sparks Protests. A German court finds four men guilty in the 1992 Berlin slaying of four Iranian opposition members. The court implicates the Iranian Committee for Special Operations, which includes Iranian president Rafsanjani and several other senior government and religious officials, in the murders. Germany and Iran expel four of each other's diplomats and recall their respective ambassadors. The European Union (EU) suspends its critical dialogue with Iran and urges member states to recall their ambassadors from Tehran. All EU countries except Greece comply. On April 29 the EU country ambassadors begin to return to Tehran, but Iran refuses to accept the German and Danish envoys.

May 10. Earthquake Kills Thousands. An earthquake in the northeast kills some twenty-four hundred people and injures six thousand others.

July 3. United States Compensates Victims. The United States reportedly pays $32.5 million to the families of the 143 victims of the July 1988 downing of an Iranian airliner over the Persian Gulf.

August 3. New President Elected. Mohammad Khatami is confirmed as president of the Islamic Republic of Iran.

August 7. United States Changes Penalties. The United States announces that it will penalize companies that spend $20 million or more a year in developing Iran's oil and gas fields instead of the $40 million originally stipulated in the Iran-Libya Sanctions Act.

December 14. President Invites Dialogue with United States. In Tehran, at his first news conference, Khatami states that he hopes to establish a dialogue with the American people.

IRAQ

February 1. Hussein's Daughters under House Arrest. The Iraqi National Accord, an opposition group, reports that Hussein's first wife, Sajida, and two daughters are under house arrest. The two daughters are widows of Hussein Kamel Hassan al-Majid and Saddam Kamel al-Majid, who were executed in February 1996.

February 3. Coup Leaders Killed. The Supreme Council for the Islamic Revolution in Iraq reports that the government has executed two brigadier generals, two colonels, a lieutenant colonel, and a captain in connection with a failed coup attempt.

March 19. Food Shipped to Iraq. Under the UN oil-for-food deal, the first delivery of food is made to Zaleho, in northern Iraq.

April 14. Russia and Iraq Sign Agreement. Russia signs an agreement with Iraq to develop the southern oil field of Kurna. Western oil companies maintain that the deal violates UN sanctions.

April 22. Iraq Violates No-Fly Zone. Iraqi helicopters violate the southern no-fly zone and UN sanctions to pick up Muslim pilgrims returning from Mecca in Saudi Arabia. Iraq picks up more pilgrims on April 25.

May 1. Chief Weapons Inspector Replaced. Australian representative to the United Nations Richard Butler replaces Rolf Ekeus as chairman of the UN committee charged with weapons inspections in Iraq.

May 5. PUK Accused by Iraq. The Ministry of Irrigation accuses the Patriotic Union of Kurdistan (PUK) of reducing water supplies flowing south through areas under their control. PUK blames the reduced supply on poor rainfall.

May 9. Refugees Face Expulsion from the United States. Thirteen Iraqi refugees, who had been employed by the U.S. Central Intelligence Agency in antiregime schemes in Iraq and subsequently received refuge in the United States, face expulsion on charges they are covert agents of Iraq.

July 13. Government Forces Attack Shrine. Opposition radio reports that an attack by government troops on the Imam al-Hussein shrine in Karbala on June 24–25 killed two hundred people.

July 20. Explosion Near Palace. Opposition radio reports that an explosive charge went off near the presidential palace in Basra, killing an unspecified number of people.

August 20. Iraq to Admit Iranian Pilgrims. Iraq announces that it will allow Iranians to visit Shiite holy sites in Karbala and Najaf. Such visits were suspended in 1980.

October 29. Iraq Orders Americans to Leave. Iraq orders all Americans working on the UN Security Council Special Commission on Iraq (UNSCOM) team to leave the country within one week. The UN responds by suspending the monitoring operation. Although UN secretary general Kofi Annan convinces Iraq to extend the deadline, he and a three-member UN delegation fail to convince the Iraqis to allow the Americans to remain. The Iraqis cite a lack of "balance" among the nations represented on the teams. The UN imposes new sanctions on Iraq on November 12, and UNSCOM chairman Butler announces that he will withdraw all inspectors by November 14. The United States orders five ships to the Persian Gulf. On November 20 Hussein allows the UNSCOM team to resume its work.

December 15. Presidential Palaces Off Limits. Iraqi authorities tell UNSCOM chairman Butler that the inspection team will never be allowed to inspect the presidential palaces.

ISRAEL

February 20. Israel Seeks Release of Spy. Israel formally requests that Egypt release Israeli Arab Azzam Azzam, whom Egypt charged with espionage on February 17. On August 31 Egypt sentences him to fifteen years hard labor.

April 17. Elder Statesman Dies. Chaim Herzog, the president of Israel from 1983 to 1993, dies at age seventy-eight near Tel Aviv.

May 9. UN Committee Accuses Israel. The UN Committee Against Torture states that extreme methods of interrogation of prisoners by Israel amounts to torture and calls on Israel to cease such practices.

June 11. Orthodox Jews Attack Conservatives, Palestinians. In Jerusalem, Orthodox Jewish men attack a group of conservative male and female Jews at the Wailing Wall. The Orthodox Jews object to men and women praying together. After the confrontation, some Orthodox youth attack Palestinians and their property.

June 15. Public Calls for Early Elections. In Tel Aviv, forty thousand people demonstrate in Rabin Square for early elections to replace Prime Minister Netanyahu.

August 25. Israel Announces Dam Plan. Israel reveals its plan to build a dam on the Yarmuk River in territory disputed with Syria.

October 25. Activists Call for Netanyahu's Resignation. In Tel Aviv and Jerusalem, an estimated two hundred peace activists hold vigils to call for Netanyahu's resignation.

November 9. Military Group Supports Leaving Lebanon. A group of military police launch "The Movement for a Peaceful Withdrawal from Lebanon" to press the government for a unilateral withdrawal from the "security zone" in southern Lebanon.

CHRONOLOGY OF EVENTS, 1945–2005 **517**

December 14. Netanyahu Supports U.S. Spy. Netanyahu releases a letter of support for Jonathan Pollard, an American serving a life sentence in the United States for spying for Israel in the 1980s.

KURDISH AFFAIRS

January 16. PUK and KDP Take Diplomatic Measures. Patriotic Union of Kurdistan (PUK) and the Kurdistan Democratic Party (KDP) agree to allow refugees to return to their homes in Iraq, withdraw from disputed areas, and turn those areas over to a monitoring force.

April 26. PUK and KIM Forces Clash. Near Iraq's border with Iran, PUK forces clash with the Kurdistan Islamic Movement (KIM). The two parties sign a cease-fire, brokered by Iran, on May 1.

May 19. KDP and PKK Members Battle. KDP forces overrun six Kurdish Workers' Party (PKK) offices in Irbil, northern Iraq.

June 26. "Operation Hammer" Ends. Turkish forces pull out of northern Iraq. They report that 113 Turkish soldiers and 3,000 PKK fighters perished in the ten-week offensive. The PKK estimates that they lost 1,912 members.

July 26. PUK and PKK Forces Attack KDP. In the Rawandez region of northern Iraq, PUK and PKK forces attack KDP positions around the village of Garawan.

August 20. Britain Extradites PKK Official. A senior official of the PKK, known only as Faysal D., is flown to Germany where he is wanted for allegedly organizing 150 attacks against offices of Turkish interests in Germany.

August 24. Turkey Returns Civilians. The Iranian news agency reports that the Turkish government has returned eight hundred Kurdish civilians—mostly women and children arrested for illegal entry into Turkey—to security forces of the KDP.

September 23. Turkey Enters Iraq. An estimated fifteen thousand Turkish soldiers, with tanks and armored vehicles, cross into the Iraqi town of Zakho from Habur, Turkey, in pursuit of PKK fighters.

September 28. KDP Ousts PKK. According to KDP radio, the KDP has conducted operations to remove PKK bases and positions from northern Iraq, forcing PKK fighters to retreat to PUK territories. The KDP also hands over PKK members to the Turkish army to be tried as prisoners of war.

October 12. Turkey Claims "Success" in Iraq. Turkish military sources report that they have killed 797 "terrorists" in cross-border operations into Iraq. Turkish sources also report that the operation has been carried out in full coordination with the KDP, led by Massoud Barzani.

October 13. PUK-KDP Cease-Fire Ends. The 1996 cease-fire between the PUK and the KDP ends in northern Iraq after a meeting of Kurdish representatives in London fails to produce an agreement.

October 17. Peace Initiative Sponsored Internationally. The United States, Turkey, and Britain issue a statement after a peace conference between Iraqi Kurdish factions. The mediators announce a truce between PUK and KDP forces.

October 24. Turkey Attacks PUK. Turkey launches air raids against PUK positions in northern Iraq with the support of the KDP.

October 24. Turkey and Iran Attack PKK. Turkish and Iranian forces carry out joint operations against PKK camps in Iran.

November 30. Turkey Engages PKK in Iraq. Turkish warplanes bomb suspected PKK bases in northern Iraq. Ground forces then cross the border to combat PKK members.

JORDAN

May 17. Press Law Inspires Demonstrations. King Hussein issues a decree that bans non-Jordanians from editing newspapers and bans journalists from writing about Jordan's military and police. In Amman, eighty protestors stage a demonstration that results in violent clashes with police on May 20.

August 26. Jordan and the United States Sign Agreements. To support Jordanian development projects, Jordan and the United States sign two agreements totaling $100 million. In a third agreement, Jordan receives $3.5 million for its population and family health programs.

LEBANON

February 16. Red Army Members Arrested. In the Biqa region, authorities arrest six suspected members of a Japanese opposition group, the Red Army. The Red Army was accused of the May 1992 Lod airport attack and of having ties with the Popular Front for the Liberation of Palestine (PFLP).

June 13. Israel Fined for Attack. The UN General Assembly votes sixty-six to two to fine Israel $1.7 million for the April 1996 attack on the Qana UN base in Lebanon.

July 30. Travel Ban Lifted. The United States lifts a decade-old ban restricting American travel to Lebanon.

LIBYA AND NORTH AFRICA

April 18. Palestinians Forced Out of No-Man's Land. At a refugee camp on the Egyptian border, Libyan authorities force some 250 Palestinian refugees, who had inhabited the camp since 1995, to return to Libya.

October 11. Americans Wanted by Libya. Libya requests that a number of Americans, including Oliver North, stand trial for "premeditated murder and offenses against public safety in Banghazi and Tripoli on 15 April 1986," when the United States bombed Libya.

PALESTINIAN AFFAIRS

February 18. Exchange Opens. In Nablus the Palestinian Securities Exchange opens.

May 20. Journalist Arrested. In Ramallah, police arrest Daud Kuttab, director of al-Quds Educational Television. The Palestinian Broadcasting Corporation (PBC) reportedly jams al-Quds broadcasts of Legislative Council meetings. Authorities release Kuttab on May 27, never having charged him.

May 26. PA Charged by Palestinian NGO. The Palestinian Human Rights Monitoring Group, a nongovernmental organization, presents a report alleging that the Palestinian Authority was responsible for forty-two cases of torture.

July 31. Legislative Council Demands New Cabinet. The Palestinian Legislative Council concludes an investigation into corruption in the Palestinian government and votes fifty-six to four in favor of a resolution calling on President Arafat to dissolve the cabinet by September.

November 13. Arafat to Declare Statehood. Arafat announces that he intends to declare Palestinian statehood in May 1999.

PERSIAN GULF STATES

February 24. Liquefied Gas Facility Inaugurated. The world's largest liquefied gas export facility, Qatar Liquefied Gas, opens.

March 22. Khobar Suspect Arrested. Canadian authorities arrest Saudi Hani Abd al-Rahim al-Sayigh, a suspect in the June 1996 Khobar bombing in Saudi Arabia.

April 4. Hizballah Leader Implicated in Saudi Explosion. Canadian court documents name Saudi Hizballah leader Ahmad Ibrahim Mughassil as the "mastermind" of the June 1996 Khobar bombing.

May 12. Internet Comes to Saudi Arabia. King Fahd reportedly approves the establishment of an Internet system in the country.

June 28. Iran Implicated in Khobar Bombing. Saudi al-Sayigh, who had been deported to the United States from Canada on June 17, links a senior Iranian official, Brigadier Ahmad Sharafi, to the Khobar incident and other plots against U.S. targets.

SYRIA

January 2. Syria Blames Israel for Explosion. The Syrian state news service reports that Israeli agents were responsible for the December 1996 bus bombing in Damascus.

January 10. Bombing Linked to Khobar, Saudi Arabia. Islamic Movement for Change claims responsibility for the December 1996 bus bombing, stating that the action was in retaliation for the execution by Syria of a suspect in the June 1996 bombing in Khobar, Saudi Arabia.

July 17. Stance Toward Iraq Eased. After seventeen years, Syria takes off the air Radio Voice of Iraq, a

transmission critical of the Baghdad regime. On July 22 the government announces that individual businessmen may travel to Iraq.

YEMEN

February 11. U.S. Citizen Kidnapped. The Murad tribe abducts U.S. citizen Joe Dell-Aria from an oil field east of San'a' in an attempt to gain leverage in a dispute with the Yemeni government.

October 30. Oil Executive Abducted. Near San'a', American oil executive Steve Carpenter is seized by unknown kidnappers, who free him unharmed on November 27.

1998

REGIONAL AFFAIRS

March 6. Saudi Arabia and Iran to Cooperate. In an interview with reporters in Tehran after a visit to Saudi Arabia, Iranian chairman of the Expediency Council Rafsanjani states that arrangements are under way to create an Iranian-Saudi cooperation commission.

April 23. Iran Submits Protest to Iraq. In Tehran, Iran's foreign minister submits a protest to Iraq's chargé d'affaires about the assassination of Shaykh Murteza Ali Muhammad Ibrahim Borujerdi, who was killed in the Southern Iraqi city of Najaf. Borujerdi was a candidate for the position of grand spiritual leader of Shiite Muslims worldwide.

May 4. Iraqi War Crimes Investigated. A U.S. envoy arrives in Kuwait to gather war-crimes evidence against Iraqi president Hussein.

July 20. Saudi Arabia and Yemen Clash over Island. Yemeni president Ali Abdallah Salih accuses Saudi Arabia of attacking Duwayma Island, a Yemeni-claimed island in the Red Sea, killing three people and injuring nine. On July 25 Yemen's foreign minister travels to Saudi Arabia for talks about the disputed territory.

August 7. U.S. Embassies Bombed. Unknown assailants bomb the U.S. embassies in Nairobi, Kenya, and Dar es Salaam, Tanzania, killing more than 130 people, including 12 Americans.

August 20. United States Bombs Suspected Complexes. The U.S. military launches about seventy-five cruise missiles from ships in the Arabian and Red Seas on two targets allegedly linked to Saudi millionaire Osama bin Laden, whom the United States suspects of involvement in the August 7 embassy bombings. One target, in Khost, Afghanistan, is an alleged terrorist training ground, and the other target is a factory near Khartoum, in the Sudan. Bin Laden is not injured in the attacks, according to Afghan sources.

August 20. Sudan Factory Innocent. The Sudanese interior minister insists in a Cable News Network (CNN) interview that the U.S. military target in his country had not manufactured components of chemical weapons as the United States alleged. On September 2 U.S. secretary of defense Cohen states that the United States was unaware that the factory produced pharmaceuticals.

September 6. United States Blames al-Qaida. In U.S. federal court papers, federal agents state that the U.S. embassy bombings in Nairobi and Dar es Salaam were the work of al-Qaida, an organization financed by Saudi millionaire bin Laden.

October 2. Syria and Turkey Argue over PKK. Turkey masses troops along its border with Syria, charging that Syria supports the Kurdish Workers' Party (PKK). Syria denies the charge and insists that it will stand up to any Turkish challenge.

October 6. Turkey Makes Demands on Syria. In Ankara, Turkish prime minister Yilmaz gives Egyptian president Mubarak a list of demands for Syria in order to avoid military conflict. Turkey wants Syria to close PKK camps, surrender PKK leader Abdallah Ocalan, and forfeit Syrian claims to the Turkish province of Hatay. Syria responds, October 13, stating that Ocalan is not in Syria and that Syria has closed all PKK camps in Syria and Lebanon.

October 15. Turkey Refuses Talks on Water. Turkey rejects a Syrian offer to hold talks on water sharing. Syria has long maintained that Turkey prevents the natural flow of fresh water into Syrian territory by damming sources.

October 21. Syria and Turkey Sign Agreement. Syria and Turkey sign an accord stipulating that Syria will not support the PKK militarily, logistically, or financially.

November 4. United States Indicts bin Laden. A federal grand jury in Manhattan hands down a 238-count indictment against bin Laden for attacks against Americans abroad.

ARAB-ISRAELI CONFLICT

January 8. Suskind Sentenced for Posters. In Jerusalem an Israeli court sentences Tatiana Suskind to two years' imprisonment for displaying posters depicting the Prophet Muhammad as a pig in June 1997.

January 13. Israeli Cabinet Makes Demands. The Israeli cabinet decides that Israel will not withdraw further from the West Bank until the Palestinians draft a new national covenant and extradite thirty-four Palestinians wanted by Israel. The cabinet also claims as vital interests Jerusalem, settlements, military bases, and "historic sites sacred to the Jewish people."

January 16. EU Insists on Role. The European Commission unanimously endorses a policy document stating that the European Union (EU) should increase its participation in the peace process negotiations and should be the "key coordinator" of all international economic aid underpinning the peace process.

January 22. United States Mediates Withdrawals. U.S. officials announce that Israel has offered to withdraw

from less than 10 percent of the West Bank in three phases over several months. Israel promises only one withdrawal before a final settlement with the Palestinians. Palestinian Authority (PA) president Arafat insists on three withdrawals before a final status agreement with the Israelis. He rejects the Israeli proposal.

February 4. Plans for Ras al-Amud Finalized. The Israeli interior ministry announces that it has approved the final plans for building Jewish housing in the Ras al-Amud neighborhood of Jerusalem on land owned by Irving Muskowitz, a retired American Jewish millionaire.

March 4. CIA Trains PA Forces. The *New York Times* reports that the U.S. Central Intelligence Agency (CIA) has been training Palestinian Authority security forces to improve the PA's ability to identify and arrest suspected terrorists and to increase the Israeli government's confidence in the PA.

March 24. Israel Ups Offer. Israeli prime minister Netanyahu compromises by telling U.S. president Clinton that the Israelis will withdraw from more than 9 percent of the West Bank. Netanyahu promises to turn over land adjacent to existing autonomous areas, not just isolated patches of the West Bank. On April 29 the Palestinian Authority approves the Clinton administration's plan for Israel to pull out of 13 percent of the West Bank, but the Netanyahu administration refuses to increase its offer further, despite repeated U.S. efforts to convince them.

April 1. Hamas Member Killed. The Palestinian Authority finds Islamic Resistance Movement (Hamas) member Muhy al-Din al-Sharif dead. Al-Sharif, wanted by Israel, had been shot to death before his car was exploded. Although Israeli authorities deny any involvement in al-Sharif's death, protests against Israel erupt throughout the West Bank and Gaza. On April 11 the PA arrests dozens of Hamas members, including one it suspects of al-Sharif's murder.

April 20. EU Helps PA with Security. In Gaza, British prime minister Blair and Palestinian Authority president Arafat announce the establishment of a joint EU-PA security committee to help the PA combat terrorism.

April 24. Netanyahu Threatens Reannexation. During an interview on Israeli television, Netanyahu states that if Arafat declares a Palestinian state in May 1999, Israel will reannex parts of the West Bank.

April 30. Cornerstone Laid at Har Homa. At the Har Homa Jewish settlement, in an area of East Jerusalem known to Arabs as Jabal Abu Ghunaym, thousands of Israelis gather to lay a symbolic cornerstone for the Jewish housing project planned for the site.

May 6. U.S. First Lady Surprises White House. Speaking to a group of Arab and Israeli teenagers, U.S. first lady Hillary Rodham Clinton says that creation of a Palestinian state is very important for the broader goal of peace in the Middle East. The next day the White House reiterates the official U.S. position on the peace process and emphasizes that Mrs. Clinton had expressed her personal views.

May 14. Palestinians March. Palestinians mark the 50th anniversary of the State of Israel with the "March of the Million" throughout the West Bank and Gaza. Nine people die when Israeli forces open fire on demonstrators.

May 26. Brief Battle in Old City. In the Arab quarter of Jerusalem's Old City, Israeli police and Palestinians clash over the Ateret Cohanim settlement, prompting Jerusalem's mayor Olmert to sign a demolition order, giving the settlers twenty-four hours to vacate the premises. Three Palestinian Authority cabinet members are among those at the building site.

June 21. Jerusalem to Expand Westward. The Israeli cabinet approves a plan submitted by Israeli city planners that would extend Jerusalem city limits westward to keep the Jewish population of the city at 70 percent. The UN Security Council issues a statement, on July 13, criticizing Israel's decision.

August 25. Settlers to Receive New Homes. Netanyahu announces plans to build new homes for Jewish settlers in Hebron.

September 9. Israel and PA Guilty of Abuses. The London-based organization Amnesty International releases a report that accuses Israel and the Palestinian Authority of human rights violations in the name of security and states that the Palestinians are the main victims.

September 15. Israeli NGOs Accuse Government. Two nongovernmental organizations, the Israeli Information Center for Human Rights in the Occupied Territories and the Center for the Defense of the Individual, publish a report accusing Israel of "deporting" Palestinians from East Jerusalem by confiscating residence permits and blocking the registration of new births.

September 16. Arafat Calls for State. In Cairo, at a meeting of the Arab League, Arafat calls on member states to support the establishment of an independent Palestinian state, with Jerusalem as its capital, on May 4, 1999. On September 28 Palestinian Authority president Arafat asks the UN General Assembly for its support in bringing about a Palestinian state by May 4, 1999.

September 27. Israeli Arabs Clash with Israeli Police. In the northern town of Umm al-Fahm, Israeli Arabs clash with Israeli riot police in an attempt to stop the Israeli army from confiscating acres of olive groves to use as a firing range. The fighting lasts for two days.

September 28. Thirteen Percent Compromise Reached. In Washington, President Clinton meets with Netanyahu and Arafat. They announce that Israel will withdraw from 13 percent of the West Bank, but 3 percent of the land will be designated a nature reserve where Palestinians cannot live.

October 15. Interim Agreement Talks Begin. At the Wye Conference Center in Queenstown, Maryland, interim agreement talks commence between Netanyahu and Arafat.

October 23. Wye Accord Signed. After nine days of negotiations at the Wye Plantation, Netanyahu and Arafat sign an interim agreement at the White House. The agreement includes an Israeli withdrawal from 13 percent of the West Bank over twelve weeks. Whereas Israel will maintain security control, the Palestinian Authority will manage civil affairs. Israel promises to release 750 Palestinian prisoners and allow the opening of the Gaza airport, an industrial zone, and two secure land routes between the West Bank and Gaza. Palestinians agree to revoke twenty-six anti-Israel clauses from the PLO charter, arrest thirty suspects wanted by Israel, lay off ten thousand of the forty thousand Palestinian police to comply with force limits, provide a computer roster of security forces to Israel to allow screening for terrorists, and provide detailed intelligence information to Israeli security.

October 30. PA Ratifies Accord. The Palestinian Authority cabinet ratifies the Wye accord during a five-hour meeting.

November 11. Israeli Cabinet Ratifies Accord. The Israeli cabinet conditionally ratifies the Wye accord. Conditions include that the Palestinian National Council vote by a majority to nullify clauses in the PLO charter calling for the destruction of Israel and that the third Israeli redeployment be from no more than 1 percent of the West Bank. On November 17 the Israeli Knesset approves the accord, voting 75 to 19 with nine abstentions.

November 20. Israel Complies with Parts of Accord. The Israeli army withdraws from 220 square miles around the West Bank town of Jenin, transferring twenty-eight towns to full or partial Palestinian control. Israel also releases 250 Palestinians from Israeli jails.

December 14. PNC Nullifies Charter Clauses. With President Clinton as witness, the PNC votes to nullify those articles of the 1964 PLO charter calling for the destruction of Israel.

December 20. Israel Suspends Wye Accord. The Israeli cabinet votes to suspend the Wye accord until the Palestinian Authority collects unlicensed weapons, abandons plans to declare statehood in May 1999, and curbs incitement against Israel.

EGYPT

January 21. Residents Clash with Police. The Antiquities Council announces plans to tear down sixty-five homes built on government land near the Valley of the Kings in Upper Egypt. Despite government promises to build a new village for those displaced, four people die when some residents clash with police.

May 19. Nasser-Era Wound Healed. The Ministry of Awqaf (religious endowments) returns to the Coptic Orthodox Church land it had seized in 1971.

August 25. Abu Nidal Held in Cairo. Egyptian authorities reportedly hold in custody Palestinian Sabri al-Banna, also known as Abu Nidal, who is wanted in Britain, Italy, and the United States for acts of terrorism. The next day, the Foreign Ministry denies the reports.

IRAN

January 16. Religious Leader Rules Out Dialogue. Ayatollah Ali Khamenei rules out dialogue with the U.S. government but praises President Mohammad Khatami for his overture to the American people during his televised interview with CNN on January 7.

February 23. EU Lifts Ban. The European Union foreign ministers agree to lift the ban on high-level contacts with Iran.

February 25. United States to Ease Visa Process. The U.S. Department of State announces that it will ease the visa process for Iranians who wish to visit the United States.

April 30. United States Accuses Iran of Terrorism. The U.S. Department of State releases a report calling Iran "the most active state sponsor of terrorism."

May 18. Iran Suspected in Argentine Bombing. Argentina's foreign minister, Guido Di Tella, orders the expulsion from the country of seven Iranians, including three diplomats, on suspicion of Iranian involvement in the 1994 bombing of a Buenos Aires Jewish cultural center. On August 7 the U.S. Federal Bureau of Investigation tells Argentina that it has concluded that Iranian embassy officials were involved in the explosion that killed eighty-six people.

June 17. United States Calls for Normal Relations. During a speech in New York, U.S. secretary of state Albright calls on Iran to join the United States in drawing up a "road map" to normal relations between the two countries. On July 1 Khatami comments that he appreciates the change in "tone" from Washington but will wait to enter into dialogue with the United States until he sees a change in "action."

August 17. Lebanon Hostages Awarded Damages. A U.S. federal judge awards $65 million to three Americans who sued the Iranian government for its role in kidnapping them in Lebanon in the 1980s.

September 22. Rushdie Death Order. In New York, Foreign Minister Kamal Kharrazi reads a statement officially renouncing the death threat against author Salman Rushdie. Britain responds by restoring full diplomatic relations with Iran, but three days later, the Iranian foreign ministry announces that the fatwa cannot be revoked. On October 12 the Fifteenth of Khordad Foundation adds $300,000 to the $2.5 million bounty on Rushdie.

November 12. "Ancient Civilizations" Meet in Athens. Following up on Khatami's call for a "dialogue of civilizations" at the UN General Assembly in September 1998, representatives from Egypt, Greece, Iran, and Italy, the "ancient civilizations," meet to outline the framework for such a dialogue.

November 19. UN General Assembly Rebukes Iran. The social, humanitarian, and cultural committee of the United Nations adopts a resolution accusing Iran of executions without due process of law and of discrimination against women and religious minorities.

November 23. American Tourists Attacked. In Tehran, members of the Fedayeen Islam pelt with stones a tourist bus carrying eleven Americans.

IRAQ

January 11. New Team Displeases Iraq. Iraq criticizes the composition of a new UN team of weapons inspectors that has arrived in Baghdad, led by American William Scott Ritter, Jr., contending that the seventeen-member team is dominated by Americans and Britons. One of the seventeen is Russian, and another is Australian. Iraq accuses Ritter of espionage and suspends the team's activities. The team leaves Iraq on January 16.

February 20. UN Increases Oil-for-Food Deal. The UN Security Council increases from $2 billion to $5.2 billion the amount of oil Iraq may sell every six months and votes to allow some of the revenue to be used to repair the country's infrastructure. On February 28, however, the Iraqi oil minister reports that Iraq cannot sell more than $4 billion worth of oil every six months unless sanctions are eased to allow the country to buy new equipment. UN secretary general Kofi Annan suggests, on April 16, that Iraq be allowed to import $300 million in equipment to improve its ability to export $5.2 billion worth of oil.

February 23. New Monitoring Agreement Signed. Deputy prime minister Aziz and Annan sign a new monitoring agreement to settle the crisis. Iraq reconfirms its commitment to the relevant UN resolutions and grants UN Security Council Special Commission on Iraq (UNSCOM) inspectors unconditional access to suspected weapons sites throughout the country. In return, the United Nations agrees to create a group of diplomats and disarmament experts appointed by Annan to aid in inspections of eight presidential palaces. The UN Security Council unanimously endorses the new agreement but does not authorize the United States to use force if Iraq does not comply.

March 5. UNSCOM Team Returns to Baghdad. An UNSCOM team, led by American Scott Ritter, resumes inspections under the new monitoring agreement.

April 9. Independent Experts Release Report. A team of experts reports to the United Nations that Iraq has failed to convince them of its elimination of biological weapons.

April 23. Iraq Demands End to Sanctions. In a letter to the UN Security Council, Aziz formally demands that sanctions be lifted immediately and without any new restrictions. The Iraqi cabinet warns the United States that it will "pay dearly" if sanctions are not lifted.

June 17. United States to Undermine Iraqi Regime. U.S. assistant secretary of state for near eastern affairs Martin Indyk announces a U.S. plan to work with seventy-three groups outside Iraq to build political opposition to President Saddam Hussein.

June 18. Iraq Violates Sanctions. The *New York Times* reports that U.S. and Turkish officials had admitted that Iraq had been smuggling large quantities of oil to Turkey in violation of UN sanctions.

August 5. Iraq Ends Cooperation with UNSCOM. The Iraqi government issues letters to Annan and the Security Council stating that Iraq is ending all cooperation with UN arms inspectors until the UNSCOM mission is restructured. Annan calls for a reassessment of UN policy toward Iraq. On August 9 UNSCOM suspends weapons inspections.

August 9. UN Special Envoy Travels to Iraq. Prakash Shah, Annan's special envoy, travels to Iraq to meet with Aziz. Shah is unable to persuade Iraq to change its stance on weapons inspections. On August 20 the UN Security Council unanimously votes to renew economic sanctions against Iraq.

August 26. UNSCOM Inspector Resigns. American UNSCOM inspector Ritter resigns, charging that Britain, the United States, and the UN Security Council have weakened their positions against Iraq, making it difficult for the inspectors to uncover Iraq's hidden weapons programs.

September 4. Oil-for-Food Program Failing. Benan Sevan, the senior official in charge of the "oil-for-food" program, reports to the UN Security Council that, due to the drop in oil prices, Iraq cannot raise enough money to buy food and medicine to meet the designated nutritional target.

September 9. Sanction Reviews Suspended. The UN Security Council votes unanimously to suspend sanction reviews and decides to review Iraqi relations with the United Nations only after Iraq allows UNSCOM and the International Atomic Energy Agency to resume work. In response, the Iraqi National Assembly votes, September 14, to end all cooperation with UNSCOM unless the UN Security Council reverses its decision.

October 6. UNSCOM Chairman Summarizes Progress. UNSCOM chairman Butler reports to the United Nations that Iraq may be close to the elimination of its chemical and ballistic weapons but not its biological weapons.

October 17. Annan Assesses Situation. Annan tells the *Washington Post* that he believes that determining the extent of Iraqi disarmament is a "political judgement" and that the UNSCOM weapons inspections teams may need to avoid confrontational inspections to regain Iraqi cooperation.

October 26. Experts Find Evidence of VX Nerve Gas. An international panel of twenty-one scientists, examining the results of French, Swiss, and U.S. tests of Iraqi missile fragments for VX nerve gas, turn in their report to the UN Security Council. They conclude that, at some point, Iraq had used detergents to wash the fragments.

October 31. Iraq Ends All Cooperation. Iraq announces that it will end all cooperation with UNSCOM arms inspectors and will close their long-term monitoring operations immediately.

November 14. Iraq Resumes Cooperation. Aziz sends a letter to the UN Security Council in which he states that Iraq will resume cooperation with UNSCOM but that UNSCOM must prove that Iraq still had prohibited weapons. He also says that Iraq would like Annan to review Iraqi-UN relations. He insists that these wishes are not conditions for Iraqi compliance. The Security Council orders UNSCOM weapons inspectors back to Iraq on November 15.

December 14. United States Called Out-of-Line. Annan asserts that U.S. calls for the overthrow of Hussein are beyond the Security Council resolution on Iraq.

December 16. Operation Desert Fox Begins, Ends. President Clinton orders a series of air strikes, named Desert Fox, on Iraqi weapons plants, intelligence agencies, and Republican Guard fortifications. British forces participate in a four-day campaign against Iraq. The Iraqis end cooperation with UNSCOM.

ISRAEL

January 4. Foreign Minister Resigns. In protest over the stagnation of the peace process and the lack of enough funding for social welfare programs, Foreign Minister David Levy resigns from the Israeli cabinet.

January 25. Citizenship Requirements Clarified. The Orthodox Chief Rabbinate agrees that Israel can recognize people converted by Conservative and Reform rabbis as Jews for purposes of citizenship but not for purposes of religious rites. On February 25 the Chief Rabbinate Council rules out cooperation with the non-Orthodox branches of Judaism on conversions and religious rites. On December 30 the district court in Jerusalem orders recognition of conversions to Judaism performed by non-Orthodox rabbis.

March 4. President Weizman Re-elected. The Knesset votes 63 to 49 to re-elect Ezer Weizman to a second five-year term as president. Weizman defeated the Likud Party's candidate, Shaul Amor.

April 29. Israel Turns Fifty. Israel celebrates "Independence Day," marking the beginning of its jubilee.

May 11. Israel Officially Recognizes Spy. Israel admits that American Jonathan Pollard had been an agent for Israel. Pollard has been imprisoned in the United States since 1987.

May 13. EU Warns Israel. The European Union formally warns Israel that it will not accept imports from Israeli settlements because the settlements "are not part of the state of Israel" and, therefore, "cannot benefit from the preferential treatment granted by [the] EU-Israel agreement." After ten days of negotiations, the EU decides that it can no longer have a political dialogue with Israel.

July 22. United States Bans Satellite Images. Because of Israel's fears that satellite images may fall into "enemy" hands, the United States prevents U.S. satellite-imaging firms from taking high-resolution images of Israel. No other country has received such an exemption.

December 9. Orthodox Students Must Serve in Military. The Supreme Court rules against the exemption from military service for Orthodox Jewish Yeshiva students.

JORDAN

January 26. Press Law Revoked. The Supreme Court revokes the May 1997 press law, which increased newspapers' minimum capital.

July 28. King Hussein Undergoes Treatment. In a televised radio address, King Hussein announces that he will seek treatment for lymphatic cancer at the Mayo Clinic in Rochester, New York.

KURDISH AFFAIRS

April 13. PKK Leader Apprehended. The Turkish army captures Semdin Sakik, the former number two leader of the Kurdish Workers' Party (PKK), after he leaves a house in Dahuk, Iraq.

May 21. Turkish Forces Gather at Iraqi Border. Thousands of Turkish soldiers amass along the Iraqi border to attack PKK forces in northern Iraq. They clash May 25.

July 18. KDP Joins Forces with Turkey. The Kurdistan Democratic Party (KDP) announces that it has signed an agreement with the Turkish foreign ministry to cooperate in countering PKK attacks in northern Iraq.

September 17. United States Brokers Agreement. In Washington, Secretary of State Albright announces that the United States has mediated an agreement between KDP leader Massoud Barzani and Patriotic Union of Kurdistan (PUK) leader Jalal Talabani to share power in northern Iraq and counter Iraqi president Hussein.

LEBANON

April 1. Israel Offers to Withdraw. The Israeli government endorses UN Resolution 425 calling on Israel to withdraw from the "zone" in southern Lebanon on the condition that Lebanon ensure border security. Lebanon rejects the offer, stating that Israel's offer goes against the UN resolution, which calls for an unconditional withdrawal.

May 24. Municipal Elections Held. Lebanon holds the first phase of municipal elections in the Central Mount Lebanon region. The elections are the first in thirty-five years at the municipal level. Hizballah candidates lose in municipal elections held in Baalbak, their stronghold.

June 21. U.S. Embassy Misses Explosion. In Beirut, three grenades explode near the U.S. embassy. Embassy officials insist that the building was not the target.

September 9. United States Takes Precautions. The United States warns all Americans in Lebanon to take the "highest level of caution" after receiving information that its embassy may be attacked.

October 15. New President Elected. After gaining Syrian backing, parliament elects Gen. Emile Lahoud, head of the Lebanese army.

November 30. New Prime Minister Chosen. Citing breaches of the 1990 Taif Accord, which stipulates that only parliamentary deputies may nominate prime ministers, Prime Minister Rafiq Hariri refuses to accept another term of office. Hariri contends that twenty-one members of parliament violated the accord by requesting that President Lahoud endorse whomever he wished. The parliament backs Lahoud's choice of Selim al-Hoss, who was prime minister during the 1975–1990 civil war.

December 9. Israelis Fly over Beirut. Israeli aircraft fly over Beirut and stage mock raids over the city.

LIBYA

April 21. Lockerbie Families and Suspects Agree. A lawyer for the two Libyan suspects from the 1988 Pan Am flight 103 bombing over Lockerbie, Scotland, claims to have reached an agreement with lawyers for the families of the victims. The agreement allegedly calls for the two Libyans to be tried in a neutral nation under Scottish law.

July 21. U.S. and Britain Assent to Special Court. U.S. Department of State spokesman James Rubin announces that Britain and the United States will consider the creation of a special court in the Netherlands to try two Libyan suspects for the downing of flight 103.

July 23. Suspects Concur, Make Demand. A lawyer for the two Libyans suspected of the Lockerbie bombing announce that the men will agree to a trial in The Hague under Scottish law but only after the United Nations lifts sanctions against Libya.

August 26. Libya Agrees to Trial. Libya releases a statement accepting the British and U.S. proposal to a Hague trial of the two Pan Am 103 suspects.

August 28. UN to Suspend Sanctions. The UN Security Council votes unanimously to suspend sanctions against Libya once it has turned over the two suspects for trial.

September 29. Libya Lists Conditions for Trial. The Libyan UN delegate says that should the two Libyan suspects be found guilty they cannot be imprisoned in Scotland, Libya cannot be asked to provide witnesses for the prosecution, and the trial cannot be held at a former U.S. military base, as planned.

October 3. Libyan Leader Drops Goal. The London-based daily *al-Hayat* reports that leader Qadhafi has replaced the Libyan goal of Pan-Arab unity with African unity.

December 15. Government Agrees to Hague Trial. The Libyan General People's Congress endorses an agreement to try the two Libyan bombing suspects in the Netherlands.

PALESTINIAN AFFAIRS

January 15. Strategic Plan Unveiled. Planning minister Nabil Shaath announces details of the Palestinian Authority's first strategic development plan, which focuses on infrastructure development over the next five years.

January 20. PA Called a "Police State." The Palestinian Human Rights Monitoring Group accuses the Palestinian Authority of acting like a "police state," reporting that seven people died in Palestinian Authority custody during 1997.

January 23. World Bank Supports Palestinian Industry. The World Bank says it will lend $10 million to the Palestinian Authority to establish the Gaza Industrial Estate, the first export-oriented industrial zone in Gaza. The venture may create up to fifty thousand jobs.

February 26. Census Results Announced. The Palestinian Central Bureau of Statistics announces the results of the Palestinian Census, reporting there are 2.9 million Palestinians living in the West Bank, Gaza Strip, and East Jerusalem. Israel refuses to acknowledge the validity of the figures.

June 14. Opposition Groups Refuse to Join Government. Arafat on June 13 invites the Islamic Resistance Movement (Hamas) to join the government, but a day later both Hamas and Islamic Jihad announce they will not.

July 7. New UN Status Accorded Palestinians. The UN General Assembly votes 124 to 4, with 10 abstentions and 26 countries absent, to give the Palestinian delegation special "super-observer" status at the United Nations, allowing the Palestinians to debate in the General Assembly, cosponsor resolutions on the Middle East, and participate in UN conferences.

August 6. Two Cabinet Members Resign. Palestinian politicians Hanan Ashrawi and Abd al-Jawad Salih resign from the cabinet to protest Arafat's failure to address issues of corruption within the Palestinian Authority.

August 30. PA Executes Prisoners. In Gaza the Palestinian Authority carries out its first executions, shooting two brothers, members of the Palestinian Security forces, who were convicted of killing two brothers from another family.

October 29. Hamas Leader under House Arrest. The Palestinian Authority places Hamas leader Shaykh Ahmad Yasin under house arrest for statements "against the Palestinian national interest." In response Hamas threatens to attack PA security forces. Arafat frees Shaykh Yasin on December 23.

November 8. Opposition Groups Will Boycott Meeting. In Damascus, leaders of Palestinian groups, such as Hamas and Islamic Jihad, announce that they will avoid any Palestinian Authority meeting on changes to the Palestine Liberation Organization charter and suggest that the PLO elect a central committee to deliberate amending the document.

November 24. Airport Opens in Gaza. The Gaza International Airport opens in Rafah, in the Gaza Strip, with a flight arriving from Egypt.

November 30. International Conference Pledges Millions. In Washington, the U.S. Department of State sponsors a one-day donor conference that raises more than $3 million in aid for the Palestinians. Canada, the European Union, Japan, Kuwait, Norway, Saudi Arabia, and the United States pledge.

PERSIAN GULF STATES

January 22. United States Deports Khobar Suspect. The U.S. Immigration and Naturalization Service announces that it will deport Hani Abd al-Rahim al-Sayigh, a suspect in the bombing of the Khobar Towers in Saudi Arabia in 1996.

June 25. OPEC Reaches Decision in Vienna. The Organization of Petroleum Exporting Countries agrees to cut petroleum production by 1.3 million barrels per day in an attempt to reverse the fall of oil prices.

October 5. UAE Awards Contracts to United States. The Michigan-based electricity utility CMS Energy announces that it has won a contract for a $700 million power plant and desalinization project, to be located northeast of Abu Dhabi in the United Arab Emirates.

October 28. Bahrain Violates Human Rights. British human rights advocates in Parliament accuse Bahrain of systematically violating human rights, asserting that dissenters are arrested, tortured, and jailed by the Security Court.

November 26. OPEC Delays Further Decreases. In Vienna, OPEC ministers delay until March 1999 any decision to stabilize the oil market through further production cuts.

SYRIA

February 8. President Dismisses Brother. President Asad fires his brother as vice president.

July 16. Asad Urges Europe Role. In Paris, during his first official visit to the West in twenty-two years, Asad blames the stalemate in the peace process on Israel and proposes that Europe play a greater role in negotiations.

December 19. U.S. Property Invaded. Demonstrators, protesting the U.S.-British air strikes on Iraq, climb the walls of the U.S. embassy to tear down the U.S. flag. Protestors also vandalize the ambassador's residence.

YEMEN

June 8. Tribe Pledges End to Kidnappings. The Bani Dabiyan tribe sends a signed document to President Ali Abdallah Salih promising to stop abducting foreigners.

July 1. Yemenis Riot over Price Increases. The *Wall Street Journal* reports that Yemeni opposition groups are claiming that one hundred people have died since riots began on June 20 over increases in the price of fuel. In one riot, a pipeline operated by the U.S. company Hunt Oil was destroyed.

July 29. Kidnapping Punishable by Death. Parliament approves a draft law imposing the death penalty for kidnapping, but tribes continue to abduct foreigners.

October 9. Court Rules on Hanish Islands. In The Hague, the Court of Arbitration rules that the Hanish Islands are the sovereign territory of both Eritrea and Yemen. Yemen is given control over four of the seven islands.

December 2. Protests Erupt in the North. In Marib, 105 miles north of the capital San'a', members of the Jahm tribe blow up a Hunt Oil company pipeline to protest the lack of development in what had been North Yemen. On December 28 members of the tribe blow up the main oil pipeline.

1999

REGIONAL AFFAIRS

April 28. United States Revises Sanctions. In a major shift in economic sanctions policy, the Clinton administration announces that it will let U.S. firms sell food and medicine to Iran, Libya, and Sudan, three countries the United States lists as sponsors of international terrorism.

July 26. Sudan and Kuwait Resume Ties. Sudan reopens its embassy in Kuwait, restoring diplomatic ties that the countries severed after Kuwait accused Sudan of supporting the 1990 Iraqi invasion of Kuwait.

October 12. Pakistani General Takes Power in Coup. General Pervez Musharraf deposes the elected government of prime minister Nawaz Sharif in a military coup.

November 14. UN Imposes Sanctions on Afghanistan. The United Nations imposes sanctions on Afghanistan, banning flights and freezing Taliban assets, after the Taliban refuses to surrender al-Qaida leader Osama bin Laden.

ARAB-ISRAELI CONFLICT

January 11. Shimon Peres Addresses PLC. In Ramallah, former Israeli prime minister Shimon Peres, in the first address by an Israeli to the Palestinian Legislative Council, affirms his support of a Palestinian state.

February 12. Arafat Favors Federation. Addressing a rally in Hebron, Palestinian Authority leader Yasir Arafat says that he still endorses the creation of a federation between Jordan and the future Palestinian state.

March 14. Israel Holds Back Water. Israel tells Jordan that because of an unusually dry winter it will reduce the amount of water diverted to Jordan. Jordan asserts that Israel's decision violates their 1994 peace treaty.

March 14. Israel Reaffirms Claim to Jerusalem. The Israeli cabinet reiterates Israel's claim to Jerusalem, issuing a statement criticizing the European Union's position that Jerusalem is a separate entity from Israel based on UN Resolution 181, which recognizes Jerusalem as an international city.

March 26. EU Supports Palestinian State. In Berlin, at an EU summit, participants issue a declaration that states the European Union's willingness to recognize a Palestinian state "in due course." Israeli prime minister Benjamin Netanyahu expresses "regret that Europe, where a third of the Jewish people perished, [saw] fit to impose a solution that endangered the state of Israel and its interests."

March 29. Netanyahu Closes Palestinian Offices. Netanyahu closes three Palestinian offices operating in East Jerusalem, insisting that they are run by the Palestinian Authority and, therefore, violate Israeli sovereignty.

July 25. Barak Orders Settlements Dismantled. Israeli prime minister Ehud Barak orders the military to dismantle a Jewish settlement north of Ramallah.

July 27. Barak and Arafat Meet. At the Erez checkpoint, Barak and Arafat set a two-week deadline for the Palestinian Authority to accept plans for an incremental transfer of West Bank territory, per the Wye River Memorandum. Barak says Israel would carry out the Wye agreement as written if the Palestinians reject the proposal.

August 18. Prisoner Negotiations Stall. Talks between Israelis and Palestinians over the release of Palestinian prisoners break down as Barak refuses to release prisoners linked to violent attacks.

August 30. Barak Extends Statehood Proposal. Barak offers to recognize a Palestinian state by 2000, in exchange for postponement of negotiations with the Palestinian Authority on Jerusalem's status and the right of return for 3.6 million Palestinian refugees.

September 5. Barak and Arafat Sign Final Status Framework. Barak and Arafat sign an agreement between the Palestinian Authority and Israel on a framework for final status talks by February 15, 2000, and a final peace agreement by September 2000. The agreement included an Israeli withdrawal from 11 percent of the West Bank, the release of 350 prisoners from Israel, and the construction of a safe-passage route for Palestinians traveling between the West Bank and Gaza.

September 8. Israeli Cabinet Approves Land Transfers. The Israeli cabinet approves the first of three West Bank land transfers, and the Knesset endorses the new peace framework.

November 10. Israel Orders Settlers Removed. Barak orders the removal of 200 Jewish settlers from Havat Maon in the West Bank, one of twelve illegal settlements scheduled for removal.

EGYPT

September 27. Mubarak Wins Fourth Term. Egyptian president Hosni Mubarak wins a fourth six-year term, winning a reported 94 percent of the vote. Opposition groups boycott the elections, demanding democratic reforms and multiparty elections.

IRAN

February 9. Intelligence Minister Resigns. Minister of Intelligence Qorbanali Dorri-Najafabadi resigns after Iranian authorities link intelligence agents to the December 1998 murders of five dissident writers.

March 22. Former U.S. Hostage Sues Iran. Terry Anderson files a $100 million lawsuit in the United States against Iran for allegedly financing and directing the Hizballah kidnappers who held him captive in Lebanon from 1985 to 1991.

April 30. United States Softens Stance. The U.S. State Department's annual report on terrorism contains subdued language on Iran in another step toward altering its views of the Islamic government in Tehran.

September 28. Students Demonstrate. Hundreds of students at Tehran University hold a demonstration, demanding the resignation of culture and Islamic guidance minister Ataollah Mohajerani and higher education minister Mostafa Moein.

November 19. UN Condemns Iran on Justice. The UN Committee on Human Rights chastises Iran for its failure to meet international standards of justice.

IRAQ

January 4. Iraq Expels Aid Workers. Iraqi authorities say they will not renew visas of British and U.S. aid workers because their safety cannot be guaranteed. The announcement follows an Iraqi statement two days earlier that British and U.S. officials working for UN aid agencies are no longer welcome in Iraq.

January 6. UNSCOM Linked to U.S. Intelligence. U.S. officials respond to a January 5 report that UN secretary-general Kofi Annan has obtained evidence alleging that the UN Security Council Special Commission (UNSCOM) on Iraq had "directly facilitated the creation of an intelligence collection system for the United States" by admitting that they had received intelligence

from UNSCOM. Commission chairman Richard Butler later asserts that he never put UNSCOM operations under the control of the United States or other supporting government.

January 6. UN Agencies Report on Desert Fox Effects. The United Nations Children's Emergency Fund (UNICEF) and the World Food Program report that the joint British and U.S. air strikes on Iraq have damaged a dozen schools and hospitals, destroyed a storehouse of rice, and wrecked a water system, cutting off water supplies to about 300,000 people.

January 20. UN Approves Equipment Purchase. The United Nations decides to allow Iraq to buy $81 million worth of equipment to increase its supply of electricity. The UN Security Council sanctions committee also approves $6.5 million worth of contracts for equipment to upgrade Iraq's oil-producing capability.

January 26. U.S. Extends Flight Crews' Powers. U.S. president Bill Clinton broadens the power of military flight crews to attack "as appropriate . . . any of the [Iraqi] air defense systems that [they] think make [allied forces] vulnerable." U.S. and British pilots continue to battle Iraqi air defense forces in the northern and southern no-fly zones.

January 30. UN Sets Up Review Panels. The UN Security Council agrees to create three panels to review Iraq's compliance with the 1991 Gulf War cease-fire demands and make recommendations to the council on how to proceed. The plan calls for panels on disarmament, humanitarian issues, and prisoners of war and missing Kuwaiti property and archives.

February 19. Grand Ayatollah of Iraq Killed. Assailants kill Muhammad Sadiq al-Sadr, the grand ayatollah of Iraq, and two of his sons in Najaf. In Baghdad and Najaf, Shiite Iraqis demonstrate.

February 28. Arab League Criticizes Air Strikes. The Arab League issues a statement calling on the United States and Britain to halt the air strikes immediately because they are causing "a loss of life, destruction of infrastructure, and an increase in tension in the region."

March 15. Iraq Violates Flight Ban. Iraq flies pilgrims to Saudi Arabia for the annual hajj in violation of the UN flight ban.

March 27. UN Disarmament Panel Submits Report. The UN panel on disarmament of Iraq reports that "the bulk of Iraq's proscribed weapons programs has been eliminated" but urges continued inspections and monitoring to prevent the reconstitution of Iraq's weapons of mass destruction programs.

March 30. UN Humanitarian Panel Decries Human Rights Abuses in Iraq; Prisoners of War Panel Calls for More Iraqi Action. Citing such issues as high infant mortality rates and lack of clean water, the UN panel on humanitarian issues concludes that Iraqis need additional revenue, more humanitarian assistance, and better distribution of aid. The panel also recommends that the Security Council lift the ceiling of allowable oil exports. The UN panel on prisoners of war and missing Kuwaiti property and archives cited Iraqi progress but called on Iraq to release all Kuwaiti and non-Iraqi prisoners, turn over remains of such people killed, allow access by International Red Cross staff to prisoners, and work to return Kuwaiti property to its rightful owners.

April 6. Iraq Executes al-Sadr Assassins. Iraq executes four of five men, including three clerics, who confessed to the February 19 murders of Muhammad Sadiq al-Sadr, the grand ayatollah of Iraq, and two of his sons.

April 8. Iraq Rejects UN Panel Reports. In an April 8 letter to the UN Security Council, Iraqi officials reject the findings of the humanitarian, disarmament, and prisoners of war panels. Iraqi officials demand the lifting of sanctions before they will allow further arms inspections.

May 24. United States Will Help Dissidents. The Clinton administration announces that it will send office equipment and provide training to Iraqi opposition groups but, despite congressional pressure, will not arm opponents of Saddam Hussein.

August 20. Iraq Holds Local Elections. Iraq holds the first local council elections since 1979, with candidates restricted to members of the Baath or independent parties.

September 20. Iraq Rejects New Inspections. Iraqi deputy prime minister Tariq Aziz says Iraq rejects any UN plans for new weapons inspections that do not involve a reduction or elimination of sanctions.

December 17. UN Approves New Iraq Resolution. The UN Security Council creates a new weapons inspection group for Iraq, the UN Monitoring, Verification, and Inspection Commission. The UN also lifts the limit on the amount of oil Iraq is allowed to sell under the oil-for-food program.

ISRAEL

January 19. Barak's Office Burglarized. In Washington, the office of Stanley Greenberg, a campaign consultant for Labor Party leader Barak, is burglarized. It had also been broken into on January 11.

February 14. Religious and Secular Jews Demonstrate. About 250,000 Orthodox Jews hold a demonstration in Jerusalem to defend the religious identity of the state. About 50,000 secular Israelis hold a pro-democracy counterdemonstration. Some 2,000 police monitor the demonstrations to prevent violence.

May 17. Barak Elected Prime Minister. Barak easily defeats incumbent prime minister Benjamin Netanyahu in prime ministerial elections, winning 56 percent of the vote to Netanyahu's 44 percent. Arab and U.S. government officials are pleased when Barak announces that he intends to negotiate a final peace with the Palestinians, withdraw from Lebanon, and reach an agreement with

Syria. Netanyahu resigns his post as head of the Likud Party.

July 18. Israel Will Buy U.S. Warplanes. Barak tells U.S. officials that Israel—in its largest arms purchase—will buy fifty new F-16 jets for $2.5 billion, with an option to purchase sixty more for an additional $2 billion.

September 2. Sharon Elected Likud Leader. Former general and foreign and defense minister Ariel Sharon is elected by a wide margin as Likud Party leader.

September 6. Court Outlaws Physical Force. The Israeli High Court outlaws Shin Bet's use of physical force during interrogations, while leaving allowances for emergency situations. Shin Bet is Israel's internal security force.

JORDAN

January 25. Hussein Appoints Son as Successor. King Hussein names his thirty-seven-year-old son, Prince Abdallah, as his successor. Three days earlier, the king had removed Crown Prince Hasan from the line of succession and appointed him king's deputy.

February 7. King Hussein Dies; Crown Prince Abdallah Crowned King. In Amman, King Hussein, ruler of Jordan since 1952, dies of cancer at the age of sixty-three. Crown Prince Abdallah is crowned King Abdallah II. He appoints his half-brother, Prince Hamza, as crown prince.

March 17. Water Emergency Inspires Loan. The World Bank agrees to lend Jordan $55 million to improve its water resources.

March 21. New Queen Named. King Abdallah appoints his wife, Rania, as queen.

October 15. Muslim Brotherhood Protest. Thousands of people participate in a peaceful demonstration organized by the Muslim Brotherhood, demanding the release of four Hamas leaders arrested in September.

November 21. Jordan Frees Hamas Prisoners. King Abdallah frees four imprisoned Hamas leaders and deports them to Qatar, where they are expected to live in exile.

KURDISH AFFAIRS

February 16. Ocalan Flown to Turkey. The Greek embassy in Nairobi, Kenya, hands over Kurdish Workers' Party (PKK) leader Abdallah Ocalan to Kenyan authorities, who later fly him to Turkey. Demonstrations by Kurds and clashes between PKK and Turkish government forces occur throughout the country after his arrest.

February 17. Kurds Storm Israeli Consulate. At the Israeli consulate in Berlin, Israeli guards open fire, killing three people and injuring sixteen, after fifty-five Kurds try to enter the consulate in response to rumors that Israel's Mossad played a role in the capture of Kurdish Workers' Party leader Abdallah Ocalan.

February 23. Ocalan Formally Charged. The Turkish government charges Ocalan with treason in a closed court session.

September 27. Turkish Troops Enter Iraq. Some 5,000 Turkish troops pursue PKK forces into northern Iraq.

LEBANON

March 5. Former Minister Indicted. Lebanese courts indict former oil minister Shabeh Barsumian for fraud and corruption.

June 2. Israeli Allies Retreat. Hearing rumors of an Israeli withdrawal from southern Lebanon, the South Lebanon Army retreats from its mountain enclave in southern Lebanon under barrages from Hizballah.

June 25. Israeli Forces Bomb Lebanon. Israeli forces bomb bridges along Lebanon's coastal highway and hit two power stations in Beirut.

August 17. Hizballah Attack Kills Two. In continued fighting between Israel and Hizballah forces, two Israeli soldiers are killed and six wounded in the security zone.

LIBYA AND NORTH AFRICA

February 9. Pilgrim Flights Approved. The United Nations approves Libyan flights of pilgrims to Saudi Arabia.

March 19. Qadhafi Agrees to Jail for Pan Am Suspects. Libyan president Mu'ammar al-Qadhafi agrees that any prison sentences for Abd al-Baset Ali al-Megrahi and Al-Amin Khalifa Fhimah, the suspects in the bombing of Pan Am flight 103, would be served in a Scottish jail under UN supervision and that Libya would post an envoy in Scotland who would have access to the prisoners.

April 5. Libya Hands Over Pan Am Bombing Suspects; UN Suspends Sanctions. In Tripoli, Libya hands over the Pam Am bombing suspects, al-Megrahi and Fhimah, to Hans Corell, the UN undersecretary general for legal affairs. An Italian plane flies them to Valkenburg, a Dutch military base, where they are taken into Dutch custody. The Netherlands then formally extradites them to Britain, where Scottish authorities take them into custody.

The United Nations suspends sanctions against Libya, allowing the resumption of air travel and the sale of industrial equipment.

July 16. Libya Pays Restitution to France. Libya gives France $33 million to pay to the families of those killed in the 1989 bombing of UTA flight 777 over Niger. Six Libyans had been convicted in absentia for the bombing.

PALESTINIAN AFFAIRS

January 31. PLC against Declaration of Statehood. The Palestinian Legislative Council demands that Palestinian Authority leader Arafat suspend plans to declare statehood unilaterally on May 4 and, instead, introduce institutional reforms.

March 17. Arafat Cracks Down. The Abu Dhabi–based publication *al-Ittihad* reports that Arafat has curbed the power of the intelligence services by requiring that military intelligence hand over all civilian detainees and refrain from arresting any civilians in the future.

April 29. Statehood Will Wait. The Palestine Liberation Organization votes overwhelmingly to defer proclaiming a Palestinian state.

November 28. Palestinian Authority Arrests Critics. Arafat asks the Palestinian Legislative Council to lift immunity for nine legislators who signed a statement critical of Arafat's rule. Palestinian police arrest seven who signed the statement.

PERSIAN GULF STATES

March 6. Bahraini Leader Dies. After thirty-eight years in power, Amir Isa bin al-Khalifa of Bahrain suffers a heart attack and dies. Al-Khalifa's son Hamad bin Isa al-Khalifa succeeds him.

September 26. Yemeni President Wins Reelection. President Ali Abdallah Salih wins overwhelming reelection. Opposition groups and pro-democracy advocates decry the election as a fraud.

November 30. Kuwait Rejects Women's Rights. In the second vote within a week, the Kuwaiti National Assembly rejects a measure giving women full political rights.

2000

REGIONAL AFFAIRS

June 19. Albright Fazes out "Rogue States." U.S. secretary of state Madeleine Albright says that states previously identified as "rogue states"—Iran, Iraq, Libya, Sudan, and Syria—will now be considered "states of concern."

August 19. Taliban Refuses to Extradite bin Laden. Taliban officials again deny U.S. demands to extradite Saudi dissident Osama bin Laden, who is accused of involvement in the August 7, 1998, bombings of the U.S. embassies in Nairobi, Kenya, and Dar es Salaam, Tanzania.

September 26. Cyprus Talks Fail. UN efforts to mediate the Turkish-Greek conflict over Cyprus fail, as Turkey refuses to recognize Cyprus as an independent country.

November 10. Cyprus Talks End Again in Failure. Attempts to mediate the dispute between Turkey and Greece over divided Cyprus again fail, despite UN secretary-general Kofi Annan's direct involvement.

November 13. Musharraf Allows Exile of Former Prime Minister. Pakistan's military leader, General Pervez Musharraf, grants former prime minister Nawaz Sharif and nineteen members of his family permission to go into exile in Saudi Arabia, where Sharif agrees to remain for twenty-one years. Sharif also agrees to stay out of Pakistani politics for that period.

December 17. Turkey Extends U.S. Base Allowances. The Turkish parliament provides a six-month extension for U.S. and British warplanes to use Turkish air bases to maintain the no-fly zone over Iraq.

December 19. UN Imposes Sanctions on Taliban. The UN Security Council votes to impose sanctions on the Taliban. The sanctions would bar military and training programs for the Taliban but not the United Islamic Force for the Salvation of Afghanistan members, who are currently battling the Taliban forces in Afghanistan.

December 20. Taliban Withdraws from Talks. In response to the imposition of UN sanctions, the Taliban withdraws from UN-sponsored talks aimed at ending the civil war in Afghanistan. The Taliban also refuses to turn bin Laden over to U.S. custody and announces a boycott of U.S. and Russian products.

ARAB-ISRAELI CONFLICT

January 11. Israeli-Syrian Talks End. Talks between Israeli prime minister Ehud Barak and Syrian foreign minister Faruq al-Sharaa in Shepherdstown, West Virginia, end without a final agreement.

February 2. Israeli Cabinet Approves Land Transfer. Israel's cabinet approves the transfer of 6.1 percent of the West Bank to Palestinian control.

February 7. Palestinians Halt Interim Negotiations. The Palestinian Authority calls off interim peace talks with Israel and instead pushes for talks on a final peace accord. Palestinian officials say they will unilaterally declare statehood on September 13 if no agreement is in place by then.

March 8. Barak and Arafat Agree to Resume Talks. Prime Minister Barak and Palestinian Authority president Yasir Arafat agree to revive peace talks in Washington, D.C., and adhere to the September 13 deadline for a final peace deal.

May 15. Fighting Escalates in West Bank and Gaza. Palestinian demonstrations marking the fifty-second anniversary of the establishment of the state of Israel spark clashes between Israeli soldiers and Palestinians in the West Bank and the Gaza Strip. Four Palestinians are killed and some 300 are wounded, while fourteen Israelis are injured. In Jerusalem, thousands of Jewish settlers gather to protest the transfer of three villages on Jerusalem's border to Palestinian control.

May 20. Clashes Continue. After seven days of rioting in the West Bank and Gaza, Barak cancels a planned trip to Washington, D.C., where he planned to continue peace talks with Arafat. More than 100 Palestinians are injured in the fighting with Israeli security forces.

July 11. Israeli-Palestinian Summit Convenes. Barak and Arafat meet U.S. president Bill Clinton at Camp David, Maryland, to continue peace talks.

July 25. Talks End in Stalemate. At Camp David, peace talks between Barak and Arafat reach an impasse.

September 28. Sharon Visits the Haram al-Sharif/Temple Mount. Likud Party leader Ariel Sharon, accompanied by more than 1,000 security personnel, leads a group of Israeli lawmakers into the Haram al-Sharif.

September 29. Violence Flares across West Bank and Gaza. Following Sharon's controversial visit to the Haram al-Sharif, violence and riots spread across Jerusalem, Gaza, and the West Bank. Fifteen Palestinians are killed and hundreds are wounded. One Israeli is killed and thirty Israeli soldiers are injured.

October 1. Fighting Spreads. Battles between Israeli soldiers and Palestinians kill twelve Palestinians and one Israeli.

October 16. Barak and Arafat Meet. In Sharm al-Shaykh, Egyptian president Hosni Mubarak and President Clinton host talks with Arafat and Barak on ways to halt Palestinian-Israeli violence.

October 17. Arafat and Barak Reach Understanding. Arafat and Barak reach an oral agreement proscribing an Israeli pullback and a reduction in Palestinian protests.

October 20. UN Votes against Israeli Force. The UN General Assembly adopts a resolution noting an "excessive" use of force by Israeli security forces against Palestinian civilians.

October 27. Violence Continues. Despite the October 17 Israeli-Palestinian cease-fire agreement, violence continues throughout the West Bank and Gaza, bringing the total number of dead to at least 137 after nearly a month of Palestinian-Israeli violence.

November 2. Arafat and Peres Meet. Arafat and former Israeli prime minister Shimon Peres meet in Gaza. Afterward, a statement issued by Barak's government confirms that both sides have agreed to implement the October 17 agreement to end hostilities.

November 7. Clinton Selects Mitchell to Head Commission. President Clinton appoints former U.S. senator George J. Mitchell to head a commission to investigate the ongoing violence between Palestinians and Israelis.

November 9. Israeli Helicopters Kill Tanzim Member. Near Bayt Sahur, Israeli gunships fire at Tanzim commander Hussein Abayat, killing him and two female bystanders and injuring ten others. The Tanzim is a Palestinian militia associated with Fatah.

December 8. Palestinians Commemorate Intifada. Fatah leaders declare a "day of rage" in commemoration of the Palestinian intifada that began 1987.

December 21. Israeli Army Admits Targeted Killing Policy. Israeli army officials acknowledge that the army has a policy of assassinating leaders of some Palestinian organizations.

December 25. Clinton Pushes Peace Proposal. U.S. officials outline President Clinton's peace plan, which includes Israel relinquishing control of the Haram al-Sharif/Temple Mount, the formation of a Palestinian state incorporating almost 95 percent of the West Bank, and Palestinians giving up the right of return.

EGYPT

February 27. Egypt Extends State of Emergency. The Egyptian parliament extends for another three years the state of emergency in place since 1981.

August 10. Authorities Free Activist. Egyptian authorities release rights activist and professor Saad Eddin Ibrahim after holding him for 45 days in detention. He had been accused of using foreign funds without government permission and forging election ballots.

November 15. Mubarak Consolidates Power. Initial results show President Mubarak's ruling party has captured 312 seats out of 444 in parliament, with opposition candidates winning 95 seats and supporters of the outlawed Muslim Brotherhood taking 17 seats.

IRAN

January 27. Council Bans Additional Candidates. The Council of Guardians announces that it has banned an additional 650 potential candidates from running in the pending parliamentary elections.

February 19. President Wins Majority. Supporters of Iranian president Mohammad Khatami win 188 seats out of 290 in the nation's sixth parliamentary elections. The results are a victory for Iranian religious conservatives, who now assume greater control of the Majlis, Iran's parliament.

March 24. U.S. Torture Victim Wins Award. A U.S. judge orders Iran to pay former hostage Terry Anderson $340 million for torture he experienced while being held captive in Iran.

April 17. Parliament Amends Press Restrictions. The Majlis amends existing press laws, barring criticism of the constitution, increasing punishments for violations of the press law, and granting wider powers to suspend newspapers.

May 18. World Bank Approves Loan for Iran. Despite objections from the United States, the World Bank approves a $232 million loan for Iran, to be used for healthcare and sewage projects.

July 1. Alleged Jewish Spies Convicted. An Iranian judge convicts ten of thirteen Iranian Jews accused of espionage, sentencing them to between four and fourteen years in prison. Two Muslims accused of being accomplices receive two-to-four-year sentences.

August 5. First Post-Revolution Female Governor. Rahmat Rohani Sarvestrani becomes the first female district governor since the 1979 revolution.

September 22. Russia Suspends Laser Sales. In response to U.S. objections, Russia suspends its sale of laser technologies to Iran.

December 23. Iranian Intelligence Officers Appear in Court. Eighteen members of the Iranian intelligence service appear in court to answer questions about the 1995 killing of five dissidents.

IRAQ

February 16. U.S. Representatives Support Some Exports to Iraq. A bipartisan group of ninety members of the U.S. House of Representatives propose a bill that would loosen sanctions against Baghdad by allowing the export of food and medical supplies to Iraq.

May 30. Farm Equipment Disbursed under Oil-for-Food Program. The United Nations releases $143 million in foreign farm equipment to Iraq under the oil-for-food program, which allows Iraq to sell $1 billion worth of oil every ninety days to finance the purchase of food and medicine.

September 22. French Airplane Lands in Baghdad. Following the reopening of the Baghdad airport, a French plane carrying medical personnel, athletes, and writers lands in Iraq. U.S. officials claim the flight is a violation of sanctions against Iraq.

October 11. International Flights Continue. Syrian and Turkish planes, following several other international aid deliveries in previous weeks, land in Baghdad to deliver medical and aid supplies.

November 28. UN Refuses Oil-for-Food Surcharges. UN officials announce that Iraq cannot add surcharges to oil sold under the oil-for-food program and place the proceeds in a non-UN-monitored account.

December 11. Iraq Agrees to Oil-for-Food Extension. The Iraqi government agrees to a six-month extension of the UN oil-for-food program.

ISRAEL

July 10. Barak Government Survives No-Confidence Vote. Prime Minister Barak's government survives a no-confidence vote shortly before Barak departs for the United States for peace talks at Camp David with President Clinton and Arafat.

September 27. Netanyahu Avoids Indictment. The Israeli attorney general decides not to prosecute former prime minister Benjamin Netanyahu on corruption charges involving taking bribes and illegal gifts during his time in office after a year-long inquiry.

October 18. Sharon Refuses Barak's Coalition Offer. Likud Party leader Sharon rejects a proposal to form a national unity government with Barak's governing party.

December 9. Barak Calls for Early Elections. Barak invokes a law requiring a special vote for prime minister within 60 days. The law allows only sitting members of the Knesset to run, thus excluding former prime minister Netanyahu, who had planned to challenge Barak.

December 13. Netanyahu Cleared to Run for Prime Minister. The Knesset grants special dispensation for former prime minister Netanyahu to run in the upcoming special elections for prime minister. Barak supports the move.

JORDAN

April 11. Jordan Joins WTO. Jordan is admitted to the World Trade Organization, following a concerted effort from King Abdallah to focus on economic growth and reform.

September 18. Tribunal Sentences Alleged Terrorists. A military tribunal sentences six of twenty-eight men to death for conspiring to attack tourist sites. The prosecution claims the men have ties to Saudi dissident Osama bin Laden.

October 24. Jordan Signs Free-Trade Pact with U.S. President Clinton and King Abdallah sign a free-trade pact in Washington, D.C., that would eliminate all trade barriers and tariffs between the two nations. The deal still requires U.S. congressional approval.

KURDISH AFFAIRS

January 12. Turkey Delays Death Sentence. Turkey decides to delay the execution of PKK leader Abdallah Ocalan, pending a ruling from the European Court of Human Rights on Ocalan's appeal.

February 9. PKK Announces End of War. With captured leader Abdallah Ocalan urging his forces to lay down their weapons, the Kurdish Workers' Party officially announces the end of its war with the Turkish government. The PKK says it will pursue its agenda through peaceful and democratic avenues.

LEBANON

May 23. Israel Completes Withdrawal. Six weeks ahead of the July 7 deadline and following months of fighting, Israel completes its military withdrawal from southern Lebanon. Hizballah assumes de facto control of the southern areas formerly under Israeli control.

July 28. UN Peacekeepers Deploy. A small group of fifty UN peacekeepers redeploys in southern Lebanon along the UN-proscribed "blue line" between Israel and Lebanon.

August 9. Lebanese Security Forces Enter the South. For the first time in more than two decades, Lebanese security forces move into the southern areas of the country previously occupied by Israel.

September 4. Hariri Party Wins Broad Support. Following elections, former prime minister Rafiq al-Hariri's party wins 18 out of 19 seats among Beirut voters, while Hizballah and Shiite candidates win all 23 seats in the southern districts.

October 23. Hariri Appointed New Prime Minister. Hariri takes post as Lebanon's new prime minister, replacing Selim al-Hoss. Hariri's party had won support from 106 of 128 members of parliament after the elections.

PALESTINIAN AFFAIRS

September 5. Amnesty Criticizes Palestinian Authority. Amnesty International issues a report criticizing the Palestinian Authority for imprisoning without due process dozens of activists who were critical of it.

PERSIAN GULF STATES

October 12. USS Cole *Bombed.* Seventeen Americans are killed in a suicide attack on the USS *Cole* in Aden.

November 7. Saudi Arabia Opens Borders to Iraq. Saudi news sources report that Saudi Arabia has opened its borders with Iraq for the first time since the Gulf War.

December 18. Bahrain Parliament Approves Reform Legislation. The Bahraini parliament approves legislation aimed at establishing an elected parliament, a constitutional monarch, and an independent judiciary. A popular Shiite movement had pushed for a restoration of parliament, sparking violence that claimed thirty-eight lives between 1994 and 1999.

SYRIA

June 10. President Hafiz al-Asad Dies. President Hafiz al-Asad dies. He had ruled Syria since 1970.

July 11. Bashar al-Asad Assumes Syrian Presidency. Bashar al-Asad runs unopposed and wins a nationwide referendum for president. Asad signals a willingness to continue peace negotiations with Israel.

July 27. Bashar Orders Prisoner Releases. Asad orders the release of some political prisoners in Syria, including members of the Muslim Brotherhood and the Communist Action League.

September 27. Syrian Activists Issue Petition. A group of Syrian activists, writers, and artists issue a petition calling for broader rights and freedom of the press in Syria. They also demand an end to the 37-year state of emergency and the release of political prisoners.

2001

REGIONAL AFFAIRS

February 5. Trial in African Embassy Bombings Begins. Four associates of Saudi dissident Osama bin Laden go on trial in a New York federal court for their alleged involvement in the August 7, 1998, bombings of the U.S. embassies in Nairobi, Kenya, and Dar es Salaam, Tanzania.

May 4. Taliban Begins Offensive against Opposition. The Taliban begins a major offensive against the forces of Ahmad Shah Massoud, the leader of the Northern Alliance opposition group, which has fought the Taliban since 1995.

June 20. Musharraf Appoints Self President. Musharraf declares himself president and head of state and formally dissolves the country's legislative bodies. The general had taken over leadership of Pakistan in

1999, after arresting then prime minister Nawaz Sharif, naming himself chief executive, and suspending Pakistan's national parliament and provincial legislatures. U.S. officials criticize Musharraf's latest move to consolidate power.

July 2. Bush Extends Taliban Sanctions. Following policies of the earlier Clinton administration, President Bush maintains U.S. sanctions against the Taliban regime. U.S. officials first imposed the sanctions after the August 1998 bombing of the U.S. embassies in Kenya and Dar es Salaam, Tanzania, attacks that U.S. officials attributed to Osama bin Laden and al-Qaida.

September 5. Bomb Kills Afghan Resistance Leader. Two suicide bombers, posing as journalists, kill Ahmad Shah Massoud.

September 11. Al-Qaida Attack World Trade Center, Pentagon. Nineteen Middle Eastern men hijack four airplanes and crash two of them into the World Trade Center towers in New York City. The third plane crashes into the Pentagon near Washington, D.C., and the fourth aircraft crashes in Pennsylvania, apparently brought down during a struggle between the hijackers and passengers. Nearly 3,000 people are killed, most in New York when the towers collapse, and thousands more are injured. Preliminary reports link Saudi dissident Osama bin Laden to the attacks.

September 12. Omar Goes Into Hiding; NATO Invokes Mutual Defense. After issuing a statement condemning the September 11 attacks, Mullah Omar goes into hiding while the Taliban regime appeals to the United States to show restraint and "mercy" on the Afghan people. U.S. officials release information linking some of the hijackers to Afghanistan.

In response to the September 11 attacks, NATO invokes its mutual defense clause for the first time. Egypt. Jordan, and Saudi Arabia offer intelligence assistance to the United States to help track down those responsible for the attacks.

September 13. Powell Accuses bin Laden. U.S. secretary of State Colin Powell says that bin Laden is the prime suspect in the September 11 attacks.

September 14. FBI Announces Terror Suspects. The Federal Bureau of Investigation releases the names of the 19 hijackers, who include fourteen Saudis, suspected of carrying out the September 11 attacks. U.S officials seek hundreds for questioning.

September 18. U.S. Asks for Lebanese Terror Suspects. U.S. officials ask Lebanon to turn over terror suspects. The United States calls for the disarmament of Hizballah.

September 21. Saudis Rebuff U.S. Airbase Requests. Saudi Arabia refuses to allow U.S. military forces to use Saudi airbases to launch attacks on Afghanistan.

October 2. Taliban Offers to Negotiate over bin Laden. Taliban leaders say they would consider handing bin Laden over if the United States presents compelling evidence of his guilt. U.S. officials indicate they will accept nothing less than the immediate surrender of bin Laden.

October 4. Blair Releases Terror Evidence. British prime minister Tony Blair releases evidence implicating bin Laden and al-Qaida in the September 11 attacks.

October 7. U.S. Campaign in Afghanistan Begins; Bin Laden Praises Attacks. The United States and Britain launch an air assault on Taliban targets and suspected strongholds in Afghanistan.

Bin Laden praises the September 11 attacks on a videotape sent to the al-Jazeera network. Flanked by the leader of Egyptian Islamic Jihad, Ayman al-Zawahiri, and Kuwaiti Sulayman Abu Ghayth, bin Laden urges further attacks on the United States and a holy war on "infidels," who he claims are killing Muslims in Palestine and Iraq.

October 10. Islamic Conference Responds to War in Afghanistan. The Organization of the Islamic Conference, comprising fifty-six Islamic states, meets in Qatar to consider the U.S. military campaign in Afghanistan. The organization warns against civilian casualties and any U.S. efforts to widen the campaign to include other Muslim nations.

October 14. Taliban Reiterates Willingness to Discuss bin Laden's Status. Taliban leaders say they will hand over bin Laden to a third country for trial if the United States halts its bombing campaign and provides compelling evidence of his involvement in the September 11 attacks.

October 19. Pakistan Approves U.S. Use of Airbases. Pakistani authorities grant the United States the right to use Pakistani airbases for logistical support during the Afghan campaign.

October 30. U.S. Ends Sanctions against Pakistan. Opening the door for military and economic aid, President Bush signs legislation ending sanctions against Pakistan.

November 11. U.S. Promises New Aid. The United States announces plans to give Pakistan more than $1 billion in assistance.

November 13. Kabul Falls. Northern Alliance forces capture the Afghan capital of Kabul four days after capturing the strategically important city of Mazar-i Sharif.

December 7. Taliban Loses Kandahar. After a swift defeat at the hands of U.S.-backed Northern Alliance fighters, the Taliban relinquishes control of Kandahar, the last city controlled by the regime. Bin Laden and Mullah Omar remain at large.

December 9. U.S. Pursues bin Laden. At Tora Bora, in the Afghan mountains, U.S. forces intensify their search for bin Laden. Heavy fighting kills hundreds of suspected al-Qaida fighters, but bin Laden continues to elude U.S. forces.

December 13. New Afghan Leader Enters Capital. Hamid Karzai, the U.S.-backed leader of Afghanistan's new interim government, arrives in Kabul in anticipation of the transfer of power on December 22.

December 22. Karzai Becomes Leader of Afghanistan. A conference of Afghan delegates chooses Karzai to head a six-month temporary administration.

ARAB-ISRAELI CONFLICT

January 2. Palestinians Object to U.S. Peace Plan. The Palestinian Authority details its objections to President Clinton's peace agreement, saying the plan fails to provide for a viable Palestinian state. In Washington, D.C., Palestinian Authority leader Yasir Arafat discusses his concerns with Clinton.

January 7. CIA Head Meets Middle East Officials. Central Intelligence Agency director George J. Tenet meets with Israeli and Palestinian security officials in Egypt in an effort to reduce violence between the two groups. In New York, President Clinton calls on both sides to make compromises and for Jerusalem to contain twin capitals, one for a Palestinian state and one for Israel.

January 11. Israeli Forces Pullback. Talks attended by CIA Director Tenet continue; Israeli forces begin a pullback from positions in the West Bank and Gaza to allow some Palestinians to travel to Jordan from the West Bank and to Egypt from Gaza. Israeli officials allow the reopening of the Gaza airport and partially lift some port blockades.

January 20. Barak Agrees to New Talks. Amid continued violence, Israeli prime minister Ehud Barak agrees to new talks with Palestinian Authority president Yasir Arafat in the hopes of brokering a peace deal or cease-fire.

January 25. Talks Resume after Break. In Taba, Egypt, Palestinian and Israeli negotiators continue talks. Palestinian officials announce the arrest of two members of the Tanzim, the armed branch of Fatah, for the killing of two Israelis on January 23.

January 27. No Final Deal, But Negotiators Hopeful. Peace talks in Egypt between Israelis and Palestinians are suspended without a deal.

February 13. Israel Kills Palestinian Officer. In the Gaza Strip, Israeli helicopters fire on a car carrying a member of Arafat's personal security service, killing the officer and a Palestinian child. Twenty other people are injured in further clashes.

February 14. Palestinian Kills Eight Israelis; Army Cracks Down. After a Palestinian bus driver crashes into a bus stop, killing eight Israelis and injuring nineteen, the Israeli army closes the Gaza airport, imposes a naval blockade, and restricts the movement of Palestinian officials.

March 4. Suicide Bomber Kills Three. A Palestinian suicide bomber kills three Israelis and injures sixty-six others in Netanya, north of Tel Aviv, touching off riots in which Israelis attack Arabs.

March 20. Sharon Meets with Bush. In Washington, D.C., Israeli prime minister Ariel Sharon meets with President Bush to discuss peace efforts in the Middle East.

March 28. U.S. Vetoes Observer Group. The United States uses its veto authority to block a UN Security Council plan to send an international observer group to the West Bank and Gaza Strip.

April 4. Palestinian-Israeli Talks Restarted. High-level Palestinian and Israeli officials renew negotiations in Greece, the first such talks since February 6 Israeli elections.

April 10. Abdallah Meets with Bush, Urges Involvement. Jordan's King Abdallah meets with President Bush and urges greater U.S. involvement in the Middle East peace process. Palestinians shell Israeli settlements and Israeli security forces retaliate with antitank missiles, killing one Palestinian and injuring seventeen others.

April 16. Israel Strikes Syria. Israeli fighter planes strike a Syrian radar station, killing three Syrian soldiers.

May 5. Mitchell Commission Calls for Settlement Freeze. The commission headed by former U.S. senator George J. Mitchell releases the report of its investigation, which calls on Israel to halt settlement construction while urging Palestinians to stop their violent uprising.

May 8. Sharon Reaffirms Settlement Commitment. Sharon vows to continue settlement expansion, in defiance of U.S. and international opinion that expanding settlements spurs further Palestinian violence and may violate Palestinian rights to sovereignty.

May 18. Violence Surges Again. Further Palestinian violence and Israeli military actions, including air strikes by F-16 warplanes, kill seven Israelis and sixteen Palestinians.

June 1. Suicide Bomber Kills Twenty. A Palestinian suicide bomber kills twenty people at a Tel Aviv nightclub. Hamas claims responsibility for the blast, while Palestinian officials condemn the bombing and call for a cease-fire. Israelis claim Arafat is ultimately responsible for the attack.

June 18. Jewish Settlers Slain. Palestinian gunmen kill two Jewish settlers in the West Bank

June 25. Sharon Demands Palestinians Halt Violence. Sharon demands that Palestinians halt violence before peace negotiations can resume.

July 10. Israel Bulldozes More Homes. In a move that draws international criticism and sparks further violence, Israel bulldozes homes and shops in a Palestinian refugee camp.

July 15. Cease-fire Talks Stall Again. Arafat and Israeli foreign minister Shimon Peres meet in Cairo for peace talks. The Israeli cabinet moves forward with a plan to construct a new town in the Halutza Sands area, formally ending the idea of a land swap with the Palestinians, an idea that had emerged during earlier negotiations.

July 19. International Calls for Observer Group. The Group of Eight and the United States call for international observers to monitor a cease-fire between the Israelis and Palestinians. In the West Bank, an Israeli militant group, the Committee for Road Safety, kills three Palestinians and wounds several others in a drive-by shooting.

July 31. Israel Attacks Hamas Office. Israeli security forces kill eight Palestinians during a raid on a Hamas office in Nablus.

August 3. UN Admits Kidnapping Tape Hidden. UN officials confirm that they hold a video recording of the Hizballah abduction of three Israeli soldiers. The officials say they withheld the tape in an effort to maintain neutrality.

August 6. Palestinian Calls for Broader Conflict. Marwan Barghouti, a member of Fatah, calls on Arafat to include Hamas and Islamic Jihad in a new government. Barghouti also calls on Arafat to intensify the intifada against Israel.

August 9. Suicide Bombing Kills 14. A Palestinian suicide bomber kills 14 people and injures 130 at a restaurant in Jerusalem. Israeli military forces occupy Orient House in East Jerusalem and destroy the Palestinian police headquarters.

August 13. Israeli Tanks Enter Jenin. Israeli tanks move into Jenin and destroy a police station.

August 25. Palestinians Attack Base, Kill Soldiers. Palestinian militants kill six Israelis at a military base in Gaza. A Palestinian is killed when Israel retaliates by demolishing Palestinian police stations.

September 9. First Israeli Arab Suicide Bomber Kills Three. An Israeli Arab suicide bomber, the first suicide bomber from within Israel, kills three and injures several others in Nahariya.

September 11. Israel Besieges Palestinian Town. Israeli military forces blockade the Palestinian town of Jenin, cutting off power and access to the community.

September 18. Arafat Orders Forces Not to Fire. Arafat orders his security forces not to fire on Israelis, even in self-defense. Sharon demands a forty-eight-hour period of no hostilities before he will allow any further talks with the Palestinians.

October 5. Israel Seizes Hebron. Israel takes control of Hebron. Five Palestinians are killed and more than a dozen wounded in ensuing battles.

October 17. Israeli Minister Assassinated. Gunmen kill Israeli tourism minister Rehavam Ze'evi, a prominent and vocal opponent of the Palestinians, in a Jerusalem hotel. The Popular Front for the Liberation of Palestine claims responsibility, saying the killing was in retaliation for the killing of their leader, Abu Ali Mustafa, in June.

October 31. Israeli Military Kills Hamas Leader. The Israeli military kills Jamil Jadalla, a senior Hamas

member who was wanted in connection with the June suicide bombing of a Tel Aviv disco that killed twenty teenagers. Five Palestinians are killed in other raids.

November 19. U.S. Plans High-Level Envoy Mission. Powell announces that the United States will send retired general Anthony Zinni and assistant secretary of state William Burns to the Middle East in hopes of brokering a cease-fire and restarting peace negotiations.

November 27. Zinni Arrives in the Middle East. U.S. envoy Anthony Zinni arrives in the Middle East.

December 2. Suicide Bomber Kills Fifteen. A Palestinian suicide bomber kills fifteen passengers on a Haifa bus.

December 12. Palestinians Ambush Bus. Palestinian militants mount an attack on an Israeli bus and several other vehicles, killing ten people and wounding more than thirty. In response, Israel severs all contact with Arafat and Israeli warplanes attack Palestinian targets.

December 14. Bush Blames Arafat for Israeli-Palestinian Violence. President Bush blames Arafat for the failing peace process and demands that Arafat stop violence by Palestinian factions. Zinni leaves Jerusalem after continued violence disrupts new peace talks.

December 16. Israel Pushes into Gaza Strip. Israeli troops and tanks enter the Gaza Strip, destroying several houses and police headquarters.

December 17. Under Pressure, Arafat Calls for End to Violence. Under intense international pressure, particularly from the United States, Arafat calls for an end to all armed attacks and suicide bombings on Israelis.

December 21. Hamas Suspends Attacks. In response to Arafat's request, Hamas representatives announce they will suspend suicide attacks against Israelis "until further notice."

EGYPT

May 21. Egyptian Court Convicts Ibrahim. The supreme security court of Egypt finds Saad Eddin Ibrahim, a vocal critic of the Mubarak regime, guilty of forgery and embezzlement and sentences him to seven years of hard labor. Western governments, including the United States, decry the sentence.

June 25. Egypt and EU Reach Trade Agreement. The European Union and Egypt sign an agreement to establish a free trade arrangement for manufactured goods. The European Union also grants agricultural trade concessions to Egypt.

July 18. Accused Homosexuals Arrested. Egyptian authorities arrest fifty-two men and charge them with suspected homosexual activity, conduct that is outlawed in Egypt. All of the accused plead not guilty.

August 5. Egypt Looks to Boost Economy. Egypt devalues its currency by 6 percent against the U.S. dollar in an effort to boost economic competitiveness and curtail the Egyptian black market.

October 16. Mubarak Orders Military Trial for Islamic Militants. Mubarak orders the immediate trial of 170 accused Islamic militants, who are suspected of plotting attacks against tourist areas, police, and Christians.

November 6. Authorities Arrest Brotherhood Members. Egyptian authorities arrest several prominent members of the Egyptian Muslim Brotherhood on charges of belonging to an organization that is seeking to overthrow the government. The fifteen detainees include professors, doctors, and other professionals.

IRAN

January 2. Intelligence Officials Confess to Killing Dissidents. Four former Iranian intelligence officers confess to participating in the 1998 killing of four dissidents.

January 27. Court Sentences Three Former Agents to Death. An Iranian military court sentences three former intelligence agents to death for their role in the 1998 dissident murders. Twelve other agents are sentenced to life in prison for their participation in the slayings.

February 28. Council Rejects Bill to Curb Police Actions. The Council of Guardians rejects a bill passed by the Majlis that would prohibit police from entering university campuses and religious institutions.

March 12. Russia Signs Arms Pact with Iran. Iranian president Mohammad Khatami and Russian president Vladimir Putin sign an agreement that would allow Russia to sell conventional arms to Iran.

March 14. Bush Renews Ban on Iranian Trade. President Bush renews the ban on U.S. trade and investment with Iran.

April 11. Members of Parliament Question Treatment of Dissidents. Some 150 members of the Majlis sign a letter condemning the treatment of dissidents and questioning the validity of the charges leveled against many of them.

April 19. Iran Launches Missiles at Group in Iraq. Iran launches fifty-six Scud missiles at a mujahidin group based in northern Iraq. One mujahidin and several civilians are killed.

May 16. Council Clears 10 Presidential Candidates. Out of 800 potential candidates, the Council of Guardians allows ten men to run in the upcoming presidential elections. The council excludes most critics of the regime and other reformers from running.

May 24. Iran Executes Accused Spy. Iran executes Muhammad Reza Pedram, who faced charges of spying for the CIA, after being caught with a fake passport in 1996.

May 30. Iran Tests Missile. Iran announces the successful test of a surface-to-surface missile. The Majlis passes a bill to end secret trials for dissidents and strengthen prisoners' rights.

June 10. Khatami Wins Reelection. President Khatami wins his bid for reelection, gathering 77 percent of the popular vote.

July 25. U.S. Senate Votes to Extend Sanctions. The U.S. Senate votes to extend sanctions against Iran and Libya.

July 19. Iran Makes Moves Toward Private Bank. Iranian officials take the first steps towards opening a private bank in Iran, Bank-e-Eqtesadi Novin, the first of its kind since the establishment of the Islamic Republic in 1979.

August 5. Khamenei Blocks Presidential Inauguration. Supreme Leader Ayatollah Ali Khamenei halts inauguration proceedings for President-elect Khatami after reformist members of parliament rejected several conservative nominees to a constitutional oversight group.

August 14. Reformists Sue Judicial Officials. Reformist lawmakers sue judicial officials for arresting journalists and political activists. The reformists claim the arrests violate the constitution.

August 18. Iranian Court Orders Intelligence Officers Retried. The supreme court of Iran orders the retrial of fifteen former intelligence officers who were tried for the killings and abuse of political dissidents in January.

October 10. U.S. Blocks Iran's Entry to WTO. The United States blocks Iran from joining the World Trade Organization.

October 31. UN Negotiator Fails to Open Iranian Borders to Afghan Refugees. UN officials are unable to persuade Khatami to open Iran's borders to almost all Afghan refugees, though some special or noteworthy hardship cases might be considered at the border.

November 13. Powell Greets Iranian Official. Powell meets Kamal Kharazi, the Iranian secretary of state, breaking a decades-long freeze between high-level officials from the two countries. The two meet at an eight-nation summit to discuss the formation of a new Afghan government.

IRAQ

January 21. U.S. Claims Arms Production Restarted. New U.S. intelligence estimates claim that Iraq has rebuilt weapons factories in Fallujah, west of Baghdad. Allied air strikes had destroyed the factories in 1998.

March 6. UN Says Iraq Charging Illegally for Oil. UN officials say that Iraq has been charging an illegal 50-cent surcharge on oil sold under the oil-for-food program and putting the surcharge proceeds into accounts not monitored by the United Nations, in violation of the program's rules.

April 26. Iraq's Oil Production Surpasses Pre-War Levels. U.S. news sources report that Iraq's oil production has surpassed pre–Gulf War levels.

June 4. Iraq Suspends Oil Production in Protest. After the UN Security Council decides to extend the oil-for-food program for only a single month and not six months, as the Iraqis requested, Iraq suspends its oil production for one month in protest, removing 2.1 million barrels a day off world oil markets.

June 27. Allied Planes Strike Iraqi Targets. British and U.S. warplanes strike targets in southern Iraq, killing three people.

July 2. UN Extends Oil-for-Food Program. The United Nations votes to extend the oil-for-food program, after Russia vetoes the British-U.S. plan to change the sanctions regime.

November 26. Bush Wants More Weapons Inspections. President Bush pushes Iraq to allow UN weapons inspectors to return, seeking assurances that the Iraqis are not working to acquire weapons of mass destruction.

November 29. UN Extends Oil-for-Food Program. The UN Security Council extends the oil-for-food program but emphasizes the need for new ways of achieving Iraqi disarmament.

ISRAEL

February 6. Sharon Wins Elections. Likud's Ariel Sharon captures more than 62 percent of the vote in nationwide prime ministerial elections, defeating incumbent prime minister Ehud Barak, who wins 37 percent of the vote.

October 1. Official Accuses Sharon of Receiving Inappropriate Campaign Funds. Israel's state comptroller issues a report saying Sharon received $1.4 million in possibly inappropriate financing during the election.

November 13. Israeli Arab MK Indicted for Remarks Supporting Hizballah. Israeli officials indict MK Azmi Bishara on charges of encouraging violence and supporting a terrorist group for voicing support of Hizballah. He is the first Israeli lawmaker charged for remarks made while in office.

JORDAN

September 24. U.S. Senate Approves Free Trade with Jordan. The U.S. Senate approves a trade agreement with Jordan that would gradually eliminate tariffs on goods sold between the United States and Jordan. Jordan joins Canada, Israel, and Mexico as the only other nations with free-trade agreements with the United States.

LEBANON

January 30. UN Extends Presence. The UN Security Council extends the United Nations Interim Force in Lebanon for six months but reduces the size of the force to 4,500 from 5,800. Lebanese officials approve of the decision.

February 16. Hizballah Attacks Israeli Forces. Hizballah fighters attack an Israeli army patrol, killing one Israeli solider and injuring two.

May 3. Lebanon Convicts More Collaborators. Military courts in Lebanon convict twenty-five people of collaboration with Israel, bringing the total number of people convicted of collaborating after Israel's withdrawal from southern Lebanon to 2,600.

LIBYA

January 31. Court Finds Pan Am Flight 103 Bomber Guilty. A Scottish court finds Libyan defendant Abd al-Baset Ali al-Megrahi guilty in the December 21, 1988, bombing of Pan Am flight 103, and sentences him to life in prison. The court acquits the second defendant, Al-Amin Khalifa Fhimah, on all charges. The bombing killed all 259 people aboard the flight and 11 people on the ground.

PALESTINIAN AFFAIRS

January 13. Palestinian Court Sentences Accused Collaborators. A Palestinian military court sentences two men to death for collaboration with Israel. Two others receive life sentences in prison for supplying information and receiving training from the Israeli security service, Shin Bet. The court heard no eyewitnesses and deliberated for less than an hour.

January 21. Report Says Palestinian Economy Suffering. Palestinian news sources report that the recent violence has caused some $2 billion in losses to the Palestinian economy.

February 11. Accused Collaborator Sentenced to Death. A Palestinian military tribunal sentences Hasan Muhammad Hasan Musalam to death for aiding Israeli security forces.

March 14. Islamic Bank Pledges Support. The Islamic Development Bank approves $60 million in direct aid to the Palestinian Authority and $10 million in grants for the Palestinian Health Ministry.

June 5. EU Provides Security Assistance to Palestinians; Suicide Bomber Attacks Tel Aviv Nightclub. The EU begins providing security assistance to the Palestinian Authority in an effort to help sustain a cease-fire. A Palestinian suicide bomber killed at least seventeen people at a Tel Aviv nightclub.

November 16. Palestinians Protest Arafat's Government. Palestinian protesters clash with police and security forces in Jenin, as demonstrators express frustration with alleged corruption within the Palestinian Authority.

December 21. Internal Strife Erupts Among Palestinian Groups. In the worst internal strife since 1994, Palestinians battle Arafat's security forces. Six people are killed.

PERSIAN GULF STATES

January 1. U.S. Announces Sale of Arms and Equipment to Saudi Arabia. U.S. officials announce that the United States intends to sell $2 billion worth of military and communications equipment to Saudi Arabia.

January 9. Yemeni Security Services Arrest Suspects. London-based news outlets report that Yemeni security services have arrested thirteen people for suspicion of their involvement in the October 2000 bombing of the USS *Cole*. The people detained are said to be members of the Islamic Jihad.

February 16. Bahrain Referendum Endorses Governmental Changes. In a nationwide referendum—the first since Bahraini independence in 1971—98 percent of Bahraini voters support the establishment of a partially elected parliament, a constitutional monarch, and an independent judiciary.

February 18. Yemenis Arrest Two in Cole *Bombing.* Yemeni authorities arrest two people in connection with the bombing of the USS *Cole.*

February 20. Violence Starts During Yemeni Elections. Armed clashes between protesters and government forces kill six during municipal elections.

April 28. Yemen Arrests Bombing Suspects. Yemeni authorities arrest three more men in the bombing of the USS *Cole.* bringing the number of arrests to thirty-one.

June 27. Saudi Arabia Sells Natural Gas Exploration Rights to Foreign Companies. Saudi Arabia completes the first stages of plans to sell natural gas exploration rights to foreign companies, provided those companies build the accompanying infrastructure to support exploration and production.

September 25. Saudis Sever Taliban Ties. The Saudi government severs diplomatic relations with the Taliban in response to the group's refusal to hand over Osama bin Laden to the United States.

SYRIA

January 22. Syria Approves Private Banks. The Syrian government approves private banks.

February 7. Bashar Approves Private Universities. Syrian president Bashar al-Asad approves private universities.

February 28. Private Syrian Newspaper Debuts. Al-Doumari, the first private Syrian newspaper in thirty-eight years, sells out its first print run in five hours.

2002

REGIONAL AFFAIRS

January 28. Pakistani Militants Claim Pearl Kidnapping. The National Movement for the Restoration of Pakistani Sovereignty claims responsibility for the January 23 kidnapping of *Wall Street Journal* reporter Daniel Pearl. The kidnappers accuse Pearl of spying for the United States and demand the release of Pakistani detainees at the U.S. naval base at Guantanamo Bay, Cuba, in return for his release.

February 12. Pakistani Authorities Arrest Pearl Suspect. Pakistani authorities announce the arrest of Shaykh Umar Said in connection with the kidnapping of journalist Daniel Pearl.

February 22. U.S. Officials Confirm Pearl's Murder. U.S. officials announce that they have received a videotape with "indisputable" confirmation that Pearl's captors have killed him.

February 27. Rumsfeld Announces Nationalities of Guantanamo Prisoners U.S. secretary of defense Donald Rumsfeld says that men from twenty-six countries are being held at Guantanamo Bay after their capture during the U.S. "war on terror."

March 3. Syrian Leader Visits Lebanon. Syrian president Bashar al-Asad meets with Lebanese president Emile Lahoud, marking the first time a Syrian president had visited Beirut since 1947.

March 28. Kuwait and Iraq End Conflict. At the conclusion of an Arab summit in Lebanon, Kuwaiti and Iraqi officials agree to formally end the conflict that dates back to the 1991 Iraqi invasion of Kuwait. Their declaration also calls for an end to U.S. sanctions of Iraq and rejects military action against Iraq.

April 11. IMF Gives Aid to Pakistan for Antiterrorism Programs. The International Monetary Fund disperses a $1.3 billion loan to Pakistan for rendering aid to the United States during its invasion of Afghanistan.

May 3. Bush Orders Resumption of Trade Relations with Afghanistan. U.S. president George W. Bush orders the reinstatement of normal trade relations with Afghanistan after a sixteen-year hiatus.

May 30. Pipeline Agreement Reached. Afghanistan, Pakistan, and Turkmenistan agree to construct a $2 billion pipeline to ship gas from Central Asia to the subcontinent.

June 11. Iraq and Qatar Sign Free Trade-Agreement. Officials from Iraq and Qatar sign a free-trade agreement.

June 30. Afghan Council Selects Karzai as Head of State. The Loya Jirga, a traditional Afghan council, chooses U.S.-backed leader Hamid Karzai to be Afghanistan's head of state.

July 1. Afghan Officials Claim U.S. Bombs Wedding. Afghan officials say a U.S. bombing mission gone awry killed more than thirty people at a wedding in the village of Dehrawad. U.S. officials claim that people on the ground were directing antiaircraft fire at U.S. warplanes.

July 15. Militants Convicted in Pearl Slaying. A Pakistani court sentences Shaykh Umar Said to death for the kidnapping and murder of journalist Daniel Pearl. Three accomplices receive life sentences.

September 2. Jordan and Israel Announce Joint Construction Deal. Jordanian and Israeli officials unveil plans to build an $800 million pipeline to resuscitate the Dead Sea. The pipeline would stretch from the Gulf of Aqaba to the Dead Sea, which is shared by both countries.

September 5. Assassination Attempt on Karzai Fails. In Kandahar, Karzai survives an assassination attempt by a lone gunman. Bomb attacks in Kabul injure dozens.

December 4. Turkey Agrees to U.S. Use of Airbases. After pressure from officials and offers of hundreds of millions of dollars for military upgrades, Turkey agrees to allow U.S. access to Turkish airbases. The United

States cannot, however, stage a ground invasion from within its borders.

ARAB-ISRAELI CONFLICT

January 3. Israel Withdraws from Some Positions. Bowing to U.S. pressure, Israeli military forces begin to withdraw from the Palestinian towns of Jenin and Nablus in the West Bank. Israeli prime minister Ariel Sharon refuses to lift a travel ban on Palestinian leader Yasir Arafat until Palestinian authorities hand over the accused killers of Israeli tourism minister Rehavam Ze'evi, who was murdered in Jerusalem in 2001.

January 10. Israel Destroys Homes; Militants Lift Cease-fire. Israeli forces destroy some fifty homes in the southern Gaza Strip. Humanitarian personnel say more than 500 Palestinians are left homeless. Islamic Jihad announces the end of a suspension of attacks on Israel.

January 18. Israel Blockades Arafat's Offices. Israeli military forces set up a blockade around Arafat's compound in Ramallah.

January 27. Female Suicide Bomber Kills Two. A Palestinian woman explodes a suicide bomb in Jerusalem, killing two people and injuring 111 others.

January 28. Palestinians Arrest Accused Weapons Smuggler. Palestinian officials arrest Fuad Shubaki in connection with a fifty-ton shipment of arms that Israel authorities had intercepted earlier in the month. U.S. officials claim Arafat was aware of the shipment.

February 5. Gunmen Storm Palestinian Courtroom. More than twenty Palestinian gunmen assault a Palestinian courtroom, killing three people who had been convicted of murdering a Palestinian security official who was suspected of killing Palestinians accused of collaborating with the Israelis.

February 6. Israeli Reservists Refuse to Serve. More than 100 Israeli reservists refuse to serve in the West Bank and Gaza; Israeli authorities suspend 48 of them from duty.

February 13. Powell Announces Arafat's Acceptance of Responsibility for Arms Shipment. U.S. secretary of state Colin Powell says that a letter from Arafat admits his responsibility for an arms shipment from Iran that Israel intercepted.

February 14. International Court Rules Sharon Ineligible for Trial. A Belgian appeals court rules that Sharon cannot be tried in Belgium on charges of war crimes brought by a foreign state. Survivors of the 1982 massacre of hundreds of Palestinians at the Sabra and Shatila refugee camps in Lebanon had launched a lawsuit against Sharon, who was Israeli defense minister at the time.

February 19. High Court Temporarily Halts Bulldozings. An Israeli high court issues an injunction halting the destruction of Palestinian homes at the Kissufim crossing point.

February 20. Violence Intensifies. Israel moves tanks into Rafah and Israeli gunships strike targets in Jenin and Rafah. An Israeli missile strike kills four members of Arafat's security service. Palestinian gunmen kill six Israelis at an army checkpoint near the Ein Arik intersection.

February 23. Arafat Arrests Three for Minister's Killing. Arafat orders the arrest of three men suspected in the 2001 killing of Israeli tourism minister Ze'evi.

February 24. Israeli Cabinet Orders Arafat Contained. The Israeli cabinet votes to restrict Arafat to Ramallah. Palestinian leaders cancel further security negotiations with Israel.

March 1. Camp Clashes Claim Palestinian and Israeli Lives. Fighting in Jenin and Balata kills five Palestinians and an Israeli soldier. Violence during a security sweep by Israel in the Jenin and Balata refugee camps kills twenty Palestinians and two Israeli soldiers.

March 3. Suicide Bombings Continue. Nine Israelis are killed and fifty-seven are wounded when a Palestinian bomber attacks a neighborhood in West Jerusalem. At a military checkpoint near Wadi al-Haramiva, a Palestinian sniper kills seven Israelis.

March 7. Israeli Incursion Kills Eleven Palestinians. Israeli military actions in the West Bank and Gaza Strip kill eleven Palestinians. In Tulkarm and Nur Shams, nine Palestinians are killed during Israeli raids. A Palestinian retaliation on a Jewish settlement in Gaza kills four Israelis.

March 11. Israel Lifts Travel Ban on Arafat; Twenty-Five Palestinians Killed in Fighting. Israel lifts a travel ban on Arafat. Nineteen Palestinians are killed when Israeli security forces enter the Jabalya camp. Six Palestinians are killed in fighting in Ramallah and the Gaza Strip.

March 12. Israel Launches Offensive in Gaza Strip and West Bank. Israeli officials order thousands of Israeli troops into the West Bank and Gaza Strip. Thirty Palestinians are killed during the advance. The al-Aqsa Martyrs Brigade claims responsibility for an attack near the Lebanese border that kills six Israelis.

March 27. Suicide Bomb Kills Twenty-Nine. At a hotel in Netanya, as dozens of Israeli families gather for Passover, a Palestinian suicide bomber kills twenty-nine people and wounds more than 100. Hamas claims responsibility for the bombing. Azmi Bishara, an Arab member of the Knesset, is accused of sedition for praising Hizballah and supporting the Palestinian uprising.

April 3. Israeli Troops Enter Nablus. Israeli military forces take control of Jenin and Salfit, and more than 100 tanks and other vehicles enter Nablus. More than 100 Palestinians take refuge in the Church of the Nativity in Bethlehem.

April 9. Some Israeli Troops Withdraw; Fighting Intense in Jenin. With U.S. officials pressuring Sharon, Israeli troops are withdrawn from Qalqilya and Tulkarm.

In Jenin, thirteen Israeli troops are killed in a booby-trapped building.

April 10. Israel Recommits to Incursions. After a suicide bombing kills eight people, Israel cancels any further withdrawals from the West Bank.

April 24. UN Postpones Jenin Investigation. The United Nations agrees to an Israeli request to delay an investigation into Israel's military actions in Jenin.

April 25. Israel Dismisses Palestinian Verdict in Minister's Slaying. Israel dismisses a Palestinian court's conviction of the Palestinians accused of murdering Israeli tourism minister Rehavam Ze'evi. The men received between one- and eighteen-year sentences.

April 28. Arafat Agrees to U.S. Plan to End Ramallah Siege. Arafat agrees to a U.S. plan to lift the blockade on his Ramallah headquarters. Under the plan, Arafat would place six Palestinians wanted by Israel for Tourism Minister Ze'evi's murder under U.S. and British custody.

April 30. Israel Cancels Jenin Inquiry. The Israeli cabinet cancels an investigation into the fighting in Jenin.

May 2. Israeli Forces Dismantle Blockade of Arafat's Compound. Israeli troops withdraw from their positions around Arafat's headquarters. The standoff ends after Israel and the Palestinians accepted a U.S. proposal to turn over several Palestinians suspected of killing Israeli tourism minister Rehavam Ze'evi.

May 5. Deal to End Bethlehem Siege Reached. After more than two months of skirmishes and several mediation attempts, the siege at the Church of the Nativity in Bethlehem ends. Some of the Palestinians who had hid in the church are arrested by Israel. Others are sent into exile.

May 8. Suicide Attack in Israel. Sharon returns early from a trip to the United States after a suicide bombing kills sixteen people at a pool club near Tel Aviv. In New York, the UN General Assembly passes a resolution condemning Israel's military action in Jenin.

May 12. Thousands Gather for Peace Protest in Tel Aviv. Tens of thousands of Israelis gather in Tel Aviv to demand Israeli withdrawal from the Palestinian territories.

June 4. Tenet Returns to Middle East. Central Intelligence Agency director George Tenet returns to the Middle East in a effort to broker a new cease-fire. In discussions with Arafat, Tenet pushes for a halt to suicide bombings and Arafat agrees to organizational changes designed to clarify lines of command in his security organization.

June 16. Israel Begins Constructing Security Fence. With suicide attacks continuing, Israel begins work on a fence between Israel and the Palestinian towns of Jenin, Tulkarm, and Qalqilya in the West Bank.

June 18. Israel Retaliates after Bus Bombing Kills Nineteen. Israeli tanks and helicopters return to Jenin after a Palestinian suicide bombing kills nineteen and wounds fifty during rush hour.

June 19. Suicide Bomber Kills Six. At a Jerusalem bus stop, a Palestinian suicide bomber kills six.

July 1. Israel Begins Barrier around Jerusalem. In Jerusalem, construction begins on a 30-mile barrier that would wall the city off on three sides and run along the border with the West Bank.

July 8. Israeli and Palestinian Officials Meet. In the first meetings between high-level officials in months, foreign minister Shimon Peres meets with Palestinian finance minister Salam Fayid to discuss the disbursement of Palestinian tax revenues frozen by Israel.

July 16. Seven Israeli Soldiers Killed. Palestinians disguised as Israeli soldiers and armed with automatic weapons kill seven Israeli soldiers and wound twenty-five.

July 29. Israeli Settlers Riot, Kill Palestinian Girl. In Hebron, an angry mob of Jewish settlers attacks Palestinian houses, killing a female Palestinian teenager. Near Ramallah, Jewish settlers kill another Palestinian.

July 30. Hebrew University Bombed. Several bombs kill seven people and injure more than 100 at Hebrew University in Jerusalem. Hamas claims responsibility for the blasts, saying the explosions were retribution for Israeli military action in the Gaza Strip.

August 2. Israel Begins Nablus Offensive. Israeli forces enter Nablus with tanks and gunships.

August 6. High Court Allows Demolitions. The Israeli High Court rules that the demolition of forty-two Palestinian homes may proceed. In New York, the UN General Assembly adopts a resolution calling on Israel to cease military action against the Palestinians.

September 5. Barghouti Trial Begins. Fatah secretary-general Marwan Barghouti goes on trial in an Israeli court on charges of coordinating terrorist attacks against Israel.

September 6. Sharon Declares Oslo and Camp David Dead. Sharon says that the 1993 Oslo agreement and the Camp David agreements are no longer relevant from the Israeli perspective.

September 19. Suicide Bomber Strikes. Following a Palestinian suicide bombing that kills five and injures ninety in Tel Aviv, Israeli forces kill five Palestinians in Ramallah.

September 22. Ramallah Compound Destroyed. Israeli forces use bulldozers to complete the destruction of Arafat's Ramallah compound, leaving the Palestinian leader surrounded by Israeli tanks and troops in the only remaining, semi-intact building. Two hundred of Arafat's advisors and staff remain with him. Across the Palestinian territories, people take to the streets to protest the Israeli action, and four Palestinians are killed.

September 24. UN Calls for End of Ramallah Siege. The United Nations adopts a resolution calling on Israel to end its siege of Arafat's compound.

September 29. Ramallah Siege Ends. After 10 days, Israeli forces withdraw from Arafat's shattered compound, dropping demands that Arafat turn over some fifty militants thought to be hiding inside.

November 21. Hamas Vows Continued Violence. After a suicide bombing kills eleven on a Jerusalem bus, Hamas announces its commitment to continuing an armed struggle against Israel.

December 8. Israeli Builds New Settlements in West Bank. The *Washington Post* reports that Israel had built forty-four new Jewish settlements in the West Bank during the previous eleven months.

December 20. Settlers Evicted. Israeli police evict 200 settlers who had taken up residence in the West Bank on a site where Palestinian militants had killed eleven people in November.

EGYPT

February 6. Donors Pledge Egyptian Aid. Thirty-seven donor nations pledge more than $10 billion in aid to Egypt over three years, with $2.1 billion in immediate aid.

March 26. Britain and Egypt Strike Oil Deal. News reports say that Egypt and Britain have reached an agreement whereby Britain would invest $5 billion in Egyptian gas and oil and that both countries would exchange energy industry expertise.

July 14. Members of Muslim Group Arrested. Egyptian authorities arrest twenty-eight members of the banned Muslim Brotherhood, claiming they were planning antigovernment activities.

July 15. IDP Plans Development Loans. The Islamic Development Bank (IDP) agrees to provide $270 million to Egypt for infrastructure and energy projects.

July 21. Muslim Brotherhood Members Arrested. Egyptian authorities arrest thirty-four members of the banned Muslim Brotherhood.

July 30. Court Sentences Brotherhood Members. An Egyptian military court sentences sixteen members of the Muslim Brotherhood to between three and five years in prison. All faced charges of attempting to overthrow the government.

August 8. World Bank Announces New Loans. The World Bank announces a new $1 billion loan to Egypt.

August 21. Court Orders Detainees Released. The Supreme State Security Court orders thirty-five members of the Muslim Brotherhood released. The men had been held without trial for more than a year and a half.

December 3. New Trial for Noted Activist. Egypt's top appeals court orders a new trial for activist Saad Eddin Ibrahim.

IRAN

January 10. Bush Warns Iran on Afghanistan. President Bush warns Iran against interfering with the fledgling government in Afghanistan. Bush also says Iran must contribute to antiterrorism efforts and turn over to U.S. custody any members of al-Qaida that flee across the border from Afghanistan.

January 20. Trial of Dissident Begins. Political activist Ezatollah Sahabi is put on trial before a closed Iranian court. Sahabi is the first of fifteen political dissidents scheduled to be tried for plotting against the government.

January 31. Iran Denies Nuclear Claims. Iranian officials deny U.S. allegations that Iran is a state sponsor of terrorism that pursues nuclear weapons.

February 11. Thousands Protest against U.S. Tens of thousands of Iranians take to the streets in Tehran to protest U.S. policies and mark the anniversary of the Iranian revolution of 1979.

February 17. Iran and Iraq Exchange Soldiers Remains. Iran and Iraq, who fought a long and bloody war in the 1980s, exchange the remains of soldiers killed on both sides of the conflict.

May 4. Iranian Courts Close Papers. Iran's judiciary bars two reformist-oriented papers for allegedly insulting the Prophet Muhammad.

May 26. Iran Announces New Missile Tests. Iran's defense minister announces the successful test of a new medium-range ballistic missile.

July 9. Demonstrators Mark Crackdown. In Tehran, thousands of protesters commemorate the third anniversary of a crackdown on student demonstrators. Despite several clashes with government forces, no serious injuries are reported.

September 17. Judiciary and President Continue Feud. The Iranian judiciary closes two reformist newspapers after President Mohammad Khatami claims conservatives are trying to block his reform agenda.

September 23. Britain and Iran Resume Relations. Britain and Iran restore diplomatic relations to the ambassadorial level after a nine-month suspension.

September 24. Khatami Requests More Power. Khatami asks parliament to grant him more power in an effort to block conservatives from closing news outlets and arresting dissidents and reformers.

November 23. Protesters Disperse. Students end two weeks of protests against the death sentence handed down to liberal academic Hashem Aghajari, who had questioned the clergy's right to rule last June.

December 8. Protestors Return. In the largest demonstration yet in support of Aghajari, thousands gather at the University of Tehran to demand clemency.

December 24. Iranians Committed to Nuclear Facility. Despite "serious concerns" from the United States, Khatami reaffirms Iran's commitment to building a nuclear power plant. U.S. officials are concerned the reactor is part of a secret weapons program, while government officials claim it is for energy production only.

December 25. Russia and Iran Agreement on Reactor Deal. Russia strikes a deal with Iran to speed construction of an $800-million nuclear reactor near Bushehr.

Iran says all spent fuel, which could be used to manufacture nuclear weapons, would be shipped to Russia.

IRAQ

January 17. Hussein Defiant in Face of U.S. Demands. President Bush reiterates demands that Iraqi president Saddam Hussein allow the return of UN weapons inspectors or face unspecified consequences.

January 26. International Team Begins Limited Arms Inspection. An inspection team from the International Atomic Energy Agency (IAEA) begins a limited inspection of nuclear facilities in Iraq. Because of their limited access, IAEA officials stress that they will not be able to determine if Iraq is attempting to establish a nuclear program.

March 6. Diplomats Level Oil-for-Food Charges. UN diplomats say that Iraq has broken the terms of the oil-for-food program, citing spy satellite photos showing civilian trucks being converted into mobile missile launchers.

March 12. Britain Offers Support for Iraq Action. British prime minister Tony Blair voices his support for U.S. plans to confront Iraq over weapons of mass destruction.

April 12. Iraq Postpones UN Inspection Negotiations. Iraqi officials postpone talks aimed at breaking the impasse over weapons inspections in Iraq.

May 7. UN Offers New Sanctions Plan. UN officials propose a new sanction regime against Iraq that would subject only those items with potential military use to UN review and oversight. It represents the biggest change in the oil-for-food program since its inception in 1996.

May 24. U.S. and Britain Bomb Air Defenses. As British and U.S. warplanes continue their enforcement of a no-fly zone over Iraq, allied warplanes attack Iraqi air defense sites south of Baghdad. Iraqi news reports two people are killed.

June 10. Iraqi Opposition Leaders Gather in U.S. Leaders of Iraqi opposition groups gather in Washington, D.C., to discuss plans to depose Hussein. Members of the Kurdistan Democratic Party-Iraq, the Kurdistani National Federation, the Higher Council for the Islamic Revolution in Iraq, and the National Reconciliation Movement attend.

July 6. Iraq Rejects New Inspections. Amid promises to keep dialogue open, Iraq rejects a UN bid for new weapons inspections.

September 12. Bush Delivers Warning to Iraq. President Bush, in a speech before the United Nations, outlines U.S. intentions for Iraq. Bush says the United States will work to build a coalition before taking action against the Hussein regime. He urges the United Nations to adopt a resolution that would authorize military action if Iraq did not allow unfettered access to weapons inspectors.

September 25. Bush Links Iraq and al-Qaida. Bush says that there is a clear link between al-Qaida and Iraq, though administration officials provide no clear evidence of such a link.

October 1. Iraq Agrees to New Inspections. After refusing to alter elements of the weapons inspections programs during negotiations with the United Nations in Vienna, Iraq agrees to allow new inspections. However, Iraqi officials insist Hussein's palaces will remain off-limits to foreign observers. U.S. official dismiss the new deal.

October 7. Bush Lays Out Iraq Plan. Bush gives a prime-time speech condemning Hussein and displaying satellite imagery that indicates Iraq is refurbishing its nuclear program.

November 26. Arms Inspectors Arrive in Iraq. A team of nineteen UN arms inspectors, led by chief weapons inspector Hans Blix, arrives in Iraq.

December 8. Iraq Delivers Report on Arms. Iraq delivers a 12,000-page report to the United Nations on the nation's weapons programs. The report says Iraq has no nuclear weapons and no plans to manufacture them.

December 12. U.S. Dismisses Iraqi Weapons Reports. U.S. intelligence officials say Iraq's arms report contains omissions and leaves many U.S suspicions unresolved, particularly regarding Iraqi plans to buy uranium in Africa. In northern Iraq, U.S. officials pledge support for Kurds.

December 17. Bush Administration Sets Inspections Deadline. The Bush administration says a final decision on war with Iraq will be made by the final week of January 2003, coinciding with the release of the inspection team's final report.

December 30. UN Tightens Sanctions. UN officials further restrict Iraqi imports of antibiotics, boats, and electronic equipment.

ISRAEL

September 30. U.S. Recognizes Jerusalem as Israeli Capital. Bush signs legislation that includes a rider recognizing Jerusalem as the de jure capital of Israel. Arab leaders and Palestinians decry the measure.

October 2. Sharon Bans Foreign Workers. Sharon issues a ban on any additional foreign workers entering Israel. The move reflects concern over high unemployment among Israelis and growing numbers of illegal foreign laborers.

November 19. Mitzna Wins Labor Party Leadership. Amram Mitzna wins the Labor Party primaries to become head of the party.

November 28. Sharon Beats Netanyahu for Likud Leadership. Sharon wins a landslide victory over foreign minister Benjamin Netanyahu for the leadership of the Likud Party.

December 30. Court Rules against Conscientious Objectors. The Israeli High Court rules that soldiers cannot refuse on moral grounds to serve in Palestinian territories. Failure to heed a call to duty warrants a sentence of thirty-five days in jail.

JORDAN

May 16. First Woman Member of Parliament Sentenced to Jail. Toujan Faysal, Jordan's first female MP, is sentenced to eighteen months in jail for accusing the government of corruption.

June 28. King Abdallah Pardons Faysal. King Abdallah grants a pardon to Toujan Faysal.

October 1. U.S. Announces New Aid. U.S. officials announce $85 million in new aid for Jordan.

October 9. Jordan Begins Privatization. The government sells a 15 percent share of government-owned Jordan Telecom, the first such sale in Jordan's history.

KURDISH AFFAIRS

October 3. PKK Leader's Sentence Commuted to Life. To remove a potential obstacle in the Turkish bid for EU accession, PKK leader Abdallah Ocalan's death sentence is commuted to life in prison.

LIBYA AND NORTH AFRICA

January 24. U.S and Libyan Officials Meet. U.S. and Libyan officials meet to discuss steps to improve relations between the two nations.

March 11. U.S. to Review Relationship with Libya. The Bush administration announces that it will review Mu'ammar al-Qadhafi's behavior, though no concrete policy changes are announced. Qadhafi hopes to have U.S. sanctions lifted.

PALESTINIAN AFFAIRS

January 11. Accused Palestinian Arms Smugglers Arrested. The Palestinian Authority arrests three men in connection with a failed attempt to smuggle fifty tons of weapons to Palestinian groups. The arrests followed demands from U.S. secretary of state Colin Powell that Arafat investigate the arms shipment. The suspects include high-ranking members of Arafat's government. Israel accuses Arafat of orchestrating the shipment. Palestinian officials maintain Arafat had no knowledge of the shipment.

May 22. Election Commission Quits. Angered by the slow pace of reforms, the Palestinian Electoral Commission resigns en masse.

May 31. Palestinian Economic Hardship Increases. The International Labor Organization reports Palestinian unemployment has risen to 43 percent in the territories. Total Palestinian economic output has fallen by 12 percent over last year.

June 13. Arafat Convenes New Cabinet Meeting. Arafat holds his first cabinet meeting after a major reorganization reduced the total of thirty-two minister positions by about a third.

July 7. Provisional Palestinian Constitution. A provisional Palestinian constitution takes effect. It protects democracy, separates the powers of the government, and affirms judicial independence.

September 11. Palestinian Cabinet Resigns to Avoid No-Confidence Vote. The members of the Palestinian Authority cabinet resign, protecting themselves and Arafat from a vote of no-confidence by the Palestinian Legislative Council.

October 2. Arafat Blocks Fatah Reformers. Arafat stymies attempts to appoint a prime minister, a position that would usurp many of Arafat's powers.

December 22. Palestinians Delay Elections. Pointing to the Israeli military actions in Gaza and the West Bank, Palestinian leaders postpone elections originally scheduled for January 20. They say elections will be held ninety days after an Israeli withdrawal from positions within Palestinian areas.

PERSIAN GULF STATES

January 1. Yemen Reaches Agreement with Tribal Chiefs. In exchange for promises that captured al-Qaida suspects would be tried in Yemen and not extradited to the United States, tribal chiefs agree to help in the search for men wanted in connection to al-Qaida.

January 2. Saudis Execute Three Convicted Homosexuals. According to kingdom press reports, three men are executed in Abha, Saudi Arabia, for homosexual acts and molesting boys.

February 14. Bahrain Declared Kingdom. Shaykh Hamad bin Isa al-Khalifa proclaims Bahrain a monarchy and declares himself king. He sets a May 9 date for municipal elections, with parliamentary elections scheduled for October 24.

March 2. Bahrain Ratifies Gender Discrimination Agreement. Bahrain ratifies the UN Convention on the Elimination of All Forms of Discrimination Against Women, although certain clauses are excepted because of potential conflicts with *sharia* (Islamic law).

May 9. Bahrain Holds Local Elections. In the first elections to include women voters and the first elections for male voters since 1975, Bahrainis vote to fill five ten-seat councils, choosing from three hundred candidates, including some thirty women. No women are elected.

July 3. Kuwaiti Minister Survives No-Confidence Vote. Yusif al-Ibrahim, Kuwait's finance minister, survives a no-confidence vote prompted by accusations that he concealed information from the assembly and rigged votes in the 1999 elections.

2003

REGIONAL AFFAIRS

January 4. Pakistan Denies Granting Permission for U.S. Military Border Crossing. Pakistani military officials say that U.S. military forces do not have permission to cross into Pakistan while pursuing suspected al-Qaida fighters from Afghanistan. Pakistan would continue to support U.S. efforts to track al-Qaida operatives down, but Pakistani troops would carry out all operations on Pakistani soil.

January 29. U.S. Coalition Launches Massive Allied Operation against Guerrillas. U.S. and allied forces kill eighteen Afghan fighters on the Pakistani border at Spin Baldak. Coalition leaders believe the guerillas are part of an antigovernment resistance group under former prime minister Gulbuddin Hekmatyar.

February 4. Karzai Commits to Elections; Opium Trade Booms. Afghan president Hamid Karzai renews his commitment to hold national elections in 2004. The United Nations reports that Afghanistan has become the world's leading opium producer, with an annual yield of 3,400 tons. The report attributes the boom in opium production to the elimination of anti-opium measures previously enforced by the Taliban.

February 19. Turkey Demands Additional Aid. In exchange for assistance during the Iraqi war, Turkey demands a $32 billion U.S. aid package in addition to the $20 billion in loan guarantees and $6 billion in grants that the United States has already offered.

March 1. Turkish Legislature Blocks American Use of Bases. Members of the Turkish parliament narrowly defeat a bill to allow 62,000 U.S. troops to use Turkey as a base of operations for an Iraqi invasion.

March 1. Top al-Qaida Commander Captured. Khalid Shaykh Muhammad, the third ranking member of al-Qaida, is captured during a joint U.S.-Pakistani raid in Rawalpindi.

March 11. Erdogan Becomes Turkish Prime Minister. Recep Tayyib Erdogan becomes Turkey's prime minister, setting the stage for another vote to allow U.S. access to military bases in Turkey.

May 6. Anti-U.S. Demonstrators Rally in Kabul. Demonstrators protest U.S. influence and policies in Kabul. The protest marks the first anti-U.S. demonstrations since the fall of the Taliban.

June 5. Taliban Supporters Battle Government. In Populazi, forty-seven fighters die in a battle between government forces and Taliban loyalists.

June 24. Musharraf Meets with Bush. Pakistani president Pervez Musharraf meets with U.S. president George W. Bush in the Pakistani president's first major trip abroad.

July 6. Violent Clashes Continue. Amid pleas from Karzai for more international security support, at least eleven people are killed in clashes between rival factions in the north. Interfactional fighting continues throughout large parts of the country, particularly outside the capital.

July 19. U.S. Special Forces Kill Twenty Alleged Taliban Members. A U.S. Special Forces patrol in southern Afghanistan kills twenty alleged Taliban fighters.

October 20. Arab Human Development Report Released. The UN Arab Human Development Report for 2003 reports that the U.S. campaign against terrorism has allowed several Arab countries to further curb freedoms and democratic movements.

December 14. Council Meets to Ratify Constitution. The Loya Jirga meets to debate and ratify a draft of the constitution, which calls for presidential elections six months after the constitution's approval and the formation of a two-house national assembly. The council comprises 500 delegates from Afghanistan's thirty-two provinces.

December 29. Pakistan Approves Musharraf's Extension. Pakistan's parliament approves a constitutional amendment granting Musharraf the authority to serve out his term until 2007 and formalizing his powers over the prime minister and parliament. In exchange, Musharraf agrees to relinquish his powers over the military in December 2004.

ARAB-ISRAELI CONFLICT

January 6. Dual Suicide Bombings Kill At Least Forty. Two suicide bombings kill twenty-three people and injure more than one hundred others. Islamic Jihad claims responsibility.

January 13. Sharon Rejects Palestinian Travel for London Peace Talks. Israeli prime minister Ariel Sharon rejects an appeal from British prime minister Tony Blair to allow Palestinian negotiators to attend peace talks in London.

January 24. Palestinian Groups Begin Negotiations. In Egypt, several Palestinian groups, including Fatah and Hamas, begin negotiations to lay the groundwork for a cease-fire.

February 5. Sharon Meets Palestinian Legislator. In an effort to halt violence, Sharon meets with Ahmad Qurei, Speaker of the Palestinian National Council.

February 15. Bomb Kills Four Israeli Soldiers. A bombing claimed by Hamas kills four Israeli soldiers near a Jewish settlement in northern Gaza.

February 18. Israelis Raid Gaza Strip. The Israel Defense Force deploys gunships and tanks in Gaza. At least seven Palestinians are killed in ensuing violence.

March 6. Israelis and Palestinians Die in Clashes. Amid continuing violence, a Palestinian suicide bomber kills 15 Israelis on a Haifa bus. Israeli forces retaliate, killing 11 Palestinians and wounding 140 in Gaza.

March 12. Hussein Pays Palestinian Families. Iraqi president Saddam Hussein disperses a total of $245,000 to Palestinian families with relatives who had been killed in Israeli-Palestinian violence. One of the twenty-three families is related to a suicide bomber.

March 20. Abbas Becomes New Prime Minister. Mahmoud Abbas (Abu Mazen) agrees to serve as the first Palestinian prime minister.

April 13. Palestinians Reject Roadmap Changes. The Palestinian Authority rejects proposed Israeli changes to the "road map" for Middle East peace, a two-year plan for Israeli-Palestinian peace. Israel demands that Palestinians give up the right of return for Palestinian refugees.

April 27. Violence Erupts Across Gaza. Responding to an April 24 suicide bombing in Tel Aviv that killed three Israelis and wounded fifty others, Israeli security forces enter Gaza. Seventeen Palestinians die and forty are wounded in ensuing battles.

May 18. During Talks, Bombing Kills Seven Israelis. Shortly after Abbas and Sharon meet for the first high-level Israeli-Palestinian talks in two years, a Palestinian suicide bomber kills seven Israelis in Jerusalem.

May 22. Sharon Endorses Road Map. Sharon endorses the "road map" for peace. Under the plan, both sides would cease violent tactics, Israel would withdraw from Gaza and the West Bank and freeze settlements construction, and Palestinians would engage in political reform and eventually create an independent state.

June 4. Leaders Meet for Talks. In Aqaba, Jordan, President Bush, Prime Minister Abbas, Prime Minister Sharon, and King Abdallah meet for talks to end violence in Israel and the Palestinian territories. No agreement is reached.

June 29. Palestinian Groups Agree to Cease-Fire. Leaders from Fatah, Hamas, and Islamic Jihad agree to a three-month cease-fire.

July 3. Israel Withdraws from West Bank and Bethlehem. In the wake of a cease-fire agreement, Israel withdraws troops around the West Bank. Palestinian security forces take control of those areas.

July 15. Cease-fire Broken. A suspected member of the al-Aqsa Martyrs Brigade attacks three Israelis, killing one, in the first act of violence since the June 29 cease-fire.

July 20. Abbas-Sharon Talks Stall. Talks in Jerusalem between Abbas and Sharon stall over the issue of Israeli pullback and prisoner releases.

August 8. Israeli Raid Kills Bombing Suspects. An Israeli raid kills two suspected Hamas bomb makers. An Israeli soldier dies in the raid.

August 19. Suicide Bombing Kills Twenty-Three in Jerusalem. A Palestinian bomber kills 23 and wounds 130 more in an attack on a bus in Jerusalem. Both Hamas and Islamic Jihad claim responsibility for the blast, which imperils the cease-fire agreement.

September 2. Israel Threatens to Remove Arafat from Power. Arguing that he is failing to stop Palestinian violence, Israeli officials threaten to remove Arafat from power, either through exile or assassination.

September 9. Suicide Bombings Kill Fourteen. Two suicide bombings in Tel Aviv and Jerusalem kill fourteen Israelis.

September 10. Israelis Attempt to Kill Hamas Leader. Israeli security forces attempt to kill the political leader of Hamas, Mahmud al-Zahar, in an air strike. Al-Zahar survives, but his eldest son and personal guard are killed.

September 15. U.S Withholds Money after Threats against Arafat. U.S. officials announce they are withholding parts of a $9 billion loan package to Israel in response to the recent Israeli threats to remove Arafat from power.

September 29. Israel Lifts Territories Blockade; Reroutes Barrier. Israel lifts the blockades of Gaza and the West Bank at the end of the Jewish New Year. Israel agrees to modify the route of the separation barrier to avoid bisecting the campus of al-Quds University in Jerusalem.

October 3. Security Barrier Moves Forward. Israel approves the next steps in the construction of a separation barrier around the West Bank.

October 5. Suicide Bomber Kills Twenty-One. At least twenty-one people die in a suicide attack by a female Palestinian at a seaside restaurant in Haifa. More than fifty people are injured. Israel launches raids on alleged Palestinian training camps in Syria.

October 15. Three Americans Killed in Bombing. A remote-controlled bomb explodes under a U.S. convoy, killing three diplomatic security advisers and wounding a U.S. diplomat.

October 20. Israeli Aircraft Retaliate for Killings. Israeli planes strike five targets in Gaza. At least eleven Palestinians are killed and more than ninety are wounded.

October 24. Palestinian Retaliation Kills Three More. Palestinian gunmen attack a Jewish settlement in Gaza, killing three people and wounding at least two. The Israeli government issues permits for the construction of 300 new homes in West Bank settlements.

November 2. Palestinians Return to Work after Travel Ban Eased. More than 6,000 Palestinian laborers crossed into Israel from the Gaza Strip. Palestinian travel of any kind had been barred after an October 5 suicide bombing in Haifa.

December 2. Israel Continues Settlement Expansion. Israeli officials announce that they have authorized the construction of 1,727 new homes in the Gaza Strip and West Bank. They confirm as well that the construction of some 1,000 homes already approved in 2003 will continue.

December 10. High-Level Palestinian-Israeli Talks Held. Israeli foreign minister Silvan Shalom meets with Palestinian foreign minister Nabil Shaath in Rome to discuss joint economic ventures and calls for foreign aid.

EGYPT

March 18. Egypt Acquits Activist. An Egyptian court reverses an earlier decision from a military court, acquitting activist Saad Eddin Ibrahim of all charges of defaming Egypt.

IRAN

February 9. Iran Plans to Expand Nuclear Program. Iranian president Mohammad Khatami announces plans for Iran to expand its nuclear program. Khatami also says Iran has begun extracting its own nuclear fuel.

February 22. Iran Agrees to More Nuclear Disclosure. In a move praised by International Atomic Energy Agency (IAEA) head Mohamed ElBaradei, Iran agrees to provide early notice of any plans to build new nuclear facilities.

March 1. Conservatives Move to Power in Elections. Reformists suffer defeat in Iranian elections, with conservatives unseating several liberal councilors on the Tehran city council. Observers attribute low voter turnout to political apathy and unhappiness with the slow pace of reform.

March 17. Iran and Iraq Release War Prisoners. Iran and Iraq release prisoners of war held since the war between the two countries in the 1980s. Iran releases 941 Iraqis, and Iraq announces it will release 349 Iranians.

March 28. Thousands Protest War in Iraq. In Tehran, tens of thousands gather to protest the U.S.-led war in Iraq.

July 30. Government Admits Journalist's Death Was Murder. Government officials concede that Canadian photographer Zahra Kazemi was beaten to death while in police custody. The 54-year-old Kazemi was arrested June 23 while photographing a student protest outside a prison in Tehran. Iranian authorities had claimed that her death was the result of a stroke.

August 13. Council Rejects Two Reform Bills. The Council of Guardians rejects two bills intended to expand civil rights. The measures called for adoption of the UN conventions on the elimination of discrimination against women.

August 26. IAEA Inspectors Find Weapons-Grade Uranium. IAEA inspectors confirm the discovery of weapons-grade enriched uranium at the Natanz nuclear facility.

September 12. Inspectors Set Nuclear Compliance Deadline. IAEA officials set October 13, 2003, as the deadline for Iran to fully comply with international pressure and confirm that it does not have a secret nuclear weapons program.

November 3. Iranian Leader Endorses Nuclear Inspections. Following announcements that Iran—in accordance with a deal brokered by Britain, France, and Germany—would suspend its uranium enrichment programs, Ayatollah Ali Khamenei endorses the agreement. The deal also would allow increased UN weapons inspections, with access to all of Iran's nuclear sites.

December 26. Earthquake Kills Thousands. An earthquake measuring 6.6 on the Richter scale kills more than 40,000 people in Bam. The United States and other international donors ease trade restrictions with Iran to render aid to victims, but Iranian authorities reject offers for direct aid and assistance from Western countries, including the United States.

IRAQ

January 9. UN Announces No WMD Found in Iraq. Chief UN weapons inspector Hans Blix says his team has found no weapons of mass destruction in Iraq. In his report, Blix faults the Iraqi government for failing to disclose older weapons programs and to provide a comprehensive list of weapons-related scientists.

January 14. UN Extends Inspections. Blix says he will expand his team and continue inspections work until March, making the expected end-of-January report an interim finding.

January 17. Chief Nuclear Inspector Hints at More Time Needed. IAEA head ElBaradei says that inspectors might need months more to assess Iraq's weapon capabilities.

January 27. Inspectors Deliver Weapons Report. Blix and ElBaradei give their weapons reports to the United Nations. Blix says Iraq has not embraced disarmament, while ElBaradei finds no evidence of a revived Iraqi nuclear program. China, France, and Russia argue that further inspections are required, while the United States says the time for inspections is over.

January 28. Bush Suggests Iraq–al-Qaida Link in State of the Union. Bush says he will look for international support when confronting Iraq, but he will not wait indefinitely for it. Bush also says the Iraqi regime has ties to al-Qaida.

February 5. Powell Makes Case before UN. U.S. secretary of state Colin Powell makes the case to the United Nations for a possible war to disarm Iraq. The presentation includes aerial photos and recordings of Iraqi officials that the United States says demonstrate Iraq's possession of weapons of mass destruction. Iraqi officials deny Powell's claims.

February 28. White House Lays Course for Iraqi Disarmament. White House officials say only total Iraqi disarmament and regime change can avert a war in Iraq.

March 16. Allies Give War Ultimatum. Bush, along with Spanish prime minister Jose Maria Aznar and British prime minister Tony Blair, gives the UN Security Council a March 18 deadline to demand Iraqi disarmament.

March 18. Bush Gives Hussein Ultimatum. Bush gives Hussein and his two sons, Uday and Qusay, forty-eight hours to leave Iraq or face a U.S. invasion.

March 20. Iraq War Begins. The U.S.-led campaign to overthrow Hussein begins. The United States targets Hussein with the first strikes, but he escapes unharmed.

March 21. Ground Campaign Begins. U.S. and British forces begin the ground campaign and move into southern Iraq.

March 23. Fierce Fighting in Nasiriya. U.S. forces encounter fierce resistance in Nasiriya.

April 3. U.S Troops Enter Baghdad. With U.S. and British forces routing most Iraqi opposition, allied troops enter Baghdad. Hussein's control of the city erodes. Looters steal ancient objects from Baghdad's museums and personal valuables.

April 11. U.S. Captures Mosul, Advance on Tikrit. U.S. forces capture Mosul in northern Iraq.

April 13. U.S. Captures Tikrit. U.S. forces capture Hussein stronghold Tikrit.

April 14. Bush Declares Major Combat Over. Bush declares major combat in Iraq over.

April 18. Anti-U.S. Protests in Baghdad. Thousands of demonstrators protest in Baghdad, demanding an end to the U.S. occupation.

April 20. Garner Arrives to Oversee Reconstruction. Retired U.S. general Jay Garner arrives in Baghdad to oversee reconstruction efforts.

May 7. Bremer Replaces Garner. Former diplomat L. Paul Bremer III replaces Garner as the top U.S. official in Iraq.

May 11. U.S. General Declares Dissolution of Baath Party. U.S. military officials declare the dissolution of the Baath Party, the backbone of Hussein's Sunni power structure. Officials later bar any former Baath Party members from serving in the public sector in postwar Iraq.

May 22. UN Lifts Iraq Sanctions. The UN Security Council adopts resolution 1483, lifting sanctions against Iraq and giving the United States and Britain control of the country until a new government is in place.

July 13. Iraqi Governing Council Formed. A group of former exiles and political leaders agrees to form the twenty-five-person Iraqi Governing Council. The council's first act is the abolition of all Iraqi national holidays and the establishment of April 9, the day Baghdad fell to U.S. forces, as the new Iraqi national independence day.

July 22. Hussein's Sons Killed. In Mosul, U.S. forces kill Uday and Qusay Hussein.

August 19. Truck Bomb Destroys UN Headquarters. A massive truck bomb destroys UN headquarters in Baghdad. At least seventeen people are killed, including Sergio Vieira de Mello, the UN special representative to Iraq.

August 29. Bomb Kills Scores of Shiite Worshippers. A car bomb kills Shiite leader Muhammad Baqir al-Hakim and seventy-five Shiite worshippers in Najaf.

September 20. Iraqi Woman Official Killed. Aqila al-Hashimi, one of only three women serving in Iraq's interim governing body, is shot by gunmen. She would die five days later.

September 21. Iraqi Administration Announces Government Reforms. Iraq's U.S.-backed government announces several economic reforms, including the liberalization of all major state industries, except for oil production.

October 27. Suicide Bombings Kill Dozens. At least 35 people are killed and 230 are wounded in suicide attacks on the headquarters of the Red Cross.

October 29. U.S. Post-Invasion Deaths Rise. Two U.S. soldiers are killed in a roadside bombing, bringing the total number of U.S. military deaths to 116, more than were killed during the initial invasion.

November 12. Suicide Bombing Kills Twenty-six at Italian Base. A suicide bombing at an Italian base in Nasiriya kills at least twenty-six people.

December 14. Hussein Captured; Suicide bombing in Khalidiyya. U.S. troops capture former Iraqi leader Saddam Hussein near Tikrit. A suicide bombing kills seventeen Iraqis and injures more than thirty outside of Khalidiyya.

ISRAEL

January 9. Newspaper Details Accusations against Sharon, Son. Ha'aretz reports that Israeli prime minister Ariel Sharon and his son received illegal campaign contributions towards Sharon's campaign for leadership of his Likud Party in 1999. Israeli attorney general Elyakim Rubinstein confirms that an investigation is underway. Sharon denies the charges.

May 4. Labor Leader Resigns. After the Labor Party's worst showing at the polls in 55 years, Amram Mitzna resigns as party leader.

July 22. Knesset Approves Settlement Dismantlement. The Knesset approves a Sharon plan to dismantle all Jewish settlements constructed over the previous two years without proper permits.

October 14. U.S. Vetoes Anti-Israeli UN Resolution. The United States vetoes a Syrian-sponsored UN resolution that would have declared illegal the security fence Israel is constructing around the West Bank.

JORDAN

January 30. Jordan Allows U.S. Forces at Bases. Jordan announces it will allow the U.S. to use its military bases in the event of a war with Iraq.

June 17. Parliamentary Elections Favor Tribal and Local Candidates. The first parliamentary election in Jordan since 1997 yields strong showings for tribal and local candidates. The Islamic Action Front wins the most seats of the major parties, with 17 of the 104 total open seats.

November 17. Abdallah Dissolves Council. King Abdallah dissolves the al-Ayan council and appoints a new fifty-five-member council. The council has powers to block legislation deemed unfavorable to the king.

Abdallah retains broad powers, including the ability to dissolve parliament and rule by decree.

LEBANON

May 30. U.S. Reopens Consulate. Twenty years after the bombing of the U.S. Marine Corps barracks in Beirut, the United States reopens its consulate.

LIBYA AND NORTH AFRICA

May 16. Bombings Kill Scores in Casablanca. Five bombings kill more than forty-one people and injure about one hundred in Casablanca, Morocco. Government officials blame al-Qaida for the attacks.

August 13. Libya Accepts Responsibility for Lockerbie Bombing. Negotiators for Libya, the United States, and Britain agree to deal in which Libya would accept responsibility for the 1988 bombing of Pan Am flight 103 over Lockerbie, Scotland, that killed 270 people. Under the agreement, Libya will pay $2.7 billion in compensation to the families of those killed.

September 12. UN Lifts Libya Sanctions. The United Nations lifts the 11-year sanction regime against the country. The United States retains its unilateral sanctions against Libya.

December 19. Libya Plans to Relinquish Nuclear Program. Following nine months of secret negotiations between British, U.S., and Libyan officials, Libya agrees to relinquish all nuclear, chemical, and biological weapons.

December 29. Weapons Inspector Reports on Libyan Arms. The UN chief military inspector says that Libya is not an immediate threat to develop nuclear weapons.

PALESTINIAN AFFAIRS

April 23. Abbas Takes Security Reins. Palestinian prime minister Abbas appoints Muhammad Dahlan as chief of security, a move that will take some control of security issues away from Arafat.

July 4. Abbas Meets with Militants. Prime Minister Abbas meets with leaders from Fatah, Hamas, and Islamic Jihad to reinforce the June 29 cease-fire agreement between Israel and the Palestinians.

July 14. Abbas and Arafat Agree to New Compromise. After Abbas threatens to resign, Arafat and Abbas agree to a powersharing structure that guarantees Arafat some continued influence over negotiations and security.

September 10. Abbas Resigns, Qurei Named as Replacement. Abbas resigns his position as prime minister. Ahmad Qurei, Speaker of the Palestinian legislature and a key negotiator in the 1993 Oslo accords, becomes prime minister of the Palestinian Authority.

October 5. Arafat Declares Emergency. Arafat, in an attempt to avoid Israeli retribution following a suicide bombing, declares a state of emergency in the Palestinian territories and installs a new government by edict. Qurei becomes prime minister in the emergency cabinet.

October 16. Palestinians Arrest Suspected Bombers. Palestinian authorities arrest seven Palestinians in northern Gaza in connection with of a bombing that killed three Americans.

December 7. Palestinian Groups Fail to Reach Deal. Palestinian groups, including Hamas and Islamic Jihad, participate in cease-fire talks in Cairo but fail to broker an end to hostilities. While some groups endorsed a complete cease-fire, Hamas and Islamic Jihad sought an end to Israeli incursions into Palestinian areas. They also argued the cease-fire should only be in regard to Israelis living within the pre-1967 war boundaries.

PERSIAN GULF STATES

April 15. Qatar Announces Constitutional Referendum. Amir Shaykh Hamad bin Khalifa al-Thani announces the first steps in a referendum on a permanent national constitution and schedules legislative elections for 2004.

April 27. Yemen Elections Largely Peaceful. Elections held in Yemen are largely peaceful with high voter turnout. The ruling General People's Congress wins 238 seats in the 301-member parliament. Opposition parties, including the Socialist Party, the Islamic Reform Party, and the Nasserite Party, say the elections were flawed by ballot rigging, fraud, and intimidation.

April 29. Qatari Voters Approve New Constitution. Qataris vote overwhelmingly for a new constitution calling for a party-elected parliament, independent judiciary, freedom of expression, and property rights.

July 6. Qatari Elections Yield Strong Results for Islamist Candidates. Liberal candidates fare poorly in Qatar's parliamentary elections, and fundamentalist Islamic candidates win gains in the fifty available seats.

October 5. Oman Holds First Elections. Oman holds its first open elections for the eighty-three seats on the sultanate's advisory council.

October 21. Oman Unveils New Government. Following open elections, Sultan Qaboos bin Said unveils the new Majlis al-Shura, raising the number of deputies to fifty-five and including seven women. The council advises the sultan but is powerless on defense, foreign policy, and security issues.

November 8. Bombing Kills 17. A car bomb kills at least 17 people and injures more than 120 at the al-Muhaya residential compound in Riyadh. Several foreign nationals are among the victims. Al-Qaida later claims responsibility for the blast.

SYRIA

October 15. U.S. House Approves Syrian Sanctions. The U.S. House of Representatives approves sanctions against Syria that would freeze Syrian assets in the United States, ban U.S. business investment and exports to Syria, and reduce diplomatic contacts.

2004

REGIONAL AFFAIRS

February 1. Pakistani Scientist Admits to Sharing Nuclear Secrets. Abdul Qadeer Khan confesses to sharing nuclear weapons technologies with Libya, North Korea, and Iran over the past fifteen years. Musharraf later pardons Khan, calling him a hero.

March 26. Karzai Postpones Elections. Citing continuing violence and unrest, particularly in outlying provinces, Afghan president Hamid Karzai decides to postpone for three months elections originally scheduled for June 2004.

October 9. Elections Start Without Major Violence. Afghanistan's first post-Taliban elections begin without major violence. Several opposition candidates call for a boycott.

November 3. Karzai Declared Winner. Despite claims of voting irregularities, government officials declare Karzai the winner of the October 9 presidential election. Parliamentary elections are delayed because of a lack of an accurate census and logistical problems.

ARAB-ISRAELI CONFLICT

January 15. Israel Seals Gaza Strip. After a suicide bombing by a female Palestinian kills four Israelis at the Erez checkpoint, Israel seals off the Gaza Strip. Prior to the attack, some 20,000 Palestinians had been crossing into Israel from Gaza for work.

January 27. Israel Reopens Workers Thoroughfare. Israel reopens the Erez checkpoint.

March 14. Suicide Bombing Kills 11. Two Palestinian suicide bombers kill eleven Israelis in Ashdod. Hamas and al-Aqsa Martyrs Brigade claim responsibility for the joint operation. In response, Israel launches military operations in Gaza.

March 21. Israel Kills Hamas Founder. An Israeli air strike targets and kills Shaykh Ahmad Yasin, the spiritual leader and founder of Hamas. Seven other Palestinians are killed with the sixty-seven-year-old leader.

April 15. Settlement Funds Frozen. The Israeli government freezes settlement funding after findings indicate that some of the funds are going to maintain illegal settlements.

April 17. Israelis Kill New Hamas Leader. An Israeli gunship kills Abd al-Aziz Rantisi, the newly designated leader of Hamas, in Gaza.

May 11. Attacks Kills Eleven Israelis. In the Gaza Strip, a car bomb kills six Israeli troops, and Palestinian gunmen kill five Israeli soldiers.

May 13. Israelis Kill Twelve Palestinians. Israeli forces kill twelve Palestinians in Gaza while searching for the remains of five Israelis killed on May 9. In three days of fighting, twenty-seven Palestinians had been killed and 280 injured.

June 30. Israeli Court Rules against Barrier. The Israeli High Court rules that the proposed route for the separation barrier between Israel and the West Bank should be changed. It is the first major court ruling on the barrier, which the court says violates the rights of local inhabitants under international and humanitarian law.

July 30. Israel Moves Barrier Route. In accordance with a High Court ruling, Israel moves the planned path for the security barrier closer to the West Bank boundary.

August 31. Sharon Details Gaza Withdrawal Plan; Hamas Retaliates for Killing. Sharon presents a plan for Gaza Strip and West Bank withdrawals to the Likud Party. The plan calls for an Israeli withdrawal to begin as early as the end of 2004. The initial phase calls for a withdrawal from Gaza and four small West Bank settlements in four stages, to be completed by September 2005. Each step of the plan will be presented to the cabinet for approval.

Palestinian suicide bombers attack two buses in southern Israel, killing at least fifteen people and wounding more than eighty. Hamas claims responsibility, saying the attacks were retaliation for the killing of Hamas leader Shaykh Ahmad Yasin.

September 30. Israel Renews Large-Scale Gaza Operations. The Israeli military launches a large-scale military operation in Gaza. At least twenty-eight people are killed and some one hundred wounded.

October 7. Bomb Explodes in Taba. A bombing at an Egyptian resort in Taba kills at least thirty-four people and injures one hundred, including several Israeli tourists.

December 27. Israel Begins Releasing Prisoners. In a gesture to the new Palestinian leadership, Israel begins releasing 159 prisoners to Egypt. Abbas calls for Israel to release the estimated 7,000 Palestinian prisoners held in Israeli jails.

EGYPT

March 25. Islamic Party Members Sentenced. An Egyptian court sentences twenty-six people to jail sentences of one to five years for their membership in the Islamic party Hizb al-Tahrir.

July 9. Egyptian Cabinet Resigns. As international and internal pressure for reform builds, Prime Minister Atef Obeid and the thirty-two other cabinet ministers resign. Mubarak appoints Ahmad Nazif as the new prime minister.

October 2. Parliament Blocks Islamic Party. Egyptian government officials block attempts to form the nation's first Islamic party. It is the third time the government has blocked the creation of the Hizb al-Wasat al-Jadid.

December 13. Egypt Signs Trade Deal with Israel, U.S. Egypt signs a trade pact that will allow the duty-free export to the United States of goods at least partly made in Israel. The pact establishes "qualified industrial zones" in parts of Alexandria, Cairo, and Port Said, where the goods are to be assembled.

IRAN

January 14. Khamenei Asks Council to Reconsider Barring Candidates. After the Council of Guardians bars dozens of incumbents from February 20 parliamentary elections, Ayatollah Ali Khamenei asks the council to reconsider the exclusion of nearly 2,000 candidates, including 83 incumbents.

January 20. Council Reinstates Some Barred Candidates. The Council of Guardians reinstates about 200 of 3,500 candidates it had previously disqualified from upcoming elections.

January 30. Council Increases Incumbent Ban. The Council of Guardians increased the number of banned incumbents to 87.

January 31. MPs Resign in Protest. More than 100 members of the Majlis resign to protest the Council of Guardians ban of incumbents.

February 24. Conservatives Win Majority in Elections. Preliminary results show conservatives won 156 of the 290 seats in Iran's parliamentary elections, with some 60 seats requiring a second round of voting.

May 29. Parliament Elects Conservative Speaker. The Iranian parliament elects Gholam Ali Haddad-Adel as Speaker of parliament. Haddad-Adel is a leader in the conservative Islamic Iran Developers coalition. He is also the first non-cleric Speaker since 1979.

June 18. IAEA Reprimands Iran for Lack of Nuclear Transparency. The International Atomic Energy Agency reprimands Iran for its lack of cooperation with international investigations regarding Iran's nuclear weapons program.

July 31. Iran Resumes Nuclear Program. In a reversal of its October 2003 pledge to European officials, Iran resumes construction of centrifuges to enrich uranium.

October 12. Outspoken Cleric Resigns. Ali Abthahi, an outspoken liberal cleric, resigns his position as vice president. He blames religious hard-liners for preventing him from implementing reforms.

November 30. Iran Refuses to Renounce Uranium. Despite international pressure and condemnation, Iran refuses to give up its uranium enrichment programs, claiming the programs are not for weapons. The announcement caps weeks of negotiations between European and international negotiators.

IRAQ

January 5. Blair Commits British Troops for Two More Years. British prime minister Tony Blair says British troops will remain in Iraq for at least two years and possibly longer if the security situation warrants.

January 7. Weapons Team Leaves Iraq. The U.S. military team tasked with finding weapons of mass destruction in Iraq withdraws, having found no evidence of banned weapons.

January 19. Shiites Call for National Elections. Thousands of Shiites demonstrate in Baghdad, calling for direct national elections.

January 23. Inspectors Say Weapons Destroyed before Invasion. David Kay, the leader of the U.S. team that hunted for weapons of mass destruction in Iraq, says that Saddam Hussein likely destroyed any weapons stockpiles before the 2003 invasion, probably in 1991.

February 1. Suicide Bombing Kills 100. Two Iraqi insurgents disguised as Muslim clerics detonate suicide bombs that kill more than 100 people and injure 225 in Irbil. The bombing inflames tensions between Kurds and other ethnic groups in the area.

March 1. Council Approves Interim Constitution. Members of the Iraqi Governing Council approve a U.S.-sponsored interim constitution. The constitution would guarantee individual civil rights for all people and bar discrimination based on sex, nationality, or religion. It also would require that 25 percent of the legislative seats be reserved for women.

March 2. Shiites Killed in Suicide Attack. A suicide bomber kills more than 100 Shiite worshippers in Karbala.

March 7. Shiite Leaders Accept Constitution. Shiite leaders signal their approval of the new constitution, despite lingering reservations from Grand Ayatollah Ali al-Sistani, a powerful Shiite cleric. Shiites had demanded greater representation in the rotating presidency and questioned the Kurdish claim to autonomy in northern Iraq.

March 20. U.S. Charges Six in Prisoner Abuse Scandal. The U.S. military charges six military police officers for mistreatment of prisoners held at the Abu Ghraib prison, west of Baghdad. Military officials suspend eleven other soldiers and order additional investigations.

March 31. Four Americans Killed in Fallujah. Angry mobs kill four U.S. contractors in Fallujah. Shiite junior cleric Muqtada al-Sadr calls for further attacks on the U.S.-led coalition.

April 4. Sadr's Forces Battle U.S. troops. Fierce fighting breaks out between Sadr's Mahdi Army and U.S. troops. Seven U.S. soldiers and forty-eight Iraqis are killed in the Sadr City section of Baghdad. The following day, U.S. leaders order al-Sadr's arrest.

April 9. Bremer Orders Cease-Fire in Fallujah. U.S. administrator L. Paul Bremer orders a cease-fire in Fallujah as leaders search for a political solution to confrontations there.

April 11. U.S. Reveals Problems with Oil-for-Food Program. A U.S. investigation indicates that Egypt, Jordan, Russia, and other countries may have overcharged for food and aid delivered under the UN's oil-for-food program.

April 12. U.S. General Requests More Troops. U.S. General John Abizaid requests that the U.S. deploy 10,000 more U.S. troops in Iraq.

April 16. Fallujah Negotiations Begin. Negotiators from the U.S. Army meet with local leaders in Fallujah in an effort to end the siege of the city.

April 21. Coalition Leaders Agree to Allow Baathists to Return. Reversing earlier policy, Bremer announces that former Baathists who did not have direct ties with Hussein are eligible for work in the new government. Elsewhere, a series of car bombings outside Basra kills more than 68 Iraqis and injures more than 200. The bombers targeted four police facilities.

April 28. Prison Abuse Photos Aired. CBS airs photographs of U.S. soldiers abusing Iraqi prisoners at the Abu Ghraib prison.

May 3. Fighting Engulfs Najaf. Insurgents loyal to Sadr battle U.S. military forces in Najaf.

May 17. Council President Assassinated. Assassins kill Izz al-din Salim, the president of the Iraqi Governing Council, at coalition headquarters in Baghdad.

June 1. Interim Administration Takes Power. The Iraqi Governing Council dissolves itself and appoints an interim administration to take power and steer the country towards general elections in 2005. The administration appoints Ghazi al-Yawar president. Iyad Allawi assumes the post of prime minister.

June 5. Al-Sadr Begins to Stand Down. The Mahdi Army begins to withdraw from Najaf and Kufa.

June 7. Allawi Outlaws Militias. Allawi says that all militias, including the Mahdi Army, are outlawed and militia leaders are banned from political office for the next three years. Sadr claims that Allawi lacks the authority to make such a decree.

July 6. Allawi Claims Broad Powers. Allawi signs a law granting himself broad martial powers, including the right to impose curfews, ban groups and demonstrations, and detain people deemed threats to security.

July 28. Violence Surges in Iraq. A bombing near a police station in Baquba kills seventy Iraqis. Elsewhere, insurgents kill two U.S. soldiers near Ramadi.

August 6. Fighting Kills Hundreds. As insurgents and U.S. Marines clash in the Sunni triangle, U.S. commanders say 300 Shiite fighters have been killed. Two marines are killed and twelve wounded.

August 8. Iraq Issues Arrest Warrant for Chalabi. Iraq issues an arrest warrant for Ahmad Chalabi, a former governing council member and key ally and intelligence source for the United States. Reports show that much of the intelligence Chalabi provided for coalition forces before the war may have been incorrect or exaggerated.

August 23. Cease-fire Takes Effect in Najaf. U.S. forces pull back from Najaf after negotiators between the Iraqi government and Sadr representatives broker a cease-fire to end nine days of fighting.

October 7. CIA Says Hussein Had No Weapons. The Central Intelligence Agency releases a report that says Hussein did not have weapons of mass destruction.

November 9. U.S. Begins Assault of Fallujah. With the approval of Prime Minister Allawi, U.S. forces launch an attack on Fallujah in an effort to stabilize the region ahead of upcoming elections.

November 13. U.S. Takes Control of Fallujah. After a week of fighting that kills at least 24 U.S. troops and about 1,000 insurgents, U.S. military commanders say they are in control of Fallujah.

December 9. Election Candidates Listed. A Shiite coalition backed by leading cleric Ayatollah Ali al-Sistani announces that 228 candidates have entered election races for Iraq's January 30 elections. The group includes the Supreme Council for the Islamic Revolution and the Islamic Dawa Party.

December 4. U.S. to Strengthen Presence for Elections. In an effort to secure Iraq before coming elections, U.S. officials announce plans to boost troop levels to 150,000.

December 21. Suicide Bomber Strikes U.S. Base. A bombing at a U.S. Army dining hall in Mosul kills twenty-four people, including fourteen U.S. soldiers. More than sixty people are wounded in the attack.

ISRAEL

January 4. Israeli Court Sentences Military Objectors. An Israeli military court sentences five Israelis who refused to serve in the Israeli army to one-year prison terms.

May 2. Likud Rebuffs Gaza Plan. In a Likud Party referendum, 60 percent of party members oppose Sharon's Gaza withdrawal plan, while 39 percent support it.

May 5. Report Claims Israel Inappropriately Funded Settlements. The Israeli government reports that $6.5 million was funneled to settlement projects in January 2000. Of the seventy-seven contracts addressed, eighteen were for outposts created without government approval.

June 6. Cabinet Agrees to Withdrawal Plan. The Israeli cabinet approves Sharon's plans to withdraw from the Gaza Strip.

June 8. Sharon Loses Majority in Knesset. Sharon loses his majority in the Knesset after the National Religious Party resigns from his governing coalition to protest the Gaza withdrawal plan.

June 13. Charges against Sharon Dropped. The Israeli attorney general drops corruption and bribery charges against Sharon, citing a lack of evidence.

July 12. Sharon Invites Labor to the Table. After several allies quit Sharon's governing coalition because of objections to the Gaza withdrawal plan, the prime minister invites the Labor Party to join his coalition.

August 18. Likud Bars Labor Governing Coalition. Likud votes to bar Sharon from adding the Labor Party to his governing coalition.

December 9. Sharon Survives Vote on Gaza Plan. Sharon wins a crucial party vote to invite the Labor Party and Orthodox Jewish parties to join his government. The victory gives Sharon a solid majority for his Gaza withdrawal plan in the face of internal opposition from the Likud Party.

JORDAN

March 23. U.S. Grants New Aid to Jordan. The United States announces an additional $134 million in aid to Jordan.

April 19. Abdallah Postpones U.S. Meeting. King Abdallah delays a planned meeting with U.S. president Bush to reflect the king's displeasure with Bush's endorsement of Israeli plans to withdraw from the Gaza Strip.

July 1. Abdallah Offers Troops for Iraq. Abdallah offers to send troops to Iraq at the new government's request. Jordan is the first Arab country to offer military aid to the newly independent country.

July 6. Jordan Finishes Economic Restructuring Plan. In accordance with a fifteen-year International Monetary Fund economic restructuring plan, Jordan reports 3 percent economic growth during the preceding year.

September 30. Arrests Bring Criticism. A spate of arrests targeting opposition groups brings international criticism of Abdallah. Jordanian authorities had detained a former cabinet minister, five former members of parliament, and a regional political official for delivering speeches calling for the end of Abdallah's reign.

LEBANON

Lebanese and Syrian Leaders Sign Accord. Lebanese prime minister Rafiq al-Hariri and Syrian president Bashar al-Asad agree to greater cooperation between the two nations' customs services and the elimination of bilateral taxes on air transport.

LIBYA AND NORTH AFRICA

January 9. Libya to Pay Victims of Airline Explosion. Libya agrees to compensate the families of French UTA flight 772, which exploded over Niger in 1989, killing 170 victims. The agreement admits no Libyan responsibility for the explosion but would provide $1 million for the families of each victim. In 1999 a French court convicted six Libyan agents in absentia of the bombing.

February 27. U.S. Lifts Travel Ban to Libya. The Bush administration lifts the travel ban on Libya.

March 2. U.S. and Morocco Agree to Free-Trade Deal. The United States and Morocco agree to a free-trade deal.

March 25. Blair Meets with Qadhafi. British prime minister Tony Blair meets with Libyan president Mu'ammar al-Qadhafi in Tripoli. The two leaders pledge to improve relations and promise to aid the United States in its fight against al-Qaida.

April 23. Bush Removes Business Roadblocks. Bush orders the removal of most of the remaining barriers to business dealings with Libya. The U.S. Department of State still lists Libya as a country that sponsors terrorism.

June 29. U.S. and Libya Renew Diplomatic Ties. The United States and Libya resume diplomatic ties after twenty-four years.

PALESTINIAN AFFAIRS

March 14. Accused Convoy Bombers Ordered Released. Citing a lack of evidence, a Palestinian court orders the release of four Palestinians who had been accused of the murder of three U.S. security personnel.

July 17. Palestinian Prime Minister Resigns. Palestinian prime minister Ahmad Qurei threatens to resigns, citing the deteriorating security situation in the Gaza Strip.

July 19. Arafat Attempts to Quell Growing Chaos. Palestinian leader Arafat attempts to quell demonstrations and protests in Gaza, asking an ousted chief of security to return in the place of Arafat's cousin, Musa Arafat, whom Yasir Arafat appointed chief of security but whom many considered corrupt.

August 12. Gaza Chaos Grows. Palestinian protesters occupy government buildings in Gaza to demand aid after rioters destroy their homes.

August 26. Arafat Rejects Reform Efforts. Arafat rebuffs efforts to reform the Palestinian Authority, refusing to sign executive orders that would restructure his administration.

November 11. Arafat Dies. Arafat dies in a French hospital after a month-long illness. The Palestine Liberation Organization elects former Palestinian prime minister Mahmoud Abbas as its new chief.

November 22. Abbas Announces Candidacy. The Fatah leadership chooses interim Palestinian leader Mahmoud Abbas to run for president of the Palestinian Authority.

PERSIAN GULF STATES

March 13. Saudi Officials Announce Election Plans. Saudi Arabia announces plans for the kingdom's first elections, in October 2004. The plan calls for municipal elections first, to be followed by general elections at a time to be determined.

June 23. Saudis Announce Amnesty for Militants. Crown Prince Abdallah says that "militants" who turn themselves in within thirty days will receive amnesty. Several do, including Khalid al-Harbi, a suspected al-Qaida member and known associate of Osama bin Laden.

August 5. Yemeni Government Battles Opposition. More than forty people are killed in fighting in the north between government forces and rebel cleric Shaykh Hussein al-Houthi.

September 15. Yemen Government Shuts Down Paper Opposition. Government officials close the Yemeni opposition paper *al-Shoura* and arrest its editor supporting al-Houthi.

September 21. Yemeni Cease-Fire Implemented. A cease-fire halts the fighting between Yemeni government forces and northern rebels that has killed more than 600 people.

September 28. Bahrain Eliminates Human Rights Center. The Bahraini government eliminates the Bahrain Center for Human Rights and arrests the group's director in response to his criticism of the government.

October 12. Saudi Officials Rule Out Women Voters. Citing logistical difficulties, Saudi officials say that women will not be able to vote in the November elections. Saudi police kill three suspected militants in Riyadh.

December 30. Militants Battle Government in Riyadh. Militants with suspected link to al-Qaida set off several car bombs in Riyadh, killing at least ten people and injuring more than twenty. Security forces kill seven they claimed were responsible for the attacks.

2005

REGIONAL AFFAIRS

February 24. Musharraf Says al-Qaida Broken in Pakistan. Musharraf says that Pakistani forces have destroyed al-Qaida's infrastructure along the Afghan border but adds that Osama bin Laden's whereabouts remain unknown.

ARAB-ISRAELI CONFLICT

January 16. Sharon Orders Military Operations. After a Palestinian suicide attack kills six Israelis at a Gaza crossing, Israeli prime minister Ariel Sharon cuts ties with Palestinian leader Mahmoud Abbas.

January 21. Palestinians Begin Policing Gaza. About 3,000 armed Palestinian police begin patrolling the northern Gaza Strip to prevent rocket fire on Israeli communities. Abbas continues negotiations with Palestinian groups to win their commitment to a cease-fire.

January 26. Israel Says It Will Halt Assassinations. Israeli officials say the military will halt the practice of targeting Palestinians for assassination.

February 8. Israeli and Palestinian Leaders Declare Cease-fire. At a summit in Sharm al-Shaykh, Israeli and Palestinian leaders announce an informal cease-fire, ending more than four years of fighting.

February 20. Jordanian Ambassador Returns to Israel. The Jordanian ambassador returned to Israel after a four-year downgrade in relations.

February 21. Israel Releases Prisoners. Israel releases 500 Palestinian prisoners in accordance with the February 8 agreement.

February 25. Suicide Attack Kills Four Israelis. In Tel Aviv, a suicide bombing kills four Israelis and prompts Sharon to halt talks with Palestinian authorities.

February 27. Sharon Halts West Bank Withdrawal. Israel decides to delay plans to turn control of five West Bank towns over to the Palestinian Authority and free 400 more prisoners, as agreed at the February 8 summit.

March 16. Israel Hands Reins of Power to Palestinians in Jericho. Israel turns over Jericho to Palestinian authorities.

March 17. Egyptian Ambassador Returns to Israel. Egypt returned its ambassador to Israel after a four-year downgrade in relations.

March 22. Tulkarm Comes under Palestinian Control. Israel completes the handover of the West Bank town of Tulkarm to the Palestinians.

March 28. Gaza Pullout Plan Survives Referendum Vote. Israel's Knesset rejects efforts to block Sharon's plan to withdraw from the Gaza Strip, vetoing a proposed national referendum.

EGYPT

January 29. Opposition Leader Detained for Forgery. Authorities arrest Egyptian legislator Ayman Nur, founder of the al-Ghad Party, on charges of forging documents to help form a new political party. Nur denies the accusations.

February 26. Mubarak Orders Election Law Review. Egyptian president Hosni Mubarak orders a review and amendment of the country's presidential election law, potentially laying the groundwork for multiple candidates to run in September's presidential election.

March 9. Parliament Agrees to Election Reform. Egypt's parliament agrees to amend the constitution to allow multi-candidate elections. The amendment requires nominees to be endorsed by members of parliament and local councils.

March 16. Opposition Candidate Plans to Run. Ayman Nur, released from prison on March 12, announces his candidacy for the presidency.

IRAN

January 9. Parliament Rejects Reformist Appointee. The Majlis rejects President Mohammad Khatami's reformist nominee to head the Transportation Ministry.

February 27. Russia and Iran Sign Nuclear Pact. Iran and Russia sign a deal to exchange nuclear fuel, targeting mid-2006 for bringing Iran's first reactor online.

March 23. Nuclear Talks with Europe Fail. Negotiations between Europe and Iran end at an impasse, with Iran refusing to scrap its uranium enrichment program.

IRAQ

January 4. Baghdad Governor Shot Dead. Militants assassinate Iraqi provincial governor Ali al-Haidari, whose jurisdiction included Baghdad.

January 6. Government Extends State of Emergency. Iraqi officials extend a state of emergency by thirty days in an attempt to quell attacks aimed at derailing upcoming elections. U.S. military commanders admit that security is poor in four of eighteen provinces.

January 17. Expatriate Iraqis Begin Registering. Exiled Iraqis begin registration for January 30 elections in fourteen countries.

January 30. Voting Begins in Iraq. In the first free elections in more than 50 years, Iraqis turn out in force to vote to fill 275 seats in the National Assembly, defying threats of violence from insurgents. Two U.S. personnel are killed in rocket attacks on the U.S. embassy in Baghdad.

February 13. Election Results Announced. Election officials report that the majority Shiite United Iraqi Alliance party has won 48 percent of the vote in legislative elections. The Kurdish Alliance won 26 percent of the vote.

February 28. Massive Car Bombing Kills 110. A car bombing kills 110 people and wounds 133 in a crowd of police and national guard recruits outside a medical clinic in Hillah, south of Baghdad.

ISRAEL

February 20. Cabinet Approves New Barrier Route, Gaza Pullout. The Israeli cabinet gives final approval to Sharon's plans for a withdrawal from the Gaza Strip and a revised route for the West Bank separation barrier more in line with Israel's original frontier.

JORDAN

January 27. Abdallah Announces Democratic Reforms. King Abdallah says he will institute limited democratic reforms, including the creation of elected councils to oversee reform.

LEBANON

January 17. Israeli Warplanes Strike Hizballah. Israeli warplanes attack suspected Hizballah targets in southern Lebanon after Hizballah members detonate a bomb in an Israeli bulldozer in a disputed area near the border.

February 14. Former Lebanese Prime Minister Assassinated. Former Lebanese prime minister Rafiq al-Hariri is killed in a massive bombing, along with 16 others. The assassination sparks anti-Syrian demonstrations in Lebanon.

February 24. Syria Committed to Withdrawal from Lebanon. Facing increasing international pressure, Syrian authorities say they are committed to withdrawing their 15,000 troops, in accordance with the 1989 Taif agreement.

February 28. Thousands Protest Syrian Rule in Lebanon. Defying a ban on protests, some 10,000 people demonstrate against Syrian involvement in Lebanon.

March 9. Hizballah Organizes Huge Pro-Syrian Rally. Under the leadership of Hizballah, hundreds of thousands gather in Beirut to praise Syria and Syrian president Bashar al-Asad.

March 10. Pro-Syrian Leader Returns. Ten days after resigning under local and international pressure, pro-Syrian prime minister Omar Karami is asked by President Emile Lahoud to form another government power.

March 11. Syrian Troops Begin Pullout. Syria begins the removal of about 15,000 troops from northern Lebanon.

March 14. Massive Anti-Syrian Demonstrations Demand Pullout. Hundreds of thousands of Lebanese gather in Beirut, demanding the removal of the Syrian-backed government. Estimates say the demonstrations exceed earlier pro-Syria demonstrations organized by Hizballah.

PALESTINIAN AFFAIRS

January 9. Palestinians Elect Abbas to Succeed Arafat. Palestinians elect Mahmoud Abbas to succeed Yasir Arafat as president of the Palestinian Authority.

PERSIAN GULF STATES

January 13. Saudi Court Sentences Dissidents. A Saudi religious court sentences fifteen Saudis, including a woman, to as many as 250 lashes each and up to six months in prison for demonstrating against the government.

January 15. New Bahraini Cabinet Sworn In. Bahraini king Shaykh Hamad bin Isa al-Khalifa names a new cabinet. Several members are supporters of his economic and political reform efforts. Several hardliners are dismissed.

February 9. Islamic Parties Successful in Saudi Elections. In the first round of Saudi city council elections, seven Islamist candidates win seats from Riyadh.

February 27. Qatar Announces New Energy Deal. Qatar's state-run petroleum company and two major international oil companies sign deals worth about $19 billion to develop liquefied natural gas for European and U.S. markets.

BIBLIOGRAPHY

The bibliography is divided into topics to help facilitate research. Most topics, however, are not discrete, so readers may want to peruse more than one topic to locate all books and articles of interest.

Egypt

Abdo, Geneive. *No God but God: Egypt and the Triumph of Islam.* New York: Oxford University Press, 2002.

Badran, Margot. *Feminists, Islam, and Nation: Gender and the Making of Modern Egypt.* Princeton, N.J.: Princeton University Press, 1995.

Baker, Raymond. *Egypt's Uncertain Revolution under Nasser and Sadat.* Cambridge, Mass.: Harvard University Press, 1978.

———. *Sadat and After: Struggles for Egypt's Political Soul.* London: I. B. Tauris, 1990.

Baron, Beth. *Egypt as a Woman: Nationalism, Gender, and Politics.* Berkeley and Los Angeles: University of California Press, 2005.

Butter, David. "Egypt: Special Report." *Middle East Economic Digest,* October 9, 1998, 23–45.

Cole, Juan R. I. *Colonialism and Revolution in the Middle East: Social and Cultural Origins of Egypt's 'Urabi Movement.* Princeton, N.J.: Princeton University Press, 1993.

Fahmy, Ninette S. *The Politics of Egypt: State-Society Relationship.* London: RoutledgeCurzon, 2002.

Giugale, Marcelo, and Hamed Mobarek. *Private Sector Development in Egypt.* Cairo: American University in Cairo Press, 1996.

Gorman, Anthony. *Historians, State and Politics in Twentieth Century Egypt: Contesting the Nation.* New York: Routledge, 2002.

Gray, Matthew. "Economic Reform, Privatization, and Tourism in Egypt." *Middle Eastern Studies* 34, no. 2 (April 1998): 91–112.

Haeri, Niloofar. *Sacred Language, Ordinary People: Dilemmas of Culture and Politics in Egypt.* New York: Palgrave MacMillan, 2003.

Haikal, Muhammed Hasanain. *Autumn of Fury: The Assassination of Sadat.* New York: Random House, 1983.

Hill, Enid. *Discourses in Contemporary Egypt: Politics and Social Issues.* Cairo: American University in Cairo Press, 2000.

Hinnebusch, Raymond A., Jr. *Egyptian Politics under Sadat: The Post-Populist Development of an Authoritarian-Modernizing State.* Rev. ed. Boulder, Colo.: Lynne Rienner, 1988.

Holt, P. M. *Egypt and the Fertile Crescent, 1516–1922.* Ithaca, N.Y.: Cornell University Press, 1966.

Hopwood, Derek. *Egypt: Politics and Society, 1945–1990.* 3d ed. London and New York: Routledge, 1993.

Kepel, Gilles. *Muslim Extremism in Egypt.* Berkeley and Los Angeles: University of California Press, 1985.

Kerr, Malcolm H., *The Arab Cold War: Gamal 'Abd al-Nasir and His Rivals, 1958–1970.* London: Oxford University Press, 1971.

McDermott, Anthony. *Egypt from Nasser to Mubarak: A Flawed Revolution.* London: Croom Helm, 1988.

Mitchell, Timothy. *Rule of Experts: Egypt, Techno-Politics, Modernity.* Berkeley and Los Angeles: University of California Press, 2002.

Petrie, Carl F., and M. W. Daly. *The Cambridge History of Egypt.* 2 vols. Cambridge: Cambridge University Press, 1998.

Pollard, Lisa. *Nurturing the Nation: The Family Politics of Modernizing, Colonizing, and Liberating Egypt, 1805–1923.* Berkeley and Los Angeles: University of California Press, 2004.

Rodenbeck, Max. *Cairo: The City Victorious.* New York: Vintage Departures, 2000.

Springborg, Robert. *Mubarak's Egypt: Fragmentation of the Political Order.* Boulder, Colo.: Westview Press, 1989.

Starrett, Gregory. *Putting Islam to Work: Education, Politics, and Religious Transformation in Egypt.* Berkeley and Los Angeles: University of California Press, 1998.

Sullivan, Denis Joseph, and Sana Abed-Kotob. *Islam in Contemporary Egypt: Civil Society vs. the State.* Boulder, Colo.: Lynne Rienner, 1999.

Vatikiotis, P. J. *The History of Egypt from Muhammad Ali to Sadat.* Baltimore: Johns Hopkins University Press, 1980.

Waterbury, John. *The Egypt of Nasser and Sadat.* Princeton, N.J.: Princeton University Press, 1983.

Iran

Abdo, Geneive, and Jonathan Lyons. *Answering Only to God: Faith and Freedom in Twenty-First-Century Iran.* New York: Henry Holt, 2003.

Ansari, Ali M. *Iran, Islam, and Democracy: The Politics of Managing Change.* London: Royal Institute of International Affairs, 2000.

Bakhash, Shaul. *The Reign of the Ayatollahs: Iran and the Islamic Revolution.* New York: Basic Books, 1984.

Bill, James A. "The United States and Iran: Mutual Mythologies." *Middle East Policy* 2, no. 3 (1993): 98–106.

Brumberg, Daniel. *The Struggle for Reform in Iran.* Chicago: University of Chicago Press, 2001.

Congressional Quarterly. *The Iran-Contra Puzzle.* Washington, D.C.: Congressional Quarterly, 1987.

Cordesman, Anthony H. *Iran's Military Forces in Transition: Conventional Threats and Weapons of Mass Destruction.* Westport, Conn.: Praeger, 1999.

Cottam, Richard W. *Iran and the United States: A Cold War Case Study.* Pittsburgh: University of Pittsburgh Press, 1988.

Cottam, Richard W., et al. "The United States and Iran's Revolution." *Foreign Policy,* no. 34 (Spring 1979): 3–34.

Fuller, Graham E. *The "Center of the Universe": The Geopolitics of Iran.* Boulder, Colo.: Westview Press, 1991.

Gieling, Saskia. "The Marja'iya in Iran and the Nomination of Khamanei in December 1994." *Middle Eastern Studies* 33, no. 4 (October 1997): 777–787.

Harris, David. *The Crisis: The President, the Prophet, and the Shah—1979 and the Coming of Militant Islam.* Boston: Little, Brown & Co., 2004.

Hooglund, Eric. "Mythology versus Reality: Iranian Political Economy and the Clinton Administration." *Critique: Critical Middle Eastern Studies,* no. 11 (Fall 1997).

Hunter, Shireen T. *Iran after Khomeini.* Washington, D.C.: Center for Strategic and International Studies, 1992.

Keddie, Nikki. *Roots of Revolution: An Interpretive History of Modern Iran.* New Haven, Conn.: Yale University Press, 1981.

Laqueur, Walter. "Why the Shah Fell." *Commentary* 67, no. 3 (March 1979): 47–55.

Lytle, Mark H. *The Origins of the Iranian-American Alliance, 1941–1953.* New York: Holmes & Meier, 1987.

Marschall, Christin. *Iran's Persian Gulf Policy: From Khomeini to Khatami.* London: RoutledgeCurzon, 2003.

Milani, Abbas. *Lost Wisdom: Rethinking Modernity in Iran.* Washington, D.C.: Mage Publishers, 2004.

Moghissi, Haideh. *Populism and Feminism in Iran: Women's Struggle in a Male-Defined Revolutionary Movement.* London: St. Martin's Press, 1994.

Nafisi, Azar. *Reading Lolita in Tehran: A Memoir in Books.* New York: Random House, 2003.

Pipes, Daniel, and Patrick Clawson. "Ambitious Iran, Troubled Neighbors." *Foreign Affairs* 72, no. 1 (America and the World 1992/93): 124–141.

Pollack, Kenneth M. *The Persian Puzzle Palace: The Conflict between Iran and America.* New York: Random House, 2004.

Pollack, Kenneth M., and Ray Takeyh. "Taking on Tehran." *Foreign Affairs* 84, no. 2 (March/April 2005): 21–34.

Potter, Lawrence G., and Gary G. Sick, eds. *Iran, Iraq, and the Legacies of War.* New York: Palgrave MacMillan, 2004.

Ramazani, Nesta. "Women in Iran: The Revolutionary Ebb and Flow." *Middle East Journal* 47, no. 3 (Summer 1993): 409–428.

Ramazani, R. K. "The Shifting Premise of Iran's Foreign Policy: Towards a Democratic Peace?" *Middle East Journal* 52, no. 2 (Spring 1998): 177–187.

Roy, Olivier. "The Crisis of Religious Legitimacy in Iran." *Middle East Journal* 53, no. 2 (Spring 1999): 201–216.

Sariolghalam, Mahmood. "Understanding Iran: Getting Past Stereotypes and Mythology." *Washington Quarterly* 26, no. 4 (Autumn 2003): 69–82.

Sciolino, Elaine. *Persian Mirrors: The Elusive Face of Iran.* New York: Free Press, 2000.

Sick, Gary. "Trial by Error: Reflections on the Iran-Iraq War." *Middle East Journal* 43, no. 2 (Spring 1989): 230–246.

al-Suwaidi, Jamal S. *Iran and the Gulf: A Search for Stability.* Abu Dhabi: Emirates Center for Strategic Studies and Research, 1996.

Takeyh, Ray. "Iran Builds the Bomb." *Survival* 46, no. 4 (Winter 2004): 51–64.

———. "Iranian Options: Pragmatic Mullahs and America's Interests." *National Interest,* no. 73 (Fall 2003): 49–56.

Vaziri, Haleh. "Iran's Involvement in Lebanon: Polarization and Radicalization of Militant Islamic

Movements." *Journal of South Asian and Middle Eastern Studies* 16, no. 2 (Winter 1992): 1–16.

Iraq

Baram, Amatzia. *Building toward Crisis: Saddam's Strategy for Survival.* Washington, D.C.: Washington Institute for Near East Policy, 1998.

Cole, Juan. "The United States and Shi'ite Religious Factions in Post-Ba'thist Iraq." *Middle East Journal* 57, no. 4 (Autumn 2003): 543–566.

Cordesman, Anthony H. *Iraq: Sanctions and Beyond.* Boulder, Colo.: Westview Press, 1997.

Diamond, Larry. "What Went Wrong in Iraq." *Foreign Affairs* 83, no. 5 (September/October 2004): 34–56.

Doran, Michael Scott. "Palestine, Iraq, and American Strategy." *Foreign Affairs* 82, no. 1 (January/February 2003): 19–33.

Farouk-Sluglett, Marion, and Peter Sluglett. *Iraq since 1958: From Revolution to Dictatorship.* New York: Methuen, 1988.

Gause, F. Gregory, III. "Getting It Backward on Iraq." *Foreign Affairs* 78, no. 3 (May/June 1999): 54–65.

Kedourie, Elie. "Iraq: The Mystery of American Policy." *Commentary* 91, no. 6 (June 1991): 15–19.

Keegan, John. *The Iraq War.* London: Hutchinson; New York: Knopf, 2004.

al-Khalil, Samir. *Republic of Fear: The Inside Story of Saddam's Iraq.* New York: Pantheon, 1990.

Lopez, George A., and David Cortright. "Containing Iraq: Sanctions Worked." *Foreign Affairs* 83, no. 4 (July/August 2004): 90–103.

Marr, Phebe. *The Modern History of Iraq.* 2d ed. Boulder, Colo.: Westview, 2004.

Orr, Robert C., ed. *Winning the Peace: An American Strategy for Post-Conflict Reconstruction.* CSIS Significant Issues 26. Washington, D.C: Center for Strategic & International Studies, 2004.

Pollack, Kenneth M. *The Threatening Storm: The Case for Invading Iraq.* New York: Random House, 2002.

Prince, James M. "A Kurdish State in Iraq?" *Current History* 92, no. 570 (January 1993): 17–22.

Tripp, Charles. *A History of Iraq.* Cambridge: Cambridge University Press, 2002.

Woodward, Bob. *Plan of Attack.* New York: Simon & Schuster, 2004.

Yaphe, Judith. "War and Occupation in Iraq: What Went Right? What Could Go Wrong?" *Middle East Journal* 57, no. 3 (Summer 2003): 381–399.

Islam

Abou El Fadl, Khaled, ed. *Islam and the Challenge of Democracy.* Princeton, N.J.: Princeton University Press, 2004.

Armstrong, Karen. *The Battle for God: Fundamentalism in Judaism, Christianity, and Islam.* London and New York: Alfred A. Knopf, 2000.

———. *Muhammad: A Biography of the Prophet.* San Francisco: HarperCollins, 1993.

Bergen, Peter L. *Holy War, Inc.: Inside the Secret World of Osama bin Laden.* New York: Free Press, 2001.

Bloom, Jonathan, and Sheila Blair. *Islam: A Thousand Years of Faith and Power.* New Haven, Conn.: Yale University Press, 2002.

Bulliet, Richard W. "The Future of the Islamic Movement." *Foreign Affairs* 72, no. 5 (November/December 1993): 38–44.

Burgat, François. *The Islamic Movement in North Africa.* Bloomington: Indiana University Press, 1993.

Burke, Jason. *Al-Qaeda.* London: I. B. Taurus, 2003.

Davis, Joyce. *Martyrs.* New York: Palgrave Macmillan, 2003.

Diamond, Larry Jay, ed. *Islam and Democracy in the Middle East.* Baltimore: Johns Hopkins University Press, 2003.

Esposito, John L. *Islam: The Straight Path.* 3d rev ed. New York: Oxford University Press, 2005.

———. *The Islamic Threat: Myth or Reality?* 3d ed. New York: Oxford University Press, 1999.

———, ed. *The Oxford Encyclopedia of the Modern Islamic World.* 4 vols. New York: Oxford University Press, 1995.

———, ed. *The Oxford History of Islam.* New York: Oxford University Press, 1999.

———, ed. *Political Islam: Revolution, Radicalism, or Reform?* Boulder, Colo.: Lynne Rienner, 1997.

———. *Unholy War: Terror in the Name of Islam.* New York: Oxford University Press, 2002.

Esposito, John L., and James Piscatori. "Democratization and Islam." *Middle East Journal* 45, no. 3 (Summer 1991): 427–440.

Esposito, John L., and John O. Voll. *Makers of Contemporary Islam.* New York: Oxford University Press, 2001.

Fakhry, Majid, trans. *The Qura'n: A Modern English Version.* Berkshire, U.K.: Garnet Publishing, 1996.

Fuller, Graham. *The Future of Political Islam.* New York: Palgrave MacMillan, 2003.

Haddad, Yvonne Yazbeck, and John L. Esposito, eds. *Islam, Gender, and Social Change.* Oxford: Oxford University Press, 1998.

Hunter, Shireen. *The Future of Islam and the West: Clash of Civilizations or Peaceful Coexistence?* Westport, Conn.: Praeger, 1998.

Kandiyoti, Deniz. *Women, Islam, and the State.* Philadelphia: Temple University Press, 1991.

Kepel, Gilles. *The War for Muslim Minds.* Cambridge, Mass.: Harvard University Press, 2004.

Lapidus, Ira M. *A History of Islamic Societies.* Cambridge: Cambridge University Press, 1988.

Lewis, Bernard. *The Jews of Islam.* Princeton, N.J.: Princeton University Press, 1984.

———. *What Went Wrong?* New York: Oxford University Press, 2003.

Mamdani, Mahmood. *Good Muslim, Bad Muslim.* New York: Pantheon, 2004.

Peters, F. E. *Children of Abraham.* 2d ed. Princeton, N.J.: Princeton University Press, 2005.

Peters, Rudolph. *Jihad in Classical and Modern Islam.* Princeton: Markus Wiener, 1996.

Roy, Olivier. *Globalised Islam.* London: Hurst, 2004.

Sachedina, Abdulaziz. *The Islamic Roots of Democratic Pluralism.* New York: Oxford University Press, 2001.

Said, Edward W. *Covering Islam: How the Media and the Experts Determine How We See the Rest of the World.* New York: Vintage Books, 1997.

Salamé, Ghassan. "Islam and the West." *Foreign Policy,* no. 90 (Spring 1993): 22–37.

Sharabi, Hisham. "Modernity and Islamic Revival: The Critical Task of Arab Intellectuals." *Contention* 2, no. 1 (Fall 1992): 127–138.

Voll, John O. *Islam: Continuity and Change in the Modern World.* 2d ed. Syracuse, N.Y.: Syracuse University Press, 1994.

Israel, the Palestinians, and the Arab-Israeli Conflict

Agha, Hussein, and Robert Malley. "Camp David and After: An Exchange (2. A Reply to Ehud Barak)," *New York Review of Books,* June 13, 2002.

———. "The Last Palestinian." *New York Review of Books,* February 10, 2005.

Avineri, Shlomo. *The Making of Modern Zionism: The Intellectual Origins of the Jewish State.* New York: Basic Books, 1981.

Aronson, Geoffrey. *Creating Facts: Israel, Palestinians and the West Bank.* Washington, D.C.: Institute for Palestine Studies, 1987.

Bar-Siman-Tov, Yaacov. *Israel, the Superpowers, and the War in the Middle East.* New York: Praeger, 1987.

Beilin, Yossi. *The Path to Geneva: The Quest for a Permanent Agreement, 1996–2004.* New York: RDV Books/Akashic Books, 2004.

Ben Ami, Shlomo. *A Front without a Rearguard: A Voyage to the Boundaries of the Peace Process.* Tel Aviv: Yediot Aharonot, 2004.

Ben-Yehuda, Hemda, and Shmuel Sandler. "Crisis Management and Interstate Conflict: Changes in the Arab-Israel Dispute." *Journal of Peace Research* 35 (January 1998): 83–109.

Bishara, Marwan. *Palestine/Israel: Peace or Apartheid: Occupation, Terrorism and the Future.* 2d ed. Halifax, Nova Scotia: Fernwood, 2002.

Boyle, Francis Anthony. *Palestine, Palestinians, and International Law.* Atlanta: Clarity Press, 2003.

Chomsky, Noam. *Fateful Triangle: The United States, Israel, and the Palestinians.* 2d ed. Cambridge, Mass.: South End Press, 1999.

Christison, Kathleen M. "Myths about Palestinians." *Foreign Policy,* no. 66 (Spring 1987): 109–127.

Cohen, Eliot A. "Israel after Heroism." *Foreign Affairs* 77, no. 6 (November/December 1998): 112–128.

Congressional Quarterly. "Palestinian *Intifada:* A Program of Nonviolent Struggle." *The Middle East.* (Washington, D.C.: CQ Press, 2000), 22–24.

Davis, Joyce. *Martyrs.* New York: Palgrave Macmillan, 2003.

Dayan, Moshe. *Breakthrough: A Personal Account of the Egypt-Israel Peace Negotiations.* New York: Knopf, 1981.

Elazar, Daniel J. *The Camp David Framework for Peace: A Shift toward Shared Rule.* Washington, D.C.: American Enterprise Institute for Public Policy Research, 1979.

Enderlin, Charles. *Shattered Dreams: The Failure of the Peace Process in the Middle East, 1995–2002.* New York: Other Press, 2003.

Fernea, Elizabeth Warnock, and Mary Evelyn Hocking, eds. *The Struggle for Peace: Israelis and Palestinians.* Austin: University of Texas Press, 1992.

Fischer, Stanley. "Building Palestinian Prosperity." *Foreign Policy,* no. 93 (Winter 1993–94): 60–75.

Foundation for Middle East Peace, "Report on Israeli Settlement in the Occupied Territories," www.fmep.org/reports.

Frisch, Hillel. *Countdown to Statehood: Palestinian State Formation in the West Bank and Gaza.* Albany: State University of New York Press, 1998.

Gilbert, Martin. *Israel: A History.* New York: Morrow, 1998.

Grossman, David. *Sleeping on a Wire: Conversations with Palestinians in Israel.* New York: Farrar, Straus & Giroux, 1993.

Haddad, Yvonne. "Islamists and the Problem of Israel." *Middle East Journal* 46, no. 2 (Spring 1992): 266–285.

Harris, William. *Taking Root: Israeli Settlement in the West Bank, the Golan, and Gaza-Sinai, 1967–1980.* New York: Wiley, 1980.

Hiltermann, Joost. *Behind the Intifada.* Princeton, N.J.: Princeton University Press, 1991.

Joffe, Josef, "A World without Israel." *Foreign Policy,* no. 146 (January/February 2005): 36–42.

Kadri, Ali. "A Survey of Commuting Labor from the West Bank to Israel." *Middle East Journal* 52, no. 4 (Autumn 1998): 517–530.

Khalidi, Rashid. *Palestinian Identity: The Construction of Modern National Consciousness.* New York: Columbia University Press, 1997.

Kuttab, Jonathan. "The Children's Revolt." *Journal of Palestine Studies* 17, no. 4 (Summer 1988): 26–35.

Lederman, Jim. "Dateline West Bank: Interpreting the Intifada." *Foreign Policy,* no. 72 (Fall 1988): 230–246.

Lesch, Ann Mosely. *Transition to Palestinian Self-Government.* Bloomington: Indiana University Press, 1992.

Lukacs, Yehuda. *Israel, Jordan, and the Peace Process.* Syracuse, N.Y.: Syracuse University Press, 1997.

Lustick, Ian S. "Israel's Dangerous Fundamentalists." *Foreign Policy,* no. 68 (Fall 1987): 118–139.

Ma'oz, Moshe. *Syria and Israel: From War to Peacemaking.* New York: Oxford University Press, 1995.

Mayer, Tamar. *Women and the Israeli Occupation: The Politics of Change.* London: Routledge, 1994.

McGowan, Daniel, and Marc H. Ellis, eds. *Remembering Deir Yassin: The Future of Israel and Palestine.* Brooklyn, N.Y.: Olive Branch Press, 1998.

Morris, Benny. *Righteous Victims.* New York: Knopf, 2001.

———. *The Birth of the Palestinian Refugee Problem, 1947–1949.* New York: Columbia University Press, 1988.

Muslih, Muhammad. *The Origins of Palestinian Nationalism.* New York: Cambridge University Press, 1988.

Oren, Michael B. "Escalation to Suez: The Egyptian-Israeli Border War, 1949–1956." *Journal of Contemporary History* 24 (1989): 347–374.

Peres, Shimon. "A Strategy for Peace in the Middle East." *Foreign Affairs* 58, no. 4 (Spring 1980): 887–901.

Peretz, Don. *Government and Politics of Israel.* 3d ed. Boulder, Colo.: Westview Press, 1997.

———. *Intifada: The Palestinian Uprising.* Boulder, Colo.: Westview Press, 1989.

Peteet, Julie. *Gender in Crisis: Women in the Palestinian Resistance Movement.* New York: Columbia University Press, 1991.

Quandt, William, ed. *Peace Process: American Diplomacy and the Arab-Israeli Conflict since 1967.* Washington, D.C.: Brookings Institution Press, 1993.

Rempel, Terry. "The Significance of Israel's Partial Annexation of East Jerusalem." *Middle East Journal* 51, no. 4 (Autumn 1997): 520–534.

Robinson, Glenn E. *Building a Palestinian State: The Incomplete Revolution.* Bloomington: Indiana University Press, 1997.

Ross, Dennis. *The Missing Peace: The Inside Story of the Fight for Middle East Peace.* New York: Farrar, Straus & Giroux, 2004.

Roy, Sarah. *The Gaza Strip: The Political Economy of De-Development.* Washington, D.C.: Institute for Palestine Studies, 1995.

Sachar, Howard M. *History of Israel.* New York: Knopf, 1976.

Said, Edward W. *Peace and Its Discontents: Essays on Palestine in the Middle East Peace Process.* New York: Vintage Books, 1996.

Segev, Tom. *1949, the First Israelis.* New York: Free Press, 1993.

Shahak, Israel. *Open Secrets: Israeli Nuclear and Foreign Policies.* Chicago: Pluto Press, 1997.

Shalim, Avi. *The Iron Wall: Israel and the Arab World.* Scranton, Pa.: W. W. Norton & Co., 2001.

Sher, Gilad. *Just Beyond Reach: Israeli-Palestinian Negotiations 1999–2001.* Tel Aviv: Frank Cass & Co., 2005.

Shikaki, Khalil. "Peace Now or Hamas Later." *Foreign Affairs* 77, no. 4 (July/August 1998): 29–43.

Shipley, David. *Arab and Jew: Wounded Spirits in a Promised Land.* New York: Penguin Books, 1987.

Shlaim, Avi. *The Politics of Partition: King Abdullah, the Zionists, and Palestine.* New York: Columbia University Press, 1990.

Sinai, Joshua. "United Nations' and Non–United Nations' Peace-Keeping in the Arab Israeli Sector: Five Scenarios." *Middle East Journal* 49, no. 4 (Autumn 1995): 629–644.

Smith, Charles D. *Palestine and the Arab-Israeli Conflict.* New York: St. Martin's Press, 1992.

Sprinzak, Ehud. "Netanyahu's Safety Belt." *Foreign Affairs* 77, no. 4 (July/August 1998): 18–28.

Swisher, Clayton E. *The Truth about Camp David: The Untold Story about the Collapse of the Middle East Peace Process.* New York: Nation Books, 2004.

Weinbaum, Marvin. "The Israel Factor in Arab Consciousness and Domestic Politics." *Middle East Policy* 2, no. 1 (1993): 87–102.

Jordan

Abu Odeh, Adnan. *Jordanians, Palestinians, and the Hashemite Kingdom in the Middle East Peace Process.* Washington, D.C.: United States Institute of Peace, 1999.

Bank, André, and Olivier Schlumberger. "Jordan: Between Regime Survival and Economic Reform." In *Arab Elites—Negotiating the Politics of Change,* ed. Volker Perthes, 35–60. Boulder, Colo.: Lynne Rienner, 2004.

Brand, Laurie A. *Jordan's Inter-Arab Relations: The Political Economy of Alliance Making.* New York: Columbia University Press, 1994.

———. "Al-Muhajirin w-al-Ansar—Hashemite Strategies for Managing Communal Identities in Jordan." In *Ethnic Conflict and International Politics in the Middle East,* ed. Leonard Binder, 279–306. Gainesville: University Press of Florida, 1999.

———. "In Search of Budget Security: A Reexamination of Jordanian Foreign Policy." In *Diplomacy in the Middle East: The Role of Regional and Outside*

Forces, ed. L. Carl Brown, 139–158. London: I. B. Tauris, 2002.

Hourani, Hani, Hussein Abu Rumman, and Nasser Ahmad Kamel. *Who's Who in the Jordanian Parliament, 2003–2007.* Amman: Sindbad, 2004.

Joffé, George, ed. *Jordan in Transition, 1990–2000.* London: Hurst, 2002.

Lowrance, Sherry R. "After Beijing: Political Liberalization and the Women's Movement in Jordan." *Middle Eastern Studies* 34, no. 3 (July 1998): 83–102.

Lynch, Marc. *State Interests and Public Spheres: The International Politics of Jordan's Identity.* New York: Columbia University Press, 1999.

Milton-Edwards, Beverly, and Peter Hinchcliffe. *Jordan—A Hashemite Legacy.* London: Routledge, 2001.

Robins, Philip. *A History of Jordan.* Cambridge: Cambridge University Press, 2004.

Ryan, Curtis R. *Jordan in Transition—From Hussein to Abdallah.* Boulder, Colo.: Lynne Rienner, 2002.

Schlumberger, Olivier, and André Bank. "Succession, Legitimacy, and Regime Stability in Jordan." *Arab Studies Journal* 10, no. 1 (April 2002): 50–72.

Tal, Lawrence. "Is Jordan Doomed?" *Foreign Affairs* 72, no. 5 (November/December 1993): 45–58.

Wilson, Mary C. *King Abdullah, Britain, and the Making of Jordan.* Cambridge: Cambridge University Press, 1987.

Kuwait

Ahmed, Ahmed A. "Kuwait Public Commercial Investments in Arab Countries." *Middle Eastern Studies* 31, no. 2 (April 1995): 293–306.

Assiri, Abdul-Reda. *Kuwait's Foreign Policy: City-State in World Politics.* Boulder, Colo.: Westview Press, 1990.

Cordesman, Anthony H. *Kuwait: Recovery and Security after the Gulf War.* Boulder, Colo.: Westview Press, 1997.

Crystal, Jill. *Oil and Politics in the Gulf: Rulers and Merchants in Kuwait and Qatar.* Cambridge: Cambridge University Press, 1990.

Ghabra, Shafeeq. "Kuwait and the Dynamics of Socioeconomic Change." *Middle East Journal* 51, no. 3 (Summer 1997): 358–372.

Jarman, Robert. *Sabah al-Salim Al-Sabah, Amir of Kuwait 1965–77: A Political Biography.* London: Centre of Arab Studies, 2002.

Joyce, Miriam. *Kuwait, 1945–1996: An Anglo-American Perspective.* London: Frank Cass, 1998.

Schofield, Richard. *Kuwait and Iraq: Historical Claims and Territorial Disputes.* London: Royal Institute of International Affairs, 1991; 2d ed. Kuwait, 1998.

Slot, Ben J., et al. *Kuwait: The Growth of a Historic Identity.* London: Arabian Publishing, 2003.

Tétreault, Mary Ann. "Kuwait: The Morning After." *Current History* 91, no. 561 (January 1992): 6–10.

———. "Kuwait's Unhappy Anniversary." *Middle East Policy* 7, no. 3 (June 2000): 67–77.

———. *Stories of Democracy: Politics and Society in Contemporary Kuwait.* New York: Columbia University Press, 2000.

Lebanon

Baroudi, Sami E. "Economic Conflict in Postwar Lebanon: State-Labor Relations between 1992 and 1997." *Middle East Journal* 52, no. 4 (Autumn 1998): 531–550.

Dagher, Carol H. *Bring Down the Walls: Lebanon's Postwar Challenge.* New York: St. Martin's Press, 2000.

Deeb, Mary-Jane. "Shia Movements in Lebanon: Their Formation, Ideology, Social Basis, and Links with Iran and Syria." *Third World Quarterly* 10, no. 2 (April 1988): 683–698.

Eban, Abba. "Camp David: The Unfinished Business." *Foreign Affairs* 57, no. 2 (Winter 1978/79): 343–354.

Ellis, Kail C., ed. *Lebanon's Second Republic: Prospects for the Twenty-First Century.* Gainesville: University Press of Florida, 2002.

Grafton, David D. *The Christians of Lebanon: Political Rights in Islamic Law.* London: I. B. Tauris, 2003.

Haddad, Simon. *The Palestinian Impasse in Lebanon: The Politics of Refugee Integration.* Brighton, U.K.: Sussex Academic Press, 2003.

Hamzeh, Ahmad Nizar. *In the Path of Hizballah.* Syracuse, N.Y.: Syracuse University Press, 2004.

Hanf, Theodor, and Nawaf Salam, eds. *Lebanon in Limbo: Postwar Society and State in an Uncertain Regional Environment.* Baden-Baden, Germany: Nomos, 2003.

Harris, William. *Faces of Lebanon: Sects, Wars, and Global Extensions.* Princeton, N.J.: Marcus Weiner, 1997.

Hof, Frederic C. *Beyond the Boundary: Lebanon, Israel, and the Challenge of Change.* Washington, D.C.: Middle East Insight, 2000.

Al-Hout, Bayan Nuwayhed. *Sabra and Shatila: September 1982.* London: Pluto Press, 2004.

Khalaf, Samir George. *Civil and Uncivil Violence in Lebanon: A History of the Internationalization of Communal Conflict.* New York: Columbia University Press, 2002.

———. *Lebanon's Predicament.* New York: Columbia University Press, 1987.

Khalidi, Walid. *Conflict and Violence in Lebanon.* Cambridge, Mass.: Harvard University Press, 1979.

Makdisi, Samir, and Richard Sadaka. *The Lebanese Civil War, 1975–1990.* Beirut: American University of Beirut, Institute of Financial Economics, 2003.

Picard, Elizabeth. *Lebanon, a Shattered Country: Myths and Realities of the Wars in Lebanon.* New York: Holmes & Meier, 2002.

Rabil, Robert G. *Embattled Neighbors: Syria, Israel, and Lebanon.* Boulder, Colo.: Lynne Rienner, 2003.

Saad-Ghorayeb, Amal. *Hizbullah: Politics and Religion.* London and Sterling, Va.: Pluto Press, 2002.

Salam, Nawaf A., ed. *Options for Lebanon.* London: I. B. Tauris, 2004.

Salibi, Kemal S. *Crossroads to Civil War: Lebanon, 1958–1976.* Delmar, N.Y.: Caravan, 1976.

El-Solh, Raghid. *Lebanon and Arabism: National Identity and State Formation.* London: I. B. Tauris, 2004.

Libya

Alexander, Nathan. "The Foreign Policy of Libya: Inflexibility amid Change." *Orbis* 25 (Winter 1981): 819–846.

Cooley, John K. "The Libyan Menace." *Foreign Policy,* no. 42 (Spring 1981): 74–83.

Gurney, Judith. *Libya: The Political Economy of Oil.* New York: Oxford University Press, 1996.

St. John, Ronald Bruce. *Qaddafi's World Design: Libyan Foreign Policy, 1969–1987.* London: Saqi Books, 1987.

Vandewalle, Dirk. *A Political History of Modern Libya.* Cambridge: Cambridge University Press, forthcoming.

The Middle East: Policies, Issues, and Events

Abdullah II, king of Jordan. "The Road to Reform." *Foreign Policy,* no. 145 (November/December 2004): 72–73.

Abi-Aad, Naji, and Michel Grenon. *Instability and Conflict in the Middle East: People, Petroleum, and Security Threats.* London: Macmillan, 1997.

Ajami, Fouad. *The Arab Predicament: Arab Political Thought and Practice since 1967.* Updated ed. New York: Cambridge University Press, 1992.

———. *Dream Palace of the Arabs: A Generation's Odyssey.* New York: Vintage Books, 1999.

———. "The Summer of Arab Discontent." *Foreign Affairs* 69, no. 5 (Winter 1990/91): 1–20.

al-Alkim, Hassan Hamdan. *GCC States in an Unstable World: Foreign-Policy Dilemmas of Small States.* London: Al Saqi, 1994.

———. "The Prospect of Democracy in the GCC Countries." *Critique: Critical Middle Eastern Studies,* no. 9 (Fall 1996).

Anderson, Betty S. "The State of 'Democracy' in Jordan." *Critique: Critical Middle Eastern Studies,* no. 10 (Spring 1997).

Atherton, Alfred Leroy, Jr. "The Shifting Sands of Middle East Peace." *Foreign Policy,* no. 86 (Spring 1992): 114–133.

Baker, Raymond William. *Sadat and After: Struggles for Egypt's Political Soul.* Cambridge, Mass.: Harvard University Press, 1990.

Barnett, Thomas. *The Pentagon's New Map: War and Peace in the Twenty-First Century.* New York: Putnam, 2004.

Bar-Siman-Tov, Yaacov. *The Israeli-Egyptian War of Attrition, 1969–1970.* New York: Columbia University Press, 1980.

Bhatia, Shyam. *Nuclear Rivals in the Middle East.* New York: Routledge, 1988.

Biswas, Asit K., et al. *Core and Periphery—A Comprehensive Approach to Middle Eastern Water.* New Delhi: Oxford University Press, 1997.

Butter, David. "Egypt: Special Report." *Middle East Economic Digest,* October 9, 1998, 23–45.

Byman, Daniel, Kenneth Pollack, and Gideon Rose. "The Rollback Fantasy." *Foreign Affairs* 78, no. 1 (January/February 1999): 24–41.

Carter, Jimmy. "The Middle East Consultation: A Look to the Future." *Middle East Journal* 42, no. 2 (Spring 1988): 187–192.

Chaudhry, Kiren Aziz. *The Price of Wealth: Economies and Institutions in the Middle East.* Ithaca, N.Y.: Cornell University Press, 1997.

Clarke, Duncan. "U.S. Security Assistance to Egypt and Israel: Politically Untouchable?" *Middle East Journal* 51, no. 2 (Spring 1997): 200–214.

Clarke, Richard. *Against All Enemies: Inside America's War on Terror.* New York: Free Press, 2004.

Coll, Steve. *Ghost Wars: The Secret History of the CIA, Afghanistan, and bin Laden: From the Soviet Invasion to September 10, 2001.* New York: Penguin Press, 2004.

Cook, Steven A. "Democracy in Arabic." *Foreign Policy,* no. 146 (January/February 2005).

Cooley, John K. *Unholy Wars: Afghanistan, America and International Terrorism.* London: Pluto Press, 2000.

Cordesman, Anthony. *The War after the War: Strategic Lessons of Iraq and Afghanistan.* Washington, D.C. Center for Strategic & International Studies, 2004.

Dann, Uriel. *The Great Powers in the Middle East, 1919–1939.* New York: Holmes & Meier, 1988.

Dawisha, Adeed. *Arab Nationalism in the Twentieth Century: From Triumph to Despair.* Princeton, N.J.: Princeton University Press, 2003.

Eickelman, Dale F., and James Piscatori. *Muslim Politics.* Princeton, N.J.: Princeton University Press, 1996.

Esposito, John L., and James Piscatori. "Democratization and Islam." *Middle East Journal* 45, no. 3 (Summer 1991): 427–440.

Freedman, Robert O., ed. *The Middle East and the Peace Process: The Impact of the Oslo Accords.* Gainesville: University Press of Florida, 1998.

Friedman, Thomas L. *From Beirut to Jerusalem.* New York: Farrar, Straus & Giroux, 1989.

Fromkin, David. *A Peace to End All Peace.* New York: Owl Books, 2001.

Goldschmidt, Arthur, Jr. *A Concise History of the Middle East.* Boulder, Colo.: Westview Press, 1991.

Gunaratna, Rohan. *Inside Al Qaeda: Global Network of Terror.* New York: Columbia University Press, 2002.

Hadar, Leon T. "What Green Peril?" *Foreign Affairs* 72, no. 2 (Spring 1993): 27–42.

Heradstveit, Daniel, and Helge Hveem, eds. *Oil in the Gulf: Obstacles to Democracy and Development.* Aldershot, U.K.: Ashgate, 2005.

Hillel, Daniel. *Rivers of Eden: The Struggle for Water and the Quest for Peace in the Middle East.* New York: Oxford University Press, 1994.

Hinnebusch, Raymond A., Jr. and Anoushiravan Ehteshami, eds. *The Foreign Policies of Middle East States.* Boulder, Colo.: Lynne Rienner, 2002.

Hof, Frederic C. "The Water Dimensions of Golan Heights Negotiations." *Middle East Policy* 5, no. 2 (May 1997): 129–141.

Hourani, Albert. *A History of the Arab Peoples.* Cambridge, Mass.: Belknap Press, 1991.

Hudson, Michael. "After the Gulf War: Prospects for Democratization in the Middle East." *Middle East Journal* 45, no. 3 (Summer 1991): 407–426.

———. *Arab Politics: The Search for Legitimacy.* New Haven, Conn.: Yale University Press, 1977.

———. *Middle East Dilemma: The Politics and Economics of Arab Integration.* New York: Columbia University Press, 1999.

———. "To Play the Hegemon: Fifty Years of U.S. Policy toward the Middle East." *Middle East Journal* 50, no. 3 (Summer 1996): 329–343.

Inbar, Efraim, and Shmuel Sandler, eds. *Middle Eastern Security: Prospects for an Arms Control Regime.* London: Frank Cass, 1995.

Indyk, Martin. "Watershed in the Middle East." *Foreign Affairs* 71, no. 1 (America and the World 1991/92): 70–93.

Kedourie, Elie. *Democracy and Arab Political Culture.* Washington, D.C.: Washington Institute for Near East Policy, 1992.

Kemp, Geoffrey, and Robert E. Harkavy. *Strategic Geography and the Changing Middle East.* Washington, D.C.: Carnegie Endowment for International Peace, 1997.

Kepel, Gilles. *Bad Moon Rising: A Chronicle of the Middle East Today.* London: Saqi Books, 2003.

———. *The War for Muslim Minds.* Cambridge, Mass.: Harvard University Press, 2004.

Khadduri, Majid. *The Gulf War: The Origins and Implications of the Iraq-Iran Conflict.* New York: Oxford University Press, 1988.

Khalidi, Rashid. *The Origins of Arab Nationalism.* New York: Columbia University Press, 1991.

———. *Resurrecting Empire: Western Footprints and America's Perilous Path in the Middle East.* Boston: Beacon Press, 2004.

Kipper, Judith, and Harold H. Saunders, eds. *The Middle East in Global Perspective.* Boulder, Colo.: Westview Press, 1991.

Korany, Bahgat, Paul Noble, and Rex Brynen. *The Many Faces of National Security in the Arab World.* New York: St. Martin's Press, 1993.

Lenczowski, George. *American Presidents and the Middle East.* Durham, N.C.: Duke University Press, 1990.

Lesch, Ann Mosely. "Contrasting Reaction to the Persian Gulf War Crisis: Egypt, Syria, Jordan, and the Palestinians." *Middle East Journal* 45, no. 1 (Winter 1991): 30–50.

Lewis, Bernard. "License to Kill: Usama bin Ladin's Declaration of Jihad." *Foreign Affairs* 77, no. 6 (November/December 1998): 14–19.

———. *What Went Wrong?* New York: Oxford University Press, 2003.

Lowrance, Sherry R. "After Beijing: Political Liberalization and the Women's Movement in Jordan." *Middle Eastern Studies* 34, no. 3 (July 1998): 83–102.

Lustick, Ian S. "Reinventing Jerusalem." *Foreign Policy,* no. 93 (Winter 1993–94): 41–59.

Makovsky, David. "Middle East Peace through Partition." *Foreign Affairs* 80, no. 2 (March/April 2001): 28–45.

Mamdani, Mahmood. *Good Muslim, Bad Muslim.* New York: Pantheon, 2004.

Maoz, Zeev, ed. *Regional Security in the Middle East: Past, Present, and Future.* London: Frank Cass, 1997.

Mattar, Philip. "The PLO and the Gulf Crisis." *Middle East Journal* 48, no. 1 (Winter 1994): 31–46.

Meriwether, Margaret Lee, and Judith Tucker, eds. *A Social History of Women and Gender in the Modern Middle East.* Boulder, Colo.: Westview Press, 1998.

Miller, Judith. "The Challenge of Radical Islam." *Foreign Affairs* 72, no. 2 (Spring 1993): 43–56.

Mueller, John, and Karl Mueller. "Sanctions of Mass Destruction." *Foreign Affairs* 78, no. 3 (May/June 1999): 43–53.

Murphy, Richard W., and F. Gregory Gause III. "Democracy and U.S. Policy in the Muslim Middle

East." *Middle East Policy* 5, no. 1 (January 1997): 58–67.

Muslih, Muhammad. "Asad's Foreign Policy Strategy." *Critique: Critical Middle Eastern Studies,* no. 12 (Spring 1998).

O'Hanlon, Michael E. *Defense Strategy for the Post-Saddam Era.* Washington, D.C.: Brookings Institution Press, 2005.

Owen, Roger. *The Middle East in the World Economy.* London: I. B. Tauris, 1993.

Parker, Richard B. *The Politics of Miscalculation in the Middle East.* Bloomington: Indiana University Press, 1993.

Peterson, J. E. *Yemen: The Search for a Modern State.* Baltimore: Johns Hopkins University Press, 1982.

Quandt, William, ed. *The Middle East: Ten Years after Camp David.* Washington, D.C.: Brookings Institution Press, 1988.

Rashid, Ahmed. *Taliban: Militant Islam, Oil, and Fundamentalism in Central Asia.* New Haven, Conn.: Yale University Press, 2000.

Reed, Stanley. "The Battle for Egypt." *Foreign Affairs* 72, no. 4 (September/October 1993): 94–107.

Rubin, Jeffrey Z. *Dynamics of Third Party Intervention: Kissinger in the Middle East.* New York: Praeger, 1983.

Rugh, William A. "The Foreign Policy of the United Arab Emirates." *Middle East Journal* 50, no. 1 (Winter 1996): 57–70.

Sadowski, Yahya. *Scuds or Butter? The Political Economy of Arms Control in the Middle East.* Washington, D.C.: Brookings Institution Press, 1993.

Salamé, Ghassan. "Islam and the West." *Foreign Policy,* no. 90 (Spring 1993): 22–37.

Savir, Uri. *The Process: 1,100 Days That Changed the Middle East.* New York: Random House, 1998.

Scheuer, Michael. *Imperial Hubris: Why the West Is Losing the War on Terror.* Washington, D.C.: Brassey's, 2004.

Shafik, Nemat, ed. *Economic Challenges Facing Middle Eastern and North African Countries: Alternative Futures.* New York: St. Martin's Press, 1998.

———. *Prospects for Middle Eastern and North African Economies: From Boom to Bust and Back?* New York: St. Martin's Press, 1998.

Sharabi, Hisham. "Modernity and Islamic Revival." *Contention* 2, no. 1 (Fall 1992): 127–138.

Simons, Geoff. *Future Iraq: U.S. Policy in Reshaping the Middle East.* London: Saqi Books, 2003.

St. John, Ronald Bruce. "Libya Is Not Iraq: Preemptive Strikes, WMD, and Diplomacy." *Middle East Journal* 58, no. 3 (Summer 2004): 386–402.

Starr, Joyce R. "Water Wars." *Foreign Policy,* no. 82 (Spring 1991): 17–36.

Telhami, Shibley. *The Stakes: America and the Middle East: The Consequences of Power and the Choice for Peace.* Boulder, Colo.: Westview Press, 2002.

Urquhart, Brian. "The United Nations in the Middle East: A Fifty-Year Retrospective." *Middle East Journal* 49, no. 4 (Autumn 1995): 572–581.

Viorst, Milton. "The Colonel in His Labyrinth." *Foreign Affairs* 78, no. 2 (March/April 1999): 60–75.

Yaniv, Avner. *Dilemmas of Security: Politics, Strategy, and the Israeli Experience in Lebanon.* New York: Oxford University Press, 1987.

Yetiv, Steven A. *Explaining Foreign Policy: U.S. Decision-Making and the Persian Gulf War.* Baltimore: Johns Hopkins University Press, 2004.

The Persian Gulf States and Middle Eastern Oil

Abir, Mordechai. *Saudi Arabia in the Oil Era: Regime and Elites, Conflict and Collaboration.* Boulder, Colo.: Westview Press, 1988.

Adelman, M. A. "Oil Fallacies." *Foreign Policy,* no. 82 (Spring 1991): 3–16.

Altorki, Soraya, and Donald Cole. *Arabian Oasis City.* Austin: University of Texas Press, 1989.

Anderson, Irvine H. *Aramco, the United States, and Saudi Arabia: A Study of the Dynamics of Foreign Policy, 1933–1950.* Princeton, N.J.: Princeton University Press, 1981.

Bahry, Louay. "The Opposition in Bahrain: A Bellwether for the Gulf?" *Middle East Policy* 5 no. 2 (May 1997): 42–57.

———. "The Socioeconomic Foundations of the Shiite Opposition in Bahrain." *Mediterranean Quarterly* 11, no. 3 (Summer 2000): 129–143.

Bidwell, Robin. *The Two Yemens.* Boulder, Colo.: Westview Press, 1983.

Carapico, Sheila. *Civil Society in Yemen: The Political Economy of Activism in Modern Arabia.* Cambridge: Cambridge University Press, 1998.

Cordesman, Anthony H. *Bahrain, Oman, Qatar, and the UAE: Challenges of Security.* Boulder, Colo.: Westview Press, 1997.

———. *Saudi Arabia Enters the Twenty-First Century.* 2 vols. Westport, Conn.: Praeger, 2003.

Dresch, Paul. *A History of Modern Yemen.* Cambridge: Cambridge University Press, 2000.

Emirates Center for Strategic Studies and Research. *The Yemeni War of 1994: Causes and Consequences.* Abu Dhabi: Emirates Center for Strategic Studies and Research, 1996.

Fandy, Mamoun. *Saudi Arabia and the Politics of Dissent.* New York: St. Martin's Press, 1998.

Gause, F. Gregory, III. *Oil Monarchies: Domestic and Security Challenges in the Arab Gulf States.* New York: Council on Foreign Relations Press, 1994.

Ghanem, Shukri M. *OPEC: The Rise and Fall of an Exclusive Club.* New York: Kegan Paul, 1986.

Al-Haj, Abdullah Juma. "The Politics of Participation in the Gulf Cooperation Council States: The Omani Consultative Council." *Middle East Journal* 50, no. 3 (Autumn 1996): 559–571.

Heard-Bey, Frauke. *From Trucial States to United Arab Emirates: A Society in Transition.* London: Longman, 1996.

Hiro, Dilip. *Desert Shield to Desert Storm: The Second Gulf War.* New York: Routledge, 1992.

Ibrahim, Ibrahim. *The Gulf Crisis: Background and Consequences.* Washington, D.C.: Center for Contemporary Arab Studies, 1992.

Ismael, Tareq Y., and Jacqueline S. Ismael, eds. *The Gulf War and the New World Order: International Relations of the Middle East.* Gainesville: University Press of Florida, 1994.

Joffe, E. G. H., et al. *Yemen Today: Crisis and Solutions.* London: Caravel, 1997.

Kapiszewski, Andrzej. *Nationals and Expatriates: Population and Labour Dilemmas of the Gulf Cooperation Council States.* Reading, U.K.: Ithaca Press, 2001.

Katz, Mark N. "Election Day in Aden." *Middle East Policy* 5, no. 3 (September 1997): 40–50.

Kechichian, Joseph A. *Oman and the World: The Emergence of an Independent Foreign Policy.* Santa Monica: RAND, 1995.

———, ed. *Iran, Iraq, and the Arab Gulf States.* New York: Palgrave, 2001.

Krimly, Rayed. "The Political Economy of Adjusted Priorities: Declining Oil Revenues and Saudi Fiscal Policies." *Middle East Journal* 53, no. 2 (Spring 1999): 254–267.

Licklider, Roy. *Political Power and the Arab Oil Weapon: The Experience of Five Industrial Nations.* Berkeley: University of California Press, 1988.

Long, David E. *The Kingdom of Saudi Arabia.* Gainesville: University Press of Florida, 1997.

Lugar, Richard G., and R. James Woolsey. "The New Petroleum." *Foreign Affairs* 78, no. 1 (January/February 1999): 88–102.

Molavi, Afshin. "Oman's Economy: Back on Track." *Middle East Policy* 5, no. 4 (January 1998): 1–10.

Molyneux, Maxine. "Women's Rights and Political Contingency: The Case of Yemen, 1990–1994." *Middle East Journal* 49, no. 3 (Summer 1995): 418–431.

Obaid, Nawaf E. "In Al-Saud We Trust." *Foreign Policy,* no. 128 (January/February 2002): 72–74.

———. *The Oil Kingdom at 100: Petroleum Policymaking in Saudi Arabia.* Washington, DC: Washington Institute for Near East Policy, 2000.

Okruhlik, Gwenn. "Saudi Arabian-Iranian Relations: External Rapprochement and Internal Consolidation." *Middle East Policy* 10, no. 2 (Summer 2003): 113–125.

Okruhlik, Gwenn, and Patrick Conge. "National Autonomy, Labor Migration, and Political Crisis: Yemen and Saudi Arabia." *Middle East Journal* 51, no. 4 (Autumn 1997): 554–565.

Peterson, Erik R. *The Gulf Cooperation Council: Search for Unity in a Dynamic Region.* Boulder, Colo.: Westview Press, 1988.

Peterson, J. E. *The Arab Gulf States: Steps toward Political Participation.* New York: Praeger, 1988.

———. "The Arabian Peninsula in Modern Times: A Historiographical Survey." *American Historical Review* 96, no. 5 (December 1991): 1435–1449.

———. *Defending Arabia.* London: Croom Helm; New York: St. Martin's Press, 1986.

———. *Saudi Arabia and the Illusion of Security.* Oxford: Oxford University Press, 2002.

———. "Succession in the States of the Gulf Cooperation Council." *Washington Quarterly* 24, no. 4 (Autumn 2001): 173–186.

Pollack, Kenneth M. "Securing the Gulf." *Foreign Affairs* 82, no. 4 (July/August 2003): 2–16.

Potter, Lawrence G., and Gary G. Sick, eds. *Security in the Persian Gulf: Origins, Obstacles, and the Search for Consensus.* New York: Palgrave, 2002.

Priess, David. "The Gulf Cooperation Council: Prospects for Expansion." *Middle East Policy* 5, no. 4 (January 1998): 17–26.

Al-Rasheed, Madawi. *A History of Saudi Arabia.* Cambridge: Cambridge University Press, 2002.

Rathmell, Andrew, and Kirsten Schulze. "Political Reform in the Gulf: The Case of Qatar." *Middle Eastern Studies* 36, no. 4 (October 2000): 47–62.

Schofield, Richard. *Territorial Foundations of the Gulf States.* New York: St. Martin's Press, 1994.

Sick, Gary G., and Lawrence G. Potter, eds. *The Persian Gulf at the Millennium: Essays in Politics, Economy, Security, and Religion.* London: Macmillan, 1997.

Stanislaw, Joseph, and Daniel Yergin. "Oil: Reopening the Door." *Foreign Affairs* 72, no. 4 (September/October 1993): 81–93.

Telhami, Shibley, and Fiona Hill. "America's Vital Stakes in Saudi Arabia." *Foreign Affairs* 81, no. 6 (November/December 2002): 167–173.

Yamani, Mai. *Changed Identities: The Challenges of the New Generation in Saudi Arabia.* London: Royal Institute of International Affairs, 1999.

Yergin, Daniel. *The Prize: The Epic Quest for Oil, Money, and Power.* New York: Simon & Schuster, 1990.

Yodfat, Aryeh. *The Soviet Union and the Arabian Peninsula: Soviet Policy toward the Persian Gulf and Arabia.* New York: St. Martin's Press, 1983.

Syria

Batatu, Hanna. *Syria's Peasantry, the Descendants of Its Lesser Rural Notables, and Their Politics.* Princeton, N.J.: Princeton University Press, 1999.

Dawisha, Adeed I. *Syria and the Lebanese Crisis.* New York: St. Martin's Press, 1980.

Drysdale, Alaisdair, and Raymond A. Hinnebusch. *Syria and the Middle East Peace Process.* New York: Council on Foreign Relations Press, 1992.

Hinnebusch, Raymond A. *Peasant and Bureaucracy in Ba'thist Syria.* Boulder, Colo.: Westview Press, 1989.

———. *Syria: Revolution from Above.* New York: Routledge, 2001.

Kienle, Eberhard, ed. *Contemporary Syria: Liberalization between Cold War and Cold Peace.* New York: I. B. Tauris, 1997.

Leverett, Flynt. *Inheriting Syria: Bashar's Trial by Fire.* Washington, D.C.: Brookings Institution Press, 2005.

Lewis, Norman N. *Nomads and Settlers in Syria and Jordan, 1800–1980.* New York: Cambridge University Press, 1987.

Perthes, Volker. *Syria under Bashar al-Asad: Modernisation and the Limits of Change.* New York: Oxford University Press for the International Institute for Strategic Studies, 2004.

Seale, Patrick. *The Struggle for Syria: A Study of Postwar Arab Politics, 1945–1958.* 2d ed. New Haven, Conn.: Yale University Press, 1987.

Van Dam, Nikolaos. *The Struggle for Power in Syria: Politics and Society under Asad and the Ba`th Party.* London: I. B. Tauris, 1996.

Wedeen, Lisa. *Ambiguities of Domination: Politics, Rhetoric, and Symbols in Contemporary Syria.* Chicago: University of Chicago Press, 1999.

INDEX